The Oxford Dictionary of
Classical Myth and Religion

The Oxford Dictionary of

Classical Myth and Religion

Edited by
SIMON PRICE AND EMILY KEARNS

OXFORD
UNIVERSITY PRESS

OXFORD

UNIVERSITY PRESS

Great Clarendon Street, Oxford OX2 6DP

Oxford University Press is a department of the University of Oxford.
It furthers the University's objective of excellence in research, scholarship,
and education by publishing worldwide in

Oxford New York

Auckland Bangkok Buenos Aires Cape Town Chennai
Dar es Salaam Delhi Hong Kong Istanbul Karachi Kolkata
Kuala Lumpur Madrid Melbourne Mexico City Mumbai Nairobi
São Paulo Shanghai Singapore Taipei Tokyo Toronto

Oxford is a registered trade mark of Oxford University Press
in the UK and in certain other countries

Published in the United States
by Oxford University Press Inc., New York

© Oxford University Press 2003

Database right Oxford University Press (maker)

First published 2003

British Library Cataloguing in Publication Data

Data available

Library of Congress Cataloging in Publication Data

Data available

ISBN 0–19–280288–7

1 3 5 7 9 10 8 6 4 2

Typeset by Kolam Information Services Pvt Ltd, Pondicherry, India
Printed in Great Britain by
Biddles Ltd

Contents

List of Maps

List of Genealogical Tables

Abbreviations

anc.	ancient	lit.	literally
b.	born	Lat.	Latin
bk.	book	m.	metre/s
c.	*circa*	mi.	mile/s
cent.	century	mod.	modern
d.	died	Mt.	Mount
Eng.	English	no.	number
Etr.	Etruscan	NT	New Testament
fem.	feminine	OP	Old Persian
f., ff.	and following	OT	Old Testament
fl.	floruit	pl.	plate
fr.	fragment	plur.	plural
ft.	foot/feet	pref.	preface
Gk.	Greek	sing.	singular
IE	Indo-European	sq.	square
kg.	kilogram/s	trans.	translation,
km.	kilometre/s		translated by

Introduction

1. Mythology: Panhellenic, Local, and Roman

Panhellenic Myths

The principal panhellenic deities, common to all Greeks, were quite limited in number: Zeus, Hera, Athena, Apollo, Artemis, Poseidon, Aphrodite, Hermes, Hephaestus, Ares, Demeter, and Dionysus were recognized all over the Greek world. These 'twelve Olympians', the number that became conventional in the fifth century BC, formed a family. Zeus, 'father of gods and men', was at its head, Hera his sister-wife, and the others his siblings or children.

The most notable tellings of Greek myths were the works of Homer and Hesiod. The Homeric narratives describe interactions between the gods and the human characters: how Apollo attacked Patroclus in battle, or how Athena gave guidance to Telemachus. Such interactions between gods and humans, and other Homeric stories about the gods, presuppose a degree of anthropomorphism: that the gods are like humans. Though this was a lasting legacy in Greece, sometimes criticized by later generations, Homer equally emphasizes that gods were also *un*like humans, in their power and their immortality. When characters in Homer talk about divine interventions, they tend to use not the names of specific deities, which the narrator uses, but indeterminate terms like a god (*theos*) or divine being (*daimōn*). Hesiod's *Theogony* is a systematic treatise on the Greek pantheon, which has at its centre the establishment of the rule of Zeus and how he mastered challenges to it by other powers (Titans, Typhon).

Homer and Hesiod were privileged texts in the expression of the Greek pantheon, but that did not mean that their stories were definitive. Neither author claims divine revelation, though both claim that the divine knowledge of the Muses, daughters of Zeus, could remedy their own ignorance. Nor was either writer comprehensive. Homer's *Iliad* focuses on four days of fighting during the ten-year Trojan war, and the *Theogony* is a genealogy of the gods, not a recounting of all the exploits known to the author. Subsequent writers, therefore, could fill in the gaps left by Homer and Hesiod—such were the other, now lost, Homeric epics of the archaic period, and (especially important for mythology) the *Catalogue of Women*, a continuation of Hesiod's *Theogony* which was accepted in antiquity as being by Hesiod. They were also at liberty to offer novel tellings of familiar tales. The tradition of telling and re-telling myths extends from the archaic period right down to the mid-fifth century AD when Nonnus composed his massive epic on Dionysus.

Ancient scholarly handbooks of mythology were composed mainly between about 250 BC and AD 150, but they could not cope with all the variants and conflicting versions. They fell into two types. One set of mythological studies collected myths to aid in understanding major Greek authors. For example, in the imperial period there circulated a huge collection of myths as background to Homer. The second category of mythological works took particular themes, such as love stories, transformation tales or genealogies. The principal surviving example is the *Library* said to be by Apollodorus, which is organized in terms of mythical genealogies, and which has been the foundation for many modern handbooks of Greek mythology.

Ancient writers, as well as modern, have thus often wished to compile 'definitive versions' of Greek myths by combining items from different sources. While this can be a helpful shorthand, it is important to realize that there can never be one complete and correct account of a myth. Rather, different authors (or artists) will represent a myth in different ways. Sometimes the attempt to produce even a reasonably consistent narrative raises more problems than it solves. For instance, it is possible to construct a genealogy of the Athenian royal house based on Apollodorus, who in turn based his information on the schematizing local historians of the late fifth and (mostly) fourth centuries BC; but to do so disregards often more prominent and older traditions of individual genealogical links, and so risks being seriously misleading. Some other genealogies make better sense, because the local traditions became standardized at an earlier date, mainly through the epic, but the point remains that we must always respect the individuality of every telling of a myth.

Local Myths

Scholars used primarily to study general, panhellenic myths, but the issue of the relation of panhellenic to local versions of myths is now of great interest. The relationship between normal and local mythologies ought to be at the centre of studies of Greek mythology, for all periods of Greek history. The significance is twofold: local myths can help to situate a community in common narratives of the past. Corinth, for example, claimed the hero Sisyphus as peculiarly Corinthian, or (at the microscopic level) the Attic village of Thoricus made the most of the claim that the story of Cephalus and Procris happened right at Thoricus. Secondly (and sometimes relatedly), local versions of panhellenic myths express sets of values which were of particular local importance.

The contexts for the local display of mythology were varied: paintings, coins, reliefs, historical works, and performances at local festivals. Advice on the composition of festival encomia is given in the third century by a treatise ascribed to Menander Rhetor. There were various possible grounds for praising a city, for example being loved by the gods, which called for use of the relevant local mythology.

Instances of being 'god-loved' may be found in what is said of the Athenians, Rhodians, Corinthians, and Delphians. Of the Athenians, it is said that Athena and Poseidon competed for their land; of the Rhodians, that Zeus rained gold on them; of the Corinthians and the Isthmus, that Helios and Poseidon competed; and of the Delphians, that Apollo, Poseidon, Themis and Night did the same.

The treatise also makes it clear that praises of cities could be delivered at various public occasions (feasts, festivals, competitions, or gladiatorial shows), and that those occasions could themselves be praised in general or in particular: for example the person honoured in the festival, whether god, hero, or emperor. Each of those could be the recipient of local stories.

The panhellenic myths of Homer and Hesiod also had their local versions, which either rooted the myths in the local community or elaborated significantly different versions of the myth. Local myths might concern the Olympians or they might relate to a further order of beings, 'heroes', normally conceived as mortals who had died and who received cult at their tomb or at a specific sanctuary. Heroes were very numerous (in Attica alone over 170 heroes were worshipped). They ranged from major Attic heroes like Erechtheus or Cecrops, worshipped in the Erechtheum on the Acropolis, down to minor and sometimes even anonymous heroes worshipped only in a particular locality (like Phytalus at Laciadae on the way to Eleusis, or Heros Iatros, the hero physician, near the Athenian Agora).

Pausanias' *Description of Greece* relates very many locally based myths, and demonstrates the vitality such stories still retained in the second century AD. For example, the Athenians told of a contest between Athena and Poseidon for the control of Attica; the event was depicted on the west pediment of the Parthenon. Poseidon created with a blow of his trident a salt spring on the Acropolis, while Athena planted there the first ever olive tree. Athena was adjudged the victor, but Poseidon in pique flooded a plain north-west of Athens, until a final reconciliation was brought about. Athena Polias became the guardian deity of the city, but the mythical contest left its material remains. The unique plan of the Erechtheum was due in part to the need to incorporate the spring within the building where Poseidon and Erechtheus, the second king of Athens, were both worshipped, and when Pausanias visited the Acropolis he was shown both the salt spring and the olive tree behind the Erechtheum, which had regenerated miraculously after the Persians had burned it in 480 BC.

Athens was far from unique in having locally rooted myths. All over the Greek world towns claimed to be the birthplace of X, or the favoured spot of Y. Some communities claimed that specific events occurred not in (say) mainland Greece, but right here. Nysa in western Asia Minor (modern Turkey) is a good case in point. A frieze from the theatre, which dates probably to the early third century AD, is a complex interweaving of the two stories: the Rape of Persephone and the birth of Dionysus, both of which are located right here in Nysa. What is interesting about the Persephone story is the divergence from the panhellenic *Homeric Hymn* tradition. That focuses on the mother–daughter relationship, the desperate grieving of the mother, and the partial recovery of the daughter. Here Demeter does give chase, but catches up with a married couple: the emphasis seems rather to be on the marriage between Persephone and Pluto. This makes perfect sense at a place whose main festival, recorded on local coins, and on inscriptions, was the Theogamia ('Marriage of the Gods'). The cult at Nysa has taken over and relocated an ancient myth, and shifted its emphasis to suit local preoccupations.

Roman Myths

Roman mythology never existed—or so it has often been claimed. There is the old theory that in the earliest period of Rome there were no *gods* as such, only primitive powers undifferentiated by personal attributes. This view is closely related to the theory of Rome as a 'myth-less' society; for if there were no gods, then it follows that there could be no stories about their deeds and adventures, or their dealings with humans—the stock-in-trade of what we think of as 'myth'. Only gradually, so the argument goes, as these powers were replaced by anthropomorphic gods, did Rome acquire some sort of mythology in the last centuries BC, largely under the influence of Greece with its huge repertoire of myths.

Other theories hold that Rome's native mythological tradition was somehow 'lost', or 'forgotten'—perhaps swamped by the influx of Greek mythology in the middle Republic, or perhaps surviving in Roman popular culture, but invisible to us.

There are many complicated issues involved here: not least, the very definition of Roman mythology, what counts as a 'myth' in any culture, and how far we can ever think of any system of myth as just an 'alien import'. But even without entering into such theoretical questions, the modern denial of Roman mythology does seem almost perverse. After all, the public imagery of late republican and Augustan Rome was largely mythological; the early books of Livy and Dionysius of Halicarnassus are full of mythological stories about early Rome; Ovid's *Fasti* consists very largely of descriptions of festivals and their associated myths. These writers would have been perplexed to be told that their myths were either trivial or merely foreign imports, and so of little significance for Roman culture and religion.

Roman myths were in essence myths of place. Greek myths, as we have seen, also related to specific cities and territories, but at the same time they were regularly linked to wider Greek, or panhellenic, mythology. In general Roman myths do not have such a wider context. Rather, the sites and monuments of the city of Rome dominate Roman mythology—from the grandeur of the Capitoline Hill to the ancient hut of Romulus still lovingly preserved on the Palatine into the imperial period. These myths recounted the history of the area of Rome itself, from earliest times to the Augustan age itself; as in Virgil's *Aeneid*, when Aeneas, guided around the future site of the city, visits so many landmarks that were to memorialize key moments in the growth of Rome through the centuries.

2. Religious Pluralism: Greek Religions, Roman Religions, Judaisms, Christianities

A central issue in understanding religious life in classical antiquity is how we should conceptualize religious differences. What we have already said about the relationship of local myths to more general myths implies a degree of pluralism in the Greek world. Not only was there no authoritative sacred book, and no powerful religious hierarchy, there was in fact a considerable variety of myths and rituals, and considerable competition between communities for possession of the most prestigious myths or cults. We must also realize that although the Greeks recognized common strands in the religious practice and thought of the Greek world, they had not invented the category of 'a religion', and the question 'What is your religion?' would not have been comprehensible to them.

Romans would have had trouble with the question too, but in Rome the position is slightly different, because of Rome's political success in dominating her neighbours and eventually the whole Mediterranean world and beyond. So Rome did not have a superior body of myths and cults against which her practices had to be measured, but equally we should not assume that there was a single 'Roman religion'. There were huge changes in the religious life of Rome, both during the Republic, and during the Empire. Gods, myths, and festivals all evolved over that period. Things changed because of changes in the social and political system of Rome. They also changed because of the changing relationship between Rome and her empire.

Outside Rome analysis of the religious life of the empire is extremely difficult. The imperial world includes an enormous variety: Roman cults borrowed from Rome, traditional Greek civic cults (as at Nysa), newly created cults (Mithraism), Jews and Christians. It has always been tempting to talk in terms of neat, abstract categories: Judaism; Christianity; Mithraism. Those categories, especially Judaism and Christianity, used to be seen as unified and exclusive entities. That is, their theological and practical positions each had a central core, consistent across place and time; round that core were a number of awkward heretical or deviant groups which could be treated as simply marginal. They were exclusive of each other and of other religious groups of the time. However, the current trends in the study of Judaism and Christianity are firmly against the normative assumptions of the old picture. So in the context of Judaism and Christianity it has become conventional to recognize diversity within each religion (so 'Judaisms', 'Christianities'). It is then a matter for debate as to whether each of those two bundles were neatly separate religions, in a way which the other religious practices of the Empire clearly were not.

Within Jewish and Christian areas of religion there were certainly some strands that excluded other groups. But this is by no means the whole picture. The evidence of inscriptions, in particular, shows us individuals happily mixing what from our perspective we might want to call Jewish, Christian, and Mithraic elements—and practices of this sort are far too widespread to be considered 'deviant'. It may be most helpful to think of groups of people exploring their place in the universe, drawing on their contemporary knowledge, which would in due course evolve into new positions. There might be family resemblances between some of these groups (so one can still recognise shared practices or ideas), but there may be resemblances to more than one family, and over time things will change.

3. Reception of Myths: Antiquity to the Present

Reflection on the standing of the stories of Homer and Hesiod is attested already in the sixth–fifth centuries BC, and the imagery of sanctuaries also demonstrates the existence of privileged stories about the gods. Difficulties arose when historians and antiquarians sought to construct narratives down to the present on the basis of mythical tales. Was it reasonable for a writer in the Classical period to treat a traditional tale about Theseus, the hero who united Attica, in the same way as one about the tyrant Pisistratus in the sixth century BC? Some writers did attempt to do just this, for example Hellanicus, writing the first history of Attica in the 420s BC; later historians of Attica, in the fourth century, were similarly committed to recounting a continuous tradition from Cecrops, the first king of Athens. But others took a more critical line to distinguish mythical from human history. Just where that line was to be drawn was simply a matter of personal judgement. Diodorus Siculus, writing his *Universal History* in the first century BC, noted that earlier historians had excluded mythology on the grounds that it contained self-contradictions and confusions (they were worried about the evidence for such stories). He himself, however, proposed to include the deeds of gods and heroes, such as Dionysus and Heracles, who were benefactors of the human race. Such inclusiveness, however, remained controversial: Dionysius of Halicarnassus, a literary critic writing a little later than Diodorus, commended the historian Thucydides' exclusion of the mythical from his narrative, while noting that local historians did not live up to Thucydidean standards.

Fifth-century writers often coped with the difficulties inherent in treating myth as history by toning down and rationalizing stories. Thus Plutarch, in his *Life of Theseus*, quotes a much earlier 'explanation' of the journey of Theseus and Pirithous to the Underworld: actually they went to the palace of the king of the Molossians, who just happened to be called Aidoneus (Hades), and his wife Persephone. Gods could always be reinvented as humans. The idea that the so-called gods were once great humans who had ruled over or helped their fellows, known as 'euhemerism' (though Euhemerus was by no means the first to propound the theory) is a particular form of rationalism which became extremely influential in the Hellenistic period and later; Christian writers found it a very useful tool with which to criticize paganism.

Another favourite strategy for dealing with myth was allegorization. The idea that 'the gods are not really like this' is first attested in Xenophanes in the late sixth or early fifth century, though it may well be older. Various forms of criticism—explicit and implicit—of mythological divine behaviour are commonplace in the fifth century. Yet the myths, it is felt, have come from somewhere old and therefore venerable. The answer to this paradox must be allegory, that the myths are not literally true—they represent symbolically another kind of truth. The gods of the myths stand for physical elements or mental qualities, and the myths are ways of talking about the universe or about human nature. This was not good enough for Plato, who pointed out that we first hear stories about the gods when we are too young to understand such symbolic interpretations, and therefore the objectionable, literal version of the myth lodges deep in our minds. For Plato, myths should be rejected, along with the poets who tell them.

Despite Plato's authority, allegorization became a tremendously popular way of working with myth from later antiquity to the Renaissance. Christian attitudes to pagan myths varied considerably, from disapproval to guarded tolerance to an approval based on a Christianizing interpretation in which the perception of allegory was essential. Ovid was extremely widely read in the Middle Ages; along with Virgil (for stories about Troy and Rome) he was the main source for classical myths in western Europe. No doubt the love of a good story was much of the secret of his success, but the understanding of the stories in an allegorical sense was general (helped now by the intricate theories of Christian scriptural commentary) and gave a sort of moral and intellectual respectability. Allegorical interpretations reached new heights of elaboration in Italy from the late fourteenth century onwards, encouraged by the wider reading of more classical texts, and in the fifteenth century by the theories of the Florentine Neoplatonists.

Modern approaches to these myths have been very varied, but all distance themselves from Plato's rejection of myths as obnoxious and therefore false stories and all assume that myths are ways of constructing meaning, whether the myths are Greek myths of gods and Titans, Christian myths of the incarnation, or New Age myths of Atlantis. No one modern method is the key to all mythologies; different approaches seem to reveal different aspects of the subject; one needs to be eclectic, depending on the material one is considering and the objectives one has, and one needs to be alert to the dangers of imposing a modern model of myth (which arose in the eighteenth-century Enlightenment) onto the Greeks.

The origins of Greek myths have interested many scholars. Though the details are largely lost to us, the origins of the Greek gods and their stories are certainly varied. The Greeks were Indo-Europeans and the names of their gods go back to Indo-European prototypes. Most clearly Zeus Pater (father) is linguistically related to Roman Dies Pater (Jupiter) and the Indian Dyauḥ Pitar (the sky), regarded in the ancient Indian sacred books, the Vedas, as the father and with the earth the origin of everything. But the Vedic Sky is not otherwise very similar to Zeus or Jupiter: etymology tells us very little, and priority should be given to the function of the deities.

The origins of myths have also been sought in their relationship to rituals. Myths of sacrifice or specific local myths are indeed sometimes said to be derived from actual ritual procedures. In one modern formulation of this old theory sacrificial rituals themselves are then traced back to the palaeolithic period by means of parallels from modern hunter-gatherer societies; parallels with animal behaviour then suggest that the need for such rituals is located at a very deep level. Much of this is wishful thinking based on a peculiar selection of Greek data and an inadmissible projecting back of the practice of contemporary 'primitives'.

A variation of this search for meaning through origins lays great emphasis on 'initiation' as a category for understanding both myth and rituals. Initiation rituals or 'rites of passage' are held to underlie many if not all myths, for example, that of the Athenian Arrhephoroi. As a matter of fact classical Greece had very few initiation rituals and so the theory hypothesized that, while rituals had been lost or transformed, myths continued to be told in the classical and later periods. Compulsive detection of initiation rituals can be rather arbitrary and in the end casts little light on Greece of historic periods.

The search for origins cannot be the end of an enquiry into myths or rituals. In fact, the borrowing of a myth from the near east does not mean that the myth had no significance for the Greeks. Aphrodite is a composite figure whose Greek configurations are different from the originals, and Hesiod's succession myths make good Greek sense in emphasizing the struggles lying behind the present sovereignty of the world. Zeus' first wife Metis ('Cunning Intelligence') was to have given birth first to Athena and then to a son who would overthrow Zeus. Zeus therefore swallowed Metis, gave birth himself to Athena (through his head), and prevented the birth of the son. Zeus' rule was not to be challenged. For us, one meaning of this might be that the study of origins has to lead to a study of contemporary significances.

The most influential contemporary studies of the synchronic meanings of myths, originating in France, have shown how Greek myths are ways of thinking about issues fundamental to society. They have explored the structures of thought and particular tellings of myths as structures that are common to many or all of the surviving versions. Analyses have been made both of texts and of images. The foundations of civilization and its defence against disorder preoccupy both Hesiod and later workings of Hesiod's story. This reading of the story is fairly unproblematic, except that, in Hesiod, the Titans are not external monsters but kin of Zeus who have to be expelled from the society of heaven. Not all foes can be so easily identified or conquered. Other myths might explore the limits of rule by one man. In the story of Oedipus, that his name is derived from his lameness suggests the unsoundness of his royal rule. In addition, major members of the panhellenic pantheon were female, an obvious fact, but one whose implications for a patriarchal society are surely surprising and far reaching. Athena or Demeter were at least sometimes classified as 'female' rather than simply as 'divine', and myths involving goddesses sometimes address social issues such as the definition of gender roles. Myths also relate to local rituals, but even so their interest is not merely as explanations of the origins of rituals, and they too have their own structure of meaning.

As we have said, none of these methodologies exhausts the ways in which myths can be read. Even the work of the Paris school, although many of its fundamentals tally well with Greek ways of thinking, has given relatively little attention to some areas which the Greeks themselves thought important. Future investigations might sensibly concentrate on the place of mythology in a *religious* system and its explorations of the nature of the divine and of divine–human relations.

4. How to Use this Book

This book is a selection drawn from *The Oxford Classical Dictionary*, 3rd edn. (Oxford, 1996). We were the two area advisers responsible for planning the substantial revisions to the second edition of that work (dating to 1970). In making the selection for this book, we have tried to include as broad a range as possible of the coverage of the main *Dictionary*. So this book is not just a dictionary of Greek mythology (though it includes many entries on this subject), nor just on Roman festivals (though it does seek to include all the major ones). Instead it covers also Greek and Roman religious places and religious officials, divination, astrology, and magic. It also includes entries on regional religions and 'mystery cults' of the Graeco-Roman world, and many entries on Judaism and Christianity in the Hellenistic and Roman periods.

We have edited the original entries to cut out untransliterated Greek, and obscure language, though the editors of the third edition had already eliminated almost all such obscurities. We have cut out in-text references (which are hard on the eye), and citations of modern works, but we offer below an Annotated Bibliography as a guide to further reading, and we have added at the end of many individual entries references to selected ancient texts. These texts are limited to those which are readily accessible and also repay independent study. That is, we have not sought to include passing allusions to gods or myths. Rather, we have given references to, for example, works by Homer, Euripides, or Ovid, which constitute important versions of myths.

Within the body of the dictionary there are full cross-references between different entries (marked by an *, or by '*see* ENTRY'). By using these you may extend your original query to other related items. If you are interested in exploring a particular topic or theme, you will also find useful the Thematic Index, which groups together (for example) all the entries on 'Myths' or 'Judaism'.

5. Acknowledgements

We are grateful to OUP for proposing this volume to us, and in particular to Rebecca Collins, at OUP, and Tom Chandler, our excellent copy-editor. We would never have got started on the process of editing the volume without the help of Tom Weber, who extracted the relevant text-files from a CD-Rom and updated the list of headwords.

6. Annotated Bibliography

Greece

S. PRICE, *Religions of the Ancient Greeks* (Cambridge, 1999), is the most accessible general introduction to the subject.

W. BURKERT, *Greek Religion: Archaic and Classical* (Oxford, 1985) (German original 1977) is the work of a master, but to be used mainly for reference.

J. N. BREMMER, *Greek Religion* (Oxford, 1994) (revised as *Götter, Mythen und Heiligtümer im antiken Griechenland*, Darmstadt, 1996) is helpful for those with prior experience and has a lot of useful bibliographical pointers.

Rome

M. BEARD, J. NORTH, and S. PRICE, *Religions of Rome*, 2 vols. (Cambridge, 1998). Vol. 1 is a history (somewhat longer and more difficult than North's book that follows); vol. 2 is a sourcebook (including monuments and images). Between them, these two books are reckoned to be the best starting points for the study of religions of Rome and her empire.

J. A. NORTH, *Roman Religion* (Greece and Rome, New Survey in the Classics 30; Oxford, 2000) is the best beginner's guide.

D. C. FEENEY, *Literature and Religion at Rome* (Cambridge, 1998), is an exciting introduction to theoretical issues concerning the relationship between literature and religion.

R. TURCAN, *The Cults of the Roman Empire* (Oxford, 1996), outlines some of the evidence for the so-called Oriental cults in the Roman empire.

W. BURKERT, *Ancient Mystery Cults* (Cambridge, Mass., and London, 1987) is interesting on the Greek roots of some of these cults.

Myths

F. GRAF, *Greek Mythology* (Baltimore and London, 1993) is helpful on panhellenic myths (though not very interested in local mythologies).

Three other books offer guidance on approaches:

J. N. BREMMER (ed.), *Interpretations of Greek Mythology* (London and Sydney, 1987).

R. BUXTON, *Imaginary Greece. The Contexts of Mythology* (Cambridge, 1994).

L. EDMUNDS (ed.), *Approaches to Greek Myth* (Baltimore and London, 1990).

P. VEYNE, *Did the Greeks Believe in their Myths?* (Chicago, 1988) (French original 1983), restates the importance of Greek mythology, especially in relation to the Roman period.

The following works by Parisian scholars have been very influential in understanding the conceptual importance of myths, and their relations to rituals:

R. L. GORDON (ed.), *Myth, Religion and Society: Structuralist Essays* by M. Detienne, L. Gernet, J.-P. Vernant, and P. Vidal-Naquet (Cambridge, 1981), is an excellent selection of their writings.

M. DETIENNE, *Dionysus Slain* (Baltimore, 1979) (French original 1977); *The Creation of Mythology* (Chicago, 1986) (French original 1981).

M. DETIENNE and J.-P. VERNANT, *Cunning Intelligence in Greek Culture and Society* (Hassocks and Atlantic Highlands, NJ, 1978) (French original 1974); *The Cuisine of Sacrifice among the Greeks* (Chicago and London, 1989) (French original 1979).

J.-P. VERNANT, *Myth and Society in Ancient Greece* (Brighton and Atlantic Highlands, NJ, 1980) (French original 1974); *Myth and Thought among the Greeks* (London and Boston, 1983) (French original 1965).

Two books on Athenian myths will guide novices:

W. B. TYRRELL, *Amazons: A Study in Athenian Mythmaking* (Baltimore, 1984).

W. B. TYRRELL and F. S. BROWN, *Athenian Myths and Institutions* (New York and Oxford, 1991).

Roman myths are discussed in Beard, North, and Price, *Religions of Rome*.

M. GRANT, *Roman Myths* (Harmondsworth, 1973) is the best general introduction.

Reception

R. S. LAMBERTON, *Homer the Theologian: Neoplatonist Allegorical Reading and the Growth of the Epic Tradition* (Berkeley, 1986), is very useful on ancient allegorization.

M. P. O. MORFORD and R. J. LENARDON, *Classical Mythology*, 6th edn. (New York and Harlow UK, 1999), 542–93, offer a brief introduction to the reception of classical mythology in later literature, art, music, and film.

J. DAVIDSON REID, *The Oxford Guide to Classical Mythology in the Arts: 1300–1990s*, 2 vols. (New York and Oxford, 1993), is the definitive handbook.

JEAN SEZNEC, *The Survival of the Pagan Gods: The Mythological Tradition and its Place in Renaissance Humanism and Art* (Princeton, 1995; French original 1940), is a classic study of one aspect of the tradition.

Judaisms

E. P. SANDERS, *Judaism: Practice and Belief 63 BCE–66 CE* (London and Philadelphia, 1992), emphasizes the centrality of the Temple in Jerusalem and its rituals.

J. LIEU, J. NORTH, and T. RAJAK (eds.), *The Jews among Pagans and Christians* (London and New York, 1992) and J. LIEU, *Image and Reality: The Jews in the World of the Christians in the Second Century* (Edinburgh, 1996) locate Jews outside Judaea in the context of contemporary religious cultures.

Christianities

E. P. SANDERS, *Jesus and Judaism* (London and Philadelphia, 1985), examines the relationship between Jesus and contemporary Judaism.

R. LANE FOX, *Pagans and Christians* (Harmondsworth, 1986), focuses on Christianity in relation to contemporary Greek civic cults.

H. CHADWICK, *Early Christian Thought and the Classical Tradition* (Oxford, 1966), is a luminous study of some borrowings by Christians from earlier, Greek thinkers.

M. EDWARDS, M. GOODMAN, and S. PRICE (eds.), *Apologetics in the Roman Empire* (Oxford, 1999), includes studies of debates between Christians, Jews, and Pagans.

A. D. NOCK, *Conversion* (Oxford, 1933), emphasizes the peculiarity of Christian conversion in comparison to paganism.

Texts

The ones that we cite can mostly be found in the Loeb Classical Library; many are also available in Penguin translations. Other translations are available (free) online in the Perseus Digital Library (http://www.perseus.tufts.edu/; UK mirror site: http://perseus.csad.ox.ac.uk). One important text, Apollodorus, is in the Loeb, but there are two newer versions:

K. ALDRICH, *Apollodorus. The Library of Greek Mythology* (Lawrence, Kansas, 1975); M. SIMPSON, *Gods and Heroes of the Greeks. The Library of Apollodorus* (Amherst, Mass., 1976).

It is common to use the following three handbooks:

M. P. O. MORFORD and R. J. LENARDON, *Classical Mythology*, 6th edn. (New York and Harlow UK, 1999); B. B. Powell, *Classical Myth*, 3rd edn. (Upper Saddle River, NJ, 2001); H. J. ROSE, *A Handbook of Greek Mythology*, 5th edn. (London, 1958, repr. 1989).

However, we warn against the homogenizing presentation of Morford and Lenardon, who make the unwary treat Hesiod and Ovid as comparable authors, and assume that there was but one main version of mythological stories.

Still widely read is:

ROBERT GRAVES, *The Greek Myths*, 2 vols. (Harmondsworth, 1955; many other editions); his narratives are lively and very readable (and indicate sources clearly), but his interpretations are wildly idiosyncratic, though not without interest.

Finally:

J.-P. VERNANT, *The Universe, the Gods and Mortals: Ancient Greek Myths told by Jean-Pierre Vernant* (London and New York, 2001; French original, 1999), is a highly attractive telling of eight key Greek myths (inspired by tales that Vernant used to tell his grandson).

Imagery and Iconography

S. WOODFORD, *Images of Myths in Classical Antiquity* (Cambridge, 2003), is the best introduction.

The *Lexicon Iconographicum Mythologiae Classicae*, 18 vols. (Zurich: Artemis, 1981–99) is an extraordinary compendium of mythological images from the whole of Graeco-Roman antiquity. The volumes are expensive, and not in many libraries, but there is also an amazing online (and free) resource on Greek iconography: the searchable database of the Beazley archive in Oxford, which has catalogued all surviving Attic pottery (http://www.beazley.ox.ac.uk).

Iconography of a later period is included in vol. 2 of Beard, North, and Price, *Religions of Rome* (discussed above).

Simon Price
Emily Kearns

August 2002

Thematic Index

All entries in the book are listed here according to broad subject areas. Many entries relate to more than one subject and sometimes appear under more than one heading.

ASTROLOGY
astrology
constellations and named stars
Dorotheus
Firmicus Maternus
Manetho
Manilius
Nechepso
Nigidius Figulus, Publius
Pleiades
Ptolemy
Septizodium (or Septizonium)
Thrasyllus
Vettius Valens

AUTHORS AND TEXTS
authors, general
Aeschylus
Aesop
Apollonius Rhodius
Apuleius
Aristides, Publius Aelius
Artemidorus
Artemon
Asclepiades
Atthis
Bacchylides
Boio
Callimachus
Carcinus (1)
Carcinus (2)
Chaeremon
Cicero
Cleidemus
Crito
Dares of Phrygia
Dorotheus
Euhemerus
Euripides
Filocalus

Firmicus Maternus
Hecataeus (1)
Hecataeus (2)
Homer
Isyllus
Jason (2)
Leon
Lycophron
Macrobius
Manetho
Manilius
Nigidius Figulus, Publius
Nonnus
Obsequens, Iulius
Olen
Orosius
Ovid
paradoxographers
Pausanias
Philochorus
Philodamus
Philon (1)
Philostorgius
Philostratus
Phlegon
Pindar
Plutarch
Porphyry
Proclus
Sallustius
Sedulius
Semos
Sophocles
Stesichorus
Tarquitius Priscus
Theagenes
Theophrastus
Varro
Vettius Valens
Virgil

authors, Christian
Ambrose
Ambrosiaster
Arnobius
Athanasius
Athenagoras
Augustine, St
Boethius
Cassian
Cassiodorus
Chrysostom, John
Clement of Alexandria
Clement of Rome
Commodianus
Cyprian
Cyril of Alexandria
Cyril of Jerusalem
Dionysius the Areopagite
Ephraem Syrus
Epiphanius
Eusebius
Irenaeus
Jerome
Justin Martyr
Lactantius
Methodius
Minucius Felix
Nemesius
Novatianus
Origen
Paul, St
Paulinus (1) of Nola
Paulinus (2) of Pella
Pelagius
Proba, Faltonia Betitia
Prudentius, Aurelius Clemens
Rufinus
Tatian
Tertullian
Theodoret
Theophilus (1)

authors, Jewish
Aristobulus
Ezechiel
Jason (2)
Jewish-Greek literature
Josephus
Philon (2)

authors, mythographers
Acusilaus
Antoninus Liberalis
Apollodorus
Conon
Fulgentius
Hellanicus
Hesiod
Hyginus
mythographers
Palaephatus
Pherecydes (1)
Pherecydes (2)

philosophers (*see also* IDEAS: philosophy)
Alcmaeon (2)
Ammonius Saccas
Anaxagoras
Anaximander
Anaximenes
Aristotle
Celsus
Cleanthes
Crantor
Diogenes (1)
Diogenes (2)
Ecphantus
Empedocles
Epictetus
Epicurus
Hermias
Iamblichus
Numenius
Oenomaus
Parmenides
Peregrinus
philosophers on poetry
Plato
Plotinus
Presocratic philosophers
Prodicus
Protagoras
Pythagoras and Pythagoreanism
Socrates
Synesius
Xenophanes

texts, general
Acts of the Pagan Martyrs

allegory, Greek
allegory, Latin
books, Greek and Roman, sacred
comedy
dithyramb
epic
Epic Cycle
epigraphy
fable
fantastic literature
folk-songs, Greek
folk-tale
forgeries, religious
libri pontificales
novel
Orphic literature
parody
phlyakes
Phoenix
Priape(i)a
pseudepigraphic literature
Tabulae Iguvinae
tragedy

texts, Christian

apocalyptic literature
Didascalia Apostolorum
Epistle to Diognetus
Vulgate

texts, Jewish

apocalyptic literature
Dead Sea Scrolls
epic, biblical
midrash
Mishnah
Septuagint
Talmud

CHRISTIANITY

Acts of the Apostles
Ambrose
Ambrosiaster
apocalyptic literature
apologists, Christian
Arianism
Arius
Arnobius
Athanasius
Athenagoras

Augustine, St
Basil of Caesarea
Boethius
Cassian
Cassiodorus
Celsus
Christianity
Chronicon Paschale
Chrysostom, John
Clement of Alexandria
Clement of Rome
Commodianus
Cyprian
Cyril of Alexandria
Cyril of Jerusalem
Damasus I
Decius
Didascalia Apostolorum
Diocletian, persecutions of
Dionysius the Areopagite
Donatists
Ephraem Syrus
Epiphanius
Epistle to Diognetus
Eusebius
Firmicus Maternus
Fulgentius
Gnosticism
Gregory (1) the Great
Gregory (2) of Nazianzus
Gregory (3) of Nyssa
Gregory (4) Thaumaturgus
Hermias
Hippolytus (2)
Irenaeus
Itinerarium Egeriae
Jerome
Jerusalem
Justin Martyr
Lactantius
Leo I, the Great
Manichaeism
martyrs, Christian
Maximinus
Melito
Methodius
Minucius Felix
Montanism
Naassenes

GODS AND HEROES

Demeter
Despoina
Dike
Dione
Dionysus
Dioscuri
Eileithyia
Eirene
Eos
Erinyes
Eris
Eros
Gaia, Gē
Hades
Hebe
Helios
Hemithea
Hephaestus
Hera
Heracles
Hermes
Hermes Trismegistus
Hestia
Homonoia
Horae
Hygieia
Hyperion
Hypnos
Iacchus
Idaean Dactyls
Ino-Leucothea
Iris
Kairos
Kasios, Zeus
Kēres
Kourotrophos
Leto
Meilichios
Morpheus
Muses
Nemesis
Nike
Nyx
Oceanus
Pallas (1)
Pan
Panacea
patrōoi theoi
Peitho

Penia
Persephone/Kore
Phanes
Phēmē
Phoebus
Plutus
Poseidon
Praxidai
Priapus
Sabazius
Selene
Soter
Telesphorus
Themis
theos
tritopatreis
Tyche
Uranus
Zeus

gods, Mesopotamian
Belus
Ishtar

gods, Persian
Ahuramazda
Anahita
Mithras
Zoroaster

gods, Roman
Aeternitas
Aion
Aius Locutius
Angerona
Angitia
Anna Perenna
Bellona
Bona Dea
Bonus Eventus
Caelestis
Caprotina
Carmen arvale
Carmentis or Carmenta
Castor and Pollux, temple of
Ceres
Concordia
Consentes Di
Consus
Cupid(o)

Leucippus [1–2]
Licymnius
Linus
Lityerses
Lotus-eaters
Lycaon [1–3]
Lycurgus
Lycus
Macar
Macareus
Machaon and Podalirius
maenads
Maia [1–2]
Maron
Marsyas
Medea
Medon
Melampus (1)
Melampus (2)
Melannipus
Meleager
Melicertes
Melissa
Memnon
Menelaus
Menestheus
Menippe, in mythology
Menoeceus [1–2]
Menoetius
Menthe or Minthe
Mentor
Merope [1–2]
Messapus [1–2]
Metanira
Metis
Midas
Minos
Minyans
Minyas
Mise
Moliones
Molossus
Momos
Mopsus
Mormo
Musaeus
Mygdon
Mylitta
Myrrha or Smyrna or Zmyrna

Narcissus
Nauplius [1–2]
Nausicaa
Neleus
Neoptolemus
Nereus
Nestor
Niobe
Nireus
Nisus (1)
Nisus (2)
Ocnus
Odysseus
Oecles or Oecleus
Oedipus
Oeneus
Oenone
Ogygus
Omphale
Ophion
Orchomenus
Orestes
Orestheus
Orion
Ormenus
Orpheus
Palamedes
Palladium
Pallas (2)
Pandareos
Pandarus
Pandion
Pandora
Panthous
Paris
Parthenopaeus
Patroclus
Pegasus
Pelasgians
Pelasgus
Peleus
Pelias
Pelops
Peneleos
Penelope
Penthesilea
Pentheus
Periclymenus [1–2]
Periphetes

festivals, Roman
  Agonium
  Ambarvalia
  Argei
  Armilustrium
  Bacchanalia
  Caristia
  Divalia (Angeronalia)
  Equirria
  Feralia
  Feronia
  Fontinalia
  Fordicidia
  Fornacalia
  Hilaria
  Larentalia
  Lemuria
  Lucaria
  ludi
  Lupercalia
  Meditrinalia
  Paganalia
  Parentalia
  Parilia
  Phlegon
  Poplifugia
  Quinquatrus
  Regifugium
  Rosalia or Rosaria
  Saturnus, Saturnalia
  Secular Games
  Sigillaria
  Tubilustrium
  Vinalia

objects, religious
  animals in cult
  birds, sacred
  cakes
  colours, sacred
  fig
  fire
  fish, sacred
  honey
  incense
  ivory
  iynx
  lamps
  lead

  ointment
  olive
  phallus
  plants, sacred
  plate, precious
  relics
  silver
  snakes
  terracottas
  water

rites, general
  betrothal
  birthday
  childbirth
  cookery
  crowns and wreaths
  exile
  gestures
  household, worship of
  incubation
  libations
  marriage ceremonies
  masks
  meals, sacred
  menstruation
  milk
  miracles
  music in worship
  mysteries
  oaths
  pilgrimage (Christian)
  prayer
  processions
  proskynēsis
  rites of passage
  ritual
  ruler-cult
  transvestism, ritual
  travel
  trophies
  votive offerings
  wine (Greek and Roman)

rites, Greek
  aparchē
  dadouchos
  first-fruits
  hymns, Greek

Abaris, legendary devotee of *Apollo from the far north, a shamanistic missionary and saviour-figure like *Aristeas whom *Pindar associated with the time of Croesus—perhaps in connection with the king's miraculous rescue from the pyre and translation to the *Hyperboreans. Herodotus, ending his discussion of the latter, tantalizes by refusing to say more than that 'he carried the arrow around the whole world while fasting' (cf. the mission of *Triptolemus, and *Demeter's search for Persephone). The arrow was a token of Apolline authority, and may have been a cure for disease; later traditions have him present it to *Pythagoras, and one source described him flying on it like a witch's broomstick.

Acamas, son of *Theseus and brother of *Demophon. Unknown to the *Iliad*, the brothers are certainly present at Troy in the *Iliu Persis* (*see* EPIC CYCLE), and free their grandmother *Aethra from her servitude there. They share other adventures in the later mythological tradition; when young, they are sent to Euboea for safety, and on their return from Troy both are connected with the seizure of the *Palladium and involuntary homicide. The usual distinguishing feature of Acamas is his interest in distant places, and as the leader of colonizing settlements he is the heroic prototype for Athenian interests in Cyprus and the Chersonesus. Acamas was one of the tribal *eponymoi of Athens.

Acarnan, who gave his name to Acarnania. He was the son, with Amphoterus, of Callirhoë (the daughter of Acheloüs) and *Alcmaeon (who had settled in the Acheloüs floodplain to escape the *Erinyes). Later, when Alcmaeon was murdered by the sons of *Phegeus, Callirhoë begged *Zeus to age her sons prematurely so they might avenge their father's murder. Their vengeance exacted, Acarnan and Amphoterus gathered settlers and inhabited Acarnania.
[Apollodorus 3. 91–3]

Acastus, in mythology, son of Pelias (*see* NELEUS); he took part in the Argonautic expedition and the Calydonian boar-hunt (*see* ARGONAUTS; MELEAGER (1)). When *Peleus took refuge with him, Acastus' wife (variously named) loved him, and being repulsed, accused him to her husband of improper advances. Acastus, therefore, stole Peleus' wonderful sword and left him alone on Mt. Pelion, where he was rescued by Chiron (*see* CENTAURS). Afterwards Peleus took *Iolcus, putting to death Acastus' wife and, by some accounts, Acastus himself.
[Apollodorus 3. 164–7, 173]

Acca Larentia, obscure Roman goddess with a festival on 23 December (*Larentalia or Larentinalia). One tradition makes her a prostitute, contemporary with *Romulus, who left her property to the Roman people; another makes her wife of *Faustulus and hence adopted mother of Romulus. Cato initially made the connection of she-wolf (*lupa*) with prostitute (*meretrix*); thus the courtesan name Faula is linked with Faustulus. The long quantity of the first syllable in Larentia suggests a connection with *Larunda and not Lar (short *a*), but this is not decisive, and the Lar as family ancestor would be appropriate (*see* LARES). *Plutarch implausibly assigned her an April festival.

Acestes, character in mythology, founder and king of Segesta (Egesta) in Sicily and of Trojan descent. In *Virgil's *Aeneid* he is the son of a Trojan mother and the Sicilian river-god Crimisus, and entertains *Aeneas and his men in Sicily; Virgil in fact makes Segesta a foundation of Aeneas and not of Acestes.

[Virgil, *Aeneid* 5. 36–41, 708 ff.]

Achaeus, hero who gave his name to the Achaeans; in mythology, son of *Poseidon, *Zeus, *Xuthus, or *Haemon.

Achates, character in mythology, faithful lieutenant of *Aeneas in the *Aeneid*; a late source ascribes to him the killing of *Protesilaus.

Acheloüs, the longest of all Greek rivers, rising in central Epirus and debouching, after a course of 240 km. (149 mi.; mostly through mountainous gorges), into the north-west corner of the Corinthian Gulf. Its lower reaches were affected by heavy alluviation and constituted the frequently disputed frontier between Acarnania and Aetolia. Acheloüs was personified early as a water- and *river-god (the son of *Oceanus and *Gaia (Gē)), from whom all seas, rivers and springs derived.

[Homer, *Iliad* 21. 194–7]

Acheron, a river of Thesprotia in southern Epirus which breaks through an impenetrable gorge into the Acherusian plain where a lake (named Acherusia) lay in ancient times. The river empties into the Ionian Sea at the ancient Glycys Limen (or 'sweet harbour'). *Homer describes the Acheron as a river of *Hades into which the Cocytus and Pyriphlegethon streams flow, the place where Odysseus consulted the spirits of the Underworld. Herodotus mentions a death oracle (*Nekyomanteion) by the banks of the river where one called forth dead spirits for consultation. Traces of such an oracle have been discovered near Mesopotamo.

[Homer, *Odyssey* 10. 513, 11]

Achilles, son of *Peleus and *Thetis; greatest of the Greek heroes in the Trojan War; central character of *Homer's *Iliad*.

His name may be of Mycenaean Greek origin, meaning 'a grief to the army'. If so, the destructive Wrath of Achilles, which forms the subject of the *Iliad*, must have been central to his mythical existence from the first. He was the recipient of *hero-cults in various places, but these no doubt result from his prominence in the epic, and do nothing to explain his origins.

In Homer he is king of Phthia, or 'Hellas and Phthia', in southern Thessaly, and his people are the Myrmidons. As described in *Iliad* 2, the size of his kingdom, and of his contingent in the Trojan expedition (50 ships), is not outstanding. But in terms of martial prowess, which is the measure of excellence for a Homeric hero, Achilles' status as 'best of the Achaeans' is unquestioned. We are reminded of his absolute supremacy throughout the poem, even during those long stretches for which he is absent from the battlefield.

His character is complex. In many ways he carries the savage ethical code of the Homeric hero to its ultimate and terrifying conclusion. When *Agamemnon steals his concubine *Briseis in *Iliad* 1, his anger at the insult to his personal honour is natural and approved by gods and men; but he carries this anger beyond any normal limit when he refuses an offer of immense compensation in *Iliad* 9. Again, when he finally re-enters the war (*Iliad* 19) after the death of his friend *Patroclus, his ruthless massacre of Trojans, culminating in the killing of *Hector (*Iliad* 22), expresses a 'heroic' desire for revenge; but this too is taken beyond normal bounds by his contemptuous maltreatment of Hector's dead body.

But what makes Achilles remarkable is the way in which his extreme expression of the 'heroic code' is combined with a unique degree of insight and self-knowledge. Unlike

Hector, for instance, Achilles knows well that he is soon to die. In his great speech at *Iliad* 9 he calls the entire code into question, saying that he would rather live quietly at home than pursue glory in the Trojan War; but it is his 'heroic' rage against Agamemnon that has brought him to this point. In his encounter with Lycaon, his sense of common mortality (the fact that Patroclus has died and Achilles himself will die) is a reason, not for sparing his suppliant, but for killing him in cold blood. Finally at *Iliad* 24, when *Priam begs him to release Hector's body, it is human feeling, as well as the gods' command, that makes him yield; but even then he accepts a ransom, and his anger still threatens to break out afresh.

Later writers seldom treated the subject-matter of the *Iliad* (though *Aeschylus did so, portraying Achilles and Patroclus as lovers). But they did provide many further details of Achilles' career, often derived from cyclic epics (*see* EPIC CYCLE) such as the *Cypria* and *Aethiopis*. As a boy he was brought up by the wise *centaur Chiron on Mt. Pelion. Later his mother Thetis, knowing that he would be killed if he joined the expedition to Troy, hid him at the court of King Lycomedes on Scyros, disguised as a girl. There he fell in love with the king's daughter Deidamia, who bore him a son, *Neoptolemus, *Odysseus discovered his identity by trickery and he joined the Greek army at *Aulis, where he was involved in the story of *Iphigenia (see *Euripides' *Iphigenia at Aulis*). On the way to Troy he wounded *Telephus. His exploits at Troy included the ambush and killing of Priam's son *Troilus, a story linked with that of his love for Priam's daughter *Polyxena. After the events of the *Iliad* he killed two allies of the Trojans: the *Amazon queen *Penthesilea, with whom he is also said to have fallen in love, and the Ethiopian king *Memnon. Finally he was himself killed by *Paris and *Apollo (as predicted at *Iliad* 22). The fight over his body, and his funeral, are described in a dubious passage of the *Odyssey*. His famous arms (described at *Iliad* 18) were

then given to Odysseus. After the fall of Troy his ghost demanded the sacrifice of Polyxena. A curious story, going back to Ibycus, is that in *Elysium he married *Medea. Several of these episodes, including the ambush of Troilus and the killing of Penthesilea, were popular with vase painters.

A late addition is the familiar motif of Achilles' heel: Thetis sought to make the infant Achilles invulnerable by dipping him in the *Styx, but omitted to dip the heel by which she held him, and it was there that he received his death-wound. This is alluded to by *Hyginus and Statius, but we have no full account until late antiquity.

[Homer, *Iliad*, *Odyssey* 24. 36–94; Sophocles, *Ajax*; Euripides, *Iphigenia at Aulis*, *Hecuba*; Apollodorus, *Epitome* 5. 3–5; Statius, *Achilleis*]

Acrisius, in mythology, son of Abas, king of Argos, and his wife Aglaïa, father of *Danaë and brother of *Proetus. After Abas' death the two brothers quarrelled; in their warfare they invented the shield. Proetus, defeated, left the country, returned with troops furnished by his father-in-law Iobates, and agreed to leave Argos to Acrisius, himself taking Tiryns; both were fortified by the *Cyclopes. *See* PERSEUS.

Actaeon, in mythology son of *Aristaeus and Autonoë, daughter of *Cadmus, and a great huntsman. Ovid gives the most familiar version of his death: one day on Mt. Cithaeron he came inadvertently upon *Artemis bathing, whereupon the offended goddess turned him into a stag and he was torn apart by his own hounds. Other (older) versions of his offence were that he was *Zeus' rival with *Semele, or that he boasted that he was a better huntsman than Artemis, or that he wished to marry Artemis. After his death his hounds hunted for him in vain, howling in grief, until the *Centaur Chiron made a lifelike image of him to soothe them.

Actaeon torn by hounds is found in many works of art from the 6th cent. In earlier pictures he sometimes wears a deerskin (as apparently in *Stesichorus), but the first vases on which he sprouts antlers are after the middle of the 5th cent. Artemis surprised bathing appears first in Pompeian paintings.

[Ovid, *Metamorphoses* 3. 138 ff.]

Acts of the Apostles The second of two volumes which continues the story of the rise and spread of *Christianity begun in the gospel of Luke. Its textual history poses peculiar interpretative problems as it is extant in two versions. Its narrative starts with Jesus' ascension in *Jerusalem and ends with *Paul preaching in Rome, where he had been taken after his appeal to Caesar (i.e. the emperor). The focus of the material on the earliest Jerusalem church around Peter and, later in the book, on the Christian career of Paul shows the concern of the author to relate the Jewish and Gentile missions and to demonstrate their basic unity. Only occasional glimpses are offered of the conflict in early Christianity which is evident in the Pauline corpus. Acts has for a long time been a cause of great controversy between those who maintain the substantial authenticity of its historical account (while allowing for its apologetic interests) and those who see the document as a work of skilful narrative propaganda whose historical value is negligible. Knowledge of contemporary Graeco-Roman institutions should not mask the difficulties in accepting the historicity of Acts, a particular problem being the reconciliation of the accounts of Paul's career in Acts, Galatians 1–2, and the Corinthian correspondence. The references to Paul's theology indicate a markedly different set of ideas from what we find in the letters to the Romans and Galatians. For this and other reasons Acts has proved to be disappointing to the historian of Christian origins as a source for early Christian history. The history of the Jerusalem church after the start of the Pauline mission is only touched on in so far as it helps the author explain Paul's career as apostle to the Gentiles. Whereas Luke's gospel portrays Jesus as a Palestinian prophet with a controversial, indeed subversive, message for Jewish

society, there is little in Acts (apart from the idealized accounts of the common life of the Jerusalem church) of that radicalism. The antagonism to Jews and the sympathetic account of Roman officials evident in the gospel of Luke is continued in Acts, and a conciliatory attitude towards Rome has been suggested. Jews in Acts are regarded as responsible for the harassment of nascent Christianity, though there are occasional glimpses of more openness to Judaism elsewhere in the book than the concluding verses would indicate.

Various suggestions have been made with regard to its (and the related gospel of Luke's) purpose. These have included an apologia for Christianity to the Roman state, an explanation for the delay of the Second Coming by stressing the role of the church in the divine purpose, an essay in anti-Jewish polemic, and a defence of Paul when his case was heard in Rome. Like his contemporary Josephus the author of Acts seeks to demonstrate that divine providence is at work, though for the latter there is nothing in the emergence of a strange Jewish messianic movement to contradict the Jewish tradition, since it is rather the inevitable continuation of it.

Acts of the Pagan Martyrs is the name given by modern scholars to about a dozen fragments of Alexandrian nationalist literature, preserved on papyri mostly written in the 2nd or early 3rd cent. AD. The majority of the fragments give, in dramatic form, reports of the hearing of Alexandrian embassies and of the trials of Alexandrian nationalist leaders before various Roman emperors. The episodes related, of which the dramatic dates range from the time of *Augustus to that of Commodus, are probably basically historical and the accounts appear to be derived to some extent from official records. But they have been coloured up, more in some cases than in others, for propaganda purposes, to caricature the emperors, to stress the fearless outspokenness of the Alexandrians, who are sometimes surprisingly rude to the emperors, and to represent their punishment, usually execution, as martyrdom in the nationalist cause. This literature is in general bitterly hostile to Rome, reflecting the tensions between Alexandria and her overlord during the first two centuries of Roman rule. These included antagonism between the Greeks and Rome's protégés, the Jews, and three episodes concern their quarrels. But despite the violent hatred expressed by the Greeks for the Jews, anti-*Semitism is only a subsidiary feature in these primarily anti-Roman compositions.

Acusilaus, of Argos, according to Josephus lived 'before the Persian Wars' (490–479 BC) and compiled *genealogies, translating and correcting *Hesiod, with ingenious conjectures but no literary merit.

Admetus *See* ALCESTIS.

Adonis Name given by the Greeks to a divine personage whom they thought to be eastern in origin (Semitic *Adon* = 'Lord'), but whose eastern prototypes (Dumuzi, Tammuz, Baal, Ešmun) are very different from the picture which became established in Greece. In mythology, Adonis is born from the incest of an easterner, whose name is variously given as Agenor, Cinyras, Phoenix, and Theias, and of Myrrha or Smyrna. He aroused the love of *Aphrodite, who hid him in a chest and entrusted him to *Persephone, but she, captivated in her turn, refused to give him back. Then *Zeus decreed that the young man should spend four months of the year in the Underworld (*see* HADES) and four months with Aphrodite—whom Adonis chose also for the final four months, left to his own decision. He was born from a myrrh tree, and dying young in a hunting accident, was changed into an anemone, a flower without scent. A festival for the young god, known as Adonia, is attested only at Athens, Alexandria, and Byblos. In 5th cent. BC Athens, women sowed seed at midsummer in broken pots and placed these on the roof-tops, so that germination was rapidly followed by withering. In this lively, noisy celebration, which has been brought into opposition with the *Thesmophoria, mourning is secondary; at Byblos, the ritual involves the whole population, expressing at two different times mourning and laments, and resurrection and joy, but there is no trace of the 'gardens of Adonis'. The festival at Alexandria, like that of Athens, presents a picture of a women's ritual including mourning, but above all rejoicing centred on the couple, Aphrodite and Adonis.

Starting from a vast comparative study, Sir James Frazer saw in Adonis an image of the succession of the seasons and of agricultural tasks, a sort of 'vegetation spirit'. Marcel Detienne, on the other hand, uses a structural analysis to demonstrate that the Greek picture of Adonis, far from being a divinization of agriculture, suggests rather the impermanent, the fragile, and the barren. Aphrodite's young lover has thus inspired a lively debate, and is still the focus of methodological problems, notably those centred on the Greek interpretation of eastern data.

[Apollodorus 3. 14. 3–4; Ovid, *Metamorphoses* 10. 300–559, 708–39; Aristophanes, *Lysistrata* 708–39; Theocritus, *Idylls* 15]

Adrastus, described in the *Iliad* as former king of Sicyon, was worshipped there at least until the 6th cent. Best known as the leader of the first Argive expedition against Thebes (and possibly the second as well), he was the only one to survive, escaping on the semi-divine horse *Arion. He had undertaken the expedition to restore one son-in-law, Polynices, to the throne, and was to have done the same for the other, *Tydeus of Calydon.

The tradition which made Adrastus king at Argos may owe something to the interpolation of a patrilineal descendant into a matrilineal regal line. His connections with cult sites other than Sicyon (Colonos Hippios, *Eleusis, Megara) derive from the influence of the epic.

Some have sought a Mycenaean origin for the Theban wars. The motif of 'seven' aggressors is found in near eastern sources. There is no canonical list of champions (*Homer names only Adrastus, *Amphiaraus, *Capaneus, Tydeus, possibly Mecisteus): perhaps the tradition of '*Seven against Thebes' was concocted to match the seven gates of Boeotian Thebes (as opposed to Egyptian, 100-gated, Thebes). The story was certainly well known to Homer's audience, and Tyrtaeus alludes to Adrastus' eloquence as a byword. The predominant role of Argos, the absence of a Corinthian champion, and the refusal of the Mycenaeans to participate suggest that the tradition developed after the Mycenaean period and before the rise of Corinth, but after that of Argos.

Aeacus, ancestral hero of Aegina, whose eponymous nymph bore him to *Zeus; to give him company, Zeus turned the island's ant population into humans, transforming murmēkes into 'Myrmidons'. As a primeval figure, he was naturally close to the gods, and unlike e.g. *Tantalus or *Ixion he retained their favour; according to *Pindar (a sedulous propagator of Aeginetan legends) he helped *Apollo and *Poseidon build the walls of *Laomedon's Troy and even settled disputes between the gods themselves. Famous for his justice and piety in life, he became a judge in the Underworld. He was the founder of the warrior clan of the Aeacidae: his sons *Peleus and *Telamon, exiled for the murder of their brother *Phocus, fathered *Achilles and Ajax (see AIAS (1)) respectively.

[Ovid, *Metamorphoses* 7. 517–660; Pindar, *Olympian Odes* 8]

aedituus (older form, **aeditumnus**), the keeper or sacristan of a consecrated building in Rome (*aedes sacra*). The word was applied to a wide range of officials, including both men of high rank charged with control of the building and those who carried out the lowly tasks of cleaning, etc.

Aëdon, in mythology, daughter of *Pandareos, the son of Hermes and Merope. She married Zethus and had two children, Itylus and Neïs. Envying *Niobe, Amphion's wife, for her many children, she planned to kill them, or one of them, at night; but Itylus was sleeping in the same room as they and she mistook the bed and so killed him. In her grief she prayed to be changed from human form, and became a nightingale (*aēdōn*).

Aegeus, Athenian hero, father of *Theseus. As son of *Pandion and brother of *Pallas (2), *Nisus (1), and *Lycus, he received at the division of Attica the area around Athens, although on one Attic vase his place is taken by Orneus, indicating that he may be a latecomer in this group. When king of Athens, he consulted the *Delphic oracle about his childlessness, but failing to understand the reply (a figurative injunction to abstain from sex until his return home) fathered Theseus on *Aethra, daughter of Pittheus, king of Troezen. Later he married *Medea, who attempted to poison Theseus on his arrival in Athens, and was therefore driven out by him. When Theseus returned from Crete, he or his steersman forgot to raise the agreed sign on the ship, and Aegeus, thinking his son was dead, threw himself off the acropolis or into the sea (in this version called 'Aegean' after him).

Aegeus had a sanctuary in Athens, and was connected with the cults of both Apollo Delphinius and Aphrodite Urania; he was also one of the tribal *eponymoi. But his popularity in the 5th cent. was largely due to his position as father of Theseus. He was the subject of (now lost) tragedies by *Sophocles and *Euripides, as well as appearing in the latter's *Medea,* and of a comedy by Philyllius.

Aegimius, a legendary king, son (or father, in one source) of Dorus, who gave his name to the Dorians. Being attacked by the *Centaurs, he asked *Heracles to help him, and in gratitude for his aid adopted *Hyllus and made him joint heir with his own sons.

aegis, divine attribute, represented as a large all-round bib with scales, fringed with snakes' heads and normally decorated with the *gorgoneion* (*see* GORGO). In Homer *Zeus' epithet *aigiochos*, and the story that the aegis was given to him by *Hephaestus suggest a primary association with Zeus, who lends it to *Apollo. It is unclear whether *Athena's aegis is also borrowed. In post-Homeric times the aegis is most closely associated with Athena, who is commonly shown wearing it over her dress; Zeus is very rarely shown with the aegis. The aegis is ageless and immortal, with a hundred tassels; its tasselled nature is reflected in its epithet *thysanoessa*. It is decorated with the Gorgon's head and the allegorical figures Phobos (Fear), Eris (Strife), Alke (Strength), and Ioke (Pursuit). Its shaking by Zeus or Apollo brings victory to the side the god supports and fear to its enemies. It protects from attack; not even Zeus' thunderbolt can overpower it. In later versions Aegis was a monster killed by Athena who then wore its skin, or the aegis was the skin of *Amalthea, the goat that had suckled Zeus, which Zeus used in the Battle of the *Titans. Herodotus argued that Athena's dress and aegis imitated the goatskin garments of Libyan women. Starting with Alexander the Great, the aegis became an element in the iconography of Hellenistic rulers and then of Roman emperors. In Athens there was probably a sacred aegis, a cult object carried by the priestess of Athena on certain ritual occasions.

[Homer, *Iliad* 2. 446–9, 5. 736–42, 15. 304–22, 17. 593–6; Diodorus Siculus 3. 70. 3–5]

Aegisthus, in mythology the son of Thyestes who survives to avenge the deaths of his brothers at the hands of *Atreus. In Aeschylus he is only a baby when Atreus kills the other boys, and perhaps for this reason survives. A version apparently Sophoclean makes him the incestuous offspring of Thyestes and his daughter Pelopia after the murder of the elder sons; an oracle had advised that a son thus born would avenge their deaths. In connection with this story, it was said that the baby Aegisthus (his name suggesting the word *aix*, goat) was exposed and fed by a she-goat. When he grew up he

learnt the truth, and avenged the murder of his brothers by killing Atreus and later, with *Clytemnestra, *Agamemnon. All this is post-Homeric: in the *Iliad* there is harmony between the brothers Atreus and Thyestes, and in the *Odyssey* Aegisthus is a baron with an estate near the domains of Agamemnon, and no reason is given for Agamemnon's murder except Aegisthus' relationship with Clytemnestra, whom he had seduced despite a warning from the gods. In all versions Aegisthus rules the kingdom securely for some years after Agamemnon's death, until he in his turn is killed in revenge by Agamemnon's son, *Orestes. By Clytemnestra, Aegisthus had a daughter, *Erigone.

The death of Aegisthus is a favourite subject in Archaic and Classical art.

[Homer, *Iliad* 1. 29–43, 2. 100–8, 3. 249–75, 4. 524–37; Aeschylus, *Agamemnon* 1583–1606]

Aegyptus *See* DANAUS

Aeneas, character in literature and mythology, son of *Anchises and the goddess Aphrodite. In the *Iliad* he is a prominent Trojan leader, belonging to the younger branch of the royal house, and has important duels with *Diomedes (2) and *Achilles, from both of which he is rescued by divine intervention. His piety towards the gods is stressed, and *Poseidon prophesies that he and his children will rule over the Trojans.

This future beyond the *Iliad* is reflected in the version in the lost cyclic *Iliu Persis* (*see* EPIC CYCLE) that Aeneas and his family left Troy before its fall to retreat to Mt. Ida, which led later to accusations of his treachery. The departure of Aeneas from Troy is widely recorded, and the image of Aeneas' pious carrying of his father *Anchises on his shoulders in the retreat is common in Greek vases of the 6th cent. BC found in Etruria, and occurs in 5th- and 4th-cent. Attic literature. The further story of Aeneas' voyage to Italy may have existed as early as the 6th or 5th cent. BC, but seems well established by the 3rd cent. Following recent excavations at *Lavinium, claims have been made for *hero-cult of Aeneas there as early as the

4th cent. BC, but these must remain unproven; it is not easy to link this with other attestations of cult for Aeneas as Jupiter Indiges.

See also GENEALOGICAL TABLES (6) HOUSE OF ROME.

The list of Aeneas' westward wanderings towards Italy is already long and contradictory by the 1st cent. BC, including cities and cults supposedly named after him in Thrace, Chalcidice, Epirus, and Sicily, and visits to Delos and Crete. A visit to Carthage, possibly involving a meeting with *Dido, is certainly part of the itinerary by the time of the Latin epic by Naevius' *Bellum Punicum* (3rd cent. BC), where it is seen as an ancestral cause of the enmity between Rome and Carthage. As Rome confronted a Greek-speaking Mediterranean world in the 3rd cent. BC, it found it politically and culturally useful to claim as its founder Aeneas, famous through his appearance in Homer but also an enemy of the Greeks; a particular stimulus was the invasion of Italy by king Pyrrhus of Epirus (280 BC), who claimed descent from Achilles and saw Rome as a second Troy. In consequence, Roman poets (e.g. Ennius), historians (e.g. Cato), and antiquarians (e.g. Varro) stressed the Trojan origins of Rome; considerations of chronology eventually led to the view that Aeneas founded not Rome but a preceding city, Lavinium, and that Rome's eponymous founder *Romulus was his distant descendant.

*Virgil's version of the Aeneas-legend in the *Aeneid* aims at literary coherence rather than antiquarian accuracy. Aeneas' wanderings, apart from the stay at Carthage, are compressed into a single book (*Aeneid* 3); his war in Latium is the subject of the second half of the poem, and he appears there and at other times to have some typological link with *Augustus, who claimed him as ancestor. The Virgilian Aeneas' central traits of *pietas* and martial courage continue his Homeric character, but he is also a projection of the ideal patriotic Roman, subordinating personal goals to national interest. And yet he never renounces his human vulnerability; he is in despair in his first appearance in the poem, he is deeply affected by love for Dido, and the poem ends not with his triumphant apotheosis, anticipated earlier, but with his emotional killing of Turnus in a moment of passion.

The success of the *Aeneid* meant that few innovations were made in the Aeneas-legend by later writers; subsequent Aeneas-narratives are clearly crafted from existing materials, principally Virgil.

[Homer, *Iliad* 5. 239 ff.; 13. 460–1, 20. 153 ff., 179–83, 230–41, 298–9, 307–8, 347–8; Dionysius of Halicarnassus 1. 44–64; Livy 1. 1–2; Virgil, *Aeneid*; Ovid, *Metamorphoses* 13. 623–14. 608]

Aeolus, (1) the Homeric ruler of the winds. Unlike Virgil, Homer makes him a human by suppressing the idea that winds are minor deities (*see* WIND-GODS). He lives in Aeolia, a floating island, in the furthest west. His six sons and six daughters have married one another. Already the 5th cent. found this incest intolerable: *Euripides (*Aeolus*) made Aeolus force his daughter *Canace to commit suicide because of her love for her brother *Macareus; Ovid paints the drama in shrill colours. In Hellenistic times he was worshipped by the Liparaeans.

[Homer, *Odyssey* 10. 1–79; Virgil, *Aeneid* 1; Ovid, *Heroides* 11]

(2) The son of *Hellen and *eponym of the Aeolians occurs first in *Hesiod but is clearly presupposed by *Homer. His original home is the north of Greece, where many of his descendants are located. (3) Son of *Poseidon and Melanippe, who is exposed together with his brother Boeotus. Their fate is the subject of Euripides' *Melanippe Desmotis* and *Melanippe Sophe*. Confusion between the various Aeoli arose early and they were accommodated into one genealogical scheme by Diodorus Siculus.

Aepytus Name of three Arcadian heroes. (1) Aepytus son of Hippothoüs entered the innermost sanctuary of *Poseidon at Mantinea, and was blinded and killed by the god. (2) Youngest grandson of (1), Aepytus son of Cresphontes, king of Messenia, was exiled when his father and brother were murdered, but returned to avenge them and take power. (3) Aepytus son of Elatus reigned over Arcadia and was buried at the foot of Mt. Cyllene.

Aerope, daughter of *Catreus, king of Crete, and given by her father to *Nauplius (2) to be sold overseas. She married *Atreus (or, in some versions, Pleisthenes) and gave birth to *Agamemnon and *Menelaus. While married to Atreus, she committed adultery with his brother Thyestes, to whom she secretly gave the golden lamb which allowed him to claim the throne. But *Zeus expressed disapproval by reversing the course of the sun.

[Euripides, *Electra* 699–746; Apollodorus, *Epitome* 2. 10–12]

Aeschylus, Athenian tragic dramatist (?525/4–456/5 BC), whose plays include influential reworkings of myths. Aeschylus, like all truly tragic writers, is well aware of, and vividly presents, the terrible suffering, often hard to justify in human terms, of which life is full; nevertheless he also believes strongly in the ultimate justice of the gods. In his surviving work (leaving aside *Prometheus*), all human suffering is clearly traceable, directly or indirectly, to an origin in some evil or foolish action—Xerxes' ill-advised decision to attempt the conquest of Greece; Laius' defiance of an oracular warning to remain childless; the attempt by the sons of Aegyptus to force the *Danaids to be their wives; the adultery of *Thyestes with Atreus' wife; the abduction of *Helen by *Paris. The consequences of these actions, however, while always bringing disaster to the actors, never end with them, but spread to involve their descendants and ultimately a whole community; some of these indirect victims have incurred more or less guilt on their own account, but many are completely innocent. In some of Aeschylus' dramas, like *Persians* or the Theban trilogy, the action descends steadily towards a nadir of misery at the end. In the *Oresteia*, however, presumably also in the Odyssean trilogy, and not

improbably in the Danaid trilogy, it proves to be possible to draw a line under the record of suffering and reach a settlement that promises a better future; each time a key element in the final stages is the substitution of persuasion for violence, as when in the *Oresteia* a chain of retaliatory murders is ended by the judicial trial of *Orestes, and the spirits of violent revenge, the *Erinyes, are persuaded to accept an honoured dwelling in Athens.

In dramas of the darker type described above, the gods are stern and implacable, and mortals often find themselves helpless prisoners of their own or others' past decisions; though they may still have considerable freedom to choose how to face their fate (compare the clear-sighted courage of Pelasgus or Cassandra with Xerxes or Agamemnon). Elsewhere, especially perhaps in Aeschylus' latest work, a different concept of divinity may appear. In the *Oresteia* ethical advance on earth, as the virtuous Electra and an Orestes with no base motive succeed the myopic Agamemnon and the monstrous Clytemnestra, is presently answered by ethical advance on Olympus as the amoral gods of *Agamemnon* and *Choephori* turn in *Eumenides* into responsible and even loving protectors of deserving mortals. Something similar may well have happened in the Prometheus plays.

Aesculapius The miraculous transferral of the god of healing *Asclepius from *Epidaurus to Rome and the origin of the important healing-cult of the Tiber island there in 291 BC constituted significant moments in Roman narratives of the history of their religion (Ovid made it his final metamorphosis); the summoning of a prestigious god from Greece, in accordance with the Sibylline Books (*see* SIBYL) and perhaps after a consultation of the *Delphic oracle, to remedy a Roman crisis (pestilence), represented a stage in the domestication of external religion and acted as a prototype for the closely related tale of the summoning of the Mater Magna in 204 BC (*see* CYBELE).

In fact the cult was becoming widely diffused at that time everywhere (even our Rome-centred stories preserve some consciousness of the contemporary importance of the cult at nearby Antium). The therapeutic tradition on the island is well attested, and survived to the point where it could be transferred to the tutelage of St Bartholomew, whose hospital there still functions. By the imperial period, in Italy and the provinces, a Roman cult is hard to disentangle from the very popular and varied combinations of healing deities blending local cults with a broadly Asclepian tradition.

[Ovid, *Metamorphoses* 15. 622–745]

Aesepus, god of the Mysian river of that name. *See* RIVER-GODS.

Aesop, as legendary a figure as Homer. What we now call *fables, i.e. stories clearly fictitious (often about speaking animals), which illustrate a point or support an argument, are first alluded to by *Hesiod. Herodotus places him in the 6th cent. BC as the slave of Iadmon, a Samian later murdered by Delphians; the legend suggests a ritual scapegoat (*pharmakos*).

A biography, serving as a context for the fables he told, may have existed already in the 5th cent., but the extant biography, written no earlier than the Roman empire, is a romance on these themes. Beginning with a miracle (*Isis grants him speech, the *Muses give him inspiration in storytelling) and concluding with a martyr's death (Delphic priests kill him because he denounces their greed), it is largely a repository of slave-savant anecdotes about Aesop and his hapless Samian master, the 'philosopher' Xanthus, followed by Aesop's career as adviser to Croesus and the king of Babylon.

Aeternitas The notion of *aeternitas*, designating perpetuity or eternity, first appears at Rome in *Cicero's day, under the influence of philosophic speculation (notably that of *Stoicism) on *aiōn* (eternity). From the beginning of the 1st cent. AD, *aeternitas* became an imperial virtue, advertising both the perpetual glory of the ruler and his power, parallel to the *aeternitas populi Romani*, and a promise of immortality. Assuming the iconography of the *Aion of Alexandria, 'Aeternitas Augusta' or 'Augusti' appears on coins and, in 66, Aeternitas even received a sacrifice after the discovery of a plot against Nero. Aeternitas is usually depicted as a veiled woman holding sceptre, globe, and phoenix, or the sun and moon (referring to eternity). But Aeternitas can also be associated with male figures.

Aëtes, father of *Medea, who deceitfully promised *Jason the Golden Fleece.

Aethra, in mythology daughter of *Pittheus, king of Troezen, and mother of *Theseus by *Aegeus. Since Theseus was often said to be son of *Poseidon, various explanations were given: Aethra was sent by *Athena (hence called Apaturia, 'the Deceitful') to the island of Hiera or Sphaeria, where Poseidon came to her; Poseidon visited her the same night as Aegeus; it was a tale invented by Pittheus to save her reputation. In the *Iliad* she is mentioned as waiting-maid to *Helen; a story as old as the *Epic Cycle and illustrated on the chest of Cypselus. Some said that she was carried off by the *Dioscuri when they came to rescue Helen from her abduction by Theseus. Her grandsons, *Demophon (1) and *Acamas, took her home when Troy fell.

Aethra is depicted in various scenes in art from the 6th cent. BC on: she is pursued by Poseidon, rescued from Troy by her grandsons, and, in a scene unknown to surviving literature, threatened by Theseus with a sword.

Aetolian cults and myths Relatively isolated, after the Archaic period Aetolia had the reputation of a rough and violent region. In cult the massive conflagration of live birds and wild animals for Artemis Laphria at Patrae (originally at Calydon) has seemed to characterize Aetolian barbarism. But archaeological evidence permits a more temperate assessment. Aetolian religion had, none the less, some distinctive, conservative features. *Artemis is a great goddess, with exceptionally comprehensive concerns, including human and natural fertility, while her male partner, usually *Apollo, is a lesser figure. This has been taken to be a continuation of a bronze age pattern. There are important early temples in pairs, a larger one usually for the goddess and a smaller one for her companion, at Calydon, Taxiarchis (the modern site name), Callipolis, and *Thermum, where alone Apollo is more prominent. At Calydon *Dionysus is associated with this pair, and he is important in local myth. *Zeus is relatively insignificant, *Poseidon unknown. Other figures are mostly female and can be seen as forms of the region's great goddess.

In myth, *Aetolus, the *eponymous ancestor of the people, and the family of *Oeneus, Althaea, *Meleager (who killed the Calydonian boar), and *Deianira, are prominent. Stories of *Heracles have him taming savage nature.

Aetolus, who gave his name to the Aetolians. *Endymion, king of Elis, had three sons: Paeon, Epeius, and Aetolus. He set them to race at Olympia, promising the kingship to the winner. Epeius won, hence the ancient name Epeii for the people of the district. Paeon left the country and gave his name to the district of Paeonia. When Aetolus was forced to leave Elis because of a blood-feud, he went to the country of the *Curetes and gained control of the region which thereafter took his name.

after-life See ART, FUNERARY, GREEK and ROMAN; DEATH, ATTITUDES TO; ELYSIUM; HADES; ISLANDS OF THE BLEST; ORPHISM; TARTARUS; TRANSMIGRATION.

Agamemnon, in mythology son of *Atreus (or, occasionally, of Atreus' son Pleisthenes), brother of *Menelaus, and husband of *Clytemnestra; king of Mycenae, or Argos, and, in Homer, commander-in-chief of the Greek expedition against Troy, taking with him 100 ships, the largest single contingent. He had a son, *Orestes, and three daughters,

Chrysothemis, Laodice, Iphianassa; *Iphigenia, whom Homer does not mention, seems to be a later substitution for Iphianassa, as does *Electra (3) for Laodice.

See also GENEALOGICAL TABLES (5) DESCENDANTS OF TANTALUS.

Homer depicts Agamemnon as a man of personal valour, but lacking resolution and easily discouraged. His quarrel with *Achilles, who withdrew in anger and hurt pride from battle when Agamemnon took away his concubine *Briseis, supplies the mainspring of the *Iliad*'s action, with Achilles' refusal to fight leading to tragedy. The *Odyssey* tells how, on Agamemnon's return home, *Aegisthus, Clytemnestra's lover, treacherously set on him and his men at a banquet and killed them all, Clytemnestra also killing his Trojan captive *Cassandra, daughter of *Priam. Eight years later Orestes came from Athens and avenged his father's murder. This whole story became a favourite one among later authors, who retold it with various elaborations and changes. Aeschylus, for instance, makes Clytemnestra a powerful and awe-inspiring female who, quite alone, kills Agamemnon after she has pinioned him in a robe while he is unarmed in his bath.

The *Cypria* (see EPIC CYCLE) is the earliest evidence of the sacrifice of Agamemnon's daughter Iphigenia. Agamemnon caught a stag, then boasted that he was a better huntsman than *Artemis, whereupon the offended goddess held the Greek fleet wind-bound at Aulis. *Calchas told them to appease her by sacrificing Iphigenia, whom they sent for on the pretext of marriage to Achilles. Here the guilt for the killing seems to be laid on the Greeks in general; moreover Iphigenia was snatched away and made immortal by Artemis, who left a deer on the altar in her place. But again matters are very different in Aeschylus, where Iphigenia is simply a child, dead, and Agamemnon himself her killer, for which Clytemnestra never forgave him.

In historic times Agamemnon had a cult in Laconia (see SPARTAN CULTS), Tarentum,

Clazomenae, Chaeronea, and Mycenae. Agamemnon appears occasionally in art from the 7th cent. BC in a variety of scenes, mostly relating to the war at Troy.

[Homer, *Iliad*; *Odyssey* 1. 35 ff., 1. 304 ff., 4. 512 ff., 11. 405 ff., 24. 96 f.; Aeschylus, *Agamemnon*; Euripides, *Iphigenia at Aulis*]

Aganippe, in mythology, daughter of the *river-god Permessus, nymph of the spring of that name on Mt. *Helicon, sacred to the *Muses.

Agapenor, in mythology, leader of the Arcadian contingent against Troy; son of *Ancaeus. On the way back from Troy he arrived at Cyprus, where he founded Paphos and a temple of *Aphrodite and settled there.

Agathos Daimon, 'good god/destiny/fortune'. He is particularly closely associated with the proper use of *wine (cf. modern toasts such as 'cheers', 'good luck'): he received small libations of unmixed wine after meals, and in Boeotia sacrifice was made to him before the new vintage was broached. But the idea expressed in his name could also be understood more broadly, as is clear from the later-attested practice of dedicating houses and small temples to him, often in association with Agathe Tyche (Good Luck); like other protective figures he was sometimes represented as a *snake. His role as a protector of houses became particularly prominent in Greek Egypt.

Agdistis, a form of the Phrygian mothergoddess; at *Pessinus*Cybele was called Agdistis. According to the myth (*see* ATTIS), she was originally androgynous. Her cult spread to various parts of Anatolia, to Egypt (by 250 BC), to Attica (with that of Attis in Piraeus 4th–3rd, cents.; at Rhamnus, 83/2 BC), Lesbos, and Panticapeum. At Lydian Philadelphia her private shrine (1st cent. BC) enforced a strict moral code. There and elsewhere Agdistis appears with *theoi sōtēres* (saviour gods). *See* ANATOLIAN DEITIES.

Agenor, Phoenician king. When his daughter, *Europa, disappeared, he sent his sons—*Phoenix (1), Cilix, and *Cadmus—to find her. They failed (*Zeus having abducted her to Crete), but founded respectively the Phoenician and Cilician peoples and Boeotian Thebes.

[Apollodorus 3. 1. 1]

Aglaurus Daughter of the Athenian king *Cecrops, Aglaurus makes her best-known appearance in myth and art alongside *Pandrosus and Herse; disobeying *Athena's instructions, the sisters opened the chest where the child *Erichthonius was kept, and what they saw caused them to hurl themselves off the Acropolis to their deaths. But there are clear signs that Aglaurus' origins are separate from her sisters. She had an independent sanctuary at the east end of the Acropolis, and unlike Pandrosus she was linked more closely with adolescents and young fighters than with babies. Her divine connections cover both *Ares, by whom she had a daughter Alcippe (*see* HALIRRHOTHIUS), and Athena, being associated especially with the goddess's festival, the *Plynteria.

agōnes (1) The term *agōn* and its derivatives can denote the informal and extempore competitive struggles and rivalries that permeated Greek life in the general fight for success and survival.

(2) Gatherings of people, usually for formal contests in honour of a god or local hero.

Before 300 BC Prior to the 8th cent. BC they seem to have been small-scale events, centring round a shrine or sanctuary. But the *agōn* at *Olympia came to acquire a special status: traditionally founded in 776 BC, by the end of the 8th cent. it was, because of the wide range of *athletics contests it offered and its lack of political ties, attracting increasing numbers of foreigners (especially from among the athletic Spartans) and was organized as a Panhellenic *agōn* (*see* OLYMPIAN GAMES). With interstate relationships assuming increased importance during the 7th cent., local *agōnes* were reorganized at other places too. The *Pythian Games became Panhellenic in 582 BC; its range of athletics events followed the Olympian model, but it preserved its identity and associations with *Apollo through its emphasis on musical competitions. With the reorganization of the *Isthmian (*c.*581) and *Nemean Games (*c.*573), a group of four Panhellenic *agōnes* came to form an athletics circuit (*periodos*), as the Olympics, World Championships, European, and Commonwealth Games do for some athletes nowadays. At Athens the Great *Panathenaea (founded 566) was also Panhellenic, but for athletes never achieved the status of the other four. Despite this development, local *agōnes* with athletics contests continued to flourish: *Pindar's victory-odes mention more than 20 local games, and a 5th-cent. Laconian inscription records 72 victories won by Damonon and his son Enymacratidas at eight *agōnes* in the Peloponnese.

Contests were often in athletics, but music, poetry, and equestrian events were also popular. *Hesiod won a poetry-singing competition in Chalcis; the Pythian Games included three types of musical contest (singing to the accompaniment of cithara or aulos, and solo aulos) and a painting competition. In Athens *tragedies, comedies, and *dithyrambs (choral songs) were performed in competitions at the City *Dionysia, and at the Panathenaea *rhapsodes competed in Homer-reciting contests. *Horse- and chariot-races were mainly entered by wealthy individuals who paid charioteers or jockeys to ride on their behalf, and hoped for political prestige from good performances. The chariot-race was often long (about 14 km. (nearly 9 mi.) at the Olympian Games) and dangerous (according to Pindar, one victor was the only one of 40 starters to finish with chariot intact). Beauty contests, drinking contests, and even a wool-carding contest are also recorded.

At the four major Panhellenic *agōnes*, victors were honoured with a wreath: olive at Olympia, laurel at the Pythian Games, varieties of *selinon* (parsley or celery) at the Isthmus and Nemea. At other venues wreaths were made of date-palms or myrtle. The victor might also be showered with leaves. On returning home he could receive more substantial rewards: free supplies of food, the privilege of a front seat when spectating at *agōnes*, and gifts. Athens was especially generous to victors: Solon is said to have passed legislation to award Athenian victors at Olympia 500 drachmae, and at the Great Panathenaea in the 4th cent. BC money, gold crowns, bulls, and large numbers of amphorae containing olive oil were awarded as prizes; 100 amphorae, *c.*4,000 litres, for a victor in the men's *stadion* race, a very valuable prize. Local *agōnes* also awarded prizes: silver cups at Sicyon, a bronze shield at Argos, and a thick cloak at Pellene.

To lose in a contest was shameful, and the incidence of failure-induced depression and mental illness is likely to have been high.

After 300 BC The spread of 'periodic' contests in the Greek style is a defining feature of post-Classical Hellenism. In the 3rd and 2nd cents. BC they were sponsored by kings (the Alexandrian Ptolemaea and Pergamene Nicephoria) and leagues (the Soteria of *Delphi, by the Aetolian Confederacy) as well as cities great and small (e.g. the plethora of Boeotian *agōnes* by *c.*50 BC). Under the Roman Principate this expansion continued; provincial cities founded new games as late as AD 275–6; by the 3rd cent. they were celebrated from Carthage to Zeugma. At Rome they were first introduced under Nero, followed by Domitian (the Capitolia of 86), Gordian III (the *agōn* for Athena Promachos of 242), and Aurelian, whose *agōn* of *Sol (274) was still celebrated in the 4th cent. under Julian. Frowned on by Christianity, Greek games (shorn of pagan ritual) none the less survived until at least 521, when Justinian banned the Olympia of Syrian Antioch.

The distinctiveness of 'sacred' games, celebrating a deity (often the principal one of a city or, under Rome, the *ruler-cult) and (at first) offering only a symbolic prize (typically a *crown), is fundamental. In the Hellenistic age the recognition of new 'sacred' games required cumbersome interstate diplomacy by the promoter (best attested with the Leucophryena of Magnesia ad Maeandrum. From 30 BC Roman emperors decided 'the gift of a sacred contest', weighing up cost, a city's record of loyalty and, in 3rd-cent. Cilicia, its support for imperial troop-movements. An élite group of 'iselastic' games emerged, often named after one of the famous games of the 'ancient circuit' (*archaia periodos*), and distinctive for the privileges which victors could demand of their home cities, notably a triumphal entry (*iselasis*), pension, and tax-immunity. Otherwise there were prize-games (*thematitai, themides*), also subject to Roman control.

'Sacred' contests comprised a sacrifice, to which other Greek cities sent representatives (*theōroi* or more often, under Rome, *synthutai*), and a profane festival (*panēgyris*), often incorporating markets and fairs, as well as the contests proper, supervised by an *agōnothetēs*. Funding of new contests relied heavily on civic benefactors; infrequently emperors—notably Hadrian—stepped in. From the 2nd cent. AD the pantomime, and from the 3rd the mime, joined the more traditional events.

Whatever the qualitative view taken of post-Classical agonistic culture, its power in the shaping of later Hellenism is undeniable, and the limits of its diffusion suggest the limits of Hellenism. *See* ATHLETICS; COMEDY (GREEK), ORIGINS OF; MUSIC IN WORSHIP; THEOROI; TRAGEDY.

Agonium, name for 9 January, 17 March, 21 May, and 11 December in the Roman calendar; also called Agonalia, Agonia, and Dies Agonales, when the *rex sacrorum* sacrificed in the *Regia*. It had no associated god and the January celebration has no character letter in extant calendars; Macrobius makes it a fixed public festival (*feriae publicae stativae*).

[Ovid, *Fasti* 1. 317–458]

agora, Greek term for an area where people gather together, most particularly for the political functions of the city-state, normally sited centrally in cities (as at Priene), or at least central to the street lines where the actual centre may be occupied by other features (such as the Acropolis at Athens); the area was sacred, and could be treated like a *temenos*; there were always temples and sanctuaries in and round the agora. In unplanned cities its shape depends on the nature of the available site, irregular at Athens, on low-lying ground bordered by rising land to west (the Kolonos Agoraios) and south (the slopes of the Acropolis). In planned cities the required number of blocks in the regular grid plan are allocated, giving a strictly rectangular shape. *See* ATHENS, RELIGIOUS TOPOGRAPHY.

Ahuramazda, 'the Wise Lord' or 'Lord Wisdom', Iranian supreme deity in the Avesta and in Old Persian inscriptions. He is the wise, benevolent god, invoked as the creator and the upholder of *aša* ('rightness, truth') by Zarathuštra and as the creator of heaven and earth by the Persian kings. In almost all inscriptions he is the only god and the special protector of kingship. Greeks equated him with *Zeus. *See* PERSIAN RELIGION.

Aias (Greek Aias, Lat. Ajax). (1) Son of *Telamon, king of Salamis, hence Aias Telamonius. He brought twelve ships from Salamis to Troy. In the *Iliad* he is of enormous size, head and shoulders above the rest, and the greatest of the Greek warriors after *Achilles. His stock epithet is 'bulwark of the Achaeans', and his characteristic weapon a huge shield of seven-fold ox-hide. He clearly has the better of *Hector in a duel after which the heroes exchange gifts, Aias giving Hector a sword-belt in return for a sword; and he is at his memorable best when with unshakeable courage he defends the Greek wall and then the ships. He is also a member of the Embassy to Achilles, when he gives a brief but effective appeal to Achilles on friendship's grounds. At *Patroclus' funeral games he draws a wrestling match with *Odysseus, strength against cunning.

The *Aethiopis* told how after Achilles' death Aias carried his body off the field of battle while Odysseus kept back the Trojans. The *Little Iliad* told how the arms of Achilles were then adjudged to Odysseus instead of Aias, who went mad with anger, killed the herds of the Greeks, believing them to be the Greek leaders, and then committed suicide. (*See* EPIC CYCLE.) *Sophocles dramatizes these later events in his *Ajax*, but at the end of the play Aias is taken to an honourable burial, in marked contrast to his treatment in the *Little Iliad*, where he is denied the customary burial honours. In the Odyssey, when Odysseus is in Hades, he meets the shade of Aias who, in anger at his loss of Achilles' arms, refuses to speak and stalks away in magnificent silence. In the Hesiodic Catalogue of Women (*see* HESIOD) and thence in *Pindar *Heracles visits Telamon and, standing on the lion-skin, prays that his new-born son may be as stout as the skin; *Zeus, in answer, sends an eagle (Gk. *aietos*) and hence the baby is named Aias. From this develops the story that Aias was invulnerable save at one point, where the skin had not touched him when (in this version) he was wrapped in it. It was later said that when he killed himself his blood flowed on the ground and there sprang up the iris (*hyakinthos*) which also commemorates the death of *Hyacinthus; hence the markings on its petals recall the hero's name (Aias–aiai, 'alas'). Aias had a cult in Salamis, Attica, Megara (?), the Troad, and Byzantium.

Scenes from Aias' life popular in art, some from the 7th cent. BC, are combats with Hector and others, dicing with Achilles, lifting Achilles' body, the argument and voting about Achilles' arms, and (an especial favourite) his suicide.

(2) Son of Oïleus or Ileus, the Locrian chieftain. In Homer Aias leads the Locrian contingent to Troy with 40 ships. He is 'much lesser' than Telamonian Aias (hence often called the Lesser Aias), quick-footed, and often paired with his great namesake as a brave fighter. He can, however, be an unpleasant character, on occasion grossly rude, hated by *Athena, and finally drowned by *Poseidon for blasphemy against the gods while scrambling ashore after shipwreck.

In the *Iliu Persis* (*see* EPIC CYCLE) he dragged *Cassandra away from the statue of Athena to rape her, and in so doing loosened the statue from its plinth. This is a favourite scene in archaic and classical art. In historic times the Locrians sent two virgins annually to serve in the temple of Athena at Ilium (Troy) in expiation of this crime, the Locrians maintaining that this penalty was imposed for 1,000 years.

[(1) Homer, *Iliad*; Sophocles, *Ajax*; Ovid, *Metamorphoses* 13. 394 ff.; Apollodorus, *Epitome* 5. 23–5, 6. 5–6

(2) Homer, *Iliad* 23. 473 ff., *Odyssey* 4. 499–511]

Aidōs *See* NEMESIS; SHAME.

Aion was for late antiquity the personification and god of indefinitely extending time. In early Greek aiōn means 'life' (often in the sense of 'vital force'), 'whole lifetime', 'generation'. It was perhaps through application to the *kosmos*, the lifetime of which is never-ending, that the word acquired the sense of eternity. There is no good evidence for cult of Aion in the Classical or Hellenistic periods. The transition from philosophy to religious practice is first suggested by a statue of Aion dedicated at *Eleusis (at some time in the 1st cent. BC or AD) by three brothers 'for the power of Rome and continuation of the mysteries'.

Aion is celebrated as 'ever remaining by divine nature the same' and closely linked with the single unchanging *kosmos*. Numerous developments occurred in the imperial period: Aion was identified with the power ruling the *kosmos* (so regularly in the *Corpus Hermeticum*, see HERMES TRISMEGISTUS; and sometimes in magical papyri, *see* MAGIC), with the sun (magical papyri), perhaps with the eternity of Rome and the emperors (*see* AETERNITAS), and much else besides; in a festival at Alexandria, probably of late foundation, an image was brought out of the inner sanctuary of the Koreion, with the announcement that 'the Maiden has brought forth Aion'. But, though the word was widespread and clearly exercised a certain fascination, it did not carry with it any very definite connotation. The identification of the lion-headed god of Mithraism (see MITHRAS) as a type of Aion remains controversial; so too does any possible influence exercised by the Iranian concept of Zurvān or primordial Time.

Aither, personification of the purer upper stratum of air (approximately the stratosphere), next to or identical with the sky; son of Erebus and Night (see NYX) (*Hesiod), or of *Chaos and Darkness; husband of Day and of Earth. See also TARTARUS.

Aius Locutius (or loquens), the divine voice, 'sayer and speaker', that shortly before the battle of the Allia (390 BC) warned of the Gauls. The warning was not heeded. As expiation a precinct (*templum) and *altar (ara) were established near *Vesta's shrine, on the via Nova, where the voice was heard.

Alastor, avenging deity or *daimōn. Personification of curse which falls on a family through guilt. The alastōr exacts punishment for murder by causing new bloodshed and ensuring continuity of guilt as in the successive generations of *Atreus' family. After killing her husband *Agamemnon, *Clytemnestra identifies with 'the ancient bitter avenger (alastōr)' of Atreus, that is the 'spirit (daimōn) thrice glutted' on the blood of Thyestes, Atreus, and Agamemnon. She dies in turn at the hands of her son, who as alastōr becomes both curse and victim. *Oedipus describes his own alastōr as the curse that lies on his land. Alastōr therefore is a suitable epithet for the *Erinyes. But the divine spirit of retribution can also work outside the family and lead Xerxes to destruction at Salamis. By the 4th cent. BC alastōr had sunk to a common term of abuse meaning 'scoundrel' or 'wretch'.

In *Homer's Iliad three minor characters are called Alastor. One is a follower of *Nestor, and the other two on the Trojan side. The first is a Lycian killed by *Odysseus,

and the other father of Tros who is killed by *Achilles.

Alba Longa, on the *Albanus mons, near modern Castel Gandolfo, traditionally founded c.1152 BC by *Ascanius, and supposed founder of other Latin cities. Alba lost its primacy in Latium perhaps in the 7th cent. BC, allegedly through its destruction by Rome: some families are said to have migrated to Rome (Iulii, Tullii, etc.), while others joined neighbouring Bovillae and preserved Alban cults and memorials until imperial times.

[Virgil, Aeneid 3. 390 f.]

Albanus mons, the Alban hills and more specifically their dominating peak (Monte Cavo, 950 m. (3,117 ft.), 21 km. (13 mi.) south-east of Rome. Until c.1150 BC the Albanus mons was an active volcano, discouraging dense population in Latium; the volcano, however, has been inactive in historical times. On the summit stood the Latin federal sanctuary of *Jupiter Latiaris where Roman consuls celebrated the feriae Latinae (see FESTIVALS (ROMAN)). Remains exist, not indeed of the temple, but of the triumphal route leading to it; here at least five Roman generals celebrated lesser triumphs after being refused regular triumphs in Rome.

Albunea, sulphurous spring and stream near Tibur with a famous waterfall, and its nymph of the same name, classed as a *Sibyl by *Varro and fancifully identified by etymology with the sea-goddess *Ino-Leucothea. The spring is the Latin equivalent of Greek poetic springs like Castalia (see DELPHI) and Hippocrene (see HELICON); it is usually identified with the modern Acque Albule. In *Virgil, Albunea is the site of the incubation-oracle (see INCUBATION) of *Faunus, but this is otherwise unattested. The name derives from the white (albus) appearance of the spring's sulphurous water. See SPRINGS, SACRED.

[Virgil, Aeneid 7. 81–102]

Alcathous, son of *Pelops and *Hippodamia, was exiled from his homeland for fratricide; finding that the kingship of Megara was on offer to whoever could kill the ferocious lion of Cithaeron, he claimed the prize (keeping the beast's tongue as proof, like *Peleus). He subsequently built the city's walls with help from *Apollo and was honoured with memorial games as a founding hero.

[Pausanias 1. 41 f.]

Alcestis, in mythology, daughter of *Pelias, wife of Admetus king of Pherae (Thessaly), who is prepared to die in his place.

Pelias promised Alcestis to whoever could yoke a lion and boar to a chariot. Admetus was assisted in this feat by his lover Apollo (cf. *Poseidon, *Pelops, and *Hippodamia), who had been punished by serfdom to Admetus for killing the *Cyclopes or the Pythian snake. But at his marriage Admetus forgets to sacrifice to *Artemis and finds the bridal chamber full of snakes. On *Apollo's advice he appeases Artemis and even obtains from the Fates the concession that someone may die in his place. In the event, only Alcestis will, but Kore (*Persephone) sends her back from death or (in tragedy) *Heracles rescues her by wrestling with Death (*Thanatos*).

Though neither Admetus nor Alcestis receives cult directly, they are intertwined with Apollo and Artemis in cult and myth. The local Artemis, Brimo or Pheraea ('of Pherae'), was a *chthonian goddess, and hints of an earlier story lie in Alcestis' marriage to 'Insuperable' (Admetus) and her Persephone-like descent and return. Admetus founded Apollo's temple at Euboean Eretria and his name is frequent amongst the Aegeidae clan who administered the cult of Apollo Carneus on Thera. Alcestis will be sung at Apollo's *Carnea festival in Sparta—as also at Athens.

Alcestis' self-sacrifice, with its hints of suttee, belongs with a sequence of folk-tale functions: (a) a young man faces early death; (b) he can only be saved if another will die for him; (c) only his wife will; (d) the lord of life and death grants life to this wife. Admetus'

task is more loosely connected with other motifs.

Alcestis is mentioned for her beauty and offspring in Homer and *Hesiod, but then the tradition is silent till Phrynichus' play *Alcestis* (early 5th cent.). The myth is best known from Euripides. Very few depictions of Alcestis in art antedate this play. The Roman age was fond of Heracles leading Alcestis back from death, with its soteriological overtones.

[Euripides, *Alcestis*; Apollodorus 1. 9. 14–15]

Alcinous, in mythology, son of Nausithous, husband of Arete, his first cousin, king of the Phaeacians in Scheria, father of *Nausicaa. He received *Odysseus hospitably and sent him to Ithaca on one of the magic ships of his people, though he had had warning of the danger of such services to all and sundry. In the Argonautic legend the *Argonauts visit Scheria (here called Drepane) on their return from Colchis; the Colchians pursue them there and demand *Medea. Alcinous decides that if she is virgin she must return, but if not, her husband *Jason shall keep her. Warned by Arete, they consummate their marriage. There was a *temenos of Alcinous on Corcyra (Corfu).

[Homer, *Odyssey*; Apollonius Rhodius 4. 993 ff.]

Alcmaeon (1) the son of *Amphiaraus and Eriphyle, who killed his mother in revenge for his father's death. Bribed by Polynices with the necklace of Harmonia, Eriphyle gave a judgement in favour of *Adrastus against her husband when adjudicating between them as to whether Amphiaraus should join the expedition of the *Seven against Thebes despite his prophetic knowledge that all the participants except Adrastus would die. Amphiaraus ordered Alcmaeon to avenge him with death; alternatively, the *Delphic oracle advised him to kill his mother. In some variants Eriphyle endangered also Alcmaeon's life, by persuading him to participate in the expedition of the *Epigoni, having been bribed by Polynices' son with Harmonia's robe. After

murdering his mother Alcmaeon became mad and wandered about pursued by the *Erinyes. In one version the oracle advised him to settle in a land that had not existed when he had killed his mother; he settled in a place silted up by *Acheloüs, and the land was named Acarnania after Alcmaeon's son *Acarnan. In a more elaborate version he was purified by *Phegeus king of Psophis whose daughter *Alphesiboea or Arsinoë he married. But the earth became barren and the oracle advised Alcmaeon to go to Acheloüs, who purified him and gave him in marriage his daughter Callirhoë; she demanded the necklace and peplos of Harmonia which Alcmaeon had given to Alphesiboea. He returned to Psophis to retrieve them, claiming that he would be cured once he had dedicated them at the Delphic sanctuary. But Phegeus and his sons found out the truth and the latter killed him. A miracle turned Alcmaeon's sons from Callirhoë into fully grown men and they avenged their father by killing Phegeus and his sons—and then dedicated the necklace and robe to Delphi and settled Acarnania.
[Thucydides 2. 102–5; Pausanias 8. 24. 7–10]

Alcmaeon (2) of Croton (5th cent. BC) wrote a philosophical book dedicated to a group of Pythagoreans (*see* PYTHAGORAS AND PYTHAGOREANISM). It mostly concerned the nature of man. Alcmaeon explained the human condition by the interplay of opposites, e.g. health as 'equal rights' of hot and cold, wet and dry, etc., disease as 'monarchy' of one of them. And he compared the immortality of the *soul to the endless circling of the heavenly bodies.

Alcmene, mother of *Heracles. Her father was Electryon, who was accidentally killed by her future husband *Amphitryon; she followed Amphitryon into exile in Thebes, but refused to sleep with him until he had avenged the death of her brothers on the Taphians and Teleboans. *Zeus came to her in Amphitryon's shape a little before the latter's return, and she gave birth to twins—Heracles by Zeus, *Iphicles by Am-

phitryon. *Hera in jealousy obstructed the birth, thus ensuring that *Eurystheus was born before Heracles and so became king of Argos. After the death of Heracles, Alcmene with the rest of her family was persecuted by Eurystheus, and in *Euripides took refuge with them in Athens, insisting on Eurystheus' death after his defeat in battle. At her own death she was taken to the *Islands of the Blest to marry *Rhadamanthys, and a stone substituted in her coffin. The stone was revered in her heroon at Thebes. Alternative traditions gave her tombs at Megara and at Haliartus (apparently a bronze age burial). She also received widespread cult in Attica, though always in connection with others in the circle of Heracles.
[Euripides, *Heraclidae*]

Aletes (1) Son of *Aegisthus, killed by *Orestes in Mycenae. His name ('Wanderer') may suggest an aetiological connection with the *aletis* rite at the Attic festival *Anthesteria, linked in mythology with his sister *Erigone. (2) Son of Hippotas, who in accordance with an oracle became king of Corinth after having been given a clod of earth when he asked for bread on a festival day.

Alexander of Abonuteichos in Paphlagonia. He was a contemporary of Lucian whose bitterly hostile account, *Alexander or the False Prophet*, remains the most important source of information, although it must now be read against the evidence of inscriptions, coins, and works of art.

Alexander claimed to have a new manifestation of *Asclepius in the form of a snake called Glycon. A number of statues and statuettes have been discovered showing Glycon as a serpent with human hair—applied by Alexander, according to Lucian. Coins reveal that the birth of Glycon, described in detail by Lucian, took place in the reign of Antoninus Pius and that his cult gained very rapid acceptance. According to Lucian, this was the result of the oracles that Glycon provided in a variety of forms. After the cult was established, Alexander, who served as Glycon's prophet, or interpreter, created mysteries from which unbelievers, especially Christians and Epicureans, were excluded. *Marcus Aurelius recognized the cult by conferring status on Abonuteichos (thereafter known as Ionopolis) and Lucian mentions several consultants from the ranks of the imperial aristocracy, including Servianus, governor of Cappadocia in AD 161, and Rutilianus, governor of Moesia around 150 and Asia between 161 and 163. Alexander also sent Marcus Aurelius an oracle of Glycon at the beginning of the German Wars (probably in 168). The cult seems to have been particularly important around the Black Sea and in the Balkans. Alexander himself married the daughter of Rutilianus, and seems to have fathered at least one child by a woman of Caesarea Trochetta. He died probably in the 170s. Lucian's attack on him dates to the reign of Commodus, while inscriptions and excavation show that Glycon continued to be honoured well into the 3rd, and, possibly the 4th, cent. AD.

Allecto, one of the *Erinyes.

allegory, Greek

Allegorical expression Elements of allegory are present in Greek literature from the earliest stage: in *Homer, in Phoenix' prayers, and *Achilles' image of *Zeus' jars; in *Hesiod, the fable of the hawk and the nightingale and the personifications of Aidos, *Nemesis, and *Dike. Larger-scale allegorical tableaux and narratives begin to be composed in the late 5th and early 4th cents.: the sophist Prodicus' Choice of *Heracles, and *Plato's myths.

Allegorical interpretation (allegorēsis) Allegorical reading of works of literature—above all the mythological poems of Homer and Hesiod, decoded as accounts of the physical world or the truths of morality—seems to begin as early as the 6th cent. BC and to be an established (if controversial) practice by the end of the 5th. Plato, though ready to construct allegories in his myths, treated allegorical interpretation as either trivial or pernicious. Throughout this early period it is hard to be sure what the balance was between 'defensive' allegoresis (rescuing the poets and their myths from charges of intellectual naïvety and impiety) and 'positive' allegoresis (claiming the poets' authority for the interpreter's own doctrines). In either case, the underlying motive force was (and would continue to be) the cultural need to maintain the authority of the revered classics in the face of new (philosophical) traditions of thought.

In the Hellenistic and Roman periods, 'defensive' allegoresis became chiefly the territory of grammarians. Crates of Mallus, working in Pergamum, within a Stoic frame of reference, seems to have been a particularly influential figure in this tradition.

In the sphere of 'positive' allegoresis, special importance is normally attached to the work of the Stoics. Zeno, Chrysippus, and others (*see* STOICISM) undeniably provided a rich set of readings and techniques for later allegorists to work with. They may, however, have thought of themselves as recovering the beliefs of early man about the world, as transmitted (and distorted) by the poets, rather than as interpreting the minds and the words of the poets themselves. It would then be only with the *Neopythagoreans and *Neoplatonists, in the 2nd cent. AD and subsequently, that the philosophical tradition produced strongly 'positive' allegorical readings, presenting the poets themselves (Homer above all) as the first and greatest philosophers. Homer was by this stage being built up, as a figure of authority to resist the rival claims of Moses and Christ, on behalf of pagan Greek culture.

allegory, Latin An awareness of the Greek traditions of allegory (*see* ALLEGORY, GREEK) entered Rome with the Hellenization of Roman culture; Ennius and *Varro adopted Greek methods with the Roman gods, and the Stoic in *Cicero supplies examples of 'etymological' allegorism on these lines, deriving e.g. *Neptunus* from *nare*. Lucretius engages extensively with physical and moral allegories of the gods and of the

Underworld; *Virgil's imitation of Homer seems to reveal an awareness of the allegorical interpretations typical of the Pergamene school (for example of the Shield of Achilles). Horace defends the claims of poetry with allegorizing interpretations of the *Odyssey* and of the tales of *Orpheus and *Amphion. *Apuleius works a Platonizing psychological allegory into his fable of Cupid and Psyche. The author of one of the surviving Greek handbooks of allegory, Cornutus, was an associate of Lucan, Persius, and the Younger Seneca, although the last is dismissive of allegory.

Personification allegory, which goes back to *Homer and *Hesiod, is developed, as in Virgil's figure of *Fama*, and in Propertius' explanation of the attributes of *Amor*; it was much extended by *Ovid in his picturesque Palace of the Sun, House of Sleep, etc., establishing a tradition that goes through Statius to the Christian Prudentius' *Psychomachia* and the fully-developed medieval use of continuous personification allegory. *See* MYTHOLOGY.

[Hesiod, *Works and Days* 197–201, 256–62; Plato, *Phaedo* 108e ff.; *Republic* 524a ff., 614b ff.; *Phaedrus* 246a ff.; Cicero, *De natura deorum* 2. 62–9; Horace, *Epistles* 1. 2, *Ars Poetica* 391 ff.; Apuleius, *Metamorphoses* 4. 28 ff.]

Aloadae, in mythology, Otus and *Ep(h)ialtes, sons of Iphimedia and not in fact Aloeus but *Poseidon. After nine years they were 9 cubits broad and 9 fathoms tall. They imprisoned *Ares in a bronze vessel for thirteen months, but *Hermes got him out. To reach heaven, they piled Ossa on *Olympus and *Pelion on Ossa, filling the sea with mountains and making land into sea. They also had designs on *Artemis and *Hera; but Artemis changed into a deer in their midst and they shot each other—an event somehow orchestrated by *Apollo on Naxos. Matching this story, their graves were found in their precinct on Naxos. They might account too for the discovery of oversize bones, whether in Crete or Thessaly.

[Homer, *Iliad* 5. 385–91, *Odyssey* 11. 305, 310–11]

Alope, daughter of Cercyon, cruel king of Eleusis, and mother of *Hippothoon.

Alphesiboea, in mythology, daughter of *Phegeus of Psophis and wife of *Alcmaeon (1). According to Propertius, she and not Callirhoë's children avenged him; perhaps a mere blunder, perhaps an unknown variant.

Alpheus, the largest river of the Peloponnese, rises in south Arcadia near Asea and flows past *Olympia to the Ionian Sea. Its main tributaries are the Arcadian Ladon and Erymanthus; the Cladeus joins it at one corner of the ancient sanctuary at Olympia. As early as Homer Alpheus was also a *river-god, son of *Oceanus; in later sources he drowns himself in the river named after him either from unrequited love for Arethusa or remorse over his fratricide. Late cult for him is attested at Olympia and Sparta.

altars Indispensable adjunct of *sacrifice in ancient religion.

Greek The chief type was the raised *bōmos* on which a wood fire was lit for the cremation of the victim's thigh-bones and spit-roasting of the entrails; *hero-cults by contrast commonly employed the *eschara*, a low altar onto which the victim's blood was made to flow; the domestic altar was for bloodless offerings (natural produce, *cakes, etc.). In Greek *sanctuaries monumental open-air *bōmoi*, usually of dressed stone (the ash altar of Zeus at *Olympia seems to have been unusual), are well attested archaeologically from the 6th cent. BC onwards; they were typically rectangular and sometimes approached by a flight of steps. Independent altars on a spectacular scale are a feature of the Hellenistic age—e.g. the so-called Great Altar of Pergamum (early 2nd cent. BC), incorporating a sculptured frieze *c.*120 m. (393 ft.) long; the tradition was continued in the Roman east with the so-called Great Antonine Altar of Ephesus (begun *c.* AD 166). In Greek myth and real life altars were traditionally places of refuge, the suppliants protected by the deity to whom the altar belonged.

Roman The Latin terms *altaria* (plur.) and *ara* (variously explained by Roman antiquarians) derive from the roots denoting 'burning' (of sacrificial offerings). Normally of stone, of varying size, from small *cippi* (stone-markers) to large structures (as the *Ara Pacis), most often quadrangular (occasionally round), and decorated with reliefs, they were dedicated to a particular deity, and stood either separately or in front of temples (inside only for incense and bloodless offerings). A separate category consists of funerary altars (also cinerary urns often had the shape of altars).

Althaemenes, in mythology, son of *Catreus, king of Crete. Warned by an oracle that he would kill his father, he left Crete for Rhodes. Long after, his father came to seek him; Althaemenes took him for a pirate and killed him.

Amalthea, the goat that suckled *Zeus after his birth, when he was hidden in a cave to prevent his father *Cronus from devouring him; later, rationalizing versions made the goat into a *nymph. The myth was connected by *Ovid with another, perhaps originally independent, tradition about a '(bull's) horn of plenty' of the nymph Amalthea. According to an ancient collection of proverbs, Zeus turned the goat into a *constellation.

[Ovid, *Fasti* 5. 111–28]

Amazons, mythical race of female warriors. The name was popularly understood as 'breastless' (*maza*, 'breast') and the story told that they 'pinched out' or 'cauterized' the right breast so as not to impede their javelin-throwing. No real etymology is known.

Epic Amazons exist in order to be fought, and ultimately defeated, by men in an Amazonomachy ('Amazon-battle'). Already in the *Iliad* we hear of *Bellerophon killing them in Lycia, their defeat at the river Sangarios (near *Pessinus), and a tomb of Myrrhine outside Troy. In a poem of the *Epic Cycle, their Thracian queen, *Penthesilea 'daughter of Ares', arrives to help the Trojans, but *Achilles kills her (and *Ther-

sites for alleging Achilles loved her). *Heracles' ninth labour was to fetch the girdle of the Amazon queen, Hippolyte, resulting in another Amazonomachy. *Theseus joined Heracles and as a result had to defeat an Amazon invasion of Attica, a story told in a late 6th-cent. BC *Theseid*.

Cult/commemoration Amazon tombs are frequent in central Greece, presumably because of local Amazonomachy myths. They are found at Megara, Athens, Chaeronea, and Chalcis—as well as in Thessaly at Scotussa and Cynoscephalae. There was an Amazoneum (shrine of Amazons, implying tombs and cult) at Chalcis and Athens. At Athens there were annual sacrifices to the Amazons on the day before the Thesea. Many Asia Minor settlements were founded by Amazons: Amastris, Sinope, Cyme, Pitana, Priene, Mytilene (Lesbos), Ephesus, Smyrna, Myrina. At Ephesus Hippolyte and her Amazons set up a *bretas* (old wooden statue) of Artemis and established an annual circular dance with weapons and shields, as performed in historical times by maidens.

Ethnography Amazons, appropriately for a group inverting normal Greek rules, live at the edge of the world. Their usual homeland is next to a river Thermodon in the city of Themiscyra in remote Pontic Asia Minor. Real Amazons would need men for procreation. Diodorus Siculus' Amazons at the Thermodon cripple their male children, but his second set, in Libya, have househusbands to whom they return (like Greek males) after their period of military service. In the *Alexander Romance*, they keep men across a river. It is part of the mythologizing of Alexander the Great that stories were quick to surface that he had met Amazons and threatened or pleasured their queen.

Matriarchy and Message Especially since J. J. Bachofen's *Mutterrecht* (1859), Amazons have been used as evidence for an actual matriarchy in prehistoric times. This has seemed an attractive counter to modern male prejudices, but mistakes the nature of myth. Women warriors and hunters are quite frequent in myth and folk-tale and inversely reflect the actual distribution of roles between the sexes. It may be that such inversion in Greece goes back to rituals of the *initiation of maidens (cf. Ephesus) and youths (cf. the Thesea), where the definition of gender roles is at issue.

Art Amazonomachies and genre studies of Amazons are represented copiously in art from the late 7th cent. on, propelled by their special importance at Athens.

[Plutarch, *Theseus* 26–7; Aeschylus, *Prometheus Bound* 723–5; Arrian, *Anabasis* 7. 13; Plutarch, *Alexander* 46]

Ambarvalia, Roman private and public field *lustration in May. The rustic calendars (*menologia rustica*) for May note: *segetes lustrantur* ('crops are purified'). The public rites symbolically lustrated all fields and are sometimes connected with the *pontifices*, sometimes with the Arval Brothers' (*see* FRATRES ARVALES) May 29 worship of *Dea Dia. Other Italic communities had similar rites. *See* TABULAE IGUVINAE.

[Virgil, *Eclogues* 5. 75, *Georgics* 1. 338 ff.; Tibullus 2. 1]

Ambrose (Ambrosius) Born *c.* AD 340, son of a praetorian prefect of Gaul, Ambrose was well educated and achieved official success under the patronage of the great prefects Petronius Probus and Quintus Aurelius *Symmachus. Until his early death, his brother Uranius Satyrus showed equal promise. His sister Marcellina became well known for her practice of consecrated virginity, dating from the time of Liberius, bishop of Rome (AD 352–66). Ambrose was appointed governor of Aemilia and Liguria in 374. Already experienced, therefore, in the affairs of Milan (Mediolanum), he was chosen to be the city's bishop in the same year, while intervening in what had become a disputed election. He died in 397.

Ambrose is famous for his confrontations with the emperor *Theodosius I. Imperial orders to rebuild in 388 a *synagogue at Callinicum destroyed by a Christian mob were rescinded after his intervention; and

in 390 he excommunicated the emperor, following the calculated massacre of thousands in the circus at *Thessalonica. But those triumphs reflected force of personality without precedent or institutional significance. Nor is it easy to judge what direct contribution Ambrose made to Theodosius' laws against *paganism. His earlier relationships with Gratian and Valentinian II, close and affectionate, did more to form and reflect his attitudes to civil authority, as also did his embassies to Trier during the usurpation of Maximus, 383–4 and 386. His abiding preoccupations in the public sphere were the defeat of *Arianism and the inhibition of pagan cult (symbolized by his successful encouragement of imperial resistance to Symmachus over the restoration of the altar of Victory in the senate-house in 384).

ambrosia (lit. 'immortality') **and nectar** are the food and drink of eternal life—usually in that order, though nectar is for eating in Alcman, and Sappho thinks of ambrosia as a drink. They are thus properly reserved for the gods, as traditional stories emphasize: e.g. *Odysseus' meals with *Calypso. *Heracles was formally served with a draught of immortal spirit by *Athena on his assumption into Olympus, but the dying *Tydeus was refused the same favour at the last moment when the goddess found him devouring his enemy's brains. One version of *Tantalus' crime claims that, having tasted divine food himself, he tried to smuggle some away for others who were not so privileged. Those who ingest such rarefied substances naturally have not blood but a special fluid called *ichor* coursing through their veins. As the ultimate preservative, ambrosia may also be administered by goddesses to their favourites by external application: it is used by *Thetis to keep *Patroclus' corpse fresh and to sustain the fasting *Achilles, and by Athena as a face cream to beautify *Penelope. Its natural fragrance is employed by Eidothea to insulate Menelaus' men from the stench of her father's seals. Doves are said to ferry it (from where?) to *Zeus.

[Homer, *Iliad* 19. 347 ff.; *Odyssey* 5. 196–9; Pindar, *Olympian* 1. 60 ff.]

Ambrosiaster (i.e. pseudo-Ambrose), the author of the *Commentary on Thirteen Pauline Letters* (except Hebrews) which has been handed down under the name of *Ambrose. Attempts at identifying the author have not yet yielded conclusive results. The commentary was written under Pope *Damasus (AD 366–84) in Rome and is regarded as an important witness to the Latin text of St *Paul prior to the *Vulgate and as an instructive example for the pre-Augustinian interpretation of Paul. The pseudo-Augustinian *Quaestiones Veteris et Novi Testamenti* probably also stem from his pen. In addition, some minor texts have been attributed to this author.

Amburbium, *lustration for Rome, seldom so named, usually linked with the *Ambarvalia's lustration of the fields. Since it appears in no *calendar it may have been a movable festival or, based on the infrequent references, all late, it may have been a rarely performed lustration which anachronistically received its name by analogy with Ambarvalia. Lucan describes an *amburbium*—but clearly an extraordinary ceremony.

[Lucan 1. 592–638]

Ammon, Hellenized name of Amun, the great god of Egyptian Thebes and chief divinity of the developed Egyptian pantheon; thus naturally identified with *Zeus (so first in *Pindar, who composed a hymn to the god and is supposed to have commissioned an image for his temple in (Greek) Thebes). Greek interest, probably mediated through the city of Cyrene (on whose coins his head is shown from the early 5th cent. with the typical ram's horns) centred on the oracular cult at the oasis of *Siwa, in the Libyan desert; Herodotus assumes its fame, and *Plutarch claims consultations by several prominent 5th-cent. Greeks including Cimon, Lysander, Alcibiades, and Nicias. In the 4th cent., in line with the growth of foreign cults, his worship is attested at Athens (where one of the two sacred triremes was renamed 'Ammonias' in his honour) and elsewhere in the Greek homeland; but it was above all Alexander the Great's visit in 331, after his victory at the Issus, which caught the ancient imagination—even if the story of Zeus Ammon's acknowledgment of his own paternity of the young king, and so of Alexander's divinity, is a later elaboration.

Ammonius Saccas, of Alexandria, Platonist philosopher, active in first half of 3rd cent. AD, famous as the teacher of *Plotinus, who studied under him 232–42, as well as of Longinus, perhaps *Origen, and others. According to *Porphyry, he was brought up as a Christian but reverted to paganism as soon as he began to think for himself. The epithet theodidaktos ('taught of God') and the nickname Saccas (sack-carrier? wearer of sackcloth?) would seem to imply a humble origin, though other interpretations have been proposed. He wrote nothing, and no distinctive features of his teaching can be established. Even the story of the vow of secrecy which his pupils, like those of Pythagoras, took and subsequently broke is not entirely free from doubt. Nevertheless the teacher who evoked from Plotinus the cry 'this is the man I was looking for' and retained him as a disciple for eleven years has some claim to be considered the Socrates of *Neoplatonism.

Amphiaraus, seer descended from *Melampus (1), resident at Argos, whence he participated in the expedition of the *Seven against Thebes. In one tradition, he died with all the other champions save *Adrastus. Since he knew that the expedition was doomed, Amphiaraus was unwilling to go, but—as pre-arranged with Adrastus—he was obliged to obey the judgement of his wife Eriphyle (sister of Adrastus), who had been bribed by Polynices with the necklace of Harmonia.

There is another version, perhaps originating with an early epic, that Amphiaraus was not killed at Thebes, but, while fleeing from the city, was swallowed up live, chariot and all, in a cleft made by *Zeus' thunderbolt.

It can be assumed that at some time between the development of the story of the Seven, and the first reference to his survival, Amphiaraus was associated with an underground oracular deity. A similar motif—pursuit, swallowing up live by the earth, and subsequent operation as an underground oracle—figures in the explanatory story of *Trophonius at Lebadea, with whom Amphiaraus shared another characteristic, direct consultation (*see* ORACLES).

Amphiaraus' major sanctuary was near Oropus, in disputed territory between Attica and Boeotia. It is unclear whether or not there was another sanctuary of Amphiaraus nearer Thebes, later abandoned in favour of Oropus. The oracle was one of those consulted by the Lydian king Croesus and Mys (for the Persian Mardonius). Amphiaraus gave Croesus the right answer.

The sanctuary at Oropus became popular during the Peloponnesian War, when the Athenians invested Amphiaraus with healing powers on the model of *Asclepius. Consultation was by *incubation: the consultants/patients bedded down on a ram-skin on the ground, and were visited by Amphiaraus as they slept.

The sanctuary, which has been excavated and is a charming place, was popular in the 4th cent. under the Athenians, under the Hellenistic Boeotian Confederacy, and under the Romans, thanks to the impetus given by Sulla, who granted it tax-free status.
[Homer, *Odyssey* 15. 243–55]

amphictiony (from *amphiktiones*, 'dwellers around') is the name given to Greek leagues connected with *sanctuaries and the maintenance of their cults. Most were concentrated in the locality of the sanctuary, but the most important, such as the amphictiony of Anthela and *Delphi, came to include representatives from much of Greece. They could punish those who offended against the sanctuary, and the Delphic amphictiony could even declare a *Sacred War against an offending state.

Amphilochus, in mythology, brother of *Alcmaeon (1), and, in some accounts, his comrade in the expedition of the *Epigoni and helper in slaying Eriphyle. After Homer he takes part in the Trojan War, and is celebrated as a diviner. He and *Calchas left Troy together by land and came to *Claros. A number of local tales (or constructions of Greek historians) connect Amphilochus with the origins of places and peoples in Asia Minor, as Poseideion on the borders of Syria and Cilicia, the Pamphylian nation, but above all the famous prophetic shrine in Mallus. Apollo killed him in Soli.

Amphion and Zethus, sons of *Zeus and *Antiope: they founded and walled seven-gated Thebes.

The story is fleshed out in now lost plays by *Sophocles and *Euripides. The brothers were born in a cave on Cithaeron and were said to have ruled Eutresis before coming to Thebes. Their mother, having been maltreated by *Dirce, was avenged by her sons. Amphion married *Niobe, with unfortunate issue; Zethus, an altogether more shadowy figure (Amphion's name can at least be connected with his walking around the site of Thebes playing his lyre and charming the stones into a wall), married the equally vague Thebe, or possibly *Aëdon. A prehistoric burial-mound immediately north of the Cadmea is probably the site variously identified as the tomb of one or the other or both.
[Homer, *Odyssey* 11. 260–5]

Amphitryon, son of Alcaeus king of Tiryns. He and his fiancée *Alcmene (daughter of Electryon king of Mycenae) were forced to flee to Thebes after he had accidentally killed Electryon. After helping the Thebans to rid themselves of the Teumessian fox, he set out to fight the Teleboans (who had killed eight of Alcmene's nine brothers), and defeated them. In his absence, *Zeus lay with Alcmene, who bore him *Heracles; in the same accouchement she bore *Iphicles to Amphitryon.

Amphitryon led the Thebans successfully in war against the Euboeans, but was less fortunate against the Minyans, fighting whom he died (Heracles subsequently freed the Thebans from their oppression). Amphitryon was buried at Thebes, jointly with *Iolaus. He seems to have been a local Theban warrior hero (the tomb is attested from the 5th cent.), whose role was partially usurped by Heracles.

[Homer, *Iliad* 14. 323–4; Plautus, *Amphitryo*; Apollodorus 2. 4. 6–7]

amulets (Lat. *amuletum*) were magically potent objects worn for protection against witchcraft, illness, the evil eye, accidents, robbery, etc.; also to enhance love, wealth, power, or victory. Houses, walls, and towns could be protected in the same way. Any kind of material might be employed: stones and metals as well as (parts of) animals and plants, since to every sort of material could be attributed an inherent 'magical' virtue (*see* MAGIC); also parts of human bodies (especially of people who had suffered a violent death: gladiators, executed criminals, victims of shipwreck, etc.) were used as amulets. Their efficacy might be enhanced by engraved figures, e.g. deities or symbols, especially on stones and gems in rings. Powerful names taken from exotic (especially Egyptian and Hebrew) myth and cult were popular: Abraxas, Solomon (e.g. in the formula: 'sickness be off, Solomon persecutes you'), magical words (e.g. *abracadabra*) and formulae, the 'great name' (e.g. Sebaoth), or lists of vowels understood as names of archangels (*see* ANGELS). Just as amulets could be applied without inscription, magical inscriptions could be effective in themselves. Signs with the inscription, 'sickness be off, Heracles lives here', could be seen on house doors. Apotropaic charms of this type have also been found in papyri.

Forms of amulets varied greatly: modern collections show hundreds of different types. Notable are rings (with gems), nails, knots, Egyptian scarabs, a hand showing an obscene gesture, phallus, vulva, eye, etc. Instructions for obtaining and preparing special materials include attention to the correct time (midnight, early morning), circumstance (*constellations), and place (crossways, burial places). Both materials and formulae are marked by wide variation and free association. The Elder Pliny gives an extensive survey, which can be supplemented by charms from later antiquity.

Belief in amulets remained active in Greece and Italy in all classes of the populations throughout antiquity and into modern times.

[Piny, *Natural History* 28–34]

Amyclae, an 'Achaean' centre on the right bank of the Eurotas river c.5 km. (*c*.3 mi) south of Sparta, mentioned in the Homeric Catalogue as in the domain of *Menelaus. Accounts vary of its resistance to the Dorians but not later than c.750 BC it, and consequently the rest of southern Laconia, fell. It was incorporated in Spartan territory as a special unit. Remains of the famous sanctuary (from the 8th cent. BC) and throne of *Apollo Amyclaeus (*see* HYACINTHUS) have been excavated on the hill of Agia Kyriaki; a deposit of over 10,000 archaic votives shows that Alexandra-*Cassandra was worshipped near by. *See* SPARTAN CULTS.

[Pausanias 3. 18. 7–19. 6]

Amycus, in mythology, king of the Bebryces, a savage people of Bithynia. He was of gigantic strength and compelled all comers to the land to box with him, the loser to be at the absolute disposal of the winner. When the *Argonauts arrived in his country, Polydeuces accepted his challenge, and being a skilled boxer overcame Amycus' brute force. In the fight Amycus was killed (so *Apollonius Rhodius) or knocked out (so Theocritus), and made to swear to wrong no more strangers, or, having lost the fight, was bound by Polydeuces.

Amymone, in mythology, daughter of *Danaus. While at Argos she went for water, was rescued from a *satyr, and seduced by *Poseidon, who created the spring Amymone in commemoration.

Amyzon, remote but important *sanctuary in Caria, north of Mylasa. Greek inscriptions have been found there dating from the time of the 4th-cent. BC Hecatomnid local ruler Idrieus, to the end of the 3rd cent.

Anacharsis, a largely legendary Scythian prince who came to exemplify the wise barbarian. Sometimes presented as an admirer of Greek ways (esp. those of Sparta), he later typifies barbarian criticism of Greek customs. He is said to have travelled extensively in Greece and elsewhere in the 6th cent. BC and gained a high reputation for wisdom. On his return to Scythia he was put to death for attempting to introduce the cult of Mater Magna (*see* CYBELE) to the Scythians. So much we are told by Herodotus, but even at this early date it is impossible to distinguish what, if anything, is historical in this legendary material. Later he was given a Greek mother and made a friend of the Athenian sage Solon, and was sometimes included among the Seven Sages. Ten letters from the Hellenistic period and some 50 sayings, a few perhaps from the Archaic period, are attributed to him. The letters especially extol the ideal simple life of the Scythians. They were much relished: *Cicero translated one of them and the figure of Anacharsis as the 'noble savage' was popularized by Abbé Barthélemy's *Voyage du jeune Anacharsis en Grèce* (1788). *See* SCYTHIAN RELIGION.

[Lucian, *Anacharsis*; Herodotus 4. 76 f.]

Anahita (Anaitis), Persian goddess of the fertilizing waters. Artaxerxes II (404–358 BC) introduced the use of cult-images into the major cities of his empire and invoked her with *Ahuramazda and *Mithras in royal inscriptions. Anahita is not mentioned in the Persepolis administrative texts. No images of Anahita from Iran are known

until Sasanid times. The cult spread to Armenia, Cappadocia, Pontus, and Lydia. In Armenia sacred *prostitution was practised. In Lydia she was assimilated to *Cybele and *Artemis, called Artemis Anaitis and Anaitis Meter in numerous monuments and inscriptions, and worshipped in temples at Sardis, Hierocaesarea, Hypaepa, and elsewhere. The name Anahita means 'undefiled, immaculate'; in Greek Anahita is sometimes equated with Aphrodite or Athena. *See* PERSIAN RELIGION; SYNCRETISM.

Anakes, 'lords', 'kings' (the latter being the meaning of *anax* in Linear B). This is the surprising title under which the *Dioscuri were invariably worshipped in Attica (as sometimes in Argos); an inscription has now confirmed that these Anake(s)/Dioscuri could be associated in cult with *Helen. Some infer from the deep embeddedness of the title in Attica that the Anakes were originally independent deities, perhaps three in number. Actual traces, however, of Anakes who are not identified with Dioscuri are faint and uncertain.

Anatolian deities Deities of prehistoric Anatolia may be inferred from such monuments as the painted shrines of neolithic Çatal Hüyük, or the figurines and 'standards' of early bronze age Alaca Hüyük, but only with the advent of writing, *c.*2000 BC, is a more complete picture available. In the Old Assyrian colony period (*c.*2000–1800 BC), deities appear as figurines or on seals, sometimes as family groups, sometimes as recognizable figures—the weather-god, the hunting-god, the nude goddess, etc., with their familiar animals, bull, stag, birds, etc. The Hittite kingdom (*c.*1650–1200 BC) provides the fullest evidence, where the iconography of seals, reliefs, figurines, etc., is amplified by the extensive texts of the Hattuša archives relating to mythology and cult. At Hattuša, overlapping pantheons are attested: the local Hattian, with that of the Hittites evolved locally, and later the imported Hurro-Mesopotamian, which gradually gained ground over the other two. The proliferation of deities reflects the need to create a national pantheon from a multitude of local cults. Weather-gods and sun-gods head the pantheons, followed by such figures as the grain-god, the stag- (hunting-) god, etc., ending with natural phenomena such as mountains and rivers, etc. Male deities are provided with female consorts, listed separately and not strongly characterized except for an Ishtar figure, who may also appear in the male list.

The end of the Hittite kingdom removes this documentation which is only partially replaced by the inscriptions of the Neo-Hittite states of south-east Anatolia and north Syria (c.1100–700 BC). Details of cult are lacking. The Hurro-Hittite weather-god and his consort continue to be worshipped, and the stag-god becomes more prominent, as do Kubaba from Carchemish and the moon-god from Harran. At this period, limited evidence may be drawn from the Phrygian monuments and inscriptions, principally relating to 'mother Kubile' (Kubaba), represented on stone monuments as a figure in a cylindrical head-dress and long robe, standing in a small shrine (*see* CYBELE).

See PHRYGIA, RELIGION OF.

Anaxagoras (probably 500–428 BC), a native of Clazomenae in Ionia; the first philosopher known to have settled in Athens. He probably arrived in Athens in 456/5 and philosophized there for 20 years or so, until his prosecution and trial on a charge of impiety (437/6). The longest and most eloquent surviving passage from his one book explains how our differentiated kosmos was created from the original mélange by the action of mind, an entirely discrete principle, unmixed with any other substances but capable of ordering and controlling them. His cosmology was a mere reworking of *Anaximenes'*, even if the claim that the sun is a huge incandescent stone shocked contemporary opinion; his explanations of physical phenomena are already reflected in *Aeschylus' Supplices* (c.463) and *Eumenides* (458).

Anaximander, of Miletus (died soon after

547 BC), was the first Greek to write a prose treatise 'On the Nature of Things' (*Peri physeōs*). He thus initiated the tradition of Greek natural philosophy by elaborating a system of the heavens, including an account of the origins of human life, and by leaving his speculation behind in written form. He was the first to make a map of the inhabited world; some sources also credit him with a *sphairos* or plan of the heavens.

Anaximander's view of the cosmos is remarkable for its speculative imagination and for its systematic appeal to rational principles and natural processes as a basis for explanation. The origin of things is the *apeiron*, the limitless or infinite, which apparently surrounds the generated world and 'steers' or governs the world process. Symmetry probably dictates that the world-order will perish into the source from which it has arisen, as symmetry is explicitly said to explain why the earth is stable in the centre of things, equally balanced in every direction. The world process begins when the opposites are 'separated out' to generate the hot and the cold, the dry and the wet. By a process that is both biological and mechanical, earth, sea, and sky take shape and huge wheels of enclosed fire are formed to produce the phenomena of sun, moon, and stars. The size of the wheels was specified, corresponding perhaps to the arithmetical series 9, 18, 27. The earth is a flat disc, three times as broad as it is deep. Mechanical explanations in terms of the opposites are offered for meteorological phenomena (wind, rain, lightning, and thunder) and for the origin of animal life. The first human beings were generated from a sort of embryo floating in the sea.

The *apeiron* is ageless, deathless, and eternal; unlike the anthropomorphic gods, it is also ungenerated. The cosmos, on the other hand, is a world-order of coming-to-be and perishing according to a fixed law of nature, described in the one quotation from Anaximander's book (perhaps the earliest preserved sentence of European prose): out of those things from which beings are

generated, into these again does their perishing take place 'according to what is need-
ful and right; for they pay the penalty and
make atonement for one another for their
wrongdoing (*adikia*), according to the ordinance of time'.

Anaximenes, of Miletus (traditionally,
active 546–525 BC) followed in the footsteps
of *Anaximander in composing a treatise in
Ionian prose in which he developed a world
system on the basis of an infinite or unlimited principle, which he identified as *aēr*. His
system differed from that of his predecessor
in several respects. Instead of suspending
the earth in the centre of the universe by
cosmic symmetry, he supported it from
below by cosmic air. And instead of leaving
the infinite starting-point for world formation indeterminate in nature, he specified it
as elemental air, which he probably conceived as a kind of vital world-breath that
dominates the world order as our own
breath-soul rules over us. Anaximenes also
offered a mechanistic explanation for world
formation and change in terms of the
condensation and rarefaction of the air. Air
becomes fire by rarefaction; by motion it
becomes wind; by condensation it becomes
water and, by more condensation, earth and
stones.

It was the Milesian cosmology as reformu-
lated by Anaximenes that became standard
for Ionian natural philosophy in the 5th
cent. Heraclitus reacts against this system
by replacing air with fire. *Anaxagoras and
Democritus follow Anaximenes in regarding
the earth as a flat disc supported by air.
Diogenes of Apollonia, the most conservative 5th-cent. physicist, retains the cosmic
air as divine principle of life and intelligence, controlling the world-order.

Ancaeus, in mythology, (1) son of Lycurgus from Tegea in Arcadia. *Pausanias identifies him with the father of *Agapenor who
led the Arcadians at Troy. He joined the *Argonautic expedition, and was the strongest
after *Heracles. His traditional weapon was
the axe. He was killed during the Calydonian

boar-hunt (*see* MELEAGER), and his death was
depicted on a famous pediment on the
temple of Athena at Tegea. (2) Another Argonaut, son of *Poseidon and Astypalaea, who
took over the job of steersman after the
death of Tiphys. The two namesakes are
often confused, and the same story explaining the proverb 'many a slip between cup
and lip' is told of both.

[Pausanias 8. 4. 10, 8. 45. 5–7; Apollonius Rhodius 2.
894]

Anchises, character in literature and
mythology, son of Capys, father of *Aeneas,
and member of the Trojan royal house. He
does not appear in person in *Homer's *Iliad*,
but the *Homeric *Hymn to Aphrodite* recounts
his union with that goddess on the slopes of
Mt. Ida. He was warned by *Aphrodite not to
reveal her identity as the mother of the
resulting child, Aeneas, but disobeyed; as
punishment, he was lamed by a thunderbolt
or blinded. Most versions of the Aeneas-
legend tell how Anchises was carried on his
son's back from Troy; some state that he
went with Aeneas to Carthage and Italy,
but in the *Aeneid* he dies in Sicily before
reaching either place. Anchises' character
in *Aeneid* is that of a frail and wise counsellor
and priest-like religious authority; mutual
affection between him and Aeneas is evident, especially when Aeneas descends to
the Underworld to see his dead father, who
offers both a philosophical revelation and a
pageant of the future of Rome.

[*Homeric Hymn to Aphrodite*. 5.286 ff.; Virgil, *Aeneid* 2–3,
6. 106–9, 684–702]

Androgeōs, son of *Minos, who died an
untimely death in Attica, either treacherously killed by his defeated rivals in the
Panathenaic Games (*see* PANATHENAEA), or
sent by *Aegeus against the Marathonian
bull and killed by it. To avenge him Minos
besieged Athens, and was only appeased by
an annual tribute of seven youths and seven
maidens to be thrown to the Minotaur
(*see* THESEUS). He was variously identified
with the hero Eurygyes at the Ceramicus or
with the 'hero at the stern' in Phaleron.

Andromache, daughter of *Eëtion king of Thebe in the Troad, and wife of *Hector. Her father and seven brothers were killed by *Achilles, and her mother ransomed for a large sum. After the fall of Troy her son *Astyanax was killed by the Greeks and she herself became *Neoptolemus' slave and concubine (from *Epic Cycle). She bore him three sons, Pergamus, Pielus, and Molossus, eponym of the Molossi. According to *Euripides, she was threatened with death by Neoptolemus' wife *Hermione during the visit to Delphi in which he was killed, but was protected by *Peleus, Neoptolemus' aged grandfather. After Neoptolemus' death or on his marriage she was handed over to Hector's brother *Helenus, lived with him in Epirus, and bore him a son, Cestrinus. After Helenus' death, Andromache went to Mysia with Pergamus, where he conquered Teuthrania and founded Pergamum.

Andromache in scenes at Troy is sometimes found in art.

[Homer, *Iliad* 6. 395 ff.; Euripides, *Andromache*; Virgil, *Aeneid* 3. 327–9]

Andromeda, in mythology, the daughter of *Cepheus, king of the Ethiopians, and his wife Cassiepeia or Cassiope. The following is the usual legend. Cassiepeia boasted that she was more beautiful than the Nereids (*see* NEREUS); they complained to *Poseidon, who flooded the land and sent a sea-monster to ravage it. On consulting *Ammon, Cepheus learned that the only cure was to offer up Andromeda to the monster, and she was accordingly fastened to a rock on the sea-shore. At this point *Perseus came by on his way from taking the head of *Medusa. He fell in love with Andromeda, and got her and her father's consent to marry her if he could kill the sea-beast. This he did; but Cepheus' brother Phineus, who had been betrothed to Andromeda, plotted against him (or attacked him by open force), Perseus showed him and his followers the head of Medusa, turning them all to stone. He and Andromeda stayed for a time with Cepheus, and left their eldest son, Perses,

with him; from Perses the Persian kings were descended. They then went on to Seriphus, then to Argos and Tiryns. Their other children were Alcaeus, Sthenelus, Heleius, Mestor, Electryon, and a daughter Gorgophone.

Andromeda, Perseus, Cepheus, Cassiepeia, and the monster were all turned into *constellations bearing their names (the monster is Cetus). This may have been foretold in Euripides' lost tragedy *Andromeda*. If so, it is one of the very few Greek star-myths which can be traced back to an earlier date than the Alexandrian period.

Andromeda being rescued by Perseus is a popular scene in art from the late 6th cent.

[Apollodorus 2. 4. 3–5; Ovid, *Metamorphoses* 5.1 ff.]

angels, 'messengers' (Gk. *angeloi*). *Hermes was considered the messenger of the Olympians, and named Angelos (once Euangelos). *Iris was ascribed the same function; for *Plato, the two are the divine *angeloi*. *Hecate was an 'angel' because she had contact with the lower world and the dead; in the early empire Hermes is once named the 'messenger of *Persephone' (1st–2nd cent. AD). By the 3rd cent. AD, with angels playing a large part in contemporary *Judaism and *Christianity, they became important too for paganism as intermediaries (along with lesser gods and demons) of the true God, not just in *Gnosticism and *Neoplatonism but also in 'mainstream' belief: thus an oracle from *Claros inscribed at Oenoanda (*c.*AD 200?) represents even Apollo as an angelic 'small part' of God. In the 2nd–3rd cents. AD abstract divinities called angels were worshipped in Egypt and Asia Minor (Lydia, Caria, and Phrygia) under such cult-titles as the Angelic Divine (Theion Angelikon) and Good Angel (Agathos Angelos).

Angerona, Roman goddess, worshipped on 21 December (*Divalia or Angeronalia) in the Curia Acculeia, or the Sacellum Volupiae, where there stood on the altar a statue of Angerona with her mouth bound and sealed. The ancients connected her name with *angina* or *angor* ('suffocation'), some moderns with *angerere*, 'to raise up', sc. the sun after the solstice.

Angitia, or the Angitiae, Marsian goddess(es) principally worshipped on the Fucine lake at Lucus Angitiae at Sulmo, where the plural of the name appears. Her native name was Anagtia; inscriptional evidence makes her a popular goddess of healing; she was subject to Hellenistic mythologizing. *See* ITALIC RELIGION.

animals in cult Numerous features of Greek religion attest links between animals and gods, usually between one animal or group of animals and one divinity. Thus *Athena is associated with various birds (in Athens especially the owl); *Dionysus is called 'bull' in an Elean hymn and seen as a bull by *Pentheus. There are traces, too, of a closer identification, in which gods (and/or their worshippers) appear in animal or part-animal form. Arcadia was in historical times the special home of theriomorphic deities (*see* ARCADIAN CULTS AND MYTHS); here we find a myth of *Poseidon's rape of *Demeter in equine form (*see* ARION, DESPOINA) along with Pausanias' reference to a horse-headed statue of Demeter, and the animal-headed figures decorating the robes of the cult-statues of Lycosura seem also to be related. But rituals involving the imitation of animals are found in other parts of the Greek world, the best-known example being probably the *arkteia* of *Brauron, where little girls played the part of bears in a ceremony for *Artemis.

By far the most important religious role of real animals in both Greece and Rome was that of sacrificial victim (*see* SACRIFICE). Animals for sacrifice were normally domesticated; pigs, sheep, goats, and cattle were the commonest species used, and it is likely that throughout antiquity most of the meat consumed from these animals would have been sacrificial meat. Deviant sacrifices, as of horses, fish, and also of wild animals more normally killed in hunting, are recorded in special contexts, but they are rare. Other sacred animals (which might also be sacrificed if appropriate) were those living in sacred enclosures and considered as consecrate to the deity: cattle, sheep, but also *snakes (like that on the Athenian acropolis), dogs (in the cult of *Asclepius), or geese (*Juno Moneta on the Capitoline). Some of these creatures had a more general religious significance: snakes were widely perceived as sacred, while dogs were normally considered impure in a religious context. The actions of some animals (especially *birds) were frequently seen as supplying omens, and prophecy from the entrails of sacrificial victims was also practised, in Greece, but more especially by the Etruscans and thence the Romans (*see* DIVINATION).

Anius, son of Apollo and king of *Delos. He prophesied that the Trojan War would last ten years. His mother Rhoeo (Pomegranate) was descended from *Dionysus through her father Staphylus ('Grape'). Anius married Dorippa and had three daughters, the Oeno-trophoi ('Rearers of Wine'): Oeno ('Wine'), Spermo ('Seed'), and Elaïs ('Olive-tree') who supplied Agamemnon's army before Troy. According to the myth (first in the *Epic Cycle), he received *Aeneas. A votive marble relief (2nd/1st cent. BC) with a dedication to Anius and with a typical funerary banqueting-scene was found near the hero's sanctuary on Delos.

Anna Perenna, Roman goddess with a merry festival on 15 March. This date on the Ides and the first full moon of the year by archaic reckoning (1 March being New Year's Day) imply a year-goddess; hence her name from the prayer *ut annare perennareque commode liceat* ('for leave to live in and through the year to our liking'). *Ovid tells three stories, one identifying her with Anna, sister of *Dido, the second with an old woman of Bovillae named Anna, who fed the plebeians during the secession to the mons Sacer; the third, after her apotheosis, provides an explanation of ribald verses via an encounter with *Mars Gradivus.

[Ovid, *Fasti* 3. 523–696]

Antaeus, in mythology, a giant, son of *Poseidon and Earth (*Gaia), living in Libya; he compelled all comers to wrestle with him and killed them when overcome. He was defeated and killed by *Heracles. That he was made stronger when thrown, by contact with his mother the Earth, seems a later addition to the story.

[Pindar, *Isthmian* 4. 56 ff.]

Antenor, in mythology, an elderly and up-right counsellor in Troy during the siege, who advised the return of *Helen to the Greeks, and in return for this (or, according to much later accounts, for betraying the city) was spared by the victors. *Pindar says his descendants held Cyrene; but in the story current in Roman times he took with him the Eneti from Paphlagonia (who had lost their king at Troy) and, settling in Venetia at the head of the Adriatic, founded Patavium (mod. Padua).

Anthesteria, a festival of *Dionysus which despite its name (suggesting *anthos*, flower) was associated particularly with the new wine. It was celebrated in most Ionian communities, but details are known almost exclusively from Athens, where it was of an importance comparable perhaps to modern Christmas. It was celebrated in the correspondingly named month Anthesterion, roughly late February. On the evening of the first day, 'Jar-opening' (*Pithoigia*), pithoi of the previous autumn's vintage were taken to the sanctuary of Dionysus in the Marshes, opened, offered to the god, and sampled. On the following day, drinking-parties of an abnormal type were held: participants sat at separate tables and competed, in silence, at draining a *chous* or five-litre measure (whence the day's name *Choes*); slaves too had a share. Miniature *choes* were also given as toys to children, and 'first Choes' was a landmark. The third day was called *Chytroi*,

'Pots', from pots of seed and vegetable bran (*panspermia*) that were offered, it seems, to the dead. On the basis of a proverb 'Away with you, Keres, it is no longer Anthesteria', it is often supposed that souls of the dead were conceived as wandering at the festival; but this is problematic, since *Kēres* are normally spirits of evil, not souls, and the proverb is also transmitted in the form 'Away with you, Carians (*Kares*)'. It was almost certainly during the Anthesteria that the wife of the *basileus* (see ARCHONTES) was somehow 'given as a bride' to Dionysus (who may have been escorted to her in image on a 'ship-chariot', a rite known from vases). A series of vases which show a mask of Dionysus on a pillar, in front of which women draw wine from mixing-bowls while others dance, may evoke a part of the same ceremony.

The main problem posed by the festival is to see how its different elements relate to one another. Recent critics have stressed the idea of 'reversal' as a unifying factor: it is clear at all events that the Anthesteria is not just an amalgam of a well-lubricated wine festival and a glum commemoration of the dead, as the Choes rite itself is marked by traits of abnormality and reversal.

anthropology and the classics currently enjoy a fairly good relationship, but one which has never been stable. In the 19th cent. the interest of evolutionary anthropology in a 'savage' period through which all societies must pass meant that studies of contemporary simple societies could be used to illuminate the classical past. After the First World War, classicists reacted against what were perceived as the excesses of the work of Jane Harrison and the Cambridge school, in which it was claimed that knowledge of 'things primitive' gave a better understanding of the Greeks. Meanwhile, in social anthropology, the rise of the static structural-functional paradigm and an insistence on an identity as 'the science of fieldwork' combined to cause a rejection of history. In the last 50 years, the divorce between the subjects has been eroded from both sides, with comparative studies increasingly valued as enabling us to escape from our intellectual heritage and the specific—though, to us, self-evident—ways it has formulated questions and sought answers.

Anthropology is a comparative science, and in this sense the classical scholar may draw on specific comparisons between societies in order to show the range of possible responses to an issue, especially one which to us seems particularly in need of explanation. By examining other societies with a similar feature, it is possible to discover how it functions. It may be possible to extrapolate from this, filling in—if only hypothetically—some of the gaps in the ancient record.

It is, however, no longer the case that classicists only turn to anthropology in desperation, when faced with a strange custom which fails to make any sense. Current work which makes use of anthropology tends to be theoretically sophisticated, and has the advantage of making theory explicit, rather than working from assumptions which, because they are left unstated, the reader cannot criticize or modify. Such work may treat the surviving sources like the anthropologist's fieldwork informants, whose words cannot be taken at face value; the fieldworker may observe one thing but be told the opposite. A fuller integration of the classics and anthropology promises a more sophisticated approach to evidence as well as a challenge to the traditional boundaries between disciplines within classics.

There remain dangers for classicists; for example, adopting concepts from anthropology after they have ceased to be used there, or failure to appreciate the disciplinary context within which a particular anthropologist's work falls. This warning also applies to the tendency in recent work to concentrate on comparisons with present-day Mediterranean societies, perceived as appropriate because of similar patterns of public/private, male/female, honour/shame; in fact, the concept of a 'Mediterranean' society has itself been questioned in anthropology, as too homogenized, taking little account of variation.

Anticlea, daughter of *Autolycus, wife of Laertes, and mother of *Odysseus and Ctimene. Her ghost tells Odysseus how she died of longing for him. She appeared in Polygnotus' picture of the Underworld at *Delphi. *Sisyphus is often said to have been Odysseus' father by her.

[Homer, *Odyssey* 11. 84–5, 152–224; cf. 15. 353–65]

Antigone (1), daughter of *Oedipus and Iocasta, sister of *Eteocles, Polynices, and Ismene.

*Sophocles' *Antigone* deals with events after the Theban War, in which Eteocles and Polynices killed one another (*see* SEVEN AGAINST THEBES). Antigone's uncle *Creon (1), the new king of Thebes, has issued an edict forbidding anyone to bury the body of the traitor Polynices. Antigone, though dissuaded by Ismene, insists on defying the edict. She is arrested and brought before Creon, and proudly defends her action. He decrees that she should be imprisoned in a tomb and left to die, although she is engaged to his son *Haemon (3). Creon is left unmoved by Haemon's arguments against such punishment, but is finally made to change his mind by the prophet *Tiresias, who reveals that the gods are angry at the exposure of Polynices and the burial of Antigone. He buries Polynices but arrives at Antigone's tomb too late: she has hanged herself, and Haemon, who has broken into the tomb, kills himself in front of his father. Creon's wife Eurydice also commits suicide, leaving Creon a broken man.

Antigone's role in the play has been the subject of endless dispute, with some critics claiming that she is wholly in the right, others that she and Creon are equally right and equally wrong. Most would now agree that she is no saint (she is harsh and unfair to Ismene, and her defiance of male authority would have shocked an Athenian audience), but still find her somehow admirable. The dispute, and the fascination, will continue.

While her story is unlikely to be pure invention by Sophocles, there is no definite evidence as to her earlier history. Facts that may be relevant are:

1. We are told that in the epic *Oedipodeia* (in the *Epic Cycle) Oedipus had children, not by his mother Iocasta, but by a woman called Euryganeia. The epic may have named the children of this union as Antigone, Ismene, Eteocles, and Polynices; Pherecydes of Athens certainly did so.

2. Mimnermus told a story about Ismene which is also mentioned in the Pherecydes fragment and illustrated on vases, but which is incompatible with her role in Sophocles (she was killed by *Tydeus, one of the attackers of Thebes). He may or may not have mentioned Antigone.

3. The *Seven against Thebes* of *Aeschylus, as we have it, ends with Antigone and Ismene mourning their brothers and Antigone defying a herald's edict against burying Polynices. But the role of the sisters in this play is thought to be a spurious addition influenced by Sophocles and by *Euripides' *Phoenician Women*.

4. According to a *dithyramb by Ion of Chios, Antigone and Ismene were burnt to death in the temple of Hera by Eteocles' son Laodamas. It is uncertain whether this is earlier than Sophocles' play.

5. *Pausanias was shown a place at Thebes where Antigone was supposed to have dragged the body of Polynices, and this has been seen as reflecting a tradition older than Sophocles' play (in which the body is not moved); but such reasoning is unreliable.

*Euripides too wrote an *Antigone*, according to which Antigone had a son, Maion, by Haemon. This must have some connection with a story in *Hyginus. Here Antigone, with the help of Polynices' widow Argeia, drags his body to the pyre of Eteocles. Antigone is arrested and Creon entrusts Haemon with the task of executing her, but instead Haemon lodges her with shepherds and pretends that she is dead. She bears him a son. Years later the son comes with her to Thebes to compete in some games, and Creon recognizes him as one of the Spartoi (descendants of the first Thebans) by a birthmark. In the end Haemon (evidently condemned by Creon) kills Antigone and himself. Probably Euripides' play dealt with the earlier part of this story (including Haemon's rescue of Antigone), while the later part (with Maion as a grown youth) comes from some later play, perhaps the *Antigone* of the younger Astydamas.

[Sophocles, *Antigone*; Hyginus 72; Sophocles, *Oedipus at Colonus*; Euripides, *Phoenician Women*; Seneca, *Phoenician Women*; Statius, *Thebais*]

Antigone (2), daughter of Eurytion son of Actor, king of Phthia. *Peleus was purified by her father after the murder of *Phocus and married her, with a third of the country for her dowry. Later she hanged herself out of jealousy.

Antigone (3), daughter of *Laomedon, king of Troy. Because she vied in beauty with *Hera, the latter turned her hair into snakes. Afterwards Hera, or the other gods, turned her into a stork, which preys on snakes.

[Ovid, *Metamorphoses* 6. 93–5]

Antilochus, in mythology, son of *Nestor, mentioned several times in the *Iliad* as a brave warrior and a fine runner. He brings *Achilles the news of *Patroclus' death, drives cleverly in the chariot-race, and courteously cedes the second prize to *Menelaus. His death is mentioned; it took place (according to the *Epic Cycle, followed by *Pindar) while he was defending his father against *Memnon, when *Paris had killed one of Nestor's horses and he called Antilochus to his help.

Antinous (1), son of Eupeithes, ringleader of *Penelope's suitors, and first to be killed by *Odysseus, whose kingship he is said to have wished to usurp.

[Homer, *Odyssey* 1. 383, 22. 8–53]

Antinous (2), from Claudiopolis (Bithynium) in Bithynia, born perhaps c.AD 110, was Hadrian's companion on his longest provincial tour and generally regarded as the emperor's 'beloved': his death by drowning in the Nile in October 130, claimed by some to have been suicide or a ritual sacrifice, was mourned extravagantly by Hadrian. Antinous was deified, the city of Antinoöpolis was founded near the place of death, and statues, cults, and festivals proliferated.

Antiochus (1) **IV** (Epiphanes) (c.215–164 BC), third son of Antiochus III, became king in 175. He sought actively to reconsolidate the remaining huge Seleucid empire, from Cilicia and Syria eastwards, after the Peace of Apamea (188) had precluded the Seleucids from their possessions north of the Taurus. His intervention in *Jerusalem, overturning Antiochus III's 'charter for Jerusalem' (following Antiochus III's capture of it from the Ptolemies), guaranteeing the worship of Yahweh and the extensive privileges of all those involved in the cult, in co-operation with an 'hellenizing party,' has, from the viewpoint of Seleucid historiography, resulted in a distorted and hostile picture of the king, presented in Maccabees 1–3 (*see* MACCABEES), whereas in reality Judaea was strategically and economically of minor importance. Antiochus was active as a benefactor of cities of Aegean Greece and of indigenous cities within the Seleucid empire. The great resources of military manpower remaining are reflected in accounts of the famous procession mounted by him at *Daphne (166/5), prior to his anabasis to the 'Upper Satrapies', a major military campaign, in which he met his death.

Antiochus (2), of Athens (not later than AD 300), author of a popular compilation of astrological lore. *See* ASTROLOGY.

Antiope, mother of *Amphion and Zethus, whom she bore to *Zeus and/or *Epopeus of Sicyon. In Hamer's *Odyssey* she is daughter of Asopus. This would locate her firmly in southern Boeotia, and fits the traditions which give her native town as Hyria, the place where she gave birth as Eleutherae, and the place where her sons lived before Thebes as Eutresis. A second version makes her daughter of Nycteus, brother of Lycus (*see* LYCUS, end). The two brothers, descended from Chthonius, one of the *Spartoi, returned from exile in Hyria when Lycus became regent for Laius. Antiope was impregnated by *Zeus, her father took umbrage, and she fled to Sicyon where she married Epopeus. Nycteus died, Lycus attacked and slew Epopeus, and led Antiope back to Thebes. *En route*, at Eleutherae, she bore her sons, who were reared by a cattleman. Antiope was imprisoned by Lycus and his wife *Dirke, but years later escaped and was reunited with her sons, who then punished Dirke and Lycus.

Subsequently Antiope was married to *Phocus and was buried at Tithorea (scene of a regular agricultural ritual): it is thought that this pairing is depicted on an Attic red-figure vase of the late 5th cent., which suggests a possible Euripidean origin for this.

The connection with Epopeus is one of several legendary threads binding Thebes to Sicyon, home of *Adrastus. There was also a river Asopus in the territory of Sicyon, which may have helped.

[Homer, *Odyssey* 11. 260–5; Pausanias 2. 5. 2-3, 9. 17. 3; Propertius 3. 15. 11–42]

anti-Semitism *See* JEWS; JUDAISM; SEMITISM, ANTI-.

Antoninus Liberalis, *mythographer, probably of 2nd cent AD, published a 'Collection of Metamorphoses' based on Hellenistic sources, e.g. the poet Nicander.

Anubis, one of several local divine guardians of the dead in Egypt, originally in the form of a jackal, later as a human figure with a dog's head. As lord of the necropolis, he supervised embalmment, and conducted the judgement of the dead. In Hellenistic times he was identified with *Hermes, as Hermanubis. Linked to the ideal funeral of *Osiris, he entered the cult of *Isis; in the inscriptions of the Serapeum at *Delos (3rd–2nd cent. BC) he has no association with death. In the Principate, he stands for the absurdity or wickedness of Egyptian religion, later for its pious strangeness.

[Plutarch, *On Isis and Osiris* 61 (375e); Virgil, *Aeneid* 8. 696–700; Apuleius, *Metamorphoses* 11. 11]

aparchē, 'first-fruits', a gift to the gods consisting in a part representing the whole, and hence named 'from the beginning' (Gk. *aparchai*, Lat. *primitiae*, Hebr. *bikkurim*). The swineherd *Eumaeus, having killed a pig for *Odysseus, cuts 'beginnings from the limbs' and burns them. 'First-fruits' are a step from nature to culture: one renounces 'firsts' for the sake of 'Those who are First'. *Aparchai* could be either burnt, deposited at sacred spots, or sunk in water. They could consist of seasonal agricultural gifts (*hōraia*), or those vowed ad hoc. Measures of wheat, barley, wine, and meat could be regulated as gifts to temples (as the Panhellenic *aparchai* in *Eleusis) and could serve, in turn, for public festivals. *See also* FIRST-FRUITS.

[Homer, *Odyssey* 14. 414–53]

Apaturia, an *Ionian festival. (*Apellai was a partial *Dorian/Boeotian equivalent.) According to Herodotus, Ionians are all those who 'derive from Athens and celebrate the festival Apaturia. All Ionians celebrate it except Ephesians and Colophonians.' Details are known almost exclusively from Athens. It is unique among Greek festivals in its special association with a particular social grouping, the *phratry, or brotherhood: the phratries celebrated it, in the autumn month Pyanopsion, at their separate centres throughout Attica, and its main function was to enrol new phratry members (who by this registration acquired a title to citizenship). It lasted three days, called (1) *Dorpia*, from the 'dinner' the *phratores* held together on assembling in the evening; (2) Anarrhysis, from the 'drawing back' of the necks of the victims sacrificed to *Zeus Phratrios and

*Athena Phratria that day; (3) *Koureōtis*, the day of admission-sacrifices brought by the relatives of prospective new members: if the *phratores* ate of the animal, the candidate was thereby acknowledged. Three types of admission sacrifice are known, the occasions of which appear to have been: *meion*, 'lesser', a preliminary offering made during early childhood; *koureion*, 'hair-cutting', on entry to the ephebate; *gamēlia*, 'marriage offering', brought by newly-married *phratores* on behalf of their wives. Whether women other than wives (mothers of future *phratores*) were acknowledged by phratries is uncertain.

Apellai was a festival of *Apollo at Sparta and elsewhere, the orthography deriving from the Doric form (*Apellōn*). The principal annual celebration of this Dorian festival corresponded to the Ionian *Apaturia, at which new members of the phratry (brotherhood) and tribe were formally admitted. The religious *calendars of many Dorian states contained the month Apellaios, as did that of *Delphi. At Sparta, the festival was monthly, on the seventh, when the Spartan assembly met.

apex, a special kind of cap worn by Roman *flamines*, *Salii, and some other priests. The word is said originally to have meant not the whole cap, but the spike or twig at the top of it, tied on with wool. The lower part of the head-dress was called the *galerus* and that of the *flamen Dialis* was the *albogalerus*, the white *galerus*, made of the skins of white victims sacrificed to *Jupiter. The *galerus* was a tight-fitting conical cap, visible in representations of *flamines* on reliefs. The *apex* achieved notoriety because *flamines* were obliged to resign if it fell off during a *sacrifice; such occasions were recorded.

Aphaea, a goddess worshipped in Aegina, where the ruins of her temple (famous for its pedimental sculptures, now in Munich) are still extant. She was identified with *Britomartis; i.e. she was of similar character to *Artemis.

Aphrodite Born from the severed genitals of *Uranus according to *Hesiod, or in the Homeric version (*see* HOMER) daughter of *Zeus and *Dione, Aphrodite is the representative among the gods of an ambivalent female nature combining seductive charm, the need to procreate, and a capacity for deception, elements all found in the person of the first woman, *Pandora. There is no agreement on her historical origins; the Greeks themselves thought of her as coming from the east, and in literature she is frequently given the name Cypris, 'the Cyprian'. The double tradition of her birth shows how the Greeks felt Aphrodite to be at the same time Greek and foreign, but also, on the level of mythology, that they perceived her as a powerful goddess whom it would be prudent to place under the authority of Zeus.

Aphrodite's cults extend very widely over the Greek world, though her temples and festivals cannot compete with those of the other great figures of the pantheon. Cyprus is the home of her most famous cults, for instance at Paphos and Amathus. There, probably in the Archaic period, the name Aphrodite became attached to an indigenous goddess who was also subject to numerous oriental influences. In Greece itself, one or more cults of Aphrodite are known in every region. She was worshipped above all as presiding over sexuality and reproduction—necessary for the continuity of the community. Thus in many cities girls about to be married sacrificed to Aphrodite so that their first sexual experience might be propitious. This is the particular sphere of Aphrodite, compared with other goddesses involved in marriage like *Hera and *Demeter, a function especially emphasized in the Argolid by the mythological connections between cults of Aphrodite and the story of the Danaids (*see* DANAUS). The close bond which the Greeks felt to exist between human fertility and the fruitfulness of the land lies behind Aphrodite's connections with vegetation and the earth in general: as Melainis at Corinth and Mantinea the 'black'

Aphrodite shows her power over the 'black earth' as well as her links with the powers of the night. In Athens, Aphrodite *en kēpois*, 'in gardens', was worshipped together with Athena at the *Arrephoria, a rite concerned with fertility and with the sexuality of the *arrhephoroi* as future wives of citizens. This Aphrodite was also worshipped by prostitutes. Epithets such as Hetaira ('courtesan') and Porne ('prostitute') show her as protectress of this profession, whose essential stock-in-trade was seduction. Corinth was particularly well known for the beauty and luxurious living of its prostitutes, who revered the local Aphrodite. All the same, it is unlikely that her sanctuary on Acrocorinth was the location of an institutionalized form of what is usually called 'sacred prostitution'. The only source (Strabo) for such a remarkable practice in a Greek context, places it in a vague past time, and is surely influenced by the eastern practices with which he was familiar. Herodotus also mentions a similar practice in several parts of the Mediterranean area, and his silence in regard to Corinth should invite caution. *See* PROSTITUTION, SACRED.

If Aphrodite was worshipped primarily by women, men also took part in her cult, notably in connection with her role as patron of seafaring (Aphrodite Euploia, Pontia, Limenia). Aphrodite is also concerned with magistrates in their official capacity, being the deity of concord and civic harmony. The title Pandemos, which is hers conspicuously in Athens, indicates her protection of the whole citizen body, but she can also be linked with a particular civic office (e.g. as Stratagis in Acarnania), and as Epistasie on Thasos. In this context, she is frequently associated with *Hermes, *Peitho, and the *Charites. Thus Plato's interpretation in the Symposium of the epithets Urania and Pandemos as indicating respectively exalted and common love is completely unfounded. The title Urania, 'heavenly', occurs frequently in cult and refers to the power of the goddess who presides over every type of union. It is with this epithet that the name Aphrodite is used as the Greek designation of foreign goddesses, a process found already in Herodotus and which accelerates with the *syncretisms of the Hellenistic period. The title also expresses one of Aphrodite's ambiguities, making her simultaneously 'daughter of Uranus' and 'the goddess who has come from elsewhere'. According to Pausanias, there were several statues showing an armed Aphrodite, particularly at Sparta. Considering the special characteristics of the upbringing of Spartiate girls, it is not too surprising that the goddess of femaleness should be given male attire, but the actual examples of the type scarcely permit us to see in her a war-goddess, except in connection with a protecting role such as she has at Corinth. Her association with *Ares, prominent in the literary tradition, has more to do with a wish to bring opposites together than with any similarity of function.

From Sappho to Lucretius, literature celebrates the power of love and the dominion of Aphrodite. Ares, *Adonis, Hermes, and *Dionysus are all at various times given as her lovers, as is the mortal *Anchises, but apart from a few isolated examples these associations do not appear in cult. *See* VENUS.

[Homer, *Iliad* 5. 370–417; Hesiod, *Theogony* 188–206, *Works and Days* 60–8; *Homeric Hymn to Aphrodite*; Lucretius 1. 30–41]

Apis, the sacred bull at Memphis in Egypt, oracular 'herald' of *Ptah, with distinctive markings. The cult probably goes back to the earliest Old Kingdom. When the bull died, the body was embalmed and borne in procession to the subterranean 'great chambers' at Saqqara. Thousands of invocations found there, requesting Apis to bless life and name, testify to the cult's appeal to Egyptians. The embalmed bull was termed Osiris-Apis, from which in the Ptolemaic period was developed the Alexandrian cult of *Sarapis.

[Plutarch, *On Isis and Osiris* 43 (368c)]

apocalyptic literature The apocalyptic literature composed by Jews and Christians in antiquity purports to offer information of God's purposes by means of revelation. In the apocalypses, understanding of God and the world is rooted in the claim to a superior knowledge in which insight of the divine through vision or audition transcends the wisdom of human reason. While an apocalyptic dimension has always formed a part of Jewish religion (evident in the material in the biblical literature which speaks of the prophet's access to the heavenly council), the writing of the extant Jewish apocalypses, most of which were preserved by Christians rather than Jews (mostly in Greek or in translations from the Greek), took place in a period which roughly spanned the career of Alexander the Great to the end of the *Bar Kokhba Revolt and may best be seen as the form the prophetic tradition took at the end of the Second Temple period. The apocalypses are linked to the prophetic writings of the Hebrew Bible (the book of Daniel is an example), though their emphasis on heavenly knowledge and the interpretation of dreams links them with the mantic wisdom of the seers of antiquity. All the apocalyptic texts are distinguished from the prophetic by the range of their imagery and the character of the literary genre. Most apocalypses go under the names of people other than the author (Revelation in the New Testament seems to be exceptional in this respect) and contain heavenly revelations mediated in different ways (heavenly ascents as the prelude to the disclosure of divine mysteries, an angelic revealer descending to earth to communicate information to the apocalyptic seer). Because in most of the extant apocalypses there is a particular focus on the destiny of the world, it is often stated that they offer evidence of an imminent expectation of the end of the world accompanied by the irruption of a new order. This is said by some scholars to contrast with a more material eschatology found in the rabbinic literature in which the future order of things evolves within history. This distinction is to be rejected as all the extant Jewish apocalypses offer an account of a hope for the future of the world which differs little from other non-apocalyptic sources.

The earliest apocalyptic material is probably found in the Enoch tradition, particularly in the collection of material known as 1 Enoch, many fragments of which have been discovered at Qumran (*see* DEAD SEA SCROLLS) and which may date from at least the 3rd cent. BC. That apocalypse contains material from a variety of sources and periods and includes legends about antediluvian heroes, revelations about astronomical calculations, geographical information, and heavenly journeys, all of which was to become typical of apocalyptic literature. There was a flowering of apocalyptic literature after the First Jewish Revolt (2 Esdras, the Syriac Apocalypse of Baruch, and the Apocalypse of Abraham being examples), when discussion of *theodicy is added to the other interests of the apocalyptists, reminiscent in many ways of the book of Job.

In the rabbinic tradition (*see* RABBIS) the perspective of apocalyptic was severely circumscribed by confining the study of certain biblical texts with cosmological and theosophic content to well-trained interpreters, though it appears to have been more widespread than our sources suggest. The contrast between the apocalyptic literature and rabbinic literature is not as great as may appear at first sight. Care needs to be taken before drawing conclusions from the content of different types of text about the existence of ideological conflicts between rabbis and apocalyptists, as the genre of the literature explains the absence of the minutiae of law from the latter. Because apocalyptic has been so consistently linked with eschatology its visionary and mystical elements have been ignored, but the mystical element of apocalyptic literature continued to be a central component of rabbinic religion. In Christianity apoca-lyptic was initially central to primitive Christianity, as the central role which visions and revelations played in the various accounts of the Christian Church's emergence in the New Testament make plain. It fell out of favour as a result of its importance in some Gnostic and Montanist circles (a fact which led to suspicion of the book of Revelation; *see* GNOSTICISM; MONTANISM), though the distinctive dualism of apocalyptic theology lies at the heart of *Augustine's *City of God*.

See PROPHECIES.

Apollo, Greek god, son of *Zeus and *Leto, brother of *Artemis, for many the most Greek of Greek gods. Among his numerous and diverse functions healing and *purification, prophecy, care for young citizens, for poetry, and music are prominent. In iconography, he is always young, beardless, and of harmonious beauty, the ideal young man and young athlete; his weapon is the bow, and his plant the laurel.

His name is absent from Linear B (while Paean, his later title and hymn, appears as *Paiawon* in the pantheon of Mycenaean Cnossus). In *Homer and *Hesiod, his myth and cult are fully developed, and his main centres, *Delos and *Delphi, are well-known (Delian altar of Apollo; Delphic shrine; stone of Cronus) though none goes back to the bronze age: Apollo's cult must have been introduced and brought to panhellenic importance during the Dark Ages. Epic poetry, where Apollo is prominent, had its decisive share in this development. The key document is the *Homeric Hymn to Apollo* (*see* HYMNS, GREEK); it consists of two aetiological parts, a Delian part which tells the story of Apollo's birth and a Delphic part about the foundation of the oracular shrine in Delphi; opinions about structure and date vary, though a date in the 7th cent. BC for the Delian, and one slightly later for the Delphic part are plausible.

The origins of Apollo are debated; after earlier theories explaining the god from the sun (following an identification as old as the 5th cent., and adding the linguistic argument that the epithet *Lykeios* would derive from the stem *luc-*, as in latin *lux*), partisans of an Anatolian, esp. Lycian, origin relied upon the same epithet and upon his mother's name being Lycian and connected with *lada*, 'earth'; the French excavations in Lycian Xanthus proved both assumptions wrong. More promising is the connection with Dorian *apella* 'assembly', i.e. annual reunion of the adult tribesmen which also introduces the young men into the community (*see* APEL-LAI). This explains his widespread role as the divinity responsible for the introduction of young initiated adults into society: he receives the first cut hair at the end of *initiation (Hesiod, mentioning Apollo together with *kourai*, 'Girls', i.e. *nymphs, and rivers), and his cult has to do with military and athletic training (cult of Apollo Lycius at Athens; the 'Wolf-Apollo' has to do with Archaic wolf-warriors) and with the citizen-right of the sons. His cult on the lonely island of Delos, where Leto gave birth after long search, became the religious focus of Archaic Ionia at least from the late 8th cent. onwards; before this date, archaeology shows a more regional, Cycladic influence. While a Delian temple of Artemis was present already in the 8th cent. (bronze age origin and continuity are contested), a temple of Apollo was built only in the mid-6th cent.; his cult centred around the famous altar of horns (parallels from Archaic Drerus on Crete, from Ephesus, and from Boeotian Hyampolis, are now archaeologically attested).

Apollo's interest in music and poetry could derive from the same source, music and poetry having an educational role in Greece. Apollo's instrument is the lyre whose well-ordered music is opposed to the ecstatic rhythms of flute and drums which belong to *Dionysus and *Cybele; according to the *Homeric Hymn to Hermes*, he received it from Hermes, its inventor. He is, together with the *Muses, protector of epic singers and cithara-players; later, he is Musagetes,

'Leader of the Muses', in Pindar and on Archaic images. When philosophy takes over a similar educational function, he is associated with philosophy, and an anecdote makes him the real father of Plato.

His own song, the *paean, is sung and danced by the young Achaeans after the sacrifice to Apollo when bringing back *Chryseis to her father: even if not necessarily a healing-song in this passage, it was understood as such later and was accordingly transferred to Asclepius as well. In the *Iliad*, Paieon could still be understood as an independent healing god; later, it is an epithet of Apollo the Healer. The Ionian Apollo Iatros ('Healer') had cult in most Black Sea cities, and as *Medicus* Apollo was taken over by the Romans during a *plague in the 5th cent. (see below). Only the rise of *Asclepius in the 5th and 4th cents. eclipsed this function, though in *Epidaurus, where Apollo took over a bronze age hill-sanctuary of Maleatas, Apollo Maleatas preceded Asclepius in official nomenclature until the imperial period. In *Iliad* 1 he is responsible both for sending and for averting the plague. The image of a god sending plague by shooting arrows points to the ancient near east where Reshep 'of the arrow' is the plague-god in bronze age Ugarit/Ras Shamra and on Cyprus; details of iconography point to a transfer from Cyprus to Spartan *Amyclae—and in the Archaic Dorian world of Crete and Sparta, the paean is first attested as an individual poetical genre; both in *Iliad* and in the cultic reality of the Spartan Apollo, paean and *kouroi* ('young men') are closely connected.

Disease is the consequence of impurity, healing is purification—in myth, this theme later crystallized around Orestes whom Delphic Apollo cleansed of the murder of his mother, and of the concomitant madness. Oracular Apollo (*see* ORACLES) is often connected with purification and plague; he decreed the Cyrenean purification laws (6th cent.) and the setting up of his statue to avert the Athenian plague of 430 BC. But this is only a small part of the much wider oracular function which Apollo had not only in his shrines at Delphi and the *Ptoion on the Greek mainland, and at Branchidae (*see* DIDYMA), *Claros, and Gryneum in Asia Minor, but also in his relationship with the *Sibyl(s) and other seers like *Bacis or *Cassandra; while the Sibyls are usually priestesses of Apollo (e.g. Erythrae, or Cumae), Cassandra refused Apollo as a lover. Apolline prophecy was usually ecstatic: the Delphic *Python was possessed by the god (in New Testament Greek, *pythōn* is 'ventriloquist'), as were the Sibyls, Cassandra, young Branchus, and Bacis; and the priest of Claros attained ecstasy through drinking water. Apollo's supreme wisdom is beyond human rationality.

In Archaic and Classical Greece, Delphi was the central oracular shrine (see the quest of Croesus to find the best oracle in Greece). Though his cult had grown out of purely local worship in the 8th cent., myth saw its foundation as a primordial event, expressing it in the theme of dragon-slaying; alternative myths gave an even longer prehistory to Apollo's taking over and his temple building. Like isolated Delos, marginal Delphi achieved international political importance in Archaic Greece simply for being marginal. But from his role as a political adviser, Apollo acquired no further political functions—and only a marginally moralistic character.

In Italy, Apollo's arrival in Rome during a plague in 433 BC was due to a recommendation of the Sibylline Books: to avert the plague, a temple of Apollo Medicus was vowed and built just outside the *pomerium*, where there had already by 449 been an *Apollinar*, presumably an open cult-place of the god. In Etruria, no cult of Apollo is attested, though his name, in the form *Aplu*, is read in mythological representations (with a Greek iconography): the form shows that the name was taken over from Latin *Apollo*, not directly from the Greek. Until the time of Augustus, the temple of Apollo Medicus was the only Roman temple of the god, and healing his main function; the

Vestals addressed him as 'Apollo Medice, Apollo Paean'. Mainly in response to Mark Antony's adoption of Dionysus, and perhaps already stimulated by the victory of Philippi which Caesar's heirs had won in the name of Apollo, *Augustus made Apollo his special god. In 31 BC, Augustus vowed a second temple to Apollo in Rome after the battle of Actium, where, from his nearby sanctuary, the god was said to have helped against Mark Antony and Cleopatra; the temple was built and dedicated in 28, close to the house of Augustus on the *Palatine, with a magnificent adjoining library. *See* DIVINATION; ORACLES.

[Homer, *Iliad* 1; *Homeric Hymns to Apollo* and *Hermes*; Apollodorus 1. 4]

Apollodorus of Athens (*c.*180–after 120 BC), studied in Athens, collaborated with Aristarchus in Alexandria, perhaps fled (in 146?), probably to Pergamum, and later lived in Athens. A scholar of great learning and varied interests, he was the last of a series of intellectual giants in Alexandria.

Works 1. *Chronicle*. Written in comic trimeters which made it easy to memorize, it covered successive periods of history, philosophical schools, and the life and work of individuals from the fall of Troy (1184) to 146/5; later it was continued to 119 or 110/9 BC. 2. *On the Gods*, a rationalistic account of Greek religion, much used by later writers, including Philodemus. 3. A twelve-book commentary on the Homeric *Catalogue of Ships*, which accounted for Homeric geography and subsequent changes. Apollodorus' authority gave rise to forgeries: a geographical guidebook in comic trimeters (1st cent. BC) and the extant *Bibliotheca*, a study of Greek heroic mythology which presents an uncritical summary of the traditional Greek mythology (1st or 2nd cent. AD). *See* MYTHOGRAPHERS; TIME-RECKONING.

Apollonius Rhodius, a major literary figure of 3rd-cent. Alexandria, and poet of the *Argonautica* (270–45), the only extant Greek hexameter epic written between

*Homer and the Roman imperial period. The poem, on the Argonautic legend (*see* ARGONAUTS), is in four long books totalling 5,835 preserved verses. It was very important at Rome, where it was translated in the 1st cent. BC, is a major influence on Catullus 64 and *Virgil's *Aeneid*, and, with the *Aeneid*, forms the basis of Valerius Flaccus' *Argonautica*.

Books 1–2 deal with the outward voyage, to recover the golden fleece, from *Iolcus in Thessaly to the Colchian city of Aia at the extreme eastern edge of the Black Sea (in modern Georgia), which is ruled over by Aeëtes, the cruel son of *Helios. The major events of this voyage are a stay at Lemnos where the local women, who have murdered the entire male population, seize the chance for procreation, and *Jason sleeps with Queen *Hypsipyle; the loss of *Heracles from the expedition; a boxing-match between *Amycus, king of the Bebrycians, and Polydeuces (*see* DIOSCURI); meeting with the blind prophet *Phineus whom the Argonauts save from the depredations of the Harpies (*see* HARPYIAE) and who, in return, tells them of the voyage ahead; passage through the Clashing Rocks (*Symplegades) which guard the entrance to the Black Sea; meeting on the island of Ares with the sons of Phrixus, who fled Greece on the golden ram. In Book 3 Jason asks Aeëtes to grant him the fleece; this the king agrees to do on the condition that Jason ploughs an enormous field with fire-breathing bulls, sows it with dragon's teeth, and slays the armed warriors who rise up from the ground. Jason succeeds in this, because, at the instigation of Jason's protector Hera, the king's daughter, *Medea, falls in love with the hero and supplies him with a magic salve to protect him and give him superhuman strength. In Book 4 Medea flees to join the Argonauts and secures the fleece for them from the grove where it is guarded by a sleepless dragon. The Argonauts flee via a great river, the Danube, which is pictured as flowing from the Black Sea to the Adriatic; at the Adriatic mouth, Jason and Medea lure her brother, Apsyrtus, who commands the pursuing Colchians, to his death, a crime for which Zeus decides that they must be purified by Medea's aunt *Circe who lives on the west coast of Italy. They reach Circe via rivers (the Po and the Rhône) imagined to link north-east Italy with the western Mediterranean. From there they sail to Drepane (mod. Corfu), Homer's *Scheria, where Jason and Medea are married, and are then driven to the wastes of Libya where they are again saved by divine intervention. They finally return home by way of Crete, where Medea uses her magic powers to destroy the bronze giant *Talos who guards the island.

The central poetic technique of Apollonius is the creative reworking of *Homer. While the Hellenistic poet takes pains to avoid the repetitiveness characteristic of Archaic epic, Homer is the main determinative influence on every aspect of the poem, from the details of language to large-scale narrative patterns, material culture, and technology (e.g. sailing) which is broadly 'Homeric'. This is most obvious in set scenes such as the Catalogue of Argonauts, corresponding to Homer's Catalogue of Ships, the description of the cloak Jason wears to meet Hypsipyle, corresponding to the Shield of *Achilles, the meeting of *Hera, *Athena, and *Aphrodite on *Olympus at the start of book 3 which finds many forerunners in Homer, the scenes in the palace of Aeëtes, corresponding to the scenes of the *Odyssey* on Scheria, and the voyage in the western Mediterranean, corresponding to *Odysseus' adventures on his way home. These scenes function by contrast: the Homeric 'model' is the base-text by which what is importantly different in the later poem is highlighted. Individual characters too owe much to Homeric predecessors, while also being markedly different from them: e.g. Jason/Odysseus, Medea/*Nausicaa and Circe. After Homer, the two most important literary influences are *Pindar's account of the Argonauts (*Pythian* 4) and *Euripides' *Medea*; the events of the tragedy are foreshadowed in a number of places in the epic—perhaps most strikingly in the murder of Apsyrtus who goes to his death 'like a tender child'—and in one sense the epic shows us that the events of the tragedy were 'inevitable', given the earlier history of Jason and Medea.

Apollonius of Tyana, a Neopythagorean holy man (see NEOPYTHAGOREANISM), whose true history and persona it is scarcely possible to grasp. According to the only full account, the highly untrustworthy 'biography' of Philostratus, he was born at Tyana in Cappadocia at the beginning of the 1st cent. AD and survived to the late 1st cent. He led the life of an ascetic wandering teacher (see ASCETICISM), visited distant lands (including India), advised cities (e.g. Sparta), had life-threatening encounters with Nero and Domitian, whose death he simultaneously prophesied, and on his own death underwent heavenly assumption. He was the object of posthumous cult attracting the patronage of the Severan emperors; pagan apologists compared him favourably to Jesus. An epigram from Cilicia (not before the 3rd cent. AD) describes him as 'extinguishing the faults of men'. Of his writings there survive some doubtfully authentic letters and a fragment of his treatise *On Sacrifices*.

apologists, Christian The term designates a number of Christian Greek and Latin authors of the 2nd and early 3rd cents. who defended the Christian faith against attacks from their pagan contemporaries. Apologists in this sense, whose writings are partly or fully preserved, are Quadratus, Aristides, *Justin Martyr, *Tatian, *Melito, *Athenagoras, and *Theophilus (1) of Antioch, who all wrote in Greek, and the Latin authors *Minucius Felix and *Tertullian. Nothing is left of the works of Miltiades and Apollinaris of Hierapolis. They all wrote at a time when the legal position of the new religious groups was unclear and the Christians were under continuous threat from their *pagan environment (see CHRISTIANITY). In a wider sense, however, later

writers such as Hermias, the author of the *Epistle to Diognetus*, *Clement of Alexandria, ps.-Justin, *Commodianus, *Arnobius, *Lactantius, and *Firmicus Maternus are also called apologists. Moreover, there are numerous writings by authors not labelled thus, which, nevertheless, serve apologetical purposes. In addition, the term is sometimes also understood to include authors writing against *Gnostics and Jews. This is, however, misleading, because these anti-Gnostic and anti-Jewish works imply other historical settings and differ considerably in content and style from the writings against pagans. The apologists proper wrote in various styles and literary genres, among which mention must be made of the *Apology*, a fictional forensic defence which may have originated in petitions to the Roman emperor(s), and the *Oration to/against the Greeks/Pagans* the precise real-life context of which is unclear. Minucius Felix composed a dialogue (*Octavius*). Likewise, the individual rhetorical strategies of these authors vary considerably. Some of them harshly attack anything non-Christian, whereas others seek to accommodate pagan ideas and concepts. The apologists had to defend themselves against popular charges such as 'Thyestean banquets' (i.e. cannibalism) and 'Oedipean intercourse' (i.e. incest) and against philosophical criticisms (*atheism and novelty and, therefore, by implication, political subversion as well). They responded by setting out their doctrine of God and Christian ethics and emphasizing their antiquity and their loyalty towards the Roman authorities. At the same time, they returned the charges brought against them and accused the pagans of idolatry and immorality. In particular, they criticized Greek and Roman myths and pointed out the contradictions among philosophers. In practice, therefore, many of these tracts go beyond pure apologetics and also serve protreptic and missionary purposes. They attempt to 'translate' the Christian faith into Greek philosophical categories and thus to make it acceptable to the pagan élite. It is not known, however, whether this literature had an immediate impact. In any case, the apologists, for the first time, tackled a variety of theological issues (e.g. the oneness of God, but also the relation between God the Father and Son (Logos), demonology, eschatology, and the immortality of the *soul) and are, therefore, important for the history of Christian dogma.

apophrades were 'impure' days of the Athenian *calendar, days associated with inauspicious rites (as e.g. of the *Plynteria, homicide trials in the Areopagus court, and, perhaps, more generally with the 'moonless' times at the end of the month. Because *pollution was thought to be abroad, temples were closed and major undertakings were avoided. The term was later used to translate Roman *dies nefasti* and *dies atri* which were, in fact, somewhat different from the Attic *apophrades*.

Apuleius, writer and orator, born c.AD 125 of prosperous parents at Madaurus in Africa Proconsularis, and educated in Carthage, Athens, and Rome; at Athens he gained enough philosophy to be called *philosophus Platonicus* by himself and others. He claims to have travelled extensively as a young man, and was on his way to Alexandria when he arrived at Oea, probably in the winter of AD 156. The story from that point is told by Apuleius himself in his *Apologia*, no doubt in the most favourable version possible; at Oea he met an ex-pupil from Athens, Pontianus, who persuaded him to stay there for a year and eventually to marry his mother Pudentilla in order to protect her fortune for the family. Subsequently, Apuleius was accused by various other relations of Pudentilla of having induced her to marry him through magic means; the case was heard at Sabratha, near Oea, in late 158 or early 159. We can deduce from the publication of the *Apologia* (see below) that he was acquitted. The *Florida* make it clear that Apuleius was active as a public speaker and philosophical lecturer in Carthage in the 160s AD, and he seems to have been made

priest of the imperial cult for his province (*see* RULER-CULT); nothing is known of him after 170. Scholars disagree on whether the *Metamorphoses* is a late or early work, though more think it late than early.

The *Apologia*, Apuleius' speech of defence against charges of *magic (see above), is an extraordinary rhetorical *tour de force*. In rebutting the charges Apuleius digresses hugely in order to show a vast range of literary and other learning, and presents himself as a committed intellectual and philosopher. The title recalls Plato's *Apology*, the argumentation Cicero at his most colourful.

The *Metamorphoses*, sometimes called the *Golden Ass*, is the only Latin novel which survives whole. On an epic scale (eleven books) and full of narratological cleverness, erotic, humorous, and sensational by turns, it is a remarkable and fascinating work. The basic story is that of the young man Lucius, who through his curiosity to discover the secrets of witchcraft is metamorphosed into a donkey and undergoes a variety of picaresque adventures before being retransformed through the agency of the goddess *Isis. This plot is punctuated by a number of inserted tales, which have in fact a close thematic relation to the main narrative; the most substantial and best-known of them is that of Cupid and Psyche ('Soul' in Greek, *see* PSYCHE), which parallels the main story of Lucius by presenting a character (Psyche) whose disastrous curiosity causes troublesome adventures before her rescue through divine agency. The last book provides a much-discussed and controversial double twist: after his rescue by Isis, Lucius' lowlife adventures are interpreted in a new religious and providential light, and the identity of the narrator seems to switch from Lucius to Apuleius himself, a final metamorphosis.

Aquae Sulis (mod. Bath). The hot springs, perhaps used in the iron age, were developed from the Neronian period and attained great elaboration, rivalling the largest Gallic establishments. The hot spring was enclosed in a polygonal reservoir in the south-east corner of a colonnaded precinct within which stood the prostyle temple with its altar axially in front. The temple carried the famous Gorgon pediment. South of the precinct the spring connected with the principal suite of baths. Many inscriptions record visitors from Britain and abroad, whilst excavation of the sacred spring has produced 130 curse-tablets (*see* CURSES), the most important such archive for Romano-Celtic religion yet published (*see* BRITAIN, ROMAN, CULTS). The site was deserted in Saxon times, the ruins being described in an 8th-cent. poem.

Ara Pacis, a monumental altar erected in the northern Campus Martius near the via Lata (Corso), considered one of the major products of Augustan public art. It was voted in 13 BC by the senate, as *Augustus records in his *Res Gestae* to commemorate his safe return from Gaul and Spain; and finished in 9 BC. The altar proper was surrounded by a walled precinct (11.6 × 10.6 m (38 × 35 ft.)) with entrances to east and west, and decorated with sculptured reliefs on two tiers. Internally there were festoons slung from ox-heads above and fluting below; externally the lower frieze was filled with complex acanthus scrolls, above which on the east and west were mythological panels, on the north and south a religious procession showing the imperial family, lictors, priests, magistrates, and representations of the Roman people. Smaller reliefs on the inner altar showing Vestals (*see* VESTA), priests, sacrificial animals, etc., continue the procession on the outer walls. Several of the sculptured slabs were brought to light about 1568, others in 1859 and 1903. In 1937–8 the site was thoroughly explored and the monument reconstructed, with most of its surviving sculptures, between the Mausoleum of Augustus and the Tiber. *See* SCULPTURE, ROMAN.

Arachne ('Spider'), daughter of a Lydian dyer who challenged *Athena to a weaving contest. No doubt her story was originally a cautionary tale like those of *Thamyris and *Marsyas, warning against the inevitable failure and dire consequences of such presumption; but in the only extant literary version (*Ovid) the emphasis is all on the insolent brilliance of the tapestry she weaves. Her catalogue of the sexual outrages of the gods, clearly designed to provoke the virgin goddess, outclasses Athena's routine effort and drives her to destroy Arachne's work and attack her. Only after the girl has hanged herself in distress does Athena transform her into a spider, fated to re-enact her compulsive web-making for ever after. It is possible that a Corinthian vase of *c.*600 BC may already show the competition scene; otherwise no other ancient representations are known.

[Ovid, *Metamorphoses* 6. 5–145]

Arcadian cults and myths Apart from *Hephaestus, all the gods common to the Greeks are found in Arcadia. But certain deities are peculiar to the region, such as Alea, who was for a long time an independent goddess, and who even when associated with and finally assimilated to *Athena always retained her importance. The same is true of *Despoina, 'the Mistress', worshipped at Lycosura, and of Anytus, her foster-father, while the Great Goddesses have their origin around Megalopolis. Some cult groupings have a distinctive composition (*Poseidon and *Demeter), while others are characteristically Arcadian in the relative importance of the individual deities (thus the daughter, Despoina or Kore (*see* PERSEPHONE) is dominant over Demeter). Different deities are preponderant in different areas. In the region of Megalopolis, *Zeus Lycaeus, who is worshipped on Mt. Lycaeon, becomes the god of the Arcadian League, while a pair of goddesses (Despoina and Demeter, or the Great Goddesses) are the most important female element. In Azania, Demeter is predominant; in the Pheneus area, *Hermes, worshipped on Mt. Cyllene. In eastern Arcadia, *Artemis, as goddess of marshy areas, is at the forefront in Stymphalus, Orchomenus, and Caphyae; Poseidon Hippius is lord of Mantinea; and Athena Alea rules over Tegea and its hinterland. *Pan is worshipped on every mountain.

The most striking cults and aetiological myths are the complex associated with Mt. Lycaeon, where human sacrifice is evoked, and those which suggest an ancient pattern of divinities in animal shape. On the peak of Lycaeon, there was an altar of Zeus Lycaeus consisting of a mound of earth and ashes, and a *temenos* into which entry was forbidden (*abaton*); transgressors would lose their shadow and would die within the year or be stoned to death. Human sacrifice, instituted by *Lycaon (3), was practised at the altar; this is attested by Plato, in the pseudo-Platonic *Minos*, in *Theophrastus, and in *Pausanias. Anyone who ate human flesh at the sacrificial feast was changed into a wolf (*see* ARCAS, LYCANTHROPY). This seems to be a genuine vestige, unique in Greece, of a ritual *cannibalism whose exact meaning escapes us. The second characteristically Arcadian feature is the appearance of theriomorphic gods; thus we find the half-animal form of Pan, with his goat's head and feet, as well as metamorphosis into animal shape and rites using animal masks. The phenomenon is illustrated in cult by the statue of Demeter Melaina ('Black') near Phigalia, who was shown with a horse's head, her hair adorned by snakes and other wild animals, and again in the same area by that of Eurynome, whose lower half was that of a fish. Part of the sculptured veil of Despoina found in the temple at Lycosura shows figures with animal masks and animal paws, dancing in honour of a goddess who has strong links with the animal world. (*See* ANIMALS IN CULT.) In myth, there is the story of Demeter's attempts at Phigalia and at Thelpusa to escape Poseidon by turning herself into a mare; to thwart this ploy, Poseidon turned himself into a stallion, and from their union was born the horse *Arion and a daughter, Despoina. At Mantinea, where there was an ancient and important sanctuary of Posei-

don Hippius, the god's epithet gave rise to a myth in which at his birth his mother Rhea gave *Cronus a foal to swallow, instead of the rock she used later at the birth of Zeus. A further type of myth particularly well developed in Arcadia was that of the divine birth (Zeus, Hermes, Pan, Athena). *See also* BASSAE; PENELOPE.

[Pausanias 8]

Arcas, eponymous hero of Arcadia (*see* EPŌNYMOI) whose name suggests 'bear' (*arktos*). He was the son of *Callisto and *Zeus, and when his mother was transformed into a she-bear he was saved by Hermes, who entrusted him to *Maia (1). The episode is located around Mt. Cyllene, and is shown on the reverse of 4th-cent. silver coins of Pheneus. Other elements of the tradition relate to Mt. Lycaeon. Some texts make Arcas the child offered to Zeus by *Lycaon (3) in a *cannibalistic feast intended to test the god's divinity. Restored to life, Arcas as an adult failed to recognize his mother in the bear Callisto and pursued her into the interior of the *abaton* (forbidden enclosure) of Mt. Lycaeon. Zeus changed him into the *constellation Boötes.

Arcas succeeded Nyctimus as king of the *Pelasgians. He introduced agriculture, which he learned from *Triptolemus, and taught the arts of making bread and clothes. He gave his name to the land, Arcadia. His wife was the *nymph Erato, his sons Azan, Apheidas, and Elatos. After his death, the oracle at Delphi (*see* DELPHIC ORACLE) ordered that his bones be moved to Mantinea, where they were the focus of a *hero-cult. A sculpture dedicated at Delphi by the Arcadian League in 369 BC showed Arcas, his mother Callisto, and his sons. *See* ARCADIAN CULTS AND MYTHS.

[Ovid, *Metamorphoses*. 2. 409 ff.]

archēgetēs Denoting genealogical origins, political beginnings, and leadership, *archēgetēs* was a cult-title of heroic progenitors of families or tribes (*see* HERO-CULT), and of heroized city-*founders (Battos of Cyrene; Euphron of Sicyon). Named or anonymous tutelary hero-*archēgetai* protected entire lands. *Apollo, the political god sanctioning and sharing in city foundation, was universally worshipped as *archēgetēs*, e.g. in Sicily (at Naxos, by both Dorians and Ionians). At Sparta (and Thera?) *archēgetai* probably signified 'kings'.

architecture, religious

Greek The development of the Archaic period centred on temples, which in terms of size and expense always constituted the most important building type in the Greek world. Some of the earliest examples such as the little temple of *c.*750 BC at Perachora retained the apsidal form, while one at Eretria (the early temple of *Apollo Daphnephoros) was curvilinear. This soon gives way to the rectangular cella, in major buildings entered by a porch at one end, balanced by a similar but false porch at the back (west Greek temples omit this in favour of an adyton, an internal room at the back of the cella) and surrounded by a colonnade. Such temples of the first part of the 7th cent. BC as that to Poseidon at *Isthmia, and to *Hera at the Argive and Samian *Heraia were, like Lefkandi, 'hundred-footers' (*hekatompeda*), with steps and wall-footings of cut stone (at Isthmia the walls imitated timber-reinforced mud-brick but were constructed entirely in limestone), but with wooden columns. It is assumed these were already anticipating the forms of the Classical orders of architecture though there is no material proof of this.

Construction in stone, employing the Doric or Ionic orders, developed in the late 7th cent. BC, when the Greeks began to have direct experience of Egypt, learning the methods of quarrying and working stone. The architectural form of temples built early in the 6th cent. BC, the temples of *Artemis at Corcyra (Doric), and the *oikos* of the Naxians, *Delos—probably a temple of Apollo—(Ionic), shows that the arrangements and details of the orders were established by then, and in the case of Doric, these clearly imitate forms evolved from the earlier wooden structures. Thereafter architecture as applied to temples is a matter of refinement and improvement, rather than radical development and change. Ionic architects (especially in the Cyclades) were already using marble in the early 6th cent. Limestone remained the normal material in the Peloponnese, even for major temples such as that of *Zeus at *Olympia (*c.*470 BC), and in the temples of Sicily and Italy, but the opening of the quarries of Pentelicon in Attica in the late 6th cent. led to the splendid Athenian marble temples of the 5th century.

Refinement concentrated on detail: the balance of proportions in all parts of the structure, in the precise form of column, capital, entablature, and above all the decorative mouldings. Colour was also used, now generally lost from temples and other normal buildings but well preserved on the façades and interiors of the built Macedonian vaulted tombs of the 4th cent. and later (such as the royal tombs at Vergina). Here the façades, which imitate temple and related architectural forms, have their painted decoration perfectly preserved because they were buried immediately after the decoration was added. In Doric, clearly, this also evolved with the wooden buildings, whose structural divisions it emphasizes. The colours are harsh, positive blues and reds, with some patterning in contrasting yellow and gold. Refinement of architectural form involves the use of subtle curves rather than straight lines for the profiles of the columns: these evolve from the cruder curvature of early Doric, perhaps itself derived from the naturalistic curvature of Egyptian plant-form columns, and curvature of the temple base or crepis carried up to the entablature may be intended to correct optical illusion, as also the slight inward inclination of columns. Ionic buildings always used slender columns; Doric, very massive at first, becomes more slender—though the continued refinement into the Hellenistic period suggests that the 5th-cent. marble forms of Periclean Athens were not recognized as ideal and the architect Ictinus' interest in the mathematical relationship of various parts, particularly the ratio $2^2:3^2$, demonstrated in the *Parthenon, is not generally imitated.

The procedures of design employed by architects are uncertain. Scale plans are known in Egypt, but their use in Greece was probably restricted by lack of drawing material and the limitations of the Greek numerical system, particularly for fractions. Procedures were more likely based on experience and tradition, details of layout being worked out *in situ*. 'Examples', probably full-scale, of detailed elements would be supplied to the quarries and craftsmen as necessary. Structural systems were simple, based on the principle of post and beam, and dimensions were restricted by the size of available timber beams, generally not more than 12 m. (39 ft.). In temple architecture there is no complexity of plan, apart from the totally exceptional *Erechtheum at Athens.

The establishment of Roman authority over the former Hellenistic kingdoms did not lead to any abrupt change in forms of architecture. The troubled years of the early 1st cent. BC must have imposed something of a moratorium on building; but with the establishment of the Augustan Principate conditions favourable to construction returned. (There was something of a false dawn under *Caesar.) Buildings in Athens are either developed from Hellenistic prototypes or conceived as Classical derivatives (the temple of Rome and Augustus on the Acropolis, based on the details of the Erechtheum). In Asia Minor the distinctive masonry style of the 2nd cent. BC continues into the 1st cent. AD. Many of the public buildings of Ephesus were reconstructed in the 1st cent. AD in Hellenistic form. Temples in the Greek areas were normally built with a stepped crepis (though they may well employ the Corinthian order); only 'official' Roman buildings such as the temple of Trajan at Pergamum are based on podia with steps only at the front. In the 2nd cent. this gives way to a more universal Roman style, ornately decorated, habitually using column shafts of smooth, coloured marbles and other stones. Even so, the construction did not employ Roman concrete techniques, though mortared work, and brickwork, occur more regularly.

Roman Roman architecture represents the fusion of traditional Greek elements, notably the trabeated orders, with an innovative approach to structural problems resulting in the extensive exploitation of the arch and vault, the evolution of a new building material, concrete, and, probably, the development of the roof truss. While the orders remained synonymous with the Greek-inspired architecture of temples and porticoes, it was the structural experiments which facilitated the creation of new building types in response to the different political, social, and economic conditions of Rome's expanding empire. Temples derived from Etruscan models, themselves influenced by Greek temples, and remained conservative in design. The great Roman development of Roman concrete architecture in the early imperial period was applied to only one temple, the *Pantheon. *See* ATHENS, RELIGIOUS TOPOGRAPHY; ROME, TOPOGRAPHY; SANCTUARIES; TEMPLE.

archontes ('rulers'), the general Greek term for all holders of office in a state. But the word was frequently used as the title of a particular office, originally at least the highest office of the state. *Archontes* are found in most states of central Greece, including Athens, and in states dependent on or influenced by Athens. In the later 5th and 4th cent. the archons' duties were particularly religious and judicial. The *archōn* was responsible for a number of religious festivals, and for lawsuits concerning family matters. The *basileus* was responsible for the largest number of religious matters, and for homicide suits. The *polemarchos* was responsible for some festivals, including the games in honour of those who had died in war, and for lawsuits involving non-citizens.

The *thesmothetai* were responsible for the system of jury-courts as a whole, and for most 'public' lawsuits (in which any citizen might prosecute). By the end of the 5th cent. it had become standard practice to identify each year by its *archōn*, and so he is sometimes referred to as the eponymous *archōn*, but that expression is not found in Greek texts until the Roman period.

[Aristotle, *Athenaion politeia* 3, 8. 1–2, 22. 5, 26. 2, 55–9; 63–6]

Ardea, a city of the Rutuli, a Latin people. Although 4.5 km (2⅔ mi.) from the sea, it served as a port for Latium. First settled in the bronze age, its elaborate defences and rich temples that long served as federal sanctuaries for the Latin League confirm the tradition that Ardea was once an important city, worthy of signing a separate treaty with Rome (444 BC).

Areithous, a mythological character, surnamed Korynētēs, i.e. Club-man, because he fought with a club of iron; his armour had been given him by *Ares. Lycurgus the Arcadian caught him in a narrow road where he had no room to swing his club, ran him through with a spear, and took his armour.

[Homer, *Iliad* 7. 138 ff.]

Ares, the Greek war-god as embodiment of the ambivalent (destructive but often useful) forces of war, in contrast to Athena who represents the intelligent and orderly use of war to defend the community.

The name is perhaps attested on Linear B tablets from Cnossus and, in a theophoric name, from Thebes. In *Homer's *Iliad*, his image is mostly negative: he is brazen, ferocious, 'unsatiable with war', his cry sounds like that of 'nine or ten thousand men', Zeus hates him, he fights on the Trojan side, his attendants are Deimos 'Fear' and Phobos 'Panic', and he is often opposed to *Athena. On the other hand, a brave warrior is 'a shoot from Ares', and the Danai are his followers. In epic formulae, his name is used as a noun ('the frenzy of fighting'); this must be metonymy, although the god's name could have originated as a personification of the warrior's ecstasy (German *wuot*). As with the ecstatic *Dionysus, the myth of his Thracian origin illustrates this position outside the ordered, 'Greek' world of the community and has no historical value.

Mythology makes Ares the son of *Zeus and *Hera (together with their daughters *Hebe and *Eileithyia), thus inscribing him in Zeus' world-order, and the lover of *Aphrodite, whose eroticism is at least as liable to subvert the communal order (as her birthlegend and some rites suggest). Offspring of Ares and Aphrodite are Deimos and Phobos, *Eros; it underlines the subversive aspect of Eros), the artificial Anteros, and Theban Harmonia. Among other children of Ares, unruly and disruptive figures abound (*Diomedes (1) the Thracian, *Cycnus (1) the brigand, *Phlegyas the eponym of the ferocious Phlegyans). *See also* ASCALAPHUS.

Cults of Ares are rare, and details for ritual lacking; what we know confirms the god's functions, and his marginality. Temples are known chiefly from Crete (Cnossus, Lato, Biannos, perhaps Olus) and the Peloponnese (Argos, Troezen, Megalopolis, Therapne, Geronthrae, Tegea), but also from Athens and Erythrae. Cretan towns offer sacrifices to Ares and Aphrodite, who appear in interstate and ephebic oaths (*see* EPHEBOI); their combination seems to be typical for Archaic bands of warriors. The Tegean women sacrifice to Ares Gynoikothoinas, 'Who feasts the women', in a ritual of reversal which fits the nature of Ares. In Athens, he has a temple in Acharnae and a priest together with Athena Areia, and the two figure in the ephebic oath as the warlike protectors of the city's young soldiers, together with the pair Enyo and Enyalius.

In Thebes, mythology makes him the ancestor of the town: *Cadmus slays the dragon whom some authors declare to be the offspring of Ares and marries Harmonia, the daughter of Ares and Aphrodite. Actual Theban cult, however, is extremely reticent about Ares: again, he as well as Harmonia seem to belong to the Archaic heritage of warfare (see above); given his nature, it would be impossible to make him the central deity of a town.

In literature from Homer onwards, Ares is identified with Enyalius, whose name Homeric formulae also use as a noun and who is attested in Mycenaean Cnossus. In cult, the two are functionally similar but distinct war-gods, sometimes with cults in the same town; Enyalius is especially common in the north-eastern Peloponnese, but receives a marginal dog-sacrifice in Sparta where his cult statue was fettered.

In Rome, Ares was identified with *Mars; the Augustan temple of Ares on the Athenian Agora (perhaps the transferred 4th-cent. temple of Acharnae) meant Mars as the ancestor of Rome; Greek Ares would have been unthinkable on an *agora.

In early art, Ares appears exclusively in mythological scenes, together with the other gods (divine assemblies, as for the wedding of Peleus and Thetis or on the Parthenon frieze). First a bearded warrior, he is later shown naked and young (Parthenon frieze), as a warlike ephebe with whom not only the Athenians connected him. *See* MARS.

[Homer, *Iliad* 5. 890 f., 13. 301, 519, 521, 15. 110–42, 17. 211; *Odyssey* 8. 267–366]

Argei On 16 and 17 March in Rome a procession went to the shrine of the puppets, i.e. to the 27 shrines (*sacraria*) of the Argei situated at various points in the four Servian regions of Rome. On 14 May the celebrants hurled the puppets from the pons Sublicius into the Tiber. This much is clear, but uncertainty surrounds almost all else. The ancients debated the number of *sacraria* (27 or 30), the god involved (if any), and commonly explained the rituals as a surrogate for human sacrifice. Modern scholars have not reached any greater agreement. Perhaps most plausible is the theory that the March setting of the puppets gathered the city's moral pollution, which is then symbolically discharged in May; this analysis of the festival's two stages and relation with the puppets of the Compitalia (*see* LARES)

accounts for more than the other modern theories.

[Ovid, *Fasti* 3. 791–2, 5. 621–62]

Argonauts, one of the earliest and most important Greek sagas, set in the generation before the Trojan War and involving heroes particularly associated with Thessaly, central Greece, and the Peloponnese.

King *Pelias of Iolcus sought to rid himself of the threat to his kingship posed by the legitimate heir, *Jason, by sending the young man off to recover the fleece of a golden ram upon which Phrixus had fled to the fabulous kingdom of the sun, Aia, ruled over by King Aeëtes. At least as early as the *Epic Cycle Aia was identified with the kingdom of Colchis at the eastern end of the Black Sea. With Athena's help Jason had a marvellous ship, the *Argo*, built; the tradition that the *Argo* was actually the first ship is first found in *Euripides. The greatest heroes of the age gathered to join Jason on the voyage. Lists differ widely, but among the most prominent Argonauts in many versions were *Heracles, who in some versions did not complete the voyage, *Orpheus, the *Dioscuri, the steersman Tiphys, Lynceus who could see even beneath the earth, *Telamon, *Peleus (father of *Achilles), the sons of the north wind *Boreas, and *Theseus. The supernatural powers of many of the Argonauts differentiate the story markedly from the Homeric epics. The main protecting goddess for the voyage was *Hera who wished to punish Pelias for neglecting to honour her. The principal events of the outward voyage were: a stop on Lemnos where the women lured the Argonauts to sleep with them in order to repopulate the island (Pindar places this on the return voyage); the mistaken killing (by Jason) of the prince of Cyzicus in the Propontis; the loss to the expedition of Heracles when his beloved squire, *Hylas, is snatched away by *nymphs and Heracles takes off to find him; a boxing-match between Polydeuces (*see* DIOSCURI) and King *Amycus of the Bebrycians; a meeting at

Thracian Salmydessus with the blind prophet *Phineus who offers information about their voyage (cf. *Circe and *Tiresias in the *Odyssey*) in return for ridding him of the foul *Harpyiae (Harpies) who refuse to allow him to eat; the passage through the *Symplegades ('Clashing Rocks') at the mouth of the Black Sea, safely accomplished (on Phineus' advice) by sending a dove through first to test the way. As a result of the *Argo*'s passage, the rocks were finally fixed fast and ceased to clash together. In Aia, Jason requests the fleece from Aeëtes, but the king sets him challenges to accomplish: he must plough with fire-breathing bulls, sow dragon's teeth, and kill the armed warriors which spring up from the ground (cf. *Cadmus). Jason succeeds with the help of Aeëtes' daughter *Medea who supplies him with protecting potions and helps him take the fleece from the grove where it is guarded by a dragon.

Accounts of the return voyage vary widely. In some the Argonauts return by the same route; in some they pass from the Colchian river Phasis into the streams of *Oceanus and around into the Mediterranean again. *Apollonius Rhodius combines various accounts into an extraordinary voyage across the Black Sea to a river system ('the Danube') which takes them to the Adriatic; from there they travel by a combination of 'the Po' and 'the Rhône' to the western Mediterranean, then back down the west coast of Italy, across to Corfu, thence to North Africa, then Crete and finally back to Thessalian Iolcus. Important events of the return voyage include the killing of Medea's young brother Apsyrtus, adventures in Libya during which the Argonauts carry their ship through the desert—they were intimately connected with the foundation legends of Cyrene—and the encounter with the bronze giant *Talos (1) who protected Crete.

The saga is of a common folkloric quest type, but also clearly expresses, and was used by Greek writers to reflect, the confrontation between what was Greek and what 'other' and hence the very qualities which represented 'Greekness'. Ancient scholars themselves saw the story as a reflection of the age of colonization and expansion or, more banally, the search for gold.

Argonauts in art Argonauts generally appear in individual episodes. Boreads pursue Harpies (*see* HARPYIAE) on an Attic bowl (*c*.620 BC), later Archaic vases and an ivory from Delphi, and a Lucanian vase. The Argo appears on the Sicyonian treasury, Delphi (*c*.560 BC), Classical vases, Etruscan gems, Roman reliefs and coins. The Classical Niobid crater may show *Hylas lost. *Amycus is most famously depicted on a Lucanian vase (*c*.420–400 BC), and the Etruscan Ficoroni chest. (*c*.300 BC). Jason and the fleece appear on Classical vases, an early imperial glass vessel, and a late imperial relief. Duris' early Classical cup showing the dragon regurgitating Jason is an otherwise unattested variation. Lost representations include the Archaic chest of Cypselus and throne at *Amyclae (Boreads), and a painting in Athens. There were also paintings by Cydias, and a statue group by Lycius, both Classical.

[Homer, *Odyssey* 12. 69–72; Pindar, *Pythian* 4; Apollonius, *Argonautica*; Apollodorus 1. 9. 16–26]

Argos, in mythology: (*a*) son of Zeus and the Argive Niobe (daughter of *Phoroneus), who gave his name to the city of Argos, part of archaic Argive mythological propaganda. His grave, not far from that of his 'brother' *Pelasgus, was in a dense sacred grove. (*b*) Argos 'Panoptes' ('All-seeing'), monster born of no agreed parents— perhaps even earthborn, with multiple eyes: four, an extra eye in the back of the head and unsleeping, or covered in eyes. *Hera has him guard *Io, but he is tricked and killed by *Hermes, who thus acquires his epithet 'Argeiphontes' (supposedly 'Argos-slayer', already in *Hesiod). In *later tradition, at death he turns into a peacock or his eyes are added to its plumage. (*c*) An *Argonaut, builder of the Argo, a favourite of Roman artists. (*d*) 'Swift', *Odysseus' dog.

Argos, cults The main cult of the state of Argos was that of *Hera (already 'Argive' in the *Iliad*), based *c*.10 km. (*c*.6 mi.) north-east of the city across the Argive plain, between *Mycenae and Tiryns. Argive ownership of this *Heraion—emphasized by an annual festival which began with a procession from the city across the plain to the sanctuary—symbolized the state's control of the territory between the two points.

At the north-west corner of Argive territory was Nemea, sacred to *Zeus and the original site of the *Nemean Games. Control of this sanctuary, originally belonging to Cleonae, passed to Argos in the 5th cent. BC. In the border area with Arcadia were a number of border sanctuaries of *Artemis. In the Argive countryside were several sanctuaries of *Demeter, and the grove of the eponymous hero *Argos.

Within the city itself, major sanctuaries were clustered around the two heights of the acropolis, around the agora, and by the gates. Thus on the Deiras were adjoining sanctuaries of *Apollo Pythaeus or Deiradiotes and *Athena Oxyderces, and on Larissa sanctuaries of Athena Polias and Zeus Larissaeus. Part way up Larissa was a sanctuary of Hera Acraea. A dedication to Enyalius (*see* ARES) (7th cent. BC) was found on this peak. Around the agora were sanctuaries of Apollo Lyceus (where public notices were posted), of *Aphrodite, Demeter, and others, including an enclosure sacred to the heroes who had died at Thebes (*c*.550 BC) (*see* SEVEN AGAINST THEBES). The east gate of the city was named after the nearby sanctuary of *Eileithyia; not far away was a sanctuary of the *Dioscuri (addressed as *Anakes in inscriptions of the 6th and 5th cent. BC).

Argos, myths of *Inachus, father of *Io, judged the contest between *Poseidon and *Hera for the place (a contest which Hera won (*see* HERAION)). The city took its name from *Argos. *Adrastus, as king of Argos, led the expedition of the *Seven against Thebes. *Acrisius, king of Argos, was father of *Danae, and brother of *Proetus. *Perseus is the son of Danae. *Danaus and the Danaids fled from Egypt to Argos, where they were received by *Pelasgus. *See* ARGOS, CULTS.

See also GENEALOGICAL TABLES (4) HOUSE OF ARGOS.

[Pausanias 2. 17–23]

Ariadne, daughter of *Minos and Pasiphaë. In Cnossus *Daedalus built her a dancing-floor, perhaps the Daidaleion on a Cnossus Linear B tablet. She fell in love with *Theseus and gave him a thread of wool to escape from the *Labyrinth after killing the Minotaur. Theseus fled with Ariadne but abandoned her on Naxos either by choice or because the gods commanded him. *Dionysus found and married her there. In another version, Ariadne was already married to Dionysus when she followed Theseus and was killed by Artemis on Dia (Naxos). Ariadne also had a tomb in the temple of Cretan Dionysus in Argos. According to one tradition she came to Cyprus pregnant by Theseus who left her there. She died in childbed and was buried in the grove of Ariadne Aphrodite. At a curious annual rite in her honour at Amathus, a young man imitated a woman in labour. Originally Ariadne was a Minoan goddess of nature whose invocatory name ('Very Holy') suggests that she was expected to appear to her worshippers in *epiphany. Her myth centres on marriage and death, combining the sorrowful and happy aspects of the annual decay and renewal of vegetation. Each part is celebrated in her two festivals on Naxos, and both elements are preserved in the Attic *Anthesteria. On the second day of the spring festival (Choes) the king (*archōn basileus*) like Theseus surrenders his wife (*basilinna*) to Dionysus for the Sacred Marriage (*see* ARCHONTES; MARRIAGE, SACRED). But the third (Chytroi) was a day of death with sacrifices to chthonian *Hermes.

Ariadne's desertion by Theseus on Naxos/Dia, her rescue by, and marriage to, Dionysus are popular themes in literature, and particularly in vase-painting from the early

5th cent. BC through all periods of Greek and Roman art until the 3rd cent. AD. Other parts of the myth occurred in the painter's repertoire as early as the 7th cent. BC. She appears assisting Theseus against the Minotaur; and on the François vase she is shown facing Theseus who leads the dance of Athenian youths and maidens whom he has rescued from the Minotaur. She can be seen with her children; or, in a Pompeian mural, sitting beside *Daedalus (?). In Polygnotus' famous Underworld Scene in the Hall of the Cnidians at *Delphi, Ariadne even appeared sitting on a rock in the Underworld gazing at her sister Phaedra.

[Homer, *Odyssey* 11. 321–5; Hesiod, *Theogony* 947–9; Catullus 64. 50 ff.; Ovid, *Heroines* 10]

Arianism, the principal Christian heresy of the 4th cent. Strictly it denotes the subordinationist teaching of *Arius concerning the Son. The council of Nicaea (325) condemned this, affirming that the Son was 'of the same substance' (*homoousios*) as the Father. While generally acceptable in the west, this formula was suspect to many easterners as suggesting that Father and Son were not distinct beings (hypostases) but an indifferentiated unity. In the prolonged debates which followed the term was applied not only to Anomoeism (from *anomoios*, or 'unlike'), the extremist Arian view that Father and Son were wholly unlike, and the watered-down Homoean (from *homoios*, or 'like') compromise that they were similar, but also to basically anti-Arian interpretations aimed at meeting the difficulties of the Nicene *homoousion*. Chief among these were (*a*) the teaching of the council of Antioch (341), which repudiated Arius and emphasized Christ's divinity in the framework of a three-hypostases theology, but ignored the *homoousion*; (*b*) the (misleadingly labelled) Semi-Arian teaching that Father and Son were 'alike in substance' (*homoiousioi*).

Apart from 350–61, when Constantius II was sole emperor, Arianism made little headway in the west. In the east he and Valens promoted the imprecise Homoean doctrine as likely to be most widely acceptable. With the accession of *Theodosius I Arianism soon found itself proscribed everywhere. It received fresh life, however, through the fact that Ulfila, missionary to the Goths, had brought Christianity to them in a radically Arian form. From the Goths it spread to other Germanic peoples, who took it with them (it had become a badge of their nationalism) when they invaded and set up their kingdoms in the west.

Aricia (mod. Ariccia), at the foot of the Alban hills (*see* ALBANUS MONS), 25 km. (15½ mi.) south-east of Rome, on the edge of a fertile volcanic depression. There are traces of early iron age occupation and, *c*.500 BC, Aricia was temporarily the leading city of Latium: it organized resistance to *Tarquinius Superbus, helped Aristodemus of Cumae to crush the Etruscans (*c*.505 BC), and supplied the Latin League with a meeting-place. Aricia is celebrated for its wealthy temple of *Diana Nemorensis, whose ruins still exist nearby in the woods surrounding Lake Nemi; its presiding priest was a runaway slave who had murdered his predecessor (*see* REX NEMORENSIS).

Arimaspeans, a fabulous one-eyed tribe from the distant north whose name Herodotus claims to be able to derive from Scythian *arima* 'one', *spou* 'eye'. He and *Aeschylus know them as a people engaged in a perpetual attempt to steal a hoard of gold guarded by griffins—just as the Indians try to take that of the giant ants. The story apparently goes back to the epic *Arimaspea* ascribed to *Aristeas.

[Aeschylus, *Prometheus Bound* 803–6; Herodotus 3. 102, 116, 4. 13, 27]

Arion In Homer Arion is the 'swift horse', 'divine in origin', of the Theban *Adrastus. His mythological origins lie in Arcadia. According to *Pausanias, he was born at Thelpusa from the union of *Demeter and *Poseidon: Demeter transformed herself into a filly to escape Poseidon, who then changed himself into a horse to unite with her. Arion belonged successively to Poseidon himself, to Copreus, *Heracles, and Adrastus. He is shown on the reverse of some Thelpusan coins, as a horse prancing towards the right.

Aristaeus, Greek culture-hero or demigod, with a bewildering number of associations. His imminent birth to *Apollo and the *nymph Cyrene is prophesied by Chiron (*see* CENTAURS) in *Pindar, celebrating him as 'a *Zeus, a pure Apollo; a delight to his friends, close escort of sheep, Hunter and Herdsman'. Scraps of evidence for his cult and myth link him to Phthia, Arcadia, and Boeotia (where he was known as *Actaeon's father) and in particular to the Aegean island of Ceos, where he was worshipped as the mediator to mankind of apiculture and *olive oil and invoked as bringer of the cooling Etesian winds in high summer. *Virgil ends the *Georgics* by telling at length the story of how once all Aristaeus' bees died; his mother referred him to *Proteus for an explanation, and he was told that this was punishment called down by *Orpheus for the death of *Eurydice, who had been bitten by a snake when trying to escape Aristaeus' attentions. He carries out a propitiatory sacrifice, and after nine days the carcasses of the bulls and heifers, left to fester, have spontaneously generated new swarms by the process of *bougonia* (birth from bulls).

[Pindar, *Pythian* 9. 59 ff.; Apollonius Rhodius 2. 500–27; Virgil, *Georgics* 4. 315–558]

Aristeas, of Proconnesus in the Propontis. Like *Abaris and *Zalmoxis, a legendary wisdom-figure associated with the cult of *Apollo, reflecting early Greek contacts with *Scythian culture (*see* SCYTHIAN RELIGION). Herodotus knew him as the author of a hexameter poem called *Arimaspea* which told of the tribes in the far north, including the eponymous *Arimaspeans; he goes on to report marvellous tales of his shamanistic feats, including the disappearance of his 'corpse' in his home town while

he was seen alive elsewhere, his subsequent reappearance after seven years (cf. EPIMENIDES); and even a rematerialization 240 years later in southern Italy, during which he informed the inhabitants of Metapontum that he had been accompanying his god in the form of a raven.

[Herodotus 4. 13 ff.]

Aristeas, Letter of, is the Alexandrian Jewish story of the making of the Greek translation of the Law (Torah) for the library of Ptolemy II Philadelphus. Aristeas, a courtier, describes to his brother Philocrates his mission on this subject to Eleazar, the high priest at Jerusalem. Eleazar expounded the rationale of the Law, and then supplied 72 scholars, six from each tribe. At a seven-day banquet, they discussed kingship and impressed the king with their philosophical wisdom. In a residence on the island of Pharos at Alexandria, they completed their work in 72 days, harmonizing their independent versions; they then gave a recitation. The Letter has a historical kernel: the ascription of the commissioning of the *Septuagint to Ptolemy Philadelphus is generally accepted; and the description of *Jerusalem is perhaps not wholly schematic. But traditional motifs are evident, especially in the discussion on kingship; and the persistent apologia for Judaism gives rise to some imaginative claims. A date in either the early or the late 2nd cent. BC is likely. Josephus paraphrases the Letter in his *Antiquities* 12. *See* JEWISH-GREEK LITERATURE; SEPTUAGINT.

Aristides, Publius Aelius (AD 117–after 181), intellectual and man of letters. Born at Hadrianotherae in Mysia, he studied in Athens and Pergamum. At the age of 26, he suffered the first of a long series of illnesses, which ended his hopes of a great public career and drove him to spend much of his time as a patient at the Asclepieum (*see* ASCLEPIUS) of Pergamum. The rest of his life was passed mainly in Asia Minor, where he made his home in Smyrna and in the intervals of illness occupied himself in writing and lecturing.

His many-sided literary output (built on an intimate knowledge of the Classical literary heritage) made him a giant in his own day and, through its subsequent popularity, a crucial figure in the transmission of Hellenism. It includes addresses delivered on public and private occasions, declamations on historical themes, polemical essays, prose hymns to various gods, and six books of *Sacred Discourses*. The prose hymns, though Aristides did not invent the genre, revealed new possibilities in both a Platonizing and an Isocratean vein, and were an influential model for later writers. The *Sacred Discourses*, finally, are in a class apart. A record of revelations made to Aristides in *dreams by the healing god Asclepius, and of his obedience to the god's instructions, they are of major importance, both as evidence for the practices associated with temple medicine (*see* MEDICINE), and as the fullest first-hand report of personal religious experiences that survives from any pagan writer.

Aristobulus, an Alexandrian Jew, probably of the second half of the 2nd cent. BC, author of a commentary on the Pentateuch which is known only through quotations by Christian writers. This has been thought by some scholars to be a much later work (of the 3rd cent. AD) falsely ascribed to Aristobulus; but this conclusion is not necessary. If the 2nd-cent. BC date be accepted, the book is the earliest evidence of contact between Alexandrian Jewry and Greek philosophy. Its object was twofold, to interpret the Pentateuch in an allegorical fashion (*see* ALLEGORY), and to show that *Homer and *Hesiod, the Orphic writings (*see* ORPHIC LITERATURE), *Pythagoras, *Plato, and*Aristotle had borrowed freely from a supposed early translation of the Old Testament into Greek. Though Aristobulus toned down the anthropomorphism of the Old Testament, his thought remained Jewish and theistic; it did not accept the pantheism of the Stoics nor anticipate the Logos-doctrine of *Philon (1). *See* JEWISH-GREEK LITERATURE.

Aristotle (384–322 BC) was born in Stagira in Chalcidice. At the age of 17 he travelled to Athens and entered Plato's Academy, remaining until Plato's death in 348/7 BC. Plato's philosophical influence is evident in all of Aristotle's work. Even when he is critical (a great part of the time) he expresses deep respect for Plato's genius. At Plato's death Aristotle left Athens, probably because of political difficulties connected with his Macedonian ties. Accepting an invitation from Hermias, ruler of Assos and Atarneus in the Troad and a former fellow student in the Academy, he went to Assos, where he stayed until Hermeias' fall and death in 345. Invited by Philip II of Macedon to Pella in 342 BC, he became tutor to Philip's son Alexander the Great. His instruction focused on standard literary texts, but probably also included political theory and history. In 335, after a brief stay in Stagira, Aristotle returned to Athens. As a resident alien he could not own property, so he rented buildings outside the city, probably between Mt. Lycabettus and the Ilissus. Here, in what was called the Lyceum, he established his own school. (The school later took its name from its colonnade or *peripatos*.)

Aristotle was little interested in the philosophy of religion. He rejected anthropomorphic *mythology, but regarded it as obvious that the gods existed and should be worshipped. His own conception of the divine was, however, untraditional: the universe depended on a supreme being who was responsible for all movement in the universe while himself being immobile.

Aristotle's work on *psychē (De anima)* is also untraditional. After criticizing materialist and Platonist accounts of *psychē*, he defends the view that *psychē* is the substance of a living thing; he argues that this substance will be not its material constituents but its species-form. His working definition is that *psychē* is the 'first entelechy of a natural organic body'. 'First entelechy' takes the place of 'form' in order to stress the fact that it is not actual functioning (e.g. seeing or thinking) that is the *psychē*, but the organiza-tion-to-function. 'Organic' seems to mean 'equipped with materials that are suitable for performing these functions'. Aristotle goes on to give more concrete accounts of self-nutrition, reproduction, perceiving, im-agining, and thinking; these inquiries are further developed in the *Parva naturalia* and, in some cases, the biological writings.

Arius (*c*.AD 260–336) was the most import-ant of early Christian heretics. Probably a Libyan by birth and a pupil of Lucian, pres-byter of Antioch in Syria, he became a leading presbyter at Alexandria. In 318 or 320/1 he began propagating subordination-ist views about Christ's person. Controversy flared up, and he was condemned at the council of Nicaea (325). Though rehabili-tated *c*.335 through the influence of Euse-bius of Nicomedia, he died shortly after. Three important letters and some fragments of his *Thalia* (verse and prose popularizations of his doctrines) survive. His characteristic teaching was that the Son or Word was a creature, created before time and superior to other creatures, but like them changeable and distinct from the Father. *See* ARIANISM.

Armilustrium Roman festival on 19 Octo-ber to *Mars which purified (*see* LUSTRATION) the army; this took place at the *Aventine's Armilustrium, which contained an altar, and involved the *Salii. Perhaps connected with the *Quinquatrus (19 March), which opened the campaign season.

Arnobius, a teacher of rhetoric at Sicca Veneria in Proconsular Numidia, said by Jerome to have taught *Lactantius and to have suddenly become a Christian (*c*.295) (*see* CHRISTIANITY). A year or two later, at his bishop's instance, he wrote seven books, *Adversus nationes*, as a proof of full conversion. He attacked those who argued, like the later opponents of *Augustine, that 'ever since the Christians have been on earth, the world has gone to ruin', and that Christ was a mortal magician, not superior to *Apollonius of Tyana or *Zoroaster. His

answer, although conventional in tenor, is not so in content, since he amasses much valuable antiquarian learning, designed to prove that Roman institutions were subject to change, and that therefore Christianity was not bad because it was new. Incidentally he reveals something of pagan beliefs cur-rent in Africa. He does not look for prefigure-ment of the Gospel even in the Old Testament. His attack on the 'new men' shows him abreast of recent developments in Platonism (*see* NEOPLATONISM); but, while he cites several dialogues and applauds *Plato's notion of God, he (characteristically) rejects the hypothesis of innate ideas. His own teaching on the soul may be of Stoic origin (*see* STOICISM). He cites the New Testa-ment little, and indeed, apart from hope of his soul's salvation through Christ and his hostility to paganism, Arnobius shows little trace of Christian theology. Writing before the council of Nicaea, he speaks of Christ as a secondary deity.

Arr(h)ephoria Athenian festival, at which a rite is performed by the *arrhēphoroi*, two or four girls between the ages of 7 and 11, chosen by the *basileus* (*see* ARCHONTES) to serve *Athena Polias. They lived on the Acropolis (*see* ATHENS, RELIGIOUS TOPOG-RAPHY), they played a ritual game of ball, and they participated in the weaving of the *peplos* (robe) offered to Athena at the *Pan-athenaea. They helped the priestess of Athena Polias. At the Chalkeia they and the priestess set up the loom for the *peplos*. They are probably represented with the priestess in the central scene on the *Parthenon frieze. At the rite marking the end of their service, at night, they put on their heads covered baskets given them by the priestess who knew no more than the girls what they contained, and through an underground passage they descended to the precinct of *Aphrodite in the Gardens, where they left what they were carrying and took and brought to the Acropolis something else covered up. After this they were replaced by others. This rite is thought to have originated in an initiatory ritual (*see* RITES OF PASSAGE); but it is also possible that it may always have been a cultic office limited to a selected few, though connected with a particular age band and the transition out of it.

art, ancient attitudes to

Evolving uses of art, Greek There was a significant distinction in the Greek world between public and private art. The major arts of sculpture and painting fall primarily, if not exclusively, into the category of public art, which had two subdivisions: works with a religious purpose, such as cult images, temple sculptures, and *votive offerings; and works with a political or cultural commemorative function, such as portraits of civic leaders, personifications of political ideas, paintings of famous battles, and victory monuments connected with public competitions (*see* AGONES). Funerary sculpture, although usually privately commissioned, was essentially public in function and also belongs to the commemorative category. Although public monuments usually had a decorative aspect, there seems to have been hardly any public art that was designed to be purely decorative. Even stage paintings in the theatre were created for public religious festivals.

Small-scale works of art which were primarily decorative, such as paintings on pottery, engravings on gems, and jewellery, belong to the category of private art.

Over time there were two major shifts of emphasis within these categories. First, beginning in the 5th cent. BC, the line between religious and commemorative-political art became blurred as traditional subjects were adapted to convey political meanings (e.g. the Amazonomachy, the Gigantomachy; *see* AMAZONS; GIANTS). The sculptures of the *Parthenon and the great altar and other Attalid dedications at Pergamum are notable examples of this trend. Second, as the idea of acquiring works of art for private delectation developed among Hellenistic monarchs, the major arts of sculpture and

painting gradually also became part of the world of private art.

Evolving uses of art, Roman Art in Rome had the same functions that it had in Greece, but private patronage of artists played a much wider role in the Roman world, and the commemorative aspect of public art tended to have a different emphasis.

Although historical subjects were occasionally depicted in Greek art, the Romans were much more consistently interested than the Greeks in using the arts to record the details of specific historical events. Public buildings, for example, frequently bore inscriptions celebrating the largess and achievements of the prominent citizens who had built them, and both paintings and relief sculptures documented military campaigns and important public ceremonies. *See* ARA PACIS.

See also ART, FUNERARY, GREEK and ROMAN; IMAGERY; SCULPTURE, GREEK and ROMAN.

art, funerary, Greek This article covers both architecture and art made specifically to mark and monumentalize the grave; for grave goods (which may be of any sort, and in Greece were rarely, it seems, custom-made for the tomb). *See* CEMETERIES; DEAD, DISPOSAL OF.

Bronze age (*c*.3000–*c*.1100 BC). The earliest monumental funerary architecture occurs in the Mesara plain of Crete, where hundreds of circular stone tholos-tombs were erected during the third millennium, each housing multiple burials. Late Minoan rulers were occasionally buried in sumptuous built tombs.

Early iron age and geometric period (*c*.1100–*c*.700). Greek monumental tomb-architecture stopped with the destruction of the Mycenaean palaces *c*.1200. Two rich 10th-cent. burials at Lefkandi in Euboea were surmounted by an apsidal building 10 m. (32 ft.) wide and 50 m. (164 ft.) long: the earliest Greek hero-shrine or heroon (*see* HERO-CULT). Such heroa were eventually to become a common feature of the Greek landscape. They assumed a wide variety of forms, from the simple triangular enclosure above the graves of seven late 8th-cent. heroes of Eretria to the heroon that Cimon built at Athens shortly after 474 to receive *Theseus' bones, lavishly embellished with frescos. *See* RELICS.

Earth mounds topped by undecorated stone slabs were popular as grave-markers in many geometric communities, but at Athens and Argos large vases performed this function after *c*.800. In other communities, most notably on Crete, the bronze age practice of burial in tholoi persists or is intentionally revived.

Archaic period (*c*.700–*c*.480). The period's chief innovations were the funerary statue and carved gravestone. *Kouroi* (standing, usually nude, youths) marked graves on Thera by *c*.630, and some argue that the type was introduced for this purpose. Funerary *korai* (standing, draped, young women) appear shortly after 600, as do painted and sculptured gravestones. At Athens, these gravestones soon became extremely lavish, until banned by sumptuary legislation, apparently *c*.490. Athletes, warriors, hunters, and elders are common subjects; women and children far less so. The less wealthy or less pretentious continued to favour earth mounds, though built tombs of stone or brick appeared around 600. These were sometimes embellished with clay plaques painted with mourning scenes.

In other areas, funerary art varied widely. *Kouroi* rarely stood over graves in central and southern Greece, but often did so in Miletus and Samos. Sarcophagi were popular in east Greece. Aeolians and Macedonians liked large tumuli, Thessalians preferred tholos-tombs; and so on.

Classical period (*c*.480–*c*.330). At Athens, the legislation mentioned above decreed that no tomb could be made by more than ten men in three days. So whereas high-quality gravestones with single figures in relief remain in vogue in the Cyclades and Thessaly, until *c*.430 Attic funerary art is restricted to white-ground lecythi: small, clay oil-flasks usually painted with domestic or mourning scenes in applied colour. Some show scenes at the tomb itself, complete with lecythi standing on the stepped bases of the simple stone slabs that now served as tomb-markers.

Around 430, for reasons perhaps relating either to the outbreak of the Peloponnesian War (431) or the plague (430), gravestones began to reappear in Athens. At first echoing Cycladic models, they soon developed a standard repertoire of subjects: athlete, warrior, mistress and maid, father and son, married couple, family group, funeral banquet, and so on. Though most are in the form of miniature shrines in high relief, low-relief slab-stones furnished a cheap alternative; stone lecythi were also popular, and unmarried women received marble water vessels. Dead and living are often linked by a handshake, and the mood is usually sombre. During the 4th cent., the steles became larger and more elaborate, until Demetrius of Phalerum banned them in 317; they were often imitated elsewhere in Greece.

In Asia Minor, Greek architects and sculptors built sumptuous tombs for local rulers. In Lycia, the most elaborate is the 'Nereid Monument' from Xanthus, now in the British Museum. Constructed *c*.380, it consisted of a square podium embellished with battle-reliefs and surmounted by a small Ionic temple; Nereids stood between the columns, and other friezes, a sculptured pediment, and acroteria decorated its entablature, cella, and roof. The Carian ruler Mausolus used many elements of this design for his Mausoleum at Halicarnassus. Begun around 365, this most grandiose of all sculptured tombs was widely imitated.

Hellenistic period (*c*.330–*c*.30). Alexander the Great's sumptuous hearse set a new standard in funerary magnificence. His own mausoleum at Alexandria has disappeared, but other royal tombs have survived. In Macedonia, kings and aristocrats were buried in vaulted chambers painted with a wide

variety of subjects: hunts, Amazonomachies, Centauromachies (*see* CENTAURS),
*Hades and *Persephone, chariot-races and
so on. There was a wide range of sculptured
monuments.

The extinction of the Attic gravestone industry in 317 prompted an exodus of sculptors to Rhodes, Macedonia, and Alexandria,
where painted or carved imitations of Attic
sculpted panels continued into the 3rd cent.
Thereafter, Alexandrians interred their dead
in underground *cemeteries, decked out
like houses with colonnaded or pilastered
façades, and often painted inside. In Cyrene,
faceless female busts set over rock-cut tombs
probably represent Persephone. A rich local
gravestone tradition develops in the Asian
cities around 200, featuring either funeral
banquets or family groups where the dead
are overtly heroized. Inscriptions also tell of
built heroa with bronze funerary statues of
the deceased, but few examples (and no
statues) survive. In Tarentum, miniature
shrines embellished with reliefs of heroic
fights, Achilles' last journey, and so on, are
popular from *c*.330–250. *See* IMAGERY.

art, funerary, Roman Early republican
tombs at Rome have none of the decorative
features of contemporary Etruscan funerary
art, but by the mid to late republic some
aristocratic tombs show a desire for elaboration. From the last years of the republic
onwards funerary art ceased to be the prerogative of the rich: even freedmen and
slaves decorated their tombs and bought funerary monuments. Inside the tomb there
were sculptured free-standing monuments,
including the containers for the remains of
the deceased—ash-chests in the early
empire and, increasingly from *c*.AD 100 onwards, *sarcophagi. The interior of the tomb
itself might be decorated with stucco,
painting, and mosaic. Stucco provided architectural and figured decoration for niches in
the walls, and was also used on the ceilings.
Painting provided colour, but also a variety
of motifs placed inside niches, on ceilings
and on walls. In the *catacombs painting
was the dominant form of decoration, but
here biblical stories and Christian symbols
replaced the pagan ones in use elsewhere.
Mosaic was used primarily for the floors of
tombs, but also appears on ceilings and walls
(the most spectacular being the ceiling decoration of the small tomb of the Iulii—tomb
M—in the Vatican cemetery, with Christ/
Helios in his chariot amid a design of vines
on a gold background).

Outside Rome, different areas of the
empire developed their own types and styles
of funerary monument and art: tombs of
many kinds were decorated with sculpture,
both statues and reliefs (e.g. the tomb of the
Secundinii at Trier, with its scenes both of
everyday life and of mythology). Tombstones or grave steles were also used in
many areas to mark the grave and commemorate the deceased.

The iconographic repertoire of Roman funerary art is particularly rich. Motifs might
refer directly to the deceased: portraiture,
whether full-length or in bust form, was
popular throughout the imperial period.
The deceased might also be represented engaged in an everyday activity, on their deathbed, or in heroized and idealized form, with
the attributes of a deity or hero, and women
might be represented with the beauty and
attributes of *Venus. Battle and hunt scenes,
designed to show the deceased's manliness,
were widely used on sarcophagi, as were
other scenes designed to suggest his virtues.
Mythological scenes were extremely popular, and a wide selection of episodes from
Greek mythology was used in all contexts,
but again especially on sarcophagi. Motifs
from the natural world (plants, birds, and
animals) abound, possibly reflecting the
desire to have one's tomb surrounded by a
luscious garden teeming with life. In addition there was a host of other motifs, such
as cupids, seasons, sphinxes, and griffins,
which could be combined in a number of
different ways. Clearly some of these designs
had a significance beyond their surface
meaning, and alluded allegorically to beliefs
in and hopes for an after-life existence:

however, this is an area of much scholarly disagreement, some maintaining that virtually all motifs used in funerary contexts have an eschatological meaning, others remaining more sceptical (e.g. some think that scenes of *Tritons and Nereids (*see* NEREUS) swimming through the sea allude to the *soul on its journey to the *Islands of the Blest, while others deny the motif any such significance). As the imperial period progressed the mystery religions (*see* MYSTERIES), with their promise of salvation, gained in popularity, and Bacchic themes (*see* DIONYSUS) and *Hercules (paradigm of a mortal attaining immortality) appeared more frequently in funerary art.

Much of the private, non-state art of Rome was funerary, and the production of sarcophagi in particular became a major industry. Although some individual choice of design was possible, and some highly idiosyncratic pieces survive, for most purposes, standardized motifs taken from pattern books were used, personalization being achieved by the addition of an inscription or portrait. Nevertheless, commemoration of the dead, on as lavish a scale as could be afforded, was a major concern for most Romans of the imperial period. *See* CEMETERIES; DEAD, DISPOSAL OF; DEATH, ATTITUDES TO; IMAGERY; SCULPTURE, ROMAN.

Artemidorus (mid/late 2nd cent. AD), of Ephesus but called himself 'of Daldis' after his mother's native city in Lydia, whose chief deity *Apollo instigated his work on predictive *dreams. His *Onirocritica*, the product of travels to collect dreams and their outcomes and of study of the numerous earlier works on the subject, is the only extant ancient dream-book. It is of interest both for its categories of dream interpretation and for its religious and social assumptions. It was influential both in the Arab world, and in Europe from the Renaissance onwards. Artemidorus also wrote *Oeonoscopica* (on *divination by birds).

Artemis Daughter of *Zeus and *Leto, *Apollo's elder twin sister, a very important Olympian deity, a virgin and a huntress, who presided over crucial aspects of life. She presided over women's transitions (*see* RITES OF PASSAGE), most crucially their transformation from *parthenos* (virgin) to (fully acculturated and fully 'tamed') woman (*gynē*), and over childbirth and *kourotrophein* (the rearing of children). She was also concerned with male activities, often (as at Sparta, see below) with their rites of transition to adulthood, also hunting and certain aspects of war. Like all deities, she had different cults in the different parts of the Greek world, but the above-mentioned concerns are part of her Panhellenic persona and recur commonly in local cults; the same is even more strongly the case with her firm association with the wild and her persona as protector of young animals as well as of hunting. It is possible to perceive that the core of her personality is a concern with transitions and transitional marginal places, such as marshes, junctions of land and water and so on, and marginal situations. There is some merit in this, but since such classifications are inevitably culturally determined, we cannot be sure whether this was indeed a core aspect of Artemis or a culturally determined construct created by our own assumptions and preferred conceptual schemata at a time when transitions and things marginal are at the forefront of scholarly discourse—especially since deities were complex beings and did not begin with one function which was then expanded.

In the Classical period Artemis' iconography crystallized into a particular version of the iconographical schema 'young *parthenos*', a version that includes several variants; usually she has a bow and arrow, and she is often associated with a deer. One of Artemis' epithets, it should be noted, is Elaphēbolos (the 'Shooter of Deer'), after which was named the month Elaphebolion. Sometimes, especially in the Archaic period, she was represented through the schema of *Potnia Thērōn*, 'Mistress of the Animals', usually winged, flanked by animals. Very rarely she is shown with wings but not as a Potnia

Thērōn, that is, not flanked by animals. Many, but not all, scholars believe that her name appears in the Linear B tablets of Pylos. One of the religious nexuses that contributed to the making of the divine persona that crystallized in the figure of the historical Greek goddess Artemis is the 'Potnia Thērōn' facet of a Minoan goddess. It is for this reason, that Artemis sometimes became associated or identified with another 'later transformation' of that goddess, *Britomartis/Dictynna.

In *Homer, Artemis was, like Apollo, on the side of the Trojans. She was a death-bringing deity, for she sent sudden death to women, as Apollo did to men. Apollo and Artemis together killed the children of *Niobe, who had boasted about the large number of children she had in comparison to Leto's two. She or Apollo, or both, killed *Tityus who had tried to rape Leto. Some of the more important myths assigning her the role of punishing deity are that of *Actaeon (whom she transformed into a stag and had torn apart by his own hounds), that of her companion *Callisto (for having lost her chastity to Zeus), and her demand that *Iphigenia be sacrificed. According to one version of his myth she killed the hunter *Orion for insulting her.

In Attica her most important cults are those of Artemis Brauronia, Munichia, Tauropolos, and Agrotera (see ATTIC CULTS AND MYTHS). As Brauronia and Munichia she was above all concerned with female transitions, especially that from *parthenos* to *gynē*. At her sanctuaries at *Brauron and Munichia little girls between the ages of 5 and 10 served Artemis as *arktoi* (bears), a pre-menarche ritual that turned girl-children into marriageable *parthenoi*. Artemis Brauronia was, in general, a women's goddess, and she included a strong kourotrophic function. Artemis Munichia was also a *kourotrophos*, and in addition she was also concerned with young men; at her festival, the *Munichia, ephebes (see EPHEBOI) sailed from Zea to the harbour of Munichia in 'the sacred ships', and held races at sea. Then they processed for Artemis

and sacrificed, celebrations said to be in commemoration and thanksgiving for the battle of *Salamis. The cult of Artemis Phosphoros ('Light-Bearer') was also associated with that of Munichia at Munichia, while the torch-bearing Artemis, the iconographical representation of Artemis as Phosphoros, is one of the most frequently encountered types among the votives, especially votive reliefs, found at Brauron. The cult of Artemis Tauropolos ('Worshipped at Taurus') at Halai Araphenides (east Attica) appears to have been associated with a boys' initiation ceremony. She ordered *Orestes to take Artemis' Tauric statue to Athens, and set it up in a sanctuary that he was to found at Halai. There Artemis was to be worshipped as Tauropolos, and at her festival (as a compensation for the aborted sacrifice of Orestes) the sword was to be held to a man's throat and blood spilled.

Artemis Agrotera had some involvement with war. The Spartans sacrificed a goat to her before battle, while the Athenians, we are told, before the battle of Marathon vowed to sacrifice to Artemis Agrotera as many goats as enemies killed. In the event they could not find enough goats, so they vowed to sacrifice 500 a year, which they did, on her festival on 6 Boedromion, which thus involved a strong element of thanksgiving for Marathon. This festival included a procession to the temple in which the ephebes took part. The sanctuary of Artemis Agrotera was peri-urban, at Agrae. The overwhelming (though not universal) scholarly opinion is that the temple of Artemis Agrotera is to be identified with the so-called Ilissus temple.

In some places, including Athens, Artemis' role as protector of women in childbirth is expressed through her epithet Loch[e]ia. Elsewhere it is expressed in her identification with *Eileithyia (cf. e.g. Artemis Eileithyia in various Boeotian cities).

At Sparta Artemis had several cults, the most important of which was that of Artemis Orthia (see SPARTAN CULTS), a cult closely associated with the *agōgē*, the long process through which Spartan boys became élite warriors and citizens. But Artemis Orthia also had other functions, not least ones pertaining to female concerns, and there was clearly a close association between Artemis Orthia and Eileithyia since many dedications to Eileithyia were found in this sanctuary.

A ritual practice broadly comparable to the Attic *arkteia* (but in much closer proximity to marriage) has been reconstructed as having been associated in Thessaly with the cult of Artemis Pagasitis at Pagasae-Demetrias and the cult of Artemis Throsia at Larissa, the *nebreia*, which consisted of the consecration of girls to Artemis for a certain period during which they were called *nebroi* (fawns).

At Patrae the festival Laphria in honour of Artemis Laphria included a procession in which the virgin priestess rode in a chariot drawn by deer and the holocaust sacrifice of many animals; these were thrown alive into the altar enclosure, and included wild animals such as deer and boar, which were not normally sacrificed in Greek religion.

The cult of Artemis at Ephesus includes Asiatic elements; but this does not make Artemis an eastern goddess.

Artemis was often identified with other goddesses whose name she sometimes bore as an epithet, for example, besides Artemis Eileithyia referred to above, Artemis *Hecate.

[Homer, *Iliad* 9. 533–49, 20. 31–40, 21. 468–513, *Odyssey* 11. 171–3, 568–81; Euripides, *Hippolytus*, *Iphigenia at Aulis*, *Iphigenia among the Taurians* 1439 ff.; Pausanias 7. 18. 8–13]

Artemon, of Miletus, wrote, under Nero, a work in 22 books on *dreams and their consequences, with special reference to cures by *Sarapis. He is criticized by *Artemidorus.

Ascalabus, in mythology, son of Misme, an Attic woman. His mother gave *Demeter, who was looking for *Persephone, a vessel of water, meal, and pennyroyal; he laughed at her for drinking it greedily, and she threw what was left of it over him, whereat he became a spotted lizard.

Ascalaphus, in mythology, (1) son of *Ares and Astyoche, who sailed with the *Argonauts, and later died at Troy. (2) Son of Orphne or Gorgyra, and *Acheron. When *Persephone was in *Hades, *Zeus agreed that she could return if she had eaten nothing. Ascalaphus had seen her eat a few pomegranate-seeds and betrayed her; Persephone turned him into an owl (*Ovid), or *Demeter did, when the stone which she had put over him was lifted by *Heracles. *See* ASCALABUS.

[(1) Homer, *Iliad* 13. 519–24, 15. 110–42. (2) Ovid, *Metamorphoses* 5. 533–50]

Ascanius, character in literature and mythology, son of *Aeneas. Not mentioned in Homer, he appears in the Aeneas-legend by the 5th cent. BC, at first as one of several sons of Aeneas. His mother in the *Cypria* (*see* EPIC CYCLE) was Eurydice; in *Virgil and Livy and thereafter she is *Creusa (2), daughter of Priam; Livy also mentions a further version, that he was the son of Lavinia. The *gens Iulia* claimed him as eponymous founder with an alternative name of 'Iulus', variously derived. In the *Aeneid* he is a projection of typical and sometimes ideal Roman youth, but still too young to play a major part; other versions tell of his subsequent career as king of *Lavinium and founder of *Alba Longa, the city from which Rome was founded. He is depicted in both Greek and Roman art.

[Livy 1. 3. 1–5; Virgil, *Aeneid* 1. 267–8]

asceticism The Greek word *askēsis* is as old as Homer and implies disciplined and productive effort. (The Romans admired ascetic practice but chiefly by absorbing the values of Greek philosophy.) At first physical by allusion—to the skill of the craftsman and the vigour of the athlete—it quickly acquired a moral sense also, clear in Xenophon. He contrasted the ascetic with the self-willed amateur, stressing submission to a tradition of instruction, and he made a connection with self-mastery, overlaying with that positive moral note the more general notion of labour. The ascetic improved upon nature, remaining in that sense a craftsman.

Asceticism was associated thereafter with philosophical rather than religious practice. Philosophers rejected ritual as a guarantee of liberation or virtue. Their moderation was distinct from the self-denial of priests, initiates, and devotees, even when that involved fasting or sexual restraint.

Linked thus with philosophy, asceticism adopted forms dictated by different schools. With Platonism ascendant, its general aim veered naturally towards truth and knowledge understood in increasingly exalted and visionary senses. Followers of *Pythagoras, believing a divine element was imprisoned in the body, recommended release through silence as an aid to contemplation, with fasting an added option (perhaps more symbolic than effective). Some Cynics may have furthered the ascetic cause, particularly when they advocated simplicity and detachment (see DIOGENES (1)). The sophists developed at their best a complex system of personal formation, in which asceticism, together with education and natural talent, had its part. Balance was called for, linked with a formal theory of the virtues, particularly prudence. The Stoics (see STOICISM) armed themselves against what they called 'passion' and relinquished some goods to safeguard others: sound judgement, therefore, mattered more than willpower. No less, in their way, the disciples of Epicurus chose some goods over others in pursuit of true happiness and should be allowed the title of 'ascetic' in a strict sense. Finally, *Neopythagoreanism from the 1st cent. BC on prompted more severe criticism of cult as a moral tool and emphasized the inner quality of true piety—an emphasis that would mirror if not reinforce the suspicion of some Christian ascetics about the usefulness of sacramental religion (see also APOLLONIUS OF TYANA). By the time of admirers such as Philostratus and Iamblichus, those different elements had begun to conflate—a process confirmed within *Neoplatonism.

Not surprisingly, therefore, asceticism made its appearance in a Christian context precisely when Christians opened themselves fully, during the 2nd cent., to the classical philosophical tradition. There was early promise, for example, in the *Second Epistle of Clement* (linking self-mastery with the Christian understanding of conversion); but the chief exemplars are *Clement and *Origen of Alexandria. Clement inherited his understanding of both concepts from *Philon (1), who was influenced here by Neopythagorean and sophistic traditions (presenting Jacob as the typical ascetic). Origen connected asceticism firmly with 'purity' and 'virginity' understood in a fully Christian sense, but only because such ideas appealed to him on other grounds.

The chief Christian theorists of asceticism sprang precisely from that Alexandrian school in the late 4th cent. and early 5th cent. AD. Their teaching, however, was modified or augmented by New Testament values, particularly that of renunciation. The classic and influential example occurs in the *Life of Antony*, a text owing much to Alexandrian tradition and marked by a surprising number of philosophical debts and allusions. There Antony, the archetype of the Christian ascetic, responds to the call of Matthew to sell all, give to the poor, and follow Jesus. It was during the later 4th cent. that reference to the word *ascesis* began to appear in Latin texts, instantly connected with 'monk' (*monachus*) and associated terms. Thus the monk inherited the mantle of the philosopher and dictated thereafter the acceptable style of strenuous self-improvement.

Asclepiades, of Tragilus (4th cent. BC), wrote an account of Greek *mythology as told in tragedy, the six books of *Tragodoumena*, just as earlier *mythographers had based such accounts on epic and lyric. He was a source for *Apollodorus but is mainly known to us from commentators on Homer.

Asclepius (Lat. *Aesculapius), hero and god of healing.

In *Homer's *Iliad*, he is a hero, the 'blameless physician', taught by the *centaur Chiron; his two sons, the physicians *Machaon and Podalirius, lead a contingent from Tricca in Thessaly. Late Archaic authors fit him into two different genealogies: in a Thessalian version alluded to in a Hesiodic poem (*see* HESIOD) and narrated more fully in *Pindar, he was the son of *Apollo and *Coronis, daughter of *Phlegyas. Coronis had become Apollo's beloved, but then married the mortal Ischys; when a raven denounced the girl to the god, he (or his sister *Artemis) killed her, but snatched the unborn baby from the pyre, and entrusted him to Chiron (*see* CENTAURS). When grown up, Asclepius became a great healer who even raised men from the dead, which provoked *Zeus into killing him with his thunderbolt. Angered, Apollo retaliated by killing the *Cyclopes who had made the thunderbolt; in order to punish him, Zeus sent him into servitude with Admetus, king of Pherae (*see* ALCESTIS). In the Hesiodic *Catalogues*, however, Asclepius is the son of Arsinoë, daughter of Messenian Leucippus, although the story probably followed about the same course as in Pindar, with Asclepius' death by lightning and Apollo's anger and servitude. Thus, already in the 6th cent. BC two local versions of the myth are well attested and show a very early double location of Asclepius; in both, Apollo is already present. A later, Epidaurian version retained 'the daughter of Phlegyas' (Coronis or Aigle) as mother but made *Epidaurus his birthplace, where the baby was exposed, nurtured by a goat, and protected by a dog (hence the sacred dogs and the prohibition of goat sacrifice in Epidaurus).

The two early local myths complicate the question of his local origin. It seems prudent to assume two Archaic foci of a healer-cult of Asclepius, in Tricca in Thessaly and in Messenia. Unlike ordinary heroes, Asclepius must have been very early emancipated from the attachment to a local grave; this allowed him to develop a god-like stature, though in most places he stayed attached to his father Apollo. Tricca had 'the oldest and most famous sanctuary' of Asclepius which is still archaeologically unknown, while the Asclepieum of Messene has revealed an important Hellenistic complex of inner-city sanctuaries briefly described by Pausanias, whose pre-Hellenistic roots are still unknown.

Expansion of Asclepius must have begun in late Archaic times; both Cos and Epidaurus became famous during the 5th cent. Cos was the home of a school of physicians which was organized in a pseudo-lineage fashion: following the lead of the Homeric *Asklēpiadai* they all called themselves the descendants of Asclepius or Asclepiadae. Local tradition insisted on a Triccan origin. The site of an early sanctuary is uncertain; when, in 366/5 BC, the city of Cos was rebuilt, Asclepius received a sanctuary in a grove of Apollo Cyparissius; the famous oath, sworn to Apollo, Asclepius, (his daughters) *Hygieia and *Panacea, 'and all gods and goddesses', belongs to the same period. At Epidaurus, Asclepius must have arrived in about 500 BC when his first sanctuary was built below the hill-sanctuary of Apollo Maleatas where cult went back to the bronze age. Epidaurus became the centre for later expansion. Already in the 5th cent., Asclepius had come to Sicyon, brought on a mule cart and in the form of his snake. Similarly, the god sent his snake to Athens where he arrived in 420/19, coming by sea to his sanctuary in the Piraeus; not long after, he was transferred by cart, together with Hygieia, to his main city sanctuary on the west slope of the Acropolis, well above the theatre of Dionysus. Perhaps already in the 4th cent. BC, a certain Archias who had found healing in Epidaurus, brought the cult to Pergamum. To cure a plague in 293 BC, the Sibylline books (*see* SIBYL) caused the Romans to fetch the god's snake by ship from Epidaurus to Rome, where the snake chose the Tiber island as its home, but a 5th-cent. dedication from Tuscany points to much earlier acquaintance with the cult elsewhere in peninsular Italy, and the architectural layout of the Hellenistic Asclepieum at Fregellae shows Coan influence. Epidaurian foundations might in their turn become foci for further Asclepiea, like the one in Cyrenean Balagrae from which derives the sanctuary on Crete at Lebena, or Pergamum mother of the Smyrnaean sanctuary. The origins of many other Asclepiea are less well documented, but not necessarily late—the Olympian dedication of Micythus of Rhegium who lived in Tegea after 467 BC dates Asclepius' Tegean cult not much later than the Coan or Epidaurian one; this sanctuary, as many others in the Peloponnese, might derive from Messenia, not from Epidaurus—though later combinations obscure the picture, like the cult of Machaon in Messenian Gerenia.

The success of Asclepius was due to his appeal to individuals in a world where their concerns became more and more removed from civic religion and even from the healer Apollo whose appeal still was discernible in his expansion to Rome in 433 BC (*see* AESCULAPIUS) and in his popularity in the Black Sea towns; with the one exception of Asclepius' transfer to Rome, it was individuals who were responsible for the expansion. The hero, 'best of the physicians', son of Apollo but still enough of a human to try to cancel death, the fundamental borderline between man and god in Greek thinking, was more easily accessible than Apollo who could proclaim lofty indifference towards man and his destiny; even as a god, Asclepius was never so distant (see the very personal attachment of Publius Aelius *Aristides in the 2nd cent. AD to Pergamene Asclepius).

Most Asclepiea share common features. The children of Asclepius, his sons Machaon and Podalirius and his daughter Hygieia, have cult in most, as has Apollo whom official inscriptions from Epidaurus always name before Asclepius. Most sanctuaries contain a sacred snake, some—like Epidaurus—also sacred dogs. A central feature of the cult is *incubation, the receiving of *dreams in which the god prescribes the healing; such dreams are preserved in the long 'Sacred Stories' (*Hieroi logoi*) of Aelius Aristides and in the accounts of more or less miraculous healings inscribed in Epidaurus, Pergamum, Lebena, and Rome. Often, actual medical therapy followed the dream. Asclepiea developed into sacred hospitals and nursing-homes, but, owing to their wide appeal, also constituted meeting-places for local intellectuals and places of philosophical instruction (as in Cilician Aegae). Besides the healing rites, other rituals are possible (initiatory dedications of ephebic hair in Paros; burnt sacrifices in Titane, with archaic cult images). Most Asclepiea were situated outside the town, sometimes on the seashore or in a lone valley, or at least in a marginal position in town. They share such sites with oracular shrines; both constituted places where man could meet the divine directly.

In iconography, Asclepius generally appears as a mature, bearded man, similar to Zeus, but with a milder expression; a beardless Asclepius is the exception. His most constant attributes are the staff (see ritual 'putting up the staff' at Cos) and the snake, often coiled about the staff. Generally, the god is standing; in the famous chryselephantine statue from Epidaurus, the god is seated, the staff in his left hand, his right extended above the head of a serpent, and beside the throne lies a dog.

[Homer, *Iliad* 4. 405, 11. 518, 21. 462–6; Pindar, *Pythian* 3; Pausanias 2. 26–8]

askoliasmos, a country sport in Attica. The players tried to keep their balance while jumping on an inflated and greasy wine-skin. It was probably played at many festivals, and should not be particularly connected with the Rural *Dionysia in Attica.

Asteria, sister of *Leto and mother, by Perses, of *Hecate. The fact that she is Leto's sister must be connected with the fact that Asteria (meaning 'starry') is also given as an ancient name for *Delos. According to *Callimachus and others, she leapt into the sea to escape the amorous pursuit of *Zeus, and so gave her name to the island.

[Hesiod, *Theogony* 409–12; Callimachus, *Hymn* 4. 36–40]

astrology, the art of converting astronomical data (i.e. the positions of the celestial bodies) into predictions of outcomes in human affairs. Astrology developed in the Hellenistic age, essentially as an import from Babylon, which equally furnished many of its astronomical parameters. Its development was connected to contemporary developments in astronomy. The history of astronomy in the 300 years between Hipparchus (working *c*.145–125 BC) and Ptolemy (working AD 146 to *c*.170) is very obscure, because the unchallenged position of the *Almagest* in later antiquity resulted in the loss of all earlier works on similar topics. However, the evidence from Indian astronomy (the *siddhāntas* based on lost Greek treatises from late Hellenistic times) and from Greek papyri shows that the process begun by Hipparchus was continued by his successors, who produced predictive mathematical models for all the heavenly bodies. This undoubtedly contributed to the enormous growth in astrology (which requires calculating the celestial positions for a given time) in the period following Hipparchus. But theoretical astronomy was characterized by a bewildering profusion of Babylonian arithmetical methods (which Hipparchus himself had not hesitated to use, even in his lunar theory), combined with geometrical planetary models which, although producing numerical results, lacked logic and consistency. This situation satisfied the professional needs of astrologers such as Ptolemy's contemporary *Vettius Valens, but was repugnant to the scientific purism of Ptolemy himself. In his magisterial *Almagest* (*c*.AD 150) he ignores (apart from an occasional contemptuous aside), the work of his immediate predecessors, singling out Hipparchus as the sole peer worthy of his imitation and criticism. Starting from first principles, and rigidly excluding arithmetical methods, he constructed an edifice of models for sun, moon, planets, and fixed stars based on a combination of epicycles and eccentrics employing uniform circular motions, the numerical parameters of which he determined by rigorous geometrical methods from carefully selected observations. These were supplemented by tables allowing the computation of all celestial positions and phenomena pertinent to ancient astronomy, to a suitable accuracy (Ptolemy regarded agreement with observation within 10′ of arc as acceptable). The result is a work of remarkable power and consistency, which dominated astronomy for 1,300 years.

By the 1st cent. BC, astrology had emerged as a sophisticated technical art, commanding widespread credence and respect. So it remained until the late empire, when its incompatibility with *Christianity led to its formal suppression (though not extinction).

There are several branches of astrology, of which the most important is genethlialogy, the art of foretelling an individual's life from the positions of the stars (i.e. sun, moon, planets, and fixed stars) at birth or conception; see CONSTELLATIONS. The basic astronomical data for calculating a 'nativity' (i.e. a horoscope) are (*a*) the positions of the seven known planets (including sun and moon) relative to one another (their 'aspects') and to the twelve signs of the zodiac, and (*b*) the position of the circle of the zodiac (and thus of the planets moving round it) relative to a second circle of twelve 'places' (mod. 'houses') whose cardinal points ('centres') are the rising- and setting-points on the horizon and the zenith and nadir. The whole may be likened to a complex clock whose seven hands (the planets) turn counter-clockwise at various mean speeds (from the moon's month to Saturn's almost 30 years) against a dial whose twelve hours are the signs of the zodiac; simultaneously, the dial and its hands together rotate clockwise (in a 24-hour period corresponding to the apparent daily revolution of the heavens) against a second, fixed dial which is the local frame of reference for the nativity, itself divided into twelve sectors (the 'places') with the rising and setting points at 9 and 3 o'clock and the zenith and nadir at about 12 and 6. The astrologer reads this clock at the time of birth and then assigns meanings, in terms of the 'native's' destiny, character, and occupation, to the various positions and relationships in the 'nativity'. In antiquity, as now, astronomical tables rather than direct observation were used.

Actual horoscopes survive from antiquity, both simple (as in papyrus fragments) and complex (as in professional treatises, e.g. the *Anthologies* of *Vettius Valens). Astrology was popular with all classes; similarly, astrologers spanned a wide social and intellectual range. At the pinnacle were men such as Tiberius Claudius *Thrasyllus and his son Tiberius Claudius Balbillus who were theoreticians and practitioners of the art, confidants and functionaries of emperors from Tiberius to Vespasian, and connected by marriage both to powerful Romans and to the Greek client kings of Commagene. Because it was so widely believed, astrology was potentially subversive of public order. Accordingly, astrologers were periodically expelled from Rome, and Augustus forbade both consultations in private and those concerning deaths (AD 11).

From a modern perspective it is the postulated link, causal or semiotic, between celestial and terrestrial events that renders astrology suspect. Most ancients took that link for granted, under a belief in a 'universal sympathy' which connects all parts of the cosmos in a harmoniously functioning whole. *Stoicism legitimized divination of all sorts, and the worship of the stars, especially the sun (*see* HELIOS; SOL), added further authority to astrology, as did the common belief in the *soul's celestial origin and destiny. Many intellectuals accordingly accepted and justified the art, including such astronomers as Ptolemy, who makes a well-reasoned case that astrology is but the application of astronomy, in a necessarily fallible way, to the sublunary environment. There were, however, sceptics and critics, among the most cogent being Sextus Empiricus and Favorinus of Arles; and low-grade practitioners preying on the superstitious attracted inevitable scorn.

Astyoche, in mythology sister of *Priam and daughter of *Laomedon. She married *Telephus and bore Eurypylus who came to the Trojan War and was killed by *Neoptolemus with many of his people, 'thanks to gifts made to a woman'. This the commentators explained as the gift either of a wife (Hermione) by *Menelaus to Neoptolemus, or by Priam to Astyoche of the golden vine which was given Tros by Zeus as compensation for the loss of *Ganymedes. In art she appears on Attic vases.

[Homer, *Odyssey* 11. 521]

Atalanta, a mythical heroine, daughter of Schoeneus, *Iasus, or Maenalus. She was exposed at birth and nursed by a bear before being brought up by hunters. When she reached maturity she chose to remain a virgin and to spend her time hunting as a companion of *Artemis (cf. CALLISTO). She killed the centaurs Rhoecus and Hylaeus, who had tried to rape her, she took part in the hunt of the Calydonian boar, where *Meleager fell in love with her, and at the games held in honour of *Pelias she defeated *Peleus in wrestling. Later, when her father wished to give her in marriage, she promised to marry the man who could defeat her in a foot-race. After several young men were defeated and put to death, Hippomenes (or Melanion, or Hippomedon) was victorious in the test, having dropped some golden apples on the track, which Atalanta stopped to pick up. Near Methydrion in Arcadia were shown 'racetracks of Atalanta'. From the marriage was born *Parthenopaeus. During a hunt, the couple made love in a sanctuary of *Zeus (or *Cybele) and as punishment for their impiety they were changed into lions.

In art Atalanta is shown sometimes as a huntress at Calydon (vases from 580 BC onwards, 4th-cent. pediment from Tegea), sometimes as an athlete at the games for Peleus. In the first type, she is usually shown wearing a short garment and sometimes an animal hide; in the second, she wears, in the 5th cent., a bodice. The episode of the foot-race is not found in art.

[Apollodorus 3. 9. 2; Ovid, *Metamorphoses* 10. 686]

Atargatis (Aramaic ʿAtar-ʿAta), the goddess of Hierapolis-Bambyce in Syria whose usual name among Greeks and Romans was the 'Syrian goddess', a mother-goddess, giver of fertility. Her temple, rebuilt *c*.300 BC by Stratonice, wife of Seleucus I of Syria, was plundered by Antiochus IV and by Crassus, but was still in Lucian's day one of the greatest and holiest in Syria; its site has yet to be found. Her consort was Hadad; his throne was flanked by bulls, that of Atargatis by lions. At Ascalon, Atargatis was represented as half woman, half fish. Fish and doves were sacred to her; the myth records that, having fallen into a lake, Atargatis was saved by the fish, or, in another version, that Atargatis was changed into a fish, and her daughter *Semiramis into a dove. Late in the 3rd cent. BC her cult appears in Egypt, Macedon, and, with civic status, at Phistyon in Aetolia and (early 2nd cent.) at Thuria in Messenia. Citizens of Hierapolis founded a shrine on *Delos in 128–127, of which Athens soon took control. Atargatis was worshipped also in a number of other Greek cities and in Rome, where Nero favoured her for a while; Roman troops took her cult to the Danubian provinces and Britain. Astrologers identified her with the constellation Virgo, and a 3rd-cent. inscribed 'creed' found in England accepts the *dea Syria* as one of several names or manifestations of the universal goddess. At Thuria her cult included mysteries. *See* EUNUCHS IN RELIGION; FISH, SACRED; SYRIAN DEITIES.

[Ovid, *Metamorphoses* 4. 44–8; Lucian, *De dea Syria*; Apuleius, *Metamorphoses* 8–9]

Ate, mental aberration, infatuation causing irrational behaviour which leads to disaster. A hero's *atē* is brought about through psychic intervention by a divine agency, usually *Zeus, but can also be physically inflicted. *Agamemnon blames Zeus, *Fate, and the *Erinyes for his delusion that made him take *Briseis and lead the Achaeans to the brink of defeat. Ate is personified as the daughter of Zeus whom he expelled from Olympus to bring harm to men. A similarly pessimistic notion of divine punishment for guilt underlies *Homer's Parable of the Prayers. In this early *allegory swift-footed Ate outruns the slow Prayers and forces men into error and punishment. In another moralizing personification Ate becomes the daughter of *Eris (Strife) and sister of Dysnomia (Lawlessness); but *Hesiod also used *atē* impersonally in the sense of punishment for hubris. *Aeschylus draws a powerful picture of *atē* both as a daemonic *force and instrument of ruin.

[Homer, *Iliad* 9. 502–12, 16. 805, 19. 87 f., 126–31; *Odyssey* 12. 371 f.; Hesiod, *Works and Days* 214 ff., *Theogony* 205 f; Aeschylus, *Agamemnon* 1124, 1433; *Choephoroi* 383, 956 ff.]

Athamas, a figure of Boeotian and Thessalian myth. In the best-known story, he was king of Boeotian Orchomenus, husband of Ino (*see* INO-LEUCOTHEA) and father of Phrixus, *Helle, *Melicertes, and Learchus. The first two were the children of Nephele ('Cloud'), Athamas' first wife; their stepmother Ino concocted a bogus oracle demanding their deaths in sacrifice in order to restore the fertility of the land, but they were borne away on a golden ram (*see* HELLE). Later, Ino and Athamas brought up the child *Dionysus, in revenge for which *Hera drove them mad. Athamas killed their son Learchus, and Ino ran from him carrying Melicertes and jumped into the sea, where mother and son were transformed into deities, Leucothea and Palaemon. In one version, Athamas was then exiled and settled in Thessaly, where he married Themisto. But another tradition places Athamas originally in Thessalian (H)alos, where he himself proposes to sacrifice Phrixus to Zeus Laphystius. The motif of human sacrifice is altogether clearer here, since in Herodotus' rather confusing account Athamas himself is later nearly sacrificed. Both stories probably have to do with the cult of Zeus Laphystius; the Thessalian one explained why a descendant of Athamas must be sacrificed if he set foot in the building with the civic hearth.

[Apollodorus 1. 9. 1–2, 3. 4. 3; Herodotus 7. 197]

Athanasius (*c*.AD 295–373) was an outstanding theologian and Church leader, and as a deacon played an influential part at the council of Nicaea (325). Appointed bishop of Alexandria in 328, he vigorously championed the Nicene doctrine of the consubstantiality (*homoousion*) of Father and Son against *Arianism, being five times deposed and exiled. Two of his exiles he spent in the west, to which he introduced monasticism. In the last decades of his life he developed the doctrine of the divinity and personality of the Holy Spirit, and did much to promote understanding between the different anti-Arian groups in the Church. His surviving writings include apologetic, dogmatic, and ascetic treatises, historical essays, and letters.

atheism The Greek for atheism is 'not to recognize (*nomizein*) the gods' or 'deny that the gods exist' or, later, 'to remove (*anairein*) the gods'. The Greek word *atheos* can be applied to atheism, but in the earliest instances it means 'impious, vicious' or 'hated, abandoned by the gods', and these senses persist along with the other; so too with *atheotēs*. Thus Christians and pagans were to swap charges of *atheotēs*, by which they meant 'impious views about the divine'.

The gods of popular polytheism were rejected or drastically reinterpreted by all philosophers from the 6th cent. BC onwards, but most preserved a divine principle of some kind (as in different ways *Plato, *Aristotle, and *Stoicism were to do). Radical atheism is hard to detect, and was never an influential intellectual position in the ancient world. *Anaxagoras and Thucydides have been suspected of it, because of their silences; a character in Critias' (or *Euripides') satyr-play (*see* SATYRIC DRAMA) *Sisyphus* argues that gods are an invention of a 'wise

lawgiver' to deter secret crime; on the other hand Democritus, whose overall system is compatible with atheism, appears to speak of gods in some fragments, and *Prodicus did not necessarily reject the divine in every form merely because he offered a rationalizing account of the origin of human belief in the gods of myth. Much the most important testimony to the reality of atheism is Plato's in *Laws*, where he speaks of contemporary thinkers who hold that the world is governed by nature or chance, not god, that morality is man-made and the best life is that according to nature. Who Plato had in mind is disputed; he goes on to say that such radical atheism was already on the wane.

Much less helpful are the claims often made in later antiquity that this or that earlier thinker (often linked together in an 'atheist list') had 'removed the gods'. Some typical atheists of these catalogues are *Protagoras, *Diagoras of Melos, Theodorus of Cyrene (who probably acquired the sobriquet *atheos* in his lifetime), *Euhemerus and *Epicurus. Too much oversimplification and polemical distortion lies beyond the lists for them to have authority: Protagoras, for instance, was a declared agnostic, a position incompatible with atheism.

A second view combated in Plato's *Laws* is that the gods exist, but are indifferent to the doings of mankind. Such 'practical atheism' had doubtless always existed, and became the declared position of Epicurus (who however urged that the gods should still be honoured); philosophical opponents asserted that only fear of public opinion had restrained Epicurus from 'abolishing the gods' altogether.

[Plato, *Apology* 26, *Laws* 10; Cicero, *On the Nature of the Gods* 1. 85, 121, 123]

Athena *Homer describes how Athena took off the finely-wrought robe 'which she herself had made and worked at with her own hands' and 'armed herself for grievous war'. This incident encapsulates the paradoxical nature of a goddess who is as skilled in the preparation of clothes as she is fearless in battle; who thus unites in her person the characteristic excellences of both sexes. At the greater *Panathenaea in Athens, she was presented with a robe, the work of maidens' hands (see ARREPHORIA), which traditionally portrayed that battle of the gods and giants in which she was the outstanding warrior on the side of the gods.

Her patronage of crafts is expressed in cults such as that of Athena Erganē, Athena the Craftswoman or Maker; it extends beyond the 'works' of women to carpentry, metalworking, and technology of every kind, so that at Athens she shared a temple and a festival with *Hephaestus and can, for instance, be seen on vases seated (in full armour!) in a pottery. Her love of battle is seen, as we saw, in myth, and also in such cults as that of Athena Victory (*Nike); she is regularly portrayed fully armed, one leg purposefully advanced, wearing her terror-inducing *aegis.

She is also closely associated with the masculine world in her mythological role as a helper of male heroes, most memorably seen in her presence beside Heracles on several of the metopes of the temple of *Zeus at *Olympia. Indeed her intervention in battle often takes the form of 'standing beside' a favourite. (She has accordingly been seen as every man's ideal elder sister, in contrast to the tomboy Artemis and sexy Aphrodite, but these modern western categories scarcely fit the Greek family.) Her virginity is a bridge between the two sides of her nature. Weaving is a characteristic activity of ordinary young girls, but a perpetual virgin, who is not subject to the distinctively feminine experience of childbirth, is a masculine woman, a potential warrior.

The warlike Athena is scarcely separable from Athena Polias, the goddess of the Acropolis (see ATHENS, RELIGIOUS TOPOGRAPHY) and protectress of cities. 'City-protecting' was most commonly performed by goddesses rather than gods; and the other great protectress was the other great warrior-goddess of the Iliad, Athena's close associate *Hera. Athena exercised this function in many cities besides Athens, including Sparta and (in the Iliad) Troy. Athens was unique only in the degree of prominence that it assigned her in this role.

A few cult titles and festivals of Athena seem to indicate interests other than those discussed so far; and it has often been suggested that her familiar classical functions have been pared down from a much broader original competence. But this is too much to deduce from stray allusions to cults the details of which are usually very little known. The 'Athena Mother' of Elis is a puzzle; and Athena's limited intrusions upon the preserves of other gods at Athens—the cult of Athena of Health (*Hygieia) for instance—may simply reflect a tendency of city-protecting gods to have a finger in every pie.

Athena is unique among Greek gods in bearing a connection with a city imprinted in her very name. The precise linguistic relation between place and goddess is teasingly difficult to define: the form of her name in early Attic inscriptions is the adjectival Athēnaia, which suggests that she may in origin be 'the Athenian' something, the Athenian Pallas for instance (Pallas Athēnaiē being a regular Homeric formula). But this account still leaves the shorter name-form Athena unexplained. Athenians themselves, of course, stressed the goddess's association with their city enthusiastically. She was foster-mother of the early king *Erechtheus/ *Erichthonius, and had competed, successfully, with Poseidon for possession of Attica. In Panhellenic mythology, however, she shows no special interest in Athens or in Athenian heroes. The association with Athens does not appear to affect her fundamental character.

Her most important myth is that of her birth from the head of Zeus. It stresses her unique closeness to Zeus, a vital quality in a city-protecting goddess, and at the same time the gap that divides her, a child without a mother, from the maternal side of femininity. In the oldest version Zeus became pregnant with Athena after swallowing *Metis;

she was thus also a kind of reincarnation of *mētis*, 'cunning intelligence'.

It has in fact been suggested that Athena's characteristic mode of action, a mode that unifies her apparently diverse functions while differentiating them from those of other gods with which they might appear to overlap, is the application of *mētis*. Her *mētis* appears obviously in her association with crafts and in her love for wily *Odysseus; more obliquely, it is argued, it is for instance to be seen in her title Hippia, 'of horses', which she acquires via a product of *mētis*, the bridle, whereas *Poseidon Hippius embodies the animal's brute strength. In warfare she would express rational force, in contrast to the mindless violence of Ares. One may doubt, however, how fundamental the opposition to Ares and the role of *mētis* in fact are in defining her military function.

Precursors of Athena have been identified in Mycenaean military or palace-protecting goddesses; the only solid evidence is a tantalizing reference in a Linear B tablet from Cnossus to A-ta-na po-ti-ni-ja.

[Homer, *Iliad* 5. 733–7, 10. 278–94, *Odyssey*; Hesiod, *Theogony* 886–90; Apollodorus 1. 3. 6]

Athenagoras, Christian *apologist from Athens and author of two extant works, *The Resurrection of the Dead*, and the *Legatio*. The latter is a defence of Christianity composed in the form of a letter to the emperors *Marcus Aurelius and Commodus. This work is an extremely important, early assertion of Christian propriety against commonplace charges that Christians were atheists and cannibals (*see* ATHEISM; CANNIBALISM). One of its most interesting features is the extensive use of classical literature to justify or explain Christian practice.

Athens, myths of *See* ATTHIS; ATTIC CULTS AND MYTHS.

Athens, religious topography

Acropolis, the central fortress and principal sanctuary of *Athena, patron goddess of the city. In the later 13th cent. BC the steep hill was enclosed by a massive wall. Within, there are Mycenaean terraces, perhaps once supporting traces of 'the strong house of *Erechtheus' (in Homer's *Odyssey*). The first monumental temples and sculptural dedications date to the 6th cent. BC. Two large Doric temples of limestone with marble trim were built, along with a half-dozen small temples or treasuries. Later quarrying has obliterated the foundations of all but one of the peripteral temples (*c.*510 BC) which stood on the north side of the hill, just south of the later Erechtheum. A marble temple, the Older Parthenon, was under construction on the south half of the hill in 480 BC when the Persians took and sacked the city. The debris from this devastation was buried on the Acropolis and no major construction took place for about a generation. In the 450s a monumental bronze statue of Athena Promachus was set up to celebrate victory over the Persians and in the second half of the 5th cent. four major buildings were constructed at the instigation of Pericles, with Phidias as general overseer. First came the *Parthenon (447–432); the Propylaea (437–432), gateway to the Acropolis, occupied the western approaches to the citadel. Soon after, an old shrine of Athena Nike (Victory) was refurbished and a small temple of the Ionic order was built just outside the Propylaea. Finally, the *Erechtheum was constructed during the last quarter of the 5th cent. Only a few buildings were added to the Acropolis in later times: a sanctuary of Braduronian *Artemis (*see* BRAURON) and the Chalkotheke, where bronzes were stored. The Roman presence in Greece is reflected on the Acropolis by the construction after 27 BC of a small round temple dedicated to Roma and Augustus and built in an Ionic order closely copying the Erechtheum.

Environs of the Acropolis Numerous sanctuaries clustered around the base of the Acropolis rock. The sanctuaries of 'the nymph' (7th cent. BC), *Asclepius (420 BC), and *Dionysus (*c.*500 BC) were on the south slope. The theatre of Dionysus was built of limestone and marble in the 330s BC and renovated several times in the Roman period. To the west was a stoa built by King Eumenes II of Pergamum (197–159 BC) and beyond that the local millionaire Herodes Atticus built a huge odeum in memory of his wife Regilla (c.AD 160). The ground east of the theatre was taken up by the odeum of Pericles (c.443 BC), a replica of the tent of Xerxes, captured by the Greeks at the battle of Plataea (479 BC). A broad street lined with tripods set up by victorious *chorēgoi* (producers) in the choral lyric contests led from the theatre around the east end and north side of the Acropolis. In this eastern area were to be found several other cults (*Aglaurus, *Dioscuri, *Theseus), as well as the *Prytaneion*, hearth of the city (all unexcavated). The north side of the Acropolis sheltered cults of *Aphrodite and *Eros, *Pan, *Apollo, and *Demeter and *Persephone (Eleusinium). The Areopagus, a low hill north-west of the Acropolis, was the seat in early times of a council and law-court as well as a shrine of the Eumenides (Furies; see ERINYES).

Agora, the civic centre of Athens, was located north-west of the Acropolis on ground sloping down to the Eridanus river. Traversed by the Panathenaic Way, the *Agora was a large open square reserved for a wide variety of public functions, lined on all four sides by the principal administrative buildings of the city. First laid out in the 6th cent. BC, it remained a focal point for Athenian commerce, politics, and culture for centuries, surviving the Persian sack of 480 BC and the Sullan siege of 86 BC. Here in the Classical period were to be found secular buildings, along with sanctuaries (Hephaisteion, Altar of the Twelve Gods, Stoa of Zeus Eleutherius, Apollo Patrous).

Pnyx, the meeting-place of the Athenian assembly (*ekklēsia*), was built on a low ridge west of the Acropolis. By the Hellenistic period most meetings took place in the theatre of Dionysus, and a small open-air sanctuary of Zeus Hypsistus was established just south-east of the *bēma* in the Roman period. North of the Pnyx the ridge was given over to the worship of the *Nymphs.

South-east Athens In this quarter of town were to be found the oldest cults of the city: Dionysus in 'the Marshes', Olympian Zeus, Gē (Earth), and Pythian Apollo. Best preserved is the colossal *Olympieum. The centre of Hadrian's worship in the Greek world, it was approached through an arch bearing inscriptions delineating the old town of *Theseus from the new Athens built by Hadrian. Nearby, to the north, a gymnasium with a sanctuary of Apollo Lyceus gave its name to *Aristotle's school, the Lyceum. Other shrines and the old Enneakrounos fountain-house lay further out, along the banks of the Ilissus river.

athletics

Greek At the core of Greek athletics was an individual's hard physical struggle in order to gain victory over an opponent; hence, it included not only (as 'athletics' implies nowadays) track and field events but also boxing, wrestling, and equestrian events (*see* HORSE-AND CHARIOT-RACES), and excluded team competitions, fun-running, and performances aimed at setting records (cf. the derivation of 'athletics' from the root *athl-*, denoting struggle, competition for a prize, and misery). Athletics was a popular activity; valuable contemporary evidence for it is provided by vase-paintings and the victory odes of *Pindar and *Bacchylides.

The first substantial description of Greek practice comes from *Homer's account of the funeral games for *Patroclus. Eight events are mentioned there (*chariot-racing, boxing, wrestling, running, javelin,* an event similar to fencing, throwing the weight, and archery); the five in italics regularly formed the central part of all later games.

From the middle of the 5th cent. the four major venues for athletics competitions were the *Olympian, *Pythian, *Nemean, and *Isthmian Games. The running-races were the *stadion* (a length of the stadium, 192 m. (630 ft.) at Olympia), *diaulos* (there and back), and *dolichos* (twelve laps at Olympia). There was no marathon or event of similar length, although Phidippides, who ran from Athens to Sparta, is said to have trained as an ultra-distance runner for the purpose of delivering messages. A race in armour, derived from military training, was introduced into athletics programmes at the end of the 6th cent., and there was a pentathlon consisting of long-jump, *stadion*, discus, javelin, and wrestling. At the Olympian and Pythian Games there were separate events for men and boys, while at the Nemean and Isthmian Games there was also an intermediate category for youths (*ageneioi*, lit. 'beardless').

Training took place in the gymnasium, or *xystos* (covered colonnade); for the running events, especially the *dolichos*, long training-runs must have been done outside the confines of these buildings. The need for athletes to have a suitable diet was widely recognized. Sometimes an athlete's father would act as his coach; often, past victors became coaches. Before the Olympia, the wise precaution was taken of making competitors swear by Zeus that for the previous ten months they had trained properly. When training or competing, athletes covered their bodies with olive oil to keep off the dust and were generally naked, though there is some disputed evidence pointing to the use of loincloths. Male sexual interest in young athletes, admired for their physique, was commonplace.

Women competed at Olympia in separate games, the Heraea in honour of *Hera; there was just one event, a shortened *stadion*-race. During the men's athletics, married women were forbidden to watch, but virgin girls were permitted, a custom perhaps derived from a conception of the games as an occasion for girls to meet future husbands.

It is hard to evaluate athletics performances, because running-races were not timed, and distances in field events not measured; one indication that standards may have been low is the fact that Pausanias records many examples of men who had

been able to win in several different types of event.

Roman At Rome colourful circus spectacles (especially chariot-racing) and ball games were the most popular sporting activities. But *Augustus promoted traditional athletics, staging athletics competitions in the Campus Martius and exhibition-running in the Circus; he himself was keen on watching boxing. Ultra-distance running was also practised. Interest in athletics was maintained by the establishing of Greek-style games at Rome and elsewhere. In (?)4 BC Tiberius won the chariot-race at the Olympian Games; from then on, Romans (mostly either eastern provincials with Roman citizenship, or those with sufficient authority to bend the rules, as Nero did in 67 BC) won at Olympia with increasing regularity. *See* AGONES.

[Homer, *Iliad* 23. 262–897, *Odyssey* 8. 120–30; Pausanias 5–6]

Atlantis, i.e. '(the island of) *Atlas', 'the island lying in the Atlantic'; the oldest surviving wonderland in Greek philosophy. *Plato is the earliest and chief source for the story, said to have been told to Solon by Egyptian priests, of a huge and wealthy island of this name outside the Pillars of Heracles which once ruled 'Libya ... as far as Egypt' and 'Europe as far as Tyrrhenia [= Etruria]' until, in an expedition to conquer the rest, its rulers were defeated by the Athenians, the island shortly after sinking overnight beneath the Atlantic after 'violent earthquakes and floods'; the unfinished *Critias* describes the island's constitution (similar to the ideal city of Plato's *Republic*) and layout of its chief city (a series of concentric circles of alternating land and water). Crantor, the first commentator on Plato, is said to have accepted the truth of the tale, an indicator of ancient controversy about Atlantis as early as *c*.300 BC. Modern speculation continues that the massive eruption of the volcano on Santorini in the late bronze age, resulting in the loss of most of the island's land mass, provided the basis for the legend. However, major discrepancies in the Platonic tale (size, date, and position) offer serious obstacles to this view.

[Plato, *Timaeus* 24e ff., *Critias*; Strabo 2. 3. 6]

Atlas, probably 'very enduring', the *Titan son of *Iapetus and brother of *Prometheus. In the *Odyssey* he is the 'deadly minded' father of *Calypso, 'who knows the depths of the whole sea, and holds the tall pillars which hold earth and heaven apart'. In *Hesiod he lives at the edge of the world beside the *Hesperides and holds up the heaven. The 'rationalizing' identification of the Titan with the Atlas mountains is first found in Herodotus (Virgil strikingly combines the mythical and rationalizing versions); a story in which he was a shepherd turned to rock by *Perseus with the Gorgon's head (*see* GORGO/MEDUSA) may go back to the 5th cent. BC. Atlas was the father of various *constellations, notably the Pleiades, and is sometimes conceived as a wise man who founded the science of astronomy; *Plato makes him the *eponymous first king of *Atlantis. From an early date Atlas was associated with Heraclean legends. Sent to fetch the golden apples of the Hesperides, *Heracles—on the advice of Prometheus— asked Atlas to get them while he held up the sky; Atlas refused to take back the sky but Heracles tricked him into doing so. Nevertheless, Atlas is often omitted from accounts of Heracles and the Hesperides, and *Euripides seems to make the Hesperides and Atlas two separate Heraclean 'labours'.

Atlas in art Atlas is depicted in art from the mid-6th cent. BC, usually with Heracles in the Garden of the Hesperides, notably on the early Classical metope from *Olympia. In Hellenistic and Roman art he supports the globe with great effort. He appeared on the Archaic chest of Cypselus, and the throne of *Amyclae. From the 5th-cent. temple of *Zeus at Acragas begins the use of 'atlantes' as architectural supports, continuing into Roman times.

[Homer, *Odyssey* 1. 52–4; Hesiod, *Theogony* 517–20; Aeschylus, *Prometheus Bound* 348–50; Euripides, *Madness of Hercules* 403–7; Virgil, *Aeneid* 4. 246–51; Ovid, *Metamorphoses* 4. 627–62]

Atreus, in mythology, son of *Pelops and *Hippodamia and brother of Thyestes. In *Homer there is harmony between the brothers, but from later epic on they had shared an implacable feud. Atreus married *Aerope, but she committed adultery with Thyestes and secretly gave him the golden lamb which carried with it claim to the kingship. *Zeus, however, expressed disapproval by reversing the course of the sun. Atreus banished Thyestes; but later, when he learnt of Aerope's adultery, he pretended a reconciliation with his brother and at a feast served up to him the flesh of the latter's own sons. At the end of the meal Atreus showed his brother the heads and hands of his sons, then once more banished him. By Aerope Atreus was father of *Agamemnon and *Menelaus; or, by another genealogy, their grandfather, who brought them up when his son and their father, Pleisthenes, died young. Atreus was finally killed by *Aegisthus, Thyestes' only surviving son.

See also GENEALOGICAL TABLES (5) DESCENDANTS OF TANTALUS.

[Homer, *Iliad* 2. 100–8; Euripides, *Electra* 699–746; Apollodorus, *Epitome* 2. 10–12; Aeschylus, *Agamemnon* 1590 ff.; Seneca, *Thyestes*]

Atrium Vestae, the whole ancient precinct next to the *Regia, east of the *forum Romanum, including the temple and sacred grove of *Vesta and the house of the Vestal virgins, although the term is now commonly used for the latter alone. Remains of its republican predecessor underlie the existing structure, built on a different orientation during Nero's reorganization of the via Sacra. Trajan added the eastern suite and probably a second storey, installing hypocausts in some rooms. There were further modifications under Hadrian, while the enlargement of the central peristyle court is Severan. Later additions were minor.

Atthis was the title given in post-Alexandrian scholarship to the genre of Greek historiography that narrated the local history of Attica. The title, derived from the name of the daughter of the mythical king Cranaus, was probably invented by *Callimachus for cataloguing purposes. The genre was probably created by *Hellanicus in the late 5th cent. It was most popular in the 4th cent.

In structure the *Atthis* was a chronicle, based upon a hypothetical list of kings (for the mythical period) and, after 683/2 BC, on the annual chief *archons. The subject-matter of an *Atthis* was typical of a local history, covering such diverse material as the origins of religious *festivals and cults, etymology of place-names, geography, ethnography, and the creation of financial and political institutions. In short, the *Atthis* was a blend of mythical fantasy and accurate historical detail, the latter especially as the account came closer to the historian's own day.

Attic cults and myths Most Greek states honoured most Greek gods; the differences between them are of emphasis and degree. As characteristic Athenian emphases one might mention: the extraordinary prominence of *Athena, unusual even for a city-protecting goddess; the international standing of the Mysteries of *Demeter and Kore (*Persephone) at *Eleusis; the rich development of local, village (deme) religion, and the related abundance of *hero-cults; the honours acquired in the second half of the 5th cent. by *Hephaestus, usually a minor figure; the comparatively modest role of *Hera.

According to one 5th-cent. observer, Athens had more festivals than any other Greek state; only a selection can be mentioned here. The great show-pieces, which attracted foreign visitors, were the *Panathenaea, the City *Dionysia (when tragedies and comedies were performed), and the Eleusinian *mysteries. Further major landmarks of the domestic year, each lasting several days, were the *Thesmophoria (Demeter and Kore), the most important women's festival; *Anthesteria, the new-wine festival; *Apaturia, the phratry festival. The other 'literary festivals' (*Lenaea, Rural Dionysia, Dionysia

in Piraeus, *Thargelia) were also very popular. Other traditional festivals that were widely or universally celebrated (sometimes impinging on domestic life, through the custom of preparing special food) or that affected many families from time to time were the *Diasia (Zeus *Meilichios), Cronia (when slaves dined with masters), *Pyanopsia (Apollo), Scira (*see* SCIROPHORIA) (Demeter: another women's festival), *Hieros Gamos* (*Zeus and Hera) and several initiatory festivals of *Artemis, chief among them the Brauronia (*see* BRAURON). 'Spectator festivals'—a newer type, on the whole—marked by competitions or an abundance of free meat, included Olympieia, Dipolieia, and Diisoteria (all for Zeus, the third in Piraeus), Epitaphia (games for the war-dead), *Thesea, *Asclepieia, *Hephaestea, *Bendidea; we should note here too an important procession in honour of the Semnai Theai (*see* ERINYES). Of several festivals of Demeter closely related to the agricultural year, the most widely diffused was Proerosia, 'pre-ploughing'. A number of other well-known festivals—the *Haloa (Demeter and others), *Arrephoria and *Plynteria (Athena), *Oschophoria (Dionysus and Athena), had restricted numbers of actual participants, symbolically important though they might be for the entire state.

The most important Attic myths concerned: the conflict of Athena and *Poseidon for possession of Attica; the birth from earth of the two first kings *Cecrops and *Erechtheus/*Erichthonius, which founded symbolically the Athenians' claim to be 'autochthonous'; the adventures of the daughters of these two kings, which acquired important aetiological associations; the arrival in Attica of *Dionysus and, especially, Demeter (the latter event being the origin of the Eleusinian mysteries); the mission of *Triptolemus, who distributed wheat worldwide; the self-sacrifice of *Codrus; and above all the varied career of *Theseus. A distinctive canon of four Athenian achievements was shaped in the special context of the Funeral Speech for the war-dead: the war of

Erechtheus against *Eumolpus of Eleusis and his Thracian allies; the war of Theseus against the invading *Amazons; succour in the cause of right given by the Athenians to the *Heraclidae and to the mothers of the *Seven against Thebes. In contrast to these public and patriotic myths is the rich cycle attaching to the misfortunes of *Cephalus and *Procris.

[Apollodorus 3. 14. 1–15. 10; Pausanias 1]

Attis, in mythology, the youthful consort of *Cybele and prototype of her eunuch devotees. The myth exists in two main forms, with many variants. According to the Phrygian tale, the gods castrated the androgynous *Agdistis; from the severed male parts an almond tree sprang and by its fruit Nana conceived Attis. Later Agdistis fell in love with him, and to prevent his marriage to another caused him to castrate himself. Agdistis is clearly a doublet of Cybele. *Ovid and others change many details, but keep the essential explanatory feature, the self-castration. In a probably Lydian version Attis, like *Adonis, is killed by a boar. The story of Atys, son of the Lydian king Croesus, who was killed by the Phrygian Adrastus in a boar-hunt is an adaptation of this, and attests its antiquity, though the Phrygian is probably the older version.

In Asia Minor Attis bears his native name only in the Neo-Phrygian inscriptions, though the high priest and, under the empire, all members of the priestly college at *Pessinus had the title Attis. Attis is sometimes called Papas or Zeus Papas.

Whatever his original character, vegetation-god or mortal lover of Cybele, in the early cult he remains a subsidiary figure, whose death is mourned but who is not, apparently, worshipped. Attis rarely appears in Greece, but was present at Rome from the time of Cybele's introduction, even if the evidence for him only becomes plentiful from c.AD 150.

Under the later empire he was invested with celestial attributes, and became a solar deity, supreme, all-powerful, and sometimes it seems a surety of immortality to his initiates. In art he is generally represented as an effeminate youth, with the distinctive Phrygian cap and trousers. See ANATOLIAN DEITIES; EUNUCHS IN RELIGION.

[Pausanias 7. 17. 10–12; Ovid, *Fasti* 4. 221–44]

Augeas See HERACLES.

augures, official Roman diviners. They formed one of the four great colleges of priests (see COLLEGIUM), instituted (so the tradition) in the regal period; originally made up of three (patrician) members, the complement was increased to nine in 300 BC when the plebeians were admitted (five plebeians, four patricians), to fifteen by Sulla, and sixteen by *Caesar. New members were admitted (for life) through co-optation; from 103 BC through popular election by the assembly of seventeen tribes from the candidates nominated by two college members. Etymology disputed: traditionally derived from 'directing the birds' (*avi* + *ger* (*o*)), but probably connected with the root *aug* (*eo*), denoting increase and prosperity (cf. *augustus*). We have to distinguish between the functions of the individual augurs and those of the college. As a college they were a body of experts whose duty was to uphold the augural doctrine (variously described as *disciplina*, *ars*, *scientia*, or law: *ius augurium* or *augurale*) which governed the observation and application of the auspices (see AUSPICIUM) in Roman public life. They passed decrees (*decreta*) either on their own initiative (mostly concerning theoretical aspects of the doctrine) or more frequently responding to questions posed by the senate or the magistrates (*responsa*). These 'replies' often dealt with cases of ritual fault (*vitium*) which would nullify the auspices or with the removal of *religio*, a ritual obstacle to an action. The senate was free either to accept or to reject the advice. Individual augurs were both experts (*periti*) and priests (*sacerdotes*). They could give *responsa* (to be distinguished from those of the college); in their capacity as priests they celebrated various rites known as *auguria*, and also (when asked) performed inaugurations of priests and temples (*templa*). They could assist the magistrates in taking the auspices (although this happened much less frequently than is generally assumed) and, in particular, an augur had the right of making a binding announcement (*nuntiatio*) of adverse unsolicited (oblative) omens, especially at the popular assemblies.

[Cicero, *On the Nature of the Gods* 1. 122, *On The Laws* 2. 20–1, 31, *Philippics* 2. 79–84]

augurium canarium, a ceremony so called by Pliny, quoting the *commentarii pontificum* (pontifical records), and *canarium sacrificium* by an Augustan jurist, who says that reddish bitches were sacrificed for crops to 'deprecate' the fierceness of the dog-star. This dog sacrifice (*sacrum canarium*, formed on *canis*, 'dog') was performed by public priests; it took place near the porta Catularia, apparently late in the summer, when the crops were yellowing. On the other hand the day or days for the sacrifice were to be fixed (Pliny) 'before the corn comes out of the sheath', hence in the spring. As it was both augury and sacrifice, the **augures* probably fixed the day for the ceremony (or in their parlance, inaugurated it), and the **pontifices* performed the sacrifice itself. The ceremony appears to have belonged to the category of apotropaic rites to prevent calamities.

[Pliny, *Natural History* 18. 14]

augurium salutis, an augural inquiry as to whether it was permissible (for the magistrates) to pray for the safety of the people. This (annual) prayer could be said only on a day free of all wars. It was attempted in 63 BC, and revived by Augustus.

[Cassius Dio 37. 24–5, 51. 20. 5; Cicero, *On Divination* 1. 105]

Augustales, members of a religious and social institution common in the cities of the western Roman empire. There are numerous variations on the title, which taken together appear in some 2,500 inscriptions. The two most common are *Augustalis* and *sevir Augustalis*. These represent two separate organizations, rarely found in the same

town but characterized by the same general features; the simple title of *sevir*, on the other hand, usually represents a very different institution. The vast majority of *Augustales* were freedmen (85–95 per cent of those attested in inscriptions), as well as Trimalchio and his friends, the only *Augustales* depicted in literature. They often acted as local benefactors, funding public entertainments and building-projects as well as paying entry fees. In return, they enjoyed the prestige of their office, which functioned almost as a magistracy. *Augustales* were entitled to honorific insignia and were often selected by the town councillors. As their title indicates, their formal responsibilities may have centred on the imperial cult (*see* RULER-CULT), in the context of which they probably organized sacrifices and games. They generally performed these duties for a year, after which they retained membership in an order (*ordo*), sometimes organized like a **collegium*, whose members held a rank just below that of the local council. The institution thus provided wealthy freedmen, who were legally barred from holding civic magistracies, with opportunities for public display and prestige.

[Petronius, *Satyricon* 30]

Augustine, St (Aurelius Augustinus) (AD 354–430), was born at Thagaste (mod. Souk Ahras, Algeria), son of Patricius, a modest town councillor of pagan beliefs, and a dominant Catholic mother, Monica. Educated at Thagaste, Madauros, and Carthage, he taught rhetoric at Thagaste, Carthage, and Rome and (384–6) as public orator at Milan, then the capital of the emperor Valentinian II. Patronized at Rome by Symmachus, the pagan orator, he hoped, by an advantageous marriage (to which he sacrificed his concubine, the mother of a son, Adeodatus—d. *c*.390) to join the 'aristocracy of letters' typical of his age. At 19, however, he had read the *Hortensius* of **Cicero. This early 'conversion to philosophy' was the prototype of successive conversions: to **Manichaeism, a **Gnostic sect promising

Wisdom, and, in 386, to a Christianized *Neoplatonism patronized by Ambrose, bishop of Milan. Catholicism, for Augustine, was the 'Divine Philosophy', a Wisdom guaranteed by authority but explored by reason: 'Seek and ye shall find', the only scriptural citation in his first work, characterizes his life as a thinker.

Though the only Latin philosopher to fail to master Greek, Augustine transformed Latin *Christianity by his Neoplatonism: his last recorded words echo *Plotinus. Stimulated by abrupt changes—he was forcibly ordained priest of Hippo (modern Bone, Algeria) in 391, becoming bishop in 395—and by frequent controversies (see DONATISTS), Augustine developed his ideas with an independence that disquieted even his admirers. He has left his distinctive mark on most aspects of western Christianity.

Augustine's major works are landmarks in the abandonment of Classical ideals. His early optimism was soon overshadowed by a radical doctrine of grace. This change was canonized in an autobiographical masterpiece, the *Confessions* (c.397–400), a vivid if highly selective source for his life to 388 and, equally, a mirror of his changed outlook. *De doctrina Christiana* (begun 396/7) sketched a literary culture subordinated to the Bible. *De Trinitate* (399–419) provided a more radically philosophical statement of the doctrine of the Trinity than any Greek Father. *De civitate Dei* (413 to 426) presented a definitive juxtaposition of Christianity with literary paganism and Neoplatonism, notably with *Porphyry. After 412, he combated in Pelagianism (see PELAGIUS) views which, 'like the philosophers of the pagans', had promised men fulfilment by their unaided efforts. In his *Retractationes* (427) Augustine criticized his superabundant output of 93 works in the light of a Catholic orthodoxy to which he believed he had progressively conformed—less consistently, perhaps, than he realized.

Letters and verbatim sermons richly document Augustine's complex life as a bishop; the centre of a group of sophisticated *ascetics, the 'slave' of a simple congregation, he was, above all, a man dedicated to the authority of the Catholic Church. This authority had enabled his restless intellect to work creatively: he would uphold it, in Africa, by every means, from writing a popular song to elaborating the only explicit justification in the early Church of a policy of religious persecution (see DONATISTS).

Augustus (63 BC–AD 14), the first emperor at Rome, who presided over the inception of much of the institutional and ideological framework of the imperial system of the first three centuries AD.

*Varro had taught the Romans to be at home in their own city, and Augustus was an eager interpreter of the process. The ancient messages of cult and civic ritual offered many opportunities, which he was making use of already in the 30s. After Actium the serious development of the cult of Palatine *Apollo as a parallel for Capitoline *Jupiter, and the restoration of dozens of Rome's ancient sanctuaries; after 12 (when he finally became *Pontifex Maximus on the death of Lepidus) the formation of the House of the Father of his Country, in 2 BC the inauguration of a replacement forum (see FORUM AUGUSTUM), to which many state ceremonies were removed; throughout the creation of a 'suburb more beautiful than the city' on the *Campus Martius, for the amenity of the populace: the reduplication of Rome's glories cleverly allowed him to be a new founder without damaging the old system, and to surpass all past builders and benefactors without the solecism of departing from or belittling their precedent. He thus underlined his relationship with the previous centuries of Roman history in a Roman history that culminated in his ascendancy. *See* ARA PACIS; PALATINE.

Aulis, small Greek city near Tanagra, on a rocky peninsula between two bays. Its most famous monument is the temple of Artemis and its neighbouring buildings. The best harbour in northern Boeotia, Aulis is most famous as the point of assembly for the

Achaean expedition against Troy. Here *Iphigenia was sent to be sacrificed for a safe voyage of the fleet, a theme developed by *Euripides, and echoed by later expeditions. For example, the Spartan king Agesilaus attempted to sacrifice there in 396 BC, before his expedition to Asia, but the Boeotians interrupted the ceremony.

Aurelius Antoninus, Marcus, the emperor (AD 218–22) **Elagabalus** Born probably in 203, he was holding the priesthood, hereditary in his mother's family, of the presiding deity of Emesa in Syria, in 218, when his mother and grandmother Iulia Maesa used him as figurehead of a rebellion against the emperor Macrinus. After the victory, he took the cult of the god by whose name he is known to Rome, which he reached in July 219. In late 220 his intention to make *Elagabalus ('deus Sol invictus') supreme god of the empire aroused open hostility at Rome when he divorced his first wife Julia Paula and married the *Vestal virgin Aquilia Severa, a 'sacred marriage' to match the union of the god with Juno *Caelestis. He was forced to adopt his cousin Alexianus, renamed Alexander (26 June 221), and to divorce Aquilia in favour of a descendant of M. Aurelius, Annia Faustina; but by the end of 221 he took Aquilia back and tried to get rid of Alexander. This provoked renewed outrage, which came to a head with his murder on 11 March 222 and replacement by Alexander. His flouting of conventions in the choice of officials, combined with disgust at the orgiastic ceremonial of the Syrian cult had proved too much for senate, praetorians, and populace alike. *See* SOL; SYRIAN DEITIES.

auspicium, literally 'watching the birds' (*avis, specio*), but the term was applied to various types of *divination. A Roman lexicon records five types of auspical signs: from the sky (*ex caelo*, mostly thunder and lightning), from birds (*ex avibus*; observed were the number, position, flight, cries, and feeding of birds), from sacred chickens, the *pulli* (*ex tripudiis*; they were kept hungry in a cage; if food dropped from their beaks when they were eating, this was an excellent sign, *auspicium sollistimum*), from quadrupeds (*ex quadrupedibus*, e.g. a wolf eating grass), and from unusual, threatening occurrences (*ex diris*). They were either casually met with (*oblativa*) or specially watched for (*impetrativa*). The first two categories could be both oblative and impetrative, the third only impetrative, the fourth and fifth only oblative. Through the auspices the gods did not foretell the future but only expressed their approval or disapproval of an action either contemplated or in progress (the latter only through the *oblativa*). They were valid for one day only, and thus pertained solely to the time of an action, not to its substance. If denied, the approval for the same undertaking could be sought again on the next day. Here resides the technical difference (often disregarded in colloquial speech) between auspices and auguries: the latter were the auspices that pertained not only to timing but also to substance. At inaugurations of priests and temples the deity gave approval not only for the day of the ceremony but also for the person or the place (*locus*) to be inaugurated. The *auguria* had no time limit, and to remove their effects a special ceremony of *exauguratio* was necessary. The auguries could be conducted only by the augurs (*see* AUGURES); any person could use the auspices, hence the division into private and public auspices. The former largely fell into disuse, though remaining in use for weddings; the *auspicia publica* were administered by the magistrates. All public acts were conducted *auspicato*, after a consultation of impetrative auspices, e.g. elections, census, military operations. The auspices of the magistrates were divided into *minora*, 'lesser' (of the lesser magistrates) and *maiora*, 'greater' (of consuls, praetors, and censors).

autochthons, in myth, are figures born literally from the earth, with no human parents. While the idea of 'mother' Earth is influential here, autochthony is not normally presented as the origin of humanity in general (the story of *Deucalion and

Pyrrha comes closest to this) but rather serves to make a statement about a particular group of people. True autochthons (as opposed to the merely earthborn, *gēgeneis*) remain in the land where they were born. Thus the autochthonous ancestor, like the founder-figure, expresses and forms the group's sense of its identity, making an implicit claim to superiority over non-autochthonous groups. The *Spartoi, the autochthonous 'sown men' of Thebes, may at one time have represented a special class in the city, while the autochthon *Erichthonius expressed the claim of all Athenians to be the true original inhabitants of Attica. There were probably very many local claims to autochthonous ancestors across the Greek world. *See also* PROPAGANDA, RELIGIOUS.

Autolycus, in mythology, maternal grandfather of *Odysseus. He 'surpassed all men in thievery and (ambiguous) swearing', by favour of *Hermes (whose son he is in later accounts).
[Homer, *Iliad* 10. 267, *Odyssey* 19. 394 ff.]

Automedon, in mythology, *Achilles' charioteer, son of Diores; hence by metonymy, any charioteer.

Aventine, the southernmost hill of Rome, overlooking the Tiber and separated from the other hills by the Murcia valley, had legendary associations with *Remus. Temples here included those dedicated to *Diana, patroness of a Latin League, and to *Juno Regina following her *evocatio* from Veii (392 BC). Until AD 49 the hill was outside the *pomerium*, which may explain why 'foreign' deities were established here. The temple of *Ceres, Liber (*see* LIBER PATER), and Libera (493 BC) was headquarters of the plebeian aedile magistrates; the hill itself was public land given to the people of Rome for settlement in 456 BC, and it remained a cosmopolitan centre of popular politics under the late republic. Under the empire, however, it became principally a centre of élite housing.

Avernus, a deep volcanic crater, now a lake, near Puteoli. Its appearance inspired the belief that it led to the Underworld. Associated monuments include the so-called Sibylline cave (*see* SIBYL).
[Strabo 5. 244]

Bacchanalia can be used to mean either 'Bacchic festival' or 'Bacchic places of worship', but usually translates the Greek *mysteries (*orgia*), with special reference to the worship suppressed by the Roman authorities in 186 BC. We have an account of the suppression in Livy and an inscribed version of the senatorial decree against the cult, in the form in which it was circulated to the allied states of Italy. These sources can be supplemented by references in Plautus' plays and now by archaeological evidence to show that the Bacchic cult, perhaps of south-Italian Greek origin, was widespread in Italy, central and south, decades before the senate chose to act against it. The form of the Italian cult seems to differ from other Hellenistic examples in admitting men as well as women to the mysteries and in increasing the frequency of meetings. It is unclear how far the cult's followers were forming a movement of protest against the Roman authorities.

The surviving decree concentrates on the structure of Bacchic cells—their oaths of loyalty, their organization and funding, their membership, their property. This suggests that it was the power of cell-leaders over worshippers, cutting across traditional patterns of family and authority, that disturbed the senate, rather than alleged criminal actions or orgiastic rites; but any allegation would have helped in the discrediting of a powerful and well-embedded cult; Livy's vivid account has valuable elements, and in substance shows knowledge of the decree itself; but its highly literary elaboration shows the influence of the senate's propaganda against the cult.

The senate's persecution succeeded at least in removing the cult from prominence, though artistic evidence shows its long-sustained influence. Later Italian evidence, especially the great Bacchic inscription of Agrippinilla, show a domesticated, family version of the cult, well subordinated to élite authority.

See DIONYSUS; MAENADS.

Bacchus *See* DIONYSUS.

Bacchylides (*c.*520–450 BC), one of the canonical nine lyric poets, of Iulis in Ceos. There survive victory odes and *dithyrambs. His patrons, apart from Hieron of Syracuse, included athletes from Ceos, Aegina, Phlius, Metapontum, and Thessaly. Several of his dithyrambs were composed for competitions at Athens, one for Sparta. The poems exploit the pathetic potential of the myths, as do those victory odes which contain a mythical narrative as their centre-piece. *Dithyramb* 2 appears to assume familiarity with *Sophocles' *Trachiniai*; *Dithyramb* 4 is unique in being a dialogue between the chorus as people of Athens and the chorus leader, their king, *Aegeus, perhaps influenced by Attic drama. Bacchylides also wrote *hymns, *paeans, processional songs (*see* PROCESSIONS), maiden-songs, dancing-songs, songs about love, and songs of praise.

Bacis, a Boeotian oracle-collector 'maddened by the *Nymphs' whose *oracles were known from the 5th cent. BC onwards (e.g. referring to the invasion of Xerxes, and to the rebuilding of Messene); collections are still known in the 2nd cent. AD. To cope with the mass of oracles from manifestly different dates, later authors assumed several Bacides. Bacis shares both possession by the Nymphs and wavering between singular and plural with the *Sibyl, with whom he is sometimes combined; both belong to the world of rather shadowy, non-official ecstatic prophecy known since the late Archaic age. *See* PROPHECIES.

Bar Kokhba, 'son of a star', is the name commonly used to denote the leader of the second Jewish revolt in Palestine (AD 132–5), to whom was applied, allegedly by Rabbi Akiba, the Messianic prophecy in the Book of Numbers (24: 17). The precise form of his real name, Shim'on (Simon) ben or (in Aramaic) bar Cosiba, which often appears in distorted form in rabbinic literature, has been given by the discovery of his letters and other documents from his camp, which designate him 'Nasi (prince) of Israel' and are dated by the era of his 'liberation of Israel'. This era, apparently dated from 1 Tishri (October) 131, is used also on the coins struck by the rebels. Little is known of the course of the revolt, but there is epigraphic evidence that a very large legionary force was needed to suppress it. The rebels relied mainly on guerilla tactics, with their focus in *Judaea. While the letters show that En Gedi was an important base, and archaeology suggests that the caves of the region were put to military use, whether the rebels ever held Jerusalem is unclear. The last stand was made at Bethar, in the sack of which Bar Kokhba was killed.

Basil of Caesarea in Cappadocia, *c*.AD 330–79 (the dates are debated). He is honoured as the chief architect of monastic life in the Greek Church. His early education was completed at Athens, where he came under the influence of Himerius and Prohaeresius. He was also instructed briefly by Libanius. Those experiences marked him out for a teaching career, upon which he may have embarked. However, the influence of Eustathius of Sebaste and of travel in the *eastern provinces inclined him to the practice of *asceticism, which he undertook in the company of his friend *Gregory of Nazianzus. His education bore fruit, nevertheless, in his *Address to Young Men*, which discussed the adaptation of the classical curriculum to Christian use and enjoyed lasting influence. His ascetic experience was distilled chiefly in his *Long Rules* and *Short Rules*.

A growing interest in Church affairs drew him into the moderate party of Basil of Ancyra and encouraged him in lifelong loyalty to Meletius of Antioch. Within the general context of the Arian controversy, those associations made him less acceptable to both Alexandria and Rome. Nevertheless, he was remembered for his courageous resistance to the Arian emperor Valens and he did much to damage the reputation of the Arian theologian Eunomius. *See* ARIANISM.

He spent the whole of his priestly and episcopal career in Caesarea. In spite of his orthodoxy, he attracted the favour of Valens, who supported financially his extensive works of charity and sent him on an important mission to Armenia in 373. As a churchman, he strongly advocated and worked for unity but in conservative terms that were less convincing to ambitious peers.

His numerous letters are an important source for eastern provincial life at the time and reveal a man of delicacy, insight, and power. His homilies are much neglected and show a skilful combination of learning, style, and clarity. His crowning achievement was his *Hexaemeron*, which *Ambrose paraphrased.

Basile, a cult figure worshipped in Athens and elsewhere in Attica. Her city shrine was held in common with *Neleus and (probably later) *Codrus, and as her name suggests one of her 'meanings' may have been that of sovereignty, especially perhaps in connection with the claim of Athens to Ionian primacy. Nothing is known of her mythology.

basileus For the *basileus* (an official) at Athens *see* ARCHONTES.

basilica, the name applied to a wide range of Roman building forms, most commonly and characteristically to the large, multi-purpose public halls which regularly accompanied the *forum in the western half of the Roman world, and corresponded roughly in function to the Greek and Hellenistic stoa. The earliest known was built in Rome by Marcus Porcius Cato in 184 BC. The name came, by extension, to be used for any large covered hall in domestic, commercial, military, or religious (e.g. Basilica Hilariana) use.

A typical basilica is a rectangular building, open either along one side or at one end, with the roof in two sections, the central part being raised over a clerestory supported on an internal colonnade. A platform, often in an apsidal niche at one end, or, less frequently, the middle of one side, contained the platform or tribunal for magistrates. This plan can be elaborated by doubling the internal colonnade, adding a gallery (Basilica Ulpia in the forum of Trajan at Rome which also has a projecting apse at both ends). Basilicas can be free-standing buildings (early examples in the Roman colony at Corinth), or placed along one side of the enclosed fora. The roofs of basilicas are supported by timber beam construction. This, and the large number of columns required to support them, are a required feature of basilical architecture. The great basilica added to the forum Romanum by the emperor Maxentius (and completed by Constantine I) of brick-faced concrete, with concrete-vaulted roofs is exceptional, and derives its form from the great central hall of the Roman imperial baths.

Basilicas of traditional type continued to be built in the 3rd cent. AD (the Severan basilica at Lepcis Magna). Since they were designed to hold large numbers of people they responded to the needs of Christian worship following the official recognition of *Christianity, and the early *churches at Rome and elsewhere are essentially basilicas with an apsidal tribunal, using the prestigious columns and timber form of construction.

Bassae, in south-west Arcadia, near Phigaleia, the site of one of the best-preserved Greek temples. This was dedicated to *Apollo the Helper (*Epikourios*). *Pausanias says it was the work of the Athenian architect Ictinus, but this attribution is now doubted. It dates to the latter part of the 5th cent. BC with an interruption due to Spartan occupation of the area during the Peloponnesian War (431–404 BC). The greater part of the temple is in the local limestone, with carved decoration applied in marble. The *orientation, followed also by its predecessor, was towards the north instead of the east, and the early sunlight, instead of entering through the main doorway, was admitted to the innermost room through an opening in the eastern side-wall. Ten engaged Ionic columns decorated the side walls of the cella internally, with a single central Corinthian column—one of the earliest of its kind, and one of the most beautiful—between the cella and the innermost room. The sculptured frieze is now in the British Museum.

Apollo with the epithet *Epikourios* may be regarded as the protector of Arcadians serving as mercenaries. The alternative explanation, that he was a helper against disease, and specifically the Athenian plague at the beginning of the Peloponnesian War, is unlikely (the plague would not have affected Bassae), though this idea has led to an excessively early date for the temple.

Baubo belongs to the main Orphic version of the Rape of *Persephone (*see* ORPHISM). She resembles *Iambe in the *Homeric Hymn to Demeter*. She and her husband Dysaules receive *Demeter at Eleusis during her search for Persephone, and their children *Eubouleus and *Triptolemus give her information about the rape. Like Iambe Baubo gives Demeter a refreshing drink (the *kykeōn*), and when she refuses it Baubo by an indecent exposure makes her laugh and accept it. (Her name can be used of the female sexual organs.) The story may be an 'explanation' of a ritual at the *Thesmophoria. Her cult is found on Naxos in the 4th cent. BC and Paros in the 1st cent. BC.

Baucis and her husband Philemon were a pair of elderly peasants who entertained *Zeus and *Hermes with the resources of their meagre larder when the gods paid an incognito visit to Phrygia (compare the story of *Orion's birth); for their piety they were spared from the flood which drowned their less hospitable neighbours. (Compare Lot and his wife in the Book of Genesis (19: 1–29).) They lived out the rest of their lives as priests of the temple into which their humble shack was transformed, and were themselves finally transfigured into an oak and a linden-tree springing from the same trunk. The tale, which has genuine roots in ancient Anatolian tree-cult (see TREES, SACRED), has its first and canonical telling in *Ovid, though a Hellenistic Greek treatment along the lines of *Theseus' stay in the hut of *Hecale or the entertainment of *Heracles by Molorcus (both recounted by *Callimachus) probably lies behind it.

[Ovid, *Metamorphoses* 8. 618–724]

Bellerophon In *Homer's account, he is son of *Glaucus (2) (or, according to *Hesiod, *Poseidon) and grandson of *Sisyphus, and a native of Ephyre (generally identified with Corinth). *Proetus, king of Tiryns, had a wife Anteia (Stheneboea in later versions) who fell in love with Bellerophon and tried to seduce him. When he rejected her advances, she falsely accused him of trying to rape her. So Proetus sent him to Iobates, king of Lycia and Anteia's father, with a sealed letter containing instructions to kill the bearer. Iobates set Bellerophon tasks likely to bring about his death, sending him to kill the *Chimaera, and to fight the Solymi and the *Amazons. When Bellerophon returned triumphant from all these tasks, and survived an ambush laid for him by Iobates, the king married him to his daughter

and gave him half his kingdom. In versions after Homer, Bellerophon accomplished his tasks with the help of the winged horse *Pegasus, which *Athena helped him to catch. According to now lost plays by *Euripides, he also used Pegasus to take vengeance on Stheneboea, and offended the gods by trying to fly on him to Olympus. In Homer, although there is no direct mention of Pegasus, Bellerophon became 'hated by all the gods', which presumably was caused by the attempt to reach Olympus. Bellerophon on Pegasus attacking the Chimaera is found in art from before the mid-7th cent. BC, where it appears first in Corinthian vase-painting.

[Homer, *Iliad* 6. 152–202; Pindar, *Olympian* 13. 63–93; Apollodorus 2. 3. 1–2]

Bellona (older form Duellona), Roman goddess of war. She had no *flamen* (see FLAMINES) and no festival in the calendar, unlike the major ancient deities; she acquired her temple as late as the 290s BC; but the presence of her name in the ancient formula of *devotio* suggests that she was nevertheless an archaic Roman goddess, whether or not belonging to the circle of Mars. Her temple was built in the *Campus Martius, outside the *pomerium*, and was a frequent meeting-place of the senate when dealing with generals returning from war. In front of it was the area used by the *fetiales* in declarations of war. Bellona was successively identified with Nerio, the cult-partner of *Mars; with Enyo, the Greek war-goddess; and with Mā, the Mother Goddess of Cappadocia.

Belus, Hellenized form of the Levantine god Ba'al and Babylonian Bel (both meaning 'lord'). Ba'al is attested from the third millennium BC on at Ebla and Ugarit. In Babylonia, Bel describes Marduk (earlier Enlil), god of Babylon and head of the pantheon certainly by the 12th cent. BC. Bol of Palmyra also came to be called Bel. For classical writers, Belus is often a way of describing an eastern supreme deity or legendary figure, sometimes seen as the founder of dynasties.

Bendis, a Thracian goddess. Little is known of the character of her cult; the geographer Strabo says—but does he know?—that it was orgiastic. Greek artists represented her as a booted huntress, rather like Artemis; she is sometimes described as 'twin-speared'. Her cult was introduced to Athens in two stages: by 430/29 BC she shared with the Phrygian Adrasteia a small treasury under the control of the Treasurers of the Other Gods; and a decree of (probably) 413/12 assigned her a priestess and founded the great festival in the Piraeus known from the opening of *Plato's Republic*, at which twin processions, of native Thracians and of Athenians, were followed by a torch-race on horseback and an 'all-night celebration'. The role played by Thracians in the Athenian public cult is confirmed by decrees issued by a body of Thracian '*orgeōnes of Bendis' in the 3rd cent. BC; in one, the origin of this unique honour is traced back to an oracle of *Dodona. The immediate motivation for the introduction of the goddess's cult is unknown; at bottom, the Athenians' interest in Bendis must be a product of their preoccupation with Thrace, which goes back to the 6th cent. See THRACIAN RELIGION.

Berenice II, daughter of Magas of Cyrene and Apama II, was born *c*.273 BC. Following the murder that she initiated of her mother's candidate Demetrius, her marriage in 246 to Ptolemy III Euergetes returned Cyrene to Ptolemaic control. She survived into the reign of her son Ptolemy IV, falling a victim to palace intrigues in 221. In the dynastic cult she and Euergetes were the Benefactor Gods; the Egyptian-style deification of their daughter Berenice is recorded in the Canopus decree of 238 BC. She is perhaps best known for 'The Lock of Berenice' commemorated by *Callimachus and Catullus. Coloured faience 'queen-vases' bearing her depiction were probably used in cult.

[Catullus 66]

betrothal

Greek enguē, was a contract between two men, the groom and the bride's father (or other male representative at law) which established that a union was a fully valid marriage. In Classical Athens, this contract was oral, more or less formulaic, aimed at assuring the legitimacy of children, and accompanied by an agreement concerning dowry; the bride herself need not be present, or even of an age to understand the proceedings, and the celebration of the marriage might be long delayed or in the end not take place. Marriages at Sparta too might involve betrothal; sources speak as well of abduction marriage (conceivably with the complicity of the bride and her family). Scattered references to betrothal in Hellenistic documents from a number of cities go some way towards confirming the suggestion that most Greeks practised *enguē*.

Roman Sponsalia in the republic consisted of reciprocal *sponsiones*, and breach-of-promise actions (in the form of actions for damages) existed. The movement of classical Roman law was in the direction of removing constraint, and the term *sponsalia* came near to an informal agreement to marry, voidable at will (except that the intending husband was required to return such dowry as had been given to him and the intending bride was expected to return the much more usual gift from her intending husband, the *donatio ante nuptias*, for gifts after marriage were excluded). The betrothal was solemnized with a kiss and the intending husband put an iron ring (*anulus pronubus*) on the third finger of his partner's left hand; it was the occasion for a party (also called *sponsalia*). See *also* MARRIAGE CEREMONIES.

bidental When lightning struck, the Etruscan and Roman ritual prescribed that the bolt be buried (often inscribed *fulgur conditum*), and the place enclosed. The ancients derived the name from the sacrificial victim (*bidens*, 'having two teeth'), but it may be a rendering of the Etruscan word for the bolt.

birds, sacred Though the Greeks and Romans did not consider any bird actually divine, many birds, like other animals, were closely associated with the gods, and all birds could bring messages from the gods by omens (see PORTENTS). *Divination from the activities of birds (often eagles or other birds of prey) is well attested in *Homer and in tragedy, where it can appear as a well-developed science. In Rome, observation of birds was one of the chief forms of divination (see AUGURES). Not only was the behaviour of wild birds watched for signs, but on military expeditions chickens were kept for the purpose.

Numerous special divine associations developed in Greece. The eagle as the bird of *Zeus was almost universal. *Athena takes the form of several different birds in Homer and local myth; her connection with owls seems to be post-Homeric and is particularly linked with Athens. *Apollo was associated with the falcon and the swan, *Hera with the peacock; this last pairing must be of relatively recent date, since the peacock was still a novelty to Greeks in the 5th cent. BC. None of these birds was considered inviolate by virtue of association with a god. In fact, the association was occasionally sacrificial: doves, which along with sparrows were *Aphrodite's sacred bird, were frequently sacrificed to her. Most of these traditions were taken over when the Roman gods were identified with Greek counterparts; there were also some native Italian associations of birds with gods, such as that of the woodpecker with *Mars (see PICUS).

birthday (Gk. *genethlios hēmera*; Lat. *natalis dies*). Among the Greeks the birthdays of several major Olympian deities (e.g. of *Artemis on the sixth, *Apollo on the seventh, and *Poseidon on the eighth) were in early times assigned to days of the month, and were treated as sacred. Throughout Greek history these 'monthly' birthdays continued to be recognized and were often the focal points of the deities' annual festivals. For humans the day of birth itself was marked by congratulatory visits and presents from relatives and friends, but in the Archaic and Classical periods there seems to have been no recurring monthly or annual celebrations of the day. Birthdays of humans first attained significance for the Greeks when they began to assimilate rulers and outstanding individuals to gods (see RULER-CULT). The philosopher *Plato, for example, shared Apollo's birthday (7 Thargelion), and after his death his followers gave him special veneration each year, probably on his birthday. In his will the philosopher *Epicurus endowed an annual banquet for his followers on his birthday (10 Gamelion). So too after his death the birthday of the Hellenistic statesman Aratus of Sicyon was celebrated annually. Under the influence of Egyptian and Asian customs, the birthdays and accession days of the Ptolemies, Seleucids, and Attalids were publicly fêted during their lifetimes throughout their kingdoms, both monthly and annually, often with offerings and games (e.g. that of Ptolemy V by the Egyptians).

The Romans, unlike the Greeks, marked only anniversaries and from earliest times annually celebrated their own birthdays and those of family members, friends, and patrons with gifts, offerings, prayers, vows, and banquets. Roman poets developed a specific type of poem for the occasion, and may have inspired a similar type of Greek poetry in the Roman period. The rituals of the Roman birthday formed part of the cult of the *genius* of a man or the *iuno* of a woman (see GENIUS). Under the empire the people celebrated annually, as an important part of imperial cult, the birthdays of past and present emperors and members of the imperial family. The Romans also marked with rituals and festivals the annual *natales dies*, or foundation days, of cults, temples, and cities.

body The history of the body questions the extent to which the body is 'natural', and asks whether all societies have experienced the body in the same way. The combined classical and Christian heritage of western civilization has assigned the body a subordinate place in its value systems, but dichotomies such as mind/body and *soul/ body are by no means universal.

One distinction between our own society and the ancient world concerns nakedness. Clothing was one of the features believed to set humanity apart from the animals. In Homer, nakedness is associated with vulnerability and shame; Odysseus covers himself before Nausicaa. For the Greeks of the Classical period, however, nudity becomes the costume of the citizen; because male nudity is seen as normal, only barbarians are represented as feeling shame when a man is seen naked. Female nudity, meanwhile, continues to be associated with vulnerability and shame; the girls of Miletus were allegedly persuaded to end a mass suicide epidemic by the threat of exposure after death. Nudity is also associated with *initiation (e.g. *Brauron) and fertility. In Athenian vase-paintings, men are represented naked in outdoor scenes, never in private domestic space. Women are generally shown naked only in private scenes when nudity is to be expected—for example, when washing—or when they are about to be killed or raped. In Etruscan art, in contrast, men wear shorts or loincloths in situations when Greek men would be shown naked—for instance when exercising. In Roman art, nudity continues to be the costume of the male hero.

From childhood, the body needed to be controlled. Roman child-nurses were advised on how to mould the shape of the body, by swaddling and massage. For men, correct control of the body was a further part of the costume of a good citizen The orator, in particular, was advised on every aspect of presentation of self. The state too had a role in controlling the body, by instilling obedience through education and, above all, through military training. From *Pandora's adornment by the gods onwards, women were represented as deceptive and frivolous, their elaborate clothing, wigs, and make-up concealing the vices underneath. Both Greek and Roman sources praise the unadorned woman, while Roman sumptuary legislation tried to set limits on the expense of women's clothing.

*Augustine draws a parallel between the ordered arrangement of the parts of the body and the ordered arrangement of the appetites of the soul. Peace and health consist of both. Within the order of nature, the soul must control the body and reason the appetites, just as master controls slave and man controls woman. Some Christians positively valued neglect of the body—seen in abstinence from food and sex (*see* CHASTITY), or lack of interest in one's appearance—as evidence of a proper rejection of this world, whereas Graeco-Roman philosophy urged the care of the body as evidence of the virtue of *enkrateia* or self-control.

Boedromia, literally 'festival of running to help in response to a cry for aid' (or of the god associated therewith), a minor Attic festival of *Apollo. Both the associated month-name Boedromion and Apollo's title Boedromios are widely attested, the festival only at Athens, and only faintly even there: in the only allusion to it in a surviving Classical text seems to imply that in the 4th cent. BC it was an optional element in the festival programme. It was probably military in flavour, being linked aetiologically with aid brought in battle. The only rites mentioned are *sacrifice and a *procession.

Boeotia, cults The Linear B archive at Thebes refers to a number of deities, four of whom were worshipped in the Graeco-Roman period: Potnia (later Demeter of Potniae, southern suburb of Thebes, of which *Demeter Thesmophoros was principal deity), *Hera, *Hermes (the chief deities of the Hellenic towns of Plataea and Tanagra respectively), and the goddess of a place near Thebes called Hapha/e (therefore [H]aphaea, possible precursor of Leucothea; *see* INO-LEUCOTHEA). *Homer knows of *Poseidon at Onchestus, *Athena of Alalcomenae, the Thebans *Dionysus, *Heracles, and *Ino-Leucothea (all, save the last, in the *Iliad*). It is possible that the Poseidon Heliconius of the Ionians was derived from the god who controlled the pass at Onchestus, at the north-east foot of the Helicon massif: his cult in Boeotia may therefore go back to the bronze age. Like the god at Calauria (where Minyan Orchomenus was a member of the *amphictiony) Poseidon at Onchestus was served by a priestess.

Athena Alalcomeneïs gave her name to the boundary sanctuary at the eastern end of the territory of Coronea; at her sanctuary just outside the town of Coronea she bore the epithet Itonia, revealing the Thessalian origins of her worshippers. From the middle of the 6th cent. BC, Itonia shared her sanctuary with a male god, first depicted as a snake, identified later as *Zeus Caraeus/Ceraeus/Acraeus ('of the mountain-tops'), Laphystius ('devourer', describing his character), and Basileus ('king', referring to the range of his powers). He was the ethnic god of the Minyans of Orchomenus and eastern Thessaly (Acraeus and Laphystius east and west of Iolcus respectively). The date at which worshippers of this Zeus and Athena moved into Boeotia is uncertain (there is reason to prefer a bronze age over a 'dark age' date: for example, the place-name Thebes, found in both Boeotia and Achaea-Phthiotis, occurs in Linear B at Thebes). However, the two may have been combined—possibly for political reasons—in the middle of the 6th cent. Later, particularly under the Hellenistic Boeotian Confederacy, Athena Itonia and Zeus Caraeus were the official gods of the confederacy: the Boeotian year began and ended (at the winter solstice) with months sacred to Zeus (Boukatios) and Athena (Alalkomenios).

Cults of *Apollo can also be traced back to the early Archaic period. He took over, directly or indirectly, a set of *oracles of the same type around the Copais (*Ptoion, Tegyra, Thurium, Tilphossa, Lebadea; see TROPHONIUS). One of these, the oracle of Trophonius at Lebadea, like that of *Amphiaraus near Oropus, belonged to an underground oracular god who was approached directly by the consultant.

Another pan-Boeotian deity whose worship covered all of Boeotia and extended across the strait to Euboea was the bi-form *Demeter, of whom traces are found as Achaea, (Demeter and Kore) Thesmophoros, Eleusinia, Megalartos/Megalomazos. She too must have belonged to a very early stratum, as did several groups of cults, known under different names in different places: female trinities, female and male pairs, warrior groups, boys who drowned.

The worship of *Artemis must also be extended back to a very early period: her function in time of war is reflected in the epithet Euclea, which apparently she bore in every Boeotian *agora.

Several Boeotian sanctuaries were regularly frequented by non-Boeotians: Amphiaraus at Oropus, *Trophonius and Zeus at Lebadea, Apollo at the Ptoion, the *Muses at the foot of Helicon. Others—*Hera called Cithaeronia (worshipped as such on Mt. Helicon as well), Demeter Achaea, Athena Itonia, Zeus Caraeus—were more important within Boeotia itself, while here and there were cults on whom the local population lavished worship and expense, but whose popularity was strictly local: *Eros at Thespiae, the hero Ptoios at Acraephnium, the *Cabiri west of Thebes (the last no doubt brought to Boeotia from Asia Minor, possibly in the 8th cent.).

[Pausanias 9]

Boethius Anicius Manlius Severinus Boethius, (*c*.AD 480–*c*.524). The Ostrogothic king Theoderic appointed this leading nobleman consul (510), and *magister officiorum* ('Chief Executive', ?522). He resisted official oppression, was implicated in a senatorial conspiracy, imprisoned, and executed. His *Consolation of Philosophy* is a prison dialogue with Philosophy, a mixture of prose and verse, owing much to Martianus Capella and *Augustine. It justifies providence on a Stoic and Neoplatonic basis (*see* STOICISM; NEOPLATONISM), without overt *Christianity; its reconciliation of free will and divine prescience is philosophically notable; it shows high literary genius, and an astounding memory for classical texts under trying conditions. Boethius' Greek scholarship was rare in Italy; he planned introductions and translations for the mathematical and logical disciplines, and complete translations of *Plato and *Aristotle. The project was never completed, and much is lost or fragmentary. Surviving works: *De arithmetica* and *Institutio musica* ; a commentary on *Cicero's *Topics*, translations and commentaries for *Porphyry's *Isagoge*, and Aristotle's *Prior Analytics*, *Categories*, and *Perihermeneias*; translations of Aristotle's *Topics* and *Sophistici elenchi*. Five treatises give Boethius' own introduction to Peripatetic logic. Literal translation and repetitive explanation made the philosophic corpus inelegant but serviceable; excepting *De syllogismis hypotheticis*, it is generally unoriginal. Boethius owed much to Alexandrian and Athenian Neoplatonists (especially *Ammonius Saccas), but personal contact is unprovable. Involved in Christological controversies which had divided Rome and Constantinople, he wrote five theological *Tractates*; the fifth, the most original, favours a formula, aimed at reconciling Monophysite heretics. Undervalued in his own day, Boethius wielded vast influence from Carolingian times onward, especially on Abelard; *De consolatione* was translated by King Alfred, Chaucer, and Elizabeth I.

Boio, short form of a woman's name (based on 'Boiotian'?). Legendary Delphian (*see* DELPHI) author of a *hymn mentioning *Hyperboreans and the prophet *Olen. Often conflated with either Boio (fem.) or Boios (masc.), author of the Hellenistic *Ornithogonia* ('Origins of Birds', cf. 'Theogony') used by *Ovid in his *Metamorphoses*.

Bona Dea (the Good Goddess—this is her title, not name, which is uncertain), an Italian goddess, worshipped especially in Rome and Latium. In Rome, she had an annual nocturnal ceremony held at the house of a chief magistrate, from which men were rigorously excluded (except in the scandal involving Publius Clodius Pulcher in 62 BC); it was led by the women of the magistrate's family with the help of the *Vestal virgins. It was a state ritual, performed in secret, 'for the welfare of the Roman people' (*pro salute populi Romani*). Some detail is recorded: the room was decorated with vine-branches and other plants; wine was brought in contained in a covered jar, but it was called milk and the jar a honey-pot. The epigraphic record presents a picture quite distinct from this secret aristocratic rite: there is no sign of secrecy; the worshippers are often slaves or freed persons; men are not infrequent dedicants. The inscriptions are quite widespread within Italy, but rare outside. The Romans evidently had their own version of the cult; it is not clear whether theirs was the original one.

Bonus Eventus, personified god of the good outcome of agricultural labour, and, by extension, other human activity. A *postiro* near the baths of Agrippa at Rome dedicated to him was probably associated with a temple; inscriptions suggest that the cult was popular.

books, Greek and Roman, sacred Books existed in Egypt long before they came into use in Greece. Systems of writing had been invented and developed for administrative purposes in both Egypt and Mesopotamia by *c*.3000 BC. Religious books were kept in temples; although temple 'libraries', i.e. chambers designated for the storage of books, have survived only in Ptolemaic temples (Edfu, Philae, ed-Tod), literary references to books and libraries suggest their existence in the Middle Kingdom (thirteenth dynasty, *c*.1700 BC), and there was a library in the Ramesseum at Thebes in Hellenistic Egypt.

In the production of books parchment played only a minor role compared with papyrus, which remained the dominant writing material throughout Greek and Roman antiquity. The carbonized papyrus roll found at Derveni, near Thessalonica, a commentary on an Orphic cosmogony, is written in small letters (*c*.2 mm. high) in a careful, skilled hand which makes the columns look almost like *stoichedon* inscriptions (i.e. exactly aligned vertically) (*see* ORPHISM). The Derveni papyrus has a strong claim to being a typical representative of a 4th-cent. book.

The most important innovation in the shape of the book was Roman in origin. The codex was created when the wooden panels of writing-tablets fastened together with thongs were replaced by parchment. At first used as notebooks, parchment codices had come into use for classical literature by the 1st cent. AD, while the normal form of the book was, in the Latin west as in the Greek east, the papyrus roll. What eventually established the codex was its adoption by the Christians; the vast majority of biblical and NT texts from the early 2nd cent. onwards are in codex form. Pagan classical authors appear in parchment and papyrus codices from the 2nd cent. AD and more frequently in the 3rd; by the 4th cent., three out of four literary texts were in codex form. Small formats (even miniature codices like the Cologne parchment codex of the life of Mani with pages of 38 × 45 mm. (1½ × ¾ in.) are also found in this period (*see* MANICHAEISM).

Boreas, the North Wind, which brings to the Greeks an icy blast from Thrace (see the fine description of *Hesiod), 'King of the Winds' for *Pindar, and the most strongly personified of the *wind-gods. This vivid characterization is owed to the story of his forcible seizing of the Athenian princess Oreithyia, daughter of *Erechtheus, from the banks of the Ilissus; from the marriage he fathered the flying heroes *Calais and Zetes. The legend probably dates to the early 5th cent. BC, when a crop of vase-paintings showing the god as a rough and hirsute winged figure (sometimes with spiky, Jack Frost hair) attest the sudden popularity of the kidnap story. Herodotus provides a possible explanation: the northerly gale which wrecked the Persian fleet before Artemisium is supposed to have been summoned

up by Athenians praying to 'their son-in-law' for aid, and they are said to have founded a cult by the Ilissus in gratitude. One might also link the tale to the marriage of the Athenian magnate Miltiades to Hegesipyle, daughter of the Thracian king Olorus, as a kind of justificatory reverse explanatory story.

[Hesiod, *Works and Days* 506 ff.; Plato, *Phaedrus* 229cd; Herodotus 7. 189]

Borsippa (mod. Birs Nimrud), *c*.20 km. (*c*. 12½ mi.) south-west of Babylon, cult-centre of Nabu, god of wisdom. The 47 m. (154 ft.) high ruins of its temple-tower (ziggurat) have attracted archaeologists: the main temple complex (Ezida) was explored by archaeologists in 1879–80 and 1902, the ziggurat in the 1980s. Borsippa flourished from *c*.2000 BC to the early Islamic period.

Bouphonia The annual 'ox-slaying' at the Athenian festival of the Dipolieia. During this rite an ox was killed, the sacrificer fled, and the sacrificial knife was cast into the sea after being tried for murder. The slain ox was stuffed and yoked to a plough.

Boutes, name of several mythological figures, the principal being (1) the family hero of the Attic lineage Eteoboutadai and first priest of *Poseidon Erechtheus; he was worshipped alongside Poseidon in the *Erechtheum. He and his brother *Erechtheus divided their father *Pandion's power so that Boutes became priest and Erechtheus king. (2) Son of Teleon, an *Argonaut, who, charmed by the *Sirens' song, plunged into the sea, but was rescued and taken to Lilybaeum by Aphrodite, by whom he became the father of Eryx.

Bouzyges, or 'Ox-yoker', in Athenian myth was the first to use oxen for ploughing, and his name was connected with one of the sacred ploughings performed in Attica. The name was also the title of the priest of *Zeus Teleios, who ceremonially pronounced (proverbial) curses against the perpetrators of certain acts. It is likely that the mythical figure was the prototype of the priest.

Brauron, site of a sanctuary of *Artemis on the east coast of Attica at the mouth of the river Eridanos. It is included in one ancient list of twelve townships united by *Theseus. Archaeological evidence indicates human presence in the area of the sanctuary and the acropolis above it from neolithic times onwards, and there is an important late Helladic cemetery nearby. In the sanctuary itself there is a continuous tradition from protogeometric on, with a temple built in the 6th cent., and an architecturally innovative *pi*-shaped *stoa with dining-rooms built in the later part of the 5th cent. Flooding in the early 3rd cent. bc led to the abandonment of the site. Some traditions associate the Pisistratids with Brauron, or with the local residential centre called Philaidai which lay a short distance inland from the sanctuary.

Cult activity at Brauron was particularly associated with the *arkteia*, a ritual, known also at the sanctuary of Artemis Munichia in the Piraeus, in which young girls between the ages of 5 and 10 'became' bears (*arktoi*). The aetiological myth for the *arkteia* related that this service was required of all Athenian girls before marriage because of an incident in which a bear belonging to the sanctuary had been killed after becoming savage with a young girl. Modern scholars suggest that the ritual was a *rite of passage which marked the physical maturation of pubescent girls and prepared them for taming by marriage by stressing their wildness. Some pottery vessels of a shape particularly used for dedications to Artemis (*krateriskoi*) excavated at Brauron show naked girls running and part of a bear, and scholars have suggested that these illustrate the ritual. The sanctuary included a cave sacred to *Iphigenia, and dedications were also made in celebration of successful *childbirth. The Brauronia was a quadrennial festival organized by officials appointed by the city by lot, and involved a procession from Athens out to Brauron. We also hear of a sacred hunt.

breast-feeding was a proof of maternal devotion and, according to some philosophers, a good woman's duty. It was acknowledged to be tiring, but it increased the mother's affection for the child, and the baby was thought to be morally, as well as physically, influenced by the milk it drank and the milk's provider. Several Greek deities have a title *Kourotrophos, meaning 'concerned with child-rearing', but no Greek or Roman goddess is specifically concerned with lactation and there are few examples in art of the 'nursing goddess'; *Isis is exceptional.

Brimo, name or title of a goddess, often identified with *Persephone, *Hecate, or *Demeter. In the Eleusinian *mysteries (*see* ELEUSIS) the *hierophantēs* proclaimed that she (viz. Demeter) had borne 'a holy child Brimos', evidently *Plutus, but this does not imply a birth in the rite.

Briseis, in mythology, daughter of Briseus of Lyrnessus and widow of Mynes; *Achilles' slave-concubine, taken from him by *Agamemnon and afterwards restored.

Britain, Roman, cults Culture in Britain developed as a hybrid of Celtic and classical features. The religions of the Mediterranean spread to Britain with the army and administrators, but the Celtic gods were worshipped across most of the province (*see* CELTIC RELIGION). However, they took on new forms, with the increased use of Romano-Celtic styles of temple architecture (first found at the end of the iron age) and the adoption of Latin epigraphy on altars and dedications. Particular gods are associated with certain regions and communities (*see* AQUAE SULIS). Many soldiers also adopted Celtic gods whom they identified with gods of the Roman pantheon (*see* SYNCRETISM). Christianity is found throughout the province in the 4th cent., although the extent of its acceptance is disputed.

Britomartis, Cretan goddess of nature whose name means 'Sweet Virgin'. She had cults mainly in north-east Crete, a festival at Olous, and cult image by *Daedalus. In myth she was pursued by *Minos and jumped into the sea to escape him, was rescued by fishermen in their nets and afterwards called Diktynna (from *diktyon* 'net'). The explanatory story confused Britomartis with another goddess called Diktynna who received worship on the Rodhopou peninsula. Both Britomartis and Diktynna were related figures and, like *Aphaea ('Unseen') on Aegina, disappeared in the cult of *Artemis as minor satellites or epithets. *See* CRETAN CULTS AND MYTHS.

Brizo, a goddess worshipped by women at *Delos, especially as protectress of sailing. Her name derives from *brizein*, 'to sleep', and she was credited with sending prophetic *dreams. Bowls of all sorts of food, except fish, were offered to her in sacrifice.

Bubastis, the local cat-goddess of Bubastis (mod. Tell Basta), also worshipped elsewhere in Egypt. Analysis of Ptolemaic cat-mummies has shown that cats bred for dedication were slaughtered at regular intervals. Egyptian animal-worship was puzzling to outsiders; one story recounts firsthand the near-disastrous fate of a visiting Roman who unwittingly killed a cat in Alexandria. *See* EGYPTIAN DEITIES.

Busiris, a legendary Egyptian king, who gave his name to Busiris in the Delta, and who, according to Ionian tradition, habitually slaughtered foreigners entering Egypt at the altar of *Zeus. He was finally slaughtered by *Heracles. The tale was popular among classical artists and authors.

Cabiri, divinities at certain mystery sanctuaries (*see* MYSTERIES), notably Thebes, Lemnos, and perhaps *Samothrace. The name is of Semitic origin from *kabir*, 'lord'. At the sanctuaries where there is adequate evidence, namely Thebes and Samothrace, it is clear that the role they play is subsidiary to that of the central deities. The latter were either a goddess and her consort, or a triad of goddess, consort, and child.

Cabiri are found throughout the northern Aegean, and on adjacent Asiatic and Thracian mainlands, and in two places in mainland Greece, Thebes and Anthedon, both in Boeotia (*see* BOEOTIAN CULTS). Their number and precise function varied with local customs and preoccupations. Thus, while numbers range from two to seven, at Thebes there were two, father and son (Cabirus and *pais* (son/child) in inscriptions, *Prometheus and Aetnaeus in *Pausanias, *Hermes and *Pan in art), a reflection of a common Boeotian dioscoric type (*see* DIOSCURI). Similarly, while at Lemnos they were smiths, at Thebes they promoted cattle-raising and viticulture as the agricultural economy developed.

Although much of the evidence for Cabiri in the Aegean and the Asian mainland is relatively late, the cults at Lemnos and Samothrace were known to *Aeschylus and Herodotus, respectively, and the Theban Cabiri are attested by name from the end of the 7th, and were probably established there by the 8th cent. BC.

Cacus For the Augustans, Cacus was a fire-breathing monster inhabiting the *Palatine hill in Rome (the *Aventine according to *Virgil, but the Scalae Caci or Steps of Cacus on the Palatine imply otherwise) whose thieving terrified the locals; he stole some of Geryon's cattle from *Heracles, who killed him. This Hellenized version relied on Heracles traditions and a false etymology from the Greek *kakos* (evil), and provided an aetiology for the cult of Heracles at the Ara Maxima. Originally a sister Caca makes him a bisexual deity, possibly *chthonian, connected with fire. There is a dubious connection with Caeculus, founder of Praeneste, of whom a miracle involving fire is related. Another tradition knew him as an Etruscan killed by Heracles.

[Virgil, *Aeneid* 8. 190–279; Livy 1. 7. 3–15; Propertius 4. 9; Ovid, *Fasti* 1. 543–86, 5. 643–52]

Cadmus, legendary Phoenician founder of Boeotian Thebes, whose origins are still disputed: Phoenicia, Egypt. Mycenaean Greece, Archaic Greece, have all been proposed.

In *Homer, he appears indirectly, as father of *Ino-Leucothea, and through the names Cadmeii, Cadmeiones given to the inhabitants of Thebes attacked by the Seven (*see* SEVEN AGAINST THEBES) and the *Epigoni. The generally accepted story is that Cadmus was sent by his father *Agenor to find his sister *Europa, who had been abducted (by *Zeus, as it turned out). He failed in his search (Europa ended up in Crete, while Cadmus went to the Greek mainland), but was ordered by Delphi (*see* DELPHIC ORACLE) to be guided by a cow and establish a city where the animal lay down. Thus he founded Thebes, having killed a dragon, and peopled the place with men sprung from the dragon's teeth (*Spartoi). His dynasty ended with Thersandrus, son of Polynices.

[Homer, *Odyssey* 5. 333; Apollodorus, *The Library* 3. 1. 1, 3. 4. 1–2, 3. 5. 4]

Caelestis, 'heavenly', the epithet of *Juno at Carthage, successor to, and inheritor of many aspects of, the Carthaginian Tinnit (Tanit). (*See* PHOENICIAN RELIGION.) The cult, with an oracle, was important in Roman Carthage, where it became an emblem of the province of Africa, and is found later at Rome and in other centres. Caelestis was closely linked with Baal, interpreted in Latin as *Saturnus, and had points of contact with other cults including the Magna Mater (*See* CYBELE). Patronage of the emperor Septimius Severus was particularly important for the cult's success, and his wife Iulia Domna was sometimes identified with her.

Caeneus, a Lapith (*see* CENTAURS), of whom three principal stories are told, mostly known to us through fragmentary and scholiastic texts. (1) He was invulnerable (*see* IN-VULNERABILITY), and therefore the Centaurs disposed of him by hammering him into the ground. (2) He set up his spear to be worshipped. (3) He was originally a girl, Caenis, loved by *Poseidon, who gave her a change of sex and (sometimes) invulnerability. He was son of Elatus of Gyrtone. His final battle was often shown in ancient art.

[Virgil, *Aeneid* 6. 448]

Caesar, Julius (Gaius Iulius Caesar, 100–44 BC). Caesar's extraordinary political career was aided by his position as *pontifex maximus* (*see* PONTIFEX/PONTIFICES), but his main significance in Roman (and wider) religion must rest on his reform of the *calendar, which regularized the festival year, and on his clear aim to be accepted as a god, which after gradual approaches he seems to have achieved shortly before his death. This was partly based on Hellenistic *ruler-cult, though there were some partial precedents at Rome also. After his death, his formal deification in 42 BC paved the way for divine honours to be given to his successors in power, and the development of an 'imperial cult'.

cakes (flour-based sweetmeats or fancy breads) were given many names in the classical languages, of which the most general were (in Greek) *pemmata*, *popana*, and in Latin *liba* (sacrificial cakes), and *placentae* (from Greek *plakountes*). The Greeks especially had a vast number of different kinds, and several monographs were written on the subject. Most were regarded as a luxurious delicacy, to be eaten with fruit after the main course at a special meal. Cakes were also very commonly used in *sacrifice, either as a peripheral accompaniment to the animal victim or as a bloodless sacrifice. Sacrificial cakes very often had a special form characteristic of the relevant divinity or rite; among the more spectacular examples are the Attic *amphiphōn*, stuck with lights and offered to *Artemis on the full-moon day, or the Sicilian *myllos*, shaped like female genitals and offered to the Two Goddesses, *Demeter and *Persephone.

Calais and Zetes, sons of *Boreas the god of the north wind and his Athenian wife Oreithyia, hence jointly the 'Boreadae'; winged like their father, they were able, as members of the Argonautic expeditionary force (*see* ARGONAUTS), to chase the Harpies (*Harpyiae) away from their persecution of the blind king *Phineus. After Heracles was left behind at Cios while searching for *Hylas, it was the Boreads who persuaded the heroes not to turn back for him; he revenged himself later by killing them both in Tenos. One of their gravestones swayed in the breeze when the north wind blew. The scene of the Harpy pursuit is popular in 6th-cent. art.

[Apollonius Rhodius 1. 211 ff., 1. 1298 ff., 2. 240 ff.]

Calauria (now Póros), a Saronic island (23 sq. km.: 9 sq. mi.) adjacent to the Argolid, and also the name of its chief city. The town lay near the island's summit (283 m.: 928 ft.);

its remains, chiefly Hellenistic, include a probable heroon (*see* HERO-CULT) of the orator Demosthenes, who died here.

The sanctuary of *Poseidon has Mycenaean tombs, 8th-cent. and later dedications, and cult buildings of *c.*520–320 BC. It was the focus of the Calaurian *amphictiony, whose members included Hermione, *Epidaurus, Aegina, Athens, and Boeotian Orchomenus. The inclusion of Nauplia and Cynurian Prasiae, neither of them autonomous after *c.*650, implies an early foundation date. Rather than a military, political, or economic union, the amphictiony was probably a cultic association of mainly local, non-Dorian towns: the sanctuary's material apogee is not matched by any known political activity. By the time of Augustus the sanctuary had been sacked by Cilician pirates and the amphictiony no longer existed. *See* AMPHICTIONY.

Calchas, in mythology son of Thestor; a seer who accompanied the Greek army to Troy. He reveals the reason for the plague on the camp and foretells the length of the war. After *Homer he is introduced into several episodes, such as the sacrifice of *Iphigenia, the building of the Wooden Horse, and generally the actions by which it was fated that Troy should be captured. An oracle had foretold that Calchas would die when he met a diviner better than himself, and this occurred when he met a seer usually identified as *Mopsus, grandson of *Tiresias. An oracle in Apulia was identified with his name.

[Homer, *Iliad* 1. 69 ff., 2. 300 ff.; Aeschylus, *Agamemnon* 201 ff., Virgil, *Aeneid* 2. 185; Pausanias 6. 3. 9]

calendar, Greek There was no single Greek calendar. Almost every Greek community had a calendar of its own, differing from others in the names of the months and the date of the New Year. All were, at least originally, lunar. The months were named after festivals held or deities specially honoured in them. Dios and Artemisios, Macedonian months, were, for example, named after *Zeus and *Artemis; Anthester-

ion at Athens from the festival *Anthesteria. Such month names are found in Linear B and in literature as early as *Hesiod. In much later times some states used ordinal numbers for their month names.

The Athenian calendar is best known. The year began, in theory, with the appearance of the first new moon after the summer solstice, and the months were Hekatombaion, Metageitnion, Boedromion, Pyanopsion, Maimakterion, Posideon, Gamelion, Anthesterion, Elaphebolion, Mounichion, Thargelion, and Skirophorion. All were named after festivals held in the month, some very obscure to us and probably to 5th- and 4th-cent. Athenians. Each month was 29 or 30 days long; an ordinary year was 354 ± 1, a leap year 384 ± 1. A leap year was created by inserting an intercalary 'second' month, usually a second Posideon.

The first day of the Athenian month was the 'new moon' (*noumēnia*), determined in theory if not always in practice by the observation or expectation of the first visibility of the new moon. The next nine days were of the 'waxing' month, and were numbered forward as with us: *Boēdromiōonos pemptē histamenou* being Boedromion 5. The 11th to the 19th were numbered forward in the style 'Boedromion 11'. The 20th was called 'former tenth' and the 21st 'later tenth' The next eight days, of the 'waning' month, were numbered backwards from the end of the month. In Athens the last day of the month was named *henē kai nea*, the 'old and new' day, but elsewhere in the Greek world was *triakas* (30th). In a 'hollow' month, having only 29 days, the omitted day was most likely the 29th.

In the 2nd cent. BC the Athenians occasionally distinguished between their purely lunar calendar (*kata theon*, 'according to the god') and their festival calendar (*kat' archonta* 'according to the archon or magistrate') which had been affected by the intercalation of individual days. Such a distinction may have been thought necessary because days were often intercalated for non-calendric purposes, as for instance to allow additional time for preparations for the City Dionysia. Dates given without the qualification *kata theon* are those of the festival calendar.

In Athens a third calendar, the 'prytany' calendar, was used, either separately or in conjunction with the two other calendars, to date government documents. From the 4th century onwards, prytany years began on the same day. Such calendars were used in Athens and elsewhere to date actions of legislative or other governmental bodies and, occasionally, events of historic importance. But the month names indicate the calendars were first invented to assure the timely performance of religious rituals and *festivals, and numerous sacred calendars, listing day, deity, sacrificial victim (*see* SACRIFICE, GREEK), and often costs, officials involved, and perquisites, survive from throughout the Greek world. Such calendars, from families, states, and smaller local units, were not records of past activities but were prescriptions for the future administration and performance of cultic activities.

calendar, Roman The original Roman calendar consisted of ten months only, March–December, and must therefore have had an uncounted gap in winter, between years. The republican calendar, represented for us by the fragmentary calendar from Antium and literary descriptions, was believed by some to have been introduced from Etruria by *Tarquinius Priscus; indeed the month-name *Iunius*, pure Latin *Iunonius*, is connected with the Etruscan form of Juno's name, *Uni*. The introduction of this calendar, however, predates the Capitoline temple (traditionally dated after the expulsion of the kings, *see* CAPITOL), for of the feast-days which it marks with large letters none is connected with that cult. January, as containing the hypothetical festival *Januar* (presumably the *Agonium of later calendars, 9 January) of the god of gates who became god of all beginnings, must have been intended to be the first month, but the revolution which expelled the kings put a stop to this and March remained the first month of

the year until 153 BC. From then the official year of the consuls and most other Roman magistrates began on 1 January; that of the tribunes of the plebs began on 10 December. Counting within each month was reckoned by the number of days before Kalends, Nones, and Ides. March, May, Quintilis (July), and October had 31 days each (Nones on 7th, Ides on 15th), February 28, and the rest 29 (Ides on 13th): total 355.

To intercalate, February was shortened to 23 or 24 days and followed by an intercalary month of 27 days. This intercalating was so clumsily done that by the time of *Caesar the civic year was about three months ahead of the solar. In his capacity as pontifex maximus (*see* PONTIFEX/PONTIFICES), he intercalated sufficent days to bring the year 46 BC to a total of 445 days, which was thus called 'the last year of the muddled reckoning'. From the next year onwards the Egyptian solar calendar was adapted to Roman use, by inserting enough days in the shorter months to bring the total up to 365 and arranging for the insertion of a day, not a month, between 23 and 24 February, in leap year (thus 23 February occurred twice; the non-existent date '29 February' is a modern absurdity). No substantial change was made thereafter until the reforms of Pope Gregory XIII, promulgated in 1582 and gradually adopted as our normal 'Gregorian' calendar (in Britain only in 1752); today the Orthodox churches use the Julian calendar for some or all purposes.

See FASTI.

[Ovid, *Fasti*; Censorinus, *De die natali* 20–2; Macrobius 1. 12–16, 1. 14. 3]

Callimachus, of Cyrene, Greek poet and scholar of the 3rd cent. BC. He was credited with more than 800 books, but, apart from the six hymns and some sixty epigrams, and a selection from the prose *Paradoxa*, only fragments now survive. Many of his works are of considerable interest to the religious historian and as sources of myth. The most important of these are the *Aetia* and the

Hecale, surviving only in fragments, and the *Hymns.*

The *Aetia* consisted of four books (some 4,000 lines in all?): a miscellany of elegiac pieces, from extended epigrams to narratives of 100–200 lines. The common subject is 'origins': the origins in myth or history of Greek cults, festivals, cities, and the like. Episodes are chosen and rehearsed with antiquarian relish. In the 'prologue' the poet answers the critics who complain that he does not compose a 'continuous poem' on the deeds of kings or heroes: poetry should be judged by art, not quantity; Apollo recommended the slender Muse, the untrodden paths; better be the cicada than the braying mule. Like *Hesiod, he had met the *Muses, in a dream, and they related the *Aetia* to him. Books 1 and 2 were structured, at least in part, by a dialogue between the poet-researcher and the Muses; books 3 and 4 are framed by the substantial court-poems *Victory of Berenice* and *Lock of Berenice*. Within books, poems may be grouped thematically. The 'epilogue' (fr. 112) recalls Hesiod's meeting with the Muses; and leads over to the 'pedestrian field of the Muses', i.e. (probably) to the *Iambi*. It is generally (but controversially) argued that the *Aetia* went through two editions: the poet in old age added 'prologue' and 'epilogue', and perhaps books 3–4 entire.

Hecale was a hexameter narrative of something over 1,000 lines. *Theseus leaves Athens secretly to face the bull of Marathon; a storm breaks; he takes shelter in the cottage of the aged *Hecale; he leaves at dawn and subdues the bull; he returns to Hecale, finds her dead, and founds the deme (local community) Hecale and the sanctuary of Zeus Hekaleios in her memory. This heroic (but not Homeric) material was deviously elaborated, with Hecale rather than Theseus at the centre. The scene of rustic hospitality became famous; talking birds diversify the narrative; the action ends in another explanation of ritual, perhaps drawn from local historians of Attica.

The *Hymns* reanimate the traditional (Homeric) form (*see* HYMNS), but probably with no view to performance. The hymns to *Zeus, *Artemis, and *Delos (nos. 1, 3, 4) elaborate the god's birth and virtues with quizzical learning and virtuoso invention. Those to *Apollo (no. 2), *Athena (no. 5), and *Demeter (no. 6) are framed as dramas, in which the narrator-celebrant draws the hearer into an imagined ritual; 6 (Doric hexameters) and still more 5 (Doric elegiacs) deliberately cross generic boundaries. How far any 'religious' intention can be discerned in them is debatable.

Callimachus wrote prose works on very many subjects, including on *nymphs. His extraordinary scholarship (his poetry even quotes its own sources), and his interest in the supposed connections of story and cult-practice make him a most valuable source of recondite information on Greek religion.

Callirhoë, the name ('beautifully flowing') given to (1) a daughter of the river Acheloüs (for her story *see* ACARNAN, ALCMAEON (1)); (2) a virgin of Calydon vainly loved by Coresus, a priest of *Dionysus; (3) a daughter of Oceanus, mother of Geryoneus; (4) an Athenian spring, later called Enneakrounos ('Nine Spouts'), whose *water was favoured for ritual uses. Both the fountain-house and the personification of the spring appear in Attic art.

[(2) Pausanias 7. 21. 1–5; (3) Hesiod, *Theogony* 287–8]

Callisto, 'very beautiful', a mythical Arcadian princess or *nymph. (*See* ARCADIAN CULTS AND MYTHS.) She was daughter of *Lycaon, and a companion of *Artemis in the chase. Loved by *Zeus, she gave birth to *Arcas and was changed by Zeus (or Artemis or *Hera) into a bear. In some versions she was shot with an arrow and killed by Artemis, while in others she was changed into a *constellation (the Great Bear) by Zeus. Despite her links with Artemis Calliste, Callisto is not simply a form of the goddess. She makes several appearances in the visual arts.

Calypso ('Concealer'?), a nymph, daughter

of *Atlas, possibly invented by *Homer. She lived on the island of Ogygie, 'where is the sea's navel', rescued *Odysseus when shipwrecked, and kept him for seven years, vainly promising immortality. Commanded by *Zeus and *Hermes to release him, she helped him to make a boat and let him go In *Hesiod, she has two sons by Odysseus, Nausithous and Nausinous, and in a fragment of the Hesiodic corpus is perhaps mother of the Cephallenians by Hermes. Later she is mother by Odysseus or Atlas of Auson, eponym of Ausonia (southern Italy). In Lucian, Odysseus writes to her after his death from the *Island of the Blest, regretting having left her and promising to return, and in Hyginus she commits suicide for love of him. She is an Oceanid, Nereid, or Hesperid, see HESPERIDES.

[Homer, *Odyssey* 1. 50, 5. 1–268, 7. 244–66; Hesiod, *Theogony* 1017–18; Lucian, *True History* 2. 35; Hyginus, *Fables* 243]

Camenae, goddesses of a spring (from which the *Vestals drew their daily water), meadow, and grove below the Caelian hill just outside the porta Capena at Rome. They included *Egeria, and were linked traditionally with the inspiration of King *Numa and in turn were identified with the *Muses. There was a shrine and a festival (13 August); the place was embellished but lost its rural atmosphere as the city spread around it.

Camilla, a legendary Volscian maiden, whose father Metabus, in flight fastened her to a javelin, dedicated her to *Diana, and threw her across the Amisenus river. After life as a huntress she joined the forces of *Turnus, engaged in battle, and was killed by the Etruscan *Arruns. *Virgil alone relates her story.

[Virgil, *Aeneid* 7. 803, 11. 539–828]

camillus, fem. **camilla,** the ancient name for acolytes in Roman cult; the normal term was *pueri et puellae ingenui patrimi matrimique*. They might be the children of the officiant, but must, as the phrase states, be below the age of puberty, be free-born, and have both parents alive.

Campus Martius comprised most of the Tiber flood-plain bounded by the Pincian, Quirinal, and Capitoline hills. Taking its name from an altar to Mars, it was originally pasture outside the *pomerium*, and therefore used for army musters and exercises and for some voting assemblies; here too armies gathered before processing in *triumph through the city. As a result, the Campus and the Circus Flaminius (221 BC), a monumentalized open space just to the south through which the procession passed, were during the republic increasingly filled with temples, porticoes, and other monuments set up to commemorate (and thank the gods for) military victories, at the same time impressing the assembled electorate: for example the temples of the Lares Permarini (179 BC) and Fortuna Huiusce Diei (101 BC), in the Porticus Minucia Vetus (107 BC), modern Largo Argentina. Later the area became predominantly one of imperial commemoration and entertainment.

Canace, tragic victim of the story presented in *Euripides' *Aeolus*. A daughter of the island-king *Aeolus (1), she was impregnated by her brother Macareus. When she gave birth and the affair came to light, her father sent her a sword with which she committed suicide; the guilty brother followed suit.

cannibalism has been called 'for Greeks, one of those extreme pollutions, often imagined, though never experienced'. (*See* POLLUTION.) Such hard evidence as there is tends to relate to sieges and is usually something the enemy does, not your own side. From Aegean prehistory, Minoan civilization provides an isolated find of human bones from *Cnossus (*c*.1500 BC) said to bear butchery-marks. Myths tell of human *sacrifice in the distant past, but not of cannibalism.

Capaneus, in mythology, son of Hipponous and father of Sthenelus; one of the *Seven against Thebes (*see also* ADRASTUS). As he climbed on the walls, boasting that not even *Zeus should stop him, he was destroyed by a thunderbolt; this is a constant in tragedy and perhaps derives from the cyclic *Thebais* (*see* EPIC CYCLE). In art he appears especially in Italy, above all Etruria.

Capitol, Capitolium, or mons Capitolinus, the smallest of the hills of Rome: an isolated mass with two peaks, conventionally known as Capitolium proper and Arx. Legend associated the hill with *Saturn, and recent archaeological work has revealed traces of bronze age settlement. It is best known as the site of the great temple begun by the Tarquins (*see* TARQUINIUS PRISCUS and TARQUINIUS SUPERBUS) and dedicated, in the first year of the republic according to tradition, to *Jupiter Optimus Maximus, *Juno, and *Minerva. At all periods, the hill was less an inhabited part of the city than a citadel and religious centre. It was successfully defended against the Gauls in 390 BC. Here the consuls sacrificed at the beginning of the year and provincial governors took vows before going to their provinces; a sacrifice here was the culmination of the triumphal procession (*see* TRIUMPH). The original platform of the temple (62 m. × 53.5 m. in area: 203 ft. × 175 ft.) still exists; but the original temple, often embellished, was burnt in 83 BC. The new temple of Quintus Lutatius Catulus (69 BC), was renovated and repaired by Augustus; it was burnt down during the course of fighting on the hill in AD 69, while the emperor Vespasian's temple perished in the fire of AD 80. The last rebuilding was undertaken by Vespasian's son Domitian. On the north summit of the hill, the Arx, lay the temple of Juno Moneta (344 BC), the *auguraculum* (an augur's observation post with primitive hut) and the Tarpeian Rock (*see* TARPEIA), which overlooked the *forum Romanum. On the col between the hills, known as *inter duos lucos*, lay the temple of Veiovis (192 BC) and the *asylum* associated with Romulus. The east face of the hill was occupied by a massive building usually identified as the Tabularium or record-office and the

approach-road from the Forum (*clivus Capitolinus*), paved in 174 BC.

Both hill and the temple of Jupiter were reproduced in many cities of Italy and (especially the western) provinces, and either hill or temple or both in *Constantinople; *Jerusalem, as refounded by Hadrian, was styled *Aelia Capitolina*. The right to erect such *capitolia* was at first probably reserved for Roman *coloniae*. See FORUM.

Caprotina, title of *Juno, from Nonae Caprotinae ('Nones of the Wild *Fig') on 7 July, to whom freedwomen and female slaves sacrificed, then fighting a mock battle with fig-tree sticks. These activities do not appear in extant calendars. The connection of fig and Juno implies an original fertility ritual.

Capys, (1) in the *Iliad*, father of *Anchises; (2) in Virgil, companion of Aeneas and founder of Capua; (3) in Livy, king of *Alba Longa.

Carcinus (1), son of the dramatist Xenocles and grandson of another Carcinus, a tragic poet of the fourth century BC who is said to have written 160 plays. Titles included *Aerope*, *Thyestes*, *Amphiaraus*, *Alope*, *Oedipus*, *Aias*, *Orestes*, *Semele*, and perhaps *Tyro*. He also wrote a *Medea* in which *Medea did not kill her children. Many of his versions will have contributed to later mythological compendia.

Carcinus (2), of Naupactus (?6th or 5th cent. BC), named by the 5th-cent. historian Charon of Lampsacus as author of the *Naupactia*, a genealogical epic (*see* GENEALOGY) elsewhere cited anonymously. It included the *Argonaut story.

Caristia (*cara cognatio*), Roman family festival on 22 February. Ovid makes it a reunion of surviving family members after the *Parentalia's rites to the departed (February 13–21), and the presence of the ancestral spirits (*Lares) supports that. Valerius Maximus adds that no outsiders were admitted and family quarrels were settled. It appears under the precise date in the calendars of *Filocalus and Polemius Silvius, under February in the *Menologia rustica*.

[Ovid, *Fasti* 2. 617–38; Valerius Maximus 2. 1. 8]

carmen, from *cano* (?), 'something chanted', a formulaic or structured utterance, not necessarily in verse. In early Latin the word was used especially for religious utterances such as spells and charms: the early laws recorded in the Twelve Tables contained provisions against anyone who chanted a *malum carmen*, 'evil spell'. *Carmen* became the standard Latin term for song, and hence poem, but the possibilities of danger and enchantment inherent in the broader sense continued to be relevant, and there is often play on the different senses.

Carmen arvale, hymn sung during the sacrifice to *Dea Dia by the *fratres arvales* (Arval Brothers). Even if known only from an inscriptional copy of AD 218, marred by errors of transcription, this hymn is of great interest, because at the least it is older than the 4th cent. BC (*Lases* for *Lares*). It has been thought to show the influence of Greek poetry. In spite of the problems that it poses, the hymn is understandable. It is addressed to the *Lares, Semones (*see* SEMO SANCUS DIUS FIDIUS), and *Mars. The first two groups of deities are invoked three times one after the other, Mars three times thrice. The *carmen* culminates in a quintuple cry of triumph (*triumpe*). In the context of the sacrifice to *Dea Dia, these divinities are requested to guarantee the integrity of the land and the harvest, so that Dea Dia can exercise her office there.

Carmen Saliare or Carmina Saliaria, the ancient hymn(s) of the *Salii in Saturnian verse, unintelligible in classical times despite commentaries by Lucius Aelius and others; the few fragments, already corrupt in antiquity, mostly illustrate obsolete diction. Of religious interest are the title *diuom deo* 'god of gods' for Janus and the name *Leucesios* or *Lucetius* '(god) of light' for Jupiter; but text and interpretation remain speculative and controversial.

Carmentis or Carmenta (the latter form Greek and seldom Latin), meaning 'full of *carmen (divine incantation)'. A Roman cult-figure connected with *childbirth (one source mentions two Carmentes, Prorsa and Postverta, in reference to the child's position in the womb), prophecy, or both, although the prohibition on leather implies childbirth. Mythologically, a prophetess, mother of *Evander paralleling *Themis of the Greek tradition, she or Evander taught original Italian writing. As a nymph, she was perhaps a water-goddess; connection with divine incantation (*carmen*) and identification with the *Camenae associated her with poetry; thus Livius Andronicus began his translation of the *Odyssey* by implicitly equating 'Camena' with 'Muse', which later literary conceits of the spring of Hippocrene on Mt. *Helicon furthered. She had a *flamen (*see* FLAMINES), which implies the cult's antiquity, a two-day festival (11 and 15 January), and a shrine at the foot of the Capitoline hill, near the Porta Carmentalis.

[Ovid, *Fasti* 1. 617–36; Plutarch, *Roman Questions* 56]

carmina triumphalia, songs sung, in accordance with ancient custom, by soldiers at a *triumph, either in praise of their victorious general or in a satiric ribaldry supposed to avert the evil eye from him.

Carnea, the main Dorian festival, honouring *Apollo Carneius. We know little about its content except at Sparta, where it took place in late summer and lasted nine days; and even here the evidence is fragmentary. The Spartan Carnea was above all a choral and musical festival of Panhellenic importance (*see* PANHELLENISM). The most picturesque rite was that of the *staphylodromoi*, 'grape runners', one of whom, draped in woollen fillets, was chased by the others: it counted as 'a good omen for the city' if he was caught. Carnea runners are also attested on Thera and at Cnidus. We also hear that the Carnea was 'an imitation of the military way of life', at which men selected by *phratries camped out and dined together in huts. *See* SPARTAN CULTS.

Carthage *See* PHOENICIAN RELIGION.

caryatides, a Greek term for column-shafts carved in the form of draped women; male equivalents were called Atlantides (*see* ATLAS). Apparently named after Caryae in Laconia, where virgins danced to *Artemis Caryatis. Of near-eastern derivation, they appear in Greece around 550 BC, and are popular on late Archaic treasuries at *Delphi; the most famous are those of the Athenian *Erechtheum. The Erechtheum accounts, however, simply call them *korai*, girls; in this case, perhaps, they were civic versions of the private *korē* statues dedicated in the past. Copies of the Erechtheum caryatids embellished the *forum Augustum, the *Pantheon, and Hadrian's villa at Tibur. Vitruvius calls them 'images of eternal servitude', and connects them with Caryae's punishment for Medism (collaborating with Persia) in the Persian Wars against Greece, but since the type is unquestionably earlier and Caryae was destroyed much later (370 BC), this must be an explanatory story invented after the fact.

Cassandra or Alexandra, in mythology daughter of *Priam and *Hecuba. In *Homer she is mentioned as being the most beautiful of Priam's daughters, and she is the first to see her father bringing home the body of *Hector. The *Iliu Persis* (*see* EPIC CYCLE) adds that during the sack of Troy she took refuge at the statue of Athena, but *Aias (2) the Locrian dragged her away to rape her, and in so doing loosened the statue from its plinth. Perhaps Homer knew of this episode, for in the *Odyssey* he says that Aias was 'hated by Athena'; but he makes no direct mention of it. Nor does he mention Cassandra's prophetic powers for which in later tradition she was famous. The *Cypria* (*see* EPIC CYCLE) first mentions her prophecies. *Aeschylus' *Agamemnon* tells how Apollo gave her the power of prophecy in order to win her sexual favours, which she promised to him. But she broke her word, so he turned the blessing into a curse by causing her always to be disbelieved. Later authors follow this form of the story; but there is another which says that she and her brother *Helenus, when children, had their ears licked by Apollo's sacred serpents while asleep and so were given their prophetic gifts. Cassandra commonly appears, in tragedy and elsewhere, as forewarning of terrible events, like the evil fate which *Paris would bring on Troy or the disasters which the Wooden Horse would cause, but having her warnings unheeded. On the basis of this, *Lycophron (*Alexandra*) puts into her mouth a forecast of mythological and historical adventures of both Trojans and Greeks from the war to his own day. After the sack of Troy, Cassandra was given to *Agamemnon as his concubine, and on his return home *Clytemnestra killed them both. There is a memorable scene in Aeschylus' *Agamemnon* where Cassandra sings of the horrors which have already polluted the house of *Atreus and foretells her own death and that of Agamemnon.

A favourite scene in Archaic and Classical art is that of Cassandra clutching the image of Athena while Aias seizes her.

[Homer, *Iliad* 13. 36, 24. 699 ff.; *Odyssey* 4. 502; Aeschylus, *Agamemnon* 1035 ff.]

Cassian, Christian writer and ascetic. Born in what is now Romania in *c.*AD 360, Cassian had the advantage of a Latin upbringing in the Greek world. Like his master Evagrius of Pontus, he travelled through Syria, Palestine, and Egypt, making extensive contact with the masters of eastern *asceticism and gaining a thorough grounding in the theory of the ascetic life.

With the Egyptian condemnation of *Origen in 399, he enjoyed the protection of John *Chrysostom in Constantinople, together with many other exiled admirers of the Alexandrian master. After an obscure interval, he settled in southern Gaul in *c.*415 under the patronage, in particular, of Proculus of Arles. He served and moulded the ascetic enthusiasms of several bishops and founded two monasteries of his own near Marseilles.

For the resulting communities he wrote his *Institutes* and *Conferences*, which gained widespread and permanent influence in the west. The *Institutes* were more practical, important for liturgical detail and for their systematic treatment of the vices, reflecting eastern practice and the theology of Evagrius. The *Conferences* reported conversations with ascetics of northern Egypt and gave new Christian vigour to the dialogue form. Their setting appeared solitary but Cassian's intentions were communal: he encouraged virtues and practices proper to community life. While respecting Egyptian tradition, he adapted it to the new monasteries of Gaul.

Cassian's writings were charged with an Alexandrian optimism. The ascetic was made in the image of God and perfection was in some sense a natural expectation based on the development of inherent qualities. Virtues formed a unity, so that any step forward would find its reward in an integrated drama of self-possession. The result was a genuine freedom—not only from inadequacy but from fear of submission to others. In making such emphases, Cassian had a role to play on a broader stage. He wrote a treatise on the Incarnation against Nestorius; and his views on freedom had a lasting influence in Gaul among those who sympathized more with *Pelagius than with *Augustine. His ascetic teaching was highly valued by Benedict and was mentioned explicitly in the latter's *Rule*. He died *c*.435.

Cassiodorus (Magnus Aurelius Cassiodorus Senator), politician, writer, and monk (*c*.AD 490–*c*.585). After a distinguished political career in Rome, he retired in 537/8 during the Gothic wars. Moving to Constantinople, he assisted Pope Vigilius in the Three Chapters controversy (550). Soon after, he withdrew permanently to his monastery of Vivarium on his ancestral estate at Scylacium. There he organized translations and manuscript copying, partly to support the Three Chapters against official condemnation, partly to promote Christian education. Vivarian texts soon circulated widely, but the monastery quickly shared in the decay of Italian civilization.

Among his works, the most influential perhaps were the following: (1) *Variae*: twelve books of state papers, edited *c*.537, an invaluable source for Ostrogothic Italy, and the structures, culture, and ideology of late-Roman government. The collection was both an apology for the Ostrogoths and their Roman collaborators, and a moral, rhetorical, and practical guide for future rulers and ministers. (2) The appended *De anima* grounded the *Variae* in religious reflections on human nature and society. (3) *Expositio Psalmorum*: this exegetical and literary commentary developed the Psalms as a Christian rhetorical handbook and encyclopaedia of liberal arts, superseding pagan classics. (4) *Institutiones*: an intellectual Rule for Vivarium (but also meant for a wider public), this short encyclopaedia and bibliography of Christian and secular studies renewed the project of Christian higher education, and depicted reading (including the liberal arts) and copying as central to monastic life. Cassiodorus did not save classical culture, as is sometimes claimed; but, especially from Carolingian times, *Variae*, *Expositio*, and *Institutiones* were widely read, and helped to maintain and integrate the Christian and Roman inheritances in western Europe.

Castor and Pollux, temple of Latin forms of the names Kastor and Polydeukes, the *Dioscuri. Their temple (*aedes Castorum* or even *Castoris*) at Rome, in the Forum (*see* FORUM ROMANUM), beside the Fountain of Juturna, was attributed to the deities' miraculous intervention in 484 BC in the battle of Lake Regillus in response to the vow of the dictator A. Postumius (they brought the news of the victory to Rome in person). Recent excavation has shown that the first temple is indeed of about this date, and that it was little smaller than the rebuildings of Lucius Caecilius Metellus Delmaticus (117 BC) and Tiberius (dedicated AD 6), lavish though the last was. This was accordingly one of the first monumental structures in the vicinity of the Forum, and long the most imposing—testimony to the importance of the cavalry in the early Roman state: the function of the Dioscuri in other Latin towns, as attested by inscriptions, and the link with the equestrian order and its annual parade, the *transvectio* of 15 July, which survived into the imperial period, leave little doubt that that was the principal association of the original cult. The temple on its high podium was a vantage-point in the Forum, and played an important part in the turbulent popular politics of the end of the republic. In the Augustan age, the brotherhood of the Dioscuri was an excuse for a display of *pietas by Tiberius towards his dead brother Drusus. Some important remains of the architecture of this phase survive.

Cults of Castor and Pollux are known from other Italian cities, such as Cora in Latium.
[Ovid, *Fasti* 1. 705–8, 5. 693–720]

catacombs, a term derived from Greek *kata kymbas*, a locality close to the church of St Sebastian on the via Appia, 3 miles south of Rome. The name may refer to the natural hollows across which the road passes or to an inn-sign, but was in use in the 4th and 5th cents. AD for the Christian cemetery associated with St Sebastian's in the form *ad catacumbas* or *catacumbae*. This famous cemetery was a series of narrow underground galleries and tomb-chambers cut in the rock. Their walls are lined with tiers (up to seven are known) of coffin-like recesses (*loculi*) for inhumation, holding one to four bodies apiece and sealed with a stone slab or tiles. The affinity to the *columbarium* type of inhumation is evident, but it seems to have been immediately derived from Jewish catacombs, where Jews, like Christians, remained a household of the faithful, united in death as in life. Catacombs were not confined to Rome: examples are known at Albano, Alexandria, Hadrumetum, Kertch, Neapolis, Malta, and Syracuse. All are associated with soft rocks, where tunnelling was easy.

The catacombs at Rome, however, are much the most extensive, stretching for at least 550 km. (340 mi.). Their distribution (some 50 are attested), along the main roads outside the city, is explained by their later growth out of, and side by side with, pagan cemeteries lying beyond the city boundaries in conformity with the law (*see* DEAD, DISPOSAL OF). That of St Priscilla, on the via Salaria, was below a burial-ground of the Acilii Glabriones, although the old view that allegedly Christian members of this consular family were buried there is now doubted. The Domitilla catacomb, on the via Ardeatina, developed from the burial vault of the Flavii. The official organization by the Church of public catacombs, mainly for the poor of Rome's Christian community, began *c*.200, when the then pope, St Zephyrinus, directed St Callixtus to provide the cemetery (Gk. *Koimētērion*), which is represented by the oldest part of the catacomb beside the via Appia that bears St Callixtus' name today. Another important catacomb near the same road is that of Praetextatus.

In the tomb-chambers (*cubicula*) of the catacombs are altar-tombs and arched recesses (*arcosolia*) for the bodies of popes and martyrs. Walls and ceilings received paintings which represent the first development of Christian art and are executed in the same technique and style as contemporary pagan work. Their subjects are biblical (scenes from the OT far outnumbering those from the NT) or symbolic (the Good Shepherd, Christ-*Orpheus, Christ as lawgiver, eucharistic and celestial banquets, figures of worshippers at prayer, etc.). A few motifs are drawn from daily life and some are frankly pagan. A remarkable and probably private catacomb, dating from the 4th cent. and discovered on the via Latina in 1955, has paintings which include a medical class and six episodes from the *Hercules-cycle (*see* HERACLES), as well as biblical scenes more elaborate and showing a much wider range of content than those in the official public catacombs. Furniture in the catacombs included carved sarcophagi, lamps, pottery, and painted-glass medallions.

The presence of these large cemeteries is explained partly by the size of the Christian community in Rome and partly by the long periods of toleration. About a century after the official recognition of the Church, the catacombs fell into disuse and became centres of *pilgrimage.

Catreus, in mythology, son of *Minos and Pasiphae, and father of *Althaemenes, Apemosyne, *Aerope, and *Clymene. Because of a prophecy that one of his children would kill him, Althaemenes and Apemosyne emigrated to Rhodes, and Catreus gave Aerope and Clymene to *Nauplius (2) the navigator and slave-trader to sell overseas. Aerope married Pleisthenes, who in this version replaces *Atreus as father of *Agamemnon; and Clymene married Nauplius himself and bore *Palamedes and Oeax. Althaemenes killed Apemosyne because he did not believe her when she claimed she had been raped by *Hermes; and also killed Catreus when visiting Rhodes, believing him to be a pirate.
[Apollodorus 3. 2]

caves, sacred The Greeks associated caves with the primitive, the uncanny, and hence the sacred. In myth they witness divine births (Zeus on Mt. Dicte), are home to monsters (the *Cyclopes), and conceal illicit sex (*see* SELENE). Remote and wild, real caves attracted the cult of *Pan and the *Nymphs, for whom several dozen cave-sanctuaries are known (e.g. those of Attica; the Corycian Cave at *Delphi) or, as openings to the Underworld, oracles of the dead: note the 'cave-like shrine' at *Taenarum). In Italy the most celebrated holy caves were the Lupercal on the Palatine (*see* LUPERCALIA) and the cave of the *Sibylat Cumae (described by *Virgil). Of imported cults, the most associated with caves was Mithraism (*see* MITHRAS), whose rites were celebrated in real or make-belief caves because the cave was considered an 'image of the universe'. That thesis is also central to *Porphyry's *On the Cave of the Nymphs*, an allegor-ical interpretation of *Homer's description in *Odyssey* book 13 of the cave near which the sleeping Odysseus is set on his return to Ithaca. Because Homer's cave has two doors, one for men and the other for immortals, Porphyry's explication is much concerned with doctrines of the entry and exit of souls into and out of the world. The cave's moistness and its dedication to water-nymphs (naiads) are related to genesis into mortal existence. *See* MINOAN AND MYCE-NAEAN RELIGION.

Cecrops, a mythical king of Athens. In most accounts he was not the first king, being son-in-law and successor to Actaeus, but Athenians clearly regarded him as their archetypal ancestral figure. No parents are recorded for him, and probably he was thought of as autochthonous (*see* AUTOCH-THONS). He was described as *diphyēs*, 'double-natured', with reference to his form as half-man, half-snake—the normal style of his depiction on red-figure vases, where he is a popular figure in many Athenian scenes. Cecrops was the father of *Aglaurus, *Pandrosus, and Herse, and of one son Erysichthon, who died young. His deeds mark him out as a civilizing figure, the one who established monogamous marriage, writing, funeral rites, and other customs which though diverse were perceived as important to contemporary, 'normal', society. The foundation of many religious cults was also ascribed to him. The historical tradition recognized a second King Cecrops, son of *Erechtheus; probably it was this Cecrops who was worshipped at Haliartus in Boeotia, and he may also have come to be identified as the tribal eponym (*see* EPONYMOI).

Celeus, as ruler of *Eleusis in the *Homeric Hymn to Demeter*, accepts the disguised Demeter as nurse of his son *Demophon (2).
[*Homeric Hymn to Demeter* 96 ff.]

Celsus, author of a comprehensive philosophical polemic against *Christianity, *The True Doctrine*, written probably between 175 and 181. The work is primarily known through *Origen's *Contra Celsum* (*Against Celsus*), which preserves most of it through direct quotation. Celsus wrote from the perspective of a Middle Platonic philosopher, though in one section of his work he also appears to have adopted the criticism levelled against Christianity by a Jew. *The True Doctrine* is important evidence for knowledge of Christian doctrine among Gentiles, as well as for the difficulty outsiders had in determining the difference between 'orthodox' Christians and *Gnostic fringe groups. The importance of Celsus' book is suggested by the fact that Origen's massive refutation was written in the 240s.

Efforts to identify this Celsus with the Celsus who is the addressee of Lucian's *Alexander* are not convincing: the author of *The True Doctrine* was a Platonist, while the recipient of the *Alexander* was evidently an Epicurean.

Celtic religion The three main sources for Celtic religion are Romano-Celtic epigraphy and iconography, the comments of classical authors, and insular Celtic tradition as represented by recorded Irish and Welsh literature. The problem they pose the modern observer is one of reconciling their very different modalities and frames of reference, and of matching insular myth to Romano-Celtic image. The iconography is largely derived from Graeco-Roman models and reflects the considerable element of religious and cultural *syncretism which obtained throughout the Romano-Celtic areas. More importantly, on mainland Europe it lacks the verbal tradition which provided its ideological context but which, being unwritten, perished along with the Celtic languages. In Ireland, however, and to a lesser extent in Wales, a rich vernacular literature has survived in writing, much of which is concerned with mythico-heroic tradition and with socio-religious institutions and ideology. But since in the pre-Norman period the writing of the vernacular was virtually confined to the monasteries, one must reckon with the fact that the

extant corpus, though in many ways deeply conservative, has nevertheless been passed through the filter of monastic, biblically-oriented, scholarship. Among the areas of pre-Christian belief and practice which seem to have best survived this process of selection and adaptation are mythico-heroic narrative in general and those traditions associated with certain key institutions such as the sacral kingship which, subject to the necessary adjustment, were accommodated under the new dispensation. One important factor in this regard was the existence of a highly organized oral learning maintained by three orders of practicians headed by the priestly fraternity of the druids and apparently replicated throughout the Celtic world. While the druids were eliminated by the Romans in Britain and displaced by Christianity in Ireland, the other two orders—the Gaulish 'vates' and bards—survived into the late Middle Ages in Ireland and Wales as privileged praise-poets maintaining the residual ideology and ritual of sacral kingship.

*Caesar names five principal gods of the Gauls—not a complete catalogue—together with their functions; unfortunately, he follows the *interpretatio Romana* in referring to them by the names of their nearest Roman equivalents. Similarly in many of the Romano-Celtic dedications the deity is assigned a Roman name, often accompanied by a native name or epithet, and since many of the latter are either infrequent or regional in distribution, some scholars have assumed that the Celtic gods as a whole were local and tribal, not national. But there is reason to believe that the Roman name often conceals a Celtic equivalent with the by-name or epithet referring to a local form of a more extended cult. What is certain is that there were gods whose cults were either pan-Celtic or enjoyed wide currency among the Celtic peoples. Caesar's Mercurius is the god perhaps called Lugus, personification of kingship and patron of the arts, whose name is commemorated in place-names throughout Europe and survives in medieval

Welsh literature as Lugh and Lleu respectively, and whose festival of Lughnasa is still widely celebrated. His Minerva corresponds to the multifunctional goddess best known as the Irish Brigit and British Brigantí/Brigantia, patron deity of the Brigantes. The horse goddess *Epona has several insular equivalents, including Welsh Rhiannon, 'Divine Queen', and Irish Macha, eponym of Armagh, the future ecclesiastical metropolis. The divine triad of Father, Mother, and Son is attested throughout the Celtic realm, with names which are substantially equivalent. Such deities indicate a greater degree of religious homogeneity among the Celtic peoples than might appear from the wide disparity of our sources, and this is borne out by the evidence of a common fund of themes, concepts, and motifs attested by insular story, continental sculpture, and classical commentator, or indeed by language and toponymy: the remarkable prevalence of triadic grouping, for example, or the cult of the centre, whether within the tribal kingdom or the greater cultural nation. Most of the Celtic gods and many of their myths are recognizably Indo-European, as has been demonstrated by Georges Dumézil and his disciples and others less committed to his trifunctional theory; in this regard it may be noted that the functions of the Celtic gods are less clearly differentiated in the literary sources than in Caesar's succinct, schematic version. The goddesses are more closely linked to land and locality: in general, as with the *matres* in particular, they promote fertility, and as a personification of a given territory, e.g. Ireland or one of its constituent kingdoms, the goddess participates in the *hieros gamos* (*see* MARRIAGE, SACRED) which legitimizes each new king, a sacred union which may form part of the symbolism of the many divine couples of Romano-Celtic iconography. Some of the more popular and widespread elements of pagan Celtic belief and ritual, such as pilgrimage, healing wells, and the rich mythology of the otherworld, were easily assimilated to the Christian repertoire or survived under the protective guise of folk culture.

[Caesar, *Gallic War* 6. 16 ff.]

cemeteries The organization of a formal cemetery, as a space reserved exclusively for the disposal of the *dead, was an important dimension of the social definition of the ancient city. Burial within the settlement had been common in many parts of the Mediterranean world in the early iron age, but after the 8th cent. BC it was rare. Cemeteries normally lined the roads leading away from cities. They usually consisted of numerous small grave-plots, which were rarely used for more than two or three generations, although some cemeteries, such as the Ceramicus at Athens, remained in use for over a millennium. Burial in a recognized cemetery was a primary symbol of citizenship in Athens.

Partly because of the impurity associated with death (*see* POLLUTION), the spatial distinction between city and cemetery held fast throughout pagan antiquity, only changing as part of the broader transformation associated with the Christian take-over of the western Roman empire. There were two parallel developments. Starting in the 3rd cent., Christians began building *basilicas over the shrines of saints, which were normally in extramural cemeteries. By the 6th cent. some of these basilicas were forming the centres for new towns: 'the city has changed address', as *Jerome put it. Meanwhile, by the 4th cent. the population of many western cities was shrinking, leaving open areas within the walls. From Britain to Africa, city-dwellers started burying in these spaces in the 5th cent. At Rome, the last-dated known burial outside the city and the first epitaph from within it both date to 567. By the 7th cent. the two processes were combining, as the first large churchyard cemeteries within settlements appeared, and by the 11th cent. this had been established as the medieval pattern.

Centaurs (Gk. *Kentauroi*; for the etymology, and their ancestry, *see* IXION), a tribe of 'beasts', as they are called in the *Iliad*, human above and horse below; the wild and dangerous counterpart of the more skittish *satyrs, who are constructed of the same components but conceived of as amusing rather than threatening creatures. In both cases it is the very closeness of the horse to humanity that points up the need to remember that a firm line between nature and culture must be drawn. *Pirithous the king of the Lapiths, a Thessalian clan, paid for his failure to absorb this lesson when he invited the Centaurs to his wedding-feast; the party broke up in violence once the guests had tasted *wine, that quintessential product of human culture, and made a drunken assault on the bride (see the west pediment of the temple of Zeus at *Olympia). 'Ever since then', says Antinous in the *Odyssey*, 'there has been conflict between centaurs and men.' Their uncontrolled lust, violence, and greed for alcohol challenge the hard-won and ever fragile rules of civilization, which are symbolically reasserted by the victories of *Heracles (whose wife *Deianira the Centaur Nessus tried to rape) and *Theseus (who sometimes fights alongside his friend Pirithous in the wedding-fight) over the savage horde. Centaurs belong to the forested mountains of Arcadia and northern Greece, the fringes of human society, so it is natural that in the Battles of the Centaurs so popular in Archaic art (e.g. the François vase) they fight with uprooted trees and boulders against armed and disciplined Greek heroes; it is with fir-trunks that they pound the invulnerable Lapith *Caeneus into the ground.

Their double-natured ambivalence is further emphasized in traditions which single out two of their number, Chiron and Pholus, as wise and civilized exceptions to the general rule. Pholus, it is true, eats his steak raw like an animal when entertaining Heracles in his Arcadian cave, but his self-control is shown by the fact that he is capable of holding his liquor—a specially aged vintage donated by Dionysus—until the other members of his tribe scent the bouquet of the wine, go berserk, and have to be shot down by Heracles. Chiron is a more complex character, blurring the human–animal boundary still further: vase-painters often make the point by giving him human rather than equine front legs and draping him in decorous robes. His bestial side is demonstrated by the way he feeds the baby *Achilles, deserted by his mother *Thetis, on the still-warm blood of the hares which in art he habitually carries over his shoulder as a portable game-larder (hence, in turn, the savagery of the hero); but he is also a source of wisdom on natural medicine, and is recorded as an educator of *Jason and *Asclepius as well as Achilles.

By the 5th cent. BC, Centaurs (like *Amazons) come to symbolize all those forces which opposed Greek male cultural and political dominance; on the *Parthenon metopes, with their heroically nude boxers and wrestlers, the triumph over Persia is a clear subtext. Of later literary treatments, *Ovid's magnificently gory, over-the-top account of the Lapith wedding is not to be missed.

[Homer, *Iliad* 1. 268, 2. 743, 4. 219, 11. 831, *Odyssey* 21. 303; Apollodorus 2. 5. 4; Ovid, *Metamorphoses* 12. 10 ff.]

Cephalus, a famous mythical hunter known to the *Epic Cycle; a hero having mythological connections with Attica (*see* ATTIC CULTS AND MYTHS), Phocis and Cephallenia. His cult is known only in Attica, where he seems to have originated from the Thoricus area. Whether he was the son of Deion(eus) of Phocis, or of Hermes and an Athenian princess, he married *Procris daughter of *Erechtheus, but was abducted by *Eos, by whom he had a son usually named Phaethon. On returning to his wife, he disguised himself in order to test her fidelity, but found it wanting. Procris fled in shame, but on her return tried the same trick, with the same result. Cephalus accidentally killed Procris when she was spying on him as he went hunting, and was brought to trial at the Areopagus by her father Erechtheus. Exiled from Attica, he took part with his invincible hound in the hunt of the Teumessian fox, and finally went to Cephallenia where he became the father of the *eponyms of the four cities of the island.

Cepheus, name of four or five mythological persons, the best known being the father of *Andromeda. Though generally called an Ethiopian from *Euripides on, he and consequently the whole legend are very variously located. Cepheus also appears in the canonical list of *constellations.

Cephissus (Gk. *Kēphisos*), the name of several rivers, the best known being the Attic and the Boeotian Cephissus. The Attic Cephissus was the main river of the plain of Athens, gathering all sources and streams of the mountains around, and emptying itself into the bay of Phaleron; its water, divided into many streams, irrigated the plain west of Athens; its clay-bed provided the material for Athenian pottery. The Boeotian Cephissus springs from the northern Parnassus, near Lilaea, and waters the plains of Phocis and northern Boeotia, debouching into lake Copais. Both were worshipped as gods and furnished with genealogies; the former's cult-statue showed him as a man with bull's horns.

Cerberus, the monstrous hound who guards the entrance to the Underworld, often called simply 'the dog of Hades', 'the dog'. Hesiod makes him a child of *Echidna and *Typhon, 'brass-voiced and fifty-headed'; three heads are more normal in literary descriptions and in art, while Attic vase-painters usually make do with two. A shaggy mane runs down his back, and he may sprout writhing snakes. Despite his impressive appearance, however, he failed to keep out *Orpheus, who lulled him to sleep with music; while *Heracles (with Athena's help) even managed to chain him up and drag him away to the upper world, where in a rerun of the conclusion to the labour of the Erymanthian boar he terrified *Eurystheus with the captive beast. The scene was already depicted in Archaic art on the so-called 'Throne of *Amyclae'; a Caeretan

hydria in the Louvre handles the theme with magnificent exuberance.

[Hesiod, *Theogony* 311 f.]

Ceres, an ancient Italo-Roman goddess of growth (her name derives from the root *ker-* 'growth'), commonly identified in antiquity with *Demeter. Her name suggests that of Cerus, found in the *Carmen Saliare*, but in cult she is found associated not with him but with *Tellus. This is shown by the juxtaposition of their festivals (*Fordicidia, to Tellus, 15 April; Cerialia, 19 April) and the fact that the *feriae sementiuae* ('sowing festivals') are celebrated in January in honour of both. The occurrence of the Cerialia on the calendars and the existence of a *flamen Cerialis* testify to the antiquity of Ceres' cult at Rome, but her whole early history is extremely obscure, particularly her relations, if any, with non-Italian (Greek) deities. One of the many difficulties is to determine whether the rite of swinging attested by the grammarian and commentator 'Probus' as used at the *feriae sementiuae* is really, as he says, borrowed from the Attic *aiōra* (*see* ERI-GONE) or an independent development. Another is the question whether the long list of minor deities invoked by the officiant on the same occasion arises out of genuinely early ideas or is a relatively late priestly elaboration. There is, however, no doubt that Ceres' most famous cult, that on the *Aventine (introduced 493 BC), is largely under Greek influence, but it is difficult to reconstruct precisely the manner of this Hellenization. She is there worshipped with *Liber Pater and Libera, the triad apparently representing the Eleusinian group of *Demeter, Kore (*see* PERSEPHONE), and *Iacchus. The temple became a centre of plebeian activities, was supervised by the plebeian *aediles Cereris*, and was connected with the *ludi Ceriales* which became a prominent feature of the Cerialia. To this Greek cult belongs also, no doubt, the annual festival conducted by the women in August, called Greek and an initiation by *Cicero; also probably Ceres' occasional association with the Underworld, the purely Roman goddess in this connection being Tellus. *See also* MUNDUS.

[Ovid, *Fasti* 1. 657 ff., 4. 393–620]

Cerynian hind *See* HERACLES.

Ceyx, son of the Morning Star, king of Trachis, friend of *Heracles, and father-in-law of *Cycnus; but most famous as husband of Alcyone. Their marriage was celebrated in the Hesiodic *Wedding of Ceyx* (*see* HESIOD), but nuptial bliss was short-lived: whether as punishment for the couple's temerity in calling each other '*Zeus' and '*Hera', or because Ceyx drowned at sea and his wife's grief was inconsolable (there is an extended, bravura account by *Ovid), the gods turned them into sea-birds. The semi-mythical 'halcyon' (traditionally identified with the kingfisher) is already associated with a plaintive, mourning cry in the *Iliad*; in the *Odyssey*, the *kēx* for whom she calls may be intended as the male of the species, or as some other diving gull.

[Apollodorus 1. 7. 4; Ovid, *Metamorphoses* 11. 410 ff.]

Chaeremon of Alexandria, where he held a priesthood: Greek writer on Egypt. He taught the young Nero. His writings treated Egyptian history, religion, customs, astrology, and hieroglyphic writings. A Stoic viewpoint is visible (*see* STOICISM).

Chaldaean Oracles, these are conventionally attributed either to a certain Julian the Chaldaean, who is alleged to have flourished in the reign of Trajan (AD 98–117), or to his son, Julian the Theurgist, who lived in the reign of *Marcus Aurelius (AD 161–80) and, according to the ancient encyclopaedic source the *Suda*, was responsible for the rain miracle in Marcus' German wars. The traditional date in the 2nd cent. AD can be defended only on the dubious assumption that there are two allusions to the oracles in the work of *Numenius, who wrote no later than the second half of the 2nd cent. Otherwise there is no reference to these texts until the late 3rd cent., when *Iamblichus quoted from them in his *On the Mysteries of the Egyptians*.

There is considerable evidence in the corpus, and from the way in which the oracles are cited by later Neoplatonists, that the text consisted of a series of oracles spoken by a variety of gods, of whom the most important was evidently *Hecate. However, at the beginning there also seems to have been a conversation between the elder 'Julian' and the soul of Plato, mediated by 'Julian' II. It also seems that the books provided some sort of explanation of the doctrines in the oracles. The doctrines appear to be based upon Platonic and Pythagorean speculation, cult, and *magic. (*See* NEOPLATONISM; PLATO; PYTHAGORAS AND PYTHAGOREANISM.)

The oracles and commentary contained in the Chaldaean book not only offered a guide to the nature of the universe, they also appear to have acted as a guide to *theurgy.

Chaos 'The very first of all Chaos came into being', says *Hesiod; it is noteworthy that he implies by the verb used that it did not exist from everlasting. What it was like he does not say; the name clearly means 'gaping void'. Later, presumably influenced by the 'all is together' theory of *Anaxagoras, it is described by Ovid as a mixture of the 'seeds' (*semina*) or potentialities of all kinds of matter.

[Hesiod, *Theogony* 116; Ovid, *Metamorphoses* 1. 5 ff.]

Charites, 'Graces', goddesses personifying charm, grace, and beauty. Like the *Nymphs and the *Horae, they vary in number, but are usually three from Hesiod, who names them Aglaea (Radiance), Euphrosyne (Joy), and Thalia (Flowering); *Homer neither names nor numbers them. *Hesiod calls them daughters of *Zeus and Eurynome, and is followed by most writers, although the mothers vary. They are closely associated with *Aphrodite in Homer, and later. In Hesiod they and the Horae deck *Pandora. They enjoy poetry, singing, and dance and perform at the wedding of *Peleus and *Thetis. As described by various writers, they make roses grow, have myrtles and roses as attributes, and the flowers of spring belong to them. They bestow beauty and charm, physical, intellectual, artistic, and moral. The Hellenistic poet Hermesianax makes *Peitho (Persuasion) one of them.

The Charites have no independent mythology, associating with gods of fertility, especially Aphrodite, whose birth they attend. Often they are shown standing, processing, or dancing, the latter sometimes in connection with *Hecate in the Hellenistic and Roman period. *Pausanias details cults and depictions of the Charites, particularly at Orchomenus in Boeotia; they also occur throughout southern Greece and in Asia Minor. Athens had a Hellenistic cult of *Demos and the Charites. Pausanias notes regional variations in their number and names, and many depictions, from aniconic images at Orchomenus, to their use as decorations on the 'Amyclaean throne' (*see* AMYCLAE) and on the Zeus at Olympia. They occur on a metope from Thermum, vases, Athenian New Style coins, and neo-Attic reliefs. The Charites were originally draped (e.g. a painting by the fourth-century artist Apelles at Smyrna), later naked. The familiar group of three naked women is Hellenistic in origin, and became standard in many Roman copies in several media.

[Homer, *Iliad* 14. 267–8, 275; *Odyssey* 8. 364–6, 18. 193–4; Hesiod, *Theogony* 53–64, 907–11, *Works and Days* 73–5; Pindar, *Olympian* 14. 3–17; Pausanias 3. 18. 9–10, 5. 11. 8, 9. 35. 1–7]

Charon, mythological ferryman, who ferries the shades across a river (usually *Acheron) or a lake (Acherusia) into *Hades proper. First attested in the fragmentary epic *Minyas*, his first known visual representations occur *c.*500 BC on two black-figure vases; a few decades later he became popular on Attic white-ground lecythi. At some date in the fifth century, Polygnotus painted him in the Nekyia in the Lesche (hall) of the Cnidians at *Delphi. In a *katabasis* (descent) ascribed to *Orpheus Charon, out of fear, ferried Heracles, who had gone to fetch *Cerberus, into Hades, and was punished for this dereliction with a year in fetters.

Charybdis, a sort of whirlpool or maelstrom in a narrow channel of the sea (later identified with the Straits of Messina, where there is nothing of the kind), opposite *Scylla (1); it sucks in and casts out the water three times a day and no ship can possibly live in it. Odysseus, carried towards it by a current when shipwrecked, escapes by clinging to a tree which grows above it and dropping into the water when the wreckage is cast out. Hence proverbially, a serious danger.

[Homer, *Odyssey* 12. 101 ff., 432 ff.]

chastity

Before Christianity Chastity, in the sense of complete abstinence from sexual activity, was not recommended in classical Greek medicine before Soranus (second century AD), nor was it normally considered a social or religious ideal. In Greek and Roman religion, certain goddesses chose to remain virgins (e.g. *Hestia/*Vesta, *Artemis/ *Diana) and priestesses of a few cults remained life virgins. Others, more commonly, could only hold the position until the age of marriage, while we also hear of priestesses who had to be 'of an age to have finished with sex'. The Gods did not, apparently, support their other human followers who emulated this behaviour, such as *Euripides' *Hippolytus (1); this play gives some evidence that such behaviour might have been associated with groups such as Orphics and Pythagoreans (*see* ORPHISM, PYTHAGORAS AND PYTHAGOREANISM).

Christian Celibacy and *asceticism are endemic to *Christianity and are typical of the distinctive outlook on life which runs throughout much of early Christian literature. The lifestyle of John the Baptist and the canonical gospels' portrayal of the celibacy of Jesus and his eschatological message set the pattern for subsequent Christian practice. While the influence of Graeco-Hellenistic ideas cannot be ruled out, particularly Platonism (*see* PLATO), the background to this form of religious observance is to be found in the ascetical practices of certain forms of sectarian Judaism. The level of purity demanded by the Qumran sect (see DEAD SEA SCROLLS) reflects the regulations with regard to sexual activity in Leviticus and the requirements laid upon men involved in a holy war in Deuteronomy (probably explaining the reference to virginity in Rev. 14: 4). Elsewhere there is evidence that asceticism was a central part of the mystical and *apocalyptic tradition of *Judaism (e.g. Dan. 10). The centrality of eschatological beliefs for Christianity meant that from the earliest period there was a marked component of Christian practice which demanded a significant distance from the values and culture of the present age. The hope for the coming of a new age of perfection in which members of the Church could already participate placed rigorous demands on those who would join. Some evidence suggests that baptized men and women thought that they had to live like angels (cf. Luke 20: 35), putting aside all those constraints of present bodily existence which were incompatible with their eschatological state. *Paul's approach in 1 Cor. 7 in dealing with the rigorist lifestyle of the Corinthian ascetics is typical of the compromise that evolved, in which there is a grudging acceptance of marriage and an exaltation of celibacy. The emerging monastic movement, therefore, drew on a long history of ascetical practice which was taken to extremes in some rigorist circles.

childbirth In Greek tradition, childbirth ritually polluted those present because blood was shed, and delivery on sacred ground was therefore forbidden (see POLLUTION). Olympian goddesses are not represented as giving birth. The deities most often invoked in labour were *Artemis*Eileithyia (sometimes regarded as separate deities) or *Hera in Greece, *Juno Lucina in Rome. Roman childbirth rituals are briefly described by *Augustine, but his source is the antiquarian *Varro rather than common practice. There are also allusions to rituals in which the father lifts the child from the earth (*tollere liberum*) or carries the child round the hearth (*amphidromia*), but these would not always be practicable—for instance, in a house with no central hearth or when the baby was born on the upper floor of a tenement—and it was the name-day celebration, approximately ten days after the birth, which publicly acknowledged the child as a family member. See also CARMENTIS, KOUROTROPHOS.

[Augustine, *City of God* 6. 9]

children Various rituals might mark the birth of a child and its acceptance into the family. In Athens a ceremony called the *amphidromia*, held probably on the fifth day after birth, signalled a child's entry into the family. Soon afterwards boys were registered in hereditary associations known as *phratries. A variety of *rites of passage for males signalled the end of childhood in the Greek world. The Roman equivalent to the *amphidromia* was the *lustratio*, 'purification', which took place on the eighth or ninth day. There was no subsequent ceremony of incorporation for Roman children. Childhood ended for boys around 16 with the putting on of the plain white adult toga in place of the *toga praetexta* with red border. There is no secure evidence of any puberty ceremonies for girls in either the Greek or Roman world, although it has been claimed that the *arkteia* functioned as such in Athens (see BRAURON). Many religious ceremonies have been interpreted by modern scholars as originally *rites of passage for age-groups (see INITIATION), but it is doubtful whether they were understood in this way in the Classical period.

Largely because of their ritual purity children played a significant role in religion, singing in choirs and even serving as priests. Especially important was the *pais amphithalēs* or *camillus, a child whose parents were both still alive and so had not been polluted by contact with the dead.

Chimaera ('she-goat'), bizarre monster slain by *Bellerophon, according to Homer composed of 'lion in front, snake behind, and she-goat in the middle'; in art the central head (sometimes a bust with forefeet) which protrudes uneasily from the lion's back may be made less laughable by allowing it to perform the fire-breathing which Homer and Hesiod describe. The latter assigns it to the monstrous family of *Typhon and *Echidna, while Homer claims it was reared by 'Amisodarus'.

[Homer, *Iliad* 6. 179–82, 16. 328; Hesiod, *Theogony* 319 ff.]

Chiron *See* CENTAURS.

Chloë, i.e. 'green', title of *Demeter as goddess of the young green crops. She had a shrine near the Acropolis at Athens and a festival, the Chloia, perhaps on Thargelion 6 (*see* ATHENS, RELIGIOUS TOPOGRAPHY; CALENDAR, GREEK).

chorēgia At Athens the *chorēgia* was a *leitourgia* (*liturgy), or public service performed by a wealthy citizen for the city. A *chorēgos* (literally 'leader of a chorus') was responsible for the recruitment, training, maintenance, and costuming of *choreutai* (members of a chorus) for competitive performance at a festival.

The *chorēgia* was central to the organization and funding of the dramatic *festivals in Athens and its local communities. The actors were appointed and remunerated by the city, but the chorus involved the main part of the expense in these productions. In the Great *Dionysia, the main dramatic festival held annually, choruses were required for each of the various genres of performance: five for comedy (with 24 *choreutai* in each), three for tragedy and satyr-play (12 or 15 *choreutai*) and ten each for the two categories of dithyramb, men's and boys' (50 *choreutai*). The competition at these festivals was as much between rival *chorēgoi* and their choruses as between poets, and the efforts of a *chorēgos* could be a crucial factor for the success of a dramatic entry.

Chorēgoi for dithyramb at the Great Dionysia were chosen by the ten *phylai ('tribes') and the *chorēgos* represented his *phylē* in the competition. *Chorēgoi* for tragedy and, until the mid-4th cent., for comedy at the Great Dionysia were appointed by the *archōn eponymos*, for the *Lenaea by the *archōn basileus*, from the richest Athenians liable for the duty. After that time comic *chorēgoi* were chosen by the *phylai*.

Christianity Classicists have traditionally found interesting both the Christian cult itself and Christian attitudes to Greek and Roman culture and the imperial state. Recent research encourages equal attention to the *Jews. Christianity began as a Jewish sect and changed its relationship with the Jewish community at a time when both groups were affected by later Hellenism. Christians laid claim to an antiquity rooted in the history of ancient Israel, while at the same time they sought the tolerance, interest, and loyalty of the pagans around them.

The first followers of Jesus inhabited a political system, the Roman empire, that regarded Jews as singular. Strategic prudence had recognized in *Herod the Great (confirmed as king of *Judaea in 40 BC) a useful ally against opponents of Roman expansion and against rivals for power in Rome itself. The Jews, *monotheists who identified closely their religion and their ethnicity, survived thus in the Roman context only because exceptions were made: suspending in this instance a characteristic readiness to absorb the religion of an alien people, Rome allowed them a controlled political independence in several territories (although Judaea itself, after Herod's death, passed under direct administration).

Many Jews lived willingly with resulting contradictions. Yet such compromise had long caused division among them. Following the conquests of Alexander the Great, greater contact with Hellenistic culture had seemed advantageous to some; but the resolution of the 'devout' and the revolt of the *Maccabees had shown that traditional values were far from dead. Now the encroachment of Rome gave new edge to revulsion from the Gentile world, and the frequent brutality of the conquerors strengthened the hand of those more dubious about the benefits of alliance.

Jesus lived, therefore, in a divided Palestine. The rule of Rome and the fortunes of her Jewish allies seemed secure; but the cruelty of Herod had kept alive strong forces of resistance and revolt. One cannot avoid asking where Jesus stood on issues of religious and political loyalty, although his native Galilee was subject to a local ruler rather than a Roman governor during his lifetime.

It is likely that Jesus reflected several tendencies in the Judaism of his day. Followers saw him variously as a forerunner of the *rabbis, holy man, wonder-worker, rebel, and prophet. Attempts to decide how he saw himself have proved difficult. When we set side by side the NT (New Testament) reports and our knowledge of Galilee at the time, the wonder-working holy man appears his most likely guise. He emphasized the imminent ending of the visible world and the judgement of God upon it. He promoted also a sense of liberty, to be enjoyed by those willing to repudiate family, career, and a sense of 'sin'. That, and the number of his followers in the volatile atmosphere of *Jerusalem at pilgrimage time, was enough to set him at odds with the Jewish high-priestly establishment, wedded to the social order required by Rome.

Those who had not known Jesus well, if at all, were less simple and less dramatic in their interpretations. The NT reveals how they broadened the religious context within which he was seen as significant, in pagan as well as Jewish terms. They also postponed the consummation he had seemed to herald. Partly as a consequence, they felt it proper to debate the value and authority of the Roman dispensation and the contrasting force of Jewish tradition. They also passed judgement on Temple and synagogue. Those characteristic centres of Jewish cult did not differ entirely from other religious traditions. In spite of strident voices defending the unique and separate quality of their life, some elements of the religious practice of the Jews

invited comparison with *paganism. Blood *sacrifice, priesthood, ritual purity, dietary law, the preservation and study of sacred texts, speculation about the nature and purposes of God and about human virtue—all took a Jewish form but also identified Judaism as a religion among others: for those categories of thought and practice were familiar to many in the ancient world. Thus Christian criticism, operating within the Jewish tradition, highlighted a potential for realignment, inviting the attachment of additional or alternative meanings to the religious practice of the Jews themselves.

At a time, therefore, when Jews were divided over the nature of their privilege and separation, one group among them began actively to seek recruits among the Gentiles. Distance from other Jews was not achieved simply. The destruction of the Temple in AD 70, occurring in the midst of the earliest Christian readjustment, was built into the Church's founding documents. The Jewish revolts of 115–17 and 132–5, however, attracted little Christian comment. The Church's distinctiveness, by then, was more obvious. Christian texts with a strong Jewish flavour, like 1 Clement (c.96) and Hermas' Shepherd (early to mid-2nd cent.), gave way to more deliberate competition for both respectability and a claim on the past. The 'apologist' *Justin Martyr (d. c.165), while defending his new religion against the Roman élite, asserted also against Jews, in his Dialogue with Trypho, Gentile claims to the heritage of Israel and a natural alliance between the OT (Old Testament) and classical cosmology.

*Origen of Alexandria (c.185–254) established in the next generation (especially after his move to Caesarea in 230) a new style of dialogue with Jews, all in pursuit of his own biblical research. The Jews in Palestine had by that time acquired new confidence, after the disasters of 66–73 and 132–5. Their rabbinic leaders had completed the publication of the *Mishnah; and, under the leadership of a Patriarch, a disciplined community had been set in place, contrasting markedly with enduring elements of Hellenistic Jewry elsewhere. Origen became the architect of a mature Christian biblical exegesis. His purpose was to demonstrate in Christianity the fulfilment of OT prophecy. He focused, as had Justin, more on the significance of Jesus than on the inadequacy of the Law. A 'spiritual' understanding was required to detect fulfilment, assisted to a limited extent by the allegory beloved of *Philon (1). Yet Origen remained dependent on the Jewish exegesis he hoped to undermine. His most notable attack on paganism, the *Against Celsus*, required extensive defence of Jewish thought. His more homiletic works addressed an enduring ambiguity in Christian life, affected by converts from Judaism only slightly less exaggerated or precise in their mixed loyalty than the Ebionites and Nazarenes of the age.

Origen's African contemporary, *Tertullian (c.160–225), is noted chiefly for rigorist theology (reflecting in part an admiration for the martyrs) and for attacks on *Gnosticism. Tertullian probably had little to do with real Jews. His work *Against the Jews* was chiefly directed against pagans. It was, rather, the gnosticizing Marcion (d. c.160) who led Tertullian to develop his views on the justice and providence of the OT God and the status of Jesus as Messiah. (Marcion, for his part, had appeared to reject the OT dispensation completely.) Displaying in the process some debt to *Melito of Sardis (d. c.AD 190) and *Irenaeus (d. c.AD 200), as well as to Justin, Tertullian thus transmitted a specifically western approach to OT exegesis that influenced his fellow Africans *Cyprian (d. 258) and *Augustine (354–430) and all Latin theology.

The real sense, however, of a seamless inclusion of the OT within the Christian tradition came with *Eusebius of Caesarea (c.260–c.340). He had been reared in the tradition of Origen. Famous for his *History of the Church*, which contributed much to a sense of continuity between the orthodox Christians of Constantine's reign and the faith and practice of the Apostolic age, his *Prepar-* *ation of the Gospel* and *Demonstration of the Gospel* are no less significant for their Christian appropriation of the Hebrew past.

The toleration of Christianity by the Roman state made it less necessary to compete with Judaism for the favour of the state and heralded a sharp decline in Jewish–Christian relations. Yet the arrogant vitriol of John *Chrysostom (c.347–407) shows that a challenge from Jewish ideas was still perceived by Christians, at least at Antioch, centuries after the death of Jesus. Unflagging antagonism remained a major engine of the Church's development, compelling it to adopt yet more distinguishing forms and attitudes of its own. The differences between Christianity and Judaism apparent or desirable in 4th-cent. eyes were, naturally, not those that had struck Hermas or Justin. Even *Jerome (d. 420), Scripture scholar though he was, found himself in circumstances very different from those of Origen. Yet the shifting quality of the debate implied a lasting insecurity of definition. Faced from within by new divisions and critics of its administration and discipline, the 4th-cent. Church was still not ready to label itself finally. Moreover, the confidence of the Theodosian Code (laws published between 429 and 438) that heresy was a thing of the past proved laughable in the light of Monophysite secession and the persistent *Arianism of barbarians in the west.

In that long process of Christian self-definition in relation to Judaism, crucial in determining the character of Christianity itself, three sensitivities stand out, concerning sacrifice, text, and morality.

The interpretation of sacrifice separated Christians at an early stage. Jews retained an attachment to priest and victim, but in the context of the desert Tabernacle rather than the Temple (almost certainly by that time destroyed). From then on, Christians saw themselves as competing for the heritage of priesthood as well as of the synagogue tradition. The Church continued to emphasize the symbolic priesthood of the heavenly Jesus and developed its own priestly caste, which presided over a eucharistic cult with strong sacrificial elements. The word 'bishop' quickly acquired an official meaning (1 Tim. 3: 1); but clear priestly association with the Eucharist (absent in the *Didache*, where the bishop is seen as teacher and prophet, and vague in 1 *Clement*, in spite of an asserted need for succession, 44) does not occur until Ignatius of Antioch (d. *c.*107), *Letter to the Philadelphians* 4 (which links 'bishop' with 'Eucharist' and 'altar'). Subsequent development was inexorable; but not every Christian assembly demanded the presence and action of a bishop or priest until the 3rd cent.

Priesthood and sacrifice implied atonement: for sacrifice had to have a purpose. *Paul had presented the execution of Jesus as an expiation for sin (Col. 1: 20, Rom. 3: 25)—the sin of Adam and the sin of individual men and women. Christianity thus adopted on its own terms the historical perspective of restoration to God's favour enshrined in the Jewish Scriptures, paying less attention to political or tribal triumph in a Messianic age and more to cosmic and psychological divisions between creatures and creator, the defeat of sin and the heavenly destiny of redeemed humanity.

Christians argued against the Jewish interpretation of the texts that they shared. Christian appropriation demanded a new sense of what drove the ancient writers. God's words and actions and the inspired utterances of prophets were now focused on Jesus. The evident meaning of older texts had often to be wrenched so far in a new direction that 'exegesis', methodical interpretation, took centuries to achieve a Christian maturity and depended in part on the literary skills of the pagan élite. Once again, Origen illustrates the process. The allegorical tradition, filtered to some extent through Philon (1), allowed him access to the 'spiritual' meaning of the Bible; but other traditional skills of criticism and analysis were required, which the rabbis were equally aware of, and which Origen just as keenly applied. Moreover, since Jesus was an historical

figure, the prophecies typical of Scripture were, after the time of Jesus himself, robbed of further purpose. 'Prophecy' suddenly attracted suspicion in place of reverence. The most famous victims of that prejudice were the Montanists of the late 2nd and early 3rd cents. (*see* MONTANISM). Their combination of ecstatic prophecy, apocalyptic expectation, and ascetic rigour (which successfully attracted Tertullian) can be found thereafter in varying proportions among many movements both critical and schismatic. Opponents favoured a closed 'canon' of Scripture (finally achieved only in the 4th cent.): no documents later than a certain date were regarded as 'inspired'. Interpretation was no longer expected to yield surprise but simply reinforced a significance already totally achieved.

The attitudes that established a textual canon were also influential in defining authority: for one had to know who was entitled to expound the significance of Scripture. Agreement on that issue kept pace with the developing style of Christian priesthood: in the end, the bishop and his assistants claimed exclusive rights to exegesis, just as they claimed the right to preside over the sacrificial cult of the church.

Finally, Christians developed a new moral theory not based on the OT; and that, too, served to separate them from Jewish contemporaries. Their emphasis was on love, as opposed to law—such were the terms in which they explained themselves, though with little justice to the Jews. They tapped other ethical traditions also: later *Stoicism especially. Increasing sophistication can be traced through the *Shepherd*, the 2nd-cent. *Sentences of Sextus*, and the *Pedagogue* of *Clement of Alexandria (*c.*150–*c.*215). The Greek ascetic tradition made its appeal to the more committed. Surprise at a failure in love would be naïve: more significant was the enduring Christian attachment to law (which made anti-Jewish polemic a tortured enterprise). With the tolerance of Constantine, the Church was ready to take advantage of the law of the state. For some time, however, it had been developing its own legal system, represented by the decrees of Church councils, of which the archetype is described in Acts 15. Other early councils, of the 2nd cent., were mustered against perceived errors such as those of Montanism or in relation to the date of Easter—a sensitive issue vis-à-vis the Jews. Evidence of gathering momentum is provided by African practice in the 3rd cent. Council decisions continued to focus mainly on ecclesiastical order; but moral prescriptions were frequently implied or stated and spilled inevitably into the lives of ordinary men and women.

The Christian cult acquired, under the same influence, an increasingly formal character. The development of a calendar, particularly relating to the ceremonies of initiation during Lent and Easter, augmented by the celebration of Epiphany and, later, Christmas and by commemorations of the martyrs, enfolded Christians in a detailed regime. A series of strictures and public ceremonies impinged upon the wayward, involving a modicum of public shame and defining the steps whereby they might be reconciled to both God and their fellows. All Christians, to a greater or lesser degree, were exhorted to undertake a life of self-discipline, marked by traditionally habitual patterns of prayer, fasting, and generosity.

While thus strengthening its self-definition against Judaism, Christianity faced the task of relating to other cults. It presented itself from an early stage as a universal religion. It did not merely invite adherence but demanded it: all men and women were thought able to achieve their destiny only within its embrace. One possible response to so aggressive an invitation was resentment; and here we touch upon the so-called 'persecution' of Christianity by the Roman state. Legal proceedings against the Church were intermittent and often moderate; violent demonstrations outside the law were unusual. The heroism revered in the *Acts of the Martyrs* seems to have been invited as often as it was imposed (*see* MARTYRS, CHRISTIAN). Nevertheless, we find occasional confrontation. The famous attack by Nero on Christians in Rome in 64 had no lasting impact or significance. The traditionally accepted oppression by Domitian in the 90s has gained its notoriety mostly from the misleading obscurity of Melito. More generally significant in political terms may have been the situation described in Pliny's *Letter* (10. 96 f.) of AD 112; but Trajan's insistence on the observance of legal procedure and the avoidance of harassment says as much as his governor's distaste. Christians in that period may have attracted suspicion partly through a presumed association with rebellious Jews. As the political hopes of the Jews began to fade and the self-effacing preoccupations of rabbinic society gathered strength, Christians were exposed as possible enemies of the state in their own right. It was then that famous martyrs made their names— *Polycarp of Smyrna and *Justin Martyr in 165 and those condemned at Lugdunum (Lyon) in 177. Yet the pleas of Melito and *Athenagoras cannot disguise the local quality of such reversals. Outbursts under Septimius Severus and Maximinus Thrax were similarly limited. It was not until the middle of the 3rd cent. that forceful opposition was sanctioned by central authority. Severe threats to the stability of the state had by that time fostered new anxieties about loyalty; but the growing strength of the Church made it less susceptible to intolerance. The short-lived brutality of *Decius (249–51) and the dissipated attacks of Valerian (253–60) were foiled by that resilience—proven as much by the Church's readmission of the weak as by its admiration for the strong. The new confidence was even more evident under the *Diocletianic persecution from 303 until Galerius' deathbed surrender in 311.

Throughout the prior period, several paradoxes had been laid bare, connected with the universal vision of the Church, the analogous breadth of Rome's claims to government, and its desire to tolerate nevertheless a variety of religious beliefs and practices. State and Church faced similar problems: how should one balance universalist demands and individual variety? The state's solution was to demand, in the interest of unity, a minimum but inescapable conformity in religious practice and to display, when it came to controlling belief, a prudent reticence. The devotee of an alien cult should not oppose, at least, the gods of Rome. The difference between loyalty to the empire and enthusiasm for local deities was more easily made clear with the growth of the imperial (*ruler-) cult (which called for the simplest obeisance) and the extension of citizenship by the Antonine Constitution of 212. Christians resolutely branded that policy a subterfuge, demanding particular rights for what they thought of in their case as absolute values, undermining at once the freedom of the individual and the authority of the state.

They pursued the same embarrassing tactics in their broader dialogue with the classical world. As they acquired the vocabulary and adopted the habits of Greek philosophy, so they began to make their own points on the issues that philosophy had traditionally addressed: the nature of the divine and the visible world, the significance of texts, the canons of moral education and behaviour, the uses of ritual, the shape of history, and the character of its major figures. Such usurpation made them eventually impossible to ignore. The stages of encroachment are represented by the very writers who composed polemic against the Jews—1 Clement, the *apologists, the Alexandrians, and the Africans—and culminate in the added reflection that came with more assured success in the 4th cent. Cappadocians and the writings of *Ambrose and Augustine. Method counted for as much as ideas: for with genre—letter, dialogue, homily, or life—Christians absorbed models as well as techniques, which affected their notions of community and conviction as much as of virtue or divinity. Thus they invaded the classrooms, libraries, temples, and debating-chambers of their adversaries long before they gained positions of public authority and power. Infuriatingly, they began to impose peculiar meanings on what the majority of their fellows had long been accustomed to say: so, while they could appear reassuringly familiar and traditional as a Mediterranean cult among others, they were constantly found to be undermining that to which they appeared to subscribe.

Christian engagement with Jewish tradition and classical culture made a distinctive contribution to the religious life of the Mediterranean world. The Christian view of God was subtle. It combined attachment to transcendence and *monotheism with a sense of personal dynamism in the godhead—potent, purposeful, and affectionate. Correspondingly, the relation of the individual to that divinity engaged every level of human experience, bodily and spiritual, from hunger, fear, and desire to insight and self-sacrifice. Such beliefs were made formal in the doctrines of the Trinity and the Incarnation, both in their way indebted to pagan and Jewish antecedents. There was also in Christianity a clear system of authority and leadership: the bishop was its own brilliant, proper, and lasting creation. Heir to Jewish priesthood and biblical learning, he provided both the focus and the generative impulse, through baptism and mission, for a stable community. The sacramental liturgy, reinforced by singing, processions, and the veneration of dead heroes and exemplars, enabled the Church to act out its beliefs through symbol and recollection. The past was especially valuable to the Christian, once correctly understood. The canon of sacred texts, the succession of priests, the interpretations of scripture, and the customs of discipline and worship all conspired to produce a vision of where time was leading the Church and rescued it from the disoriented ambiguities of *Gnosticism. Finally, Christians developed their own morality, founded on the conviction that each person was created by God and destined for his lasting company; a morality that valued, therefore, the whole human being, refined by continence, expanded by selfless generosity, and rewarded by bodily resurrection.

Such, at least, was the 'orthodox' view; but it was never taken for granted. 'Orthodoxy' was established only slowly and was constantly challenged by men and women who claimed the title 'Christian'. The nature of their dissent or variety sprang in part from the fact that they had found other ways of relating to Jewish and pagan tradition. A more anthropomorphic view of God, indifference to sacramental worship, suspicion of the clergy and preference for charismatic leadership and personal inspiration, a love of myths and symbols in the place of literal history, mistrust of the *body and a corresponding desire for 'spiritual' experience and fulfilment—all such emphases diffracted the pattern of Christian development, yet seemed no less Christian for that. It is neither possible nor just to isolate groups that represented those tendencies precisely: that was the ploy of their enemies. What seemed clear choices in the cause of self-definition, especially when they attempted to exclude either pagans or Jews, were normally made in circumstances of confusion, which they by no means brought to an end. The tidy writings of Irenaeus and *Epiphanius of Salamis (d. 403) teem with supposedly undesirable eccentrics; but those 'heretics' may have seemed to others at the time no more than ordinary Christians. The image of the Gnostic or the Montanist, of the Encratite or rigorist ascetic, often the product of prejudice and horror, can disguise a more complicated variety that represented nevertheless the Christian norm.

We cannot content ourselves, therefore, with a straightforward account of Christian triumph over pagan and Jew. It was simply that certain answers to fundamental questions began to seem more acceptable to some Mediterranean people—answers in a debate pursued by some in all parties about the nature of creation, the destiny of the cosmos and the individual, the status of sacred texts, the substantiality of the visible world, the use of ritual and law, and the proper styles of religious authority. The new answers were thought to deserve the label 'Christian'; but what had happened was that the controlling element in a whole society had changed its mind about the meaning of history and experience.

Can we be sure about the scale of that development? It is impossible to judge the size of the Christian population at any one time. Surviving reports are marred by hyperbole, ignorance, and convention. Archaeology and inscriptions are statistically haphazard and impervious to individual sentiment. Suffice it to say that within certain urban communities, particularly in the east, Christians formed a sizeable minority and occasionally even a majority in the late 3rd cent. The difficult question is why. Breeding and friendship must have played a large part in the expansion of Christianity—perhaps always larger than that of convincing oratory. What remains textually of Christian address was not necessarily disseminated broadly. We know little more about the reception of the Christian message than we do about that of any ancient document. With the advent of toleration, it is likely that expediency, laziness, and fear played as much a part then as they do now. Talk of 'superstition' is misleading. Features of religious life supposedly attractive to a superstitious mind had always been available in traditional cult. The change of allegiance demands more subtle explanations. *See* JUDAISM; PAUL, ST.

Chronicon Paschale ('Easter Chronicle'), a universal history from Creation to *c.*AD 630. A particular concern is the establishment of chronological connections between Church feasts and the Creation and Incarnation; there are several computations and each year is dated by different methods. The anonymous narrative amalgamates Old and New Testament, Jewish, Christian, and secular material. The sixth-century AD author John Malalas was an important source for mythological events.

Chryseis, in *Homer's *Iliad* the daughter of Chryses, priest of *Apollo at Chryse in the Troad, who has been captured and awarded to *Agamemnon. On Agamemnon's refusal to let Chryses ransom her, Apollo sends a plague on the Greek camp. *Calchas explains the situation and Chryseis is returned, but Agamemnon takes Achilles' concubine *Briseis for himself, thus causing *Achilles' anger.

[Homer, *Iliad* 1. 11 ff.]

Chrysostom, John (*c.*AD 354–407), bishop of Constantinople. Though educated at Antioch by the pagan rhetorician Libanius, John turned to *asceticism at home and later became a hermit. Ordained deacon at Antioch in 381 and priest (386), and pre-eminently a preacher, he reluctantly became bishop of *Constantinople (398). Trouble with the empress Eudoxia, Theophilus of Alexandria, and Asiatic bishops resenting his extension of Constantinople's quasi-patriarchal authority, caused his deposition by the Synod of the Oak (403). He was banished, recalled, banished again to Armenia (404), and died in exile (407).

Most eloquent of preachers (hence his name Chrysostom, 'the golden-mouthed') but not an outstanding theologian, he expounded Scripture in the Antiochene tradition according to its historical sense, practically and devotionally. He has left commentaries on Genesis, the Gospels of Matthew and John, the *Acts of the Apostles and all the Epistles of *Paul. Denunciation of luxury, care for the poor, and interest in education are characteristic. The *Liturgy of Chrysostom* is not his work.

chthonian gods, literally gods of the earth, *chthōn*, a subdivision of the Greek pantheon. In this usage, *chthonios* gets its meaning from a contrast, implicit or explicit, with 'Olympian' or 'heavenly' gods. Gods can be chthonian in two ways.

1. *Chthonios* was applied as a cult-title to individual gods, notably *Hermes, *Demeter, *Hecate, *Zeus, and (once) Ge (*Gaia), Earth, herself. This usage goes back, in the case of Zeus, to *Homer and *Hesiod. The epithet was normally given to a god who was connected with both the upper and the lower worlds, and served to show that in a particular ritual context it was the chthonian aspect that was being appealed to. The case of Zeus Chthonios is more complicated, since in some contexts he seems to be less 'Zeus when active in the Underworld' than a distinct figure, 'the Underworld equivalent to Zeus', i.e. Hades.

2. A general division between Olympian and chthonian gods is sometimes made, first apparent to us in *Aeschylus. In such references the *chthonioi* are not listed; if pressed to do so, unnaturally, a Greek would doubtless have named *Hades/Pluton, *Persephone, the Eumenides (*see* ERINYES), and similar figures, and probably the heroes too. Scholars often, more questionably, extend the list to include powers such as Zeus *Meilichios who are not explicitly associated with the earth but share characteristics with those which are.

In modern accounts, the Olympian/ chthonian distinction is often elevated into a fundamental principle structuring the whole of Greek mythology and ritual. But the Olympio-chthonian gods of type (1) straddle the great divide; and the modern distinction between Olympian and chthonian forms of sacrificial ritual distorts a different distinction that the ancients drew, between 'divine' and 'heroic' forms of sacrifice. (Divergences from the standard type of sacrifice did indeed occur in the cult of the chthonians, but not always, and not there alone.) The point is not simply that the question 'Olympian or chthonian?' is sometimes unanswerable, but that in many contexts the Greeks might simply not have felt the need to ask it.

churches (early Christian) The first Christians met in the private houses of the faithful. Gradually, as local Christian communities became more established both in numbers and in wealth, they might acquire their own church-houses, using them specifically as places of worship and for other religious activities, such as the granting of charity and the instruction of converts. Externally these buildings looked just like other private houses, though internally they might be adapted for their new function, for instance by combining rooms to create a large enough space for worship. The best example of an early church-house is that excavated at Dura-Europus on the Euphrates: an ordinary town house, built around AD 200, adapted for Christian use before 231, and destroyed when the city walls were reinforced in 257. Before the conversion of *Constantine I, and his conquest of the empire between 312 and 324, some Christian communities may already have commissioned halls specifically for worship, and certainly small shrines, such as the 2nd-cent. *aedicula* over the supposed tomb of St Peter in Rome (*see* VATICAN), were already being built over the bodies of the martyrs.

However, the accession of an emperor with Christian sympathies and the granting of security, wealth, and privileged status to the Church transformed church building. Large buildings were constructed inside towns, to serve as halls of worship for the rapidly expanding Christian community, and outside, to glorify the shrines of the martyrs and to serve as the focus for Christian burial-grounds. The pace of building differed according to circumstance. For instance, in Rome itself massive investment by Constantine rapidly gave the city one huge intramural church (St John Lateran) and a string of martyr-churches outside the walls (St Peter's, S. Agnese, S. Lorenzo, SS. Marcellino e Pietro, and the first church of St Paul). However, in many provincial towns the earliest substantial church buildings may often have been of the late 4th, or even of the 5th cent.

The Christians wished their buildings to look different from pagan shrines, and their principal need was for large halls that could contain many people worshipping together, unlike pagan temples which were mainly conceived of as homes for the gods

and their statues, and internally as the focus of rituals involving few people at a time. The principal influence on early Christian architecture was, therefore, not the pagan *temple, but the great secular meeting-hall of antiquity, the *basilica. Christian basilicas varied greatly in detail (i.e. with or without aisles, galleries, apses, transepts, etc), but all shared in common the aim of containing many people at one time, with an architectural, decorative, and liturgical focus on one end of the building, where the clergy officiated at the altar (which in many cases was sited over the body of a saint). Alongside the prevalent rectangular basilicas, other types of church existed, such as centrally planned and domed churches, of which the most famous examples are the 4th-cent. S. Lorenzo in Milan (Mediolanum), and the 6th-cent. S. Vitale in Ravenna and S. Sophia in *Constantinople.

Probably because more happened inside churches than inside temples (which were often the backdrop to ceremonies performed outside), the main focus of decoration tended to be internal. Many late antique churches, like S. Vitale at Ravenna, are plain structural shells on the outside, but inside are lavishly decorated with marble fittings, veneer, and floor- and wall-mosaics; and would once also have been filled with gold and silver plate and fittings, and with drapes of precious fabrics.

Cicero (Marcus Tullius Cicero, 106–43 BC). Among Cicero's philosophical works are two written in 45–44 BC which are very largely concerned with theological questions. First is *De natura deorum* in three books, each devoted to the view of a different school (*Epicurean, *Stoic, Academic) on the nature of the gods and the existence of the divine, its role in human culture and the state. Having allowed Cotta to present the sceptical Academic view in book 3, after Velleius' presentation of the Epicurean in book 1, and Balbus' of the Stoic in book 2, Cicero rounds off the debate with a typically Academic expression of his own opinion: that the Stoic's argument is more likely to be right (3. 95). In the second, the two books of the *De divinatione*, published just after Caesar's murder, Stoic beliefs concerning Fate and the possibility of prediction are examined, with more use of anecdote and quotation perhaps indicative of a popular exposition. In this case Cicero displays no sympathy with the views of the Stoics, whose commitment to the validity of *divination was based on complex principles of logic and cosmic sympathy. Cicero's pious reaffirmation (2. 148) of his belief in the existence of a divine being, maintaining that it is prudent to keep traditional rites and ceremonies, belies his concerns in matters of theology and religion for the state above all else.

Cineas, (?) Thessalian *founder of Ai Khanoum (in modern Afghanistan) to whom, as *archēgetēs*, *hero-cult was paid, on the evidence of an interesting verse inscription put up at the instance of *Aristotle's pupil Clearchus of Soli.

Cinyras, legendary king of Cyprus; in *Homer's *Iliad*, he is the donor of *Agamemnon's magnificent inlaid corslet, and thereafter becomes a byword for wealth. Some authors make him an immigrant from Syria, and he is strongly associated with the cult of *Aphrodite at *Paphos, whose priests traced their descent back to him. His devotion to the goddess did not however save him from being tricked into bed by his daughter *Myrrha; though *Apollodorus makes the child of that incestuous union, *Adonis, a legitimate son by his wife Metharme.

[Homer, *Iliad* 11. 20 ff.; Apollodorus 3. 14. 3; Tacitus, *Histories* 2. 3]

Circe, powerful sorceress of mythology, daughter of *Helios and the Oceanid Perse. *Homer places her island of Aeaea at the extreme east of the world, but as early as *Hesiod she is associated also with the west and frequently placed at Monte Circeo on the coast of Latium; this is standard in later authors. In the *Odyssey*, Circe transforms a group of *Odysseus' men into pigs (though they retain human intelligence); Odysseus rescues them by resisting the goddess' magic, thanks to the power of the plant 'moly' which *Hermes gives him. Odysseus and his men stay with her for a year, after which she dispatches them to the Underworld to consult *Tiresias. On their return she gives them more detailed instructions as to how to confront the perils of the homeward journey. In the cyclic *Telegonia* (*see* EPIC CYCLE), her son by Odysseus, Telegonus, accidentally killed his father when raiding Ithaca, and she herself married *Telemachus. As Aeëtes' sister, she has a prominent role in Apollonius' *Argonautica* in which she cleanses *Jason and *Medea after their treacherous killing of Medea's brother Apsyrtus; it is probable that Apollonius was not the first poet to associate her with the Argonautic voyage (*see* ARGONAUTS). Moralists frequently interpreted Circe as a symbol of luxury and wantonness, the pursuit of which turns men into beasts.

[Homer, *Odyssey* 10. 135–545, 12. 8–164; Hesiod, *Theogony* 1011–16; Apollonius Rhodius, *Argonauts* 4. 557–752]

city-founders *See* FOUNDERS, CITY.

Claros, *oracle and grove of *Apollo belonging to the city of Colophon. The oracle appears to have been founded by the 8th cent. BC, as stories about its foundation appear in the *Epigoni*, attributing the foundation to Manto, *Hesiod mentions the site in connection with a contest between the seers *Calchas and *Mopsus, and it is mentioned as a residence of Apollo in the Homeric *Hymn to Apollo*. The sanctuary was discovered in 1907, and an excavation, begun under the direction of Louis Robert in the 1950s, turned up the oracular chamber under the temple and numerous inscriptions relating to its operation. On the basis of these inscriptions and literary texts, we know that there were 'sacred nights' upon which the consultations would take place, when there would be a procession of consultants to the temple of Apollo with sacrifices and singing of hymns. Consultants would then hand over questions to the priests who would descend into the adytum (innermost sanctuary), through the blue marble-faced corridors underneath the temple, to a place outside the room in which the divine spring flowed. Within this room the *thespiōdos*, a man, would drink from the spring and utter his responses to the questions of each consultant. These would then be written down in verse by the *prophētēs* and delivered to the consultants. An inscription of Hellenistic date confirms Tacitus' statement that the Colophonians imported people of Ionian descent to act as prophets (*thespiōdoi*), though he confuses the issue by mentioning only one official instead of two.

Inscriptions are now revealing the nature of Claros' clientele among the cities of Asia Minor and further afield in greater detail. These inscriptions, along with various discussions in the literature of the empire, reveal that Claros was one of the most important oracular sites in Asia Minor from roughly the 3rd cent. BC to the mid-3rd cent. AD. A number of responses are preserved on inscriptions and in fragmentary texts.

[Tacitus, *Annals* 2. 54. 2–3; Aelius Aristides, *Sacred Tales* 3. 10–11; Iamblichus, *On Mysteries* 3. 11]

Cleanthes of Assos (331–232 BC), student of Zeno and his successor as head of the Stoa (*see* STOICISM). His religious spirit is distinctive; after the writings of Chrysippus established a Stoic orthodoxy, this came to seem less central. We have a long fragment of his *Hymn to Zeus*, which allegorizes the active principle of Stoic physics and displays a distinctive use of the ideas of the pre-Socratic philosopher Heraclitus. He was interested in the detail of Stoic physics, and wrote on the nature of the cosmos, stressing the role of fire. His version of ethics uncompromisingly stressed the distinctive value of virtue and downplayed the importance of factors like pleasure. He denied the usefulness of moral rules unless based on an understanding of basic principles, and even in consolatory writings urged the import-ance of understanding general principles, rather than their applications.

Cleidemus, or Cleitodemus (writing between 378 and 340 BC), expert in ceremonial ritual (**exēgētēs*), was considered in antiquity the first 'atthidographer' or local historian of Attica (*see* ATTHIS). His work was probably titled *Prōtogonia*. It comprised no more than four books. We have 25 fragments. Those from the first two books concern the mythical period to 683/2; those from books 3 and 4 more recent history. Like other atthidographers he wrote with a democratic and patriotic bias. From the fragments we can see that he rationalized myth and used etymology.

Clement of Alexandria (Titus Flavius Clemens) was born *c.*AD 150, probably at Athens and of pagan parents. He was converted to *Christianity and after extensive travels to seek instruction from Christian teachers received lessons from Pantaenus, whose instructional school in Alexandria was then an unofficial institution giving tuition to converts. Clement affects a wide acquaintance with Greek literature, since his writings abound in quotations from *Homer, *Hesiod, the dramatists, and the Platonic and Stoic philosophers (*see* PLATO; STOICISM). However, it is clear that he made much use of anthologies of favourite passages. His *Protrepticus* is a copious source of information about the Greek *mysteries, though his wish to represent them as a perversion of Scriptural teachings must have led to misrepresentation. After ordination he succeeded Pantaenus as head of the school some time before 200, and held the office till 202, when, on the eve of the persecution under Septimius Severus, he left Alexandria and took refuge, perhaps with his former pupil Alexander, then bishop of Cappadocia and later of Jerusalem. Clement died between 211 and 216.

Much of his writing is lost, but the following survive nearly complete: (1) The *Protrepticus* or 'Hortatory Address to the Greeks' (*c.*190), designed to prove the superiority of

Christianity to pagan cults and way of life. (2) The *Paedagogus* or 'Tutor' (*c.*190–2), an exposition of the moral teaching of Christ, not only in general, but also with application to such details as eating, drinking, dress, and use of wealth. (3) The *Stromateis* or 'Miscellanies' (probably *c.*200–2) in eight books, the first seven attempting a construction of Christian philosophy with its centre in Christ the *logos* and the word of Scripture; book 5. 9, with its justification of *allegory as a way of saying what cannot be spoken, points the way to negative theology; the eighth book is a fragment on logic. (4) The *Excerpta ex Theodoto*, which follow in one MS, is a collection of dicta by a Valentinian heretic, of whom Clement, who calls himself a Gnostic, seems not to disapprove (*see* GNOSTICISM). (5) *Eclogae propheticae* are also attached to this MS. (6) The *Quis dives salvetur?* is a homily urging detachment from (though not necessarily renunciation of) worldly goods. Clement added little to dogma, but his philosophy points the way to *Origen, and, as in the case of the latter, prevented his being regarded as a saint.

Clement of Rome, author of an epistle (*c.*AD 96) from the Roman Church, rebuking the Corinthian Church for arbitrarily deposing clergy. This letter is remarkable, in a largely pacifist Church, for its use of martial imagery. Clement has been identified improbably with *Flavius Clemens and more probably with Peter's successor as bishop of Rome. The *Clementina* say that he is of Caesar's household, but associate neither him nor Peter with Rome.

The chief of the numerous works attributed to him are (1) the *Second Epistle*, a mid-2nd-cent. sermon on virginity of uncertain origin; (2) *Apostolic Constitutions*, eight books of law and liturgy, *c.*375, of which the seventh contains Hellenistic–Jewish prayers; and (3) the *Clementine Romance*, which combines an apologetic dialogue featuring Clement as the adversary of *Apion with an account of Peter's legendary encounter with Simon Magus. The plot which brings the two

together substitutes domestic separation and reunion for the erotic stereotypes of pagan novels. This romance survives in two 4th-cent. versions, neither of which fully represents the original, which appeared between the 2nd and 4th cents.

Cleobis and Biton, the two Argive brothers mentioned by the Athenian 'wise man' Solon to the Lydian ruler Croesus, in Herodotus' story, as among the happiest of mortals. Their mother, presumably as *Cicero says, a priestess of *Hera, found that her oxen were not brought in time for a festival, and they drew her cart the 45 stades (*c.*8 km: *c.*5 mi.) to the temple. She prayed to the goddess to grant them the greatest boon possible for mortals, and Hera caused them to die while they slept in the temple. The Argives honoured them with statues at *Delphi. A pair of *kouros*-statues from Delphi, long thought to be inscribed with their names, may, according to a controversial rereading, represent the *Dioscuri.
[Herodotus 1. 31; Cicero, *Tusculans* 1. 47]

Clitumnus, a river near Trebiae in Umbria, famous for the white sacrificial cattle on its banks. It flowed into the Tinia, and subsequently into the *Tiber. Shrines of the personified Clitumnus and other deities adorned its source, attracting numerous tourists. *See* RIVER-GODS.
[Virgil, *Georgics* 2. 146; Pliny, *Letters* 8. 8; Suetonius, *Caligula* 43]

Cloelia, a Roman girl given as hostage to Porsenna. She escaped across the Tiber to Rome, by swimming or on horseback, but was handed back to Porsenna who, admiring her bravery, freed her and other hostages. An equestrian statue on the via Sacra later celebrated her exploit. Critics who dismiss the story as legend believe that the statue was dedicated to a goddess (*Venus Equestris?) and that later Romans wrongly associated it with Cloelia.

clubs Greek clubs, sacred and secular, are attested as early as the time of Solon, one of whose laws gave legal validity to their regulations, unless they were contrary to the laws of the state;. Although we hear of political clubs at Athens in the 5th cent. BC, in the Classical period the societies known to us are mostly religious, carrying on the cult of some hero or god not yet recognized by the state, such as the votaries (see ORGEONES) of Amynus, *Asclepius, and Dexion, the heroized *Sophocles. In Hellenistic times, clubs become much more frequent and varied, and though many of them have religious names and exercise primarily religious functions, their social and economic aspects become increasingly prominent and some of them are purely secular. Among the religious guilds a leading place is taken by the Dionysiac artists (see DIONYSUS, ARTISTS OF). See also THIASOS.

The Latin words corresponding most closely to the English 'club' are *collegium and sodalitas (see SODALES). The former was the official title of the four great priestly colleges, *pontifices, *septemviri epulones, *quindecimviri sacris faciundis, and *augures, and the word had religious associations even when the object of the club was not primarily worship. Few, if any, collegia were completely secular. Some took their name from a deity or deities, e.g. *Diana et *Antinous, *Aesculapius and Hygia (see HYGIEIA), *Hercules, *Silvanus, and their members were styled cultores. Even when their name was not associated with a god, collegia often held their meetings in temples and their clubhouse (schola) might bear the name of a divinity. The collegia illustrate the rule that all ancient societies from the family upwards had a religious basis. Collegia are associated with trades and professions (merchants, scribes, workers in wood and metal) and also with districts (vici) of the city of Rome. The annual festival of the districts was the Compitalia, held at the turn of the calendar year, which celebrated the *Lares of the Crossroads.

Plutarch attributes to *Numa Pompilius the foundation of certain collegia but it is doubtful whether many existed before the Second Punic War (218–201 BC). There were no legal restrictions on association down to the last century of the republic though the action taken by the senate against the Bacchanales (see BACCHANALIA) in 186 BC shows that the government might intervene against an objectionable association. Although many collegia were composed of men practising the same craft or trade, there is no evidence that their object was to maintain or improve their economic conditions. In most cases they were probably in name burial clubs, while their real purpose was to foster friendliness and social life among their members.

Clymene, name of a dozen different heroines (for one see CATREUS), the best known being the mother of *Phaethon, wife of Merops, king of Ethiopia. Meaning simply 'famous', it is a stopgap name, like Creusa, Leucippus, etc., used where there was no genealogical or other tradition.

Clymenus (1) Euphemistic epithet ('Renowned') of *Hades/Pluton, esp. as the husband of Kore (see PERSEPHONE). Pluton was worshipped by this title in his cult at Hermione in the Argolid; his temple stood opposite that of *Demeter Chthonia, whose foundation was ascribed to Clymenus, son of Phoroneus, and to his sister Chthonia. The variant form Periclymenus appears to have been literary rather than cultic. (2) Homonym shared by a dozen mythological figures. (a) The Argive (or Arcadian) Clymenus, son of Teleus (or Schoeneus), abducted and violated his daughter *Harpalyce just after her marriage to *Alastor. In revenge, she served the flesh of her younger brother, or that of the offspring from the incestuous union, to her father at a banquet. Harpalyce was transformed into a bird, the chalkis; Clymenus committed suicide. Hyginus has Harpalyce killed by Clymenus. (b) Boeotian, son of Presbon and king of the *Minyans at Orchomenus. He was murdered by Theban brawlers at the festival of *Poseidon at Onchestus. His son Erginus, an *Argonaut, attacked Thebes and was killed by *Heracles; his grandsons *Trophonius and Agamedes built the first stone temple for *Apollo at *Delphi. (c) Son of Orchomenus, perhaps the same as the son of Presbon. (*d*) Father of Eurydice, *Nestor's wife. Usually identified with the king of Orchomenus (*see b* and *c* above) in modern accounts. (*e*) Aetolian, son of Oeneus and Althaea. (*f*) Cretan, son of Cardys from Cydonia and in one version founder of the *Olympian Games.

[(2a) Parthenius, *Erotika Pathemata* (*Love Stories*) 13; Hyginus, *Fables* 206, 238, cf. 242, 246; (*b*) Pausanias 9. 37. 1–4; Apollodorus 2. 4. 11]

Clytemnestra (Clytaem(n)estra, Gk. *Klytaimnestra* or *Klytaimestra*; the shorter form is better attested); daughter of *Tyndareos and *Leda; sister of *Helen and the *Dioscuri; wife of *Agamemnon; mother of a son, *Orestes, and of three daughters, named by *Homer Chrysothemis, Laodice, and Iphianassa, although *Iphigenia, whom Homer does not mention, seems to be a later substitution for Iphianassa, as does *Electra for Laodice. During Agamemnon's absence at Troy she took his cousin *Aegisthus as a lover, and on Agamemnon's return home after the ten-year war they murdered him, along with his Trojan captive, *Cassandra. Years later Orestes avenged his father's murder by killing both Clytemnestra and Aegisthus.

Her legend was a favourite one from Homer on, and given a variety of treatments. Homer makes her a good but weak woman led astray by an unscrupulous Aegisthus, and 'hateful' or 'accursed' only in retrospect. Agamemnon is killed by Aegisthus, while Clytemnestra kills Cassandra. Here there is no direct mention of her own murder by Orestes, although it is implied. *Stesichorus blames *Aphrodite, who made Tyndareos' daughters unfaithful because he had neglected her. But it is *Aeschylus' Clytemnestra, in his *Oresteia* of 458 BC, who dominates the extant literature which incorporates this legend. Prior to Aeschylus, Aegisthus and Clytemnestra were, as far as we can tell, joint partners-in-crime in Agamemnon's murder, with Aegisthus taking the dominant role. In the *Agamemnon*, Clytemnestra has nursed grief and rage down the long years because of her husband's sacrifice of

their daughter Iphigenia at Aulis, then on his return home kills him entirely on her own, and with a fierce joy, after netting him in a robe while he is unarmed in his bath. Here she is an immensely powerful figure, a woman 'with the heart of a man', while Aegisthus' role has dwindled into comparative insignificance, and he becomes a blustering weakling (although already in the *Odyssey* he is described once as 'feeble Aegistheus') who appears on stage only at the end of the play. *Sophocles and *Euripides in their *Electras* still make her the more prominent figure, but tend to increase the relative importance of Aegisthus again; in Sophocles she is depicted as a truly evil woman, but Euripides treats her more sympathetically, making her somewhat sorry for all that has happened. When the time comes for her death at Orestes' hands, in Aeschylus she tries to resist him and threatens him with the *Erinyes, whom her ghost afterwards stirs up against him; in the two other tragedians she simply pleads for her life, although Euripides, unlike Sophocles, also introduces the Erinyes into the legend.

Her part in other legends is small: she brings Iphigenia to Aulis, supposedly to marry *Achilles; and according to Hyginus, whose probable source is Euripides, she gives advice to *Telephus when he comes in search of Achilles to heal his wound, which enables him to get a hearing from the Greeks.

Clytemnestra appears occasionally in art from the 7th cent. BC, though usually in scenes where she is not the main character, such as the murder of Aegisthus by Orestes; depictions of her own death are rare.

[Homer, *Odyssey* 3. 263 ff., 11. 422; Aeschylus, *Agamemnon, Choephori, Eumenides*; Sophocles, *Electra*; Euripides, *Electra, Iphigenia at Aulis* 607 ff.; Hyginus, *Fables* 101. 2]

Codrus, supposedly king of Athens in the 11th cent. BC. According to the story current in the 5th cent. his father Melanthus, of the Neleid family (*see* NELEUS), came to Attica when expelled from Pylos by the Dorians, and, after killing the Boeotian king

Xanthus in single combat during a frontier war, was accepted as king of Athens in place of the reigning Theseid Thymoetes. During the reign of Codrus the Dorians invaded Attica, having heard from *Delphi that they would be victorious if Codrus' life was spared; a friendly Delphian informed the Athenians of this oracle. Codrus thereupon went out dressed as a woodcutter, invited death by starting a quarrel with Dorian warriors, and so saved his country. He was succeeded by his son Medon, and the kingship remained in the family until the 8th cent.; alternatively, Codrus was the last king and his descendants were archons (see ARCHONTES). Other sons of Codrus, in particular Androclus and Neleus, led the colonization of Ionia from Athens. This last detail makes Codrus a hinge-figure in the controversial tradition according to which the Pylians who colonized Ionia had gone there not direct but via Athens: the existence of this tradition, which is sometimes seen as essentially an Athenian imperial fiction of the 5th cent., in the century before is implied by Herodotus' statement that the family of the 6th-cent. Athenian tyrant Pisistratus were, like Codrus and Melanthus, 'Pylians and Neleids'. A sizeable shrine of Codrus, Neleus, and Basile in Athens is known from a decree of 418/17 BC. A vase of *c*.450 shows the king, dressed as a hoplite, in conversation with Aenetus.

Colchis The triangular region on the east coast of the Black (Euxine) Sea, fenced around by the mountains of the Caucasus range. In myth, it was the destination of Phrixus on the Golden Ram, of which the fleece was the object of the *Argonauts' quest. Colchis' king was *Aeëtes, whose daughter *Medea fled with *Jason. Local kings traced their ancestry to Aeëtes, whose name remained current in the region throughout antiquity.

collegium (1) Magisterial or priestly: a board of officials. The name *collegium* was especially applied to the two great priesthoods of the *pontifices and the *augures and

to the *duoviri* (later *decemviri* and *quindecim-viri*) *sacris faciundis*, who had charge of the Sibylline oracles (see SIBYL) and of what the Romans called the 'Greek ritual' (*ritus Graecus*) in general. The lesser priesthoods were known as *sodalitates* (see SODALES). Collegiality, in which members possess equal authority and are subject to mutual control, here had the added dimension of expertise in recondite lore and tradition.

(2) Private: any private association of fixed membership and constitution (see CLUBS).

Colonos, a small Attic deme or local community 0.5 km. (⅓ mi.) north of the Acropolis, near Plato's Academy. The deme seems to have been particularly rich in sanctuaries of gods (*Poseidon Hippios, *Athena Hippia, and probably *Demeter and the Eumenides, see ERINYES) and of heroes (*Theseus, *Adrastus, *Pirithous, *Oedipus), although we know of these only from literary sources. The sanctuary of Poseidon may have been a gathering place for members of the Athenian cavalry, a group whose commitment to democracy was often felt to be suspect, and it was at Colonos in 411 BC that the assembly was held which voted democracy out of existence. The natural beauty of the place, now almost entirely lacking, was lovingly described by Colonos' most famous demesman, *Sophocles.

[Sophocles, *Oedipus at Colonus*, esp. 670 ff.; Thucydides 8. 67; Pausanias 1. 30. 4]

colours, sacred Three colours are especially important for sacral purposes in antiquity: white, black, and red, the last understood in the widest possible sense, to include purple, crimson, even violet.

White is in general a festal colour, associated with things of good omen, such as sacrifices to the celestial gods (white victims are regular for this purpose in both Greece and Rome). See for instance *Homer, *Iliad* 3. 103, where a white lamb is brought for sacrifice to *Helios; the scholiast rightly says that as the Sun is bright and male, a white male lamb is brought for him, while Earth, being dark and female, gets a black ewe-lamb. *Virgil speaks in the *Georgics* of the white bulls pastured along *Clitumnus for sacrificial purposes. It is the colour of the clothing generally worn on happy occasions, and of horses used on great festivals such as (probably) that of Demeter and Persephone at Syracuse. In Rome, white horses drew the chariot of a *triumphator*. See LEUCIPPUS.

Black on the contrary is associated with the *chthonian gods, mourning, and the dead (hence the *Erinyes wear sombre clothing, as infernal powers). There are, however, exceptions. At Argos, white was the mourning-colour, although Plutarch's assertion that white was the colour of Roman mourning will hardly pass muster. Hence to wear black at a festival was both ill-mannered and unlucky. The above facts easily explain why 'white' and 'black' respectively mean 'lucky' and 'unlucky' when used of a day, etc. The natural association of white with light and black with darkness is explanation enough, but it may be added that white garments are conspicuously clean (and appropriate for prayer), black ones suggest the unwashed condition of a mourner; *see* DEAD, DISPOSAL OF.

Red has more complicated associations. It would seem to suggest blood, and therefore death and the Underworld (hence, e.g., the use of red flags in cursing), but also blood as the source or container of life (hence a red bandage or wrapping of some kind is common in ancient, especially popular medicine), and also the ruddy colour of healthy flesh and various organs of the body (hence it is associated with rites of fertility on occasion, e.g. statues of *Priapus). Perhaps because red, or purple, is the colour of light, red is on occasion protective, e.g. the *praetexta* or red-purple stripe on the toga of Roman magistrates and children. But it is also associated with the heat of summer, *see* AUGURIUM CANARIUM. Red (and red hair) may also represent shamelessness and evil.

Other colours are of little or no sacral importance, but it may be noted that the veil (*flammeum*) of a Roman bride, often stated to be red, is distinctly called yellow (*luteum*) by Lucan and Pliny.

columbarium A type of tomb, popular in early imperial Rome, so called because of its similarity to a dovecote, the proper meaning of the word. Often totally or partially subterranean, such tombs had niches (*loculi*) arranged in rows in the walls with pots (*ollae*) sunk into them to contain the ashes of the dead. These provided comparatively cheap but decent burial for the poorer classes: the occupants of each niche could be identified by an inscription, and might be commemorated by more expensive memorials (such as a portrait bust or marble ash-chest). The largest *columbaria* could hold the remains of thousands and were built to accommodate the slaves and freedmen of the Julio-Claudian imperial households (e.g. the columbaria of the freedmen of *Augustus and Livia Drusilla on the via Appia, now virtually destroyed, or the three well-preserved *columbaria* of the Vigna Codini). Smaller *columbaria* appear to have been built by speculators or burial clubs (*see* CLUBS), with the niches allocated to individuals not related to one another (as in the columbarium of Pomponius Hylas), though some, such as those in the Isola Sacra cemetery and at Ostia, were family tombs.

comedy

comedy (Greek), Old 'Old Comedy' is best defined as the comedies produced at Athens during the 5th cent. BC. The provision of comedies at the City *Dionysia each year was made the responsibility of the relevant magistrate in 488/7 or 487/6 BC; Aristotle's statement that before then comic performances were given by 'volunteers' is probably a guess, but a good one. Comedies were first included in the *Lenaea shortly before 440 BC. Before and after the Peloponnesian War of 431–404 BC five comedies were performed at each festival; there is evidence that this was reduced to three during the war, but this question is controversial. In the 4th cent. comedies were performed also at the

Rural *Dionysia, and it is likely, given the existence of early theatres in several Attic villages, that such performances were widespread before the end of the 5th cent. No complete plays of any poet of the Old Comedy except Aristophanes survive.

Mythology and theology are treated with extreme irreverence in Old Comedy; some plays were burlesque versions of myths, and gods (especially Dionysus) were made to appear (e.g. in Aristophanes' *Frogs* and Cratinus' *Dionysalexandros*) foolish, cowardly, and dishonest. Yet the reality of the gods' power and the validity of the community's worship of them are consistently assumed and on occasion affirmed, while words and actions of ill-omen for the community are avoided. It is probable that comic irreverence is the elevation to a high artistic level (Demodocus' tale of *Ares and *Aphrodite in book 8 of *Homer's *Odyssey* may be compared) of a type of irreverence which permeates the folklore of polytheistic cultures. The essential spirit of Old Comedy is the ordinary man's protest—using his inalienable weapons, humour and fantasy—against all who are in some way stronger or better than he: gods, politicians, generals, artists, and intellectuals.

comedy (Greek), Middle The term 'Middle Comedy' is a convenient label for plays produced in the years between Old and New Comedy (*c*.404–*c*.321 BC). This was a time of experiment and transition; different types of comedy seem to have predominated at different periods; probably no single kind of play deserves to be styled 'Middle Comedy' to the exclusion of all others. The defeat of Athens in 404 BC vitally affected the comic stage; the loss of imperial power and political energy was reflected in comedy by a choice of material less intrinsically Athenian and more cosmopolitan. The variety of subject, especially in contrast with New Comedy, is striking. Plays with political themes were still produced, mainly but not exclusively in the early part of the period, and politicians were frequently ridiculed, if rarely criticized

outright. As in Old Comedy, philosophers were pilloried and their views comically misrepresented; *Plato and the Pythagorean sects (*see* PYTHAGORAS AND PYTHAGOREANISM) seem to have been the commonest victims. In the earlier part of the period mythological burlesque played a prominent role, doubtless continuing Old-Comedy traditions. There may have been two main types of such burlesque: straight travesty of a myth, with or without political innuendo, and parody of tragic (especially Euripidean) versions. The aim was often to reinterpret a myth in contemporary terms; thus *Heracles is asked to select a book from *Linus' library of classical authors, and *Pelops complains about the meagre meals of Greece by contrast with the Persian king's roast camel. Popular also were riddles, descriptions of feasting, and the comedy of mistaken identity.

comedy (Greek), New, comedy written from the last quarter of the 4th cent. BC onwards, but ending its creative heyday in the mid-3rd cent., composed mainly for first performance at Athens. Menander, though not the most successful in his own lifetime, was soon recognized as the outstanding practitioner of this type of drama. Although Athenian citizenship and marriage-laws are integral to many of the plays, the presentation of characters, situations, and relationships is true to such universal elements of human experience that the plays could be enjoyed then as now by audiences far removed from Athens. Political references are rare and subordinate to the portrayal of the private and family life of fictional individuals; there are social tensions (between rich and poor, town and country, citizens and non-citizens, free and slave, men and women, parents and children), but they are not specific to one time or place. Love or infatuation (always heterosexual) plays a part and is regularly shown triumphing over obstacles in a variety of contexts. But this is not the only ingredient; Menander excelled at the sympathetic portrayal of many kinds of personal relationship and of the problems that arise from ignorance, misunderstanding, and prejudice. These generate scenes that the audience can perceive as comic because of their own superior knowledge, enjoying the irony of the situation; but Menander often plays games with his audience's expectations as well.

comedy (Latin) This term has come to be synonymous with *fabula* palliata (i.e. *fabula*, 'drama in a Greek cloak (*pallium*)'), the type of comedy written at Rome by Plautus and Terence (2nd cent. BC), usually adaptations of (Greek) New Comedy; their plays are the only complete Latin comedies to have survived from antiquity. Almost certainly a masked drama from the start, it shows Greek characters in a Greek setting, and in general the authors are believed to have preserved many of the essential elements of plot from their Greek originals. But Roman details sometimes intrude, particularly in Plautus, who adapted the Greek plays with considerable freedom.

comedy, Greek, origins of In many preliterate cultures there are public occasions on which people pretend humorously to be somebody other than themselves, and it is a safe assumption that comedy, so defined, was of great antiquity among the Greeks (possibly of incomparably greater antiquity than tragedy). The word *kōmōdoi*, *kōmos*-singers, presupposes *kōmos*, which is a company of men behaving and singing in a happy and festive manner. It appears that, so far as was known in the 4th cent., a humorous adult male chorus was an archaic feature of the City *Dionysia, and it is probable that comedy was a specialized development from this. The question: 'when did the *kōmos*, first develop a *dramatic* character?' is not answerable. The practical question is: 'how far back, and to what parts of the Greek world, can each ingredient of Old Attic Comedy be traced?'

The earliest and best-known theory about the origin of comedy is in *Aristotle's *Poetics*: that it began 'from the prelude to the phallic

songs'. As it is hardly to be supposed that Aristotle had any information on the nature and content of phallic songs 200 years before his own day, it seems that having (reasonably) decided that the origins of both tragedy and comedy were to be sought in festivals of *Dionysus, and having derived tragedy from the leader–chorus relationship in the serious and heroic *dithyramb, he looked for a similar relationship in something gay and ribald, and found it in the phallic songs of his own day (he says: 'the phallic songs which are still customary in many cities'). It is possible that the germ of part of Old Comedy lay in words or verses uttered in mockery of the public by men who accompanied the phallus in the procession in Dionysiac festivals at Athens. It must, however, be remembered that phallic songs as known to Aristotle may have been deeply influenced by literary comedy.

Commodianus, Christian Latin poet, probably from 3rd-cent. Africa, but assigned by some to the 4th or 5th cent. and to other locations; perhaps of Syrian origin. In the *Instructiones*, 80 short poems mostly in acrostic form, he attacks paganism and Judaism and admonishes Christians; the *Carmen apologeticum* or *De duobus populis* is an exposition of Christian doctrine with didactic intent. His language and versification have been much vilified; in particular, he shows scant regard for classical prosody. The character of his verse, however, is better attributed to a desire to innovate and write poetry with appeal for ordinary uneducated Christians than to incompetence.

Compitalia *See* CLUBS; LARES.

Concordia The cult of personified harmonious agreement (Gk. *Homonoia*) within the body politic at Rome (a useful ideological slogan, as for instance *concordia* of the senate and equites in the politics of *Cicero) is an effective diagnostic of its absence. The first temple overlooking the *Forum from the lower slopes of the Capitoline was attributed to Marcus Furius Camillus as peacemaker in the troubles associated with the Licinio-Sextian legislation of 367 BC; a major rebuilding by Lucius Opimius in 121 commemorated the suppression of Gaius Sempronius Gracchus and his followers, and the grandest rebuilding by Tiberius (vowed 7 BC, dedicated as Concordia Augusta, AD 10, foreshadowing various usages under the empire), on coins (*concordia* of provinces, soldiers, or armies) and in municipal contexts (e.g. the monument of Eumachia at Pompeii) to proclaim loyalty and political acquiescence in difficult times) was intended to celebrate a really elusive solidarity within Augustus' household. Some remains of the lavish marble architecture of the last temple survive. There were other minor sanctuaries of this cult at Rome, also linked to republican political disturbances.

Condate, a common place-name in the Celtic provinces of the Roman empire, meaning 'confluence', and perhaps reflecting the Celts' reverence for watercourses. *See* CELTIC RELIGION.

Conon, author of 50 mythical 'Narratives' (*Diegeseis*) dedicated to King Archelaus Philopator (or Philopatris) of Cappadocia (36 BC–AD 17). A summary is preserved by the Byzantine scholar Photius, who calls him 'Attic in style, pleasant and charming in his constructions and phrases, often somewhat compressed and recondite'. Part of the original seems to be extant on a papyrus of the 2nd cent. AD. The stories are localized, and include foundation myths, love stories, and aetiologies or stories explaining cults.

consecratio Roman law (civil and pontifical) distinguished between things belonging to gods and things belonging to humans (*res divini* and *humani iuris*); the former were subdivided into *res sacrae* and *res religiosae*. A third category was the *res sanctae* which were *quodammodo divini iuris*, only in a certain sense governed by divine law. 'Sacred (*sacrae*) things' belonged to a deity; they were transferred from the human into the divine sphere by the twofold act of **dedicatio* and *consecratio*, performed by a magistrate assisted by a **pontifex*. Things given to gods by private persons the pontifical law did not regard as (technically) sacred. Furthermore the *immobilia* (temples, altars) could be consecrated only on 'Italian soil'; in the provinces they were only *pro sacro*. 'Religious (*religiosae*) things' were objects affected by *religio*, i.e. reverence or fear, in particular graves. As examples of 'holy (*sanctae*) things' walls (*muri*) and gates (*portae*) are given in legal sources, but all inaugurated places were *loca sancta*, i.e. all *templa* (*see* TEMPLUM), hence also city walls as they followed (at least originally) the line of **pomerium*, the inaugurated boundary (*see* AUGURS). They were under divine protection, but they did not belong to a deity; in a broader sense all things protected by a sanction, divine or human, were described as *sancta*. As most temples were consecrated and inaugurated, they were 'sacred', 'holy', and also 'religious'; the Curia and Rostra (inaugurated but not consecrated) were 'holy' and 'religious'; graves were 'religious', and 'holy' only in so far as protected by a sanction. A thing (or person) was given to the deity as a permanent possession through *dedicatio* and *consecratio*, or could be forfeited to it for destruction through the ritual of *consecratio capitis* (without *dedicatio*), which proclaimed a person an accursed outlaw, *homo sacer*; also the goods of a (religious) offender could be consecrated by a tribune or magistrate; he would pronounce the formula of *sacratio* with his head covered (*capite velato*), incense burning on a portable altar (*foculus*), and the flute-player drowning ill-omened sounds.

Consentes Di Twelve deities (six male, six female), perhaps those worshipped at the **lectisternium* of 217 BC, whose gilded statues stood in the Forum in the late republic, like the Twelve Gods whose altar stood in the Agora at Athens. The relationship of these to the modest monument on the slopes of the Capitoline hill, whose rebuilding in AD 367 is recorded in an inscription which calls it the 'Porticus Deorum Consentium', is not clear.

[Varro, *On Country Matters* 1. 1. 4]

Constantine I, 'the Great' (Flavius Valerius Constantinus, *c.*AD 272/3–337), emperor whose promotion of *Christianity was crucial in its emergence as the dominant religion in the Roman Empire. Son of the emperor Constantius I, after his father's death Constantine had to overcome various rivals for power. In 312 he invaded Italy and marched on Rome, defeating the usurper Maxentius. The senate welcomed Constantine as liberator and made him senior Augustus. He took over the rule of Italy and Africa, and disbanded the praetorian guard which had supported Maxentius.

Two years earlier it had been given out that Constantine had seen a vision of his tutelary deity the sun-god *Apollo accompanied by Victory (*see* NIKE; VICTORIA) and the figure XXX to symbolize the years of rule due to him. By the end of his life Constantine claimed to have seen a (single) cross above the sun, with words 'Be victorious in this'. At the last battle with Maxentius, Constantine as the result of a dream sent his soldiers into battle with crosses (and no doubt other symbols) on their shields; heavily outnumbered, he was nonetheless victorious. No more, yet no less, superstitious than his contemporaries, he saw the hand of the Christian God in this, and the need to maintain such support for himself and the empire. From that moment he not merely restored Christian property but gave privileges to the clergy, showered benefactions on the Church, and undertook a massive programme of church building. At Rome a basilica was provided for the Pope where the barracks of the mounted branch of the praetorians had stood, and other churches, most notably St Peter's, followed. His religious outlook may have undergone later transformations, and was affected by his encounters with problems in the Church. In Africa he confronted the Donatist

schism: the *Donatists objected to the largess for their opponents and appealed to him. To the *vicarius* (effectively governor) of Africa, a 'fellow worshipper of the most high God', he wrote (314) of his fear that failure to achieve Christian unity would cause God to replace him with another emperor. Sincerity is not determinable by historical method; it is, in any case, not incompatible with a belief that consequential action may have political advantage. He had been present at Nicomedia when persecution began in 303; he knew that the problem with Christianity was that its exclusiveness stood in the way of imperial unity. If he threw in his lot with the Christians, there could be no advantage if they were themselves not united. Following a papal council in 313, his own council at Arles (Arelate) in 314, and his investigation into the dispute, he saw the refusal of the Donatists to conform as obtuse. From 317 he tried coercion; there were exiles and some executions. Totally failing to achieve his object, he left the Donatists to God's judgement (321). Weakness in the face of a movement widespread in Africa was seen when the Donatists seized the basilica Constantine built for the Catholics at Cirta; he left them in possession and built the Catholics another one.

On 8 November 324 Constantine made his third son Constantius II Caesar and largely for strategic reasons, founded *Constantinople on the site of Byzantium. The city's dedication with both pagan rites and Christian ceremonies took place on 11 May 330. From the beginning it was 'New Rome', though lower in rank. Pagan temples and cults were absent, but other features of Rome were in time reproduced (Constantius II upgraded the city council to equality with the Roman senate). To speak of the foundation of a capital is misleading; yet a permanent imperial residence in the east did in the end emphasize division between the empire's Greek and Latin parts.

Resident now in the more Christianized east, his promotion of the new religion became more emphatic. He openly rejected *paganism, though without persecuting pagans, favoured Christians as officials, and welcomed bishops at court, but his actions in Church matters were his own. He now confronted another dispute which was rending Christianity, the theological questions about the nature of Christ raised by the Alexandrian priest *Arius. To secure unity Constantine summoned the council which met at Nicaea in 325 (later ranked as the First Ecumenical Council), and proposed the formula which all must accept. Dissidents were bludgeoned into agreement; but *Athanasius' view that his opponents had put an unorthodox interpretation on the formula was seen by Constantine as vexatious interference with attempts to secure unity. Even if his success in this aspect was superficial, he nevertheless brought Christianity from a persecuted minority sect to near-supremacy in the religious life of the empire.

Constantinople Constantinople was founded by *Constantine I on the site of Byzantium in AD 324, shortly after his victory over Licinius near by. There are hardly any sources before the 6th cent., and these are already full of myths: e.g. that Constantine started to build at Troy and brought the *Palladium from Rome. When he claimed to 'bestow an eternal name' he probably meant his own! The city was styled 'New Rome' from the start, but it is not likely that Constantine had any thought of superseding Rome. He was simply building his own tetrarchic capital: the New Rome motif took on new significance after the sack of Rome (410) and the disappearance of the western empire.

Though claimed by *Eusebius as a Christian foundation never stained by *pagan worship, several pagan temples were left untouched. But Constantine at once built a number of martyr shrines and churches, notably the Holy Apostles, where he and many of his successors were buried. The bishop of Constantinople soon acquired great prestige, and in 381 the council of Constantinople declared that 'he should have the primacy of honour after the bishop of Rome because it was the New Rome'. In 451 he acquired patriarchal jurisdiction over the dioceses of Thrace, Asiana, and Pontica. Already before the close of the 4th cent. we find the first stages in the growth of Byzantine monasticism.

constellations and named stars From the earliest times the Greeks, like many other peoples, named certain prominent stars and groups of stars. *Homer and *Hesiod both speak of the Pleiades, the Hyades, Orion, Boötes, the Bear ('also called the Wain'), and the 'Dog of Orion' (i.e. Sirius). These are the only stars and star-groups known to have been named in archaic times, and although it is likely that some of the later constellations were identified before the 4th cent. BC, the division of the *whole* visible sky into constellations seems not to precede Eudoxus in around 360 BC. However, the twelve signs of the zodiac were introduced from Mesopotamia long before then; the iconography and nomenclature of some of those constellations betray their Babylonian origin.

Like other peoples of antiquity, the Greeks identified some star-groups with mythological beings. Thus Hesiod calls the Pleiades 'daughters of Atlas', and the Hesiodic corpus seems already to reflect the idea that mythological figures were in some cases translated to the sky in a kind of *metamorphosis. The identification with such figures was, at least in the system of Eudoxus, embedded in the very name of some constellations: for instance the whole *Perseus myth is reflected in the names of the constellations Perseus, *Andromeda, Cetus, Cassiopeia, and *Cepheus. But it was only in Hellenistic times that systematic attempts were made to connect all constellations with traditional mythology. The most influential work of this kind was the *Catasterisms* of the 3rd-cent. BC Alexandrian scholar Eratosthenes. A later epitome of this survives, which shows it to be the source of much in the similar work of *Hyginus. Although we possess only a small part of the extensive ancient literature on astral mythology, even this is enough to show that there was no 'standard' version, but that different myths were often attached to the same constellation. For instance the sign Gemini, which gets its name from the Babylonian Maš-Maš ('twins'), was identified not only with the famous divine twins Castor and Pollux (*see* DIOSCURI), but also with the Theban heroic twins *Amphion and Zethus, and even with the half-brothers *Heracles and *Apollo.

Consus, a Roman god of the granary (from *condere* 'to store') whose festivals (Consualia) on 21 August and 15 December coincided, respectively, with the gathering of the harvest and the onset of winter. The ancients commonly supposed his name to have something to do with *consilium*. Horses as funerary animals were added under Etruscan influence, and led to a misidentification with *Poseidon Hippios. He seems connected with two festivals of *Ops: Opiconsivia (25 August) and Opalia (19 December). Since corn was often stored underground, this may account for his subterranean altar in the Circus Maximus, uncovered only on his festival days. He had a temple (Aedes Consi) on the *Aventine, probably vowed or dedicated by Lucius Papirius Cursor about 272 BC. His characteristic offering was first-fruits. Horses and donkeys were garlanded and rested on his festival.
[Ovid, *Fasti* 3. 199 f.]

conventus, 'assembly', is technically used (as well as for provincial assizes) for associations of Italians abroad. By the early 2nd cent. BC Italians (especially in the east) united for religious and other purposes under elected *magistri*.

conversion The term implies rejection of one way of life for another, generally better, after brief and intense insight into the short-comings of self or the demands of circumstance. Ancient religious cult did not require such radical or sudden shifts. Devotees could embrace one allegiance without re-nouncing others. Observance was intensified by addition rather than by exchange, even in the case of initiation to a mystery. A. D. Nock, made much of the account of Lucius in *Apuleius (the allusions are to Isis). Lucius' *metamorphosis owed more to miracle, however, than to will-power, although the conversion of others may have been invited.

It is common to suggest that only *Christianity, and to a lesser extent *Judaism, could muster a sharp sense of exclusive loyalty, so that adherence to either cult demanded rejection of some other practice. Two considerations undermine that view.

First, the characteristic word for conversion in the NT, *metanoia*, was used also by Classical philosophers. Its chief meaning was to come to one's senses in a new and different way. While *Marcus Aurelius, for example, and Plutarch generally retained the narrow sense of inconstancy or regret, other texts are more dramatic. In the words used by the Stoic Hierocles, 'conversion is the beginning of philosophy'. Such writers could take their cue, in any case, from the classic insights of *Plato.

Latin was strikingly weak in its corresponding word-power. *Conversio* remained resolutely wedded to its physical origins and even in a moral sense had more to do with association than with psychological attitude. There was among the Romans a contrasting admiration for *constantia*, in the sense of steadfastness, whereby those deserving moral approbation were as likely to maintain the gifts and inclinations of their breeding as to renounce their past in favour of novel commitments.

Second, the literature of Christian conversion frequently describes a change of heart based on existing association with the Church. The classic example of *Augustine echoes the experience of many men and women in the century before him. Antony and *Basil were already sprung from pious Christian families. *Ambrose, by contrast, although similarly placed, was embarrassed to find himself on the verge of baptism and episcopacy with no respectable conversion to his name.

The perceived meanings of conversion, therefore, prompt us to attach equal importance to breeding or intimate friendship in the growth of the Christian community. Baptism, even when postponed because of its demands, was not identified with conversion. The term should be reserved for the experience of a narrower body of men and women, who felt a need to carry religious commitment to new heights not far removed from the ambitions of pagan philosophers. Mass attachment to the Church after Constantine, on the other hand, was more circumspect than passionate. The sermons addressed by bishops to their expanding flocks are telling in their exhortations. The level of intensity they recommended was clearly greater than their cautious hearers had achieved.

convivium *See* EPULUM.

cookery The religious importance of *sacrifice gave cooking a powerfully expressive role in ancient society: the order of the exposing of meat to different sources of heat, especially boiling and roasting, mattered ritually. The public meat-cook (*mageiros*) was a man; other food preparation was among the private, household tasks of an adult woman. Food could be prepared at the hearth of the city and consumed as a public activity, like the meals of the Athenian *prytaneion*; it was more normally regarded as a household matter. But the staples of domestic diet, especially grains (of which there was a considerable variety) could also be cooked in special forms as offerings (a wide range of sacred breads and *cakes is known). *See* SACRIFICE.

Corinthian cults and myths Corinth, not having a Mycenaean past, lacked a heroic tradition of its own, borrowing legendary figures from the Argolid (*see* ARGOS, CULTS and ARGOS, MYTHS OF) and the east (e.g. *Bellerophon(tes), *Medea). None of the myths is intimately connected with the major gods of the city, whose principal urban cults were those of *Aphrodite on Acrocorinth, *Apollo, and *Demeter Thesmophoros. The urban centre also possessed hero sanctuaries (their incumbents as yet unidentified, but probably connected with the founding families of the city) and one or more sacred springs, of which Peirene is the best known.

The principal extra-urban cults were of *Hera Akraia at *Perachora (with an urban branch) and of *Poseidon at Penteskouphia (west of the city) and at Isthmia. The last became the site of one of the four panhellenic festivals of the so-called 'circuit', at which contestants took part in games (*see* PANHELLENIC SANCTUARIES). Poseidon was the protecting deity of the whole land of Corinthia, having won it in myth from Athena; his son *Sinis was killed by *Theseus.

Strong eastern influence is to be seen both in the legends and especially in the nature of the urban cult of Aphrodite. Not only was she the *poliouchos* ('protecting the city'), but her cult at Corinth was notorious as a centre for sacred *prostitution. Also unusual was the relative prominence of *Helios in myth and cult.

Greek Corinth was destroyed in 146 BC, and no doubt much evidence for pre-Roman cult went with it. The Roman city continued to worship Aphrodite, Poseidon, and Demeter, to whom were added gods from Rome and Asia.

Coronis, daughter of *Phlegyas, and mother of *Asclepius according to the common tradition. She was loved by *Apollo; while pregnant with his child, she was (lawfully or not) united with Ischys, son of Elatus. A raven denounced them to Apollo in *Delphi and was turned from white to black (Pindar, however, says Apollo knew it by his omniscience); the god had Coronis and Ischys killed. But when she was on the funeral pyre, he took the unborn child from her and gave him to the *Centaur Chiron to bring up. The local Epidaurian legend omits the union with Ischys and has 'the daughter of Phlegyas' expose her baby son in the woods of *Epidaurus where a dog finds and a goat nurtures him; hence the sacred dogs and the prohibition on goat sacrifice in Epidaurus. *See* ASCLEPIUS.

[Pindar, *Pythian* 3; Ovid, *Metamorphoses* 2. 542–632; Pausanias 2. 26. 3]

Corybantes, nature spirits, often confused with the *Curetes. Like them they danced about the new-born *Zeus, and they functioned together in *Despoina's cult at *Lycosura . They guard the infant *Dionysus in Orphic myth (*see* ORPHISM) and dance to the sound of flutes in the orgiastic cults of *Dionysus and of *Cybele.

Corythus, the name of several obscure mythological persons, including (1) son of *Zeus and husband of *Electra (2) daughter of Atlas; his sons were Dardanus and Iasius (Iasion) (*see* DARDANUS). (2) Son of *Paris and *Oenone. His story is variously told; the least unfamiliar account is in *Parthenius. He came to Troy as an ally; *Helen fell in love with him and Paris killed him. Nicander, quoted by Parthenius, calls him son of Paris and *Helen.

[Parthenius, *Erotika Pathemata* (*Love Stories*) 34 (from *Hellanicus and Cephalon of Gergis)]

Cotys, Cotyto, a Thracian goddess (*see* THRACIAN RELIGION) worshipped in her homeland and later in Corinth (*see* CORINTHIAN CULTS AND MYTHS) and Sicily (*see* SICILY AND MAGNA GRAECIA, CULTS AND MYTHOLOGY) with orgiastic, Dionysiac-type rites (*see* DIONYSUS) of music and dance. In Athens Eupolis, contemporary and rival of Aristophanes, made her Corinthian devotees and their notorious rites the subject of his comedy *Baptae* ('Baptists').

Cragus, a Lycian god identified with *Zeus, humanized into a son of Tremiles (*eponym of the Tremileis or Lycians), after whom Mt. Cragus was named.

Crantor of Soli in Cilicia (*c.*335–275 BC), philosopher of the early *Academy, and the first Platonic commentator. His influential commentary on *Plato's *Timaeus* sided with those who denied a literal creation of the world. It included a detailed mathematical interpretation of the harmonic intervals constituting the world soul. His ethical writings were much admired. One famous passage depicted a contest between the various Goods, with Virtue the eventual winner. *See also* ATLANTIS.

Creon (1), of *Thebes, son of *Menoeceus (1), brother of Iocasta. (*See* OEDIPUS.) He offered her and the kingdom to anyone who would rid Thebes of the *Sphinx. After Oedipus' fall and again after the death of *Eteocles, he became king or regent of Thebes. During the attack by the *Seven against Thebes, he lost his son *Menoeceus (2). Another son, *Haemon (3), was either killed by the Sphinx or took his own life after the suicide of *Antigone (1), his espoused, or on a later occasion. Creon was almost as unfortunate in his daughters, whom he gave in marriage to *Heracles and *Iphicles. The former, Megara, was killed by Heracles in a fit of madness. Creon was killed by *Theseus in a battle over the burial of the Seven.

Creon (2), a king of *Corinth whom *Medea killed by magic and fled, leaving her children behind to be killed by the Corinthians. *Euripides has her kill Creon's daughter (*Jason's betrothed) with a poisoned costume and murder her own children

Although the name 'Creon' means simply the 'lord' or 'ruler', and is used to fill in gaps in genealogies, it is a measure of the skill and artistry of *Sophocles and *Euripides that they make these two figures into credible, if not lovable, human beings.

[(1) Sophocles, *Oedipus Tyrannus*, *Oedipus at Colonus*, *Antigone*; Statius, *Thebaid* 12. 773 ff.; (2) Euripides, *Medea*]

Cretan cults and myths Most reflect the island's important bronze age past. Diodorus Siculus records the tradition that the Greek gods had their origin in Crete and thence visited the world to confer their benefactions on mankind (*see* EUHEMERUS). *Zeus Cretagenes was worshipped in the central Cretan cities of Gortyn, Lato, and Lyttus, and in the west. Legend placed his birth in a Cretan cave on Mt. Ida or Dicte (Psychro). He also died in Crete, and from Hellenistic times his tomb was shown on the island, prompting *Callimachus' outburst in his *Hymn to Zeus* that all Cretans are liars. The cult was old, since Zeus Dictaeus already appears on a Linear B tablet from Cnossus. Zeus Welkhanos represents the fusion with a native youthful male accompanying the Minoan goddess of nature. Coins from Phaestus (5th/4th cent. BC) show the young god sitting in a tree and holding a bird in his lap. The Theodaesia were celebrated in central and eastern Crete in honour of Zeus' periodic *epiphany. It was an occasion of renewal and of initiation of the youth to full citizenship. It recalls the renewal of *Minos' kingship by Zeus in a cave every nine years.

*Apollo Delphinius had cults in Cnossus (as Delphidios), Hyrtacina, and Dreros. The connection with dolphins attested in the *Homeric Hymn to Apollo* probably arose from the local adaptation of a pre-Greek name. The substance of the cult also concerned initiation of the young. The Archaic Delphinium at Dreros combined the Minoan form of the bench-shrine with the interior sacrificial hearth of the Mycenaean megaron. The temple contained bronze figures of the trinity of *Leto, Apollo, and *Artemis. Leto's (Dorian form, *Lato*) cults at Gortyn and Phaestus (as Phytia) celebrated the withdrawal of young men from the *agela* or training group on reaching manhood and marriageable age. At the Ecdysia festival they stripped off the girlish clothes of their childhood. The implications of sex change are reflected in myth, while the attendant institutionalized homosexuality gave much offence to other Greeks.

Three Minoan goddesses who were absorbed by Artemis but retained important cults in historic times are *Eileithyia in her cave at Amnisus, *Britomartis ('Sweet Maid') near Lyttus and at Olous, with a wooden image said to be by *Daedalus in her temple, and Dictynna at Lisus and Cydonia. Myths were told around Dictynna's hellenized name: she either invented hunting nets (*diktya*) or fled into fishermen's nets to escape Minos' attentions. Athena's cult as Tritogeneia in Cnossus, and as Wadia ('Sweet Athena') in Castri, also had a Minoan background, as did that of Aphrodite and *Hermes at Kato Symi. *Asclepius' cult was popular in Crete in Hellenistic times. His main sanctuary at Lebena attracted visitors throughout Crete and from across the Libyan sea. *See* MINOAN AND MYCENAEAN RELIGION.

*Demeter's sacred marriage with *Iasion in a thrice-ploughed field, which produced the divine child Plutus, preserved a Minoan sacred ritual. Similar origins accounted for the story of Europa's abduction by Zeus in the shape of a bull, and the myth of *Ariadne who died in more ways than any other heroine. Crete's best known legends of *Minos, of the Athenian Daedalus who built the labyrinth of Cnossus, and the annual Athenian tribute of seven youths and maidens until *Theseus slew the Minotaur, mirror Cretan influence in the Aegean during the bronze age. Minos built the first fleet, and when his grandson *Idomeneus joined the Achaean expedition against Troy, there were 100 cities on the island, according to the *Iliad*.

Minoan Crete pioneered the working of metal in the western Aegean giving rise to the myths about the Dactyles, *Curetes, and the bronze robot *Talos (1) who burnt Crete's enemies in his fiery embrace.

For Cretan bull, *see* HERACLES.

[Diodorus Siculus 3. 61. 1–3, 5. 46. 3, 64–5, 76. 3; Ovid, *Metamorphoses* 9. 666–797]

Creusa, the feminine form of *Creon, 'ruler'. The name is borne by several mythical characters. (1) Daughter of *Erechtheus of Athens, wife of *Xuthus, and mother of *Achaeus, *Ion, and Diomede, according to *Hesiod. *Sophocles' *Creusa* presumably concerned this Creusa, and may have been identical with his *Ion*. She is also an important character in *Euripides' *Ion* (in which *Apollo was father of Ion by Creusa). (2) Daughter of *Priam, wife of *Aeneas, and mother of *Ascanius. According to

*Virgil she was lost in the flight from Troy and her ghost then prophesied the future. In earlier authors the wife of Aeneas had been called Eurydice and had escaped with him. (3) Alternative name for Glauce, daughter of the Corinthian *Creon (2), especially in Latin authors.

[(1) Euripides, *Ion*; (2) Virgil, *Aeneid* 2. 730–95]

Crito of Argos, a *Neopythagorean philosopher, of whose *On Wisdom* the anthologist Stobaeus quotes fifteen lines of Doric prose, about the mind as created by God so as to enable man to contemplate God.

Cronus, the youngest of the *Titans, sons of *Uranus (Heaven) and *Gaia (Earth). His mythology is marked by paradoxes. According to one myth he castrated his father at the instigation of his mother. From his marriage with his sister *Rhea the race of the (Olympian) gods was born: *Hestia, *Demeter, *Hera, *Hades, *Poseidon, and *Zeus. Fearing to be overcome by one of his children he swallowed them on birth, save only the last, Zeus, saved by Rhea, who wrapped a stone in swaddling-clothes which Cronus swallowed instead. The infant Zeus was hidden in Crete, where he was protected by the *Curetes. Later, by the contrivance of *Gaia, Cronus vomited up all his children and was overcome by them after a desperate struggle. He was incarcerated in Tartarus. Later authors give roughly the same story, differing mainly on his place of exile, clearly under the influence of the second group of Cronus myths.

In these Cronus is pictured as king of the *golden age, a utopian wonderland. He maintains this role in the hereafter at the borders of the earth, as the ruler of the *Islands of the Blest. Another variant posits him on a far away island, asleep and inactive. Later he becomes the model for the Italic god *Saturnus, civilizer of Latium and Italy.

The stark contradiction between the extreme cruelty manifested in the first version and the utopian blessings in the second, both found in Hesiod, has fostered conjectures concerning different origins. While Cronus as king of the golden age was supposed to have been an authentic Greek (or at least Indo-European) contribution, the cruel tyrant was assumed to have been derived from another culture. Indeed, similar myths of swallowing fathers can be found all over the world, but none as close as the Hurrian–Hittite myth of Kumarbi, first published in 1945. Scholars generally agree that Hesiod must have (indirectly) borrowed the theme from this near-eastern myth. This, however, does not suffice to explain the blatant inconsistencies in the presentation of one divine person in a single work by Hesiod, the more so since the same inconsistency returns in ritual.

Since Cronus is predominantly a mythical god, rites, cults, and cult-places are scarce. *Olympia boasted an ancient cult. His festival, the Cronia, celebrated in Athens and a few other places after the harvest, is a carnevalesque feast of exultation and abundance at which masters and slaves feast together. One source even reports that masters served their servants during the festival. However, other (legendary) cult practices involve horrible human sacrifices, while foreign gods associated with human sacrifice, like Bel, are consistently identified with Cronus. Though pre-Greek and Asia Minor influences cannot be discarded, the central contradiction in both myth and ritual seems to reveal the very essence of their message and function; both refer to exceptional periods in which stagnation and reversal of the normal codes find expression in both positive and negative imagery.

[Hesiod, *Theogony* 137–8, 154 ff., 453 ff., *Works and Days* 111, 169; Macrobius, *Saturnalia* 1.10]

crowns and wreaths (Gk. *stephanos*, *stephanē*, Lat. *corona*). Among the Greeks, these were among the most frequent offerings made to the Gods in the form of their cult-statues. They were also worn by humans for a variety of ceremonial purposes: by priests when *sacrificing (and by sacrificial animals), by members of dramatic choruses, orators, and symposiasts. They served as prizes at games and as awards of merit. Originally made from the branches of trees and plants, each having a specific connotation (e.g. olive/*Olympian victory, funerals; vine and ivy/*Dionysus; rose/*Aphrodite, symposium), crowns began to be made in gold and occasionally silver. Less solid examples were made for funerary use, and some are preserved in the archaeological record. Gold crowns occur frequently in the epigraphic sources relating to Athens and *Delos, where, however, the figures given represent their cost in silver drachmae rather than their weight in gold. The crown-making stage was often bypassed, and the recipient simply pocketed the money. Usage was very similar among the Romans, who in addition awarded crowns and wreaths as decorations for valour.

cults See under name of region.

culture-bringers, mythical figures who are credited with the inventions of important cultural achievements. Around the 6th cent. BC the Greeks started to ascribe a number of inventions to gods and heroes. So *Athena Polias planted the first *olive-tree, and as Ergane she invented weaving; *Demeter taught sowing and grinding corn; *Dionysus was connected with viticulture (see WINE), and *Apollo thought up the *calendar. Of the heroes, Argive *Phoroneus invented fire, and the Rhodian *Telchines metal-working; pan-Hellenic *Heracles founded the *Olympian Games. In Athens, *Prometheus became highly important; to him it owed politics, logic, architecture, meteorology, astronomy, arithmetic, literature, etc.—in short all *technai*, as he himself says in the *Prometheus Bound* attributed to Aeschylus.

In the 4th cent., interest shifted towards inventors of political traditions and finding new names for all kinds of inventors. The first development reflects the growing importance of philosophy, the latter the growing consciousness of local traditions.

Especially the sophists developed a great interest in the origin of culture, witness *Protagoras' lost *On the Original State of Man*. *Prodicus went so far that he considered Demeter and Dionysus to have been deified because of their inventions. His views were an instant success and he was followed by (among others) *Euhemerus, whose Zeus takes a great interest in 'inventors who had discovered new things that promised to be useful for the lives of men'. Euhemerus was translated into Latin by the famous 2nd-cent. BC poet Ennius, but the Romans on the whole showed little interest in culture-bringers.

[Aeschylus, *Prometheus Bound* 436–506]

Cupid, Lat. *Cupido* ('desire'), literal translation of Greek *Eros and therefore his Roman counterpart in literary treatments. Unlike Eros, however, Cupido had virtually no existence in cult.

Curetes, young, divine male warriors of Crete. They attend upon Zeus, the *megistos Kouros* of the Dictaean Hymn of Palaiokastro who leads them (*daimones, see* DAIMON) up Mt. Dicte. As nature spirits and associated with the mountain goddess Rhea (compare the *Idaean Dactyls), they protect the fruit of the fields. Their name is in fact identical with *kouroi* (boys, young men), and they are the male equivalent of the *Nymphs, themselves often called *Kourai*. Curetes and Nymphs were born together and acted as joint witnesses to Cretan oaths.

In their best-known myth the Curetes are connected with the birth of *Zeus *Kretagenes* and dance noisily about his cave on Dicte, or Ida, while clashing their shields either to drown the infant's cries or to frighten off his father *Cronus. In the same manner the Curetes protect *Leto's children from jealous Hera. Their lively armed dance, like Zeus' leaps in the epigraphically preserved Dictaean Hymn, promoted the growth of fields and flocks.

The find of bronze shields (8th–6th cent. BC) in the Idaean cave suggests that human *kouroi* annually performed war dances there in a kind of initiation ritual of young men (cf. the role of the *Anakes, and *Dioskouroi* ('sons of Zeus', *see* DIOSCURI) who

were identified with the Curetes in Phocis). The dancers re-enacted Zeus' birth and death (the Curetes buried the god in his cave in one source). The confusion with other collective divine groups such as *Cabiri and *Corybantes, and an association with Dionysiac cult (*see* DIONYSUS), hint at orgiastic elements in the armed initiatory rites. The number and names of Curetes varied in tradition, like their complex genealogy. *See also* CRETAN CULTS AND MYTHS.
[Callimachus, *Hymn* 1. 52–4; Apollodorus 1. 1. 7; Diodorus Siculus 5. 70]

curses A curse is a wish that evil may befall a person or persons. Within this broad definition several different types can be distinguished, according to setting, motive, and condition. The most direct curses are maledictions inspired by feelings of hatred and lacking any explicit religious, moral, or legal legitimation. This category is exemplarily represented by the so-called curse tablets (Gk. *katadesmos*, Lat. *defixio*), thin lead sheets inscribed with maledictions intended to influence the actions or welfare of persons (or animals). If a motive is mentioned it is generally inspired by feelings of envy and competition, especially in the fields of sports and the (amphi)theatre, litigation, love, and commerce. Almost without exception these texts are anonymous and lack argumentation or references to deserved punishment of the cursed person(s). If gods are invoked they belong to the sphere of death, the Underworld, and witchcraft (*Demeter, *Persephone, *Gaia, *Hermes, *Erinyes, *Hecate). In later times the magical names of exotic demons and gods abound. Spirits of the dead are also invoked, since the tablets were often buried in graves of the untimely dead as well as in *chthonian sanctuaries and wells. The tablets might be rolled up and transfixed with a needle and sometimes 'voodoo dolls' were added. These tablets first appear in the 6th cent. BC with often simple formulas ('I bind the names of …') and develop into elaborate texts in the imperial age. More than 1,500 have been recovered.

Also included in the well-known collections of *defixiones*, yet a distinct genre, are prayers for justice or 'vindictive prayers'. Often inscribed on lead tablets, but also in other media, they differ from the binding curses in that the name of the author is often mentioned, the action is justified by a reference to some injustice wrought by the cursed person (theft, slander), the gods invoked belong to the great gods (including for instance *Helios), and they are supplicated in a submissive way to punish the culprit and rectify the injustice. This variant becomes popular only in the Hellenistic and Roman periods and is found all over the Roman empire, but especially in *Britain.

Both these types of curse are concerned with past and present occurrences. Another type refers to future events. Conditional curses (imprecations) damn the unknown persons who dare to trespass against certain stipulated sacred or secular laws, prescriptions, treaties. They are prevalent in the public domain and are expressed by the community through its representatives (magistrates, priests). The characteristic combination of curse and prayer, a feature they share with judicial prayer, is already perceptible in the Homeric term *ara*. The culprit thus found himself in the position of a man guilty of sacrilege and so the legal powers could enforce their rights even in cases where only the gods could help. A special subdivison in this category is the conditional self-curse as contained in oath formulae. Here, too, the person who offends against the oath invokes the curse he has expressed himself and the wrath of the gods. Similar imprecations, both public and private, are very common in funerary inscriptions against those who violate graves, especially in Asia Minor. All these curses may be accompanied with ritual actions, and most of them have left traces in literature, especially in 'curse poetry'.

Curtius, the hero of an aetiological myth invented to explain the name of lacus Curtius, a pit or pond in the Roman *Forum, which by the time of *Augustus had already dried up. Three Curtii are mentioned in this connection: (1) Mettius Curtius, a Sabine who fell from his horse into a marsh while fighting against *Romulus; (2) C. Curtius, consul of 445 BC who consecrated a site struck by lightning; (3) and most important, the brave young knight M. Curtius who, in obedience to an oracle, to save his country, leaped armed and on horseback into the chasm which suddenly opened in the Forum.

Cybele (Gk. *Kybelē*; Lydian form *Kybēbē*), the great mother-goddess of Anatolia, associated in myth, and later at least in cult, with her youthful lover *Attis. *Pessinus in Phrygia was her chief sanctuary, and the cult appears at an early date in Lydia. The queen or mistress of her people, Cybele was responsible for their well-being in all respects; primarily she is a goddess of fertility, but also cures (and sends) disease, gives oracles, and, as her mural crown indicates, protects her people in war. The goddess of mountains (so *Mētēr oreia*; Meter Dindymene), she is also mistress of wild nature, symbolized by her attendant lions. Ecstatic states inducing prophetic rapture and insensibility to pain were characteristic of her worship.

By the 5th century BC Cybele was known in Greece, was early associated with *Demeter and perhaps with a native 'Mother of the Gods', but except possibly for such places as Dyme, Patrae, and private cult associations at Piraeus, where Attis also was honoured, it is likely that the cult was thoroughly Hellenized. Cybele was officially brought to Rome from Asia Minor in 205–204, but under the republic, save for the public games, the Megalesia, which were celebrated by the aediles and the old patrician families, and processions of the priests of Cybele with the participation of the *quindecimviri sacris faciundis*, she was limited to her Palatine temple and served only by oriental priests. The consultation of the Sibylline books (*see* SIBYL) and the cult of Cybele were under the control of the quin-

decimviri sacris faciundis. The cycle of the spring festival, mentioned in public documents from Claudius' reign, while not fully attested till AD 354, began to take form then. The rites began on 15 March with a procession of the Reed-bearers (*cannophori*), and a sacrifice for the crops. After a week of fastings and purifications, the festival proper opened on the 22nd with the bringing of the pine-tree, symbol of Attis, to the temple. The 24th was the Day of Blood, commemorating the castration and probably the death of Attis. The 25th was a day of joy and banqueting, the *Hilaria, and after a day's rest the festival closed with the ritual bath (*Lavatio*) of Cybele's image in the Almo. The relation of this spring festival to the Hellenistic mysteries of Cybele is uncertain. Of the later mysteries, in which Attis figured prominently, we again know little. The formulae preserved mention a ritual meal; the carrying of the *kernos*, a vessel used in the *taurobolium* ('bull-sacrifice') to receive the genitals of the bull; and a descent into the *pastos*, probably an underground chamber where certain rites were enacted; but one can also think in terms of a metaphor for *initiation.

The ritual of the *taurobolium* originated in Asia Minor, and first appears in the west in the cult of Venus Caelesta (properly Caelestis) at Puteoli in AD 134. From the Antonine period, numerous dedications to Cybele and Attis record its performance in this cult 'ex vaticinatione archigalli' (i.e. with official sanction), on behalf of the emperor and the empire. From Rome the rite spread throughout the west, notably in Transalpine Gaul. It was performed also on behalf of individuals, and was especially popular during the pagan revival, AD 370–90. In the rite, the recipient descended into a ditch and was bathed in the blood of a bull, or ram (*criobolium*), which was slain above him. It was sometimes repeated after twenty years; one late text has 'taurobolio criobolioq. in aeternum renatus', 'reborn into eternity through the *taurobolium* and *criobolium*' (a concept possibly borrowed from Christianity), but in general the act was considered rather a 'thing done' for its own value than as a source of individual benefits. There has been much speculation, ancient and modern, about Cybele and her cult, but these theories are either late allegorizations or in the latter case, inspired by the modern 'myth' of the Great Mother.

A belief in immortality was perhaps part of the cult from early times, and the after-life may at first have been thought of as a reunion with Mother Earth. Later, Attis became a solar god, and he and Cybele were regarded as astral and cosmic powers; there is some evidence that the soul was then thought to return after death to its celestial source.

Thanks to its official status and early naturalization at Rome and in Ostia, the cult spread rapidly through the provinces, especially in Gaul and Africa, and was readily accepted as a municipal cult. Its agrarian character made it more popular with the fixed populations than with the soldiery, and it was especially favoured by women.

Cybele is generally represented enthroned in a *naiskos* ('shrine'), wearing either the mural crown or the *calathos* ('basket'), carrying a libation-bowl and drum, and either flanked by lions or bearing one in her lap.

See also AGDISTIS; ANAHITA; ANATOLIAN DEITIES; ATTIS; EUNUCHS.

[Catullus 63; Dionysius of Halicarnassus, *Roman Antiquities* 2. 19. 3 ff.; Ovid, *Fasti* 4. 179–372; Clement of Alexandria, *Protrepticus (Exhortation)* 2. 15; Julian, *Orations* 5. 9. 168d–169d]

Cyclopes are one-eyed giants. In *Homer they are savage and pastoral, and live in a distant country without government or laws. Here *Odysseus visits them in his wanderings and enters the cave of one of them, Polyphemus, who imprisons him and his men and eats two of them raw, morning and evening, until they escape by blinding him while in a drunken sleep, and getting out among the sheep and goats when he opens the cave in the morning. Polyphemus is the son of *Poseidon, and the god, in answer to his prayer for vengeance, opposes the homecoming of Odysseus in every possible way, bringing to pass the curse that he may return alone and find trouble when he arrives. The blinding is a popular theme of early vase-painting. Elsewhere, notably in Theocritus, we find an amorous Polyphemus, who lives in Sicily and somewhat ludicrously woos the nymph *Galatea, without success.

But in *Hesiod the Cyclopes are three, Brontes, Steropes, and Arges (Thunderer, Lightener, Bright). They are divine craftsmen who make *Zeus his thunderbolt in gratitude for their release from imprisonment by their father *Uranus (Heaven; their mother is Earth). They often appear as *Hephaestus' workmen, and often again are credited with making ancient fortifications, as those of Tiryns, and other cities of the Argolid. Their only known cult is on the Isthmus of Corinth, where they received sacrifices at their altar. The story of the blinding of the one-eyed 'Polyfoumismenos dragon' in his cave is still told in Greece.

[Homer, *Odyssey* 9. 105–542; Hesiod, *Theogony* 139–46, 501–6; Callimachus, *Hymn* 3. 46–79; Theocritus 11]

Cycnus, the Greek for 'swan' and the name of more than ten mythical figures. (1) A son of *Ares who robbed travellers bringing offerings to *Delphi. The pseudo-Hesiodic (*see* HESIOD) *Shield of Heracles* tells how *Heracles and *Iolaus encountered Cycnus and Ares in the sanctuary of *Apollo at Pagasae in Thessaly, and, when Cycnus would not let them pass, did battle and killed him, with the encouragement of Athena. *Stesichorus's *Cycnus* added other details: the brigand had planned to build a temple (to Apollo, apparently, but this has been questioned) with the skulls of his victims, and Heracles fled before him as long as he was aided by Ares. The battle was a very popular subject in 6th-cent. art. (2) A son of *Poseidon killed by *Achilles at the start of the Trojan War. The episode was treated in the *Cypria* (*see* EPIC CYCLE) and apparently in a lost play of *Sophocles. *Ovid provides details: Cycnus was invulnerable, so *Achilles strangled him, and he was transformed into a swan.

(3) A king of the Ligurians and relative or lover of *Phaethon. He lamented beside the Po for Phaethon's death and was transformed into a swan. (4) Ovid has yet another Cycnus transformed into a swan in *Metamorphoses* 7. 371–9.

[(1) Hesiod, *Shield of Achilles* 57–121, 320–480; (2) Ovid, *Metamorphoses* 12. 71–145; (3) Virgil, *Aeneid* 10. 189–93; Ovid, *Metamorphoses* 2. 367–80]

Cyparissus (in Greek, *Kyparissos*), i.e. Cypress, in mythology son of *Telephus, a Cean (in Ovid), who grieved so much at accidentally killing a pet stag that the gods turned him into the mournful tree; or a Cretan, who was so metamorphosed while fleeing from the attentions of *Apollo, or Zephyrus.

[Ovid, *Metamorphoses* 10. 106–42]

Cypria *See* EPIC CYCLE.

Cyprian (Thascius Caecilius Cyprianus), *c*.AD 200–58. Son of rich parents probably from the upper ranks of local society rather than of Roman senatorial rank, he became bishop of Carthage (248) soon after baptism and was quickly beset by *Decius' persecution (248), for which his writings are a major source. His letters and tracts, from which much of the old Latin Bible can be reconstructed, deal mainly with difficulties within the Christian community resulting from the persecution, especially the terms and proper authority for restoration of apostates and the avoidance of a split between the rival advocates of laxity and rigour. In 256–7 his theology led to a split with Rome, whose bishop Stephen recognized the baptism of *Novatianus' community (since 251 separated on rigorist grounds). In Valerian's persecution (257) he was exiled to Curubis, but returned to Carthage and on 14 September 258 was executed there, the authorities treating him with the respect due to his class. More an administrator than a thinker, he writes with the effortless superiority of a high Roman official, liking correct procedure and expecting his clergy and people, whom he calls *plebs* (and in practice his episcopal colleagues), to accept his authority. He speaks of bishops as magistrates, judges on behalf of Christ, and his language finds many analogies in Roman law. His application of juridical categories to the conception of the Church permanently influenced western Catholicism. His *Life* by his deacon Pontius, the earliest Christian biography, aims to show him as the equal of the glorious martyr Perpetua, pride of African Christianity.

Cyril of Alexandria (d. AD 444), bishop from 412 after his uncle Theophilus. He continued Theophilus' suppression in Egypt of all 'error' (*paganism, *Judaism, heresy), though his monks probably had not his approval for their murder of the Neoplatonist philosopher Hypatia (*see* NEOPLATONISM) in 415. Polemic in his Old Testament commentaries presupposes the continuing vitality of pagan cult in Egypt. He replaced the Isis-cult at Menuthis by translating thither relics of SS Cyrus and John. About 435–40 he wrote twenty books (only 1–10 extant in full) refuting *Julian point by point, so that his refutation is the principal source for reconstructing Julian's work, besides containing many quotations from *Porphyry, *Hermes Trismegistus, and other pagan sources. In 430–1 his zeal for orthodoxy and the honour of Alexandria led him to attack Nestorius of Constantinople, who was deposed at the council of Ephesus (431). But the resulting schism between Antioch and Alexandria could be healed (433) only by cautious concessions on Cyril's part, and in the controversy between the defenders of the one-nature and the dual nature of Christ at the council of Chalcedon (451) both sides were able to appeal to his statements, the interpretation of which became an issue in theological debate under Justinian.

Cyril of Jerusalem, bishop from *c*.AD 350 to his death in 387 (although banished three times from his see). His 24 *Catechetical Lectures* are an important source for liturgical history and for the topography of 4th-cent. *Jerusalem. Cyril promoted the theological significance of holy places, and was instrumental in the development of a 'stational' liturgy; he was also a keen defender of the ecclesiastical status of Jerusalem as the prime see of Christianity, provoking opposition from the provincial metropolitan bishop of (Syrian) Caesarea.

Cythera, an island off Cape Malea in the Peloponnese. In myth it was a birthplace of *Aphrodite, who had a sanctuary there and is frequently called 'Cytherean'. *See also* PAPHOS.

dadouchos, the torchbearer, the second most important priest of the *Mysteries (after the *hierophantēs) at *Eleusis, was chosen for life from the lineage of the Kerykes. He was distinguished by a head-band with a myrtle wreath, a robe (probably) of purple, and his torches: his main task had to do with providing light, a central feature of the cult. The *dadouchoi* were frequently drawn from distinguished families; the appointment was considered a very great honour; and at times there was considerable competition for it. *See* ELEUSIS.

Daedalus, a legendary artist, craftsman, and inventor. *Homer calls artful works *daidala* and associates them with *Hephaestus. The Caananite–Ugaritic artisan-god Kothar (*ktr*) probably stands behind both. Homer locates Daedalus himself in Crete (a place with early contact with the east), ascribing to him the 'dancing-ground' of *Ariadne at Cnossus; the Cnossian Linear B *da-da-re-jo* ('Daedalus' place') may corroborate the association. Later sources add the Minotaur's *labyrinth, a statue of *Aphrodite, Ariadne's thread, and the bull that captivated Pasiphae—enraging her husband, *Minos, who imprisoned Daedalus.

His escape with his son Icarus on waxen wings may appear in Greece *c.*560 BC, on a vase from Athens, and in the west *c.*470, on an inscribed Etruscan gold amulet. Icarus flew too close to the sun and his wings melted, but Daedalus crossed safely to Sicily, where he was protected by King Cocalus, whose daughters boiled the pursuing Minos alive in a steam bath. There Daedalus was

credited with numerous marvels, including a fortress near Acragas, the platform for Aphrodite's temple on Mt. *Eryx (where he also made a golden ram or honeycomb for the goddess), and his own steam bath at Selinus. Greek encounters with Phoenicians already in Sicily perhaps inspired these tales.

Attic 5th-cent. dramatists wrote satyr-plays and comedies about his adventures, and Aeschylus turned him into a maker of 'living' statues. Next he was credited with the invention of the walking pose for male statues, whose Egyptian connections were soon noticed. Connoisseurs constructed a family tree of Greek and Sicilian pupils, and local pride labelled many primitive statues with his name. His association with the 'Daedalic' style of sculpture is, however, purely modern.

By *c.*500, the Athenians had begun to claim him for themselves. The Athenian politician Cleisthenes named a village of the tribe Cecropis after him, and an Athenian antiquarian had him escape to Athens, not Sicily, and be protected by *Theseus. He was soon incorporated into Attic genealogy via *Erechtheus' son Metion; *Socrates even calls him an ancestor. New legends appeared: jealous of his nephew *Talos (2) for inventing the saw, potter's wheel, and compass, he killed him, was tried by the Areopagus, but escaped to Crete, whereupon his adventures with Minos began.

A chameleon-like figure mutating with changing political and cultural circumstance, he gained a new lease of life in Rome, where his Sicilian flight caught *Ovid's imagination, and was popular in

Roman painting. A source of inspiration into the 20th cent. (James Joyce and Michael Ayrton), this episode even prompted a self-proclaimed 'New Daedalus' to make the first human-powered flight from Crete to Thera in 1988.

[Herodotus 7. 170; Diodorus Siculus 4. 76–9; Plutarch, *Theseus* 19; Apollodorus, *Epitome* 1. 12–15; Ovid, *Metamorphoses* 8. 183 ff.; *Tristia* 2. 105 f.]

Daeira, an obscure Attic goddess associated with fertility and identified, in confusing testimonia, with *Persephone, other Underworld figures, or even *Demeter. She received cult in some Attic localities, apparently had a shrine at *Eleusis, but was not worshipped in the *Mysteries.

daimōn Etymologically the Greek term *daimōn* means 'divider' or 'allotter'; from *Homer onwards it is used mainly in the sense of operator of more or less unexpected, and intrusive, events in human life. In Homer and other early authors, gods, even Olympians, could be referred to as *daimones*. Rather than referring to personal anthropomorphic aspects, however, *daimōn* appears to correspond to supernatural power in its unpredictable, anonymous, and often frightful manifestations. Accordingly, the adjective *daimonios* means 'strange', 'incomprehensible', 'uncanny'. Hence *daimōn* soon acquired connotations of Fate. *Hesiod introduced a new meaning: the deceased of the *golden age were to him 'wealth-giving *daimones*' functioning as guardians or protectors. This resulted in the meaning 'personal protecting spirits', who accompany each human's life and bring either luck or harm. A lucky, fortunate person was *eudaimon* ('with a good *daimōn*': already in Hesiod), an unlucky one was *kakodaimōn* ('with a bad *daimōn*': from the 5th cent. BC).

*Plato used all the earlier meanings of the term and introduced a new one. He describes guardian-*daimones* who accompany man during his life and after his death function as prosecutor or advocate. In a related sense the *daimōn* becomes a transcendental stake in man, his divine 'Ego', also identified with his *Nous* ('Mind'), which man receives from god, an idea already developed by *Empedocles. Completely new is Plato's concept of *daimones* as beings intermediate between god and men. This notion was adopted by all subsequent demonologies. A pupil of Plato, Xenocrates, argued for the existence of good and evil *daimones*. This is essentially the picture accepted by the Stoa (*see* STOICISM) and in Middle and New Platonism (esp. *Plutarch, *Porphyry, and *Iamblichus). In later antiquity the existence of semi-divine beings helped to solve problems connected with the emergence of monotheistic ideas and the inherent problems of *theodicy. It also offered a solution to the question of the true nature of the old polytheistic gods. They now acquired the status of (good) *daimones* (*see* ANGELS).

All three solutions were gratefully adopted by Christian theologians: the angels from their own biblical heritage took over the positive functions of good and beneficent intermediaries; all *daimones*, now revealing the true nature of the pagan gods, were interpreted as both the embodiment and the cause of evil and sin against the will of God.

Damasus I, Pope AD 366–84. Damasus organized bloody riots to defeat his rival Ursinus. Elegant and vigorous, cultivated and unscrupulous, this 'matrons' earpick' increased the wealth and status of his church, but generally avoided confrontation with pagan senators. He requested his adviser *Jerome to begin the *Vulgate, and restored martyrs' tombs on which the calligrapher *Filocalus, his 'follower and admirer', engraved his epigrams. He advanced Rome's disciplinary and credal authority, basing it, against *Constantinople's, on apostolic succession; his buildings and martyr-cults gave Rome new glory as the Christian capital.

Damia and Auxesia, goddesses of fertility (*see* DEMETER and PERSEPHONE/KORE), worshipped at *Epidaurus, Aegina, and Troezen. Herodotus says that the cult at Epidaurus was instituted on the advice of Delphi (see DELPHIC ORACLE) after a crop-failure, and the cult statues were later stolen by the Aeginetans. The Aeginetan cult involved sacrifices and female choruses who sang ritual abuse against local women. The Epidaurian rites were similar. The Aeginetan statues were kneeling, probably as birth-goddesses. The explanatory story for this was that they fell on their knees when the Athenians tried to carry them away unsuccessfully. Women dedicated their brooches to them. At Troezen Damia and Auxesia were Cretan girls, stoned to death in a revolt, and honoured in the Lithobolia (stone-throwing festival). This and the ritual abuse resemble what occurred in other fertility cults. Damia was identified with the Italian *Bona Dea.

Danaë, in mythology daughter of *Acrisius, king of Argos, and *Eurydice. Acrisius imprisoned her, but *Zeus visited her in the form of a shower of gold, and Danaë gave birth to *Perseus. Acrisius cast mother and baby adrift in a chest, but they landed safely on the island of Seriphus. In later years Perseus rescued Danaë from persecution by Polydectes, king of Seriphus, by turning him to stone with Medusa's head. According to *Virgil, she went to Italy. Scenes of Danaë with the shower of gold, or with the chest, are found not infrequently in art.

[Apollodorus 2. 4. 1; Virgil, *Aeneid* 7. 371–2, 408–13]

Danaus and the Danaids Danaus was the son of *Belus, the brother of Aegyptus, who gave his name to the Egyptians, and the brother-in-law of *Phoenix (1), who gave his name to the Phoenicians. He himself gave his name to the Danaans, a word of unknown origin used commonly by Homer and other poets to mean the Greeks.

He was the father of 50 daughters, the Danaids. They were the subject of a long epic poem, the *Danais*, of which we know little except that it described them preparing for a battle in Egypt. From other sources we learn that they were betrothed to their cousins, the 50 sons of Aegyptus, and that, to

escape this marriage, they fled with their father to *Argos (whence their ancestor *Io had fled to Egypt) and were received as suppliants by its king, *Pelasgus.

Their reception and their pursuit by the sons of Aegyptus are the subject of the *Suppliants* of *Aeschylus. This is generally thought to have been the first play of a connected tetralogy of which the other plays were *Egyptians*, *Danaids*, and the satyric *Amymone*. It is uncertain how the story was treated in the rest of the tetralogy, since other sources contradict each other on many details. It is agreed, however, that Pelasgus failed to protect the Danaids from the Egyptians (probably they defeated and killed him in a battle), and that Danaus ordered his daughters to kill their new husbands on their wedding night. All obeyed except one, Hypermestra, who spared her husband Lynceus (probably out of love), and became the ancestor of subsequent kings of Argos. Surviving accounts of this story include Horace (a famous evocation of Hypermestra's heroism) and Ovid (a letter from Hypermestra to Lynceus), as well as treatments by scholiasts and *mythographers; and lost accounts include plays by Phrynichus (*Egyptians*, *Danaids*) and Aristophanes.

We do not know how Aeschylus resolved the issues, except that *Aphrodite had a role in *Danaids* and made a speech in favour of love. *Euripides mentions a prosecution of Danaus by Aegyptus, and *Pindar says that Danaus found new husbands for his daughters by offering them as prizes in a foot-race. A frequent motif in Latin literature is that of the Danaids' punishment in the Underworld, where they continually pour water into a leaking vessel. But this is not demonstrably earlier than the Roman period (the water-carriers seen in earlier vase-paintings of *Hades need not be Danaids).

The myth of *Amymone and *Poseidon is a separate story, linked by their water-carrying to that of the other Danaids.

[Aeschylus, *Suppliants* and *Prometheus Bound* 853–69; Apollodorus 2. 1. 4; Horace, *Odes* 3. 11; Ovid, *Heroines* 14]

dancing From earliest times, the dance played an important role in the lives of the Greeks, and was sometimes regarded by them as the invention of the gods. It was generally associated with music and song or poetry in the art called *mousikē* and frequently made use of a body of conventionalized *gestures. The dance had a place in religious festivals, in the secret rites of *mysteries, in artistic competitions, in the education of the young, and even in military training, especially in Sparta. People danced at weddings, at funerals, at the 'naming-days' of infants, at harvests, at victory celebrations, in after-dinner merrymaking, in joyous dance processions (*kōmos*) through the streets, in animal mummery, and even in incantations. Performances by professional dancers were enjoyed, especially at the symposium; such dancers were almost all slaves and prostitutes.

Among particularly famous dances of the Greeks were the *geranos* (a nocturnal serpentine dance the name of which is probably derived from the hypothetical root *ger-*, 'to wind', and not from the word for 'crane'); the pyrrhic and related dances by men and boys in armour; the *partheneion*, a song-dance performance by maidens; the *hyporchēma*, a lively combination of instrumental music, song, dance, and pantomime; the skilful 'ball-playing' dance; and the uproarious *askōliasmos*, performed on greased wine-skins. In the worship of *Dionysus the wild *oreibasia*, or 'mountain-dancing' of frenzied women, by Classical times was toned down into a prepared performance by a *thiasos*, or group of trained devotees.

In the Athenian theatre, the *tyrbasia* of the cyclic choruses, the lewd *kordax* of comedy, the stately *emmellia* of tragedy, and the rollicking *sikinnis* of the satyr-play were distinctive. The actors in the farces (*phlyakes*) of Magna Graecia apparently at times burlesqued the dignified dances of the religious festivals.

The Romans were much more restrained than the Greeks in their use of the dance. Some of them, including *Cicero, openly expressed contempt for dancers. There are records of a few ancient dances used in religious ceremonies—e.g. the leaping and 'three-foot' dances (*tripudia*) of the armed *Salii and the *fratres arvales*, and the 'rope dance' of maidens in honour of *Juno. Etruscan and Greek dancers, from the 4th cent. BC on, exerted some influence, and the introduction of various *oriental cults brought noisy and ecstatic dances to Rome. Dancing by professionals, usually slaves, often furnished entertainment at dinner-parties. With the coming of the pantomime, popular interest in the dance became great. *See* MASKS; MUSIC IN WORSHIP.

[Plato, *Laws* 7. 814e–817e; Athenaeus 1. 25–7, 37–40, 14. 25–30; Lucian, *On the Dance*; Livy 27. 37. 12–15]

Daphne ('Laurel'), daughter of a river-god (usually the Ladon, in Arcadia), a wild virgin huntress who caught *Apollo's eye. Failing to outrun the god in her attempt to avoid ravishment, at the point of capture she prayed for help from *Zeus (or her father) and was metamorphosed into a bay-tree; Apollo, clasping the trunk in frustrated passion, had to content himself with adopting her foliage as his cultic plant.

[Ovid, *Metamorphoses* 1. 452–567; see also Pausanias 8. 20, who summarizes a Hellenistic Greek version]

Daphne, a park 9 km. (5½ mi.) south of Antioch in Syria, at natural springs supplying the city's water. Its inviolate *temenos*, with a temple of *Apollo and *Artemis, was dedicated by King Seleucus I and served by priests appointed by the kings; it saw the celebrated festival and procession staged by *Antiochus (1) IV in 166 BC. Pompey enlarged its area, and under the Principate it seems to have been imperial property and, in the 4th cent. AD, the site of a palace. Famed for its natural beauties (the emperors protected its famous cypresses), it was a favourite and somewhat disreputable resort of the Antiochenes; in the 4th cent. a controversial festival (the Maiumas?) celebrated there was considered immoral by the local orator Libanius and on one occasion banned. A theatre, several villas, and mosaics have been excavated.

Daphnis, a Sicilian herdsman, named from the laurel-tree (*daphnē*), he was the son, or favourite, of *Hermes and loved by the nymph Echenais who demanded his fidelity. When he was made drunk by a princess and lay with her, the *nymph blinded him. This version was attributed, probably wrongly, to the lyric poet *Stesichorus. Daphnis consoled himself by inventing pastoral music or perhaps was the first subject of the genre when other herdsmen sang of his misfortunes. In another version, he dies when *Aphrodite, angry because he will love no one, instils in him a powerful passion to which he refuses to yield.

[Theocritus, *Idylls* 1. 64–142, 8; Virgil, *Eclogues* 5; Diodorus Siculus 4. 84]

Dardanus, ancestor of the Trojan kings. In *Homer we have the genealogy *Zeus–Dardanus–Erichthonius–Tros.

See GENEALOGICAL TABLES (2) HOUSE OF TROY.

According to Homer, Dardanus was Zeus' favourite of all his sons by mortal women. Later authors give two accounts of him. (*a*) He was from Samothrace, the son of Zeus and *Electra (2), daughter of *Atlas, and brother of *Iasion. Either because he was driven out by *Deucalion's flood or because Iasion was killed by a thunderbolt for assaulting *Demeter Dardanus left Samothrace and came to the mainland. Here King *Teucer (1) welcomed him and gave him part of his kingdom and the hand of his daughter Batia in marriage. After Teucer's death Dardanus called the country Dardania. (*b*) He lived in Italy, and was son of Electra (2) and *Corythus (1) and brother of Iasius (Iasion). Either the brothers separated, Iasius going to Samothrace and Dardanus to the Troad, or Dardanus killed Iasius. There are also three other accounts, that he was an Arcadian, a Cretan, and a native of the Troad. The constants are that he was Electra (2)'s son and founded Dardania.

[Homer, *Iliad* 20. 215 ff., 304–5; *Odyssey* 5. 125 ff.; Apollodorus 3. 12. 1]

Dares of Phrygia, Trojan priest of *Hephaestus in the *Iliad* and supposed author of a pre-Homeric account of the Trojan War. The extant Latin *History of the Fall of Troy by Dares of Phrygia* (5th or 6th cent. AD) is represented in a fictional prefatory epistle from the historian Sallust to Cornelius Nepos as a translation of this work by the former. It is undistinguished and derivative, but was much read in the Middle Ages.

Dea Dia, a goddess worshipped by the *fratres arvales* who celebrated her main festival in May. Her function and character are, in many respects, obscure. The etymology of 'Dia' suggests an original connection with the brightness of the sun; but she was also connected with agricultural prosperity. See CARMEN ARVALE.

dead, disposal of Correct disposal of the dead was always a crucial element in easing the *soul of the deceased into the next world. However, the forms of burial varied enormously. Great significance was attached to the choice of inhumation, cremation, or some other rite, but there is rarely any reason to see a direct correlation between specific methods and specific racial, class, or religious groups.

Greece In prehistory there was enormous variation. An inhumation burial is known from mesolithic times in the Franchthi cave (Argolid), while in Thessaly cremation cemeteries go back to early neolithic. In the early bronze age rich grave goods were sometimes used, particularly in the multiple inhumation tombs of the Cyclades and Crete. In the late bronze age, there was for the first time considerable uniformity on the mainland, with multiple inhumations in rock-cut chamber-tombs being the norm. In early Mycenaean times a few people were buried in spectacular tholos-(beehive) tombs. Very large cemeteries of chamber-tombs have been found at Mycenae and other sites. This pattern extended as far north as Thessaly, but in Macedonia and Epirus individual inhumation in stone-lined cist-graves, grouped together under mounds of earth, was normal. After the destruction of the Mycenaean world *c*.1200 BC, regional variations returned in the 'Dark Age'. Inhumations in cists with the body contracted were normal at Argos; cremation on a pyre with just a handful of the ashes scattered in the grave at Lefkandi on Euboea; on Crete, chamber-tombs with multiple inhumations until about 1000, and then multiple cremations with the ashes placed in urns. At Athens, adult rites changed frequently—inhumations in cists in the 11th cent.; cremations with the ashes in urns, *c*.1000–750; inhumations in earth-cut pit-graves, *c*.750–700; cremations in the grave itself, *c*.700–550; and then inhumations in pit-graves, tile-covered graves, or sarcophagi from about 550 onwards. Early archaeologists associated both cist burial and cremation with the Dorian invasion at various times, but these correlations are not convincing.

There were, however, a few generally observed rules. Cremation with the ashes placed in a metal urn (usually bronze), in the Homeric style, tended to be associated with warrior burials throughout antiquity. Children were rarely cremated, and in most places infants were buried inside amphoras or storage pots. Starting in the 6th cent. there was a general trend towards simpler burials, which may have been accompanied by sumptuary laws. Inhumation in pit-graves or tile graves was adopted for adults in most parts of Greece by the 6th or 5th cent. The main exception was western Greece, where adults were inhumed in giant storage pots from the Dark Age to Hellenistic times.

Rich grave goods and elaborate tomb markers went out of style everywhere for most of the 5th cent., but returned around 425. There was a great flowering of funerary sculpture at Athens in the 4th cent. Funerary spending escalated still further after 300, and in the 3rd–1st cents. BC the massive

'Macedonian'-style vaulted tombs, often with painted interiors, are found all over Greece. The most spectacular of these are the late 4th-cent. royal tombs, possibly of Philip II and his court, at Vergina in Macedonia. Athens was an exception to this general pattern. Demetrius of Phalerum banned lavish tombs, probably in 317, and indeed no monumental burials are known from Attica between then and the 1st cent. BC. In Roman times inhumation was the strict rule throughout the whole Greek east, although the precise forms varied—from tile graves at Athens to chamber-tombs at Cnossus, built tombs at Dura Europus, and spectacular rock-cut tombs at Petra. Greek settlers in the near east, from Egypt to Bactria, generally adopted rites very similar to the local population's practices.

Rome Burial customs in prehistoric Italy were as varied as those in Greece. The earliest graves found at Rome date to the 10th cent. BC, and include both urn cremations and inhumations. There is, however, no reason to see these as belonging to different racial groups. Roman burials were until about 100 BC generally rather simple, in marked contrast to their neighbours the Etruscans, who built complex chamber-tombs which often housed cremations in unusual urns, accompanied by rich grave goods. From the 8th cent. on the customs of southern Italy were heavily influenced by Greek settlers, and inhumation generally replaced cremation. Impressive local traditions of tomb-painting developed, particularly in Campania.

At Rome itself, few burials are known from republican times, suggesting that rites were so simple as to leave few archaeological traces. Across most of Europe in the 5th–3rd cents. the bulk of the population was disposed of relatively informally, often by exposing the body on platforms. In Italy there is some evidence for mass burial of the poor in huge open pits. The use of these *puticuli* at Rome is attested in the late republic, and a few were excavated in the 1880s. By the

3rd cent. BC some of the rich were being cremated with their ashes placed in urns and buried in communal tombs. By the 1st cent., cremation was the norm, and apparently even the ultra-conservative Cornelii gave up inhumation in 78 BC. At about the same time, Roman nobles began building very elaborate tombs modelled on those of the Greek east, with monumental sculptures and elaborate stone architecture.

The spiralling cost of élite tombs ended abruptly under Augustus, who built himself a vast mausoleum. Other nobles were careful to avoid being seen as trying to rival the splendour of the imperial household. Simpler tombs, organized around modest *altars, came into fashion for the very rich, while the not-quite-so-rich and the growing number of funerary clubs (see CLUBS (collegia)) adopted the *columbarium (a word meaning 'dovecote', coined by modern scholars). The earliest example dates to c.50 BC, but they became common after c.AD 40. They were barrel-vaulted brick and masonry tombs with niches for urns, usually holding 50–100, although one example found at Rome in 1726 held 3,000 urns.

Urn cremation was adopted all over the western empire in the 1st and 2nd cent. AD, although there were always significant local variations. By about AD 150, the empire can be divided into a cremating, Latin-using west and an inhuming, Greek-using east. But during the 2nd cent. members of the Roman élite adopted inhumation, probably as a conscious emulation of Hellenistic practices, and in the 3rd cent. this rite gradually swept across the whole west. The change has no obvious links to *Christianity or any other religious movement. However, it was certainly convenient for the spread of Christianity, which generally opposed cremation, which destroyed the body and posed difficulties for some visions of the day of resurrection. By the late 4th cent., certain practices found widely in western cemeteries—an east–west orientation, the use of lime on the walls of the grave, and the decline of grave goods—might indicate the presence

of Christians. At Rome itself, there was a general shift around 300 away from traditional cemeteries in favour of *catacombs and burial within *basilicas.

See further ART, FUNERARY, GREEK and ROMAN; CEMETERIES; DEATH, ATTITUDES TO.

Dead Sea Scrolls, documents made of leather and papyrus, and, in one case, of copper, found between 1947 and 1956 in caves near Qumran by the Dead Sea. The scrolls, written by Jews, are mostly in Hebrew and Aramaic, but a small number are in Greek. Many are fragments of biblical texts from the Old Testament and from Jewish religious compositions otherwise only preserved through Christian manuscript traditions. The scrolls were written in the last centuries BC and 1st cent. AD.

Of particular significance in the study of Judaism in this period are the texts composed by sectarians, who are probably to be identified with Jews who used the nearby site at Qumran as a religious centre. These texts include community rules, hymns, liturgical texts, calendars, and works of bible interpretation. Among this last group is found the *pesher* type of interpretation, characteristic of this sect and rarely found elsewhere in Jewish literature, in which the real meaning of scriptural passages is alleged to lie in hidden allusions to more recent events.

The Community Rule (1QS, also called the Manual of Discipline), a composite work found in various manuscripts in different caves, laid down the rules for initiation into the community and for living within it. The Rule of the Congregation or Messianic Rule (1QSa) gives regulations for the eschatological integration of the 'congregation of Israel' into the sectarian community. The Damascus Rule (CD) is also attested in a medieval manuscript (the Zadokite Fragments) discovered in Cairo in 1896. The War Rule (1QM) is a rather different text which regulates the behaviour of the 'sons of light' in the eschatological war against the 'sons of darkness'. The Temple Scroll (11QT) contains a systematic statement of the regulations pertaining to the Temple cult, derived from the Pentateuch but with frequent non-biblical additions which are presented as the direct words of God. Numerous fragments of the scrolls are still unedited and it is certain that more sectarian material will be recognized in the remaining material.

How many of those documents were originally composed by adherents of one particular sect is debated. If the scrolls were deposited in the caves for safe keeping, they may have been placed there by more than one group, perhaps after the destruction of the Jerusalem Temple in AD 70. The contents of the Copper Scroll (3Q15), a prosaic list of the hiding-places of an immensely valuable treasure, might support this hypothesis, but finds of multiple copies of some sectarian texts in different caves may suggest that only one sect was responsible for placing them there. In that case doctrinal differences between texts must be accounted for by supposing either variant branches of the sect or a gradual development of the sect's ideas over time.

Many attempts have been made to connect the scrolls to the Jewish groups of this period known from other sources. Most such attempts assume that the scrolls were deposited by the inhabitants of the site at Qumran, where excavation revealed a small community, isolated in the desert, with a deep concern for ritual purity. The most plausible of such identifications is with the *Essenes, who are known primarily from descriptions by ancient authors (both Jewish and pagan). However, the classical evidence is equivocal and contradictory, and some aspects of the Essene society depicted there do not fit the evidence from the scrolls, so that those who hold this hypothesis have to consider the scrolls community as Essenes of a peculiar type. It may be better to take the sectarian material in the scrolls as evidence of a type of Judaism otherwise unknown. *See* JUDAISM.

deae matres, 'mother goddesses', whose cult is widely attested in monuments and inscriptions of the Celtic and Germanic regions of the Roman empire, from northern Italy to Britain. Their role as fertility goddesses is suggested not only by their titles but also by their most common attribute, baskets of fruits and other provisions. There was, however, considerable local variation both in epithets and in iconography, indicating that their general character took many particular forms. The most distinctive representation is of a triad, typical of Celtic thought, although individual goddesses, pairs, and groups of four or more are also common. In some cases they are associated with springs, while in others they are depicted nursing infants. The title *matronae* ('matrons') was preferred in northern Italy and on the lower Rhine, while their epithets, found in many parts of the empire, often incorporate tribal or local names. *See* CELTIC RELIGION.

death, attitudes to

Greek The Greek attitude towards *Hades is best summed up by *Achilles, 'I'd rather be a day-labourer on earth working for a man of little property than lord of all the hosts of the dead'. The Homeric dead are pathetic in their helplessness, inhabiting draughty, echoing halls, deprived of their wits (*phrenes*), and flitting purposelessly about uttering batlike noises. Athenian lawcourt speeches urge the jury to render assistance to the dead as if they were unable to look after their own interests. The precise relationship between the living body and the *psychē* (spirit of the dead) is unclear, since the latter is only referred to in connection with the dead. The necessity of conducting burial rites and the insult to human dignity if they are omitted are frequently mentioned in literature. Except in philosophy and *Orphism, belief in a dualistic after-life is largely absent from Greek eschatology. In Homer the Underworld judge *Minos merely settles lawsuits between the litigious dead. Only gross sinners (e.g. *Tantalus, *Tityus, and *Sisyphus) receive retributive punishment (*see* TARTARUS), while the favoured few end up in the Elysian Fields (*see* ELYSIUM). Fear of the after-life was therefore largely absent. (*See also* SIN.) Though powerless in themselves the dead had access to the infernal powers, notably Pluto (Aedoneus) and Persephone, for which reason folded lead plaques (*katadesmoi*) inscribed with *curses bearing the name of the person to be 'bound down' were occasionally placed in graves.

The deceased's journey to the next world was effected by elaborate ritual conducted by the relatives of the deceased, primarily women. The funeral, from which priests were debarred for fear of incurring *pollution, was a three-act drama which comprised laying out the body (*prothesis*), the funeral cortège (*ekphora*), and the interment. We only rarely hear of undertakers (*nekrothoptoi*, *nekrophoroi*) and other 'professionals'. We know of no burial 'service' as such. Cremation and inhumation were often practised concurrently in the same community, with no apparent distinction in belief. From c.500 BC intramural burial was forbidden in Athens. No tomb-cult was practised in early times, but in Classical Athens women paid regular visits to the grave. Offerings included cakes and *choai*, i.e. *libations mainly of pure water. The attention that the dead received from the living in this period was judged to be so important that it constituted a reason for adopting an heir. In the Archaic period a funeral provided a perfect showcase for the conspicuous display of aristocratic wealth, power, and prestige, and many communities passed legislation designed to limit its scope and magnificence.

Funerary ritual was substantially modified for those who died in their prime, the unburied dead, victims of murder, suicides, heroes, etc. Special sympathy was felt towards those who died at a marriageable age but unmarried. To underline their pathos, a stone marker in the form of a *loutrophoros* (i.e. vase used in the wedding bath) was placed over the grave. Victims of murder were vengeful and malignant, as indicated by the grisly

practice of cutting off their extremities (*see* MASCHALISMOS). Most powerful were the heroic dead, who even in the 2nd cent. AD still received blood sacrifice. *See* HERO-CULT.

Geometric vases depict only the *prothesis* and *ekphora*, whereas Athenian white-ground *lēkythoi* (oil flasks) frequently depict tomb-cult. *Hades is rarely represented in Greek art (an exception is the painter Polygnotus' lost painting, the *Nekyia*) or in literature (Homer's *Odyssey*, book 11 and Aristophanes' *Frogs* are notable exceptions; cf. too '*Orphic' gold leaves). Though the belief in Hades as the home of the undifferentiated dead predominated and never lost its hold over the popular imagination (cf. its persistence as a theme in epitaphs), other concepts include the transformation of the dead into stars (e.g. Castor and Pollux), their absorption into the upper atmosphere or aether, the Pythagorean and Platonic belief in *transmigration, and the indistinct 'blessedness' promised to initiates in the mysteries of *Eleusis. *See* CONSTELLATIONS; PYTHAGORAS.

Roman In the Roman tradition death is conceived of essentially as a blemish striking the family of the deceased, with the risk of affecting all with whom it had contact: neighbours, magistrates, priests, and sacred places. For this reason ritual established a strict separation between the space of the deceased and that of the living. Cypress branches announced the blemished house, and on days of sacrifices for the dead sanctuaries were closed.

The time of death spanned above all the period when the deceased's corpse was exposed in his or her home, its transport to the cemetery, and its burial. These operations were usually completed after eight days. The transformation of the corpse was achieved in the course of 40 days. The deceased did not, in the course of the funerary ritual, arrive at life eternal, but joined, as it were, a new category: those members of the community, the *di *manes*, who lived outside towns on land set aside for this purpose and managed by the *pontifices*. The legal status of these tombs was that of the *religiosum* (*see* ROMAN RELIGION, TERMS RELATING TO). The *di manes* were thought of as an undifferentiated mass or (rather) a collective divinity (Romans spoke of the *di manes* of such-and-such a person), and received regular cult during the *Parentalia of 13–21 February and at other times. The immortality which they enjoyed was conditional on the existence of descendants, or at least of a human presence (a proprietor of the land on which the tomb was located, or a funerary *collegium*: *see* CLUBS), since it was the celebration of funerary cult, in the form of sacrifices, which ensured the deceased's survival.

The unburied dead were called *lemures* and thought of as haunting inhabited areas and disturbing the living. Usually anonymous (being no longer integrated into any social context) they none the less received cult at the *Lemuria in May, supposedly to appease them.

Along with these forms of survival, conceived generally as menacing and undesirable, there existed a third belief about life after death—deification. Combining Roman tradition with Hellenistic practices and ideas deriving from Hellenistic philosophy, the deification of exceptional individuals was instituted at Rome after Julius *Caesar's assassination. Thereafter elevation to the status of a god (*divus*) by a *senatus consultum* became the rule for emperors and some members of their families (*see* RULER-CULT).

To these traditions was added, from the last centuries of the republic on, a series of Hellenistic concepts, ranging from speculation about the immortality of the soul to images of hell. Verse epitaphs prove that these ideas were rarely exclusive and coherent. We are dealing with speculations rather than beliefs capable of shaping a person's whole existence.

See CEMETERIES; DEAD, DISPOSAL OF.

[Homer, *Odyssey* 11, 24. 1–204; Aristophanes, *Frogs*; Lucretius 3]

Decius (Gaius Messius Quintus Decius), emperor AD 249–51, born in Pannonia, but of an old senatorial family, had already achieved high office before being appointed by Philip to restore order on the Danube. His success, and Philip's unpopularity, caused his troops to declare him emperor and compel him to overthrow his patron. In 250 the Carpi invaded Dacia, the Goths, under Kniva, Moesia. Decius was defeated near Beroea. The following year, in an attempt to intercept the Goths on their way home, he and his son Herennius were defeated and killed at Abrittus.

Decius was a staunch upholder of the old Roman traditions. His assumption of the additional surname of Trajan promised an aggressive frontier policy; and his persecution of Christians (the first attempt by the state to impose a sacrifice test on all the inhabitants of the empire) resulted from his belief that the restoration of state cults was essential to the preservation of the empire. (*See* CHRISTIANITY.) However, his approach was outdated and his reign initiated the worst period of the 3rd-cent. 'crisis'.

dedicatio Transfer of a thing from the human into the divine sphere was accomplished through the act of *dedicatio* and *consecratio*, the former indicating surrender of an object into divine ownership, the latter its transformation into a *res sacra*. Dedications of temples, places, and altars (*aedes*, *terra*, *ara*) were legally binding only if performed by competent authorities: (*a*) the magistrates with *imperium*; (*b*) with respect to temples, the board of two men acting in their stead (*duumviri aedi dedicandae*) elected by the people (as duumvirs were often appointed the magistrates who had vowed the temple while in office, or their relatives); (*c*) the aediles, but only from the fines imposed by them (*pecunia multaticia*); (*d*) any person specifically selected by the people, as stipulated by a *lex Papiria*, perhaps of 304 BC. At dedications of temples, the dedicant held a doorpost and pronounced (without interruption, hesitation, or stumbling) a formula dictated to him by a pontiff (*see* PONTI-

FEX/PONTIFICES), with other pontiffs often present. It contained a precise description of the object, the ground on which it stood, and the conditions of its use, with a written record as the title-deed (*lex dedicationis*).

dedications *See* VOTIVE OFFERINGS.

deformity Far fewer congenitally deformed persons would have survived infancy than is the case today because the Greeks and Romans had little compunction about withholding the necessities of life from those they deemed incapable of leading an independent life.

The belief that the birth of a congenitally deformed infant was an expression of divine ill will is already present in *Hesiod. *Oath-breaking was supposedly punished by the birth of a deformity. However, there is no evidence to indicate that any Greek community took official notice of abnormal births, nor that such births constituted a distinctive category of *divination. By contrast the Romans regarded the birth of a deformed child or animal as portentous in the extreme, as is demonstrated by the fact that *monstrum* ('portent') is etymologically related to *monere* ('to warn'). Prodigies were recorded on a yearly basis in the pontifical records and have survived in the writings of Livy. According to Livy 'the most abhorred *portents of all' were the hermaphrodites (*see* HERMAPHRODITUS), for whom distinctive rites of expiation were introduced in 207 BC.

Few individuals of whom we have record are known to have been congenitally deformed. The absence of physical blemish was a requirement for holding both Greek and Roman priesthoods (*see* PRIESTS).

From earliest times reports of persons exhibiting gross deformities were widely circulated, as the name of the Cyclops Polyphemus ('much talked about') suggests, though we should note that *Homer never specifically describes the giant's celebrated single eye (*see* CYCLOPES).

Deianira, in mythology daughter of *Oeneus and Althaea, and wife of *Heracles, won by him in combat from another suitor, the river *Acheloüs. Originally she may well have been a bold-hearted and aggressive character who deliberately murdered Heracles, but *Sophocles portrays her as a gentle, timid, and loving woman who unintentionally brings him to death. Once, years earlier, when the *Centaur Nessus assaulted her, Heracles shot him with an arrow poisoned with the Hydra's blood. Dying, Nessus told Deianira to gather some blood from around his wound, assuring her that it was a potent love-charm. She did so and kept it for years, during which she bore Heracles several children. Now, in the play, Heracles brings Iole home as his concubine, and Deianira, to regain his love, sends him a robe smeared with the 'love-charm'. He is carried home, dying from the poison, and she kills herself. Deianira with Nessus is a popular scene in art from the 7th cent. BC.

[Sophocles, *Women of Trachis*]

Deiphobus, in mythology, son of *Priam and *Hecuba, and one of the more powerful Trojan fighters. *Athena impersonated him so as to deceive *Hector and bring about his death. After *Paris was killed, Deiphobus married *Helen; he went with her to examine the Wooden Horse; and after the capture of Troy, *Menelaus and *Odysseus went first to his house, where the fighting was hardest. He was killed and mutilated by Menelaus after being, according to *Virgil, betrayed by Helen. Deiphobus is sometimes found in art in scenes of the war at Troy.

[Homer, *Iliad* 13. 156 ff., 402 ff., 22. 227 ff.; *Odyssey* 4. 274 ff., 8. 517 ff.; Virgil, *Aeneid* 6. 494 ff.]

Deiphontes, in mythology, a descendant in the fifth generation of *Heracles. He married *Hyrnetho, daughter of *Temenus king of Argos, and was favoured by him above his own sons, who therefore murdered their father and strove with Deiphontes, with results variously described by different authors.

deisidaimonia Although originally the term had a positive meaning ('scrupulousness in religious matters'), it is predominantly used in a derogatory way and denotes an excessive pietism and preoccupation with religion, first and most explicitly in Theophrastus' sixteenth *Character*. He defines *deisidaimonia* as 'cowardice vis-à-vis the divine' and gives the following characteristics: an obsessive fear of the gods, a bigoted penchant for adoration and cultic performance, superstitious awe of *portents both in daily life and in *dreams, and the concomitant inclination to ward off or prevent possible negative effects by magical or ritual acts, especially through continuous *purifications. Later, *Plutarch gives largely the same picture, tracing its origin to erroneous or defective knowledge about the gods. This is also the opinion of Roman observers like Lucretius, *Cicero, and the younger Seneca, who use the Latin word *superstitio, which Ennius and Plautus had already associated with negative notions such as private *divination, *magic, and more generally *prava religio* ('bad religion').

The latter notion in particular forbids us from simply identifying *deisidaimonia* and *superstitio* under the collective label 'superstition'. To a far greater extent than the corresponding Greek term, Latin *superstitio* became a judgemental term used by the dominant 'orthodox' religion to classify 'other', especially foreign and exotic, religions of which it disapproved (e.g. foreign, esp. Egyptian, rites, and Jewish rites). It acquired the function of a social marker through pejorative reference to the other's 'bad religion'. This use was adopted (and reversed) by the Christians especially in their condemnation of the retention of *pagan beliefs and of the magical application of Christian myth and ritual. *See* ORIENTAL CULTS AND RELIGION.

Delos, a small island (3 sq. km; 1⅕ sq. mi.) between Myconos and Rheneia, regarded in antiquity as the centre of the Cyclades. Composed of gneiss and granite, it is barren and almost waterless and was incapable of supporting its inhabitants.

Delos, the only place to offer shelter to *Leto, was said to be the birthplace of *Apollo and *Artemis, as recounted in the Archaic *Homeric Hymn to Apollo* (*see* HYMNS (GREEK)). This was the basis of its historical importance. It was also the burial-place of the *Hyperboreans. *Anius was its heroic founder, son and priest of Apollo, later associated with the Trojan cycle.

Early Bronze-Age occupation on Mt. Cynthus was succeeded by a Mycenaean settlement on the low ground later occupied by the sanctuary. Two Mycenaean graves were later identified as the tombs of the *Hyperborean maidens (the Theke and the Sema). Continuity of cult into historic times is unlikely.

Delos was colonized by Ionians *c*.950 BC but the sanctuary's prominence originates in the 8th cent. It became the principal cult centre of the Ionians of the Cyclades, Asia Minor, Attica, and Euboea, and was perhaps the centre of an Ionian *amphictiony. Naxos and Paros were its most conspicuous patron communities in the early Archaic period. In the later 6th cent. first Pisistratus of Athens and then Polycrates of Samos asserted their authority. The Athenians purified the island by removing burials within view of the sanctuary and perhaps built a temple of Apollo (the *pōrinos naos*). Polycrates dedicated Rheneia to Apollo, providing the basis for the sanctuary's subsequent wealth. Delos emerged unscathed from the Persian Wars (490–479 BC) and subsequently became the meeting-place and treasury of the Delian League. After their removal to Athens in 454 BC the Athenians assumed administration of the sanctuary but did not impose tribute. In 426 BC Athens carried out a second purification, clearing all burials and depositing their contents in the Purification Trench on Rheneia. Henceforth women about to give birth and the dying had to be removed to Rheneia. They also reorganized their quadrennial festival (the Delia), celebrated with particular splendour by Nicias in 417 BC, perhaps to inaugurate the new temple of Apollo. In 422 BC the Delians were expelled by Athens on a charge of impurity but were soon recalled. Its independence following liberation in 405 BC was short-lived, administration of the sanctuary reverting to Athens from 394 BC.

Athenian domination lasted until the Macedonian king Antigonus' foundation of the League of Islanders in 314 BC, championed by the Ptolemies in the early 3rd cent. but redundant after the failed Chremonidean War of Athens against Macedon. For a century and a half Delos was independent and functioned as a normal city-state, with an archon as its chief magistrate and the sanctuary's administration entrusted to a board of *hieropoioi* (religious officials). This was a period of extensive new public building, some provided by foreign patrons (e.g. the stoas of Antigonus II Gonatas and Philip V of Macedon). These and the festivals instituted by successive Hellenistic kings were more a display of religious patronage than an assertion of political domination. Although Delos' population remained relatively small (*c.*3,000–4,000) it began to develop as a commercial centre, attracting foreign bankers and traders, Italians prominent among them.

Independence ended in 166 BC when Rome handed control of Delos to Athens. Its inhabitants were expelled and replaced by Athenian settlers. Delos was made a free port to the detriment of Rhodian commerce. In conjunction with its commercial growth in the later 2nd and early 1st cent. its population expanded enormously and it became increasingly cosmopolitan, merchants and bankers from Italy and the Hellenized east forming distinct communities. Delos became the most important market for the slave trade. Although Athenians filled the civic posts (chief magistrate, the *epimelētēs*), guilds and associations of the foreign communities and trading groups administered their own affairs. Sacked in 88 BC by Archelaus, the general of Mithradates VI of Pontus, and again in 69 BC by pirates, Delos never recovered its former greatness. By the end of the 1st cent. BC its importance as a sanctuary as well as a commercial centre were lost. Its decline, which became a standard topic in

Roman literature, owed as much to shifts in trading-patterns as the destructions. A small community survived into late antiquity.

The cults of Apollo, Artemis, and Leto were naturally the most prominent and among the most ancient, though none need be earlier than the 8th cent. Apollo was the focus of the annual Ionian festival (the *panēgyris*) celebrated with games, singing, and dancing. Individual cities sent delegations to the major festivals and some, such as Andros, Ceos, and Carystus, had their own *oikoi* (buildings) within the sanctuary. It was administered by boards of officials responsible for managing the property of Apollo and guarding the temple treasures, as well as maintaining the buildings of the officially recognized cults. However, as in any normal community, the gods charged with other communal concerns were given due attention, each having its own cult and annual festival. From the late 3rd cent. and especially after 166 BC foreign cults multiplied, reflecting the cosmopolitan character of the city. Most were of oriental origin, such as *Sarapis, *Isis, and the Syrian gods Hadad and *Atargatis, but Italian divinities, such as the *Lares compitales*, also occur and, from the early 1st cent. BC, a *synagogue served the Jewish community. Many were private and not officially recognized.

Among the more curious cult rituals were the sacred offerings sent to Delos by the Hyperboreans, passed from city to city along a fixed route, apparently modified under Athenian influence to pass through Attica. The serpentine dance (*geranos; see* DANCING; PYGMIES), initiated by *Theseus and the Athenian youths returning from Crete, was performed at the Altar of Horns. The poet *Callimachus alludes to self-flagellation around the altar and gnawing the trunk of the sacred olive.

The archaeological exploration of Delos, conducted by the French school since 1873, has unearthed the sanctuary and large parts of the ancient city. Its public buildings, commercial installations, and residential quarters, combined with a mass of epigraphic documentation from the 4th cent. BC, give a detailed picture of its political, religious, social, and economic history. Nevertheless, the identification of many of the monuments is disputed.

Most of the ancient cults lay in the low ground on the sheltered west side of the island. Here were the temples of Apollo, the Artemision, and, to the north, the Letoon, as well as the Dodekatheon (sanctuary of the twelve gods) and others not securely identified. In the same area are the buildings of various cities, *dining-rooms, and the altars; the site of the Altar of Horns (the *keratinos bōmos*), reputedly built by Apollo himself, is debated. The Heraion, one of the earliest temples, stood apart at the foot of Mt. Cynthus, whose peak was crowned by a sanctuary of Zeus and Athena. The cult of Anius was housed in a building in the north-east. Originally the sanctuary was approached from the north, passing the Lion Terrace, but subsequently it was entered from the south. The later cults, especially those of oriental origin, were for practical and religious reasons concentrated below Mt. Cynthus and around its peak. The synagogue, on the north-east coast, was isolated from the other sacred areas. Many of the associations named after a particular divinity (e.g. the Poseidoniasts of Berytus and the Hermaists) combined cult with commercial and social functions (*see* CLUBS).

The sanctuary of Apollo was also the focus for the city's political institutions, with buildings for council and assembly. Associated with the social and religious life of the city were the hippodrome, stadium, and gymnasium on the low ridge north-east of the sanctuary. North of the Sacred Lake were two palaestras and on the lower slopes of Cynthus, in the old town, was the theatre. Around the sanctuary and encroaching on the sacred precincts were many of the commercial establishments, such as the markets of the Delians and the Italians. Warehouses fringed the shore south of the port. Residential areas surrounded the sanctuary on the north, east, and south. No trace of the early

city remains. The old town of the 3rd cent., with its unsystematic plan of winding streets and irregular houses, lay to the south at the base of Mt. Cynthus. The expansion of habitation in the later 2nd and early 1st cent. matched the increase in population after 166 BC. Houses of this period are larger, more regular, and organized on a rectilinear street grid. Their affluence testifies to the wealth of the city. Many contain mosaics and traces of wall-paintings and the largest have colonnaded courts. Some 15,000 clay sealings found in one house are all that remains of a private archive. Delos remained unwalled until 69 BC when, following the pirate sack, Triarius constructed a wall encompassing the main sanctuary and the residential areas to its north and south. The city's vast necropolis covered the south-east shore of Rheneia.

Delphi (*See also* DELPHIC ORACLE; PYTHIAN GAMES.) Delphi, one of the four great *pan-Hellenic *sanctuaries (the others are *Isthmia, *Olympia, and *Nemea), is on the lower southern slopes of *Parnassus, *c.*610 m. (*c.*2,002 ft.) above the gulf of Corinth.

Before 300 BC There was an extensive Mycenaean village in the *Apollo sanctuary at the end of the bronze age; the area was resettled probably during the 10th cent., and the first dedications (tripods and figurines) appear *c.*800. The settlement was probably relocated after the first temple was built (late 7th cent.). The first archaeological links are with Corinth and Thessaly. The 6th-cent. *Homeric Hymn to Apollo* (*see* HYMNS, GREEK) says Apollo chose Cretans for his Delphic priests, and early Cretan metal dedications have been found, but Cretan material could have come via Corinth, and Cretan priests may have been invented because Crete was distant (i.e. this is a way of stressing the end of local domination). The first *Pythian Games were held in either 591/0 or 586/5.

The sanctuary, for which our main literary evidence is *Pausanias, consisted of a *temenos* enclosed by a wall. Inside it were the monuments dedicated by the states of Greece to commemorate victories and public events, together with about twenty 'treasuries' (the oldest are those of Cypselid Corinth, and Sicyon, c.560; Cnidus, c.550; and Siphnos, c.525), a small theatre, and the main temple of *Apollo to which the Sacred Way wound up from the road below. The Persian Wars (490–479 BC) were architecturally celebrated with special panache, and heroes like the Athenian Miltiades were commemorated more assertively here than was possible back at democratic Athens. The first temple was destroyed by fire in 548 BC; debris, including many votives (notably statuary of gold and ivory), was buried under the Sacred Way. This destruction led to an architectural reorganization of the *temenos*. The great new temple was constructed in the late 6th cent. with help from the Alcmaeonids of Athens, and was itself destroyed by earthquake in 373. A new temple was built by subscription.

Delphi was attacked by the Persians in 480 and by the Gauls in 279 BC, but suffered little damage. Excavations were begun by French archaeologists in 1880, when the village of Kastri was moved from Delphi to its present site some way away. Apart from the revelation of the main buildings of the enclosure and the remains of numerous buildings (such as the base of the Serpent Column and Lysander's monument for the Spartan victory at Aegospotami), there have been notable finds of sculpture: the metopes of the Sicyonian building and the metopes of the Athenian treasury, the frieze of the Siphnian treasury, pedimental sculptures of the 'Alcmaeonid' temple, the bronze Charioteer, and the remnants of Lysippus' memorial for a Thessalian dynast (the 'Daochos monument'). Below the modern road and the Castalian Spring are public buildings (palaestra, etc.), the mid-7th-cent. temple of Athena Pronaia, the 4th-cent. tholos, and the treasury of Massalia (c.530), in the area called the Marmaria, where there are also boulders which have fallen from the rocks above (the Phaedriades).

The affairs of the sanctuary were administered by an ancient or ostensibly ancient international organization, the Delphic *Amphictiony, run by the amphictionic council, whose duties included the conduct of the pan-Hellenic *Pythian Games, the care of the finances of the sanctuary, and the upkeep of the temple. Influence at Delphi could be exercised in various ways and (mostly) via this amphictiony: by imposing fines for religious offences, by declaring and leading *sacred wars, and by participation in prestigious building projects. Thus from the age of Archaic tyranny to the Roman period, Delphi (like other panhellenic sanctuaries but more so, because of its centrality and fame) was a focus for interstate competition as well as for contests between individuals. The amphictiony, we are told, fought a war against Crisa and defeated it; this is the First *Sacred War, the historicity of which has been doubted, but the traditional date for its end (c.590 BC) coincides with the beginning of a period of transformation, a serious upgrading of the sanctuary, not the least of its manifestations being the building of several treasuries. The first Pythian Games were held to celebrate the amphictiony's victory. Other Sacred Wars took place subsequently, of which the fourth ended in 338 with the victory of Philip II of Macedon at the battle of Chaeronea. The four sacred wars are only the moments when interstate competition flared up into overt military clashes. But even 'conventional' wars like the Peloponnesian Wars between Athens and Sparta and their allies (431–404 BC) had a religious aspect: Sparta's foundation of Heraclea Trachinia during the Peloponnesian War was arguably an attempt to increase Sparta's influence in the amphictiony. And at all times in Greek history, control of Thessaly was desirable because Thessaly had a built-in preponderance of amphictionic votes. In the 3rd cent. BC the power of Aetolia was linked to its possession of Delphi, and significantly Rome's first alliance with a Greek state (212 or 211) was with Aetolia. It is not true that the oracle's influence had diminished as a result of its suspect position in the Persian Wars. Its influence continued, only its 'political' role inevitably diminished in the radically changed circumstances of the Hellenistic and Graeco-Roman world.

Delphi was also a community, which issued decrees that survive on stone. But one decree suggests abnormality in that the *phratry of the Labyadae is found handling some of the business (e.g. rules about conduct of funerals) which would elsewhere have been the concern of the community proper rather than of a kinship group.

After 300 BC New Hellenistic powers used patronage of Delphi to gain legitimation; the Aetolian Confederacy certainly, and perhaps Attalus I of Pergamum, made dedications promoting their victories against the Gauls as pan-Hellenic services (*see* SOTERIA). The appropriation (168 BC) by the victorious Lucius Aemilius Paullus of a monument destined for King Perseus of Macedon announced *de facto* Roman domination of the sanctuary. Although the emperor *Augustus reformed the amphictiony (mainly to serve the interests of the newly founded Nicopolis) and Domitian repaired the temple (AD 84), the only emperor to take a real interest in Delphi was Hadrian, who held the city's archonship twice, toyed with enlargement of the amphictiony, and sponsored building; whether the orchestrator of Roman Delphi's beautification in a debated passage of Plutarch is Hadrian or the author himself, a priest of Apollo under Trajan, is debated. A regional Greek interest in the cult endured into the 3rd cent. AD, but international attention was now confined largely to tourism and the Pythian Games. Delphi was still a 'sacred city' in the fourth century under Constans; the steps in the installation of *Christianity remain obscure.

[Pausanias 10. 5–31]

Delphic oracle *Oracle of *Apollo. Dating originally to the very end of the 9th cent. BC, it developed into the most important Greek oracle. It was consulted by communities as well as individuals, and played an important role in the formation of the Greek communities and in colonization; it gave guidance on *pollution, 'release from evils', (rarely) laws, and, above all, cult. The story that Apollo was not the original owner of the oracle, but replaced an earlier deity (different versions naming different deities, but all including *Gaia or *Themis, or both) does not reflect cult history; it is a myth, expressing the perception that at Delphi the *chthonian, dangerous, and disorderly aspects of the cosmos have been defeated by, and subordinated to, the celestial guide and lawgiver. Apollo's oracle has tamed the darker side of the cosmos—both at the theological (Gaia's defeat) and at the human level: it therefore gives people divine guidance through which they can cope with this side of the cosmos.

The oracular consultation took place in the adyton (innermost sanctuary), in which stood the *omphalos marking the centre of the world as determined by Zeus, who released two eagles, one from the east and one from the west, which met at Delphi. Another story makes the omphalos Python's (*see* APOLLO) or *Dionysus' tomb. Also in the adyton grew a laurel-tree, but the chasm with the vapours is a Hellenistic invention. The enquirer had to pay a consultation tax called *pelanos* (which had begun as a bloodless offering and kept the name when it became a monetary contribution). At the altar outside the temple was offered the preliminary sacrifice before the consultation, the *prothysis*, which on regular consultation days was offered by the Delphic community on behalf of all enquirers. On other days it was offered by the enquirer—to be more precise, on behalf of the enquirer by the local representative of his city: non-Delphians were treated at the Delphic oracle as foreigners, worshipping at the sanctuary of another community. If the preliminary ritual was successful, i.e. if the animal had reacted as it should when sprinkled with water, it was sacrificed, and the enquirer entered the temple, where he offered a second sacrifice, depositing either a whole victim or parts of one on a *trapeza*, offering-table, at the entrance of the adyton. He then probably went with the *prophētai* (interpreters) and other cult personnel to a space from which he could not see the Pythia in the adytum. The Pythia, who had prepared herself by *purification at the Castalian Spring, burnt laurel leaves and barley meal on the altar called *hestia* ('hearth') inside the temple (which came to be seen as the common hearth of Greece); crowned with laurel, she sat on the tripod, became possessed by the god, and, shaking a laurel, prophesied under divine inspiration—a state which may correspond to what in non-religious explanatory models would be considered a self-induced trance. Her pronouncements were then somehow shaped by the *prophētai*. Exactly what form the Pythia's pronouncements took and what the *prophētai* did are matters of controversy. One possibility is that she felt that she received partial signs transmitting fragmentary visions—*not* gibberish—and that the *prophētai* interpreted these, shaping them into coherent, if ambiguous, responses; this was not an attempt to hedge their bets, but a result of the ambiguity inherent in the god's signs and the Greek perception that ambiguity is the idiom of prophecy, that there are limits to man's access to knowledge about the future: the god speaks ambiguously, and human fallibility intervenes and may misinterpret the messages.

The most important of the oracle's religious personnel (consisting of Delphians) were: the Pythia, an ordinary woman who served for life and remained chaste throughout her service; the *prophētai*; the *hosioi*, who participated in the ritual of the consultation and shared tasks with the *prophētai*, and the priests of Apollo. The Pythia is not mentioned in the oldest 'document' informing us about the Delphic cult and oracle, the *Homeric Hymn to Apollo* (*see* HYMNS (GREEK)), where the god gives oracular responses 'from the laurel-tree', an expression that corresponds closely to that ('from the oak-tree') used in the *Odyssey* for the proph-

ecies at *Dodona, where the oak-tree spoke the will of *Zeus, which was interpreted by priests. A similar practice involving the laurel may perhaps have been practised at Delphi at an early period. Whether *divination by lot was practised at Delphi as a separate rite is a matter of controversy.

Demeter, the Greek goddess of corn, identified in Italy with *Ceres. The second part of her name means 'mother', and *de* (or *da*) was thought to mean 'earth' in antiquity, but the Greeks had a separate goddess of the Earth, and Demeter came later in the pantheon, as granddaughter of Gē (*Gaia) and sister of *Zeus. An alternative modern theory connects *de* with *deai*, the Cretan word for 'barley' (cf. *zeia* 'spelt'), but this is linguistically doubtful. She is, however, certainly the goddess who controls all crops and vegetation, and so the sustainer of life for men and animals. In early epic corn is called 'Demeter's grain', and in a Homeric simile 'blonde Demeter' herself winnows grain from chaff. Her daughter by Zeus, *Persephone (Attic Pherrephatta), was called simply *Kore*, 'the Girl', and the two were so closely linked that they were known as 'the Two Goddesses' or even sometimes as 'the Demeters'. Because the life of plants between autumn and spring is one of hidden growth underground, Persephone was said to have been carried off by her uncle *Hades, lord of the Underworld, and compelled to spend the winter months with him as his wife, returning to the upper world with the flowers of spring. Thus as Kore she was a deity of youth and joy, the leader of the *Nymphs, with whom she looked after the growth of the young, but as Hades' wife she was also queen of the dead, governing the fate of souls, and thus an awesome and dread goddess.

As deities of agriculture and growth, associated with a settled rhythm of life, Demeter and Kore were regarded as important influences in the development of civilization. Their title Thesmophoros was traditionally interpreted as due to their role as givers of law and morality. The Greek religious *calendar was closely linked to the farmer's year, and many of their festivals coincided with the seasonal activities of ploughing, sowing, reaping, threshing, and storing the harvest. One of the most important and widespread, the *Thesmophoria, normally took place in autumn (11–13 Pyanopsion in Athens), near to sowing-time, and included ceremonies intended to promote fertility. Like many festivals of Demeter, it was secret and restricted to women. Their secrecy seems to have been due primarily to the sense of awe and fear generated by contemplation of the powers of the earth and Underworld.

The most important festivals of Demeter and Kore were the ceremonies of initiation known as '*mysteries', the most famous of which were those of *Eleusis. By guaranteeing to initiates the favour of the goddesses, they offered above all the promise of a better fate after death, but they also promised prosperity in life, personified by *Plutus (Wealth), who was the child of Demeter, born from her union with the Cretan hero *Iasion 'in a thrice-ploughed field'.

Many legends told how, when Demeter was searching for her daughter after Hades had carried her off, she received information or hospitality from the local inhabitants of different places in Greece, and in gratitude taught them how to practise agriculture and to celebrate her rituals. The chief claimants for this honour were Eleusis and Sicily (*see* SICILY AND MAGNA GRAECIA, CULTS AND MYTHOLOGY), her most important cult centres. The oldest and best-known version of the myth is the *Homeric Hymn to Demeter* (*see* HYMNS (GREEK)), an epic poem probably of the Archaic period. This tells how, after Kore was carried off, Demeter wandered the earth in search of her, disguised as an old woman, until she came to Eleusis where she was welcomed by the family of King *Celeus. She became the nurse of his baby son *Demophon (2), and tried to immortalize him by anointing him with *ambrosia and holding him in the fire at night to burn away his mortality. She was interrupted by *Metanira, Celeus' wife, and so prevented from making him immortal. Instead, she revealed her true identity, promised Demophon heroic honours after death, and ordered the Eleusinians to build her a temple and altar. She then withdrew to her new temple and caused a universal famine, until Zeus was forced to order Hades to release her daughter. Hades, however, gave Persephone a pomegranate seed to eat, and because she had tasted food in the Underworld she was compelled to spend a third part of every year there, returning to earth in spring. Demeter then restored the fertility of the fields and taught the princes of Eleusis how to perform her mysteries, whose absolute secrecy is stressed. The poem closes with the promise of divine favour to the initiates both in life and after death.

The Great Mysteries at Eleusis were celebrated in early autumn (Boedromion), and were preceded by the Lesser Mysteries at Agrae, just outside Athens, in spring (Anthesterion). Some modern scholars have rejected the predominant ancient view which connected Persephone's absence with winter, arguing that her descent should coincide with the storing of seed-corn in underground granaries after harvest, during the period of summer dryness, to be taken out in autumn for sowing. This fits some near-eastern myths of a similar type about a disappearing deity, but the story was never understood in this way by the Greeks, and the traditional explanation agrees much better with the agricultural condition of Greece itself.

The famine, in the *Homeric Hymn*, reflects another form of the belief that the death of vegetation has a divine cause. Persephone's absence and Demeter's anger and grief both combine to create sterility. The hymn assumes the existence of agriculture already before the Rape, but the Athenians in the Classical period claimed that Demeter had given to *Triptolemus, one of the princes of Eleusis, the gifts of corn and the arts of agriculture, and that he then travelled over the world teaching these to other nations (*see* CULTURE-BRINGERS).

Sicily was always regarded as especially consecrated to the Two Goddesses, and in the Hellenistic and Roman periods versions of the myth of Kore which placed her Rape and Return here became popular. She was said to have been carried off from a meadow near Enna in the centre of the island, and to have disappeared underground at the site of the spring Cyane near Syracuse, where an annual festival was held. Other major festivals took place at the times of harvest and sowing.

In Arcadia Demeter was worshipped with *Poseidon. The Black Demeter of Phigaleia and Demeter Erinys of Thelpusa were both said to have taken the form of a mare and to have been mated with by Poseidon in horse-shape, and at Phigaleia she was shown as horse-headed. Their offspring were *Despoina ('the Mistress') and (at Thelpusa) the horse *Arion. At Phigaleia she was also said to have caused a universal famine because of her anger both with Poseidon and over the loss of her daughter.

These motifs of Demeter's anger and a consequent famine recur in the story of *Erysichthon, who incurred her wrath by trying to cut down a grove sacred to her, although warned by the goddess in disguise not to do so. She punished him with an insatiable hunger which ruined all his household.

A unique genealogy of Demeter makes her the mother of *Artemis: Herodotus says that this was due to *syncretism with Egyptian mythology.

In art Demeter is shown both on her own and with Persephone, with related figures of cult such as Hades and *Triptolemus, and in groups with the other Olympian deities. Particularly popular scenes are those of the Rape and Return of Persephone, and the Mission of Triptolemus. She carries a sceptre, ears of corn and a poppy, or torches, and she and her daughter are often portrayed as closely linked and similar in iconography.

[Homer, *Iliad* 5. 499–502; Hesiod, *Theogony* 453–506; *Homeric Hymn to Demeter*]

Demodocus, a blind and respected first-class bard at *Alcinous' court—an image which Homer offers of his own trade. He sings the adultery of *Ares and *Aphrodite, a comic pendant to the contrasts in *Iliad* 5, and sings the (tragic) Trojan War so realistically that Odysseus weeps. He was depicted on Bathycles' throne of Apollo at *Amyclae (*c*.530 BC).

[Homer, *Odyssey* 8]

Demophon (1) Son of *Theseus, often found paired with his brother *Acamas. Both were sent to Euboea for safety, and from there (in the *Epic Cycle) went to Troy, where they freed their grandmother *Aethra from captivity. Each is named as lover of *Laodice (1) in Troy and Phyllis in Thrace, and each, on his return to Athens, was linked with an involuntary homicide centring on the *Palladium. Where their myths diverge, Acamas tends to act as colonizer while Demophon succeeds Theseus as king of Athens. It was in his reign that the Palladium (in various versions) came to Athens, and it may be that the important sanctuary of Demophon was part of the Palladium cult complex.

(2) Eleusinian hero, identified in the *Homeric Hymn to Demeter* (*see* HYMNS (GREEK)) with the infant son of *Celeus and *Metanira, nursling of *Demeter, who attempted to make him immortal by placing him in the fire. The attempt failed when interrupted by Metanira, and instead Demeter decreed the institution of a mock battle in his honour—a not uncommon heroic rite. Later, Demophon's role as young boy favoured by the goddesses is taken over by *Triptolemus.

Derveni *See* BOOKS, GREEK AND ROMAN, SACRED; DIONYSUS (Derveni crater); ORPHIC LITERATURE; ORPHISM.

Despoina, 'The Mistress', an Arcadian goddess worshipped at *Lycosura together with her mother *Demeter, her foster-father Anytus, and *Artemis; there was an altar to her father, *Poseidon Hippios, near the temple. The cult group inside the temple of Despoina was the work of Damophon of Messene, early 2nd cent. BC. Important fragments remain. We do not know Despoina's actual name, since it was kept secret from those who were not initiates of her mysteries. Her character is related to that of Kore (*Persephone) in Attica; she and Demeter were a paired mother and daughter, and her iconography shows the Eleusinian features (*see* ELEUSIS) of *kistē* (basket) and sceptre. But the figures of dancers with animal masks on her clothing, and the brutal nature of the *sacrifice made to her in the sanctuary at Lycosura place her in a fully Arcadian context and bring out her links with the animal world. *See* ARCADIAN CULTS AND MYTHS.

[Pausanias 8. 25, 37, 42]

detestatio sacrorum, renunciation of family rites. A Roman head of household (*sui iuris*) performed religious rites (*sacra*). These rites were peculiar to each family group. If such a person agreed to be transferred by official adoption (*adrogatio*) into another's family, he had to submit to a pontifical examination prior to proceedings in the *comitia calata* (the 'summoned assembly'). On the *pontifices* being satisfied that, so far as possible, other members of the family existed to continue that family's rites, the individual concerned proceeded to make formal renunciation of his existing family rites.

Deucalion, in mythology, the Greek Noah, son of *Prometheus, married to Pyrrha daughter of Epimetheus. When *Zeus floods the earth in anger at the sins of the age of bronze (in particular, of *Lycaon (3)), Deucalion and Pyrrha, on the advice of Prometheus, build a chest (*larnax*) and live there for nine days and nine nights. When they come to land, they repopulate the earth by casting stones over their shoulders, from which people spring. Greek *genealogy begins with Deucalion's son *Hellen ('Greek'). Deucalion is held to have founded the temple of Olympian Zeus in Athens (*see* OLYMPIEUM) and there was an annual sacrifice commemorating the final ebbing away of the waters

down the crevice there. Deucalion and Pyrrha first came to land at sites such as: Othrys in Phthiotis (Thessaly) where Deucalion is king, Opus in Locris or its port Cynus (site of Pyrrha's grave—Deucalion's is in Athens). The purpose of the flood is to create a new beginning for a new world-order. It is scarcely accidental that a son of Prometheus the fire-bearer stars in the flood, or that both are so involved with the creation of mankind. He is depicted once in Roman art.

[Apollodorus 1. 7. 1-2; Ovid, *Metamorphoses* 1. 163–413]

deus, divus These two words, deriving from the same hypothetical form (*deiwo-*), designate two different types of Roman divinity. A *deus* (fem. *dea*, plural *divi* under the republic) was immortal and had never experienced mortal existence; but a *divus*—from the beginning of the Principate at least—was a divinity who obtained this status posthumously and by human agency. Although deification is above all a public phenomenon relating to dead emperors and empresses (*see* RULER-CULT), apotheosis existed equally in a private context. The Romans believed that the world was full of divinities, living in the skies, on earth, in water, or underground. Some were known and entered into permanent relations with humans, while others did not manifest themselves, although this does not mean that the Romans neglected them: when they needed to invoke all the divinities present in a locality, e.g. for an expiation, these anonymous deities were designated by the title 'God-or-goddess' (*Sive deus sive dea*). Sometimes these anonymous deities emerged from the shadows and appeared to the Romans, who then conferred on them a name and a cult, just as they attributed a cult and the name *divus* to deceased persons whose deeds and exceptional powers had revealed their divine nature.

As regards the mode of action of the gods, modern opinions differ. According to one, going back to 19th-cent. ethnology, divinities overlap and can be mutually assimilated since they preside over fields as vast and indeterminate as fecundity and fertility. In opposition to this view is a more rigorous conception of the divine function, according to which a divinity possesses, in a given religious sysem, a precise divine function which he or she exercises in different contexts; in conformity with the principles of polytheism, a divinity often collaborates with others, without becoming confused with them, even if they are very closely associated. This approach thinks in terms of power and divine functions rather than the 'sacred' and the 'sacred force'.

devotio Ritual to devote either enemies or oneself (or both) to gods of the Underworld and death. Allegedly, in ancient times enemy cities were devoted (*devoveri*) to gods of the Underworld (*Dis pater*, **Ve(d)iovis*, **manes*), after the **evocatio* (calling out) of their protective deities. The prayer (*carmen devotionis*) quoted on the occasion of the *devotio* of Carthage calls the enemies substitutes (*vicarios*) for the Roman commander and his army, who are thus saved. A better-known variant of this genuine *votum* is the type of *devotio* only attested for Publius Decius Mus (and less unequivocally for his son and grandson, around 300 BC). Here, the Roman commander linked the sacrifice of his own life, through an act of self-**consecratio*, with the *devotio* of the enemies. The prayer by which Decius devoted the enemy army and himself to the *di manes* and **Tellus* is recorded. After various ritual preparations, the Roman general, on horseback and wearing special clothing, the *cinctus Gabinus*, rode into the midst of the enemy to seek a voluntary death. Despite a number of ritual prescriptions (possibility of substitution by an ordinary soldier, regulations if this soldier or the general were not killed), it is doubtful whether this type of *devotio* ever belonged to the fixed body of Roman ritual institutions.

Diagoras, of Melos, lyric poet active in Athens in the last decades of the 5th cent. BC. Renowned for his '*atheism', he mocked the **mysteries of Eleusis—perhaps in

reaction to the capture of Melos by the Athenians. He was condemned to death, and fled. Fragments of his poem survive, but they contain no trace of 'atheism'. In the Arabic tradition also Diagoras was notorious for his atheism.

Diana (hypothetical root *dyw*- 'the bright one' (cf. **Jupiter*), originally a moon goddess), an Italian goddess anciently identified with **Artemis*, from whom she took over the patronage of margins and savageness. But the modalities of this evolution remain puzzling (moonlight as the contrary of daylight, and so of civilized life?). Her cult was widespread. One of her most famous shrines was on Mt. Tifata near Capua in southern Italy; the name Tifata means 'holm-oak grove', which suits Diana's character as a goddess of the wilderness. Most famous of all was her ancient cult near **Aricia* (on the shore of the volcanic lake known as the 'Mirror of Diana', below the modern Nemi, i.e. *nemus*, 'grove'). Her temple stood in a grove, which was recorded as dedicated to her by Egerius Baebius (?) of Tusculum, leader of the Latins. It was therefore an old religious centre of the Latin League and it is probable, though direct proof is lacking, that the foundation of her temple (probably preceded by an altar) on the **Aventine* hill in Rome traditionally by king Servius Tullius, was an attempt to transfer the headquarters of this cult to Rome, along with the headship of the league. *See further* REX NEMORENSIS, and for the Massiliote and Ephesian connections of the Aventine temple, *see* ARTEMIS.

That she was later largely a goddess of women is shown by the processions of women bearing torches (symbols of her name and original function) in her honour at Aricia, also by the character of many of the votive offerings there, which have clear reference to children and childbirth. Her links with women, along with slaves and asylum, seem to inscribe her within the frame of her real field of action—namely, margins.

At Aricia she was associated with **Egeria*,

and Virbius, an obscure male deity (*see* HIPPOLYTUS (1)). Identifications with foreign deities are common all over the west.

[Catullus 34; Ovid, *Fasti* 2. 153–92]

Diasia, an ancient and major Athenian festival of Zeus *Meilichios, held at Agrae just outside the city on 23 Anthesterion (roughly, late February). Athenians attended *en masse*, and sacrificed 'not animal victims, but local kinds of offerings' (*cakes?); animals were, however, offered too, as some are listed in calendars to be sent up for the festival from outlying villages. It was celebrated 'with a certain grimness', appropriate no doubt to Zeus Meilichios; and it lacked the publicly provided spectacle characteristic of many later-founded Attic festivals. But we hear of relatives dining together, and it was also an occasion to buy toys for children.

Dictynna See BRITOMARTIS and CRETAN CULTS AND MYTHS.

Didascalia Apostolorum (*The Catholic Teaching of the Twelve Apostles of the Redeemer*), a Church order originally written in Greek, but completely preserved only in Syriac translation. It claims apostolic authorship, but was, in fact, written probably by a bishop in northern Syria in the first half of the 3rd cent. AD for a Gentile Christian community. Its principal aim is moral instruction and canonical regulation for the maintenance of the constitution and order of the Church. In addition, it is a valuable source for the history of Christian penance.

Dido, legendary queen of Carthage, daughter of a Phoenician king of Tyre, called Belus by *Virgil. According to the 4th/3rd-century historian Timaeus, the earliest extant source for her story, her Phoenician name was Elissa, and the name Dido ('wanderer') was given to her by the Libyans. Her husband, called Sychaeus by Virgil, was murdered by her brother *Pygmalion (2), now king of Tyre, and Dido escaped with some followers to Libya where she founded Carthage. In the earlier tradition, in order to escape marriage with a Libyan king (Iarbas in Virgil) Dido built a pyre as though for an offering and leapt into the flames. The story of the encounter of *Aeneas and Dido (chronologically difficult given the traditional dating of Carthage's foundation four centuries after the destruction of Troy) probably appeared in the republican Roman epic by Naevius, the *Bellum Poenicum*. According to the late republican antiquarian *Varro it was Dido's sister Anna who killed herself for love of Aeneas. In the classic version in Virgil's *Aeneid* Aeneas lands on the coast of Carthage after a storm and is led by Venus to Dido's new city; Dido's infatuated love for the stranger is consummated in a cave during a storm while they are hunting. Mercury (*see* MERCURIUS) descends to remind Aeneas of his mission to travel to Italy; as Aeneas departs obedient to the call of fate, Dido kills herself on top of a pyre that she has built. Her curse on the Trojans will eventually be fulfilled in the historical wars between Carthage and Rome. Many readers also detect a more recent historical allusion to the charms of Cleopatra VII in the Virgilian Dido. She has enjoyed a vigorous afterlife, in art, in literary reworkings from Ovid through to Chaucer and Marlowe, and in numerous operas including Purcell's *Dido and Aeneas* and Berlioz's *Les Troyennes*. Her chastity has also been defended against Virgil by partisans including *Tertullian and Petrarch.

[Virgil, *Aeneid* 1, 4; Ovid, *Heroines* 7]

Didyma, oracular shrine of *Apollo (*see* ORACLES), located about 16 km. (10 mi.) south of Miletus. In the Archaic period, it was administered by a priestly lineage, the Branchidae, and rose to great prominence in the 6th cent. BC. Three prose oracular responses survive from this period, as does one dedication. In 494 the shrine was destroyed by Darius I of Persia and the Branchidae were exiled to Sogdiana.

The oracle was refounded in the time of Alexander the Great (probably in 331 BC), and rapidly re-emerged as an extremely important site. It made significant contact with the Seleucids, and, during the brief Ptolemaic control of Miletus, with the Ptolemies as well. In the imperial period, it ranked with *Claros as one of the great oracular centres of Asia Minor.

Excavations have revealed a massive structure begun when the oracle was refounded. The total building measures 118×60 m. (387×196 ft.) at the platform. A dipteral (double) Ionic colonnade contains 108 columns and a further 12 in the pronaos (forecourt). The western wall of the pronaos is broken by an 8-m. (26-ft.)-wide entrance raised 1.5 m. (5 ft.) above the floor of the pronaos. The cella (roofed chamber) contains two Ionic columns to support the roof, and opens on the north and south sides to small chambers containing staircases, which may have given access to a terrace at the level of the cella roof. The western end of the cella is pierced by three doors leading to a great staircase giving access to the adyton or innermost sanctuary (never roofed). Within the adyton there is a small *naiskos* (chapel) surrounding the sacred spring. The priestess gave her oracles here.

Oracles could be given on a limited number of days. The absolute minimum was once every four days, and the interval was probably far greater—possibly some months. The session itself began with a three-day fast by the prophetess, during which time she apparently resided in the adyton. On the appointed day, the prophetess would take a ritual bath and enter the *naiskos*, while those who wished to put questions to her sacrificed outside and choruses sang hymns to the gods. Within the *naiskos*, the prophetess sat on an axle suspended over the sacred spring and, when a question was put to her, she would dip her foot (or her dress) into the spring, but not drink from it, before giving her answer. These answers would probably have been in prose and would then have been turned into verse by the priests. The priests were appointed by the city of Miletus.

Didyma's fate seems to have been sealed by an oracle given in AD 303, advising the emperor Diocletian to initiate his empire-wide persecution of the Christian church. *Constantine I closed the oracle, and executed the priests; it appears not to have functioned thereafter. A number of responses from the imperial period have, however, been discovered on inscriptions and in literary sources.

Dike, personification of Justice, daughter of *Zeus and *Themis, and one of the *Horae, with *Eunomia and *Eirene. She reports men's wrongdoing to Zeus, and sits beside him. In Aratus and Roman poets she is the *constellation Virgo or Astraea, who left the earth when the Age of Bronze began. In Archaic art she punishes Injustice (e.g. chest of the tyrant Cypselus), and later she is shown with a sword in Underworld scenes.

[Hesiod, *Theogony* 901–3, *Works and Days* 256–62; Aratus, *Phaenomena* 96–136]

dining-rooms Reclining on couches while dining was introduced in Greece from the near east, probably around 700 BC. Special rooms were built in sanctuaries to accommodate the couches along the lengths of the wall, often on a slightly raised plinth. Floors are durable (cement or mosaic), presumably to allow for swabbing down. Each couch had a low table alongside. Such rooms were referred to by the number of couches they held. Eleven is a frequent number, the resulting dimensions (*c.*6.3 m. (*c.*21 ft.) square) thus giving a reasonable size for general conversation across the room. Dining-rooms for ritual feasting in *sanctuaries may be larger, and may consist of very large halls for over 100 couches.

Diocletian, persecutions of (Gaius Aurelius Valerius Diocletianus), Emperor AD 284–305. Many legal decisions show Diocletian's concern to maintain or resuscitate Roman law in the provinces. He was an enthusiast for what he understood of Roman tradition and discipline, to reinforce imperial unity: hence he decreed the suppression of the Manichees (*see* MANICHAEISM). This policy forms the backdrop to the persecution of Christians, undertaken possibly on the insistence of Galerius. (*See* CHRISTIANITY.) Earlier attempts had been made to purge the court and the army, but the first persecuting edict, issued at Nicomedia (23 February 303), was designed to prevent the Church from functioning, by requiring the burning of Scriptures and the demolition of churches, and the banning of meetings for worship; recusants were deprived of any rank, and thus made liable to torture and summary execution and prevented from taking action in court; imperial freedmen were re-enslaved. In Gaul and Britain Diocletian's colleague Constantius contented himself with demolishing churches, and the later edicts were not promulgated outside the areas controlled by Diocletian and Galerius. The second edict imprisoned all clergy; the third released them, but they were to sacrifice first. The fourth edict ordered a universal sacrifice, but implementation was patchy except in Palestine and Egypt.

Diogenes (1) the *Cynic (*c*.412/403–*c*.324/321 BC). Accused with his father, moneyer at *Sinope, of 'defacing the currency' (a phrase which was to yield a potent metaphor), Diogenes was exiled some time after 362 and spent the rest of his life in Athens and Corinth. He evolved a distinctive and original way of life from diverse, mainly Greek, elements: the belief (espoused by certain types of holy men and wise men) that wisdom was a matter of action rather than thought; the principle of living in accordance with nature rather than law/convention; the tradition, perhaps sharpened by contemporary disillusionment with the city-state, of promulgating ideal societies or constitutions; a tradition of 'shamelessness' (reflected by the symbol of the dog in literature and by the supposed customs of certain foreign peoples); Socratic rejection of all elements of philosophy except practical ethics; Socrates' pursuit of philosophy in the agora rather than in a school; an anti-intellectual tradition; the tradition (variously represented by *Odysseus, *Heracles, the Spartans, and to some extent by Socrates) of physical toughness as a requirement of virtue; the image of the suffering hero and the wanderer (Odysseus, Heracles, various tragic figures); the tradition of mendicancy (represented both in literature and in life); the life of *asceticism and poverty (as represented by various wise men and holy men and labourers); the tradition of the wise or holy man who promises converts happiness or salvation; and various humorous traditions (the jester's practical and verbal humour; Old Comedy's outspokenness and crudity; Socrates' serio-comic wit).

Diogenes pursued a life as close as possible to the 'natural' life of primitive man, of animals, and of the gods. This entailed the minimum of material possessions (coarse cloak, staff for physical support and protection, purse for food) and of sustenance (obtained by living off the land and by begging); performance in public of all natural functions; training in physical endurance, and a wandering existence in harmony with natural conditions. Freedom, self-sufficiency, happiness, and virtue supposedly followed. It also entailed not merely indifference to civilized life but complete rejection of it and of all forms of education and culture as being not simply irrelevant but inimical to the ideal life. Hence Diogenes' attacks on convention, marriage, family, politics, the city, all social, sexual, and racial distinctions, worldly reputation, wealth, power and authority, literature, music, and all forms of intellectual speculation. Such attacks are imposed by the Cynic's duty metaphorically to 'deface the currency'. Hence the modern implications of the word 'cynic' are misleading. Indeed, humane attitudes came easily to Diogenes (e.g. his advocacy of sexual freedom and equality stemmed from rejection of the family).

Diogenes' missionary activity entailed what his aggressiveness sometimes obscured: recognition of the common humanity of Cynics and non-Cynics. 'Philanthropy' (concern for one's fellow human beings) is integral to Cynicism and essential to Diogenes' celebrated concept of 'cosmopolitanism' (the belief that the universe is the ultimate unity, of which the natural and animal worlds, human beings, and the gods are all intrinsic parts, with the Cynic representing the human condition at its best, at once human, animal, and divine).

[Diogenes Laertius 6. 70–3]

Diogenes (2) of Oenoanda in Lycia, author of a massive Greek inscription presenting basic doctrines of Epicureanism. The inscription was carved in a *stoa, probably in the 2nd cent. AD. The inscription occupied several courses of a wall c.80 m. (263 ft.) long. In the lowest inscribed course was a treatise on ethics dealing (inter alia) with pleasure, pain, fear, desire, *dreams, necessity, and free will; beneath its columns was inscribed a selection of Epicurus' Primary Tenets and other maxims. Immediately above was a treatise on physics, the surviving sections of which include criticisms of rival schools and discussions of epistemology, the origins of civilization and language, astronomy, and theology. Above these main treatises were more maxims, letters of Epicurus (one, addressed to his mother, concerns her anxious dreams), at least three letters written by Diogenes to Epicurean friends, and Diogenes' defence of old age. Fragments survive also of Diogenes' instructions to his friends.

Diogenes records that he was ailing and aged when he set up the inscription, and that he was moved by a desire to benefit his fellows at home and abroad as well as future generations. Although most of the inscription remains buried, the recovered fragments illuminate Epicurean theory and the activity of the school under the Roman empire. See EPICURUS.

Diomedes, in mythology (1), son of *Ares and Cyrene, barbarous king of the Thracian Cicones or Bistones; owner of a team of man-eating mares which were kept supplied with human victims by their groom. *Heracles fed the stable-lad, and in some versions the

king himself, to the animals and drove them back to Greece as his eighth labour, though not before the horses had killed Abderus, one of the hero's companions; the story provided a foundation-myth for the city of Abdera. The king's punishment was depicted on the Archaic 'throne' at *Amyclae near Sparta and on Greek vases. (2), Son of *Tydeus and Deipyle the daughter of *Adrastus; one of the chief Achaean warriors in the Trojan War and leader of a contingent of 80 ships from Argos and Tiryns. In the Iliad, his great charge leads to the death of *Pandarus, the removal of *Aeneas from looming defeat by his mother *Aphrodite, and the wounding of the goddess herself and of Ares the war-god; later we are shown a more restrained side of his character as he declines to fight with his hereditary xenos ('guest-friend') *Glaucus of Lycia. Throughout the poem, but especially in the second half, he offers shrewd and bold advice to the Greek war-council. In the funeral games for *Patroclus he wins both the chariot-race and (against *Aias (1)) the spear-fight. He is particularly associated with *Odysseus in various actions, killing Dolon and *Rhesus, and in the poems of the later *Epic Cycle sharing in the murder of *Palamedes, bringing *Philoctetes back from Lemnos, and stealing Athena's talismanic statuette, the *Palladium, from the Trojan citadel.

Other traditions assign him a part in the expedition of the *Epigoni against Thebes, where his father had fought, and in the restoration of the kingship of Calydon to its rightful line. But on his safe return from Troy he had found his wife Aegialea unfaithful; emigrating to Italy, he ended his days with King Daunus in Apulia.

[Homer, Iliad 5–6, 10]

Dione, consort of *Zeus at *Dodona, where she had a cult as Naïa beside Zeus Naïos. Her name is the feminine equivalent of Zeus and recalls diwija/diuja in Linear B, although *Hera already appears beside Zeus on a Linear B tablet from Pylos. Dione is the mother of Aphrodite in Homer, a fresh-water *nymph, daughter of *Oceanus and *Tethys, in Hesiod, or first generation *Titan. But outside Dodona her influence was limited.

Dione appears on Epirote coins of the 3rd and 2nd cent. BC. On the reverse of a tetradrachm of Pyrrhus, king of Epirus (c.297 BC), she is shown with sceptre and wearing a headdress (*polos*). Attic vase-painters of the 5th cent. sometimes added her to the circle of *Dionysus' followers, showing Athenian interest in the northern sanctuary of Zeus during the Peloponnesian War.

[Homer, *Iliad* 5. 370–417]

Dionysia Many festivals of *Dionysus had special names, e.g. the *Anthesteria, the *Lenaea, etc. This article concerns those Attic festivals known as (*a*) 'the Rural Dionysia', and (*b*) 'the City or Great Dionysia'. Festivals of Dionysus were widespread throughout the Greek world, but we know most about the Attic ones, for which almost all surviving Greek drama was written.

(*a*) The Rural Dionysia were celebrated, on various days by the different villages of Attica in the month of Posideon (roughly December). They provided an opportunity for the locality to reproduce elements of the City Dionysia, and we hear of performances of *tragedy, *comedy, and *dithyramb. There survive various inscriptions concerning the proceedings, notably from Piraeus, *Eleusis, Icarion, and Aixone. In Aristophanes' *Acharnians* Dicaeopolis goes home to celebrate the festival: he draws up a little sacrificial procession in which his daughter is *kanephoros* ('basket-bearer'), two slaves carry the *phallus, Dicaeopolis himself sings an obscene song to Phales, and his wife watches from the roof. The song may be of the kind from which, according to Aristotle, comedy originated.

(*b*) The City Dionysia belonged to Dionysus Eleuthereus, who was said to have been introduced into Athens from the village of Eleutherae, on the borders of Attica and Boeotia. At Eleutherae there was a cult of Dionysus Melanaigis ('of the black goatskin'),

who was said to have driven the daughters of Eleuther mad, and to have appeared at a duel between Xanthus and Melanthus. The festival is generally regarded as having been founded, or at least amplified, during the tyranny of Pisistratus (mid-6th cent.). But in fact the archaeological, epigraphic, and literary evidence is so uncertain as to be no less consistent with a date for its foundation right at the end of the 6th cent., just after the establishment of democracy, in which case the title Eleuthereus would perhaps have been taken to connote political liberty.

The festival was celebrated at the end of March, when the city was again full of visitors after the winter. A preliminary procession brought the image of Dionysus to the theatre (on the south slope of the Acropolis), in commemoration of his original arrival from Eleutherae (our evidence for this does not predate the late 2nd cent. BC). Then, on 10 Elaphebolion, a splendid procession followed an unknown route to the sacred precinct (adjacent to the theatre), where animals were sacrificed and bloodless offerings made. In the procession were carried phalli, loaves, bowls, etc., and the resident foreigners were dressed in red. The theatrical performances took place from the 11th to the 14th. Their precise arrangement is unknown, but normal practice in the Classical period was as follows. Three tragedians competed, each with three tragedies and a satyr-play (*see* SATYRIC DRAMA). There were five comic poets, each competing with a single play. And each of the ten tribes provided one dithyrambic chorus for the men's contest and one for the boys'. At some point before the performance of the tragedies the sons of citizens killed in battle were paraded in full armour in the theatre, and so was the tribute brought by Athens' allies. Various fragmentary inscriptions survive with the remains of lists of the annual performances (or victors). *See also* TRAGEDY and COMEDY (GREEK), ORIGINS OF.

[Aristophanes, *Acharnians* 241–79]

Dionysius the Areopagite, an Athenian

converted at Athens by St *Paul. Four treatises—*The Celestial Hierarchy, The Ecclesiastical Hierarchy, The Divine Names*, and *The Mystical Theology*—and ten letters are ascribed to him. These works, the product of a single mind, belong almost certainly to the early 6th cent. AD and were first cited (and ascribed to Paul's convert) in 532. They display an enthusiasm for the *Neoplatonism of *Proclus, while theologically they belong to a Syrian milieu, mistrustful of Chalcedonian Christology. Their heady brew of Neoplatonic philosophy and biblical and liturgical symbolism became immensely popular in the Middle Ages: they exercised a powerful influence both in the east and the west. The author sees the cosmos as a vast theophany in which divine revelation draws all rational creatures back through love into harmony with the unknowable God by a process of purification, illumination, and union: this harmony is displayed in the celestial hierarchy of angelic powers, whose order reflects the threefold nature of the Trinity, and achieved through the similarly triadic sacramental structure of the Church. Scholars are divided as to whether Dionysius' allegiance is fundamentally pagan and Neoplatonic or authentically Christian.

Dionysus (Linear B *Diwonusos*, Homeric *Diōnysos*, Aeolic *Zonnusos*, Attic *Dionysos*) is the twice-born son of *Zeus and *Semele. His birth alone sets him apart. Snatched prematurely from the womb of his dying mother and carried to term by his father, he was born from the thigh of Zeus. Perceived as both man and animal, male and effeminate, young and old, he is the most versatile and elusive of all Greek gods. His myths and cults are often violent and bizarre, a challenge to the established social order. He represents an enchanted world and an extraordinary experience. Always on the move, he is the most epiphanic god (*see* EPIPHANY), riding felines, sailing the sea, and even wearing wings. His most common cult name was *Bakch(e)ios* or *Bakchos*, after which his ecstatic followers were called *bakchoi* and *bakchai*.

Adopted by the Romans as *Bacchus*, he was identified with the Italian *Liber Pater. Most importantly, while modern scholars regard Dionysus inevitably as a construct of the Greek imagination, in the eyes of his ancient worshippers he was a god—immortal, powerful, and self-revelatory.

Throughout antiquity, he was first and foremost the god of *wine and intoxication. His other provinces include ritual madness or *ecstasy (*mania*); the *mask, impersonation, and the fictional world of the theatre; and, very differently, the mysterious realm of the dead and the expectation of an afterlife blessed with the joys of Dionysus. If these four provinces share anything in common that illuminates the nature of this god, it is his capacity to transcend existential boundaries. Exceptionally among Greek gods, Dionysus often merges with the various functions he stands for and thus serves as a role model for his human worshippers. In the Greek imagination, the god whose myths and rituals subvert the normal identities of his followers himself adopts a fluid persona based on illusion, transformation, and the simultaneous presence of opposite traits. Both 'most terrible and most sweet to mortals' in Attic tragedy, he was called 'Eater of Raw Flesh' on Lesbos as well as 'Mild' on Naxos in actual cult.

The name Dionysus appears for the first time on three fragmentary Linear B tablets from Pylos (in the Peloponnese) and Khania (north-west Crete) dated to c.1250 BC. The tablets confirm his status as a divinity, but beyond that they reveal little about his identity and function in Mycenaean religion. One of the Pylos tablets may point to a tenuous connection between Dionysus and wine; on the Khania tablet, Zeus and Dionysus are mentioned in consecutive lines as joint recipients of libations of honey. But thus far no physical remains of his cult have been identified with absolute certainty. A Dionysiac connection has been claimed for several archaeological discoveries; none convinces. The most spectacular is the discovery in the early 1960s of a large number of terracotta statues in a late Cycladic shrine at Ayia Irini on Ceos. Tentatively dated to 1500–1300 BC, these fragmentary, nearly life-sized figures represent mature women who stand or, perhaps, dance. A much later deposit of Attic drinking-vessels was found in the same room; among them is a scyphus of c.500 BC inscribed with a dedication to Dionysus by one Anthippus of Iulis. According to the excavators, the temple was in continuous use from the 15th to the 4th cent. BC. This remarkable find does not prove, however, that Dionysus was worshipped on the site before the Archaic period, let alone continuously from the bronze age to the Classical period. Given the prominence of women in *Minoan religion generally, it is equally far-fetched to identify these figures as Dionysus' female attendants, whether *nymphs, nurses, or *maenads. Yet typical features of Dionysus and his religion—including wine and ivy; divine epiphanies and ecstatic forms of worship; women dancing, handling *snakes, or holding flowers; the divine child and nurturing females; and bulls with and without anthropomorphic features—are all prominent in Aegean, especially Cretan religion and art. The earliest Dionysus may indeed be sought in the culture of Minoan Crete (see MINOAN AND MYCENAEAN RELIGION).

If we had more information on the bronze-age Dionysus, he would probably turn out to be a complex figure with a substantial non-Greek or Mediterranean component. Absolute 'Greekness' is a quality that few, if any, Greek gods can claim. This is especially true of their names. If Dionysus signifies 'nysos (son?) of Zeus', as some linguists believe, the god's name would be half Greek and half non-Greek (not Thracian, however, as its occurrence in Linear B demonstrates). But such etymological neatness is just as improbable as a divine name derived from the god's genealogy. Hardly more plausible is the derivation from nysai, the dubious designation for three nymph-like figures on a vase fragment by Sophilus. Attempts to derive the name Semele from Phrygian, bak-chos from Lydian or Phoenician, and thyrsos—the leafy branch or wand carried by the god and his followers—from Hittite, though highly speculative, reflect the wide spectrum of potential cross-cultural contacts that may have influenced the early formation of Dionysus and his cult.

In Archaic epic, Dionysus is referred to as a 'joy for mortals' and 'he of many delights'. The source of all this pleasure is wine, the god's ambivalent 'gift' which brings both 'joy and burden'. Dionysus 'invented' wine, just as *Demeter discovered agriculture (see CULTURE-BRINGERS). By a common substitution, the wine-god is also synonymous with his drink and is himself 'poured out' to the other gods as a ritual liquid. *Libations of mixed or, occasionally, unmixed wine accompanied every animal *sacrifice; wineless libations were the exception. In vase-painting, Dionysus is never far from the wine. Surrounded by cavorting *satyrs and silens, nymphs, or maenads he presides over the vintage and the successive stages of wine-making on numerous black-figure vases. Holding in one hand a grapevine and in the other one of his favourite drinking-vessels, either a cantharus or a rhyton, he is often depicted receiving wine from a male or female cupbearer such as Oenopion, his son by *Ariadne, or pouring it on an altar as a libation, or lying on a couch in typical dining posture. Yet he is never shown in the act of consuming his own gift. His female followers, too, keep their distance from the wine, at least in maenadic iconography. While maenads may carry drinking-vessels, ladle wine, or pour it, they are never shown drinking it.

Longus' Dionysiac novel 'Daphnis and Chloe' culminates in the celebration of the vintage on the Lesbian estate of Dionysophanes, whose name evokes the divine *epiphanies of Dionysus. Wine festivals were celebrated in many regions of the Greek world; in Elis as well as on Andros, Chios, and Naxos, they were accompanied by wine miracles. The oldest festival of Dionysus, the Ionian-Attic *Anthesteria, was held each spring. In Athens, the highlight consisted of the broaching of the new wine followed by a drinking-contest. On this occasion, as on others, citizen women were excluded from the ceremonial drinking of wine. The admixture of wine and water was allegorized as the nurturing of Dionysus by his mythical nurses, or more ominously, as the 'mixing of the blood of *Bakchios* with fresh-flowing tears of the nymphs'. In Attica, myths were told which connected the arrival of Dionysus and the invention of the wine with the murder of *Icarius. Here and elsewhere, Dionysiac myths emphasize the darker aspects of the god, and the perversion of his gifts.

Of Dionysus' four provinces, wine is the most dominant; it often spills over into the other three. Drunkenness can cause violence and dementia. Yet the ritual madness associated with Dionysus in myth and cult had nothing to do with alcohol or drugs. Seized by the god, initiates into Bacchic rites acted much like participants in other possession cults. Their wild dancing and ecstatic behaviour were interpreted as 'madness' only by the uninitiated. As numerous cultic inscriptions show, the actual worshippers did not employ the vocabulary of madness (*mania, mainesthai, mainades*) to describe their ritual ecstasy; rather, they used the technical but neutral language of *bakcheia* and *bakcheuein*. The practitioners of *bakcheia* were usually women; the exception is Scyles, the 'mad' Scythian king who danced through the streets of Olbia—an early centre of the Dionysus cult—as a *bakchos*. While men, too, could 'go mad' for Dionysus, they could not join the bands (*thiasoi*) of maenadic women who went 'to the mountain' (*eis oros*) every other year in many Greek cities to celebrate their rites. Their notional leader was always the god himself, who appears already in the Homeric version of the *Lycurgus myth—the earliest reference to maenadic ritual—as Dionysus *mainomenos*, 'the maddened god'. Known mainly from post-classical inscriptions and prose authors like *Plutarch and

*Pausanias, ritual maenadism was never practised within the borders of Attica. Athenian maenads went to *Delphi to join the Delphic Thyiads on the slopes of Mt. *Parnassus. Halfway between Athens and Delphi lies Thebes, the home town of Dionysus and 'mother city (*mētropolis*) of the Bacchants', from where professional maenads were imported by other cities.

In poetry and vase-painting, Dionysus and his mythical maenads tear apart live animals with their bare hands (*sparagmos*) and eat them raw (*ōmophagia*). But the divinely inflicted madness of myth was not a blueprint for actual rites, and the notion that maenadism 'swept over Greece like wildfire' is a Romantic construct that has to be abandoned along with the suggestion that the maenads sacramentally consumed Dionysus in the shape of his sacred animal. The 'delight of eating raw flesh' appears in maenadic myth, where it can escalate into *cannibalism. In the entire cultic record, however, omophagy is mentioned only once. In a maenadic inscription from Miletus, the following directive occurs: 'Whenever the priestess performs the rites of sacrifice on behalf of the [entire] city, no one is permitted to "throw in" (deposit?) the *ōmophagion* before the priestess has done so on behalf of the city'. Although the ritual details escape us, a piece of raw meat was apparently deposited somewhere for divine or human consumption. The mere reference to eating raw flesh is significant, given that sacrificial meat was normally roasted or cooked. In this instance, the perverted sacrifice, a mainstay of Dionysiac myth, has left its mark also on Dionysiac cult.

Dionysiac festivals were ubiquitous throughout the Greek world; in Athens alone there were seven such festivals in any given year, five of which were dedicated chiefly to Dionysus—*Oschophoria, Rural *Dionysia, *Lenaea, Anthesteria, and City *Dionysia. The name Oschophoria commemorates the ritual carrying of vine branches hung with bunches of grapes. The Lenaea and both Dionysia featured performances of tragedy and comedy. Apart from the new wine, the Anthesteria celebrated the spring time arrival of Dionysus from across the sea. Less is known about two other Dionysiac festivals at Athens, the *Theoinia* and the *Iobakcheia*. Festivals of Dionysus were often characterized by ritual licence and revelry, including reversal of social roles, cross-dressing by boys and men (*see* TRANSVESTISM, RITUAL), drunken celebrants in the streets, as well as widespread boisterousness and obscenity. In Athens as throughout Ionian territory, monumental *phalli stood on public display, and phallus-bearing processions paraded through the streets. But, unlike *Pan or the *Hermes of the *herms, Dionysus himself is never depicted with an erection. The god's dark side emerged in rituals and aetiological myths concerned with murder and bloodshed, madness and violence, flight and persecution, and gender hostility (as during the Agrionia). Throughout the Athenian Anthesteria festival, merrymaking predominated, but it was punctuated by ritual reminders of a temporary suspension of the normal structures of daily life—the invasion of the city by spirits of evil, or by the dead, or by strangers called 'Carians'; the silent drinking at separate tables, explained by the myth of the matricide *Orestes' arrival in Athens and the fear of pollution it provoked; the 'sacred marriage' (*hieros gamos*) of the wife of the *archon basileus* to Dionysus (*see* MARRIAGE, SACRED); and the cereal meal prepared on the festival's last day for the dead or for Hermes Chthonios (*see* CHTHONIAN GODS) and the survivors of the Great Flood (*see* DEUCALION).

Tragedy and comedy incorporate transgressive aspects of Dionysus, but they do so in opposite ways. While comedy re-enacts the periods of ritual licence associated with many Dionysiac festivals, tragedy dramatizes the negative, destructive traits of the god and his myths. *Aristotle connected the origins of tragedy and comedy with two types of Dionysiac performance—the *dithyramb and the phallic song respectively. Yet, in his own analysis of the tragic genre, he ignored not only Dionysus but also the central role of the gods in the drama. In addition to the mask worn by the actors in character, including the disguised god himself in both *Euripides' *Bacchae* and Aristophanes' *Frogs* the choral dance is the most palpable link between Attic drama and Dionysiac ritual. Tragic and comic choruses who refer to their own dancing invariably associate their choral performance with Dionysus, *Pan, or the maenads. Despite Aristotle's silence, tragedy in particular has a lot to do with Dionysus. The tragedians set individual characters, entire plays, and indeed the tragic genre as a whole in a distinct Dionysiac ambience.

The god so closely associated with exuberant life is also connected with death, a link expressed as 'life–death–life' in one of the Dionysiac-*Orphic bone inscriptions from Olbia. '*Hades and Dionysus are the same' according to the early philosopher Heraclitus. On a south Italian funerary vase, Dionysus and Hades are shown in the Underworld each grasping the other's right hand while figures from Dionysiac myth surround them. A sacred tale ascribed to *Orpheus and modelled on the *Osiris myth describes the dismemberment of Dionysus Zagreus by the *Titans and his restoration to new life; his tomb was shown at Delphi. According to another myth, Dionysus descends to the Underworld to rescue Semele from Hades; Aristophanes' comic parody in *Frogs* of the god's descent to the Underworld has Dionysus retrieve *Aeschylus. In a related ritual, the Argives summoned Dionysus ceremonially 'from the water' with the call of a trumpet hidden in thyrsi 'after throwing a lamb into the abyss for the gatekeeper', i.e. for Hades. Dionysus loomed large in the funerary art and after-life beliefs of Greeks and Romans alike. In many regions of the ancient world, tombs were decorated with Dionysiac figures and emblems like the maenad, the cantharus, and the ivy, or bore inscriptions with a Dionysiac message.

The tombstone of Alcmeionis, chief maenad in Miletus around 200 BC, announces that 'she knows her share of the blessings'—a veiled reference to her eschatological hopes. Found in tombs from southern Italy to Thessaly, the so-called Orphic gold tablets contain ritual instructions and Underworld descriptions for the benefit of the deceased. Two ivy-shaped specimens refer to a ritual rebirth under the aegis of Dionysus, and to wine-drinking in the after-life; a third identifies the dead person as a Bacchic initiate (mystēs) (see DEATH, ATTITUDES TO; ORPHIC LITERATURE; ORPHISM).

No other deity is more frequently represented in ancient art than Dionysus. Until about 430 BC, Dionysus is almost invariably shown as a mature, bearded, and ivy-wreathed adult wearing a long robe often draped with the skin of fawn or feline, and occasionally presenting a frontal face like his satyrs; later he usually appears youthful and beardless, effeminate, and partially or entirely nude. From his earliest depictions on Attic vases (c.580–570 BC) to the proliferating images of the god and his entourage in Hellenistic and Roman imperial times, Dionysiac iconography becomes more varied while remaining remarkably consistent in its use of certain themes and motifs. Major mythical subjects comprise the Return of *Hephaestus and the Gigantomachy (see GIANTS); Dionysus' birth and childhood; his punishments of *Lycurgus, *Pentheus, and the impious sailors whom he turns into dolphins; and his union with Ariadne (as on the Derveni crater of c.350 BC from Macedonia). Cult scenes in vase-painting include those on the so-called Lenaea vases, which show a makeshift image of Dionysus—fashioned from a mask attached to a pillar—surrounded by women carrying or ladling wine. It is unclear whether these settings refer to a single festival or represent an artistic montage of authentic ritual elements. The Hellenistic friezes of his temples at Teos and Cnidus displayed the *thiasos of satyrs, maenads, and *centaurs; in the theatre at Perge, we find scenes from the god's mythical life. Most conspicuously, sarcophagi of the imperial period abound with scenes from Dionysiac mythology such as the god's birth and his Indian triumph—the theme of *Nonnus' monumental epic Dionysiaca (5th cent. AD).

The very existence of Dionysus in the Mycenaean pantheon came as a complete surprise when it was first revealed by Michael Ventris in 1953 (see MINOAN AND MYCENAEAN RELIGION). Already in antiquity Dionysus was considered a foreign god whose original home was Thrace or Phrygia and who did not arrive on the Greek scene until the 8th cent. BC. The Thracian origin of Dionysus achieved the status of scholarly dogma with the second volume of Rohde's Psyche (1894). In Rohde's view, the Thracian Dionysus invaded Greece, where his wild nature was ultimately civilized and sublimated with the help of the Delphic *Apollo, a process commemorated in the myth of Dionysus' exile abroad, the resistance with which his cult was met upon its arrival in Greece, and his ultimate triumph over his opponents. Rohde's Dionysus—barbarian but happily Hellenized, occasionally wild but mostly mild—appealed to successive generations of scholars from Jane Harrison to E. R. Dodds. Wilamowitz derived Dionysus from Phrygia and Lydia rather than Thrace, while Nilsson adopted a theory of multiple foreign origins. As early as 1933, however, Walter F. Otto dissented, emphasizing instead the Greek nature of Dionysus as the epiphanic god who comes and disappears. According to Otto, the myths of Dionysus' arrival—with their dual emphasis on resistance to his otherness as well as on acceptance of his gifts—articulate the essential aspects of the god's divinity rather than the historical vicissitudes of the propagation of his cult. Otto's version of a polar and paradoxical Dionysus categorizes the diversity of Dionysiac phenomena, thus making them more intelligible. It has been argued, after Otto, that the 'foreign' Dionysus is a psychological rather than a historical entity which has more to do with Greek self-definition and the

'Dionysus in us' than with the god's actual arrival from abroad. More recently, Dionysus has emerged as the archetypal 'Other'—in a culturally normative sense—whose otherness is an inherent function of his selfhood as a Greek divinity. However, if such abstractions are pushed too far, Dionysus ceases to be the god he was to the Greeks—present in his concrete manifestations, and in the perplexing diversity of his myths, cults, and images—and becomes a modern concept.

[Euripides, *Bacchae*; Aristophanes, *Frogs*; Apollodorus 3. 4. 2–3, 3. 5. 1–3; Ovid, *Fasti* 3. 713–90; Longus, *The Pastoral Story of Daphnis and Chloe*; Nonnus, *Dionysiaca*]

Dionysus, artists of, generic name for the powerful guilds into which itinerant Greek actors and musicians formed themselves from the 3rd cent. BC, chiefly those (a) 'in *Isthmia and *Nemea', by 112 BC based on Argos and Thebes; (b) 'in Athens', first attested in 279/8 BC; (c) of Egypt, based in Alexandria; and (d) 'in Ionia and the Hellespont', at first centred on Teos. Their formation reflects the demand for Attic-style drama from the 4th cent. onwards, in both Greece and the Hellenistic kingdoms, where they came under royal patronage. On occasion organizing dramatic performances on a city's behalf, they chiefly served to secure benefits for members, notably personal inviolability in their travels and exemption from military service and local taxes. Like independent cities they had their own assemblies, magistrates, and ambassadors; a cultic community (sacred, of course, to *Dionysus), each had its own *temenos, priest, and festivities. Roman emperors, notably Hadrian, took over as patrons and may have encouraged amalgamation into the 'world-wide' guild attested from AD 43 until the reign of Diocletian and probably surviving much longer. *See* CLUBS.

Diopeithes, decree of (c.432 BC), provided an impeachment procedure against impiety. *Plutarch, our only source, says it attacked 'those who fail to respect (*nomizein*) things divine or teach theories about the heavens'.

Its object was the philosopher *Anaxagoras, and ultimately his friend Pericles.

Dioscuri, 'sons of Zeus', a regular title (already found in 6th-cent. BC inscriptions, of Castor and Polydeuces (Pollux), who on the human plane are also Tyndaridae, sons of *Tyndareos. They are the brothers of *Helen, Tyndareos' daughter, in *Homer, where they are once treated as being dead; but once they are 'alive' even though 'the corn-bearing earth holds them', and the author explains that they are honoured by *Zeus and live on alternate days, 'having honour equal to gods'. Here and in *Hesiod they are sons of Tyndareus and *Leda; later, as in *Pindar, Polydeuces is son of Zeus, his twin Castor of Tyndareos, and at Polydeuces' request they share his immortality between them, living half their time below the earth at Therapnae near Sparta, the other half on *Olympus. Very probably the same conception of their double nature as sons both of Zeus and of Tyndareos underlies all these passages, different though the particular emphases are. Similarly ambiguous parentage characterizes another great god/hero, *Heracles (as also *Theseus). Sometimes they are Dioscuri and Tyndaridae in successive lines of texts.

Other Greeks recognized Sparta as the centre of their cult. But they were also immensely popular in Attica, for instance, and in effect throughout Greece and Greek Italy (where the Spartan colony of Tarentum was another centre of the cult). At Thebes, however, the oath 'by the two gods' evoked a local pair of twins, *Amphion and Zethus.

Very broadly, they were gods friendly to men, 'saviours', in a variety of spheres. Their characteristic mode of action is the *epiphany at a moment of crisis. Such interventions are regularly also an expression of their trustworthiness, their eagerness to help those who help or put their trust in them. The poet Simonides was denied his fee by the Thessalian prince Scopas, on the grounds that his poem had paid more honour to the Dioscuri than to the mortal patron. A little later, two youths summoned Simonides outside during a banquet in Scopas' palace; the roof collapsed, killing all within. The Italian Locrians, at war with the people of Croton, appealed to Sparta for help, and were offered and accepted the assistance of the Dioscuri. This showed faith; in the battle that ensued at Sagra, two gigantic youths in strange dress were seen fighting on the Locrian side, and the Locrians achieved total victory (there are other battle *epiphanies of the Dioscuri, of which that at Lake Regillus is the most celebrated). The Dioscuri were closely associated with athletic competitions, and here too it is their reliability as helpers that Pindar stresses. Above all they brought aid at sea, where their saving presence in storms was visible in the electric discharge known as St Elmo's fire.

A characteristic rite was performed in their honour, that of *theoxenia, 'god-entertaining'. Individuals in their own houses, states at their public hearths or equivalent places, set a 'table' to which they then summoned the Dioscuri; votive reliefs sometimes show them arriving at the gallop over a table laid with food. Such 'table-offerings' were quite common in Greek cult, but normally they were made in the shrine of the god or hero concerned. The domestic setting in the case of the Dioscuri creates an added intimacy.

The Dioscuri are distinctive also in the extent to which they are associated with characteristic sacred symbols (about most of which we can say little more than they stress the idea of twinness). Both in art and literature they are constantly associated with horses; and on votive reliefs they appear with some or all of: the *dokana*, two upright pieces of wood connected by two cross-beams; a pair of amphorae of characteristic shape; a pair of bossed shields; a pair of snakes. They also often wear felt caps, above which stars may appear.

In myth, they had three main exploits. When Theseus kidnapped Helen, they made an expedition to Attica, recovered her, and carried off Theseus' mother *Ae-

thra. They took part in the Argonautic expedition (see ARGONAUTS), and on it Polydeuces distinguished himself in the fight against *Amycus. Their final exploit on earth was the carrying off of the two daughters of Leucippus ('white horse'!), the *Leucippides, Phoebe and Hilaeira. Thereupon the nephews of Leucippus, *Idas and Lynceus, pursued them. In the resulting fight Castor and both his pursuers were killed; the sequel of the shared immortality has already been mentioned. On the basis of these adventures the Dioscuri can be seen as ideal types of the young male; but a consistent connection between them and a particular age group cannot be observed in cult.

In art they appear before the middle of the 6th cent. BC on metopes of the Sicyonian building at *Delphi, with the Argo (ship of the Argonauts), and rustling cattle with Idas. In Attic black-figure pottery they are shown with Tyndareos and Leda. Later the most popular subjects are: the rape of the Leucippides; the Dioscuri as Argonauts; at the *theoxenia*; at the delivery to Leda of Nemesis' egg containing Helen.

Similarities have often been noted between the Dioscuri and the divine twins of other mythologies, above all the Vedic Aśvins, who like them are closely associated with horses.

[Homer, *Iliad* 3. 237–44; *Odyssey* 11. 300–4; *Homeric Hymn to the Dioscuri*; Pindar, *Nemean* 10; Theocritus, *Idylls* 22. 137 ff.]

Diotima, actual or fictitious priestess (see PRIESTS) at Mantinea (c.440 BC), from whom *Socrates pretends in *Plato's *Symposium* to have learnt his theory of love.

Dipolieia See ATTIC CULTS AND MYTHS; BOUPHONIA; SACRIFICE, GREEK; ZEUS.

Dipylon, the name used to refer to the double gateway in Athens' city wall leading into the Ceramicus and to the cemetery immediately outside the wall in that area. The gateway comprised a rectangular courtyard open on the land side, closed by two double doors on the city side; each corner was enlarged to form a tower;

a fountain-house adjoined the gateway on the city side. The complex dates from immediately after the Persian Wars, but was rebuilt in the 3rd cent. BC. The road from the *Agora to the Academy passed through this gate. Some 75 m. (246 ft.) south-west a similar smaller gateway protected the passage of the Sacred Way to *Eleusis. Between the two gates stood the Pompeium, the marshalling-place for the Panathenaic procession (*see* PANATHENAEA). From the 11th cent. BC onwards the area was the principal burial-ground of Athens. The best impression of the cemetery is given by *Pausanias, who observed here the tombs of those who fell in war and individual monuments to Harmodius and Aristogiton, Cleisthenes, Pericles, and other prominent politicians.

[Pausanias 1. 29]

Dirae *See* ERINYES.

Dirce, gave her name to the spring/river at Thebes. She was done to death by *Amphion and Zethus, sons of Antiope whom she had mistreated. A Theban rite, where the outgoing cavalry commander swore in his successor at Dirce's tomb, reflects local tradition. *See* THEBES, MYTHS OF.

dithyramb, choral song in honour of *Dionysus; the origins of dithryramb, and the meaning of the word itself, have been the subject of speculation since antiquity. There are three phases in the history of the genre: (1) pre-literary dithyramb; (2) the institutionalization of dithyramb in the 6th cent. BC; and (3) the latest phase, which began in the mid-5th cent.

Already in phase (1) dithyramb was a cult song with Dionysiac content. It was sung by a group of singers under the leadership of an *exarchōn*. Phase (2) has its roots in the cultural and religious policies of the Athenian tyrants and the young Athenian democracy. Allegedly is was *Arion in late 7th-cent. Corinth who was the first to compose a choral song, rehearse it with a choir, and produce it in performance, and who finally gave the name 'dithyramb' to this new kind of choral song. Lasus of Hermione is connected with dithyramb at Athens: he organized a dithyrambic contest in the first years of the democracy. Each of the ten Athenian tribes entered the competition with one chorus of men and one of boys, each consisting of 50 singers. The financing of the enterprise (payment for the poet, the trainer of the chorus (*chorodidaskalos*), and the pipe-player; and the cost of equipping the chorus) was the responsibility of the *chorēgos* (*see* CHOREGIA). The winning *chorēgos* could put up a tripod with a dedicatory inscription in the Street of the Tripods. The dithyrambic contest was a competition between the tribes, not the poets, who are never mentioned on the victory inscriptions. Dithyrambs were performed at the following Athenian festivals: the City or Great *Dionysia, the *Thargelia, the (Lesser) *Panathenaea, the Promethiea, the Hephaestia (*see* HEPHAESTUS). The first victor at the Dionysia at Athens was the otherwise unknown Hypodicus of Chalcis (509/8 BC). In the first part of the 5th cent. Simonides (with 56 victories), *Pindar, and *Bacchylides were the dominant dithyrambic poets. Pindar's dithyrambs are recognizable as such by their Dionysiac character. The standard content of a Pindaric dithyramb included some mention of the occasion which had given rise to the song, and of the commissioning city; praise of the poet; narration of a myth; and some treatment of Dionysiac theology. By contrast, *Bacchylides' dithyrambs, with the exception of Io, lacked these topical allusions. Hence the difficulties of classification which have been felt since scholars working in Hellenistic Alexandria: there was a discussion between Aristarchus and *Callimachus over whether the *Cassandra* of Bacchylides was a dithyramb or a *paean. From the mid-5th cent. (phase 3), dithyramb became the playground of the musical avant-garde. Melanippides, Cinesias, Timotheus, and Philoxenus are the best-known exponents of phase (3): they introduced astrophic form (i.e. their poems were not arranged according to strophe and antistrophe), instrumental and vocal solos, and 'mimetic' music. In the course of the 4th cent., a recognizably dithyrambic manner and idiom developed, and penetrated other lyric genres also. Songs with dithyrambic content were composed, like Philoxenus' *Banquet*; and in 4th-cent. Middle Comedy we find fairly long passages in dithyrambic style. In the Hellenistic period dithyrambs were performed at the festivals of the Delia and Apollonia on Delos; and at the City Dionysia in Athens until the 2nd cent. AD. But post-Classical fragments (citations) allow no confident judgement about these compositions.

Divalia (Angeronalia), Roman festival on 21 December to the goddess *Angerona. The inscribed calendar of Praeneste describes her statue's mouth as bandaged and connect this with Rome's 'secret name'.

divination

Greek Divination is at the heart of Greek religion: *Sophocles in a famous ode can represent a challenge to *oracles as a challenge to religion itself, and the pious Xenophon in listing the benefits conferred on man by the gods regularly gives special prominence to guidance through 'sayings and dreams and omens' and sacrifices. His *Anabasis* presents in fact much the best panorama of the place of divination in an individual's experience. Before joining Cyrus's expedition, which he realized might lead him into political difficulties, Xenophon had, on Socrates' advice, consulted the *Delphic oracle. At a moment of crisis, he received a dream from, as he thought, Zeus the King, containing both a threat and a promise: 'what it means to see such a dream one can judge from the consequences' (i.e. the rest of the *Anabasis*). A bird-omen which he had witnessed on leaving Ephesus had been interpreted by a seer as being of similarly mixed significance. During the campaign, the army regularly took omens from sacrifice, before marching off or joining battle for instance (see, above all, his account of a four-day delay caused by bad omens), and Xenophon also records

the consultative sacrifices that he performed whenever an important decision, personal or collective, had to be made. Through divinatory sacrifice Xenophon could, as it were, consult an oracle wherever he found himself, posing the question in exactly the form in which he might have put it to an oracle: 'is it more beneficial and advantageous to stay with King Seuthes or to depart?', for instance. He also mentions an omen from a sneeze. *See* DREAMS.

Xenophon thus presents at least five ways in which the will of the gods was revealed (whether spontaneously or in response to a mortal inquiry): at fixed oracular shrines, through dream-interpretation, observation of birds, sacrifice, and 'chance' omens such as a sneeze or an encounter or something said casually at a significant moment. Lesser methods can easily be added, such as the form of inspired prophecy known as 'belly-talking', or the 'sieve-divination' that Theocritus introduces in a poem to characterize a rustic. All Xenophon's five forms are already found in *Homer, except the very important technique of divination by sacrifice, which probably entered Greece from the near east in the early Archaic period (with the consequence that bird divination dropped somewhat in significance). Also influential were the collections of verse oracles deployed by 'oracle-mongers'; these were commonly ascribed to mythical seers such as *Bacis, *Musaeus (1), and the *Sibyl, but 'ancient oracles of *Apollo' could also be among them. As well as such 'oracle-mongers' and the staff at oracular shrines, professional diviners included dream-interpreters and above all seers, *manteis,* who specialized in sacrificial divination but no doubt claimed a broader competence. We hear of 'books on divination' bequeathed by a seer to a friend who then took up the art and grew rich, and the literature on *dream interpretation, of which *Artemidorus's *Onirocritica* is a late example, is said to go back to a work by the 5th-cent. sophist Antiphon. *See* PROPHECIES.

Professional seers were always exposed to ridicule and accusations of charlatanism, but anthropology teaches that societies which depend on seers also regularly deride them; attacks on individual seers are to be sharply distinguished from a more general scepticism. The philosophical debate on the subject is splendidly presented in *Cicero's *De divinatione*. *Xenophanes, the Epicureans, (*see* EPICURUS), the Stoic Carneades and others denied the possibility of divination. Some Peripatetics defended 'inspired' prophecy such as the Pythia's (*see* DELPHIC ORACLE) or that through dreams, while rejecting inductive divination from signs; most Stoics (notably Posidonius) vigorously defended both types, basing their justification upon the powers of gods, fate, and nature or the doctrine of 'sympathy' between the different parts of the world. *See* STOICISM.

Roman All divination stems from the belief that gods send meaningful messages. These messages were classified in a variety of intersecting ways: according to the character of signs through which the message was conveyed, and whether these signs were sent unasked or were actively sought; the time-frame to which a sign was taken to refer (future, present, past) and the content of the message itself (prediction, warning, prohibition, displeasure, approval); and, most importantly, whether the message pertained to the private or public sphere, the observation and interpretation of the latter category of signs forming part of Roman state religion.

The divine message was either intuitively conveyed or required interpretation. *Cicero adopts the division of divination (elaborated by the Stoics, *see* STOICISM) into two classes, artificial (external) and natural (internal). The latter relied upon divine inspiration (*instinctus, adflatus divinus*), and was characteristic of prophets (*vaticinantes*) and dreamers (*somniantes*). The former was based on art (*ars*) and knowledge (*scientia*). To this category belonged the observation

of birds, celestial signs, entrails, unusual phenomena, also astrology and divination from lots. But inspired utterances (*see* SIBYL) and dreams also required interpretation.

The Roman state employed three groups of divinatory experts: the *augures* (augurs), the board of priests for the performance of sacred rites (*see* QUINDECIMVIRI SACRIS FACIUNDIS), who were in charge of the Sibylline books (*see* SIBYL), and the *haruspices*. The first two were the official state priests; the haruspices were summoned as needed. Their special province was the observation of the entrails of sacrificial victims (haruspicy or extispicy), especially the liver (hepatoscopy). Both the augurs and haruspices observed and interpreted the bird and celestial signs (*auspicia*, particularly *fulmina* and *tonitrua*, lightning and thunder), but they treated them differently. For the augurs they were the auspices expressing divine permission or prohibition concerning a specific act; they were indicative of the future only in so far as faulty auspices, and especially wilful disregard of auspices, might cause divine anger (which, however, could manifest itself in a variety of unpredictable ways). But for the haruspices (and also for the non-Roman augurs) the very same signs could be indications of specific future happenings.

All signs were either solicited or unsolicited. The latter could function either as unsolicited *auspicia oblativa* or as prodigies. The former referred solely to a concrete undertaking, the prodigies on the other hand to the state of the republic. They were indications that the normal relationship with the deity, the 'peace of the gods' (*pax deum*), was disturbed. Particularly potent were unusual occurrences (*monstra, ostenta*). In the case of adverse auspices the action in question was to be abandoned; in the case of prodigies it was imperative to find out the cause of divine displeasure (this task often fell to the haruspices) and to perform various ceremonies of appeasement (*procuratio*). *See* PORTENTS.

The Roman state did not officially employ

astrologers (occasionally they were even banned from Rome) or dream-interpreters, but their services were sought by many, including the emperors (*see* ASTROLOGY). Predictions were made also from involuntary motions, sneezing, and from lifeless objects, particularly from (inscribed) lots (*sortes*) drawn from a receptacle and interpreted by the *sortilegi*, with centres elsewhere in Italy at Praeneste, Tibur, Antium, and the fountains of Aponus near Patavium and of *Clitumnus in Umbria. Also the works of poets were so used, particularly *Virgil (*sortes Vergilianae*).

Popular divination was often scorned as charlatanry (allegedly a haruspex could not but laugh on meeting another haruspex), and the government was particularly suspicious of astrologers and inspired prophets. In the Christian empire all forms of divination were prohibited and persecuted, though never eradicated.

Divitiacus (1st cent. BC), an Aeduan Druid, whose career typifies the political division that exposed Gaul to conquest. His policy of inviting Roman aid against aggressors (unsuccessfully in 61 BC against Ariovistus alone, successfully in 58 against both the Helvetii and Ariovistus) enabled him to emerge victorious over his bitter rival, his brother Dumnorix. *Cicero and *Caesar used their personal contacts with him to form the Roman view of Druidism. *See* CELTIC RELIGION.

Dodona, the sanctuary of *Zeus Naïos in Epirus (north-west Greece), and reputedly the oldest Greek *oracle. The god's temple-sharer is *Dione Naïa, and both are shown together on coins. Settlement on the site probably began in the prehistoric period, but there is no evidence of an early Earth (or any other) oracle. Also stories of a mantic gong or oracular spring rising from the roots of Zeus' sacred oak are later inventions. Traditionally oracular responses emanated from the rustling leaves of the sacred oak or from doves sitting in the tree. Oracular doves are shown on two Epirote coins.

*Odysseus claimed to have gone to Dodona in order to 'hear Zeus' will from the lofty oak' *Achilles prayed to the Pelasgian Zeus at Dodona whose prophets the Selli 'sleep on the ground with unwashed feet'. These mysterious male prophets may have been identical with the people called Tomari (after Mt. Tomaros), but by the mid-5th cent. BC the oracle was operated by three priestesses who later on themselves were called 'the Doves'. Their method of issuing responses in a trance was borrowed from *Apollo's inspirational oracle at *Delphi. Rarely consulted officially by states, the Dodonian oracle generally offered advice on private problems. The enquirer scratched his question on a lead tablet and was answered with a simple 'yes' or 'no'. Thousands of tablets survive and can be seen in the museum at Ioannina. In the reign of Pyrrhus, Dodona was made the religious centre of his kingdom and the festival of the Naïa was instituted. The sack by the Aetolians in 219 BC was followed by a restoration, but the sanctuary never really recovered from the Roman ravaging of Epirus in 167 BC. The festival of the Naïa was revived and lasted till the 3rd cent. AD. A simple tree-sanctuary remains on the site, and the ruins of a small 4th-cent. temple stand beside the recently restored large theatre (17,000 seats) of the 3rd cent. BC. *See* DIVINATION.

Donatists The Donatists were members of a puritanical church of the martyrs in 4th- and early 5th-cent. Roman Africa. Their schism from the African Catholics derived from the events of the Great Persecution under the emperors *Diocletian and Maximian (303–5). African clergy who complied with imperial demands to surrender Christian scriptures were dubbed *traditores* or 'surrenderers'. Moderates and rigorists clashed over the procedure for readmitting *traditores* to communion, arguing over how far the Church on earth must be a 'mixed body' containing both righteous and sinners. The death of Mensurius, bishop of Carthage, accentuated divisions. When Carthaginian Christians elected the archdeacon Caecilian bishop in Mensurius' stead, a strong party of dissenters, backed by Numidian bishops, countered by electing Majorinus as rival bishop (probably 307, but perhaps 311/12). At his death, Majorinus was succeeded by the cleric Donatus, possibly of Casae Nigrae in Numidia.

In the winter of 312/13, the emperor *Constantine I ordered the return to Caecilian of confiscated Church property and exempted Caecilian's clergy from a number of fiscal burdens. The opposition appealed to Constantine for arbitration by Gallic bishops as to who was rightful bishop of Carthage. Constantine commissioned Miltiades, bishop of Rome, himself an African, to convoke an episcopal tribunal which decided for Caecilian and condemned Donatus (October 313). The Donatists now asserted that one of Caecilian's consecrators, Felix of Abthugni, had been a *traditor* and therefore incapable of performing a valid consecration. While their complaints were again rejected at the council of Arles (August 314), it was not until February 315 that Felix was cleared, and only in November 316 did Constantine declare Caecilian lawful bishop. By then Donatus' church had won wide acceptance throughout Africa, but apart from a precarious foothold in Rome the movement did not spread outside Africa. For the remainder of the century, the Donatists incurred only intermittent persecution and, despite the exile of Donatus by the emperor Constans (347), apparently remained the majority church until *c*.400.

By the 340s there emerged in southern Numidia Donatist extremists who became known as Circumcellions, probably through their association with the shrines of martyrs (*cellae*). The Circumcellions, whose social origins remain unclear, perpetrated violent attacks against creditors and landlords. Beneath these seemingly social and economic grievances, however, lay a fundamental religious fanaticism manifested clearly in the Circumcellions' vigorous pursuit of martyr-dom by any means, including suicide. Donatist bishops alternately disavowed the Circumcellions and employed them against their Catholic enemies, prompting intervention by imperial forces.

The Donatists' support of the revolt of Firmus (372–5) left them virtually unscathed, but an internal schism involving Maxentius (392–3) and their backing of Gildo's failed revolt (398) laid the Donatists open to counter-attack by African Catholics and imperial officials. St *Augustine devoted considerable energies to overcoming the schism. A series of imperial rescripts banned the movement (405), and in 411 a conference of more than 500 bishops, presided over by the imperial commissioner Marcellinus, went against them. Years of persecution followed, ended only by the arrival of the Vandals in 429. Thereafter, Donatists and Catholics seem to have reconciled themselves to a peaceful coexistence of divergent traditions within a single ecclesiastical (Catholic) structure.

Theologically the Donatists were rigorists, following the tradition of *Tertullian and *Cyprian, holding that the Church of the saints must remain holy. They insisted on rebaptizing converts and held that sacraments dispensed by a *traditor* were not only invalid but infected the recipients. Donatist theologians included Macrobius, Donatist bishop of Rome, and Tyconius, whose work influenced St Augustine. Despite their appeals to Constantine (313) and Julian (361), the Donatists also accepted a theory of worldly government which practically equated the Roman empire with the apocalyptic image of Babylon. Cultural and economic divisions seem to have contributed to the ecclesiastical controversy, with the Catholics drawing support from the more urbanized and Latinized Proconsular Africa and the Donatists from the more rural and native Numidia and Mauretania.

Donatism produced its own art forms, but not, so far as is known, a Bible in a language other than Latin. With the Coptic and Syrian Churches, it is an example of cultural and religious groupings by regions which characterized both halves of the empire from the late 3rd cent. onwards.

Dorian festivals In contrast to the abundance of *Ionian festivals, only one has a claim to be a marker of Dorian identity, the *Carnea (Karneia). A festival of that name is attested in Sparta, Thera, Cyrene, Argos, Cos, and Cnidus, a month name *Karneios* much more widely; according to Thucydides, *Karneios* was a 'sacred month' for Dorians, and *Pausanias speaks of worship of Apollo Karneios as common to all Dorians. The month *Hyakinthios* is also often found in Dorian communities, but the corresponding festival Hyacinthia is attested only for Sparta (*see* HYACINTHUS; SPARTAN CULTS). Other festivals or associated month names such as Agrionia and *Apellai that are common in Dorian states also appear in Aeolian regions. Negatively, Herodotus claims that *Thesmophoria were not celebrated by Dorians of the *Peloponnese; *see* TRIOPAS.

Dorotheus, of Sidon (1st or beginning of 2nd cent. AD), astrological poet who had great vogue with the Arabian astrologers.

dreams fascinated the ancients as much as they do us, though it is illegitimate to employ Freudian categories in interpreting ancient dreams: their categories must not be ignored in favour of our own culturally relative theories. Most ancients accepted that there were both significant and non-significant dreams (according to *Homer and *Virgil, true dreams come from gates of horn, delusory dreams from gates of ivory). This basic division might itself be subdivided, most elaborately into a fivefold classification: non-predictive dreams, subdivided into *enhypnia* caused by the day's residues and *phantasmata* or distorted visions that come between sleeping and waking states; predictive dreams subdivided into: *oneiroi* that need symbolic interpretation, *horamata* or prophetic visions, and *chrēmatismata* or advice from a god. The last category is well attested epigraphically by *votives

put up by people as the result of successful advice or instructions from a god received in a dream, and in the remarkable diary kept by Aelius *Aristides which included numerous visions of *Asclepius and other gods. Dreams were indeed an important aspect of diagnosis in sanctuaries of Asclepius (*see* INCUBATION).

The idea that dreams could be significant, but might need professional interpreters, is found from Homer onwards. Dream-books were written from the 5th cent. BC onwards; the only surviving example from antiquity is that by *Artemidorus.

Philosophers and others discussed whether dreams had a divine origin. The Hippocratic author of the treatise *On the Sacred Disease* urged that dreams were caused merely by disturbances in the brain, and the author of *On Regimen* 4 explained how to use dreams for medical diagnosis. *Plato argued that some dreams came from the gods and were reliable sources of knowledge, *Aristotle that physiological explanations applied, while *Epicurus and Lucretius located dreams in a theory about the nature of sense perceptions. For *Cicero the possibility of prophetic dreams was an example of *divination that worked in practice, but which was impossible to justify theoretically. Cicero also used a dream narrative (the Dream of Scipio) as part of his *Republic*, the part to which *Macrobius devoted his commentary.

Christian texts also developed the importance of dream visions, in a variety of styles: the Book of Revelation or the *Shepherd* of Hermas both stand as reports of visions; the *Martyrdom of St Perpetua* includes a vivid first-hand report of a dream vision she had of her martyrdom; the bishop *Synesius, *On Dreams* (AD 405–6) offered an allegorical interpretation of dreams. Eight handbooks of dream interpretation survive from the Byzantine period.

[Homer, *Iliad* 1. 62–7, 2. 1–40, 5. 148–51; *Odyssey* 19. 560–7; Virgil, *Aeneid* 6. 893–8; Ovid, *Metamorphoses* 11. 592–649]

Druids *See* MONA; CELTIC RELIGION.

Dryope, daughter of *Dryops or of Eurytus, was mother by *Apollo of Amphissus,
who gave his name to the city of Amphissa.
She was transformed either into a *nymph
associated with a spring or a lotus-tree—
Celtis australis.

[Ovid, *Metamorphoses* 9. 330–93]

Dryops, who gave his name to the Dryopes;
his parentage is variously given, and the history of his people, allegedly *Pelasgian (i.e.
pre-Hellenic), obscure, but they are stated to
have emigrated widely (from the Spercheius
valley to *Parnassus, the Argolid, Arcadia,
etc.); hence perhaps the differing stories
which make him the son of gods or men
belonging to several of these regions. *See
also* DRYOPE.

Echidna, one of many female monsters in Greek mythology. She was daughter of *Phorcys and Ceto, was half-woman, half-snake, and was mother by *Typhon of several of the monsters killed by *Heracles and others. The name may also be generic: Herodotus traces the descent of the Scythians to the union of an *echidna* ('serpent') with Heracles.

Echion ('snake-man'), (1) one of the surviving Sparti or 'sown men' (*see* CADMUS); he married Agave and was father of *Pentheus. (2) Son of Hermes and Antianeira, daughter of Menetus. He and his twin brother Erytus joined the *Argonauts. Their home was Pangaeus (Pindar) or Alope (Apollonius). They joined the Calydonian boar-hunt, *see* MELEAGER (1).

[(2) Pindar, *Pythian* 4. 180; Apollonius Rhodius 1. 51 ff.; Ovid, *Metamorphoses* 8. 311]

Echo There are two mythological explanations of echoes, neither very early. (*a*) Echo was a *nymph vainly loved by *Pan, who finally sent the shepherds mad and they tore her in pieces; but Earth hid the fragments, which still can sing and imitate other sounds. (*b*) *See* NARCISSUS.

[Longus, *Daphnis and Chloe* 3. 23]

eclipses Solar and lunar eclipses, ranking with the most impressive celestial phenomena, were widely considered ominous, even though by the 5th cent., well-informed Greeks like Thucydides understood that solar eclipses can take place only at new, and lunar ones at full moon. *See* PORTENTS.

Ecphantus, a 4th-cent. BC Pythagorean from Syracuse (or perhaps Croton), held that indivisible bodies (monads), moved by a divine power referred to as 'mind' and 'soul', constitute the world, which is spherical and governed by providence. A Neopythagorean treatise *On Kingship* is falsely attributed to him; it exalts kingship as naturally superior, the mediator between the gods and man, an essential link in a divinely organized universe. This work, variously dated between the 3rd cent. BC and the early 3rd cent. AD, shows Jewish and/or Gnostic influence (*see* GNOSTICISM; PYTHAGORAS AND PYTHAGOREANISM).

ecstasy In Classical Greek the term *ekstasis* may refer to any situation in which (part of) the mind or body is removed from its normal place or function. It is used for bodily displacements, but also for abnormal conditions of the mind such as madness, unconsciousness, or 'being beside oneself'. In the Hellenistic and later periods the notion is influenced by the Platonic concept of 'divine madness', a state of inspired possession distinct from lower forms of madness and as such providing insights into objective truth. *Ekstasis* now acquires the notion of a state of trance in which the soul, leaving the body, sees visions (as for instance in Acts 10: 10; 22: 17). In later, especially *Neoplatonist theory (Plotinus, Porphyry), *ekstasis* is the central condition for escape from restraints of either a bodily or a rational-intellectual nature and thus becomes the gateway to the union with the god (*unio mystica*); *see* DIONYSUS.

Eëtion, king of the city of Thebe in the

Troad, and father of *Andromache. *Achilles sacked the town and killed him along with his seven sons, but gave him a warrior's burial.

[Homer, *Iliad* 6. 395 ff.]

effatus *See* AUGURES.

Egeria, water goddess, worshipped with *Diana at Aricia and apparently with the *Camenae outside the porta Capena in Rome. Her name may be connected with *egerere* ('to deliver') or with the *gens Egeria*. Pregnant women sacrificed to Egeria for easy delivery. She was allegedly *Numa's consort and adviser, appropriate for the connection between prophecy and Egeria and the Camenae as water divinities.

[Virgil, *Aeneid* 7. 762–4, 775; Livy 1. 21. 3, 38. 1]

Egyptian deities The Graeco-Roman view of Egyptian religion is sharply fissured. Despite Herodotus' more neutral stance, many writers of all periods, and probably most individuals, found in the Egyptians' worship of animals a polemical contrast to their own norms, just as, conversely, the Egyptians turned animal-worship into a symbol of national identity. The first Egyptian divinity to be recognized by the Greek world was the oracular *Ammon of the *Siwa oasis; but *oracles have a special status. The only form of Late-period Egyptian religion to be assimilated into the Graeco-Roman world was to a degree untypical, centred on anthropomorphic deities—*Isis, *Sarapis, and Harpocrates—and grounded in Egyptian vernacular enthusiasm quite as much as in temple ritual. The other gods which became known in the Graeco-Roman world, *Osiris, *Anubis, *Apis, *Horus, *Bubastis, Agathodaemon (*see* AGATHOS DAIMON), Bes, etc., spread solely in their train. Moreover, especially in the Hellenistic period, a nice balance was maintained between acknowledgement of their strangeness (Isis *Taposirias*, *Memphitis*, *Aigyptia*, etc.) and selection of their universal, 'hearkening', 'aiding', 'saving' roles.

From the late 4th cent. BC, these cults were most commonly introduced into the Greek world, primarily to port- and tourist-towns, by (Hellenized) Egyptians, i.e. immigrant metics. Sometimes they were introduced by Greeks who had served or lived in Egypt. There is a growing consensus that they were often indirect beneficiaries of Ptolemaic political suzerainty. Within a generation or two they became sufficiently attractive to Greeks of some social standing to be able to press for recognition as *thiasoi* (*see* THIASOS): it was when they proselytized among the citizen body that they were regulated by city governments and incorporated as civic deities. Full-time Egyptian priests were then obtained for larger temples, and subordinate *synodoi* (associations) formed, e.g. *melanephoroi* (lit. 'the black-clad'), *pastophoroi* ('shrine-carriers'), analogous to a development widespread in Late-period Egypt. In many smaller communities the Greek model of annual priesthoods was adopted. (*See* PRIESTS.) In the west, Isis reached Campania from *Delos in the late 2nd cent. BC. At Rome the situation was initially volatile: the private *Isium Metellinum* (75–50 BC) and an illegal shrine on the Capitol were pulled down in 53 BC. The first public temple was the *Iseum Campense* (43 BC). The cults attracted members of the local upper class in the 1st cent. AD, spreading from Italy unevenly into the western empire. Neither slaves nor the poor are much in evidence.

[Herodotus 2. 35–67; Cicero, *On the Nature of the Gods* 1. 29. 81 f.; Diodorus Siculus 1. 86–90]

Eileithyia (Cretan *Eleuthia*), Minoan goddess of birth. She had numerous cults throughout Greece and the Cycladic islands but mainly in Laconia (with two temples at Sparta), and in Crete where she was chief goddess of Lato. Her name is obscure, probably non-Greek, so that etymologies, including the tempting connection with (*Demeter) Eleusinia remain conjectural. Eileithyia occurs beside the place-name Amnisos on a Linear B tablet (*ereutija*). She had a cave sanctuary there which Odysseus claims to have seen on his visit to king

*Idomeneus of Cnossus. Inside the goddess was worshipped in the form of a stalagmite during middle Minoan (palace period), and her cult was remembered until Roman times. Eileithyia Inatia had another cave-cult at Tsoutsouros (Inatos) with votive figurines of pregnant and parturient women. In Greek myth Eileithyia is the daughter of *Hera and often Eileithyiae (in the plural) are associates of *Artemis (Artemis Eileithyia) in their function as goddesses of *childbirth. Eileithyia helps or hinders a birth in epic, and the Eileithyiae may be synonymous with birth pangs.

The winged figure seen assisting at the birth of Athena depicted on a 7th-cent. BC Tenean relief pithos may be Eileithyia, but the scene has been variously interpreted. The goddess is often shown in scenes of divine births from Archaic times, although her iconographic form and attributes were never clearly defined. *See* CRETAN CULTS AND MYTHS; MINOAN AND MYCENAEAN RELIGION.

[Homer, *Iliad* 11. 271–3, 16. 187, 19. 103, 119; *Homeric Hymn to Apollo* 97; Hesiod, *Theogony* 922]

Eirene, peace personified. In poetry *Hesiod has her and her sisters ('Observance of the Laws' and 'Justice'), daughters of Zeus and Themis, watch over the field crops of men. She receives a lyric prayer in *Euripides' fragmentary *Cresphontes* and appears often elsewhere. She is the title (but silent) character of Aristophanes' *Peace*, produced in 422/1 BC, just days before the Peace of Nicias. Her cult is known only for Athens. Plutarch has the Athenians build an altar for her about 465 to commemorate peace with the Persians, probably mistakenly. The Common Peace of 371 was commemorated by an annual state sacrifice to her and by a statue by Cephisodotus of her carrying the child *Plutus ('Wealth').

[Hesiod, *Works and Days* 901–3; Isocrates 15. 109–10; Plutarch, *Cimon* 13. 6; Pausanias 1. 8. 2]

eiresiōnē, an olive branch carried by singing boys at the *Pyanopsia and perhaps the *Thargelia at Athens, and at an unknown festival of *Apollo on Samos. At the Pyanop-

sia, a public *eiresiōnē* was deposited at a temple of Apollo, others at house doors (where they remained, probably, till the next year). The branch was hung with figs, fruits, and other symbols of agricultural abundance, and according to the song brought 'figs and fat loaves' and other good things with it; householders were expected to give the boys a present in return.

Elagabalus, deus Sol invictus ('Invincible Sun-god Elagabalus'), oracular deity of Emesa in Syria, his sacred symbol a conical black stone. His cult was established in Rome from the later 2nd cent. AD. In 218 his hereditary priest at Emesa became emperor as Elagabalus and made the god the supreme official deity of the empire with precedence over Jupiter. This short-lived promotion (including translation of the sacred stone to the *Palatine) was ended by the emperor's assassination, although the cult survived to enjoy the patronage of Aurelian (270–75). *See* ORIENTAL CULTS; SOL.

Elatus ('Driver'), the name of several minor mythological figures: (1) a Trojan ally killed by *Agamemnon (*Iliad* 6. 33); (2) one of *Penelope's wooers (*Odyssey* 22. 267); (3) the *eponym of Elatea in Phocis (Pausanias 8. 4. 2–4); (4) a Centaur (Apollodorus 2. 85); (5) a Lapith, father of Polyphemus the *Argonaut; (6) father of Taenarus eponym of *Taenarum.

Electra (Dorian form Ālectra), in mythology: (1) daughter of *Oceanus and *Tethys, wife of Thaumas, mother of *Iris and the Harpies (*Harpyiae). (2) Daughter of *Atlas and Pleione, and one of the Pleiades; mother by Zeus of *Dardanus and *Iasion.

(3) Daughter of *Agamemnon and *Clytemnestra, and sister of *Orestes. She does not appear in epic, the first certain mention of her being in the *Oresteia* of *Stesichorus, although she was said to be the Laodice mentioned in book 9 of the *Iliad*, renamed because of her long unwedded state. Our major source for her story is Athenian tragedy, where she plays a central role in

Orestes' vengeance on Clytemnestra and her lover *Aegisthus for the murder of Agamemnon. Her first appearance is in the *Choephori* of *Aeschylus, where she is unalterably hostile to her mother and Aegisthus, welcoming her brother, joining with him in an invocation to Agamemnon's ghost, but not actively involved in the killings. In fact here the focus is still mainly on Orestes, with Electra disappearing from view once the vengeance begins. But her role is very much developed in *Sophocles and *Euripides.

In Sophocles' *Electra*, the main focus of the play is Electra herself, a steadfast, enduring figure, passionately grieving her father's murder and passionately set on revenge. She rescued Orestes, then a young child, from his father's murderers, and now longs for his return. The move from despair to joy in the scene where she laments over the urn, believing it to hold the ashes of her dead brother, then learns that the man beside her is in fact the living Orestes himself, gives us perhaps the most moving recognition scene in extant tragedy. She is a strong and determined character who, when she believes Orestes dead, is willing to kill Aegisthus entirely unaided; then, when it comes to the murder of Clytemnestra, she urges Orestes on, shouting out to him at the first death-cry of her mother, 'Strike, if you have the strength, a second blow'.

In Euripides' *Electra* she is even more active in the murder: Orestes is weak and indecisive, and it is Electra who is the dominant figure, driving him to kill Clytemnestra and even grasping the sword with him at the moment of murder, although afterwards she is as full of remorse as before she was full of lust for revenge. In Euripides' *Orestes* she appears as a desperately faithful nurse and helper to her mad brother, abetting him and his comrade Pylades in their attacks on Helen and Hermione. In some accounts she later marries Pylades, where she also meets Orestes and Iphigenia at Delphi and nearly murders the latter, who she thinks has murdered him).

There is no certain representation of Electra in art before the beginning of the 5th cent. BC, where she is present at the murder of Aegisthus; later her meeting with Orestes at the tomb of Agamemnon became popular.

[(1) Hesiod, *Theogony* 265 ff.; (2) Apollodorus 3. 10. 1, 12. 1; (3) Sophocles, *Electra*; Euripides, *Electra*, *Orestes*; Hyginus, *Fables* 122]

Eleusinia, a festival of games, celebrated at *Eleusis, never (in local Attic sources) the Eleusinian mysteries. The games were celebrated on a grand scale every fourth year (the third of the Olympiad), on a lesser scale two years later (the first of the Olympiad). There was a procession, and the prize was a certain quantity of grain from the Rarian field (the part of the plain of Eleusis on which allegedly grain was first cultivated). The Eleusinia and *Panathenaea were the most important agonistic festivals (*see* AGŌNES) at Athens.

Eleusis, the most famous deme or local community in Athens after Piraeus, on a land-locked bay with a rich plain, was a strong prehistoric settlement but merged with Athens sometime before the 7th cent. BC. There was an important theatre of *Dionysus there, and the sanctuary of *Demeter and Kore (*see* PERSEPHONE) was the site of many festivals of local or national importance (*Eleusinia, *Thesmophoria, Proerosia, *Haloa, Kalamaia), but the fame of Eleusis was due primarily to the annual festival of the *Mysteries, which attracted initiates from the entire Greek-speaking world. Within the sanctuary of the Two Goddesses the earliest building that may be identified as a temple is 8th cent. Its replacement by increasingly larger buildings (two in the Archaic period, two attempted but not completed in the 5th cent.), culminating in the square hall with rock-cut stands built under Pericles, the largest public building of its time in Greece, bears eloquent witness to the ever increasing popularity of the cult. The unusual shape of this temple reflected its function as hall of initiation (usually called Anaktoron, sometimes Telesterion).

Destroyed by the Costobocs in AD 170, it was soon rebuilt under *Marcus Aurelius, who also brought to completion the splendid entrance, a copy of the *Propylaea on the Athenian Acropolis. In this he followed the initiative of Hadrian, who was primarily responsible for the physical renewal of the sanctuary in the 2nd cent. The sanctuary evidently ceased to exist after AD 395.

Elysium (Elysian Fields or Plain), a paradise inhabited by the distinguished or (later) the good after their death. The name appears first in *Homer's *Odyssey*, where it is the destination of *Menelaus as husband of Helen. It is situated at the ends of the earth and is the home of *Rhadamanthys; a gentle breeze always blows there, and humans can enjoy an easy life like that of the gods. Such a destiny is unique in Homer, and, as in the case of the clearly comparable *Islands of the Blest, Elysium tends to be reserved for the privileged few, although the base broadens with time. A typical later description of such a place is in the Underworld book of Virgil's *Aeneid*. The name Elysium perhaps derives from Gk. *enēlysios*, 'struck by lightning', death by lightning being regarded as a kind of apotheosis.

[Homer, *Odyssey* 4. 563 ff.; Virgil, *Aeneid* 6. 637 ff.]

Empedocles (c.492–432 BC), a philosopher from Acragas in Sicily. Most details of his life are uncertain. Book 8 of the compiler Diogenes Laertius provides the largest selection of legends. Much of our biographical information (especially the manner of his death and claims that he was a doctor and prophet and considered himself a god) may have been extrapolated from his poetry. There is no reason to doubt his aristocratic background, that his family participated in the *Olympian Games, that he was involved in political life, or that he was active in both the religious and the philosophical spheres. He apparently travelled to mainland Greece to recite at the Olympian Games and visited Thurii in southern Italy soon after its foundation in 443 BC. Pythagoreanism was clearly a philosophical inspiration. Equally important was *Parmenides, whose thought shaped the basic ideas underlying Empedocles' philosophy. There is no evidence that he was familiar with the work of Zeno, Melissus, or the atomists; he probably knew the work of *Anaxagoras, certainly that of *Xenophanes.

According to Diogenes Laertius, he was the author of two poems, *On Nature* and *Purifications*. Other authors refer to one poem or the other, not both. The relationship between these two poems is problematic, with no consensus about the distribution of the fragments. Hence the suspicions that *On Nature* and *Purifications* are alternative titles for a single work. Our sources also mention works of dubious authenticity: medical writings in prose and verse, tragedies, a hymn to *Apollo, an *Expedition of Xerxes*. But the surviving fragments can be fairly well accommodated in the work(s) on natural philosophy and religion.

Empedocles is important for various philosophical positions, among them:

1. *His response to Parmenides*, who argued that no real thing could change or move and that the world was static. Empedocles accepted that *real* objects did not change; but against Parmenides he claimed that there could be several such things, his four 'roots' or elements, which moved under the influence of Love and Strife. All six of Empedocles' realities were often personified as gods. The events of the world's history result from the interaction of these entities.

2. *Introducing the notion of repeated world cycles*. The influence of Love and Strife alternated; hence the history of the cosmos was cyclical. The principal controversy about the details of the cosmic cycle centres on whether or not there is a recognizable 'world' during each half (under the increasing power of Love and under that of Strife). When Love is supreme, the world is a homogeneous whole; when Strife has conquered, the elements are completely separated.

3. *The claim that there are only four basic forms of perceptible matter*: earth, water, fire, and air. Unlike *Aristotle, who adopted his view,

Empedocles thought that these forms of matter were unchangeable.

4. *A theory of reincarnation and the transmigration of the soul.* Despite the claim that *transmigration occurs, there is no clear indication of whether the *daimones* (spirits) which move from body to body survive for ever or only until the end of the current world cycle. His claim that even human thought is identifiable with the blood around the heart points to the physical nature of the transmigrating *daimōn*. Orphic and Pythagorean views are also relevant (*see* ORPHISM; PYTHAGORAS AND PYTHAGOREANISM).

Empusa, a Greek bogey-woman who, in Aristophanes' *Frogs* takes the form of, in succession, a cow, mule, beautiful woman, and dog. The shaman *Apollonius of Tyana rescued a young philosopher from her amorous and deadly clutches. She is often identified with *Hecate or the *Lamia.

[Aristophanes, *Frogs* 285–95; Philostratus, *Life of Apollonius* 4. 25]

Endymion, a handsome mortal with whom the moon-goddess, *Selene, fell in love; according to one scholiastic source, which adds much other detail, the story was already alluded to in Sappho. He now sleeps eternally in a cave on Mt. Latmus in Caria, where his lover visits him periodically—no doubt during the dark phase of the lunar month. Other versions located him in Elis, and linked him with the *Olympian Games; another even claimed he had tried to rape *Hera, like *Ixion.

Enipeus, god of a river in Thessaly or Elis, loved by *Tyro, daughter of *Salmoneus. As she wandered beside it, *Poseidon took the form of the river-god and possessed her, making a wave curve over them to hide them. She was mother of *Pelias and *Neleus.

Enyalius *See* ARES.

Eos (in Greek *Ēōs, Eōs*), the personified goddess of the dawn, daughter of Theia and the sun-god *Hyperion. In *Homer her formulaic epithets are 'rosy-fingered' and 'saffron-robed', reflecting the pale shades of the dawn sky; and while the Sun himself has a four-horse chariot, Eos, to mark her subsidiary status, is content with a chariot and pair (the team are named as Lampus, 'Shiner', and Phaethon, 'Blazer').

Her mythology centres on her role as a predatory lover: she carries off the handsome hunters *Cephalus and *Orion as they stalk their own prey in the morning twilight, or seizes the Trojan prince Tithonus to be her heavenly gigolo. It is the latter whose bed she leaves when day breaks in book 5 of the *Odyssey*, and by whom she became the mother of *Memnon , the eastern warrior-prince and Trojan ally. She begged immortality for Tithonus from *Zeus, but forgot to ask for eternal youth to go with it, so that he shrivelled away until nothing was left but a wizened, piping husk (hence the origin of the cicadas); she locked him into a room and threw away the key. The explanation of these stories, in which a goddess's love is used as a metaphor for death, may perhaps be found in the Greek practice of conducting funerals at night, with the *soul departing at daybreak.

In art she is usually winged, first appearing in the 6th cent. BC in scenes concerning the death of her son: she balances *Thetis in the *psychostasia* ('weighing') of the fates of *Achilles and Memnon or at the fight itself, or (on Duris' fine cup in the Louvre) she weeps over his corpse in a moving *pietà*. For the 5th cent. the favoured theme is the pursuit and abduction of Cephalus and Tithonus, not always clearly distinguished.

[Homer, *Odyssey* 5.1, 121 ff., 23. 246; Hesiod, *Theogony* 372; *Homeric Hymn to Aphrodite* 218 ff.; Ovid, *Metamorphoses* 7. 690 ff.]

Epeius, in mythology, (1) son and successor as king of Elis of *Endymion. (2) Son of Panopeus, and builder, with Athena's help, of the Wooden Horse. In the *Iliad* he is a poor warrior, but an excellent boxer and winner of the boxing match at Patroclus' funeral games; later he casts the weight very badly. In *Stesichorus he is a water-carrier to *Agamemnon and *Menelaus (1), and *Athena pities his hard toil.

[(1) Pausanias 5. 1. 4; (2) Homer, *Iliad* 23. 664–99, 839–40; *Odyssey* 8. 493]

ephēboi originally meant boys who had reached the age of puberty, and was one of several terms for age classes. In 4th-cent. BC Athens it came to have a special paramilitary sense, boys who in their eighteenth year had entered a two-year period of military training. But it is unlikely that there was no system of training before the 4th cent., and traces of the later 'oath of the ephebes', an interesting document in which the youths swear by deities including *Ares and *Aglaurus have been detected in e.g. Thucydides and *Sophocles. And structuralist accounts of the ephebate bring out its (ancient?) function as a rite of passage; they point to the marginal character of service on the frontiers and to the civic exemptions and exclusions to which ephebes were subject, i.e. ephebes were made non-hoplites in preparation for being real hoplites (heavy-armed citizen soldiers). Analogous to an extent was the Spartan training system, the *agōgē*, although this covered the ages 7–29; similar systems existed in many other cities, notably those of Crete.

Ep(h)ialtes (1) a giant; (2) one of the *Aloadae; also (3) a demon of nightmare.

Ephraem Syrus, c.AD 307–73, was born at Nisibis in Mesopotamia where he lived until Jovian's surrender of the city to the Persians (363) forced him to move to Edessa. He wrote (mainly verse) in Syriac; he could read Greek and was influenced by Hellenistic rhetoric. His 'hymns' contain many historical references, e.g. to the death of *Julian the Apostate and the surrender of Nisibis, to the sufferings of the Church under Julian and the restoration of Church life under the Persians, and to the Arian controversy (*see* ARIANISM). Greek adaptations of his verses were current during his lifetime, and the fame he enjoyed is attested by *Jerome. A small but increasing proportion of his works has been critically edited.

Ephyra *See* NEKYOMANTEION.

epic The purely metrical ancient definition of epic or *epea/epē* ('words') as verse in successive hexameters includes such works as *Hesiod's didactic poems and the philosophical poems of the Presocratics. In its narrower, and now usual, acceptance 'epic' refers to hexameter narrative poems on the deeds of gods, heroes, and men, a kind of poetry at the summit of the ancient hierarchy of genres. The cultural authority of epic throughout antiquity is inseparable from the name of *Homer, generally held to be the earliest and greatest of Greek poets; the *Iliad* and the *Odyssey* establish norms for the presentation of the heroes and their relation with the gods, and for the omniscience of the inspired epic narrator. According to Herodotus (2. 53), Homer and Hesiod established the names, functions, and forms of the Greek gods, and Homer was generally held in the highest esteem throughout antiquity. The *Iliad*, *Odyssey* and the Cyclic poems (*see* EPIC CYCLE) provided the chief early tellings of myth.

Epics on mythical or legendary subjects continued to be produced in the 5th cent. BC and the Hellenistic period, and were taken up in Rome from the 3rd cent. BC. Although the historical and panegyrical functions of epic particularly appealed to the Romans, epics were also written on legendary and mythological themes (*Virgil's *Aeneid* combines both). The presentation of the gods in later epic is in effect a constant dialogue with Homer.

epic, biblical, a late antique genre in which material from the Bible is versified in hexameters. Six major texts survive, the earliest being (1) the *Evangeliorum libri IV* (four books of the gospels) of Iuvencus. (2) The *Heptateuchos* of 'Cyprianus Gallus' versifies the first seven books of the Old Testament, and may originally have extended further. (3) The *Carmen Paschale* of Caelius *Sedulius consists of four books which synthesize the Gospel narratives, preceded by a résumé of Old Testament miracles. A prose version of the same material was written to accompany the poem. Provenance is uncertain, but the works are usually dated to AD 425–50. (4) The *Alethia* of Claudius Marius Victorius, a teacher of Marseilles, is a three-book paraphrase of the earliest portion of Genesis, written *c*.430. (5) Alcimus Avitus, born of a noble family *c*.450 and appointed bishop of Vienne *c*.490, wrote a five-book epic *De spiritalis historiae gestis*, treating Genesis 1–3, the Flood, and the Crossing of the Red Sea. (6) The *De actibus Apostolorum* of the Italian subdeacon Arator treats the material of Acts in two books, devoted respectively to SS. Peter and Paul. It received public readings in Rome in 544.

It is sometimes argued that these texts were produced in order to make Christian material stylistically acceptable to educated pagans, and hence to aid conversion, but this is never explicit in the poems themselves, and hard to believe for the later works. Moreover, it is difficult to draw the generic boundaries between these poems and other contemporary texts which involve much biblical narrative while clearly having a theological orientation—Dracontius' *Laudes Dei* and *Prudentius' Apotheosis* and *Hamartigenia*.

Epic Cycle (Gk. *epikos kyklos*), a collection of early Greek epics, artificially arranged in a series so as to make a narrative extending from the beginning of the world to the end of the heroic age. Apart from the *Iliad* and *Odyssey* (*see* HOMER), we possess only meagre fragments of the poems involved, and our knowledge of what poems were involved is itself incomplete. We are best informed about those that dealt with the Trojan War and related events: there were six besides the *Iliad* and *Odyssey*, and summaries of their contents are preserved in some Homer manuscripts as an extract from the *Chrestomathia* of *Proclus. *Apollodorus and *Hyginus (*see* MYTHOGRAPHERS) draw on a related source for their accounts of the Trojan War. There are also epigraphic sources such as the so-called 'Tabula Iliaca'.

The poems were composed by various authors, mainly or wholly in the 7th and 6th cents. BC. (Earlier dates given by chroniclers are valueless.) The Cycle is not mentioned as a whole before the 2nd cent. AD. But a Trojan Cycle, at least, seems to have been drawn up not later than the 4th cent. BC, since Aristoxenus knew an alternative beginning to the *Iliad* evidently meant to link it to a preceding poem. Indeed, some of the Trojan epics seem designed merely to cover an allotted span of events; Aristotle criticizes the *Cypria* and *Little Iliad* for their lack of a unifying theme.

The cyclic poems (this term by convention excludes the *Iliad* and *Odyssey*) were sometimes loosely attributed to Homer; but Herodotus rejects this for the *Cypria* and queries it for the *Epigoni*, and later writers generally use the names of obscurer poets or the expression 'the author of (the *Cypria*, etc.)'. The poems seem to have been well known in the 5th and 4th cents., but little read later; no papyrus fragment of them has been identified. *Proclus' knowledge of them is demonstrably indirect.

The poems known or presumed to have been included in the Cycle, and the poets to whom they were ascribed, were as follows.

(1) In first place stood a *theogony. Comparison with Apollodorus and *Orphica* indicates that an Orphic theogony was chosen, but doctored. *See* ORPHIC LITERATURE.

(2) *Titanomachia*: Eumelus or Arctinus of Miletus. *See* TITANS.

(3) *Oedipodia* (6,600 lines): Cinaethon of Lacedaemon. *See* OEDIPUS.

(4) *Thebais* (7,000 lines): Homer (but more often anonymous). Highly esteemed by *Pausanias, who says that even the 7th-cent. poet Callinus knew the poem as Homer's; but if the name is correct, Callinus may only have alluded to the legend and to 'earlier singers'. On the subject of this and the following poem, *see* THEBES, MYTHS OF; ADRASTUS.

(5) *Epigoni* (7,000 lines): Homer, or in one source Antimachus. Cited by Herodotus and parodied by Aristophanes. The first line survives, and implies another poem preceding. *See* EPIGONI.

(6) *Cypria* (11 books): Homer, Stasinus of Cyprus, or Hegesias of (Cyprian) Salamis. The poem dealt with the preliminaries of the Trojan War (wedding of Peleus and Thetis, judgement of Paris, rape of Helen) and all the earlier part of the war down to the point where the *Iliad* begins. Fr. 1 implies no poem preceding. It was familiar to Herodotus, *Euripides, *Plato, and *Aristotle. The title seems to refer to the poem's place of origin.

(7) *Iliad*: There were alternative versions of the beginning and end which linked it with the adjacent poems.

(8) *Aethiopis* (5 books): Homer or Arctinus. The main events were the deaths of *Penthesilea, *Thersites, *Memnon, and Achilles. The title refers to Memnon's Ethiopians; there was an alternative title *Amazonia*.

(9) *Little Iliad* (4 books): Homer, Lesches of Mytilene or Pyrrha, Thestorides of Phocaea, Cinaethon, or Diodorus of Erythrae. The suicide of *Aias (1), the fetching of *Philoctetes and *Neoptolemus, the Wooden Horse, *Sinon, the entry into Troy. (The last part, which overlaps the *Iliu Persis*, is omitted by Proclus, and may have been omitted from the poem when it formed part of the Cycle.) The poem must have acquired the name *Ilias* independently of our *Iliad*, and then been called 'little' (*mikra*) to distinguish it.

(10) *Iliu Persis* (i.e. 'Sack of Troy') (2 books): Arctinus or Lesches. The Trojan debate about the horse, *Laocoön, the sack of Troy, and departure of the Greeks. *Aeneas left the city before the sack, not as in *Virgil. The same title was given to a poem of *Stesichorus.

(11) *Nostoi* (5 books): Homer, Agias (or Hegias) of Troezen, or Eumelus. The returns of various Greek heroes, ending with the murder of Agamemnon, Orestes' revenge, and Menelaus' homecoming. The *Odyssey* alludes to these events—so much that it cannot have been intended to accompany the *Nostoi*—and its poet knew 'the Return of the Achaeans', as a theme of song. Stesichorus also wrote *Nostoi*.

(12) *Odyssey*: Aristophanes of Byzantium and Aristarchus put the end of the poem at 23. 296, and so perhaps counted what followed as part of the *Telegonia*.

(13) *Telegonia* (2 books): Eugammon of Cyrene or Cinaethon. An element of romantic fiction was conspicuous here (*see* ODYSSEUS). The appearance in a Cyrenean poet of Arcesilaus as a son of Odysseus suggests a 6th-cent. date, and *Eusebius dates Eugammon to 566.

Various other early epics were current in antiquity, and some of them may have been included in the Cycle.

Epictetus (mid-1st to 2nd cent. AD), Stoic philosopher from Hierapolis in Phrygia; in early life a slave of Nero's freedman Epaphroditus in Rome. He set up a school at Nicopolis in Epirus, where his reputation attracted a following which included many upper-class Romans. Arrian published the oral teachings (*Discourses*, *Diatribai*) of Epictetus. Four books of these survive, along with a summary of key teachings known as the *Manual* (*Encheiridion*). These writings and his personal reputation made an impact on the emperor *Marcus Aurelius; the *Manual* has been an important inspirational book in both ancient and modern times.

Though Epictetus shows considerable familiarity with the technicalities of *Stoicism, in the *Discourses* he places great emphasis on the need to put philosophical sophistication to work in reforming moral character; learning is of little value for its own sake. From the religious point of view, he is interesting chiefly for his powerful belief in divine providence. He interprets the rational, cosmic deity of Stoicism in a more personal sense with an emphasis on the need to harmonize one's will with that of the deity.

Epicurus (b. Samos, 341 BC; d. Athens, 270 BC), moral and natural philosopher. The compendium-writer Diogenes Laertius reports that Epicurus wrote more than any of the other philosophers—about 300 rolls. Most of these are now lost. Fragments of his 37 books *On Nature* survive in the volcanic ash at Herculaneum, and efforts to restore and interpret them, begun around 1800, are now in progress with renewed vigour. But present-day knowledge and appreciation of Epicurean philosophy depends very largely on the great Latin epic poem of his later follower, *Lucretius' De rerum natura (On the Nature of Things)*. His school, known as the Garden, was much libelled in antiquity and later, perhaps because of its determined privacy, and because of Epicurus' professed hedonism. The qualifications that brought this hedonism close to *asceticism were ignored, and members of rival schools accused the Epicureans of many kinds of profligacy. In Christian times, Epicureanism was anathema because it taught that man is mortal, that the cosmos is the result of accident, that there is no providential god, and that the criterion of the good life is pleasure.

Epicurus taught that the purpose of philosophy is practical: to secure a happy life. Hence moral philosophy is the most important branch, and physics (in which he embraces an atomist theory) and epistemology are subsidiary. In moral philosophy, he starts from the premise 'We say that pleasure is the beginning and end of living happily'. Since it is a fact, however, that some pleasures are temporary and partial, and involve pain as well, it is necessary to distinguish between pleasures, and to take only those which are not outweighed by pains. Pain is caused by unsatisfied desire; so one must recognize that those desires that are natural and necessary are easily satisfied; others are unnecessary. The limit of pleasure is the removal of pain; to seek always for more pleasure is simply to spoil one's present pleasure with the pain of unsatisfied desire. Pleasure of the *soul, consisting mainly of contemplation or expectation of bodily pleasure, is more valuable than bodily pleasure. The ideal is *ataraxia*, freedom from disturbance. The study of philosophy is the best way to achieve the ideal. By teaching that the soul, made of atoms as the body is, dies with the body, it persuades us that after death there is no feeling: what happens after our death, like what happened before

our birth, is 'nothing to us'. By teaching that the gods do not interfere and that the physical world is explained by natural causes, it frees us from the fear of the supernatural. By teaching that the competitive life is to be avoided, it removes the distress of jealousy and failure; by teaching one how to avoid intense emotional commitments, it frees us from the pain of emotional turmoil.

Gods exist, atomic compounds like everything else, but take no thought for this cosmos or any other, living an ideal life of eternal, undisturbed happiness—the Epicurean ideal. It is good for men to respect and admire them, without expecting favours or punishments from them; thus they are deprived of their central position in many thought-systems, and most of their important functions. Both creation, as in *Plato's *Timaeus*, and the eternity of the cosmic order, as in *Aristotle's world picture, are rejected: natural movements of atoms are enough to explain the origin and growth of everything in the world. A theory of the survival of the fittest explains the apparently purposeful structure of living things.

Epidaurus, one of the small states of the Argolic Acte, on a peninsula of the Saronic Gulf. It is remarkable for the sanctuary of *Asclepius, some 7 km. (4⅓ mi.) inland, towards Argos, near a small sanctuary of Apollo Maleatas, with a small Doric temple: the small sanctuary of Apollo was enlarged *c.*330 BC with a massive terrace wall. The healing-cult of Apollo's son Asclepius, elevated to divine status, seems to have been given particular impetus by the effects of the plague at the time of the Peloponnesian War, developing considerably in the 4th cent. The temple, peripteral but not large, was built *c.*370 BC. Adjacent to it was the *abaton*, where the sick spent the night in hope of a healing visitation from the god (*see* INCUBATION), and the circular *thymelē* or tholos, probably to be regarded as the cenotaph of Asclepius as a hero. After a decline in the later Hellenistic period, and spoliation in the 1st cent. BC, the sanctuary revived in the 2nd cent. AD, when many buildings were reconstructed or replaced. The sanctuary ceased to function in the 4th cent. *See also* ISYLLUS.

Epigoni, sons of the '*Seven against Thebes': as with the latter, the names and number vary (Homer names *Diomedes, Sthenelus, Euryalus, *Alcmaeon, and *Amphilochus). The sons succeeded where their fathers had failed, drove the Cadmeans out of Thebes, and restored *Thersander to the throne sought by his father Polynices. All of the Epigoni but one (Aegialeus, son of *Adrastus, sole survivor of the first expedition) survived. This happened in the same generation as, but before, the Trojan War.

[Homer, *Iliad* 4. 406–10; Apollodorus 1. 377–9]

epigraphy, the study of inscriptions engraved on stone or metal. In almost every field of classical studies epigraphy acts as an invaluable supplement (sometimes corrective) to literary sources, and that of religion is no exception.

Dedications form the second largest category among Greek inscriptions. Together with temple laws, oracles, prayers, and regulations concerning religious and agonistic festivals (the latter always having a religious component) they offer us a wealth of detailed knowledge about the Greek religious mentality, the organization and function of cults, the status of priests and, in general, the place of religion in civic life. In particular, the texts known conventionally as sacred laws provide magnificent insights into the workings of *sanctuaries— their financial operations, the functions and emoluments of priests and other sacred officials, and the prescribed behaviour of the worshippers both in and outside the temple. Confession inscriptions, typical of Lydia/ Phrygia in Asia Minor, inform us about ancient ideas of *sin and the types of human behaviour eliciting divine punishment (often in the form of disease), and ultimately leading to confession of guilt and the erection of a stele. Funerary epigrams and

epitaphs, sometimes with with curse- and fine-formulas, when collected and studied as a group, provide valuable insights into views on after-life and popular ethics.

Similarly among inscriptions in Latin, religion is the subject of some formal documents, e.g. regulations for sanctuaries and temples, calendars of festivals, accounts of official ceremonies such as the Augustan and Severan *Secular Games and the *acta* of the *fratres arvales*. There are also many dedications to many deities, a striking demonstration of the effort and expenditure continuously invested in Roman religion. Something can be seen from them, for instance, of the character of particular cults, the survival of some older cults, the introduction of new ones like ruler-cult or Mithraism, and the interaction of Roman with local cults. Recent large finds of lead curse-tablets at Bath (*see* AQUAE SULIS; BRITAIN, ROMAN, CULTS) have stimulated interest in these widespread devices for harnessing divine power to the dedicators' interests in recovery of property, success in love, victory in the races, etc.

Christian inscriptions begin as a group hardly, if at all, differentiated from the pagan texts of their time, but develop formulas and other new features, especially after the conversion of *Constantine I. The earlier texts are often ordinary tombstones or pilgrims' *graffiti*. Later they include more ambitious items, such as building inscriptions for churches. The set of verse *elogia* on popes and martyrs, written by Pope *Damasus (366–84) and finely cut by *Filocalus in letters which may have been especially designed for the purpose, form a landmark in this development of a specifically Christian epigraphic tradition. They show something of early Christian society, the organization of the Church, the survival of pagan features, and the emergence of new ideas, including heresies.

Epimenides, of Crete, holy man of the late 7th cent. BC, supposed to have been called in to purify Athens after the sacrilege of the

Cylon affair, in which the followers of the would-be tyrant were killed, though suppliants at an altar; *Plato, however, puts him a century later. As in the case of *Aristeas, any genuine traditions were quickly obscured by legends and miraculous tales, such as those of his great age (157 or 299 years), his out-of-the-body experiences, the boyhood nap from which he awoke to discover that 57 years had elapsed or the *asceticism which enabled him to survive on an appetite-suppressant of his own devising. Many early epic works were attached to his name, including oracles, a *Theogony, and an Argonautic poem.

Epiphanius, c.AD 315–403, born in Eleutheropolis, Palestine. He became a monk, and in 367 bishop of Salamis (Constantia) in Cyprus. Regarding *Origen as the source of *Arianism, he attacked both in his Ancoratus (373) and Panarion (374–6), which includes the chief Greek philosophies among its 80 heresies. Ignorant and suspicious of Greek culture, he feared that *allegory would deny the historicity of Scripture and the resurrection of the body. Nevertheless his De gemmis and De mensuris et ponderibus allow typology, the latter also an important source on Greek versions of the Old Testament.

epiphany occurs in both myth and cult when a god reveals his presence or manifests his power to a mortal or group of mortals, who 'see' or 'recognize' the god. Gods may appear in anthropomorphic form (as extraordinarily beautiful or larger than life; in the likeness of their cult statue; or disguised as ordinary mortals), as a disembodied voice, or as animals. Divine epiphanies take the form of waking or *dream visions; they may be accompanied by miracles or other displays of power (Gk. aretai), be protective or punitive; they may be sudden and spontaneous, or occur in response to a prayer. The concept is much older than the term. As early as the Minoan period, scenes of divine epiphany in cultic settings appear on seal rings. From Homer onwards, epiphany scenes constitute an essential element of epic narrative (for instance *Athena in book 1 of the Iliad and in the Odyssey) and hymnic poetry (self-revelation of *Demeter, *Aphrodite, and *Dionysus in their respective Homeric *Hymns; Callimachus, Hymns 2, 5, 6). Stage epiphanies are more frequent in tragedy (Athena in Aeschylus' Eumenides and Sophocles' Ajax and as deus ex machina in Euripides', Ion; Dionysus in Euripides' Bacchae) than comedy, but we find divine prologues in Menander and Plautus. From the 4th cent. onwards, epiphany emerges increasingly as a function of cult: we find, for instance, a dedication to Athena consequent on an epiphany. Throughout the Hellenistic period, collections of divine epiphanies promoted faith and served religious propaganda in the cults of such gods as *Asclepius, *Apollo, Athena, as well as *Isis and *Sarapis. In contrast to the importance of omens (see PORTENTS), epiphany is not a feature of Roman state religion. However, Roman poets and historians freely adapted Greek epiphanic conventions. Separate trajectories lead from divine epiphany to *ruler-cult, from the epopteia ('watching') of the Eleusinian *mysteries to the sublimation of epiphany in *Neoplatonism, and from the pagan concept of divine self-manifestation to Christian and *Gnostic forms of revelation.

[Aelius Aristides, Hieroi Logoi (Sacred Tales); and texts mentioned above]

Epistle to Diognetus, Greek Christian apology of uncertain authorship, date (perhaps 3rd cent. AD), and provenance (perhaps Alexandria). It contains an exposition of the Christian doctrine of God, of the Christian life in the world, and of the reasons for and the time of the salvation of the sinner brought about by the coming of the Son of God. The ending (chs. 11–12) is perhaps secondary.

epithets, divine

Greek In considering the very numerous surnames or epithets of gods it is necessary first to distinguish between those appearing only as literary (especially epic) ornaments and those known to have been used in cult. Thus we have no proof that *Athena was ever addressed in ritual as *glaukōpis* ('grey-eyed'); it is her stock epithet in *Homer, *Zeus' pet-name for her. It seems unlikely that *Ares was prayed to as *brotoloigoa* ('ruinous to mortals'); he is so addressed by Athena, which is a very different thing, and it is his stock epithet. But there are many borderline cases, hard to decide. We have no instance of Athena being called Pallas in cult, yet it is not easy to suppose that so familiar a name was never used for her by worshippers; Zeus' stock epithet, 'cloud-gatherer', appears in the vocative, *nephelēgereta*, in epic in many places where it is syntactically a nominative, strongly suggesting that its form had become fixed by some ancient liturgical phrase, which, however, is quite lost to us. The immediate function of the epithet in epic is often to form with the proper name a convenient metrical unit. Now and then an epithet is used to avoid mentioning an ill-omened name; *Hades in *Sophocles' *Oedipus at Colonus*, and often, is Zeus *Chthonios* ('of the earth'), and in *Aeschylus' *Supplices* he is even Zeus *allos* ('other', 'another').

But coming to those epithets which are guaranteed by their occurrence in liturgical formulas, dedications, and the official names of temples, we may distinguish the following classes. (1) Purely local, meaning that the deity in question is worshipped, or has a temple or altar, at such-and-such a place. Thus *Apollo *Dēlios* is simply Apollo who is worshipped in *Delos, and differs from the Pythian (*see* DELPHI), or any other similarly named Apollo, not otherwise than as Our Lady of Lourdes does from Our Lady of Loreto. *Dionysus *Kydathenaieus* is nothing but the Dionysus who has a cult in the Attic locality Kydathenaion. Such titles may tell us something of the history of the cult, if the title does not fit the immediate locality; a *Demeter *Eleusia* worshipped at Pheneos in Arcadia (*see* ARCADIAN CULTS AND MYTHS) manifestly has something to do with the famous cult at *Eleusis, and the local legend said as much. (2) Titles indicating association with another god. These are often of some historical importance, and at times puzzling. Apollo Carneius has behind him a history of identification; 'Hephaestian' Athena need surprise no one, in view of the resemblance of some functions of the two deities (*see* HEPHAESTUS); but it is less easy to see why she had a temple at Megara under the title *Aiantis*. (3) Undoubtedly the largest and most important class of epithets, however, have reference to the functions of the god or goddess, either in general or with reference to some particular occasion on which his or her power was manifest. Thus, Zeus has a great number of titles denoting his control of the weather and all that depends on it; he is *Brontōn*, Thunderer, *Keraunios*, God of the thunderbolt, *Ombrios*, Sender of rainstorms, *Hyetios*, Rainer, and as a natural consequence *Geōrgos*, Farmer; also *Ourios*, God of favourable winds, and so forth. Similarly, *Aphrodite has epithets denoting her power over the sexual life of mankind, as *Ambologēra*, 'Delayer of old age'; her connection with love whether licit or illicit, for example *Pandēos* 'Goddess of the whole people', in her Athenian worship as a deity of marriage; and on the other hand *Hetaira*, 'Companion', Courtesan, and even *Pornē*, Prostitute. These last belong to an extremely curious subclass in which the characteristics of the worshipper are transferred to the deity; both signify the goddess who is worshipped by harlots. *Hera is similarly called *Pais*, *Teleia*, and *Chēra* at her three shrines in Stymphalus, in other words Maid, Wife, and Widow; she naturally received the worship of women of all ages and conditions. The local legend was somewhat at a loss to explain the third title, since Zeus cannot die, and invented a quarrel between the two leading to a separation; clearly the sense of such epithets was no longer remembered in the time of *Pausanias, who records the tradition.

Epithets referring to the higher (moral or civic) qualities of a deity are not uncommon, though less so than those which are due to his or her natural functions. It is to be noted that there is a tendency in later ages to read such qualities into an old title; thus Athena *Pronaia* at Delphi, so named from the fact that her shrine was in front of the temple (*naos* of Apollo), had so decided an inclination to become *Pronoia* that some manuscripts of have been infected by it. As genuine examples may be instanced Apollo *Archēgetēs* ('Founder') (*see* APOLLO), Athena *boulaia* (of the *boulē*, or council).

Late hymns, for instance those of the *Orphic collection, have a strong tendency to heap up epithets, including the most unheard-of and fanciful.

Roman Each deity had its name, but this name could be hidden or unknown (hence the formula in addresses 'whether god or goddess', *sive deus, sive dea*). If it was known, and could be uttered (as the hidden name could not), it was often accompanied by epithets and surnames (*cognomina*). They are either descriptions used informally or true names occurring in actual cult (attested in formulas, dedications, and names of temples), although strict distinction is not always possible. We can distinguish several classes of epithets and surnames: (1) Purely literary descriptions, e.g. of *Mars by *Virgil as harsh, wicked, untamed, savage, or powerful in arms, *durus, impius, indomitus, saevus, armipotens*. (2) Popular descriptions derived either from a special feature (often iconographic) of a deity, e.g. *Hercules Bullatus, 'Wearing a bulla' (an amulet worn by young boys), Puerinus, 'Youthful', Pusillus, 'Small' (also Monolithus, 'Made of a single stone'), or from a story concerning a deity, e.g. *Minerva Capta, 'Captured', because she was transported to Rome after the capture of Falerii Veteres in 241 BC. (3) Geographical and local descriptions, e.g. *Bona Dea Subsaxana, because she had her shrine *sub Saxo*, 'under the Rock' (of the *Aventine), *Diana Aventinensis, Tifatina, *Fortuna Praenestina, or *Venus Erycina, after their temples on the Aventine, in Tifata, *Praeneste, and *Eryx (Erice in Sicily), such descriptions often functioning (especially in dedications)

as regular surnames, as was the case e.g. with *Jupiter Dolichenus ('of Doliche' in Syria). (4) Descriptions indicating association with another deity attested in archaic prayers (*comprecationes*), e.g. *Lua Saturni, Herie Iunonis*, the second name standing in the genitive, thus indicating that the first deity was an emanation of the second or was acting in its sphere, cf. *Moles Martis*, 'Oppressions' of Mars. (5) Epithets referring to the civic standing of a deity: Jupiter Optimus Maximus, 'the Best (and) the Greatest, *Juno Regina, 'the Queen'. (6) Most numerous are epithets describing the function of a deity or its particular manifestation: *Apollo Medicus, 'Healer', *Bona Dea Nutrix, 'Nurse', Jupiter Tonans, 'Thunderer', Stator, 'Stayer' (he stopped the advance of the enemy, as related in Livy), Mars Ultor, 'Avenger' (he helped *Augustus to avenge the murder of *Caesar), Venus Verticordia, 'Changer of Hearts' (she averted women's minds from lust to chastity). Deities for whom the most epithets are attested are Jupiter (over 100), Fortuna, Juno (over 40), Hercules, Mars, Venus (over 30), *Lares, *Mercurius, Silvanus (over 20). A complete list of Roman divine epithets is yet to be compiled.

[Ovid, *Fasti* 3. 835–48, 5. 147–58]

Epona, a Celtic goddess known from dedications that spread from Spain to the Balkans, and northern Britain to Italy. Her name derives from the Celtic word for 'horse', and the most common iconography of the goddess shows her seated side-saddle on a horse; Latin writers mention her as the goddess of the stable. She is also at times depicted with fruits or a cornucopia, attributes that link her with the mother goddesses. Her original cult area was in north-eastern Gaul, and monuments are very frequent in the regions of the Aedui (near Dijon), the Treveri (around the Mosel), and east of the Rhine to the border. The wider dispersal is due largely to devotees in the army, often members of the cavalry, but she also has a festival in a civic calendar of 27 BC from northern Italy. *See* CELTIC RELIGION.

eponymoi are those, usually gods or heroes, after which something is named or thought to be named. Most frequently place-names—regions or cities—are considered to be named from an eponymous hero, such as *Arcas for Arcadia, or the heroine Sparte/Sparta for the city of the same name. Historical characters also gave their names to cities (Antioch, Alexandria). The phenomenon was common all over the Greek world and also in Roman Italy.

Divisions of the populace also had heroic eponyms. In Athens, the *eponymoi* (with no further qualification) were the ten heroes who gave their names to the ten Cleisthenic tribes (*phylai*) created in 508/7 BC. These heroes, who were said to have been picked by *Delphi from a list of a hundred submitted, all had separate, presumably pre-existing cults, to which members of the new tribes gradually became in some measure attached; they had also, apparently, a collective cult in the *Agora, where statues of the ten were situated and tribal notices posted.

Epopeus/Epops, an old mythical figure, whose name suggests a relationship with *Zeus Epopetes. According to the *Cypria* (see EPIC CYCLE) he was king of Sicyon and seduced the Boeotian *Antiope; the result, *Amphion and Zethus, is mentioned in a 6th-cent. source, though more often they are said to be sons of Zeus. The epic poet Eumelus said that he was son of Aloeus, son of *Helios, and father of Marathon, the eponym of the Attic region of that name (see MARATHON).

epulones See SEPTEMVIRI EPULONES.

epulum Roman religion involved special forms of the feast, generally called *epulum* rather than the more general word *convivium*. In 399 BC the *lectisternium* was introduced, a ritual in which images of the gods were arranged as banqueters on couches, and for which the priestly college (see COLLEGIUM) of the *septemviri epulones* seems to have had responsibility. Other *collegia* such

as the *fratres arvales dined together according to complex rituals. The Saturnalia (see SATURNUS) was a traditional carnevalesque feast of inversion.

Equirria, two Roman festivals of horseracing on 27 February and 14 March. The first was founded by *Romulus and the second was connected with the martial festival of the October Horse. (See MARS.)

[Ovid, *Fasti* 2. 857 ff., 3. 517 ff.; Varro, *On the Latin Language* 6. 13]

Erechtheum, the third outstanding building on the Athenian Acropolis, begun in 421 BC and finished, after a lapse, in 407 BC; built of Pentelic marble, with friezes of black *Eleusis stone to take applied white marble relief sculpture. Exact details of its construction are known from a contemporary inscription. The main structure is divided into four compartments: the largest (east cella) has a six-columned Ionic portico; the west end is closed by a wall with engaged columns and corner piers. At this end is a unique and boldly projecting (though small) south feature—the 'porch of the maidens', with draped female figures (*caryatides) serving as supports—and, nearly opposite on the north side, a still more boldly projecting porch with Ionic columns (partly reassembled in early 20th cent.) standing on a lower level and having the tallest order of the whole composition.

The temple replaced to some extent the large 6th-cent. temple of *Athena whose foundations can be seen between it and the *Parthenon. We know from *Pausanias that the Erechtheum housed a number of ancient cults (this may partly account for its complicated form) and many sacred spots and objects—the venerable image of Athena Polias, a golden lamp made by the 5th-cent. sculptor Callimachus, a salt well and the mark of *Poseidon's trident, an altar of Poseidon and *Erechtheus, and altars of Butes and *Hephaestus. Near the west end of the building were shrines of *Cecrops and *Pandrosus, and the original sacred olive of Athena. A minority view denies the usual identification of the famous 5th-cent. building with the Erechtheum of Pausanias.

[Pausanias 1. 26. 5–27. 3]

Erechtheus, a cult figure worshipped on the Athenian Acropolis, formally identified with *Poseidon but often regarded as an early king of Athens. The confusion surrounding his identity and status is compounded by his closeness to *Erichthonius, from whom he may not have been consistently distinguished much before the 4th cent. BC. The Iliadic Catalogue of Ships mentions an Erechtheus who was born from Earth, brought up by Athena and installed in her sanctuary, and who is worshipped with sacrifice of bulls and rams; this gives the kernel of his myth and cult. His cult title (at least in the earlier period) 'Poseidon Erechtheus' may result from a character like that of *Poseidon the earthshaker (Gk. erechthō = tear, smash). About Erechtheus the king, the most consistently told tradition was that of the war against *Eleusis. This he won by killing the enemy leader *Eumolpus, son of Poseidon, but was thereupon himself killed by a blow of Poseidon's trident. (See HYACINTHIDES.) With *Cecrops, Erechtheus is seen as the prototype ancestor of all Athenians, who are poetically named Erechtheidai; but he was also one of the tribal *eponymoi, in which capacity he was probably conceptualized more as a typical hero than as the quasi-divine figure of the original cult.

Erichthonius, an Athenian hero connected with the Acropolis and its cults. It is possible that he was originally identical with *Erechtheus, the older attested name, a hypothesis strengthened by the lack of clear evidence for a separate cult. He is distinguished from his near homonym by the emphasis placed on his birth and infancy. *Hephaestus attempted to rape *Athena, but succeeded only in spilling his seed on her thigh; she wiped it off with a piece of wool (erion), and dropped it on the ground, whereupon the Earth conceived Erichthonius, after his birth handing him over to Athena—the last episode being a popular subject on red-figure vases. Athena shut the child in a chest or basket and in turn entrusted him to the daughters of *Cecrops, who with disastrous results disobeyed her instructions not to look inside (see AGLAURUS; PANDROSUS). Almost certainly the myth relates to rituals performed on the Acropolis, in particular the *Arrhephoria. By the late 5th cent. BC historical tradition clearly distinguished Erichthonius the *autochthon from his grandson Erechtheus, and attributed the institution of various religious practices, notably the celebration of the *Panathenaea, to him.

Eridanus (Gk. Ēridanos), mythical river (see PHAETHON), having Electrides (Amber-) Islands at its mouth. Named by *Hesiod as a real river, the Eridanus was placed first in unknown northernmost Europe, or in western Europe, flowing into the northern Ocean. Herodotus and Strabo doubted its existence. *Aeschylus called it 'Spanish', meaning the Rhône. Greek authors from the time of *Pherecydes (2) agreed to identify the Eridanus with the Po, and Roman writers followed suit (since there are no islands at the mouth of the Po, some authors sought these in the east Adriatic). The description of the Eridanus as an amber-river may embody the memory of an early amber-route from Jutland up the Elbe and Rhine (Rhenus) and down the Rhône (Rhodanus) or across the Alps to north Italy.

Erigone, name of two figures in Attic mythology, both associated with the aiōra ('swing') rite of the *Anthesteria. In the first story, subject of the (lost) poetic narrative of the Hellenistic scholar Eratosthenes, she is daughter of *Dionysus' host *Icarius (2), who hanged herself on finding her father's body. When other girls began to follow suit, her curse was appeased by the institution of the aiōra, swinging representing a modified form of hanging. The second version makes her daughter of *Aegisthus and *Clytemnestra, who brought *Orestes to trial for their murder and on his acquittal hanged herself. In other tellings, she was the mother of Orestes' illegitimate son Penthilus, or she was nearly killed by him but rescued by *Artemis, who made her a priestess in Attica. Myth and cult combine to place Erigone in a group of heroines and goddesses associated with hanging.

[Hyginus, *Fables* 122]

Erinyes, chthonian powers (*see* CHTHONIAN GODS) of retribution for wrongs and blood-guilt especially in the family. They (sometimes singular) are mentioned very often in *Homer, *Hesiod, and the tragedians. Individually or collectively they carry out the curses of a mother or father, or they are personified curses without moral significance. Outside the family, Erinys blinds a man's reason, and, as *daimōn* beneath the earth, she protects a solemn oath. She also looks after beggars and generally ensures the natural order of things, like guarding the rights of an elder brother (Zeus in Homer's *Iliad*, book 15, for instance) or silencing *Achilles' horse Xanthus, given a voice by *Hera. Heraclitus extends the Erinyes' control over the cosmic order. Also the concept of Erinyes as the souls of the dead is a moral development from their primary chthonian nature. Their negative function as powers of death predominates in popular imagination and is reflected in epitaphs. *Aeschylus in *Eumenides* calls them daughters of Night (*see* NYX) and introduces them to the stage repulsively dressed in black, with snakes for hair but wingless. According to Hesiod's genealogy, which is closer to their divine chthonian origins, they spring from Earth (*see* GAIA), made pregnant by *Uranus' blood.

In *Arcadian cult Erinys was identified with *Demeter. Together with *Poseidon she produced the horse Arion. Her background and nature resembled that of Medusa (*see* GORGO), loved by Poseidon and mother of Pegasus. The connection with horse and water illustrates Erinys' dual nature as chthonian goddess of vegetation and death. The latter allied her with other agents of death like the Harpies, Keres, Moirai, and Melainai (Black Ones).

Erinys' name occurs in Linear B, as *erinu*. Her link with Potnia (Potniai) in Boeotia also hints at a prehistoric past, as does the Gorgoneion on a late Minoan vase from Cnossus. On the other hand, their cult as Semnai ('August') at Athens, Eumenides ('Kindly') in Sicyon, and their identification with the Ablabiai ('Harmless') at Erythrae may suggest attempts at neutralizing the Erinyes' dark powers through euphemisms.

The Eumenides occur on a number of votive stones from the Argolid. Three Erinyes together with Hecate and an image in the Underworld on an Attic black-figure *lekythos* of about 470 BC seem to belong to the same iconographic tradition that relates to the chthonian function of these figures. In the vast majority of instances, however, representations of the Erinyes were based on the theatre of Aeschylus and remained popular in this form in Greek, Etruscan, and Roman art. In later writers there are only three of them and their names are Tisiphone, Allecto, and Megaera. *See* CURSES.

[Homer, *Iliad* 3. 279, 9. 454, 571, 11. 280, 15. 204, 19. 87, 259, 409; *Odyssey* 2. 135, 15. 234, 17. 475; Hesiod, *Theogony* 185, 472; Aeschylus, *Choephori* 1048–50, *Eumenides*; Apollodorus 3. 6. 8; Pausanias 1. 28. 6, 8. 25, 42]

Eris, 'Strife' (Discordia in Latin), often personified as a goddess in poetry. She appears in several Homeric battle scenes, in one of which she is described as the sister of *Ares. *Hesiod in the *Theogony* makes her the daughter of Night (*Nyx) and mother of Toil, Pain, Battles, Bloodshed, Lies, Ruin, and the like. In the *Works and Days*, however, he declares that there is not just one Eris but two, a bad Eris who fosters war and a good Eris who stimulates men to work through a spirit of competition.

Eris is given a mythical role by the *Cypria* (*see* EPIC CYCLE): at the instigation of Zeus she attended the wedding of *Peleus and *Thetis and there created rivalry between *Athena,

*Hera, and *Aphrodite, which led to the Judgement of *Paris and thus to the Trojan War. Much later sources (first *Hyginus) say that she was angry at not being invited to the wedding and created the rivalry by tossing the 'Apple of Discord' among the guests as a prize for the most beautiful.

[Homer, *Iliad* 4. 440–5, 11. 3–14; Hesiod, *Theogony* 225–32; *Works and Days* 11–26; Hyginus, *Fables* 92]

Eros, god of love. Eros personified does not occur in Homer, but the Homeric passages in which the word *erōs* is used give a clear idea of the original significance. It is the violent physical desire that drives *Paris to Helen, *Zeus to Hera, and shakes the limbs of the suitors of *Penelope. A more refined conception of this Eros who affects mind and body appears in the Archaic lyric poets. Because his power brings peril he is cunning, unmanageable, cruel; in Anacreon he smites the lovestruck one with an axe or a whip. He comes suddenly like a wind and shakes his victims (Sappho, Ibycus). Eros is playful, but plays with frenzies and confusion. He symbolizes all attractions which provoke love. He is young and beautiful, he walks over flowers, and the roses are 'a plant of Eros' of which he makes his crown. He is sweet and warms the heart.

With Himeros ('Desire') and Pothos ('Longing'), Eros is a constant companion of *Aphrodite, although he can appear with any god, whenever a love story is involved. *Hesiod seems to have transformed the Homeric conception of Eros. Although he describes Eros in terms almost identical with Homer as the god who 'loosens the limbs and damages the mind', he also makes him, together with Earth (*see* GAIA) and Tartarus, the oldest of all gods, all-powerful over gods and men. With Eros as a cosmic principle, *Parmenides found a place for him, perhaps as the power which leads contrasts together. This philosophic conception contributed to the Epicurean picture of omnipotent Eros, took abstruse mythological shape in Orphic cosmogonies (*see* ORPHIC LITERATURE; ORPHISM), and

formed the background for Plato's discussions of Eros in *Symposium* and *Phaedrus*.

Hellenistic poets continue the more playful conception of Anacreon, the tricks Eros plays on mortals, the tribulations of those who try to resist him, and the punishments he receives for his misdeeds. His bow and arrows, first mentioned by *Euripides, play a great part in these accounts. Frequently a plurality of Erotes is introduced, because both love and the god who symbolized it could multiply.

Eros had some ancient cults and much individual worship. He was always the god of love directed towards male as well as female beauty. Hence his images in the gymnasia, his cult among the Sacred Band (a military unit composed of pairs of lovers) in Thebes, and the altar in Athens erected by Hippias' lover. As a god of fertility Eros is celebrated in the very old cult at Thespiae in Boeotia, and in the joint cult with Aphrodite on the north slope of the Athenian Acropolis. In Thespiae Eros was represented by an aniconic image; in Athens phallic symbols have been found in the sanctuary. In both cults festivals were celebrated; that in Thespiae, called Erotidia, incorporated art, athletics, and equestrianism. Altars to Eros at the Academy in Athens and the gymnasium at Elis were matched by ones to Anteros, whom Eros sometimes wrestles. In Philadelphia, worshippers called themselves Erotes; other cult centres include Leuctra, Velia, and Parium in Mysia.

Eros in Archaic art is hard to differentiate from other winged males. An Attic plaque shows him wingless. On vases, he appears alone, carrying lyre or hare, or in myth, especially accompanying Aphrodite, winged, boyish, sometimes with bow and arrows. During the Classical period he increasingly associates with women, in domestic scenes or weddings. He appears in military and athletic scenes, and was painted by Zeuxis and Pausias. The weighing of two Erotes occurs occasionally. Scopas' group of Eros, Pothos, and Himeros at Megara is an early sculpture. In the Hellenistic period, he is a putto, common in terracottas and with Psyche.

[Alcman 36, 101; Ibycus 6; Sappho 136; Theognis 1231; *Anacreonta* 53. 42; Hesiod, *Theogony* 120–122; Euripides, *Iphigenia at Aulis* 548–9; Pausanias 1. 30. 1, 6. 23. 3, 9. 27. 1–5; Athenaeus 13. 561]

Erymanthian boar *See* HERACLES.

Erysichthon, a mythological figure usually located in Thessaly, whose story is best known from *Callimachus' Sixth Hymn. Despite warnings, he cut down a grove sacred to *Demeter, and was punished by insatiable hunger, to satisfy which he was forced to ruin himself and his household. In some versions he had a daughter Mestra who had received from her lover *Poseidon the power of changing into whatever shape she chose; she therefore supported her father by being sold in various animal forms and escaping to be resold.

The Attic hero Erysichthon was son of *Cecrops, who was associated with *Delos and died young. The two may sometimes have been identified.

[Callimachus, *Hymn* 6; Ovid, *Metamorphoses* 8. 846–74]

Erytheia, 'the red, or blushing, one', i.e. sunset-coloured. Name of (1) one of the *Hesperides; (2) the daughter of Geryon, and also his island.

Eryx, an Elymian settlement and a mountain (Monte San Giuliano, 751 m. (2,464 ft.) above sea-level) above Drepana (mod. Trapani) in western Sicily. Dependent on nearby Segesta in the 5th cent. BC, Eryx was occupied later by the Carthaginians. Phoenician masons' marks are found on the defensive walls, and Punic legends appear on the coinage from the 4th cent. Phoenician associations are also indicated by the rite of sacred *prostitution in the cult of Astarte-*Aphrodite-Venus on the acropolis rock. The Romans stressed the Elymian–Trojan associations of the cult: *Virgil makes *Aeneas visit Eryx and found the temple. The cult enjoyed great popularity during the republic and widespread diffusion (sanctuaries of Venus Erycina were established at Rome in 217 and 184 BC, as well

as elsewhere), but it declined in the early empire, despite Claudius' repair of the temple. Today nothing survives of the sanctuary, which underlies a 12th-cent. castle.

[Virgil, *Aeneid* 5. 759 f.; Diodorus Siculus 4. 83. 4; Suetonius, *Claudius* 25. 5]

Essenes, Jewish religious group known to have flourished in Judaea in the 1st cent. AD. The doctrines and customs of the Essenes were described in detail by *Josephus and *Philon (1), and in a short notice by Pliny the Elder. References in Christian literature were mostly derived from Josephus. The Essenes lived in regimented communities dedicated to pious *asceticism. They were to be found above the Dead Sea, according to Pliny, or in all the towns of *Judaea, according to Josephus, who mentions two kinds of Essene, one group which was celibate, and others who married. Some relationship between the Essenes and the sectarians at Qumran by the Dead Sea who produced some of the *Dead Sea Scrolls is plausible but impossible to prove. If the Qumran sectarians were indeed Essenes, there must have existed even more varieties of Essenism and doctrines must have changed over time. According to Josephus and Philon, the Essenes were noted for their communal solidarity and discipline, their strict interpretation of the Law of Moses, and their devotion to their beliefs to the point of martyrdom, but the descriptions in these writers may have been overidealized in order to impress a non-Jewish audience. *See* JUDAISM.

Eteocles, the older son of *Oedipus. According to the Cyclic *Thebais* (*see* EPIC CYCLE), after the blinding and retirement of their father, he and his brother Polynices twice insulted him, once by setting before him certain vessels which had belonged to Laius, and then by giving him a portion of meat less honourable than a king deserved. *Oedipus therefore cursed them. The two brothers agreed to reign in alternate years, Eteocles taking the first year, Polynices leaving Thebes for Argos. At the end of his year Eteocles refused to give up the throne; Polynices returned with his father-in-law *Adrastus and the 'Seven'; in the ensuing battle, the two brothers met and killed each other (*see* SEVEN AGAINST THEBES).

[Aeschylus, *Seven against Thebes*]

Eteoclus, son of Iphis, Argive hero (*see* ARGOS). At a fairly early stage of the tradition he seems to have replaced *Parthenopaeus as one of the *Seven against Thebes (*see* ADRASTUS). Then *Aeschylus or his authority included both him and Parthenopaeus, apparently so as to be able to leave Adrastus out of the actual assault; hence later writers use the same list.

[Aeschylus, *Seven against Thebes* 458 ff.; Sophocles, *Oedipus at Colonus* 1316; Euripides, *Suppliant Women* 872]

Ethiopia was a name usually applied by the Greeks to any region in the far south (but north of the equator). Perhaps originally designating radiance reflected by dwellers in the east from the morning star, it soon came to mean the land of the 'Burnt-faced People'. An ethnic connotation is found already in *Homer, and as geographical knowledge increased a distinction was made between western and eastern Ethiopians. Ethiopia was favoured by the gods, who in both *Iliad* and *Odyssey* go to dine there, and hence has an important place in utopian literature. In later Classical literature (Heliodorus, *see* NOVEL) Ethiopia is again a quasi-mythical land, but with the addition of ethnographic details culled from the encyclopaedists.

[Homer, *Iliad* 1. 423–5; *Odyssey* 1. 22–4]

Etruscan discipline *See* HARUSPICES.

Etruscan religion Our primary sources are archaeology (reliefs, tomb paintings, statues, mirrors, altars, temples, funerary urns) and Etruscan inscriptions, especially the 'liturgical' texts such as the linen wrappings on the Zagreb (Agram) mummy (a ritual calendar) and the Capua tile (a list of sacrifices). Aulus Caecina, *Tarquitius Pris-

cus (both of Etruscan origin), *Nigidius Figulus, and Fonteius Capito produced at the end of the Republic antiquarian treatises containing translations from Etruscan ritual books; in the Empire Umbricius Melior in the 1st and Cornelius Labeo in the 3rd cent. dealt with the Etruscan discipline. The surviving fragments often show a curious mixture of Etruscan, Egyptian, and Chaldaean tenets, and of Hellenistic and Neoplatonic philosophy. Of extant authors especially important are *Cicero, Martianus Capella, and Johannes Lydus; and there are mentions in *Varro, the younger Seneca, the elder Pliny, Pompeius Festus, *Arnobius, *Macrobius, *Fulgentius, and the commentaries on *Virgil.

Etruscan religion, unlike Greek and Roman, was a revealed religion. The revelation was ascribed to the semi-divine seer *Tages, and to the *nymph Vegoia. Their teaching, with later accretions, formed a code of religious practices, *Etrusca disciplina*. It included *libri haruspicini, fulgurales*, and *rituales. See* HARUSPICES.

The haruspical books dealt with inspecting the entrails (*exta*) of victims, especially the liver. A bronze model of a sheep's liver found near Piacenza (Placentia) has its convex side divided into 40 sections (16 border, 24 inner), inscribed with the names of some 28 deities. The liver reflected the heavens. Its sections corresponded to the abodes of the gods in the sky (esp. the 16 border sections to the 16 regions of the celestial *templum*; see the references to Pliny and Martianus Capella below, the latter description of the dwelling-places of the gods showing striking parallels with the regions of the liver), and thus the haruspex distinguishing the favourable and inimical part of the liver (*pars familiaris* and *hostilis*) and paying attention to the slightest irregularities was able to establish which gods were angry, which favourable or neutral, and what the future held.

The fulgural books concerned the interpretation of thunder (bolt) and lightning (*fulgur, fulmen*); the portentous meaning depended on the part of the sky from which they were coming. Nine gods threw thunderbolts (*manubiae*), Jupiter (*Tin*) three kinds: foretelling and warning (*praesagum* or *consiliarium*), frightening (*ostentatorium*), and destroying (*peremptorium*). The first he sent alone, the second on the advice of his counsellors (*Consentes Di*), and the third with the approval of *dei superiores et involuti*, 'the higher and veiled gods' = the Fates. There existed various other subdivisions of thunderbolts, but the 'brontoscopic calendar' indicating the significance of thunderbolts for every day of the year (preserved by Lydus, and attributed to Nigidius) appears to exhibit rather Chaldaean than Etruscan wisdom.

The ritual books contained 'prescriptions concerning the founding of cities, the consecration of altars and temples, the inviolability (*sanctitas*) of ramparts, the laws relative to city gates, also how tribes (*tribus*), *curiae*, and centuries are distributed, the army constituted and ordered, and other things of this nature concerning war and peace'. The *libri Acheruntici* dealt with the underworld, and the *Ostentaria* were the manuals for the interpretation of portents.

The Etruscan word for 'god' is *ais* (pl. *aiser*). We know a great number of Etruscan deities, but their functions and relations often remain obscure. They mostly bear Etruscan names, but were early subjected to Greek influences. The highest was the thundergod *Tin/Tinia* (*Zeus/*Jupiter); there is no compelling evidence that he formed with *Uni* (*Juno) and *Men(e)rva* (*Minerva, assimilated to *Athena) a triad worshipped in tripartite temples (as on the *Capitol). *Voltumna* (*Velthumna, Vortumnus/*Vertumnus*), perhaps =*Tin* of Volsinii, presided over the league of twelve Etruscan cities. *Cath/Cavtha* and *Usil* were solar deities (*see* HELIOS; SOL), *Cel* a goddess of Earth (Gē, *Gaia; *Tellus) and *Thesan* of dawn (*Eos, Aurora), *Tiv* a moon god, and *Neth/Nethuns* (*Neptunus) a water god. *Vetis/Veive* corresponded to *chthonian *Vediovis/Veiovis*, but *Maris* (a youthful male deity) was not a counterpart of *Mars (as a war-god

there appears *Lar/Laran*), and *Velch/Velchans* (originally a vegetation god?) was assimilated only late to Vulcan (*Volcanus). It was *Sethlans* who was identified with *Hephaestus, *Turms* with *Hermes, *Fufluns* with *Dionysus (who also appears as *Pacha*= Bacchus), and *Turan* (a mother goddess) with *Aphrodite. *Apollo (*Aplu*), *Artemis (*Aritimi/Artumes*), and *Heracles (*Hercle*) kept their Greek names, but sometimes assumed new features. In the tablets from *Pyrgi *Uni* is conflated with the Punic Astarte (perhaps corresponding to Roman *Matuta Mater). Most prominent were various underworld and funerary deities: *Thanr, Calu*, and their attendants *Charun* (*Charon) and *Tuchulcha*, and the female winged demon *Vanth*.

Etruscan religious expertise made a lasting impression upon the Romans. Livy called the Etruscans 'a nation (*gens*) more than any other devoted to religious rites, all the more as it excelled in the art of practising them'. The Christian *Arnobius proclaimed Etruria 'begetter and mother of superstitions'.

[Cicero, *On Divination*, esp. 1. 72, 2. 49; *De haruspicum responso* (*On Response from Etruscan Soothsayers*); Pliny, *Natural History* 2. 143–4; Martianus Capella, 1. 41–61; Johannes Lydus, *De ostentis* (*On Portents*) 27–38]

Eubouleus, 'the good counsellor', was a major god in the Eleusinian *mysteries, and played an important role in the myth presented in the secret rite: he brought Kore back from the Underworld. In art he is a torch-bearer and usually stands next to Kore (*see* PERSEPHONE) after her return, or between Theos and Thea (as *Hades and *Persephone were called in the mysteries) before her return. In related myth (not dramatized in the cult) he is a swineherd, son of Dysaules and brother of *Triptolemus, who gave *Demeter news of the rape of Kore; in one version his pigs were swallowed up with Kore, which is why piglets are thrown into pits at the *Thesmophoria. But he evidently was not worshipped at the Attic Thesmophoria. Outside Attica Eubouleus appears as (1) an epithet of *Zeus as god of earth and fertility, worshipped at local

Thesmophoria; (2) a euphemistic title of Hades; and (3) the name of one of a group of 'Orphic' Underworld deities (*see* ORPHISM).

Eudorus, in mythology, a Myrmidon captain, son of *Hermes and Polymele.

[Homer, *Iliad* 16. 179 ff.]

Euhemerus, of Messene, perhaps wrote while in the service of Cassander (311–298 BC), but was perhaps active as late as 280 BC. He wrote a *novel of travel which was influential in the Hellenistic world. The substance of the novel is known from fragments, especially in Diodorus Siculus (see below) and from an epitome by *Eusebius. Euhemerus described an imaginary voyage to a group of islands in the uncharted waters of the Indian Ocean and the way of life on its chief island, Panchaea. The central monument of the island, a golden column on which the deeds of *Uranus, *Cronus, and *Zeus were recorded, gave the novel its title *Hiera Anagraphē*, 'Sacred Scripture'. From this monument Euhemerus learnt that Uranus, Cronus, and Zeus had been great kings in their day and that they were worshipped as gods by the grateful people. Earlier authors had written of imaginary utopias, but the utopia of Euhemerus was particularly relevant to the position of those Hellenistic rulers who claimed to serve their subjects and on that account to receive worship for their services (*see* RULER-CULT). Euhemerism could be interpreted according to taste as supporting the traditional belief of Greek epic and lyric poetry which drew no clear line between gods and great men; as advancing a justification for contemporary ruler-cults; or as a work of rationalizing *atheism. At the same time Euhemerus was influenced by the beliefs of the wider world which had been opened up by the conquests of Alexander the Great, and his novel reflected the awareness of new ideas in an exciting situation.

The theory of god and man which was advanced by Euhemerus was not original (*see* CULTURE-BRINGERS; PRODICUS), and it seems to have made little impression on later Greeks, but Diodorus, apparently taking the romance for fact, embodied it in his sixth book, which survives in fragments. In Latin it had more success after the publication of the *Euhemerus* of the great 2nd-cent. BC poet Ennius, and euhemerizing accounts of such mythological figures as *Faunus exist. The Christian writers, especially *Lactantius, liked to use it as evidence of the real nature of the Greek gods. Euhemerus' name survives in the modern term 'euhemeristic', applied to mythological interpretation which supposes certain gods (e.g. *Asclepius) to be originally heroes. *See also* HECATAEUS (2); LEON; PHILON (2).

Eumaeus, *Odysseus' faithful swineherd, a man of royal birth but carried off as a child by Phoenician sailors and sold to Laertes. He gives Odysseus refuge on his return to Ithaca disguised as a beggar, and later helps him kill the suitors (*see* PENELOPE).

[Homer, *Odyssey* 14, 15. 403 ff.]

Eumenides *See* ERINYES.

Eumolpus, the 'fair singer', was the mythical ancestor of the Eleusinian clan (*see* GENOS) of the Eumolpidae, as Keryx was of the Kerykes. He appears first in the *Homeric Hymn to Demeter* as one of the rulers of *Eleusis instructed by the goddess in the *mysteries. According to the Eumolpidae he was the son of *Poseidon and the first *hierophantēs*. In art he holds a sceptre, like the *hierophantēs*, who with his melodious voice, saw himself as re-enacting the role of Eumolpus. According to *Apollodorus, he was son of Poseidon and Chione daughter of *Boreas. The story of her throwing him into the sea, in shame, may perhaps be an explanation of a ritual in which the hierophant consigned his former name to the sea. The various ancient genealogies of Eumolpus and his adventures in *Ethiopia and Thrace reflect in large part attempts to reconcile the Eleusinian *hierophantēs* with the homonymous Thracian king who led the Eleusinians against the Athenians;

but the latter story evidently is no older than the 5th cent. BC, perhaps invented by *Euripides.

[*Homeric Hymn to Demeter* 184, 475; Apollodorus 3. 201 ff.]

Euneōs and Thoas, sons of *Jason and *Hypsipyle, whose best-known exploit was to free their mother from captivity at Nemea. The fact that their great-grandfather was *Dionysus appears to be significant: they brought wine to the Achaeans at Troy, and the Attic *genos Euneidai was closely associated with the cult of Dionysus Melpomenos.

[Homer, *Iliad* 7. 468–71; Euripides, *Hypsipyle* (fragments)]

eunomia ('good order') In mythology, Eunomia is daughter of *Dike.

eunuchs in religion In the Classical period, religious eunuchs are a feature of several Anatolian cults of female deities, extending across to Scythia and to the southern foothills of the Taurus mountains, but independent of Babylonian and Phoenician practices (*see* ANATOLIAN DEITIES). As a whole the institution created a class of pure servants of a god (compare Matt. 19: 12). Its significance derives from a double contrast, with the involuntary castration of children for court use and the normal obligation to marry. The adult self-castrate expressed in his body both world-rejection and -superiority.

Two forms may be distinguished. (1) A senior, or even high, priest in a temple, e.g. the eunuchs of *Hecate at Lagina in Caria; the Megabyz(x)us of *Artemis at Ephesus; the *Attis and Battaces, the high priests of Cybele at *Pessinus. (2) A member of an itinerant (at Rome restricted) group of servants of the goddess (Gk. *mētragyrtai*), not priests, who might or might not be eunuchs. The best known are the galli (also Gk. *bakēloi*) of the cults of *Cybele and *Atargatis (the fanatici of Ma-Bellona were not castrated). Catullus' *Attis* (poem 63) has led to excessive emphasis upon subjective meaning. Self-castration was a (decisive) step into a status

'between worlds', parallel to poverty, homelessness, self-laceration, ecstatic dancing. Cross-dressing (esp. earrings) and face-whitening advertised the anomalous state (*see* TRANSVESTISM, RITUAL). The value of eunuchism probably shifted over time, e.g. from the 2nd cent. AD towards negative *asceticism. Some Phrygian *Montanists picked up the theme in a radical Christian idiom. *See also* ORIGEN.

[Herodotus 4. 67; Catullus 63; Justin Martyr, *Apologia* 29. 2; Eusebius, *Life of Constantine* 3. 55. 2 f.]

Euphemus, an *Argonaut, son of *Poseidon, connected with the foundation legend of *Cyrene. According to *Pindar he was given a clod of earth with instructions to drop it into the sea at *Taenarum; his descendants in the fourth generation would then rule over Libya. But the clod was washed overboard at Thera, and instead Libya was colonized from that island in the seventeenth generation.

[Pindar, *Pythian* 4; Apollonius Rhodius 4. 1730–64]

Euphorbus, in mythology, a Dardanian, son of Panthoos, who wounded *Patroclus, and was afterwards killed by *Menelaus. *Pythagoras claimed to have been Euphorbus in a former incarnation and to recognize his shield.

[Homer, *Iliad* 16. 806 ff., 17. 45 ff.; Horace, *Odes* 1. 28. 9 ff.]

Euripides, Athenian tragic playwright. Euripides was born probably in the 480s. He first took part in the dramatic competitions of the City *Dionysia at Athens in 455 BC, but his first victory came only in 441. Though he was felt to be noteworthy and in some respects he was apparently popular, in his lifetime he won only four victories at the Dionysia (and one posthumous one). Soon after his last competition at the Dionysia in 408 he left Athens on a visit to Macedon, as guest of the Hellenizing king Archelaus; he never returned and died in Macedon.

In his ninety or so plays, Euripides covered an immense amount of mythological material, often recasting it in new forms to suit his dramatic purposes. Like his dramatic predecessors, he drew both on the Trojan and Theban cycles of myth (*see* EPIC CYCLE) and on other, more local narratives (for instance *Alcestis*, *Medea*, *Hippolytus*); several of his plays are either set in Athens or have a strong Athenian reference. In turn, later mythographers derived a great deal of material from Euripides, so that far more than the surviving nineteen of his plays have contributed to our knowledge of mythology.

Among his contemporaries, Euripides had a reputation as a radical, devoted to 'new' ways of thought and expression; clearly this was not undeserved. Many modern scholars have seen him as deeply critical of traditional religion, and this too has some foundation. Gods are often shown in an embarrassing or apparently unfavourable light, and human characters comment frequently that gods *ought* not to behave in ways that are (to human ways of thinking) morally questionable, while the plot invariably shows that they do. But the distance between Euripides and his predecessors and older contemporaries in this regard has been much exaggerated. *Aeschylus is deeply questioning about the justice of Zeus, the author of *Prometheus Bound* (see PROMETHEUS) even more so; neither does the 'pious' *Sophocles present cosy pictures of divine–human relationships—justice, in our sense, seems often to be totally lacking from his dramas, and *Hyllus, at the end of *Trachiniae*, speaks quite as bitterly about the gods as any Euripidean character. The fact is that virtually all fifth-century mythological narrative is engaged, implicitly or explicitly, in questioning the role of the gods and their relationship with human beings. Euripides simply returns to the topic more often than some authors, and (in keeping with his practice in other areas) makes his observations more explicit, more pointed and more obviously paradoxical. That said, his plays contain a wealth of material dealing with the moral difficulties of myth, the perceived unresponsiveness of the gods, and alternative conceptions of div-

inity, which bears witness to the immense variety of viewpoints in religious thinking which were current in 5th-cent. Athens.

Perhaps paradoxically, Euripides seems to have been fonder than any other dramatist of bringing the gods onto stage. This device is used often in the prologue, and most often in the closing scenes of the play, where the *deus ex machina* becomes almost his trademark. Usually the god makes a prophecy about some aspect of the future, which we either assume or know will come true; often the prophecy relates to the foundation of a cult which is still current in the audience's own time. These endings vary a great deal in their dramatic effect, and there is frequently an uncomfortable or dissonant aspect to them.

Europa, in mythology, is usually said to be the daughter of the Phoenician king *Agenor, though Homer makes her the daughter of *Phoenix. *Zeus saw her when she was playing with her companions on the seashore and was filled with desire for her. So he turned himself into, or sent, a beautiful bull, which approached her and enticed her by its mildness to climb on its back. At once it made off with her and plunged into the sea, then swam to Crete. There Zeus made love to her, and she bore him two or three children, *Minos, *Rhadamanthys, and, in post-Homeric accounts, *Sarpedon. She was then married to Asterius, king of Crete, who adopted her sons as his own. Zeus gave her three presents: the bronze man *Talos (1) to guard the island, a hound which never missed its quarry, and a javelin which never missed its mark. These last passed afterwards to Minos, thence to *Procris and so to her husband *Cephalus. Agenor, anxious about Europa, sent his sons *Cadmus, *Phoenix, and Cilix to find her, and their mother Telephassa went too. But when they failed to find Europa they all chose to settle elsewhere, and Agenor never saw them again. The bull whose form Zeus had taken became the *constellation Taurus.

Europa with the bull was a favourite theme in art from the 6th cent.

[Homer, *Iliad* 14. 321; Moschus, *Europa*; Apollodorus 3. 1. 1; Ovid, *Metamorphoses* 7. 681 ff.]

Eurycleia, *Odysseus' nurse, who recognizes Odysseus on his return to Ithaca by the boar's scar on his leg, abets his killing of the suitors, and exults at their deaths. Subject of ancient, esp. Roman, art.

[Homer, *Odyssey* 19. 392 ff., 21. 380 ff., 22. 407 ff.]

Eurydice, 'broad-judging'. The best-known bearer of this name was the wife whom *Orpheus either brought back from the Underworld or lost again in the process. The story is first referred to by *Euripides and *Plato, but the name Eurydice first occurs on 4th-cent. BC pottery and in literature not until the *Epitaphios Bionos* attributed to Moschus; it may have stood on a late 5th-cent. relief of which Roman copies survive. The Hellenistic poet Hermesianax calls Orpheus' wife Agriope. It is uncertain whether Virgil's version, in which Eurydice was killed by a snake as she was fleeing from *Aristaeus, was original to him. As early as the *Epic Cycle *Aeneas' wife was called Eurydice, and there are clear similarities between the hero's loss of Creusa in *Aeneid* bk. 2 and Orpheus' loss in *Georgics* bk. 4.

[Euripides, *Alcestis* 357–62; Plato, *Symposium* 179d; Virgil, *Georgics* 4]

Eurypylus, a minor Iliadic figure sometimes identified with an important hero of Patrae, having connections with both *Artemis and *Dionysus. At the fall of Troy Eurypylus received a chest containing an image of Dionysus, and on opening it went mad. He was told at *Delphi to establish the worship of the god in the chest wherever he found a 'strange/foreign sacrifice'; the condition was fulfilled by the human sacrifice given to Artemis Triclaria at Patrae, and on the establishment of the cult of Dionysus Eurypylus was cured. At the same time human sacrifice in the Artemis cult was abolished, another oracle having declared that it would cease when a foreign king arrived with a foreign god. In cult as well as myth Eurypylus links both deities: his tomb was in the sanctuary of Artemis Laphria, but he was worshipped at the festival of Dionysus Aesymnetes.

[Pausanias 7. 19. 1–20]

Eurystheus, in mythology, son of Sthenelus and Nicippe, and granted rule of the Argolid by *Zeus through *Hera's trickery. *Heracles was enslaved to him while he performed his twelve Labours, on the orders of the *Delphic oracle and as a punishment for killing his wife and children in a fit of madness. In art Eurystheus is depicted as a coward, hiding fearfully in a great jar when Heracles delivers e.g. the Erymanthian boar. Even after Heracles' death, Eurystheus persecuted his descendants.

[Homer, *Iliad* 19. 95–125; Euripides, *Heraclidae (Children of Heracles)*]

Eurytion, in mythology, (1) Geryon's herdsman, *see* HERACLES. (2) A *Centaur; getting drunk and misbehaving at *Pirithous' wedding-feast, he began the quarrel between Centaurs and men. (3) Brother of *Pandarus. (4) *See* PELEUS.

[(2) Homer, *Odyssey* 21. 295 ff.; (3) Virgil, *Aeneid* 5. 495 ff.]

Eusebius, of Caesarea (*c*.AD 260–339), prolific writer, biblical scholar and apologist, effective founder of the Christian genres of Church history and chronicle, and the most important contemporary source for the reign of *Constantine I. His intellectual formation at Caesarea in Palestine owed much to the influence of Pamphilus (martyred 310), by whom he was apparently adopted, and to their joint use of the library of *Origen. From his election as bishop of Caesarea *c*.313 until his death in 339, Eusebius played a significant role in ecclesiastical politics in the eastern empire.

Eusebius wrote biblical commentaries, in which the profound influence exerted on him by Origen is tempered by his own historical perspective; his *Onomasticon*, 'a biblical gazetteer', is an important source for the historical geography of Palestine. The two editions (?before 303 and 325–6)

of his lost *Chronicle*, represented by
*Jerome's Latin version and by an Armenian
translation, synthesized Old Testament,
near eastern, and Graeco-Roman history
into a continuous chronological sequence
accompanied by chronological tables. The
object, as in his *Ecclesiastical History*, was to
demonstrate that God's plan for salvation
subsumed the whole of history. The same
thinking lay behind his *Preparation for the
Gospel* and *Proof of the Gospel* (after 313), apologetic works in which pagan philosophy is
refuted and the Roman empire seen as the
necessary background for the coming of
Christ and the establishment of Christianity.
The *Preparation* reveals Eusebius' immense
debt to the library of Origen, with its many
citations from Greek historians, *Philon (1),
and especially Middle Platonist philosophy.
An early work, *Against Hierocles*, attacks the
comparison of the pagan *Apollonius of
Tyana with Christ; in the *Preparation* the
main target is *Porphyry, whose anti-
Christian arguments Eusebius systematically set out to refute. The later *Theophany*
(325–6 or later), extant in Syriac translation,
and his last works repeat many of the same
apologetic themes. His *Life of Constantine*,
left unfinished at his death, sought to
create the impression of a harmonious
and consistent imperial religious policy
from the accession of Constantine (306) to
the reign of his three sons, beginning in
September 337.

Euthymus, an early 5th-cent. boxer and
Olympian victor (*see* OLYMPIAN GAMES), best
known for the story of his victory over the
malevolent hero of Temesa. In Pausanias'
account this hero, one of *Odysseus' companions, had been lynched after raping a
local girl, but continued to demand a virgin
as wife each year; Euthymus, coming to Temesa, fell in love with that year's victim,
fought and banished the hero, and married
the girl. The story combines several familiar
motifs, in particular that of the ending of
human sacrifice. Euthymus himself, like several contemporary athletes, became the

object of heroic or even divine cult; *see*
HERO-CULT.

[Callimachus, *Aetia (Origins)*, frs. 98–9; Aelian, *Varia
Historia* 8. 18; Pausanias 6. 6. 4–11]

Evadne (Gk. *Euadnē*), in mythology, (1) a
daughter of *Poseidon, who became by
*Apollo mother of *Iamus, ancestor of the
prophetic clan of the Iamidae in *Olympia.
(2) Daughter of Iphis and wife of *Capaneus,
one of the *Seven against Thebes. She
burned herself on his funeral pyre.

[(1) Pindar, *Olympian* 6. 29 ff.; (2) Euripides, *Suppliant
Women* 980 ff.]

Evander was in origin probably a minor
hero or divinity of Arcadia (*see* ARCADIAN
CULTS AND MYTHS). Some attributed him
human parents (Echemus of Tegea, and Timandra, daughter of Tyndareos) but he was
more commonly regarded as a son of
*Hermes by a nymph (Themis or Nicostrate).
Through Hermes he was descended from
Atlas and hence could be credited with kinship with *Aeneas through *Dardanus (so
Virgil) and also with *Atreus.

Independent Greek evidence for Evander
or his cult is (at best) scanty. He appears
predominantly in Roman (or Rome-
orientated) sources as fleeing Arcadia,
landing at the site of Rome on the advice of
his mother (identified with *Carmentis) and
(usually) being allowed to settle on the *Palatine by Faunus. The legend was probably
based on, and explained, the name of the
Palatine (supposedly derived from Pallan-
teum in Arcadia, or from Pallas, variously
described as Evander's grandfather, son, or
grandson, or from Pallantia, Evander's
daughter) and the sanctuary and ritual of
the Lupercal (identified as the cult of the
Arcadian 'wolf-god', Lycaean *Pan; *see* LUPER-
CALIA). An etymological association of Evander and *Faunus (both names being
interpreted as 'beneficent') may also be involved but is not directly attested.

The legend has no historical foundation
but served to emphasize Rome's Greek cultural credentials. Quintus Fabius Pictor attributed to Evander the introduction of the

alphabet to Rome, and as he brought *Hercules to Italy, he may, like later sources, have placed the Hercules–Cacus episode and consequent foundation of the Ara Maxima under Evander. Some later authors elaborated this civilizing Greek input (*Varro and perhaps Cato the Censor) even made Evander responsible for an Aeolic substrate in Latin, and Ateius Philologus traced to him the (Greek) name of Rome itself. Others, however, such as Livy and Virgil, limit severely its significance for Rome's future cultural identity.

[Virgil, *Aeneid* 8; Dionysius of Halicarnassus, *Roman Antiquities* 1. 31 ff.]

evocatio A ritual by which, in the course of a war, a Roman general would attempt to deprive the enemy of divine protection, by formally offering their protecting deity a new home and cult at Rome. The clearest recorded case is the evocation of *Juno Regina from the Etruscan city of Veii in 396 BC—a process which led to the establishing of her cult on the *Aventine hill in Rome. There has been some debate over how long this ritual continued to be practised, and (in particular) whether the record of the evocation of Juno from Carthage in 146 BC is anything more than antiquarian invention. The discovery of an inscription at Isaura Vetus (in modern Turkey), apparently recording an *evocatio* in *c.*75 BC, suggests that the ritual survived at least to the late republic. There are, however, changes from earlier practice: in 75 BC the deity seems to have been offered a home not in Rome, but in provincial territory.

[Livy 5. 21 ff.]

exēgētēs, an interpreter or expounder, usually of sacred lore. The Athenians traditionally considered *Apollo Pythios (i.e. Apollo of *Delphi) their *exēgētēs*. At Athens exegesis of the *patria*, sacred and ancestral law, was an old custom, but from *c.*400 BC they entrusted it to officials specif-ically appointed for the task: (1) one *exēgētēs* elected by the people from the **eupatridai*; (2) one *exēgētēs* chosen by the Pythia (*see* DELPHIC ORACLE), called *exēgētēs Pythochrēstos*; (3) three *exēgētai* of the Eumolpidae (*see* EU-MOLPUS), who expounded the *sacra* of the *mysteries. The Athenian *exēgētai* were generally concerned with the unwritten sacred law, but they often pronounced on secular and domestic questions (e.g. duties and obligations) untouched by statutes and of possible religious implications. Other cities too had *exēgētai*, official or unofficial.

exile Exile (Gk. *phygē*, literally 'flight') is permanent or long-term removal from one's native place, usually as a punishment imposed by government or other superior power. In Greece it was from earliest times a standard consequence of homicide, and was as much a religious way of getting rid of a source of *pollution as a punishment. Thus *Zeus in *Homer's *Iliad* is said to make men exiles, driving them like a gadfly over the face of the earth. An element of this concept probably remained, though in later times exile took on a much more secular significance.

[Homer, *Iliad* 24. 532 f.]

Ezechiel, author of the *Exagoge*, a tragedy in Greek about Moses and the escape of the Israelites from Egypt. Nothing is known of his life, but he must have been a Hellenized Jew active between the late 3rd and early 1st cent. BC, probably at Alexandria. He is credited with 'Jewish tragedies' in the plural, but we know only the *Exagoge*, of which 269 lines are preserved. It is based on the *Septuagint version of Exodus 1–15, but includes some free invention and aspires, with mixed success, to Euripidean style. Though obviously untypical, it provides valuable evidence for Hellenistic tragedy. *See* JEWISH–GREEK LITERATURE.

fable, a short story in the popular tradition of Greece and other ancient culture. Fables found their way into literature as illustrative examples; later they were compiled into collections.

They usually deal with a conflict in which animals speak and intervene, but the characters may also be plants, sundry objects, men, or gods. Fables normally deal with the triumph of the strong, but also portray the cunning of the weak and their mockery of, or triumph over, the powerful. Fables also stress the impossibility of changing nature; some give aetiological explanations. Most often there is a comic element; sometimes the 'situation' of a protagonist is depicted, from which the audience may draw analogies.

It is therefore impossible to offer a fixed definition. The boundaries of fable intermesh with those of myth, animal proverbs, anecdotes, tales, and *chreiai* (witty sayings). Fable is normally fiction, but does at times use anecdotes about real characters. It reflects popular literature and may satirize the values and abuses of the dominant social classes.

Greek fable undoubtedly originated in Greece, but clearly absorbed foreign traditions, particularly Mesopotamian fable (itself based on Sumerian fable); compare, for instance, the fable of the eagle and the serpent in the Akkadian *Etana*. The Greeks themselves attributed the origin of certain fables to Libya or Egypt. In its turn, Greek fable influenced Indian fable. From the time of Lucilius (2nd cent. BC) through to the Middle Ages Greek fable gave rise to numerous fables in Latin.

In Greek literature fable appears as an example, used alongside myth and the historical or fictitious anecdote, from the time of *Hesiod, who talks of 'The Hawk and the Nightingale'. Thereafter it is found above all in the writers of iambics (Archilochus, Semonides), and was used by elegists (Theognis), lyric poets (Simonides) and playwrights. It appears in prose in Herodotus and is a favourite medium of the Socratic writers. It was associated with *Socrates and is used in *Plato, Xenophon, Antisthenes, and *Aristotle.

From the end of the 5th cent. BC, the authority of fable was often attributed to *Aesop, whom a dubious historical tradition identifies as a Phrygian slave in Samos. Yet it is clear that from the 5th century onwards there was a legend, seemingly influenced by the Assyrian story of Ahikar, of a person named Aesop who was connected with *Delphi. Aesop emerges as a popular character who tells anecdotes, jokes, and fables, and gives lessons in wisdom.

family, religion of *See* HOUSEHOLD, WORSHIP OF.

fantastic literature, or fiction of the unreal, took two forms in antiquity: (*a*) fantasies of travel beyond the known world; (*b*) stories of the supernatural. Both look back to the Phaeacian tales in the *Odyssey*, which became a byword for the unbelievable.

From the Hellenistic period we know of a series of descriptions of imaginary lands, such as those by *Euhemerus, *Hecataeus of Abdera, and Iambulus. Their primary purpose was social and moral comment, but they often seem to have been authenticated by an adventure story, which provided entertainment but also drew attention to the question of how literally they were to be believed. Antiphanes of Berge's account of the far north was so transparently fictitious that 'Bergaean' became synonymous with 'fantasist'. Although these works were criticized as falsehoods, some recognized that undisguised fiction represented an area of licence for the imagination. Fantasies of this kind are parodied in the space-travel of Lucian's True History, but, despite his satirical programme, Lucian's invention acquires its own fantastic momentum.

Tales of the supernatural also make doubt and belief their central theme. Lucian's Philopseudes tells stories of ghosts and magic, including the Sorcerer's Apprentice, while mocking those who believe them. Fantastic episodes occur in the *novels, notably of Iamblichus and *Apuleius, whose characters share the reader's hesitation as to the nature of the phenomena. The fragments of *Phlegon of Tralles contain the story of an amorous revenant, while Philostratus narrates the detection of a vampire. There was a collection of ghost stories by the neoplatonist Damascius (b. c.AD 458), but most literature of this kind has been lost, except for some papyrus fragments.

The two strands of fantasy united in the Wonders beyond Thule of Antonius Diogenes, which combined travel beyond real geography with witchcraft, *Pythagorean philosophy, and self-conscious authentication, all arguably intended to subvert the reality of the perceptible world. See PARADOXOGRAPHERS.

fasti, the calendar of dies fasti, dies comitiales, and dies nefasti, which indicated when a specific legal process organized by the urban praetor (the legis actio) and assemblies might or might not take place; it received definitive publication by Cnaeus Flavius in 304 BC. Vulgarly, dies nefasti came to be thought of as ill-omened days. We know of the sacral calendars of Marcus Fulvius Nobilior (consul 189 BC) and Verrius Flaccus (at *Praeneste), and have fragments of the pre-Julian calendar of Antium (84–55 BC) and twenty calendars mainly of the Augustan and Tiberian periods; also two 'rustic' almanacs, and in book form the calendar of AD 354 and the calendar of Polemius Silvius (AD 448-9). The Fasti of Hydatius (covering 510 BC–AD 478), and the *Chronicon Paschale (7th cent. AD) are chronicles of events.

The word fasti also includes other listings: fasti consulares (of eponymous magistrates), fasti triumphales (of triumphs), and fasti sacerdotales (of priests), including the fasti of the feriae Latinae (festival of *Jupiter celebrated by the Latins). Of fasti consulares we have the exemplar from Antium (84–55 BC) and the so-called fasti Capitolini, which were inscribed on an arch in the forum Romanum 18-17 BC; the ludi saeculares (*Secular Games) were added, until AD 88. Fasti triumphales were also inscribed on the same arch, from Romulus down to the last 'republican' triumph, that of Lucius Cornelius Balbus in 19 BC.

The authenticity of the fasti consulares and triumphales has been much debated. The reconstruction for the 5th cent. BC was necessarily speculative, perhaps politically tendentious, and includes both omissions and interpolations; it was sounder in its main lines for the 4th cent., and from c.300 BC appears consistently accurate, presumably using full regular records. This suggests that the inclusion of magistrates' names and cult notices may have followed directly on the publication by Cnaeus Flavius.

See also OVID.

fasting (Gk. nesteia, Lat. ieiunium) is the temporary abstinence from all food for ritual, ascetic, and medicinal purposes. Alien to Roman practice except for the ieiunium in the cult of *Ceres, which was considered a Greek import, it was infrequent in Greek cult, where feasting was more central than fasting. The Greeks, who used the meat of sacrificial animals, amongst other food-stuffs, as offerings to the gods and as meals for human worshippers (*see* SACRIFICE, GREEK), did not recognize extended periods of ritual fasting on the scale of the Muslim Ramadan or Christian Lent. In the few cults that made fasting a ritual requirement, its observance was always brief, lasting up to an entire day, and in exceptional circumstances up to three days.

According to the Christian writer *Clement of Alexandria, those initiated into the Eleusinian *mysteries declared that they had performed the required rites preliminary to initiation by reciting the following 'password': 'I fasted, I drank the ritual drink (*kykeōn*), I took from the chest (*kistē*), and having worked [with the sacred implements] I removed [them] into the basket and from the basket into the chest'. In fact, the initiation proper was preceded by a whole day of fasting, which ended at nightfall with the drinking of the *kykeōn*. The initiates' fast, like their breaking of it, had a mythical precedent in the fasting of *Demeter herself, who roamed the earth for nine days abstaining from *ambrosia and nectar, and even from bathing. Later, at Eleusis, 'wasting away with longing for her deep-bosomed daughter, she sat unsmiling, tasting neither food nor drink', until the jests of *Iambe prompted her to laugh and to drink the *kykeōn*. Similarly, *Achilles refused food after the death of *Patroclus. In Greek culture, as in many others, self-neglect was an outward sign of extreme grief and mourning. Fasting was equally integral to another women's festival of Demeter, the *Thesmophoria. On its second day, called 'the Fast' (*Nēsteia*) by the Athenians, the participating women 'fasted like mullets', a fish known for its empty stomach. On this day, the 'gloomiest day' of the festival, the subversive women in Aristophanes' *Thesmophoriazusae* hold their assembly while keeping a strict fast. In addition to fasting, the celebrants at the Thesmophoria

had to be sexually abstinent for several days. Fasting and sexual abstinence often went hand in hand as techniques designed to promote ritual purity (*see* PURIFICATION, GREEK) and, conceivably, to heighten spiritual awareness. More importantly, for the Greeks they signal a ritual departure from the social conventions of normal life.

A short fast may have been observed by male initiates in the cult of the Thracian goddess Cotys. Fasting was also practised as a preparatory rite in mystery religions of the oriental type (especially those of *Isis and Mater Magna; *see* CYBELE), as well as in *magic. Abstention from certain kinds of food—all or some meats; particular fish, such as the red mullet; or vegetables like mint and beans—is related to fasting. *Pythagoras is said to have taught men 'to abstain from eating animate creatures'. *Porphyry's *On Abstinence from Living Things*, a treatise on vegetarianism inspired by Theophrastus' *On Piety*, refers to similar food taboos from various parts of the Mediterranean world. Esoteric groups like the 'Orphics' (*see* ORPHISM) and Pythagoreans were vegetarians and surrounded their daily lives with other dietary prohibitions, many of which corresponded to the rules of conduct imposed on members of some private cults. Christian ascetics abstained from wine and meat, and often kept prolonged fasts more rigorous than any observed by pagan holy men. *See* ASCETICISM.

fate The common Greek words for fate mean 'share', 'portion': *moira, aisa, moros, morsimos, heimartai*. One's share is appointed or falls to one (*potmos, peprōmenon*) at birth. The most important share is man's universal fate of death. *Moira, aisa, potmos*, etc. either expressly or by implication primarily refer to death from which even the gods cannot protect man. In *Homer's *Iliad* *Zeus considers saving his son *Sarpedon and favourite *Hector from imminent death, but *Hera and *Athena dissuade him from upsetting the natural order of things. Exceptions to this predominantly negative idea of fate are rare: *Agamemnon is *moirēgenēs* ('favoured by fate') and *olbiodaimōn* ('of blessed lot'), or Zeus knows the good and evil *moira* of mortal men.

The workings of fate can appear irrational. At one moment the Pythia (*see* DELPHIC ORACLE) tells Lydian enquirers that 'no one, not even the god, can escape his appointed *moira*', at the next *Apollo postpones the sack of Sardis for three years to help Croesus. Nevertheless a governing principle of proper order attaches to the basic meaning of 'share' in *moira*, *aisa*, and their derivatives, even when they do not obviously refer to fate. They can describe a section of land, share of booty, a part of the night, or portions of meat. *Moira* already occurs in Linear B in the sense of 'share'. The developed notion of due order determined all shares, including that of fate and death, which fitted into a kind of prescribed order of the world.

In Homer the decisive factors were tradition, social hierarchy (cf. Agamemnon's epithet of *moirēgenēs*), and seniority (the *Erinyes support the elder brother). Any action or speech that followed such carefully defined criteria was said to be 'in accordance with *moira*'. The impersonally appointed fate often meant little more than the orderly sequence of the plot. It was, for example, fated for *Odysseus to return to Ithaca eventually. Consequently this fate can be transgressed by any infringement of the rules of society. So the Cyclops Polyphemus (*see* CYCLOPES) did not act 'in accordance with fate' when he ate his guests. Examples are legion in both Homeric epics. Of interest is an added moral dimension where not only the *moira* of the plot brought the suitors down but also their wicked deeds. Zeus explains that *Aegisthus caused his own suffering by acting 'beyond *moira*' in marrying *Clytemnestra and killing Agamemnon. This sense of order extended to the entire cosmos whose proper running was guaranteed by fate, generally with the gods' co-operation. The Archaic philosopher Heraclitus said that 'if the sun should overstep his bounds, the Erinyes will find him out'.

The impersonal *moira* and *aisa* were not natural agents of fate. That role normally fell to the *daimōn, an often malign being who could be blamed for sudden unexpected happenings. Etymologically *daimōn* means 'giver of share', yet neither his status or nature is clearly defined in epic. He tends to occur in the plural and is all but synonymous with the general *theos*, *theoi* who give good and bad fortune to men. In later literature and philosophy the *daimōn* stands for a man's personal fate. In *Plato's myth of Er man chooses his own *daimōn*, but more usually it is allotted to him. However, the distinction between individual fate and character virtually disappears.

The Moirai, like the related *Horae, Erinyes, and possibly the goddess *Nemesis, possessed more colourful identities in popular belief and as *chthonian cult figures. It is difficult to know which preceded the other: deity or concept. Both existed from early times. Certainly the idea of a personal Moira or Aisa (who lacked cult) was already familiar to Homer and Hesiod as an agent that binds its victim, overcomes him, or leads him to his death. The imagery reflects funeral inscriptions, as does the concept of Moira, Aisa, or the Klothes as spinners of fate (cf. the related popular notions of the weaving and singing of fate). The Moira that, together with Zeus and Erinys, cast confusion into Agamemnon's mind also suggests a cultic origin. The Moirai appear on the François vase (6th cent. BC) and on the still earlier Cypselus chest. However, their genealogy as daughters of Zeus and *Themis and personification in the trinity of Clotho, Lachesis, and Atropos were the fruit of Hesiodic theology (*see* NYX).

There is no conflict between this concept of fate and the gods. When Zeus weighs two 'dooms' (*kēres*) against each other, the image does not imply his dependence on a superior agency of fate. The golden scales are a *façon de parler*, a poetic device, to raise the tension at a critical moment in the narrative by appearing to create a momentary doubt regarding the outcome of an event which always firmly remains in the control of Zeus. On the contrary, Zeus and the other Olympians ensure the orderly sequence of events like Odysseus' return, or they may influence the moment of a hero's death, and in that respect they can be said to be masters of human fate (cf. Zeus' epithet *Moiragetēs*, 'guide of fate'). Fate gradually assumed a wider significance, until the Presocratics, Heraclitus, and the Stoics elevated Heimarmene to an absolute power, the 'orderly succession of causes' and the same as *anankē* ('necessity'). Neoplatonists equated *heimarmenē* with *physis* ('nature'), in order to exempt man's soul from the stranglehold of fate. The problematic relationship of *heimarmenē* with *pronoia* or providence and free will could only be resolved through faith. In fact the cults of *Mithras and *Isis promised their followers release from the constraining power of *heimarmenē*.

The notion of a universal power of fate was less evident in Roman thought. The Parcae became goddesses of fate through assimilation with the Moirai. Originally a goddess of birth, Parca appeared under three different guises as Nona, Decima, and Morta, presumably in relation to the month of a birth and perhaps to stillbirth.

The etymology of *fatum* (*fari*, to speak) suggests a primary connection with *oraculum*—the spoken word of the gods—but that is historically misleading. In literature *fatum* was a frequent euphemism for *mors* or *calamitas*, but it merely echoed Greek concepts. The personified plural Fata were modelled on the three Moirai who appear on coins of Diocletian and Maximian but with the legend, *Fatis victricibus*, 'to the conquering Fates'. Parcae and Fata were also virtually indistinguishable in Roman literature and art. The Fatae in dedicatory inscriptions seem to be Romanized foreign (Celtic) figures. *See also* FORTUNA/FORS; STOICISM; TYCHE.

Faunus (apparently from the root of *favere*, 'kindly one', a euphemism), a god of the forests, was especially connected with the mysterious sounds heard in them, hence his titles (or identification with) Fatuus and Fatuclus, both meaning 'the speaker'. His dwelling-place, wild forests, made him a protector of transhumant flocks. His first temple, dedicated on the Tiber island in 193 BC, was built with money from a fine imposed on the *pecuarii* ('drovers'). From this time on he was identified with *Pan, to the point that his original traits can no longer be separated from those of the Greek god. 'Wild', *agrestis*, he is endowed in ritual (*see* LUPERCALIA) and myth with a lubricity earning him the surname Inuus ('Fructifier') and recalling the adventures of Pan and his power to excite irrepressible desire. Like him, Faunus also pursues women in their dreams. Finally, his opposition to civilized society allowed him to be claimed as one of the mythical kings of early Latium, son of *Picus or *Mars, or one of the gods of Arcadian *Evander. He had female counterparts, Fauna (of whom we know practically nothing; *see* BONA DEA) and Fatua. He was on occasion oracular.

[Virgil, *Aeneid* 7. 45–103]

Faustulus, a mythical figure, shepherd of King Amulius, husband of *Acca Larentia, who found *Romulus and Remus being suckled by the she-wolf. In a further rationalization his wife was the she-wolf herself (*lupa*, loose woman, prostitute). He reared the twins, and when Remus was brought before the Alban king Numitor (*see* ALBA LONGA) for an act of brigandage, told Romulus the whole story, whereupon the twins and their grandfather killed Amulius.

[Livy 1. 4. 6 ff.]

Febris, patron goddess of fever (without doubt, malaria), belonging to a group of baleful divinities invoked by the Romans to stop them from exercising their powers. She possessed three cult places in Rome: on the *Palatine, the Esquiline, and the Quirinal hills. We know almost nothing about her cult. According to Valerius Maximus, cured persons deposited in her sanctuary charms (*remedia*) which had been in contact with their bodies, perhaps because they passed for representations of the power of the goddess. In the 2nd–3rd cents. AD, the sick invoked as well the goddesses Tertiana or Quartana; in the 1st cent. BC they were not yet deified.

Felicitas, a goddess of good luck, not heard of till the middle of the 2nd cent. BC, when a temple was dedicated to her on the Velabrum hill in Rome; another was planned by *Caesar and erected after his death where the original Senate House had stood. She is associated with *Venus Victrix, *Honos, and Virtus at Pompey's theatre; with the *Genius Publicus and Venus Victrix on the *Capitol. Thereafter she is important in official cult under the emperors, appearing frequently on coins (*Felicitas saeculi*, 'Good Luck of the Age', with figure of the goddess) and in addresses to the gods in dedications etc., immediately after the Capitoline triad (*Jupiter, *Juno, and *Minerva).

Feralia, Roman festival on 21 February which concluded the ancestors' festival (*Parentalia) which had begun on 13 February. Each household made offerings at the graves of its dead. It is marked *NP* (i.e. probably a time when legal business should not be done) in imperial calendars but *F* (i.e. a time when the courts were open) in the republican calendar. There is no evidence for a public ritual.

[Ovid, *Fasti* 2. 533–70; Cicero, *Letters to Atticus* 8. 14. 1]

Feronia, an Italian goddess, of presumably *Sabine origin. She was officially received in Rome during the 3rd cent. BC (before 217) and given a temple in the Campus Martius on 13 November. Her principal place of worship was the grove of Capena, Lucus Feroniae, near Mt. Soracte. Her cult, however, is shown by inscriptional and other evidence to have been widespread in central Italy. The etymology of her name is problematic. Of her cult and function almost nothing is known. Strabo says that a ceremony of firewalking was performed in her precinct, but this seems to be a confusion with the so-

called Apollo of *Soracte. Near Tarracina slaves were set free in her shrine. It is likely that the function of Feronia was to convert the savage forces of nature for human use.

festivals

Greek Greek festivals were religious rituals recurring, usually every year, two years, or four years, at fixed times in the calendar. Unlike *sacrifices and other *rituals performed for specific occasions (e.g. *marriage) or in times of crisis, they were intended, in general terms, to maintain or renew the desired relationship with supernatural powers. In the Classical period it was believed that this relationship was maintained by rendering honour, at the appropriate time and in the appropriate manner, to the deity.

Festivals proper (*heortai*) should be distinguished from annual sacrifices (*thysiai*), however large, and the many other rituals that together formed the religious calendar. *Heortai* are described as pleasant and joyful religious experiences with an abundance of good food, good company, and good entertainment, a combination seen in many Mediterranean religious festivals today. The atmosphere and characteristics of *thysiai* and other rituals varied greatly, sometimes being very sombre, depending on the deity, purpose, and cult personnel involved. But the study of festivals has traditionally investigated the dating and description of all calendrically recurring rituals, and that is the sense in which 'festival' is usually understood in Classical scholarship.

The festivals of Athens are best known, and their origins, like those of all Greek festivals, are multifarious, with, for example, some going back to very ancient times (e.g. *Bouphonia), some instituted to honour contemporary Hellenistic kings (e.g. Ptolemaieia). Over the centuries new elements were added to old festivals (e.g. the *Panathenaea) and separate festivals on consecutive days may have coalesced into one (e.g. *Anthesteria). Many were of one day only (e.g. *Thargelia); some, like the City

*Dionysia in Athens, ran five or six days. Athens had at least 60 days a year devoted to annual festivals.

The religious concerns of the Greeks were many, and the variety of the festivals and rituals reflects this. Rarely, furthermore, does a single festival address only one concern. Despite the risk of great oversimplification, we may isolate some major types of developed festivals. Festivals with competitions, each eventually assigned to an Olympian deity, consisted initially of a *pompē* (procession), a *thysia* (sacrifice), an *agōn* (contest, *see* AGŌNES), and a banquet, in that order. The contests might be 'gymnastic' (human and animal races of various types, boxing, wrestling, etc.) or of the Muses (lyre- and pipe-playing, recitations, dancing, and drama), or both. The original *agōn* at *Olympia was, according to myth, simply a 200-m. (*c.* 220-yd.) foot-race. As contests were added, some were placed before the procession, and by the 5th cent. BC the programmes had become very large. Such festivals were the model for those established by monarchs in the Hellenistic period.

Periodic fertility rituals, many of great antiquity, were often performed by women, often in secret. Some were genuine *mysteries (as at Eleusis). Those centred on agriculture naturally occurred at critical times in the farming cycle, e.g. at ploughing (Proerosia), at seeding (*Thesmophoria), and at harvest (Anthesteria), with rituals appropriate to the deity and crop in question. Because concepts of human, animal, and crop fertility were intertwined, sympathetic *magic played a role. For this reason, and because of their secrecy and the combining of two or more festivals, the rituals of fertility festivals are particularly complex and opaque.

Through certain annual rituals, again of great antiquity, the Greeks initiated young people into adult society, in Athens particularly at the *Apaturia for young men and at the Brauronia (*see* BRAURON) for young women. The rituals differed significantly from city to city, but generally followed the pattern of separation, liminal experience,

and reintegration characteristic of such *rites of passage.

A festival presumes a group, in the Greek context the smallest being a village (or 'deme' in Athens), the usual the city-state, a few confederations of states, and the largest (rare) all the Greeks. By the Classical period the city-state had absorbed many village festivals and now financed and administered them. Through festivals a city-state like Athens might celebrate its own origins (the Synoecia), its national identity and accomplishments (Panathenaea), or even, in later times, its military victories. The festivals could be integrated, mythologically, into the legendary history of the city, as, at Athens, the *Oschophoria and Deipnophoria were tied to *Theseus' expedition to Crete. In all festivals the roles and often even dress of the participants maintained traditional divisions of citizen status, gender, age, and office; and thus a festival could provide cohesion to the group but simultaneously reassert traditional social orders. But, on the other hand, a few festivals, the Cronia in Athens and the Hybristica in Argos provided a temporary reversal of the social order, with slaves acting as masters or women as men. Confederations of states with both tribal and geographical ties had cult centres with their own festivals, e.g. the Panionia (*see* PANIONIUM) for *Poseidon at Mycale in Ionia. It was not until the 4th cent. that philosophers such as Isocrates used the pan-Hellenic festivals at Olympia, *Isthmia, and *Delphi as examples and occasions for promoting a sense of shared identity among all Greeks.

Roman (Lat. *feriae*). The basic notion included not only the honouring of the gods, but also restrictions on public life: the courts were closed, some agricultural work was restricted, and in some cases holidays given to other workers. Festivals were of various kinds: some fixed by the regular calendar of the *fasti* (*stativae*) (*see* CALENDAR, ROMAN); movable festivals (*conceptivae*), such as the *feriae sementivae* dedicated to *Tellus and

*Ceres, were held annually on days appointed by priests or magistrates; special festivals (*imperativae*) were ordered, again by magistrates or priests, because of a specific event, a prodigy, a disaster, or a victory. A major element in many public festivals was the accompanying games (*see* LUDI). Besides public festivals, the period assigned to private ceremonial might be classed as *feriae*—e.g. birthdays or the ten days of mourning (*denicales*).

fetiales, priests of the Latin states, concerned with the procedures and laws of declaring wars and making treaties. Our information comes from Rome, where they formed a college (*collegium*) of twenty members, who advised the senate on issues of peace and war, and had their own legal tradition (the *ius fetiale*). The institution presupposes that similar priests, with whom Roman *fetiales* interacted, existed in the other Latin states.

Livy gives an account of their ritual in the form of a narrative, no doubt an antiquarian reconstruction, but perhaps based on priestly sources. In making a treaty two *fetiales* were sent out, who met with *fetiales* from the other side; one carried herbs (the *verbenarius*), the other (the *pater patratus*), having heard the new treaty read out, pronounced a curse that would operate against the Romans, should they be first to break the treaty. The other side did the same. The sacrifice of a pig with a special stone knife confirmed the transaction.

In the case of a declaration of war, the *pater patratus* entered the territory of the state against whom the Romans claimed a grievance and made a public declaration of the claim, calling on *Jupiter to witness the justice of the Roman case. If satisfaction had not been offered within 33 days, the Roman senate and people proceeded to declare war and this was conveyed by the *fetialis* again travelling to the boundary, making the declaration, and throwing a symbolic spear into enemy territory. The consequence of these proceedings was that the war was a just war (*bellum iustum*).

Whether or not this ritual was literally followed in the Archaic period, we meet it in the later republic completely transformed by the distances to be travelled, the lack of enemy *fetiales*, the requirements of diplomacy, and so on. For instance, the symbolic spear-throwing took place inside Rome, on ground near the temple of *Bellona ritually regarded as non-Roman. But the *fetiales* were still being consulted prominently in the 2nd cent. BC; there is no reason to believe they had ceased to exist in the late republic and no evidence as to what if anything their Augustan 'revival' revived.

There has been much debate as to whether the fetial doctrine of the 'just war' inhibited aggressive war-declarations by Rome, and led to defensive attitudes and a consequent lack of consciously imperialist policies. The theory seems to rest on a confusion of ritual propriety (which was what the *fetiales* looked for) with power politics (which were not their concern). But undoubtedly Roman historians, and therefore surviving accounts, were influenced by the expectation, implicit in fetial doctrine, that Rome's wars derived from enemy misbehaviour and Roman piety.

Fides, the Roman personification of good faith. Although her temple (on the *Capitol, near that of *Jupiter, with whom she is closely connected) is no older than 254 BC, her cult is traditionally very old, said to have been founded by *Numa, although it should be noted that Jupiter himself once discharged her function. Livy also gives details of her ritual; the *flamines, meaning probably the *flamines maiores*, drove to her shrine in a covered carriage drawn by two beasts, and the sacrificer must have his hand covered with a white cloth. A pair of covered hands is indeed her symbol, as often on coins commemorating the *fides* of the Emperor, the legions, etc., in imperial times. Since giving the hand is a common gesture of solemn agreement, the symbolism is natural.

fig 218

fig The fig-tree is an underrated food source and sweetener in antiquity. The irritant, latex-like sap of fig trees was thought to have medicinal qualities. Figs also featured in religious ceremonies, for example the rites of Artemis Orthia in Sparta (*see* SPARTAN CULTS) where boys were beaten with their branches or the Attic *Thargelia, celebrated in May at fig fertilization time, when the *pharmakoi*, 'scapegoats' (*see* PHARMAKOS), wore 'black' and 'white' (male and female) figs.

Filocalus (Furius Dionysius Filocalus), calligrapher of Pope *Damasus I (AD 366–84), produced many of Damasus' inscriptions in the Roman *catacombs. He is perhaps also the author of the *Chronicle of 354*, which contains various tables, lists, and chronicles relating to the history and geography of the city of Rome and the Roman empire, a world chronicle, a calendar of traditional *festivals, a list of Roman bishops and martyrs, and a list of the popes until Liberius.

fire has special status in ancient myth, religion, cosmology, physics, and physiology. According to Greek myth, *Prometheus stole it from the gods for mortals with dire consequences, and the name of the god *Hephaestus is often synonymous with it. Fire figures prominently in the cosmologies of Heraclitus, *Parmenides, the Pythagoreans (*see* PYTHAGORAS AND PYTHAGOREANISM), and *Empedocles, to name only a few. In Stoic physics (*see* STOICISM), fire is the one element which remains constant even when one particular world-order comes to an end. The Stoic *Cleanthes insisted that fire, as heat, gave the whole world its coherence. Fire is normally essential to animal sacrifice, *see* SACRIFICE, GREEK.

Firmicus Maternus (Iulius Firmicus Maternus) of Syracuse, wrote (AD 334–7) an astrological treatise, *Mathesis*, in eight books, the first containing an apologia for *astrology. In this book he promised to provide a Latin summary of the wisdom of Babylonian and Egyptian astrologers. In doing so he reveals considerable ignorance of the technical aspects of the subject; the panegyric on the emperor *Constantine I is however of considerable interest, as is the discourse on the lingering death of *Plotinus. He later converted to *Christianity and wrote *Concerning the Error of Profane Religions*, a blistering attack upon traditional cult in which he urged the emperors Constantius II and Constans to eradicate paganism (343–50). The most interesting features of this work are his effort to contrast pagan symbolism with Christian, his accounts of the origins of some ancient cults, and the insight that he offers into the impact of Constantinian legislation against traditional cults in the western empire.

first-fruits (Gk. *aparchai*; *see also* APARCHĒ). The custom of offering firstlings to the gods from the produce of agriculture, hunting, or fishing was widespread in ancient Greece, ranging in scale from simple gifts in humble agrarian settings to organized donations made in the context of the Eleusinian *mysteries. One common form is known as *panspermia*, the bringing of a mixture of fruits at various festivals, sometimes cooked in a pot (at the *Thargelia and *Pyanopsia). *Thalusia* are, according to the lexicographers, the *aparchai* of the fruits and the first loaf baked after the threshing. Firstlings of animal sacrifice are offered by *Eumaeus in the *Odyssey*. At the mysteries *aparchai* of wheat and barley are requested of all Athenians, allies, and even other Greeks, to be delivered after the spring harvest, and were sold to provide sacrifices and a dedication. In the opinion of the Greeks first-fruits were brought in order to ensure fertility. They survive in ecclesiastical usage in Greece today under the ancient name *kolliva*.

fish, sacred Fish, hard to classify biologically and inhabitants of the alien world of water, had a considerable role in ancient religion (*see* HECATE): in diet, they were sometimes taboo (various species to Pythagoreans, *see* PYTHAGORAS AND PYTHAGOREANISM, and in Egypt), and sometimes ingredients in ritual meals (as in Samothrace). They were kept in *sanctuaries, and sometimes used to provide *oracles (as at Sura in Lycia). The most famous fish observances were connected with the Syrian cult of *Atargatis, which spread to other areas (one inscription is a set of regulations for the care of the fish of this cult at Smyrna): the priests ate the fish, which were prohibited to other worshippers. Fish became important in early Christianity, perhaps in a Syrian tradition, but also because of the acrostic ICHTHYS (I(ēsous) Ch(ristos) th(eou) hy(ios) s(ōtēr): Jesus Christ, Son of God, Saviour).

flamines, Roman priests within the college of the *pontifices. There were three major, and twelve minor flamines, each of them assigned to the worship of a single deity, though this did not preclude their taking part in the worship of other deities, as when the flamen Quirinalis conducted the ritual for *Robigus on 25 April. The three major ones were the flamen Dialis, Martialis, and Quirinalis—of *Jupiter, *Mars, and *Quirinus. These three gods probably formed the most ancient and senior triad of Roman gods, representing the three Indo-European functions of law, warfare, and production. Of the twelve deities served by a minor flamen, we know ten, including *Ceres, *Flora, and *Volcanus; but next to nothing is known of their priests' duties.

The three major flamines were always patricians and chosen by the members of the pontifical college, never elected. The Dialis in historic times was bound by an elaborate system of ritual rules, marking the holiness of his person and protecting it from pollution. These meant that he and his wife (the flaminica) had perpetual religious obligations. If the rules originally applied to other flamines as well, they had been much relaxed by the later republic, for they could hold high office, even up to the consulate; successive pontifices maximi did, however, dispute the right of the flamines to abandon priestly duty, leave Rome, and so hold provincial commands, like other politician-priests; in

the case of the Dialis, this right was still disputed when the priesthood lapsed, for unknown reasons, between 87 and c.12 BC. In this gap, we know that the rituals were maintained by the pontifices. Since the flaminate was the only priesthood devoted to a specific deity, it was the natural model for the new priesthood devised first for Caesar and then for successive emperors after their deaths. Specific rules and privileges were borrowed from old to new flamines, but not the full set of restrictions. See RULER-CULT.

flight of the mind The philosopher Parmenides spoke of his own ascent to knowledge as a journey in a heavenly chariot, and the mind's capacity to explore the universe was adduced by later thinkers as a proof of its innate divinity. When the *soul was conceived as separable, the image could be taken literally: in *Plato's Phaedrus (246c–248c) a pageant of celestial chariots is an allegory for the initial state of souls, and in such works as Cicero's Somnium Scipionis ascent to the stars is the destiny of the good soul after death. Cicero depends on Plato's Timaeus, perhaps through Posidonius; but Maximus of Tyre appeals to the legend of *Aristeas as evidence that the soul is immortal and capable of flight. The motif is found in popular theosophy (e.g. Hermetica; see HERMES TRISMEGISTUS), while parody in *Hermias, Lucretius, Horace, and even perhaps Aristophanes suggests that it was frequent in Pythagoreanism (see PYTHAGORAS AND PYTHAGOREANISM). In the pseudo-Platonic Axiochus a discourse on immortality is said to have translated the hearer's mind to the upper regions, the metaphorical flight being made to anticipate the soul's ascent to heaven, and once again a parody in Lucretius may imply that the thought is common.

flood See DEUCALION.

Flora (Oscan Flusia), an Italian goddess of flowering or blossoming plants, mainly cereals (also found in Agnone, Vittorino, and Furfo, as well as Rome). The antiquity

of her cult in Rome is proved by the existence of a *flamen Floralis* (*see* FLAMINES), but
her festival is not in the 'calendar of Numa'
and therefore was movable (*see* FESTIVALS).
Flora had an old temple on the Quirinal,
dedicated on 3 May, but, shortly after the
foundation of the Floralia in 241–240 BC,
and on the advice of the Sibylline books,
she was given a second temple in 238 close
to the Circus Maximus. Its dedication day
was 28 April. The games (*ludi Florales*) were
celebrated annually from 173 BC. These included farces (*mimi*) of a highly indecent
character. She is often considered a foreign,
heavily Hellenized, goddess, but there is no
decisive reason for seeing Flora as a foreign
goddess.

[Ovid, *Fasti* 5. 183–378]

folk-songs (Greek) The Greeks, like other
peoples, had their folk-songs, often rooted
in ancient popular and ritual traditions.
However, it is impossible to give dates to
the songs or to construct a history. They
may be roughly classified as follows: (*a*) to
gods; (*b*) ritual songs; (*c*) occupational;
(*d*) apotropaic songs; (*e*) love-songs.

folk-tale As an identifiable and critically
useful category of prose narrative the folk-
tale owes its broad characterization to a generalized abstraction of the typical themes,
plots, structures, and characters of the popular stories collected by the Grimm brothers
in Germany in the early 19th cent. and by
A. N. Afanasiev in Russia 50 years later.
These orally transmitted folk-tales, polished
and perfected over centuries by generations
of peasant storytellers, tap into deep strata
of psychological and social wisdom, and are
badly served by their relegation to the nursery, as 'Fairy Tales', in modern societies. As
a general rule, the stories engage protrepti-
cally and optimistically with the problems
faced by the powerless (poor, young, unre-
garded) male hero in his attempts to assert
himself in a world of hostile forces, aided by
animal or supernatural helpers; the goal and
climax consists in maturity and marriage.
Encouraging or consolatory templates for

female behaviour make a natural complement. But the range is wide, and the invention fertile. Aarne and Thompson attempted
to gain an overview by laboriously classify-
ing themes and motifs ('Learning to play
fiddle: finger caught in cleft'), but an altogether more acute and sophisticated analytical approach was carved out by Vladimir
Propp, who brilliantly showed how the apparently random proliferation of narrative
possibilities could be reduced to an elegant
algebra of permitted moves and structural
sequences. Greek (and to a smaller extent
Roman) tales offer a cornucopia of such
themes, whose extent can only be hinted at
here. The careers of *Perseus and *Bellerophon are perfect exemplifications of the
basic type (which can be traced even further
back, to 13th-cent. Egypt, as with *The Tale of
Two Brothers*). The Odyssean episode of the
hero trapped in the giant's cave (*see* CYCLO-
PES; ODYSSEUS) finds parallels from Finland
to Mongolia, and though some of these may
be secondary refractions of the famous
Homeric account, it beggars belief that *all*
other versions fall into this category; early
oral diffusion of the powerfully attractive
theme, from some undetermined source,
seems probable. Herodotus too adapts many
folk-tales to the purposes of his Histories,
notably the pranks of the unnamed trick-
ster-thief who pitted his wits against the
Pharaoh Rhampsinitus, and who survives as
the *Meisterdieb* of the Grimms' collection;
cf. also e.g. Herodotus' tales of Perdiccas,
Euenius, *Arion, or Democedes. Even 5th-
cent. drama draws up plots from the folk-
tale reservoir (*Sophocles's lost *Polyidus*, *Euripides' *Alcestis*), and the same is true of Hellenistic poetry (*Erysichthon, and Acontius
and Cydippe, in *Callimachus). There is at
least a prima facie case for supposing
that some ancient Greek tales have managed
to retain their core structure intact through
constant retellings right down to modern
times. In Latin, the classical example is
the Cinderella-like story of Cupid and
Psyche, recounted in a much elaborated
version by *Apuleius. Even this brief sketch

should make it clear that while this is a rich and underexploited field of research at least two obstacles stand in the way of any attempt to focus the subject more precisely: first, the impossibility of marking off Greek 'folk-tale' from myth, legend, saga, popular history, and biography, etc.; secondly, the fact that since our knowledge of the form in Graeco-Roman culture is by definition confined to preserved *literary* texts the relevant material is necessarily contaminated with features determined by its generic context.

Fontinalia, Roman festival on 13 October to Fons, god of *springs, at Rome outside the porta Fontinalis.

food, religious *See* CAKES; SACRIFICE; WINE.

Fordicidia (Sabine *Hordicidia*), Roman *festival on 15 April, when a *forda* (pregnant cow) was sacrificed to *Tellus. It and the *Fornacalia were the only festivals which in historic times were organized on the basis of the archaic political units the *curiae*.

[Ovid, *Fasti* 4. 629–72]

forgeries, religious The idea of literary property had already evolved by the 5th cent. BC, when Herodotus doubted the Homeric authorship of the epics *Epigoni* and *Cypria* (*see* EPIC CYCLE). Even then, and even when bibliographic scholarship developed in the 3rd cent. BC, *pseudepigraphic literature continued to circulate. Forgeries form a subclass: works written, or at least attributed (it is often unclear which), with intent to deceive. Claiming religious or mythical authority was one motive for forgery. Solon and Pisistratus allegedly interpolated the Homeric text in Athens' interest; Onomacritus inserted an oracle of his own among those of *Musaeus. Gaps in the record invited filling: Musaeus and *Orpheus, many Pythagorea and Epicharmea (*see* PYTHAGORAS AND PYTHAGOREANISM). A Lycian temple displayed a letter (on papyrus) written by *Sarpedon from Troy. The seven books on pontifical law by King *Numa Pompilius found in 187 BC must have been

a forgery, i.e. a work written by someone other than Numa and deliberately passed off as the king's.

Fornacalia, one of the movable *festivals (*feriae conceptivae*), tied to the Quirinalia (17 February) and celebrated then. It was called 'fools' festival' according to *Ovid because those too stupid to know their *curiae* (subdivision of the people) celebrated then instead of on the proper day, proclaimed by the relevant official. This makes it a festival of the *curiae*, not the people. It consisted of ritual either to benefit the ovens (*fornaces*) which parched grain, or to propitiate the obscure goddess Fornax.

[Ovid, *Fasti* 2. 257–32]

Fortuna/Fors, the goddess of Chance or Luck, Greek *Tyche, of great importance in Italian and Roman religion, but not thought by the Romans to be part of the oldest level of their religious system (no feast-day in the oldest calendar, and no *flamen*; *see* FLAMINES). Instead, her introduction was importantly attributed to the rather anomalous figure of King Servius *Tullius, who was associated with several of the more important of her numerous cults at Rome. Oracles of Fortuna existed outside Rome at Antium and at *Praeneste, where the important cult of Fortuna Primigenia ('the First-born') was much embellished in the 2nd cent. BC during the age of Roman and Italian success in Mediterranean conquest and its economic rewards. Fortuna-cults combined political achievement and a patronage of procreation; for the latter see, for example, a dedication by a local woman to Praenestine Fortuna as daughter of *Jupiter, to secure procreation, and note the existence of an important cult of Fortuna Muliebris, 'Women's Luck'.

At Rome the most important early cults of Fortuna were that of Fors Fortuna on the right bank of the *Tiber and that of the forum Boarium. Here Fortuna was twinned with the cult of *Matuta Mater (the goddesses shared a festival on 11 June), and the paired temples have been revealed in the excavations near the forum Boarium: the cults are indeed archaic in date. The cult statue was draped in two togas, which rendered it practically invisible. Praenestine Fortuna Primigenia was adopted at the end of the 3rd cent. BC in an important cult of Fortuna Publica Populi Romani (the 'Official Good Luck of the Roman People') on the Quirinal hill outside the porta Collina. No temple at Rome, however, rivalled the magnificence of the Praenestine sanctuary. The Fortune that won battles or wars was also the object of a number of cults, and the goddess in various guises was important to the presentation of late-republican leaders and the emperors (*Augustus' cult of the 'Fortune of Return' (from duty in the provinces), Fortuna Redux, is an example).

[Ovid, *Fasti* 6. 569–636]

forum, an open square or market-place in a Roman town, hence the name of several Roman market towns such as Forum Appii, Iulii, etc. In contrast to the forum Boarium (cattle market) and Holitorium (vegetable market) at Rome, the *forum Romanum was also a place of public business, a role later shared with the imperial fora. Public fora of this kind, combining political, religious, judicial, and commercial functions, formed the focal point of most Roman towns particularly in the western empire. A typical forum, as at Pompeii, was a long, rectangular open space flanked by a variety of public buildings, including variously temples, basilicas, speakers' platforms, senate-house, and other public offices, as well as inns and restaurants, often in an informal arrangement with colonnades on two or more sides; the open space was adorned with honorific statues and other minor monuments. The imperial fora at Rome provided models for more monumental complexes, most common in the European provinces (e.g. Tarraco (mod. Tarragona), Spain; Augusta Raurica (mod. Augst), Switzerland) but also found in North Africa (e.g. Lepcis Magna). These were symmetrical colonnaded squares, dom-

inated by either a major temple (usually either a *capitolium* (temple of the Capitoline triad *Jupiter, *Juno, and *Minerva) or dedicated to the imperial (*ruler-cult) or a transverse *basilica across one short end, or both. *See* AGORA; CAPITOL.

forum Augustum or Augusti, dedicated in 2 BC, the vast precinct (110×83 m.: 361×272 ft.) of *Mars Ultor in Rome, vowed by the future emperor *Augustus at the battle of Philippi. The marble Corinthian temple, with eight columns across the front, stood on a lofty podium at the north end; the interior of the cella, flanked by columns, terminated in an apse housing a colossal statue of Mars; in the cella there were also statues of *Venus, and Divus Julius. Caesar's sword and many works of art were kept there. The temple was set against a high precinct wall of fire-resistant marble, which cut off the neighbouring district, the Subura. Broad flights of steps flanking the temple led from the Subura into the forum through *triumphal arches, dedicated under the emperor Tiberius to Drusus and Germanicus. The forum area was flanked by Corinthian porticoes enriched with coloured marble, and crowned by a tall attic decorated with *caryatides copied from the *Erechtheum at Athens; behind these were large semicircular exedrae. Statues of *Romulus and of *Aeneas adorned the exedrae, while others representing the Julian family and Roman state heroes decorated the porticoes; laudatory inscriptions from the bases of the statues survive. Here youths assumed the *toga virilis* (the symbol of manhood) and provincial governors ceremoniously departed or returned.

[Ovid, *Fasti* 5. 545–98]

forum Romanum, the chief public square of Rome, surrounded by monumental buildings, occupied a swampy trough between the hills of the Palatine, Velia, Quirinal, and Capitol. The edges of the marsh were covered with cemeteries of early iron age settlements on the surrounding hills, until the area was made suitable for building in the late 7th cent. BC by the canalizing of the Cloaca Maxima, and the deposition of considerable quantities of fill. The *Regia and temple of *Vesta were traditionally associated with this period, while the earliest dated monuments are the temples of *Saturnus (497 BC) and *Castor (484 BC). The forum became the centre of Roman religious, ceremonial, and commercial life, as well as the political activities which took place in the adjacent Comitium; balconies were in 338 BC built above the shops surrounding the forum, to allow for the viewing of the gladiatorial shows which took place there. Butchers and fishmongers were, however, soon relegated to separate buildings, as more monumental buildings were constructed around the forum. *Basilicas were introduced from184 BC onwards.

In 121 BC the temple of Concord was restored, following the assassination of C. Sempronius Gracchus and his supporters. The temple of Castor was rebuilt in 117. Much of the present setting, however, is due to Sulla, Julius *Caesar, and *Augustus. Sulla rebuilt the senate house on a larger scale to accommodate the senate of 600 members; Caesar planned a new basilica Iulia, which, like his Curia Iulia, was finished by Augustus. After Caesar's assassination a column was erected to mark the site of his pyre and later (29 BC) replaced by the temple of Divus Iulius; this, and the adjacent Parthian arch of Augustus (19 BC), had the effect of monumentalizing the east end of the forum. New Rostra (speakers' platforms) in front of the temple of Divus Iulius faced the 'old' Rostra, rebuilt by Caesar and then Augustus. Many ancient monuments were restored: the Regia (36 BC), the basilica Aemilia (14 BC), and the temples of Saturnus (42 BC), Castor (AD 6), and *Concordia (AD 10).

Comparatively few changes were made to the topography of the forum under the empire; the imperial fora, the *Campus Martius, and the *Palatine provided more scope for emperors keen to make their mark on the city. New temples were, however, dedicated to deified emperors and empresses (Augustus, Vespasian, Antoninus Pius, and Annia Galeria Faustina), while Domitian set up an equestrian statue of himself in AD 91; and the arch of Septimius Severus was built in AD 203. A major fire in AD 283, however, provided an opportunity for a major reconstruction under Diocletian, with a row of monumental columns set up in front of the basilica Iulia, and the Curia rebuilt.

founders, city Founders were chiefly important before Alexander the Great in the case of colonies, founded under the leadership of an *oikistēs*, whose achievements frequently led to his posthumous worship as a hero (*see* HERO-CULT). In 5th-cent. BC Athens oikists were state officials who returned home after completing their task, as with Hagnon at Amphipolis. Among Hellenistic founders of cities (*ktistēs* was now the preferred term) kings naturally loomed largest, although not all attended in person the founding rituals like Alexander the Great. As a device for asserting a Hellenic ancestry compatible with the cultural and ethnic preferences of the ruling power, city-founders acquired a new significance in the Hellenistic and Roman empires: thus Cilician Mallus gained tax-exemption from Alexander on the strength of mutual kinship through Argos. Precisely because such claims had a political value, their 'truthfulness' must be assessed cautiously, especially when they were set in the mythic past and demand belief in otherwise unattested mainland Greek colonization of Asia. In the Roman east, stimulated by the *Panhellenion, city-founders were celebrated in local coinages and monuments as important sources of civic prestige; orators were advised to measure their praise according to the order 'god, hero, or man'. '*Ktistēs*' by now was also an honorific title applied to civic benefactors, especially patrons of building. *See also* ARCHĒGETĒS.

fratres arvales (Arval Brothers), a priestly college in Rome. Our detailed knowledge of the brotherhood comes from their inscribed records (now known as the *Acta fratrum* *arvalium*), found mostly on the site of their sacred grove 8 km. (5 mi.) outside Rome on the *via Campana* (mod. La Magliana). The earliest surviving inscription dates from 21-20 BC, while the only republican reference to the arvals is found in *Varro. It is a reasonable conjecture that the brotherhood was an ancient priesthood of the city, which had ceased to function by the end of the republic and was revived under *Augustus.

The college consisted of twelve members chosen from senatorial families by co-optation; the reigning emperor was always a member. The president (*magister*) and the other main official (*flamen, see* FLAMINES) were elected annually. Their main ritual obligation was the festival of the goddess *Dea Dia, to whom their grove was dedicated. In the course of this festival the brothers sang the famous 'song' of the Arval Brothers, the *Carmen arvale.* Their other rituals mainly concerned the imperial house: annual vows 'for the safety of' the reigning emperor, sacrifices on his birthday, on his recovery from illness, etc.

Their grove has been partly excavated; it housed not only a temple of Dea Dia, but a variety of other cult buildings (a 'tetrastyle' dining-room; a shrine of the imperial cult; a bath-building; even a circus). These buildings appear not to have been dismantled until the very end of the 4th cent. AD, even though the inscribed texts cease some time before (a fragment survives from 304; but the main series stops in the mid-3rd cent.).

Fulgentius, (Fabius Planciades Fulgentius), a late 5th-cent. Christian writer from somewhere outside Rome, possibly Carthage, to whom are attributed the *Mythologiae*, a set of allegorical interpretations of various pagan myths, the *Expositio Vergilianae*

continentiae secundum philosophos moralis, an allegorical interpretation of the *Aeneid*, and the *Expositio sermonum antiquorum*, an explanation of 62 obsolete words illustrated by citations of a wide range of authors. The three works, which share a single manuscript tradition, are marked by considerable foolishness of thought and by an extremely mannered style. Many of the citations Fulgentius makes of earlier Greek and Latin authors have been thought bogus. The *De aetatibus mundi et hominis*, a summary of world history, sacred and profane, is attributed by its manuscript tradition to a 'Fabius Claudius Gordianus Fulgentius'. It resembles in quality of thought and style the mythological and lexicological works attributed to Fabius Planciades Fulgentius. All four works, and in particular the *Mythologiae*, were much read in the Middle Ages. They were then attributed to a Fulgentius, bishop of Ruspe (AD 467–532), the author of a number of sermons and rhetorically but soberly expressed refutations of *Arianism and Pelagianism (*see* PELAGIUS). Some scholars still accept this attribution.

Furies *See* ERINYES.

Furrina, Roman goddess whose relatively early importance is reflected in the festival of the Furrinalia (25 July) and the existence of a *flamen Furrinalis* (*see* FLAMINES). Her cult at Rome was located in a sacred grove on the slopes of the Janiculum hill in Transtiberim. The site, in a well-watered cleft in the hillside, became an important cult place in the Syrian tradition in the later empire (*see* SYRIAN DEITIES), and its remains offer an interesting case history of the constant process of reinterpretation of the forms of cult in the religious tradition of the city.

Gaia, Gē, the Earth, a primordial goddess. In *Hesiod, the original entity was *Chaos, then came Gaia and other beings like *Eros. Gaia had many children from her son *Uranus, including the *Titans. In the conflict between the *Olympians and the Titans she assists *Zeus by telling him what he needs to do to win. But after the defeat of the Titans she produces, from her union with *Tartarus, the monster *Typhon who was a threat to the order of the Olympians, but was defeated by Zeus. The Olympians chose Zeus as their ruler on Gaia's advice. She is generally ambivalent: she can be deceitful and threatening, dangerous, and gives birth to creatures that pester gods and men. But she is also a positive nurturing figure. In Athens there was an important cult of Gē Kourotrophos; the sanctuary of Gē Kourotrophos and *Demeter Chloe was near the entrance to the Acropolis. Besides offerings to Gē and to Gē Kourotrophos and other mentions of the latter, there also appears in sacrificial *calendars, a figure called simply *Kourotrophos, who may have been identical to Gē Kourotrophos, though we cannot be certain. A popular episode in Attic art is the representation of the birth of *Erichthonius, where Gaia is shown as a woman emerging from the ground, handing the baby Erichthonius to Athena. The story that Gaia was the original owner of the *Delphic oracle is not a reflection of cult history, but a myth. The earliest evidence for a cult of Gaia at Delphi is early 5th cent. BC. At *Olympia the sanctuary of Gaia (Gaion) had an ash altar of Gaia and it was said that in earlier times there had been an oracle of Gē there.

Galatea (Gk. *Galateia*, perhaps 'milk-white'), name of a sea-nymph, first in *Homer's *Iliad*; her legend was apparently first told by the early 4th-cent. Sicilian poet Philoxenus. Polyphemus (*see* CYCLOPES) loved her, and wooed her uncouthly; the story is a favourite especially with pastoral writers (Theocritus, Bion, Moschus, Virgil) and also Ovid. In this last, the earliest surviving passage which adds anything important to the story, Galatea loved a youth, Acis, son of Faunus (Pan?) and a river-nymph. Together they listened in hiding to Polyphemus' love-song, but when he had finished he rose to go and caught sight of them. Galatea dived into the sea, but Polyphemus pursued Acis and hurled a huge rock at him. As it fell on him and crushed him, Galatea turned him into a river, which bore his name ever after. The whole may well be a local Sicilian tale. The resemblance between Galatea's name and *Galates*, a Gaul, seems to underlie a less-known version in which she finally accepted Polyphemus' attentions and had by him a son, Galas or Galates—a pseudo-historical or pseudo-mythical explanation of the ancestry of the ghouls. The love-story appears in Roman art, especially wall-painting.

[Homer, *Iliad* 18. 45; Ovid, *Metamorphoses* 13. 738 ff.]

Galinthias, friend or servant of *Alcmene. When, at *Hera's command, *Eileithyia and the Moirai (*see* FATE) were delaying the birth of *Heracles, she broke their spell by shouting that Alcmene had given birth.

Galinthias was punished by being turned into a weasel. In its first occurrence known to us, probably belonging to the 2nd century BC, the story is told as explanation for a Theban ritual. It is also told by *Ovid of Galanthis. Other sources tell of the weasel, not the person.

Ganymedes (the name suggests *ganos*, 'sheen' (esp. of wine) + *mēdea*, ambiguously 'cunning', and 'genitals'); handsome young Trojan prince (son of Tros in the *Iliad*, of *Laomedon in the *Epic Cycle and *Euripides) carried off to *Olympus by *Zeus, as his compatriot Tithonus was by *Eos the dawn-goddess. His kidnapping is usually said to have been effected by Zeus himself, either in person (as on the fine 5th-cent. BC terracotta from *Olympia), or in the shape of his associated bird, the eagle. As reparation, his father received either a marvellous breed of horses or a golden vine. Though early versions emphasize the boy's beauty, Zeus' motivation is given as the need for a noble and presentable wine-steward; a homoerotic interest on the god's part does not become explicit until later, but Attic vase-painting and Hellenistic art stress this aspect (hence 'catamite', from *catmite* in Etruscan via Latin *catamitus*).

Gello, vicious female spirit (like *Empusa, *Lamia, and *Mormo) that steals children, in ancient, medieval, and modern Greek belief, first attested in Sappho (7th/6th cent. BC). Supposedly she was a woman from Lesbos who died untimely. In modern times the name has been associated with *Gallū*, Sumerian/Akkadian term for a demon. *See* FOLK-TALE.

genealogy, the enumeration of descent from an ancestor. Legendary pedigree was particularly important in Greece. Before fighting, *Homeric heroes boast of their ancestry, citing between two and eight generations of ancestors. *Hesiod's poetry is preoccupied with legendary ancestry; even aristocrats in Classical Athens (which put more stress on recent achievements) claimed descent from important local and Homeric heroes, and thence from the gods. The politician and orator Andocides was descended from *Odysseus and therefore *Hermes, Alcibiades from Eurysaces (and *Zeus), *Plato from Solon and *Codrus. Other groups, cities, colonies, or tribes might trace descent from a single legendary figure (*see* FOUNDERS, CITY), and genealogies were sometimes akin to king-lists, for instance in Sparta, or assimilated with lists of office-holders. Some of the first prose writers recorded (or worked out) genealogies, mostly legendary, as well as their chronological implications: *Hecataeus (1) (*c*.500 BC), *Acusilaus, *Pherecydes (2), *Hellanicus. Genealogies and their enumeration were evidently popular despite *Plato's criticisms. They reflect the enormous significance attributed by the Greeks to origins and the original ancestor in determining the character of future generations. Prestige, status, even moral character, might be derived from the original progenitor, preferably legendary, heroic, or divine. (The Romans, more interested in their recent ancestors, only adopted the Greek penchant for legendary ancestry in the course of Hellenization from the 2nd cent. BC.) Political and tribal affiliations might, similarly, be seen in genealogical terms. Given the value of the original ancestor, it is therefore unsurprising that the intervening links were sometimes vague or forgotten, and it may be the professional genealogists who did much to create continuous and coherent stemmata. However, intermediate ancestors would also, obviously, carry prestige or opprobrium, and unsuitable ancestors would drop from view. Such is the moral or political importance of ancestry, that genealogy tends to reflect the current position or claims of a family, and thus it is usually the least reliable of historical traditions. Numerous inconsistencies would arise from the symbolic reflection of current status in past genealogy, and it is these contradictions which the genealogists were in part trying to resolve.

genius, lit. 'that which is just born'. The *genius*, once understood as the deification of the power of generation, is now defined as 'the entirety of the traits united in a begotten being'. It is a deified concept, its seat in the forehead, and is not far from the notion of the self. The *genius* forms the 'double' of the male, and is both born and dies with him. The same idea was developed for the 'double' of a woman (the *iuno*). This divine being, distinct from its human 'double', was the object of a cult. Although in common parlance every male, slave or free, seems to have a *genius*, in family-cult only one *genius* was honoured in each *household, that of its head, the *paterfamilias*, particularly on the occasion of marriage, but also in the ordinary worship at the shrine of the *Lares. Visual depictions of such scenes may show, for instance, a large serpent, bearded and therefore male—a well-known convention in Roman art—beneath a scene of sacrifice, or two such serpents, one beardless—i.e. female, presumably the *iuno* of the *materfamilias*. The *genius* of the *paterfamilias* was also invoked as a witness during oath-taking by family members.

The *genius* was not limited to individual humans. Divinities equally, at least ones with an official 'birth' or entry into the body of communal cults, possessed a *genius* or a *iuno*. By extension every locality and establishment where the Romans exercised an activity had a *genius* which expressed the totality of its traits at the moment of constitution. The cult of the *genius* of the *paterfamilias*, a pillar of domestic and client relationships, was used by *Augustus to link Roman citizens closely to his person: associated with the *Lares Augusti* in crossroads-shrines, invoked with the *genius* of the *paterfamilias* at private banquets, the *genius Augusti*, double of the living emperor, rapidly became an important element in Roman *ruler-cult. It was generally represented (like the *iuno* of the empresses) by a toga-clad male with the features of the ruler, carrying a cornucopia and often a patera (dish for *libations). In the speculations of

grammarians and philosophers the *genius* was assimilated to the Greek *daimōn.

genos The word *genos* (pl. *genē*) was widely and variously used in Greek of all periods to denote 'species', 'category', 'race', 'family', etc. Probably from its use to denote '(noble) lineage', it came to be used in the 4th cent. BC in a quasi-precise sense to denote a set of families or individuals who identified themselves as a group by the use of a collective plural name. Some such names were geographical (e.g. Salaminioi, 'from Salamis') or occupational (e.g. Bouzygai, 'ox-yokers'), but most were patronymic in form (e.g. Amynandridai, Titakidai), implying the descent of their members—the *gennētai*—from a fictive or real common male ancestor. About 60 such groups are known. Since certain 5th-cent. inscriptions define the responsibilities and privileges of various *genē* in matters of cult, *genē* may primarily have been the groups or lineages which provided the holders of certain major hereditary priesthoods. However, not all *genē* are known to have 'possessed' priesthoods or other cultic privileges, and it is often supposed that the word was used to refer to diversely constituted groups. But like most groups in Greek cities, even the *genē* which were not priestly in origin will have celebrated common *sacrifices, as the nearly complete festival *calendar of the Salaminioi shows.

Geryon *See* HERACLES.

gestures Among both the Greeks and Romans, certain gestures and postures were appropriate to religious ritual. The commonest *prayer gesture, which the Greeks considered to be in universal use, was that of stretching the hands outwards and upwards—towards the sky, they explained. When praying to the dead or to a *chthonian deity, the palms of the hands might face downwards. Standing was the usual posture, but kneeling was not unknown, especially in desperate or strongly emotional circumstances, in which cases prayer becomes assimilated to the supplication of a powerful human. Reliefs depicting cult scenes show that more elaborate hand gestures may have been used by priests and worshippers in certain cults. *See* PROSKYNESIS.

Giants, a mythological race of monstrous appearance and great strength. According to *Hesiod they were sons of Gē (Earth) from the blood of *Gaia/*Uranus which fell upon earth; he describes them as valiant warriors. *Homer considers them a savage race of men who perished with their king Eurymedon. The prevailing legend of the fight of the gods and the Giants was formulated in Archaic epics and was embroidered by many later writers. A substantial account is given by *Apollodorus. When the gods were attacked by the Giants they learned that they could win only if they were assisted by a mortal. They called in *Heracles, who killed the giant Alcyoneus and many others with his arrows. *Zeus, who led the gods, smote with his thunderbolt Porphyrion who attempted to ravish *Hera; *Athena killed Pallas or Enceladus; *Poseidon crushed Polybotes under the rock that became the island of Nisyros; *Apollo shot Ephialtes; *Hermes slew Hippolytus; *Dionysus killed Eurytus and many other Giants besides who were caught in his vine; and *Hephaestus aided the gods, throwing red-hot iron as missiles. The Giants were defeated and were believed to be buried under the volcanoes in various parts of Greece and Italy, e.g. Enceladus under Etna. Bones of prehistoric animals were occasionally believed to be bones of giants.

The Battle of the Giants was one of the most popular myths in Greece and the names of participants and the episodes of the battle vary from writer to writer and from representation to representation. Zeus, Heracles, Poseidon, and later Athena, are the usual protagonists. In its early stage the myth seems to represent a variation of the popular motif of the tribe that attempted to dethrone the gods; in a more advanced stage of culture the myth was interpreted as

the fight of civilization against barbarism.

In art the Giants are first shown as warriors or wild men, later as snake-legged monsters. The most famous sculptural renderings are found on the Archaic treasury of the Siphnians at *Delphi and on the Hellenistic altar of Pergamum.

[Homer, *Odyssey* 7. 59; Hesiod, *Theogony* 185; Apollodorus 1. 6. 1]

Glauce, feminine of the adjective *glaukos* ('grey'), the colour of the sea, hence applied to water divinities. A spring Glauce at Corinth (*see* CORINTHIAN MYTHS AND CULTS) is named, as often, after a mythic maiden who committed suicide there. She develops into the daughter of the king 'Creon' ('ruler') whose marriage to *Jason (1) in *Euripides' *Medea* sets the plot in motion. (*See also* CREUSA (3).)

Glaucus, a name given to several, apparently unrelated, characters, of whom the following stand out:

(1) Glaucus son of Hippolochus, with his cousin *Sarpedon led the Lycians at Troy. He subsequently fell fighting over the body of *Achilles. Glaucus claimed descent through his grandfather *Bellerophon from Glaucus (2). The Lycian connection would be in harmony with other Corinthian links with the east.

(2) Glaucus son of *Sisyphus, of Ephyre (that is, probably, Corinth). Identified by *Asclepiades of Tragilus as the Glaucus of Potniae who was eaten by his horses at the funeral games for *Pelias (*Pausanias identifies him as the Taraxippus, 'Horse-scarer', at Isthmia). The story may go back to *Aeschylus' lost play *Glaucus Potnieus*. Most sources locate the horses' (usually mares) stables at Potniae south of Thebes (*see* THEBES, MYTHS OF), but why this should be so is not clear.

(3) Glaucus infant son of *Minos and Pasiphae, who fell into a jar of honey and was drowned. His body was recovered by the seer *Polyeidus, who revived him, gave him the gift of prophecy but later revoked it.

(4) Glaucus Pontius or Thalassius, a sea-

daimōn with prophetic powers. Located, at least since Aeschylus' *Glaucus Pontius* in the vicinity of the Euboean strait. He was a mortal deified, usually by eating a magical herb. He may have had cult in the Marathonian region of Attica. The people of Boeotian Anthedon claimed him as one of their own.

[(1) Homer, *Iliad* 2. 876, 6. 152–21, etc.; (2) Pausanias 6. 20. 19; (4) Euripides, *Orestes* 362–5; Ovid, *Metamorphoses* 13. 903–6; Pausanias 9. 22. 6–7]

Gnosticism is a generic term primarily used of theosophical groups which broke with the 2nd-cent. Christian Church (*see* CHRISTIANITY). A wider, more imprecise use of the term describes a syncretistic religiosity diffused in the near east, contemporaneous with and independent of Christianity. In recent years (especially following the full publication of the Coptic Gnostic texts discovered at Nag Hammadi in Upper Egypt in 1946), the diversity of beliefs in the various 'Gnostic' sects has been increasingly emphasized, with some scholars unwilling any longer to use 'Gnosticism' as a collective term at all, or even the broad grouping into 'Valentinian' and 'Sethian' traditions, but no new consensus has yet emerged. Many ingredients of 2nd-cent. Gnosticism are pre-Christian, but there is no evidence of a pre-Christian religion or cultic myth resembling Christianity as closely as the systems of Basilides, Valentinus, and *Manichaeism, all of which owed the essentials of their beliefs to Christianity, or even as the doctrine of Simon Magus, which provided a rival religion of redemption with a redeemer replacing Christ.

The principal characteristics of the 2nd-cent. sects are (1) a radical rejection of the visible world as being alien to the supreme God and as incompatible with truth as darkness with light; (2) the assertion that elect souls are divine sparks temporarily imprisoned in matter as a result of a precosmic catastrophe, but saved by a redeemer, sent from the transcendent God, whose teachings awake the sleepwalking soul to a consciousness of its origins and destiny, and also

include instructions how to pass the blind planetary powers which bar the *soul's ascent to its celestial home. The first proposition has close affinities with late Jewish *apocalyptic; for the second the Gnostics claimed, with some reason, large support in the dialogues of *Plato.

To explain how humanity came to need such drastic redemption, many Gnostics expounded Genesis 1–3 as an allegory of the fall of a female cosmic power, normally termed Sophia, a primal 'sin' (arising from restlessness or inquisitiveness) which led to the making of this visible world by an incompetent or malevolent creator. So the natural world betrays nothing of a beneficent creative intention. This cosmogony provided the ground for an ethic which in most sects was rabidly ascetic, but in a few groups (especially Carpocrates') produced a religion of eroticism, supported by privileging grace in St *Paul's antithesis of law and grace and by an extreme predestinarianism.

The principal sources of Gnosticism are the Platonist dualism of the intelligible and sense-perceptible (material) realms, in which matter is invested with quasi-demonic properties by what was seen by later Platonists as an evil world-soul, Hellenized forms of Zoroastrianism (chiefly attested in *Plutarch's interpretation of *Isis and *Osiris), Mithraism (*see* MITHRAS) with its theme of the soul's ascent through the seven planets (modified to form part of the Ophite Gnostic system as described in *Origen), *Judaism which, besides the Book of Genesis, contributed the apocalyptic themes of the conflict between angelic powers and of the deliverance of the elect from this evil world, Hermeticism (Hermetic tracts feature in the Nag Hammadi corpus), and above all *Christianity. The evidence of the Pauline Epistles (esp. Galatians, 1 Corinthians, Colossians) shows the author (who may not always be Paul) using language often close to that of Gnosticism, and at the same time strenuously resisting Gnostic tendencies in the churches. The fact that some of the proto-Gnostic elements in the Epistles can also be found in *Philon (1) suggests that extreme liberalizing Judaism was a material cause of Gnostic origins. Nevertheless, the Jewish element is not strong in all the systems, and in many there is an anti-Semitic spirit. From the 2nd cent., attitudes resembling Gnosticism appear in pagan texts, especially in *Plutarch's theosophical tracts, the Hermetic corpus, *Numenius of Apamea, the *Chaldaean Oracles, and alchemists like Zosimus. It is entirely possible that some Gnostic influence passed from Numenius to *Plotinus and *Porphyry. Plotinus' passionate attack on the Gnostics (*Enneads* 2. 9) reads like the work of a man who not only had to purge his own circle but felt within himself the power of Gnostic attitudes; and the *theurgy of later *Neoplatonism is near to some of the grosser forms of 2nd-cent. Gnosticism combated by the Church. See HERMES TRISMEGISTUS; ZOROASTER.

In Christianity Gnosticism produced a sharp reaction against its rejection of the doctrines of the goodness of the creation and the freedom of man. The capacity of individual sects for survival was also weakened by the syncretistic acceptance of all religious myths as valid and true (see SYNCRETISM). Nevertheless, Gnosticism had a strikingly successful future in Manicheism, one form of which still survives in the Mandaeans of Iraq.

gods For an introduction, see GREEK RELIGION. There was sometimes made a distinction between heavenly Gods, who lived on *Olympus (for a list see OLYMPIAN GODS), and earthly Gods and heroes, both of whom were associated with the earth (see CHTHONIAN GODS, HERO-CULT). See also GENEALOGICAL TABLES (1) GREEK GODS. Sacrifices were one way that the differences between these beings might be expressed ritually (see ALTARS; SACRIFICE, GREEK). The term for a Greek God was *theos, for a Roman deus. Traditionally, the Gods were described in human form (anthropomorphically), and such depictions were dominant throughout antiquity, but from the Archaic period

onwards intellectuals challenged anthropomorphism in favour of more abstract views of deity (see ARISTOTLE; NEOPLATONISM; PLATO; STOICISM). Jews and Christians had an idea of the divine which stressed the oneness of God, and sometimes drew gratefully on arguments already employed by pagan intellectuals (see APOLOGISTS, CHRISTIAN; CHRISTIANITY; MONOTHEISM; JUDAISM). Within Christianity fierce debates arose in the 4th cent. because of the difficulty of talking both about the oneness of God and the uniqueness of Jesus (see ARIANISM).

golden age, an imagined period in early human history when human beings lived a life of ease, far from toil and sin. The most important text is *Hesiod's *Works and Days*, which talks of a 'golden *genos*', i.e. species or generation, as the first in a series: reference to a golden *age* occurs first in Latin. The motif was widespread in ancient literature and parodied in comedy from the 5th cent. BC. The golden age is associated especially with *Cronus or *Saturnus and is marked by communal living and the spontaneous supply of food: its end comes with a series of inventions that lead to the modern condition of humanity (typically first plough, first ship, first walls, and first sword). Rationalist thinkers tended to reject the model in favour of 'hard' primitivism or a belief in progress, but the function of the myth was always to hold up a mirror to present malaises or to presage a future return to the idyll.

[Hesiod, *Works and Days* 109–26; Aratus, *Phaenomena* 100–14; Ovid, *Metamorphoses* 1. 89–112]

Golden Fleece See ARGONAUTS; JASON (1); MEDEA; PELIAS.

Gorgo/Medusa, female monsters in Greek mythology. According to the canonical version of the myth related by *Apollodorus, *Perseus was ordered to fetch the head of Medusa, the mortal sister of Sthenno and Euryale; through their horrific appearance these Gorgons turned to stone anyone who looked at them. With the help of *Athena, *Hermes, and *nymphs, who had supplied him with winged sandals, *Hades' cap of invisibility, and a sickle (*harpē*) Perseus managed to behead Medusa in her sleep; from her head sprang Chrysaor and the horse *Pegasus. Although pursued by Medusa's sisters, Perseus escaped and, eventually, turned his enemy Polydectes to stone by means of Medusa's head.

*Hesiod already knows the myth which shows oriental influence: the Gorgons' iconography has been borrowed from that of Mesopotamian Lamashtu; Perseus saved *Andromeda in Ioppe-Jaffa, and an oriental seal shows a young hero seizing a demonic creature whilst holding a *harpē*. Gorgons were very popular—often with an apotropaic function, as on temple-pediments—in Archaic art, which represented them as women with open mouth and dangerous teeth, but in the 5th cent. they lost their frightening appearance and became beautiful women; consequently, the myth is hardly found in art after the 4th cent. BC.

Perseus' adventure was already popular in Etruria in the 5th cent. Roman authors concentrated especially on Medusa's frightening head.

Perseus was connected with *initiation in Mycenae, and his slaying of Medusa probably has an initiatory background: the reflection of the young warrior's test. Actually, descriptions of the Gorgo's head relate features of the Archaic warrior's fury: fearful looks, gaping grin, gnashing of teeth, violent war cry. The popularity of the Gorgo's head, the Gorgoneion, on warriors' shields also points to its terrifying effects. The myth of Perseus and Medusa, then, is an important example of the complex interrelations in the Archaic age between narrative and iconographical motifs, between Greece and the orient.

[Hesiod, *Theogony* 270–82; Apollodorus 2. 4. 1–2; Ovid, *Metamorphoses* 4. 604–5. 249; Lucan 9. 624–733]

Graeae (Gk. *Graiai*, 'Crones'), supporting actors in the cast of the *Perseus *folk-tale. *Hesiod makes them daughters of the monstrous pair *Phorcys and Ceto, like the Gorgons; and their role is to be pale precursors and minimally equipped counterparts of that powerful trio (*see* GORGO). While their sisters are characterized by their writhing snaky locks, gnashing fangs, and deadly glare, these feeble hags are greyhaired from birth and can muster only a lone tooth and a single eye between them, which they must use in turn; Perseus intercepts the eye as it is handed from one to another, thus forcing them to reveal the next stage of his quest. Hesiod knows two names, Pemphredo and Enyo; Aeschylus has the more usual three-sister pattern (*Charites; cf. *Harpyiae), and the third name is later given as Deino.

[Hesiod, *Theogony* 270 ff.; Aeschylus, *Prometheus Bound* 794 ff.; Apollodorus 2. 4. 2]

Greek religion Despite the diversity of the Greek world, which is fully reflected in its approach to things divine, the cult practices and pantheons current among different communities have enough in common to be seen as essentially one system, and were generally understood as such by the Greeks. This is not to say that the Greeks were familiar with the concept of 'a religion', a set of beliefs and practices espoused by its adherents as a matter of conscious choice, more or less to the exclusion of others; such a framework was not applied to Greek religion before late antiquity, and then under pressure from Christianity. Boundaries between Greek and non-Greek religion were far less sharp than is generally the case in comparable modern situations, but they were perceived to exist. The tone is set by Herodotus, who characterizes 'Greekness' (*to hellēnikon*) as having common temples and rituals (as well as common descent, language, and customs). Thus, despite his willingness to identify individual Persian or Egyptian deities with Greek ones (a practice followed by most Greek ethnographers), and indeed despite his attribution of most of the system of divine nomenclature to the Egyptians, he still sees a body of religious thought and practice which is distinctively Greek. Many modern scholars go further and see a certain overall coherence in this body which enables us to speak of a 'system' despite the lack of formal dogma or canonical ritual.

Origins The system, then, as known to Herodotus, had clearly developed over a long period. The origins of some ritual acts may even predate the human species itself. More definitely, we can clearly trace some Greek deities to Indo-European origins: *Zeus, like *Jupiter, has evolved from an original Sky Father, while the relation between the *Dioscuri and the Aśvins, the twin horsemen of the Indian Vedas, is too close for coincidence. Another source of input will have been the indigenous religious forms of Greece, originating before the arrival of Greek-speakers. Sorting such elements from 'Greek' ones in the amalgam we call Minoan-Mycenaean religion is an impossible task; it is easier to trace Minoan-Mycenaean elements in the religion of later periods. See MINOAN AND MYCENAEAN RELIGION. Most obviously, many of the names of the major Greek gods are found already in Linear B, but recent discoveries also indicate that some elements of classical cult practice have their roots in this period. It remains true, however, that the total complex of cult presents a very different aspect.

At various periods the religion of Greece came under substantial influence from the Near East. Much in the traditions of creation and theogony represented for us in *Hesiod has very striking parallels in several west Asian sources, probably reflecting contact in the Minoan-Mycenaean period. Cult practice, however, does not seem to have been open to influence from the east much before the Geometric period, when we begin to find the construction of large temples containing cult images, a form which is likely to owe more to near-eastern/west Semitic culture than to the Bronze Age in Greece. Elements of the classical form of sacrificial ritual can also be derived from the east. A final 'source' for later Greek religion is formed by the poems of *Homer and Hesiod, who though they did not, as Herodotus claims, give the Gods their cult titles and forms, certainly fixed in Greek consciousness a highly anthropomorphic and more or less stable picture of divine society, a pattern extremely influential throughout antiquity despite its frequent incompatibility with ritual practices and local beliefs.

General characteristics Turning to the analysis of Greek religion as it appears in the post-Geometric period, we find in common with most pre-modern societies a strong link between religion and society, to the extent that the sacred/secular dichotomy as we know it has little meaning for the Greek world. Greek religion is community-based, and to the extent that the *polis* or city-state forms the most conspicuous of communities, it is therefore *polis*-based. The importance of this connection began to wane somewhat in the Hellenistic period and later, but to the end of antiquity it remains true to say that Greek religion is primarily a public religion rather than a religion of the individual. Reciprocally, religious observances contributed to the structuring of society, as kinship groups (real or fictitious), local habitations, or less obviously related groups of friends constructed their corporate identity around shared deities and cults. One major difference in the socio-religious organization of Greece from that of many other cultures concerns priestly office, not in the Greek world a special status indicating integration in a special group or caste, but rather parallel to a magistracy, even where, as often, a particular priesthood is hereditary. *See* PRIESTS.

Cult Specific religious practices are described more fully under separate headings (*see also* RITUAL); the following is a very brief résumé. Probably the central ritual act in Greek cult, certainly the most conspicuous, is animal *sacrifice, featured in the overwhelming majority of religious gatherings. Its overlapping layers of significance have been much debated, but it is clear that sacrifice relates both to human–divine relations (the celebration of and offering to a deity) and to a bonding of the human community (the shared sacrificial meal). The act might take place at most times, but on certain dates it was celebrated regularly at a particular sanctuary, usually in combination with a special and distinctive ritual complex; the word '*festival' is loosely but conveniently applied to such rites, whether panhellenic like the *Olympian Games or intimate and secret like the *Arrephoria in Athens. Festivals, at least those of the more public type, articulated the calendar year and provided an opportunity for communal recreation. A more specialized type of gathering was provided by rites known as *mysteries, participation in which was usually felt to confer special benefits, often a better fate after death. Secrecy was a prominent characteristic of these rites, and the experience was often a profoundly emotional one. There were of course more basic methods of communicating with the divine. Most obviously, *prayer was an indispensable part of any public ritual, but was also used on other occasions, often by individuals. *Votive offerings were a very common individual religious act throughout the Greek world. On a day-to-day basis, individuals would greet deities whose shrines they were passing, and might also show piety by garlanding an image (*see* CROWNS AND WREATHS) or making a personal, unscheduled sacrifice—often bloodless, consisting of *cakes or other vegetarian foods, or a pinch of incense. Sometimes they might experience a divine *epiphany in the form of a dream or a waking vision. Both individuals and city-states might make use of various types of *prophecies; methods were very various, but generally the process was understood as another form of divine–human communication.

Gods and other cult figures The pantheon certainly showed some local variations, but presented a recognizable picture throughout the Greek world. Zeus, *Demeter, *Hermes, for instance, were names to which any Greek could respond. Again, the fundamental qualities or 'personality' of a deity remained to some extent consistent across different areas of Greece, but exceptions spring readily to mind; *Persephone (Kore), typically an underworld goddess, is at Locri Epizephyrii in southern Italy more concerned with human fertility and the life of women, while the normally strong connection of *Artemis with her brother *Apollo is virtually absent in her Arcadian manifestations (*see* ARCADIAN CULTS AND MYTHS). Looking at this another way, we might speak of a multiplicity of deities in different locations, who share their name with others of partially similar character. This analysis, although incomplete, accounts better for the existence of certain local deities who are not, or not completely, identified with the great Panhellenic gods. Thus for instance at Aegina and elsewhere we find *Damia and Auxesia, clearly goddesses very roughly of the Demeter–Kore type, but too different to be readily identified with them. Cretan *Britomartis appears both as herself and as a form of Artemis. More generally, we might ask in what sense, and to what extent, *Hera of Samos is identical with Hera of Argos, or indeed within the same city whether Apollo Pythios is 'the same' god as Apollo Agyieus. From one point of view it could be said that every sanctuary housed a 'different' god. On the other hand, the desire to schematize was clearly a strong centripetal force, as was the anthropomorphizing concept of the gods exemplified and promoted by the Homeric poems and their milieu. The boundaries of divine individuality could be drawn in quite different ways depending on context and circumstance.

See also GENEALOGICAL TABLES (1) GREEK GODS.

An anthropomorphic view of the Gods also encouraged a concept of a divine society, probably influenced by west Asian models and very prominent in Homer. Prayer formulae locate deities in their sanctuaries or favourite place on earth, but much mythology creates a picture of a group of Gods living more or less together in (albeit rather eccentric) family relationships. Since their home was traditionally *Olympus, the Gods most prone to this presentation were the 'Olympians', by and large those who were most widely known and worshipped. Sometimes these deities were schematized into the 'Twelve Gods', a group whose composition varied slightly and might include such figures as *Hades/Pluto (widely known, but not situated on Olympus) and *Hestia, the hearth (Olympian, but scarcely personified), whose presence is due to their Homeric or Hesiodic status as siblings of Zeus. (The twelve on the *Parthenon frieze are *Aphrodite, Apollo, *Ares, Artemis, *Athena, Demeter, Dionysus, *Hephaestus, Hera, Hermes, *Poseidon, Zeus.) However, any local pantheon would also exhibit deities who were not so universally known or who, though the object of widespread cult, were scarcely perceived as personal mythological figures. As examples of the former we could adduce Eleusinian *Da(e)ira or Arcadian *Despoina; of the latter, such well-known divinities as *Gaia/Gē (who seems scarcely affected by her presentation in Hesiod) and *Kourotrophos. There were also 'new', 'foreign' Gods such as *Adonis or *Sabazius who were difficult to place in the pre-existing framework of divine personalities; and there were deities like the *Cabiri who had a Panhellenic reputation although their cult remained confined to a very few locations. More localized still were the 'minor' figures of cult such as *nymphs and heroes (*see* HERO-CULT), for here there was much less tendency to assimilate figures with others more universally known. True, local heroes were sometimes identified with characters in Panhellenic mythology, but such identifications often remained speculative and were by no means the invariable rule. Nymphs and heroes were generally

thought of as residing in one specific place, and though in that place their powers were often considerable, they were usually perceived as ranking lower than gods. They were however a characteristic and indispensable part of the circle of superhuman beings.

Later developments The above sketch is based mainly on evidence from before the 3rd cent. BC. Much of the picture is applicable also to Greece in the Hellenistic and Roman periods; religious thought and practice were constantly evolving rather than undergoing sudden transformation. But during the period of Alexander the Great and his successors, the Greek world acquired a vastly greater geographical extent, and at the same time the significance of the *polis* was gradually changing. These changes inevitably had an influence on religious development. Overall, it seems that many distinctive local practices were giving way to wider trends. It is easy to exaggerate the extent to which this occurred; *Pausanias, writing in the 2nd cent. AD, still found a vast diversity of cult in old Greece. On the other hand, it is undeniable that the worship of certain 'new' deities was steadily gaining in popularity over the Greek world as a whole. One of the most spectacular examples is the cult of *Tyche (Chance, Fortune), while also conspicuous in the later period were Egyptian and Anatolian deities such as *Isis, *Sarapis, and *Men, whose cults showed a large admixture of Greek elements. The payment of divine honours to rulers (*see* RULER-CULT), originating with Alexander, soon became standard, modifying pre-existing religious forms in a new direction.

Greek religion, terms relating to The semantics of Greek and Latin in this regard are very different from those of modern European languages. In Greek, the most important word denoting the sacred was *hieros*, denoting basically something which is consecrated to a god, although its use in Homer may reflect an original meaning 'strong'. A related sense is 'connected with cult'; thus *hiera* are religious rites, or materials, especially victims, for them. Contrasting with *hieros*, both *hosios* and *eusebēs*, with their corresponding abstract nouns, cover some of the meaning of 'religion', 'religious'. *Hosion* seems to mean primitively 'usage', 'custom', hence 'good, commendable, pious usage' or the feelings which go with it. It tends to specialize into meaning that which is proper and lawful with regard to holy things, or to traditional morality; it is, for instance, *anhosion* to commit murder. Its sense of 'lawful' can, however, further develop into 'that which is permitted, as not sacred or taboo', and thus may contrast with *hieros*, coming to mean almost 'profane, secular.' *Eusebēs*, literally 'reverent', does not necessarily indicate reverence towards the gods unless a qualifying phrase is added; in this respect it is like Latin *pius* (*see* PIETAS). A word belonging essentially to the religious vocabulary in Classical times is *themis*, since that which it is or is not *themis* to do is respectively allowed or disallowed by religious custom; but the word is also used of traditional, non-religious custom, particularly in *Homer. Words for reverence include *aidoumai*, 'to feel respect' and *sebomai/ sebō*, 'to honour'; what is honoured may be *semnon* or (less often) *hagion*. The latter word, though probably distinct in etymology, seems to have been felt as related to *agos*, 'curse'; in both cases, something outside normal every-day life is being described. Related too is *hagnos*, 'pure', referring generally to a particular state of remoteness from pollutions such as those of sex and death, appropriate for the gods and for dealings with them. *Deisidaimōn* varies between 'pietistic' (traditionally 'superstitious') and 'pious', but is more often pejorative (*see* DEISIDAIMONIA). As regards cult acts, the simple word *timē*, 'honour', is common; a worshipper is often said to 'attend on' or 'serve' the gods (*therapeuein* and synonyms, rarely *douleuein*, to be a slave). To be a regular worshipper, e.g. of the particular gods of the state, is *nomizein*, which may also mean to believe in their existence. Occasionally *thrēskeuein* has the

former sense; *thrēskeia* is a common, though mostly late, word for worship. *Latreia, latreuein* are also found. A *teletē* or *telos* is any rite, though in Hellenistic Greek it tends to mean a mystical rite or even secret doctrine (*see* TELETĒ).

Gregory (1) **the Great,** pope AD 590–604, of senatorial and papal family; probable prefect of Rome *c.*573; subsequently monk; deacon, 578; *apocrisiarius* (lit. 'delegate', a church official) at Constantinople, 579–585/6 (despite his poor Greek); then adviser to Pope Pelagius II. When pope, despite ill-health, he valiantly administered a Rome stricken by flood, plague, and famine, shrunken in population and isolated and threatened by Arian (*see* ARIANISM) and pagan Lombards. He reorganized papal estates for Rome's supply, centralizing their administration through appointments, paid imperial troops, appointed officers, and negotiated with the Lombards. He devotedly served the Byzantine empire as the 'holy commonwealth', but sometimes acted independently of emperor and exarchs. Warfare and political fragmentation limited his powers, but expectation of the Day of Judgement sharpened his sense of spiritual responsibility for the world. As churchman, he upheld ecclesiastical discipline in Italy and Dalmatia, maintained authority in the vicariate of Illyricum, restructured the dioceses of his dwindling patriarchate, and laboured to convert Jews and *pagan rustics. He urged Church reform on the Merovingians, reviving the vicariate of Arles at their request. He struggled (against imperial opposition) to end the Three Chapters schism in Venetia and Istria, and (with small success, and perhaps small need) to suppress African *Donatism. He worked to convert the Lombards through queen Theodelinda, and organized a mission to the Anglo-Saxons (596). In the east, he maintained papal appellate jurisdiction, and was friendly with the patriarchs of Alexandria and Antioch. With Constantinople, he quarrelled over its patriarch's title Oecumenical, wrongly seen as challenging

Rome's primacy. Generally, though, he was sensitive to local religious traditions.

A contemplative at heart, he saw episcopal duties as a necessary, but uncongenial extension of his monastic vocation into the secular world. His diaconal appointments favoured monks, alienating Rome's secular clergy. No original theologian, he was an eloquent moralizer and mystic, striving to make sense of his beleaguered world, and transmitting much patristic thought to the Middle Ages. His *Moralia in Iob* proved enormously popular; his *Cura pastoralis* remains a mirror for priest and bishop. His *Dialogues* (whose authenticity has been challenged) inspiringly portrayed the Italian Church as ascetic, preaching, thaumaturgic, but episcopally controlled. His *Homiliae in Ezechielem*, preached to the besieged city, movingly lament Rome's decay. He defended sacred art, reformed the Roman liturgy, and perhaps established a choir school. He conventionally condemned bishop Desiderius of Vienne for inappropriately teaching classical culture, and suspected its influence on potential monks, but conventionally acknowledged its utility in biblical studies; his straightforward, rhythmically skilful prose shows rhetorical training. (Many letters, though, are chancery-drafted.) A chief founder of the papal states, and of papal prestige in the post-Roman west, his leadership, and vigorous sense of Rome's political and Christian traditions, justified his epitaph as 'God's consul'.

Gregory (2) **of Nazianzus** (AD 329–89) was educated at Athens in the company of *Basil of Caesarea, of whom he composed a crucial portrait in his *Oration* 43. He shared for a short period Basil's enthusiasm for practical *asceticism but did much to encourage his friend to take up controversial writing and pastoral office.

His own career was marred by indecisiveness: he was never able to define an acceptable balance between the 'philosophic life' and engagement in ecclesiastical affairs. He was probably inhibited by his father's hopes (the elder Gregory was a bishop also) and by Basil's success, which he could not help admiring in spite of differences between them. That inadequacy was highlighted by his brief tenure of the see of *Constantinople, upon which he was suddenly thrust in 381 and which he almost as suddenly abandoned. Events allowed him, however, to influence the ecumenical council of that year and contribute to the resulting defeat of *Arianism. His historical significance springs from his detailed, honest, and lively letters, a series of polished and thoughtful orations (some of theological importance), and relatively uninspired poetry that nevertheless contains valuable autobiographical information.

Gregory (3) **of Nyssa** (c.AD 330–95) was the master figure of Greek Christian theology. Deeply learned in Platonism and in the thought of *Origen, he imparted to that tradition a strong mystical flavour of his own, while safeguarding its orthodoxy. He was unable to engage in controversy without elevating the debate to timeless significance (and his criticism of Eunomius added much to the work of his brother *Basil of Caesarea).

It would be wrong, however, to regard him as a remote seer. He was married, and capable of pursuing secular interests for a number of years. Even in Church affairs, in spite of misgivings on Basil's part, he had practical interests and pastoral skills. His theology, therefore, was more than academic. He saw world and divinity associated dynamically, allowing human beings to develop the 'image of God' within them and to become in the process 'like unto God' (such were his key notions). His view of the relation between freedom and grace was correspondingly integrated and helped to save the eastern Church from the polarities that afflicted *Augustine.

His works were representative and influential, Christianizing further almost every traditional genre. Particular value may be attached to his *Life* of his sister

Macrina, which propounded a doctrine of 'philosophy', offered useful illustration of the ascetic life, and prompts reflection on virginity and the place of women in the early Church.

Gregory (4) **Thaumaturgus** (c.AD 213–c.275) was born of a prominent family of Neocaesarea, Pontus (formerly Cabeira; mod. Niksar). He studied law at Berytus (Beirut), but when visiting Caesarea (Palestine) was converted to Christianity by *Origen. His parting panegyric of gratitude describes Origen's methods of instruction. On returning to Pontus he successfully preached Christianity as bishop of Neocaesarea. His memory was venerated a century later by *Basil of Caesarea and *Gregory (3) of Nyssa, the latter of whom wrote a *Life* on the basis of Pontic folk-traditions which ascribed to him extraordinary prodigies as 'the wonder-worker'. Of particular interest, both for contemporary historical conditions and for the liturgical development of the 3rd-cent. Church, is the 'Canonical Letter' written in the aftermath of the Gothic invasions of Pontus in the mid-250s, in which various grades of penance were laid down for Christians who had exploited the invasions for their own advantage.

Hades, son of *Cronus and Rhea and husband of *Persephone, is 'Lord of the dead' and king of the Underworld, the 'house of Hades', where according to *Homer he rules supreme and, exceptionally, administers justice. After Homer, Hades is not only the god of the dead, but also the god of death, even death personified. Hades refers normally to the person; in non-Attic literature, the word can also designate the Underworld. Cold, mouldering, and dingy, Hades is a 'mirthless place'. The proverbial 'road to Hades' is 'the same for all'. *Aeacus, son of *Zeus, 'keeps the keys to Hades'; the same is said of Pluton, *Anubis (love charms from Roman Egypt), and Christ (book of Revelation 1. 18). The 'gates of Hades' are guarded by 'the terrible hound', *Cerberus, who wags his tail for the new arrivals, but devours those attempting to leave. Hades, too, was sometimes perceived as an eater of corpses. Without burial, the dead cannot pass through Hades' gates. Once inside, they are shrouded in 'the darkness of pernicious Hades'.

Like the *Erinyes/Eumenides ('Angry/Kindly Ones') and *Demeter ('Earth-mother'), Hades lacked a proper name; as in the case of other nameless *chthonians, his anonymity was a precaution. He was referred to by descriptive circumlocutions as 'chthonian Zeus', 'the chthonian god', 'king of those below', 'Zeus of the departed' and 'the other Zeus', 'the god below', or simply 'lord'. As the Lord of the Dead, he was dark and sinister, a god to be feared and kept at a distance. Paradoxically, he was also believed to 'send up' good things for mortals from his wealth below; he is a 'good and prudent god'.

The two opposite but complementary aspects of his divinity are reflected in a host of positive and negative epithets. Of the latter, Hades, 'the invisible one' according to ancient etymology, recalls the darkness of his realm. The 'wolf's cap of Hades', worn by *Athena in the *Iliad* and by Aita/Hades in Etruscan art, makes its wearers invisible. Other negative epithets are 'hateful', 'implacable and adamant', 'tearless' and 'malignant'. Epithets which euphemistically address his benign and hospitable aspects include *Clymenus ('Renowned'), *Eubouleus ('Good Counsellor'), Euchaites ('the Beautiful-haired One'), Eukles ('Of Good Repute'), Hagesilaos ('Leader of the People'), Pasianax ('Lord over All'), Polydektes or Polydegmon ('Receiver of Many'), Polyxeinos ('Host to Many'), and Pluton ('Wealth'). Originally a divinity in his own right, during the 5th cent. BC Pluton became Hades' most common name in myth as well as in cult.

Hades was not a recipient of cult. Like *Thanatos, he was indifferent to prayer or offerings. The abnormal cult of Hades at Elis, with a temple open once a year, then only to the priest, and his sanctuary at Mt. Minthe near Pylos are the exceptions that prove the rule. But throughout the Greek world—at *Eleusis, Sparta, Ephesus, Cnidus, and Mytilene, among numerous other places—he received cult in his beneficial aspect as Pluton, often alongside his consort *Persephone. The couple were widely worshipped as Pluton and Kore; at Eleusis, they were also known as Theos and Thea, 'God and Goddess'. Pluton is related to the Eleusinian cult figures *Plutus and Eubouleus as well as to other friendly chthonians such as Zeus Meilichios and Zeus Eubouleus (*see* CHTHONIAN GODS). In various curse tablets, however, he is invoked along with *Demeter and Kore or, more menacingly, with the *Erinyes, *Hecate, *Hermes, Moirai (*fates), and Persephone; *curses in the name of Hades and Persephone are less common. So-called Plutonia marked entrances to the Underworld.

Apart from the story of Persephone's abduction by him, few myths attach to Hades. By giving her the forbidden food of the dead to eat—the pomegranate—he bound Demeter's daughter to return periodically to his realm. Their union was without issue; its infertility mirrors that of the nether world. When the sons of Cronus divided the universe amongst themselves, Hades was allotted the world of the dead, Zeus obtained the sky, and Poseidon the sea. As ruler of the dead, Hades was always more ready to receive than to let go. Two kindred gods, Demeter and *Dionysus, as well as heroes like *Heracles, *Theseus, and *Orpheus descended alive to Hades and returned to earth. Ordinary mortals went there to stay; *Alcestis, *Eurydice, and *Protesilaus were among the few allowed to leave. Heracles wrestled with Thanatos, and wounded Hades with his arrows. Hades' mistress Minthe (*see* MENTHE) was changed into the mint plant by Persephone.

Alcestis' death vision of Hades, who comes to get her, is dim but frightening; according to Euripides, 'Someone is leading me, leading me away—don't you see?—to the hall of the dead. He stares at me from under his dark-eyed brow. He has wings— it's Hades!'. In Greek art, Hades and Pluton— differentiating between the two is not always possible—are wingless human figures lacking any terrifying aspects. Zeus-like and bearded, Hades-Pluton is a majestic, elderly man holding a sceptre, twig, cornucopia, pomegranate, or large two-handled vessel. On some vases, Hades is shown averting his gaze from the other gods.

Unlike Hades, Thanatos is represented with wings. Conceptually and iconographically, Dionysus and *Sarapis in their chthonian aspects have affinities to Hades-Pluton.

Hades was the universal destination of the dead until the second half of the 5th cent. BC, when we first hear of the souls of some special dead ascending to the upper air (*aithēr*), while their bodies are said to be received by the earth. Notably, the souls of the heroized daughters of *Erechtheus 'do not go to Hades', but reside in heaven. The various Underworld topographies found in Homer and Virgil, in the esoteric gold leaves containing descriptions of Hades, and in the Christian apocryphal *Apocalypse of Peter* reflect changing constructs of the afterlife. *See* DEATH, ATTITUDES TO; TARTARUS.

[Homer, *Iliad* 5. 394–402, 15. 187–93; *Odyssey* 11; Hesiod, *Theogony* 453–506; Euripides, *Alcestis*; Apollodorus 1. 5; Virgil, *Aeneid* 6]

Haemon (1) Eponym (*see* EPONYMOI) of Haemonia, i.e. Thessaly, and father of Thessalus. (2) Grandson of *Cadmus: leaving Thebes on account of homicide, he came to Athens, and his descendants went successively to Rhodes and Acragas. (3) Son of the Theban *Creon: early epic seems to place him in the generation of *Oedipus: he was apparently killed by the *Sphinx, and his son Maeon was one of the Thebans who ambushed *Tydeus. The tragedians place him later, as the fiancé or lover of *Antigone. (4) The same name is given to other minor figures in the *Iliad*.

Halirrhothius, an Attic hero, son of *Poseidon. He raped *Aglaurus' daughter Alcippe and was therefore killed by her father Ares, thus precipitating the latter's trial by the Areopagus court. A less well-known tradition brings him into the context of the rivalry between *Athena and *Poseidon: sent by Poseidon to chop down Athena's olive-trees, he accidentally lopped off his own leg and died.

Haloa An Attic, perhaps exclusively Eleusinian (*see* ELEUSIS), *festival of *Demeter and *Dionysus (and perhaps *Poseidon) conducted largely by women on the 26th day of the winter month of Posideon. *Haloia* probably derives from *halōs*, in the sense of 'worked land, garden plot' rather than the unseasonal 'threshing-floor'. Records at Eleusis of the purchase of firewood for the Haloa suggest that a bonfire, as well as manipulation of sexual symbols, ribaldry, drinking and feasting, encouraged revivification at a dead time of year.

Harpalyce (1), a mythical Thracian princess brought up by her father as a warrior. On one occasion she saved his life in battle, but when finally he died she became a brigand, and was eventually caught and killed. She received heroic honours in the form of a mock battle at her tomb. (2) daughter of *Clymenus (2a) of Argos, given in marriage to Neleus' son Alastor but raped by her father, to whom in revenge she served up her younger brother at a feast. She was thereupon transformed into a bird.

Harpyiae, Harpies, 'snatchers', personify the demonic force of storms and are always represented as winged women. In *Homer they serve to explain the traceless disappearance of *Odysseus or the sudden death of the daughters of *Pandareos. Their names—Podarge or Aello and Okypete—reflect their speed. Usually, as in Hesiod, there are only two, but later sources—perhaps under influence of the theatre—sometimes mention three Harpies or leave their number unspecified. The fast messenger of the gods, *Iris, is their sister. The main role of the Harpies in myth occurs in the context of the *Argonauts: they plague the Thracian king *Phineus by snatching away his food before being chased off by the sons of *Boreas. The episode already occurs in *Hesiod and becomes very popular in Hellenistic times: *Apollonius of Rhodes relates it in detail.

[Homer, *Iliad* 16. 148–51; Apollonius Rhodius 2. 234–434; Virgil, *Aeneid* 3. 209–67]

haruspices, Etruscan diviners. The Etruscan word for the general concept of 'priest'

is unknown; the *haruspices* are represented as wearing the conical cap, similar to the *pilleus* (apex), in Rome the headgear of *flamines*. In Roman sources the *haruspices* appear as interpreters of *fulgura* (thunderbolts), *ostenta* (unusual happenings), and above all *exta* (entrails, especially liver). They were members of the Etruscan aristocracy (to be distinguished from private itinerant diviners). When need arose they were on the senate's orders called from Etruria to explain prodigies and *portents, especially when thunderbolts struck public places; they would give a formal reply, and propose a remedy. They always appear as a group, and this presupposes some sort of organization. An inscription dating to the end of the republic or beginning of the empire is the first document attesting the college of 60 *haruspices*; it may go back to the mid-2nd cent. when the senate decreed that sons of Etruscan nobles should be trained in the art of divination. The college (presided over by a special official) was reorganized under the emperor Claudius; the *haruspices* and their doctrine were placed under the supervision of the *pontifices*. Individual *haruspices* were attached to Roman magistrates and, later, emperors; and there also existed public *haruspices* in various Roman cities. With *Constantine I began the persecution of the *haruspices*; after a short revival under *Julian they were banned by *Theodosius I (AD 392), though their art lingered for a long time. *See also* DIVINATION; ETRUSCAN RELIGION; TAGES.

healing gods In all times, illness has been a major crisis both in the lives of individuals and communities; to overcome such a crisis has been a major task of religion. Specific divinities became patrons of human healers or were renowned for their special ability to help individuals, some presiding over healing springs; a frequent strategy was to regard illness as the result of *pollution and then to try to cure it with cathartic rituals; *see* PURIFICATION.

In Greece, the main divinity responsible for healing was *Apollo who already in the *Iliad* sent the plague and took it away again; behind this function, there lie ancient near-eastern conceptions. Apollo remained a healer throughout the Archaic and Classical ages; in Ionian cities (and their colonies), he often bore the epithet 'physician'; as Apollo Medicus, his cult was introduced to Rome in 433 BC. In the course of the 5th cent., Apollo's role as a healer was contested and slowly replaced by the much more personal and specialized hero *Asclepius, whom myth made Apollo's son and whose fame radiated chiefly from his Epidaurian sanctuary; in his main sanctuaries (*Epidaurus, Cos, Pergamum), Asclepius succeeded Apollo who, however, still retained a presence in spite of the fame of his son. The ritual of Asclepius developed *incubation as a specific means to obtain healing in *dreams.

Other divinities could, under given circumstances, heal as well. When a specific illness was understood as possession, as in the case of epilepsy (the 'sacred disease'), the god or hero who had caused the possession held also the key to its healing. For some diseases *Demeter was thought useful as well, as was the mighty 'averter of evil' Heracles. Besides, many places had local heroes whom people could ask for healing, like the Oropian seer *Amphiaraus (with incubation) or the Athenian 'Hero Physician'. Among the functions of local *nymphs, there was also help with female sterility and birth.

Rome followed the course set by Greece, introducing first Apollo Medicus, then, in 204 BC, Asclepius from Epidaurus; later, as in Greece, nymphs and Hercules were thanked for help, as were the Egyptian gods *Isis and *Sarapis; Rome also venerated the goddess Febris, 'Fever'. Besides, and from time immemorial, Italy had a large number of local shrines, often of female, motherly divinities who were supposed to heal; one of their main concerns, to judge from the large amount of anatomic *votive gifts, was with female fertility. Chiefly in the ancient Celtic provinces of Gaul and Britain, cults at healing springs were important (*see* CELTIC RELIGION); their divinities kept their Celtic names or were identified with Roman gods, like Apollo or, in Roman Bath, Minerva (Sulis); *see* AQUAE SULIS.

See APOLLO; ASCLEPIUS; DISEASE; INCUBATION.

Hebe, a personification of *hēbē*, the standard Greek word for 'adolescence, puberty'. Hebe is normally a daughter of *Hera and *Zeus, and thus a sister of *Ares and *Eileithyia; only in a late-attested tradition of uncertain origin is she born of Hera alone, made fertile by a lettuce. She is often mentioned and depicted as cupbearer of the gods and as bride of *Heracles; this marriage is always viewed from the perspective of the groom, to whom it brought reconciliation with Hebe's mother Hera, a home on *Olympus, and eternal youth (i.e. godhead). She occasionally appears in cult, normally in association with the circle of Heracles, as in the village Aixone in Attica where a temple of Hebe seems to have been the centre of a cult complex in which *Alcmene and the *Heraclidae were also honoured; at Phlius and Sicyon she was identified with figures also known as Ganymeda and Dia.

[Homer, *Odyssey* 11. 601–4; Hesiod, *Theogony* 921–3, 950–5; Euripides, *Children of Heracles* 847–58; Apollodorus 2. 7. 7; Pausanias 2. 13. 3–4; Strabo 8. 6. 24, 382c]

Hecale, *eponymous heroine and object of cult in the Attic village of Hecale. In her honour *Theseus founded a cult of Zeus Hekaleios, because she had entertained him kindly on his way to fight the bull of Marathon; by the time he returned she had died. *Callimachus wrote a very influential hexameter narrative poem about her, of which significant fragments survive; his main source was Philochorus, the historian of Attica.

Hecataeus (1), son of Hegesander, of Miletus, the most important of the early Ionian prose-writers. He was a senior figure in the planning of Ionian Revolt against Persia (500–494 BC).

Besides improving *Anaximander's map of the world, which he envisaged as a disc encircled by the river *Oceanus, he wrote a pioneering work of systematic geography, the *Periēgēsis* or *Periodos gēs* ('Journey round the World'), divided into two books, *Europe* and *Asia* (which included Africa). This offered information about the places and peoples to be encountered on a clockwise coastal voyage round the Mediterranean and the Black Sea, starting at the Straits of Gibraltar and finishing on the Atlantic coast of Morocco, with diversions to the islands of the Mediterranean and inland to Scythia, Persia, India, Egypt, and Nubia.

His *mythographic work, the *Genealogies* (or *Histories* or *Heroologia*) occupied at least four books (*see* GENEALOGY). We have fewer than 40 fragments; they reveal a rationalizing approach to the legends of families claiming a divine origin (including, apparently, his own). As is shown by his treatment of the stories of Geryon and *Cerberus, he evidently believed that behind the fabulous elaborations of tradition lay historical facts distorted by exaggeration or by literal interpretation of metaphors. His opening proclaims his intellectual independence: 'Hecataeus of Miletus speaks thus. I write what seems to me to be true; for the Greeks have many tales which, as it appears to me, are absurd.'

[Herodotus 2. 143, 5. 36, 124–6]

Hecataeus (2), of Abdera, *c.*360–290 BC, author of philosophical ethnographies, pupil of Pyrrhon the sceptic, visited Egyptian Thebes under Ptolemy I (305–283).

Works (1) *On the *Hyperboreans*, fictitious travelogue on a northern people dwelling on an island on the utmost borders of the world: model for *Euhemerus of Messene. (2) *Aegyptiaca*, idealizing account of the country and people, the exemplary nature of the Egyptian way of life and form of government. Hecataeus' enthusiasm bordered on 'Egyptomania'. The digression on the Jews in Diodorus Siculus is the first mention of Jews in a Greek author—the work *On Jews* referred to

in Flavius Josephus is not genuine. (3) *On the Poetry of Homer and Hesiod*, now lost.

[Diodorus Siculus 40. 3. 8]

Hecate was a popular and ubiquitous goddess from the time of *Hesiod until late antiquity. Unknown in *Homer and harmless in Hesiod, she emerges by the 5th cent. as a more sinister divine figure associated with magic and witchcraft, lunar lore and creatures of the night, dog sacrifices and illuminated *cakes, as well as doorways and crossroads. Her name is the feminine equivalent of Hekatos, an obscure epithet of *Apollo but the Greek etymology is no guarantee that her name or cult originated in Greece. Possibly of Carian origin, and certainly outlandish in her infernal aspects, she is more at home on the fringes than in the centre of Greek polytheism. Intrinsically ambivalent and polymorphous, she straddles conventional boundaries and eludes definition.

In Hesiod's *Theogony*, she is the granddaughter of the *Titans *Phoebe and Coeus, daughter of Perses and *Asteria, and first cousin of Apollo and *Artemis. In a remarkable digression Hecate is praised as a powerful goddess who 'has a share' of earth, sea, and sky—but not the Underworld—and who gives protection to warriors, athletes, hunters, herders, and fishermen. As with all gods, she may choose to withhold her gifts. But, because her functions overlap with those of other divinities, she lacks individuating features. Furthermore, the Hesiodic Hecate contrasts sharply with the goddess's later manifestations, which tend to be much more menacing. Where and how this differentiation occurred remains uncertain.

Throughout her long history, Hecate received public as well as private cult, the latter often taking forms that were anything but normal. She was worshipped in liminal places, and sacrifices to her were as anomalous as the goddess herself. The earliest archaeological evidence is a dedication to Hecate on a circular altar in the precinct of Apollo Delphinios at *Miletus; she had her own shrine 'outside the gates'—as opposed to the Coan cult of Hecate 'in the city'—where she received libations of unmixed wine. In Athens *Hermes Propylaios and Hecate Epipyrgidia ('On the Ramparts') watched the entrance to the Acropolis. Similarly, altars and cult images of the trimorphic Hecate (hekataia) stood in front of private homes and especially at forks in the road, after which she was named triodītis and Trivia.

The documentation for the Hecate cult in Classical Athens is particularly rich and varied. Her favourite food offerings consisted of a scavenging fish (see FISH, SACRED) tabooed in other cults—the red mullet—of sacrificial cakes decorated with lit miniature torches, and, most notoriously, of puppies. The illuminated cakes were offered at the time of the full moon. So-called 'suppers of Hecate'—consisting of various breadstuffs, eggs, cheese, and dog-meat—were put out for her at the crossroads each month to mark the rising of the new moon. On an Attic vase, a woman deposits a puppy and a basket with sacrificial cakes in front of burning torches. Attested for Athens, Colophon, Samothrace, and Thrace, dog sacrifices to Hecate were alimentary as well as cathartic. During Hellenistic and Roman times, she was worshipped as the regional mother-goddess at her main Carian sanctuary at Lagina near Stratonicea. There, the ritual carrying of a sacred key was part of her cult, of which the clergy included a priest and priestess as well as *eunuchs. On the temple frieze, she carries to *Cronus the stone that represents the newborn *Zeus; in another scene, she participates in the Gigantomachy (see GIANTS). No dogs were sacrificed in the Lagina cult, but the puppy sacrifices, prominent in Hittite and Carian purification rituals, point to an early Anatolian connection. See ANATOLIAN DEITIES.

Hecate was identified with other divine figures such as Ereschigal, the Babylonian goddess of the Underworld; the Thessalian Enodia and *Brimo; the Sicilian Angelos;

*Persephone; *Iphigenia and especially Artemis. In Athens, too, she was worshipped as Artemis Hecate and as Kalliste, another of Artemis' cult titles. Sacrifices to Artemis Hecate and to *Kourotrophos were performed in Hecate's shrine at Erchia in Attica. Hecate was also associated with various male gods, including Apollo Delphinios, *Asclepius, Hermes, *Pan, Zeus *Meilichios, and Zeus Panamaros.

Like all *chthonian divinities, Hecate was perceived as simultaneously terrible and benign. Her 'good' side is addressed by her Hesiodic epithet 'nurturer of the young' (*kourotrophos, echoed in later sources). In Aeschylus, the title 'Hekata' refers to Artemis in her association with childbirth and young animals. The Hecate seen in Eleusinian myth and cult is propitious and caring. She assists *Demeter in her search for Persephone (Kore), and after the reunion of mother and daughter becomes Kore's 'minister and attendant'. Attic vase-painters included Hecate in their depictions of the return of Kore and the mission of *Triptolemus; in the Attic deme of Paiania, Hecate's cult and priestess were attached to the local Eleusinion. In later versions of the myth, Hecate is another daughter of Demeter and retrieves Persephone from the Underworld. Mystery cults (see MYSTERIES) of Hecate also existed, as on Aegina and Samothrace; a woman initiate claims on her tombstone to have been immortalized in death as the 'goddess Hecate'.

Although Hecate lacked a mythology of her own, her nocturnal apparitions, packs of barking hell-hounds, and hosts of ghost-like revenants occupied a special place in the Greek religious imagination. As 'the one of the roadways' (Gk. enodia), she protected the crossroads as well as the graves by the roadside. She also guarded the gates to Hades. According to one of the hymns to *Selene-Hecate embedded in the Paris magical papyrus, Hecate keeps the keys that 'open the bars of Cerberus' and wears 'the bronze sandal of her who holds *Tartarus'. A permanent fixture of the Greek and Roman

Underworld, in *Aeneid*, book 6, she gives Virgil's *Sibyl, a priestess of Apollo and Hecate, a guided tour of Tartarus. Because of her association with the chthonian realm and the ghosts of the dead, Hecate looms large in ancient *magic. Sorceresses of all periods and every provenance, such as *Medea, Simaitha, and Canidia, invoke her name as one who makes powerful spells more potent. On curse tablets (*see* CURSES) dating from the Classical to the imperial period, Hecate is conjured in conjunction with *Hermes Chthonios, Gē (*see* GAIA) Chthonia, Persephone, or Pluton (*see* HADES). In a specimen from Hellenistic Athens, Hecate Chthonia is invoked 'along with the maddening *Erinyes'. In the *theurgy of the *Chaldaean Oracles adopted by the Neoplatonists, Hecate, though still linked to demons, has become an epiphanic celestial deity (*see* EPIPHANY) and cosmological principle—the Cosmic *Soul—accessible through ritual as well as contemplation.

Representations of Hecate in art fall into two broad categories—her images are either single-faced or three-faced. The earliest example of the former type may be a late 6th-cent. inscribed terracotta figurine of a woman seated on a throne, dedicated by 'Aigon to Hecate'. After *c*.430 BC, the goddess of the crossroads is often represented as a standing female figure with three faces or bodies, each corresponding to one of the crossing roads. The trimorphous Hecate is said to be the creation of Alcamenes. She is often shown wearing the *polos* (divine headdress) and holding torches in her hands, and occasionally with a phiale, a sword, snakes, boughs, flowers, or a pomegranate. Central to her cult, the three-faced image of Hecate is depicted on two Attic vases from the Classical period. On the Altar of Zeus at Pergamum, Hecate and her dog attack a serpentine giant; her single body supports three heads and three pairs of arms. Exceptionally, on a vase with the death of *Actaeon, a winged Hecate urges on his maddened dogs while Artemis looks on. On an equally unique vase, Hecate has man-eating dogs for feet and is accompanied by three *Erinyes.

Greek wordsmiths went to great lengths in their efforts to verbalize the triple aspects of the trimorphic goddess. In one of the comedies of Chariclides, she is humorously invoked as 'lady Hecate of the triple roads, of the triple form, of the triple face, enchanted by triple-fish [mullets]'. A curse tablet from the imperial period addresses her similarly as 'Lady Hecate of the heavens, Hecate of the Underworld, Hecate of the three roads, Hecate of the triple face, Hecate of the single face'. Playing with sacred *numbers added to her mystery.

[Hesiod, *Theogony* 411–52; *Homeric Hymn to Demeter* 22–63, 438–40; Aristophanes, *Wealth* 594–600; Apollonius Rhodius, *Argonautica* 3. 477–8, 528–30, 861f., 1035–41, 1207–24; Theocritus, *Idylls* 2. 12–16; Horace, *Satires* 1. 8. 33; Virgil, *Aeneid* 6. 35, 247, 564–5]

Hecatoncheires, hundred-handed monsters, Cottus, Briareos, and Gyes, sons of Heaven and Earth, aided *Zeus against the *Titans. Briareos (called Aegaeon by men) was brought by *Thetis to protect Zeus against *Hera, *Poseidon, and *Athena.

Hector, in mythology son of *Priam and *Hecuba, husband of *Andromache and father of Astyanax, and the greatest of the Trojan champions. In *Homer's *Iliad* he first appears leading the Trojans out to battle; he reproaches *Paris for avoiding *Menelaus, and arranges the truce and the single combat between the two. He takes a prominent part in the fighting of books 5 and 6, but in the latter goes back to the city for a while to arrange for offerings to be made to the gods. He thus meets Andromache and Astyanax on the city walls in one of the best-known scenes of the *Iliad*, then returns with Paris to the battle. In book 7 he challenges any Greek hero to single combat, and is met by the greater *Aias (1), who has rather the better of the encounter; they part with an exchange of gifts. In book 8 he drives the Greeks back to their camp and bivouacs on the plain. In the long battle of books 11–17 he takes a prominent part, leading the main attack on the fortifications of the Greek camp which nearly succeeds in burning the Greek ships. During the battle he is struck down with a stone thrown by Aias, but restored to strength by *Apollo at the command of Zeus. He kills *Patroclus, and strips him of his arms despite the efforts of the Greeks. After the appearance of *Achilles at the trench, full of rage at Patroclus' death, Hector again bivouacs on the plain, against the advice of *Polydamas. After the Trojan rout on the following day, he alone refuses to enter Troy, but stands his ground and waits for Achilles despite the entreaties of his parents. At Achilles' approach he flees, but after a long chase halts, deceived by Athena into thinking that *Deiphobus has come to his aid. In the subsequent fight he is killed, and with his dying words begs Achilles to return his body to Priam, then predicts Achilles' own death. But Achilles, still overcome with rage and hatred, drags Hector's body behind his chariot, though the gods keep it safe from harm. Finally, when Priam comes by night to the Greek camp to beg for the return of his son, Achilles' anger is eased and replaced by pity. The body is ransomed, an eleven-day truce is agreed, and the *Iliad* ends with Hector's funeral. Later poets add nothing of importance to Homer's account.

Hector is depicted in art from the 7th cent. on, setting out for battle, fighting Aias or some other hero, meeting his death at Achilles' hands, and his body being dragged and ransomed.

[Homer, *Iliad*; Apollodorus, *Epitome* 4. 7]

Hecuba, wife of *Priam, and daughter of Dymas king of Phrygia, or of Cisseus. The name of her mother was one of the problems posed by the emperor Tiberius. She was the mother of nineteen of Priam's fifty sons, including *Hector and *Paris.

In *Homer she is a stately and pathetic figure, coming only occasionally into the foreground. In Euripides she is more prominent. The first half of his *Hecuba* deals with the sacrifice of her daughter *Polyxena, the second with her revenge on the Thracian

king Polymestor, who has murdered her youngest son Polydorus. Turning from victim to savage avenger she blinds Polymestor and kills his sons, and he makes a curious prophecy of her end: on the ship transporting her to Greece she will be transformed into a bitch and then plunge into the sea. In Euripides' *Trojan Women* she is again the central character, battered by a succession of woes, and incidents include her moral victory in a debate with Helen and her allotment as a prize to *Odysseus. For her role in *Alexandros* see PARIS.

[Homer, *Iliad* 6. 251–311, 22. 79–92, 24. 193–227, 283–301, 747–60; Euripides, *Hecuba*, *Trojan Women* 860–1059, 1260–86; Apollodorus 3. 12. 5; Ovid, *Metamorphoses* 13. 422–575; Seneca, *Trojan Women*]

Helen, daughter of *Zeus and *Leda (or Zeus and *Nemesis, according to an early variant); wife of *Menelaus of Sparta; the beautiful woman whose abduction by Paris was the cause of the Trojan War.

Helen was also worshipped (at Sparta and on Rhodes) as a goddess associated with trees (*see* TREES, SACRED). It is generally agreed that she must have been a goddess before she was a mortal heroine, but the connection between these two different incarnations is obscure. It has been suggested that the repeated seductions of the mortal Helen are derived from temporary absences of the goddess in the cult myths.

In *Homer she is entirely human. As we see her in the *Iliad*, she is deeply conscious of the shame of her position at Troy, though it is unclear how far she is responsible for this. *Hector and *Priam treat her kindly; the Trojan elders marvel at her beauty; and she is in general a sympathetic character. In the *Odyssey*, after her return to Sparta, she is seen as a respectable wife and queen, though Menelaus' curious story of her role in the episode of the Trojan Horse presents a less complimentary picture.

Later writers supply further mythical details: how she was born from an egg (Zeus having visited *Leda in the form of a swan); how she was abducted by Theseus but rescued by her brothers, Castor and

Polydeuces (see DIOSCURI); how she was wooed by all the greatest heroes of Greece before her marriage to Menelaus. She now generally stands condemned for having willingly accompanied Paris to Troy. A story often illustrated on vases is that Menelaus, after the capture of Troy, intended to kill her, but dropped his sword on seeing her breasts. In a much-debated episode in *Virgil's Aeneid it is *Aeneas who thinks of killing her.

The 6th-cent. poet *Stesichorus wrote a poem in which he held Helen to blame, but then, we are told, was punished with blindness for having slandered a goddess. His sight returned when he wrote a recantation (two recantations by one account) saying that she never went to Troy at all: the gods lodged her in Egypt for the duration of the war and put a phantom Helen in her place. This version is then rationalized by the historian Herodotus.

The tragedians, especially *Euripides, often condemn Helen for her adultery. An attempt at self-defence is refuted by *Hecuba in a debate in *Trojan Women*, and she is presented as vain and shallow in *Orestes*. In his *Helen*, however, Euripides follows the version of Stesichorus' recantation: Menelaus, returning from Troy with the phantom Helen, is astonished to find the real Helen in Egypt, and the pair then escape by trickery from the wicked king Theoclymenus, son of *Proteus.

The sophist Gorgias composed a *Defence of Helen* as a light-hearted rhetorical exercise, and this is carried further in an encomium by Isocrates.

[Homer, *Iliad* 3. 121–244, 383–447, 6. 343–69, 24. 761–76; *Odyssey* 4. 120–305; Virgil, *Aeneid* 2. 567–88; Herodotus 2. 112–20; Euripides, *Trojan Women* 860–1059, *Orestes* 71–131; Apollodorus 3. 10. 4–9, *Epitome* 6. 29–30; Isocrates 10]

Helenus, in mythology, son of *Priam, warrior and prophet. In the *Iliad* he gives prophetic advice to *Hector, and is wounded by *Menelaus at the battle of the ships. Captured by *Odysseus, he prophesied the fall of Troy if *Philoctetes was brought there with his bow. After the fall of Troy he was carried off by *Neoptolemus, who gave him *Andromache as his wife. They settled in Epirus and made 'a little Troy'; there they were visited by *Aeneas, to whom Helenus prophesied his future wanderings.

[Apollodorus, *Epitome* 5. 9–10, 6. 12–13; Virgil, *Aeneid* 3. 294–505]

Helicon, mountain in south-west Boeotia sacred to the *Muses. Running from Phocis to Thisbe in Boeotia, it stretched northwards to Lake Copais and southwards to the Corinthian Gulf. Its most famous feature is the Valley of the Muses, the site of Ascra, the unbeloved home of *Hesiod. Thespiae celebrated a festival of the Muses, and the oldest tripod dedicated was reputedly that of Hesiod. The Thespians also established a festival of Love there. Above the Grove of the Muses was Hippocrene, a *spring supposedly created when *Bellerophon's horse struck the ground with his hoof.

Heliopolis (mod. Baalbek) was the religious centre of a local Ituraean kingdom, after whose dissolution it became a Roman colony (15 BC). The cult of the Heliopolitan triad, *Jupiter, *Venus, and *Mercury, became widespread in the Roman world. The huge 1st-cent. AD temple of Jupiter-Hadad (Ba'al-Hadad having been worshipped here earlier), its two courtyards (completed AD 244–9), the adjacent Antonine-period temple of Mercury-Bacchus (see DIONYSUS), and another small circular temple are among the most impressive monuments of the Syrian school of Hellenistic architecture.

Helios, the sun. In early Greece Helios was always treated with reverence but received little actual cult. The philosopher *Anaxagoras' announcement that the 'sun was a red-hot mass' caused outrage and it was not uncommon to salute and even pray to the sun at its rising and setting, but Aristophanes can treat the practice of sacrificing to sun and moon as one that distinguishes barbarians from Greeks. Hence evidence for actual cults is scarce and usually cannot be shown to be ancient. The exception was

*Rhodes, where Helios—subject in fact of the original 'colossus of Rhodes'—was the leading god and had an important festival, the Halieia; the myth explaining this prominence is told in *Pindar. In *Homer he is invoked and receives an offering as witness to an oath, and his all-seeing, all-nurturing power is often stressed in poetry.

For his most important myth *see* PHAE-THON. He is regularly conceived as a charioteer, who drives daily from east to west across the sky (a conception with both Indo-European and near-eastern parallels). His journey back each night in a cup is already attested in 6th-cent. BC poetry.

The identification of the Sun with *Apollo was familiar in the 5th cent. BC but did not become canonical until much later: *Aeschylus in *Bassarides* probably associated it with *Orpheus, the religious innovator, and a passage in *Euripides where it appears unambiguously for the first time also mentions (whether for this reason or another is unclear) 'those who know the secret names of the gods'. (The identification is also attested for the scientists *Parmenides and *Empedocles.) The 'visible gods' of heaven acquired new prominence in the astral religion of *Plato, and *Cleanthes the Stoic named the sun the 'leading principle' of the world. Through indirect influence from philosophy, worship of Helios probably became more common in the late Hellenistic period and after. But it was not until the later Roman empire that Helios/*Sol grew into a figure of central importance in actual cult.

[Homer, *Iliad* 3. 277, *Odyssey* 8. 270–1, 12. 127–41, 260–419; Hesiod, *Theogony* 371–4, 956–62; Pindar, *Olympian* 7. 54–76; Ovid, *Metamorphoses* 1. 750–2. 380, 4. 169–270]

Hellanicus of Lesbos (c.480–395 BC) was a *mythographer, ethnographer, and chronicler of major significance. Though his background was in the tradition of Ionian enquiry begun by *Hecataeus (1), he deserves to be ranked with Herodotus and Thucydides in the effect he had on the development of Greek historiography. He wrote extensively, but only some 200 fragments have survived.

His five works of mythography (the study of myth as history)—*Phoronis*, *Deukalioneia*, *Atlantis*, *Asopis*, and *Troika*—brought together in a form that was definitive for later scholarship the efforts of earlier mythographers to collate and integrate the disparate corpora of *mythoi* into a coherent and chronologically consistent narrative. The effect of this creative activity upon the whole classical tradition is incalculable.

His ethnographic works (studies of peoples and places) were even more extensive, ranging from areas in Greece (Thessaly, Boeotia, Arcadia, and Lesbos) to foreign countries (Egypt, Cyprus, Scythia, and Persia). They were, however, less influential, partly because they were largely unoriginal, partly because they were overshadowed by the great work of Herodotus.

His other area of interest was the Universal Chronicle. Hellanicus pioneered the use of victor lists (Carnean Games; *see* CARNEA) and of magistrates (priestesses of *Hera at Argos) to establish a common chronology for Greek history.

He combined all his talents late in life in Athens to create the first local history of Attica (*Atthis*), based upon his ordering of the succession of mythical kings and the list of annual chief magistrates. His *Atthis* (called *Attike Syngraphe* by Thucydides) covered in two books all Athenian history to the end of the Peloponnesian War. Its tone was influenced by Athenian national propaganda. Thucydides criticized Hellanicus but used his *Priestesses*.

Helle, daughter of *Athamas and sister of Phrixus, who, while escaping with her brother from their stepmother Ino, fell into the sea from the flying ram with the Golden Fleece which was carrying them to *Colchis; the sea was thereafter known as Helle's sea or Hellespont.

Hellen, *eponymous ancestor of the Hellenes, son or brother of *Deucalion. His sons were Dorus, *Xuthus (father of *Ion), and *Aeolus (2), the ancestors of the Dorians, Ionians, and Aeolians.

Hemithea, in mythology a daughter of Staphylus, was established by *Apollo as a healing deity at Kastabos in southern Caria. Her sanctuary has been identified on a spur of the Eren Dağ. The temple, in the Ionic order with 6 by 12 columns, was built in the late 4th cent. BC, and the cult was at its height in the following period of Rhodian domination.

Hephaestus, Greek god of *fire, of blacksmiths, and of artisans. The name, of uncertain etymology, has no certain attestation in Linear B, though there is the possibility of reading a theophoric name in Minoan Cnossus.

In *Homer, Hephaestus is so closely connected with fire that earlier scholars felt tempted to derive the god from the element: he owns the fire and helps fight Scamandrus with it; in a formula, his name is used to stand for fire. On the other hand, he is the divine master-artisan who fabricates *Achilles' shield and miraculous automata, self-moving tripods, golden servant maidens, or watchdogs for king *Alcinous. In the divine society of Homer, he is an outsider: he works, even sweats; he is laughed at when he tries to replace *Ganymedes; he is married to *Aphrodite but cuckolded; his feet are crippled (in Archaic iconography they are turned backwards): the outsider even lacks divine bodily perfection. His mother *Hera had conceived him without a male partner, as Gaia had done with some monsters; seeing the crippled offspring, she cast him out of *Olympus, and he grew up with the sea goddesses Eurynome and *Thetis; or Zeus had thrown him out because he had sided with Hera, and he had landed on Lemnos where the indigenous Sinties tended him. But he is not to be underestimated: his works evoke wonder; when serving the gods he intentionally provokes laughter; and he takes his cunning revenge on *Ares and Aphrodite and on Hera, and is brought back into Olympus. Thus, the Homeric picture preserves among an aristocratic society the physiognomy of a cunning blacksmith whose professional skills are highly admired and secretly feared, and whose social skills should not be underrated. It is very much the position blacksmiths have in Archaic societies. With the exception of Athens (see below), later mythology continues without fundamentally new concepts. His workshop was located beneath active volcanoes, especially Etna on Sicily, and the *Cyclopes were assigned to him as his workmen; he was also connected with natural fires, like the one on Lycian Olympus. That he had created mankind, according to Lucian, is but a witty extrapolation from his role in the creation of *Pandora.

Foremost among his cult places is the island of Lemnos where he landed when thrown out from Olympus. One of its two towns is called Hephaestia, with a sanctuary whose priest was eponymous (see EPONYMOI). He is connected with the mysteries of the *Cabiri whose father he was and whose ritual structure may derive from secret societies of blacksmiths. The Homeric Sinties were regarded as pre-Greek Thracians or Etruscans and the cult in the Lemnian sanctuary of the Cabiri begins before the Greek settlement; thus, non-Greek elements play a role in this cult, reinforcing the marginality of Hephaestus.

Better known is the Athenian cult where he is connected with Athena, the goddess of cunning intelligence. In his sanctuary above the *Agora ('Theseion'), which was built after 450 BC, there stood a group of Hephaestus and Athena Hephaestia, set up in 421/0 by the sculptor Alcamenes. At the same time, the festival Hephaestia in honour of Hephaestus and Athena was reorganized as a *penteteris* (festival celebrated every fifth year) with a splendid torch-race and lavish sacrifices: the splendour of the festival reflects the position of artisans in the Athenian state. The same holds true for the Chalkeia on the last day of Pyanopsion, a festival dedicated to Athena and Hephaestus when the artisans went in procession through the town. The god was also important in the

*Apaturia when the participants in their best robes and with torch in hand offered a hymn and a sacrifice to the god. Here and in the Hephaestia, the torch alludes to the theme of new fire (which is also present in the Lemnian cult). Athenian mythology tells of Hephaestus' abortive attempt to rape *Athena; from his spilled semen grew *Erichthonius, the ancestor of the autochthonous Athenians—the myth explains Hephaestus' role in the Apaturia and the theme of (new) beginnings.

He was very early identified with Roman *Volcanus and with Etruscan Sethlans (*see* ETRUSCAN RELIGION).

In Archaic iconography, Hephaestus appears especially in the scene of his return to Olympus under the guidance of *Dionysus. He is also shown helping Zeus to give birth to Athena (east pediment of the *Parthenon) and in the assembly of the gods. The statue of a standing Hephaestus by Alcamenes with a discreet indication of his limp was famous.

[Homer, *Iliad* 1. 571–600, 18. 373–9, 417–21, 21. 328–82; *Odyssey* 8. 267–366; Apollodorus 1. 3. 5–6]

Hera This major figure in the pantheon, daughter of *Cronus and wife of *Zeus, is already attested by name (as *Era*) on two Mycenaean tablets, one from Thebes, the other from Pylos, where she appears together with Zeus. Boeotia (*see* BOEOTIA, CULTS) and especially the Peloponnese are precisely the two regions of Greece where the cult of Hera is most prevalent. According to *Homer, Hera's favourite cities were Argos, Sparta, and Mycenae; several cults are actually attested at Sparta, and her most famous sanctuary was on the hill dominating the Argive plain, where there was a temple perhaps from the 8th cent. BC. Sanctuaries with buildings at least as ancient are known at Perachora (in the territory of Corinth), Tiryns (on the site of the megaron of the Mycenaean palace), and *Olympia. Of island sites, the best known is the sanctuary on Samos, where the main building, rebuilt in the 6th cent. BC, was mentioned by Herodotus, who comments on its magnificence.

Thus, the most ancient and important temples were those of Hera. Her cults also spread at an early date to the Greek colonies of the west, where later she became identified with the Roman *Juno. Her sanctuaries (*see* HERAION) at Croton and Paestum were much frequented.

In the Classical period, Hera's distinguishing feature compared with other goddesses is her double connection with royalty and marriage. In this way she is closely associated with Zeus, who made her 'last of all, his flourishing wife'. Her queenliness and noble beauty are abundantly stressed in her epithets and in artistic representations. The ancient formula *potnia Herē* is succeeded by that of *basileia*, 'queen'. She is described as 'golden-throned', and is often thus represented, sometimes seeming to surpass her husband in importance: at Olympia, an Archaic statue showed Zeus standing beside Hera enthroned, while in the Argive Heraion the famous gold and ivory statue by the sculptor Polyclitus represented the god in the form of a cuckoo perched on the sceptre held by the goddess—in her other hand she held a pomegranate; and on her head-dress were figures of the *Charites and the *Horae. One of *Plato's myths clearly underlines her royal qualities: according to this the followers of Hera are those who seek in love a 'kingly nature'.

Marriage is stressed constantly in Hera's myths and cults. It is attested by epithets such as Gamelia, Gamostolos, Syzygia, Zeuxidia, and especially Teleia, sometimes in connection with Zeus Teleios. Rituals in her honour connected with a sacred *marriage are recorded in various places, notably in Athens, where this marriage served as a social and institutional paradigm: at the festival of Theogamia, celebrated in Gamelion, the divine couple were given the title of 'magistrates of marriages'. In Crete, the marriage was re-enacted annually by the river Theren 'in imitation of weddings'. But Hera was not only the patron of marriages; she was often given the title of *Parthenos*, 'girl', and associated with prenuptial rites, including sometimes the lying together of the two sexes. Marital separation, suggested by Hera's mythology, is also evoked in cult, particularly at Plataea and at Stymphalus, where Hera was called simultaneously *Pais* 'child', *Teleia* 'wife', and *Chēra* 'widow' or 'separated', thus covering the whole life of women, with its turning-points. An Argive ritual, whereby every year the statue of Hera was bathed in a spring at Nauplia to restore the goddess's virginity indicates the recurrent nature of these separations.

*Motherhood, though part of Hera's personality, is little stressed, particularly in cult. Her children are *Ares, *Hebe, and *Eileithyia, goddess of childbirth, whose name she bears at Argos; in her sanctuary at Paestum, she is sometimes shown as a *kourotrophos. She suckled *Heracles, a scene often shown on Etruscan mirrors, but her relationship with the hero, whose name could be taken to mean 'glory of Hera', is ambivalent. She acted as nurse to monsters born to Earth, the Lernaean Hydra and the Nemean lion; in addition she was the sole parent of the monster Typhon and also, according to Hesiod, Hephaestus, whom she produced in anger, to defy her husband. But these episodes by their exceptional nature in fact illustrate Hera's close links with the marriage bond, which she herself protects and guarantees.

The marriage of Zeus and Hera is part of a complex symbolism including the natural world of plants and animals. This is shown by Hera's oldest sanctuaries, which are often situated in fertile plains away from urban settlements. The statue of Polyclitus mentioned above is relevant here. The sacred marriage described by Homer, despite the alterations due to epic, still bears traces of this natural symbolism, and we also find mentioned the flourishing garden at the edge of the Ocean, which served as marriage-bed for the two deities. We can see a relationship between the goddess called Boöpis ('ox-eyed') and herds of cows, and also with horses, especially in connection with a sacred marriage. Io, changed into a heifer by Zeus in bull form, was the priestess

of Hera at Argos, where Hera's rule extended over the animal herds of the plain (*see* CLEOBIS AND BITON). At *Olympia, where Hera Hippia ('of horses') was worshipped alongside *Poseidon Hippios, contests among girls had been established in honour of the goddess by Hippodamia in thanks for her marriage to Pelops. These facts may be linked with two other chthonian features, isolated as they are: the oracles of Hera, at Perachora and Cumae, and the funerary cult given to *Medea's children in one of Hera's sanctuaries at Corinth.

Hera was also worshipped as protector of cities and other social groups, especially at Argos and on Samos; the poet Alcaeus calls her 'mother of all', in a hymn of invocation where she appears between Zeus and Dionysus. It is in this context that she is sometimes shown armed. At Argos the prize at the games held during the Heraia festival was a shield. Despite this protecting function, it is noteworthy that literary presentations, from the *Iliad* onwards, tend to stress the destructive and capricious side of Hera's nature.

As with most of the Greek pantheon, Hera's origins are unclear. There is no certain etymology for her name; if the modern consensus sees Linear B *Era* as the feminine of *hērōs*, this itself has given rise to differing interpretations. The supporters of an Indo-European origin from the hypothetical root *yer* explain the name variously as meaning 'heifer', 'the goddess of the year', or 'a girl of marriageable age'. Others incline towards a pre-Greek origin for both Mycenaean words. But a solution to the problem of the name would not explain the whole issue of Hera's origin. Associated as she is with Zeus from the Mycenaean period onwards, it is clear that Hera preserves certain characteristics of an Indo-European divine couple; but in her sovereign power, tending towards the universal, it is difficult not to see traces of an Aegean great goddess.

[Homer, *Iliad* 1. 536–611; Hesiod, *Theogony* 313–32, 453–506, 921–9; *Homeric Hymn to Hera*; Pindar, *Nemean* 1. 33–72]

Heracles, the greatest of Greek heroes. His name is that of a mortal (compare Diocles), and has been interpreted as 'Glorious through *Hera'. In this case, the bearer is taken as being—or so his parents would hope—within the protection of the goddess. This is at odds with the predominant tradition (see below), in which Heracles was harassed rather than protected by the goddess: perhaps the hostility was against worshippers of Heracles who rejected allegiance to the worshippers of Hera on whom the hero depended. This could have happened when Argos had established control over the *Heraion and Tiryns (possibly reflected in an apparent falling-off of settlement at Tiryns late in the 9th cent. BC). Some of the inhabitants of Tiryns might have emigrated to Thebes, taking their hero with him. Traditionally Heracles' mother and her husband (*Alcmene and *Amphitryon) were obliged to move from Tiryns to Thebes, where Heracles was conceived and born. However, there is no agreement over the etymology of the name, an alternative version deriving its first element from 'Hero'.

Heracles shared the characteristics of, on the one hand, a hero (both cultic and epic), on the other, a god. As a hero, he was mortal, and like many other heroes, born to a human mother and a god (Alcmene and *Zeus; Amphitryon was father of *Iphicles, Heracles' twin: the bare bones of the story are already in *Homer). Legends arose early of his epic feats, and they were added to constantly throughout antiquity. These stories may have played a part in the transformation of Heracles from hero (i.e. a deity of mortal origin, who, after death, exercised power over a limited geographical area, his influence residing in his mortal remains) to god (a deity, immortal, whose power is not limited geographically). See HERO-CULT.

Outside the cycle of the Labours (see below), the chief events of Heracles' life were as follows: Hera pursued him with implacable enmity from before his birth, which she managed to delay until after that of *Eurystheus. She then sent serpents to

Thebes to attack Heracles in his cradle, but the infant strangled them. Later, she drove him mad and caused him to murder his Theban wife, Megara, and their children (there are different versions). In his youth, Heracles led the Thebans in their successful revolt against *Orchomenus. He also took part in an expedition against Troy and sacked Oechalia, accompanied the *Argonauts, founded the *Olympian games, and ultimately died by burning on Mt. Oeta (death came as a relief against the poison given him inadvertently by his wife *Deianira, who had hoped to regain his love thereby: the dying *Centaur Nessus, from whom Heracles rescued his wife, had given her the poison as a love potion. She used it when Heracles took up with Iole).

The Labours themselves (twelve is the canonical number, but there is little agreement on the full complement) support, by their geographical distribution, the contention that, however popular Heracles became in other parts of the ancient world, his origins were in the Peloponnese, and more specifically in the Argolid. He was sent to perform them by Eurystheus of Argos, to whom he was bound in vassalage. Six belong to the northern part of the Peloponnese, and might be taken to represent either a gradual spread of Argive ambitions in that region, or, with equal likelihood, the growing popularity of Heracles over a steadily widening area. These tasks were to deal with (1) the Nemean lion (northern border of the Argolid; *see* NEMEA); (2) the Lernaean Hydra (south-west Argolid); (3) the Erymanthian boar (north-west Arcadia); (4) the hind of Ceryneia (Achaea); (5) the Stymphalian birds (north-east Arcadia; *see* STYMPHALUS); (6) the stables of Augeas (Elis). The other Labours are situated at the ends of the habitable world or beyond: the Cretan bull to the south, the horses of the Thracian *Diomedes to the north, the quest for the belt of the *Amazon queen to the east, the search for the cattle of Geryon to the west, the apples of the *Hesperides at the edge of the world, and *Cerberus in the world of the dead. Many but not all of the Labours are already depicted in Greek art of the geometric and early Archaic periods. Also early to appear are two feats outside the canon, a fight against *Centaurs, and a struggle with *Apollo for the Delphic tripod. The encounters with Centaurs take place in Arcadia and Thessaly; the fight with Apollo might reflect a struggle for political control over *Delphi between its inhabitants and those of Malis (Trachis and Mt. Oeta).

The iconography of Heracles was firmly established by the Archaic period, but even before then it is possible to identify him from the subject-matter. The major identifying symbols were the lion-skin cape and hood (flayed from the Nemean lion), his club, and his bow and arrows.

Throughout his life and many adventures, Heracles was guided closely by *Athena, by whom he was introduced to *Olympus after his death. The apotheosis of Heracles was represented in literature and art by giving him—after his death—a wife in the person of *Hebe, i.e. 'youth', or rather the embodiment of the prime of life, for it is the permanent possession of this boon which most distinguishes gods from men. The story is attested definitely by the 6th cent. BC. In popular cult, Heracles was recognized and invoked as a god from at least late in the 6th cent. Herodotus writes approvingly of those Hellenes who worshipped Heracles both as an immortal Olympian and as a hero. The practice must have been common, if not widespread (*Pindar calls Heracles a 'hero god').

As in the case of Apollo, his divine rival for the Delphic tripod, the cult of Heracles spread at least partly through the absorption of local cult figures—in Heracles' case, mostly heroic—of similar nature. Individuals adopted Heracles as a more or less personal patron; at the communal level, he presided over ephebes, young men, as their ideal in warfare and their patron in military training, whence his patronage of the gymnasium (a role often shared with *Hermes), and over the young in general. He was primarily associated with the activities of men rather than women, which may explain the regulations barring women from his rites or even his *sanctuaries. Occasionally, however, the character of the local hero whom Heracles had deposed might override the general practice, as in the case of the western Boeotian Charops Heracles, who was served by a priestess.

The geographical distribution of his cults is, as one might expect, as wide as that of his legends. Interestingly, evidence from Tiryns and Argos, although early in the former, is sparse. That he was established at Thebes by the Homeric period cannot be doubted, although the earliest contemporary evidence for cult occurs in the 5th cent. He was worshipped fairly widely throughout Boeotia, and neighbouring Attica.

One of the earliest places to produce archaeological evidence for a cult of Heracles is the sanctuary on Mt. Oeta, site of his immolation. Another important early site is at Thasos, where evidence extends from soon after the foundation of the colony. The Thasian cult exemplifies several features of the worship of Heracles: first, his treatment as a god; second, his function as champion or protector of the community (particularly its urban centre); third, the tendency to syncretize (*see* SYNCRETISM) Heracles with other deities, local or otherwise, in the case of Thasos, the other being Melqart of Tyre.

The sanctuary at Thasos, which may be typical, included not only a sacrificial area, but also a temple and extensive dining-facilities (the last often illustrated in vase-painting and so probably typical); descriptions of other Herakleia would lead us to expect the existence of extensive athletic facilities as part of the complex. All of this public devotion to bodily well-being would have helped to produce the impression of Heracles as a boisterous glutton.

As noted above, Heracles was adopted by individuals or states as a symbol or protecting deity, to which numerous towns named after him bear eloquent testimony. Boeotian Thebes used Heracles as its symbol from at least the second half of the 5th cent. BC, if not earlier. In the preceding century Pisistratus of Athens may have made Heracles his personal divine protector and legitimator of his actions. The Macedonian royal family ('Argeads') claimed lineal descent from Heracles for similar motives. Most notoriously, however, the Dorian rulers of the Peloponnese sought to legitimate their claims to sovereignty by tracing their descent to Heracles through his sons, the *Heraclidae, who, as the tale was told, 'returned' to the Peloponnese from the north to claim their inheritance.

[Sophocles, *Women of Trachis*, *Philoctetes*; Euripides, *Madness of Heracles*; Apollodorus 2. 4. 8–7. 8; Diodorus Siculus 4. 9–39; Virgil, *Aeneid* 8. 175–279; Propertius 4. 9]

Heraclidae, the children of Heracles. The myth of the return of the descendants of *Heracles to the Peloponnese functioned, above all, as a charter myth for the division of the Peloponnese between different Dorian states. The fullest accounts are of the late Hellenistic period, but the myth was already familiar in all essentials in the 5th cent. BC; the poet Tyrtaeus in the 7th cent. had already told how *Zeus had granted Sparta to the Heraclidae who left 'windy Erineos' in the Dorian heartland of north Greece.

*Eurystheus, persecutor of Heracles, continued to persecute the exiled sons of Heracles after their father's death; the Athenians in particular gave them aid. After various adventures, the Heraclidae enquired of Delphi (*see* DELPHIC ORACLE) when they could return, and were told to do so at the third harvest. *Hyllus supposed this to mean the third year, but failed and was killed in single combat against a Peloponnesian champion at the Isthmus. A hundred years later his descendant *Temenus again inquired, and got the same reply, which was now interpreted for him as meaning the third generation. The Dorians therefore tried again, in three companies, led by Temenus, Cresphontes, and the sons of Aristodemus, Eurysthenes, and Procles. They

entered by Elis, taking, again by oracular advice, the 'three-eyed man' for their guide; he turned out to be Oxylus of Aetolia, whose mule, or horse, had only one eye. Conquering the Peloponnese, they divided it into three parts, of which Cresphontes took Messenia, Temenus Argos, and the sons of Aristodemus Lacedaemon, thus founding the dual kingship of Sparta. In the fighting Tisamenus, son of *Orestes and grandson of *Agamemnon, was killed, thus ending the line of the Pelopidae.

Several incidents of the myth had a life independent of the explanatory function of the whole. Athenian writers in particular made much of the support given to the Heraclidae in Attica, and several Athenian villages even paid *hero-cult to them and the companions of their wanderings, *Iolaus and *Alcmene.

[Euripides, *Heraclidae*; Diodorus Siculus 4. 57–8; Apollodorus 2. 7. 8–8]

Heraion, sanctuary of *Hera. The most important are the Heraion of Argos, and the Heraion of Samos. Both are situated at some distance from the cities which controlled or dominated them. The Argive Heraion is at an important but abandoned late bronze age site, which may have influenced its selection; the Samian Heraion also may have had earlier significance. Both developed early, having peripteral temples by at latest the first half of the 7th cent. BC. These had stone footings, with wooden columns. Both sanctuaries include structures designed for the crowds of worshippers, particularly porticoes from which to view the religious activities, and processional ways linking them physically and symbolically with the city-centre. *See* SANCTUARIES.

heralds (*kērykes*) in *Homer were important aides of the kings, used for such tasks as maintaining order in meetings, making proclamations, and bearing messages. They were under the protection of *Hermes, were inviolable, and carried a herald's staff as a symbol of authority. In later Greece they retained much of their importance, assisting magistrates in assemblies and lawcourts and bearing messages to other states. In this capacity they are to be distinguished from ambassadors (*presbeis*), who were not similarly inviolable but who might be authorized not only to transmit formal messages but also to negotiate. Heralds could circulate freely even during wars, and so were sometimes sent to open negotiations by requesting permission to send ambassadors. The Roman public crier (*praeco*) was a more humble attendant of magistrates.

Hercules, from *Hercles*, Italic pronunciation of the name *Heracles. His is perhaps the earliest foreign cult to be received in Rome (perhaps from Tibur), the Ara Maxima, which was his most ancient place of worship, being within the *pomerium* of the archaic Palatine settlement. It was probably desired to make the forum Boarium, in which it stood, a market-place under the protection of a god better known than the local deities. The theory of some ancients that he is identical with *Semo Sancus Dius Fidius is untenable, and seems ultimately to rest on nothing better than the interpretation of *Dius Fidius* as *Iovis filius*. His cult had become very popular with merchants, no doubt because of his supposed ability to avert evil of all kinds (see HERACLES) and the long journeys involved in his Labours and other exploits. It was common to pay him a *tithe of the profits of an enterprise; this was not confined to commercial dealings but included spoils of warfare.

His worship at the Ara Maxima had some interesting features. No other god was mentioned; no women were admitted; dogs were excluded. The sacrificial meat had to be eaten or burnt daily: hence the popularity of the sanctuary. The ritual was originally in the hands not of the *pontifices* but of two clans, the Potitii and Pinarii, of whom the former were senior; in 312 BC, it passed to the state; thereafter an annual sacrifice was celebrated on 12 August by the urban praetor (attested in inscriptions from the later 2nd cent. AD). It was performed in Greek fashion. The exclusion of women is found also in his cult at *Lanuvium.

He had numerous other places of worship at Rome. The most important, after the Ara Maxima, are a sanctuary of Hercules Cubans within Caesar's Gardens, temples of Hercules Custos near the Circus Flaminius (probably *c*.220 BC), of Hercules Victor (or Invictus) near the porta Trigemina (the surviving round temple, anniversary on 13 August), of Hercules Musarum near the Circus Flaminius (*c*.187 BC), of Hercules Pompeianus near the Circus Maximus, of Hercules Victor (dedicated on the Caelian hill in 142 BC), and of Hercules, a round temple in the forum Boarium, decorated with frescoes.

Identification or comparison with Hercules was common among the later emperors, especially Commodus.

[Propertius 4. 9]

Hermaphroditus, half-male, half-female divinity, his cult first attested in the 4th cent. BC at Athens. Diodorus makes him the offspring of *Hermes and *Aphrodite; *Ovid provides a lengthy aetiology (the prayers of the nymph Salmacis that she and her beloved might never be parted are dramatically granted). A favourite subject of Hellenistic and Roman artists, he is invariably depicted with developed breasts and male genitals, his physique soft and boyish. At republican Rome natural hermaphrodites (*androgyni*) were considered ill-omened prodigies (see PORTENTS) and were liable to ritual drowning at birth.

[Diodorus Siculus 4. 6. 5; Ovid, *Metamorphoses* 4. 285 ff.]

Hermes Already attested among the Mycenaean pantheon (tablets from Cnossus in Crete, Pylos, and Thebes; see MINOAN AND MYCENAEAN RELIGION), the god has no original connection with the *herma* or cairn of stones, as was once thought. Myths about Hermes are mostly concerned with his childhood, told in the *Homeric Hymn to Hermes* (last third of the 6th cent. BC; see HYMNS). He was the son of *Zeus and the *nymph *Maia, born on Mt. Cyllene in Arcadia. On the day of his birth, he left his cradle, found a tortoise which he made into a lyre, then went to Pieria where he stole 50 cows belonging to *Apollo, which he led backwards to a cave where he sacrificed two and hid the others, before returning to Cyllene; finally he made up the quarrel with Apollo. Later, he invented the syrinx (pipe) and was taught *divination by Apollo. Apart from these stories of his childhood, Hermes plays only a secondary part in other myths. He has no recognized wife, but two sons, Eudorus (in the *Iliad*) and *Pan, are attributed to him. He is characterized by a great variety of functions. Above all, he is a messenger god, who carries out the orders of Zeus. In this capacity, he appears as a subordinate deity, giving the ultimatum of Zeus to *Prometheus, for instance, or acting as his go-between when he is enamoured of *Ganymedes. He is generally well-disposed, and negotiates the ransom of Hector with pleasantness and good humour. His titles stress his speed and beneficence. He is also the god who guides: he shows transhumant shepherds the way and leads teams of animals; he guides people, especially travellers, for whom he marks out the route in the form of a pillar or herm (see below). He takes divine children to safety (thus he gives *Dionysus to the Nymphs of Nysa, as depicted in the famous statue by Praxiteles, and *Arcas to Maia), and is generally a patron of children (*Heracles, *Achilles); he also helps heroes such as *Perseus, for whom he obtains the bronze sickle used by the hero to decapitate Medusa (*see* GORGO), and Heracles. He leads *Hera, *Aphrodite, and *Athena to *Paris, the judge in their beauty contest. As god of movement, he is leader of the Nymphs and the *Charites. Finally as *psychopompos* (one who escorts *souls), he leads the dead to *Hades, summoning them to the journey beyond, taking them by the hand and accompanying them on to *Charon's boat.

Another aspect of Hermes is that of a god of abundance, fertility, and prosperity. He is the patron of herdsmen and of the fruitfulness of herds and flocks; he is himself a cowherd and shepherd. This form of Hermes is called Nomios, 'pastoral' and Epimelios, 'presiding over sheep', and is often shown in art as Hermes *kriophoros* ('ram-bearing'), especially in Arcadia and Boeotia. He is also sometimes a 'lord of animals', of horses in particular. More generally, he is the god of every kind of prosperity. The herm, a quadrangular pillar topped with a head, with tenons on its sides and a phallus on the front, was very popular from the end of the 6th cent. onwards, and not only recalls Hermes' powers of fertility but, as an apotropaic talisman, also guarantees the success of all sorts of undertakings. (*See* HERMS.) It is found in towns both at the threshold of houses and inside them, and became a sort of mascot bringing luck both to cities and to individuals (the mutilation of the herms at Athens was perceived as a bad omen on the eve of the Sicilian expedition). In the same context, Hermes is also the god of trade (on Delian seals of the Hellenistic age he appears holding a purse).

Hermes is an ingenious god, expert in both technology and magic. From his birth onwards, he was skilled in trickery and deception, and in the *Homeric Hymn* he is 'prince of thieves'. Even in cult, he is attested as trickster and thief (Hermes Dolios at Pellene in Achaea and Hermes Kleptes in Chios). But most often he uses his power in mischief, illusion, and mystery. He creates a lyre out of the shell of a tortoise, he puts on his feet sandals which erase footprints. He is an expert in knots and chains. Like a magician he knows how to put the enemy camp to sleep, and to call up the dead. As a corollary, this god of *mētis* (prudence, cunning) and of mediation has no part in violence. He is the least warlike of the gods; he is dragged into the battle with the *Giants, and linked with murder only in the story of *Argos. He prefers persuasion to weapons, and appears frequently as patron of orators. He can also be a musician: he is the inventor of the syrinx, and accompanies the dances of the Nymphs and the Charites. Only in a late period, as Trismegistus ('thrice-greatest'), does he come to preside over mystical revelations, as the successor to the Egyptian god Thoth and god of the 'hermetic' (*see* HERMES TRISMEGISTUS). A final function of Hermes, attested above all from the 4th cent. BC, is that of god of athletes—one linked, no doubt, to the youthful appearance and charm which the god assumed for seductions. In this role he is frequently associated, particularly in the gymnasium, with *Heracles. He even became, in the Hellenistic period, the god of the school and of education.

Hermes' main aspects are shown in his physical appearance and iconography. His attributes are the caduceus, the herald's sign which he almost always carries, the traveller's hat (*petasos* or *pilos*), with or without wings, and the winged sandals which evoke his quality of speed. He is generally bearded in the earlier period, but an unbearded type develops from the 4th cent. onwards. He is clothed in a cloak, a *chlamys* or a *chlaina*, with sometimes a furry leopard-skin. Side by side with this very frequent representation of the god of herds and flocks, the god of music, the messenger and guide, or the *chthonian god, we find the herm (see above), whose identity as Hermes is sometimes stressed by a caduceus painted on the shaft. This form, attested in sculpture as well as on vases, was very popular and could symbolize most of the functions of the god. In some cases, especially to indicate Hermes as god of the gymnasium, the pillar wears a cloak.

The cult of Hermes is particularly widely diffused in the Peloponnese, where *Pausanias mentions numerous myths, rituals, cults, and herms. Passing over the more ordinary examples (Pellene, Pheneos, and Mt. Cyllene, Megalopolis, Tegea, Corinth, Argos), we may point out the oracular ritual in front of a pillar of Hermes at Pharae in Achaea. In Athens, Hermes had a very ancient cult (cf. the *xoanon* or ancient statue dedicated on the Acropolis by *Cecrops), and in the form of the herm he was present everywhere in the city. The Hermaia, a young boys' festival, were celebrated in his honour. His cult is also attested in Boeotia (at Tanagra) and in the Cyclades: at *Delos he is the god of the gymnasium. At Cydonia in Crete, the Hermaia were a popular festival where slaves took the part of their masters. Hermes was not a major divinity, but because he was essentially kindly, he was one of the most familiar gods in the daily lives of the Greeks.

[Homer, *Iliad* 20. 31–40, 21. 497–501; *Homeric Hymn to Hermes*]

Hermes Trismegistus, the Hellenistic *Hermes, Egyptianized through contact with the Egyptian Thoth. 'Trismegistos' derives from the Egyptian superlative obtained through repetition (Hermes appears as 'Great, Great, Great' on the Rosetta stone), which is later simplified through the substitution of the prefix *tris* ('three-fold') in the Roman period. According to *Clement of Alexandria he was the author of 42 'fundamental books' of Egyptian religion, including astrological, cosmological, geographical, medical, and pedagogic books as well as hymns to the gods and instructions on how to worship. The extant corpus of Hermetic writings (in Greek, Latin, and Coptic) includes astrological, alchemical, iatromathematical, and philosophic works. Some elements in some of the philosophical books (especially the *Asclepius* and *Corpus Hermeticum* 16) are overtly anti-Greek in sentiment, but the basic content of the works is thoroughly Hellenic and offers an insight into 'popular Platonism' in the Roman world as spread through small groups of literate people who gathered around a teacher for instruction. Hermes also appears frequently in the Greek magical papyri, a reflection of Thoth's role as the god of *magic, and may be connected with late antique *theurgy.

Hermias, otherwise unknown Christian author of the *Satire on the Profane Philosophers*. This small Greek treatise of uncertain date (perhaps *c*.AD 200) aims at exposing the contradictions of the teachings of the major philosophical schools as regards the nature of the soul and the universe.

Hermione, in mythology daughter of *Menelaus and *Helen. According to *Homer, Menelaus betrothed her to *Neoptolemus while he was away at Troy, and the wedding took place after the war. The marriage, however, was childless; according to *Euripides' *Andromache*, Hermione blamed this on spells cast by *Andromache, Neoptolemus' concubine won at Troy, and would have had both Andromache and Molossus, her son by Neoptolemus, put to death if old *Peleus, Neoptolemus' grandfather, had not intervened to save them. Neoptolemus was then murdered by *Orestes while at *Delphi enquiring why Hermione was childless, and she was carried off by Orestes, to whom in this version she had originally been promised. According to another play by Euripides (*Orestes*), however, she was never married to Neoptolemus. Almost all authors agree that she became Orestes' wife, and mother of his son Tisamenus.

[Homer, *Odyssey* 4. 1–14; Euripides, *Andromache* 966–81; Ovid, *Heroines* 8]

herms were marble or bronze four-cornered pillars surmounted by a bust. Male herms were given genitals. Herms originated in piles of stones used as road- and boundary-markers, but early on developed into the god *Hermes. As representations of Hermes they were viewed also as protectors of houses and cities. The Athenians claimed credit for the developed sculptural form, and herms were particularly common in Athens, at crossroads, in the countryside, in the Agora, at the entrance of the Acropolis, in sanctuaries, and at private doorways. The sacrilegious mutilation of the herms in 415 BC led to the exile of Alcibiades. Other deities, e.g. *Aphrodite, were also occasionally represented as herms, and the Romans in copying Greek portrait statues converted some into herm form.

Hero and Leander, mythological lovers. Hero was priestess of *Aphrodite at Sestus on one side of the Hellespont; Leander lived at Abydos on the other side, saw her at a festival, fell in love with her, and used to swim the Hellespont at night to see her until a storm put out the light by which she guided him, and he was drowned; Hero leapt from her seaside tower onto his corpse.

Originally perhaps a local Hellespontine tale, the story was probably popularized by one or more Hellenistic poets and later was well known to Roman writers. The most detailed extant treatment is that of Musaeus (5th/6th cent. AD), a learned Christian and/or *Neoplatonist. His 343-line hexameter miniature epic, which owes much in diction to the contemporary epic writing of *Nonnus, contains many contextual and linguistic allusions to *Homer, and employs to fine effect the motifs of light and darkness: Hero's lamp is equated with the life of her lover in an ingenious variety of ways. The poem inspired Marlowe's *Hero and Leander* and many other later works.

[Virgil, *Georgics* 3. 258–63; Ovid, *Heroines* 18–19]

hero-cult Heroes were a class of beings worshipped by the Greeks, generally conceived as the powerful dead, and often as forming a class intermediate between gods and men. Hero-cult was apparently unknown to the Mycenaeans; features suggestive of the fully developed phenomenon have been found in 10th-cent. BC contexts, but it is not until the 8th cent. that such cults become widespread and normal. The reasons for its rise have been much debated, but seem likely to be somehow connected with more general social changes at that date.

Although Greek authors expect the phrase 'heroic honours' to convey something definite, there was in practice much variation in the type of cult given to heroes. At one end of the spectrum it could have a strong resemblance to the offerings given to a dead relative; at the other, it might be barely distinguishable from worship paid to a god. Many features cited by ancient and modern authorities as typical of heroic *sacrifice occur also in divine cults with a '*chthonian' aspect: holocaust sacrifice on a low altar, using dark animals, performed at night.

Such rites, characteristic of the form of sacrifice known as *enagismos*, certainly seem designed to contrast with 'normal' sacrifice, *thusia*, in the strict sense, but there are too many examples of heroic sacrifices which do not conform to this pattern to be dismissed as anomalies (*see* SACRIFICE, GREEK). Epigraphic evidence, in particular the Attic sacrifice calendars, shows that very often the hero's offering was distinguished from the god's simply by its lesser value, but even this is not universal, especially where the hero represents an old divinity or forms the focal point of a festival. Again, while heroes' sanctuaries tended to be smaller and less splendid than those of gods, often indeed occupying a small space within a divine precinct, a few heroes, such as *Hippolytus (1) at Troezen, had sanctuary complexes as impressive as those of any god. Hero-shrines were often—not always—constructed around tombs, real or supposed, and the hero had a very close connection with that particular place, being far more localized than a god. The only real exception to this is *Heracles, who is in any case as much god as hero.

Concepts of heroes were as variable as their cult, if not more so. There is some evidence that heroes as a class were viewed as at least potentially malign, to be placated with apotropaic ritual rather than worshipped in the normal sense, but this is true only rarely of individual heroes, who more often appear as patrons or saviours of their city, as helpers in sickness or personal danger, and generally as benefactors. The traditions of their lives, deaths, and actions after death, however, usually contain some element of singularity or paradox. Many cult heroes were identified with the characters of heroic epic, but bronze age credentials were not necessary: the newly dead might be given heroic honours, generally by oracular command, if they conformed to one of the heroic patterns, for instance by instituting a divine cult or founding a city. Still other heroes were probably never very clearly identified by their worshippers, but went by appellations such as 'the hero in the salt-pan' or 'the reed-man'. Heroines in particular might appear in groups named only for their place of cult, and in such cases seem closer to *nymphs than to the powerful dead. In other instances a heroine or heroines, often nameless, may be associated with a hero and receive sacrifice with him, generally an offering of lesser value; but there was no shortage of named heroines such as *Aglaurus or *Iphigenia who were independent of male heroes.

From the 4th cent. onwards there was a tendency in many parts of the Greek world for mourners to depict the ordinary dead in heroic forms, to call them 'hero', and even on occasion to establish regular heroic cult and a priesthood. The exceptional nature of the older heroes was thus undermined, and the changed political circumstance of the Hellenistic and Roman periods further reduced the relevance of the many heroic cults which were closely connected with a sense of civic identity. A number of old cults flourished still in the time of *Pausanias, but perhaps the majority had fallen into disuse.

Herod the Great (*c*.73 BC–4 BC), son of the Idumaean Antipater, was through him made governor of Galilee in 47 BC and then, with his brother, designated tetrarch by Mark Antony. Herod escaped the Parthian invasion of 40, and, while the Parthian nominee, the Hasmonean Antigonus, occupied the throne, Herod was declared king of Judaea by Antony and the senate. In 37, having married Mariamme, granddaughter to both of the feuding Hasmoneans, Hyrcanus and Aristobulus, Herod took *Jerusalem, with the assistance of Caius Sosius. Octavian, whom Herod supported at Actium, confirmed his rule, adding a number of cities. In 23, Herod received territories north-east of the Sea of Galilee—Trachonitis, Batanea, and Auranitis. Herod's rule meant that the kingship and high priesthood were now again separate in Judaea, though the latter was in the king's gift: he promoted a new high-priestly class, centred on a handful of diaspora families, who thus acquired great wealth and standing. The palace élite, of mixed ethnic affiliation, also grew. Herod was an able administrator and a skilful financier. He taxed the country heavily, but also developed its resources, to which end his artificial harbour at Caesarea contributed. Spectacular building projects were a hallmark of his reign, including the rebuilding of Samaria as Sebaste, a characteristic string of fortress-palaces, most notably Masada, and Herodium, also his burial place. Jerusalem acquired an amphitheatre as well as a theatre, whose decorations aroused the suspicion of some Jews. But his greatest undertaking, the rebuilding of the Temple, was left entirely to priests, to preserve purity. There, offence was given by a golden eagle put over the gate at the very end of his reign, a time when tensions with the *Pharisees, earlier his friends, were running high. Lavish donations outside Palestine established Herod as a benefactor on an empire-wide scale, as well as a flamboyant philhellene; the *Olympian games and the city of Athens were among the beneficiaries. Through his personal good offices, his visits to Rome, and the mediation of Nicolaus of Damascus and of Marcus Vipsanius Agrippa, Herod long retained Augustus' confidence. He may have been exempt from tribute. But, in 9 BC, an unauthorized war against the Nabataeans incurred imperial displeasure. Also increasingly unacceptable was his savagery towards the large family produced by his ten wives: intrigues led him to execute his favourite, Mariamme I, in 29, her two sons in 7, and his eldest son and expected heir a few days before his death. Serious disturbances then allowed Roman intervention, and the division of his kingdom between his remaining sons, Herod Antipas, Archelaus, and Philip, was formalized.

Hesiod, one of the oldest known Greek poets, often coupled or contrasted with *Homer as the other main representative of early epic. Which was the older of the two was much disputed from the 5th cent. BC on:

Homer's priority was carefully argued by the Hellenistic scholar Aristarchus, and generally accepted in later antiquity. Hesiod's absolute date is now agreed to fall not far before or after 700 BC. Of his life he tells us something himself: that his father had given up a life of unprofitable sea-trading and moved from Aeolian Cyme to Ascra in Boeotia; that he, as he tended sheep on Mt. *Helicon, had heard the *Muses calling him to sing of the gods; and that he once won a tripod for a song at a funeral contest at Chalcis. For his dispute with Perses see below (2). He is said to have died in Italian Locris, but his tomb was shown at Orchomenus in Boeotia. For the story of his meeting and contest with Homer see the poem *Certamen Homeri et Hesiodi*. The poems anciently attributed to him are as follows (only the first three have survived complete, and only the first two have a good claim to be authentic):

1. The *Theogony* The main part of the poem, which is prefaced by a hymn to the Muses (cf. the *Homeric Hymns*), deals with the origin and genealogies of the gods (including the divine world-masses Earth, Sea, Sky, etc.), and the events that led to the kingship of *Zeus: the castration of *Uranus by *Cronus, and the overthrow of Cronus and the *Titans, the 'former gods', by the Olympians. This 'Succession Myth' has striking parallels in near eastern Akkadian and Hittite texts, and seems originally to have come from the near east. Hesiod's version shows some stylistic awkwardness and inconcinnity, but is not without power. Interlaced with it are the genealogies, which run smoother. The first powers born are *Chaos, Earth (see GAIA), and (significantly) *Eros. From Chaos and Earth, in two separate lines, some 300 gods descend; they include personified abstracts, whose family relationships are clearly meaningful. There is an interesting passage in praise of the un-Homeric goddess *Hecate, further myths, notably the explanatory tale of *Prometheus, and a detailed description of Tartarus. The poem ends with the marriages of Zeus

and the other Olympians, and a list of goddesses who lay with mortal men. This last section, which refers to *Latinus and led on to the *Catalogue* (below, 4), is agreed to be post-Hesiodic, though opinions vary as to where the authentic part ends.

See also THEOGONY and GENEALOGICAL TABLES (1) GREEK GODS.

2. The *Works and Days*. This poem, apparently composed after the *Theogony*, would be more aptly entitled 'the Wisdom of Hesiod'. It gives advice for living a life of honest work. Hesiod inveighs against dishonesty and idleness by turns, using myths (Prometheus again, with the famous story of *Pandora; the five World Ages), parable, *allegory, proverbial maxims, direct exhortation, and threats of divine anger. The sermon is ostensibly directed at a brother Perses, who has bribed the 'lords' and taken more than his share of his inheritance; but Perses' failings seem to change with the context, and it is impossible to reconstruct a single basic situation. Besides moral advice, Hesiod gives much practical instruction, especially on agriculture (the year's 'Works'), seafaring, and social and religious conduct. There is a fine descriptive passage on the rigours of winter. The final section, sometimes regarded as a later addition, is the 'Days', an almanac of days in the month that are favourable or unfavourable for different operations. Some ancient copies continued with an *Ornithomanteia*, a section on bird omens. The poem as a whole is a unique source for social conditions in early Archaic Greece. It has closer parallels in near eastern literatures than in Greek, and seems to represent an old traditional type. (*Virgil's *Georgics*, though much influenced by Hesiod, are shaped by the Hellenistic tradition of systematic treatment of a single theme.)

It has always been the most read of Hesiodic poems. There was even a 'tradition' that it was Hesiod's only genuine work; but he names himself in the *Theogony*, and links of style and thought between the two poems confirm identity of authorship. Both bear the marks of a distinct personality: a surly, conservative countryman, given to reflection, no lover of women or of life, who felt the gods' presence heavy about him.

3. The *Shield* is a short narrative poem on *Heracles' fight with Cycnus, prefaced by an excerpt from the fourth book of the *Catalogue* giving the story of Heracles' birth. It takes its title from the disproportionately long description of Heracles' shield, which is based partly on the shield of Achilles in the *Iliad*, partly on the art of the period *c.*580–570 (this proves that the Hellenistic scholar Aristophanes of Byzantium was right in denying the poem to Hesiod). Disproportion is characteristic of the work; the Homeric apparatus of arming, divine machination, brave speeches, and long similes is lavished on an encounter in which two blows are struck in all. Parts of the description of the shield betray a taste for the macabre.

4. The *Catalogue of Women* or *Ehoiai* was a continuation of the *Theogony* in five books, containing comprehensive heroic *genealogies with many narrative annotations. Numerous citations and extensive papyrus fragments survive. The poem was accepted as Hesiod's in antiquity, but various indications point to the period 580–520 BC.

5. Other lost poems. (*a*) Narrative: *Greater Ehoiai* (genealogical); *Melampodia* (at least three books; stories of famous seers); *Wedding of *Ceyx*; *Idaean Dactyls*; *Aegimius* (at least two books; alternatively ascribed to Cercops of Miletus or Clinias of Carystus). (*b*) Didactic: *Precepts of Chiron* (addressed to *Achilles; see CENTAURS); *Astronomy* (risings and settings—and myths?—of principal stars); *Greater Works*. A few fragments of most of these poems survive.

Hesione in mythology, (1) an Oceanid (*see* NYMPHS), wife of *Prometheus. (2) Wife of *Nauplius (1) and mother of *Palamedes, Oeax, and Nausimedon. (3) Daughter of *Laomedon. After her rescue from the sea-monster by *Heracles, she was taken prisoner by him when he captured Troy, given as the prize of valour to *Telamon, and granted leave to save any prisoner she chose; she therefore bought (*epriato*) her brother Podarces for a nominal price, and he was henceforth called *Priamos* (*Priam). By Telamon she became mother of *Teucer (2).

[Apollodorus 2. 23, 136, 3. 146, 162]

Hesperides, the daughters of Night (*Nyx) and Erebus (according to *Hesiod) or, in later versions, of Hesperis and *Atlas, or of Ceto and Phorcys, were guardians of a tree of golden apples given by Earth to *Hera at her marriage. From the same tree came the apples thrown down by Hippomenes (or Melanion) in his race against *Atalanta. The garden of the Hesperides was popularly located beyond the Atlas mountains at the western border of the Ocean. The number of the sisters, renowned for their sweet singing, varies from three to seven. Names attributed to them include Aigle, Erytheia, Arethusa, Hespere, and Hesperethusa. In some accounts they were associated with the *Hyperboreans. *Heracles succeeded in taking the apples after slaying Ladon, the dragon who guarded the tree. The subject was popular in Greek art, especially on painted pottery.

Hesperus (Gk. *Hesperos*; Lat. *Vesper*, *Vesperugo*), the Evening Star; shown in art as a boy carrying a torch. Early tradition makes him the son of Astraeus (or *Cephalus) and *Eos, but later he was associated with *Atlas as his son or brother. He disappeared from Mt. Atlas in a whirlwind after climbing up to observe the stars. As father of Hesperis, he was grandfather of the *Hesperides.

Hestia, the goddess of the hearth, closely related to *Vesta. Respect for and worship of the hearth are characteristic of the Greeks from earliest times. In the Mycenaean age the king's throne-room was the architectural centre of the palace, and in the very centre of that room was a low, round hearth, *c*.4 m. (13 ft.) in diameter. After the fall of monarchies, the kings' hearths as political

centres and sites for asylum and the entertainment of foreign visitors were succeeded by official state hearths housed in public buildings called *prytaneia*. There, at least in some cities, the fire was kept continuously burning. To unify Attica Theseus eliminated the various local *prytaneia* in favour of a single *prytaneion* in Athens. As a token of continuity a mother city sent to a newly founded colony fire from its own hearth. Similarly each family had its own hearth where small offerings were placed at meal times. Newborns, brides, and new slaves were initiated into the family by various rituals at or around the hearth. In Argos the death of the head of the family required the extinguishing of the hearth fire and the fetching of new, unpolluted fire. Analogously, after the Persian occupation of much of Greece in 480 BC, *Delphi ordered the Greek states to extinguish their fires, because they had been polluted by the Persians (*see* POLLUTION), and take new fire from the *prytaneion* at Delphi.

Although one of the twelve Olympians, Hestia has little mythology, unable as she was to leave the house. She is not mentioned by *Homer, for whom *histiē* is simply 'fireplace'. *Hesiod and authors after him make her a daughter of *Cronus and Rhea. She 'liked not the works of *Aphrodite', rejected *Apollo and *Poseidon as suitors, and swore herself to lifelong virginity. Zeus accordingly granted her (according to the *Homeric Hymn to Aphrodite*) 'to sit in the middle of the house, receiving the "fat" of offerings', to be honoured in all temples, and to be a goddess 'senior and respected among all men'. The *hymns reflect cult realities. It may well have been the duty of the maiden daughters of the family to tend the hearth. Even at sanctuaries and sacrifices of other gods Hestia regularly received a preliminary offering; in *prayers and *oaths she was usually named first. 'To begin from Hestia' became a proverb. But Hestia's extremely close tie to one physical object, the hearth, is uncharacteristic of Greek gods and probably limited her development in both myth and cult. In art she appears as a veiled young woman, heavily draped.

[*Homeric Hymn to Aphrodite* 21–32; *Homeric Hymn to Hestia*; Pindar, *Nemean* 11. 1–7; Aristophanes, *Birds* 865–88 (parody)]

hierodouloi The term *hierodoulos* is variously used to describe slaves who are technically the property of a god and live on land owned by temples, slaves who are attached to the service of a god through a gift or civic decree, and slaves who were manumitted through a fictitious sale to a god; occasionally, it is applied to devotees of a cult who refer to themselves as 'slaves of the god'.

Hierodouloi of the first sort are better described as 'serfs of a divinity', rather than as 'slaves' in the classical sense. They are attached to villages belonging to a divinity. This status, in Anatolia, can be traced to the Hittite period, and seems to be analogous to that of the Sirkirtu in Mesopotamia (*see* ANATOLIAN DEITIES). This ancient Anatolian system survived well into the Roman imperial period, and conferred immunity from imperial taxation in so far as the temples to which they were attached were immune. According to the jurists of the Severan period, such *hierodouloi* appear to have been characterized as 'freedmen'. It is possible that sacred slaves of this sort also existed during Mycenaean times; they are attested in Egypt into the imperial period.

In the Greek world, slaves, like other property, could be given to a divinity. Although such slaves could be called *hierodouloi*, their status was categorically different from that of the *hierodouloi* previously discussed since they acquired their condition through attribution rather than birth. Such slaves passed under the control of the city controlling the sanctuary, and their condition was determined by the civic authorities. They may best be regarded as 'public slaves of the god'.

Manumission through consecration to a divinity should not be confused with either status described above; it took two forms: unconditional freedom and conditional freedom. A slave who was manumitted on terms of conditional freedom was bound to continue in the service of a former master for a set period of time (usually until a master's death). Under both systems, the god acted as a guarantor of the former slave's new status.

The final usage of the term has nothing to do with status, being merely a rhetorical form used to express devotion to a god.

hieromnēmones, type of religious official, found in many Greek states. *Aristotle classifies them with the civil registrars of public and private documents, and temples frequently served as record offices. Their functions varied widely: some appear as archivists, others as financial officers, some managed the festivals or controlled temple properties, and in several cities, e.g. Issa and Byzantium, they were the chief magistrates. They usually formed a college, and the position was one of responsibility and honour. Best known are the *hieromnēmones* who represented their states in the Delphic–Pylaean amphictiony (*see* AMPHICTIONY; DELPHI). Their number was normally 24, but varied considerably under the Aetolian domination (*c.*278–178 BC). Their exact relationship to the other delegates, the *pylagorai* (in the Aetolian period called *agoratroi*), is not clear. The duties of the *hieromnēmones* are set forth in a law of 380 BC. Their tenure of office varied from state to state: in the 4th cent. the Thessalian *hieromnēmones* served for several years, the Athenians one year, while the Malians sent different *hieromnēmones* for each of the semi-annual meetings; a Chian decree of 258–254 stipulates that their delegate should serve one year and be ineligible for reappointment. There were *hieromnēmones* in charge of 'the (?) treasury' and 'the grain' at Italian Locri; *hieromnēmōn* could also be a functionary of a private cult association. The term was sometimes used to translate the Latin *pontifex.

hierophantēs, chief priest of the Eleusinian *mysteries, was chosen for life from the hieratic clan of the Eumolpidae (*see* EUMOLPUS). He was distinguished by a head-band, myrtle wreath, and a robe probably of purple, and like many priests he carried a sceptre. Among Athenian priests he was the most revered. An impressive, melodious voice was an important requirement for appointment. Before the celebration he sent forth heralds to proclaim truce for the period of the mysteries. He opened the ceremonies with a proclamation that barbarians, murderers, and the defiled must keep away. In presenting the mysteries to the initiates he was assisted by the *dadouchos* and two *hierophantides*; at a climactic moment in the rite he emerged from the hall of initiation (the Anaktoron, or Telesterion) amidst a brilliant flood of light. He also took part in other state festivals and had some minor public duties. Starting in the 2nd cent. BC he practised hieronymy, i.e. he suppressed his own name (upon entering office he threw it into the sea in a special ceremony) and replaced it with 'Hierophantes'. See ELEUSIS.

Hierophantai also occur in cults of *Demeter and *Dionysus elsewhere (e.g. at Gela, Lerna, Phlius, Andania), some of which were modelled to a certain extent on the Eleusinian mysteries.

Hilaria Roman festival on 25 March, one of a series of five festivals to the Mater Magna or *Cybele (15–26 March), when she rejoiced in *Attis' resurrection. It apparently belongs to the later empire. *Filocalus' calendar gives a 3 November Hilaria associated with an Isis festival (28 October–1 November).

Hippodamia (1), daughter of King Oenomaus of Pisa (later *Olympia) in the Peloponnese. Her suitors were forced to engage in a chariot-race with her father, second prize being decapitation; eventually *Pelops cheated his way to victory and won her. (2) Bride of the Lapith *Pirithous, whom the drunken *Centaurs tried to seize at the marriage feast.

Hippolyte *See* HERACLES.

Hippolytus (1), son of *Theseus and an *Amazon (Antiope or Hippolyte), was de-voted to the hunt and to the virgin *Artemis, ignoring Aphrodite, who responded by afflicting Hippolytus' stepmother Phaedra with a passion for him. When he rejected her, she accused Hippolytus to Theseus (just returned from the Underworld) of making advances to her, and killed herself. *Poseidon, responding to the prayer of Theseus, sent a bull from the sea which caused the death of Hippolytus in a chariot crash as he left Troezen for exile.

The story was a famous one. It was dramatized in lost tragedies by *Sophocles (*Phaedra*) and *Euripides (*Hippolytus Calyptomenus*), in both of which it seems that Phaedra is, as in the much later play by the younger Seneca (*Phaedra*), lustful and unscrupulous. In a second, surviving version by Euripides (*Hippolytus Stephanephorus*) on the other hand, Phaedra has a strong sense of modesty which struggles with her passion, and it is the nurse rather than Phaedra herself who approaches Hippolytus. The myth was also handled by *Ovid. In one version Hippolytus is restored to life by *Asclepius (as early as the epic *Naupactica*) and taken to *Diana's sanctuary at *Aricia in Italy, where he is identified with her attendant Virbius.

In cult Hippolytus is also associated with *Aphrodite. At Athens she had a shrine 'at Hippolytus' on the Acropolis. At Troezen, the place of his death, he had a precinct containing a temple of Aphrodite and a hero-cult in which girls about to marry lamented for him and offered him their hair. Hippolytus embodies the persistence of virginal resistance to marriage, a resistance which the girls themselves must abandon. In *Pausanias' time the Troezenians refused to show his tomb, and maintained that he had become the constellation Auriga. The name 'Horse-looser' may derive from the unharnessing of horses in a sacrificial context in the Troezenian cult of Poseidon. The first of the myth's many depictions in classical art (on 4th-cent. Apulian vase-painting) were probably prompted by Attic drama.

[Euripides, *Hippolytus*; Ovid, *Heroines* 4; Virgil, *Aeneid* 7. 765–82]

Hippolytus (2), *c.*AD 170–*c.*236, styled bishop of Portus and (probably) rival to Callistus of Rome (217–22), whom he reckoned a heretic because he denied that Christ was distinct from God. He died in exile in Sardinia under the emperor Maximinus' persecution. Though allegedly reconciled, he is more often named than quoted in later writing. A statue of him in Rome gives a list of his works, but the attribution of almost every work that goes under his name has been disputed. Book 1 of the *Refutation of all Heresies* (the *Philosophumena*) was once ascribed to Origen; books 4–10 were found in the last century, and, along with the *De Universo* and the *Chronicle*, have been assigned to one Josippus. The work yields valuable fragments of the Presocratic philosophers, but he assimilates them blatantly to the Christian heresies which he attempts to trace to them. The *Chronicle* extends to 234, and, like the massive *Commentary on Daniel*, was written to quench apocalyptic expectation.

Hippothoon or Hippothon, a hero located at *Eleusis, son of *Poseidon and Alope the daughter of Cercyon. His mother was the subject of several tragedies, including one (now lost) by Euripides. He was one of the ten Attic tribal *eponymoi.

Homer The ancient world attributed the two epics, the *Iliad* and the *Odyssey*, the earliest and greatest works of Greek literature, to the poet Homer. Against this general consensus a few scholars in Hellenistic Alexandria argued for different authorship of the two poems; and modern critics, in the 150 years after Wolf (1795), went further and questioned the unity of authorship of each poem. However, the difficulties on which these 'analysts' based their discussions have been resolved through a greater understanding of oral poetry, and now most scholars see each as the work of one author. Whether he was the same for both remains uncertain. They have a great deal of common phraseology, but the *Odyssey* is less archaic in language and more repetitive in content, it

views the gods rather differently, and for a few common things it uses different words. Such changes might occur in the lifetime of one person. As nothing reliable is known about Homer, perhaps the question is not important.

There is some agreement to date the poems in the second half of the 8th cent. BC, with the *Iliad* the earlier, about 750, the *Odyssey* about 725. This was the age of colonization in the Greek world, and it may be no accident that the *Iliad* shows an interest in the north-east, towards the Black Sea, while much of the *Odyssey* looks towards the west. In *Odyssey* book 6 many have seen an echo of the founding of a Greek colony. As to Homer himself, the *Iliad* at least suggests a home on the east side of the Aegean Sea, for storm winds in a simile blow over the sea from Thrace, from the north and west, and the poet seems familiar with the area near Miletus as well as that round Troy. Moreover, the predominantly Ionic flavour of the mixed dialect of the poems suits the cities of the Ionian migration on the other side of the Aegean. Chios and Smyrna have the strongest claims to have been his birthplace.

2. The *Iliad* is the longer of the two by a third, consisting of over 15,600 lines, divided into 24 books. The book division seems to have been later than the original composition, although the books do in many cases represent distinct episodes in the plot (e.g. books 1, 9, 12, 16, 22, 24). There is now broad agreement that we have the poem virtually as it was composed, with the exception of book 10, where the evidence for later addition is strong. For the rest, an individual intelligence is shown by the theme of the anger of *Achilles, begun in the quarrel with *Agamemnon in 1, kept before us in the Embassy of 9, transferred from Agamemnon to *Hector in 18, and resolved in the consolation of *Priam, Hector's father, in 24; also by the tight time-scale of the epic, for, in place of a historical treatment of the Trojan War (*see* TROY, MYTHS OF), the *Iliad*, from book 2 to 22, records merely four days of fighting from the tenth year, separated by

two days of truce. Even the beginning and end add only a few weeks to the total.

Thus the action is concentrated, but the composition subtly expands to include the whole war, with echoes from the beginning in books 2 to 4, and the final books repeatedly looking forward to the death of Achilles and the fall of Troy. The centre is occupied by a single day of battle between 11 and 18, with the Trojans temporarily superior, Greek leaders wounded, their strongest and most mobile fighter (Achilles) disaffected, only Ajax (see AIAS (1)) and some warriors of the second rank holding the defence. The turning-point is in 16, when *Patroclus, acting on a suggestion from *Nestor in 11, persuades Achilles to let him go to the rescue of their comrades, and thus starts the sequence that leads to his own death (16), Achilles' return (18), Hector's death (22), and the conclusion of the epic (24).

3. High among the qualities of the *Iliad* is a vast humanity, which justifies comparison with Shakespeare. The poet understands human behaviour and reactions. There are numerous well-differentiated portraits of leading figures, introduced on the Greek side in the first four books, whose successes in action reinforce their heroic status, and whose personal feelings and relationships are expressed in the very frequent speeches. Figures of the second rank (e.g. Meriones, *Antilochus) support the leaders; and a large number of minor characters, who appear only to be killed, add a sense of the pathos and waste of war, through background details, particularly reference to families at home. The Trojans have their leaders too, but their efforts are essentially defensive, and the desperate situation of their city, and the threat to the women and children, contrast with the more straightforward heroics of the Greeks. Three women of Troy, *Hecuba, *Andromache, and *Helen, appear at key moments in books 6 and 24, the first two also in 22.

There is also what Alexander Pope called 'invention', a constant brilliance of imagination infusing the reports of action, speeches of the characters, and descriptions of the natural world. The language has a kind of perfection, due to a combination of phrases worn smooth by traditional use and the taste and judgement of the poet; and features which had been technical aids to the oral bard seem to have assumed the form of art in the *Iliad*—the use of formulae and repeated story patterns, ring-composition in the construction of speeches, the pictorial effects of extended similes.

4. The *Odyssey*, about 12,000 lines long, was probably composed in its present form in imitation of the already existing *Iliad*. Its 24 books show exact construction. Four books set the scene in *Ithaca ten years after the end of the war, and send Odysseus' son *Telemachus to two of the most distinguished survivors, *Nestor at Pylos and *Menelaus at Sparta, in search of news of his father. The next four show Odysseus himself released from the island of *Calypso and arriving at the land of the Phaeacians (see SCHERIA), a half-way house between the fairy-tale world of his adventures and the real world of Ithaca which awaits him. There, in 9 to 12, he recounts his adventures to the Phaeacians. That completes the first half; the second is devoted to Odysseus' return home, the dangers he faces, and his eventual slaughter of the suitors of his wife *Penelope. In book 15, the two strands of the first half are brought together, when Telemachus returns from Sparta and joins his father.

For reasons difficult to guess, the quality of composition fades at the end, from 23. 296, which the Alexandrian scholars Aristophanes and Aristarchus confusingly describe as the 'end' of the *Odyssey*. However, at least two parts of the 'continuation' (i.e. what follows 23. 296) are indispensable for the completion of the story—the recognition of Odysseus by his old father Laertes, and the avoidance of a blood feud with the relatives of the dead suitors.

5. The *Odyssey* is a romance, enjoyable at a more superficial level than the heroic/tragic *Iliad*. We can take sides, for the good people

are on one side, the bad on the other. Even the massacre of the suitors and the vengeance on the servants who had supported them are acceptable in a story of this kind. The epic depends very much more than the *Iliad* on a single character; and Odysseus has become a seminal figure in European literature, with eternal human qualities of resolution, intellectual curiosity, and love of home. Apart from books 9 to 12, the settings are domestic, Ithaca, Pylos, Sparta, and Scheria (the land of the Phaeacians). The effect of this is that the gentler qualities of politeness, sensitivity, and tact come into play, as in the delicate interchanges between Odysseus and *Nausicaa (the princess on Scheria) and her parents. On the other hand, the boorish behaviour of the suitors shows a break-down of the social order.

For many readers the adventures are the high point. The *Lotus-eaters, Cyclops (*see* CYCLOPES), king of the winds, cannibal giants, witch *Circe, *Sirens, *Scylla (1), and Charybdis are part of the folk-tale element in western consciousness. They are prefaced by a piratical attack on a people in Thrace, near Troy, and concluded on the island of the Sun, an episode which results in the elimination of Odysseus' surviving companions, leaving him alone to face the return home. In the middle, in book 11, comes the visit to the Underworld, where he sees figures from the past and receives a prophecy of the future.

The combination of precision of observation and descriptive imagination is on a par with the *Iliad*; examples are Odysseus in the Cyclops' cave, Odysseus in his own house among the suitors of his wife, the recognition by his old dog *Argos (*d*). One gets the impression, however, more strongly with the *Odyssey* than the *Iliad*, that the tale has been told many times before, and some superficial inconsistencies may be the effect of variant versions (e.g. the abortive plans for the removal of the arms in 16).

6. The dactylic hexameter has a complex structure, with from twelve to seventeen syllables in the lines, and some precise metrical requirements. Milman Parry demonstrated that features of composition, notably pervasive repetition in the phraseology, derive from the practice of illiterate oral bards, who would learn the traditional phrases (formulae) in their years of apprenticeship. This explains many aspects that worried analytical critics since the days of the Alexandrian scholars; for repetition of a half-line, line, or sequence of lines had been taken by readers used to the practice of later poets as evidence for corruption in the text, and an adjective used inappropriately had seemed to be a fault, instead of the inevitable consequence of the use of formulae.

Of equal significance to the repetition of formulaic phrases in the composition of oral poetry is the repetitive, though flexible, use of what are called typical scenes, patterns in the story, sometimes described as 'themes'. These range from the four arming-scenes in the *Iliad* (in books 3, 11, 16, 19), scenes of arrival and departure, performance of sacrifices, descriptions of fighting, to the repeated abuse directed at Odysseus in the second half of the Odyssey. Such 'themes' performed a parallel function to the formulae, giving the experienced bard material for the construction of his songs in front of an audience.

Virtually all scholars now accept that oral poetry theory has added to our understanding. Difference remains about whether Homer himself was an illiterate bard, or whether his position at the end of a long tradition shows a bard using the possibilities of literacy while still retaining the oral techniques. The ultimate problem of the survival of the two epics is inextricably bound up with this question. Three possibilities divide the field. Either the poet composed with the help of writing, the Greek alphabet having become available at just the right time; or the poems were recorded by scribes, the poet himself being illiterate; or they were memorized by a guild of public reciters (*rhapsodes) for anything up to 200 years (there being evidence for a written text in Athens in the 6th cent. BC).

7. The language in which the poems are composed contains a mixture of forms found in different areas of the Greek world. The overall flavour is Ionic, the dialect spoken on Euboea, other islands of the eastern Aegean such as Chios, and on the mainland of Asia Minor opposite them. Attic Greek was a subdivision of Ionic, but Atticisms in the epic dialect are rare and superficial. Second in importance to Ionic in the amalgam is Aeolic, the dialect of north Greece (Boeotia and Thessaly) and the northern islands such as Lesbos. Where Aeolic had a different form from Ionic, the Aeolic form mostly appears as an alternative to the Ionic in the epic language when it has a different metrical value. More deeply embedded are certain words and forms which belonged to the dialect of southern Greece in the Mycenaean age, sometimes described as Arcado-Cypriot, because it survived into historical times in those two widely separated areas of the Greek world.

The historical implications of all this are obscure. The geographical location during the Mycenaean age of the speakers of what later became Ionic and Aeolic was necessarily different from that in historical times; and the dialects themselves obviously developed differently in different areas. What is clear, however, is that the linguistic picture is consistent with that presented by oral theory. Some features are very ancient (often preserved in the formulaic phrases), some quite recent. An important conclusion is that late linguistic forms are not to be seen as post-Homeric interpolations, but more probably come from the language of the poet himself, while earlier ones had reached him through the tradition. It is noted that the similes in the *Iliad* contain a high proportion of 'late' forms.

8. The assumed date of the Trojan war falls in the 13th cent. BC, towards the end of the Mycenaean age; for the Mycenaean palaces on the mainland were destroyed from about 1200. There is thus a gap of some four and a half centuries between the date of composition of the *Iliad* (about 750) and the legendary past which is its setting. The 8th cent. is essentially more important for the epics than the 13th; but the history of the Mycenaean age and of the shadowy times that lay between is naturally of the greatest interest. Here archaeologist and historian combine. We have the extraordinary discoveries of Schliemann at Mycenae, and the excavations at Troy itself by Schliemann (1870–90), Blegen (1932–8), and Korfmann (1981–). Archaeological evidence from the 13th cent. has come to the surface. It is, however, unsafe to assume too close a connection with Homer. For the passage of time, and a retrospective view of a heroic age, have moved the picture nearer to fiction than reality. Only fossilized memories of the Mycenaean age survive in his work.

After the destruction of the palaces a long Dark Age intervened, lightened to some extent by the discovery at Lefkandi in Euboea of a city with important trade connections in the 10th and 9th cents. It must have been during the Dark Age that heroic poetry developed and spread, even if (as seems probable) it originated in the Mycenaean age. Historians see in the epics reflections of the society and political aspirations of this period, even of the 8th cent.

9. Hexameter poetry continued after Homer, with *Hesiod and the *Homeric Hymns* (see HYMNS (GREEK)), and the poems of the *Epic Cycle, which described the two legendary wars of the heroic age against Thebes and Troy. The Theban epics are lost, but for the Trojan we have summaries of the contents of six poems (*Cypria, Aethiopis, Little Iliad, Sack of Troy (Iliu Persis), Returns (Nostoi), Telegony (Telegonia)*), which had been fitted round the *Iliad* and *Odyssey* to create a complete sequence from the marriage of *Peleus and *Thetis to the death of Odysseus. The summaries, attributed to 'Proclus' (perhaps a grammarian of the 2nd cent. AD), are found in some manuscripts of the *Iliad*. These cyclic epics were obviously later than the Homeric poems, and from a time when oral composition had ceased and public performance was by rhapsodes, not traditional bards.

Their significance for us is that they represent the subject-matter of heroic poetry as it was before Homer; for the *Iliad* itself, being the individual creation of a poet of genius, was not typical. Thus, by a time reversal, the partially known later material can make some claim to priority over the earlier. A school of 'neoanalysts' argues that episodes in books 8 (rescue of Nestor), 17 (recovery of the body of Patroclus), 18 (mourning of Thetis), and 23 (funeral games) echo situations connected with Achilles in the repertoire of the oral bards, which later appeared in the cyclic *Aethiopis*. The importance of this is that it seems to give us an insight into the creativity of the *Iliad* poet.

homonoia, lit. 'oneness of mind', a political ideal first met in Greek writers of the later 5th cent. BC, essentially signifying either (1) concord or unanimity within the city-state and especially the avoidance of civil strife or (2) the achievement of Panhellenic unity against the barbarian (i.e. Persia or Macedonia). The ideal was sufficiently powerful (because so rarely attainable) to attract theoretical praise and, from the 4th cent. BC on, personification (a woman) and worship, as with the Panhellenic cult of the 'Homonoia of the Hellenes' at Plataea. *See* CONCORDIA.

honey, the chief sweetener known to the ancients, who understood apiculture and appreciated the different honey-producing qualities of flowers and localities. It was used in medicines, e.g. for coughs, ulcers, and intestinal parasites. It had a very important role in religion, cult, and mythology. Its religious associations derive from the idea that it was a *ros caelestis* ('heavenly dew'), which fell on to flowers from the upper air for bees to gather. According to poets it dripped from trees in the *golden age. It was used in *libations to the dead, in rites for *Persephone and *Hades, for *Hestia, and in the cult of *Mithras. In literature honey was given to infants to impart qualities such as wisdom or eloquence. The infant *Plato was fed with honey by bees.

*Zeus was called Melissaios from a similar legend of his Cretan birth.

Honos and Virtus, deities at Rome personifying military courage and its reward; their cult was selected for two major commemorative temples by successful generals: Marcus Claudius Marcellus after his conquest of Syracuse (dedicated after some controversy by his son in 205 BC), and Caius Marius after the Cimbric War. We know little of the latter (though it was large enough to hold the senate-meeting at which *Cicero was recalled from exile), but Marcellus' temple outside the porta Capena was of some importance: richly equipped with his spoils, it survived well into the imperial period.

Horae, goddesses of the seasons. *Hesiod makes them daughters of *Zeus and of *Themis ('Divine Law') and names them *Eunomia ('Good Order'), *Dike ('Justice'), and *Eirene ('Peace'). But according to *Pausanias in *Attica they bore names relating to growth and the effects of the seasons: Thallo ('Blooming') and Karpo (from Gk. *karpos*, 'crop, fruit'), and the antiquarian writer Philochorus says that offerings to them were boiled, not roasted, to encourage the goddesses to avert excessive heat. Often they remain anonymous. They guard the gates of *Olympus, and are regularly linked with the birth, upbringing, and marriages of gods and heroes; common associates are the Graces or *Charites, *Demeter 'bringer of the Seasons', *Helios and *Apollo, *Aphrodite, and *Dionysus.

In the great procession of Ptolemy II Philadelphus in the 3rd cent. BC marched four Horae, each bearing their appropriate fruits. Such differentiated 'season Horae' were a favourite theme of Graeco-Roman art thenceforth. The new motif remained potentially in relation with religion, because the orderly procession of the seasons was a signal proof of the divine order of the world.

[Homer, *Iliad* 5. 749–81; *Homeric Hymn to Aphrodite* 5 ff.]

Horatii The Horatii were triplets who, in an

ancient Roman legend, fought as champions against the Curiatii, also triplets, in order to decide the outcome of a war between their respective cities, Rome and *Alba Longa. The view of the surviving sources is that the Horatii were Roman, but Livy, most interestingly, tells us that earlier historians had disagreed about which brothers belonged to which city. Two of the Horatii, and all three Curiatii, were killed; on returning home the surviving Horatius killed his sister, when she wept for one of the Curiatii to whom she had been betrothed. Horatius was convicted of murder, but was allowed by King Tullus *Hostilius to appeal to the people, who acquitted him. The story thus offered a precedent for the right of appeal, and was also associated with many ancient monuments and relics in and around Rome. The oath of the Horatii is the subject of a painting exhibited in 1785 by J.-L. David, but David appears to have made up the idea of the oath, though the men depicted are certainly the famous legendary Horatii.

[Livy 1. 24–6]

Horatius Cocles In one of the most famous of all Roman legends, Horatius and two companions held the Sublician bridge in Rome against the invading army of Lars *Porsenna until it could be demolished, whereupon he swam back to safety across the Tiber. An archaic statue of a one-eyed man, which stood in the Volcanal in the Comitium in the *forum Romanum, was thought by the Romans to represent Horatius (his surname, Cocles, means 'one-eyed').

[Polybius 6. 55. 1–4; Livy 2. 10–11]

horse- and chariot-races In the funeral games for *Patroclus the chariot-race is the premier event. The heroes drive two-horse chariots normally used in battle over an improvised cross-country course, round a distant mark and home again. Similar funeral games for other heroes are recorded; and heroes as well as gods were remembered at the Panhellenic festivals. Malicious ghosts (*Taraxippoi*, 'horse-frighteners') sometimes panicked the horses. But, despite the story

of the race by which *Pelops won his bride and kingdom (*see* HIPPODAMIA), equestrian events were not the oldest in the historic Olympia festival (*see* OLYMPIAN GAMES). Four-horse chariots were introduced in the 25th Olympiad (680 BC); ridden horses in the 33rd; and other equestrian events at irregular intervals thereafter. Regular hippodromes were now used. No material remains survive; but literary evidence shows that competitors raced to a marker about 550 m. (1,805 ft.) distant, round which they made a 180° left-hand turn before galloping back to round another marker. The number of laps varied (twelve for the four-horse chariots). Over 40 teams might take part, and the sport was dangerous, though elaborate arrangements (at least at Olympia) were made to ensure a fair start. Owners, not drivers or riders, received the glory, and equestrian events were supported by tyrants, and commemorated by epinician poets.

At Rome, a horse-race preceded the sacrifice to *Mars (whether considered as a war- or fertility-god is disputed) of the *equus October*. The chariots that drew vast crowds to the Circus Maximus and its provincial equivalents were managed by factions, whose distinguishing colours—white, red, blue, and green—were thought by *Tertullian to represent the seasons. The date at which the factions were formed is uncertain. Blue and green eventually predominated. Horses (supplied by large stud-farms) and drivers became famous, many names being preserved in inscriptions, including leaden curse-tablets; *see* CURSES. Races resembled the Greek ones but with no more than twelve entries. A raised barrier (*spina*) connected the turning-points. For emperors—Gaius's support of the Greens is notorious—the races provided occasions for public display; for men-about-town opportunities to impress girlfriends.

[Homer, *Iliad* 23. 262–538; Pindar, *Olympian* 1, 2; Ovid, *Art of Love* 1. 135]

Horus (Egyptian *Ḥrw*, 'he is far off'), one of the most important Egyptian gods (*see* EGYPTIAN DEITIES), soon equated, like other falcon-headed deities, with the sun-god Re. His main centre was Edfu in Upper Egypt, where the fullest (Ptolemaic) version of the myth is found. Horus was very early a royal god, and played with *Set ('the two brothers') a key role in the mythic establishment of an ideal pharaonic order based on the resolution of their conflict. In the first Edfu myth, Horus as the Winged Disc harpoons his enemies from Upper to Lower Egypt. But in the Osiris-cycle, Horus became *Isis' son, and heir of the dead *Osiris, whom he avenged. In this form, as Harsiësis, he may be contrasted with the older or 'great' Horus. A Horus child 'with the finger in his mouth' occurs already in the Pyramid Texts, but no official cult can be traced until the late New Kingdom, when, perhaps at Egyptian Thebes, Harsiësis became, or was ousted by, Harpocrates (Egyptian Ḥr-pᵌ-ḥrd, 'Horus the child'). Motifs from two minor divinities, Šed and Neper, were combined with Harsiësis to create a deity with three manifestations: the sun in its first two hours above the horizon (Harpocrates as Creator on the lotus), a god of fertility, and the infant of the divine pair Isis and Osiris. Harpocrates' main cults in the Hellenistic, but chiefly Roman, period were at Pelusium in the Delta, and in the Fayūm. The 'great' Horus appears in the Graeco-Roman period mainly as a rider, recalling the Isiac festival of his victory over Set. Outside Egypt, Harpocrates, as nursling of Isis, predominates overwhelmingly.

Hostilius, Tullus, the sixth king of Rome (conventionally 672–641 BC). The supposed derivation of Hostilius from *hostis* ('enemy') prompted his depiction as a martial figure. He reputedly campaigned against Fidenae, Veii, and the Sabines (*see* SABINI), but early accounts of his reign were dominated by the conflict with *Alba Longa (determined by the duel of the *Horatii and Curiatii), the destruction of Alba itself, and the incorporation of its citizens in the Roman state. This sequence is probably a fiction based on later Roman legitimation of her hegemony in Latium as Alba's supposed successor, her supervision of Alban cults, the claims of certain Roman lineages to be of Alban origin, and the later absence of a 'city' of Alba Longa; its historicity is not demonstrated by changes in settlement patterns in the Alban hills from the later 9th cent. BC on. The ascription to Hostilius of the first senate-house, and the associated assembly area is an aetiological fiction, although the first level of the assembly area goes back at least to the late 7th cent. and architectural terracottas imply an important structure here by *c*.600 BC.

household, worship of The domestic cult of a Greek family concerned the protection and prosperity of the house and its occupants, with daily small offerings and prayers to *Zeus Ctesius (protector of the stores), Zeus Herceius (protector of the wall or fence surrounding the house), and *Apollo Agyieus (of the streets) whose image stood at the house's street entrance. The hearth, as *Hestia, was sacred, and at mealtimes a bit of food was placed there as a *first-fruits offering. Similarly, before drinking wine, libations were poured on the floor to Hestia or at formal banquets to Zeus and the heroes, to the *Agathos Daimon, or to other deities. In these family cults the rituals seem of primary importance and hence were widespread while the deities honoured varied from place to place. The father served as priest for the family, however, and that may partially explain the regular appearance of Zeus, father of the gods. The admission of new members to the family (brides, babies, and slaves) was marked by initiation rites, often involving the hearth and featuring fertility symbols. Death brought to the household a pollution which was effaced only by the passage of a set period of time.

The Roman domestic cult was similar, centred on the hearth (*Vesta), with somewhat more elaborate table ritual, and with *Janus watching the door, the *di Penates* (*see* PENATES, DI) guarding the stores, and the *Lar*

Familiaris (*see* LARES), of obscure origin, offering more general protection. Like their Greek counterparts these deities remained numinous, without distinct personality or mythology. The functions of the Lares and Di Penates overlapped to the degree that they were regularly confused or generalized. They were housed, along with the *genius* of the *paterfamilias* and other particularly favoured deities, in the *lararium*, many examples of which are known from Pompeii.

[Antiphon 1. 16–20; Isaeus 8. 15–16; Plautus, *Aulularia* (*The Little Pot*) 1–27, *Mercator* (*The Merchant*) 830–7]

houses, Greek Private houses of the Classical and Hellenistic periods were basically the same throughout the Greek world. Most rooms opened onto one or more sides of a small, rectangular courtyard, as did a doorway to the street, often preceded by a short passage. Windows were few and small and living areas were not visible from the street. An upper storey, reached by a ladder or, more rarely, a built stairway, was common but is often hard to detect. Construction was in mud-brick or rubble on stone socles. Interior walls were plastered and often painted simply, mostly in red and white. Floors were of beaten earth. In most houses, on the ground floor, one or two rooms with heavier floors and provisions for bathing, heating water, and cooking can be identified, but cooking could take place on simple hearths or portable braziers in any room or in the courtyard. The concept of the hearth and its goddess, *Hestia, symbolized the identity and cohesion of the household (*oîkos*) but formal, fixed hearths were not common, nor were *altars for domestic ritual.

houses, Italian The first really copious evidence is the 3rd–2nd-cent. BC houses of Pompeii, which show a regular plan and a systematic division of urban space, but a very considerable variety of size and levels of wealth, the House of the Faun being absolutely outstanding by the standards of anywhere in the Mediterranean world. In these

houses it is relatively easy to identify the features which Vitruvius, our principal literary source, regarded as canonical, but their evolution in different parts of Italy should not be taken for granted. The traditional houses of the centre of Rome seem also to have adhered to the basic pattern of atrium with rooms round it; where more space was available, this traditional arrangement could be combined with peristyles and gardens, offering scope for planned suites of rooms, interesting light effects, and amenities such as ornamental plantings or fountains, and providing more flexible spaces for living, entertaining, politics, and the cultural activities which were integral to upper-class life. The politicians of the late republic were credited with various changes to the use of houses; and luxury in domestic appointments was thought to have taken off dramatically in the 1st cent. BC; but the setting for both processes seems to have been the traditional 'Pompeian/Vitruvian' house.

The salient feature of this traditional plan was the atrium—a rectangular space open to the sky at the centre, columned in the more elaborate forms, with wide covered spaces on each of the four sides, one of which gave onto the outside world through a vestibule. Originally the site of the family hearth, whose smoke caused the blackening (*ater*) which gave the place its name, this was also the abode of the household deities, and housed the copies of the funerary masks which were the sign of the family's continuity and identity (*see* IMAGINES; LARES). The adjacent rooms, including a *tablinum* and *cubicula*, were in fact flexible in their use, and this flexibility is the key to the understanding of all Roman domestic space, even in very much more elaborate dwellings. A *triclinium* for convivial dining was an early and frequent adjunct, but meals could be taken in a variety of different rooms, if they were available, according to season and weather.

hubris, intentionally dishonouring behaviour, was a powerful term of moral condemnation in ancient Greece; and in Athens, and perhaps elsewhere, it was also treated as a serious crime. Most often it refers to the insulting infliction of physical force or violence. The common use of *hubris* in English to suggest pride, over-confidence, or any behaviour which may offend divine powers, rests, it is now generally held, on misunderstanding of ancient texts, and concomitant and over-simplified views of Greek attitudes to the gods have lent support to many doubtful, and often over-Christianizing, interpretations, above all of Greek tragedy.

Hubris is not essentially a religious term; yet the gods naturally were often supposed to punish instances of it, either because they may feel themselves directly dishonoured, or, more frequently, because they were held to uphold general Greek moral and social values. Nor is it helpful to see Greek tragedy centrally concerned to display the divine punishment of hubristic heroes; tragedy focuses rather on unjust or problematic suffering, whereas full-scale acts of *hubris* by the powerful tend to deprive them of the human sympathy necessary for tragic victims.

Hyacinthides or Parthenoi ('Maidens'), cult titles of a group of heroines in Athens identified as daughters of *Hyacinthus or daughters of *Erechtheus, sacrificed for the safety of the city and in some versions metamorphosed into the star-group *Hyades. The 'Daughters of Erechtheus' story occurs in *Euripides' *Erechtheus*; it is unclear how much is Euripidean invention, but the details given about their cult (*dances by young girls in their honour, restrictions on entry into the sanctuary, a ban on *wine) are presumably accurate, and it is likely to have been concerned with the city's escape from crisis.

Hyacinthus, Dorian god or hero at *Amyclae near Sparta. His festival Hyacinthia (*see* DORIAN FESTIVALS) and month Hyakinthios recur in many other Dorian locations. A pre-Greek figure (cf. the suffix *-nth-* of his name), he merged with Apollo probably before the end of the bronze age. Hence the popular

myth in which Apollo kills his young favourite with an unlucky throw of the discus. In Alexandrian tradition (also in Attic vase-painting) Zephyrus caused Hyacinthus' death by blowing the discus off course. A flower (iris) sprang from the boy's blood with the letters *AI AI* ('alas, alas') inscribed on its leaves. Hyacinthus' death was an important element of the three-day Hyacinthia at Amyclae. The hero received a preliminary sacrifice on the first day at his tomb which formed the base of Apollo's 6th-cent. BC altar/throne with relief sculptures by Bathycles including Hyacinthus' translation to heaven with his sister *Polyboea (2). *See* SPARTAN CULTS.

Originally Hyacinthus may have been a dying nature-god like *Adonis. As the youthful male associate of a goddess of nature, he symbolized the annual cycle of vegetation. Memories of his past function are preserved in the Cnidian cult of Artemis Hyakinthotrophos. Though bearded at Amyclae, Hyacinthus, like other Divine Children, is more frequently portrayed as a beautiful youth. As the beloved of Apollo and Zephyrus, who is often shown in lively pursuit of his loved one, Hyacinthus became a popular subject for Attic vase-painters of the early 5th cent. BC.

[Euripides, *Helen* 1469 ff.; Apollodorus 3. 116]

Hyades ('the Rainers'), a group of five stars in Taurus, so named because their acronychal rising and setting (respectively 17 October and 12 April according to the astronomer Eudoxus) are at rainy times of the year; called Suculae in Latin, as if from Greek *hys* 'pig'. Mythologically they were nurses of *Dionysus; but the story, which seems to go back to *Pherecydes, is very confused in the forms which we have. Another account is that they are sisters who cried themselves to death when their brother Hyas was killed hunting. *See* CONSTELLATIONS; HYACINTHIDES.

hybris *See* HUBRIS.

Hydra *See* HERACLES.

Hygieia, personified Health, said to be daughter of *Asclepius and associated with him in cult; in the Hippocratic oath her name follows immediately on his, and they share many later dedications. Her first attestation is a statue set up in *Olympia, together with an image of Asclepius, by Micythus of Rhegium who lived in Tegea after 467 BC; still earlier is the epithet *Hygieia* given to Athena in Athens, attested from the late 6th to the late 5th cent. BC. Here, Hygieia was introduced by Telemachus together with Asclepius in 429/19—without entirely ousting the cult of *Athena Hygieia. Ordinarily, her cult is subordinated to that of Asclepius, with the one exception of Titane near Sicyon where she had an Archaic image hidden by women's dedicated hair and garments, reminiscent of the cult of Iphigenia in *Brauron. The *hymn of Licymnius of Chios which addresses her as 'Mother most high' and connects her directly with *Apollo underlines this unusual independence.

Hyginus Two extant Latin works are attributed to an otherwise unknown person.

(*a*) *Genealogiae*, a handbook of mythology, compiled from Greek sources, probably in the 2nd cent. AD. The work was abbreviated, perhaps for school use, and has suffered later accretions; its absurdities are partly due to the compiler's ignorance of Greek. The usual title *Fabulae* (*Fables*) is due to the first edition by Micyllus (Basel, 1535), now the only authority for the text; the manuscript which he used is lost. *See* MYTHO-GRAPHERS.

(*b*) A manual of astronomy, based on Greek sources, possibly by the same author.

Hylas, son of the Dryopian Theiodamas, after whose murder by *Heracles he became Heracles' protégé. He accompanied the *Argonauts but disappeared during a stop at Cius in Mysia: he went to fetch water and the *nymph or nymphs of the spring fell in love with him and dragged him into the water. His companions searched for him in vain, and Heracles forced the locals to go on searching and, to ensure their compliance, took as hostages boys from noble families whom he settled at Trachis. This is the explanatory story for a Cian ritual involving a sacrifice and ritual search in which the priest called 'Hylas' three times and was answered by the echo. In most versions Hylas was Heracles' beloved; in some he was Polyphemus' (*see* CYCLOPES).

[Apollonius Rhodius 1. 1207 ff.; Theocritus, *Idylls* 13. 36 ff.]

Hyllus, in mythology, eldest son of *Heracles by *Deianira or Melite. *See* HERACLIDAE.

Hymenaeus The cry *hymēn ō hymenaie* (with variants) was traditional in Greek wedding songs. It presumably arose as a mock lament for the bride's hymen in the anatomical sense (though this has been disputed), but it was soon taken as an invocation of a marriage-god. *Pindar relates that Hymenaeus died on his wedding night and was lamented, like *Linus and Ialemus, by a goddess; in Euripides Hymen is a son of *Aphrodite. These conceptions are later elaborated, and Hymenaeus or Hymen is often found as god of marriage in Roman literature.

[Aristophanes, *Peace* 1332–56; Euripides, *Trojan Women* 310–25; Catullus 61]

hymns (Greek) 'Hymn' is a simple transliteration of a Greek word; but the relation of Greek to English hymns is not at all simple. *Hymnos* has at least three meanings: (1) a song of any kind; (2) any song in honour of a god; (3) a particular type of song in honour of a god. Use (1), the first attested, is standard in Archaic poetry; (2) would perhaps have been judged normal by a Greek of the Classical period; (3) distinguishes the hymn from other forms of song in honour of gods, such as the paean, the *prosodion* (processional), and the 'proem' (below), which would all count as *hymnoi* by use (2). Hymns in this narrow sense may have been principally what the late rhetorician Menander was to call 'cletic' or summoning hymns. As a working definition, (2) is the most useful, because the various forms differentiated in (3) probably shared numerous features of style and content (see below: but about some of these forms we know very little). They are, then, best seen as species within a genus which it is convenient to call 'hymn'.

Modern hymns are written to be performed, communally, on a potentially unlimited number of occasions. The ancient hymn proves less easy to define by reference to the circumstances of performance. The only complete specimens that survive from before the year 400 BC are the *Homeric Hymns*, hexameter compositions ranging from a handful of lines to several hundred. In early sources they are described as 'preludes', because originally at least they were sung as introductions to other hexameter compositions (such no doubt as heroic epic). It is commonly supposed that the longer *Homeric Hymns* had grown into works that stood on their own; the further supposition is often added that they were recited at a festival of the god whom they honour (a possibility that, however, has internal support only in the case of the *Hymn to Delian Apollo*); but, being hexameter works, they were of course not performed chorally. (Other composers of supposedly Archaic hymns known to *Pausanias—*Olen, Pampho, *Orpheus, *Musaeus—also used hexameters.) Similarly, the fragmentary hymns of Alcaeus, if they were presented at festivals at all, were surely, like the rest of his work, sung by a single voice. Another possible context of performance for a short hymn was the symposium.

The hymns of the early choral lyric poets are lost, a few scraps aside, with the important exception of substantial fragments of *Pindar (*Paeans* in particular) and to a lesser extent of *Bacchylides. For Pindar, the *paean is an occasional poem, written to be performed on a particular occasion by a particular chorus; and to a remarkable extent it is given over to glorification, sometimes through mythological exempla, of the country from which the chorus derives. Thus in Pindar's hands it comes to resemble the epinician ode unexpectedly closely. The early *hymnoi* that most recall our hymns are in fact the imitations of the form embedded in drama, above all in the parabases of Old Comedy.

The picture changes after 400, because the character of our evidence changes: from the 4th cent. and the Hellenistic and Roman periods there survive more than ten hymns that were piously inscribed on stone in sanctuaries. Most have a clear relation to cult practice: two have musical notation, one is preceded by instructions for use, another is known in four copies of varying date and provenance. All are comparatively restricted in length, simple in structure, and devoted to praise of the god; not all, however, were necessarily intended for choral rather than solo performance. Guilds of *hymnōdoi* are also widely attested epigraphically in the Roman period. Conversely, many hymns were also composed that were not, in all seeming, intended for performance: instances are as diverse as the *Hymns* of *Callimachus, *Cleanthes' *Hymn to Zeus*, hymns to Fortune and to Nature and to Rome, and in due course show-piece compositions such as the prose hymns of Aelius *Aristides. A special place belongs to the *Orphic Hymns*, a collection of 87 short hexameter poems composed for use, it is generally supposed, by an Orphic society in Asia Minor in or near the 2nd cent. AD: the one surviving ancient Greek hymn-book; *see* ORPHIC LITERATURE.

Typical features of hymns include: lists of the god's powers and interests and tastes and favourite places (often showing distinctive stylistic features); accumulations of the god's *epithets; portrayals of the god engaged in characteristic activities; greetings, summonses, and *prayers to the god; and, most important of all, accounts of how the god was born and acquired his or her 'honours' and functions. For the hymn, the fundamental form of 'theology' is '*theogony'.

hymns (Roman) *See* CARMEN, and the various particular entries beginning CARMEN, e.g. CARMEN ARVALE.

Hyperboreans, legendary race of *Apollo-worshippers living in the far north, 'beyond the North Wind' (*Boreas); first mentioned in *Hesiod's *Catalogue*. For *Pindar their land is an earthly paradise presided over by the god, who overwinters there; only heroes like *Perseus or *Heracles might reach it. Elsewhere it functions as a magical place to which things may conveniently disappear (Apollo's first Delphic temple; *see* DELPHI; Croesus from his pyre), or from which they may mysteriously materialize (the straw-wrapped offerings to Apollo which were passed down a long chain of real-world intermediaries before eventually reaching *Delos). The Delian cult has attracted much speculation; it may perhaps have been a local attempt to trump the Delphic Daphnephoria.

[Pindar, *Pythian* 10. 30 ff.; *Olympian* 3. 16 ff.; Herodotus 4. 33–5; Bacchylides 3. 57 ff.; Callimachus, *Hymn* 4. 281–99]

Hyperion, a *Titan, husband of his sister Theia and father by her of the Sun, Moon, and Dawn (*Hesiod). Often the name is used as an epithet of the Sun himself (*Odyssey*).

Hypnos, the god of sleep in Greek mythology. Hypnos is fatherless, son of *Nyx and brother of *Thanatos. According to *Hesiod he lives in the Underworld and never sees the sun, but in contrast to his brother he comes softly and is sweet for men. In *Homer, however, Hypnos lives on Lemnos and gets from *Hera the Charis (*see* CHARITES) Pasithea as wife. He is human at first, but changes into a bird of the night before he makes Zeus fall asleep. Throughout antiquity Hypnos was usually thought of as a winged youth who touches the foreheads of the tired with a branch, or pours sleep-inducing liquid from a horn. Myths about Hypnos are few: he helps to bury *Sarpedon and is said to have fallen in love with *Endymion whom he made to sleep with open eyes. He had a cult in Troezen. In art, Hypnos carried by Nyx was shown on the chest of Cypselus; on vases, he and Thanatos carry *Memnon, Sarpedon, and human warriors to the grave. A beautiful Hellenistic statue known through several copies shows Hypnos gliding over the ground and pouring sleep-bringing liquid from his horn.

[Homer, *Iliad* 14. 225–362, 16. 666–83; Ovid, *Metamorphoses* 11. 592–649]

Hypsipyle (a) Because the women of *Lemnos neglected the rites of *Aphrodite, she made them stink, and their husbands left them to take concubines from Thrace. They then murdered all the males on the island, except that Hypsipyle hid her father King Thoas, son of *Dionysus, and got him out of the country (cf. Hypermestra amongst the *Danaids). She now governed Lemnos and received the *Argonauts when they came. The women mated with them, and Hypsipyle had two sons (*see* EUNEŌS) by *Jason. The myth is interpreted as the counterpart of a new year ritual where women form a temporary separate society (as in the *Thesmophoria) and a ship (represented by the Argonauts) bears new fire from *Delos, allowing households to be re-formed. (b) 'Later', Hypsipyle as a slave is sold to Lycurgus king of *Nemea, whose wife employed her as nurse to her child Opheltes or Archemorus. While she shows a watering-place to the passing army of the *Seven against Thebes, a snake kills Opheltes. Amphiaraus secures her pardon and the *Nemean Games are founded in the child's honour.

(a) and (b) are clearly in origin two different Hypsipyles, one from Lemnos and one from Nemea.

[(a) Apollonius Rhodius, *Argonautica* 1. 609–909; Ovid, *Heroines* 6; (b) Euripides, *Hypsipyle*; Statius, *Thebaid* 4. 715 ff.]

Hypsistos 'Most High', one of the commonest divine *epithets in late antiquity. The most important application was one familiar from a wide range of literary and epigraphic texts, beginning in the Hellenistic period, whereby 'highest god' was the standard way of referring in Greek to the god of *Judaism. Dedications to 'highest god' are, however, found in places where no Jewish or Christian presence is yet attested, and a broader disposition to exalt a particular god, temporarily at least, as 'highest' is doubtless to be recognized. The widespread cult of 'Highest God' in Anatolia perhaps represents a compromise or synthesis between Jewish, Christian, and pagan tendencies, of the kind continued by the 'Hypsistarian' sect of Cappadocia in the 4th cent. AD.

In many cults, as in one established on the deserted Pnyx in Athens in the 2nd cent. AD (*see* ATHENS, RELIGIOUS TOPOGRAPHY), dedications to 'Highest God' or plain 'Highest' alternate with others to 'Highest *Zeus'; in such cases there is usually still less reason to suspect Jewish worshippers. This Athenian 'Highest Zeus' is a healer, while in a flourishing Macedonian cult first attested in the 1st cent. BC dedications are regularly made 'on behalf of' members of the dedicant's family. The functions implied are not those of the Classical *Zeus, associated with high places and even termed 'highest' (though he was occasionally 'highest' in poetry, and often Hypatos in cult), and it looks as if this 'Highest Zeus' of post-Classical worship is normally a product of *syncretism (in Macedonia the influence of *Sabazius has been suggested). How many distinct figures underlie the various 'Highest Zeus'es of late antiquity remains to be clarified.

Hyrnetho/Hyrnatho, gave name to the Argive tribe Hyrnathioi (who were the non-Dorian, or not fully Dorian, tribe of Argos), *Temenus' daughter and Deiphontes' wife. After her brothers had had their father killed for favouring her and *Deiphontes, in some versions of the myth Hyrnetho and Deiphontes succeeded Temenus; in others, the kingdom was split between them and Hyrnetho's brothers, who tried to persuade her to leave Deiphontes and abducted her when she refused. Deiphontes came to her rescue but one of her brothers killed her while dragging her away. Deiphontes buried her in a heroon (*see* HERO-CULT) at *Epidaurus and established a cult. She also had a grave at Argos.

[Pausanias 2. 19, 23, 26, 38]

Iacchus, patron god of the initiates in their procession to *Eleusis in the *mysteries. In origin he was probably a personification of the ritual cry *iakkh' ō iakkhe* sung by the initiates as they marched (*see* HYMENAEUS). In art he is a torch-bearer, seen conducting (or in the company of) initiates, usually divine initiates (*Heracles, *Dionysus, *Dioscuri). In the mysteries the procession of initiates, led by a priest called Iacchagogus (i.e. leader of Iacchus), was given a day of its own (Boedromion 20; the escort of the sacred objects by priestesses, priests, and magistrates of Athens took place on the preceding day). Late traditions made Iacchus the son of *Demeter, of *Persephone, and of Dionysus, or the partner of Demeter, but evidently none of this was derived from the mysteries.

The name Iacchus, like Bacchus, was also used of Dionysus, frequently in literature, but in cult there was never confusion between the Eleusinian god of initiates and Dionysus, who was not worshipped in the mysteries. The important sanctuary of Dionysus at Eleusis caused some confusion between him and Iacchus among non-Athenian writers in antiquity and even more among modern scholars.

Ialmenus, in mythology, son of *Ares and *Astyoche; leader, with his brother *Ascalaphus, of the contingent from Aspledon and Orchomenus at Troy.

Iambe, eponym of the iambic rhythm, made the mourning *Demeter laugh at *Eleusis by her jesting in the *Homeric Hymn to Demeter* (see HYMNS (GREEK)). She comes from Halimous on the Attic coast in the Hellenistic poet Philicus' *Hymn to Demeter*, and is connected with jesting by women at the *Thesmophoria. She was also said to be the daughter of *Echo and *Pan, and a Thracian. *See* BAUBO.

Iamblichus (*c.*AD 245–*c.*325), *Neoplatonist philosopher, born at Chalcis in Coele Syria (mod. Qinnesrin), probably studied with *Porphyry in Rome or Sicily; later he founded his own school in Syria (?at Apamea). Extant writings: (1) A compendium of Pythagorean philosophy (largely compiled from extracts derived from earlier writers, Platonic, Aristotelian, and Pythagorean), of which the first four books survive: *On the Life of Pythagoras*, *Protrepticus* (believed to contain material from Aristotle's lost *Protrepticus*), *On General Mathematical Science*, *On Nicomachus' Arithmetical Introduction*; (2) The 'Reply of Abammon to Porphyry's *Letter to Anebo*', known as *On the Mysteries*. Iamblichus' lost writings (of which fragments survive) include a work *On the Soul*; one *On the Gods*, probably used by *Macrobius and *Julian; an extensive exposition of Chaldaean theology; letters; and commentaries on Plato and Aristotle which were fundamental sources for later Greek Neoplatonist commentators.

Iamblichus' successors (in particular Syrianus and Proclus) credit him with determining the direction taken by later Neoplatonic philosophy. He established a standard school curriculum; imposed a systematic method of interpreting Plato; extended the use of mathematical ideas in philosophy; refined Neoplatonic metaphysics; and incorporated in Neoplatonic philosophy what he took to be the 'theologies' of the ancients (Egyptians, Persians, Chaldaeans, Orphics (see ORPHISM), *Pythagoreans), their demonology and their rites, in particular Chaldaean *theurgy.

Iamus, legendary ancestor of the prophetic clan of the Iamidae at *Olympia (see DIVINATION). *Pindar makes him son of *Apollo and *Evadne (1), daughter of *Poseidon and Spartan Pitane. At his birth Evadne left him in a bed of pansies and he was fed on honey by snakes. As a young man he prayed to Poseidon and Apollo, and Apollo told him to go to Olympia where he received the gift of divination. The most famous Iamid of Pindar's time was Tisamenus of Elis, who was given Spartan citizenship: this is probably what led to the link between Iamus and Pitane. The clan continued at Olympia well into the 3rd cent. AD.

[Pindar, *Olympian* 6. 28–73; Herodotus 9. 33–6]

Iapetus, a *Titan cast by Zeus into the depths of Tartarus. In *Hesiod's *Theogony*, son of Earth (see GAIA) and Heaven (see URANUS), father of *Prometheus, Epimetheus, *Atlas, and *Menoetius—by an Oceanid Clymene or Asia, or by *Themis. His name appears not to be Greek, and may derive from the Near East, a version of Japheth son of Noah (Genesis 9–10).

[Hesiod, *Theogony* 134, 507 ff.]

Iasion (or Iasius) was loved by *Demeter, slept with her 'in a thrice-ploughed field', and was killed by *Zeus' thunderbolt. In *Hesiod's *Theogony* this happened in Crete, and their child was *Plutus, the earth's wealth. This suggests the agricultural symbolism of the myth.

His birth was recorded in the Hesiodic *Catalogue*. Later he was son of Zeus and *Electra (2), and brother of *Dardanus and Harmonia, and played a part in the Samothracian mysteries (see MYSTERIES; SAMOTHRACE), as husband of *Cybele and father of Corybas and Plutus. Italian legend made him son of *Corythus (1), and a migrant from Italy to Samothrace. *See also* IASUS, IASIUS.

[Hesiod, *Theogony* 969–74; Diodorus Siculus 5. 48–9; Virgil, *Aeneid* 3. 167 f.]

Iason *See* JASON.

Iasus, Iasius, names of various legendary figures, including Arcadian Iasus, son of *Lycurgus and father of *Atalanta, perhaps the same as Arcadian Iasius who won the first horse-race at Olympia; Iasius or Iasus, king of *Minyan Orchomenus and father of Amphion whose daughter Chloris married *Neleus; one of the *Idaean Dactyls; and various early kings of Argos. Sometimes equated with *Iasion, *Demeter's lover.

[Homer, *Odyssey* 11. 281–6]

Icarius (1), father of *Penelope. Though the name is well established in *Homer's *Odyssey*, little is said about the person. Later tradition places him in Sparta, as son of *Oebalus or Perieres. Unwilling to allow Penelope to depart with her new husband, he followed her on the journey until *Odysseus told Penelope to choose between them; for reply, she veiled her face to indicate embarrassment and modesty, and Icarius abandoned his attempt, realizing that she preferred to go with Odysseus. (2) Attic hero probably worshipped in the village Icaria, evidently the possessor of a rich sanctuary. In a common story-type, he gave hospitality to *Dionysus, who taught him how to make wine. However, when he gave some to his neighbours they thought he had poisoned them and so killed him. (For the sequel, *see* ERIGONE.) The story is not attested before the Hellenistic scholar Eratosthenes.

[(1) Apollodorus 3. 10. 5–6]

Icarus *See* DAEDALUS.

Idaean Dactyls, the 'Fingers' of Mt. Ida in Phrygia or, according to some, Crete. First mentioned in the *Phoronis* epic (see EPIC CYCLE) as attendants of the Mother Goddess Adrasteia, they are small fabulous beings who discovered the working of iron. Their name is explained in various explanatory stories through their size (cf. German 'Däumling', Tom Thumb), or number: five or ten (five brothers and five sisters).

According to *Apollonius Rhodius, the *Nymph Anchiale bore them in the Dictaean cave clutching the earth with her fingers in her birth-pains. In an Elean tradition they are Heracles (not Alcmene's son), Paeonaeus, Epimedes, *Iasius, and Idas (or Acesidas).

Identified with the *Curetes, they guard the infant *Zeus in the Dictaean cave; but they are also related to the *Corybantes (offspring of the Dactyls in Phrygia), *Cabiri, *Telchines, and other dwarfish sprites. Their history began in prehistoric times in the sphere of a Mother Goddess connected with the early working of metal, an eastern invention that travelled west via Cyprus, Rhodes, and Crete. The novel skill was invested with magic powers in popular imagination, which also credited the Dactyls with inventing the *mysteries, organizing the first *Olympian Games, and teaching *Paris music. *See also* HESIOD.

[Apollonius Rhodius 1. 1129 ff.; Pausanias 5. 7. 6]

Idaeus, 'connected with Ida', and so (*a*) a title of *Zeus (*Iliad* and on Cretan coins and (usually in a dialect form) inscriptions); (*b*) a stock name for sundry little-known Trojans or Cretans; (*c*) magic name for a finger, perhaps the index.

Idas and Lynceus, prominent figures in early Peloponnesian legend, sons of Aphareus, king of Messenia (though *Poseidon is sometimes credited with the paternity of Idas). As the 'Apharetidae' they form a Messenian heroic pair to rival their Spartan cousins, the *Dioscuri; when the latter tried to steal their brides, the daughters of *Leucippus (1) (*see* LEUCIPPIDES), a fight led to the death of all but Polydeuces. *Pindar's version is more respectful to the sons of *Zeus, loading the blame onto the Apharetidae and making cattle, not women, the cause of the violence. Earlier Idas, the dominant brother, had competed with *Apollo for Marpessa, daughter of the river Euenus, daring to draw his bow against the god in the *Iliad*, where he is called 'mightiest of men'; when Apollo carried her off (on the chest of

Cypselus; in another tradition Idas is the kidnapper, using a winged chariot lent by Poseidon), Zeus arbitrated the dispute and allowed Marpessa to decide between her suitors; she preferred security to glamour, and chose Idas.

The brothers participated together in both the great ventures of their epoch, the Argonautic expedition (in which *Apollonius presents Idas as a hot-tempered braggart; *see* ARGONAUTS) and the Calydonian boar-hunt (*see* MELEAGER). Lynceus' contribution is his 'lynx-eyed', even X-ray vision.

[Theocritus, *Idylls* 22. 137 ff.; Pindar, *Nemean* 10. 60 ff.; Homer, *Iliad* 9. 558 ff.; Bacchylides 20]

Idmon, 'the knowing one', name of several skilful persons, especially a seer, son of *Apollo or Abas, who accompanied the *Argonauts although he knew he would not return alive; he was killed by a boar in the country of the Mariandyni.

Idomeneus, in mythology son of *Deucalion and grandson of *Minos. He was one of the suitors of *Helen, and later led the Cretan contingent to Troy with 80 ships. He is a major figure in the *Iliad*, older than most of the other Greek leaders, but a great warrior, and one of the nine who volunteered to stand against *Hector in single combat. Meeting with a great storm on his journey home after the war, he vowed that if he returned safely he would sacrifice to *Poseidon the first living creature which met him when he landed in Crete. This turned out to be his own son. When he fulfilled, or tried to fulfil, the vow, a plague broke out, and to appease the gods he was forced to leave Crete for Italy.

[Homer, *Iliad* 2. 645–52, 13. 210–515, 7. 161 ff.]

Iliona, in mythology, eldest daughter of *Priam and *Hecuba. Wife of Polymestor (*see* HECUBA), she saved the life of *Polydorus in a variant version by passing him off as her son, Polymestor thus murdering his own child.

[Virgil, *Aeneid* 1. 653–4]

Ilus, in mythology, (1) son of *Dardanus.

(2) His grand-nephew, son of Tros and father of *Laomedon. He founded Ilium on the site of ancient Troy, being guided to the site by a cow (cf. CADMUS) and received the *Palladium from heaven.

[(2) Apollodorus 3. 12. 1–3; Ovid, *Fasti* 6. 419–30]

imagery The identification of scenes in sculpture, painting and the minor arts has long been a major activity of classical archaeology, although it has traditionally been accorded less emphasis than the identification of artists' hands. In all the figurative arts conventional schemes were developed, sometimes under the influence of near-eastern iconography, for portraying particular mythological figures and episodes. Individual artists exploited conventional imagery not simply by replicating it, but by playing variations on a theme or by echoing the conventional scheme for one episode when portraying a different one. An extreme form of this is iconographic parody.

The origins of particular iconographic schemes, and the reasons why the popularity of scenes changes over time, are rarely clear. Ceramic vessels may owe some of their imagery to lost gold or silver *plate, and some vases can reasonably be held to take over the imagery of lost wall-paintings or of famous sculptures, such as the Tyrannicides group, although it is also possible in some cases that vase-painting influenced subsequent sculptural imagery. Influence from drama has also frequently been alleged: few images in Attic vase-painting represent scenes from tragedies on stage in any straightforward way, but direct representation of scenes from comic drama is popular in 4th-cent. BC south Italian pottery. In the Greek world, public sculpture often carried broadly political meaning, using the otherness of more or less fantastic figures, *Centaurs or *Amazons, to define the behaviour of the good citizen. Whether particular mythical images on pottery also carry political significance, and the popularity of particular scenes at particular times is a result of their value as political propaganda, is more

hotly debated. At Rome, sculptural style as well as imagery was used to convey political points, particularly during the empire, and the Classical and Hellenistic Greek and republican Roman heritage was manipulated to political ends.

Images were an extremely important part of religious cult. Cult statues sometimes incorporated whole programmes of mythical imagery, as in the *Athena Parthenos (*see* PHIDIAS). In the Roman world religious imagery became increasingly complex, and more or less arcane symbolic programmes are associated with mystery cults. Christianity, with its use of types and antitypes drawn from pagan mythology as well as from both Old and New Testaments, further enriched the interpretative range of familiar imagery. *See* ART, ANCIENT ATTITUDES TO; ART, FUNERARY; MYTHOLOGY.

imagines wax portrait-masks of Romans who had held the higher magistracies, were prominently displayed in shrines in the family mansion, with lines of descent and distinctions indicated. They were worn by actors impersonating the deceased in full ceremonial dress at public sacrifices and family funerals, at first only of male descendants, after *c*.100 BC gradually of female descendants as well. The families 'known' (Lat. *nobiles*) to the public through these processions formed the *nobilitas*, though the term was later restricted in application. By the early empire, and probably even in the late republic, the *imagines* of all qualified men to whom the deceased was related by birth or marriage seem to have been displayed at his funeral, and the right to keep the deceased's *imago* was assumed by his family. The custom lasted, no doubt with further changes, into the late empire.

[Polybius 6. 53; Pliny, *Natural History* 35. 6 ff.]

impiety, official action against *See* INTOLERANCE, RELIGIOUS.

Inachus, an Argive river and *river-god, father of *Io. He was made judge between *Poseidon and *Hera when both claimed

Argos, and decided in favour of Hera, whose cult he introduced; Poseidon therefore dried up his waters. He is often represented as a mortal, ancestor of the Argive kings, and therefore the earliest figure in Greek legend.

[Apollodorus 2. 13; Pausanias 2. 15. 4–5]

incense is the general name given to a variety of aromatic gum-resins which, when heated, produce a fragrant odour. Often used interchangeably with frankincense (Gk. *libanos* (probably a direct loan from South Arabian *libān*, from the Semitic root *lbn*, meaning 'white, milky'), Lat. *tus/thus*), it is the oleo-gum-resin extracted chiefly from the species *Boswellia sacra* Flückiger and *Boswellia carterii* Birdwood, of the family Burseracea. Incense was widely burnt as a religious offering in the ancient world, as an accompaniment to acts of divination, on the occasion of a burial, and as a gesture of homage (e.g. on the occasion of Alexander the Great's entry into Babylon). See subsection below, *Incense in religion*. The natural distribution of frankincense-producing *Boswellia* is restricted to Dhofar and eastern Hadhramaut, in southern Arabia; the island of Socotra; the Coromandel coast of India; and northern Somalia. Sappho preserves the earliest Greek reference to *libanos*, while Herodotus contains the earliest Greek reference to specifically Arabian frankincense, and Theophrastus obviously had first-hand accounts of the frankincense-producing area of southern Arabia to draw on in drafting his detailed treatment of it. Arabian frankincense was always the most important variety in the ancient world, and given the large quantities of frankincense consumed it is natural that a lively trade should have developed in this commodity. In the earlier periods it was transported overland by, among others, Sabaean, Minaean, and Gerrhaean merchants to Gaza, and thence on to the cities of the eastern Mediterranean. In the Roman era, maritime trade seems to have been more important. The *Periplous Maris Erythraei* identifies the port of Qana as the principal point of frankincense export by sea in ancient south Arabia.

Incense in religion Fragrance of burning wood, herbs, spices, and resins fulfilled ritual functions on three levels: first, to neutralize odours of burning sacrificial flesh, hair, hoofs and horns, etc. (*see* SACRIFICE); secondly, to generate appropriate mood and ambience; thirdly, metaphorically, incense was an expression of the intangible yet distinctly felt presence of the divine as well as the 'rising' to heaven of either prayers or souls of the dead. Myrrh and frankincense were most common in Greek religion, probably imported from southern Arabia since the 8th cent. BC via Phoenicia and Cyprus and retaining their Semitic names. The more expensive and finer incense gradually came to replace fragrant wood. In Greece incense-burning was particularly associated with *Aphrodite. Granules of incense were thrown directly onto the altar or burnt separately in special braziers.

incubation, *ritual sleep in a sanctuary (*see* SANCTUARIES) in order to obtain a dream, mostly for healing.

Incubation is known from sanctuaries of *Asclepius, but also from other healing sanctuaries like the *Amphiaraion at Oropus or oracular shrines like the Daunian ones in Italy of *Calchas and Podalirius. Such sanctuaries mostly had specific halls where patients slept during the night, with high walls to prevent casual (or intentional) prying. Aristophanes gives a detailed description of a night in the Asclepieum in the Piraeus, a Pergamene inscription adds details, while the healing inscriptions from *Epidaurus, Lebena, Rome, and Pergamum, although directly aimed at promoting the cult, allow some insights into the nature of the *dreams, as does the diary of Aelius *Aristides.

Incubation is possible only in a culture which believes that at least some dreams can always open communication with a superhuman world; thus, the experience of incubation is always formulated as a real meeting with the god (or his divine assistants), and the sanctuary is a place where the god 'reveals himself in person to man'. The structure of the ritual concurs: the ritual setting takes care that all dreams allow this meeting. Preliminary cleansing rites and offerings in the evening are a preparation for entering the doubly sacred space (a consecrated space inside the sacred space of the sanctuary) where man and god converse: these preliminaries comprise cleansing ablutions (*see* PURIFICATION) before entering the precinct, sacrifices when entering the sleeping-hall—bloodless cakes for Asclepius, a ram for *Amphiaraus, Podalirius, or Calchas; in Pergamum, Mnemosyne ('memory' in order to remember the dream) was among the recipients. In the sleeping-hall, one slept on a *stibas* (a makeshift bed of twigs), or on the hide of the sacrificial animal, not on a bed; one donned a white robe, an olive wreath, having previously removed all rings, girdles, and belts. The *stibas*, a 'natural' bed, belongs also to Bacchic mystery cults (*see* DIONYSUS; MYSTERIES) where similar experiences took place; the white robe, wreath, and absence of all bonds express the new, non-human sphere; the animal hide belongs to the god, not to the sacrificer. During the night, the god and his helpers appeared, gave advice, and performed cures. When leaving the hall in the morning, one had to pay a fee to the temple treasury.

Incubation survived the advent of *Christianity, and was absorbed into the cult of Byzantine saints as a means of obtaining healing—a phenomenon which survived up to modern times.

See ASCLEPIUS; HEALING GODS; MACHAON AND PODALIRIUS.

[Aristophanes, *Wealth* 653–747]

indigetes or -ites, indigitamenta, 'invoked deities'. Both words, as well as the corresponding verb *indigitare*, are fairly common and there is no doubt that they mean respectively a class of Roman gods and a list of gods. The lists of *indigitamenta* known from the fragments of *Varro's *Antiquitates divinae*, for the most part are antiquarian compilations without cultic value, with the exception of the deities invoked during the sacrifice to *Ceres and during some expiations of the *fratres arvales*. These lists of minor deities whose name is reduced to their function are subordinated to the major divinities whose activity they second. Nowadays there is agreement that the *indigitamenta* do not represent a primitive stage in formation of personalized deities.

The epithet *indiges* was applied to the god *Sol and to Jupiter who, at *Lavinium, was gradually assimilated to Aeneas.

initiation is the set of rituals which transforms girls and boys into adults. In Greece, these rituals were the combined product of the Indo-European heritage and indigenous traditions, as the Minoan frescos show. In historical times full rituals can be found only in Sparta and Crete, but scattered notices from other cities and the mythological tradition about the 'career' of heroes, such as *Achilles and *Theseus, suggest that puberty rites once existed all over Greece. *Apollo and *Artemis were the most important gods connected with these rites.

The Greeks had no term for initiation, but various cities used the term *agōgē*, literally 'the leading of a horse by one's hand', and related words. This view reflects itself not only in Archaic poetry, where boys and girls are often addressed as foals and fillies, but also in mythological namings: youths connected with initiation regularly have names with the element *hippos* (horse): *Leucippus (1–2), *Leucippides, Melanippe, etc. Clearly, youths were seen as wild animals, who had to be domesticated before entering adult society.

Regarding girls, our best information comes from Sparta, where their 'education' prepared them for motherhood through physical exercises and dancing in choruses.

Aristocratic girls had to pass through a lesbian relationship to mark the contrast with
their final destination, marriage; a similar
custom existed on Lesbos where Sappho
instructed aristocratic girls. Special stress
was laid on the enhancing of the girls'
physical beauty: not unusually, a beauty
contest concluded the girls' initiation. *See
also* BRAURON.

Male puberty rites survived into the 4th
cent. BC on Crete, where at the age of 17,
after an informal training, sons of aristocrats together with boys of lower classes
were gathered into bands, *agelai* or 'herds
of horses', which were supervised by their
fathers. Here they received a training in
dancing, singing, hunting, fighting, and
letters. The rites were concluded with a
brief stay in the countryside, where the aristocratic youth passed through a homosexual
affair. The festivals in which the new adults
showed off to the community belong to the
most important ones of Crete.

Similar rites existed in Sparta, but their
character changed after the Messenian
Wars. The *agōgē* was extended by the introduction of age classes and became increasingly harsh when Sparta's position started to
depend on a decreasing number of citizens.
In Athens the original initiatory structures
had disintegrated in the course of the Archaic age, but its 'military service', the *ephēbeia*, still displays various initiatory features.

In Rome, boys' initiation did not survive
into the republic, but the traditions about
*Romulus and Remus with their band of
youths and run-away criminals strongly suggest its one-time existence, as does the myth
of Caeculus of *Praeneste. *See also* RITES OF
PASSAGE and (for a different sense of migration) MYSTERIES.

Ino-Leucothea is a goddess connected with
*initiation and rites of reversal. The names
are already combined by *Homer, but Ino
appears independently in myth, as do Leucothea and her festival Leucathea in cult.
Leucothea was worshipped in 'the whole
of Greece' (according to Cicero), but it is

difficult to get a clear idea of her festivals,
which often seem to have contained features
of dissolutions of the social order: her sanctuary at *Delos was connected with a phallic
procession, and in Chaeronea slaves and Aetolians were excluded. In Teos the young
men became adult during the Leucathea,
here the first month of the year. This initiatory aspect of Leucothea may well have led
to her identification with Ino, who is also
connected with initiation: she founds a contest for boys in Miletus and raises *Dionysus,
in a typical initiatory way, 'as a girl' in
Euboea. It is probably also this connection
with growing up which made Aristotle
assign the famous temple at Pyrgi to Leucothea, but Strabo to *Eileithyia. The story
of Ino's raising of Dionysus and *Hera's subsequent anger, which caused her death,
sometimes together with her son *Melicertes, was a favourite theme in tragedy
and comedy.

[Euripides, *Medea* 1282–9; Apollodorus 3. 28; Ovid,
Metamorphoses 4. 416–542, *Fasti* 6. 489–550]

inscriptions *See* EPIGRAPHY.

instauratio When a religious ceremony
was interrupted or wrongly performed (*vitium*) it had to be repeated from the beginning. We hear particularly of *instauratio* of
games (*ludi*) and the Latin Festival (*feriae Latinae*). To pontifical *instauratio sacrorum* ('of
rites') corresponded augural repetition and
renewal of vitiated auspices; *repetitio auspi-
ciorum* ('repetition of auspices') concerned
primarily military auspices of a commander
(*see* AUSPICIUM); *renovatio* ('renewal') was accomplished through abdication of all curule
magistrates.

interpretatio Romana, lit. 'Latin translation', a phrase coined by Tacitus and used to
describe the Roman habit of replacing the
name of a foreign deity with that of a Roman
deity considered somehow comparable. At
times this process involved extensive identification of the actual deities, while in other
cases, the deities, though sharing a name,
continued to be sharply distinguished.

Different Latin names could sometimes be substituted for the same foreign name, depending on which characteristic of the god was chosen as the basis for comparison. The earliest of these 'translations' were from Greek: thus 'Zeus' was translated by 'Iuppiter' (*see* ZEUS; JUPITER). The process continued as the Romans came into contact with other cultures, so that the German 'Wodan' was called '*Mercurius' by Roman writers. Only in a few cases were foreign divine names adopted directly into Latin, e.g. '*Apollo' and '*Isis'. *See* SYNCRETISM.

intolerance, religious For most Greek states our evidence is too poor and patchy for us to be able to say much. We know a little about 5th-cent. BC Athens. It is often thought of as an 'open society' but the tolerance of that society had limits. There is some evidence for literary censorship, though of a haphazard and perhaps ineffective sort. Between 440 and 437 BC there were formal restrictions on ridicule in theatrical comedy. On the other hand there were no 'witch-hunts' against intellectuals, though *Anaxagoras and other associates of Pericles were prosecuted in the courts. Anaxagoras' ostensible offence was impiety, and the decree of *Diopeithes, if historical, would provide hard evidence for public control of religious teaching. (*See also* ATHEISM; DIAGORAS; THEODICY.) Alcibiades and others were punished severely for parodying the Eleusinian *mysteries, but the offending action was not necessarily 'the product of earnest intellectual inquiry'. The reasons for *Socrates' execution in 399 are still disputed by scholars, but political considerations were surely at least as relevant as religious: Socrates was critical of the democracy and its institutions, and had taught prominent oligarchs. Aeschines in the mid-4th cent. explicitly makes the latter point, which could not be made openly in 399 because of the amnesty granted to oligarchs compromised by involvement with the extreme oligarchs, the Thirty Tyrants.

The most notable (actually unique) instance of Hellenistic religious persecution was *Antiochus IV's treatment of the *Jews. Roman attitudes to foreign religions were generally cosmopolitan; *see* ROMAN RELIGION. The suppression of the *Bacchanalia in 186 BC was exceptional. For Roman treatment of Jews *see* JEWS; for persecution of Christians see CHRISTIANITY. *See also* SEMITISM, ANTI-.

invulnerability was commonly ascribed to the legendary heroes in the 'cyclic' epic tradition (*see* EPIC CYCLE), but is rigorously excluded from the Homeric poems (*see* HOMER) as quite incompatible with the principle that the great warriors are genuinely fighting for their lives. However, most examples have an 'escape clause'; there is one vulnerable spot, or one weapon which can wound. *Achilles, famously, had been dipped in the Styx by his mother Thetis, and his skin could only be pierced where she had suspended him by the heel. *Aias (1) was wrapped as a baby in the skin of the Nemean lion (itself invulnerable, until *Heracles had the idea of strangling it, and skinning it with its own claws), and could only be wounded in his armpit, where the hide had failed to make contact. The Lapith hero *Caeneus fights with two swords because the invulnerability granted to him by *Apollo meant he could dispense with a shield; the *Centaurs eventually neutralize him by battering him into the ground. Early artistic representations of the Centauromachy and the deaths of Aias and Achilles show that these cyclic versions were widely popular. Cities, similarly, may be impregnable until their talisman can be captured (Troy's '*Palladium'); and a country may be invincible if it can guard the secret grave of an enemy hero buried on its territory. *See* CEPHALUS.

Io, in mythology, priestess of *Hera at the Argive *Heraion, daughter of Iasus (*see* IASUS, IASIUS) or the river *Inachus. *Zeus seduces her but when Hera discovers, she is transformed into a white cow by Zeus or by

Hera, and tethered to an olive-tree in the Heraion grove with the monster *Argos (b) 'All-seeing' as guard. Hermes kills Argos, but Hera inflicts a gadfly upon the bovine Io, who now wanders distraught around the world (in Aeschylus past the remote Caucasus to receive a lecture from the enchained *Prometheus) until finally she comes to Egypt, where with a touch (*ephaptein*) of his hand Zeus restores her and presently Epaphus is born to her, the ancestor of *Danaus who will return to Argos with the Danaids, his daughters. Because of her bovine shape, Io was identified with the Egyptian *Isis (who had assumed the bovine characteristics of Hathor). In rationalized versions, she was kidnapped by Phoenician traders, and the Egyptians sent Inachus a bull in compensation.

Her *metamorphosis belongs to a pattern of association of girls reaching maturity with animals (cf. the Proetides at nearby Tiryns; *see* PROETUS) and has been argued to reflect rites of transition into adulthood (*see* INITIATION; RITES OF PASSAGE). But it is also a story of the priesthood at the Heraion, of *genealogy (Danaus), and of growing awareness of the non-Greek world. Sociologically, the story is interesting for its projection of frenzy and marginalization onto the girl reaching maturity.

In art the monster Argos covered in eyes and the bovine Io provided unusual subjects, popular in Greek colonies too. The influential 4th-cent. BC painting by Nicias was perhaps imitated by murals at Pompeii.

[Apollodorus 2. 1. 3–4; Aeschylus, *Prometheus Bound* 561–886; Ovid, *Metamorphoses* 1. 583–750]

Iolaus, younger companion and helper of *Heracles, was identified as the son of his half-brother *Iphicles and often appeared with Heracles in cult. He was worshipped notably at Thebes and in Sicily and Sardinia, where he was said to have led a colonizing expedition. His distinguishing feature in myth and cult is his connection with youth; even as an old man he was rejuvenated for one day in order to defeat *Eurystheus.

[Euripides, *Children of Heracles* 843–63; Diodorus Siculus 4. 24. 4–6, 29–31, 38]

Ion, a heroic name, especially that of the ancestor of the Ionians. The early tradition appears to agree in making him son of *Xuthus and grandson of *Hellen; Athenian claims to primacy among the Ionians are expressed in the tradition that his mother was *Creusa (1), daughter of the Athenian king *Erechtheus. The more familiar story that his true father was *Apollo is not certainly attested before *Euripides; this version not only eliminates all non-Athenian ancestry, but also indicates Ionians as superior to Dorians by making Dorus, along with Achaeus (already Xuthus' son in *Hesiod) son of Creusa and Xuthus.

In Attica, Ion has connections both with the Gargettus area, where there is a village Ionidai, and with the east coast, but he eventually became a central figure in both cult and myth; as well as his parentage, Athenian writers record the help given by him to Erechtheus in the Eleusinian War, and the contribution made by him to Attic unification. He was also invoked in connection with the Ionians of the Peloponnese.

[Euripides, *Ion*]

Ionian festivals Festivals constitutive of the *Ionians on several levels of identity.

Festivals which were specific to the Athenian and Ionian festival-calendars were already in antiquity used as an argument for a common origin; they date back to before the Ionian migration (10th cent. BC). They include *Anthesteria, *Apaturia, *Boedromia, *Lenaea, *Plynteria, *Pyanopsia (or Pyanepsia or Kyanepsia), and *Thargelia. Some festivals are only marginally important, as Boedromia (attested only through the month-name) or Pya-/Kyanepsia. The Anthesteria attest a cult of *Dionysus already before the emigration, the Apaturia point to the social importance of lineage rites. Exceptionally, common rituals confirm the connection, such as the expulsion of the *pharmakos* at the Thargelia or the ship-cart procession attested for the *Dionysia in Athens, in Archaic Clazomenae(?), and in Roman Smyrna.

The Ionians themselves articulated their identity in two festivals. In the Archaic age, first the Cycladic, then later (by mid-7th cent.) all Ionians met at the festival of Delian Apollo. *See* DELOS. The (mainly Asia Minor) Ionian cities held their common festival, the Panionia, in the *Panionium, a sanctuary of Poseidon Heliconios in the territory of Melie or, after the destruction of Melie *c*.700 BC, of Priene. During the Persian occupation, the cult was continued by Ephesus, to be reactivated in the Panionium in the 4th cent; a sacred law from this period attests the primacy of Zeus *Boulaios*, i.e. the prime function of political meeting. During the Hellenistic and imperial epochs, ruler-cult became important for the Panionia; the imperial Panionia were again held in the major towns.

Iphicles, in mythology, twin brother of *Heracles, also called Iphiclus. He was Heracles' companion on some exploits and father of Heracles' better-known companion *Iolaus. Two other children of his were killed by Heracles in his madness.

[Apollodorus 2. 61 ff.]

Iphigenia, the daughter of *Agamemnon and *Clytemnestra (or, according to the less common version, of *Theseus and *Helen). *Artemis demanded her sacrifice as the price for sending a fair wind to the Greeks waiting at *Aulis to sail for *Troy. In some versions Artemis was angry because Agamemnon had killed a deer—and boasted that he was a better hunter than Artemis. In another version he had killed a sacred goat kept in Artemis' grove and made the same boast. In a less common version it is the non-fulfilment of a vow that caused Artemis' wrath; in *Apollodorus it was caused both by Agamemnon's boasting and by the fact that *Atreus had not sacrificed the golden lamb to her, though he had vowed to sacrifice to her the most beautiful animal in his flocks. According to one version Agamemnon sent for Iphigenia on the pretext of

marriage to *Achilles. In Aeschylus it is suggested that she died at the altar—or at least that the spectators thought she did. In most versions Artemis snatched her away and saved her; a hind replaced her and was sacrificed in her place. Alternatively she was replaced by a bear, and in one of this version's variants the sacrifice took place at *Brauron not Aulis; in one version she was replaced by a calf. In *Hesiod's *Catalogue* Artemis replaced Iphimede (as she is called there) by an *eidōlon*; Iphimede becomes Artemis *einodia*, which is understood by *Pausanias to mean that she became *Hecate. In the epic *Cypria* (*see* EPIC CYCLE) Iphigenia is carried off to Tauris in the Black Sea and made immortal by Artemis. In the Hesiodic *Catalogue*, the *Cypria*, *Stesichorus, and Herodotus, she then becomes divine. In the version in *Euripides she becomes a priestess of Artemis, first in the Taurid and then at Brauron. In the Taurid she was forced to preside over human sacrifices; on recognizing her brother (*Orestes) in one of the prospective victims she fled with him and Artemis' statue, which Athena instructed them to take to Attica. At *Brauron she was associated with the rite of the *arkteia*, had a heroon, and received *hero-cult; the clothes of women who died in *childbirth were dedicated to her. Her relationship to Artemis varies in the different cults. In some, as at Brauron and at Aegira, she is distinct from Artemis; in others she is identified with Artemis. She had a heroon also at Megara, where, in the local version of the myth, she was alleged to have died. One version combines the priesthood in the Taurid with immortality conferred by Artemis at Leuce, where Iphigenia married Achilles. According to Herodotus, the Taurians sacrifice shipwrecked men and any Greeks they capture to a goddess Parthenos whom they identify with Agamemnon's daughter Iphigenia.

[Aeschylus, *Agamemnon* 218–49; Herodotus 4. 103; Euripides, *Iphigenia in Tauris*; Apollodorus, *Epitome* 3. 21-2]

Iphis, in mythology, (1) father of *Eteoclus,

one of the *Seven against Thebes, and of *Evadne (2), wife of *Capaneus. (2) A young Cypriot, who loved Anaxarete, a noblewoman of that island. She would have none of him, and he finally hanged himself at her door; she looked, unmoved, from her window, and was turned by Aphrodite into stone. The resulting image was called Aphrodite *prospiciens* 'looking out'.

[Ovid, *Metamorphoses* 14. 698 ff.]

Irenaeus (*c.*AD 130–*c.*202), sometimes called the first systematic Christian theologian, was born in Asia Minor, had contacts in youth with *Polycarp of Smyrna, but spent most of his active life in Gaul, becoming bishop of Lyons *c.*178. He was thus an important link between east and west, and intervened at Rome on behalf of the Montanists (*see* MONTANISM) at Lyons (177/8) and the Quartodecimans (Fourteen-Dayers) of Asia (190), who observed Easter on 14 Nisan, the day of the Passover, rather than the following Sunday. Only two of his numerous works survive, the vast anti-Gnostic (*see* GNOSTICISM) *Adversus haereses* (mainly in a Latin translation) and the short *Proof of the Apostolic Preaching* (in an Armenian translation). His constructive exposition of Christian theology developed out of his critique of Gnostic systems, and was characterized by stress on traditional elements in Christianity.

Iris, goddess of the rainbow and messenger of the gods. She is usually employed by *Zeus in *Homer's *Iliad*, once by *Hera, whose officious minister she later becomes. Elsewhere in the *Iliad* she summons *Boreas and Zephyrus (*see* WIND-GODS) on her own initiative to help *Achilles, and resists their boisterous advances, but the poet Alcaeus makes her mother of *Eros by Zephyrus. She is 'wind-footed' and 'storm-footed' in the *Iliad*, where the rainbow portends war or storm, and *Hesiod makes her daughter of Thaumas and *Electra (1), and sister to the *Harpyiae or Harpies (storm-winds). She is sometimes described as amorous, but Theoc-

ritus calls her 'still virgin' as bedmaker to Zeus and Hera.

In Archaic art (François vase, etc.) she has winged boots and short chiton like *Hermes, but later is winged, with long or short dress, and carries a herald's staff. She appears in many divine or heroic scenes as messenger, as servant of Hera (as on the Parthenon frieze), and sometimes as a lone traveller beset by *satyrs or *Centaurs.

[Homer, *Iliad* 17. 547–52, 18. 165 ff., 23. 198 ff.; Hesiod, *Theogony*, 265 ff.; Euripides, *Madness of Heracles* 822 ff.; Callimachus, *Hymn* 4. 66 f., 215 ff.; Theocritus, *Idylls* 17. 133 f.]

Ishtar, Mesopotamian goddess of love and war, variously described as daughter of Sin (moon-god) or of Anu (sky-god), with various attributes according to different city traditions. At Uruk she was identical with Sumerian Inanna, lover of Dumuzi (Tammuz); at Dilbat she was the planet Venus; at Kish she was warlike; at Arbela her oracle was famous in the 7th cent. BC and her temple there organized loans far abroad; at Nineveh her Hurrian-influenced entourage included demons of disease. Probably all her temples were centres for cult prostitution of various kinds (*see* PROSTITUTION, SACRED). Her name was used as a generic term for goddess, sometimes in the plural, facilitating *syncretism with other goddesses in the pantheon. She is often depicted as naked, or with a lion, with weapons, or with the rod-and-ring of kingship. She plays major roles in literary texts, such as the Epic of Gilgamesh and in Ishtar's Descent to the Underworld.

Isis (Egyptian *As* or *Ast*, Gk. *Isis, Eisis*), 'mistress of the house of life', whose creative and nurturing functions made her the most popular divinity of the Late period in the Egyptian Fayûm and delta. As such she absorbed, or was equated with, many other divinities, acquiring a universal character expressed in Greek as 'invoked by innumerable names'. The hieroglyphic form of her name, whose meaning is disputed, connects her with the royal throne and with *Osiris: his centre at Busiris was close to hers in the twelfth nome. A connected narrative of her myth appears late, doubtless under Greek influence. In the Egyptian versions, the myth generally begins with Set's murder of her brother and husband, Osiris, whom she and her sister Nephthys revive by mourning. Impregnated by Osiris after his resurrection, Isis gives birth to *Horus, who, after 'redeeming his father', ascends his throne, and later attacks and rapes, even beheads, Isis. In return, Isis chops off his hands. In the theology of the New Kingdom she has several linked roles: as a goddess who protects the coffin, she is 'mother', 'wet-nurse', of the dead, and brings about rebirth; as midwife, she protects women in giving birth and suckling—she is often the 'king's wet-nurse'; equated with Sothis (Sirius), she brings the Nile flood and the new year; equated with the snake-goddess Renenutet, the goddess of harvest, she is 'mistress of life'; as magician and protector, as in the Graeco-Egyptian magical papyri, she is 'mistress of heaven'. *See* MAGIC.

In Egyptian popular religion of the Hellenistic and Roman periods, these roles are simplified to three: protector of women and marriage; goddess of maternity and the new-born (Isis suckling Harpocrates (*see* HORUS) or *Apis); guarantor of the fertility of fields and the abundance of harvests. Herodotus' identification of Isis with *Demeter, and the later view of Isis and Osiris as inventors of arable farming, reproduce only the last of these motifs. The version of Isis that was attractive in the Graeco-Roman world universalized this popular representation: dispenser of life, protector (especially of the family), healer, deliverer, and so mistress of the universe. A more complex account of Isis was available through the aretalogies, or hymns of praise. Six Greek versions are known. They are now generally regarded as variants of a first-person praise-scheme produced (in the 2nd cent. BC) at Memphis in Egypt by Hellenized priests, deliberately excluding many features of Egyptian Isis. But the earliest surviving example, from Maroneia near Abdera (*c*.100 BC), merely alludes to the scheme, and is thus a bridge to the more numerous '*hymns' (ten known, including that in Apuleius). Isidorus, the author of the three earliest surviving hymns (1st cent. BC), from the Egyptian temple at Medīnet Mādī, speaks expressly of 'interpreting' Egyptian texts for Greek use. No credence is now given to the old view that the Egyptian cults offered a deeper spirituality through personal salvation: the mysteries of Isis, whatever their origin, were always secondary. Discussion of Isis' success has centred on two themes, both vaguely Weberian. A 'political' view comes in two forms. (1) The world-affirmation inherent in Egyptian Isiac religion made it attractive as a personal religion both to successful Egyptian emigrants and to a 'broad church', including local élites; even if often incorporated into the civic calendar, it remained sufficiently marginal to retain authority through the god's personal demand on the worshipper. (2) The motif of personal subjection to and dependence upon Isis is combined with that of freedom from fate. This paradox reproduces the negotiation between free cities and absolute Hellenistic kings/Roman emperors; the Egyptian cults validated this uneasy relation for individuals. The second theme is that of women: though not dominant, women were important, as suggested by Augustan poetry. Isis may have given a religious overtone to a positive view of female sexuality. *See* EGYPTIAN DEITIES.

[Diodorus Siculus 1. 13–27; Plutarch, *On Isis and Osiris*; Apuleius, *Metamorphoses* 11; Propertius 2. 33a; Tibullus 1. 3; Ovid, *Amores* 2. 13]

Islands of the Blest (*Fortunatae insulae*) were originally, like the 'Gardens of the *Hesperides', the mythical winterless home of the happy dead, far west on Ocean shores or islands. Comparable is *Homer's description of *Elysium; in both cases entry is reserved for a privileged few. The islands were later identified with Madeira or more commonly with the Canaries, after their discovery (probably by the Carthaginians).

[Homer, *Odyssey* 4. 563 ff.; Hesiod, *Works and Days* 171; Pindar, *Olympian* 2. 68 ff.]

Isthmia (sanctuary of *Poseidon), a Corinthian *Panhellenic shrine 16 km. (10 mi.)
east of Corinth, beside the modern Athens–
Corinth road. A hippodrome and hero shrine
(West Foundation) lie 2 km. (1⅓ mi.) south-
west, with additional cults in the Sacred
Glen.

The sanctuary was established c.1050 BC in
an area of Mycenaean settlement. The first
temple (a peripteral i.e. colonnaded building
with wall-paintings), c.690–650, had a
30-metre altar and *temenos wall. It was rebuilt after fires in c.470–460 and 390. The
first stadium (early 6th cent. BC) accords
with the traditional foundation date (582
BC) for the *Isthmian Games; a larger stadium (further south-east) was built c.300 BC.
Chariot- and horse-races were prominent (see
HORSE- AND CHARIOT-RACES), and there was a
special four-lap foot race called the hippios
('equestrian'). Musical contests are attested
from the 3rd cent. BC, and were held in a
theatre (established by 390). Isthmia was a
major assembly place; it was at the games
in 196 BC that Titus Quinctius Flamininus
announced the freedom of the Greeks. A
bath (originating c.4th cent.) survives in
Roman form.

After Lucius Mummius sacked Corinth in
146 BC, Isthmia was abandoned and the
games transferred to Sicyon; returned to
the Roman colony c.2 BC, they were resumed
at Isthmia c.AD 50–60, when the theatre was
renovated, followed, by 100, by the temple
and temenos wall. A heroon of Palaemon (see
MELICERTES) dates from the mid-1st cent. AD;
the first, Hadrianic, temple of Palaemon was
transferred during the reign of *Marcus Aurelius. Cult activity ceased during the 3rd
cent. AD.

On the Rachi ridge to the south is a small,
mainly Hellenistic, settlement (abandoned
c.200 BC).

Isthmian Games The Isthmian Games (see
ISTHMIA) were held in honour of *Poseidon,
the prize being originally a crown of pine,
but during the Classical period one of dry
celery. They were said to have been founded
to commemorate the death of *Melicertes
(or Palaemon), *Ino's son, or (according to
Athens) by *Theseus after he had killed the
robber *Sinis. They were held biennially in
April or May.

Isyllus (late 4th cent. BC), of *Epidaurus,
author of six poems in various metres
found in inscriptions at Epidaurus. Poems
1 and 3 are dedications. In poem 2 the poet
praises himself for the introduction of a
procession to Phoebus (i.e. *Apollo) and
*Asclepius at Epidaurus. Poem 4 is a *paean
to Apollo and Asclepius, poem 5 a *hymn to
Asclepius.

Italic religion In a strict sense this concept
refers to religions of various Indo-European
tribes forming the Italic linguistic league,
Umbrians, Sabello-Oscans (Sabines, Samnites, and a number of others such as Ves-
tini, Marrucini, Paeligni, Marsi, Frentani,
Campani, Lucani, and Latins. In a broader
sense it may also include the cults of the
Veneti in the north-east, and those of the
speakers of Messapic (cognate with the Illyrian) in the south-east (Apulia); excluded
are the religions of the Etruscans, Greeks,
Ligurians, and Celts. The cults of the Indo-
European settlers were first amalgamated
with the pre-existing Mediterranean elements, and later exposed to Etruscan and
(from the 8th cent.) Greek influences.

Roman and Italic religion belonged to the
same cultural universe; hence after the
Roman conquest, and the gradual extinction
of the Italic languages and their replacement
by Latin, the Italic cults were relatively
easily assimilated to the Roman cult.
Roman authors provide precious information, especially *Varro, *Ovid's Fasti, Pompeius Festus, and the ancient commentaries
on *Virgil. Archaeological evidence (cultic
statuary, temples, tomb paintings, funerary
urns, votive offerings) presents a vivid picture of religious life; it has been enriched
particularly by excavations in the sanctuaries of *Fortuna Primigenia in Praeneste,
*Juno in Gabii, the precinct of Thirteen
Altars in *Lavinium, Mater *Matuta in

Satricum, a (Samnite) sanctuary at Pietrab-bondante, *Mefitis in Rossano di Vaglio (in Lucania).

But above all we have inscriptional evidence in Italic languages (4th–1st cents. BC), with numerous dedications to various deities. The principal documents are:

1. The Umbrian *Tabulae Iguvinae*, seven bronze tables from Iguvium describing in great detail various religious ceremonies, lustration, sacrifices, and auspication (nothing as detailed exists either in Latin or Greek).

2. The Oscan Table from Agnone in Samnium (c.mid-3rd cent. BC, and thus predating all Latin literary texts), a list of seventeen deities who possessed altars in the precinct of *Ceres, and to whom sacrifices were made on certain days (to some deities on the feast of *Flora).

3. The so-called *iúvila* inscriptions, Oscan gravestones from Capua (4th–3rd cents. BC), indicating the name(s) of the deceased, and recording or prescribing the dates of (annual) sacrifices, e.g. 'this is the *iúvila* of Sp(urius) Kaluvius and (his) brothers. At the feast (*fíisiaís*, cf. Lat. *feriae*) of *púmperiai prai-mamerttiai* (i.e. taking place in the month that precedes the month of March, so circumscribed because it was devoted to the cult of the dead and its real name was regarded as inauspicious) (blood) sacrifices (*sakrasias*; *kersnasias* were bloodless) were made in the presence of (or in the year when) L(ucius) Pettius (was) the chief magistrate (*L. Pettíeis meddíkiaí*)'.

4. Oscan lead imprecations, also from Capua, very similar to Greek or Latin specimens, one of them mentioning (in dat.) *Keri arent[ikai]*, Ceres the Avenger.

Still our knowledge of Italic pantheon and cult is fragmentary. Common to all Italic peoples were *Jupiter as the chief sky-god and *Mars as the war-god. In Iguvium together with the obscure *Vofionus* they formed a triad, all bearing the epithet *Grabovius* (perhaps 'of the oak'). Next the cult of *Hercules and of the *Dioscuri. Very prominent were female (most often fertility) de-

ities, Juno (esp. in Latium, in Lanuvium, Ardea, Gabii, Tibur, Tusculum), and in the Faliscan Falerii; *Ceres (partially identified with Demeter); *Herentas* (= *Venus); *Mefitis* (also identified with Venus); *Angitia (particularly among the Marsi and Paeligni), often associated with Ceres; *Fortuna in Latin Praeneste, where she was called *Primigenia*, and in Antium; *Reitia* among the Veneti, often with the epithet *sainatis*, 'healer', later identified with Juno; Umbrian *Cubrar Mater*, and in Picenum *dea Cupra*; further *Diana, esp. in Latium, where her grove (*nemus*) at *Aricia (Nemi) was the centre of the Latin League, and in Campania (mount Tifata near Capua). In the Table of Agnone a striking feature is deities representing various aspects of Ceres. These names are followed by the adjective *Kerríi-* = *Cerealis*, 'of Ceres', i.e. Ceres as Nurse, Nymph, *Perna*(?), *Flora* ('Bloom'), *Imbres* ('rain water') and 'Mother(s)'. There appears also 'Daughter of Ceres', and 'Hercules of Ceres'. Next Jupiter (*Diúvei*) in his two functions, *Verehasiúí* (*Iuvenis*? *Frugifer*?) and *Regaturei* ('Irrigating'?), and other deities. Most of these deities (as also those in Iguvium) have no direct counterparts in Rome, but their name-forms and minute specialization recall those innumerable Roman gods who according to the pontifical doctrine presided over every stage and aspect of life. In Rome their names and functions (with the exception of four deities recorded in the acts of Arvals; *see* FRATRES ARVALES) have been preserved by antiquarians and church writers; in the Table of Agnone we meet them not as an antiquarian curiosity but as part of a flourishing cult. *See also under* SANCTUARIES.

Ithaca, in *Homer's poetry the island homeland of *Odysseus and the capital of his kingdom. Judging from the suitors who tried to win this realm by marrying *Penelope, it also included Dulichium, Same, and Zacynthus. From ancient times, the Homeric island was identified with modern Ithaca, a small narrow island between Cephallenia and Leucas off the Acarnanian coast. Because

Homer's descriptions and modern topography do not always match, some scholars still debate the 'Ithaca question', although most would accept the verdict of the ancients. The recent excavation of a large Mycenaean-style tholos-tomb on Cephallenia may now shift the debate to that island.

Although excavations at Aetos (at the narrow strip of land in the island's middle) and Pelikata (near Stavros by Polis Bay) have not produced a clear Mycenaean palace-complex like that at Pylos, they have revealed two bronze age settlements, both inhabited during the Mycenaean period. Finds of Corinthian, Cretan, and Rhodian pottery (from a sanctuary on the slopes of Mt. Aetos and from the cave near Polis Bay) reveal the island as a staging-post for Greek trade to Italy, up to, and perhaps even after, the foundation of Corinthian colonies. The cave at Polis Bay was the site of cult activity from the bronze age to Roman times: inscriptions reveal the worship of *Athena, *Hera, the *Nymphs, and Odysseus and bits of twelve splendid geometric tripods recall the ones brought home by Odysseus from Phaeacia i.e. *Scheria. Curiously, Ithaca played no major role in the events of Classical Greece.

Itinerarium Egeriae, an account of a pilgrimage to the Holy Land in AD 381–4 (including visits to Egypt, Sinai, and Mesopotamia), written from Constantinople for a western audience described as *sorores*, probably a circle of pious Christian laywomen in Spain or Gaul to which Egeria belonged. Although the text displays admiration for eastern monks, it is only later tradition which makes Egeria herself a nun. The sole manuscript, apart from fragments, was discovered at Arezzo in 1884. The text is incomplete, but provides detailed information about the Church liturgy of *Jerusalem and the holy places, as well as a record of the pilgrim's journey to biblical sites in the Sinai peninsula and elsewhere in the Holy Land, and to the monks and martyr-shrines of Edessa. *See* PILGRIMAGE.

Iustitia, Roman equivalent of *Dike;

mostly in poetry, but she had a temple from 8 January AD 13 and was among the virtues celebrated by *Augustus' famous golden shield set up in the Senate-house and inscribed with the emperor's virtues in 27 BC. In inscriptions she sometimes has the title Augusta.

Iuventas, goddess, not of youth or youthful beauty in general, but of the *iuvenes*, those who had just put on their togas and were now men of military age (contrast HEBE). She controlled the admission of males into the community and protected them as *iuvenes*. She had a shrine in the vestibule of *Minerva's cella in the Capitoline temple, and is said to have been there before the temple was built, she and *Terminus refusing to leave. When any young man took the toga of manhood, it seems that a contribution was made to her temple chest. A sacrifice to *Spes and Iuventas commemorated the day of Octavian's assumption of the toga of manhood.

ivory, a material derived from the tusk of the Asiatic or African elephant or the tooth of the hippopotamus. Capable of being carved in the round, or in relief, used as inlay, as a veneer, turned on a lathe, or even moulded, ivory was a multi-purpose commodity that was imported into the Mediterranean from North Africa and the Levant. The Old Persian for the Nile delta meant 'The Tusks'. There were flourishing schools of ivory-working in bronze age Crete. Rich finds of ivory inlays at Nimrud, Arslan Tash, and other near-eastern sites have echoes in ivory objects found at Ephesus, Samos, Delphi, and in Laconia. At all periods, furniture was decorated with ivory plaques. Ivory was used for the flesh parts of cult statues (e.g. *Phidias' gold and ivory *Athena Parthenos and his *Zeus at *Olympia), and for temple doors.

Ixion, legendary king of Thessaly, was a primal offender against divine order. *Pindar records two crimes: not only was he the world's first parricide (victim unspecified; one early source apparently named him as his father-in-law Eïoneus), but after *Zeus had purified him (*see* PURIFICATION) he reoffended by attempting to rape his benefactor's wife *Hera. His intended victim was however substituted by Zeus with a cloud-image, which conceived Centaurus ('Pokewind', named as usual after the father), sire of the *Centaurs. His punishment was to be crucified on a fiery wheel which revolves throughout eternity—i.e. presumably the sun; Ixion is condemned to become part of the operating mechanism of Zeus' universe, as *Sisyphus heaves the sun-disc up to the zenith only to see it roll back down, and as *Atlas and *Prometheus support the weight of the sky at its western and eastern limits.

[Aeschylus, *Eumenides* 441 f., 717; Pindar, *Pythian* 2. 21 ff.]

iynx, a bird ('wryneck'—so named for its mating-gesture) sharing its name with a mythological figure and the wheel to which it was affixed as an implement of erotic magic. Iynx, the daughter of *Peitho or *Echo, employed magic to seduce *Zeus either for *Io or for herself. Offended, *Hera turned her into a bird. As early as the Archaic period, a love-charm in the form of a spoked wheel with a spread-eagled iynx fastened to it was suspended and spun to attract a love-object. *Pindar attributes the iynx-wheel's invention to *Aphrodite and its first use to *Jason, who secures *Medea's love with its magic. By Theocritus, the bird has vanished from the wheel, but has left its name behind: Simaitha spins a birdless iynx to beguile Delphis.

[Pindar, *Pythian* 4. 214; Theocritus, *Idylls* 2]

Janus, god of door and gate (*ianua*) at Rome (the term also for the type of honorific gateway that we misleadingly call 'triumphal arch'). Like a door, he looked both ways, and is therefore depicted as a double-headed and bearded man (the image chosen for many early Roman coins). More generally he controlled beginnings, most notably as the eponym of the month January (he was named first in prayer, e.g. Livy's account of the *devotio* of Publius Decius Mus), and was linked with the symbolism of the gate at the beginning and end of military campaigns (the bad omen of the departure of the Fabii from Rome before their destruction at the battle of the Cremera involved going through the right-hand *ianus* or arch of the city-gate instead of the left). This was most famously expressed in the ritual of the closing of the temple of Janus Geminus in the Forum in times of complete peace: under *Numa, in 235 BC, three times under *Augustus, and more frequently in the imperial period. Domitian transferred the cult to a new shrine in the forum 'Transitorium'.

This shrine (as depicted on coins) was little more than a gateway itself. It was probably *geminus*—'twin'—in being a four-way arch, like the 'arch of Janus' which survives in the forum Boarium (the porta triumphalis through which victorious generals crossed the *pomerium* into the city probably had this shape). There are serious topographical problems about the nature and relationship of the other ancient shrines of Janus along the *via Sacra, which may have been related to crossings of the early watercourses in the

area. A sanctuary in the forum Holitorium was Gaius Duilius' monument for his victory at Mylae (260 BC).

Janus was a god of considerable importance (*divom deus*, god of gods, in the *Carmen Saliare*). *Ovid describes his cosmic significance. The *rex sacrorum* sacrificed to him in the *Regia on the *dies Agonalis* of 9 January.

[Varro, *On The Latin Language* 7. 27; Livy 8. 9. 6; Ovid, *Fasti* 1. 101 f.]

Jason (1), in mythology, son of Aeson and Alcimede, and leader of the *Argonauts in their quest for the golden fleece; the Greek form *Iasōn* was sometimes etymologized in antiquity as 'the healer'. In the most common version, Jason was brought up in the Thessalian countryside by the *Centaur Chiron after *Pelias took the throne of Iolcus in place of Aeson. When Jason returned to Iolcus to claim his inheritance, Pelias, forewarned by an oracle to beware of a man wearing only one sandal, recognized the danger and devised the expedition to recover the golden fleece from the kingdom of Aia in the extreme east. The expedition itself follows a pattern of *rite-of-passage stories in which young men must undergo terrible ordeals before claiming their rightful inheritance; *Apollonius Rhodius' Jason, in particular, resembles the tragic *Orestes in the hesitation he feels in the face of what he must do. The expedition is successfully completed with the assistance of *Hera, who wished to punish Pelias for neglecting to honour her, and Aphrodite who makes the Colchian princess *Medea fall in love with Jason. Already in the *Odyssey* Jason is 'dear to

Hera', and Apollonius explains that he once carried her across a torrent when she was disguised as an old woman; later sources combine this incident with the fateful loss of a sandal. After Jason and Medea had taken revenge upon Pelias, they fled to Corinth, where they lived until Jason decided to marry Creon's daughter; in the version made famous by *Euripides' *Medea*, Medea then killed their common children and his new bride. There are various accounts of Jason's death, of which the most colourful are that he killed himself in despair, that he was killed when a plank from the rotting *Argo* fell on him as he slept, and that the stern-piece which he had dedicated to Hera fell on him when he entered her temple. Along with many other Argonauts, he was said to have taken part in the Calydonian boar-hunt; *see* MELEAGER.

[Homer, *Odyssey* 12. 72; Pindar, *Pythian* 4; Euripides, *Medea*; Apollonius Rhodius, *Argonautica*; Diodorus Siculus 4. 55. 1; Apollodorus 1. 8. 2; Ovid, *Metamorphoses* 8. 302]

Jason (2), of Cyrene, wrote, before 124 BC, a Greek history in five books about Judas Maccabaeus and his brothers. The author of 2 Maccabees describes his own work as an abridgement of Jason (2 Macc. 2: 19–25). Jason's cultural background is presumed to lie in the important Greek-speaking Jewish communities of Cyrenaica. *See* MACCABEES.

Jerome (Eusebius Hieronymus, *c*.AD 347–420), biblical translator, scholar, and ascetic. Born into a Christian family at Stridon in Dalmatia, he was educated at Rome at the school of Aelius Donatus, and later studied rhetoric. During a stay at Trier (Augusta Treverorum), where he had probably intended to enter imperial service, his *Christianity took on greater meaning, and around 372, fired with ascetic zeal (*see* ASCETICISM), he set out for the east. After two years or more at Antioch, he finally withdrew to the desert of Chalcis to undertake the penitential life of a hermit monk. Here he began to learn Hebrew, with immense consequences for biblical scholarship. But after no more than

a year or so he returned to Antioch, where he was ordained priest. Back in Rome in 382, he quickly won the confidence of Pope *Damasus, at whose request he commenced work on what was to become the core of the *Vulgate version of the Bible. There too he formed friendships with several aristocratic women who had dedicated themselves to Christianity and were living austere and simple existences. His association with the widow Paula in particular combined with other factors to put him in a bad light with the generality of Roman Christians, and following Damasus' death he was effectively hounded from the city (385). Paula followed him to Palestine, where, at Bethlehem, they founded a monastery and a convent. Here Jerome remained for the rest of his life, devoting himself to the ascetic way and to Christian learning.

Jerome was a prolific writer. In addition to his translations of Scripture, he produced numerous commentaries on books of the Bible, for which he drew heavily on previous commentators such as *Origen. Polemical works on a variety of religious issues reveal a bitter and vitriolic side to his nature. His surviving correspondence, which discloses a network of connections across the whole Mediterranean world and in high places, is of the greatest interest for the study of 4th- and 5th-cent. Christianity. Other works of importance include his translation and expansion of *Eusebius of Caesarea's *Chronicle* of world history, and the *De viris illustribus*, a catalogue of 135 mainly Christian writers.

The famous *dream in which Jerome saw himself accused of being not a Christian but a 'Ciceronian' (*see* CICERO), and which seems to have resulted in his giving up reading pagan literature altogether for many years, is a reflection of the tension felt by many Christians of the time between their religious beliefs and their classical heritage. Over a long period Jerome himself succeeded in resolving this conflict, and perhaps more than any other of the Latin Fathers he can be seen as a man of the classical world who happened to be Christian.

His classicism is evident not only in his frequent quotations from classical literature, but often in his style. While his scriptural translations and exegetical works tend to be simple and unadorned, other texts display the full fruits of rhetorical training and the verve of a great natural talent steeped in the best writings of an earlier age. If his enduring importance lay most of all in the Vulgate, in his teaching on celibacy, and in his contribution to western monasticism, he also ranks among the finest writers of Latin prose.

Jerusalem (Gk. *Hierosolyma* and *Hierousalēm*) was repopulated and the Temple reconstructed with the blessing of the Persian king Cyrus, some 50 years after the destruction of 587 BC, by Jews returning from the Babylonian exile. In the 440s, the walls were rebuilt and their completion marked by a great celebration of the Tabernacles festival, described in the Book of Nehemiah. Palestine as a whole came into Alexander the Great's empire after the battle of Issus, and there are traditions that he visited the Temple and paid his respects to the high priest. A schematic sketch of Ptolemaic Jerusalem occurs in the Letter of *Aristeas, where it is dominated by a temple on a hill. Attempts to stamp on Jerusalem the forms of a Greek city, apparently with the added name Antioch, were set in motion by the Hellenizers under *Antiochus (1) IV, who himself established a pagan cult in the Temple in 168/7; but within three years the shrine was rededicated by the *Maccabees. A capacious Seleucid citadel, whose location is still undetermined, dominated the city, and was occupied by Hellenizing Jews until its demolition by Simon in 142. In 135/4 Antiochus VII Sidetes besieged Jerusalem, and John Hyrcanus was accused of ransacking the tomb of David on Mount Zion to pay for its defence. Under the Hasmoneans (*see* JEWS), the city became a major centre, expanding to the west and north. During Pompey's siege of 63, to settle the war between the two Hasmonean brothers, Aristo-

bulus held out in the Temple, and in the aftermath Pompey personally inspected the shrine and removed Temple treasures, including the famous golden vine; but little physical damage was inflicted. The capture and pillaging of Jerusalem by the Parthians in 40 led to Gaius Sosius' siege and recapture in 37 and the installation of *Herod the Great.

Herod transformed Jerusalem: the city acquired a theatre, hippodrome, and amphitheatre, all now vanished; a palace defended by three massive towers (the lower courses of 'Phasael' are in the present Tower of David); the Antonia fortress, of which the paved courtyard and other installations remain. Above all, starting in 20/19 BC, the Temple was reconstructed, in white stone, with copious gold covering. The biblical prescriptions were still followed, but the height was doubled and the surrounding courts expanded. The Temple mount was erected on a vast retaining platform, of which the 'Western wall' ('Wailing wall') and adjoining extensions are a remnant, as well as the traces of a great course of stairs, 'plaza', and shops exposed by excavation at the south-east corner. The valley between this and the élite residential quarter in the upper city was bridged. There the excavated houses, with their copious ablution cisterns, bear witness to the sophisticated but religiously correct lifestyle of the high priestly and lay élite of Second-Temple Jerusalem. The landmark monumental tombs standing in the Kedron valley confirm the impression. Diaspora benefactors (*see* JEWS) had contributed to the Temple, and Jewish pilgrims converged from far afield during the three 'foot festivals'. The inscription of the Theodotus synagogue, rare evidence of a pre-70 *synagogue in Jerusalem, speaks about the reception of visitors. Some Diaspora Jews had tombs in Jerusalem, including the converted royal family of Adiabene. For the elder Pliny, Jerusalem was 'by far the most famous city of the east'.

In the revolt of AD 66, after the reduction of other parts of the country, Jerusalem became the centre first of the faction-fighting between the rival rebel leaders and then of unified resistance. The destruction of the city and the Temple by Titus in 70, after a five-month siege, was a major turning-point in its history. The walls were razed, leaving only the three towers. The priestly class all but disappeared. After the revolt, the camp of the tenth legion (Legio X *Fretensis*) was located at Jerusalem. After the *Bar Kokhba Revolt, Hadrian refounded the city as a military colony, Aelia Capitolina, but there is little conclusive evidence of large-scale reconstruction. Christian sources claim that Jews were barred. In any event, Jewish religious life perforce ceased to be focused on Jerusalem. The Christian holy places were not developed until *Constantine I. The church of the Holy Sepulchre was dedicated in 335, and a second great *basilica was built on the Mount of Olives, to mark the supposed site of the Ascension. Again, a pilgrim trade benefited the city; and in the 5th cent. the empress Eudocia included Mount Zion and the original City of David within its walls. *See* PILGRIMAGE (CHRISTIAN).

Jesus *See* CHRISTIANITY.

Jewish-Greek literature originates with the Greek translation of the Hebrew Pentateuch (Torah; *see* ARISTEAS, LETTER OF), made in the 3rd cent. BC. A unique, literal style was adopted, Hebraized in syntax and distinctive in vocabulary. The first versions were revised, and the rest of the Hebrew Bible was translated, together with numerous Apocryphal books, over succeeding centuries, to constitute what we know as the *Septuagint. Jews heard and read the Bible in Greek not only in the Diaspora (*see* JEWS), but also in various contexts in Palestine: a Greek scroll of the Minor Prophets was found at Nahal Hever on the Dead Sea (*see* DEAD SEA SCROLLS), and Qumran has yielded Greek biblical fragments. Such texts served the many Jews whose primary means of expression was Greek, as well as bilingual groups accommodating to a Greek environment.

In the case of certain, sometimes canonical books, the Greek translation is free enough to have become a creation in its own right. The translation of Ecclesiasticus (the book of Ben Sira) was made in Egypt under Ptolemy VII Euergetes (i.e. before 116 BC) by the author's grandson, who ruminates in his preface on the problems of turning one language elegantly into another, addressing himself to scholars living 'in a foreign land'. First Esdras is an imaginative version of the Book of Ezra, which survives alongside a literal one. Passages which seem to have been original compositions in Greek were sometimes added to Semitic texts: the Greek Esther has substantial digressions of Hellenistic type, supplementing the story's drama and romance; in a postscript in some manuscripts, the translator says that his work was taken to Egypt and describes himself as Lysimachus son of Ptolemy from *Jerusalem.

A varied literary culture evolved around the Greek Bible, in general dependent upon biblical material for content, style, or both. While this literature was read largely by Jews, and subsequently by Christians, some authors aspired also to a Gentile audience. There is no real evidence to suggest, however, that any of them were aiming at proselytization.

Alexandria was the first and principal home of this creativity, as emerges from the marked Egyptian orientation of many fragments. But it is clear that Jewish literature in Greek was also written in the cities of Asia Minor, in Cyrene, and in other major Diaspora centres. Biblical themes were adapted to diverse Greek literary genres. Precise dates for the earliest works are hard to come by, since much of this literature survives only in small fragments, cited by *Eusebius in the *Praeparatio evangelica* or by *Clement of Alexandria, from the anthology of the 1st-cent. BC Roman polymath Alexander Polyhistor.

In prose, history, in the widest sense, was the dominant mode. At the end of the 3rd cent. BC Demetrius ('the Chronographer') offered comparative dates for biblical events. Eupolemus, sometimes identified with Judas Maccabaeus' ambassador to Rome of the same name (*see* MACCABEES), gave more picturesque renderings of biblical episodes, with accretions from Jewish oral interpretation (*midrash). Artapanus made Moses the founder of Egyptian religion and identified him with *Musaeus and with *Hermes. *Joseph and Asenath* is a novelistic account (*see* NOVEL) of Joseph's love for Potiphar's daughter and her adoption of the mysteries of Judaism. Cleodemus Malchus, of whom only a short fragment survives, presented the Libyan people as descendants of Abraham as well as of Hercules. Comments on Abraham and on the Egyptians, ascribed by *Josephus to *Hecataeus (2) of Abdera (who did write on the Jews) are believed to derive from a Hellenistic-Jewish work, nowadays known as Pseudo-Hecataeus.

*Aristobulus gave his exegesis a philosophical slant, dedicating to Ptolemy (probably Ptolemy VI Philometor) a partly allegorical interpretation of the Torah which anticipates *Philon (1). He is sometimes identified as the teacher of Ptolemy who is named as the recipient of a letter from Jerusalem in the preface to 2 Maccabees (1: 10). With copious quotation of Greek poetry, genuine and spurious, he presented Moses as the father of Greek philosophy. The Wisdom of Solomon, of uncertain date and provenance, in form adopts the oriental proverbial mode, but describes in philosophical language, tinged with echoes of the Greek Bible, the rule in the world of a personified wisdom sprung from God.

Among verse writers, Philon the Epic Poet recounted stories of Abraham, Joseph, and Jerusalem in his work, while Theodotus focused on the town of Shechem, and especially the rape of Dinah. *Ezechiel the Tragedian's drama on the Exodus, influenced by *Aeschylus and *Euripides, may well have been designed for performance. Perhaps as late as the 1st cent. AD, a generalized Jewish ethic was put into hexameter by Pseudo-Phocylides, with, however, a marked lack

of interest in specific religious practices. In a quite different mould are the Jewish prophetic texts amongst the heterogeneous collection of Greek Sibyllines (*see* SIBYL), which derive from a broad geographical and chronological span.

History-writing on contemporary or at any rate post-biblical themes was also practised. First Maccabees is a translation from the Hebrew, in which the influence of the historiography of Samuel and Kings is still dominant. But 2 Maccabees is a paraphrase of an independent Greek historical work on the same subject. (*See* JASON (2).) Third Maccabees recounts a fictitious persecution of the Jews in Alexandria supposedly at the hands of Ptolemy IV Philopator; while 4 Maccabees embeds an account of the fictitious deaths of the seven Maccabean martyrs and their mother in an amalgam of rhetoric and philosophy characteristic of the 'Second Sophistic' (*c.*AD 60–230, a period when declamation became the most valued literary activity in the Greek world).

*Philon (1), *Josephus, and Josephus' contemporary Iustus of Tiberias also belong to the tradition of Jewish-Greek literature. Composition did not cease with the destruction of the Temple in AD 70. We must suppose that Jews were still writing in Greek at the same time as Christians were adopting the earlier products of this tradition as their own.

Jews (in Greek and Roman times). The Jews at the beginning of the period were an ethnic group with distinctive religious practices. In the course of the period, the religious definition acquired new emphasis, and significant numbers of Jews became Jews by conversion rather than birth.

Palestine A demographically mixed region, this was understood to be the homeland of the Jews throughout the period, though in fact housing a minority of them. More precisely, the Jews belonged to the small area around *Jerusalem known in Greek as *Ioudaia*, whence the name *Ioudaioi*. However, the two revolts against Roman rule brought about the physical exclusion of the Jews from their centre.

From 538 to 332 BC the Jews of Palestine were a part of the Persian empire. The high priest seems to have been the highest Jewish official. A century of Ptolemaic rule followed Alexander the Great's death. In 200 Palestine passed into Seleucid hands, and the pressure of Hellenism was manifested, first in dissension within the high priestly families, and then in *Antiochus (1) IV's installation of a pagan cult in the Temple (168/7 BC), which was resisted by the *Maccabees. Only in 142 BC was the Seleucid garrison expelled from Jerusalem. For the next 80 years, the Jews were ruled by the hereditary Hasmonean high priests, attaining complete autonomy after the death of Antiochus in 134 BC. The expansion of Jewish territory involved a phenomenon new to Judaism, the conversion of the neighbouring peoples, Idumaeans and Ituraeans, at least partly by force.

Pompey's intervention in 63 BC, occasioned by a quarrel between the two sons of the defunct queen, Alexandra Salome, led to the installation of one of them, Hyrcanus, and to the reduction of the kingdom, with the freeing of the conquered Greek cities. In 57 the area was organized into five self-governing communities, with Hyrcanus remaining as leader until his removal by the Parthians and the appointment of the Idumaean convert *Herod as ruler.

In AD 6 *Judaea was annexed, together with Samaria and Idumaea, to form the Roman province of Judaea, administered by equestrian officials (prefects, later procurators). A census in that year crystallized opposition and generated an ideology of resistance. Called by *Josephus the 'fourth philosophy', this tendency was evidently the source of the subsequent, more famous rebel groupings, *sicarii* and *zealots. A pattern of procuratorial misgovernment enlisted the sympathies of the Jewish crowd in Jerusalem and of the poor in Galilee to the anti-Roman cause. The high-priestly and landowning élites criticized Rome only under extreme provocation, as

when the emperor Gaius attempted to have his statue placed in the Temple (39/40). The installation of Marcus Iulius Agrippa I (41–4) by Claudius was to prove merely a brief interlude in the regime of the procurators. Famines, banditry, and the breakdown of the working relationship between the Jewish ruling class and Rome marked the years before the outbreak of the First Jewish Revolt in 66. The Temple sacrifices for the emperor's welfare were terminated, and a provisional government in Jerusalem appointed regional leaders (including the historian Josephus), chose a populist high priest by lot, abolished debt, and issued its own freedom coinage. But the Jews were deeply divided politically. In Galilee the conflict between pro- and anti-war elements made resistance ineffectual. In besieged Jerusalem, three rebel factions conducted a civil war until the last stages of the siege.

In 70 the Judaean victory of Vespasian and Titus, confirmed by the burning of Jerusalem and the (perhaps accidental) destruction of the Temple, was crucial in consolidating the Flavian seizure of power. Much was made of '*Judaea capta*' in Flavian propaganda, culminating in the *triumph over the Jews. Jewish-owned land in Judaea was expropriated.

From 70 the province of Judaea was governed by legates and a legion was stationed in Jerusalem. Jewish religious and cultural life centred for a generation on Jamnia (Jabneh), an enclave on the Judaean coast, where a new definition of Judaism without a Temple was evolved by the first *rabbis.

The revolt in the Diaspora under Trajan, in 115–18, produced disturbances in Palestine, suppressed by Lusius Quietus. Of greater significance was the second great revolt in Palestine, led by *Bar Kokhba. Its long-term causes are ill-documented, but the immediate triggers were Hadrian's prohibition of circumcision, and his plan to turn Jerusalem into the Roman *colonia* of Aelia Capitolina. After the costly suppression of this revolt, in 135, the name of the province became Syria

Palaestina, another legion was stationed in Galilee, and, according to Christian sources, Jews were altogether excluded from Jerusalem. A further revolt occurred under Antoninus Pius, in spite of his exemption of the Jews from Hadrian's ban on circumcision.

During the 3rd cent. Jewish life flourished in Galilee: *synagogues began to proliferate, in villages as well as towns; rabbinic influence on daily life grew; and Jews played their part in some of the newly refurbished cities, notably Caesarea. The patriarch, located successively in several Galilean towns, operated as the representative of the Jews of Palestine and was closely associated with the rabbis. Greek was widely used by the educated élite, though the first great rabbinic compilation, the *Mishnah, was written in Hebrew, c.200. Prosperous Jews from the Syrian and Phoenician Diaspora were buried, alongside rabbis, in heavily figurative sarcophagi, in the spacious vaults and catacombs of Beth Shearim.

This vigorous community life, and the building of synagogues, continued into the era of Christianization (*see* CHRISTIANITY) in the Holy Land which followed the conversion of *Constantine I, when sites associated with biblical events became focuses of *pilgrimage. But from then on there were spiritual claims to Jerusalem, Judaea, and Galilee which rivalled those of the Jews.

A destructive Jewish revolt in Palestine, allegedly centred on a supposed Messiah, is ascribed by one source to the reign of Gallus Caesar (350/1). This may have been a protest against Christian anti-Jewish legislation. But it was left to a pagan emperor, *Julian the Apostate, to plan for the rebuilding of the Jewish Temple and the restoration there of the blood sacrifices. An earthquake, a fire, and various supernatural manifestations put a stop to the construction; and a year later (363) Julian was dead.

The Diaspora The dispersion of the Jews began in 586 BC, when Nebuchadnezzar took the inhabitants of Jerusalem into captivity. Many of them did not return when permitted by Cyrus of Persia in 538, but remained voluntarily in Babylonia, where flourishing communities existed for centuries, producing in late antiquity the greatest monument of rabbinic learning, the Babylonian *Talmud. During the Hellenistic period, many Jews migrated from Palestine and also from Babylonia, settling around the eastern Mediterranean, especially in Syria, Asia Minor, and Egypt. Jewish military colonists had lived at Elephantine for centuries, and now they were joined by new military and civilian settlers in both countryside and town. The community at Alexandria became the most important in the Diaspora, the splendour of its synagogue a byword, its mixed Jewish-Greek culture highly creative. Numbers alone made the Jews prominent inhabitants of the city. But by the 1st cent. AD there were sizeable communities in most of the cities of the eastern Mediterranean. The *Acts of the Apostles is important testimony to the local prominence of synagogues.

Expansion to Italy and the west began later, but the community in Rome was established by the mid-2nd cent. BC. Jews taken as slaves after the various wars in Palestine swelled the numbers of the Diaspora, as in due course did the voluntary attachment of pagans to the Jewish synagogues of Rome. Inscriptions from the Jewish *catacombs of Rome reveal the existence of eleven synagogues in the 2nd to 4th cents. AD, whose names suggest an earlier, in some cases an Augustan, foundation.

Diaspora Jews retained their identity and the basic religious practices of Judaism—male circumcision, observance of the sabbath, and other festivals (notably Tabernacles) and the avoidance of non-kosher meat. Until AD 70, their allegiance to the Temple and to Jerusalem as their mother city was signalled by the payment of the Temple tax and by the practice of pilgrimage at the major agricultural festivals.

At the same time, inscriptions concerning Jewish benefactions and commemorations from many cities in the eastern Roman empire make it clear that the Jews adapted to their varied environments. Greek was their native language. In Cyrenaica, at Berenice, there were Jewish town-councillors and Jewish ephebes (*see* EPHEBOI) as early as the 1st cent. AD. In the 3rd cent. the phenomenon is quite common. Non-Jews expressed attachment to the Jewish synagogue by becoming benefactors, 'God-fearers' (or sympathizers), and proselytes. The 4th-cent. Jewish inscription from Aphrodisias shows an association of Jews and proselytes subscribing to a memorial together with a separate group of 'God-fearers', including councillors.

The advocacy of Hyrcanus and the Herodians (*see* HEROD), together with their own diplomacy, gained for Jewish communities in the Roman provinces the patronage successively of *Caesar, of Antony, and of *Augustus. In their disputes with their neighbours, they were assisted by Roman decrees which upheld their right to observe their customary practices; and these decrees were adopted empire-wide as precedents. Synagogues, though classed as *collegia* (associations: *see* COLLEGIUM), were exempted by Caesar from his general ban. The right to raise, deposit, and transmit the Temple tax was upheld. Sometimes, special food markets were permitted, sometimes exemption granted from court appearances on the sabbath or from military service which rendered sabbath observance impossible. Christian authors were later to describe Judaism as a *religio licita* ('legitimate religion') in the Roman empire on the basis of these arrangements (*see* ROMAN RELIGION). Furthermore, after the destruction of the Temple, the two-drachma (half-shekel) tax paid by all adult Jewish males to the Temple was extended to women and children, diverted to *Jupiter Capitolinus, and deposited in the new *fiscus iudaicus* or 'Jewish treasury'. Domitian's exactions were notoriously harsh, but Nerva issued coins announcing his removal of the abuses. Implicit in the taxation was an official acknowledgement of the existence of Jewish communities, and this also contributed to the Christians' sense that the Jews had been 'legalized'.

Periodic expulsions of the Jews from the city of Rome were short-lived and did not undermine their standing elsewhere. Three expulsions of the Jews are recorded: in 139 BC; by Tiberius in AD 19; and by Claudius. The authorities' fear of disturbance and of un-Roman practices, rather than overt proselytizing, was the immediate cause of anti-Jewish measures, as of those against other alien cults and practices. The Jews do not appear to have been actively seeking converts during this period. It was not until the reign of Septimius Severus (193–211) that conversion to Judaism was forbidden; even then, there was no Jewish 'mission'.

In spite of—or because of—Jewish acculturation, friction between Jews and their neighbours was not uncommon. In Alexandria, anti-Semitic literature was produced in the Hellenistic period (*see* SEMITISM, ANTI-); but the Roman annexation of Egypt shook a centuries-long political equilibrium, redefining the privileges of Alexandrian citizens, and excluding the Jews from them. In AD 38, a visit of Marcus Iulius Agrippa I to Alexandria sparked the first pogrom in Jewish history, when synagogues were burnt, shops looted, and the Jews herded into a ghetto. Trouble returned in 66, at a time when the outbreak of revolt in Palestine also provoked Greek–Jewish violence in a number of Syrian cities. The failure of the revolt saw further attacks on urban Jews.

In 115 the Jews of Cyrenaica rose against their pagan neighbours and against the Roman authorities, inflicting considerable damage and targeting pagan temples. The uprising, which suggests considerable frustration, spread to Alexandria and other parts of Egypt; and to Cyprus, where it was furthered by a charismatic leader. The rebellion in 116 in Trajan's new Mesopotamian province, coinciding with these events, brought in the Jews of Babylonia. The revolts were suppressed by Quintus Marcius Turbo with considerable effort. An era of more peaceful co-existence for the Jewish Diaspora ensued, and the increasingly high profile of Jewish communities in some cities is attested by excavated remains of synagogues. The case of Sardis is particularly noteworthy, where a massive synagogue adjoined the city's main baths-complex, and was refurbished several times, well into the Christian era. The legal restrictions placed on Jews by the Christian emperors of the 4th and 5th cents. did not in the first instance crush the activities of the synagogues.

Josephus (Flavius Iosephus, b. AD 37/8), was a Greek historian but also a Jewish priest of aristocratic descent and largely Pharisaic education (see PHARISEES), and a political leader in pre-70 *Jerusalem. Though a zealous defender of Jewish religion and culture, his writing is largely hostile to the various revolutionary groups, whom he regarded as responsible for the fall of the Temple: his theology centres on the idea that God was currently on the Romans' side. Participation in a delegation to Rome (*c.*64) impressed on him the impracticality of resistance. When the Jerusalem leaders put him in charge of Galilee, he played an ambiguous role. He was besieged at Jotapata, but when captured, evaded a suicide pact and, he claims, was freed when his prophecy of Vespasian's accession came true. He remained close to Titus until the fall of Jerusalem, making several attempts to persuade the besieged city to surrender. He was given Roman citizenship, and, after the war, an imperial house to live in in Rome, a pension, and land in Judaea.

He first wrote an account of the war, now lost, in Aramaic for the Jews of Mesopotamia. Most, if not all, of the seven books of the Greek *Jewish War* appeared between 75 and 79. The first book and a half sketch Jewish history from the Maccabean revolt (see MACCABEES) to AD 66. Much of the rest is based on Josephus' own experience, together with eyewitness reports from others and, probably, the diaries (*commentarii*) of Vespasian and Titus. The triumph at Rome

over *Judaea capta* is described in detail. The *Jewish Antiquities*, in twenty books, published in 93/4, is a history of the Jews from the Creation to just before the outbreak of revolt, ostensibly for Greek readers. The biblical history of the first ten books depends not only on the Hebrew and Greek Bibles, but also on current Jewish oral interpretation. For the post-biblical period, works of Jewish-Hellenistic literature such as the Letter of Aristeas (see ARISTEAS, LETTER OF), 2 Esdras, and 1 Maccabees (see MACCABEES) are adapted. In the later part, there is a substantial dependence on the histories of Nicolaus of Damascus. The famous passage on Jesus is partly or even wholly an interpolation. Appended to the *Antiquities* was the *Life*—not a full autobiography, but a defence of Josephus' conduct in Galilee, responding to his critics, especially Iustus of Tiberias. The *Against Apion* was an apologia for Judaism in two books, demonstrating its antiquity in comparison with Greek culture, and attacking anti-Semitic writers, from the 3rd cent. BC to *Apion. Josephus' writings were preserved by the early Church. *See* JEWISH-GREEK LITERATURE.

Judaea first appears in the Hellenistic period as the name for the primarily Jewish territory (see JEWS) around *Jerusalem. Acquiring, under the Hasmoneans (see JEWS), much enlarged borders and a substantial non-Jewish population, especially in the coastal cities, the territory was reduced by Pompey after 63 BC, and was then reorganized by Gabinius, the governor of Syria, into five districts. Growing again under *Herod, Judaea became a Roman procuratorial province after the banishment in AD 6 of Herod's successor there, Archelaus. Eleven regions are listed by Josephus, and a slightly different list is given by Pliny. The term Judaea might also be used loosely, as in Luke–Acts where it sometimes simply denotes the part of Palestine inhabited by Jews, excluding even Caesarea. After 70 Judaea was put by Vespasian under an imperial legate, with a permanent legionary garrison. The Jewish population dwindled after the *Bar Kokhba Revolt of 135. Nevertheless, Judaea figures regularly in the *Mishnah, in connection with rabbinic regulations, often in association with Galilee and Peraea (trans-Jordan).

Judaism Judaism in Graeco-Roman antiquity is better known than any other ancient religion apart from Christianity, primarily because of the survival to modern times of traditions about ancient Judaism through rabbinic and Christian literature. However, this same factor creates its own problems of bias in the selection and interpretation of evidence.

The main sources of knowledge about Judaism are the Old and New Testaments and other religious texts preserved in Greek within the Christian Church: the apocrypha and pseudepigrapha, and the writings of *Philon (1) and *Josephus. The works composed in Hebrew and Aramaic produced by the rabbis after AD 70 stress rather different aspects. A fresh light has been shone on Judaism by the chance discovery of Jewish papyri in Elephantine and especially by the *Dead Sea Scrolls, which revealed the incompleteness of the later Jewish and Christian traditions even about the 1st cent. AD, the period for which most evidence survives. Pagan Greek and Latin writers emphasized the aspects of Judaism most surprising to outsiders but many of their comments were ignorant and prejudiced.

Many of the basic elements of Jewish worship were shared with other religions of classical antiquity. The prime form of worship was by sacrifices and other offerings in the Jerusalem Temple. In this respect the Jewish cult differed from most in the Greek and Roman world only in the exceptional scrupulousness of its observance; in the assumption of most Jews that sacrifices were only valid if performed in Jerusalem, even though this meant that the sacrificial cult was for many only known from a distance; in the role of the priestly caste, who inherited the prerogative to serve in the sanctuary under the authority of an autocratic high priest who at certain periods also operated as political leader of the nation; and in their strong sense of the special sanctity of the land of Israel and the city of *Jerusalem and its shrine.

Of the special elements of Judaism noted in antiquity, most striking to pagans was the exclusive *monotheism of Jews: most Jews worshipped only their own deity and either asserted that other gods did not exist or chose to ignore them. Equally strange was the lack of any cult image and the insistence of most Jews by the Hellenistic period that Jewish sacrificial worship was only permitted in the Jerusalem Temple, despite the existence of Jewish temples at Elephantine in Egypt in the 5th cent. BC and at Leontopolis in the Nile delta from the mid-2nd cent. BC to AD 72, and the Samaritan temple on Mt. Gerizim, which was destroyed only in the 120s BC.

Jews were in general believed by outsiders to be specially devoted to their religion, a trait interpreted sometimes negatively as superstition, sometimes positively as philosophy. The foundation of this devotion lay in the Torah, the law governing all aspects of Jewish life which Jews considered had been handed down to them through Moses on Mt. Sinai as part of the covenant between God and Israel. The Torah is enshrined in the Hebrew bible, and pre-eminently in the Pentateuch (the first five books). Jews treated the scrolls on which the Torah was recorded with exceptional reverence; if written in the correct fashion, such scrolls were holy objects in themselves. The covenant, marked by circumcision for males, involved the observance of moral and ethical laws as well as taboos about food and sacred time (especially, the sabbath).

The main elements of Judaism as here presented were already in place by the 3rd and 2nd cents. BC, when the final books of the Hebrew bible were composed, but the Jewish religion was to undergo much change over the following centuries. One new development was the gradual emergence of the notion of a canon of scripture treated as more authoritative than other writings.

Agreement about the authority of particular books did not lead to uniformity, or even the notion of orthodoxy. The Hebrew bible left many opportunities for diversity of interpretation. The extent of variety, at least up to AD 70, is clear from the Dead Sea scrolls. Disagreements may have been fuelled in part by diverse reactions to the surrounding Hellenistic culture. The continuation of variety after c.AD 100, after which Christians ceased to preserve Jewish texts and Judaism is known almost only through the rabbinic tradition, is uncertain.

From the 2nd cent. BC self-aware philosophies began to proclaim themselves within Judaism: *Pharisees, *Sadducees, and *Essenes, and perhaps others. These groups differed on correct practice in the Jerusalem cult as well as on quite fundamental issues of theology, such as the role of fate and the existence of an afterlife. However, apart perhaps from the Dead Sea sectarians, who saw themselves as the True Israel, all these Jews believed that they belonged within a united religion: Josephus, who described the three main Jewish philosophies in detail, elsewhere boasted that Jews are remarkable for their unanimity on religious issues, The earliest followers of Jesus are best considered in the context of such variety within Judaism.

In the Hellenistic and early Roman periods some aspects of the biblical tradition were particularly emphasized by Jews. Ritual purity as a metaphor for holiness was stressed by Jews of all persuasions: *mikvaoth* (ritual baths) have been excavated in many Jewish sites in the land of Israel, both Pharisees and Essenes elaborated complex elucidations of the biblical purity rules, and restrictions on the use of gentile foodstuffs became more widespread.

Some Jews indulged in speculation about the end of days, which was variously envisaged as a victory of Israel over the nations under God's suzerainty or the total cessation of mundane life. In some texts a leading role

was accorded to a messianic figure, but ideas about the personality and function of a messiah or messiahs varied greatly, and the extent to which messianic expectations dominated Judaism in any period is debated. Much of the extant eschatological literature is composed in the form of apocalyptic, in which a vision is said to have been vouchsafed to a holy seer. All the apocalyptic texts from the post-biblical period are either anonymous or pseudepigraphic, reflecting a general belief that the reliability of prophetic inspiration had declined since biblical times. *See* APOCALYPTIC LITERATURE.

Religious ideas of all kinds within Judaism were generated or confirmed by study and *midrash of the biblical books. According to Josephus, making a defence and summary of Judaism, Jews were uniquely concerned to learn their own law. The primary locus of teaching was the synagogue, where the Pentateuch was read and explained at least once a week, on the sabbath. Buildings for such teaching, and probably for public prayer, are first attested in Egypt in the 3rd cent. BC. In the late-Roman period some *synagogue buildings were designed with monumental architecture similar to pagan temples and were treated as sacred places.

The increased ascription of sanctity to synagogues was in part a reaction to the destruction of the Jerusalem Temple by Roman forces under Titus in AD 70 (*see* JEWS). The destruction, at the end of the great Jewish revolt of AD 66–70, was eventually to have important consequences for the development of Judaism, although new theologies were slow to emerge: Josephus in the nineties AD still assumed that God is best worshipped by sacrifices in Jerusalem, and about a third of the *Mishnah, redacted c.AD 200, is concerned with the Temple cult.

In the diaspora the Temple had in any case always dominated more as an idea than as an element in religious practice, since only occasional pilgrimage was ever possible. The synagogues at Dura Europus and Sardis may reveal Judaisms based on synagogue liturgy. An honorific inscription probably of the 4th cent. AD from Aphrodisias in Caria reveals that, in that Jewish community at least, gentile God-fearers may have participated in Jewish religious institutions.

The Judaism of the *rabbis differed from other forms of Judaism mainly in its emphasis on learning as a form of worship. Rabbinic academies, first in Yavneh (Jamnia) on the coast of Judaea immediately after AD 70, but from the mid-2nd cent. mainly in Galilee and (from the 3rd cent.) in Babylonia, specialized in the elucidation of Jewish law, producing a huge literature by the end of antiquity. Their most important products, were the Mishnah, composed in Hebrew c.AD 200, and the two *Talmuds, redacted (mainly in Aramaic) in Palestine in c.AD 400 and in Babylonia in c.AD 500; but they also produced a large corpus of midrashic texts commenting on the bible, and they or others in late antiquity composed the Hekhalot texts, which attest to a continued mystical tradition. *See* CHRISTIANITY.

Judas Maccabaeus *See* MACCABEES.

Julian 'the Apostate' (Iulianus Flavius Claudius), emperor AD 361–3, was born at *Constantinople in 331, the son of a half-brother of *Constantine I, Julius Constantius. After his father's murder in dynastic intrigues of 337, Julian was placed by Constantius in the care of an Arian bishop (*see* ARIANISM) and from 342 was confined for six years on an imperial estate in Cappadocia. He impressed his Christian tutors there as a gifted and pious pupil (*see* CHRISTIANITY), but his reading of the Greek classics was inclining him in private to other gods. In 351, as a student of philosophy, he encountered pagan Neoplatonists (*see* NEOPLATONISM) and was initiated as a theurgist by the philosopher Maximus of Ephesus. For the next ten years Julian's *pagan 'conversion' remained a prudently kept secret. He continued his studies in Asia and later at Athens until summoned to Milan by Constantius to be married to the emperor's sister Helena

and proclaimed Caesar with charge over Gaul and Britain (6 November 355). Successful Rhineland campaigns against the Alamanni and Franks between 356 and 359 proved Julian a talented general and won him great popularity with his army. When Constantius ordered the transfer of choice detachments to the east the army mutinied and in February 361, probably with tacit prompting, proclaimed Julian Augustus. Constantius' death late that year averted civil war and Julian, now publicly declaring his paganism, entered Constantinople unopposed in December. A purge of the imperial court quickly followed, drastically reducing its officials and staff. In his brief reign Julian showed remarkable energy in pursuit of highly ambitious aims. An immediate declaration of general religious toleration foreshadowed a vigorous programme of pagan activism: the temples and finances of the ancestral cults were to be restored and a hierarchy of provincial and civic pagan priesthoods appointed, while the Christian churches and clergy lost the financial subsidies and privileges gained under Constantine and his successors. Though expressly opposed to violent persecution of Christians, Julian overtly discriminated in favour of pagan individuals and communities in his appointments and judgements: measures such as his ban on the teaching of classical literature and philosophy by Christian professors and his encouragement of charitable expenditure by pagan priests mark a determination to marginalize Christianity as a social force. His attempts to revive the role of the cities in local administration by restoring their revenues and councils and his remarkable plan to rebuild the Jewish Temple at *Jerusalem are best appraised in the light of this fundamental aim.

Julian's military ambitions centred on an invasion of Persia intended to settle Rome's long-running war with Sapor II. To prepare his expedition he moved in June 362 to Antioch, where his relations with the mainly Christian population deteriorated markedly during his stay. The expedition set out in March 363 but despite some early successes it was already in serious difficulties when Julian was fatally wounded in a mêlée in June 363. He left no heir (Helena died childless in 360, and Julian did not remarry), and after his death the reforms he had initiated quickly came to nothing.

Julian's personal piety and intellectual and cultural interests are reflected in his surviving writings, which show considerable learning and some literary talent. They include panegyrics, polemics, theological and satirical works, and a collection of letters, public and private. Of his anti-Christian critique, *Against the Galileans*, only fragments remain. His own philosophic ideology was rooted in Iamblichan *Neoplatonism (*see* IAMBLICHUS) and *theurgy. How forcefully it impinged on his public religious reforms is controversial: on one view, they were directed more to the founding of a Neoplatonist 'pagan Church' than to a restoration of traditional Graeco-Roman polytheism, and their potential appeal to the mass of contemporary pagans was correspondingly limited.

Juno, an old and important Italian goddess and one of the chief deities of Rome. Her name derives from the same root as *iuventas* (youth), but her original nature remains obscure. The argument that she developed from the *iuno* attributed to individual women is probably mistaken, since that concept apparently arose during the republic on the analogy of the *genius. On the other hand, her roles as a goddess of women and as a civic deity were both ancient and widespread, and it is difficult to give priority to either. Juno was widely worshipped under a number of epithets throughout central Italy. Some of her important civic cults in Rome were in fact imported from this region. Thus in the 5th cent. BC Juno Regina was brought from the Etruscan town of Veii and received a temple on the *Aventine. Also apparently Etruscan in origin was the Capitoline Triad (*see* CAPITOL) of *Jupiter, Juno, and *Minerva;

the Capitoline Juno was by the late republic also identified as Regina ('Queen'), and regularly carried that epithet in the imperial period. Another imported cult was that of Juno Sospita, the chief deity of *Lanuvium (mod. Lanuvio), which from 338 BC onwards was administered jointly with Rome. The distinctive iconography of this goddess, who wears a goatskin and carries a spear and shield, indicates a martial character; Dumézil believed that her full epithet, Sospita Mater Regina, confirmed his thesis that Juno was originally trivalent, with influence over military prowess, fertility, and political organization. The cult of Juno Lucina, the goddess of childbirth, appears both in Rome and in other parts of Latium. The foundation-day of her temple on the Esquiline, 1 March, was traditionally celebrated as the Matronalia, when husbands gave presents to their wives. Peculiar to Rome is Juno Moneta, whose cult dates to the 4th cent. BC. The ancient association of her epithet with *monere* (to warn) is usually accepted, but its origins are unknown. The first mint in Rome was later located in or near her temple on the *arx* or citadel, hence the derivation of 'money' from Moneta. Other epithets, such as Pronuba, belong more to poetry than cult. The Roman conception of Juno's character was deeply affected by her identification with similar goddesses of other cultures. The most important was the Greek *Hera: her mythology and characteristics were largely adopted for Juno, who was thus firmly established by the time of the playwright Plautus (early 2nd cent. BC) as the wife of Jupiter and the goddess of marriage. The great goddess of Carthage (*see* PHOENICIAN RELIGION), Tanit, was also identified at a relatively early date with Juno, but had much less influence on her character. Apart from her part in the Capitoline Triad, Juno played a relatively minor role in the provinces. The exceptions are northern Italy, where the mother goddesses were sometimes called *iunones*, and Africa, where Juno *Caelestis was heir to the cult of Tanit.

Jupiter (*Iuppiter*), sovereign god of the Romans, bears a name referring to the 'luminous sky' (*Dyew-pater*), the first member of which is etymologically identical with that of *Zeus. He was known to all Italic peoples.

Even if associated with the sky, storms, and lightning, Jupiter was not just a god of natural phenomena. These expressed and articulated, in fact, his function as sovereign divinity. Jupiter was sovereign by virtue of his supreme rank and by the patronage derived from exercise of the supreme power. His supreme rank was signified by the fact that the god or his priest was always mentioned at the head of lists of gods or priests, and that the climactic point of the month, before the waning of the moon, was sacred to him in particular. In addition, the Roman symbol of power, the sceptre (*sceptrum*), belonged to him and functioned as his symbol. This privilege was described by the traditional epithets of *optimus maximus*, 'the best and the greatest', or by the title *rex* 'king' given him by the poets. His patronage of the exercise of sovereign power expressed itself in the fact that no political action could be accomplished without his favourable and prior judgement, expressed through the auspices (*see* AUSPICIUM) and in the celebration of the *triumph, representing the fullest exercise of Roman supremacy. Between these two poles the figure of Roman Jupiter must be constructed.

In rituals as well as in mythical narratives, the exercise of sovereignty by Jupiter, which made him into a deity with a political function, is presented under two aspects. On the one hand Jupiter was patron of the violent aspect of supremacy. As well as falling lightning, the Roman triumph, ending at his temple, represented the inexorable side of this power. From this point of view it is understandable that the grape and its product, *wine, were placed under his patronage (*see* VINALIA). But Jupiter was also a political god, who agreed to exercise power within the limits imposed by law and good faith. It was he who took part in the institution of *templa* (*see* TEMPLUM), those inner spaces in which the important activities of the Roman people took place (*see* AUSPICIUM), and patronized the *nundinae*, traditional days of popular assembly. It was he too who, by means of the auspices, conferred legitimacy on the choices and decisions of the Roman people. Finally, he was the patron of *oaths and treaties, and punished perjurers in the terrible manner appropriate.

From the end of the regal period, the most brilliant of Jupiter's seats was his temple on the *Capitol, which he shared with *Juno Regina (in the cella or chamber to the left) and *Minerva (in the right-hand cella). This triad constituted the group of patron deities of the city of Rome, whose well-being was the subject of an annual vow; under the empire, vows for the health of the ruler and his family were celebrated on 3 January. The first political action of the new consuls was the acquittal of these vows, formulated the previous year, and their utterance afresh. The anniversary of the Capitoline temple was celebrated during the Ludi Romani (4–19 September) on the Ides of September (13 September). On the Ides of November, during the Ludi Plebei or Plebeian Games (4–17 November), a great banquet was celebrated on the Capitol (*Iovis epulum*: *see* SEPTEMVIRI EPULONES), reuniting the Roman élite around the supreme god, along with Juno and Minerva. It was to the Capitol as well, and specifically to the *arx*, that the procession concluding the 'rites of the Ides', *sacra idulia*, ascended. Finally, the Ludi Capitolini, celebrated in honour of Jupiter Feretrius (15 October) their date of foundation uncertain, point to a third ancient sanctuary of Jupiter on the Capitol. Jupiter Feretrius, whom it is difficult to separate from Jupiter Lapis or 'Stone', was invoked in treaties; the famous flint used in the most solemn oaths was kept there, as well as the *sceptrum* by which oaths were taken. A tradition reactivated by *Augustus attributed to Jupiter the 'first' *spolia opima*.

Jupiter was frequently associated with other deities. From a very early period an association thought by many to reflect

Indo-European ideas linked him with *Mars and *Quirinus. On the Capitol he shared his temple with Juno and Minerva. Near this temple were found deities who fell in some sense within his orbit: *Fides and the problematic *Semo Sancus Dius Fidius, patrons of good faith and oaths.

The special priests of Jupiter were the *flamen Dialis* and his wife (*see* FLAMINES) and, where the auspices were concerned, the *augures (interpretes Iovis optimi maximi*, 'interpreters of Jupiter Best and Greatest').

[Macrobius, *Saturnalia* 1. 15. 14, 16. 30; Livy 1. 24. 8, 30. 43. 9, 41. 14. 7 ff.; Gellius, *Attic Nights* 1. 21. 4]

Jupiter Dolichenus (Iupiter Optimus Maximus Dolichenus), high god of Doliche in Commagene, now Dülük, near Gaziantep, eastern Turkey. The original temple on top of Dülük Baba Tepe has not been excavated, but the god's stance on a bull, holding lightning-bolt and double-axe, indicate clearly his ancestry in the Hittite storm-god Teshub. All three connote the transcendent but ambivalent power of natural forces. At Rome, he is invoked as *conservator totius poli*, 'he who maintains the whole firmament'. There are no literary texts. No monument from the Persian occupation or the Hellenistic period is known: the cult first spread in the 2nd cent. AD, well after Rome's absorption of Doliche into Syria (?31 BC or AD 17). Two votive triangles for processions found at Dülük confirm that such cult objects, like most other aspects of the cult in the west, derive directly from Doliche. But the modest western sanctuaries show no common pattern. The counterpart of Iupiter Optimus Maximus Dolichenus is usually named *Juno Sancta/Regina. Two other pairs also occur: Sun and Moon, and the Castores, who appear Hellenized as the *Dioscuri, or as figures emerging from rock or pedestal.

Known adherents in the west almost all bear names suggesting first- or second-generation immigration. Organization is enigmatic. Priesthoods seem to have been numerous but temporary. Worshippers, *fratres* (literally 'brothers'), were admitted to the sacred feasts only after a period of instruction as *candidati* ('candidates'), each group of which had a *patronus* ('patron'). Those outside these groups were termed *colitores* 'worshippers'. The function of *scriba/notarius* ('scribe', 'notary') suggests that written records were important. Though women might be *colitores*, none is known to have been priest or full member.

Outside Rome itself, the cult spread mainly in the Rhine–Danube area and Britain (*see* BRITAIN, ROMAN, CULTS). Up to a point, it was a religion of military loyalty, especially under the Severans. Many sanctuaries were plundered by Maximinus Thrax AD 235–8) and never rebuilt. Though the *Aventine temple was used into the 4th cent. AD, the sack of Doliche by Sapor I in 252 evidently undermined the cult.

Justin Martyr (*c*.AD 100–65), a Christian *apologist, flourished under Antoninus Pius and died a martyr in Rome after his condemnation as a Christian (*see* CHRISTIANITY) by the prefect of the city Quintus Iunius Rusticus. At the beginning of his *First Apology* he tells us that he was born at Flavia Neapolis (the ancient Shechem in Samaria) of *pagan parents. He seems never to have been attracted to *Judaism, though he knows seven Jewish sects. His account of his early disappointments in philosophy is conventional, but he was certainly a Platonist (*see* PLATO) when converted to Christianity. The Stoics (*see* STOICISM) he knew and admired, but more for their lives than for their teachings, and his conversion owed much to the constancy of Christian confessors.

After leaving Samaria, he set up a small school in Rome, and wrote two apologies, nominally directed to Antoninus Pius. One (*c*.155) defends Christianity in general against popular calumny and intellectual contempt; the second (*c*.162) is inspired by acts of persecution following denunciations of Christians to the authorities. It reveals that Christians served in the army and that Christian wives sometimes divorced their pagan spouses. Justin's pupil *Tatian attributes his death to information given by Crescens, a Cynic rival.

Justin's work is not so much a synthesis of Christianity, paganism, and Judaism as an attempt to discover an underlying homogeneity. This he effects by his doctrine of the Logos, which, as Christ, was present in many Old Testament epiphanies, and guarantees the unity of scriptural inspiration. (So he maintains in his *Dialogue with Trypho*, the first great work of Christian typology).

In the *Apologies* he anticipates *Clement of Alexandria and the Alexandrian school by arguing that a 'spermatic *logos*', identical with or related to Christ, instructs every man in wisdom, so that even pagan philosophers foreshadowed Christian truth. Like the other apologists, he accepts the civil authorities, and at once explains and enhances the attraction of Christianity for Greek-speaking intellectuals of the period.

Kairos, personified Opportunity. He had an altar at *Olympia, and the 5th-cent. author Ion of Chios called him the youngest son of *Zeus (i.e. Opportunity is god-sent) in a *hymn possibly composed for this cult. A cult existed at Velia (Elea) in southern Italy by the mid-5th cent. BC. In the early 4th-cent. poet Antimachus, Kairos is one of *Adrastus' horses. He has no mythology, but was a favourite subject in art, especially from the time of Lysippus (mid–late 4th cent.), whose bronze statue showed him between youth and age, tiptoeing, with a razor and scales, representing the fleeting nature of Opportunity (and the precision of the sculptor). Describing the statue (echoed in imperial reliefs and gems), the epigrammatist Posidippus says he had his hair over his eyes but was bald behind, since Opportunity can be grasped as he approaches, but never once he has passed. In literature, Kairos also encompasses time (differentiated from Chronos) and the seasons.

kanēphoroi were usually young women who bore baskets or vessels (*kana*) in religious processions. In the Panathenaic procession the young women were chosen from noble houses, and were required to be of good family, unmarried, and of unsullied reputation; hence 'to be fit to carry the basket' is to live chastely, and to reject a candidate was a grave insult. Serving as *kanēphoros*, as with other religious tasks, such as the little bears of Artemis of *Brauron, was thus not a normative *rite of passage for young girls but a mark of special prominence. They were dressed in splendid raiment; hair and garments were decked with gold and jewels; they were powdered with white barley-flour and wore a chain of figs. They carried vessels of gold and silver, which contained all things needed in the sacrificial ceremony: *first-fruits, the sacrificial knife, barley-corns, and garlands. (*See* SACRIFICE.) The sacred utensils were kept in the Pompeion, the 'procession house'. *Erichthonius was said to have introduced *kanēphoroi* at the *Panathenaea. Certainly the institution was very old, and its object was doubtless to secure the efficacy of the sacrificial materials by letting them touch nothing that was not virginal and therefore lucky and potent.

Kanēphoroi are also found in other Attic cults, e.g. those of *Apollo, *Dionysus, and *Isis, and in the cult of *Zeus Basileus at Boeotian Lebadea (*see* TROPHONIUS).

[Aristophanes, *Lysistrata* 642–7; Thucydides 6. 56. 1; Menander, *Epitrepontes* (*Arbitration*) 221]

Kasios, Zeus, an oriental god connected with Mt. Kasion (mod. Jabal al-Aqraʿ) near Antioch. In Ugaritic texts this mountain, called ṣasapānu, is the abode of Baʿal, a weather-god like *Zeus. Kasios/Ḫazzi plays a part in the Hurrian-Hittite Ullikummi myth and figures in Zeus' conflict with the dragon *Typhon. Zeus Kasios is also associated with a mountain near Pelusium in Egypt.

Kēres, in post-Homeric usage, powers of evil. They pollute and make unclean, like the *Harpyiae or Harpies, and are associated with ills of all kinds such as disease, old age and death, and troubles in general. They are in varying degrees personified, sometimes being treated as the bringers of evil and sometimes as the evil itself. In *Homer, *kēr* and *kēres* seem less like malignant agents, more like impersonal fates; but the fate of which they are the vehicle is always evil, almost invariably in fact that of death. In *Iliad* 22, *Zeus weighs the fates of death of *Hector and *Achilles, to decide which hero is to perish; later in the book, Achilles counters Hector's prediction of his death with 'I shall suffer my fate [lit. receive *kēr*], when Zeus chooses to bring it to pass'. Even Homer once, in an exceptional context, shows a personified 'dire *Kēr*' manhandling the dead and dying on the battlefield. In art, to judge from literary descriptions, Kēres could be a blend of human and bird of prey, rather like Harpies or *Sirens; they are hard to identify on surviving monuments.

It used to be argued that *kēres* were 'originally' *souls of the dead, largely because souls were supposedly banished at the end of the Athenian festival *Anthesteria with the formula 'away, Kēres, Anthesteria is over'. But (even if the reading *Kēres* rather than the variant *Kāres*, 'Carians', is correct) it does not follow that *kēres* means souls just because in a particular context souls could be addressed as such, perhaps abusively: 'away, hobgoblins'.

[Homer, *Iliad* 18. 535, 22. 210–11, 365; Hesiod, *Theogony* 213–22; Pausanias 5. 19. 6]

Kore *See* PERSEPHONE/KORE.

Kourotrophos, 'child-nurturer', appears to be known both as a divine epithet and as an independent goddess over much of the Greek world. Although lacking in mythology, she is evidently an important figure of cult, appearing frequently in sacrifice groups connected with fertility and child care.

Kronos *See* CRONUS.

Labraunda, sanctuary of *Zeus Labraundos in Caria, between Mylasa (to which it was linked by a sacred way) and Amyzon, occupying a mountainous and beautiful position. Herodotus calls the god Zeus Stratios but the inscriptions mostly have Zeus Labraundos or Labraundeus, a part-Greek part-indigenous deity; cf. *Sinuri. The 4th-cent. BC Hecatomnid satraps built lavishly at the sanctuary, laying it out afresh. Thereafter there was a gap in building activity until Roman imperial times. There are also inscriptions from Labraunda in Carian, a reminder of Caria's mixed culture.

Labyrinth (Gk. *labyrinthos*), a complex building constructed by *Daedalus for king *Minos of Crete and commonly identified with the Minoan palace of Cnossus. The labyrinth's confusing system of passages, from which no one could escape, concealed the *Minotaur which fed on human victims until destroyed by *Theseus. The hero imitated its twists and turns in a ritual dance on *Delos. Later the name was applied to a quarry at Gortyn with many chambers and to other labyrinthine structures at Nauplia, Lemnos, and in Egypt. The maze-like design occurs on Cretan coins and in Greek vase-painting, and proved popular in Roman mosaics (there is a Pompeian graffito with the inscription: *Labyrinthus. Hic habitat Minotaurus*, 'Labyrinth. Here lives the Minotaur'). Similar designs can already be seen on Minoan seals and frescos of the second palace at Cnossus. A Minoan fresco from Tell el-Dab'a (anc. Avaris) in Egypt (Hyksos period,

16th cent. BC) combines the characteristic pattern with a bull and acrobats.

A plausible derivation of the non-Greek word from (Lydian) *labrys* 'double axe' connects the labyrinth with a potent Minoan religious symbol and weapon of Zeus Labraundeus (see LABRAUNDA). Linear B mentions a labyrinth (*dapurito-*) of Potnia.

[Apollodorus 3. 1. 4, *Epitome* 1. 7–11; Plutarch, *Theseus* 15, 21; Pausanias 1. 27. 10]

Lactantius (Lucius Caelius (Caecilius?) Firmianus also called Lactantius), *c.*AD 240–*c.*320, a native of North Africa, pupil of *Arnobius, one of the Christian *apologists (see CHRISTIANITY). Under Diocletian (see DIOCLETIAN, PERSECUTIONS OF) he was officially summoned to teach rhetoric at Nicomedia; the date of his conversion is uncertain, but is earlier than the persecution of 303, when his Christianity caused him to lose his position at Nicomedia. He remained there until he moved to the west in 305; in extreme old age he was tutor (*c.*317) to Crispus, eldest son of *Constantine I.

Of Lactantius' numerous works on various subjects, only his Christian writings survive. He began these after the outbreak of the persecution. The *De opificio Dei* demonstrates providence from the construction of the human body. The *Divinae institutiones* (303–13), begun as a reply to attacks on *Christianity by the philosopher and official Hierocles, was intended to refute all opponents past, present, and future. The order of composition of the books, like the date of the *Epitome*, is uncertain. The work shows knowledge of the major Latin poets, and above all of Cicero, but little of Greek apart from spurious Orphic and Sibylline poems. The *De ira Dei* (after 313) makes anger, as a disposition rather than a passion, an essential property of God. The *De mortibus persecutorum* (317/8) is designed to show that the fate of persecutors is always evil, and may therefore have exaggerated the role of the co-emperor Galerius in inspiring the persecution of his own times. One poem by Lactantius, the *Phoenix*, also survives.

At the Renaissance Lactantius, the most classical of all early Christian writers, came to be known as the Christian Cicero. Except in the *Epitome*, he shows little philosophic knowledge or ability, and has little of importance to say on Christian doctrine or institutions. The latter defect, at least, can be explained as the accustomed reserve of the Christian apologist when writing for hostile or unbelieving readers.

Laestrygones, cannibal giants encountered by *Odysseus. They inhabit 'the lofty city of Lamus', ruled by King Antiphates, who eats two of Odysseus' men. The nights are so short there that one can earn a double wage, which suggests the distant north (as one ancient scholar observed). Greek tradition located them in Sicily, especially Leontini, but the Romans placed them at Formiae in Campania. Horace playfully connects Lamus with the family of the Aelii Lamiae.

[Homer, *Odyssey* 10. 80–132; Horace, *Odes* 3. 17]

Lamia, best known as the name of a nursery bogey, like *Empusa, *Mormo, and *Gello, who stole or ate children. In myth she was a beautiful Libyan, daughter of Belus and Libya, whose children by *Zeus were killed in jealousy by *Hera. She then assumed a monstrous form and began to seize and kill the children of other women.

Lampon, 5th-cent. BC Athenian seer, evidently prominent; he was attacked by the comic poet Lysippus and is mentioned in Plutarch's *Life of Pericles* (ch. 6), when *Anaxagoras advanced a naturalistic interpretation of a *portent expounded by him.

lamps in the classical world were made of various metals and of pottery. They might be placed on stands, or be suspended on chains or cords. Olive oil was the usual fuel. They were not only used for practical lighting purposes, but served as *votive offerings in sanctuaries and as tomb-furniture. The epigraphic record (*see* EPIGRAPHY) shows that sanctuaries frequently possessed gold and silver lamps, while lamps of cheaper materials were also dedicated. From the 4th cent. we find pottery lamps made in North Africa bearing Christian symbols.

Laocoön, a Trojan prince, brother of *Anchises and priest of *Apollo Thymbraeus or *Poseidon. Of his story as told by Arctinus (*Iliu Persis*; *see* EPIC CYCLE), *Bacchylides, and *Sophocles (*Laocoön*), we know little. In the standard version, he protested against drawing the Wooden Horse (*see* EPEIUS (2)) within the walls of *Troy, and two great serpents coming over the sea from the island of Tenedos killed him and his two sons (or in other versions Laocoön and one son, or only the sons). According to Hyginus, the serpents were sent by Apollo to punish him for having married in spite of his priesthood, in Quintus Smyrnaeus and *Virgil, by *Athena on account of his hostility to the Horse.

In art, Laocoön is the subject of the famous marble group in the Vatican showing father and sons in their death-agony. It was made by three Rhodian sculptors. The group was exhibited in the palace of Titus, and was said by Pliny the Elder to have surpassed all other works of painting and sculpture. The death of Laocoön is shown on two wall-paintings from Pompeii, and late Imperial gems. Two south Italian vases show Laocoön as devotee of *Apollo Thymbraeus.

[Virgil, *Aeneid* 2. 40–56, 199–231; Apollodorus, *Epitome* 5. 17–18; Hyginus, *Fables* 135. 1]

Laodice, in mythology, a stock name for women of high rank, meaning 'princess' (*see* CREON; CREUSA), e.g. (1) a daughter of Priam (*see* ACAMAS; DEMOPHON (1)), (2) a daughter of *Agapenor; she founded the temple of Paphian *Aphrodite in Tegea; (3) in the *Iliad*, daughter of *Agamemnon, later replaced by *Electra.

[(2) Pausanias 8. 53. 7, cf. 5. 3; (3) Homer, *Iliad* 9. 145]

Laomedon, a legendary king of *Troy, son of *Ilus (2) and Eurydice, and father of several children, including *Priam and *Hesione (3). He was renowned for his treachery: he had the walls of Troy built for him by *Apollo and *Poseidon, but then refused to pay them the agreed wage. As punishment, Apollo sent a plague and Poseidon a sea-monster which could only be appeased by the sacrifice of Hesione. But *Heracles saved her and killed the sea-monster, at which once again Laomedon refused to pay an agreed reward, this time the divine horses which *Zeus had once given him in exchange for *Ganymedes. In due course Heracles returned to Troy with an army, captured the city with the help of *Telamon (1), and killed Laomedon and all his sons except *Priam, giving Hesione to Telamon as a concubine and leaving Priam to rule Troy. Laomedon was buried at the Scaean gate, and it was said that Troy would be safe while his grave remained undisturbed.

[Apollodorus 2. 5. 9, 6. 4]

Larentalia, Roman festival on 23 December of funeral rites (called *Parentalia in the *Fasti Praenestini*) at the supposed tomb of the goddess *Acca Larentia on the Velabrum in Rome. Acca, connected with Greek and Sanskrit roots for 'mother', may be the *Lares' mother.

[Cicero, *Brutus* 1. 15. 8; Varro, *On the Latin Language* 6. 23–4; Macrobius, *Saturnalia* 1. 10. 11 ff.]

Lares (older *Lases* in the Arval hymn: *see* CARMEN ARVALE). There are two principal theories of origins; it is impossible to prefer one.

1. According to the first, the Lares are considered ghosts. The theory from the *Lar familiaris*, connecting him with the cult of the dead on two grounds: (a) if a bit of food falls on the floor during a meal, it is proper to burn it before the Lares. Since ghosts notoriously haunt the floor, the food, therefore, has gone to the ghosts' region and is formally given to them. (b) At the Compitalia it was customary to hang up a male or female puppet for each free member of a household, a ball for each slave, that the Lares might spare the living and take these surrogates. This seems a precaution against ghosts and accords with the crossroads as favourite places for ghosts. This theory had languished until the publication of an inscription which by linking 'Lar' with 'Aeneas' appears to support the Lar as a deified ancestor. Although the reading *Aineia* has been questioned, the inscription's site (crossroads, cave with sulphur spring) supports the ancestor/ghost theory.

2. The second theory asserts that the Roman dead are honoured not in the house but at their graves; the hearth is the place of *Vesta and the di *Penates and the Lar (*familiaris*) was a later intruder. He reconciles this with the ceremonial at the crossroads by observing that a *compitum* is properly and originally the place where the paths separating four farms meet. This has no ghostly associations, but regularly had a chapel of the Lares. Thus the *Lar familiaris* (in origin, Lar of the servants, rather than of the household generally) would have come to the house via farm-slaves.

The Lares, whatever their origins, expand (apart from purely theoretical developments of their name to signify ghost or *daimōn) (a) into guardians of any crossway, including one in a city: hence arose in Rome the *collegia compitalicia*, associations (*see* CLUBS; COLLEGIUM) of mostly freedmen, who tended the shrines, and ran the festival, the compitalia; *Augustus restored those colleges which had been banned in the late republic, adding his own *genius; (b) into guardians of roads and wayfarers, *Lares viales*, including travellers by sea, *Lares permarini*; (c) into guardians of the state in general, *Lares praestites*; (d) into a variety of sometimes obscure associations.

Some later stories feature the Lares. *Ovid reports their begetting by *Mercurius on Lara—possibly his own invention. In one version of the birth of King Servius *Tullius, from a *phallus arising from ashes and impregnating the servant Ocrisia with a flame, later appearing around his head marking him for the kingship, his father is the *Lar familiaris*. Since the cult of the *Lar familiaris* ultimately became universal, *lar* or *lares* is used like *penates*, by metonymy, for 'home'.

[Ovid, *Fasti* 2. 599 ff., 5. 129 ff., 6. 631 ff.; Dionysius of Halicarnassus, *Roman Antiquities* 4. 2; Pliny, *Natural History* 28. 27, 36. 204]

Larunda, obscure Roman goddess, perhaps Sabine (according to *Varro) and *chthonian. She was honoured on 23 December on the Velabrum. The long quantity of the first syllable suggests a connection with *Acca Larentia and not Lar (short *a*; *see* LARES). Some equated her with Lara, mother of the *Lares, others with *Maniae*, woollen puppets, implying the *Lares compitales* (*see* LARES). Certainty seems impossible.

[Varro, *On the Latin Language* 5. 74, 9. 61; Ovid, *Fasti* 2. 599 ff.]

Latini The Latins were the inhabitants of Latium Vetus, Old Latium, bounded to the north-west by the rivers Tiber and Anio and to the sea by the Apennines and Monti Lepini. From very early times they formed a unified and self-conscious ethnic group with a common name, a common sentiment, and a common language; they worshipped the same gods and had similar political and social institutions. Archaeological evidence shows that a distinctive form of material culture (the so-called 'Latial culture') was diffused throughout all of Latium Vetus from the final bronze age (*c.*1000 BC) onwards. The Latins' shared sense of kinship was expressed in a common myth of origin; they traced their descent back to *Latinus (the father-in-law of *Aeneas) who after his death was transformed into *Jupiter Latiaris and worshipped on the Alban mount (*see* ALBANUS MONS). Even if this version of the legend is relatively late, the annual festival of Jupiter Latiaris (the *feriae Latinae*) was extremely ancient. The main ritual event was a banquet, at which representatives of the Latin communities each received a share of the meat of a slaughtered bull (*see* SACRIFICE, ROMAN). Participation in the cult was a badge of membership; it was regularly attended by all the Latin peoples, including the Romans, well into the imperial period. Similar cult centres existed at *Lavinium, Aricia, and Tusculum, and these too may have been common to all the Latins from an early date.

Latinus, eponymous hero of the *Latini. *Hesiod makes him son of *Circe and *Odysseus and king of the Tyrrhenians (i.e. Etruscans); he is later said to be the son of *Faunus or even *Hercules. Callias in the 4th cent. BC reports that he married Rhome, a Trojan companion of *Aeneas, and was the father of *Romulus; other early versions have him either giving his daughter to Aeneas in marriage or dying in battle against him. *Virgil's *Aeneid* shows Latinus as honourable but aged and powerless, dominated by his queen Amata and by *Turnus, who declare war on Aeneas although Latinus has already given him his daughter Lavinia in marriage. Latinus survives the war, and his abortive peace treaty with Aeneas anticipates the future reconciliation between Trojans and Latins.

[Hesiod, *Theogony* 1011–16; Dionysius of Halicarnassus, *Roman Antiquities* 1. 43. 1; Livy 1. 1. 5–11; Virgil, *Aeneid* bks. 7, 12]

Lavinia *See* LATINUS; TURNUS.

Lavinium (mod. Pratica di Mare), where *Aeneas landed in Latium, a large town of the Latin League (*see* LATINI), whose federal sanctuary it became in the 6th cent. BC: thirteen large archaic altars survive *in situ*, dating between the 6th and 2nd cents. BC. Nearby was a 4th-cent. hero-shrine, built over a 7th-cent. tumulus-tomb, and probably linked with Aeneas. Finds attest direct links with the Greek world, and Lavinium may have played an important role in transmitting Greek influence to Rome. The Romans revered Lavinium for its Trojan associations, its *Venus temple common to all Latins, its cults of *Vesta and *Penates, and its loyalty in the Latin War. After the 3rd cent. BC, it became, however, of little importance.

[Dionysius of Halicarnassus, *Roman Antiquities* 1. 64. 5]

laws, religious The most general type of religious law is an aspect of international law.

Here some approach to statutory law can be seen in the amphictionic laws (*see* AMPHICTIONY), and the relations of states to each other were regulated by treaties. Nevertheless, international law remained essentially customary and, in contrast to the laws of individual states, which also had once been customary, was never officially recorded or codified. The importance of religion is seen in the amphictionic oath, the fetial rites (*see* FETIALES), and the practice of ratifying treaties by *oaths.

Certain Panhellenic practices were relatively well developed by Homeric times (*see* HOMER), when *heralds and ambassadors were considered inviolable and the sanctity of sworn agreements was recognized. Similar evidence is supplied for early Italy by the fetial code with its demand that every war be a just war. Greek practice was soon expanded by the amphictionic oath and the truces for the Panhellenic games (*see* PANHELLENISM; and ISTHMIAN, NEMEAN, OLYMPIAN, and PYTHIAN GAMES). There was general acceptance of the inviolability of *sanctuaries (*asylia*). Hellenistic cities often asked for and usually got recognition of *asylia* for sanctuaries in their territory. Such sanctuaries were used for refuge; hence the later meaning of 'asylum'.

At Rome, the interpretation of all law was originally in the hands of the *pontifices*, until perhaps the 4th cent. BC; they continued to advise on sacred law.

See also SANCTUARIES; WAR, RULES OF.

lead in the Greek world was often used for small offerings to the gods, such as those found in the sanctuary of *Artemis Orthia at Sparta (*see* SPARTAN CULTS). It was also the material on which *curses were commonly

inscribed among both Greeks and Romans; in this case it may be supposed to be endowed with special qualities.

lectisternium, a Roman version of Greek *klinē* and *theoxenia*, a banquet for gods whose images were placed on a cushioned couch or couches. The ceremony (supervised by priests but also involving public participation) was meant to propitiate gods and repel pestilence or enemy. It was first celebrated in 399 BC at the behest of the Sibylline books (*see* SIBYL) for *Apollo, Latona, *Hercules, *Diana, *Mercury, and *Neptune, later for *Iuventas, *Juno, *Saturnus, Magna Mater (*see* CYBELE), and (in 217) the twelve great gods. In private cult *lectisternia* are attested in connection with birth rites. *See* EPULUM.

[Livy 5. 13. 4–8; Dionysius of Halicarnassus, *Roman Antiquities* 12. 9]

Leda, mother of the *Dioscuri (Castor and Pollux/Polydeuces) and *Helen (as well as *Clytemnestra and the minor figures Timandra and Phylonoe), wife of *Tyndareos, daughter of King Thestius of Pleuron in Aetolia. She is a mythic not a cult figure. Genealogically she supports the linking of the descendants of Tyndareos with Aetolia, as found in the earliest genealogical authors and reinforced by the hero-shrine of the eponym Pleuron in Sparta. Most striking is the myth that *Zeus in the form of a swan copulated with Leda, who subsequently produced an egg containing Helen and Polydeuces, an egg displayed in Sparta. Castor, thus the mortal twin, was born to Tyndareos on the same night. In a different version, stemming from the cult of *Nemesis at Rhamnus (Attica) and its local Helen, Nemesis transforms herself to escape Zeus and finally in the form of a goose is fertilized by Zeus in the form of a swan (in the *Cypria*, *see* EPIC CYCLE); Leda only finds the egg, or has it brought to her.

Egg births are not unfamiliar in mythologies, but generally give rise to the world or to mankind. The Orphic god (*see* ORPHISM) *Phanes emerged from an egg, and in

Egypt the earth-god Geb, whose attribute is the goose, laid the cosmic egg. The story is rather out of place in Greek mythology and might seem specially incredible, as suggested by its treatment in *Euripides' *Helen*, and the *Nemesis* of the comic poet Cratinus.

For art Leda offered an exotic theme: Leda and the swan, or even Leda discovering the egg. From the Attic vase-painter Exekias on she was available to accompany the Return of the Tyndarids.

[Euripides, *Helen* 17 ff., 257–9; Apollodorus 3. 10. 7; Pausanias 3. 13. 8, 16. 1]

Lemuria, Roman private *ritual on 9, 11, and 13 May to propitiate apparently anonymous, dangerous, and hungry ghosts (*lemures*), then prowling about houses. The ritual's midnight time and tossing of black beans have been taken as 'magical', but this view relies on false anthropological assumptions. Sometimes distinguished from the ancestral spirits of the *Parentalia (13–23 February) on the basis of malignancy versus benevolence, but *Ovid in the *Fasti* contradicts this.

[Ovid, *Fasti*. 2. 547 ff.; 5. 419 ff.]

Lenaea, a Dionysiac festival (*see* DIONYSUS) celebrated in Athens on the 12th day of the month Gamelion (January–February), which in other Ionian calendars is called Lenaion. The name is derived from *lēnē*, '*maenad'. The official Athenian name, 'Dionysia at the Lenaion', proves that it took place in this sanctuary, which was probably in the agora. Officials of the Eleusinian mysteries (*see* ELEUSIS; MYSTERIES) joined the *basileus* (the magistrate discharging the religious duties of the one-time king, *see* ARCHONTES), in the conduct of the festival. We hear of a procession, and there are various slight indications of mystic ritual. The rituals depicted on the so-called 'Lenaea vases' may have occurred at this festival. Notices in the lexicographers and compilers Hesychius and Photius indicate that drama was performed in the Lenaion before the Athenians built their theatre; but probably dramatic contests at the Lenaea were formally organized

only from about 440 BC. In the 5th cent. it seems that the contests in comedy were arranged much as at the City *Dionysia, but that the tragic contests at the Lenaea were less prestigious, with only two tragedians competing, each with two tragedies. *See* TRAGEDY, GREEK.

Leo I, the Great, pope AD 440–61. As deacon, though an unoriginal theologian, he influenced Popes Celestine I and Sixtus III on doctrine, and served in secular diplomacy. As pope, he purged Manichaeans (*see* MANICHAEISM) from Rome, in partnership with senate and emperor, and attacked Pelagians (*see* PELAGIUS) and *Priscillianists. He intervened against the view that Christ had only one nature; the council of Ephesus (449) had spurned his Christological work, but it was accepted at Chalcedon (451). He annulled Chalcedon's equation of Rome and Constantinople, but improved contact with Constantinople. Proclaiming the authority of St Peter, through interventions and administrative restructurings, and despite worsening communications, he strengthened papal power in the Balkans and crumbling western provinces. His buildings, iconography, liturgies, cult of St Peter, and encouragement of charity and observance of the Christian calendar enhanced Rome's sacred status. Confronting Attila (451) and Gaiseric (454), he helped to turn back the Huns and minimize the Vandal sack. His surviving letters (many drafted by others) and 96 sermons are lucid and forceful, with imperial and liturgical resonances.

Leon of Pella (?late 4th cent. BC), wrote a book on the Egyptian gods, in the form of a letter from Alexander the Great to his mother Olympias, in which the gods are represented as in origin human kings, the discoverers of agriculture and other means of human subsistence. *See also* EUHEMERUS; CULTURE-BRINGERS.

Leto (Gk. *Lētō or Lātō*, Lat. *Latona*), a Titaness (*see* TITAN), daughter of Coeus and *Phoebe in Hesiod.

In myth, though she occupies a position of relative prominence in the *Iliad*, her main role is to be mother of *Apollo and *Artemis. Local legends locate the birth in various places. The main version is the one given in the Delian part of the *Homeric Hymn to Apollo* where the island of *Delos allows Leto to give birth to her twins on condition that it would became Apollo's main cult place (or that the island, now floating, would become stable, a typical motif in foundation legends); grasping the palm-tree, Leto is delivered of Apollo (and, in later authors, of Artemis as well). One version adds that Leto had come as a she-wolf from the *Hyperboreans to Delos: this connects her with Apollo Lykeios, Apollo 'Of the Wolves'. Another important place was Ephesus where the birth legend, with emphasis on Artemis, was connected with the local cult of the *Curetes and influenced by the myth of Rhea giving birth to *Zeus. Minor sanctuaries held similar claims, e.g. the oracular shrine of Tegyra, the sanctuary of Zoster (east coast of Attica) or the Letoon of Xanthus in Lycia.

Formerly scholars derived Leto from Lycia. The excavations in the Letoon of Xanthus show that it belonged to an indigenous 'Mother' who in the 5th cent. BC was identified with Greek Leto, as she was identified in other places with other Anatolian goddesses, often as 'Mother Leto'. Her Greek cult is often closely connected with that of Apollo and Artemis, as on Delos, where she had her own sanctuary, or in *Didyma, while she is curiously absent from cult in *Delphi.

In some sanctuaries, her cult is more independent. In certain Greek cities (Delos, Ephesus, or Chios), she has a priestess, while her Anatolian cults usually have a priest. (*See* PRIESTS.) In Roman times, some Anatolian cities celebrated Letoa, festivals and contests for a former local deity. In several places, Leto is connected with the same care for younger members of society that otherwise is characteristic of Apollo and Artemis. In Chios, Leto received the dedications of parents for the victory of their daughter; there is evidence from Chios for girls' athletics which must have their roots in the world of *initiation. For Leto Phytia in Phaestus on Crete, a myth tells of the transformation of a girl into a young man in order to explain the ritual of Ekdysia whose dependence on initiatory ritual is undisputed (*see* CRETAN CULTS AND MYTHS). The Athenian Demotionidai (*see* PHRATRIES) put up the list of their new members in the local Letoon; and the strange epithet *kyanopeplos*, 'with a dark cloak' in Hesiod might be explained by the usually black or dark cloaks of ephebes (*see* EPHEBOI).

The Delian Letoon contained a small wooden image, one of the rare representations of Leto alone. The triad is attested already in the Daedalic (*see* DAEDALUS) statuettes from 7th-cent. BC Dreros on Crete and is the common image both in temples and in vase-painting.

See ANATOLIAN DEITIES; APOLLO; ARTEMIS.

[Hesiod, *Theogony* 406–8, 918–20; *Homeric Hymn to Apollo* 25–178; Aristotle, *History of Animals* 580ª15; Callimachus, *Hymn* 4; Ovid, *Metamorphoses* 6. 333 ff.; Antoninus Liberalis 17; Strabo 14. 1. 20, 639 f.]

Leucippides Phoebe and Hilaeira, the daughters of *Leucippus (1), were cousins both of the Spartan *Dioscuri and of the sons of the Messenian king Aphareus, *Idas and Lynceus; engaged to marry the latter, they were seized at the altar by Castor and Polydeuces (*see* DIOSCURI) and a violent fight (expressing the enmity between the two neighbouring regions of the Peloponnese) ensued.

[Pindar, *Nemean* 10; Theocritus, *Idylls* 22. 137 ff.]

Leucippus, 'person who keeps white horses', hence 'rich man, noble'. Name of fifteen mythological characters, but especially (1) father of Hilaeira and Phoebe, *see* LEUCIPPIDES; (2) a young Cretan, turned from a girl into a boy by a miracle of *Leto.

[Antoninus Liberalis 17]

libations, *ritual pouring of *water, *wine, oil (*see* OLIVE), *milk, or *honey in honour of gods, heroes, or the dead. Libations are an act of surrender, preceding human participation in meals and other acts. They mark commencements and endings, such as mornings and evenings; at the banquet, the group pours threefold libations to *Zeus and the Olympians, to the heroes, and to Zeus Teleios, 'He who Finishes'. *Dionysus 'himself' (i.e. wine) is poured to gain divine favour. Libations express blanket-propitiation when associated with the unknown and new: having arrived in foreign *Colchis, the *Argonauts pour a libation of 'honey and pure wine to Earth (*Gaia) and the gods of the land (*epichōrioi*) and to the souls of dead heroes', asking for aid and a favourable welcome. The more common term, *spondē*, usually associated with wine, refers also to the cry of invocation and to the solemn act it accompanies, such as the signing of truces. In iconography sacrificial acts may end with a libation over the fire on the altar (*see* SACRIFICE). Common is the 'departure of the hoplite', where a woman is seen to the right, holding a libation vessel; the scene affirms the link between the group, the gods, the house, and the act. *Spondē* is controlled: libation is poured from an *oinochoē* (wine-jug) to a bowl (*phialē*), then onto an altar or the ground. *Choai*, 'total libations', often wineless (*aoinoi*), are characterized by greater quantities, especially for the dead, *chthonian and nature deities, such as *Nymphs, *Muses, and *Erinyes.

[Hesiod, *Works and Days* 724–6; Euripides, *Bacchae* 284–5; Apollonius Rhodius, *Argonautica* 2. 1271–5]

Liber Pater, Italian god of fertility and especially of *wine, later commonly identified with *Dionysus. There has been much discussion of his origins and possible relation to *Jupiter Liber, but there is no doubt that he was an independent god in Rome by the time (5th cent. BC?) at which the archaic festival calendar (in capital letters in the *Fasti*) became fixed, for his festival (the Liberalia, 17 March) appears there. He never had a major temple of his own in Rome, but formed part of the *Aventine Triad, *Ceres, Liber, and Libera, whose joint

temple was founded in 493 BC, possibly under south Italian influence, and became a great centre for the plebeians in the 5th and 4th cents. BC. Liber and Libera (like other early Roman deities) seem originally to have formed a pair; they were concerned with seeds and therefore with the promotion of fertility both agricultural and human. At Liber's festival, a *phallus was paraded through the fields and into town, accompanied by the singing of crude rustic songs, according to *Augustine. *Virgil also mentions the crude songs, together with *masks of Dionysus, hung on the trees. At the Liberalia, too, Roman boys commonly put on the toga of manhood; this is not satisfactorily explained in the sources, but it seems natural to assume that Liber was seen as the patron of the boy's transition (*see* RITES OF PASSAGE) into fertility.

[Virgil, *Georgics* 2. 385–96; Ovid, *Fasti* 3. 771–90; Augustine, *City of God* 7. 21]

Libertas, 'freedom', personified deity at Rome, linked with *Jupiter in the cult of Jupiter Libertas and the censors' headquarters, the Atrium Libertatis; worshipped alone on the *Aventine in a temple built by Tiberius Sempronius Gracchus (238 BC). Her ideological connection with the freedoms of the ordinary citizen is apparent: freedom opposed both to the state of slavery and to *domination* by the powerful. The term was often used in the late republic and early empire to designate the liberty of the politician to develop his career without interference, and so came to focus various types of resistance to the more autocratic aspects of the early Principate. But *Augustus had made a point of restoring the temples of both Libertas and Jupiter Libertas, and the slogan *libertas Augusta* was the final response.

[Livy 24. 16. 9]

Libitina, Roman goddess of burials, which were registered at her grove on the Esquiline. Some writers identify her with *Venus, apparently a confusion with Lubentina.

[Varro, *On the Latin Language* 6. 47; Dionysius of

Halicarnassus, *Roman Antiquities*. 4. 15. 5; Plutarch, *Roman Questions* 23]

libri pontificales, general name for the records kept by the college of **pontifices* at Rome. An idea of part of their contents may be formed from the surviving, inscribed, *commentarii* (records, memoranda) of the Arval Brothers (*see* FRATRES ARVALES) and the *acta* of the *Secular Games; but these are records of rituals performed at particular dates, whereas the pontifical records will have contained in addition rules of procedure and directions for the performing of rituals, including the texts of prayers, vows, and other formulae. So much is clear from the quotations and references preserved in the antiquarian tradition; but hardly any verbatim quotations can be trusted, so that the method of organizing the records and even the question whether there was any organization, remain highly arguable.

Licymnius, brother of *Alcmene and so uncle of *Heracles, killed by Heracles' son *Tlepolemus. His tomb was at the gymnasium of Argos (*see* ARGOS, MYTHS OF), but he was also recognized as *eponym of Licymna, the acropolis of Tiryns.

[Homer, *Iliad* 2. 653–70; Pausanias 2. 22. 8; Plutarch, *Life of Pyrrhus* 34; Strabo 8. 373]

Linus, an old song sung either at the vintage as on the Shield of Achilles in the *Iliad*, where it is performed by a boy accompanied by the lyre and by a cheerfully dancing and shouting group of young people, or a song of lament using the ritual cry *ailinos* ('alas for Linus'), which was interpreted as a mournful song in honour of Linus. Linus was also a mythical person for whom various *genealogies exist, e.g. son of *Apollo and Psamathe, a local princess of Argos: after she exposed him, he was devoured by dogs and the city was plagued by Apollo till satisfaction was made. He had strong connections with music: (*a*) he invented the *thrénos* (dirge); (*b*) he was killed by Apollo in a music contest, because he had boasted that he was as good a singer as the god; (*c*) he was the music

teacher of *Heracles and was killed by his pupil; (*d*) he was generally considered a great composer and citharode. The Linus song was widely sung under different names in the near east (*see* LITYERSES).

[Homer, *Iliad* 18. 570; Herodotus 2. 79; Apollodorus 2. 63; Pliny, *Natural History* 7. 204; Pausanias 1. 43. 7–8, 9. 29. 6 f.]

liturgy (Greek) The liturgy (*leitourgia*, 'work for the people') is an institution known particularly from Athens, but attested elsewhere, by which rich men were required to undertake work for the state at their own expense. Apart from the trierarchy, which involved responsibility for a ship in the navy for a year, Athenian liturgies were connected with *festivals. They included the **chorēgia* ('chorus-leading': the production of a chorus at the musical and dramatic festivals), the gymnasiarchy (responsibility for a team competing in an athletic festival), *hestiasis* ('feasting': the provision of a banquet), and *architheōria* (the leadership of a public delegation to a foreign festival). At state level there were at least 97 in a normal year, at least 118 in a year of the Great *Panathenaea, and there were in addition some liturgies at the level of the deme or local community.

lituus, curved staff (without a knot) of the **augures* which they used to delineate their field of vision (**templum*). It also appears in Umbria and Etruria, and earlier in Asia Minor. It is frequently represented on republican coins.

[Cicero, *On Divination* 1. 30; Livy 1. 18. 7; Ovid, *Fasti* 6. 375].

Lityerses, personification of a Hellenistic reapers' song. (*See* LINUS.) Said to be the bastard son of King *Midas, he lived in Phrygian Celaenae and forced passing travellers to compete with him at harvesting. When they tired, he whipped them, cut off their heads, and bound the bodies in a stook. He was killed by *Heracles.

Locrian Maidens, the *See* AIAS (2).

Lotus-eaters (Gk. *Lōtophagoi*), a mythical

people (the ancients liked to locate them in North Africa) living on the lotus plant, which induces forgetfulness and makes its eaters lose all desire to return home. Those of *Odysseus' men who ate the lotus had to be dragged back to their ships by force.

[Homer, *Odyssey* 9. 82–104]

Lucaria, Roman *festival on 19 and 21 July celebrated in a grove between the via Salaria and the *Tiber where the Romans had hidden when fleeing the Gauls. The 18 July, day of the defeat at the Allia, occasioned this explanation of the rite. *Plutarch indicates that revenue from public groves was called *lucar*, while an inscription confirms that the word originally meant 'grove'. Lucaria must originally have involved clearing groves and propitiating their spirits, as suggested by a passage in Cato.

[Cato, *On Agriculture* 139–40]

Lucretia, wife of Lucius Tarquinius Collatinus, was raped by Sextus, the son of *Tarquinius Superbus; her subsequent suicide because of her dishonour was the catalyst for the expulsion of the Tarquins by Lucius Iunius Brutus. The legend, probably originally distinct from that of Brutus but already linked with it in the first Roman historian, Quintus Fabius Pictor, utilizes Greek notions to explain the overthrow of tyranny; but, particularly in Livy, Lucretia becomes a paradigm of the Roman *matrona* (married woman), heroic in her resolute adhesion to the code of female chastity. But she may also be seen as the victim not only of male violence but also of the ideology of a patriarchal society.

[Livy 1. 57–9]

ludi (games). Games of an informal nature and schools of instruction were called *ludi*, but more particularly the word referred to the formalized competitions and displays held at religious *festivals, which counted as religious rites just as much as sacrifices and processions. The numbers of days devoted to *ludi* in Rome increased over time: 57 in the late republic; 77 in the early 1st

cent. AD; 177 in the mid-4th cent. AD. There were three types of *ludi*. First, *ludi circenses*, which consisted of chariot-racing, held in the circus in the Campus Martius and eventually in the Circus Maximus (which could seat 150,000 people). Dionysius of Halicarnassus give a full account of the prior procession. Secondly, *ludi scaenici*, originating in 364 BC as pantomime dances to flute, later including plays, first at the Ludi Romani of 240 BC. Under the empire performances chiefly consisted of mime and pantomime. The cost was usually shared between state and presiding magistrate. Admission was free, with special seats designated for senators and others; women and slaves were admitted, but sat separately, at least from *Augustus onwards. Plays were staged, initially in temporary settings associated with particular sanctuaries (by the temple of *Apollo in the Prata Flaminia; on the *Palatine next to the temple of Magna Mater; *see* CYBELE) and from the mid-1st cent BC onwards in permanent theatres (which became increasingly common throughout the empire). Augustus' *Secular Games included both the 'archaic' games 'on a stage without a theatre and without seats', and more 'modern' games (in a purpose-built wooden theatre and in Pompey's theatre). Thirdly, fights involving gladiators and *venationes* (wild animal combats), which under the republic were given under private auspices. These were staged in the republic in the Forum and elsewhere, but from 29 BC in the amphitheatre of Titus Statilius Taurus and from AD 80 in the Colosseum (which could seat 50,000, with standing-room for another 5,000). Outside Rome, specialist amphitheatres were built and, in the Greek world, existing theatres adapted for the safety of the spectators.

[Dionysius of Halicarnassus, *Roman Antiquities* 7. 70–3]

Luna, Roman moon-goddess. *Varro names her among a number of deities introduced by Titus *Tatius and therefore of Sabine origin (*see* SABINI). The latter statement may be doubted, but the existence of an early cult of Luna remains likely, though Wissowa objects that no trace of it is to be found. This may be mere accident; in historical times she certainly had a cult with a temple on the *Aventine, first mentioned in 182 BC (anniversary on 31 March), but founded between 292 and 219, and another on the *Palatine, which was illuminated all night long.

[Varro, *On the Latin Language* 5. 68, 74]

Lupercalia, a Roman *festival (15 February), conducted by the association (*sodalitas*, *see* SODALES) of Luperci (cf. *lupus*, 'wolf'). It included odd rites: goats and a dog were sacrificed at the Lupercal (a cave at the foot of the *Palatine where a she-wolf reared *Romulus and Remus); the blood was smeared with a knife on the foreheads of two youths (who were obliged to laugh), and wiped with wool dipped in milk; then the Luperci, naked except for girdles from the skin of sacrificial goats, ran (probably) round the Palatine striking bystanders, especially women, with goat-skin thongs (a favourite scene in the iconography of Roman months). The rite combined purificatory *lustration and fertility magic, but no interpretation is fully satisfactory. It was at the Lupercalia that Antony, consul and Lupercus, offered a royal diadem to *Caesar (44 BC). The festival survived until at least AD 494 when Gelasius I, the bishop of Rome, perhaps banned Christian participation and transformed it into the feast of Purification of the Virgin.

[Varro, *On the Latin Language* 6. 13, 34; Ovid, *Fasti* 2. 19–36, 267–452; Dionysius of Halicarnassus, *Roman Antiquities* 1. 32. 3–5 and 80. 1; Plutarch, *Life of Antony* 12, *Romulus* 21, *Caesar* 61]

lustration (*lustratio*), is the performance of *lustrum*, a ceremony of *purification and of averting evil. The main ritual ingredient was a circular procession (*circumambulatio*, *circumagere*, often repeated three times); hence a derived meaning of *lustrare*, 'to move around something'. The instruments of purification, such as torches and sacrificial animals (in particular the *suovetaurilia*), were carried or led (by attendants specially selected on ac-

count of their propitious names) round the person(s) or the place to be purified, often to the accompaniment of music, chant, and dance. *See* SACRIFICE, ROMAN. The victims were sacrificed at the end of the ceremony, and their entrails, *exta*, inspected. We hear of *lustratio* of fields, of the village, of the Roman territory (= *Ambarvalia) and the city (= *Amburbium), and of an army (represented on Trajan's Column) and fleet, always before, not after, a campaign or battle; here also belong the old rites of *Armilustrium and *Tubilustrium. But the most important was *lustratio* (by the *suovetaurilia*) of the Roman people as the concluding part of the census, performed on the Campus Martius by one of the censors (selected by lot). The deity invoked was primarily *Mars, also *Ceres and *dii patrii*, 'ancestral gods'. The ceremony excluded evil, and kept the pure within the circle, but it also denoted a new beginning, especially for the Roman people at the census or for an army when a new commander arrived or when two armies were joined together. The etymology (and the exact meaning of *lustrum condere*) is disputed: perhaps connected with *lavare* 'to wash', *luere* 'to wash, cleanse', or *lucere*, 'to shine', hence *lustrare* 'to illuminate' (with fire or torches carried at the procession; *fire was also used at the lustrations of Iguvium (Gubbio); *see* TABULAE IGUVINAE, ITALIC RELIGION).

[Cato, *On Agriculture* 141; Virgil, *Georgics* 1. 338 ff.; Tibullus 2. 1; Livy 1. 44. 2, 23. 35. 5; Appian, *Civil Wars* 5. 401; Varro, *On Country Matters* 2. 1. 10]

lycanthropy (or werewolves). Those who ate human flesh at the human sacrifice offered on Mt. Lycaeon in Arcadia (*see* ARCADIAN CULTS AND MYTHS) and were believed to be changed into wolves. Here *Lycaon would have been the first werewolf. Various stories speak of athletes who lived as wolves for nine years but regained their human form after abstaining from human flesh during this period and subsequently were victorious in contests: thus Demaenetus. A comparable episode is given by the Elder Pliny and *Augustine. But the best-known literary werewolf is probably that of Petronius in the *Satyricon* (*see* NOVEL). Modern scholars suggest that the phenomenon might indicate the existence of a group of 'wolfmen' devoted to the worship of a wolf-god, or a rite of passage as at Sparta (*see* INITIATION).

[Plato, *Republic* 8. 565d; Pliny, *Natural History* 8. 81–2; Pausanias 6. 8. 2; Porphyry, *On Abstinence* 2. 27. 2; Augustine, *City of God* 18. 17; Petronius, *Satyricon* 61–2]

Lycaon, mythological characters whose name seems to include the Greek word for wolf, *lykos*. (1) Son of *Priam and Laothoe, killed by *Achilles. (2) Father of *Pandarus. (3) Son of *Pelasgus and king of Arcadia (*see* ARCADIAN CULTS AND MYTHS). According to *Apollodorus he had 50 sons; *Pausanias gives the names of 28 of them, all of whom except Nyctimus and Oenotrus founded settlements in Arcadia. Some of his actions depict Lycaon as a *culture-bringer and pious ruler: he founded *Lycosura, and gave *Zeus his epithet Lycaeus, instituting the festival Lycaia in his honour. But his sacrifice to Zeus Lycaeus of a newborn child shows him in a different light. For Pausanias the act appears to be a simple, though horrific, sacrifice; other sources compound Lycaon's impiety by having him entertain Zeus to a feast and offer the god human flesh to test his divinity (already in a fragment attributed to Hesiod). Sometimes the responsibility for the feast is attributed to Lycaon's sons. Zeus punished the transgressors with a thunderbolt, or sent a flood, or changed Lycaon into a wolf (*see* LYCANTHROPY).

[(1) Homer, *Iliad* 21. 34–135; (2) Homer, *Iliad* 2. 826–7; (3) Apollodorus 3. 8. 1; Pausanias 8. 2–3]

Lycophron The name of Lycophron is attached to the author of the probably Hellenistic poem *Alexandra*, the bulk of which is composed of a recitation of mythological and historical events cast in the form of a prophecy by *Cassandra. Although his style is obscure and allusive, he is a useful mythological source, especially for Italian legends and those connected with the returns of *Odysseus and the other heroes from *Troy.

Lycosura, a small town with an important sanctuary in south-west Arcadia (*see* ARCADIAN CULTS AND MYTHS), situated in the hills west of the main Megalopolitan basin, belonged to the Parrhasians, but on the foundation of Megalopolis was allowed, because of its sanctuary, to survive as a separate *polis surrounded by Megalopolitan territory. Though claiming to be the earth's oldest city, its known history and archaeology run from the 4th cent. BC. The sanctuary and surrounding area have been excavated (but not traces of the walled town). Lycosura was an important religious centre with cults of several deities, but the most significant was *Despoina, who had an imposing Doric temple and colossal cult statuary by Damophon of Messene. Unfortunately the dates of both the temple and the statuary are disputed, suggestions ranging from the 4th cent. BC to the Hadrianic period; both may belong to the early 3rd cent. BC. The cult centre still flourished in the 2nd cent. AD.

Lycurgus, a mythological personage, according to *Homer, a son of Dryas, who attacked *Dionysus, driving him and his nurses before him till the god took refuge in the sea; thereafter Lycurgus was blinded and died soon, having first massacred his family in a divinely induced madness. His death is vaguely placed on Mt. Nysa. Later, as in a fragment of *Aeschylus, he is an Edonian; he and others elaborate the story in various ways. *Apollodorus and *Hyginus say Dionysus drove him mad, and further embroider the story of his sufferings and death; their sources are uncertain. The myth was popular in art, e.g. (the massacre) on Greek and South Italian painted pottery (5th–4th cents. BC).

[Homer, *Iliad* 6. 130 ff.; Apollodorus 3. 5. 1; Hyginus, *Fables* 132]

Lycus, 'wolf', a common heroic name. In Attic tradition, Lycus was one of the sons of King *Pandion who at their father's death divided Attica between them. Herodotus makes this Lycus the *eponym of the Lycians, while *Pausanias connects him with the cult of *Apollo Lycius. It is not clear whether this figure was identified with the Lykus whose shrine was situated near a lawcourt and who appears as a sort of patron of jurors in Aristophanes' *Wasps*. A Theban Lycus (*see* THEBES, MYTHS OF) was husband of *Dirce, who with her mistreated *Antiope and was killed by her children *Amphion and Zethus.

[Herodotus 1. 173. 3; Pausanias 1. 19. 3; Aristophanes, *Wasps* 389–94]

Macar, sometimes called *Macareus, in mythology a Lesbian king, but usually a son of *Helios and so a Rhodian. His name, very strange for a mortal because a stock divine *epithet, has been interpreted as a corruption of the Phoenician Melqart.

[Homer, *Iliad* 24. 544]

Macareus, when not identical with *Macar, is usually the name of a son of *Aeolus (1) (which see for his incestuous love of his sister *Canace). Several minor figures have the same name, e.g. a son of *Lycaon (3); a Lapith (*See* CENTAURS).

Maccabees The name Maccabee, probably meaning 'the hammer', was the appellation of Judas son of Mattathias, leader of the Judaean Revolt of 168/7 BC against *Antiochus (1) IV Epiphanes. (*See* JEWS.) The name was given also to Judas' fellow rebels, his father and his four brothers. They were the leaders of the traditionalists, reacting against a process of Hellenization in Jerusalem masterminded by a section of the Jewish aristocracy. The high priesthood was usurped by Jason, a member of the Oniad clan, from his brother Menelaus. But the ultimate provocation to the Maccabees was the king's installation of a garrison in the city and a pagan cult in the Temple, and his consequent attempt to suppress Judaism on a wide front. After Mattathias' public killing of an apostate Jew in the act of sacrifice, the Maccabees took to the hills to conduct a guerrilla war, eventually winning concessions from the regent Lysias on behalf of the young Antiochus V. Judas rededicated the Temple on 25 Kislev (December) 164 BC,

a date already marked within a few years of the events as the festival of Hanukkah. But he continued to resist the Hellenizers in Jerusalem and successive Seleucid armies. A memorable victory against Nicanor, the Seleucid general, in 161 was followed by the defeat and death of Judas in 160, in battle against Bacchides, after which his brother Jonathan continued the struggle.

The term Maccabees is also applied to the two Greek books in which the revolt and its sequel are narrated and to two associated books (*see* JEWISH-GREEK LITERATURE). Finally, the name is sometimes given to the seven children and their mother, whose legendary martyrdom in the persecution of Epiphanes, described in 2 Maccabees 7 and embellished in 4 Maccabees, was remembered in rabbinic literature and gave rise to a cult at Antioch and to a long-lasting Christian tradition (as well as to the word 'macabre').

Macedonia, cults and myths *Hesiod first mentioned 'Makedon', the eponym of the people and the country, as a son of *Zeus, a grandson of *Deucalion, and so a first cousin of *Aeolus (2), Dorus, and *Xuthus; in other words he considered the 'Macedones' to be an outlying branch of the Greek-speaking tribes, with a distinctive dialect of their own, 'Macedonian'. The claim of the Macedonian kings to be Temenids, descended from *Heracles and related to the royal house of Argos (*see* ARGOS, MYTHS OF) in the Peloponnese, was recognized at *Olympia.

Nowadays historians generally agree that

the Macedonians form part of the Greek people; hence they also shared in the common religious and cultural features of the Hellenic world. Consequently most of the gods worshipped in Greece can also be found in Macedonia. However, regional characteristics have to be noted. Especially in the areas bordering on Thrace and among the Paeonians in the north—though these had early contacts with the Macedonians in the centre—local deviants in cult and religion have been attested.

The cult of *Zeus was one of the most important cults in Macedonia. Its places of worship on *Olympus, at the foot of the mountain at Dion, and at Aegae (Vergina) were extremely popular. As father of Makedon he was the Macedonians' eponymous ancestor. The cult of *Artemis was widely practised. Although most of the evidence dates to Roman times one may assume the existence of older religious practices. In the areas in contact with Thrace it is determined by the Thracian cult of Artemis and the worship of *Bendis, probably themselves types of a deity of fertility and vegetation. Herodotus says that women in Thrace and Paeonia always brought wheat-straw in their offerings to Artemis Basileia. In central Macedonia Enodia is attested, on horseback and holding a torch. She has frequently been associated with Artemis. By comparison the cult of *Apollo is not as widespread. Here too local deviants can be found. In Thessalonica, where *Pythian Games were held in honour of Apollo Pythius, the cult of Apollo is even connected with the *Cabiri.

The cult of *Dionysus, whom the Paeonians called Dyalus, was especially popular. However, the sites are unevenly distributed. On the basis of the borders of the later Macedonian provinces there are fewer monuments for Dionysus in the south-west, while one of the cult centres was in the area of the Pangaeus—a region admittedly also settled in by the Thracians.

Zeus, *Apollo, *Heracles, Dionysus, *Athena, and other such gods appear on coins of the 5th and 4th cents. BC. This evidence, however, ought not to be overestimated since these gods were depicted chiefly in order to demonstrate the close links with the Greek world. Especially important was Heracles not only as the ancestor of the Macedonian royal family, but also fulfilling manifold other functions, e.g. as the patron of hunting. Other cults of not inconsiderable importance were those of *Helios, among the Paeonians worshipped as a disc, *Selene, the *Dioscuri, healing deities—represented by *Asclepius and *Hygieia—*river-gods, *nymphs, the Pierian *Muses, and a strange *snake. Alongside the cult of Dionysus and the Samothracian *mysteries (see SAMOTHRACE); *Orphism too was not unknown (see ORPHIC LITERATURE).

The so-called Thracian Rider (see RIDER-GODS) is attested on votive tablets in north and east Macedonia. However, in contrast to Thrace the Hero on Horseback is frequently depicted on Macedonian tombstones. The numerous deifications of the dead as e.g. *Aphrodite, Artemis, Athena, Dionysus, *Eros, *Hermes, and Heracles belong in this context. These monuments, as well as most of the rider-statues and the votive reliefs depicting various deities, generally date to the second half of the 2nd and the first half of the 3rd cent. AD.

Machaon and Podalirius, sons of *Asclepius and physicians already in *Homer, but sons of *Poseidon in the *Iliu Persis* (see EPIC CYCLE). In the *Iliad*, they lead the contingent from Tricca in Thessaly (focus of the later cult of Asclepius), Ithome, and Oechalia. Their names have an epic ring, Machaon being 'Warrior', Podaleirios apparently 'Lily-foot'. Machaon tends *Menelaus, but is also active as a fighter and is wounded by *Paris; Podalirius is too busy in the battle to tend *Eurypylus. Their further feats at Troy consist mostly of healing or fighting: they heal *Philoctetes in Sophocles (other sources name only one of them), Machaon is killed by Eurypylus, Podalirius survives the war and settles in one of several places, especially in Caria or southern Italy. They had a cult, both separately (Machaon at Gerenia in Messenia (*see* MESSENIAN CULTS AND MYTHS), Podalirius an *oracle in Daunia, on Monte Gargano) and together, generally with their father.

[Homer, *Iliad* 2. 731-3, 4. 200-19, 11. 505-20, 11. 836; Sophocles, *Philoctetes* 1333 f.; Lycophron, *Alexandra* 1047; Pausanias 3. 26. 9]

Macrobius (Macrobius Ambrosius Theodosius), 5th-cent. AD Latin author whose works contain useful information on a variety of topics relating to religion and mythology.

(1) *Commentarii*. The bulk of the work is a philosophical exposition of *Cicero's *Somnium Scipionis* (*Dream of Scipio*). Macrobius discourses on *dreams, on number-mysticism, *oracles, moral virtue, astronomy, music, geography, and the *soul (vindicating *Plato against *Aristotle); he praises Publius Cornelius Scipio Aemilianus for uniting all the virtues, and the *Somnium* for uniting all the branches of philosophy. The main source is *Porphyry, in particular his commentary on *Timaeus*; but direct knowledge of *Plotinus has been established. Despite frequent inconsistencies and misapprehensions, the work was a principal transmitter of ancient science and Neoplatonic thought to the western Middle Ages. *See* NEOPLATONISM.

(2) *Saturnalia*. This work is cast in the form of dialogues on the evening before the Saturnalia (16 December, *see* SATURNUS, SATURNALIA) of AD 383(?) and during the holiday proper. The guests include the greatest pagan luminaries of the time. After a few legal and grammatical discussions the night before, the three days are devoted to serious topics in the morning, lighter ones, including food and drink, in the afternoon and evening. Having ranged over the Saturnalia, the calendar, and famous persons' jokes, the speakers devote the second and third mornings to *Virgil, represented as a master of philosophical and religious lore and praised almost without reserve in matters of rhetoric and grammar, including his use of

earlier poets, Greek and Roman. The guests then turn to physiology, with special reference to eating and drinking. The work expresses the nostalgia of the Christianized élite in a diminished Rome for the city's great and pagan past; the new religion is ignored. The *Saturnalia* was less read in the Middle Ages than the *Commentarii*, but returned to favour in the Renaissance.

maenads, women inspired to ritual frenzy by *Dionysus. Maenadic rituals took place in the rough mountains of Greece in the heart of winter every second year. Having ceremonially left the city, maenads (probably upperclass women) would walk into the mountains shouting the cry 'to the mountains'. Here they removed their shoes, let their hair down, and pulled up their fawn-skins. After a sacrifice of *cakes, they started their nightly dances accompanied by drum and *aulos* (in sound more similar to the oboe than the flute). Stimulated by the high-pitched music, the flicker effects of the torches, the whirling nature of the dances, the shouting of *euhoi*, the headshaking, jumping, and running, the maenads eventually fell to the ground—the euphoric climax of their *ecstasy.

Maenadic ritual strongly stimulated the mythical imagination: the *Bacchae* of *Euripides shows us women who tear animals apart, handle *snakes, eat raw meat, and are invulnerable to iron and fire. Most likely, in Euripides' time maenads did not handle snakes or eat raw meat; however, their ecstasy may well have made them insensible to pain. Myth often exaggerates ritual, but the absence of contemporary non-literary sources makes it difficult to separate these two categories in the *Bacchae*, where they are so tightly interwoven.

Maenadism was integrated into the city and should not be seen as a rebellion. It enabled women to leave their houses, to mingle with their 'sisters', and to have a good time. This social aspect, though, could only be expressed through the worship of Dionysus. To separate the social and religious aspect is modern not Greek. *See* WOMEN IN CULT.

Most likely, maenadism already occurs in *Homer's *Iliad*. In Athenian art it became popular on pots towards the end of the 6th cent. and again in the 4th cent. BC, with a selective interest expressed in the intervening period by painters of larger pots. Among the tragedians *Aeschylus pictured maenads in various of his lost plays, e.g. the *Bassarai*, as did Euripides, especially in the *Bacchae*. Given these changing periods of interest in maenadism in literature and art, we should be wary in privileging the *Bacchae* by ascribing to it a special influence on later maenadic ritual or by tying it too closely to contemporary new cults. The demise of maenadism started in the Hellenistic period and was complete by the 2nd cent. AD.

See also BACCHANALIA.

[Homer, *Iliad* 22. 460–1; Euripides, *Bacchae*; Livy 19. 8–18]

magi *See* MAGUS.

magic

1. The concept Antiquity does not provide clear-cut definitions of what was understood by magic and there is a variety of terms referring to its different aspects. The Greek terms that lie at the roots of the modern term 'magic' (*magos, mageia*) were ambivalent. Originally they referred to the strange but powerful rites of the Persian magi (*see* MAGUS) and their overtones were not necessarily negative (thus *Plato speaks of 'the magian lore of *Zoroaster'). Soon, however, *magos* was associated with the doubtful practices of the Greek *goēs* ('sorcerer') and hence attracted the negative connotations of quack, fraud, and mercenary. Through *Aristotle, *Theophrastus, and Hellenistic authors this negative sense also affected the Latin terms *magus, magia, magicus*. However, in late antiquity, especially in the *Greek Magical Papyri*, the term *magos* regained an authoritative meaning, somewhat like wizard, and was also embraced by philoso-

phers and theurgists (*see* THEURGY). Since in these late texts prayer, magical formulae, and magical ritual freely intermingle, they challenge modern distinctions between magic and religion (and science). However, definitions being indispensable, we here employ a broad description of the 'family resemblance' of magic: a manipulative strategy to influence the course of nature by supernatural ('occult') means. 'Supernatural means' involves an overlap with religion, 'manipulative (coercive or performative) strategy', as combined with the pursuit of concrete goals, refers rather to a difference from religion.

2. Sources Greek and Roman literature provides abundant examples of magical practice in both narrative and discursive texts. Myth affords many instances. Besides gods connected with magic (*Hermes and *Hecate), we hear of *Telchines, skilful but malignant smiths well versed in magic. The *Idaean Dactyls were masters of medical charms and music. Thracian *Orpheus was a famous magician, and so were *Musaeus, *Melampus, and others. But, as elsewhere, the female gender predominates. The most notorious witch was *Medea. Thessaly boasted an old tradition of witchcraft, the Thessalian witches being notorious for their specialism of 'drawing down the moon'.

The earliest literary examples come from *Homer. The witch *Circe uses potions, salves, and a magic wand to perform magical tricks and teaches *Odysseus how to summon the ghosts from the nether world. Folk magic glimmers through in a scene where an incantation stops the flow of blood from a wound. *Hesiod offers an aretalogy (*see* MIRACLES) of the goddess *Hecate. Tragedy contributes magical scenes (e.g. the calling up of the ghost of Darius in *Aeschylus' *Persians*, as well as whole plays (*Euripides' *Medea*), while comedy ridicules magicians (many examples in Aristophanes and Menander). Theocritus' Second Idyll, *Pharmakeutria* ('Drug- or Poisonmonger', hence 'Sorceress') became a model for many later witch scenes, describing the gruesome preparation of a love potion). Similarly, magical motifs in Greek epic tradition (e.g. *Apollonius Rhodius, *Argonautica*) were continued by Roman epic (*Virgil and Lucan). Exceptionally informative is *Apuleius' *Metamorphoses*, which contains many a picturesque magical scene.

Another illuminating work by Apuleius belongs to the sphere of critical reflection. His *Apologia* (*De magia*) is a defence against the charge of magic and provides a full discussion of various aspects of ancient magic. Other discussions can be found in the satirical works of e.g. *Theophrastus and Lucian. Although early philosophers like Heraclitus, *Pythagoras, *Empedocles, and Democritus were often associated with magical experiments, Greek philosophy generally rejected magic. *Plato wants the abuse of magic (*pharmakeia*) to be punished, and Sceptics, Epicureans (*see* EPICURUS), and Cynics never tired of contesting magic. The shift towards a more positive appreciation in late antiquity, in, for example, Hermetic writings (*see* HERMES TRISMEGISTUS), *Iamblichus, and *Proclus (*see* (1) above), was effected by a new cosmology, also apparent in new demonologies, in *prophecies, and *astrology.

3. Objectives As to the intended effects, a rough distinction can be made between harmful 'black' magic and innocent or beneficial 'white' magic, although the boundaries cannot be sharply drawn. For the category of black magic curse-tablets are the most conspicuous evidence (*see* CURSES). Numerous other forms of black magic were widely applied and feared: incantations; the use of drugs and poison (significantly *pharmakon* may refer to magic, poison, and medicine); the practice of 'sympathetic magic', for instance the use of 'voodoo dolls' melted in fire or pierced with needles; and 'contagious magic', the destruction of the victim's hair, nails, part of his cloak, or other possessions as 'part for all', with the aim of harming the victim himself.

Some of these practices can function in 'white' magic as well. Its main objectives are protection against any kind of mishap, the attraction of material or non-material benefits, and the healing of illness. The first two are above all pursued by the use of *amulets or phylacteries, the last by the application of all sorts of materia medica, often activated by charms and ritual (*see* (4) below); also by means of *purifications, exorcism, or divine healing.

Mixtures occur: love magic is generally pursued for the benefit of the lover, not for that of the beloved, who is sometimes bewitched in a very aggressive manner and by gruesome means. Other types of magic (e.g. prophecy) are more or less neutral, although uncanny aspects may render them suspect (e.g. nekyomancy or the consultation of spirits of the dead; *see* NEKYOMANTEION).

4. Techniques Magic is essentially based on secret knowledge of sources of power. The most important are (*a*) utterances, (*b*) material objects, and (*c*) performance.

(*a*) Utterances may consist of inarticulate sounds, cries, various types of noise (e.g. the use of bells), hissing, or whistling. More common are powerful words and formulae. One important category consists of strange, uncanny words not belonging to the Greek or Latin idiom: the 'Ephesian letters' (so called from their alleged origin in Ephesus), also referred to by terms such as *onomata asēma* ('meaningless names'), or *voces magicae* ('magical names/words'), whose (alleged) foreign origin and lack of normal communicable meaning were believed to enhance their magical power. Another category of effective words consists of Greek or Latin expressions in which the illness or the cure is compared with a model taken from myth or legend (esp. Homer, Virgil, the Bible) or nature. Stylistic and prosodic devices, such as metre, anaphora, repetition, and rhyme, add emphasis and efficacy to the formulae, as do other magical devices such as writing normal words from right to left or with foreign letters. A copious stock of magical formulae is provided by the so-called *Greek Magical Papyri*, a corpus of papyrus texts from Egypt that contain extended formulae with magical words and names of great gods and demons, including lists of vowels understood as names of archangels, who are invoked or even forced to assist the practitioner.

(b) There is practically no limit to the selection of magical ingredients: any object or material may have a magical force—iron, (precious) stones, pieces of wood, parts of animals, nails, hair, the blood of criminals. Most important are herbs and plants, where magic and folk medicine often coalesce in the wisdom of the root-cutter and herbalist. Drawings of foreign gods and demons may be added and, especially in black magic, 'voodoo dolls', sometimes transfixed with needles, could have a role.

(c) In the application of these objects and as independent magical acts, various performative actions play a part. The magical objects must be manipulated in a special way, various gestures are prescribed, etc.

These three technical aspects are often combined, exemplarily so in the famous cure of a fracture in Cato's *De Agricultura*: a knife is brandished and two pieces of reed are brought together over the fracture while a charm is sung: *motas vaeta daries dardares astataries dissunapiter* (untranslatable).

5. Social setting The social and legal standing of magic is basically ambivalent. (Secret) wisdom and expertise in the application of supernatural means was indispensable and widely resorted to, hence highly valued. Many official 'religious' rites, especially in Rome, contained 'magical' elements, which were accepted because and as long as they were publicly executed on behalf of the state. In the private sphere, however, magic's very secretiveness and association with asocial or even antisocial goals fostered suspicion and condemnation. Already in the 5th cent. BC, the author of *The Sacred Disease* made a clear distinction between religious and magical strategies and censured the latter. Plato (*see* (2) above) wanted the abuse of magic to be penalized in his ideal state; the Romans, as early as 450 BC, actually did so in the law code known as the Twelve Tables. Under the first emperors many laws were issued to repress the growth of magical practices, and the 4th cent. AD saw a renaissance of anti-magical legislation. In this period, however, magic was practically identified with *prava religio* ('bad religion') and **superstitio* ('superstition'), which, together, served as conveniently comprehensive (and vague) classificatory terms to discredit social, political, and/or religious opponents.

[Homer, *Odyssey* 10. 274 ff., 19. 457; Hesiod, *Theogony* 411–52; Aeschylus, *Persians* 619–842; Theocritus 2; Horace, *Epode* 5; Virgil, *Eclogue* 8, *Aeneid* 4. 494 ff.; Ovid, *Heroines* 6. 9; Apollonius Rhodius, *Argonautica*; Lucan, *Pharsalia* 6. 413–830; Apuleius, *Metamorphoses*, *Apologia*; Plato, *Laws* 933b; Cato, *On Agriculture* 160; [Hippocrates], *The Sacred Disease* 2. 12 f., 4. 36 ff.]

magistri We have to distinguish between (a) *magistri*, the presidents of various associations (*see* CLUBS), religious, funerary, and professional (*collegia*) or territorial, and (b) the boards of *magistri* (**collegia magistrorum*) who acted as supervisors of shrines, such as the *magistri* attested in Capua, **Delos, and Minturnae (mod. Minturno) in the last century of the republic. The cult of *Lares compitales* (*see* LARES) was in the late republic and under Augustus supervised by the *magistri* of *vici*. Also the state priesthoods of **quindecimviri, *fratres arvales, *Salii, Luperci (*see* LUPERCALIA) (and **haruspices) possessed as administrative officers the (normally) annually elected *magistri*. They also performed sacrifices, often assisted by **flamines*.

Magna Mater *See* CYBELE.

magus/magi (Gk. *magos*, Old Persian *ma-kuš*). Only Herodotus calls the magi a Median tribe. In the pre-Hellenistic Greek tradition they are reciters of **theogonies, explainers of **dreams, royal educators and advisers. Magi are experts in the oral tradition rather than a class of priests, although they partake in sacrifice. In the Persepolis administrative texts and in other cuneiform documents magi often occur without a religious context. The Avesta does not mention magi. In the later Greek tradition the term frequently refers to specialists in exotic wisdom, astrology, and sorcery. See MAGIC; PERSIAN RELIGION.

[Herodotus 1. 10, 132; Plato, *Alcibiades* 122a; Plutarch, *Artaxerxes* 3; Strabo 15. 1. 68, 3. 15]

Maia (1) daughter of *Atlas, and one of the Pleiades (*see* PLEIADES); her name means simply 'mother' or 'nurse', and she may once have been a goddess of the *kourotrophos* type; but apart from conceiving *Hermes with Zeus and bringing him to birth in a cave on Mt. Cyllene in Arcadia, she retains little independent identity. (2) Roman goddess associated with *Volcanus, to whom the *flamen Volcanalis* sacrificed on 1 May (*see* FLAMINES); yet the connection with the fire-god is puzzling, since her name appears to come from the root *mag*, and points to growth or increase; cf. the by-form Maiesta, and the month-name, appropriate to a season when all plants are growing. By a natural conflation with (1) she was associated with *Mercurius, and worshipped also on 15 May, the anniversary of his temple; apparently her title in this role was *invicta* (unconquered).

[(1) *Homeric Hymn to Hermes.* (2) Aulus Gellius, *Attic Nights* 13. 23. 2; Macrobius, *Saturnalia* 1. 12. 18]

makarismos, or 'calling blessed', is a useful term for expressions of the form 'Blessed is the mortal who has seen these rites' (*Homeric Hymn to Demeter* 480). As in that instance, where the reference is to the Eleusinian *mysteries (*see* ELEUSIS), such language is particularly commonly used in religious contexts (so also e.g. in *Euripides, *Bacchae* 72 ff., and on the Orphic 'gold plates'; *see* ORPHISM), and it is plausible that initiates in mystery cults were at a certain stage so acclaimed. But the religious use is only a specialization of a broader formula of congratulation, seen for instance in *Odysseus' complimentary words to the lovely Nausicaa in *Homer, *Odyssey* 6. 154: 'Thrice blessed are your father and lady mother.'

Mandulis, Hellenized (i.e. Greek) form of the name of the god Merul or Melul, whose cult was centred at Talmis in Nubia. The name is unknown in pharaonic Egypt, and his shrine at Talmis was built under the Ptolemies, with further work done under *Augustus and Vespasian. The temple attracted considerable attention in the Roman empire. The range of dated texts at the temple runs from the reign of Vespasian to AD 248/9. According to one of these texts, Mandulis revealed himself to be the 'Sun, the all-seeing master, king of all, all-powerful *Aion'.

manes, Roman spirits of the dead; probably a euphemism from old Latin *manus* ('good'). The singular form did not exist. (1) Originally, the dead were undifferentiated, with a collectivity expressed as *di* (gods) *manes*; Cicero quotes the ancient ordinance 'let there be holy laws of the dead'. Graves had the formulaic dedication *Dis Manibus Sacrum*, 'sacred to the *di manes'*. They were collectively worshipped at three festivals (*Feralia, *Parentalia, *Lemuria), individually on the dead person's birthday. From this come two derivatives: (a) the poets used *manes* topographically for 'realm of the dead': (b) *Manes* represents all Underworld gods. (2) Later in a special, still collective sense, *di manes* were identified with the *di parentes* ('family ancestors'). (3) *Manes* could represent an individual's *soul. This usage is first found in Cicero, then frequently in Augustan writers. In the empire it became customary on inscriptions to add to *Dis Manibus Sacrum* the name of the dead person in the genitive or dative.

Manetho (fl. 280 BC), Egyptian high priest at Heliopolis in the early Ptolemaic period, wrote a history of Egypt in three books (*Aigyptiaka*) from mythical times to 342. The human history was divided into 30 human dynasties (a 31st was added by a later hand), which still form the framework for ancient Egyptian chronology. The original, which contained serious errors and omissions, is lost and the fragments preserved in Christian and Jewish writers are frequently badly corrupted. Nevertheless, his importance in the preservation of Egyptian historical tradition is great, and his influence has been generally benign.

There also exist under the name of Manetho six books of didactic hexameters on *astrology entitled *Apotelesmatika* ('Forecasts'). Probably they were composed between the 2nd and 3rd cents. AD. The sole extant text transmits them in confused order: books 2, 3, and 6 are together a complete poem, and book 4 is another; books 1 and 5 are heterogeneous fragments. The author of the long poem gives his own horoscope (6. 738–50), from which it can be calculated that he was born in AD 80. By claiming knowledge of Egyptian sacred writings and addressing 'Ptolemy', the writer of book 5 seeks extra credibility by implying that he is the famous Manetho; and the whole collection came to be attributed to the same source. The poems are bald catalogues of the likely duties, characteristics, and sexual proclivities of those born under the various combinations and conjunctions of planets and star-signs. The writer of book 4 is notable for his many new compound nouns and adjectives; but in general these poets have little to recommend them.

Manichaeism, a developed form of *Gnosticism founded by the Syriac-speaking Babylonian Mani (AD 216–76). At first influenced by a baptismal Gnostic sect such as the Mandaeans (some of whose hymns the Manichees used), he left the sect at the age of 24, after two visions convinced him that he was a manifestation of the Holy Spirit promised by Jesus. After visiting India he returned to the Sasanid empire, where he enjoyed friendly relations with the Sasanian royal family and aristocracy including King Sapor I; but Mazdean opposition under Bahram I led to his execution. A systematic catechism (*Kephalaia*), preserved in Coptic, was edited in his name. His doctrine was a religion of redemption in which dualistic myth provided a rationale for an ascetic ethic. A precosmic invasion of the realm of light by the forces of darkness had resulted in the present intermingling of good and evil, the divine substance being imprisoned in matter. In Jesus the Son of God came to save his own soul, lost in Adam. The Elect, to whom all worldly occupations and possessions were forbidden, participated in redemption, and were destined for deliverance from transmigration. The community also included an inferior order of Hearers who by keeping simple moral rules could hope for rebirth as one of the Elect.

Proscribed in the Roman empire as a subversive foreign cult by Diocletian (whose edict is preserved) and later emperors, it was attacked by Neoplatonists (Alexander of Lycopolis c.300, Simplicius c.540; see NEO-PLATONISM) and by Christians (Hegemonius, Titus of Bostra, Serapion of Thmuis, *Ephraem Syrus, *Epiphanius, *Augustine). Nevertheless, and despite repeated suppression by imperial legislation, it spread rapidly in the west. Augustine, whose *Confessions* are a prime document of Manichaean influence in the Roman empire, was a Hearer for nine years. Eastwards, the advent of Islam drove it across central Asia to survive in China till the 14th cent. Important texts and paintings were found (1895–1912) at Turfan in Chinese Turkestan, and many Coptic papyri in Egypt in 1933. In the medieval west the legacy of Manichaeism passed to the Paulicians and Bogomils. Significant new material on the early religious experience of Mani, including his break with the baptismal sectarians and his first missionary journeys, is provided by the account of his life in Greek in the so-called Cologne Mani-Codex, published in 1970.

manifestation, divine See EPIPHANY.

Manilius (Marcus Manilius), Stoic author (*see* STOICISM) of the *Astronomica*, a didactic astrological poem whose composition spans *Augustus' final years and Tiberius' succession. The technical content is as follows. Book 1: an introductory theodical account of creation and an astronomy influenced by the Hellenistic poet Aratus; book 2: the characteristics, conjunctions, and twelvefold divisions (*dodecatemoria*) of the zodiacal signs, the relationship of cardinals and temples to different areas of human life; book 3: a different circular system of twelve lots (*sortes*) of human experience, its adjustment, the calculation of the horoscope at birth, length of life, tropic signs; book 4: zodiacal influences at birth, the tripartite division of signs into decans, the 360 zodiacal degrees and their influence, the partition of the world and its nations among the signs, ecliptic signs; book 5: the influence on character of extra-zodiacal constellations at their rising, a lacuna, stellar magnitudes. The proem to 5 demonstrates that Manilius settled for a five-book structure, though he may have abandoned an earlier plan for seven books to include a thorough treatment of planetary influences which can only have received about 200 lines in the lacuna at 5. 709 ff. Manilius' astrological sources are unclear. Egyptian, Hermetic, and Posidonian influences have been mooted (*see* HERMES TRISMEGISTUS; STOICISM), and some material only reappears in Arab astrological writings.

The *Astronomica* are no more a practical treatise than are *Virgil's Georgics. Religious philosophy and political ideology are the driving forces. A blistering attack on Lucretius' republican Epicurean poem (*see* EPICURUS) underlies the poet's passionate Stoic hymns to the mystical order governing the multiplicity and diversity of creation. *Astrology allows Manilius to link heavenly macrocosm with earthly and human microcosm and he claims the authority of a divinely inspired ascent to justify his vision. His hexameters are fine and his poetic range unusual. *See* ASTROLOGY; CONSTELLATIONS AND NAMED STARS.

Marcius, the alleged author of prophetic verses (*see* PROPHECIES) circulating at Rome in the 3rd cent. BC. In 213 BC, verses attributed to him predicting the disaster at Cannae were circulated at Rome, as were verses to the effect that Rome would only be rid of

the foreign enemy if it founded games in honour of *Apollo. A subsequent consultation of the Sibylline books (*see* SIBYL) confirmed this prediction, leading to the foundation of the Ludi Apollinares.

Subsequent ancient scholarship produced several tales about Marcius (and more than one Marcius). According to Livy, he (singular) was simply 'a famous prophet'. *Cicero mentions the brothers Marcius, 'famous prophets', in two places, and says that 'Marcius' wrote in verse; the elder Pliny says that Marcius was the most famous Roman to write in verse; while Ammianus Marcellinus refers to 'Marcius' as a quintessentially Roman prophet, on a par with *Amphiaraus. In late antiquity, Symmachus says that Marcius wrote his oracles on the bark of trees, and Servius that he took dictation from the Sibyl. The one point that seems certain is that the prophecies of Marcius were in Latin.

[Cicero, *On Divination* 1. 89, 115, 2; Livy 25. 12. 4–12; Pliny, *Natural History* 7. 33; Ammianus Marcellinus 14. 1. 7; Symmachus, *Epistles* 4. 34; Servius, Commentary on *Aeneid* 6. 72; Macrobius, *Saturnalia* 1. 17. 25]

Marcius, Ancus, the fourth king of Rome (traditionally 640–617 BC), reputedly established a settlement at Ostia (which archaeological investigation has not (yet) confirmed) and exploited the nearby salt-pans. He is also credited with the preceding conquest of Politorium, Tellenae, Ficana, and Medullia, but archaeological evidence refutes his alleged destruction of Ficana and Politorium (if Politorium is modern Castel di Decima). Roman tradition further fleshed out his anonymous reign with the institution of the fetial procedure (*see* FETIALES), annexation of the Janiculum, and construction of the Marcian aqueduct (certainly anachronistic) and Sublician bridge. Ennius characterized him as 'good' (*bonus*; often with the sense 'conservative'), but his supposed settlement of the *Aventine perhaps contributed to his alternative portrayal as a populist, reflected in *Virgil's Underworld pageant of heroes.

[Ennius, *Annales* 137 Skutsch; Virgil, *Aeneid* 6. 815 f.]

Marcus Aurelius, emperor AD 161–80. His leaning to philosophy, already manifest when he was 12, became the central feature of his life. Marcus is most famous for a work his subjects never saw, the intimate notebook in which he recorded (in Greek) his own reflections on human life and the ways of the gods, perhaps before retiring at night. The title *Meditations* is purely modern: 'to himself', found in our manuscripts, may not go back to the author, but is surely accurate. Internal evidence suggests that he was past his prime when he wrote, and that at least parts were composed during his lengthy campaigns against the German tribes. It seems to have survived almost by accident; it was unknown to the writers of his time and for long afterwards, but seems to have surfaced in the 4th cent. Although Marcus is called a Stoic, his *Meditations* are eclectic, with elements of Platonism and Epicureanism as well. In general the closest analogies for the thought are with *Epictetus, but Marcus is interested less in sustained exposition. The style, often eloquent and poetic, can also be compressed, obscure, and grammatically awkward. All of this is understandable if he was writing memoranda for his eyes alone.

Although divided by moderns into twelve 'books', the work seems not to have a clear structure. Brief epigrams are juxtaposed with quotations (usually of moral tags, occasionally of longer passages) and with more developed arguments on divine providence, the brevity of human life, the necessity for moral effort, and tolerance of his fellow human beings.

In the rest of the work, though technical discussion of Stoic doctrine is avoided, certain recurrent themes stand out: the need to avoid distractions and concentrate on making the correct moral choice; the obligation of individuals to work for the common good; the unity of mankind in a world-city; insistence on the providence of the gods, often combined with rejection of the Epicurean alternative that all is random movement of atoms. *See* STOICISM.

Mariccus, a Boian of humble stock who declared himself divine 'liberator of the provinces of Gaul', and attracted a large following, before being suppressed on the orders of Vitellius (AD 69). His activities reflect the uncertainty created by the fall of Nero, and indicate persisting popular hostility to Rome. However, his failure points up the absence of genuine Gallic nationalism soon evident in the collapse of the 'Gallic empire' of Iulius Classicus, Tutor, and Sabinus in 70.

Maron, in *Homer's *Odyssey* son of Euanthes and priest of *Apollo at Ismarus in Thrace (later to be called Maroneia). He gave *Odysseus the wine with which he made Polyphemus drunk (*see* CYCLOPES), along with other gifts of gold and silver, as thanks for protecting him and his family. According to the ancient commentaries on the *Odyssey* he was a grandson of *Dionysus; in *Euripides he is son of Dionysus.

[Homer, *Odyssey* 9. 197 ff.; Euripides, *Cyclops* 143–5]

marriage, sacred *Hieros gamos*, holy wedding, was a name given to a festival in Athens, but in modern times the phrase has been given a much wider meaning, and is often used to denote the presentation—conceptual, mythical, or ritual—of a solemn sexual union involving at least one divine partner. The clearest case of a sacred marriage is that of *Zeus and *Hera, marriage indeed being central to Hera's 'meaning'. Rituals which re-enact or allude in some way to this marriage seem to be attested in several parts of Greece: in Athens (the Theogamia or *hieros gamos*), at Cnossus, and possibly at Plataea in the curious festival called Daedala, which is explained as the fake marriage, interrupted by Hera, of Zeus with a log dressed as a bride and called Plataea. The great Hera sanctuaries of Argos (*see* ARGOS, CULTS AND MYTHS) and Samos (*see* HERAION) may also have celebrated a kind of sacred marriage. Although the description of Zeus and Hera's union in *Iliad* 14 (347–51), where the event is marked by rainfall and the growth of lush vegetation, has led scholars to interpret the scene as a marriage of Sky and Earth resulting in the fruitfulness of nature, it is likely that on the ritual level the divine marriage was concerned not so much with fertility as with the social aspects of human marriage, forming a legitimating model for the institution.

It is possible that the myth of the abduction of *Persephone and its related rituals should also be understood as a sacred marriage, one dramatizing the darker side of the bride's experience. Rather different, however, is the annual 'marriage' of *Dionysus with the (human) *basilinna*, the wife of the official called *basileus* or 'king', at the Athenian *Anthesteria. This is clearly a sacral act, perhaps sealing the relationship between the 'stranger' Dionysus and the Athenian people, but it seems not to be called *hieros gamos*.

marriage ceremonies

Greek Ceremonies were not identical all over Greece. For example, at Sparta they included a mock abduction. But they were shaped by largely similar perceptions about the ceremony and the deities concerned with it. Thus, *Artemis was concerned with the girl's transition to womanhood, *Hera, especially as Hera Teleia, with the institution of marriage, *Aphrodite with its erotic aspect. The evidence is more plentiful for Athens, where it includes images on vases, some of which (e.g. the *loutrophoroi*, 'water-carriers') were actually used in the wedding ceremony. What follows is centred on Athens. But the main elements were common to all; thus, the form of the preliminary *sacrifices and offerings may have varied from place to place, but such sacrifices and offerings were made everywhere. After a ritual bath, in water carried in *loutrophoroi* from a particular spring or river, in Athens Callirhoë, the bride and groom were dressed and (especially the bride) adorned. Then the banquet took place at the house of the bride's father, during

which (almost certainly) there took place also the rite of the Anakalypteria, the bride's unveiling in front of the groom, followed by gifts to the bride by the groom. Probably also during the banquet, a *pais amphithales* (boy with mother and father still living; *see* CHILDREN) carried a winnowing-basket full of bread and said, 'I escaped the bad, I found the better'. After the banquet, in the evening, a procession went from the bride's house to that of the groom, an important part of the ceremony, and a favourite image on vases with nuptial scenes. The couple went on foot or in a carriage, with the *parochos* (the groom's best friend). The bride's mother carried torches; the procession included the bride's attendants, musicians, and others who shouted *makarismoi* to the couple. The bride was incorporated in her husband's house through the rite of *katachysmata*, the same rite as that by which newly acquired slaves were received into the house: when she first entered the house she was led to the hearth where nuts, figs, and other dried fruit and sweetmeats were showered over her and the bridegroom. They then went to the bridal chamber to consummate the marriage while their friends sang epithalamia outside. On the day after they were sent gifts called *epaulia*.

Roman The favourite season was June. Usually on the previous day the bride put away her *toga praetexta*, the dress of childhood—she had come of age. Her dress and appearance were ritually prescribed: her hair was arranged in six locks, with woollen fillets, her dress was a straight white woven tunic fastened at the waist with a 'knot of Hercules', her veil was a great flame-coloured headscarf and her shoes were of the same colour. Friends and clients of both families gathered in the bride's father's house: the bridegroom arrived, words of consent were spoken, and the matron of honour (*pronuba*) performed the ceremony of linking bride's and bridegroom's right hands. This was followed by a *sacrifice (generally of a pig), and (in imperial times) the marriage contract (involving dowry) was signed. Then the guests raised the cry of *Feliciter!* ('Good Luck!'). There followed the wedding feast, usually at the expense of the bridegroom. The most important part of the ceremony then took place: the bride was escorted in procession to the bridegroom's house (*deductio*), closely accompanied by three young boys, whither the bridegroom had already gone to welcome her. The bridegroom carried her over the threshold to avert an ill-omened stumble; in the house she touched fire and water, was taken to the bedchamber and undressed by *univirae* (women who had known only one husband), and the bridegroom was admitted. Meanwhile an epithalamium might be sung. This is a generalized account of an upper-class wedding as it appears in literature. There could be many variations of detail and there could be different forms of marriage.

[Plutarch, *Roman Questions*, nos. 1, 2, 6, 7, 9, 29, 30, 31, 65, 85, 86, 87, 105, and 107]

Mars (*Mavors, Mamars*, Oscan *Mamers*, Etruscan *Maris*; reduplicated *Marmar*), next to *Jupiter the chief Italian god. Months were named after him at Rome (*Martius*, mod. Eng. March), *Alba Longa, Falerii, *Aricia, Tusculum, *Lavinium, and among many Italic peoples. At Rome his festivals came in March and October, with the exception of the first *Equirria (27 February). They were the *feriae Marti* on 1 March (old New Year's Day), second Equirria (14 March), *agonium Martiale* (17 March), *Quinquatrus (19 March; afterwards extended to five days and supposed to be a festival of *Minerva), and *Tubilustrium (23 March). All these may be reasonably explained, so far as their ritual is known, as preparations for the campaigning season, with performance of rites to benefit the horses (Equirria), trumpets (Tubilustrium), and other necessaries for the conduct of war. On 1, 9, and 23 March also, the *Salii, an ancient priesthood belonging to Jupiter, Mars, and *Quirinus, danced a sort of war-dance in armour of the fashion of the bronze age and sang their traditional hymn, addressed apparently to all the gods, not to these three only. This is intelligible as further preparation for war. In October the Equus October came on the Ides (15th). A *horse-race took place in the Campus Martius; the off horse of the winning team was sacrificed and his head contended for by the inhabitants of the via Sacra and the Suburra. On the 19th was the *Armilustrium, presumably the purification of the soldiers' arms before putting them away for the winter (*see* LUSTRATION). In this month again the Salii performed their dances ('moving their *ancilia*', the *ancilia* being archaic shields shaped like the figure 8). Before commencing a war the general shook the sacred spears of Mars in the Regia, saying 'Mars vigila', 'wake up, Mars'; it is most probable that these were the original embodiments of the god. His priest is the *flamen Martialis* (*see* FLAMINES) and his sacred animals the wolf and woodpecker (*see* PICUS). It is therefore not remarkable that he is usually considered a war-god and was equated with *Ares. Scholars have hesitated over the function of Mars. Often interpreted as a god of vegetation, Mars is now considered a war- and warrior-god, who exercised his wild function in various contexts, e.g. by his presence on the border of a city, a territory, a field, or a group of citizens. This border-line was materialized, before an action or a period of time, by a *lustration, i.e. a circumambulation of three victims—a boar, a ram, a bull (*suovetaurilia)—which were then sacrificed.

His mythology is almost entirely borrowed from Ares, the only exception being the comic tale of how he was deceived into marrying *Anna Perenna. Under *Augustus he obtained an important new title, Ultor, 'Avenger', in recognition of the victory over *Caesar's assassins.

[Ovid, *Fasti* 3. 89–95, 675 ff.]

Marsyas, a silenus or *satyr. He invented the *aulos* ('double-oboe') or found it, cast aside by *Athena because playing it distorted her face, and challenged *Apollo on his *kithara* ('lyre') to a competition. He lost and, suspended from a tree, was flayed alive by Apollo, suffering the proverbial punishment of being 'flayed for a (wine)skin (*askos*)'. The moment at which Marsyas catches sight of the abandoned *aulos* was captured in a much-copied bronze statue-group by Myron *c*.450 BC, which perhaps stood on the Acropolis, and Zeuxis *c*.400 BC painted a 'Marsyas Bound'. Vases from the later 5th cent. on depict the contest and the punishment. The 5th-cent. poet Melanippides wrote a dithyramb *Marsyas*, but there were no tragedies on the theme.

The sense of the contest is unclear. It has been thought to demean the Boeotian love of the *aulos* (appropriate around 450 BC), to reflect the sophistic love of *agōnes* ('competitions'), or to assert the cultural superiority of the *kithara* over the *aulos*.

The story was given a setting at Celaenae in southern Phrygia, a major road junction, where a local tributary of the Maeander was named the 'Marsyas' and the *askos* of Marsyas was displayed in the cave from which the river springs. This Marsyas later helped repel Gauls with water and flute-music. Beside Celaenae grew the new settlement of Apamea (Kibotos) whose coins in the imperial age alluded to the spring and flutes.

The myth needs a connection with an Apollo cult. The inventive Alexandrian scholar Ptolemaeus Chennus alleged that Marsyas was born on the day of an Apollo festival and that his flaying is an intriguing coincidence with the flaying of sacrificed animals on that day. Fluting and flaying are certainly part of *sacrifice.

[Apollodorus 1. 4. 2; Herodotus 5. 118, 7. 26. 3; Xenophon, *Anabasis* 1. 2. 8; Pausanias 10. 30. 9]

martyrs, Christian played an important role in the ideology of early *Christianity. The *Acts of the Martyrs*, inspired in part by Jewish resistance to Seleucid rule (*see* MARTYRS, JEWISH) memorialized and heroized some of those who died for their faith

in various persecutions (*see* CYPRIAN; DECIUS; DIOCLETIAN; MAXIMINUS; POLYCARP).

martyrs, Jewish The ideology of Jewish martyrdom goes back to the conflicts betweeen Jews in Jerusalem and *Antiochus (1) IV Epiphanes of Syria. The books of *Maccabees (*see* JEWISH-GREEK LITERATURE) and the book of Daniel (written now, but set in the Babylonian period) heroize such Jewish resistance. Those who fought Rome in the revolt of AD 66–70 and in the revolt led by *Bar Kokhba saw themselves as standing in this tradition.

martyrs, pagan *See* ACTS OF THE PAGAN MARTYRS.

Masada is a small isolated plateau 457 m. (1,499 ft.) high, on the western shore of the Dead Sea, and accessible from there only by the tortuous 'snake path'. *Herod the Great, having secured his family in its fortress during the Parthian invasion of 40 BC, later made it the most spectacular of his own fortress residences, with two ornate palaces, one built onto the northern rock terraces. Archaeology supplements *Josephus' detailed description of the architecture, revealing also a garrison-block, baths, storage rooms for quantities of food and weapons, cisterns, a surrounding wall, and (probably) a *synagogue. After the murder of their leader, Menahem, in Jerusalem early in the Jewish Revolt, *sicarii* (Jewish rebels) occupied Masada; and it was the last fortress to hold out after the fall of *Jerusalem, succumbing in AD 73 or 74 to a six-month siege by Flavius Silva. (*See* JEWS.) The eight Roman camps and circumvallation are visible, as well as the earth ramp which supported a platform for artillery. Josephus' graphic account of the mass suicide of the 960 defenders, with their leader, Eleazar ben Yair, after the breaching of the wall, supposedly based on the testimony of two women survivors, has aroused some scepticism. But the remains of the revolutionaries' years of occupation of the site are at any rate extensive. These include domestic and personal objects, as well as Greek papyri and biblical texts of the Qumran type.

[Josephus, *Jewish War* 7. 252–3, 275–406]

maschalismos, the practice, mentioned in tragedy, of cutting off the extremities of a murder victim and placing them under the corpse's armpits (*maschalai*). The ancient commentators invoke the wish to avoid *pollution, or explain the action as an attempt to incapacitate the corpse and prevent it from taking vengeance, but parallel practices elsewhere suggest that mutilation for the sake of ridicule may have been an equally prominent motive; certainly the references to its use on the dead *Agamemnon suggest it was a humiliation, the antithesis of proper burial rites. Compare also the mutilation of the living Melanthius in Homer's *Odyssey*. Whether the practice was common in real life we have no means of knowing.

[Homer, *Odyssey* 22. 474–7; Aeschylus, *Choephori* 439; Sophocles, *Electra* 445]

masks, as in many other pre-modern cultures, were used in Greece and Rome in cult and in dramatic representations. We have terracotta representations of grotesque masks worn in adolescent rites of passage in the cult of *Artemis Orthia in Sparta (*see* SPARTAN CULTS), and depictions of the wearing of animal masks in the cult of *Demeter and Despoina at *Lycosura in Arcadia (*see* ARCADIAN CULTS AND MYTHS). Masks were often worn in the cult of *Dionysus, and the masks of *satyrs and of Dionysus were sometimes not worn but at the centre of ritual action. Notable among the figures imagined in terms of a frightening mask is the *Gorgon. In Roman religion a notable use was of the *imagines, ancestral masks displayed in the atrium of a noble family and worn by the living at funerals (along with the mask of the deceased). Whereas the Greek word for mask (*prosōpon*) also means face, the Latin *persona* probably derives from the Etruscan *phersu*, a masked figure, who is depicted in a 6th-cent. BC tomb.

Greek drama probably inherited the mask from Dionysiac ritual, but there are obvious dramaturgical advantages in the use of masks, especially where the audience is (as often in ancient theatres) at some distance from the action. We have depictions of dramatic masks from the 5th cent. BC onwards, and a classification of dramatic masks by Iulius Pollux, written in the 2nd cent. AD but based on earlier Alexandrian scholarship. Numerous terracotta representations of theatrical masks have been discovered on the island of Lipari. Masks were used in all the major dramatic genres (although there is some evidence to the contrary for Plautus. A common material was linen, and they generally covered the whole head. On the whole the masks of tragedy (naturalistic in the Classical period) and New Comedy represented types rather than individuals.

[Pollux, *Onomasticon* 4. 133 ff.]

Matuta Mater, goddess of the dawn, sometimes assimilated to *Leucothea, had an ancient temple in the forum Boarium, beside that of *Fortuna. During her festival, the Matralia of 11 June, matrons made a *cake, expelled a slave from the temple, and recommended to the goddess the children of their sisters over their own. The meaning of the rituals and of the goddess's name has prompted a difference of views between G. Dumézil and H. J. Rose. Dumézil sees Matuta as a goddess of the dawn and has proposed an interpretation of the known elements of the Matralia based on comparison with Vedic mythology. Rose wanted to recognize a goddess of growth. Other interpretations base themselves on the assimilation to Leucothea (*see* INO-LEUCOTHEA). Matuta Mater also had a temple at Satricum in Latium.

[Lucretius 5. 656; Ovid, *Fasti* 6. 475]

Maximinus (Gaius Galerius Valerius Maximinus) originally named Daia, born in Illyricum *c.*AD 270, son of a sister of Galerius, was rapidly promoted in the army, and made Caesar when Galerius became Augustus (305). Charged with governing Syria and Egypt, he was resentful that Galerius made Licinius Augustus (308). Spurning the title *filius Augustorum* ('son of the Augusti'), he had his troops proclaim him Augustus; Galerius recognized this (309/10). On Galerius' death (311), as senior Augustus he seized Asia Minor while Licinius occupied Galerius' European territories; war with Licinius was averted, but to balance the latter's alliance with Constantine (*see* CONSTANTINE I) he drew closer to Maxentius. Learning of the latter's defeat, and that the senate had made Constantine senior Augustus, he crossed the Hellespont. Defeated by Licinius near Adrianople (30 April 313), he fled and committed suicide at Tarsus. Like Galerius, he was an ardent *pagan. In 306 and 308 he ordained that all in his dominions should sacrifice: city magistrates and census officials drew up lists and individuals were called on by name. From 307 he used the death penalty only rarely, but mutilated recusants and sent them to the mines; outside Egypt there were relatively few executions. When Galerius ended the persecution, Maximinus acquiesced but in autumn 311 recommenced. With little genuine support, he incited cities and provinces to petition against the Christians. 'Acts of Pilate' and confessions of ex-Christians to incest were published as propaganda. To revive paganism he organized the pagan priesthood hierarchically. The persecution was relaxed and then called off just before his defeat.

meals, sacred, either as part of a religious festival or functioning as religious festivals. The notion that a divinity is a participant in the meal with mortals distinguishes these meals from those in which acts of devotion are part of the standard ritual of dining because the act of devotion is the occasion for the meal.

The notion that a divinity could share in a meal with mortals was common to many cultures in the ancient Mediterranean and near east (we are insufficiently informed about the cult practices of Celtic, Germanic, and indigenous African peoples to say anything about their beliefs in this regard). In some cases (banquets with the god *Sarapis,

for instance), invitations would be issued in the name of the divinity, e.g. 'Sarapis invites you to dine at his temple'; in other cases the invitation would be issued by a priest. *Homer may illustrate the ideology of these events when he specifically says that the gods could be seen eating with the Phaeacians. In all such cases, it is generally understood that a god would participate with humans at a sacrificial banquet. The underlying principle was that the divinity shared the sacrificial food with those who had offered the sacrifice. Under such circumstances a specific portion of the sacrificial meal that was thought to be appropriate to the divinity in question was set aside, burned, or otherwise disposed of (it might be buried in the case of *chthonian gods, or thrown into the sea in the case of maritime immortals). It was not uncommon for a place to be set at the table for the divinity, and for the divinity to be the titular master of the banquet: thus numerous references in the sources to such items as 'the table of *Zeus', the 'couch of Sarapis', or 'the meal of the gods'. In some ceremonies certain priests might themselves eat the god's food (e.g. the festival of the Iobacchi at Athens) where individuals ate the portion of the divinity whom they represented in the procession, and would thus be thought to partake directly of the divinity. This belief is most familiar in the Christian Eucharist.

The concept of the 'sacred meal' is of great importance in classical polytheism since it represented the direct involvement of the divinities in the life of a community and generated numerous associations of worshippers (*see* THIASOS) who celebrated their own meals with divinities for their own benefit, in addition to those meals held in conjunction with state cults. It is also symbolic of the essential connection between group dining and the concept of community in the ancient world. *See* SACRIFICE, GREEK and ROMAN; SANCTUARIES.

[Homer, *Iliad* 1. 423–4, *Odyssey* 1. 22–6, 7. 201–3]

Medea, in mythology, granddaughter of

*Helios, and daughter of Aeëtes, king of Colchian Aia (*see* COLCHIS), and his wife Eidyia; ancient writers frequently associate her name (perhaps rightly) with *mēdesthai*, 'to devise', and she became the archetypal example of the scheming, barbarian woman. Already in our earliest testimony, *Hesiod's *Theogony*, she is associated with the completion of *Jason (1)'s challenges in Aia in his quest for the golden fleece, and leaves Aia with him to live in Iolcus, but her mastery of drugs and potions, a skill she shares with her aunt *Circe, is not mentioned. This passage appears in a catalogue of goddesses who slept with mortal men, and Medea was clearly always conceived as a divine being. In one Archaic legend she married *Achilles in the Elysian Fields (*see* ELYSIUM) after the hero's death. In the best known account, that of *Pindar, *Pythian* 4 and *Apollonius Rhodius' *Argonautica*, Jason succeeds in gaining the golden fleece because Medea is made to fall in love with him and supplies him with a potion to protect him in the tasks Aeëtes sets him; she then charms the dragon which guarded the fleece so that Jason could steal it. In a story first attested for *Pherecydes (2) and *Sophocles, Medea protected the *Argonauts from the pursuit of the Colchians by killing her baby brother, Apsyrtus, and scattering his limbs either in the palace itself or at the later Tomis ('the cutting') on the Black Sea coast. Apollonius, however, makes Apsyrtus a young man, and Medea plots his murder by Jason on an Adriatic island. On their return to Iolcus, Medea rejuvenated Jason's aged father, Aeson, (first in the cyclic *Nostoi, see* EPIC CYCLE), and in some versions also Jason himself; as the instrument of Hera's revenge, she then punished *Pelias by persuading his daughters to cut him up and boil him so that he too could be rejuvenated. After this, Jason and Medea fled to Corinth (*see* CORINTHIAN CULTS AND MYTHS), the setting of *Euripides' famous *Medea* which, more than any other text, influenced later traditions about and iconographic representations of Medea. If Euripides did not actu-

ally invent Medea's deliberate killing of Jason's new bride and her own children to punish Jason for abandoning her, he certainly gave it fixed form; in earlier tradition Medea had sought to make her children immortal, and in the historical period they were the object of cult in Corinth (alluded to in Euripides). Her association with that city, attested in a complex variety of stories, goes back at least to the early Archaic period; in his epic *Corinthiaca*, Eumelus (*c*.700) made Aeëtes king first of Corinth and then of Colchis, and the Corinthians subsequently summoned Jason and Medea from Iolcus.

Medea fled from Corinth to Athens in a chariot of the Sun (*Helios) drawn, according to a tradition at least as old as the 4th cent. BC, by dragons; there she took shelter with King *Aegeus. When Aegeus' son, *Theseus, came to Athens from *Troezen, Medea recognized him and sought to remove a threat to her position by attempting to poison him or having him sent to fight the bull of *Marathon, or both; fragments of *Callimachus's *Hecale* refer to these stories.

In art, Medea first appears on an Etruscan vase of *c*.630 BC showing the cauldron of rejuvenation, with which she tricks the Peliads (i.e. daughters of *Pelias) on Attic vases from a century later, and on a Roman copy of a Classical relief, probably from the Altar of the Twelve Gods in the Athenian Agora. The slaughter of the children appears mainly on south Italian vases, also a painting by Timomachus, mid-1st cent. BC. From the later 5th cent., Medea usually wears eastern garb and carries potions. She appears in the capture of *Talos (1). Her snake-chariot is shown. She appears with Theseus. In Roman art, she appears particularly on *sarcophagi, contemplating the murder of her children.
[Hesiod, *Theogony* 992–1002; Pindar, *Pythian* 4; Euripides, *Medea*; Apollonius Rhodius, *Argonautica*]

medicine In the ancient world, medicine was never a profession in any strict modern sense; the vast amount of medical literature which survives from the pens of educated, philosophically literate men does not necessarily present a balanced view of the range and diversity of medical traditions, which seem to have competed on more or less equal terms. The pluralism of ancient medicine is very striking.

From earliest times, therapies might involve incantation (for example, to staunch the flood of blood from a wound sustained fighting a wild boar, in the Odyssey), or the use of analgesic drugs in the Iliad, or the magical herb *moly* to defend *Odysseus against *Circe's witchcraft, down to the use of *amulets and charms by the so-called 'purifiers' (*kathartai*; see PURIFICATION) and *magoi* (*see* MAGUS). In the absence of formal qualifications, anyone could offer medical services, and the early literary evidence for medical practice shows doctors working hard to distinguish their own ideas and treatments from those of their competitors. Some Hippocratic treatises, like *On the Sacred Disease*, indicate by their hostility the importance of medical services offered by 'rootcutters', drug-sellers, and purveyors of amulets, incantations, and charms.

Medicine with a more strictly religious base was also practised, for which shrines and temples to the god *Asclepius formed one important focus. Most of the detailed evidence we have for temple medicine comes from later writers and inscriptions; and it is not altogether clear when Asclepius, rather than his father Apollo, began to become the object of veneration. That the practice of temple medicine was widespread in the 5th and 4th cents. BC, however, seems clear from the extended parody in Aristophanes' *Plutus*. The most important temple was at *Epidaurus. Many inscriptions from here detail the practical help and advice that the faithful received from the god as they slept in the temple precincts (it was called *enkoimēsis*, Lat. *incubatio*, '*incubation'). All manner of problems were solved here, not all of them strictly medical—monuments erected by grateful patients record cures for lameness, baldness, infestations with worms, blindness, aphasia, and snakebite.

One case involves the god repairing a broken wine-cup brought to the temple by a worried slave. It is widely believed that the development of the cult of Asclepius at Epidaurus received a new impetus after the great plague at Athens.

Relations between temple medicine and the medicine of the Hippocratic corpus are difficult to determine. One later tradition has it that disciples of Hippocrates established a rival temple to Asclepius on Cos but there is considerable disagreement over the antiquity of the cult here; there was another at Tricca in Thessaly, and throughout antiquity the medical, magical, and religious seem to have coexisted in this context. In Greek and Roman temple sites, many stone and terracotta votive objects survive— models of affected parts of the body which the god was able to cure. Important later accounts of experiences of temple medicine are preserved in the *Sacred Orations* of Publius Aelius *Aristides (2nd cent. AD), and the importance of *dreams is shown by the *Onirocritica* of *Artemidorus of Daldis (2nd cent. AD). In many cases, it seems, diagnoses of physicians could be rejected in favour of those acquired through dreams.

See HEALING GODS.

[Homer, *Iliad* 11. 837–48, *Odyssey* 10. 203–347, 19. 452–8; Aristophanes, *Plutus* (*Wealth*) 653–744; Aelius Aristides, *Sacred Tales*; Artemidorus, *Oneirocritica* (*Dream Book*)]

Meditrinalia, Roman festival on 11 October, from *mederi* ('be healed'), that is to say, by tasting old and new *wine. The *Vinalia Priora (23 April) appropriately involved new wine; Meditrinalia probably 'healed' by mixing new wine with old.

[Varro, *On the Latin Language* 6. 21]

Medon, name of several mythological persons, the only one of importance being the herald in *Homer's *Odyssey*, who warns *Penelope of the suitors' plot against *Telemachus and is spared by *Odysseus.

[Homer, *Odyssey* 4. 677 ff., 22. 357 ff.]

Medusa *See* GORGO.

Mefitis, Italic goddess, protectress of fields and flocks and provider of water, associated with sulphurous vapours. Her sanctuaries were widespread in Italy, from Cremona in the north to the Esquiline in Rome, and to Rossano di Vaglio, in Lucanian territory, and Amsanctus, in the region of the Hirpini Samnites, in the south.

[Varro, On the Latin Language 5. 49; Tacitus, Histories 3. 33]

Meilichios, a cult epithet meaning roughly 'who can, but needs to, be propitiated'. The primary Meilichios was *Zeus. He was a god of individuals and of semi-familial groups more often than of cities, a frequent recipient of private dedications, and a giver of wealth. *Sacrifices to him were often of non-standard type (wineless *libations, victims burnt whole), and his festival at Athens, the *Diasia, was marked by 'a certain grimness'. He was sometimes associated in cult with the Eumenides (*Erinyes), and could be portrayed as a giant *snake. Moderns therefore categorize him as a '*chthonian' god, one threatening but powerful to confer benefits.

[Xenophon, Anabasis 7. 8. 1–6]

Melampus (1), mythical seer and ancestor of the Melampodids, Greece's most renowned family of seers. The young, unmarried seer Melampus won a bride for his brother Bias, and for himself a part of a kingdom with its kingship. The kernel of this myth belongs to the older strata of Greek mythology, as Melampus' knowledge of the language of snakes and woodworms demonstrates. But his kingship is almost certainly the invention of the Melampodids, who probably tried to strengthen their position by this myth. Melampus is also connected with girls' *initiation. He is the king's son who with a band of youths catches the daughters of *Proetus and cures them of madness. Melampus was worshipped in Arcadia (see ARCADIAN CULTS AND MYTHS), witness his Melampodeon and the personal name Melampodorus.

[Homer, Odyssey 11. 281–97, 15. 231–6]

Melampus (2) (3rd cent. BC), author of two extant works on *divination, On Divination by Palpitation and On Birthmarks.

Melanippus, one of the Theban champions who opposed the *Seven Against Thebes. Aeschylus tells us only that he was a descendant of the Spartoi and defended the Gate of *Proetus against Tydeus. But a fuller story, attested in Statius and *Apollodorus, and illustrated on 5th-cent. BC vases, must already have existed in epic. Here Melanippus wounds *Tydeus but is killed by him or by *Amphiaraus. Amphiaraus or *Capaneus brings the head of Melanippus to Tydeus, who sucks out the brains. *Athena, who had intended to give immortality to Tydeus, withholds the gift in disgust, and he dies.

Herodotus records that the 6th-cent. ruler Cleisthenes of Sicyon, being at war with Argos, brought an image of Melanippus from Thebes and transferred to him certain rites that the Sicyonians had previously paid to his enemy, the Argive *Adrastus.

The same name is borne by several other figures in myth and epic.

[Aeschylus, Seven against Thebes 407–16; Apollodorus 3. 6. 8; Statius, Thebaid 8. 716–66; Herodotus 5. 67]

Meleager, in mythology son of *Ares or of *Oeneus, king of the Aetolians of Calydon, and Althaea. He was the great hero of the Calydonian boar-hunt, the story of which is first found in Homer, told by *Phoenix (2) during the Embassy to *Achilles. Oeneus forgot to sacrifice to Artemis, and she, in anger, sent a great wild boar to ravage the country. Meleager gathered huntsmen and hounds from many cities and killed the boar. The goddess then stirred up strife between Aetolians and Curetes (here a tribe, not divinities) over the head and hide of the boar, and a violent battle ensued. From this point on, Homer seems to develop the traditional story in order to create a paradeigma (example) paralleling Achilles' situation, the better for Phoenix to persuade him back to battle. While Meleager fought, all went well for the Aetolians, but when he withdrew from battle (out of anger with his mother, who had cursed him for the 'slaying of a brother') the Curetes attacked their city more and more violently. Meleager was offered gifts and was entreated to return to battle by priests, his father, mother, and sisters; but he refused. Only when his wife Cleopatra entreated him did he go and fight, but then too late to receive the offered gifts. Elsewhere the fact of his death is mentioned, but not the manner of it. In other epic versions he is killed by Apollo.

In later legend the manner of his death changes. Shortly after his birth the Moirai (*see* FATE) had said that he would live until a brand then on the fire burned away. His mother extinguished the brand and kept it safe for many years until, after the boar-hunt, Meleager killed her two brothers, either accidentally, or in anger when, after he had given the hide of the boar to *Atalanta with whom he was in love, they took it away from her. At this Althaea threw the brand into the fire and Meleager died, whereupon she killed herself.

The hunt of the Calydonian boar was a popular subject in art from the 6th cent. BC.

[Homer, *Iliad* 9. 529 ff., 2. 642; Bacchylides 5. 93 ff.; Apollodorus 1. 8. 2–3; Ovid, *Metamorphoses* 8. 268 ff.; Pausanias 10. 31. 3]

Melicertes was flung by his mother Ino (*see* INO-LEUCOTHEA), when pursued by *Athamas, into the sea. A dolphin carried his body ashore; he received a new name, Palaemon, and the *Isthmian Games were instituted in his honour. His cult took place in *Poseidon's sanctuary and received new impetus in Roman times, when a temple and precinct were built under Hadrian; the temple is illustrated on coins of the period.

[Pausanias 1. 44. 7–8]

Melissa, Greek word for 'bee'. Like its Hebrew equivalent Deborah, this is occasionally found as a proper name, also as a title, especially of priestesses of *Demeter; of *Artemis; of Rhea, besides the Asianic cult of the Ephesian Artemis, whose regular symbol is a bee; that, however, her priest-

esses were called *melissai* is not quite certain. One or two minor heroines of mythology are so named, the best known being the sister of *Amalthea; both were daughters of Melisseus king of Crete, who was the first to sacrifice to the gods. While her sister fed the infant *Zeus with milk, she provided honey for him, and was afterwards made the first priestess of the Great Mother, meaning presumably Rhea. Columella mentions a 'very beautiful woman Melissa whom Jupiter turned into a bee', generally taken to refer to the same story. *See* HONEY.

[Columella, *On Country Matters* 9. 2. 3; Lactantius, *Divinae Institutiones* 1. 22]

Melito (d. *c*.AD 190), bishop of Sardis, addressed a defence of Christianity to *Marcus Aurelius (only fragments extant), in which he sees Christ's birth as providentially coinciding with Augustus' establishment of the Roman peace. A sermon on the Eucharist (preserved in three Greek papyri, a Coptic papyrus, some Syriac fragments, a Georgian version, and a Latin epitome), is both an early essay in typology and a rhetorical exercise.

Memnon, a mythical king of *Ethiopia, was the son of *Eos and Tithonus. He went with a large force to Troy to assist *Priam, his uncle; and there, wearing armour made by *Hephaestus, he killed many Greeks including *Antilochus, the son of *Nestor, who died saving his father's life. Finally he fought with *Achilles while the two mothers, Eos and *Thetis, pleaded with *Zeus for their sons' lives. Memnon was killed, and Eos asked Zeus to show him some special honour. Either he was made immortal (*Aethiopis*; *see* EPIC CYCLE), or Zeus turned the smoke from his funeral pyre into birds, which circled the pyre and then, separating into two groups, fought and killed each other, falling into the flames as offerings to the hero. After this, fresh flocks of birds, named Memnonides, gathered annually at Memnon's tomb, and fought again and died again. The dew was said to be the tears shed by Eos in grief for her son.

Many ancient writers connect Memnon with Susa. On his march to Troy, he was said to have left several great plaques along his route, and Herodotus notes that this has caused him to be confused with Sesostris. He also has unmistakable connections with Egypt: there was a Memnoneion at both Egyptian Thebes and Egyptian Abydos, a little to the north of Thebes; and the 'Colossi of Memnon' were huge statues inscribed with the name of Amenophis III, which, when the first rays of the dawn struck it, was said to emit a musical note, as though it were Memnon greeting his mother's light.

Memnon's final combat with Achilles and his body carried away by Eos were favourite themes in Archaic and Classical vase-painting. He is given regular heroic features, but often has black African attendants.

[Hesiod, *Theogony* 984–5; Homer, *Odyssey* 4. 187 f.; Pindar, *Pythian* 6. 28–42; Ovid, *Metamorphoses* 13. 576–622; Pausanias 1. 42. 3, 10. 31. 7; Herodotus 2. 106]

Mēn (Gk. *Mēn*, also *Meis*), one of the most important gods of west Anatolia (*see* ANATOLIAN DEITIES). Etymology uncertain, but the name must derive from a native language. From its home territory of Mysia Abbaitis and west Phrygia (*see* PHRYGIA, RELIGION OF), the cult spread south and east to Pisidia and Lycaonia, and down the Hermus valley. The earliest iconography was formed in Attica (*see* ATTIC CULTS AND MYTHS), where a few dedications by metics ('resident aliens') from the 4th–3rd cent. BC survive. Almost all the other evidence is Anatolian, from the Principate (no significant literary evidence). The *c.*370 surviving inscriptions suggest a high god (*Tyannnos*, *Ouranios* (heavenly), *Megas* (great)) invoked to obtain healing, safety, and prosperity, confirmed by the iconography of Mēn riding a horse, or carrying spear or sceptre. His most characteristic sign is the crescent moon, either alone or behind his shoulders; as moon-god, Mēn was linked with the Underworld, agricultural fertility, and the protection of tombs. The cult was highly local: Mēn almost always bears a native local epithet, and sometimes the name of the local cult-founder too.

Different aspects of the god seem to be stressed in each area. There were several large temple-estates with tied villages.

A quarter of the epigraphic evidence comes from the temple of Mēn Ascaenus near Antioch in Pisidia, revealing the gradual assimilation of the Roman military colonists into local religious life. Many of these votives 'testify' to the god's intervention. Mēn is also the god whose power is most commonly written up in the 'confession texts' of Maeonia (border of Lydia/Mysia). Typically they recount how the dedicant was punished with misfortune after committing an offence against the god (e.g. impurity) or a neighbour (especially theft). (*See* SIN.) These steles are important evidence for the symbolic role of inscriptions (*see* EPIGRAPHY).

Mendes, a he-goat often represented on Egyptian monuments as a ram and identified by Herodotus as the Greek god *Pan, was the god of Mendes (mod. Djedet) in the north-east Delta where a cemetery of sacred rams has been uncovered. The cult was widespread in Hellenistic Egypt. An important hieroglyphic inscription, the Mendes Stele, from 270 BC records the divinization and entry into the Mendes temple of Arsinoë II as a full Egyptian goddess (*see* RULER-CULT); local taxes financed the cult. By decree her worship was thus joined to that of the chief god of each temple throughout Egypt.

Menelaion, the Laconian shrine of *Menelaus and *Helen at ancient Therapne; from *c.*700 BC it occupied a commanding position on a spur high above the Eurotas, 2.5 km. (1½ mi.) south-east of Sparta. A high rectangular terrace reached by a ramp, and retained by massive rectangular conglomerate ashlars, surrounded a *naiskos* ('small temple') built on a conspicuous knoll. Excavations (1900, 1909–10, 1973–7) recovered dedications for Helen and for Menelaus. The site survived until the 1st cent. BC. There was an extensive bronze age settlement on the spur. Though occupied in early and middle Helladic times, its ascendancy was in the 15th cent., when an embryonic Mycenaean palace was built, the earliest of its kind on the Greek mainland. The 'palace' was demolished and rebuilt on a new axis soon after its completion. 'Palace' and size of settlement combine to suggest that here, and not at the Palaeopyrghi site by the Vaphio tholos 5.5 km. (3½ mi.) south-south-east, was the Mycenaean centre of the upper Eurotas valley. Parts of the site were burnt c.1200 BC; it was abandoned shortly afterwards. Doubtless its significance was understood by the later builders of the Menelaion. See SPARTAN CULTS.

[Herodotus 6. 61; Isocrates 10. 63; Polybius 5. 18. 21; Pausanias 3. 19. 9]

Menelaus, younger brother of *Agamemnon and husband of *Helen; king of Sparta (though *Aeschylus makes him share his brother's palace at Argos.). The abduction of his wife by *Paris caused the Trojan War. In *Homer's *Iliad* he is sometimes effective in battle (notably in book 17, where most of the other Greek leaders are absent), and he defeats Paris in a duel. He is consistently portrayed, however, as a (relatively) 'gentle warrior', inferior to the best fighters but honourable and courageous (in book 6 he wishes to spare the Trojan Adrestus until overruled by Agamemnon, and in book 7 he volunteers for a hopeless duel with the far stronger *Hector). In *Odyssey* book 4 he is seen at Sparta as a wealthy and hospitable king and recounts his adventures on his way home from Troy. These include his visit to Egypt and his encounter with *Proteus, who prophesied that instead of dying he would finally be translated to *Elysium.

In tragedy his character deteriorates, like that of Helen. In *Euripides' *Trojan Women* he is a weak man, who clearly lacks the resolve to kill his guilty wife, while in *Sophocles' *Aias* and Euripides' *Andromache* and *Orestes* he shows varying degrees of unpleasantness. He is a sympathetic character, however, in Euripides' more light-hearted *Helen*. Herodotus, surprisingly, makes him sacrifice two Egyptian children.

He shared a tomb and cult with Helen at Therapne near Sparta (*see* MENELAION).

[Homer, *Iliad* 3. 340–82, 6. 37–65, 7. 94–122, 17. 588; *Odyssey* 3. 276–302, 4. 561–9, 15. 56–181; Herodotus 2. 119; Apollodorus 3. 10. 8–11. 2, *Epitome* 2. 15, 3. 9, 3. 28, 5. 21–2, 6. 1, 6. 29]

Menestheus, leader or joint leader of the Athenian forces at Troy in the account in *Homer's *Iliad*. He is remarkable for his lack of prominence in the story, and in later Athenian accounts is at least partially eclipsed by the sons of *Theseus (*see* ACAMAS; DEMOPHON (1)).

Menippe, in mythology, (1) a daughter of *Nereus. (2) Mother of *Orpheus. (3) Daughter of *Orion, who killed herself to fulfil an *oracle of *Apollo and avert a famine.

[(1) Hesiod, *Theogony* 260. (3) Ovid, *Metamorphoses* 13. 685–704]

Menoeceus, in mythology, (1), descendant of *Echion (1), one of the *Spartoi, and father of *Creon (1) and Iocasta. His charioteer Perieres killed the *Minyan king *Clymenus (2b) thus starting the war between Orchomenus and Thebes (*see* THEBES, MYTHS OF), which ended with the defeat of the former by *Heracles and the Thebans. (2) Son of *Creon (1), who sacrificed himself that Thebes might survive the assault of the Seven; *see* SEVEN AGAINST THEBES.

[(1) Sophocles, *King Oedipus* 69–70; Apollodorus 2. 4. 11. (2) Euripides, *Phoenicians* 905–1018, 1090–2]

Menoetius, son of Actor and Aegina, and one of the *Argonauts. He was father of *Patroclus, and lived at Opoeis in Locris; but, when Patroclus accidentally killed a comrade in a dice game, Menoetius brought him to *Peleus' house in Phthia to grow up with *Achilles.

[Homer, *Iliad* 23. 84–90]

Mens, personified Roman deity of good counsel (*gnōmē* or *euboulia* in Greek), whose temple on the Capitoline (*see* CAPITOL) was vowed after the disastrous defeat at Trasimene (217 BC) and dedicated in 215. It was restored by Marcus Aemilius Scaurus at a time (after 115 BC) of popularist criticism, when senatorial good counsel was in need of some advertisement. More generally, the cult of Mens Bona was popular in the imperial period among slaves and freedmen.

menstruation In contrast with many religious systems, among the Greeks and Romans relatively little emphasis seems to be laid on menstruation as an impurity (*see* POLLUTION) or religious barrier.

Ritual laws including prohibitions on contact with menstruation as well as death, *childbirth, and intercourse are known from the Hellenistic era. Yet not all officiating priestesses were of an age before menarche or after menopause.

There is some evidence for belief in the special properties of menstrual blood. In a passage which may be a later interpolation, *Aristotle describes the clouding effect on a mirror of the gaze of a menstruating woman. Some Roman writers attributed further magical powers, not all negative; Pliny passes on the belief that it increases agricultural fertility and can cure a number of diseases.

Mommsen's suggestion that the use of *rhakos* in the inventories of Artemis Brauronia should be interpreted as a dedication of menstrual rags after menarche is erroneous (*see* BRAURON); this probably indicates only that the condition of dedicated garments had deteriorated.

Menthe or Minthe, i.e. spearmint or green mint (*Mentha viridis*). She was *Hades' mistress (a Naiad (*see* NYMPHS), daughter of *Peitho, according to one late source). *Persephone trampled her underfoot, and she was transformed into the plant named after her, which smells sweeter when trodden upon.

[Strabo, 8. 3. 14; Ovid, *Metamorphoses* 10. 729–30]

Mentor, in mythology, an old Ithacan (*see* ITHACA), friend of *Odysseus, who left his household in his charge. At several points in the Odyssey, *Athena takes his shape to help *Telemachus.

[Homer, *Odyssey* 2. 225 ff., 401; 24. 548]

Mercurius (Mercury), patron god of circulation, known as well in Campania (at Capua and in the *Falernus ager* and Etruria (the Etruscan deity Turms, *see* ETRUSCAN RELIGION). According to ancient tradition, in 495 BC Mercury received an official temple on the south-west slope of the *Aventine, its anniversary falling on 15 May. He was foreign in origin in the view of some scholars (Latte), but others see him as an Italic and Roman deity (Dumézil, Radke). On any view his cult was old, and it had close links with shopkeepers and transporters of goods, notably grain; also, at the *lectisternium* of 399 BC he was associated with *Neptunus, and, at that of 217 BC, with *Ceres. But his function was not simply the protection of businessmen or 'the divine power inherent in *merx* [merchandise]'. If all the evidence for his cult is taken together, he emerges, like the Greek *Hermes, as the patron god of circulation, the movement of goods, people, and words and their roles. Mediator between gods and mortals, between the dead and the living, and always in motion, Mercury is also a deceiver, since he moves on the boundaries and in the intervening space; he is patron of the shopkeeper as much as the trader, the traveller as well as the brigand. Hence it is not astonishing that Horace, with a certain malice, assigns to *Augustus the traits of this ambiguous mediator.

[Ovid, *Fasti*. 5. 681–90; Horace, *Odes* 1. 2. 41 ff.]

Merope, in mythology, (1) a Pleiad (*see* CONSTELLATIONS AND NAMED STARS), wife of *Sisyphus; she is the nearly invisible star of the group, for she hides her face for shame at having married a mortal, while all her sisters mated with gods. (2) Wife of Cresphontes king of Messenia; *see* AEPYTUS. (3) Wife of *Polybus (1) of Corinth, Oedipus' foster-father; *see* OEDIPUS. (4) Daughter of Oenopion; *see* ORION.

[(1) Apollodorus 1. 9. 3; Hyginus, *Fables* 192. 5 (3) Sophocles, *King Oedipus* 775 (4) Apollodorus 1. 4. 3]

Messapus, (1) eponym (*see* EPONYMOI) of Messapia in southern Italy. (2) In Virgil,

Etruscan ally of *Turnus, son of *Neptunus. *Virgil innovates in his parentage, and probably takes his name from (1). The earlier poet Ennius claimed descent from him.

[(1) Strabo 9. 2. 13 (2) Virgil, *Aeneid* 7. 691–705]

Messenian cults and myths Since the Messenians were subject to Sparta from the Third Messenian War to the refoundation of Messenia as a state in 370/69 BC, little is known of their traditions in the early period. There are few excavated sanctuaries (e.g. Pharae, Corone), and most of the evidence is from Hellenistic times or even, in the case of *Pausanias and of imperial coins, from the age of the Antonines or the Severi.

Among the older cults, we can pick out that of *Zeus Ithomatas (i.e. of Ithome) at Messene, which was already important during the Messenian Wars. On the Laconian border and common to both territories was the sanctuary of Artemis Limnatis at Kombothekra, whose origins date back to legendary times. Archaeology has made known to us the temples of Apollo Corythus near Corone, and of the *river-god Pamisus, near Thuria. And the cult of Hagna and *Demeter at Andania, best known for a cult ordinance of 92/1 BC (*see* EPIGRAPHY) may also go back to an early period.

Other cult figures seem to belong to the period of Spartan domination, like the *Dioscuri at Messene, or *Apollo Carneius (*see* CARNEA). But most of the gods are represented: at Messene, Pausanias mentions *Zeus *Soter (linked with the 4th-cent. foundation of the city), *Poseidon and *Aphrodite, *Artemis Laphria (whose epithet comes from Naupactus in western Locris), *Eileithyia, the *Curetes, Demeter, *Asclepius, *Sarapis, and *Isis, while inscriptions give in addition Artemis Oupesia, the imperial cult, etc. In addition, excavations at the Asclepieum (formerly thought to be the civic agora) have revealed a temple and cult-room of Artemis Orthia overseen by a sacred council of 'elders of Oupesia', (an alternative name for the goddess) and the Sebasteum

or chamber for the Roman imperial cult. Elsewhere in Messenia, we can point to Athena as city-goddess at Corone and Thuria, and Aphrodite as 'Syrian Goddess' (*see* ATARGATIS) at Thuria. *Hero-cult is also found (the semi-mythical Aristomenes (below), the heroine Messene). The chief characteristic of Messenian myths is an evident wish to confer antiquity on cults; hence local legends which place the births of Zeus and Asclepius in Messenia. Other myths, such as that of Caucon at Andania, are concerned with the establishment of cults, or with the central figure of Aristomenes, who in the tradition of the Second Messenian War symbolizes the Messenian wish for freedom. His saga, mixing epic elements from the Hellenistic poet Rhianus with themes of tragedy, was put together in order to create a glorious past as a foundation for Messenian identity.

[Pausanias 4]

Messiah, messianism *See* CHRISTIANITY; JUDAISM.

metamorphosis, a type of tale focusing on a miraculous transformation into a new shape. Tales of transformations of a divine or human being into an animal, plant, or inanimate object were very popular throughout antiquity. Already attested in *Homer, they were given a literary form later. Collections of these tales are known to have existed from the Hellenistic period onwards. Nicander of Colophon (2nd cent. BC) wrote *Heteroioumena* 'things made different', Parthenius of Nicaea (1st cent. BC) *Metamorphōseis*. These and similar collections are now lost except for a book of excerpts by *Antoninus Liberalis. They provided the model and material for *Ovid's *Metamorphoses*, recording some 250 transformations from the creation of the world to the reign of *Augustus. After Ovid the most famous literary metamorphosis is that in *Apuleius' *Metamorphoses* (2nd cent. AD), relating the transformation of Lucius into an ass and his final, miraculous, restoration to human shape by the goddess *Isis. Outside the realm of fiction, magicians (and gods) were generally believed to be able to change their own shapes and those of others.

Metanira, in mythology, wife of *Celeus, king of *Eleusis; she received *Demeter hospitably, but spoiled her plan to make Metanira's child immortal by screaming when she saw him laid on the fire; see DEMETER. She had a cult in Eleusis near the well where Demeter sat.

[Homeric Hymn to Demeter; Pausanias 1. 39. 2]

Methodius, according to (an unreliable) tradition, bishop of Olympus in Lycia and martyr (d. c.AD 311), author of the Greek treatises The Banquet, or On chastity modelled on *Plato), Aglaophon, or On the Resurrection (against *Origen; fragments), On the Freedom of the Will (against *Gnosticism; fragments), On the Life and the Reasonable Action (in Old Slavonic translation), and of several other writings.

Metis, intelligence personified. According to *Hesiod she was the wife of *Zeus, who swallowed her when she was pregnant, since he knew she would first bear *Athena and then another child, who would become ruler of the universe. She was also connected with the birth of *Hephaestus. The myth explains the close connection of Zeus and Athena with mētis.

[Hesiod, Theogony 886–900]

mētropolis ('mother-city') The 'mother-city' of a Greek colony (apoíkia) usually nominated the *founder (oikistēs), conducted rituals of *divination and departure, organized a body of settlers, and formulated the charter of their individual status. Customs, nomima, were to be those of the mother-city; they could include cults, *calendar, script, dialect, names and number of tribes (see PHYLAI) and other social divisions, titles of officeholders, and so on. Three salient facts of the civic identity of colonies seem to emerge, stressing the importance attached to the mētropolis: the identity of the mother-city, the date of foundation, and the name of the founder. The annual founder's cult in the colony probably commemorated, simultaneously, both the independence of the colony and its metropolitan, dependent origins. Taking sacred fire from the common hearth at the *prytaneion of the mother-city to light a new fire in the colony, a rite analogous both to marriage and military sacrifices, similarly stressed both continuity and new sovereignty. Kinship-links were both real and metaphorical: descendants could point out graves of ancestors in the mother-city, and citizens from colonies could participate in cults and sacrifices in the mētropolis, a right usually denied to strangers. Religion was often the only, albeit meaningful, expression of continuing relations. See ARCHĒGETĒS; FOUNDERS, CITY.

Mezentius, king of Caere in Etruria, whose aid was invoked by *Turnus against *Aeneas. According to the story, told in the Origins of Cato the Censor, Mezentius helped the Rutulians in exchange for the first-fruits of the vintage; the Latins (see LATINI) then promised their first-fruits to *Jupiter, who gave them victory, Mezentius himself being killed by *Ascanius in single combat. In the Aeneid of *Virgil, Mezentius appears as a bloodthirsty and impious tyrant, and is killed by Aeneas. Attempts to interpret the story as a reflection of historical events, such as the war between Veii and Rome, or a supposed Etruscan conquest of Latium in the 6th cent. BC are misguided. The story remains a legend, although an inscription on a 7th-cent. Etruscan vase from Caere attests to the presence there of a family of Mezentii in the Archaic age.

[Cato, Origins 1. 9–12; Virgil, Aeneid 7–10; Ovid, Fasti 4. 877–900]

Midas, legendary king of Phrygia, a comical figure famous in Greek tradition for his interview with Silenus (see SATYRS AND SILENS), his golden touch, and his ass's ears. Eager to learn the secret of life, the universe, and everything, he captured the wild nature-spirit Silenus by spiking the pool at which he drank—on the borders of Macedonia, according to Herodotus—with wine; the *daimōn* was brought before him bound (a scene attested in Greek art from *c*.560 BC) and revealed either the existence of a world beyond our own divided between the two races of the Blest and the Warriors, or the melancholy insight, which became proverbial, that the best thing for mankind was never to be born, otherwise to leave this world as soon as possible. Virgil's 6th *Eclogue* is a variant on this theme.

*Dionysus, grateful for Silenus' safe return to the wild, offered to grant the king any wish; Midas asked that everything he touched should turn to gold, but regretted his request when it became apparent that this made it impossible for him to eat or drink. The unwanted gift was washed off into the source of the Lydian river Pactolus, which thereafter carried gold dust down in its streams. A second divine encounter confirmed Midas' lack of judgement: invited to judge a musical contest between *Apollo and *Pan (or, according to Hyginus, *Marsyas), he preferred Pan, and was rewarded by the god with the ironical gift of donkey's ears. A turban hid his shame from all except his barber who, unable to contain the secret, told it to a hole in the ground; but reeds grew over the spot, and their wind-blown whispering propagates the unhappy truth for all time: 'Midas has ass's ears.'

Behind the character of legend there probably lies the historical king (of 'Mushki') whom the Assyrians knew as Mita; the eastern evidence is compatible with the traditional dates given for Midas by *Eusebius, 738–696/5 BC. The excavation of the largest of the tomb-mounds outside the Phrygian capital Gordium recovered a skeleton which may be his; it shows no sign of auricular abnormality.

[Herodotus 8. 138; Ovid, *Metamorphoses* 11. 90–193; Aelian, *Miscellany* 3. 18; Pseudo-Plutarch, *Consolation to Apollonius* 27]

midrash, a type of exegesis of scriptural texts practised by *Jews. The genre of midrash is characterized by the use of an explicit citation of, or clear allusions to, a passage in an authoritative text in order to provide a foundation for religious teachings often far removed from the plain meaning of the passage employed. In halakhic midrash such teachings comprise legal rulings. In aggadic midrash scriptural passages are exegeted for their own sake or for homiletic sermons. Midrashic techniques are found embedded in much post-biblical Jewish literature but they also engendered a large body of works devoted to this technique alone.

Midrashic exegesis is found already within the Hebrew Bible, where the books of Chronicles act as a midrash on the books of Samuel and Kings. Various types of midrash are attested in Jewish writings from the Hellenistic period, notably the *pesher*, found only among the *Dead Sea Scrolls, in which biblical texts are treated as complex codes from which the secret meaning has to be explicated, and the *Liber Antiquitatum Biblicarum*, attributed in the Renaissance to *Philon (1) of Alexandria but actually composed in Hebrew by an unknown Jew, probably in the 1st cent. AD. But most extant midrashim were produced and preserved by *rabbis from the 2nd cent. AD to the medieval period.

In rabbinic midrash, the rules of interpretation were eventually subjected to codification, but in earlier texts the authors were often creative, particularly in the use of exegesis to support legal views already reached for reasons independent of biblical support. Rabbinic midrashim reflect varied interests. On the whole, the halakhic midrashim are earlier (2nd and 3rd cents.), the aggadic midrashim are later (3rd to 6th cents., and on into the Middle Ages), but the distinction between these genres is not precise. All the midrashim contain teachings passed down from earlier generations (sometimes in oral form), and it is extremely difficult to give a date and place for the final redaction of many of the texts found in the medieval manuscripts.

The main extant halakhic (legal) midrashim from the Roman period are the *Mekhilta de Rabbi Ishmael* and the *Mekhilta de Rabbi Shimon bar Yohai* (both on Exodus), *Sifra* (on

Leviticus), and *Sifre* (on Numbers and Deuteronomy), all probably compiled in Palestine by the early 3rd cent. AD. Of the exegetical and homiletic midrashim, *Lamentations Rabbah* may have been redacted in the 4th cent., *Genesis Rabbah*, *Leviticus Rabbah*, and *Pesikta de Rab Kahana* in the 5th cent., all probably in Palestine. However, all these texts certainly include material from earlier generations and may contain insertions from later periods. *See* RABBIS; JUDAISM.

milk Although fresh milk was not very important in the Greek and Roman diet, it was used in religious ceremonies as a first-fruit offering (*see* APARCHĒ) and as a *libation. When used for these purposes, it was often considered a sign of an early or primitive origin for the rite in question, especially when the more commonly used *wine was absent.

Minerva (archaic *Menerva*), an Italian goddess of handicrafts, widely worshipped and regularly identified with *Athena. Altheim believed her actually to be Athena, borrowed early through Etruria (*see* ETRUSCAN RELIGION); but most scholars think her indigenous, and connect her name with the root of *meminisse* ('to remember') etc. At all events there is no trace of her cult in Rome before the introduction of the Capitoline Triad, where she appears with *Jupiter and *Juno in an Etruscan grouping. Apart from this she was worshipped in a (possibly) very ancient shrine on mons Caelius, which was called Minerva Capta by *Ovid, from the taking of Falerii in 241 BC. But it seems that this name was derived from a statue captured in Falerii and offered to the Caelian Minerva. A much more important cult lay 'outside the *pomerium' on the *Aventine; it was supposedly vowed in 263 or 262 BC. The Aventine Minerva was of Greek origin and was the headquarters of a guild of writers and actors during the Second Punic War (218–201 BC) and seems to have been generally the centre of organizations of skilled craftsmen. Minerva's worship spread at the expense of *Mars himself, the *Quinquatrus

coming to be considered her festival, apparently because it was the *natalis* ('anniversary') of her temple; it was also extended to five days, from a misunderstanding of the meaning ('fifth day after' a given date). 13 June was called the *Quinquatrus minusculae* ('Lesser Quinquatrus') and was the special feast-day of the professional flute-players (*tibicines*).

[Ovid, *Fasti* 3. 812, 835 ff., 6. 651 ff.]

Minoan and Mycenaean religion

Bronze age Cretan (Minoan) religion assumed what we may take to be its canonical form with the second palaces in the middle bronze age. From the latter half of the second millennium BC (late bronze age) the Mycenaeans appear to have been politically dominant in Crete and Greece and clearly took over some Minoan cult traditions, although as a whole their religious system seems to show as many differences as similarities. Both civilizations sprang from centralized urban theocratic societies along contemporary eastern models. The earliest evidence of communal religious activity in Crete derives from early bronze age tombs (3rd millennium BC), mainly the round *tholoi* of the Mesara, and from caves which had been used for habitation and burial since neolithic times. A probable cult complex at the Early Minoan II settlement of Myrtos consisted of a rectangular bench-type sanctuary with what may be the earliest female cult idol (Lady of Myrtos). The shrine may have been associated with an open area for cult, foreshadowing the central court of the later Minoan palace with shrines leading off from it. (Even after the palaces disappeared the arrangement of open space and adjoining shrines was retained.) At Cnossus the western side of the court opened onto a complex of sanctuaries. Pillar crypts there, and lustral basins in the Throne Room and elsewhere in the palace, perhaps recall the stalagmites and spring water basins of the natural cave shrines. The palace was one of the major foci of religious ritual, often containing several cult complexes; it seems likely that much activity there had in some way to do with cult. The other major types of cult-place, especially in the First Palace Period, were cave sanctuaries and peak sanctuaries, which are often thought to have functioned in relation to the palace or similar administrative centre. It is possible that this is reflected in topography: the cult cave at Amnisos and the mountain sanctuary on Juktas south of Cnossus looked directly at the palace, while the Kamares cave on the southern slope of Mt. Ida was also visible from, and aligned with, the palace of Phaestos. Visibility seems in general to have been an important criterion for the siting of peak sanctuaries. *See* CAVES, SACRED.

Minoan gems showed sacred enclosures in the open with one or more trees as central features. Like the related pillars and baetyls (sacred stones), these are likely to have been potent religious symbols rather than objects of cult themselves. Bull horns, aptly named 'horns of consecration' by A. Evans, indicated the sacred nature of what was placed between them. Sacred buildings were generally decorated with a pair or entire row of stylized horns. A cultic role may also be implicated in the famous bull-leaping games which took place in the central court of the palace. There is no unequivocal evidence of bull-cult, however, or of a bull-god, any more than of a snake- or bird-deity. Animals did however play an important part in Minoan religion. In a ritual context they could suggest a numinous presence, or they could symbolize divine powers of regeneration, chthonic and protective forces. The most important symbol was the double axe. In votive form it appears in caves like Arkalochori, in peak shrines (Juktas), in palace sanctuaries, standing between horns of consecration but also in tombs and engraved on pillars. Its meaning has been variously interpreted, but the Minoan religious context and later tradition suggest that the axe represented the instrument of sacrifice. Going a stage further in speculation, we might guess that it was both lethal weapon and symbol of new life arising from the blood of the sacrificial victim. Certainly it could be set up in the tomb or used at the ritual in honour of the dead, as on the Ayia Triada sarcophagus. Specialized cultic vessels like the so-called snake tubes to direct libations to the dead show a deep respect for the influence of chthonic powers.

Whether the Minoan world was acquainted with permanent anthropomorphic cult images, like those of contemporary near-eastern and later Greek societies, is not yet established with certainty. Even small iconic idols (e.g. the faience figurines of a goddess—or priestess?—holding *snakes from the Cnossian Temple Repositories) were relatively rare in the later palace period until the appearance in Late Minoan IIIB of what may be a new format of representing the goddess (see below). Homer and Linear B documents identify the name of the birth-goddess *Eileithyia in the Amnisos cave and the type of cult practised there. It is still debated whether Minoan religion, like the systems of the contemporary near east and of the Mycenaeans and later Greeks, was clearly polytheistic, or whether, as Evans was the first to suggest, essentially a single goddess, accompanied by a youthful male associate, was worshipped in different forms. To judge by the iconography, goddesses were more prominent than male deities. They could have been called on by an invocatory title such as Potnia ('Lady', 'Mistress'), *Ariadne ('Holy One'), *Europa ('Far Seeing'), or Pasiphae ('All Seeing'). Such names, surviving in tradition, suggest a close Homeric-type *parousia* or joint presence of worshippers and divinity who was expected to appear in direct *epiphany. This is borne out by the religious scenes in frescos and on gems. Minoan ritual shared some basic features with Greek practice in the manner of their *prayer, use of *altars, and burnt *sacrifice, in their elaborate processions with offerings of gifts, including spring flowers or even a peplos-type garment. Lively ceremonial dances celebrated the various stages of the annual cycle of nature. The seasonal renewal of crops, hope for new life from the death of the old, were primary motivating forces of Minoan religion. (*See* CRETAN CULTS AND MYTHS.)

Mycenaean religious life outside Crete first manifested itself in the Shaft Graves of Mycenae in the 16th cent. BC. Depictions of rituals on finds from the graves are identical with Minoan forms. It has been argued that the meaning of symbols had changed or been lost to Mycenaean perception. However, there are further traces of Minoan religious traditions on the mainland at Asine, Mt. Kynortion, while on Crete itself, apart from Cnossus, the rural sanctuary of Kato Symi may perhaps show a fusion of traditions. Here continuity of cult suggests that 'Minoans' and 'Mycenaeans' could have worshipped side by side in a place whose holiness endured into historical times, when it was dedicated to *Hermes and *Aphrodite. Comparable in some ways is the sanctuary at Ayia Irini on Ceos, laid out in the middle bronze age and continuing in use into Hellenistic times as a temple of *Dionysus. Bronze-Age clay statues of Minoan appearance were found here, but no trace of such typical Minoan ritual objects as double axes, horns of consecration, clay tubes, etc. Conversely, Mycenae itself has yielded ritual figures of 'apotropaic' appearance which have as yet no parallel from Minoan Crete. The characteristic Minoan cave and peak sanctuary, as well as the lustral basin, had no exact parallels on the mainland. The Mycenaean palace, which succeeded its Cretan model, may have confined its worship to the megaron. Open sanctuary areas were distinctive developments at the end of the bronze age. At Mycenae such a cult centre competed with the palace, but elsewhere modest bench-type shrines on their own and as part of hypaethral (roofless) precincts replaced the palace sanctuaries. This happened in Tiryns, for example, in the 'Unterburg', and in Crete in the *Piazzale dei Sacelli* at Ayia Triada. The format of the bench shrine proved popular until Hellenic times. Curiously in Crete cave sanctuaries enjoyed a renaissance at the end of the bronze age.

They, too, went on into Roman times and became places of Christian *pilgrimage. Modern Cretan chapels still show the birth of the infant Christ in a cave.

The Mycenaeans of the late bronze age showed a preference for anthropomorphic divine representation in apparent contrast with Minoan iconic forms. Some relatively large goddess figures survive from Mycenae, Tiryns, and Phylakopi on Melos, together with countless stylized figurines. A new cult assemblage at the end of the Bronze Age emphasized the growing importance of the god beside distinctive idols of the goddess with her arms upraised. He resembles the oriental Warrior God whose iconographic type spread west across the Aegean and provided the model for early Archaic sculptures of Zeus and Poseidon. The increasing prominence of male deities is reflected in Linear B, which was familiar with *Zeus, *Poseidon, Enyalius (*see* ARES), *Paean, Dionysus, Hermes, and probably *Ares. Other names of Olympians, beside the general *theos* ('god') and 'all the gods', are *Hera, *Artemis, *Athena, and perhaps *Demeter. These stand beside the invocatory titles Potnia, Wanassa ('Queen'), and Wanax ('Lord', 'King'), and beside other divine names which did not survive in later use. None can be safely identified from the iconography. But they probably reflect both Minoan and Mycenaean cult figures, although their status and function remain uncertain. The documents bear out the Homeric tradition (*Odyssey* 3) of Poseidon's pre-eminence at Pylos in *Nestor's time. At Cnossus Zeus has the greater prominence. His probable epithet of Dictaeus (*dikatajo diwe*(?)) reveals his link with the Minoan Divine Child who was born in the Psychro Cave on Mt. Dicte. But in Pylos he was already linked with Hera. Other theophoric names, as well as religious titles such as 'slave of the god' remain deeply obscure. But the many unknown elements in the script hint at the complexity of Aegean bronze age religion. Much of it continued into later Greece, notably features in the administration of cult, in ceremonial ritual, paraphernalia, and the characteristic festal calendar. However, given the many factors that influence the development of Greek religion, the precise ratio of old to new will never be known.

Minos (Gk. *Minōs*), legendary king of Crete who lived three generations before the Trojan War. The island's Bronze Age civilization has been named Minoan after him. He was a son of *Zeus and *Europa (daughter of Agenor, or of *Phoenix (1)) whom Zeus had carried to Crete from Tyre or Sidon in the shape of a bull. According to another tradition, which implies a prehistoric Dorian presence on Crete, he was the son of Asterius (Asterion) and descendant of Dorus. In a contest for the kingship Minos prayed to *Poseidon to send him a bull from the sea for sacrifice. The god complied, but the bull was so handsome that Minos kept it for himself. Poseidon therefore caused Minos' wife Pasiphae to fall in love with the bull, and from their unnatural union the Minotaur, half-man, half-bull, was born and kept in the *labyrinth built by *Daedalus. Labyrinth occurs in Linear B as *dapurito*, and has been connected with the double axe (*labrys*), a Minoan religious symbol, and with the palace of Cnossus. The myth probably conceals bronze age cult involving Zeus, the bull, and Minos, although the king was not divine.

Minos may have been a dynastic title rather than an individual: Diodorus distinguishes between two with that name over three generations. Minos was the most royal of mortal kings according to a fragment of *Hesiod, the favourite of Zeus who granted him kingship and renewed it every nine years in his cave on Mt. Ida. With his brother *Rhadamanthys he gave the first laws to mankind, and acted as judge of the living and the dead. Minos' reputation as first 'thalassocrat' (possessor of sea power) recalls Minoan influence in the bronze age. Attic legend called him cruel. He made war on Megara (*see* NISUS (1)) and Athens to avenge his son *Androgeus, and he forced the Athenians to send an annual tribute of seven young men and women to be sacrificed to the Minotaur until *Theseus slew the monster. Minos died violently in Sicily. He had followed the fugitive Daedalus to the court of Cocalus, king of Camicus, whose daughters scalded him to death in his bath. His companions built him a large tomb, but the bones were later returned to Crete in the reign of Theron of Acragas (d. 472 BC).

The Minotaur appears on Minoan neopalatial seals (once on the mainland at Midea) but without mythological context. The legend of the killing of the Minotaur by Theseus remained a popular subject in Greek painting from the Archaic period, but King Minos was rarely represented on his own in art, generally as judge of the dead. *See* MINOAN AND MYCENAEAN RELIGION.
[Homer, *Iliad* 13. 449, 14. 321; *Odyssey* 11. 568, 19. 179; Herodotus 1. 171. 3, 3. 122, 7. 170; Plato, *Laws* 624d; [Plato], *Minos* 318d; Diodorus Siculus 4. 60–79, 5. 78. 1; Apollodorus 3. 1, 3. 15, *Epitome* 1. 15; Plutarch, *Theseus* 15–19]

Minotaur *See* DAEDALUS; LABYRINTH; MINOS; THESEUS.

mint *See* MENTHE.

Minucius Felix (Marcus Minucius Felix), fl. AD 200–40, author of a dialogue in elegant, ironic Latin between a Christian, Octavius, and a *pagan, Caecilius Natalis of Cirta (perhaps identical with a Caecilius Natalis mentioned in Cirta inscriptions of *c*.210–17). The pagan case uses Marcus Cornelius Fronto's discourse against *Christianity. The Christian rejoinder uses Stoic matter (*see* STOICISM) from *Cicero and Seneca, and has a long-disputed relation to *Tertullian's *Apologeticum* which must be one of dependence. The target is philosophical scepticism which lacked the honesty to abandon polytheism. *See* APOLOGISTS, CHRISTIAN.

Minyans (*Minyai*), the descendants of *Minyas, a proto-Greek population-group believed in Classical times to have inhabited

Aegean lands in the heroic age (*see* DRYOPS; PELASGIANS), with centres at Boeotian Orchomenus and Iolcus. Western Peloponnesian communities of so-called Minyans existed in the lifetime of Herodotus (4. 148). In myth they appear outside the mainland mainly linked to the itinerary of the Minyan *Argonauts (Teos, Lemnos, Cyrene, etc.).

Archaeologists since Schliemann call 'Minyan' a grey, wheel-made pottery ubiquitous on the pre-Mycenaean mainland of Greece from *c*.1900 BC and once, but now no longer, thought to mark that phantom, 'the coming of the Greeks'.

Minyas, known almost entirely from legendary genealogies: the epic, *Minyad*, survives only in fragments, which tell us nothing about him. He was the *eponym of the *Minyans, who were based in Boeotian Orchomenus (the tholos-tomb there being called the Treasury of Minyas), with strong connections to parts of Thessaly, and others to the south-west Peloponnese: it was the Minyans of Iolcus who dispatched the *Argo*; the Minyan *Athamas reigned—according to varying traditions—at Orchomenus and at Halus; *Neleus of Pylos wed Chloris daughter of Amphion son of *Iasus, a former king of Orchomenus.

miracles Stories of the power of the gods were common throughout antiquity, many of them rooted in personal devotion, as appears, for instance, from votive inscriptions expressing gratitude for a miraculous recovery. A large group is linked with particular cults and cult places allegedly founded following miraculous deeds by the deity involved, who thus showed his/her divine power. Early instances can be found in the *Homeric *Hymns*, for example those to *Dionysus, *Demeter, and *Apollo. From the 4th cent. BC onwards there is a rapid increase in miracle-stories, and the connection with *epiphany receives ever more emphasis. Under the title *Epiphaneiai* collections of miracles abounded, the term *epiphaneia* signifying both the appearance and the

miraculous deeds of the god; *see* EPIPHANY. Among the epigraphic evidence the miracles performed by *Asclepius in Epidaurus (4th cent. BC) are particularly significant. Slightly earlier, literature reveals a new impetus in the *Bacchae* of *Euripides. Miracles (healing, punitive, and other) are now explicitly pictured as divine instruments to exact worship, obedience, and submission. In the same period the term *aretē*—literally the 'virtue' of a god—develops the meaning 'miracle', which entails the rise of so-called *aretalogiai*, aretalogies: quasi-liturgical enumerations of the qualities, achievements, and power (all could be referred to by the term *dynamis*) of a specific god. All these features abound in and after the Hellenistic period in the cults of great foreign gods, for instance *Sarapis and *Isis, and no less in Christian texts. The fierce competition between, and radical demand of devout submission to, these new gods fostered a propagandistic tendency to publicize the gods' miraculous deeds. 'Miracle proved deity' and as such it was often welcomed with the exclamation *heis ho theos* ('one/ unique is the god'), thus contributing to the shaping of 'henotheistic' religiosity, in which any one god of the pantheon may be taken as supreme at different times.

Mise, an obscure goddess, first mentioned in the writer of mimes Hero(n)das, where the name of the festival, *kathodos* ('descent'), suggests chthonian ritual (*see* CHTHONIAN GODS). The forty-second Orphic hymn (*see* ORPHIC LITERATURE) says she is bisexual and seems to identify her with both *Dionysus and *Demeter; she may well be Asianic.
[Hero(n)das 1. 56]

Mishnah, a collection of legal opinions which became the foundation document of rabbinic Judaism. Compiled in *c*.AD 200 in Palestine by the patriarch Judah ha-Nasi and his school, the Mishnah comprises the legal statements of the *tannaim*, i.e. *rabbis, and the sages they considered to be their forebears, from Hellenistic times to the early 3rd cent. AD. This material, expressed in a spare post-biblical Hebrew, is arranged in 63 tractates divided into six orders: *Zeraim* ('seeds'), dealing with agricultural matters; *Moed* ('set times'), on the observance of festivals; *Nashim* ('women'), primarily on relations between women and men; *Nezikin* ('damages'), on civil and criminal law; *Kodashim* ('holy things'), on sacrifices in the Jerusalem Temple; *Tohorot* ('purities'), on the transfer, avoidance, and removal of ritual pollution. The division into tractates was already more or less established by the 3rd cent., but their arrangement within each order varies in different manuscript traditions. Tractate *Abot* ('Fathers'), a collection of wisdom sayings by a range of rabbis included within the order *Nezikin*, belongs to a different literary genre from the rest of the Mishnah. It includes a few quotations by rabbis of the generation after Judah ha-Nasi, and may have been added to the Mishnah after its initial redaction.

Since the legal opinions expressed by the rabbis cited in the Mishnah frequently contradict each other explicitly, it is unlikely that the compilation was intended simply as a law code. On the other hand, the redactor imposed a clear literary structure on the material and did not simply collect earlier traditions. It may be best to view the work as a teaching manual.

The imprint of the editor is clear in all tractates despite the persistence of minor textual variants for several centuries after Judah ha-Nasi. Such variants are best explained by the oral transmission of the text within rabbinic academies by professional reciters who painstakingly committed it to memory (hence the name 'Mishnah', from the Hebrew root *shnh* ('repeat')). The date when the Mishnah was written down is uncertain. It may have been only after the compilation of the *Talmuds (i.e. *c.*AD 500), or even later.

According to later rabbinic tradition there existed already at the time of the redaction of the Mishnah compilations of rabbinic legal materials of which Judah ha-Nasi

made use. Of such non-Mishnaic collections from this period, only the Tosefta survives; it was compiled probably in *c.*AD 250 and has a literary form similar to the Mishnah. Other tannaitic material was preserved in early works of *midrash and as independent traditions (*beraitot*) in the Talmuds.

Since the Mishnah was not composed as a work of historiography, its use as a source for Jewish social, political, and religious history in the period before AD 70 is hazardous, but the text contains much information about the social history of Palestine in the 2nd cent. AD. The attribution of legal opinions in the Mishnah to particular rabbis is in general reliable, so that it is possible to reconstruct from the text the development of rabbinic law between AD 70 and 200. *See* RABBIS; JUDAISM.

Mithras, an ancient Indo-Iranian god adopted in the Roman empire as the principal deity of a mystery cult which flourished in the 2nd and 3rd cents. AD. Iranian Mithra was a god of compact (the literal meaning of his name), cattle-herding, and the dawn light, aspects of which survive (or were re-created) in his western manifestation, since Roman Mithras was a sun-god ('deus sol invictus Mithras', 'invincible sun god Mithras'), a 'bull-killer', and 'cattle-thief', and the saviour of the sworn brothers of his cult.

The cult is known primarily from its archaeological remains. Over 400 find-spots are recorded, many of them excavated meeting-places. These and the *c.*1,000 dedicatory inscriptions give a good idea of cult life and membership. Some 1,150 pieces of sculpture (and a few frescos) carry an extraordinarily rich sacred art, although the iconography remains frustratingly elusive in default of the explicatory sacred texts. Literary references to Mithras and Mithraism are as scarce as the material remains are abundant.

Mithraism was an organization of cells. Small autonomous groups of initiates, exclusively male, met for fellowship and worship in chambers of modest size and distinctive design which they called 'caves' ('Mithraea', like 'Mithraism' and 'Mithraist', are neologisms). A cave is an 'image of the universe', and according to *Porphyry the archetypal Mithraeum was designed and furnished as a kind of microcosmic model. Mithraea were sometimes sited in real *caves or set against rock-faces (e.g. at Jajce in Bosnia) or were made to imitate caves by vaulting or decoration or by sequestering them in dim interior or underground rooms (see the Barberini, San Clemente, and Santa Prisca Mithraea in Rome, those at Capua and Marino, and the many Mithraea of Ostia, among which the 'Seven Spheres' Mithraeum with its mosaic composition of zodiac and planets arguably exemplifies Porphyry's cosmic model). The Mithraeum is the antithesis of the classic temple, totally lacking in exterior decoration and space for solemn public ritual. The Mithraeum's most distinctive (and unvarying) feature is the pair of platforms flanking a central aisle. It was on these that the initiates reclined for a communal meal. Visual representations (see esp. the Santa Prisca frescoes and the relief from Konjic in Bosnia) show that this meal was the human counterpart of a divine banquet shared by Mithras and the sun-god (the latter appearing on the monuments as a separate being) on the hide of the bull killed by the former in his greatest exploit.

As is now known from the Santa Prisca frescos and the pavement of the Felicissimus Mithraeum in Ostia, initiates were ranked in a hierarchy of seven grades, each under the protection of one of the planets: Raven (Mercury), 'Nymphus' (Venus), Soldier (Mars), Lion (Jupiter), Persian (Moon), 'Heliodromus' (Sun), Father (Saturn). It is generally accepted that this was a lay hierarchy, not a professional priesthood. Mithraists, as their monuments attest, remained in and of the secular world. It is unlikely that the full hierarchy was represented in each Mithraeum, although probable that most were presided over by one or more Fathers. The disparate connotations of the various ranks, the two idiosyncratic coinages ('Heliodromus' and 'Nymphus'—the latter would mean, if anything, 'male bride'), and the unique planetary order all bespeak an unusually inventive and evocative construct.

Actual Mithraea or traces of the cult have been found in virtually every quarter of the Roman empire, though with two notable areas of concentration. The first was Rome itself and its port of Ostia. In Ostia, some 15 Mithraea have been discovered in the excavated area that comprises about half of the town's total. At Rome some 35 locations are known, and more will have existed, but individual Mithraea were small, and even if all were in service contemporaneously they would accommodate no more than 1 per cent of the population—scarcely the great rival to Christianity that inflated views of the cult have sometimes made it. The other area of concentration was the empire's European frontier from Britain to the mouth of the Danube. As inscriptions confirm, Mithraism's typical recruits were soldiers and minor functionaries, e.g. employees of the Danubian customs service headquartered at Poetovio (mod. Ptuj in Slovenia). Many were freedmen or slaves. Mithraism did not generally attract the upper classes (except as occasional patrons) until its final days as the rather artificial creature of the pagan aristocracy of 4th-cent. Rome. It was always better represented in the Latin west than the Greek east.

By the middle of the 2nd cent. AD the cult was well established. The routes of its diffusion and its earlier development are much debated, problems complicated by the question of transmission from Iran. Did the cult develop from and perpetuate a stream of Zoroastrianism, or was it essentially a western creation with 'Persian' trimmings? (*See* PERSIAN RELIGION; ZOROASTER.) There is no agreement, because there is so little evidence. Almost the only firm datum is *Plutarch's remark that the Cilician pirates suppressed by Pompey had secret initiatory rites (*teletai*) of Mithras which had endured to his own day. These may have been a prototype of the developed *mysteries.

The cult's theology and its sacred myth must be recovered, if at all, from the monuments. Principal among these is the icon of Mithras killing a bull, which was invariably set as a focal point at one end of the Mithraeum. Mithras is shown astride the bull, plunging a dagger into its flank. The victim's tail is metamorphosed into an ear of wheat. Mithras is accompanied by dog, snake, scorpion, and raven; also by two minor deities, dressed like him in 'Persian' attire and each carrying a torch (one raised, the other inverted), whose names, Cautes and Cautopates, are known from dedications. Above the scene, which is enacted in front of a cave, are images of *Sol and *Luna. This strange assemblage challenges interpretation. Clearly, the killing is an act of sacrifice, but to what end? It has been seen variously as an action which creates or ends the world (support for both can be adduced from Zoroastrian sources) or which in some sense 'saves' the world or at least the initiates within it. The line from Santa Prisca 'et nos servasti […] sanguine fuso' ('and who saved us with the shed blood') probably refers to the bull-killing Mithras as saviour, though one must beware of reading into this 'salvation' inappropriate Christian connotations.

The bull-killing has also been interpreted as an astrological allegory, the initial warrant for this being the remarkable correspondence, certainly not an an unintended coincidence, between elements in the composition and a group of constellations. But there is no consensus on the extent to which learned astrological doctrines should be imputed to the cult, let alone on their theological or soteriological function. One view is *astrology was central and that its function was to provide the specifics of a doctrine of the soul's celestial journey (descent to earth and ascent to heaven), initiation into which, Porphyry says, was the ritual enacted in Mithraea.

The bull-killing is but one episode, albeit the most important, in a cycle of Mithraic myth represented (frustratingly, in no set order) on the monuments. Other episodes are Mithras' birth from a rock, the hunt and capture of the bull, and the feast celebrated with Sol. The banquet scene is sometimes shown on the reverse of bull-killing reliefs, as salvific effect from salvific cause. There are fine examples in the Louvre (from Fiano Romano), Wiesbaden (from Heddernheim), and—still, one hopes—Sarajevo (from Konjic). See MYSTERIES.

[Plutarch, *Life of Pompey* 24; Porphyry, *On the Cave of the Nymphs* 6, 15–16, 17–18, 24–5, *On Abstinence from Animal Foods* 4. 16; Tertullian, *On the Soldier's Crown* 15; Origen, *Against Celsus* 6. 22]

Moliones, the twin sons of Molione and Actor, her mortal husband. In *Homer they are sons of *Poseidon (or they are born from a silver egg in early lyric). They were conjoined twins in a fragment of *Hesiod; in the *Iliad* they are named Cteatus and Eurytus, are married, and have sons. In Homer they fight *Nestor, elsewhere they fight *Heracles and are killed by him at Cleonae, where *Pausanias saw their tomb.

'Conjoined twins' appear on vases and brooches of the second half of the 8th and early 7th cents. BC, and according to *Pausanias on the 6th-cent. throne of *Amyclae. Their identification as the Moliones is disputed: they may rather be inseparable twins or sworn brothers.

[Homer, *Iliad* 2. 620–1, 11. 750–3; Apollodorus 2. 7. 2; Pausanias 2. 15. 1]

Molossus, son of *Neoptolemus (son of *Achilles) and the captive *Andromache, and eponymous ancestor (*see* EPONYMOI) of the Molossians in Epirus.

[Euripides, *Andromache* 1243–51]

Momos, fault-finding personified, a literary figure, hardly mythological (though he occurs in *Hesiod among the children of Night, *see* NYX) and quite divorced from cult. He advises *Zeus to foment the Trojan War (in the *Cypria*; *see* EPIC CYCLE). *Callimachus makes use of him as the mouthpiece of views which he opposes, while in Lucian he amusingly voices the author's satires on the conventional, popular Stoic, theology (*see* STOICISM), or otherwise makes fun of his fellow gods. He is a figure in a fable, also cited by Lucian.

[Hesiod, *Theogony* 214; Callimachus, *Hymn* 2. 113; Lucian, *Zeus Rants* 19 ff., *Nigrinus* 32, *Hermotimus* 20, *Vera Historia* (*True Histories*) 2. 3]

Mona (mod. Anglesey). As a centre of Druidism (*see* CELTIC RELIGION) it was attacked by Suetonius Paulinus (AD 60/1), who then withdrew to tackle the revolt of Boudicca. It was reduced by Gnaeus Iulius Agricola in 78/9. A collection of iron age metalwork from Llyn Cerrig Bach is probably associated with the cult.

monotheism Apart from the influence of developed *Judaism and *Christianity, no such thing as monotheism in the strict sense, i.e. the refusal to use the predicate 'god' of any but one being, existed in classical antiquity; even theistic philosophers, such as *Plato, *Aristotle, or the Stoics (*see* STOICISM), acknowledged the existence of subordinate deities (even if no more than planetary gods) beside the supreme one. Locally, it was usual enough to refer to one particular deity as 'the god' or 'the goddess', e.g. *Athena at Athens, *Apollo at *Delphi. But a further tendency towards monotheism may be detected, at any rate in Greek popular religion as interpreted by non-philosophical authors. This takes the form of the increasing supremacy of *Zeus. Even in *Homer he is much stronger than all the other gods put together; later authors tend to use 'Zeus', 'the gods', 'God' indiscriminately, e.g. *Hesiod, where within six lines the same act is ascribed, first to 'the gods', then to Zeus. To *Aeschylus Zeus is the supreme moral governor of the universe, though even there the existence of other gods is clearly recognized. Hellenistic writers favour vague phrases like *to theion*, *to daimonion*, 'the divine' (*see* DAIMON). In the philosophical tradition, especially that of Platonism, an attitude of virtual monotheism is taken up, though there the single organizing principle of the universe is very much an impersonal force. *See* ANGELS.

[Homer, *Iliad* 8. 18–27; Hesiod, *Works and Days* 42, 47; Aeschylus, *Agamemnon* 160 f.]

Montanism was a prophetic movement among Christians in Asia Minor. It emerged in Phrygia, probably c.AD 172 (according to *Eusebius, in year twelve of *Marcus Aurelius), since the conflicting evidence of *Epiphanius is otherwise unreliable. Montanus is a shadowy figure, and his sect owed its growth to the prophetesses Prisca and Maximilla, who proclaimed the approaching descent of the New Jerusalem near the Phrygian village of Pepuza. Their message seems to have been purely eschatological, with a strong emphasis on the glory of martyrdom, the attainment of ritual purity by rigorous fasts and penances, and freedom from the encumbrances of daily life. The movement was forcefully opposed throughout Asia Minor by bishops who denied the validity of prophecy through women or in *ecstasy. Yet, despite the failure of the original prophecies, it gained a firm hold in the country areas of Asia Minor, where an important series of Montanist inscriptions openly proclaiming the Christian beliefs of those commemorated have been found in the Tembris valley of northern Phrygia. Dating to 249–79 they are the earliest undisguisedly Christian inscriptions outside the Roman *catacombs. Montanism became an organized Church whose hierarchy included the ranks of patriarch and *koinōnos* ('companion' of Christ) as well as bishops, presbyters, and deacons. It persisted in Asia Minor until the 8th cent., but had a brilliant flowering in North Africa, where it won the allegiance of *Tertullian about 207. The martyrology of Perpetua and Felicitas is perhaps of Montanist origin. The sect had a great appeal for anyone who maintained a strong opposition between Christianity and the institutions of the world; hence, no doubt, its greater frequency in rural areas.

[Eusebius, *Church History* 5. 16 f.; Epiphanius, *Against Heresies* 48]

months *See* CALENDAR, GREEK and ROMAN.

moon *See* ASTROLOGY; CALENDAR, GREEK and ROMAN; LUNA; MENSTRUATION; PHOEBE; SELENE.

Mopsus, famous mythological seer, who is already the *Argonauts' seer in a papyrus fragment of Archaic epic. He is the son of Ampyx or Ampycus, comes from Titaresos (i.e. *Dodona), and dies on the journey, bitten by a serpent in Libya. Another tradition makes him the son of Manto, daughter of *Tiresias. This Mopsus founds the oracle of *Claros and then emigrates to Cilicia, where the city of Mopsuestia carries his name ('hearth of Mopsus'). Here he defeats *Calchas in a contest of *divination. As a Hittite inscription mentions a 'Muksus' and the 7th-cent. BC Luwian–Phoenician inscription at Karatepe the 'house of Mopsus', this Mopsus probably derives from Anatolia. But how does this fit with the name *mo-qo-so* in Linear B? Was there a family of seers called Mopsus?
[Apollonius Rhodius, *Argonautica* 4. 1502 ff.; Pausanias 7. 3. 2]

Mormo, a vicious female spirit (like *Empusa, *Gello, and *Lamia) used to frighten children, whose name is perhaps connected with Latin *formido* ('fear'). According to the ancient commentators, she was a queen of the *Laestrygones who lost her own children and so murders other children, or a Corinthian who ate her own children.

Morpheus, in Ovid a son of Sleep, who sends dream visions of human forms (Gk. *morphai*). Medieval and later authors use the name more generally for the god of *dreams or simply of sleep.
[Ovid, *Metamorphoses* 11. 633–8]

mountain cults Mountains as such were not worshipped in classical Greece or in Italy, but they were places of special cult, to the point that Mt. Maenalus in Arcadia was considered sacred to *Pan in its entirety. The location of a sanctuary was rarely the exact summit of the mountain (*Zeus Lycaeus on Mt. Lycaeon is an exception), but more often in the passes or on the slopes. The sanctuary could include a temple, as at *Bassae, or might be more rustic and simple (the cave at Phigalia, the Corycian cave above *Delphi; *see* CAVES). Worshippers were mainly shepherds, depicted on their votives. The deities most frequently worshipped were *Zeus, the weather-god, *Artemis, goddess of the animal world and of boundaries, *Hermes, a country god and patron of shepherds, *Apollo, another pastoral god, and Pan, the divine herdsman and hunter of small game. Overall there are no special cult acts proper to mountain sites. However, two rituals at Mt. Lycaeon, unparalleled elsewhere, can be linked to the wildness of the place: the magic ritual attached to the spring Hagno, performed with an oak branch by the priest of Zeus after a long period of drought to cause rain, and the human sacrifice practised at the Lycaea on the top of the mountain, the origin of which was traced to *Lycaon (3). Certain types of myths have a more particular connection with mountains, such as those of the births of gods (Zeus on Lycaeon, or in Crete on Mt. Ida, Hermes on Cyllene). The mountain solitude and the presence of divinities of nature in the form of *kourotrophos-type nymphs would give the young gods a secluded and suitable upbringing before their integration into divine society.
[Pausanias 8. 36–8]

mundus (etymology uncertain), the world, the ornament (cf. Gk. *kosmos*), also a round pit at Rome, *mundus Cereris*, with its upper part vaulted, and the lower giving access to the Underworld. It was open (*mundus patet*) on 24 August, 5 October, and 8 November. On these days (*dies religiosi*) no public business (unless necessary) or marriages could be transacted. It is unlikely that this *mundus* was identical with the foundation pit *Romulus excavated in the Comitium (or the *Palatine) to deposit clods of earth and first-fruits. *See also* PITS, CULT.
[Macrobius, *Saturnalia* 1. 16. 18]

Munichia (1) (or Munychia), mod. Kastella, is a steep hill to the north-east of Piraeus which rises to a height of 86 m. (282 ft.).

Directly below is Munichia Port and to the south-east Zea Port. The theatre of Dionysus on its north-west flank was used for dramatic festivals, deme (local) assemblies, and in 411 and 404 for political rallies. Its most prominent shrines were those of *Artemis Munichia (see MUNICHIA (2)) and *Bendis.

Munichia (2), an Attic festival held on the 16th of the month Munichion (roughly, early May) in honour of the *Artemis of *Munichia (1). There was sacrifice and a procession, in which *cakes ringed with 'little torches', like birthday cakes, were brought to the goddess (who was herself a *phōsphoros*, 'light-bringer' or saviour). The festival came also to serve as a commemoration of the Greek victory at the battle of Salamis (480 BC). In addition, archaeological evidence now supports the ancient reports that young girls served as *arktoi*, 'bears', at Munichia as well as at *Brauron.

Munichus (later Munychus), eponym of *Munichia (1), the acropolis of *Piraeus, where he received refugees from Boeotian Orchomenus and founded the temple of *Artemis Munichia. Though he is connected with *Theseus, appearing in the fight against the *Amazons on a red-figure vase, he is distinct from Munitos, son of *Acamas or *Demophon (1).

Musaeus, a mythical singer with a descriptive name ('He of the Muses'). He belongs particularly to *Eleusis, where he is either autochthonous (see AUTOCHTHONS) or an immigrant from Thrace, the country of mythical singers. He is father or son of *Eumolpus, the eponymous hero of the chief sacerdotal family of Eleusis, and his wife Deiope has her grave beneath the Eleusinian Telesterion or initiation hall; the couple and their son Eumolpus are shown on a red-figure vase of the Meidias Painter.

He is closely connected with *Orpheus, whom he follows together with *Hesiod and *Homer in a canonical list of the quintessential Greek poets. *Plato called Orpheus and Musaeus descendants of the Moon; to others, Musaeus is Orpheus' son, disciple, or, after his identification with Moses, teacher (in Hellenistic Jewish writers). Like Orpheus, Musaeus is said to have invented the hexameter or even the alphabet.

Like Orpheus, Musaeus became, in the late 6th cent. BC, the exponent of apocryphal poetry; their works share some titles. Among Musaeus' works are *oracles, collected around 500 BC by Onomacritus, whom Hipparchus, the son of Pisistratus, exiled for having added a forgery. (*See also* DIVINATION.) More important are poems which make him the chief exponent of an Attic and Eleusinian '*Orphism'. *Plato alludes to a poem (or poems) on eschatology used by 'Orphic' vagrant priests, later sources know a *Theogony* (see THEOGONY) and a *Hymn to Demeter* used in the Attic family cult of the Lycomidae. A vase in the Louvre depicts a young Musaeus learning epic (theological) poetry from his teacher *Linus, while a cup in Cambridge perhaps shows Musaeus writing down the utterances of Orpheus' singing head.

See ORPHEUS; ORPHIC LITERATURE.

[Herodotus 7. 6. 3; Plato, *Republic* 364e; Pausanias 4. 1. 5]

Muses, goddesses upon whom poets—and later other artists, philosophers, and intellectuals generally—depended for the ability to create their works. They were goddesses, not lesser immortals, not only because of their pedigree(s) and their home on *Olympus. They are called goddesses from the earliest sources on, and their attitude to mankind is identical to that of gods: they do not hesitate to destroy a mortal who dares to usurp their place (so *Thamyris in Homer's *Iliad*, whom they maimed and deprived of his skill), and they are divinely contemptuous of humankind (it does not matter to them whether the poetry they inspire is true or false). Muses appear both singly and in groups of varying sizes. Homer, for example, addresses a single goddess or Muse but knows there are more (the Thamyris story). The canonical nine and their names probably originated with *Hesiod.

They were: Calliope (epic poetry), Clio (history), Euterpe (flute-playing), Terpsichore (lyric poetry and dancing, esp. choral), Erato (lyric poetry), Melpomene (tragedy), Thalia (comedy), Polyhymnia (hymns and pantomime), and Urania (astronomy). But their names, functions, and number fluctuated.

The earliest sources locate the Muses at Pieria, just north of Olympus, and on Olympus itself; they are associated with so-called 'Thracian' bards, *Orpheus, Thamyris, and *Musaeus. That region appears to have been their first home. A southern group, the Muses of *Helicon, is identified by Hesiod with the Muses of Olympia and Pieria, perhaps because of an underlying connection between the two regions (compare Mt. Leibethrion and its nymphs in the Helicon massif with Leibethra in Pieria in Macedonia), but possibly because the young poet himself saw fit to make the association as a means to enhance his own reputation.

Hesiod's influence led eventually—but possibly not before the 4th cent. BC—to the establishment of a formal cult and sanctuary below Mt. Helicon in the Vale of the Muses. This may have been the first 'Mouseion' (*Museum: it housed, in the open air, statues of both legendary and historical notables, and possibly contained an archive of poetic works), and it is not surprising that a Ptolemy (probably Ptolemy IV Philopator, whose queen Arsinoë III was worshipped as the Tenth Muse) was among the benefactors when part of the musical *agōn, the Mouseia, was reorganized towards the end of the 3rd cent. BC.

Philosophers, traditionally beginning with *Pythagoras, adopted the Muses as their special goddesses, in some cases organizing their schools as *thiasoi under their patronage. From Hellenistic times they were a popular subject, individually or as a group, in sculpture (especially sarcophagi) and mosaics

There is no satisfactory etymology for the word.

[Homer, Iliad 2. 594–600; Hesiod, Theogony 1–45, 75–104]

Museum (Gk. *Mouseion*), originally a place connected with the *Muses or the arts inspired by them. *Euripides speaks of the *mouseia* of birds, the places where they sing. When a religious meaning was attached an altar or a temple was built to mark the spot. But the predominant significance of the word was literary and educational. Thus Mt. *Helicon had a Museum containing the manuscripts of *Hesiod and statues of those who had upheld the arts. Almost any school could be called 'the place of the Muses'.

music in worship Both in Greece and Italy music, vocal and instrumental, formed an important part of worship at all periods. To begin with *Homer, the embassy sent to Chryse in book 1 of the *Iliad* spend the whole day after their arrival singing a hymn (*paiēōn*) to *Apollo, who is pleased with it. This *paean remained typical of his worship, and the quintuple rhythm characteristic of it was named after it. In like manner the *dithyramb was appropriated to *Dionysus. Neither of these, however was exclusively the property of Apollo or Dionysus; e.g. paeans were composed to *Asclepius. The singing of some kind of *hymn appears regularly to have accompanied any formal act of worship, and instrumental music (strings and wind) also is commonly mentioned: *see* SACRIFICE, GREEK.

Much the same is true for Italy. Hymns are continually met with, some traditional, as those of the *Salii (*see* CARMEN SALIARE) and arval brothers (*see* CARMEN ARVALE). Instrumental music was so regular and necessary an accompaniment of ritual (according to Cicero, the proceedings are vitiated 'if the pipe-player suddenly falls silent') that the '*collegium of pipe-players and lyre-players at public sacrifices' formed an ancient and important guild with a holiday of its own; *see* *MINERVA. One reason for this was doubtless to drown any slight noises which might be of ill omen.

Very little is known of the style of this music, but it is fairly certain that there was no prohibition of the introduction of new forms.

[Homer, *Iliad* 1. 472–4; Cicero, *De haruspicum responso* 23]

Mycenae, myths of Mycenae is very prominent in *Homer, but other versions of related legends give greater prominence to Argos or Sparta (*see* ARGOS, MYTHS OF; SPARTAN CULTS). *See* AEGISTHUS; AGAMEMNON; CLYTEMNESTRA.

See also GENEALOGICAL TABLES (5) DESCENDANTS OF TANTALUS.

Mygdon In the *Iliad*, *Priam relates that he went as an ally to a Phrygian army gathered under Mygdon and Otreus to fight the *Amazons on the Sangarius. The Coroebus in book 2 of *Virgil's *Aeneid* was Mygdon's son, according to the *Rhesus* attributed to Euripides. Mygdon is apparently the *eponym of the Thracian or Phrygian Mygdones.

[Homer, *Iliad* 3. 184 ff.; [Euripides], *Rhesus* 539]

Mylitta is the Greek transcription for the Assyrian goddess Mullissu (Sumerian *Ninlil*). She was the spouse of Aššur (the Assyrian Enlil) in Assyria. Herodotus, who associated prostitution with her cult (*see* PROSTITUTION, SACRED), identified her with *Aphrodite.

[Herodotus 1. 199]

Myrrha, or Smyrna, or Zmyrna, legendary Levantine beauty who conceived an incestuous passion for her father (Theias of Assyria or *Cinyras of Cyprus) and, consequently, *Adonis; she was transformed into a tree whose bark weeps the eponymous *myrrh. Ovid's account was no doubt influenced by the lost poem of Gaius Helvius Cinna, praised in Catullus 95.

[Ovid, *Metamorphoses* 10. 298 ff; Antoninus Liberalis, *Metamorphoses* 34]

mysteries For much of the last hundred years the term 'mystery religions' has been current, denoting a special form of personal religion linking the fate of a god of Frazer's 'dying-rising' type with the individual believer. The two scholars whose authority made soteriology the central issue were Fr. Cumont (1904) and R. Reitzenstein (1910).

The concealed agendum was the question of the uniqueness, and by implication, validity, of Christianity; at the same time, it was the model of that religion which provided the agreed terms of discussion. In this perspective, the earliest and most influential Greek mystery cult, of *Demeter and Kore (*see* PERSEPHONE) at *Eleusis, appeared a crude forerunner of more developed mystery religions from the near east, which in the Hellenistic period filled a spiritual vacuum left by the etiolation of Archaic and Classical civic cult. 'Mystery' was taken to be the essence of oriental religiosity.

This entire scenario, and with it the coherence of the notion 'mystery', has now been seriously eroded. U. von Wilamowitz and C. Schneider showed in the 1930s that mysteries in the Greek (Eleusinian) sense were unknown in the homelands of the oriental cults, and were only attached to them on their entry into the Graeco-Roman world. M. P. Nilsson later made a similar point about Dionysiac mysteries (*see* DIONYSUS); and it is now agreed that all the 'oriental' divinities were thoroughly Hellenized in the process of being assimilated. The validity of Frazer's typology of the dying-rising god (*Osiris, *Attis, *Adonis) was undermined in the 1950s by H. Frankfort and others. The nature of the soteriology of mystery cults has been critically reviewed by the 'School of Rome' since the 1960s, especially by U. Bianchi and his pupils, and redefined as 'the mass of benefits and guarantees which the worshipper expected from the celebration of the cult' (Sfameni Gasparro). In the light of this revisionism, the uniqueness of the claims of Pauline *Christianity (*see* PAUL, ST.) against the background of Judaic Messianism (*see* JUDAISM) has been re-emphasized, and the issue of the Christianization of the Roman empire opened to fresh debate. The category 'mysteries' is looking decidedly limp. For it is clear that they cannot be considered independent movements, let alone religions, but as merely an ingrained modality of (Greek, later Graeco-Roman) polytheism—they have been compared with a pilgrimage to Santiago di Compostela in the Christian context. And they are only a specialized, often highly local, form of the cult of ill-assorted divinities. Their prominence in modern scholarship is quite disproportionate to their ancient profile.

The most useful recent typology of Graeco-Roman mysteries as forms of personal religious choice is that of Bianchi and others. Three modes are distinguished: 'mystery' proper, an entire initiatory structure of some duration and complexity, of which the type (and in many cases the actual model, e.g. Celeia near Phlius or the mysteries of *Alexander of Abonuteichos is Eleusis; 'mystic' cult, involving not initiation but rather a relation of intense communion, typically ecstatic or enthusiastic, with the divinity (e.g. Bacchic frenzy (*see* DIONYSUS), or the *galloi* of *Cybele); and 'mysteriosophic' cult, offering an anthropology, an eschatology, and a practical means of individual reunion with divinity—the primitive or original form is *Orphism, consistently represented as a 'mystery', the most typical, Hermeticism and Gnosis (*see* GNOSTICISM), though these are late Egyptian and Judaeo-Christian forms of religiosity. Bianchi himself has sought to provide an element of thematic unity by adapting Frazer's 'dying-rising god' typology: these cults are all focused upon a 'god subject to some vicissitude'. This tack has rightly been criticized, but the scheme as a whole has value.

Of their very nature, ideal types simplify to offer insight. The real world is always much more confused. The word *teletē*, which often denotes initiatory rituals of the Eleusinian type, could also be applied to any kind of unusual rite in some way analogous. One of the costs of conceptual clarity is the exclusion from consideration of numerous minor cults of Greece and Asia Minor, such as the *teletē* of *Hera at Nauplion, where she bathed annually to 'become a virgin'. 'Mystery' shifts uneasily between indigenous term and analytical concept. Further complications are the intermingling of the

three types in practice and the clear evidence of changes over time: early Orphic lore cannot be neatly distinguished from Bacchic 'mystic' experience; Orphic texts are intimately connected with the formation of Eleusinian myth; the cult of Cybele and Attis is marked by 'mystic' *ecstasy but also, in the Hellenistic period and after, by mysteries of uncertain content analogous to those of Eleusis, and, from the 2nd cent. AD, by a fusion of sacrifice, substitute-castration, and personal baptism—the *taurobolium* ('bull-sacrifice'); the cult of *Mithras may have taken on a 'mysteriosophic' tone.

The variety of mystery cults makes them exceptionally difficult to summarize both briefly and accurately. The aim of the 'mystic' form is best contrasted with that of the collective, integrative, political value of sacrificial civic religion: the individual seeks through possession/'madness' to transcend the constraints of the everyday and become a member of a privileged but temporary community of bliss (seen in *Euripides' *Bacchae*, for instance). Religious imagery and style offer a complex counterpoint to those of civic cult. A brusquer world-rejection inspired the 'mysteriosophic' form, based upon a myth accounting for the separation between god and man, flesh and spirit, evident in the gold plaques from Pelinna in Thessaly (late 4th cent. BC; *see* ORPHISM). The 'mystery' type is much more integrated into dominant social values. The model form, the Eleusinian mysteries, was a full and regular part of Athenian civic cult from the late 6th cent. BC, institutionalizing many aspects of religious aspiration otherwise excluded from public ceremonial: collective purification, the dramatic representation of mythical narrative, the opportunity for awe, fear, wonder, scurrility, and humour (the *gephyrismoi* (ritual abuse) at the bridge over the Cephissus), explicit exegesis by the *mystagōgoi*, the privilege bestowed by an open secret 'that may not be divulged', and public reaffirmation of a *theodicy of moral desert linked to good fortune. In this perspective, the offer of a blessed existence after death, found already in the *Homeric Hymn to Demeter*, received no special emphasis, being apparently a projection of experience into the world beyond, rather than a compensation for sorrows in this one. The point probably holds for all mystery cults, indigenous or 'oriental', until the 3rd cent. AD. *See* CABIRI.

[*Homeric Hymn to Demeter*; Aristophanes, *Frogs* 324–459; Euripides, *Bacchae* 64–169; Strabo 10. 3. 7; Pausanias 2. 14. 1–4, 2. 38. 3]

mythographers The first comprehensive collection of heroic myths was the *Catalogue of Women* ascribed to *Hesiod, and myths formed a substantial element in the writings of the genealogists (*Hecataeus (1), *Acusilaus, *Pherecydes (2) of Athens, *Hellanicus) in the 5th cent. BC, and the Atthidographers (*see* ATTHIS) in the 4th. *Asclepiades of Tragilus, a pupil of Isocrates, treated the myths of tragedy in particular, and compared them with earlier versions.

But the main mythographic collections date from Hellenistic or early imperial times, and fall into two broad categories. The first type attempts to collect relevant myths to elucidate major authors such as *Homer, *Pindar, the tragedians (*see* TRAGEDY), and the Hellenistic poets. Scattered in the ancient commentaries on *Pindar, *Euripides, Theocritus, *Apollonius Rhodius, and *Lycophron are rich collections of mythography. The most remarkable such collection consists of hundreds of stories (*historiai*) in the scholia to the *Iliad* and *Odyssey*, which papyrus discoveries now show to have been an independent book (dubbed the 'mythographus Homericus') in antiquity; only later was it incorporated with the commentaries.

The second category comprises independent collections of myths organized around a particular theme and attributed (usually falsely) to a famous name, such as the star-myths of Eratosthenes (*see* CONSTELLATIONS AND NAMED STARS), the love stories of Parthenius, the 'Tales from Euripides' of Dicaearchus, the narratives of *Conon and the *Metamorphoses* of *Antoninus Liberalis.

The greatest of these is the *Library* ascribed to *Apollodorus of Athens (the genuine Apollodorus had a scholarly interest in myths, but cannot be the author of this handbook). It contains a continuous account of Greek myths from the Creation to the Dorian invasion, arranged by family genealogies; the Hesiodic *Catalogue of Women* is a likely structural model, although the sources are seldom named, and (for individual details) may be countless.

In Latin, *Ovid's *Metamorphoses* offered in poetry a comprehensive mythography (although of a very different sort) to match the *Catalogue of Women*, and several works in Latin either translate or imitate Greek predecessors: mythographic narratives are found in Servius and other commentaries, and traces of earlier sources can be glimpsed in the *Fabulae* and *Astronomia* of *Hyginus (another suspicious attribution) and the miscellanies of *Fulgentius and the so-called *Mythographi Vaticani*.

mythology is the field of scholarship dealing with myth but also a particular body of myths. Myth goes back to the Greek word *mythos*, which originally meant 'word, speech, message' but in the 5th cent. BC started to acquire the meaning 'entertaining, if not necessarily trustworthy, tale'. The Romans used the word *fabula*, which was also used in modern discussions until *c*.1760, when the Göttingen classicist C. G. Heyne (1729–1812) coined the word *mythus* in order to stress the inner veracity of myth. No universally accepted definition of myth exists, but Walter Burkert's statement that 'myth is a traditional tale with secondary, partial reference to something of collective importance' gives a good idea of the main characteristics of myth.

Let us start with the problem of tradition. *Homer already mentions the *Argonauts, the Theban Cycle, and the deeds of *Heracles. The presence in Linear B texts of the formulae 'Mother of the Gods' and 'Drimius, son of *Zeus' suggests a divine genealogy, and the myths of *Achilles, *Helen, and the cattle-raiding Heracles all seem to go back to Indo-European times (and Heracles maybe further back than that). The connection with central institutions or pressing problems of society—*initiation, marriage, food—makes their continuity persuasive: Achilles' myth can hardly be separated from rites of initiation, whereas wedding poetry probably stands in the background of Helen's mythology. *See* INITIATION; RITES OF PASSAGE.

Other myths were certainly also of considerable age, such as the birth of Athenian *Erechtheus from the seed of *Hephaestus or the birth of the famous horse *Arion from the union of *Poseidon with the goddess Erinys (*see* ERINYES). It is typical of Greek myth that Homer and other Archaic poets tended to suppress such strange and scandalous details, which survived only in locally fixed traditions. The trend of Greek mythology was firmly anthropomorphic and away from the fantastic.

Another ancient complex was constituted by initiatory myths. Strikingly, all early Panhellenic expeditions—the Trojan War (*see* TROY), *Jason and the Argonauts, and the Calydonian Hunt (*see* ATALANTA; MELEAGER)—contain many male initiatory elements, just as the myths of *Iphigenia, *Io, *Europa, and the daughters of *Proetus reflect the final transition into womanhood. Although many other Indo-European peoples had initiatory myths, its prominence is one of the distinctive features of Greek mythology.

A more recent complex of myths came from the east. The Indo-Europeans had at the most only rudimentary theogonical and cosmogonical myths. It is not surprising, therefore, that in this area Greece became very much indebted to the rich mythologies of Anatolia and Mesopotamia. *Cronus' castration of his father *Uranus ultimately derives from the Hurrians, having passed through Hittite and Phoenician intermediaries; the division of the world between Zeus, Poseidon, and *Hades through the casting of lots, as described in book 15 of the *Iliad*,

derives from the Akkadian epic *Atrahasis*; and when *Hera, in a speech to deceive Zeus, says in book 14 that she will go to *Oceanus, 'origin of the gods', and *Tethys, the 'mother', she mentions a couple derived from the parental pair Apsu and Tiamat in the Babylonian creation epic *Enuma Elish*. New clay tablets will surely present further surprises in this direction.

The fertile contacts with the east probably took place in the early iron age. Somewhat later, the foundations of colonies in the Mediterranean and the Black Sea (*c*.750–600 BC) led to the last great wave of mythological inventions. In particular, the myths about the return of the heroes after the Trojan War, but also the expedition of the Argonauts, enabled many colonies to connect their new foundations to the Panhellenic past as created through these great myths. It is surprising how quickly traditional story-patterns here transformed historical events.

It is clear that poets were always prepared to assimilate or borrow new material. Another way of 'staying in business' was to vary the traditional myths by introducing new details—e.g. new names and motivations—or by restructuring the myth into a different direction. Whereas archaic myth concentrated more, for example, on dynasties and heroic feats, in a later, more regulated society, myth tended to concentrate on relations within the family and, especially in Athenian tragedy (*see* TRAGEDY), on the relation between individual and city or the value of democratic institutions.

Rome, on the other hand, was situated at the margin of the 'civilized' world and was late to assimilate Greek myth (see further below). When the Roman élite started to write down its history at the end of the 3rd cent. BC, it had one fixed mythological complex at its disposal: the foundation of Rome by *Romulus and Remus. A few names, such as *Janus and *Picus, hint at the sometime existence of other myths, but nothing suggests an originally rich mythology, and the absence of divine tales has even led some scholars to the suggestion that the Romans lacked a mythology altogether. Moreover, the 'brain drain' of neighbouring élites into Rome did not favour the survival of Italic myths: the founding of *Praeneste by Caeculus is the only full myth from Latium that we still have. The foundation myths show that the temporal horizon was not the creation of gods or men but the birth of the native city; the foundation of the city was also the most important mythological theme in public declamations in imperial times (*see* FOUNDERS, CITY).

Unlike Rome, which lacked a native expression for poets and poetry, Greece knew many poets who were the main producers of mythology; the tradition of formal narrative prose, which existed as well, is only discoverable in bare outlines. Poets performed at courts or local festivals in various genres, which successively became popular: epic in the 8th cent., choral lyric in the 6th and, finally, tragedy, the last public performance of myth, in the 5th. Yet myths were also related in other contexts. Temple friezes, sculptures, and vases made myth as a subject visible virtually everywhere. Women told myths during weaving-sessions, according to Euripides in his *Ion*; old men will have related them in the *leschai* (club-like meeting-places), and mothers and nurses told them to children, as Plato relates in *Laws*. 'Indoctrination' by mothers and nurses will have been a significant, if usually neglected, factor in the continuing popularity of myth all through antiquity.

The uses of myth varied over time, but the entertainment value was always important. Indeed, Homer himself points to the delight of songs. Choral lyric, with its combination of music, dance, and song, must have been quite a spectacle, and for the thousands of spectators Athenian tragedy was a welcome break in the winter months. Other uses included the foundation of the social and political order. Myth explained how in Athens males had arrived at their dominant position through the chaos caused by women; how cities originated, such as Thebes through a struggle against a dragon, or how tribal groupings arose, such as the Ionians from *Ion and the Aeolians from *Aeolus (2). It explained why, for example, the Spartans ruled their extended territory, or why Athens could claim Aegina.

Myth also helped the Greeks to define the world around them and their own place in relation to the gods. By situating murderous women on mountains, by letting girls in their prime play on flowery meadows, or by ascribing the ancestry of the leading family to a river-god, these features of the landscape were assigned negative or positive values. Moreover, by relating the unhappy endings of love affairs between gods and humans, for example *Semele being burnt to ashes through the appearance of Zeus in full glory, myth stressed the unbridgeable gap between mortals and immortals.

Finally, the aetiological function of myth was substantial. Many myths explained the birth or function of rituals; even the tragedian *Euripides often recounted the origins of vital Attic cults. Other myths highlighted or 'explained' unusual features of ritual: the myth of the Lemnian women concentrated on the separation of the sexes but totally left out the new fire, which was actually very prominent in the corresponding ritual. The exaggeration by myth of the ritual separation of the sexes into the mythical murder shows up an important difference between myth and *ritual: myth can depict as real what in ritual has to remain symbolic. Over time, myth could free itself from one specific ritual and be connected with other ones, or the ritual could disappear while the myth continued to be narrated: in the 2nd cent. AD the traveller *Pausanias recorded many myths of which the rituals had already long disappeared.

Myth was originally the product of an oral society, but the arrival of writing brought important changes. Poets had now to share their leading intellectual roles with philosophers and historians—authors who wrote in prose and did not have to subject their opinions to the scrutiny of a public. The new intellectuals soon started to systematize and criticize mythological traditions. On the other hand, the force of tradition weighed heavily and that explains why the two most popular strategies in dealing with mythology were rationalization, which in our sources starts with *Hecataeus (1) of Miletus (c.550–480 BC), and allegorization, which probably started with the late 6th-cent. rhapsodist *Theagenes of Rhegium; the adoption of this approach by the Stoics (see STOICISM) caused its survival until late antiquity. In this way, intellectuals could have their mythological cake and eat it.

These developments strongly diminished the public influence of poets as prime producers of mythology. In Hellenistic times, the myths recorded and adapted by *Callimachus and his contemporaries were directed at a small circle of connoisseurs not the general public. However, it was these poets who exercised an enormous influence in Rome, where in the last two centuries of the republic and during the early Principate a proliferation of mythical themes can be noted—to the extent that in *Ovid one ritual can receive several aetiological myths. However, it is hard to say what degree of authority, if any, these myths had in Rome.

In the Hellenistic and early imperial period scholars started to collect myths in order to elucidate allusions in the Classical authors; most important in this respect was the collection of mythological commentaries on Homer which circulated as a separate book at least from the 1st to the 5th cent. AD. Other collections concentrated on one theme, such as Eratosthenes' book of star-myths (see CONSTELLATIONS AND NAMED STARS), or the famous *Library* ascribed to *Apollodorus, which organized the mythological material by families (see MYTHOGRAPHERS). It is especially these collections which have ensured modern knowledge of the less familiar myths of Greece.

The modern study of Greek mythology started in France in the 18th cent., but the centre of interest soon shifted to Germany, where there was more philological expertise. It was the insights of Heyne in particular—myth as history, myth as explanation of natural phenomena, myth as the product of a specific people—which dominated the field in the 19th cent. However, the excesses of the naturalist interpretation were an important factor in the shift of scholarly interest away from mythology towards ritual at the end of the 19th cent. Since the middle 1960s interest in Greek myth has revived, notably through the work of Walter Burkert. The focal points of the new approaches are the relationship between myth and ritual and the explanatory and normative functions of myth. Roman myth has also profited from this revival, but the scarcity of material and the élite's view of myths as *fabulae*, 'fictional stories', make it difficult to see what exactly the place of myth was in Roman society. The differences between Greek and Roman mythology still await further analysis.

Naassenes, Christian splinter group that took its name from the Hebrew word for serpent (*nahash*), Hellenized (i.e. turned into Greek) as *naas*; the word in Hebrew had the same numerical value as the word for Messiah. In Greek, the serpent was connected by false etymology with the word for temple (*naos*), and the Naassenes believed that nothing mortal or immortal, animate or inanimate could exist without Naas. They taught that the universe derived from an hermaphroditic monad (Adam), who produced three elements as offspring, Nous (Mind), *Chaos, and *Psyche. The three elements of Adam descended into one man, Jesus, who revealed knowledge, *gnōsis*, to humans. Just as Adam and Naas created without sex, they also preached strict sexual abstinence. They seem to have claimed that their doctrine originated with James, the brother of Jesus, who had revealed it to Mariamme. Numerous quotations from their works, including a Naassene hymn, are preserved in *Hippolytus' (2) *Refutation of all Heresies*.

Naiads *See* NYMPHS.

names, religious Name-giving among the Greeks is associated in our sources with the ceremony of the Amphidromia, and is assigned variously to the fifth, seventh, or tenth day after birth. Among names originating in an enormous range of concepts, 'theophoric' names form a special class, recognized as such in antiquity. These were based not only on gods' names, but also on their cult titles, and on months named after them. Adjectival derivatives of a deity's name (*Apollonios/a, Dionysios/a, Demetrios/a*)

were among the most common of Greek names. Compound forms were likely to carry notions of giving/given (*-dōros, -dotos*) birth (*-genēs, -geneia*), repute or favour (*-klēs/ kleia; phanēs/phaneia; charēs/charis*, etc.). Thus, based on the name of *Zeus, with the root *Dio-*: Diodoros, Diodotos, Diogenes, Diokles, Diophanes, Diochares, Diognetos, etc. Some theophoric names reflect a local cult, for example Karneades, Karnis, etc. common at Cyrene, a centre of the cult of *Apollo Carneius (*see* CARNEA). Non-Greek deities were also absorbed into nomenclature, as is shown by the spread, from the late 3rd cent. BC, of the names Serapion, Serapias, Serapis, etc., derived from the Egyptian god *Sarapis. With time, however, these and other names became neutralized, as the survival into the Christian period of names deriving from pagan deities shows. In fact, the common Greek practice of naming after family members means that we cannot at any period assume that an individual has been named directly with reference to the god referred to in the name.

Roman nomenclature was quite different from Greek, and had little room for theophoric names. A few are found among cognomina, the last of the three names borne by a male Roman citizen, and are sometimes of Greek origin: thus Diodorus, Hermes, and (with a more Roman flavour) Saturninus and Romulus. The influence of *Christianity on name-giving was slight before the last centuries of antiquity. Explicitly Christian names came into use slowly, starting from the 4th cent.; but the majority of names used by the Christian communities in the west were still firmly anchored in the old pagan world (names such as *Aphrodite, Eros, Hermes* remained common). Biblical names, such as *Iohannes* or *Petrus*, as well as names of martyrs (*Laurentius*), became popular only from the 5th cent.

Narcissus, in mythology, a beautiful youth, son of *Cephissus (the Boeotian *river-god) and Liriope, a *nymph. He loved no one till he saw his own reflection in water and fell in love with that; finally he pined away, died, and was turned into the flower of like name. *Ovid, who preserves the fullest version, claims that Narcissus was punished for his cruelty to *Echo: he repulsed her and she so wasted away with grief that there was nothing left of her but her voice. Variants are found in *Conon, where the rejected suitor is male, and *Pausanias, who has a rationalizing version. The story appealed to Roman taste: it is depicted in nearly 50 murals from Pompeii alone.

[Ovid, *Metamorphoses* 3. 342 ff.; Pausanias 9. 31. 7-8]

nature *See* ANIMALS IN CULT; ASTROLOGY; BODY; CONSTELLATIONS AND NAMED STARS; PHYSIOGNOMY.

Nauplius, (1) eponym of Nauplia near *Argos (2); son of *Poseidon and *Amymone. (2) His descendant, often confused with (1) (Nauplius (1)-*Proetus–Lernus–Naubolus–Clytoneus–Nauplius (2)), an *Argonaut, navigator, and slave-trader. He was given *Catreus' two daughters, Clymene and *Aërope, to sell overseas, but married Clymene and fathered *Palamedes and Oeax. He was also given Aleus' daughter Auge, after she gave birth to *Telephus (1), to sell overseas, but instead gave her to Teuthras, king of Teuthrania, who married her. To avenge the death of Palamedes, he caused some of the Greek leaders' wives to be unfaithful; then later he was instrumental in wrecking the Greek fleet on its return from *Troy, when he lit false beacons at Cape Caphareus in Euboea. *See also* HESIONE.

Nausicaa, in *Homer's *Odyssey* the young daughter of *Alcinous, king of the Phaeacians (*see* SCHERIA), and Arete. In book 6, moved by *Athena in a dream, she goes to the river-mouth to do the family washing, and is playing ball with her maids when the shipwrecked *Odysseus comes out of hiding and begs her help. He is almost naked, and the maids run away in fear; but Nausicaa, given courage by Athena, stands her ground and promises him her help. She gives him food, drink, and clothing, shows him the way to the city, and advises him on how to behave to her parents. She admits to herself that she would like to marry him, and Alcinous is ready to agree to this, but Odysseus is eager to return home to *Penelope. He bids farewell to Nausicaa, assuring her that he owes her his life and will remember her always. According to a later story, she married *Telemachus.

[Homer, *Odyssey* 6, 7. 311 ff., 8. 457-68]

Nechepso, pseudonymous author, with Petosiris, of an astrological treatise in at least fourteen books, written, perhaps in Egypt, by a late Hellenistic Greek who used the Egyptian names to convey a spurious antiquity. Its great influence is shown by the frequent citations in later astrological works. *See* ASTROLOGY.

nectar *See* AMBROSIA.

Nekyomanteion The most famous oracle of the dead was situated on the river *Acheron in Thesprotia. According to Herodotus it was consulted by Periander, the 6th-cent. tyrant of Corinth, who wished to contact his dead wife Melissa; the story shows that he was successful. In the 1960s, S. Dakaris excavated a 3rd-4th-cent. complex which he believed to be the Nekyomanteion, but his interpretation has now been refuted.

Judging by Herodotus' account, the aim of consultation was to make contact with a particular dead person in order to retrieve some information they had had while living. The earlier account in the *Odyssey* of *Odysseus' journey to the Underworld to obtain a prophecy relevant to himself might therefore seem to be different in intent. In fact, however, he receives information from his mother *Anticleia about the state of his home at the time of her death, and the main purpose of his visit is to get a prophecy from *Tiresias, who was a prophet in his lifetime. There is no implication that the ordinary dead had actual prophetic powers.

See ORACLES.

[Herodotus 5. 92]

Neleus, son of *Tyro and *Poseidon, twin of *Pelias, with whom he is exposed but saved by a herdsman or an animal. After a quarrel, he leaves Pelias as king of Iolcus and either conquers or founds Pylos in Messenia. Here he fathers twelve sons, with *Nestor the youngest. He reigns without playing a major role in the wars of Nestor's youth. But when he refuses to cleanse *Heracles from the murder of Iphitus (*see* POLLUTION; PURIFICATION), Heracles conquers Pylos and kills all the sons, except Nestor. Exposure and miraculous survival are typical for founders of dynasties and empires (*Romulus, Darius, Moses), while the geographical dislocation hides the combination of different local traditions. The later events, as they appear already in the *Iliad*, are determined by Pylian story telling about the youth of Nestor.

Neleus had cult in Attica, together with *Basile, was believed the ancestor of the noble families of the Medontidae, Paeonidae, and Alcmaeonidae, and founder of Erythrae, Miletus, or the entire *Ionian dodecapolis ('twelve cities': *see* IONIAN FESTIVALS), and he had a grave in *Didyma. Athenian tradition made him a younger son of *Codrus who emigrated to Ionia after a quarrel with his brother; at least some Ionian traditions preferred to derive him from Pylos. *See* ATTIC CULTS.

[Homer, *Iliad* 7. 132–56, 11. 670–762; *Odyssey* 11. 235–9; Pausanias 7. 2. 6]

Nemea Fertile upland valley in the northwest Argolid sandwiched between the territories of ancient Phlius and Cleonae; legendary scene of *Heracles' encounter with the lion; site of the Panhellenic sanctuary of *Zeus, its accompanying festival (*see* NEMEAN GAMES) wandering between here and Argos, where it remained for good from *c.*50 BC. American excavations have revealed remains of an Archaic heroon (*see* HERO-CULT), perhaps for Opheltes, and a 6th-cent. temple; this last was replaced in the late 4th cent. by the temple still partly standing, evidently built to mark the festival's (temporary) return *c.*330 BC under Macedonian patronage, along with the stadium, baths, and guest-house; a row of nine treasury-like buildings, evidently 'club-houses' or *leschai* for foreign states, dates from the early 5th cent. By the mid-2nd cent. AD the temple was roofless. A small Christian *basilica of the 5th–6th cent. and the settlement which it served have been found.

[Pausanias 2. 15. 2–3]

Nemean Games These were held in the sanctuary of *Zeus at *Nemea. They were said to have been founded by *Adrastus of Argos, in memory of the child Opheltes, killed there by a snake during the expedition of the *Seven against Thebes, or by *Heracles after he had killed the Nemean lion. They were reorganized as a Panhellenic festival in 573 BC, held in July every second and fourth year in each Olympiad, and were at first managed by Cleonae, later by Argos. The prize was a *crown of fresh celery.

Nemesis, both goddess and abstract concept from *nemein* (to deal or distribute); often a personified moral agent ('Retribution') like Lachesis and Praxis. She was daughter of Night (*Nyx), according to *Hesiod, and born after the Moirai (*see* FATE) and *Keres as 'an affliction to mortal men' An Attic tradition names *Oceanus as father, perhaps to indicate that she belonged to an older generation of gods. *Homer did not know the goddess, although he was familiar with *Themis. In Homer we find the abstract noun given a negative sense of anger, disgrace, and censure which is absent from the verb but reflected in Hesiod's genealogy.

The moral element becomes more distinct in Hesiod's juxtaposition of Nemesis beside Aidos, echoing Homer, *Iliad* book 13, in which she expresses public indignation and Aidos the offender's sense of shame.

Nemesis' oldest cults were Ionic: at the Attic village of Rhamnus (6th cent. BC), and in Smyrna where she was worshipped in dual form. Her first Rhamnusian temple was destroyed by the Persians and replaced in the late 5th century. A smaller temple belonged to *Themis whose 4th-cent. marble statue was dedicated by Megacles. Agoracritus' (or perhaps Phidias') image of Nemesis—its fragmentary remains now partly excavated—held an apple branch in her left hand and a bowl, decorated with Ethiopians, in her right. A crown on her head showed figures of *Nike and deer. In myth Zeus pursued her in the shape of a fish and various animals; he finally changed into a swan and she into a goose. She laid an egg which a shepherd found and took to *Leda who nurtured *Helen after she was hatched. This account from the *Epic Cycle shows Homeric influence (Nemesis feels *aidōs* and *nemesis*); but her affinity with animals and connection with *Artemis may point to an original chthonian divine nature, as may her festival the Nemeseia. *See* CHTHONIAN GODS. Like Themis, Nemesis' cultic past is obscured by her nature as indignant avenger. Both as an impersonal and personified power, she is merciless, envies good fortune, and punishes *hubris. There is a Nemesis of gods, men, and even of the dead. As relentless Fate, she is identified with Adrasteia and guards against excess, hence her attribute of an ell or measuring-rod. Later she shared cult with *Tyche.

[Hesiod, *Theogony* 223, *Works and Days* 200; Homer, *Iliad* 6. 351, 13. 122; Pindar, *Pythian* 10. 44, *Olympian* 8. 86; Herodotus 1. 34; Apollodorus 3. 10. 7; Pausanias 1. 33. 2–8, 7. 5. 3]

Nemesius (fl. *c*.AD 400), bishop of Emesa in Syria, perhaps identical with the former advocate to whom, as governor of Cappadocia Secunda (*c*.386/7), *Gregory (2) of Nazianzus addressed four letters and a protreptic poem inviting him to become a Christian. His essay in Christian Platonism, *On the Nature of Man*, is remarkable not only for its wide reading in medical and philosophical sources, e.g. Galen and *Porphyry, but also for its Christian standpoint and its thesis that the spiritual life of man is conditioned by the body's natural limitations.

Nemi *See* ARICIA; REX NEMORENSIS.

Nemrut Dag (Mt. Nemrut), the highest mountain in Commagene, its peak—commanding spectacular views over south-east Turkey—the site of a monumental *hierothesion* (mausoleum-cum-cult-centre) built *c*.40 BC by the Commagenian king Antiochus I; of interest for its grandiose divinizing (*see* RULER-CULT) of this Roman client king and for its mix of Greek and Persian imagery and religious ideas (*see* SYNCRETISM). The complex comprised a vast tumulus (probably the royal burial-mound) flanked by two terraces for sculpture, each repeating the same row of colossal enthroned divinities (8–9 m. (26–9 ft.) high), among them Antiochus himself, and the same two series of inscribed relief-slabs portraying respectively his Persian and Macedonian ancestors. In two long (Greek) inscriptions (duplicates), Antiochus expounded his lifelong piety and prescribed details of the cult.

nenia A dirge containing lamentation and praise of a deceased person. It was sung to a flute accompaniment by a hired mourner (*praefica*), whose assistants made responses before the house of mourning, during the funeral procession, and beside the pyre. Nenia or Naenia was also the goddess of funerary lamentation, according to Christian sources. She had a temple in front of the porta Viminalis.

neōkoros ('temple warden'), originally a temple official; from the late 1st cent. AD formalized as a title for a city which held a provincial temple to the Roman emperor. Ambitious cities could claim by the 3rd cent. AD to be 'thrice *neōkoros*', e.g. Ephesus. *See* TEMPLE OFFICIALS.

Neoplatonism, a modern term for *Plotinus' renewal of Platonic philosophy (*see* PLATO) in the 3rd cent. AD. It became the dominant philosophy of the ancient world down to the 6th cent. The following phases may be distinguished in its history. (*a*) After the Sceptical period of Plato's Academy, philosophers in the 1st cent. BC, notably Antiochus and Posidonius, initiated a revival of dogmatic Platonism. This revival (called today 'Middle Platonism') became widespread in the 2nd cent. AD when such writers as Albinus (Alcinous) and *Numenius, having recourse sometimes to Aristotelian and Stoic ideas, drew from Plato's dialogues a systematic philosophy. (*b*) Working in this intellectual context, Plotinus developed an unorthodox, compelling interpretation of Plato, a philosophy containing profound metaphysical and psychological ideas which provided his successors with a fruitful basis of reflection. Plotinus' *Enneads* (published posthumously, *c*.300–5) are Neoplatonism's most important philosophical product. (*c*) Plotinus' school at Rome did not survive his death in 270. However his closest pupils (*Porphyry, Amelius Gentilianus) did much to promote his philosophy. Porphyry published Plotinus' biography and works, on which he commented. He also innovated, in particular in metaphysics and in integrating Aristotle's logic into Neoplatonism, contributing also to the influence of Neoplatonism among Latin writers, pagan and Christian, such as Marius Victorinus, Calcidius, *Augustine, and *Macrobius. Plotinus and Porphyry were also read in the east and used by *Eusebius of Caesarea and *Gregory (3) of Nyssa. (*d*) *Iamblichus, who founded an influential school in Syria, introduced a new phase. In particular his systematic harmonization of Neoplatonic metaphysics with supposedly ancient pagan theologies made Neoplatonism suitable to the needs of the pagan reaction led by the emperor *Julian. *Sallustius' *On the Gods and the World* (ed. and trans. A. D. Nock (1926)) summarized the Neoplatonic interpretation of pagan religion, whereas Eunapius made out of the lives of his Neoplatonic teachers a pagan hagiology. (*e*) Iamblichean philosophers contributed to the emergence of a Neoplatonic school at Athens (Syrianus, *Proclus, Damascius, Simplicius, etc.) which produced works of learning and philosophical sophistication and had close relations with a Neoplatonist school in Alexandria (Hypatia, *Synesius, Hierocles, *Ammonius Saccas, John Philoponus, etc.) from which came important commentaries on *Aristotle. The emperor *Justinian closed the Athenian school in 529. Its members took temporary refuge in Persia, whereas the Alexandrian school, perhaps through an understanding with the Church, continued on for another century. Neoplatonism strongly influenced Byzantine thought (through *Dionysius the Areopagite, Michael Psellus), Islamic philosophy, medieval Latin thinkers (through Augustine, John the Scot) and the Renaissance (through Ficino, Pico).

Neoptolemus, son of *Achilles and Deidamia; also known (but not to *Homer) as Pyrrhus.

The *Odyssey* of Homer relates how, after the death of Achilles, *Odysseus fetched Neoptolemus from Scyros to *Troy, where he distinguished himself in counsel and battle and was one of the warriors in the Wooden Horse. After his return to Greece he married *Hermione, daughter of *Menelaus and *Helen. Cyclic epics (*see* EPIC CYCLE) told how, in the sack of Troy, he killed *Priam and (according to the *Little Iliad*) the infant *Astyanax (but the *Capture of Troy* attributed this to Odysseus), and chose *Andromache as his prize. The 6th-cent. poet Ibycus made him responsible for the sacrifice of *Polyxena, as he is in *Euripides' *Hecuba*, and in the younger Seneca's *Trojan Women*.

He had a tomb at *Delphi. *Pausanias is probably wrong in claiming that this did not receive cult honours until after the hero had been seen helping to repulse an attack by Gauls in 279/8. Of his death at Delphi various accounts are given. *Pindar says that *Apollo was angry with him for killing Priam at the altar of *Zeus Herkeios and swore that he would not return home; so, after a visit to Molossia (where the royal house in historical times claimed descent from him), he came to Delphi and was killed by the god during an argument with the temple servants. In a later ode, however, apparently wishing to correct the *Paean with a version more favourable to Neoptolemus, Pindar does not mention Apollo's anger and says that Neoptolemus was killed, to the Delphians' distress, in a quarrel over sacrificial meat.

Yet another account is given by *Euripides' *Andromache*: his death at the hands of the Delphians is brought about by the treachery of *Orestes, his rival for the hand of Hermione. *Virgil, who depicts him as a monster of savagery in the sack of Troy, has him killed by Orestes in person, a version dubiously referred to the *Little Iliad* (*see* EPIC CYCLE).

*Sophocles in *Philoctetes* makes Neoptolemus a companion of Odysseus on the expedition to fetch *Philoctetes from Lemnos. Here he is an essentially honourable youth, persuaded at first to assist in the plots of Odysseus but then finding his true nature through pity for Philoctetes.

Various episodes from his career are depicted on vase-paintings, especially the killing of Priam or Astyanax in scenes of the sack of Troy.

[Homer, *Odyssey* 4. 5–9, 11. 505–37; Sophocles, *Philoctetes*; Euripides, *Hecuba* 523–68, *Andromache*; Pindar, *Paean* 6. 98–120, *Nemean* 7. 34–47; Pausanias 1. 4. 4; Virgil, *Aeneid* 2. 526–8, 3. 330–2]

Neopythagoreanism, a renewed interest in Pythagorean ideas and practices (*see* PYTHAGORAS AND PYTHAGOREANISM) that took widely different forms, appears first in the Hellenistic period with the emergence of apocryphal texts, often inspired by Platonic, Aristotelian, or Stoic sources (*see* PLATO; ARISTOTLE; STOICISM), usually decked out in Doric dialect, and claiming to be the work of Pythagoras or of Pythagoreans such as

Archytas, Timaeus of Locri, Ocellus. Individuals described as 'Pythagoreans' appear in the 1st cent. BC in Alexandria (Eudorus) and Rome (*Nigidius Figulus, his circle, and others) and are found in the 1st cent. AD (Moderatus of Gades, *Apollonius of Tyana) and in the 2nd (Nicomachus of Gerasa, Numenius, *Alexander of Abonuteichos). Some were philosophers who, in the context of a revival of dogmatic Platonism and inspired by Pythagorizing in Plato's Academy, took an interest in Pythagorean metaphysics, mathematics, and number symbolism. Thus Eudorus and Moderatus spoke of an ultimate Pythagorean cause, the 'One', source of numbers and of all else. The Pythagorean way of life, which had a strong religious bent and involved ascetic and vegetarian practices, was followed by Moderatus and by Apollonius, whose activities as magician show another Neopythagorean tendency also found in Alexander of Abonuteichos. Much of Neopythagoreanism and the legend of Pythagoras as a source of religious revelation were incorporated in *Neoplatonism by *Porphyry and by *Iamblichus. Neopythagoreanism also exercised influence on Jewish thought through *Philon (2) and Christian thought through *Clement of Alexandria.

Neptunus, Italic god of *water. He extended his protection to watercourses and to expanses of water threatened by evaporation in the heat of summer as well as to human activities linked with water; hence, under the influence of *Poseidon, he could become patron of journeys on water. During *sacrifice (Roman), the cooked *exta* ('entrails') were thrown into water; it is in virtue of this capacity that the identification of *Consus with 'Neptunus Equester', i.e. Poseidon Hippios or Horsey Poseidon, takes place. The etymology of his name is quite uncertain; in Etruscan it is Neθun(u)s. His festival is of the oldest series (Neptunalia, 23 July); we know concerning its ritual only that arbours, *umbrae*, of boughs were commonly erected, but it may be conjectured that its object was to obtain sufficient water at this hot and dry time of year. Neptune is attested at Rome before the first *lectister-nium (399 BC); his association there with *Mercurius seems to refer to the circulation of merchandise. His cult-partner is Salacia; she may be the goddess of 'leaping', i.e. springing water (*salire*), but was identified with Amphitrite as he was with Poseidon.

Nereus, an old sea god, son of *Pontus and father by the Oceanid Doris of the Nereids; *see* NYMPHS. He lives with the Nereids in the depths of the sea, particularly in the Aegean. *Hesiod and *Pindar extol his righteousness. Like other 'Old Men of the Sea' he has great wisdom and even the gift of prophecy. These abilities bring him into strenuous contest with *Heracles. Pindar's contemporary *Bacchylides and *Pherecydes relate that Heracles had to catch Nereus unawares in order to learn the whereabouts of the golden apples (*see* HESPERIDES). The 5th-cent. epic poet Panyassis makes Nereus give the bowl of the Sun to Heracles. In his contest with Heracles Nereus transforms himself into fire, water, and many other shapes. In addition to his 50 or 100 daughters, he is said by Lucian to have educated *Aphrodite.

The earliest representations of him are of the early 6th cent. BC, as a fishtailed old man fighting Heracles and mutating. Vases from the mid-6th cent. to the early Classical show him fully human and holding a fish rather than mutating, distinguished from *Triton, whom he watches fighting Heracles. Nereus attends the wedding of *Peleus and *Thetis on the François vase, and *c.*510–425 watches them wrestle. Some late Archaic vases show Nereus riding a hippocamp (i.e. a monster with a horse's body and a fish's tail), others Heracles destroying Nereus' house, sometimes in his presence. His only post-Classical appearance is on the Pergamum altar, where he is named, helping Doris and *Oceanus.

[Homer, *Iliad* 1. 357–9, 18. 35–8; Hesiod, *Theogony* 233–6; Pindar, *Pythian* 9. 93–6; Bacchylides, *Dithyramb* 17; Apollodorus 2. 5. 11; Horace, *Odes* 1. 15. 3–5]

Nestor, in mythology the youngest son of

*Neleus and Chloris, and the only one to survive the massacre by *Heracles. He was king of Pylos, and in the *epic cycle went with *Menelaus around Greece to assemble the heroes ready for the expedition against *Troy, then himself accompanied them with 90 ships and his sons *Antilochus and *Thrasymedes, even though he was at that time a very old man. Homer portrays him as a highly respected elder statesman, the archetypal wise old man, but one still strong and valiant in battle. He is always ready with advice: he tries to make peace between *Achilles and *Agamemnon, and later suggests the Embassy to Achilles, giving the ambassadors many instructions, he also suggests the spying raid on *Hector's camp in which Dolon is killed; he even offers to his son Antilochus advice on chariot-racing which he himself admits is superfluous. He is much given also to long, rambling stories of the distant past, rich in reminiscences of his own achievements: how he excelled in war against the *Centaurs and the Epeians, killed the Arcadian hero Ereuthalion and almost killed the *Moliones, and performed outstandingly at the funeral-games of Amarynceus. But he is always listened to by his comrades with patience, and indeed with respect (see Agamemnon's comments in *Iliad* book 2).

The *Aethiopis* (*see* EPIC CYCLE) told how *Memnon killed Antilochus, who died to save his father's life. The *Odyssey* records that, at Achilles' funeral, Nestor stopped the panic of the Greeks at the wailing of *Thetis and her attendants. After the fall of Troy he realized that disaster impended and sailed safely home to Pylos, where he entertained *Telemachus who was seeking news of *Odysseus. No tradition about the manner of his death has survived.

[Homer, *Iliad* 1. 250 ff., 2. 77, 370 ff., 591 ff., 9. 111 ff., 10. 204 ff., 11. 635 ff., 23. 306 ff.; *Odyssey* 3. 4 ff., 24. 47 ff.; Pindar, *Pythian* 6. 28–42]

night *See* NYX.

Nigidius Figulus, Publius (praetor 58 BC), scholar and mystic, 'after Varro the most learned of men' (Gellius), friend of *Cicero, active supporter of Pompey, died in exile in 45. He displayed an enthusiasm for Pythagoreanism (see PYTHAGORAS AND PYTHAGOREANISM) and along with it *astrology, and was said to engage in *magic. He wrote comprehensive works on grammar, theology (in particular De dis, 'On the Gods'), and various branches of natural science. His scholarship was too abstruse to win public esteem and he was eclipsed by his contemporary, M. Terentius *Varro. Fragments of his works survive in Gellius and other writers.

Nike, the goddess of Victory, is first mentioned by *Hesiod as daughter of the Titan (see TITANS) Pallas and *Styx, and sister of Zelos, Kratos, and Bia ('Rivalry', 'Strength', and 'Force'). With these she was honoured by *Zeus because she fought with the gods against the *Titans. She is popular with the authors of 5th-cent victory odes: *Bacchylides depicts her standing next to *Zeus on *Olympus and judging the award for areta (virtue) to gods and men, and according to *Pindar the victorious athlete sinks into the arms of Nike. Here Nike is already victory of an athletic, not only a military, contest.

Nike has no mythology of her own, and in cult may be assimilated with other gods, like Zeus at *Olympia or *Athena at Athens, where from c.566 BC, she had an altar on the Acropolis, and subsequently a Classical temple. *Pausanias calls this Nike wingless, adding that the Athenians and Spartans had a wingless Nike so that she would always stay with them. In art, her winged appearance is readily confused with orientalizing figures, and subsequently with *Iris, especially when she holds a kērykeion (*caduceus). She appears from the early 6th cent., on vases, freestanding or as acroteria, always in the bended-knee pose. She may have two or four wings. The Nike of Archermus (supposedly the first to give Nike wings) c.550 BC and that of Callimachus c.480, are representative.

In the Classical period, her iconography is fully developed, attributes including gar-

land, jug, phiale, and thymiatērion (censer). She is particularly popular on vases after the battle of Marathon, often alone, or pouring a libation over an altar, for both gods and men; also in athletic and military contexts, sometimes holding weapons, or decorating a *trophy. She strides, runs, or flies. Sculptural representations attempt to evoke flight, such as the Nike of Paros (c.470) where she hovers or alights; so too the Nike of Paeonius at Olympia of c.420. She was shown alighting on the hand of the Athena Parthenos and the Zeus at Olympia (where she was also an acroterion). The sculpted parapet of her temple on the Acropolis (c.410) shows her as messenger of Victory, setting a trophy, administrating libations, leading bulls to sacrifice, and, characteristically, binding her sandal. She appears as charioteer on Classical vases, especially south Italian.

In the Hellenistic period, Nike is used for political ends by Alexander the Great and his successors (the Diadochi) on coins and gems. The striding type is represented by the Nike of *Samothrace (c.306–250), and continues in attachments to Canosan vases and terracotta statuettes to the 1st cent.

[Hesiod, Theogony 383–4; Bacchylides 11. 1; Pindar, Nemean 5. 42; Pausanias 1. 22. 4, 3. 15. 7, 5. 14. 8]

nimbus, a circular cloud of light which surrounds the heads of gods or emperors and heroes. The belief that light radiates from a sacred or divine person is a common one and the nimbus only a special form which was developed in classical religion and art. Assyrian art, for instance, represents some gods with rays around their shoulders, and Greek art shows deities of light, such as *Helios, with a radiate crown. Greek vases and Etruscan mirrors of the 5th cent. BC afford the earliest examples of nimbus, often combined with the crown of rays. This hybrid form is also found at Palmyra in the 1st cent. AD. Under the Roman empire the plain, smooth form tends to prevail. In Pompeian wall-paintings it is still associated primarily with the deities of light, such as

*Apollo-Helios and *Diana, but almost all pagan gods of any importance are occasionally represented with a nimbus; in the 2nd and 3rd cents., for example in the mosaics of Antioch and Africa, its use becomes more indiscriminate. In late ancient art emperors, consuls, and other dignitaries, and sometimes even portraits of dead commoners have the nimbus. In Christian art only Christ was represented with the nimbus at first, but it was soon extended to the Virgin, the major saints, and angels.

Niobe, in mythology, daughter of *Tantalus and wife of *Amphion of Thebes. They had a large family, though the number varies in different accounts: six children of either sex according to *Homer (the oldest mention of Niobe, which seems to imply that the story was well known and that she was already a stock type of bereavement), seven of either sex according to Ovid, five or ten in other versions. Niobe boasted that she was superior to *Leto, who had only one son and one daughter, *Apollo and *Artemis. So Leto called on her children to avenge the insult, whereupon Apollo shot down all Niobe's sons and Artemis her daughters. Sometimes it was said that there were either one or two survivors. Homer seems to have adapted the story of Niobe to suit *Priam's situation: after the children were killed they lay unburied for nine days because *Zeus had turned the people to stone, then on the tenth day the gods themselves buried them (cf. HECTOR). Niobe, 'worn out with weeping', ate, just as Priam is being urged to eat, and then became a rock on Mt. Sipylus in Magnesia, an image of everlasting sorrow with water flowing down her face like tears. The rock, according to *Pausanias, was a natural formation looking something like a woman. Niobe remains to this day a symbol of grief.

In art the deaths of the children and the grief of their mother are a favourite subject.

See also GENEALOGICAL TABLES (5) DESCENDANTS OF TANTALUS.

[Homer, *Iliad* 24. 604 ff.; Apollodorus 3. 5. 6; Pausanias 1. 21. 3; Ovid, *Metamorphoses* 6. 182-3]

Nireus, after *Achilles the best-looking man in the Achaean expedition against *Troy, became in later poetry a byword for male beauty. No certain representation in art is identified.

Nisus (1), legendary king of Megara and evidently an important hero there, according to ancient thought-patterns giving his name to its harbour, Nisaea. His life and the fate of his city depended on his red or purple lock of hair; this was cut off by his daughter Scylla in order to betray the city to the besieging general *Minos, either for a bribe or, according to *Ovid for love. Nisus was turned into a sea-eagle, Scylla into the bird *ciris* pursued by him. The story is told at length in the pseudo-Virgilian poem *Ciris*. Nisus was also worshipped in Athens, where he was made into a son of *Pandion, who received the Megarid (the territory of Megara) when his father divided *Attica among his four sons.

[Aeschylus, *Choephori* 612-22; Ovid, *Metamorphoses* 8. 1-151.]

Nisus (2), Trojan hero in *Virgil's *Aeneid*, son of Hyrtacus, sympathetically presented as the devoted older lover of the young and headstrong Euryalus. In book 5 he helps Euryalus to victory in the foot-race, and dies avenging him in the night-episode in book 9.

[Virgil, *Aeneid* 5. 286-361, 9. 176-502]

Nonnus, of Panopolis in Egypt (fl. AD 450-70), the main surviving exponent of an elaborate, metrically very strict style of Greek epic that evolved in the imperial period. His huge *Dionysiaca* is in 48 books, the sum of the books of the *Iliad* and *Odyssey*; Nonnus' stated intention is to rival *Homer, and to surpass him in the dignity of his divine, not human, subject. The poem describes at length the antecedents of *Dionysus' birth, the birth itself, and the new god's fight for recognition as a member of the pantheon in the face of hostility from Hera; the central section (books 13-40), which describes the war of Dionysus and his Bacchic forces against the Indians and their king Deriades, is Nonnus' equivalent of the *Iliad*. Nonnus' highly rhetorical and extraordinarily luxuri-ant style is an attempt to create a new type of formulaic composition, recognizably similar to that of Homer but with greater variety and with far more lexical permutations. In his mythological learning and countless allu-sions to earlier poetry he is a true successor to Hellenistic writers of the Callimachean school (*see* CALLIMACHUS); the episodes that describe Dionysus' love affairs with youths and nymphs are influenced also by the *novel.

Nonnus' other extant work is a hexameter version of St John's Gospel. Stylistic analysis suggests that it may be earlier than the *Dio-nysiaca*; but the *Dionysiaca* clearly lacks final revision. These two facts have led scholars to make ingenious conjectures about Nonnus' life, religion, and possible conversions. But there is evidence that amongst intellectuals in the 5th cent. it was not felt contradictory for a Christian to write heavily classicizing verse.

Nortia, an Etruscan goddess (*see* ETRUSCAN RELIGION). The Etruscan name-form is uncer-tain. In her temple at Volsinii each year a nail was affixed; Livy compares the old Roman custom of the *praetor maximus* affixing on the Ides of September a nail in Jupiter's temple, and interprets these yearly nails (*clavi an-nales*) as markers of years. They could serve that purpose, but the goal of the rite (with Mesopotamian and Hittite parallels) was rather to fix the fates for the coming year. Nortia was identified with *Fortuna and *Nemesis. *Necessitas* and the Etruscan *Athrpa* appear with nails of destiny. Akin to this rite was the practice of driving nails to ward off disaster or pestilence.

Novatianus, Roman presbyter and 'anti-pope'. On failing to be elected to the see of Rome in AD 251, he had himself consecrated counter-bishop to Cornelius, perhaps from a mixture of personal and theological mo-tives, and certainly under pressure. His schismatic church of *katharoi* ('pure ones'), which lasted for centuries, was strongly rig-orist, refusing all reconciliation to those who lapsed or committed serious sins. Surviving works, written in stylish Latin, include at least two letters in the Cyprianic corpus (30, 36; perhaps 31), an impressive treatise on the Trinity, and another on Jewish dietary laws; the *De spectaculis* ('On Spectacles') and *De bono pudicitiae* ('On the Excellence of Chas-tity') attributed to *Cyprian are now also widely accepted as his. His debt to *Stoicism has been exaggerated. He was apparently martyred under Valerian.

novel The surviving Greek novels, all from the imperial Roman period, are concerned primarily with the obstacles to a happy ro-mantic union between hero and heroine, and deal with religious matters only in pass-ing. The same may be said of Petronius' *Satyrica*, though its style and subject-matter are otherwise quite different. The other remaining Latin novel is the *Metamorphoses* of *Apuleius. This is written in eleven books and concerns the metamorphosis of a young man into a donkey and his comic adventures before retransformation by the goddess *Isis. It contains a number of inserted tales, the most famous being that of *Cupid and *Psyche in two books. The *Metamorphoses* has marked Isiac and Platonic elements; in the final book, the conversion of Lucius to Isiac cult and the resulting reassessment of his adventures (11. 15. 1–5), coupled with the apparent revelation that the narrator is no longer Lucius but Apuleius himself (11. 27. 9), provide a problematic conclusion in both ideological and narratological terms.

Christian texts in Latin make use of the ancient novel for fictionalized hagiography: the pseudo-Clementine *Recognitiones* (4th cent. AD), translated from an earlier Greek original, shows many novelistic elements in its melodramatic story of the young Clem-ent, Peter's successor as bishop of Rome, as does *Jerome's similar *Life of St Paul the First Hermit* from the same period. *See also* DARES OF PHRYGIA.

novensides, a group of Roman deities of totally unknown function. According to one theory this group was supposed to embrace, in contrast to the *di* *indigetes, divinities newly installed at Rome (*nov-en-sides*, 'newly settled-in'). A second hypothesis, in view of the spelling *novensiles*, attested in the literary sources, derived their name from *nuere*: hence 'mobile, active' deities. More recently these two interpretations have been dropped in favour of a connection with *novem*, 'nine', already made in antiquity. The epigraphic testimony from the land of the Marsi, along with the literary references to their *Sabine origin, suggests that these 'nine gods' were originally from central Italy and were introduced fairly early to Rome, a colony of which, Pisaurum, mentions them. But others give them an Etruscan origin.

Numa (Pompilius Numa), legendary second king of Rome (traditionally 715–673 BC), from whom the Aemilii, Calpurnii, Marcii, Pinarii, and Pomponii later claimed descent. Reputedly a *Sabine from Cures, he supposedly created much of the basic framework of Roman public religion through his institution of cults, rituals, priesthoods, and calendar reforms. Already in Ennius' *Annales* (early 2nd cent. BC) he claimed to have received instruction from *Egeria and (an originally distinct?) Greek or Graecizing tradition, going back at least to 181 BC (when alleged 'books of Numa' were discovered and destroyed), made him a pupil of *Pythagoras. Rationalistic historians reinterpreted Egeria as a political fiction and the discarding of the Pythagoras story on chronological grounds enables *Cicero and Livy to stress Numa's native credentials. Accounts of Numa's reforms (including e.g. the encouragement of settled agriculture) are hardly historical and are elaborated according to individual taste: Livy, for example, discards stories of divine instruction and miraculous encounters with deities to focus on religion as a matter of human ordinance and an ethico-political instrument. Alleged 'laws of Numa' will be (at best) supposedly ancient ordinances preserved by the *pontifices.

numbers, sacred, certain numbers taken to represent or control divine actions. The derivation of such numbers can be extremely complex, deriving at times from natural phenomena, at times from linguistic coincidence, this last being the result of the use of letters for counting in a majority of ancient societies, in turn resulting in the practice of numerology, or the representation of a person or concept by the sum of the letters in a word. Thus in Aramaic, the name of Nero Caesar, written as *nrwn ksr*, is 666, and in the *Sibylline Oracles* (*see* SIBYL) emperors are often represented by the sum of the letters in their names.

Interest in the number seven seems to derive from the belief that there were seven planets, in five from the number of fingers on a hand (and, possibly, ten for similar reasons), in three, possibly from the tripartite division of the cosmos into air, land, and sea, and twelve from the numbers of signs in the zodiac. Multiples of these numbers may also be regarded as significant (e.g. nine), as could numbers that exceeded a significant number by one (e.g. 13). After the adoption of the Julian calendar (*see* CALENDAR, ROMAN), the number 365 seems also to have attracted considerable attention.

In addition to calculations based upon numbers derived from nature, there were calculations based upon broader eras of human history. Here the number ten seems to have been of particular interest in the Roman world as the number of *saecula* (ages) before an eschatological catastrophe (the succession of nine, or, more often, ten *saecula* derived from Etruscan speculation), even though there was considerable dispute as to how *saecula* should be counted. The Egyptian scheme of the Great Year (1,461 ordinary years) was derived from the fact that the Egyptian year was a quarter-day too short, and thus the calendar corresponded exactly with the natural year only once every 1,461 years. In Judaeo-Christian thought, a belief in a 'sabbatical millennium' developed out of the view that a day of the Lord lasted for a thousand years, and that he had created the world in six days resting upon the seventh. This scheme generated much heated debate so long as schemes based upon the age of the world were used.

numen, the 'expressed will of a divinity', a term generating much modern debate. Basing themselves on the pre-deist theories of the beginning of this century, some scholars supposed that by *numen* the Romans meant an impersonal divine force. This conception has since been challenged, in particular on grammatical grounds. In fact, until the beginning of our era (and later), *numen* is always construed with the genitive of the name of a divinity (a term like *deus*, or with the adjective *divinus*), and can only mean 'the expressed will of a divinity'. This assent was indicated notably by the *nutus*, an inclination of the head. Such at any rate was the interpretation of the ancient grammarians. The concept of *numen*, which without doubt was very old, serves to represent the action of both mortals and immortals. The *numen* of a divinity shows the actual and particular will of this deity, and it is different both from his or her person and *genius* (which describes the capacity for action of a being or a thing at the moment of its constitution). In general the *numen* concerns the gods and, under the empire, the ruling emperor, but exceptionally it applies to the senate and the Roman people, endowed like the ruler with a quasi-divine power of action. The *numen Augusti* received a cult from the beginning of our era, its function being to represent the exceptional power of the ruler, and enabling the attribution of divine honours to him in his lifetime. Later on, writers considered the *numen* as an 'integral part of the particular will of the deity'— i.e. as a synonym of divinity, taking the manifestation of power for the divinity who exercises it. This usage was never general, however, and only applied in earlier times. *See* RULER-CULT.

Numenius, of Apamea (2nd cent. AD), leading Platonist (also referred to as a Py-

thagorean). Substantial fragments of two of his works survive: a metaphysical dialogue *On the Good* and a history of the Academy designed to show how much it had corrupted *Plato's teaching. This teaching was Pythagorean, he claimed, relating it to the ancient wisdom of the Brahmans, Magi (*see* MAGUS), Egyptians, and Jews whose scriptures he interpreted allegorically. He shared ideas with *Gnosticism and with the *Chaldaean Oracles*. His metaphysics includes a first god (the Good, which is absolutely transcendent) and a second god who imitates the first and organizes the world. Matter is evil, as is life in the body for our soul. He had considerable influence on *Plotinus, who was accused of plagiarizing from him, on *Origen, *Porphyry, and later *Neoplatonists. *See* NEOPYTHAGOREANISM.

Numicus (or Numicius) (mod. Fosso di Pratica), the creek near *Lavinium in Latium where *Aeneas allegedly perished. He was subsequently venerated in the sanctuary of *Sol Indiges at the mouth of the river, where he is supposed to have landed. Finds show that the sanctuary was in existence by the 5th cent. BC. *See* RIVER-GODS.

nymphaeum In the Classical Greek world a nymphaeum was a shrine to the *Nymphs, often a rural cave or grove with no architectural adornment. Several sculptured reliefs dedicated to *Pan and the Nymphs are known from Classical Attica (*see* CAVES, SACRED).

The Nymphs were with *river-gods the guardian spirits of sources of pure *water. When the tyrant Theagenes of Megara diverted fresh water for his city, he sacrificed to the river-god at the point where the waters had been captured. By the Roman imperial period such sentiment was more publicly expressed at the urban terminus of aqueducts, where the waters were filtered into a fountain, often richly decorated with statues and inscriptions recording the generosity, piety, and social status of the donor, and in many instances referring to the river or spring from which the waters originated. The most intelligible surviving example was built by Tiberius Claudius Atticus Herodes in the sanctuary at *Olympia about AD 150. The modern term *nymphaeum* applied to such buildings derives from late antique usage; in the early empire urban fountains were called *munera*, onerous burdens to those who held public office. Ornate fountains were built in many wealthy cities of the Roman empire, notably Miletus, Lepcis Magna, and Carthage. Grotto-nymphaea were built as rustic conceits in some late republican and early imperial villas of the Roman Campagna and the bay of Naples. Some sacred nymphaea survived in remote areas: several Greek sites were noted by *Pausanias, who commended their oracular or healing powers; many were associated with baths.

nymphs A varied category of female divinities anthropomorphically perceived as young women (the word *nymphē*, means also 'bride'). They inhabit and animately express differentiated nature: *water (rivers, springs, the sea), mountains, trees, and 'places' (regions, towns, states). Their ubiquitous presence in popular imagination, folklore, art, myth, and cult, provides a vivid illustration of ancient pantheism.

Cult of nymphs, particularly associated with caves, is mentioned already in *Homer and corroborated by archaeology. In the Polis cave at *Ithaca, there was a cult both to *Odysseus and the nymphs; in western Crete (*see* CRETAN CULTS AND MYTHS), at Lera was a cave sacred to *Pan and the nymphs. The grotto on Mt Hymettus above Vari (*Attica) was sacred to Pan, *Apollo, and the nymphs; at the Corycian cave in Phocis were found hundreds of small vessels (aryballoi), thousands of figurines, and 16,000 knucklebones. (*See* CAVES, SACRED.) Nymphs were closely associated (mythically perceived as daughters or lovers) in worship with *river-gods, such as the archetypical *Acheloüs. They received both animal and cereal *sacrifices; *wine was usually forbidden in their worship. Nymphs are intim-

ately, albeit vaguely, linked with productive and life-enhancing powers. Although mostly belonging to the countryside or to particular spots (streams, groves, hills), nymphs appear also in official state cult. *Dionysus' nurse, Nysa (a place-name), had a state cult at Athens led by official 'hymn-singers', *hymnē-triai*. Pandemos was the 'All the People' nymph in Athens. There was a fountain-house sacred to the nymphs in the Athenian Agora. At Cos magistrates were responsible for 'ancestral sacrifices' to the nymphs. At Thera each Dorian tribe (Hylleis and Dymanes; *see* PHYLAI) had its own nymph. In Illyrian Apollonia the crackling of *incense (burning on the altar of the nymphs) served for divination.

The association with other gods, such as Pan (especially), *Hermes, and *Artemis appears both in cult and myth. Apollo and Dionysus are addressed as 'Nymph-leaders', *nymphagetai*. Often regarded as daughters of Zeus, nymphs were also perceived as belonging to an earlier stratum: the Meliads, nymphs of ash trees, emerged from the drops of blood of *Uranus' castrated genitals. Nymphs are either lovers or mothers of gods, heroes, or satyrs; as virgins they roam the woods and mountains with Artemis. *Eponymous nymphs (or mothers of eponymous heroes), such as Aegina and Aeacus, or Satyra (Satyrion) the mother of Taras (both the name of a river and the city, the later Tarentum), filled up the landscape.

Nymphs may have other nymphs attending them (*Calypso). They are either immortal or endowed with super-human longevity. They are often named after their respective elements: Hamadryads die with the particular trees with which they are identified; Oreads are mountain-nymphs; Naiads and Hydriads, water-nymphs, often daughters of the river-god, e.g. Asopus; the Nereids are nymphs of the calm sea (daughters of the Old Man of the Sea, *Nereus); Alseids reside in groves (*alsos*); Oceanids are daughters of *Oceanus and *Tethys; other nymphs were named after geographical features, such as the Leimoniads, nymphs of meadows, or the Acheloids, nymphs of the river Acheloüs.

Most nymphs are benevolent, although they may abduct handsome boys (*Hylas). They bring flowers, watch with Apollo and Hermes over the flocks, and, as patronesses of healing springs (for instance, in the Asclepieum at Athens), they aid the sick. (*See* SPRINGS, SACRED.) As divinities of woods and mountains they may help hunters. Folk-tales, similar to those about fairies and mermaids, are told about nymphs. A man who sees them becomes 'possessed by nymphs'. They punish unresponsive lovers, as did the nymphs who blinded *Daphnis. *See also* NYMPHAEUM.

Nyx, personification of night. In Greek mythology she was a great cosmogonical figure, according to Homer feared and respected even by *Zeus. In *Hesiod she is born of *Chaos and mother of Aether, Hemera, and lesser powers. Frequent touches in the description recall her nocturnal aspect, but this is scarcely seen in the Orphic *theogonies, where her influence over creation is immense (cf. ORPHIC LITERATURE; ORPHISM). In the Rhapsodies she is daughter of *Phanes and succeeds to his power. When in turn she hands the sceptre to her son *Uranus she continues to advise the younger generations, Uranus, *Cronus, and especially *Zeus, in the task of world-making. Her influence is due to her oracular powers, exercised from a cave. There are signs that in an earlier Orphic version Phanes was absent and Nyx the primal power. The theogony of Aristophanes' *Birds* makes her prior to Eros (= Phanes), and this supposition suits the awful dignity of Nyx which Homer and '*Orpheus' alike emphasize, and the vague reference of *Aristotle to *theologoi* who derive everything from Night. Nyx was primarily a *mythographer's goddess, with little cult, but one may mention her connection with *oracles, which is not confined to Orphic literature. In Greek and Roman art her identification is problematic as she has no canonical form (fig. N on the Parthenon's east pediment, for example, may either be Nyx or *Selene).

oaths An oath (Gk. *horkos*, Lat. *iusiurandum*) was a statement (assertory) or promise (promissory) strengthened by the invocation of a god as a witness and often with the addition of a *curse in case of perjury. A defendant in a lawsuit, for example, might swear by a god that his testimony was truthful and might specify the punishment for perjury. If the oath was false, the god, by effecting the provisions of the curse, would punish the individual, not for lying in court but for committing perjury. Throughout antiquity oaths were required of signatories to treaties, of parties to legal disputes, commercial and private contracts, conspiracies, and marriages, of governmental officials, judges, and jurors, and, particularly by the Romans, of soldiers (*sacramentum*), and, under the empire, of citizens to affirm their allegiance to the emperor.

Virtually any deity could be invoked as a witness, but in formal oaths the Greeks often called upon a triad of gods representing the sky, earth, and sea (*Helios or *Zeus, Gē (*see* GAIA) or *Demeter, and *Poseidon); the Romans upon *Jupiter (Dius Fidius) and 'all the gods'. Everyday language was apparently sprinkled with casual oaths, and Greek women often invoked *Artemis, the men Zeus or *Heracles; Roman women named Castor and the men Hercules or Pollux (*see* DIOSCURI). The gods themselves swore by the *Styx. The punishment for perjury, when specified, might suit the particular circumstances of the oath-taker, but often called for 'the complete destruction of the perjuror and his family'. An oath itself could be strengthened by being taken in a *sanctuary or by an act of sympathetic *magic. As an example of the latter, in *Homer's *Iliad* the combatants, as they prayed to Zeus and poured a *libation to accompany their oath, said, 'Whoever first causes suffering contrary to this oath, may their brains flow to the ground like this wine.' Animal *sacrifice was performed for the same purpose.

The maintenance of oaths was an essential element of public and personal piety. The Spartans imagined that their defeats at Pylos and elsewhere were caused by their disregard of an oath, and *Plato saw in the growing disregard of oaths signs of a breakdown of belief in the gods (*see* ATHEISM).

[Homer, *Iliad* 3. 295 ff.; Thucydides 7. 18. 2; Plato, *Laws* 12. 948b–e; Euripides, *Medea* 492–5]

Obsequens, Iulius, tabulator of Roman prodigies (*see* PORTENTS), most plausibly dated to the 4th or early 5th cent. AD. His collection covered prodigies from 249 to 12 BC, and is extant for 190–12. It is based on Livy, though comparison with books 37–45 shows that he exercised selectivity; he also notes the events which he thought the omens presaged or reflected. There is little basis for the common view that he knew Livy only or largely in epitome.

Oceanus, son of *Uranus (Sky) and Gē (*Gaia, Earth), husband of *Tethys (a combination probably derived from the Babylonian creation-epic *Enuma Elis*), and father of the Oceanids and river-gods; the name has no Indo-European etymology and is probably a loan-word. The Homeric Oceanus is the river encircling the whole world, from which through subterranean connections issue all other rivers; its sources are in the west where the sun sets. Monsters such as Gorgons (see GORGO/MEDUSA), *Hecatoncheires, *Hesperides, Geryoneus, and outlandish tribes such as *Cimmerians, Aethiopians (see ETHIOPIA), and *pygmies, live by the waters of Oceanus.

In Greek theories of the world Oceanus is conceived as the great cosmic power, water, through which all life grows, and in Greek mythology as a benign old god. Sometimes the elemental, sometimes the personal, aspect is more emphasized. The belief that sun and stars rise and set in the ocean is expressed mythologically in the statement that stars bathe in Oceanus, and the Sun traverses it in a golden bowl by night to get back to the east. (See HELIOS.) The rise of rational geographical investigation in Herodotus and others narrowed the significance of Oceanus down to the geographical term of 'Ocean'.

In art Oceanus appears early (François vase), is represented on the famous Gigantomachy (see GIANTS) of Pergamum, and becomes really common in Roman times, especially on sarcophagi (see ART, FUNERARY, ROMAN), with Earth as a counterpart. See TITAN.

[Homer, Iliad 3. 3, 14. 201, 246, 302, 18. 489; Odyssey 1. 22, 2. 13; Hesiod, Theogony 133, 364]

Ocnus ('Hesitancy' personified), a proverbial figure made famous by Polygnotus' Underworld mural in the Cnidian leschē (club-house for the citizens of Cnidos) at *Delphi. The painter showed him seated in *Hades, plaiting a straw rope which a donkey, behind him, ate up as fast as he could weave it; presumably, since for the Greeks the future lies 'behind', the allegorical point was that chronic indecision can lead only to futile consequences (though *Pausanias was told by the locals that Ocnus, in life, had been a hard-working man whose wife spent all his money). It may also be relevant that 'donkey' (onos) is the Greek for windlass; as if winches 'ate' rope. His eternal labour recalls that of the

Danaides (see DANAUS); he looks like a popular moralist's humorous, scaled-down version of the great criminals in hell.

[Pausanias 10. 29. 1]

October horse See MARS.

Odysseus (Latin Ulixes from one of several Greek variants; hence English Ulysses), king of *Ithaca; son of *Laertes and *Anticlea; husband of *Penelope; hero of *Homer's Odyssey.

In Homer's Iliad, despite his out-of-the-way kingdom, Odysseus is already one of the most prominent of the Greek heroes. He displays martial prowess (e.g. at 11. 310–488, where he delays the rout of the Greeks), courage and resourcefulness (e.g. in the Doloneia of book 10, a late addition), and above all wisdom and diplomacy (e.g. at 2. 169–335, where he prevents the Greek army from disbanding, and in the embassy to *Achilles, especially 9. 223–306). He shows little of the skill in deceit which is characteristic of him in the Odyssey, but such epithets as 'much enduring' and 'cunning', which occur in both epics, must refer to his exploits after the Trojan War, and show that these were always his principal claim to fame.

In the Odyssey he is in some ways the typical 'trickster' of folktales, who uses guile and deception to defeat stronger opponents. His maternal grandfather is the knavish *Autolycus (19. 392–466). Besides spear and sword he uses the bow, which was often considered a less manly weapon, and he even procures arrow-poison (1. 261–2). He not only resorts to trickery by necessity but sometimes revels in it, as when he boasts of his triumph over the Cyclops (9. 473–525; see CYCLOPES); and his lying tales on Ithaca are elaborated with relish, as *Athena observes (13. 291–5). But Homer was concerned to make him a worthy hero, not just for a folktale, but for an epic. Books 1–4, where his son *Telemachus takes centre-stage, are largely devoted to building up our sense of his greatness: he is the ideal king, whose return is necessary to establish order on Ithaca, and a friend deeply honoured by

*Nestor and *Menelaus. When we first see him in book 5—longing for home after his long detention by *Calypso, then no sooner released than shipwrecked—the emphasis is on his noble patience and endurance. At his lowest point, naked and destitute on the shore of *Scheria in Book 6, he is still resourceful, and can be seen by the princess *Nausicaa as an ideal husband (6. 239–45). Even in the fantastic and magical episodes which he relates as bard-like storyteller to the Phaeacians in books 9–12 (the Lotus-Eaters, the Cyclops, the Bag of the Winds, the *Laestrygonians, the witch *Circe, the visit to the Underworld, the *Sirens, *Scylla and *Charybdis, the Cattle of the Sun), there is pathos as well as adventure. When he finally reaches Ithaca he spends much of the rest of the poem (books 17–21) in the most humiliating condition, disguised as a beggar in his own house; but in his final revenge over Penelope's suitors, although he takes the crafty and necessary precaution of removing their weapons (19. 1–52), the main emphasis is on his strength in stringing the great bow and the skill with which he wields it (books 21–2).

(For the works mentioned in the following paragraph *see* EPIC CYCLE.) A later epic, the *Telegoneia* of *Eugammon of Cyrene, continued the story with further travels and martial adventures for Odysseus, who was finally killed unwittingly by Telegonus, his son by Circe. Other early poetry seems to have presented him less favourably. In the *Cypria* he feigned madness to evade his obligation to join the Trojan expedition, but the trick was exposed by *Palamedes. In revenge he and *Diomedes (2) later brought about Palamedes' death. In the *Little Iliad* Odysseus and Diomedes stole the *Palladium, a Trojan talisman; and by some accounts Odysseus tried to kill Diomedes on the way back. The dispute with *Aias over the arms of Achilles, first mentioned at *Odyssey* 11. 543–51, was related in the *Aethiopis* and *Little Iliad*, and *Pindar claims that Odysseus won the arms by dishonest trickery. The killing of the infant Astyanax was attributed to *Neoptole-

mus by the *Little Iliad* but to Odysseus by the *Capture of Troy*.

The tragedians tended to be similarly unfavourable. *Sophocles, while presenting a noble and magnanimous Odysseus in *Aias*, makes him an unprincipled cynic in *Philoctetes*. *Euripides depicts the Homeric Odysseus straightforwardly in *Cyclops*, but made him a villain in his lost *Palamedes* (as does the sophist Gorgias in his *Defence of Palamedes*), and his character in other plays (on stage in *Hecuba*, reported elsewhere) is in keeping with this. His detractors now often call him the son, not of Laertes, but of the criminal *Sisyphus, who had allegedly seduced Anticlea before her marriage.

*Virgil's references to Ulixes in *Aeneid* 2 follow the Euripidean conception (ignoring a tradition which made him a founder of Rome and father of *Latinus), as does Seneca in his tragedy *Troades*. The dispute over the arms of Achilles, treated as a rhetorical debate by Socrates' associate Antisthenes, is again so treated by *Ovid, *Metamorphoses* 13.

At a few sites Odysseus was honoured as a cult hero, evidently because of his prestige in epic. His name has been found on a dedication on Ithaca.

In art he is always a popular figure. The more spectacular adventures are illustrated especially often in the Archaic period (the blinding of Polyphemus (*see* CYCLOPES) and the escape under the ram are found as early as the seventh century). Later these are joined by quieter subjects, such as the embassy to Achilles and the dispute over the arms. From the 5th cent. Odysseus is often depicted in a conical hat, the *pilos*.

Oebalus, an early Spartan king, who had a hero-shrine (*see* HERO-CULT) at Sparta (*see* SPARTAN CULTS). He has no legend, merely a place in several mutually contradictory genealogies. Hence *Oebalius*, *Oebalides*, etc., in Latin poetry often mean Spartan, and the name itself is now and then used for some minor character of Spartan or Peloponnesian origin.

[Pausanias 3. 5. 10]

Oecles or Oecleus, in mythology, father
of *Amphiaraus, as for instance in *Aeschylus' *Seven against Thebes*.

Oedipus, son of Laius, the king of Thebes
who killed his father and married his
mother. The name appears to mean 'with
swollen foot', but the reason for this is obscure, as the explanation given by ancient
authors—that his feet were swollen because
his ankles were pierced when he was exposed as a baby—looks like rationalizing
invention.

*Homer's *Iliad* mentions him only in the
context of the funeral games held after his
death, implying that he died at Thebes and
probably in battle. Homer's *Odyssey*, however, tells how he unwittingly killed his
father and married his mother Epicaste (the
later Iocasta), but the gods soon made this
known (this version allows no time for the
couple to have children) and Epicaste
hanged herself. Oedipus continued to reign
at Thebes, suffering all the woes that a
mother's *Erinyes can inflict.

Of the epic *Oidipodia* (*see* EPIC CYCLE) we
know little except that it mentioned the
*Sphinx (also mentioned in Hesiod), who
killed *Haemon (3) son of *Creon (1) and
must have been killed (perhaps in fight) by
Oedipus, and that Oedipus had children, not
by his mother, but by a second wife, Euryganeia. The children must have included
*Eteocles and Polynices, and probably also
*Antigone (1) and Ismene.

Another epic, the *Thebais*, told how Oedipus, now probably blind, twice cursed his
sons, first when Polynices disobeyed him
by serving him wine in a gold cup on a silver
table, and again when his sons served him
the wrong joint of meat. He prayed that they
would quarrel over their patrimony and die
at each other's hands, and the epic went on
to describe the Theban War that ensued. *See*
SEVEN AGAINST THEBES.

It is uncertain when Oedipus was first said
to have had children by his mother, and
when the motif of his exile arose. In a fragment of *Stesichorus the mother of Eteocles

and Polynices attempts to mediate between
them, presumably after the death of Oedipus, but she could be either Iocasta (Epicaste) or Euryganeia. Pindar may allude to
Oedipus in exile.

In 467 *Aeschylus produced a tetralogy
consisting of *Laius*, *Oedipus*, the surviving
Seven against Thebes, and the satyr-play *Sphinx*.
Though much is debatable, the outlines of
the Oedipus story can be gathered from fragments and from allusions in the *Seven against
Thebes*. Laius learned from the *Delphic
oracle that to save the city he must die childless. Overcome by lust, however, he begot
Oedipus, and sought to have the baby exposed. Oedipus somehow survived to kill
his father at a fork in the road near Potniae.
He came to Thebes and rid the city of the
man-eating Sphinx, probably by answering
its riddle. He married Iocasta, became an
honoured king, and begot Eteocles and Polynices. The patricide and incest came to light
(we do not know how, but the prophet *Tiresias may have played a role), and Oedipus in
his anguish blinded himself and cursed the
sons born of the incest: they were to divide
their patrimony with the sword. In the *Seven
against Thebes* Oedipus is dead, having probably died at Thebes.

*Sophocles' *Antigone* mentions how Oedipus blinded himself and died and Iocasta
hanged herself. But Sophocles' *Oedipus Tyrannus* (*King Oedipus*) became the definitive
account. Here Laius received an *oracle
from *Apollo that his son would kill him,
so he ordered a shepherd to expose the
infant Oedipus on M. Cithaeron. The shepherd, however, took pity on the baby, and
Oedipus survived to be brought up as the son
of *Polybus, king of Corinth, and his wife
Merope. An oracle warned him that he
would kill his father and marry his mother,
so he fled from Corinth. At a junction of
three roads near Daulis he killed Laius in a
quarrel, not knowing who he was. Coming
to Thebes he answered the riddle of the
Sphinx, married Iocasta, and became king.
When the play opens, the city is being rav-
aged by a plague, caused, so the oracle

reveals, by the polluting presence of the killer of Laius (*see* POLLUTION). Oedipus, an intelligent and benevolent king, pronounces a *curse on the unknown killer and begins an investigation, which ends in the discovery of the whole truth. Iocasta hangs herself and Oedipus blinds himself with pins from her dress. The ending is problematic, as Oedipus does not go into the immediate exile foreshadowed earlier but remains, for the moment, in the palace.

*Euripides too wrote an *Oedipus*, in which the king was blinded by the servants of Laius, not by his own hand. In Euripides' *Phoenissae* he is self-blinded and is still living in the palace at the time of his sons' death.

At the end of his life Sophocles returned to Oedipus with his *Oedipus at Colonus*. Here the blind man, led by Antigone, comes to the grove of the Eumenides (*see* ERINYES) at *Colonos near Athens, where he knows that he must die. Protected by *Theseus, he resists the attempts of Polynices and Iocasta's brother Creon, who banished him from Thebes, to bring him back there for their selfish purposes. He curses his sons for their neglect, and finally, called by the gods, he dies mysteriously at a spot known only to Theseus, where his angry corpse will protect Athens against Theban attack. Tombs and *hero-cults of Oedipus are reported from Colonos and from Athens itself (among other places), but the antiquity of these, and their relation to Sophocles' play (where he has *no* tomb), are uncertain.

Roman authors of an *Oedipus* tragedy included *Caesar. The *Oedipus* of Seneca is based on Sophocles' *King Oedipus*. The role of Oedipus in Statius' *Thebaid* is derived from Euripides' *Phoenissae*.

In art the confrontation with the Sphinx is often portrayed, other episodes more rarely.

[Homer, *Iliad* 23. 679, *Odyssey* 11. 271–80; Hesiod, *Theogony* 326; Sophocles, *King Oedipus, Oedipus at Colonus*]

Oeneus, mythical king of Calydon in Aetolia (*see* AETOLIAN CULTS AND MYTHS) and father by Althaea of *Meleager and *Deianira. His name (from *oinos*, *wine) and the story in Hyginus that Deianira's real father was *Dionysus suggest that he was a hero associated with that god. His second wife Periboea was the mother of *Diomedes (2)'s father *Tydeus, whose paternity is variously given; either Tydeus or Diomedes took the aged Oeneus' side in a quarrel over the throne with his brother Agrius.

An Attic (*see* ATTIC CULTS AND MYTHS) hero Oeneus was among the tribal *eponymoi*; he was said to be son of Dionysus or of Pandion, but we know nothing else about him.

[Hyginus, *Fables* 129; Apollodorus 1. 8. 4–6; Pausanias 2. 25. 2]

Oenomaus *See* HIPPODAMIA (1); PELOPS.

Oenomaus of Gadara (fl. *c*.AD 120), a Cynic philosopher; seemingly the *pagan philosopher 'Abnimos' of the *Talmud, so perhaps a Hellenized *Jew. He wrote: 'Exposure of the Charlatans' (or 'Against the Oracles'), a witty and inventive polemic extensively preserved by *Eusebius; various works effectively known by title only; and tragedies (lost). An ambitious and important literary voice of later Cynicism, he imitated *Diogenes (2) and other Cynic authors. He himself became a literary influence on Lucian, a philosophical influence on 4th-cent. Cynics, a target of *Julian's vilification and a source for Christians of arguments against paganism.

Oenone, a *nymph of Mt. Ida, loved by *Paris. When he deserted her for *Helen she was bitterly jealous, and on learning that he had been wounded by *Philoctetes with one of *Heracles' arrows, she refused to cure him. Relenting too late, she came to *Troy and found him already dead, then hanged herself or leapt upon his funeral pyre.

[Apollodorus 3. 154–5]

Ogygus (etymology and meaning uncertain), a primeval king, generally of Boeotia, but also in various sources said to be of Lycia; of Egyptian Thebes; of the Titans (*see* TITAN). The first Deluge was in his time according to *Eusebius.

[Pausanias 9. 5. 1]

oil *See* OLIVE.

ointment (Gk. *myron*, Lat. *unguentum*) was used for medical and cosmetic purposes, and in religious ceremonies and funeral rites (*see* DEAD, DISPOSAL OF), in which the restorative, the aromatic, the sacrificial, and the sumptuary combined in varying degrees. Vegetable oils and animal fats served as the vehicles for herbal remedies and fragrant salves, lotions, and unguents. Exotic ingredients, such as cassia, cinnamon, frankincense and myrrh were inevitably more costly and carried greater status. *See* INCENSE.

Olen, mythical poet, before *Musaeus; a *Hyperborean or Lycian; said to have brought the worship of *Apollo and *Artemis from Lycia to *Delos, where he celebrated their birth among the Hyperboreans in hymns which continued to be recited there; individual Delian hymns of Olen are mentioned by *Pausanias in several places.
[Herodotus 4. 35; Callimachus, *Hymn* 4. 304–5]

olive The olive, which is probably native to the Mediterranean region, was of extreme importance to the ancient economy. In Attica, the olive was an important symbol of *Athena and Athens. Athena was said to have produced an olive-tree as her gift to the people of Athens, thus winning her contest with *Poseidon for the land. Some trees, called *moriai,* were sacred (connected with *Zeus as well as Athena), and oil from these trees was given as prizes at the Panathenaic Games (*see* PANATHENAEA).

Olive oil was used for food, medicine, lighting, perfume (*see* OINTMENT), and bathing, as well as athletics. In religious practice it was used to anoint sacred *stones and for *libations.

Olympia, *panhellenic sanctuary of *Zeus located in hill country beside the river *Alpheus in Elis.

1. Before 500 BC There is evidence of extensive prehistoric settlement in the vicinity. Votives (tripods and figurines) in an ash layer in the Altis indicate cult activity at least from the late 10th cent. (perhaps with an early ash altar). The first Olympiad was traditionally dated 776 BC. According to *Pindar, *Heracles founded the *Olympian games; an alternative tradition, also found in Pindar, attributed the foundation to *Pelops after his victory over Oenomaus (see next article). A sequence of wells on the eastern side of the sanctuary beginning in the late 8th cent. served visitors.

The first temple (ascribed to *Hera) was built *c.*590. A row of eleven treasuries (primarily of West Greek, i.e. Italian and Sicilian, states) lay under Cronus Hill. The first phase of the stadium (*c.* mid-6th cent.) consisted of a simple track west of the later stadium, extending into the Altis. The first *bouleuterion* (council-chamber) was built in *c.*520. From at least the 6th cent., sanctuary and festival were managed by Elis.

2. Classical The Greeks of the west (see (1) above) always had close connections with Olympia. But Olympia, the paramount athletic sanctuary, was properly panhellenic. Thus the Persian Wars of 490–479 BC were commemorated at Olympia, though less spectacularly than at *Delphi; for instance the Athenians dedicated at Olympia a helmet 'taken from the Medes'; another splendid helmet-dedication by the Athenian general Miltiades might be from Marathon but is probably earlier. The battle of Plataea prompted a colossal bronze Zeus, inscribed with a roll of honour of the participating states, including Ionian Athens in second place after Sparta. But the Dorian character of Olympia is marked, even if we deny political symbolism to the labours of *Heracles depicted on the temple metopes of the mid-cent. Zeus temple, the second to be built within the Altis. Thus the Olympian Games of 428 were turned by Sparta into an overtly anti-Athenian meeting. But Athens was never, even in the Peloponnesian War (431–404 BC), formally denied access to Olympia, any more than to *Delphi; and to balance the Spartan victory dedication over Messenians from the 490s (?) we have, from the 420s the lovely *Nike of Paeonius— a dedication by Athens' friends the Messenians of Naupactus. We do hear of a classical exclusion from the Olympic games, but of Sparta not Athens, in book 5 of Thucydides, a rare Thucydidean glimpse of the continuing political importance of *athletics.

3. Hellenistic and Roman Hellenistic kings affirmed by their dedications Olympia's panHellenic standing. New buildings included a palaestra, gymnasium, and (c.100 BC) the earliest Roman-style baths found in Greece. Roman domination, signalled by the dedications of Lucius Mummius (146 BC), at first saw Olympia decline in prestige: by 30 BC the games had dwindled into an essentially local festival. Imperial patronage prompted a marked revival: Marcus Vipsanius Agrippa repaired the temple and both Tiberius and Germanicus won chariot-races, to be outdone by Nero, who performed in person at irregularly convened games (67) including (uniquely) musical contests. In the 2nd cent., with the popularity of the games never greater, Olympia once more attracted orators, as well as cultural tourism (*Phidias' statue of Zeus was among the Seven Wonders of the ancient world); facilities saw a final expansion, including a *nymphaeum, attracting conservative attack. From fear of the barbarian incursions, the sanctuary was fortified (c.268) at the cost of many classical monuments. Cult survived well into the 4th cent. A Christian *basilica was built c.400–450; the temple was only toppled by earthquake in the 6th cent.

[Pausanias 5; Thucydides 5. 49–50; Lucian, *On the Death of Peregrinus* 19]

Olympian Games These were held in the precinct of *Zeus (the Altis) at *Olympia, once every four years in August or September. They were in honour of Zeus, and were said to commemorate the victory of *Pelops in his chariot-race with king Oenomaus of Pisa (a catalogue of the winners down to AD 217 is preserved by *Eusebius). They were

abolished in AD 393 by the emperor Theodosius I.

The original contest was the *stadion*, a sprint of about 200 m. (656 ft.). Other contests were added between the late 8th and 5th cents. BC, including races for chariots and single horses (*see* HORSE- AND CHARIOT-RACES). Early victors were often from Sparta, but by the 6th cent. competitors were coming from all over the Greek world. In the 5th cent. the festival lasted five days. The main religious ceremony was the *sacrifice of a hecatomb on the great altar of Zeus. The contests were preceded by a procession from Elis (the host-city) to Olympia, and a ceremony at which athletes and officials swore an oath to observe the rules of the games, and they were followed by victory celebrations, with processions and banquets. From 472 BC the main sacrifice was preceded by the pentathlon and horse-races, and on subsequent days there were the boys' contests, men's foot-races, wrestling, boxing, *pankration, and finally the race in armour. The prizes were crowns of wild *olive.

[Pindar, *Olympian* 1. 67–88, 10. 24–77]

Olympian gods, Olympians *See* APHRODITE; APOLLO; ARES; ARTEMIS; ATHENA; DEMETER; DIONYSUS; HEPHAESTUS; HERA; HERMES; POSEIDON; ZEUS (these are the twelve on the *Parthenon frieze; but *see* GREEK RELIGION, *Gods and other cult figures*).

Olympieum, the temple of *Zeus Olympius at Athens; begun by Antistates, Callaeschrus, and Antimachides, architects employed by the 6th-cent. BC tyrant Pisistratus, but abandoned after the latter's death, and the expulsion of his son, Hippias, and not resumed until *Antiochus (1) IV Epiphanes employed the Roman architect Cossutius to continue the work. It was completed for Hadrian. The Pisistratean building was planned as a Doric temple. Cossutius changed the order to Corinthian, but in general seems to have adhered to the original plan, dipteral at the sides, tripteral at the ends. The stylobate measured

41.11 × 107. 89 m. (135 × 354 ft.), and the Corinthian columns were 4.88 m. (16 ft.) in height. The capitals are carved from two blocks of marble. Vitruvius says the temple was open-roofed (hypaethral), which may have been true in its unfinished state at that time. It would have been roofed when completed by Hadrian to contain a gold and ivory cult-statue. Hadrian certainly is responsible for the impressive buttressed peribolos wall, decorated with Corinthian columns on its interior, and with a gateway of Hymettan marble on its north side.

Olympus, the highest mountain in the Greek peninsula, dominating the Aegean to the east and, to the north and south, the Macedonian and Thessalian plains. Rising at one point to 2,918 m. (9,577 ft.), with several other heights exceeding 2,900 m. (9,518 ft.), it forms a ponderous limestone cupola relieved by an aureole of lesser mountains and foothills pierced by valleys. Considered to be the throne of *Zeus and home of the gods, it held an important place in religion, mythology, and literature. While the Olympus of the *Iliad* is clearly a mountain, in some other texts, including the *Odyssey*, it seems to fluctuate between mountain and sky.

Omphale, daughter of Iardanus and queen of Lydia. According to a not always totally reliable messenger in *Sophocles' *Trachiniae*, *Heracles killed Iphitus, son of Eurytus of Oechalia, by treachery, and *Zeus decreed that he should expiate this crime by being sold in slavery to Omphale. Having endured this humiliation for a year, Heracles sacked Oechalia in revenge. Other details are given elsewhere: after the killing of Iphitus *Apollo refused to give Heracles an oracle, so Heracles carried off the *Delphic tripod. The quarrel was halted by Zeus, and Apollo then decreed that Heracles should be sold to Omphale for three years (not one year in this version) and the price should be paid to Eurytus. *Hermes took him to her, and during his servitude he performed various exploits. Others again say that as Omphale's slave Heracles had to dress

as a woman and perform women's work (a paradox popular with Hellenistic and Roman authors), and that he was her lover and had one or more children (Lamus according to *Ovid, other names elsewhere) by her.

[Sophocles, *Trachiniae* 248–80; Apollodorus 2. 6. 2–3; Ovid, *Heroines* 9. 53–118]

omphalos, the navel. Metaphorically, the centre of a geographical area, e.g. the sea, a city (= the agora), the world. Title to the last was claimed by *Delphi, at least by early in the classical period (e.g. *Pindar, *Bacchylides, *Aeschylus), and reinforced by identification with a concrete object, namely an egg- (or navel-) shaped stone. The geographer Strabo gives the fullest description of the Delphic omphalos: it was covered by wreaths and had two images on it representing the two birds sent by *Zeus, one from the west, one from the east, meeting at Delphi. This stone was in the temple. The marble stone seen by *Pausanias—and preserved to this day—is a man-made object, the wreaths depicted in relief. It stood on the esplanade outside the temple.

Burkert takes the omphalos to represent a sacrificial stone (*see* SACRIFICE) over which a fleece or goatskin was spread. Hermann associates it with a pre-Greek chthonic goddess (*see* CHTHONIAN GODS). The earliest known depiction of an omphaloid object is on a Tyrrhenian amphora of the second quarter of the 6th cent., showing *Hector and *Achilles fighting over the body of *Troilus. Here it is draped with a cross-hatched covering and labelled 'altar'. The event took place in the sanctuary of *Apollo Thymbraios: the use of the omphalos to identify the site not only reflects the influence of Delphi, but also confirms the sacrificial function of the omphalos.

[Strabo 9. 3. 6; Pausanias 10. 16. 3]

Opheltes *See* NEMEA; NEMEAN GAMES.

Ophion, Orphic god (*see* ORPHISM), husband of Eurynome and ruler of the universe before *Cronus.

Ops, personified Abundance, seen by the Romans as very ancient, was honoured above all during the Opiconsiva of 25 August and the Opalia of 19 December, in conjunction with the god *Consus. Ops consiva was patron of the reserved (*condere, Consus*) portion of the harvest (*ops*). This important function earned her a shrine in the *Regia, a temple on the *Capitol (where she bears the epithet *opifera*, bearer of abundance), and, after her late association with a reinterpreted *Saturnus, an altar in company with Ceres, 'at the forum', on the Vicus iugarius (10 August AD 7), no doubt coinciding with a time of famine.

[Varro, *On the Latin Language* 5. 74; Livy 39. 22. 4]

oracles Among the many forms of *divination known to the Greeks, the responses given by a god or hero when consulted at a fixed oracular site were the most prestigious. Such oracles were numerous. Herodotus lists five in mainland Greece and one in Asia Minor which king Croesus supposedly consulted in the 6th cent. BC, and at least another five (including one 'oracle of the dead') appear in his pages; *Pausanias mentions four lesser local oracles, and at least five more can be added from epigraphical evidence.

Healing oracles, those of *Asclepius above all, are a specialized group, though even these never confined themselves exclusively to medical questions. The business of a general purpose oracle is best revealed by the lead question-tablets found at *Zeus' oracle at *Dodona. The majority of enquiries are from individuals; of the minority addressed by states, most ask whether a particular alteration to cult practice is acceptable, or more generally by what sacrifices divine favour is to be maintained; one or two concern political issues. Individuals enquire, for instance, whether their wife will conceive (or conceive a son), whether a proposed marriage or journey or change of career is wise, whether a child is legitimate; they also ask about health problems, and more generally about ways of winning and keeping divine favour. The kind of answer envisaged is either 'yes' or 'no' or 'by sacrificing to X'.

According to *Plutarch, similar everyday questions about 'whether to marry or to sail or to lend', or, from cities, about 'crops and herds and health' ('and cults', he might have added) formed the staple of Delphi's business in his day (*see* DELPHIC ORACLE). Before about 400 BC, states had certainly also consulted Delphi about political issues, but even then a decision, to go to war for instance or dispatch a colony, had normally been made by the state before approaching the oracle. What was sought was a divine sanction. And since no mortals were endowed with religious authority in the Greek system, all oracles at all dates had an especially important role in sanctioning adjustments to cult practice.

Techniques by which responses were given were very various. The most prestigious was 'inspired' prophecy, the sayings of a priest or more commonly a priestess who spoke, probably in a state of trance, in the person of the god. This was the method of several oracles of *Apollo in Asia Minor and almost certainly of that of Delphi too, though a process of drawing bean-lots seems also to have played some part there. The prophetic dream was characteristic of healing oracles such as those of Asclepius and *Amphiaraus, though not confined to them: the consultant slept a night or nights in the temple (*incubation), during which the god in theory appeared in a dream and issued instructions (or even, in pious legend, performed a cure direct). The oracle of Zeus at *Olympia worked by 'empyromancy', signs drawn from the flames on Zeus' *altar. To consult the hero *Trophonius at Lebadea, the client made a simulated descent to the Underworld: how the revelation then occurred is not recorded. Nor do we know anything certain about the practice at Zeus' oracle at Dodona.

Apart from the Egyptian–Libyan oracle of *Ammon at the oasis of *Siwa in the Sahara, which many Greeks consulted as an oracle of Zeus from the 5th cent. BC onwards, the great oracular shrines were Greek. In Italy, the oracle of the *Sibyl at Cumae is well-known from *Virgil, who describes an ecstatic form of prophecy (see ECSTASY). Also prominent was the lot-oracle of *Fortuna Primigenia at *Praeneste. On extraordinary occasions the Roman government or ruler consulted the Sibylline books (see SIBYL).

Late antiquity The first two centuries AD witnessed a great flourishing of oracular shrines throughout the Greek-speaking portion of the Roman empire. These oracles took many different forms. *Delphi, *Didyma, and *Claros delivered responses from a god through a prophet, whose words were interpreted for consultants by priests at the shrine. At Mallus in Cilicia and the sanctuary of *Amphiaraus at Oropus (for example), the consultant slept (after a period of some preparation) in the shrine, hoping to have a dream of the god (also interpreted by priests). Other oracles, such as that of Bel at Apamea appear to have worked by indicating passages in Classical literature. Lot-oracles of various sorts are known from southern Asia Minor and Egypt. The oracle of Glycon (see ALEXANDER OF ABONUTEICHUS) offered a variety of methods of consultation.

Many responses are concerned with cult activity and personal crises; others, however, appear to have been more philosophic and provided important material for some pagan opponents of Christianity—they were taken as proof that the gods existed and as a proper guide to religious belief. Two oracles, of Didyma and Zeus Philios, the last opening at Antioch under *Maximinus Daia (305–13), also played significant roles in the great persecutions of the early 4th cent. Christians argued in turn that these responses were the work of demons, and those oracular shrines that survived the problems of the 3rd cent. appear to have been closed very soon after *Constantine I's defeat of Licinius in 324.

[Herodotus 1.46; Sophocles, *King Oedipus* 498–501; Plutarch, *The Oracles at Delphi no longer given in verse, The Obsolescence of Oracles*; Pausanias 1. 34, 4. 32, 7. 2, 21–22, 25, 9. 37–40, 10. 5–31, 33, 35; Virgil, *Aeneid* 6. 9–101]

Orchomenus (*a*) *Eponym of the Boeotian Orchomenus, whose genealogy was disputed; he was variously son of *Zeus and the Danaid Isonoe (see DANAUS AND THE DANAIDS) and father of *Minyas; son of Minyas; his brother, and so son of Eteocles (not the Theban). (*b*) Eponym of the Arcadian Orchomenus.

Oreads See NYMPHS.

Oreithyia See BOREAS.

Orestes, in mythology son of *Agamemnon and *Clytemnestra, and avenger of his father's murder by his mother and her lover *Aegisthus. Homer says that Orestes killed Aegisthus, having returned home from Athens in the eighth year after Agamemnon's death, and implies that he also killed Clytemnestra. The vengeance was an entirely praiseworthy deed, for which he won great reputation; no regrets are expressed by anyone at his having to kill his mother, and there is no hint of any pursuit by the *Erinyes, who later play so important a part in the legend. Clytemnestra was simply 'hateful', and Orestes, as head of the family, would necessarily have been her judge and executioner.

*Stesichorus wrote an *Oresteia* running to at least two books, but few fragments are left. We know, however, that he included a recognition scene between Orestes and *Electra, and also the pursuit by the Erinyes, against whom *Apollo provided Orestes with a bow. But it is 5th-cent. tragedy which provides the fullest details of Orestes' legend. At the time of Agamemnon's murder Orestes was taken to Strophius, king of Phocis and brother-in-law of Agamemnon, and brought up by him together with his own son Pylades, who later accompanies Orestes when he returns secretly home, on the instruction of Apollo, to avenge his father's death. Here he encounters his sister Electra, and they recognize each other with mutual joy. In *Aeschylus' *Choephori*, brother and sister join together in an invocation to Agamemnon's ghost, but the focus of this play is still mainly on Orestes, and Electra is not actively involved in the killings. Orestes gets access to the palace as a stranger, bringing news of his own death, and can scarcely bring himself to kill Clytemnestra. After her murder he is at once pursued by her Erinyes, who form the Chorus of the following play (*Eumenides*) where Orestes is put on trial and finally absolved by the homicide court on the Areopagus, once Athena has given the casting vote in his favour. She also calms the Erinyes, who are to be settled in a shrine with the beneficent title of the Eumenides, 'the Kindly Ones'.

Electra's role in helping her brother is developed by *Sophocles and *Euripides: in Sophocles' *Electra* she urges Orestes on from outside the door while he is inside killing their mother, and in Euripides' *Electra* she is by far the more dominant figure, driving the weak and indecisive Orestes to kill Clytemnestra and even grasping the sword with him when his own hand fails. Here in Euripides, quite unlike Sophocles' play, brother and sister are entirely overcome with guilt and remorse once the deed is done; here too, again unlike Sophocles' version, the Erinyes will pursue Orestes. Elsewhere in Euripides we are aware of these Furies as the imagined phantoms of Orestes' guilty conscience (*Orestes*); and his release from their pursuit is a long process involving a journey to the land of the Tauri (*Iphigenia in Tauris*). In his *Andromache*, Orestes murders *Neoptolemus and carries off *Hermione, whom he later marries, having by her a son, Tisamenus.

Various local traditions are recorded: for instance *Pausanias was shown an altar which Orestes set up in commemoration of his being freed from the Erinyes by the verdict of the Areopagus (as in Aeschylus), a stone at *Troezen on which he had been purified, and another at Gythium in *Laconia where he was cured of madness; also a place near Megalopolis where he had bitten off a finger in his madness and so been cured.

Orestes, killing Aegisthus, was a popular scene in art, occurring possibly in the 7th cent., and with certainty from the 6th. Also popular was Orestes' meeting with Electra at Agamemnon's tomb. *See also* RELICS.

[Homer, *Odyssey* 1. 29 ff.; 298 ff.; 3. 303 ff.; Aeschylus, *Choephori, Eumenides*; Sophocles, *Electra*; Euripides, *Orestes, Electra, Iphigenia in Tauris, Andromache*; Pausanias 1. 28. 5, 2. 18. 6, 31. 4, 3. 22. 1, 8. 34. 1–3]

Orestheus, in mythology, a king of Aetolia (*see* AETOLIAN MYTHS AND CULTS), grandfather of *Oeneus and son of *Deucalion. He had a bitch which brought forth a stick; this he buried and from it sprang a vine. From its branches, *ozoi*, the Ozolian Locrians were named, and Orestheus called his son Phytios, 'Plant-man'. For the connection of the family with *wine *see* OENEUS.

orgeōnes are members of a society devoted to the rites (*orgia*) of a particular hero or god; they are in effect confined to Attica. A group of *orgeōnes* was an organized corporation with a precinct (sometimes leased out when not in use), funds, a constitution and officers; it met periodically (in several attested cases once a year) to *sacrifice and feast, to pass decrees, and to enrol new members. *See* CLUBS.

A complication arises with a law, probably of the 5th cent., which required *phratries to grant membership to (among others) *orgeōnes*. This seems to show that groups of *orgeōnes* were not wholly private bodies but had some relation to sub-structures of the city. On the most plausible view, the law did not force phratries to admit persons of lower status, but rather confirmed that those already admitted after scrutiny to more exclusive groups should be given phratry membership without more ado. If *orgeōnes* enjoyed such privilege, it is natural to wonder whether their cults (like those of their grander relatives the *genē*: *see* GENOS) were in some sense public. Not all *orgeōnes* can have benefited from this law, however; for of the attested groups at least one consisted of non-citizens, the Thracians who, exceptionally, organized a procession in the Athenian public cult of *Bendis (*see* THRACIAN RELIGION). Several groups of prosperous citizens who are *orgeōnes* of heroes (such as the healer Amynos) may represent the old type envisaged by the law; other groups that honoured gods—Mother, *Asclepius, *Dionysus, the Syrian goddess (*see* ATARGATIS)—were perhaps *orgeōnes* only in a looser sense.

oriental cults and religion Although eastern influences, real or imagined, were by no means absent from Greek mythology and cult prior to Alexander the Great, the term 'oriental religions' typically designates the cults of a variety of divinities originating in Anatolia and the Fertile Crescent, which, spreading beyond their homeland, arrived in Italy and the western Mediterranean between the late 3rd cent. BC and the 3rd cent. AD. Though the outlandish character of individual cults was noted in antiquity, the term corresponds to no ancient distinction. For its modern use, we may usefully invoke Edward Said's conception of Orientalism. Here the central thesis is that the concepts 'Europe' and 'Orient', as polar opposites, have been created by Europeans (mainly in the context of European imperialism, but with some roots going back to Greek writers) to provide a positive, strong image of Europe, with which eastern civilizations can be negatively contrasted. The 'Orient' is thus presented as lacking all desirable, active characteristics: it is effeminate, decadent, corrupt, voluptuous, despotic, and incapable of independent creative development.

The history of the term may be roughly divided into three phases. From the Renaissance to *c.*1900, it was used casually to account for 'decadence', whether of Italo-Roman religion or paganism in general. For one strand of post-Renaissance Humanism, exemplified by Gibbon, it embraced Christianity. F. Cumont's *Les Religions orientales dans le paganisme romain* (1906), however, was the first attempt to give the notion explanatory power: he assimilated religious movements from Asia Minor, Egypt, Syria, and Persia to one another as mystery religions concerned with a promise of afterlife. As such, they prepared the way for Christianity. Cumont himself, by including *astrology and *magic, and by introducing Bacchic cult (*see* DIONYSUS) into the 4th edition (1929), muddied the claim. A. D. Nock's *Conversion* (1933) began a process of reaction. Do the similarities between these cults outweigh their differences? What was the role of post-mortem salvation? Is the contrast civic cult/personal religion satisfactory? Why exclude *Christianity? There have been uneven attempts to rework Cumont's term. *See* MYSTERIES.

orientation The patterning of the human environment according to generally accepted calibrations of ambient space took a number of forms in ancient Mediterranean cultures, and particularly in religious contexts, such as the laying out of *sanctuaries according to the cardinal points (that is to solar phenomena: there is little evidence of lunar or stellar orientations), or to face parts of ritually or mythically important landscapes (note the orientation of sanctuaries in Latium towards the *Albanus mons). A connection between the sunrise quarter and the right hand was found in Greek practice, and an eastward orientation is common but not mandatory for *temples (e.g. the *Parthenon). Conversely the west was inauspicious and used in cursing, though many Anatolian goddess-temples faced west (*see* ANATOLIAN DEITIES). Roman augury (*see* AUGURES) was one of the most developed of such systems, with a complex division of the sky and the land beneath it from the observer's viewpoint, which was closely related to the cardinal points and to the practices of land division.

Origen (Origenes Adamantius), probably AD 184 or 185–254 or 255, was born at Alexandria of Christian parents. Educated by his father Leonides (who perished in the persecution of 202 under Septimius Severus) and later in the Catechetical School of Alexandria under Pantaenus and *Clement (of

Alexandria), he became a teacher himself, with such success that he was recognized, first informally, then in 203 officially, as head of the school. He learned pagan philosophy from one Ammonius. The story of his self-castration in accordance with Matthew 19: 12 is supported by *Eusebius, but doubted by *Epiphanius. His career as a teacher was interrupted in 215 by Caracalla's massacre of Alexandrian Christians. He withdrew to Palestine, but after a time was recalled by his bishop, Demetrius. Through his extensive literary work he now acquired such influence in the eastern Church as to become its unofficial arbiter, and, on a journey to Greece in this capacity, allowed himself to be ordained priest. Demetrius, who had not given his consent, took offence at this and perhaps also at parts of Origen's teaching. On obscure grounds, Origen was banished from Alexandria and deposed from the presbyterate, but the decision was ignored in Palestine, and Origen settled at Caesarea in 231. He continued his labours until, after repeated torture in the Decian persecution (250–1; see DECIUS), his health gave way and he died at Tyre at the age of 69.

Origen's works were voluminous and of wide scope, but only a fraction has survived. He was a pioneer in textual criticism of the Bible, exegesis and systematic theology. His chief work in the critical sphere was the Hexapla, setting out in six columns the Hebrew text of the OT, a transliteration, and various Greek versions. He also wrote commentaries on the greater part of Scripture, where he sought, though not consistently, a moral sense pertaining to the soul and a typological sense to instruct the spirit, occasionally discarding the historical sense where data were in conflict. In the doctrinal and apologetic area, he wrote the De Principiis and the Contra Celsum. The latter, written c.249, replies in detail to the learned attack of the Middle Platonist *Celsus, which probably appeared in 176. This is the only extant work in which Origen avows his philosophic education. Two of Origen's devotional works, the De oratione and Exhortatio ad mar-

tyrium have come down to us complete. The Philocalia is a collection of excerpts from Origen's writings by *Gregory (2) of Nazianzus and *Basil of Caesarea. It preserves the original Greek of many passages otherwise known only in Latin, and shows what the Cappadocians found valuable in his teaching. But Origen had already come under attack by Methodius for his denial of a carnal resurrection, and at the end of the 4th cent. he was condemned by Epiphanius and (eventually) Jerome. The translations by his champion Rufinus are often freer and more periphrastic than those of Jerome, in the interests of orthodoxy and of clarity. Despite this advocacy, Origen was finally condemned under Justinian at the Council of Constantinople (553).

Orion, of whom various tales are told, was a mighty hunter and prodigious lover (father of fifty sons by as many *nymphs: he also pursued the *Pleiades, and assaulted *Merope (1) and *Artemis), who was favoured and/or punished by the gods (in particular Artemis), and eventually transformed into the *constellation. One version of the myth (that he was beloved of *Eos, for which reason Artemis killed him in Ortygia) was known to *Homer, who also has Odysseus see Orion in the underworld, gathering the beasts he had slain in his lifetime. On the shield of *Achilles, the Bear keeps a watchful eye on Orion. *Hesiod also knew the constellation.

Orion's tomb was shown to *Pausanias at Tanagra, where there was also a place called the Pole, at which *Atlas (father of the Pleiades) sat and meditated. Both Euphorion and Corinna associate Orion with Tanagra, and one of the stories of his parentage makes him son of Hyrieus. According to another he was a son of *Poseidon and Euryale.

[Homer, Odyssey 5. 121–4, 11. 572–5; Apollodorus 1. 4. 3–5; Pausanias 9. 20. 3]

Ormenus, name used by *Homer for miscellaneous Trojan warriors introduced to be killed, and for miscellaneous grandfathers, of *Phoenix (2) in the Iliad and of

*Eumaeus in the *Odyssey*. Also, the *eponym of a city Ormenion, the later Orminion on the Gulf of Pagasae, with which the topographical writer Demetrius of Scepsis speciously associated Phoenix in the light of his grandfather.

[Homer, *Iliad* 2. 734, 8. 274, 9. 448, 12. 187; *Odyssey* 15. 414]

Orosius, a young presbyter who arrived in Africa from north-west Spain (Braga) in AD 414; his memorandum (*Commonitorium*) against the *Priscillianist and Origenist heresies (*see* ORIGEN) led *Augustine to address a reply to him on the subject. On Augustine's commendation he moved on to *Jerome in Bethlehem. While in the Holy Land he argued against the Pelagians (*see* PELAGIUS), and received a portion of the recently discovered remains of St Stephen to take back to the congregation in Braga; unable to make the crossing to Spain, he left these relics with the Christians of the island of Minorca. Returning to Africa, with Augustine's encouragement he compiled the seven books of his *Histories against the Pagans*, stretching from the Creation to the history of Rome down to AD 417—an apologetic response (*see* APOLOGISTS) to the *pagan argument that the coming of Christianity had brought disaster to the world.

Orpheus, the quintessential mythical singer, son of *Apollo and a Muse (*see* MUSES), whose song has more than human power. In archaic Greece, Orpheus appears among the *Argonauts whom he saves from the *Sirens by overcoming their song with his own; other early attestations exalt the power of his song. In the 5th cent. Orpheus enlarges his field of competence: his powerful song encompasses epic poetry, healing songs, oracles, and initiatory rites.

His main myth is his tragic love for *Eurydice (1), narrated by *Virgil and *Ovid but known already in some form in the 5th cent. BC. In Virgil's version Eurydice, newly wed to Orpheus, died of a snakebite, and the singer descended to Hades to bring her back. His song enchanted *Hades; Eurydice was allowed to return provided Orpheus did not look back when leading her up; he failed, losing Eurydice for ever. He retired into wild nature where his lamenting song moved animals, trees, and rocks; finally a band of Thracian women or Bacchic *maenads (*see* DIONYSUS) killed him. The first representation of Eurydice, Orpheus, and *Hermes is the relief from the Athenian Altar of the Twelve Gods: earlier is the allusion in *Euripides' *Alcestis* (438 BC). Orpheus' death at the hands of maenads is presented in *Aeschylus' drama *Bassarae* as the result of Dionysus' wrath (470/460 BC). Vases depicting Thracian women murdering him are somewhat earlier, without giving a reason for the killing; later, it is the aloofness of the widowed (and turned homosexual) singer which provokes the women. But even after his death, Orpheus' voice was not silenced: his head was carried by the sea to the island of Lesbos where for a while it gave prophecies.

Generally, Orpheus is called a Thracian. A grave and a cult belong not to Thrace but to Pieria in Macedonia, north-east of Mt. *Olympus, a region which formerly had been inhabited by Thracians and with which the Muses had some relations. It may have been a recent invention, or point to the original home of Orpheus who has no certain place in the web of Greek mythological *genealogy.

An important consequence of his miraculous song was his authorship of the so-called Orphic poetry: as early as the late 6th cent. the powerful singer who went down into Hades was thought especially competent to sing about eschatology and theogony. Pythagoreans (*see* PYTHAGORAS AND PYTHAGOREANS) and adherents of Bacchic mystery cults adopted him as their figurehead, and the Neoplatonist philosophers (*see* NEOPLATONISM) especially discerned deep theosophical knowledge in these poems and promoted Orpheus to the role of prime theological thinker.

In art the myth of Orpheus is treated from c.550 BC to late antiquity (main themes: as

Argonaut; murder; in Hades; with the animals).

See MUSAEUS; ORPHIC LITERATURE; ORPHISM.

[Euripides, *Alcestis* 357–62; Virgil, *Georgics* 4. 453–525; Ovid, *Metamorphoses* 10. 1–11. 84]

Orphic literature, the pseudepigraphical literature ascribed to *Orpheus. Neoplatonist authors especially cite hexameters from different poems attributed to Orpheus 'the theologian', and an entire corpus of hymns is preserved. The fragments of his poetry have often been collected and the remains of a 4th-cent. papyrus commentary on a theogony of Orpheus, found in 1962 in the remains of a funeral pyre in Derveni (Macedonia), considerably enlarged the corpus of texts.

The main texts attributed to Orpheus are *theogonies. The Neoplatonists (*see* NEOPLATONISM) relied chiefly on the 'Rhapsodic Theogony', a late Hellenistic work incorporating earlier theogonies; at least four earlier works are known, the earliest of which one goes back to the first half of the 5th cent. BC. They follow the Oriental succession scheme established by *Hesiod, but extend it in both directions: *Uranus and *Gaia, Hesiod's first ruling couple, are preceded by Night (*see* NYX) and Protogonos or Phanes, and *Zeus' reign was succeeded by that of *Dionysus. The decisive invention is a double birth myth of Dionysus. Dionysus is the incestuous offspring of Zeus and his daughter *Persephone; *Hera, in anger, ordered the Titans (*see* TITAN) to kill the young god, which they did; they cooked and ate the boy. Zeus in turn killed the Titans with his thunderbolt. From the ashes of the burning Titans sprung mankind; from the heart of Dionysus which had been saved, Zeus reproduced with *Semele the second Dionysus. This myth is told only in Neoplatonist sources, and the consequence that man has a double nature, from the Titans and from the divine child they had eaten, is the one drawn by Olympiodorus, not by the Orphic poet. Still the story explains why man's nature is wicked

(he is an offspring of the wicked Titans), and why Dionysus could intercede on man's behalf with Persephone after death (Dionysus alone, if anyone, can assuage his mother's wrath against the offspring of the Titans). These elements are present already in Classical times—in a much-discussed fragment of a Pindaric threnos or dirge (*see* PINDAR), the overcoming of Persephone's 'ancient grief' is vital for the human *soul to attain the supreme stage in metempsychosis. *Plato knows man's Titanic nature, and in a gold tablet from Thessaly (Pelinna, *c*.320 BC), the dead person has to appeal to Dionysus' help before the tribunal in the underworld.

Incidentally, these references show the role Orphic poetry played in Bacchic mystery cults, and their syncretistic nature. Other Orphic texts (as those of *Musaeus) contained ritual prescriptions (*teletai*, 'rites': *see* TELETĒ). Others again were concerned with eschatology and especially with Eleusinian mythology (*katabasis*, 'descent to Hades'; *see* ELEUSIS), as were the related ones, by Musaeus and *Eumolpus. In Classical times, Pythagorean Orphica were important; Pythagoras himself was said to have published poems under the name of Orpheus. An author of the 4th cent. BC gave a list of Pythagoreans responsible for Orphica; some titles seem to indicate poems about cosmogony and natural history.

The corpus of 87 *hymns stands somewhat apart. They centre again round Dionysus and presuppose the Orphic theogony, and they seem to have been used in actual rituals: they must have belonged to a local Dionysiac community. Details of cult and language point to western Asia Minor (Pergamum) as place and the late Hellenistic or early imperial epoch as date of origin; such groups are well attested in this region and epoch. Even more loosely connected to Orpheus are two poems from late antiquity, under Orpheus' name, the *Orphic Argonautica* and the *Lithica*. In the *Argonautica*, Orpheus narrates the myth of the *Argonauts, with some superficial knowledge of Orphic cosmogony. The *Lithica* reveal the secret qualities of stones; it was only the Byzantine Tzetzes who attributed them to Orpheus as a specialist in arcane lore.

See DIONYSUS; ORPHEUS; ORPHISM; PYTHAGORAS AND PYTHAGOREANISM.

Orphism, a set of beliefs and religious practices thought to derive from Orphic literature. The concept is modern; it develops ancient and Florentine Neoplatonist ideas (*see* NEOPLATONISM) about the crucial role *Orpheus had as a theologian of all mystery cult (*see* MYSTERIES) in Greece. Reacting to F. Creuzer (1771–1858) who, though he denied that Orpheus was a historical figure, still thought that Orphic literature contained the essential knowledge of Eleusinian and Dionysiac mysteries (*see* ELEUSIS; DIONYSUS), C. A. Lobeck (*Aglaophamus*, 1829) had distinguished Eleusis, Bacchic (i.e. Dionysiac), and Samothracian mysteries (*see* CABIRI; SAMOTHRACE) from the Orphica; this opened the way to assimilate Orphic literature to Pythagoreanism and to see Orphism as a religious movement on its own, beginning in the late archaic age and combining ideas from Dionysian mysteries and Pythagorean philosophy. Formulated by E. Rohde (*Psyche*, 1894) and refined, among others, by M. P. Nilsson, A.-J. Festugière, and W. K. C. Guthrie, the concept of Orphism as a religious movement and part of a wider mystic and ascetic movement of late archaic Greece, or even as 'Orphic religion', gained general acceptance in 20th-cent. scholarship. However, Wilamowitz had pointed out that to the Greeks, there existed only Orphic literature and lowly religious quacks called *orpheotelestai*, 'initiators according to Orpheus'; I. M. Linforth, later G. Zuntz and esp. W. Burkert went on to deny the existence of Orphism as a religious movement in the strict sense of the word, and recent archaeological finds have helped to change previously accepted opinion about Orphism.

Orphism is basically Orphic literature; it comprised, besides the dominant theogonical (*see* THEOGONY) and eschatological poems, ritualistic texts, *hymns sung in ritual and prescriptions about specific *initiation and other rites. They were used by two sets of people, followers of Bacchic mystery groups, and individual ritual specialists, the itinerant *orpheotelestai*. The specialists used rituals to heal demonic possession, to harm by *magic, and to bring about eschatological hopes; they belong to the wide group of initiators, cathartic priests, and soothsayers attested from archaic Greece to imperial Rome, who often had oriental origins (*see* ORIENTAL CULTS AND RELIGION) and who performed outside the bounds of *polis* religion (the religion of the city-state). Bacchic rituals begin to have distinctive eschatological beliefs and rituals at least in the early 5th cent.; an inscription from Cumae attests an exclusive burying ground, bone tablets from Olbia in south Russia show Bacchic belief in an afterlife (or even metempsychosis) and connect this with Orpheus, Herodotus connects Bacchic burial customs with Orpheus and derives them via Pythagoras from Egypt. By the end of the century, the first gold leaf appears in a woman's grave in south Italian Hipponium (Vibo Valentia); it prescribes what the deceased must to do in the nether world in order to join the other 'initiated bacchoi'. More such leaves are known from northern Greece, southern Italy, and Crete, ranging from the 4th cent. BC to a late Roman one. Some follow the Hipponium pattern, others describe an underworld tribunal under *Persephone where the deceased has to give the correct answer; a series from Thurii attests belief in metempsychosis (*see* SOUL) and is influenced by south Italian Pythagoreanism; a text from Pelinna in Thessaly shows Dionysus as decisive helper with Persephone, which recalls the Orphic anthropogony. Vase paintings from southern Italy confirm the connection of Orpheus with eschatology and Dionysus, as does a terracotta group of Orpheus overcoming the Sirens from a Tarentine grave. The general impression is that many Bacchic mystery groups in the ancient world, ranging in time from the 5th cent. BC to the 2nd cent. AD and later, derived part of their beliefs and rituals from Orphic literature, without however striving for a unified doctrine or abstaining from other influences, like Pythagoreanism.

See MYSTERIES; ORPHEUS; ORPHIC LITERATURE; PYTHAGORAS AND PYTHAGOREANISM.

Ortygia, old name of *Delos ('Quail Island'); its *nymph was identified with *Asteria. But as some half-dozen other places were also called Ortygia, it is by no means certain that all references, especially in *Homer, are to Delos.

Oschophoria (*Ōschophoria*), an Attic festival celebrated early in the autumn month Pyanopsion, and organized by the *genos* of Salaminioi. The main rites were (1) a procession from a temple of *Dionysus to the shrine of *Athena Skiras at Phaleron, led by two young men 'outstanding in wealth and nobility' (Salaminioi?), dressed as women and carrying ōschoi, i.e. bunches of grapes on the branch; (2) (probably) a race along the same course between ephebes of each tribe (*see* EPHĒBOI; PHYLAI), also holding ōschoi, the winner of which received first taste of a special five-ingredient brew; (3) a banquet, with which female 'dinner-bearers' were involved. The libations were accompanied by a mixed cry, of joy, *eleleu*, and of grief, *iou iou*. The elements of abnormality in the rite (*transvestism, and the ambiguous cry) were explained mythologically by reference to incidents accompanying the homecoming of *Theseus.

Osiris (Egyptian *Wsìr*), the Egyptian god whose death and resurrection provided the model for the fate of each Pharaoh, and, from the Middle Kingdom, also of non-royal persons. The association with Pharaoh is most marked at Abydus in Upper Egypt. In the Pyramid Texts, he is killed by his brother *Set, but his body is prevented by *Isis and Nephthys from rotting, and restored to life. The myth gradually grew in complexity, esp.

in the Late Period, when it is the subject of an interesting essay by *Plutarch.. In iconography, Osiris, as 'lord of the west', appears as a mummy holding crook and 'flail', most commonly in the New Kingdom as judge with *Anubis at the 'weighing of the heart'. The basis of the Hellenistic/Roman Osirian *mysteries however was probably the 'festival of Choiak', the celebration of Osiris' death and resurrection. In the Roman period (from the 1st cent. BC), the Osiris Canopus, a jar with the head of Osiris carried in processions, becomes the preferred public form, alluding to the water of life given by Osiris. *See* EGYPTIAN DEITIES.

[Plutarch, *De Iside et Osiride* (*On Isis and Osiris*)]

Ouranos *See* URANUS.

Ovid (Publius Ovidius Naso, 43 BC–AD 17), poet, is important as a source for religious and mythological lore chiefly because of two poems, the *Metamorphoses* and the *Fasti*, and to an extent the *Heroides*.

Heroides, 'Heroines' Of the 'single *Heroides*' 1–14 are letters from mythological female figures to absent husbands or lovers; *Heroides* 15, whose Ovidian authorship is in doubt, is from the historical but heavily mythologized Sappho. The heroines tend to be well known rather than obscure: some of the interest of the letters lies in locating the point at which they are to be 'inserted' into prior canonical works, usually epic or tragic. The 'double *Heroides*' (16–21) are paired letters.

Metamorphoses, 'Transformations'. An unorthodox 'epic' in fifteen books, Ovid's only surviving work in hexameters, composed in the years immediately preceding his exile in AD 8. The poem is a collection of tales from classical and near-eastern myth and legend, each of which describes or somehow alludes to a supernatural change of shape (*see* METAMORPHOSIS). Metamorphic myths enjoyed an especial vogue in Hellenistic times and had previously been collected in poems (all now lost) by Nicander, by the obscure Boios or Boio, and by Parthenius. In Ovid's hands metamorphosis involves more than just a taste for the bizarre. Throughout the poem (and with programmatic emphasis in the opening cosmogony) the theme calls attention to the boundaries between divine and human, animal and inanimate, raising fundamental questions about definition and hierarchy in the universe. As narrative it brilliantly captures the infinite variety and patterning of the mythological tradition on which it draws (and which, for many later communities of readers, it effectively supersedes).

Fasti, 'Calendar'. A poetical calendar of the Roman year with one book devoted to each month (*see* CALENDAR, ROMAN). At the time of Ovid's exile it was incomplete, and only the first six books (January–June) survive. The poem's astronomy (1. 2) is influenced by Aratus' *Phaenomena*, its aetiological treatment of history and religion (1. 1) by Callimachus. These debts show Ovid at his most overtly Alexandrian; but he is applying Callimachean aetiology to distinctively Roman material, and the poem has long been mined for its detailed information about the perceived roots of Roman religion and ritual.

Paean (Gk. *Paian*). Originally a healing god later equated with *Apollo and *Asclepius, also a ritual exclamation (Gk. *paian*) and a name for the song addressed to these gods. In Archaic and Classical times it is used in various religious, political, and personal situations, the common function being to create a dialogue between man and god, the latter being petitioned or thanked for well-being and salvation. Typical situations for paean-singing were: (1) a religious festival (esp. for Apollo), (2) illness or plague, where Apollo is addressed in his role as Healer, (3) a military action, (4) a sympotic or drinking-party context, where all sang it in unison after the *libations and before the symposium, (5) on public occasions such as the ratification of peace. Paeans were not confined to Apollo, but were also sung to *Zeus, *Poseidon, *Dionysus, Asclepius, and *Hygieia. From the 4th cent. BC the songs become more formalized and are also addressed to individuals such as Lysander and Titus Quinctius Flamininus. *See also* HYMNS.

pagan, paganism The Latin word *paganus* means literally one who inhabits a *pagus*, a dispersed settlement. By imperial times, the term was applied to one who stayed at home or lived a civilian life. Christian reference implied one who was not a 'soldier of Christ'. *Paganismus* was first used in the 4th cent. by Marius Victorinus and *Augustine. Traditional usage nevertheless persisted, even in Christian authors.

Both expressions, in the Christian era, may have been colloquial. *Paganus* occurs more in sermons than in treatises, where it appears to demand explanation—the implication being that the more sophisticated were aware of a misleading facility. Literary usage had long preferred *gentes* (peoples) and associated forms. Such also was the custom in the older Latin version of the Bible, with Greek analogues in the *Septuagint, which suggests that a readiness to group all other believers under one heading owed something to the exclusiveness of the *Jews. *Orosius and *Prudentius were wrong in supposing an allusion to mere rusticity and in any case referred to *gentiles/gentilia* as well.

Use of the terms in English has encouraged the risky assumption that religious belief and practice, outside the Christian and Jewish spheres, formed a unity. Christian convenience and a late Roman inclination to *syncretism contributed to the habit. The English word 'paganism' was transferred from Latin at least as early as the 14th cent. In more modern times it has been applied to non-European peoples, with a suggestion of 'natural religion'.

Such language ignores only with prejudice the sheer variety of ancient cult. A modern and objective writer might justify its use by the undoubted desire of men and women, especially among the more philosophical from the 3rd cent. AD, to stress the exalted nature of an ultimate and single god and to associate as divinities the different objects of local devotion. The prayer of Lucius in *Apuleius is a useful example of the latter. *Plotinus' 'flight of the alone to the alone' is notorious and *Julian carried that quasi-monotheistic process to a cultic peak. Even apparently less reflective men were increasingly eclectic in their practical observance. We may have our suspicions about the historicity of the erudite catholicity of the emperor Severus Alexander, who supposedly revered in private a statue of Christ along with those of Abraham, *Orpheus, and *Apollonius of Tyana; but the capacity for shared perception in a few Christian sources and the charming tolerance of bishop Pegasius of Ilium attested in Julian are less open to doubt. Deliberate competition with Christianity is difficult to document, except in Julian's case.

For those who continue to baulk at the taint of judgement in the word, alternatives (like 'polytheism', which is not always accurate) have been hard to identify and harder to enforce.

[Apuleius, *Metamorphoses* 11. 2; Plotinus, *Enneads* 6. 9; Julian, *Hymn to King Helios, Epistles* 49, 78]

Paganalia, Roman public festival of the *pagi* (village communities). Listed as one of the movable feasts (*feriae conceptivae*) by Macrobius; anachronistically attributed to Servius *Tullius by Dionysius of Halicarnassus. Sometimes linked with the 24–6 January Sementivae, but *Varro, while noting both festivals' agricultural basis, clearly differentiates the Paganalia as one 'that the entire *pagus* might celebrate in the fields'. Wissowa connects it with the Compitalia of January 3–5. Certainty on its date of celebration thus becomes impossible.

[Varro, *On the Latin Language* 6. 24, 26; Dionysius of Halicarnassus, *Roman Antiquities* 4. 15. 1–4; Ovid, *Fasti* 1. 655–704; Macrobius, *Saturnalia* 1. 16. 6]

Palaemon *See* ISTHMIA; MELICERTES.

Palaephatus, *mythographer, wrote (? in the late 4th cent. BC) a *Peri apiston*, 'on incredible things', extant only in an excerpt, in which myths are rationalized. It had considerable influence in the Byzantine period. The name Palaephatus is perhaps a pseudonym.

Palamedes ('the handy or contriving one'), a proverbially clever hero, son of *Nauplius (2) and Clymene. Tradition from the *Cypria* onwards (*see* EPIC CYCLE) makes *Odysseus his enemy because he was forced by Palamedes to serve in the Trojan War (*see* TROY): Odysseus pretended to be mad to avoid going to Troy, but Palamedes exposed him, either by putting the infant *Telemachus in front of his ploughshare or by threatening the baby with a sword. Odysseus saved his son, and thus gave himself away. In revenge he later forged a letter from *Priam to Palamedes, promising him a sum of gold if he would betray the Greeks, then buried this same amount of gold in Palamedes' quarters. *Agamemnon read the letter, found the gold, and handed over Palamedes to the army to be stoned. His father Nauplius avenged his death by causing some of the Greek leaders' wives to be unfaithful, and later by lighting false beacons at Cape Caphareus in Euboea, with the result that the Greek fleet was wrecked.

Palamedes was credited, alongside *Cadmus, with having invented certain letters of the *alphabet and the games of draughts (*pessoi*) and dice to help while away the Trojan War.

[Apollodorus, *Epitome* 3. 7–8, 6. 7–8; Hyginus, *Fables* 95. 2, 105, 277. 1; Pausanias 2. 20. 3]

Palatine, the chief of the seven hills of Rome, traditionally the site of the oldest settlement there; in legend, the home of *Evander and *Romulus. Tradition assigns fortifications to the hill, and this seems to be confirmed by recent archaeological work. Early settlement is represented by two archaic cisterns and rock-cut post-holes for Iron Age huts; one example, above the Lupercal (*see* LUPERCALIA) and forum Boarium, is identified as the 'hut of Romulus' which was preserved in historic times. Temples on the hill included those dedicated to *Victoria (294 BC) near the Clivus Victoriae, Victoria Virgo (193), and the Magna Mater (191; *see* CYBELE). Many aristocratic houses occupied the hill and the slopes which led down to the Forum, from the late 6th cent. BC onwards; the house of Quintus Hortensius Hortalus was acquired by *Augustus and became the nucleus of a group of palace-buildings which included a portico and libraries as well as the new temple of *Apollo.

[Dionysius of Halicarnassus 1. 87; Livy 1. 7; Tacitus, *Annals* 12. 24]

Palici (Gk. *Palikoi*), Sicel (indigenous Sicilian) twin-gods of the small lake (Lago dei Palici) near Menaeum in the Sicilian interior, which sends up a considerable amount of natural gas. Allegedly a suspected person might go to the lake and swear he was innocent; if he lied, he lost his life by the power of the gods (the gases are in fact somewhat poisonous); if not, he returned safe and might claim damages from his accuser. Their legend was that a local *nymph, Thalia, being pregnant by *Zeus, begged to be swallowed up in the earth to escape Hera; this was granted to her, and when she bore twins they made their way up through the pools known as Delloi. Traces of the sanctuary described by Diodorus Siculus are extant.

[Diodorus Siculus 11. 89. 8; Macrobius, *Saturnalia* 5. 19. 15 ff.]

Palinurus, in mythology, helmsman of *Aeneas. In *Virgil's *Aeneid* he is overcome by the god Sleep (Somnus), falls overboard, is washed up on the shore of Italy, and there killed by local inhabitants; his loss is negotiated by *Venus as the price to *Neptunus of the Trojans' safe arrival in Italy. Aeneas sees his ghost in the Underworld, and promises to bury him at the site of his death, named after him as Cape Palinurus, modern Capo Palinuro in Lucania, where a settlement of the 6th cent. BC has been excavated.

[Dionysius of Halicarnassus 1. 53. 2; Virgil, *Aeneid* 5. 779 ff., 6. 337 ff.]

Palladium Miraculous guardian statues were common in ancient cities, but none was more famous than the Trojan Palladium, a small wooden image of armed *Athena. It fell from the sky, and the safety of *Troy depended on its possession. *Odysseus and *Diomedes (2) carried it away, thus enabling the sack of Troy. There are several variants of the story, but in the canonical Roman tradition (dating perhaps to the late

4th cent.) it was *Aeneas who rescued the Palladium and brought it to *Lavinium, whence it ultimately reached Rome. *Ovid adduces both legends, but others tried to reconcile them: the image stolen by the Greeks was only a copy, or Diomedes came to Italy and returned the Palladium to Aeneas. Also other cities claimed the Trojan Palladium: Athens, Argos, Sparta, and in Italy Heraclea, Luceria, Siris, and Lavinium. In Rome it was kept as a 'pledge of Rome's fate' in the innermost part of *Vesta's temple, where only the chief Vestal could enter; when in 241 BC the temple burnt, the pontifex maximus Lucius Caecilius Metellus (*see* PONTIFICES) saved the Palladium, but (so some authorities) lost his sight. It was still there in AD 191, but *Augustus may have placed it (or its copy) temporarily in Vesta's chapel in his *Palatine house.

[Ovid, *Fasti* 6. 419–60; Dionysius of Halicarnassus 1. 68–9; Virgil, *Aeneid* 2. 162–79; Silius Italicus, *Punica* (epic on 2nd Punic War) 13. 36–70]

Pallas (1) (Pallas, genitive Pallados), a name of *Athena, apparently said to be derived either from a playmate of the same name accidentally killed by the goddess or from a giant Pallas (genitive Pallantos) whom Athena overcame.

[Apollodorus 1. 6. 2, 3. 12. 3]

Pallas (2), an Attic hero, one of the four sons of *Pandion among whom Attica was divided. His division was usually said to be the Paralia (south coast), but he was evidently also, rather awkwardly, the eponym of the inland deme (settlement) of Pallene. Together with his sons, who were *Giants, he opposed *Theseus, but their ambush near Gargettus was unsuccessful and they were killed. The story has an oblique relation to the regional factions of the late 6th cent. BC.

The name was borne also by other characters in myth, notably the son of *Evander and protégé of *Aeneas, killed by *Turnus.

[Virgil, *Aeneid* 8. 104 ff., etc.]

Pan, a god whose original home was *Arcadia. His name, attested on Mt. Lykaion in the dative form *Paoni*, is certainly derived from the root pa(s), and means 'guardian of flocks' (cf. Lat. *pascere*). His appearance is mixed, half man and half goat, not surprising in a region where divine theriomorphism is well attested (*see* ARCADIAN CULTS AND MYTHS). His usual attributes of syrinx and *lagobolon* (a device for catching hares) mark him out as a shepherd. Pan became a kind of national god of Arcadia, being shown in the 4th cent. on the reverse of coins of Zeus Lycaeus type of the Arcadian League. Starting at the beginning of the 5th cent., Pan spreads into Boeotia and Attica, continuing in the 4th cent. to reach the rest of the Greek world.

The principal myths concern his birth, and there are no fewer than fourteen different versions of his parentage. Most often his father is *Hermes, another Arcadian god, but the name of his mother varies, though most often she is a *nymph, in harmony with the god's rustic nature. In some versions Pan's mother is *Penelope. Otherwise, there are few stories about Pan before Hellenistic times: he loves the nymphs *Echo, Pitys, and *Syrinx, of whom the last two escape him, and *Selene, the moon.

Pan's activities and functions are basically concerned with the pastoral world. He is a shepherd god and protector of shepherds, who sacrifice in his honour kids, goats or sheep, and who dedicate to him statuettes showing herdsmen, with or without offerings. He is also a hunting god, concerned with small animals such as hares, partridges, and small birds, while it is *Artemis who presides over larger game. This function is illustrated by an Arcadian ritual, whereby after an unsuccessful hunt, young men would beat Pan's statue with squills. In this way they would stimulate Pan's powers of fertility and direct it towards the animal domain. Pan is also linked to the world of those soldiers patrolling the rocky, lonely places where he lives. During the Persian Wars (490–479 BC), he intervened among the Athenian ranks at Marathon. Herodotus has the story of his appearance to the runner Phidippides, who was near Mt. Parthenion in

Arcadia on his way to Laconia to get help from the Spartans; he offered to help the Athenians, in return for which the cult of Pan was established in Athens. From the Hellenistic period onwards, Pan is the god responsible for sowing panic (*panikon*) in the enemy, a sudden, unforeseeable fear. Soldiers therefore pay cult to him. In the case of the individual, too, Pan can exercise a type of savage and violent possession (*panolepsia*). In Attica, Arcadia, and at the Corycian cave at *Delphi, Pan is credited with oracular and prophetic powers. *See* CAVES, SACRED; ORACLES; VOTIVE OFFERINGS.

The Greeks liked to worship Pan, together with Hermes and the nymphs, in sacred *caves, recalling the figure of the Arcadian goatherd. But in his homeland of Arcadia, though he is fond of mountains, well away from human habitation, Pan does not live in caves, and he is not absent from cities. Little is known of his public cult. In Athens, it involved the sacrifice of a castrated goat and a *torch-race. Individual offerings are typified by votives such as vases, golden grasshoppers, oil-lamps (in the cave at Vari in Attica), and reliefs, which show the God in his cave in front of his worshippers, playing the syrinx and accompanied by Hermes, three nymphs, and sometimes the river *Achelous (*see* RIVER-GODS). In the *Dyskolos* of Menander, the mother of Sostratos organizes a religious celebration in honour of Pan at *Phyle, in Attica, after the god appears to her in a *dream. The sacrifice of a sheep is followed by a meal, and the happy and rowdy celebration continues all night at the cave, with drinking and dancing in the presence of the god.

The ancients quite early associated Pan with the word *pan*, 'all'. From this, wordplay leads to the association which made Pan in the Roman period into a universal god, the All. It is in this context that we should see the well-known story in *Plutarch, which has sometimes been linked with the rise of Christianity, of a mysterious voice announcing the death of 'great Pan'. Despite these developments, as *Pausanias bears witness, in cult the god remained the god of shepherds.

[*Homeric Hymn to Pan* 47; Herodotus 6. 105. 2–3; Menander, *Dyskolos*; Theocritus, *Idylls* 7. 106–8; Plutarch, *Moralia* 419 ff.]

Panacea (Gk. *Panakeia*), 'All-Healer', daughter of *Asclepius.

Panathenaea, the great civic festival of Athens in honour of its patron goddess *Athena, celebrated in Hekatombaion (roughly August). Its core was the great procession, evoked on the *Parthenon frieze, in which representatives of different sections of Athenian society and even metics (resident non-Athenians) marched or rode from the Ceramicus through the agora to the acropolis (*see* ATHENS, RELIGIOUS TOPOGRAPHY). There followed large sacrifices, the meat from which was publicly distributed. The night before, choirs of boys and maidens had celebrated a 'night festival' (*pannychis*). Every four years, the Panathenaea was extended to become the 'greater Panathenaea'. Only then, probably, did the procession bring to Athena the famous Panathenaic robe, embroidered with scenes from the battle of Gods and Giants. The greater Panathenaea also included major athletic and musical competitions (*see* AGŌNES), open to all Greece and lasting several days, winners in which received money prizes or olive oil contained in the distinctive Panathenaic prize amphoras. The games were added to the Panathenaea in the 6th cent. (in or near 566), doubtless to set it on a par with other recently founded panhellenic athletic festivals (Pythia, Isthmia, Nemeia; *see* PYTHIAN, ISTHMIAN, and NEMEAN GAMES). In the 5th cent. Athens' allies were required to participate in the procession, which thus became a symbol of imperial power.

Pandareos, name of either one or two obscure mythological persons, the father of *Aëdon, and, if this is not the same Pandareos, the father of two daughters whose story is told in the *Odyssey*; the ancient commentators add much detail. Their names were Cleothera and Merope, and they were left orphans (the ancient commentator says *Zeus killed their father and mother because Pandareos had stolen his dog from Crete). *Hera, *Athena, *Artemis, and *Aphrodite befriended them, brought them up, and gave them all manner of good qualities; but while Aphrodite was visiting Zeus to arrange their wedding, the *Harpyiae carried them off and gave them to be servants to the *Erinyes.

[Homer, *Odyssey* 20. 66 ff.]

Pandarus, a Trojan, son of *Lycaon (2), and an archer favoured by *Apollo. Urged on by *Athena, he breaks the truce between the Greeks and Trojans by shooting at and wounding *Menelaus; wounds *Diomedes (2), and is killed by him while fighting alongside *Aeneas.

[Homer, *Iliad* 2. 826–7, 4. 86 ff., 5. 95 ff., 166–296]

Pandion, a Megarian hero and a mythical king of Athens, later identified as the name of two Athenian kings. For Athenians, his Megarian connections would have bolstered aggressive territorial claims, linked with the tradition of the division of Attica (including the Megarid, i.e. the territory of Megara) between his four sons. He was also one of the tribal *eponymoi. See also* NISUS (1).

Pandora, whose name combines 'all' and 'gifts', was a goddess connected with the earth, but she is better known as the first human female, the cause of all man's woes. If the name has any relevance here, it sounds ironic; but the two Pandoras may in fact be connected through the idea of the earth as first ancestor. In the account of the Hesiodic poems (*see* HESIOD) *Zeus caused Pandora to be created in order to punish *Prometheus and the human race. She was fashioned out of clay by *Hephaestus, given 'gifts' by 'all' the *Olympian gods, and sent as a gift herself to Prometheus' brother Epimetheus. Here she opened a large jar and released all manner of evils into the world; only Hope was left to counterbalance these.

[Hesiod, *Works and Days* 53–105]

Pandrosus, daughter of the Athenian king *Cecrops, to whom with her sisters

*Aglaurus and Herse the infant *Erichthonius was entrusted. In some versions she was the only sister not to disobey *Athena's command not to open the chest in which the baby was concealed, which probably reflects her close association with Athena and the *Arrephoria rite and her role as a nurse of children. Pandrosus had a sanctuary on the Athenian acropolis separately from her sisters, but may have been worshipped together with them elsewhere in Attica.

panhellenic sanctuaries Although the idea that what the Greeks have in common as Greeks, and what distinguishes them from barbarians, is more important than what divides them is not a necessary axiom before the Persian Wars (490–479 BC), certain religious places and festivals, such as the Panhellenic games (*see* AGONES). The four great panhellenic *sanctuaries were *Delphi, *Olympia, *Isthmia, and *Nemea, though there were panhellenic aspects to e.g. the *Panathenaea at Athens.

Panionium, meeting place of the Ionian League from very early (early 7th cent. BC?), where the common festival (Panionia) of the twelve member-cities took place and their representatives met to discuss common policy in time of need. The historian Herodotus places it on Mt. Mycale; for security it was later moved near Ephesus (by 426/5 BC: the festival was then called Ephesia), before returning (373 BC?) to Mt. Mycale, where it was still celebrated under the Roman Principate. Sacrifice was made to Heliconian *Poseidon; the priesthood was reserved for men from Priene. The site has been excavated: there was no temple, it seems, but an altar, 18 m. (59 ft.) long (*c*.500 BC); also a council-house.

pannychis, an 'all-night' festival, with rites appropriate for the deity but often including banquets, hymns, and dances, as in Athens for *Athena Polias at the *Panathenaea and for *Artemis at the Tauropolia. In comedy such night festivals could be made the occasion of illicit sexual encounters.

Pannychis was also a common name for a *hetaira* or upper-class prostitute.

Pantheon, a temple in the *Campus Martius dedicated to all the gods. The first Pantheon, built by Marcus Vipsanius Agrippa in 27–25 BC, was completely rebuilt early in the reign of Hadrian, but retained Agrippa's name in the dedicatory inscription; it was later repaired by Septimius Severus and Caracalla. The building was entered from a long rectangular forecourt through a traditional octastyle Corinthian portico (33.1 × 13.6 m.; 108 × 45 ft.) of red and grey granite columns, 48 Roman feet (11.8 m.; 38 ft.) high, although the original design may have been for 60 (Roman) ft. columns. A rectangular block links this to the circular cella, 43.3 m. (142 ft.) in both diameter and height, lit from a single central oculus, 9 m. (29½ ft.) in diameter. The cylindrical wall of the brick-faced concrete rotunda (6.2 m. (20 ft.) thick) supporting the dome is divided into eight piers by the doorway and alternating semi-circular and rectangular recesses at the lower level with internal key-shaped chambers above, all linked by a complex series of relieving arches extending to the haunches of the dome. The six lateral recesses were divided off by marble columnar screens crowned by a continuous entablature while small aedicules framing statue niches decorated the piers between them. Richly coloured marble veneer, substantially preserved in the lower zone, decorated the interior; a small section of the attic decoration has been restored to its original form. The great bronze doors are ancient. The play of light from the oculus across the vast surface of the richly coffered dome is largely responsible for the building's enduring fascination.

Panthous (or Panthoos), Trojan elder in *Homer's *Iliad*; his son *Polydamas is protected by *Apollo, who may have rescued Panthous himself from Troy. *Virgil makes Panthous priest of Apollo, killed at Troy's fall.

[Homer, *Iliad* 3. 146, 15. 522; Pindar, *Paean* 6. 73 ff.; Virgil, *Aeneid* 2. 318 ff.]

pantomime, popular art-form under the Roman empire in which a solo dancer (Lat. *pantomimus*, Gk. *pantomimos*) represented mythological themes without voice, supported by instrumental music and a chorus. The apparent meaning is 'one who imitates everything', but the distinctive quality of pantomime is that the artist did everything by imitation, as in modern mime. The art (called the 'Italian dance' in the Greek east) was introduced at Rome in 22 BC by the Cilician Pylades and Bathyllus of Alexandria; Hellenistic antecedents are suggested too by e.g. the *pantomimos* of an inscription from Priene of *c.*80 BC. Pylades' innovation, according to himself, was to add the orchestra and the chorus. Bathyllus seems to have specialized in light themes related to comedy or satyric drama, such as *Pan playing with a satyr; Pylades' style is said to have been 'high flown, passionate' and related to tragedy. Tragic subjects were in fact a favourite, and Greek inscriptions grandly describe pantomime-performers as 'actors of tragic rhythmic dance'. A highly sophisticated art, demanding much from both performers and spectators, pantomime was essentially serious, and so enjoyed a higher status than the mime.

Performance took place in the theatre or privately. The artist, usually a handsome, athletic figure, wore a graceful silk costume permitting free movement and a beautiful mask with closed lips. Behind him stood the chorus, the musicians and the *scabillarii*, who beat time by pressing with the foot on the *scabillum*, a wooden or metal instrument fastened underneath the sandal. Beside the artist there sometimes stood an assistant—perhaps an actor with a speaking part. The dancer might in one piece have to appear in five different roles, each with its own mask. The dancer's power to convey his meaning by steps, postures, and above all gestures was aided by certain conventions, e.g. there was a traditional dance for 'Thyestes devouring his children' (*see* ATREUS). The songs of the chorus were of secondary importance; surviving fragments are in Greek. Men of letters

such as Lucan and Statius wrote libretti for the pantomime. Pantomime-artists were popular in both halves of the empire. In the east they performed not just in special shows but also in *agōnes*, including, eventually, such old sacred festivals as the *Pythian Games. In late antiquity the pagan content of the pantomime drew the fire of church fathers, especially John *Chrysostom; but it still flourished in the 6th century.

[Lucian, *On Dance*; Libanius, *In Defence of Dance*]

Paphos, city-kingdom of south-west Cyprus. Palaepaphos (mod. Kouklia) built on a coastal bluff, site of a famous sanctuary of *Aphrodite, by tradition born nearby of sea-foam (*see also* CYTHERA). Alternative cult-founders are the pre-Greek *Cinyras, ambivalent friend of Agamemnon, (the Paphos royal house was Cinyrad throughout its history) and *Agapenor of Tegea, post-Trojan War settler. Archaeology supports both traditions. The first temple (pillar-hall and temenos) is 12th-cent. BC; contemporary tombs nearby contain imported and local Mycenaean pottery. 11th-cent. chamber tombs suggest Aegean colonization; so does a grave-gift inscribed in the Cypriot syllabary with the Greek name Opheltes.

paradoxographers Interest in the unexpected or unbelievable (*paradoxa, thaumasia, apista*) is prominent in the *Odyssey* and Herodotus. Collections of marvels attributed to 4th-cent. authors (*Aristotle, Theopompus, Ephorus) are not genuine, but paradoxography as a distinct literary genre came into existence in the 3rd cent. with *paradoxa* by *Callimachus and his pupil Philostephanus, Antigonus of Carystus, Archelaus of Egypt, Myrsilus of Methymna, and others. In the Roman period there are substantial collections of marvels by Isigonus and *Phlegon, and several anonymous collections survive in medieval manuscripts. The material is taken from geography, botany, zoology, and human culture. Several ancient writers dabbled in the subject (*Cicero, Michael Psellus) and others (*Varro, Pliny the Elder, Aelian) used paradoxographers as sources.

Parcae See FATE.

Parentalia, Roman festival of ancestors on the *dies parentales* (13–21 Feb.), the last of which was a public ceremony (*Feralia), while the rest were days for private devotions to the family dead (*di parentum, parentes*). These were *dies religiosi* (*see* FASTI) during which the magistrates did not wear the *praetexta* characteristic of their office, temples were closed and no weddings celebrated, but not all were *nefasti* (*Lupercalia, 15th, Quirinalia, 17th, 18th–20th all *comitiales*). Often distinguished from the *Lemuria by benevolence, but *Ovid implies otherwise.

[Ovid, *Fasti* 2. 533 ff.]

Parilia, Roman festival of the god, or goddess (both genders are attested), Pales, held on 21 April. In early times it seems to have been a ritual concerned with the flocks and herds of the Roman community; *Ovid describes the lighting of bonfires (through which the celebrants were supposed to jump) and the purification of the animals (with material made by the *Vestals from the ashes of the calf of the *Fordicidia and blood of the October Horse; *see* MARS). By the late republic it was also identified as the 'birthday' of the city of Rome; and in the 2nd cent. AD it gained the alternative title 'Romaia'.

[Cicero, *On Divination* 2. 98; Varro, *On Country Matters* 2. 1. 9; Ovid, *Fasti* 4. 721 ff.; Athenaeus 8. 361 e–f]

Paris, also called Alexandros (his usual name in *Homer), son of *Priam and *Hecuba. Homer refers several times to his abduction of *Helen, which was the cause of the Trojan War (*see* TROY, MYTHS OF). At an earlier stage in the development of the legend he was perhaps the principal warrior on the Trojan side. Even in the *Iliad* he is sometimes effective in battle, and he will be responsible, with *Apollo's help, for the death of *Achilles. In general, however, he is seen as greatly inferior to *Hector, who taunts him as handsome but unwarlike in several places. He uses the bow, which tends to be regarded as an unmanly weapon. He is defeated in a duel by *Menelaus, has to be rescued by *Aphrodite, and then consoles himself by making love to Helen.

The *Cypria* (*see* EPIC CYCLE) told the story of the Judgement of Paris, often mentioned in subsequent literature. Incited to rivalry by *Eris, the goddesses *Hera, *Athena, and Aphrodite appointed Paris to decide between them. They were brought to him by *Hermes, and, bribed by the promise of Helen, he chose Aphrodite as the most beautiful. The story is mentioned in *Iliad* book 24, in a passage which some scholars (from ancient times onward) reject on the grounds that Homer shows no knowledge of the Judgement elsewhere; but others argue that he did know of it but in general suppressed it as unsuitable for his epic.

According to the *Little Iliad* (*see* EPIC CYCLE) Paris was killed by *Philoctetes.

*Sophocles and *Euripides each wrote an *Alexandros*, and the Roman poet Ennius an *Alexander*. We are now well-informed about Euripides' influential play: Hecuba, before the birth of Paris, dreamt that she had given birth to a fire-brand (this motif goes back to *Pindar). So the child was exposed, and Hecuba initiated athletic games (*agōnes*) in his memory. But he survived and was brought up among herdsmen. Grown to manhood, he was brought to Troy, where he competed in the games himself, winning several events. His brother *Deiphobus, furious at being defeated by a mere herdsman, urged Hecuba to kill him, and *Cassandra, recognizing him, prophesied disaster for Troy; but his identity was revealed and his life was spared.

The motif of the *nymph *Oenone, who loved Paris when he lived as a herdsman on Mt. Ida, was abandoned by him for Helen, and later refused to cure him of the wound that killed him, was known as early as *Hellanicus, and is exploited by *Ovid in book 5 of his *Heroides* (*Heroines*).

In art various episodes from his career are represented. The Judgement is especially popular, and is identifiable as early as the 7th cent.

[Homer, *Iliad*, esp. 3. 38–57, 313–82, 383–447, 6. 325–31, 13. 660–720, 768–73, 22. 359–60, 24. 27–30]

Parmenides of Elea is said to have legislated for his native city and (c.450 BC) to have visited Athens in his sixty-fifth year. His philosophical poem, in hexameters, survives in large fragments. It opens with the narration of a journey taken by the initiate poet-speaker, apparently from the world of daily life and light to a mysterious place where night and day cross paths and opposites are undivided. Here he is greeted by a goddess whose instruction forms the remainder of the work. She urges him to cease relying on ordinary beliefs and to 'judge by reason the very contentious refutation' of those beliefs that she offers. Her address attends closely to logical rigour and connection. The proem is suffused with religious language, and one might conjecture that an initiation in reason is being substituted for the perception-suffused initiations of religious cult.

Every aspect of this difficult argument is disputed; one can only offer one plausible account. Central to the goddess's teaching is the idea that thought and speech must have an object that is there to be talked or thought about. This being the case, if something is sayable or thinkable, it must *be*: 'You cannot say or think that it is not.' On this basis, she concludes not only that nothingness or the non-existent cannot figure in our speech, but also that temporal change, internal qualitative variation, and even plurality are all unsayable and unthinkable—on the grounds that talk about all these will commit the speaker to making contrasts and entail the use of negative language. Thus, whatever can be talked or thought about must be 'without birth or death, whole, single-natured, unaltering, and complete'.

A subsidiary argument invokes an idea of sufficient reason to rule out cosmogony: if what is had a beginning in time, there must have been some reason for that beginning. But what reason could there be, if (by hypothesis) there was nothing there previously?

Having described the 'Way of Truth', the goddess then acquaints her pupil with the deceptive contents of mortal beliefs. The cosmogony that follows is not intended to have any degree of truth or reliability. It is presumably selected because it shows the fundamental error of mortals in its simplest form. The decision to 'name' two forms, light and night, commits mortals to contrastive negative characterizations.

Parnassus, outlying spur of the Pindus range, running south-east and rising to 2,457 m. (8,063 ft.). It separates the (Boeotian) *Cephissus valley from that of Amphissa and runs into the Corinthian Gulf at Cape Opus. Its limestone mass is mostly barren, but its lower slopes are well watered; they carry the Phocian towns on its eastern flank and the plain of Crisa with the high valley of *Delphi on the south. The best ascent is from Daulis; the passes which cross its spurs run from Cytinium to Amphissa and from Daulis to Delphi via 'the cross-roads' of *Sophocles, *King Oedipus* 733 (where Oedipus killed Laius), where it is joined by the route from Lebadea (*see* TROPHONIUS) to Delphi. It was a sacred mountain, especially to the Dorians

parody (Gk. *parōdia*). Parody entails imitation, but an imitation which is intended to be recognized as such and to amuse. By exaggerating distinctive features, it may simply invite ridicule and criticism of the original; or it may exploit the humour of incongruity, coupled with exaggeration for ease of recognition, by combining the language and style of the original with completely alien subject-matter. Most parody found in our texts is itself based on literary texts, such as epic, tragedy, or other 'serious' genres, but we find parody of religious ritual for instance in Aristophanes' *Birds* and *Thesmophoriazusae*. Mythology could also invite burlesque or parodic treatment, as in *Ovid and Lucian.

It is unclear whether the profanation of the Eleusinian *Mysteries in 415 BC really involved parody of the ritual, as alleged in some modern accounts.

Parthenon The Parthenon was the temple of *Athena built on the highest part of the Acropolis at Athens south of the Archaic temple (see ATHENS, RELIGIOUS TOPOGRAPHY). The name ('virgin chamber') is properly that of the west room, but is generally extended to the entire building. The title Parthenos (virgin) describes Athena; she was Polias, protector of the city. It was begun in 447 BC in the time of Pericles; the temple and cult statue were dedicated in 438, but work continued, notably on the pedimental sculptures, until 432. A temple had been begun on the site after Marathon (490), but work was abandoned on the approach of the second Persian war (480–79). What had been built was destroyed by the Persians when they captured the city.

The Periclean building adapts the foundations and platform of this earlier structure, and, possibly, some of the marble elements prepared for it. It was built to house the gold and ivory *statue by *Phidias, who must have been responsible for at least the design of its sculptural decoration; it is unlikely that he also directed the architectural design, which was determined more by the existing foundations than the statue it was to house.

The architect was Ictinus together with Callicrates. In the Parthenon the Doric order is seen at its most perfect in proportions and in refined details, though there are some unusual features. The material is fine marble readily available from the quarries of Pentelicon a few miles north-east of Athens and generally used in the important Athenian buildings of the Periclean period. The temple measures about 69.5 × 30.8 m. (228 × 101 ft.) on the top step. It has eight columns at the ends, and seventeen on the sides. The inner structure has a porch of six columns at each end. The larger eastern room had a two-tiered inner colonnade running not only along the sides but round the western end, behind the great cult statue; recent study has shown that there were windows high to the sides of the east door. The smaller western room opened off the back porch, and had its roof supported by four Ionic columns; it served as a 'treasury'.

The *sculpture was more elaborate, more unified in theme, and more relevant to the cult than in most temples. It was also more extensive: every metope is carved, while the porch colonnades have instead a continuous frieze, extended abnormally the entire length of the cella outer walls. The metopes must have been made first, and then the frieze. The pediments were the latest addition. They showed, in the east, Athena newly sprung from the head of *Zeus, and in the west, the contest of *Poseidon and Athena for the land of Attica. The metopes, in high relief, showed mythical combats, on the south side, best preserved, Lapiths and *Centaurs, on the east, Gods and *Giants, on the west, Greeks and *Amazons, on the north—less certainly, since this side is very badly preserved—Trojan scenes (see HOMER; TROY, MYTHS OF). Some of these themes were echoed in the minor decoration of the cult statue. The frieze, in low relief, comprises a Panathenaic procession (see PANATHENAEA). It has been suggested this depicts or honours the young Athenian citizens who died at the battle of Marathon. A general allusion on these lines is certain. The whole temple, like its predecessor, is best interpreted as a thank-offering (after a false start) for the final, successful outcome of the wars with Persia, and it is clear that the reliefs allude to this, to the glorification of the Greek, and specifically Athenian, contribution to the victory.

The temple was subsequently converted into a church, dedicated to the Virgin, and then a mosque. It remained almost intact, though reroofed, until 1687, when a Turkish powder-magazine in it was exploded by the besieging Venetians. Earlier reconstruction work has been dismantled, and a thorough programme of conservation is being carried out, which has led to the identification of many of the fallen fragments.

Parthenopaeus, one of the *Seven against Thebes. Sometimes he is Argive,

brother of *Adrastus , sometimes Arcadian, the son of *Atalanta. With *Telephus, he was exposed on Mount Parthenion, and he accompanied Telephus to Mysia. He was victorious in the archery contest at the games founded at *Nemea in honour of Archemorus-Opheltes (*see* NEMEAN GAMES). He took part in the expedition of the Seven against his mother's wishes, and was killed in front of Thebes by *Periclymenus (or Asphodicus or *Amphilochus).
[Apollodorus 1. 9. 13, 3. 6. 3 ff., 9. 2 ff.]

Pasiphae *See* MINOS.

patricians formed a privileged class of Roman citizens. The word is probably connected with *patres* ('Fathers'), a formal collective term for patrician senators. In the republican period patrician status could be obtained only by birth; and it may be surmised that in early times both parents had to be patricians, if the law of the Twelve Tables which stated that patricians could not legally marry plebeians was a codification of long-established practice rather than an innovation; this law was repealed in 445 BC. It is also possible, but not certain, that patrician *marriages had to be by *confarreatio*.

The origin of the patriciate is disputed. Tradition made it the creation of *Romulus, but also suggested that it was augmented by the admission of aristocratic clans from outside Rome, such as the 'Trojan families' (including the Iulii) who were brought to Rome after the sack of *Alba Longa, and the Claudii, a Sabine clan (*see* SABINI) that migrated to Rome at the beginning of the republic.

We know that the patricians originally monopolized all the important priesthoods (*see* PRIESTS), and it is most probable that they were essentially a group defined by religious prerogatives. Although by 300 BC the patricians had lost their monopoly of office and of the major priestly colleges (*see* COLLEGIUM), they continued to exercise power out of all proportion to their numbers. Until 172 BC one of the two annual consuls was always a patrician, and they continued to hold half the places in the major priestly colleges as of

right. Other priesthoods, such as the *flamines maiores*, the *rex sacrorum*, and the *Salii, remained exclusively patrician.

Patroclus, in mythology, son of *Menoetius. Having accidentally killed a playfellow, the young Patroclus took refuge with *Peleus. He and his father were kindly received, and Patroclus, who was somewhat older than *Achilles, was assigned to him as a personal attendant. For the rest *see* ACHILLES.
[Homer, *Iliad*, esp. books 9, 11, 16, 23]

patrōoi theoi, in Greek, literally 'gods associated with a father', hence commonly 'ancestral' or 'inherited gods'. There is a clear similarity between the use of the epithet here and in phrases such as *hiera patrōa*, ancestral shrines, and *ousia patrōa*, a man's patrimony: gods, like their altars, are in sense inherited property (whence the names of *patrōoi theoi* are often followed by a possessive genitive or other similar construction). Two usages can be distinguished: (1) in patriotic appeals and similar contexts, the *patrōoi theoi* seem to be the whole established pantheon of the state; (2) particular gods are *patrooi* to particular groups or individuals; put in other terms, particular individuals or groups traditionally worship at particular shrines (which they own). Thus in the Thesmophorion (*see* THESMOPHORIA) of Thasos a series of altars have been found bearing inscriptions such as '[altar] of *Zeus Patroos of the Neophantideis' (a kinship group), 'of Zeus Alastoros Patroos of the Phastadeis'. At Athens, candidates for the archonship (*see* ARCHONTES) were asked 'if they possessed an *Apollo Patroos and a Zeus of the Courtyard, and where these shrines were'. Here the cult of a particular *patroos* is in principle universal or at least widespread, though diffused through the separate altars of a series of individual groups; and it was primarily in this sense that Apollo could be said to be *patroos* to the Ionians, or Zeus to Dorian states.

Patrōoi theoi normally belonged, it seems,

to hereditary extended groups based on fictitious kinship such as the *patra* on Thasos and the *phratry and *genos* at Athens; but individual families could probably also have *patrōoi* of their own. One Leocrates was accused by the orator Lycurgus of having exported his *hiera patrōa*, 'ancestral shrines', in a crisis.

Zeus *patrōos* is occasionally spoken of as if he were 'Zeus who protects the rights of fathers'; this is an exceptional interpretation of the epithet, not its basic meaning. More common and influential (in modern accounts too) is the idea that an ancestral god is also an ancestor god: we are told for instance that it is as father of the Ionian ancestor *Ion that Apollo is *patrōos* to the Ionians; so too with the Zeus *patrōos* of the Dorians (via *Heracles). But the virgin Athena is a *patrōa* on Thasos, and there are other like cases; the idea of paternity is not, therefore, fundamental. The emotional appeal of the *patrōoi* (the strength of which is visible above all in Lycurgus' speech against Leocrates) derives primarily not from the idea of parenthood but from that of tradition, continuity, the transmission to one's children of that which was one's parents'.

Paul, St St Paul was a convert (*see* CONVERSION) from Pharisaic to Messianic Judaism as a result of a mystical experience (Gal. 1: 12 and 16) when he believed himself called to be the divine agent by whom the biblical promises about the eschatological ingathering of the pagans would be fulfilled. That transference of allegiance led him to renounce his previous religious affiliations (Phil. 3: 6 f.), even though the form of his religion remains in continuity with apocalyptic *Judaism. We know him as the result of letters which he wrote over a period of about ten years to maintain communities of Jews and gentiles in Rome and several other urban centres in a pattern of religion which enjoined faithfulness to Jesus Christ as the determining factor in the understanding of the Mosaic Law. This subordination of the Law inevitably led to conflict with Jewish and Christian opponents who suspected

him of antinomianism and apostasy. His doctrine of justification by faith was hammered out as a way of explaining his position in relation to the Jewish Law. He commended Christianity as a religion which was both the fulfilment of the Jewish tradition and also the negation of central precepts like food laws and circumcision, though he was emphatic in his rejection of idolatry. In his letters we have clear evidence of the emergence of identifiable Christian communities separate from Judaism with a loose adherence to the Jewish tradition as interpreted by Paul. At the end of his life he organized a financial offering for the poor in Jerusalem from the gentile churches he had founded. According to *Acts his journey to Jerusalem with this collection preceded his journey to Rome where later Christian tradition suggests that he died in the Neronian persecution. The letters in the New Testament which are widely assumed to be authentic are Romans, 1 and 2 Corinthians, Galatians, Philippians, 1 Thessalonians, and Philemon, and possibly Colossians and 2 Thessalonians. Ephesians, and 1 and 2 Timothy and Titus are probably not by Paul. This last group of documents indicates the direction of the Pauline tradition after the apostle's death when accredited teachers began to be ordained to ensure the preservation of the apostolic traditions and institutions in the face of emerging *gnosticism and antinomianism. *See also* CHRISTIANITY; PHARISEES.

Paulinus (1) of Nola (AD 353/4–431), born at Bordeaux, was a favourite pupil of the poet and rhetor Ausonius. After governing Campania (381) and Magnus Maximus' usurpation in Gaul (383–8), he turned to a Christian ascetic life with his wife Therasia first in Spain then, from 395, as a priest and bishop at Nola (*see* ASCETICISM). His poems, mostly in hexameters, celebrated the cult of St Felix of Nola and made him a leading Christian Latin poet. Over fifty of his letters also survive, revealing a wide network of correspondents, including *Augustine. Emotional, devout, often prolix, and occasionally humorous, Paulinus is an important witness to the religious character of his age.

Paulinus (2) of Pella, a Gallo-Roman aristocrat, wrote the *Eucharisticon*, a Christian poem of thanks for his misfortunes, c.AD 460, when in his eighties. The grandson of the poet Ausonius, he was born at Pella but reared at Bordeaux. He experienced the Germanic invasions of 407 and served with the usurper Priscus Attalus (414–15) in Aquitaine. His two sons died young and he was reduced to poverty by barbarian inroads and the dishonesty of his relations but later made a partial recovery when he unexpectedly received payment from a Goth who had settled on his land.

Pausanias from Magnesia ad Sipylum (?) (fl. c.AD 150), travel writer, wrote an extant *Description of Greece* (*Perriēgēsis tēs Hellados*) claiming to describe 'all things Greek'; in fact limited essentially to the province of Achaia with the omission of Aetolia and the islands. Contents: 1. Attica, Megara; 2. Argolis etc.; 3. Laconia; 4. Messenia; 5–6. Elis, Olympia; 7. Achaea; 8. Arcadia; 9. Boeotia; 10. Phocis, Delphi.

His chief concern in his selective account was with the monuments (especially sculpture and painting) of the Archaic and Classical periods, along with their historical contexts, and the sacred (cults, rituals, beliefs), of which he had a profound sense. His work is organized as a tour of the *poleis* (city-states) and extra-urban sanctuaries of Achaia, with some interest in topography, but little in the intervening countryside. His concern for objects after 150 BC is slight, although contemporary monuments attracted his attention, especially the benefactions of Hadrian. He wrote from autopsy, and his accuracy (in spite of demonstrable muddles) has been confirmed by excavation. Although his approach was personal, his admiration for old Greece (Athens, Sparta, Delphi, and Olympia figure prominently) and its great patriots belongs to the archaizing enthusiasm for the Greek motherland

fanned by the literary movement known as the Second Sophistic and Hadrian's organization of Greek cities, the Panhellenion, which attracted many overseas (especially Asian) Greeks to old Greece; presumably Pausanias wrote partly with these in mind.

Pax, the personification of (political) peace, (*see* EIRENE). Scarcely heard of before *Augustus, she comes (as Pax Augusta) to represent one of the principal factors which made the imperial government both strong and popular, the maintenance of quiet at home and abroad. The most famous, but not the only, monuments of the cult were the *Ara Pacis Augustae and the Flavian Templum Pacis, dedicated AD 75.

Pegasus, the immortal winged horse who carries the thunder and lightning of *Zeus; he was born from Medusa's severed neck (*see* GORGO) when she was pregnant by *Poseidon. Pegasus was caught and tamed at the fountain of Pirene at Corinth (*see* CORINTHIAN CULTS AND MYTHS) by the hero *Bellerophon, with the help of *Athena Chalinitis or of Poseidon. He helped Bellerophon to kill the *Chimaera, the *Amazons, and the Solymi. Bellerophon took vengeance on Stheneboea by flinging her off Pegasus from a great height into the sea; and in turn was himself flung off when he tried to fly on him to *Olympus. Pegasus was said to have created various springs from the earth by a stamp of his hoof, including Hippocrene on Mt. *Helicon near the *Muses' sacred grove, and another spring of that name at Troezen. Pegasus' birth is represented in the early archaic pediment of Corcyra, and he appears on early coins of Corinth, the city with which he is most closely connected by legends. With Bellerophon he is a popular subject in art from before the mid-7th cent., where their attack on the Chimaera first appears in Corinthian vase-painting. In Roman times Pegasus became a symbol of immortality.

[Hesiod, *Theogony* 278–86; Apollodorus 2. 3. 1–2; Pausanias 2. 4. 1, 31. 9; 9. 31. 3]

Peitho, the personification of 'Winning Over', more loosely, 'Persuasion', that makes woman available to man in the context of love and marriage. Her divine status is not fixed, allowing *Euripides' wilful lines: 'There is no shrine of Peitho except words, and her altar is in human nature.' Thus she appears as a minor figure in the entourage of *Aphrodite (like Pothos and Himeros—'longing' and 'desire'), e.g. on vases from the early 5th cent. onwards, or as an epithet of Aphrodite or *Artemis. More substantially, she has a shrine at Sicyon connected with Apollo and Artemis, whilst at Argos there is a shrine of Artemis Peitho founded by Hypermestra (see DANAUS AND DANAIDS). At Athens *Theseus established the worship of Aphrodite Pandemos and (of?) Peitho, where she has a priestess and receives annual sacrifices. Her name is used at Argos for the aunt or wife of the culture-hero *Phoroneus (see CULTURE-BRINGERS), and in *Hesiod for an Oceanid (see NYMPHS) and a Lady Peitho. The existence of Peitho from early times perhaps shows something about men's awareness of the independent minds of women.

[Pausanias 1. 22. 3, 2. 7. 7, 21. 1; Isocrates 15. 249]

Pelagius Now agreed to have been British by birth, educated in rhetoric and possibly in law, Pelagius settled in Rome after AD 380. Noted for his *asceticism, though formally neither monk nor priest, he enjoyed (like *Jerome, Priscillian (see PRISCILLIANISTS), and *Rufinus) the patronage of Christian aristocrats, especially women, and responded similarly to their interest in scripture. His *Letter to Demetrias* is a vivid monument. His commentaries on the Epistles of *Paul are straightforward and polished, following in a Roman tradition dating to Marius Victorinus and including *Ambrosiaster, reminiscent of the 'Antiochene' school, but informed also by Latin translations of *Origen. He was inevitably engaged with protagonists of the controversy over Origen's theology. His asceticism was moderate, his attachment to freedom intense. He aroused the scorn of Jerome for the one and criticized *Augustine on account of the other. Anxious to maintain a balance between *Manichaeism and a disparagement of virginity, he rejected current views of original sin, defending the justice of God and the individual's ability to rise by deliberate choice above moral weakness. Protected in Rome by his patrons, he left the city at the time of the Gothic sack in AD 410, taking brief refuge in Africa and seeing his supporter Cælestius condemned at the Council of Carthage in 411. Pelagius moved east and was supported at synods by John of Jerusalem in 415. Western enemies in both Africa and Rome were relentless, however, and were reinforced by imperial condemnation in 418. The remaining course of his life and the circumstances of his death are unknown. The soundness of his judgement has been hard to suppress, in spite of Augustine's reputation, and was proliferated in numerous pamphlets and defended by Julian of Eclanum.

Pelasgians, a mythic population-group mentioned by *Homer as Trojan allies 'from Larisa' (apparently in Thrace). In Homer's Greece, *Achilles' domain includes 'Pelasgian Argos', and Achilles worships 'Pelasgian *Zeus' of *Dodona; in the *Odyssey*, Pelasgians are among the mixed population of Crete. Thus installed in the heroic age as a group with an Aegean home, 'Pelasgians' became a descriptive category for the original peoples of the Aegean more generally, as with Herodotus, who ascribes the minority-language of the Crestonians in Chalcidice a Pelasgic origin; since the Athenians claimed to be autochthonous (see AUTOCHTHONS), they too were 'Pelasgians'. Myths of Pelasgian colonization in (especially central) Italy, including Rome, essentially reflect the desire to Hellenize, first Etruscan, then Roman, origins. *See also* PELASGUS.

[Homer, *Iliad* 2. 684, 840, 15. 233, 17. 301; *Odyssey* 19. 177; Herodotus 1. 57, 6. 137–40]

Pelasgus, eponym of the *Pelasgians, the mythical pre-Hellenic inhabitants of Greece.

A hero of that name is found in Arcadia, Argos, and Thessaly, i.e. the regions said to have been occupied by the Pelasgians. The Arcadians claimed Pelasgus as their first-born man, king, and godlike *culture-bringer. According to one genealogy, he was the son of *Niobe and *Zeus, father of *Lycaon (3) who in turn had fifty sons, the eponymous founders of the Arcadian cities. The Argive Pelasgus was king at the time of the arrival of *Danaus and the Danaids; he welcomed *Demeter during her search for *Persephone and built a temple for her as Pelasgis. His daughter Larissa gave her name to the Argive citadel. Son of Larissa and *Poseidon in Thessalian legend, Pelasgus left his native Peloponnese with his brothers *Achaeus and Phthius and settled in Thessaly, from then on called Haemonia. They divided the land into three parts which were named after them Achaea (i.e. Achaea Phthiotis), Phthiotis, and Pelasgiotis.

[Apollodorus 3. 8. 1; Pausanias 2. 22. 1, 8. 2. 1]

Peleus, in mythology son of *Aeacus, king of Aegina, and Endeis. He and *Telamon killed their half-brother *Phocus, at which their father banished them both, and Peleus went to Phthia, where he was purified (see PURIFICATION, GREEK) by Eurytion, son of Actor, and married his daughter *Antigone (2). But at the Calydonian boar-hunt (see ATA-LANTA; MELEAGER) he accidentally killed Eurytion and was again exiled. This time he reached Iolcus, where *Acastus son of Pelias purified him, and he took part in Pelias' funeral games in which he wrestled with Atalanta. But Astydamia, Acastus' wife, fell in love with him; and when he refused her advances she sent a lying message to Antigone that Peleus was about to marry Acastus' daughter Sterope. Antigone hanged herself. Astydamia then lied to Acastus that Peleus had tried to rape her. Acastus, unwilling to kill the man whom he had purified, instead took him hunting on Mt. *Pelion and hid his sword while he slept, thus leaving him defenceless against the *Centaurs. Either the gods sent Peleus a sword or Chiron gave him

back his own sword. So he escaped, and took vengeance on Astydamia by capturing Iolcus and cutting her to pieces. He was given the extraordinary privilege of marriage to the goddess *Thetis, though he had to win her by wrestling with her while she changed into many different shapes—fire, water, wind, tree, bird, tiger, lion, snake, and cuttle-fish. The gods came to their wedding-feast and brought gifts. But Thetis left Peleus because he interfered when she tried to make their son *Achilles immortal by burning away his mortality. In old age Peleus was alone and afflicted, but finally in death was reunited to Thetis and made immortal.

His wrestling at the funeral games of Pelias, his wrestling with Thetis, their wedding, and his bringing the infant Achilles to be brought up by Chiron, are favourite subjects in 6th- and 5th-cent. art (the last already in the mid-7th cent.); he also appears in pictures of the Calydonian boar-hunt.

[Apollodorus 3. 12. 6–13. 6; Homer, *Iliad* 24. 486–9; Euripides, *Andromache*]

Pelias, in mythology, son of *Tyro and *Poseidon and father of *Alcestis; his name was etymologized from the dark mark on his face left by the kick of a horse when he was exposed as a child. Already in *Hesiod he is portrayed as an evil man; when king of Iolcus he devised the expedition for the Golden Fleece to rid himself of *Jason (1)'s rightful claims to his throne (see ARGONAUTS). After the expedition Jason and *Medea persuaded his daughters to cut him up so that Medea could rejuvenate him by boiling; thus did *Hera punish him for neglecting to honour her. The funeral games in his honour were a famous subject for Archaic epic and vase painting.

[Hesiod, *Theogony* 995–6; Apollodorus 1. 9. 8]

Pelion, a mountain of over 1,615 m. (5,300 ft.) in Thessalian Magnesia. It was the reputed home of the centaur Chiron (see CENTAURS).

Pelops, father of *Atreus, a hero worshipped at *Olympia and believed to be the *eponym of the Peloponnese. As a child, he was killed and served up by his father *Tantalus, in order to test his guests the Gods. Only *Demeter, mourning the loss of her daughter, failed to notice, and ate part of his shoulder; the other Gods restored him to life and replaced his shoulder with ivory. Later, he wooed *Hippodamia, daughter of Oenomaus of Pisa, the area round Olympia. Oenomaus had promised his daughter to any man who could carry her off in a chariot and escape his pursuit; unsuccessful contenders would be killed. Though skilled in horsemanship through the favour of his former lover *Poseidon, Pelops won (in the usual version) by bribing Oenomaus' charioteer Myrtilus to loosen the linchpins on his master's chariot. Oenomaus was thus killed, but in dying cursed Pelops; or he was cursed by Myrtilus, whom he killed on the homeward journey, either because he was ashamed by the manner of his victory or because Myrtilus loved Hippodamia. The curse took effect only in the next generation; Pelops himself prospered greatly, and had six sons by Hippodamia.

*Pindar speaks of Pelops' burial near the great altar at Olympia 'amidst blood-offerings', but no burial was found in the tumulus there, and *Pausanias records that the hero's bones were kept in a chest near the temple of *Artemis Kordax at Pisa. However, just as Pelops' myth suggests a connection with the *Olympian games, so his cult was most prominent at Olympia, where he had a large sanctuary inside the Altis grove; numerous archaic dedications were found here. There was a ritual opposition between this cult and that of Olympian *Zeus, whereby those who had eaten meat sacrificed to Pelops were refused entry to the precinct of Zeus (presumably for a specified time, or until purified; *see* PURIFICATION, GREEK).

In art, Pelops appears at Olympia itself, where the preparations for the chariot-race are the subject of the east pediment of the temple of Zeus, and the preparation and race are found occasionally in 5th- and 4th-cent. vase-painting

[Pindar, *Olympian* 1. 90–3; Pausanias 6. 22. 1]

Penates, di, Roman spirits connected with the inner part (*penus, penitus,* etc.) of the house; the name only exists in the plural and as an adjective with *di* (gods). They were worshipped in *Vesta's temple and also on the Velia. Roman legal scholars theorized about and expanded on the content of the *penus,* and it is tempting to parallel this with the expanding province of the Penates: officials sacrificed to them and they received offerings as *Publici* and of the imperial house. Moderns assert they were regularly conjoined with the *Lares, but the ancient evidence does not support this.

Although *Virgil's *Aeneid* crystallized the tradition of a Trojan/Greek origin, the precise Greek origins and route to Rome remain disputed. At *Lavinium they were equated with the *Dioscuri and represented by statues. But they had aniconic representations at another shrine there, according to Timaeus. The former group probably influenced the Velia shrine, the latter the Vesta temple.

[Cicero, *On the Nature of the Gods* 2. 67; Dionysius of Halicarnassus, *Roman Antiquities* 1. 67; Tacitus, *Annals* 15. 41. 1]

Peneleos (*Pēneleōs* or *Pēneleos*), son of Hippalcimus or Hippalcus; one of the Boeotian leaders in the *Iliad.* In other sources we learn that he was killed by *Eurypylus, wooed *Helen, and was an *Argonaut.

[Homer, *Iliad* 2. 494]

Penelope, daughter of *Icarius (1) (*Tyndareos' brother), wife of *Odysseus, and mother of *Telemachus. In *Homer's *Odyssey* she faithfully awaits Odysseus' return, although pressed to marry one of the many local nobles. She pretends that she must first finish weaving a shroud for Laertes, Odysseus' father, which she unravels every night for three years, until detected by a maid and forced to complete it. Finally, twenty years after Odysseus' departure, in despair she resolves to marry the suitor who can string Odysseus' bow and perform a special feat of archery. Odysseus, who has returned disguised as a beggar, achieves this and kills the suitors with the bow. She tests his identity by another trick concerning their marriage-bed and they are reunited. Homer portrays her as a model of fidelity, prudence, and ingenuity, and most later writers echo this view.

In the *Telegony* (*see* EPIC CYCLE) Odysseus, Penelope, and Telemachus are immortalized by *Circe after Odysseus' death. Telemachus marries Circe, Telegonus Penelope. Italus is their son in *Hyginus. In the epic *Thesprotis* Penelope bears Odysseus a second son, Ptoliporthes, on his return from Troy (sometimes called Arcesilaus). But in Arcadian legend Odysseus expels her because of infidelity and she dies at Mantinea, where *Pausanias saw her tomb. In another version she is seduced by the suitor Amphinomus and killed by Odysseus. Arcadian legend seems also to be behind the odd tradition which made her the mother of *Pan, by *Apollo or *Hermes, or even by all the suitors! (*See* ARCADIAN CULTS AND MYTHS.)

In art she is shown mourning Odysseus' absence (seated at her loom with head on hand, elbow on knee), at the departure of Telemachus, receiving gifts from the suitors, conversing with Odysseus, at the foot-washing scene, and at the suitors' death. Zeuxis is said to have portrayed her character (*mores*) in a painting.

[Homer, *Odyssey*, esp. 2. 93 ff., 19. 137 ff., 24. 128 ff., 23. 174–206; Herodotus 2. 145; Apollodorus, *Epitome* 7. 38; Pausanias 8. 12. 5–6; Hyginus, *Fables* 127]

Penia, poverty personified, differentiated from *ptōcheia* or destitution; an allegorical and not a cult figure, though described humorously as a local divinity by characters in Herodotus.

[Herodotus 8. 111. 3]

pentathlon, a contest at the *Olympian Games and elsewhere, with five events (long-jump, running, discus, javelin, wrestling).

Penthesilea, in mythology daughter of *Ares and the *Amazon queen Otrere. She accidentally killed her comrade Hippolyte in the battle which followed *Theseus' marriage to Phaedra, then went to *Troy to be purified (*see* PURIFICATION, GREEK) of her blood-guilt by *Priam. As a consequence, she led an army of Amazons to Troy to help Priam after *Hector's death. Here, according to the *Aethiopis* (*see* EPIC CYCLE), she performed valiantly in battle until finally overcome and killed by *Achilles. She was buried by the Trojans, and Achilles grieved over her; whereupon *Thersites jeered at him for being in love with her and Achilles killed him. Since in this version Thersites was of good family—son of Agrius brother of *Oeneus, and thus a kinsman of *Diomedes (2)—a dispute arose and Achilles had to sail to Lesbos to be purified.

Penthesilea's death at Achilles' hands is often shown in art from the mid-6th cent., and was the subject of one of the panels painted by Panaenus round Phidias' Zeus.

[Apollodorus, *Epitome* 5. 1–2]

Pentheus, in mythology son of Agave, daughter of *Cadmus, and her husband *Echion (1). *Euripides' *Bacchae* gives the most familiar version of his legend. The disguised *Dionysus returns from his conquests in the east to Thebes (*see* THEBES, MYTHS OF), where the young king Pentheus is refusing to recognize his deity or to allow his worship. Pentheus imprisons Dionysus, in ignorance of his true identity and seeing him simply as a corrupting influence on the women of Thebes; but Dionysus escapes, and, by making Pentheus mad, inveigles him up on to Mt. Cithaeron to spy on the *maenads there. Pentheus, deranged and himself dressed as a maenad, is torn to pieces by the women led by his mother Agave. She carries his head home in triumph, believing it to be that of a lion killed in the hunt, where she is gently brought to sanity and grief by Cadmus.

Pentheus with the maenads is found occasionally in vase-paintings from the late 6th cent. on, but these seem to reflect a different tradition in which an armed Pentheus went into battle against the maenads.

Perachora (ancient *Peiraion*), the promontory opposite Corinth, in Corinthian territory. At the western extremity, sited on a narrow shelf of land by a small harbour is the sanctuary of *Hera Akraia (oracular according to Strabo; *see* HERAION; ORACLES), of considerable importance in the Archaic period, attracting offerings from a wide area. A small apsidal temple of *c.*750 BC must have resembled the terracotta models found among the offerings. The final temple of *c.*525 BC is abnormally long and narrow because of the restricted site. Other buildings include a formal dining building *c.*500 BC and a two-storey stoa of *c.*300 BC. There are complex waterworks, by the sanctuary and in the area above its 'sacred valley'.

Peregrinus (later called Proteus), from a wealthy family in the Roman colony of Parium. A Cynic philosopher, he is the subject of a satirical essay by Lucian, *On the Death of Peregrinus*, unfortunately preserving most of what is known about him, including dubious allegations of parricide and pederasty. Visiting Palestine, he became a Christian convert (*see* CONVERSION). Returning to Parium, he gave away his property to his fellow-citizens; apostasy led to a period of study in Egypt under the Cynic Agathobulus. According to Lucian a visit to Rome ended with banishment for verbal abuse of the emperor (Antoninus Pius). Based in Achaia, he made speeches at *Olympia exhorting a Greek revolt and attacking the ex-consul Tiberius Claudius Atticus Herodes, a local benefactor. He achieved posthumous fame by self-immolation at the *Olympian Games of AD 165. Although Lucian paints him as a mad charlatan, Aulus Gellius thought him a man of 'dignity and fortitude'.

[Lucian, *On the Death of Peregrinus*; Aulus Gellius, *Attic Nights* 12. 11. 1]

Periclymenus, in mythology, (1) son of *Poseidon and a daughter of *Tiresias. One of the Theban defenders against the *Seven against Thebes; according to the epic *Thebais* (*see* EPIC CYCLE) and *Euripides (*Phoenissae*), he killed *Parthenopaeus, and *Pindar tells how he would have killed the seer *Amphiaraus, had not Zeus intervened. (2) Son of Pylian *Neleus. His grandfather, Posei-

don, gave him the power of *metamorphosis which made him a great warrior; he was finally killed by *Heracles with the assistance of *Athena.

Peripatetic school The name belongs to a series of philosophers of whom *Aristotle was the first and by far the most significant. Geographically the school was located in a sanctuary dedicated to *Apollo, called the Lyceum, a public space outside the city wall of Athens but within easy walking distance (the Academy of *Plato was another such place). As in other similar places, there were 'walks' (*peripatoi*). The name 'Peripatos' stuck to the school begun there by Aristotle, formerly a member of the Academy, when he returned to Athens in 336.

In the time of Aristotle and Theophrastus, the foundations were laid for systematic, co-operative research into nearly all the branches of contemporary learning. There is evidence of continuous philosophical activity until the 1st cent. BC, when Athens was captured by Sulla and the Peripatetic library removed to Rome. After this, Peripatetic philosophy was not specifically located in Athens, and was not sharply distinguished doctrinally from the Academy and *Stoicism; the Epicureans were opposed to them all.

Periphetes ('famous', 'notorious'), name of several minor mythological figures, especially of a brigand, also called Corynetes ('club-wielder'), killed by *Theseus on his way to Athens. He was son of *Hephaestus and Anticlea, according to Apollodorus, who adds that he lived in *Epidaurus, was weak in the legs (or feet) and killed all passers-by with an iron club. This Theseus took from him and afterwards carried (another resemblance between Theseus and *Heracles). *Hyginus says he was son of *Poseidon.

[Apollodorus 3. 16. 1; Hyginus, *Fables* 38. 1]

persecution, religious See CHRISTIANITY; DIOCLETIAN; INTOLERANCE, RELIGIOUS; MARTYRS, CHRISTIAN; MARTYRS, JEWISH; SEMITISM, ANTI-.

Persephone/Kore, goddess, *Demeter's daughter by *Zeus, *Hades' wife and queen of the underworld. Her most important myth is that of her abduction by Hades, her father's brother, who carried her off when she was picking flowers in a meadow and took her to the underworld. Demeter's unsuccessful search for her daughter (which took her to *Eleusis) and consequent withdrawal from her normal functions caused the complete failure of crops; men would have starved if Zeus had not intervened. When Demeter did not respond to the persuasion of the divine messengers he sent to mediate, Zeus sent *Hermes to persuade Hades to release Persephone, which he did; but Hades tricked Persephone and made her eat some pomegranate seeds, with the consequence that she could not leave Hades for ever, but had to spend part of the year with her husband in the underworld and part of the year with her mother in the upper world. The story is told in the *Homeric Hymn to Demeter* (see HYMNS (GREEK)), a text which has a complex relationship with what may well have been the most important cult involving Persephone and Demeter, that of the Eleusinian *mysteries, the celebration of which included a ritual search for Kore with torches.

In the images Kore/Persephone is represented as a young woman, often with the addition of attributes, among which torches, stalks of grain, and sceptres are common, while some, like the cock at Locri Epizephyrii, are found especially in the iconography of particular cults.

The name Kore ('Maiden') stresses her persona as Demeter's daughter, Persephone that as Hades' wife. (Her name also occurs in other forms, for example, Phersephone, or, in Attic, Pherrephatta.) The myth of her rape was perceived as, among many other things, a polarized articulation of some perceptions pertaining to marriage from the viewpoint of the girl. Her cult in some places, notably Locri Epizephyrii, stresses this aspect. Her wedding had an important place in Locrian cult and myth and she was

worshipped also as the protector of marriage and the women's sphere, including the protection of children. Demeter does not seem to have had a prominent place in the Locrian cult. Persephone's wedding and the flower-picking that preceded the abduction were also celebrated in other places, as, for example, in Sicily, where her flower-picking and marriage were celebrated, and in the Locrian colony of Hipponium. The Sicilians also celebrated the bringing down of Kore to the underworld.

Of course she also had an awesome and dread aspect as the queen of the underworld. Everyone will eventually come under her authority. But she was not implacable, and she and Hades listened to reasonable requests, such as that to return to the upper world to request the performance of proper burial or other rites—a trait abused and exploited by the dishonest *Sisyphus who refused to return to Hades.

She was often worshipped in association with Demeter; a most important festival in honour of the two goddesses was the *Thesmophoria, which was celebrated by women all over the Greek world (Demeter also bore the cult-title Thesmophoros, 'law-giving'). At Cyzicus Persephone was worshipped with the epithet Soteira (Saviour) and her festival was called Pherephattia or Koreia or Soteria. (The title seems also to have been found in Arcadia). Not surprisingly, Persephone had an important place in the texts inscribed on the gold leaves that were buried with people who had been initiated into *Orphism. In one strand of belief Persephone was the mother of Dionysus-Zagreus.

Perseus, a mythological hero. The following is the usual legend. *Acrisius, brother of *Proetus, being warned by an oracle that his daughter *Danaë's son would kill him, shut her away in a bronze chamber. *Zeus visited her there in a shower of gold. Acrisius, learning that she had borne a son, whom she called Perseus, set mother and child adrift at sea in a chest. They drifted to the island of Seriphus, where a fisherman called Dictys rescued them and gave them shelter. When Perseus became a young man, Polydectes, the king of Seriphus and Dictys' brother, having fallen in love with Danaë contrived to send him away to fetch the head of the Gorgon Medusa (*see* GORGO). This Perseus achieved, with the help of *Athena and *Hermes through whom he acquired the necessary implements of sickle, bag, cap of darkness for invisibility, and winged shoes. While returning home he came upon *Andromeda about to be devoured by a sea-monster, fell in love with her, rescued and married her. When they returned to Seriphus he used the Gorgon's head to turn Polydectes and his followers into stone for persecuting Danaë. He now gave the head to Athena, who put it in the centre of her *aegis, and returned the bag, cap, and shoes to Hermes. Leaving Dictys as king of Seriphus, he came with his wife and mother to Argos to see his grandfather. But Acrisius, learning of this and still fearing the oracle, hurried away to Pelasgiotis. Perseus followed, and, while competing in the funeral games of Teutamides, king of Larissa, he threw the discus and accidentally struck and killed Acrisius, thus fulfilling the oracle. Leaving Argos to the son of Proetus, Megapenthes, he became king of Tiryns and founder of the Perseidae dynasty. The adventures of Perseus, and particularly those relating to the beheading of Medusa, are favourite themes in art from the 7th cent.

[Apollodorus 2. 4. 1–5]

Persian religion Two religious complexes are discernible in the first millennium BC in Iran.

1. The eastern Iranian tradition of Zarathuštra (*see* ZOROASTER), with the Avesta as its sacred writings. The Older Avesta consists of the Gāthās (*c*.1000 BC) and the *Yasna Haptaŋhāiti*, which were transmitted orally for many centuries. The remainder of the Avestan texts are dated later (5th cent. BC at the earliest) on linguistic grounds. The texts were written down in Sasanian times (AD 224–661) when Zoroastrianism became the state religion. This tradition cannot be provided with a historical or archaeological context.

2. The western Iranian religion of the Achaemenids is attested in iconography, epigraphy, and in administrative texts; no sacred texts were preserved. *Ahuramazda is the only god invoked by name in the OP inscriptions (until Artaxerxes II) and is portrayed as a winged deity on reliefs and seals (although some interpret this figure as the *khvarnah*). Sanctuaries have not yet been identified in the Achaemenid residences, although Darius I claims to have restored the sanctuaries (OP *āyadanā*) destroyed by Gaumata. Two altar-plinths at Pasargadae remain the only (uninformative but certain) cult structures. Evidence for cult-practices consists of tomb-reliefs where the king worships the sacred *fire. Around the residences, the picture is more diversified. Persepolis administrative tablets mention several Iranian gods, as well as Elamite Humban and Babylonian Adad, who receive rations for sacrifices from the royal treasuries. Mithra (*see* MITHRAS) occurs frequently in names such as Mithradates, but is otherwise unattested until Artaxerxes II. There is no evidence that the cult of Ahuramazda was imposed on subjects or even particularly favoured in Fārs.

Research has focused excessively on the question whether the Achaemenids were Zoroastrians. This presupposes thorough understanding of the contents of the older Avesta, although these texts contain many incomprehensible parts and modern translations differ considerably, and insight into the relationship between the older Avesta and pre-Avestan Iranian religious developments. As now argued, it is preferable to regard both complexes of data as part of developments as yet incompletely understood.

The often-supposed Iranian influence on Presocratic Greek philosophy remains largely speculative. Herodotus' description of Persian cult is substantially correct, although he confuses Mithra with *Anahita. Sacrifices to fire, earth, and water mentioned in Greek sources are partly confirmed by the Persepolis tablets. Fire-worship was known from personal observation in Asia Minor. Herodotus and *Plato emphasize the importance of 'truth' (Avestan *aša*, OP *arta*) to the Persians (although Plato mistakes Ahuramazda for Zarathuštra's father). *Aristotle on the two opposing principles of good (Oromasdes) and evil Añgra-Mainyu (Ahriman, Gk. *Areimanios*) and *Plutarch on the relations between them give valuable information on the development of Iranian religious thought. In general, Greek literature contains useful information on Persian religious developments, provided it is analysed with due attention to the period and place it refers to.

[Herodotus 1. 131–2; Plato, *Alcibiades* 122a; Strabo 15. 3. 13–14; Plutarch, *Moralia* 369d–370c; Pausanias 5. 27. 5–6]

Pessinus, mod. Ballıhisar, was one of the most important cult centres of the goddess *Cybele in Phrygia; the temple, built and adorned with marble porticos by the Attalids, was controlled by priests (*galli, archigalli*). In 204 BC the sacred stone of the goddess was taken to Rome. The Galatians assumed control over the priesthood, and in imperial times Pessinus became the centre of the Tolistobogian tribe. The cult of Cybele was maintained until AD 362, when the emperor *Julian visited the sanctuary and attempted to revive it. Excavations to date have yielded no trace of the main sanctuary, but have uncovered a temple of the imperial cult from the time of Tiberius and the central street of the city, which ran along the valley of the river Gallus and served as a canal during periods of high rainfall, when flood water swept through the city from the slopes of nearby Mt. Dindymus.

[Livy 29. 10. 4]

Phaea, the ferocious Sow of Crommyon, killed by *Theseus, first called Phaea in the *Epitome* attributed to *Apollodorus. It is named by (or maybe 'after') the old woman who reared it. Crommyon was a village belonging to Corinth (previously to Megara).

The deed invites association with *Heracles' slaughter of the Erymanthian boar and is depicted on 17, mainly red-figure, vases (often including the old woman egging the sow on), as well as on a metope of the Hephaisteion (*see* ATHENS, RELIGIOUS TOPOGRAPHY, *Agora*), as once it had on the Athenian treasury at *Delphi. It presumably entered literature with the lost late 6th-cent. BC epic *Theseid* (*see* EPIC CYCLE).

[Bacchylides 17 (18). 23–5; Euripides, *Suppliants* 316–17; Apollodorus, *Epitome* 1. 1; Plutarch, *Theseus* 9; Diodorus Siculus 4. 59; Hyginus, *Fables* 38 (a boar, by confusion with Erymanthian/Calydonian boars); Ovid, *Metamorphoses* 7. 435]

Phaeacians *See* SCHERIA.

Phaedra *See* HIPPOLYTUS (1).

Phaethon, in mythology, son of *Helios (the Sun-god) and the heroine Clymene. Learning who his father was, he set out for the East to find him, and arriving at his palace, asked him a boon. The Sun granting him in advance anything he liked, he asked to guide the solar chariot for a day. But he was too weak to manage the immortal horses, which bolted with him and were likely to set the world on fire till *Zeus killed Phaethon with a thunderbolt. He fell into the *Eridanus, and his sisters, mourning for him, turned into amber-dropping trees. Fragments of *Euripides' play *Phaethon* survive.

[Euripides, *Hippolytus* 735 ff.; Ovid, *Metamorphoses* 1. 750 ff.]

phallus, an image of the penis, often as erect, to be found in various contexts, in particular (*a*) in certain rituals associated with fertility, notably Dionysiac *processions (*see* DIONYSUS), as for instance the Attic rural Dionysia (*see* ATTIC CULTS AND MYTHS), where there might be groups of 'ithyphallics' and 'phallus-bearers', or in Rome 'for the success of seeds' at the Liberalia (*see* LIBER PATER); (*b*) as a sacred object revealed in the Dionysiac *mysteries, as in the Villa of the Mysteries fresco at Pompeii; *Iamblichus mentions it as a symbol of secret doctrine; (*c*) in the costume of comedy, satyric drama, and various low theatrical

genres; *Aristotle says that comedy originated in phallic songs (see COMEDY, GREEK, ORIGINS OF); (d) on permanent display, often as part of a statue such as those of *Priapus or the *herms identified with *Hermes; (e) as apotropaic: e.g. the Elder Pliny says that it guards not only babies but also triumphal chariots (against envy). In general its appeal is as an expression of fertility and regeneration but also of masculine strength (e.g. in the case of the herms marking boundaries).
[Aristophanes, *Acharnians* 243; Iamblichus, *On the Mysteries* 1. 11; Varro in Augustine, *City of God* 7. 21]

Phanes, a god in several Orphic theogonies, 'the one who makes (or is) manifest', born from an egg fashioned by *Cronus in the *Aither, also called *Prōtogonos*, the First-born. He is the first ruler and the creator of all, bisexual, invisible but radiant with light, gold-winged, and has the heads of various animals. His daughter with whom he mates is Night (see NYX), who bears *Gaia and *Uranus. He is also called *Eros, Bromios, *Zeus, *Metis, and Erikepaios. See ORPHIC LITERATURE; ORPHISM.

Phaon, a mythical ferryman, made young and beautiful by *Aphrodite, who also hid him among lettuces like her beloved *Adonis. Sappho among others is said to have loved him, finally leaping from the cliff at Leucas (mod. Lefkada) for his sake: the story, which echoes other legends, appears first in Attic *comedy.

Pharisees, an influential religious group among *Jews in the late Hellenistic and early Roman periods. Explicit references to Pharisees are found in *Josephus and the New Testament and in Christian writings dependent upon them. The evidence found there can be supplemented from rabbinic references to Jewish religious figures before AD 70, since some of those to whom they referred may have been Pharisees. There may also be allusions to Pharisees in the *Dead Sea Scrolls. Pharisees are mentioned in Josephus' histories as a political party in the time of the Hasmonean ruler John

Hyrcanus (135–104 BC). After a period of opposition to Alexander Janneus (103–80 BC), their influence over the Hasmonean dynasty reached a peak during the rule of his widow Alexandra Jannaea (80–67 BC). Under *Herod the Great (37–4 BC) the Pharisees won the support of some members of the royal court, but in general they seem to have stopped interfering in Judaean politics as a group, although individual Pharisees sometimes had prominent political roles. The last attestation of anyone describing himself as having been a Pharisee at some stage in his life was Josephus in the 90s AD.

The sources on the Pharisees are largely second-hand accounts and hence are too contradictory to permit a clear and convincing analysis of their beliefs and influence. No one source is satisfactory, and discrepancies abound. Josephus described the Pharisees as a philosophy within Judaism, equivalent to the Stoics (see STOICISM) among the Greeks. According to his account, Pharisees taught that there is a life after death and that man controls his own destiny, although fate also plays a role in human fortunes. In contrast to the *Sadducees, they accept ancestral traditions in interpreting the law. Josephus' account may have been coloured by his own Pharisaic leanings and by a desire to appeal to his gentile Greek readers. In one passage, he described the Pharisees as particularly influential among Jews with regard to prayers and sacrifices. In the Gospels, Pharisees appear as opponents of Jesus, attacked for hypocrisy, in particular in the scrupulous observance of biblical laws about the sabbath, the tithing of agricultural produce and the avoidance of pollution. In the *Acts of the Apostles the Pharisee Gamaliel is portrayed as a powerful opponent of the Sadducees in a meeting of the sanhedrin in Jerusalem, and as the teacher of St *Paul. Paul's own writings are those of a former Pharisee, but how much his theology reflects Pharisaic rather than common Jewish or novel Christian ideas is debated. Rabbinic texts may refer to Pharisees when they report the teachings of those Jewish sages before AD 70 whom they see as their forebears. In particular, the sayings of Hillel (fl. *c.* AD 10–30) and his descendants are probably to be accounted those of Pharisees, since Hillel's family included both Rabban Gamaliel (mentioned as a Pharisee in the New Testament) and Simon son of Gamaliel (described as a Pharisee by Josephus). Many of those rabbinic traditions about the sages before AD 70 which are specifically attributed to named individuals concern purity, tithing and the sabbath; some deal with the rules governing dining clubs (*haburoth*) in which purity and tithing regulations were carefully observed by all members. However, it cannot be securely deduced from this that sages before AD 70 were believed by later rabbis to have had no other religious interests, since many traditions on moral and ethical issues, on civil and criminal law, and on the conduct of worship in the Jerusalem Temple, were preserved anonymously. Many such teachings may have been promulgated before AD 70 by Pharisees, but there is no evidence to confirm or disprove the possibility.

There is no agreement among scholars about the best way to reconcile this confused evidence. It may be that the self-description 'Pharisee', which probably derives from the semitic root *prs* ('separate'), was adopted by a large group in which some (in rabbinic terminology, *haberim* ('fellows')) were particularly zealous over purity and tithing while others were less so. The only figure given in ancient sources for the number of Pharisees is the 6,000 who refused to take an oath of loyalty to Herod in 12 BC. *See* JUDAISM.

[Josephus, *Jewish War* 2. 162–6; *Jewish Antiquities* 17. 42, 18. 12–15]

pharmacology From earliest times, drugs formed an important part of medicine, and *Homer has the first record of good drugs and bad drugs (poisons). Folklore incorporated many data on toxic substances, and in the legends Homer's *Circe and *Euripides'

*Medea link *magic with poisons. There is simultaneously another understanding of drugs and their actions: *Pindar reflects *Asclepius' medicine as curative with drugs, surgery, and magical incantations. Thus mythology reflects in a partly exaggerated form real perceptions.

[Homer, *Odyssey*; Euripides, *Medea*; Pindar, *Pythian* 3]

pharmakos, a human scapegoat. During the *Thargelia, but also during adverse periods such as plague and famine, Athenians and Ionians expelled scapegoat(s), who were called 'offscourings', in order 'to purify' the cities. These *pharmakoi* were chosen from the poor and the ugly, received a very special treatment in the *prytaneion* ('townhall': at Massalia, Marseilles), were led in a procession to the sound of unharmonious music around the city, beaten with wild or infertile plants like the squill, and finally pelted with stones and chased over the border of the city-state. Corresponding myths speak about aristocrats, princesses, or kings sacrificing themselves for the city. Clearly, myth exaggerates, but saviours have to be important: with a less valuable sacrifice the city cannot be saved. Comparable rites among Hittites and Israelites suggests a near-eastern origin. *See* POLLUTION.

Phegeus, in mythology, father of Arsinoë, wife of *Alcmaeon (1); his sons murdered Alcmaeon when he remarried (*see* CALLIRHOË). An undatable but probably late story says *Hesiod stayed for some time at his court and was put to death by his sons, who suspected him of seducing their sister.

[Apollodorus 3. 7. 5; Pausanias 8. 24. 8–10; Ovid, *Metamorphoses* 9. 411–18]

phēmē, in Greek, a rumour of unknown origin which springs up among the people at large; unprompted and unguided popular opinion. According to *Hesiod it is a god, and is never quite in vain.

[Hesiod, *Works and Days* 763–4]

Pherecydes (1) of Syros, fl. 544 BC, reputed to be the first writer of Greek prose. His subject was the birth of the gods and the creation of the cosmos. Fragments and testimonia attest the following features: (1) Zas (*Zeus) was the first god, and with him *Cronus and Chthonie (Gē, 'Earth', *see* GAIA); (2) subsequent gods were born from five (or seven) 'recesses' (*mychoi*: their cosmogonic significance is variously interpreted); (3) Zas married Chthonie in a formal ceremony, and presented her with a robe he had decorated with Earth and Ogenos (Ocean: *see* OCEANUS), providing the model for a human marriage-ritual; (4) Cronus battles Ophioneus ('the snake'). Points of comparison exist with Hesiod's *Theogony*, the 'Orphic' cosmogony in the papyrus from Derveni (*see* ORPHIC LITERATURE), and near-eastern cosmogonies. Biographical fragments attribute to Pherecydes world travels, miracles, and an uncanny death. His belief in the immortality of the soul led writers on the history of philosophy to make him the teacher of *Pythagoras.

Pherecydes (2) of Athens, 'the genealogist' (later confused with (1)), wrote copious *Histories*, mythical and genealogical, commended by Dionysius of Halicarnassus. *Eusebius' date for him is 456 BC (Olympiad 81. 1).

[Dionysius of Halicarnassus, *Roman Antiquities* 1. 13. 1]

Phidias, Athenian sculptor, son of Charmides, active *c*.465–425 BC; reputed pupil of Hegias and Hageladas. His early works included the colossal bronze *Athena Promachos on the Acropolis; her spear-point and helmet-crest were supposedly visible from *Sunium. His Athena Lemnia, perhaps preserved in Roman copy, and his Marathon group at *Delphi may also be early; some attribute the Riace bronzes to the latter.

Phidias' reputation rested chiefly on his chryselephantine Athena Parthenos and his *Zeus at *Olympia. Both were of gold and ivory over a wooden core, with embellishments in jewels, silver, copper, enamel, glass, and paint; each incorporated numerous subsidiary themes to demonstrate the divinity's power. *Plutarch puts Phidias in charge not merely of the Athena but of Pericles' entire building programme. He certainly belonged to Pericles' inner circle, and at the least probably directed the *Parthenon's exterior sculpture. The Athena recapitulated several of its themes. Almost 12 m. (39 ft.) high and draped in over a ton of gold, she was begun in 447 and installed in 438; descriptions by Pliny and *Pausanias have enabled the identification of many copies. Her right hand held a *Nike, and her left a spear and a shield embellished outside with the Amazonomachy and inside with the Gigantomachy (*see* AMAZONS; GIANTS). Lapiths and *Centaurs adorned her sandals, and her base carried the birth of *Pandora in relief. A Gorgoneion (*see* GORGO) occupied the centre of her *aegis, and a *sphinx and two Pegasi (*see* PEGASUS) supported the three crests of her helmet; griffins decorated its cheek-pieces.

Plutarch reports that Pericles' enemies prosecuted Phidias for embezzling the Parthenos' ivory and for impiety, and that he died in prison; *Philochorus dated his trial to 438, but says that he fled to Olympia, where the Eleans killed him after he made the Zeus. This seems more likely, for his workshop there belongs to the 430s and has yielded tools, terracotta moulds (for a colossal female statue), and even a cup bearing his name. As Strabo and Pausanias describe it, the Zeus was even larger than the Parthenos. Enthroned, he held a Nike in his right hand and a sceptre in his left; coins and vase-paintings reproduce the composition. The throne was richly embellished with Graces (*see* CHARITES), Seasons (*see* HORAE), Nikai, sphinxes and Theban children, the slaughter of the children of *Niobe (of which marble copies survive), and an Amazonomachy; paintings by Panaenus (Phidias' brother) on the screens between its legs included Hellas (Greece) and Salamis, some of the Labours of *Heracles, *Hippodamia and *Sterope (1), and *Achilles and *Penthesilea. Another Amazonomachy adorned Zeus' footstool, and the statue's base carried the birth of *Aphrodite.

Ancient critics regarded Phidias as the greatest and most versatile of Greek sculptors. His pupils dominated Athenian sculpture for a generation, and Hellenistic and Roman neo-classicism looked chiefly to him. Attributions (all copies) include the Medici Athena, the 'Sappho-Ourania', the Kassel Apollo, and the Mattei-Sciarra Amazon.

[Plutarch, *Pericles* 13, 31 f.; Pausanias 1. 24, 5. 10. 2 ff.; Pliny, *Natural History* 36. 18; Strabo 8. 353 f.]

Phidippides, a long-distance courier (*hē-merodromos*) who Herodotus says ran from Athens to Sparta in 490 BC to enlist help for the battle of Marathon, reaching his destination 'next day'; a possible feat, since the winner of a race over the same ground in 1983 managed to cover the distance (*c*.240 km.; *c*. 149 mi.) in under 22 hours. On the way Phidippides encountered the god *Pan, who asked him why the Athenians did not yet honour him with a state cult; this was subsequently put right. Later sources confuse his run with that of a messenger who brought the news of the Marathon victory back to Athens; they also call him Philippides (as do some manuscripts of Herodotus).

[Herodotus 6. 105 f.]

Philammon, legendary musician and poet, son of *Apollo according to a fragment attributed to *Hesiod, and famous citharode (lyre-player and singer) in the time of *Orpheus and the *Argonauts. He won the citharodic contest at the Pythian festival (*see* PYTHIAN GAMES), instituted choruses singing about the birth of *Leto, *Artemis, and Apollo, and according to *Pherecydes (2) was first to use choruses of maidens. He also founded the *mysteries at Lerna.

[Pausanias 2. 37. 2, 10. 7. 2]

Philemon and Baucis *See* BAUCIS.

Philochorus (*c*.340–260 BC), son of Cycnus, was a truly Hellenistic man. The mini-biography of him in the Byzantine encyclopaedia *Suda* reveals a man of religion (he was official prophet and diviner in 306), a patriot, who was arrested and put to death

by Antigonus Gonatas for supporting Ptolemy Philadelphus, and a scholar-historian, who wrote at least 27 works, of which the most famous was his *Atthis*. His scholarly interests ranged from local history of Attica (*see* ATTIC CULTS AND MYTHS), *Delos, and Salamis to chronography (Olympiads), cult (monographs on *Prophecy, Sacrifices, Festivals,* and the *Mysteries at Athens*) and literature (studies on *Euripides and Alcman). He was the last writer of histories of Attica and the most respected, to judge from the number of times his work was cited. A modern authority considered him the first scholar to write an *Atthis*, though this may be unfair to his predecessors.

The *Atthis* was seventeen books long. We have over 170 fragments. From these we can form a good impression of the structure and character of his work. It was arranged in the standard chronological format of the genre, by kings and archons (magistrates), and presented its information in succinct factual notices in unadorned prose. Despite his professional interest in religion, Philochorus only devoted two books to the early period down to Solon, and two more to the end of the 5th cent. The 4th cent., which had been treated in detail by Androtion, was also reduced to two books. The remaining eleven books covered the 60 years from 320–260. So, Philochorus' main interest was the period of his mature years. But nothing of significance has survived from these books, because this period did not interest the later scholars who cited him.

In his research Philochorus used documents and his own experience for his own time. For the earlier period he used the *Atthis* of Androtion, as is shown by the frequency with which the two are cited together. By contrast he did not approve of the *Atthis* of his immediate predecessor, Demon, which he criticised in a monograph entitled *Atthis against Demon.* The fragments show that Philochorus was familiar with the works of Herodotus, Thucydides, Ephorus, and Theopompus. His *Atthis* was a source for the Hellenistic chronographers.

Philoctetes, in *Homer the son of Poeas and leader of seven ships to *Troy, but left behind in Lemnos suffering from a snake-bite. The *Epic Cycle adds that while the Greeks were sailing to Troy they sacrificed in Tenedos, and there Philoctetes was bitten and left behind because of the stench of his festering wound. Ten years later *Odysseus captured *Helenus, the Trojan seer, and learned from him that Troy could only be taken if Philoctetes was present, so *Diomedes (2) fetched him from Lemnos. He was healed by *Machaon, then fought a duel with *Paris and killed him. *Aeschylus, *Sophocles, and *Euripides each wrote a *Philoctetes*, but only Sophocles' play survives. Sophocles adds that Philoctetes had the bow and inescapable arrows of *Heracles given to him (or to his father, according to *Apollodorus) for lighting the pyre on Mt. Oeta. Without the bow Troy would not fall, so *Neoptolemus is ordered by Odysseus to obtain it by trickery. But Neoptolemus' basic honesty causes complications in the plot, and the play ends with Heracles *ex machina* ordering Philoctetes to Troy. Homer's *Odyssey* says that Philoctetes returned safely home after the war; but some later accounts say that he wandered to southern Italy and founded cities there. He certainly had *hero-cult in more than one place in Italy.

[Homer, *Iliad* 2. 718–23, *Odyssey* 3. 190; Sophocles, *Philoctetes*; Apollodorus 2. 7. 7]

Philodamus of Scarphea, author of a *paean to *Dionysus apparently performed, by demand of the Pythia (*see* DELPHIC ORACLE), at the Delphic festival of *Theoxenia and inscribed in the sanctuary in 340/39 BC. A paean to Dionysus, rather than *Apollo, is a novel hybrid; but at Delphi the two gods were traditionally closely associated, and the paean itself interweaves themes of Dionysiac legend with such local concerns as the rebuilding of Apollo's temple.

Philomela, daughter of *Pandion and sister of Procne, transformed into a bird. The earliest version of the story, found in the *Odyssey*, makes the nightingale daughter of *Pandareos, who killed her own son in a fit of madness. In the more familiar version, crystallized by *Sophocles' lost play *Tereus*, the story began when Procne's husband Tereus raped Philomela and then attempted to guarantee her silence by cutting out her tongue. Philomela depicted her story in a piece of weaving which she sent to Procne, whereupon the latter took revenge by killing Itys, her son by Tereus, and serving him up to his father. Tereus pursued the two women to punish them, but was turned into a hoopoe, while Philomela became a swallow and Procne a nightingale (or vice versa).

[Homer, *Odyssey* 19. 518–23; Apollodorus 3. 14. 8; Ovid, *Metamorphoses* 6. 424–674]

Philon (1), 'Philo', often known as Philo Judaeus, philosopher, writer and political leader, was the leading exponent of Alexandrian-Jewish culture, and, together with *Josephus, the most significant figure in *Jewish-Greek literature. Philo's voluminous works were a formative influence on *Neoplatonism and on Christian theology, from the New Testament on. His family was prominent in the Jewish diaspora and in the service of Rome in the east. The only fixed date in Philo's own life is AD 39/40, when, as an old man, he led the Jewish embassy to Gaius (Caligula). Apart from those events, he himself seems to have confined his activities to the Alexandrian Jewish community. He made a pilgrimage to *Jerusalem, but need not otherwise have had much contact with Palestine. Virtually all his surviving works were apparently preserved in the library of Caesarea, built up by *Origen and then by *Eusebius, who catalogues most of them in his *Church History*. Some three-quarters of the corpus consists of exposition of the Pentateuch, in three series, whose order of writing is obscure: *Quaestiones*, which are brief catechetical commentaries in the form of questions and answers, *Legum allegoria*, a more extended and systematic exegesis, and *Exposition*, which sets out the Mosaic laws. The *Life of Moses* was perhaps a separate enterprise, as also the *De vita contemplativa*, which describes the way of life of a group of Egyptian Jewish ascetics called the Therapeutai. Two tracts, *In Flaccum* and the *De legatione ad Gaium*, probably originally one composite work, give a graphic account of the persecutions of the Jews under Gaius and of their political consequences. The *In Flaccum* gives much space to the divine punishment inflicted on the persecutors of the Jews.

Philo operated within the Greek philosophical tradition and deployed an elaborate Greek literary language. At the same time, he was at home with the Greek Bible on which his commentaries were based. The sole authority of the Mosaic law was fundamental to him. The spuriousness of his Hebrew etymologies suggests, but does not prove, that he did not know Hebrew. His ontology was markedly Platonic: to provide a medium for the operation of a perfect God upon an imperfect world, he introduced a range of mediating beings, notably Powers and Reason (*logos*). Philo's ethics are close to *Stoicism, but for him true morality is imitation of the Deity.

Philon (2) of Byblos (Herennius Philon), scholar, born *c*.AD 70 and died *c*.AD 160, composed in Greek a learned work on Phoenician history, providing a markedly euhemeristic account (*see* EUHEMERUS) of *Phoenician religion. Extensive fragments of this history were preserved by *Eusebius. Philon's claim to have translated much of his material directly from the ancient writer Sanchuniathon, who had devoted a treatise in the Phoenician language to theology, cosmogony, and the origins of civilization, should be regarded with considerable scepticism, since Philon's versions of the ancient myths have clearly been moulded to conform to Hellenistic expectations. On the other hand, similarities between the stories ascribed by Philon to Sanchuniathon and the evidence for Phoenician myths discovered in Ugaritic texts demonstrate that some of the material used by Philon may derive from

genuine Phoenician traditions, which have, however, been modified over the intervening centuries.

Philon's other writings included a work *Concerning the Acquisition and Selection of Books*, a work *Concerning Cities and the Illustrious Men each of them Produced*, and another *Concerning the Reign of Hadrian*.

[Eusebius, *Praeparatio evangelica* 1. 9. 22]

philosophers on poetry The engagement of philosophers with poetry (and therefore with myth) was a recurrent and vital feature of the intellectual culture of Graeco-Roman antiquity. By around 380 BC, *Plato could already refer to 'a long-standing quarrel between philosophy and poetry'. Early Greek philosophy, while closely related to poetry (*Xenophanes, *Parmenides, and *Empedocles wrote in verse, with various debts to poetic tradition), set itself to contest and rival the claims of 'wisdom', *sophia*, made by and on behalf of poets. Xenophanes, repudiating anthropomorphic religion, cast ethical and theological aspersions on the myths of *Homer and *Hesiod; Heraclitus expressed caustic doubts about the idea of poets as possessors and teachers of insight. Philosophy and poetry could be considered competing sources of knowledge and understanding. The stage was set for lasting debates about their relationship.

Plato, while emulating poetry in his myths and in features of his dramatic writing, produced a far-reaching critique of poetry's credentials as an educational force within Greek culture. Though sometimes scantily concerned with complexities of context, he responds to an existing tendency to regard poetic works as carrying normative significance: the putative 'truth' of poetry, which he so frequently (though not invariably) impugns, was in part a matter of paradigmatically interpreted images of human behaviour and morality. Plato's anxieties over poetry are based, besides, on an awareness of its immense psychological power, especially in the theatre. Yet despite the *Republic*'s proposals for severe political censorship,

Plato's dealings with poetry remain ambivalent and deeply felt: he quotes, echoes, and competes with it throughout his dialogues. But his critique rests, from first to last, on the premiss of philosophy's superior wisdom and judgement.

*Aristotle too is committed to the superior range of philosophical thought, but much readier than Plato to allow the independent cultural value of poetry. In the *Poetics*, he asserts that poetic standards are not identical to those of *politikē* (ethics/politics), and the treatise as a whole, respecting generic traditions and recognizing the status of poetry as a distinct art (*technē*), elaborates categories that focus upon the internal organization of poetic works.

By the later 4th cent., philosophical schools had established an institutional status which made their relationship to a traditional education in *mousikē* (poetry and music) an urgent question. Both *Epicurus and Zeno, founder of *Stoicism, are said to have rejected such conventional *paideia*. Yet the attitudes of their schools towards poetry were more complex and divergent than this suggests. Epicurus followed Xenophanes and Plato in attacking poetic myths as purveyors of false religious beliefs, to which the proffered antidote was his own natural philosophy. He asserted the need for philosophical judgement of poetry: 'only the wise man can discourse correctly about music and poetry'. Epicureans acquired a reputation for rejecting poetry. According to *Plutarch, Metrodorus, *Epicurus' follower, provocatively declared it unnecessary to know even the openings of Homer's epics. But the possibility of a more positive evaluation remained available, given the school's commitment to pleasure as the criterion of value.

Stoicism, by contrast, was solidly tied to a moralistic view of poetry—a view influenced by Plato, yet largely unplatonic in its inclination to 'save' poetry, wherever possible, either by allegorical interpretation or by exploiting the principle, propounded by Zeno himself, that not everything in poetry need be judged in terms of truth.

Interpretative control, even to the point of appropriation, was perhaps the dominant tendency in ancient philosophy's dealings with poetry; Aristotle and Philodemus stand out as exceptionally liberal. Appropriation, but also reconciliation, reached a climax in the Neoplatonic reinterpretation of Homer as a fount of esoteric wisdom, symbolically expressed (*see* NEOPLATONISM). Thus, on the threshold of a new Christian synthesis of learning and culture, the 'ancient quarrel' was temporarily silenced.

Philostorgius (*c.*AD 368–*c.*440 (?)), ecclesiastical historian; born in Boryssus (Cappadocia), into a clerical family who had been won over to neo-*Arianism (Eunomianism). By the age of 20, he was in *Constantinople where he spent much of his life. An adherent of Eunomius, he wrote in continuation of *Eusebius of Caesarea an ecclesiastical history to AD 425 in twelve books, each beginning with a letter of his name. It is now fragmentary, surviving in an extended epitome by Photius, and in other fragments, especially the *Passio of Artemius*. The work is valuable in presenting an alternative view of church history from the time of *Constantine I, with praise for Constantius II and condemnation in apocalyptic tones of the policies of *Theodosius I and II, together with secular material and geographical digressions partly based on his own travels. Other (lost) works of Philostorgius include a refutation of *Porphyry, an encomium on Eunomius and a life of Lucian of Antioch.

Philostratus Lucius Flavius Philostratus ('the Athenian') enjoyed both a distinguished local career and a place in the circle of Iulia Domna, wife of Septimius Severus. She commissioned his *Life of *Apollonius* (2) of Tyana, a philosophic holy man of the 1st cent. AD; later he produced *Lives of the Sophists*, and he is probably the author of most of a number of minor pieces, including the *Hēroikos*, a dialogue on the heroes of the Trojan War and their cults, a treatise 'On Athletic Training' and 'Erotic Epistles'; he died under Philip the Arab (AD 244–9).

The *Life of Apollonius* offers pagan hagiography under a sophistic veneer, and remains suspect both in sources and details; the *Lives of the Sophists* offer the foundation for our knowledge of the so-called Second Sophistic (when declamation become the most valued literary activity in the Greek world): they are sketches, sometimes affected and tendentious, of prestigious public speakers in action. The *Hēroikos* offers an entertaining *aperçu* into how a sophistic writer might extend and 'correct' still vibrant Homeric materials. The first *Eikones* are often charming mythological sketches, purporting to instruct a child on the content of perhaps imaginary pictures; the later set are more perfunctory.

Philyra, 'Linden-tree', an Oceanid (*see* NYMPHS) loved by *Cronus, who, being surprised by Rhea while making love to her, turned himself and Philyra into horses. Their child was the *centaur Chiron, whose monstrous shape horrified the mother so that she prayed to change her own form, and thus became the tree called after her. The myth is consistently located in northern Greece.

Phineus, a Thracian seer-king, whose myth derives from the Peloponnese. According to a fragment of *Hesiod, Phineus had been blinded because he had shown Phrixus the way or because he had preferred a long life over eye-sight. *Apollonius of Rhodes adds that he revealed the plans of the gods against their will. They penalized him through the Harpies (*see* HARPYIAE), who stole or defiled all his food. When the *Argonauts came, he made a compact with them: he would prophesy the further course of their adventures, if they would deliver him from the Harpies. This was achieved by the sons of Boreas, whose action already appears on 6th-cent. vases.

In his *Phineidaei* and *Phineus* (twice) *Sophocles probably preferred a different version. After a first marriage with Cleopatra, daughter of *Boreas, Phineus remarried. His new wife so slandered her stepsons that Phineus

either blinded them himself or let her do so. When the Argonauts arrived in Thrace, the sons of Boreas liberated their cousins against the will of Phineus, who now directed his army against the Argonauts and was killed by *Heracles. The stepmother was handed over to her father and executed.

Phlegon of Tralles, a freedman of Hadrian, author of a work covering all the Olympiads, from the first to that of AD 140. He also wrote works on Sicily, Roman festivals, Roman topography, and wondrous events.

Phlegyas, *eponym of the Phlegyae, a Thessalian people, son of *Ares (his mother's name varies). He is also represented as living near Lake Boebeis, or in Boeotian Orchomenus, while the Epidaurian legend (*see* EPIDAURUS) brings him to the Peloponnese. He was father of Coronis, the mother of *Asclepius or of *Ixion. Virgil puts him in *Tartarus. [Apollodorus 3. 5. 5; Pausanias 2. 26. 4, 9. 36. 1]

phlyakes, farces (also called *hilarotragōdiai*, 'cheerful tragedies') which were performed in southern Italy and also perhaps at Alexandria in the 4th and 3rd cents. BC. The chief authors of these ludicrous scenes from daily life or from mythology were Rhinthon, Sciras, and Sopater of Paphos; vase-pictures illustrate an earlier (?pre-literary) stage in their development.

Phocus, in mythology, son of *Aeacus by the *nymph Psamathe, who took the shape of a seal, *phōkos*; hence the name of her son. He proved a distinguished athlete, thus arousing the jealousy of the legitimate sons, *Peleus and *Telamon; they drew lots to see which should kill him, and Telamon, to whom the task fell, murdered him while they were exercising; Aeacus found out and banished them both. [Apollodorus 3. 158]

Phoebe, in *Hesiod one of the race of *Titans, daughter of Gē (*Gaia) and *Uranus and mother by Coeus of *Leto. Both name (*see* PHOEBUS) and kinship suggest an Apolline connection (*see* APOLLO), although the use of the name for Artemis/Diana, or for the moon, appears to be confined to late authors. The name belongs also to a heroine, sister of Hilaeira (*see* LEUCIPPIDES).

Phoebus i.e. radiant; name or description of *Apollo. *See also* PHOEBE.

Phoenician religion Phoenician religion originally did not differ much from Canaanite religion (as known from evidence from Ugarit in northern Syria), but it evolved under Greek influence in the Hellenistic and Roman periods. By the 1st cent. BC there had developed an important role for civic gods ('Lord of Byblos', 'Melqart of Tyre', 'Astarte, Baal and Esmun of Sidon'), and nature gods (including *Adonis), and a sense of local traditions remained strong. In the 2nd cent. AD *Philon (2) of Byblos published (in Greek) what he claimed to be a translation from Phoenician of an ancient work on Phoenician mythology. Phoenician ties were also felt by Phoenician colonies. In the 2nd cent. BC Carthage was still sending offerings of first fruits (*see* APARCHE) to her mother city Tyre.

Greeks from an early date constructed ties between Phoenician and Greek culture and religions. *Cadmus, founder of Thebes, was said to come from Phoenicia; Herodotus was so interested in claims for the antiquity of cults of *Heracles that he made a special trip to an ancient temple of Heracles at Tyre, and from there to Thasos because there was a shrine to Heracles said to have been founded by Phoenicians (compare the 10th cent. BC Phoenician temple at Kommos on the south coast of Crete); and *Pausanias relates an argument with a man from Sidon about Phoenician and Greek ideas of deity.

[Herodotus 2. 44; Pausanias 7. 23. 7–8]

Phoenix (1) *Eponym and founder of the Phoenicians, son of Agenor. In *Homer, however, he is the father of *Europa; and in *Hesiod his wife Cassiepea bears him Cilix, Phineus, and Dorcylus. (2) In *Iliad* book 9, an ambassador sent by *Agamemnon together with *Odysseus and *Aias (1) to persuade *Achilles to give up his wrath. Phoenix has been appointed by *Peleus to accompany Achilles to *Troy and teach him heroic values. In an extensive and powerful oration, he illuminates Achilles' situation through a story of his own conflict with his father Amyntor over a concubine, leading to his reception by Peleus, and by a story of *Meleager's withdrawal from fighting in anger at his mother. *Sophocles wrote a *Phoenix*, as did *Euripides whose influential version accounts for *Apollodorus's story that Amyntor blinded Phoenix and Peleus had him healed by the *centaur Chiron. In *Sophocles' *Philoctetes* (and probably earlier in Lesches' *Little Iliad*, *see* EPIC CYCLE) he is again an ambassador with Odysseus, to persuade *Neoptolemus to enter the war, and the latter buries him *en route* for the Molossians (*see* MOLOSSI) in Hagias' *Nostoi* (returns of the Heroes); *see again* EPIC CYCLE.

[(1) Homer, *Iliad* 14. 321; Apollodorus 3. 1. 1. (2) Homer, *Iliad* 9, 16. 96; Apollodorus 3. 13. 8]

Phoenix (*De Ave Phoenice*), poem in 170 elegiac lines on the fabulous bird whose life, eternally renewed through death, was a potent symbol for both pagans and Christians. The ascription to *Lactantius has been questioned, but there are strong hints of Christian authorship.

Phorbas, a common heroic name; many of its bearers seem particularly associated with violence. One was a Lapith (*see* CENTAURS). Another was a brigand who forced travellers to *Delphi to box with him and so killed them; eventually he was killed by *Apollo. At least one Phorbas was also worshipped in Athens, though in myth there are two figures: one was a foreign ally of *Eumolpus, killed by *Erechtheus in the Eleusinian war, the other an associate of *Theseus, his charioteer or tutor and inventor of wrestling.

Phorcys, in mythology, son of *Nereus and Earth i.e. *Gaia. Marrying his sister Ceto, he became father of the *Graeae and *Gorgo. Other children are ascribed to him in various sources, as Thoosa, mother of the Cyclops,

Polyphemus (*see* CYCLOPES), and the *Sirens. In general he is the father or leader of sea-monsters, such as the *Tritons.

[Hesiod, *Theogony* 237, 270 ff.; Virgil, *Aeneid* 5. 824]

Phoroneus, a very ancient figure of Argive tradition (*see* ARGOS, MYTHS OF). He was son of *Inachus and Melia; father of Apis and the Argive Niobe, the first earthly love of *Zeus; and king of the whole Peloponnese, with numerous descendants. He was reputedly the first to gather together scattered families into cities. The Argives credited him with the discovery of fire, and kept a flame burning in his memory.

[Apollodorus 2. 1; Pausanias 2. 15. 5, 19. 5]

Phosphorus (*Pōsphoros* = *Heōsphoros*, light-bearer, dawn-bearer; Lucifer), son of *Eos, the Dawn, and Astraeus, a Titan; personification of the morning star which announces the approach of dawn, and thus 'light-bearer', bringer of the light of day, i.e. the planet Venus, and the only planet mentioned in *Homer or indeed in Greek literature before the 4th cent. BC. Phosphorus was father of *Ceyx, king of Trachis.

[Homer, *Iliad* 23. 226; Hesiod, *Theogony* 381; Apollodorus 1. 7. 4]

phratries (*phratriai*, with dialectal variations), in Greek states, groups with hereditary membership and probably normally associated with specific locality(ies). The members were 'phrateres', related to words which in other Indo-European languages mean 'brother'. Phratry names often, but not always, had the patronymic ending *-idai*. The relationship between a phratry's *eponym and its members, however, is largely obscure.

Ionian Greeks, including Athenians, conceived of the institution as part of their Ionian heritage. Like the Ionian *phylai*, their origin was attributed to *Ion, and celebration of the phratry festival *Apaturia was regarded as a criterion of Ionian identity.

We know much more about phratries at Athens than anywhere else. Phratry membership, along with certain other qualifica-tions, was necessary for a native-born Athenian citizen. The phratry apparently played a major role in controlling matters relating to legitimacy of descent, including access to citizenship and inheritance of property. A variety of subgroups (possibly sometimes known as *thiasoi*) is found in Athenian phratries: *genē*, groups whose members were *orgeōnes* and others.

While phratries might pursue common activities throughout the year, phratry admissions normally took place at the annual phratry festival, Apaturia, at which there was also religious observance, especially cult of *Zeus Phratrios and *Athena Phratria, feasting and e.g. competitions. Phratry subgroups might contain priests, but it is unclear whether there were also separate phratry priests.

Phrygia, religion of Religion in Phrygia (west-central Anatolia) is well documented through thousands of inscriptions from its cities and above all from the village-communities, which were the most characteristic form of settlement. They show it to have been a blend of Greek and indigenous traditions: apart from funerary texts, the commonest type of inscriptions are religious dedications to Greek and *Anatolian deities. Phrygian religious life, which doubtless perpetuated traditions which stretched far back into Anatolian prehistory, can be described and analysed in considerable detail. Alongside those of *Zeus and various mother goddesses, the most widespread cults were for the Anatolian god *Mēn, and for deities associated with righteousness, vengeance, and justice, including the abstract couple 'Holy and Just' (*see* ANGELS). They enjoined a strict moral code of behaviour, and it is no coincidence that Jewish and early Christian communities flourished on Phrygian soil in the 2nd and 3rd cents. AD.

Phylacus, protector-hero of *Delphi, whose sanctuary was near that of *Athena Pronaia. Together with Autonous, he appeared in heroic form and attacked the Persian invaders in 480 BC, and in some accounts he joined three other heroes for the same purpose at the attack of Brennus and the Celts in 279 BC.

[Herodotus 8. 38–9; Pausanias 10. 23. 2]

phylai The Greek word *phyle*, usually but misleadingly translated 'tribe', was widely but not universally used in the Greek world to denote the principal components or divisions of the citizen body. Their origins are unclear, but typically they functioned as military units and as constituencies for the election of magistrates. Usually, they were under the patronage of particular gods or heroes, thus often finding an explanation for their origins in mythology, and they might also be associated with particular cults.

Two sets are well attested in the Archaic period: the Dorian tribes Hylleis, Dymanes, and Pamphyloi, known as such in 7th-cent. Sparta and elsewhere, and the Ionian–Attic tribes Geleontes, Hopletes Argadeis, Aigikoreis, Oinopes, and Boreis, known in Archaic Athens (the first four), some Aegean islands and Ionia. The Dorian tribes were supposed to be named from the sons of Heracles (*see* HERACLIDAE), the Ionian tribes, according to *Euripides in *Ion*, after those of *Ion. At some point in their history, many states reorganized their tribal system, the best known such restructuring being that of Cleisthenes in Attica in or just after 508/7 BC. The new system was used in all military and administrative contexts, but the old still existed for some religious purposes. However, the new tribes were named after local heroes (*see* EPONYMOI), and were involved in the worship of their patron.

Phylas, name of four minor mythological persons, the least unknown being a king of the Dryopes (*see* DRYOPS). He sinned against the shrine at *Delphi, and consequently *Heracles overthrew him and gave his people to *Apollo as serfs. Many of them, either escaping or being sent by Apollo's command, went to the Peloponnese, where they settled at Asine and other places. Heracles had by Phylas' daughter a son Antiochus, after whom the Attic tribe (*see* PHYLAI) Antiochis was named. *See* EPONYMOI.

Phyle, a small Attic community with a fort controlling one of the major routes through Mt. Parnes to Boeotia. In the depth of a gorge to the east is a Cave of *Pan (*see* CAVES, SACRED), from which remains from the Middle Helladic period onwards have been recovered. Close to it lay the fictional plot of land of Menander's *Dyscolus*, in which Pan speaks the prologue and apparently directs the action.

Physiologus ('The Natural Scientist'), an exposition of the marvellous properties of some 50 animals, plants, and stones, with a Christian interpretation of each (e.g. the pelican, which kills its offspring then revives them after three days with its own blood, figures the salvation of mankind through the Crucifixion). Both place and date of composition are disputed: perhaps Syria, perhaps Egypt; perhaps as late as the 4th cent. AD, perhaps (more likely?) as early as the 2nd. In any event, the work draws heavily on earlier traditions of Greek natural historical writing, particularly that of the *paradoxographers, with their concentration on the marvellous in nature and on occult natural sympathies and antipathies. The *physiologus* of the title is not the (entirely anonymous) author, but the (equally anonymous) authority from whom he claims to derive his information; it is however unclear whether he drew on a single source or on several. No neat separation of the entries into borrowed (pagan) 'information' and superimposed Christian interpretation is possible, as in many cases the 'information' has already been reshaped to fit its new context (e.g. in the highlighting of the number three, to allow reference to the Trinity and the three days of the Passion).

The work enjoyed extraordinary popularity in late antiquity and the Middle Ages. After the first version there were two subsequent (shorter) re-editions in Greek, between the 5th and the 11th cents. At least two, possibly three separate Latin translations were made, beginning perhaps as early as the 8th cent., and there were translations into Armenian, Georgian, Slavic, Syriac, Coptic, and Ethiopic. Illustrated versions were also produced. Via the Latin translation, it had a profound influence on medieval Bestiaries.

Phytalus, a hero associated with the sacred fig-tree at Laciadae in Attica, he was said to have been taught the culture of *figs by *Demeter. His descendants purified *Theseus (*see* PURIFICATION, GREEK) after his shedding of blood on the road from Troezen to Athens, clearly a story legitimating certain sacral duties performed by the *genos Phytalidai.

[Plutarch, *Theseus* 23; Pausanias 1. 37. 2–4]

Picus, king of pre-Roman *Latium, son of *Saturnus, and father of *Faunus, later transformed into a woodpecker (*picus*) by a jealous *Circe which afterwards appeared in a dream to Rhea Silvia (*see* ROMULUS AND REMUS) and brought food to the Twins. *Ovid's account utilized Aemilius Macer's *Ornithogonia*, which relied on Boeus' (Boeo?) account; thus Italic traditions are conflated with *Alexandrian.

Of the early historians, Quintus Fabius Pictor knew the woodpecker as *Mars' bird (*picus Martius*), while Valerius Antias knows Picus as a king, thus indicating early variability of the human/bird traditions. Further, some felt the Picentes (inhabitants of Picenum) were descended from Picus, although this probably relies on folk etymologies. The *Picus Martius* was clearly associated with prophecy and according to Ovid had to be bound, a prophetic commonplace (*see* PROTEUS). The *Tabulae Iguvinae* name spelt to be drawn from fields sacred to it, and augural Picus may be reflected in the names of St Picentia and Tiora Matiene or Martiana. These many conflations make certainty impossible.

[Virgil, *Aeneid* 7. 47–9, 171, 189–91; Ovid, *Metamorphoses* 14. 308–415, *Fasti* 3. 37, 291–4; Plutarch, *Roman Questions* 21]

pietas is the typical Roman attitude of dutiful respect towards gods, fatherland, and parents and other kinsmen. According to Cicero, '*pietas* is justice towards the gods'; and 'religion is the term applied to the fear (*metus*) and worship (*caerimonia*) of the gods. *Pietas* warns us to keep our obligations to our country or parents or other kin'. Pietas, personified, received a temple in Rome (vowed 191 BC, dedicated 181); it was destroyed in 44 BC. She is often represented in human form, sometimes attended by a stork, symbol of filial piety; during the empire, Pietas Augusta appears on coins and in inscriptions. Some Romans adopted as cognomen the term Pius; *Virgil's 'Pius *Aeneas' significantly expresses the Roman ideal in his religious attitude, in his patriotic mission, and in his relations with father, son, and comrades. The decision to construct an Ara Pietatis Augustae was taken in AD 43. *See* ROMAN RELIGION, TERMS RELATING TO.

[Cicero, *On The Nature of The Gods* 1. 116]

Pietrabbondante, a cult centre of the Pentri Samnites, in the Abruzzi mountains of Molise. It has been quite erroneously identified as Bovianum Vetus, and lies close to the citadel site of Monte Saraceno, with defences of the 4th cent. BC. The sanctuary, which has commanding views, was established in the 3rd cent. BC, and was apparently destroyed by Hannibal. A small Ionic temple was then built. An inscription in Oscan mentions Samnium, suggesting that it was a national shrine; another records a *meddix tuticus* (chief magistrate of the Samnites), Cnaeus Staiis Stafidins. Between *c.*120 and 90 BC, a second much larger temple, of Latian form, and a Hellenistic-type theatre, were added to the sanctuary. It went out of use, however, at the end of the Social War (between Rome and her Italian allies, 91–87 BC), although the site was frequented down into the 4th cent. AD.

piety *See* CHRISTIANITY; GREEK RELIGION; INTOLERANCE, RELIGIOUS; JUDAISM; PIETAS; PRAYER; RITUAL; ROMAN RELIGION; SACRIFICE.

pilgrimage (Christian) Despite the New Testament's disavowal of the localized cults of Judaism and the surrounding pagan world—the need was for holy lives rather than holy places—early Christians still clung to their sacred sites. Jesus' followers preserved some memory of the location of his tomb in *Jerusalem and (at least by the mid-2nd cent.) of his birthplace in Bethlehem; while further afield the burial places of martyrs on the outskirts of their cities attracted local gatherings. In maintaining these recollections of their sacred past, the first Christian pilgrims tried to assert some communal identity in a world indifferent or hostile to their faith.

As the first emperor to favour Christianity, *Constantine I actively promoted holy places through imperial church-building in the Holy Land, as well as at the shrines of Peter and *Paul and other Roman martyrs; and his mother Helena Augusta personified the official interest in sacred sites by visiting Palestine as part of a tour of the eastern provinces (*c.*AD 327). Pilgrimages to the Holy Land were no longer just a local preserve, but might bring travellers from the opposite end of the empire. The earliest such journey on record is that of an unknown pilgrim from Bordeaux, who reached Jerusalem in 333: the surviving document is both a 'secular' itinerary of the route and the account of a pilgrimage round the biblical sites of the Holy Land. The religious significance attached not to the journey itself, but to its objective of locating and—with the aid of the 'eyes of faith' and a very literal reading of the text—entering into the scriptural past of both Old and New Testaments.

In 381–4 the western pilgrim Egeria journeyed round the Holy Land and Egypt (*see* ITINERARIUM EGERIAE). Besides visiting martyr-shrines *en route*, she endeavoured to search out 'on the ground' the places of the Bible, attempting e.g. to retrace the movements of the children of Israel out of Egypt. Holy men were as much an object of pilgrimage for her as holy places: the monks who now populated the region

formed part of Egeria's scriptural landscape, perceived as successors of the Holy Land's biblical occupants. These 4th-cent. Christian travellers engaged in a species of devotional tourism, which had eyes only for the biblical past re-created in the contemporary Holy Land. The many other associations of pilgrimage—ascetic (*see* ASCETICISM), therapeutic, penitential—would emerge only later.

Pindar, lyric poet, native of Cynoscephalae in Boeotia, was born probably in 518 BC; his last datable composition (*Pythian* 8) belongs in or shortly after 446. The Alexandrian editors divided Pindar's works into 17 books: *hymns, *paeans, *dithyrambs (2 books), *prosodia* (processional songs, 2 books), *partheneia* (maiden-songs, 3 books), *hyporchemata* (dance songs, 2 books), encomia, *threnoi* (dirges) and *epinicia* (victory songs, 4 books). Of these, the only books to survive intact are the choral victory songs composed for the formal celebration of victories in the four panhellenic athletic festivals (*see* AGONES). Here, the longer odes usually have three sections, with the opening and closing sections devoted to the victor and his success and the central section usually containing a mythic narrative. Within each section there are certain conventional features. Recurrent themes are the impossibility of achievement without toil, the need for divine aid for success, the duty to praise victory, the vulnerability of achievement without praise in song, the importance of inborn excellence and the inadequacy of mere learning. The effect of this moralizing is to give the ode a pronounced didactic as well as celebratory quality.

Pindar usually chooses myths dealing with the heroes of the victor's city. As with most Greek lyric, the myth is not narrated in full. Usually a single incident is selected for narration, with other details dealt with briskly. Even the lengthy quasi-epic myth of *Pythian* 4 proceeds by a series of scenes, not an even narrative. Audience familiarity with the myth is assumed. Unlike his contemporary

*Bacchylides, Pindar regularly adopts an explicit moral stance with reference to the events narrated. The role of myth in the odes varies. Sometimes the myth has only a broad relevance to the victor, in that the deeds of the city's heroes highlight the tradition which has produced the victor's qualities. On occasion myth presents a negative contrast to the victor (such as the *Tantalus myth in *Olympian* 1, the *Orestes myth of *Pythian* 11). Often it appears to reflect an aspect of the victory or the victor's situation as developed in the direct praise.

The fragmentary nature of the rest of the corpus makes it difficult to generalize about other genres. The same moralizing quality is present. The structure where ascertainable corresponds to the tripartite structure of the victory odes. The myth is in most cases uncontroversial, since it arises from the location and occasion of the performance.

To judge by his poems, Pindar adhered throughout his life to a conservative set of standards. His thought impresses not for its originality but the consistency and conviction with which he presents the world view of the aristocrat of the late Archaic period. Though he criticizes some common versions of certain myths (for instance in *Olympian* 1), he does so on the grounds of reverence and seemliness, rather than any radical rethinking of the nature of divinity. His religion is the traditional Olympian religion (*see* GREEK RELIGION), combined in *Olympian* 2 and the dirges with elements of mystery cult and Orphico-Pythagorean belief (*see* ORPHISM; PYTHAGORAS AND PYTHAGOREANISM).

Pirithous (*Pe(i)rithoos* or -*thous*), in mythology, a Lapith (*see* CENTAURS), son by *Zeus of *Ixion's wife Dia. *Homer knows of him as fighting the *Centaurs, presumably in the Lapith–Centaur quarrel mentioned in the *Odyssey*, and a doubtfully genuine verse mentions him in *Hades. In the first and last of these passages he is associated with *Theseus, whose close friend he is in later authors. Hence, as our mythological tradition is largely Attic (*see* ATTIC CULTS AND

MYTHS), he tends to appear as little more than the pendant of his friend. He is actually an Athenian according to one ancient commentator on Homer.

One of the few adventures which are his rather than Theseus' is his wedding-feast. Marrying *Hippodamia, daughter of Butes, he forgot, according to one account, to include *Ares among his guests). For that or some other reason (the simplest is that they were very drunk, as in the *Odyssey* passage, where one Centaur is responsible for the disturbance) the Centaurs abused his hospitality by offering violence to Hippodamia, and a great fight began (a story which the *Olympia pediments and *Parthenon metopes show to have been well known in the 5th cent., if not before) ending in the victory of the Lapiths.

For the rest, Pirithous took his share in the carrying off of *Helen, the war against the *Amazons, and finally Theseus' descent to *Hades, which, indeed, in one account was undertaken to get *Persephone as wife for Pirithous, in return for his services in the matter of Helen. Theseus in most accounts escapes; Pirithous generally does not.

The fight of Lapiths and Centaurs appears in early Archaic art (François vase and elsewhere) as a pitched battle in armour. The brawl at the feast first appears in the early Classical period, in Attic vase-painting, and the west pediment of the Temple of *Zeus at Olympia; no doubt also in the picture in the Theseum at Athens probably by Micon. Pirithous is also shown aiding Theseus to abduct Helen, pictured from the mid-6th cent. Theseus and Pirithous were shown in the underworld by the 5th-cent. painter Polygnotus, and in a few surviving works from the mid-5th cent.

[Homer, *Iliad* 1. 263 ff., 14. 317–18; *Odyssey* 11. 631, 21. 295 ff.; Ovid, *Metamorphoses* 12. 210 ff.; Hyginus, *Fables* 79. 2]

pits, cult The Greeks placed in pits (*bothroi*) offerings and libations to the dead and to those deities (*chthonian) thought to reside in the earth or in the underworld. Offerings in pits could form part of funerary or tomb cult or of a fertility ritual (e.g. the *Thesmophoria in Athens) and could be used to honour or invoke the dead or deity for a variety of purposes, including prophecy, as in the underworld book of the *Odyssey*. Water and blood used in rites of *purification could also be buried. In the cults of Olympian deities (*see* GREEK RELIGION) worn-out or broken dedications and other consecrated objects as well as the bones and ashes of sacrificed animals were buried in pits. Because such things, however useless, had been consecrated to the deity, they were still sacred and hence were buried within the *sanctuary. *See also* the Roman MUNDUS.

[Homer, *Odyssey* 11. 24 ff.]

Pittheus, legendary king of Troezen in the northern Peloponnese; quick to grasp the meaning of the *Delphic oracle to the Athenian king *Aegeus, he got him drunk and put him to bed with his daughter Aethra, thus becoming the grandfather of *Theseus and creating a family tie between his own small state and the powerful city over the water.

plants, sacred Plants are associated with particular gods by virtue of their special properties of *purification and healing (*see* PHARMACOLOGY), or because of their symbolic value usually connected with fertility and growth. Thus corn is sacred to *Demeter who taught its cultivation to man. Similarly the vine belongs to *Dionysus as the god of *wine. Mugwort (*parthenis* or *artemisia*) is a healing plant connected with *Artemis in her function as goddess of *childbirth. The sexual symbolism of the pomegranate as the attribute of *Persephone and *Hera, goddess of women and marriage, is well known. In ritual plants symbolized the annual death and rebirth of vegetation, as in the pre-Greek cult of *Hyacinthus. The papyrus flower, lily, and crocus have the same significance in the Minoan frescoes of Thera.

Corn also symbolized the recurring cycle of vegetation in the Eleusinian *mysteries (*see* ELEUSIS), but acquired moral and political overtones after 600 BC under Orphic influence (*see* ORPHISM) and as a result of Athenian propaganda. Plants had *magic and medicinal properties: the withy (*lygos*, *agnus castus*) bound the image of *Artemis Orthia in Sparta and of Samian Hera during the Tonaea festival on the island of Samos. The use of the *lygos* in Demeter's *Thesmophoria was intended to reduce the sexual drive of the women worshippers. The *moly* plant cured *Circe's spell in *Homer's *Odyssey*. But it is doubtful if such plants were intrinsically sacred, any more than the wild olive awarded to the Olympic victor (*see* OLYMPIAN GAMES), the bay leaves of the *Pythian Games or the wild celery of the *Nemean Games.

plate, precious (Greek and Roman) Vessels of gold and silver are frequently mentioned in literary texts. Greek temple inventories list large quantities of plate and they frequently provide information about the weights of items. Herodotus also records the gold and silver dedications made by various Lydian kings such as Gyges, Alyattes, and Croesus. As silver and gold can be reworked, few items of ancient plate have survived in their original form. Likewise sanctuaries as depositories of such wealth were frequently looted; the inscribed dedication on a silver *phiale* found in a grave at Kozani was to *Athena at Megara. Practice was similar in the Roman world.

Plato Although some of his early dialogues, notably *Euthyphro*, might appear to question society's normal assumptions about religion and its relationship with morality, in his works on politics (*Republic* and *Laws*) Plato shows a keen appreciation of the role of traditional religion in the functioning of the state. However, his more original 'religious' thought relates mainly to the concept of the *soul and its relationship to the cosmos. Throughout the dialogues Plato expresses many versions of the idea that a person's soul is an entity distinct from the living embodied person, attached to it by a relation which is inevitable but unfortunate. In the *Phaedo* several arguments for the soul's immortality show that Plato is dealing indiscriminately with a number of different positions as to what the soul is: the principle of life, the intellect, the personality. The latter two are the ideas most developed. Soul as the intellect is the basis of Plato's tendency to treat knowledge as what transcends our embodied state; in the *Meno* learning a geometrical proof is identified with the person's soul recollecting what it knew before birth. Soul as the personality is the basis of Plato's use of myths of *transmigration of souls and afterlife rewards and punishments. In the middle dialogues these two ideas are united: the *Phaedrus* gives a vivid picture of souls caught on a wheel of ongoing rebirth, a cycle from which only philosophical understanding promises release.

Plato's use of the idea that souls are immortal and are endlessly reborn into different bodies is a metaphorical expression of a deep body–soul dualism which also takes other forms. He tends to draw sharp oppositions between active thinking and passive reliance on sense-experience, and to think of the senses as giving us merely unreflected and unreliable reports; the middle dialogues contain highly coloured disparagements of the world as revealed to us through the senses. However, there is also a strain in Plato which sets against this a more unified view of the person. In the *Symposium* he develops the idea that erotic love can be sublimated and refined in a way that draws the person to aspire to philosophical truth; in the *Phaedrus* he holds that this need not lead to repudiation of the starting-point. In the *Republic* the soul has three parts, two of which are closely connected with the body; but in the final book only the thinking part achieves immortality.

The *Timaeus*, an account of the natural world cast in the form of a description of how it was made by a creator god, treats the world itself as a living thing, with body and soul, and a fanciful cosmic account is developed. Other later dialogues, particularly the *Philebus*, also introduce the idea

that our souls are fragments of a cosmic soul in the world as a whole. Many aspects of the *Timaeus'* cosmology depend on the assumption that the world itself is a living thing.

For later developments of Plato's thought, *see* PLATONISM, MIDDLE; NEOPLATONISM.

Platonism, Middle The Platonism of the period between Antiochus of Ascalon (d. *c*.68 BC) and *Plotinus (b. AD 205), characterized by a revulsion against the sceptical tendency of the New Academy and by a gradual advance, with many individual variations, towards a comprehensive metaphysic, including many elements drawn from other schools. In logic and ethics, especially, these philosophers oscillated between the poles of Aristotelianism and *Stoicism, but in their metaphysics, after Antiochus, at least, they remained firmly transcendentalist, drawing varying degrees of inspiration from the Pythagorean tradition; *see* PYTHAGORAS AND PYTHAGOREANISM. The only surviving corpus of work is that of *Plutarch, but there are useful summaries of Platonist doctrine by Alcinous and *Apuleius. The Jewish philosopher *Philon (1), and the Christians *Clement of Alexandria and *Origen, are deeply influenced by contemporary Platonism, and are often good evidence for its doctrines.

Pleiades Name of a group of seven stars (*see* CONSTELLATIONS AND NAMED STARS), attested in *Homer and *Hesiod, and early identified with the daughters of *Atlas. *See* MAIA; MEROPE (1); ORION; STEROPE.

Plotinus *c*.AD 205–269/70), Neoplatonist philosopher. Recent writers see in Plotinus the most powerful philosophical mind between *Aristotle and Aquinas or Descartes; and in his work a logical development from earlier Greek thought, whose elements he organized in a new synthesis designed to meet the needs of a new age. These needs influenced the direction rather than the methods of his thinking: its direction is determined by the same forces which resulted in the triumph of the eastern religions of salvation, but its methods are those of traditional Greek rationalism. Plotinus attached small value to ritual, and the religious ideas of the near east seem to have had little direct influence on the *Enneads*, though certain parallels with Indian thought have been explained by postulating contact with Indian travellers in Alexandria. To *Christianity Plotinus makes no explicit reference; but in the *Enneads* there is an eloquent defence of Hellenism against Gnostic superstition (*see* GNOSTICISM).

Plotinus holds that all modes of being, whether material or mental, temporal or eternal, are constituted by the expansion or 'overflow' of a single immaterial and impersonal force, which he identifies with the 'One' of the *Parmenides* and the 'Good' of the *Republic* (*see* PLATO), though it is strictly insusceptible of any predicate or description. As 'the One', it is the ground of all existence; as 'the Good', it is the source of all values. There is exact correspondence between degrees of reality and degrees of value, both being determined by the degree of unity, or approximation to the One, which any existence achieves. Reality, though at its higher levels it is non-spatial and non-temporal, may thus be pictured figuratively as a series of concentric circles resulting from the expansion of the One. Each of these circles stands in a relation of timeless dependence to that immediately within it, which is in this sense its 'cause'; the term describes a logical relationship, not an historical event. Bare Matter (*hylē*) is represented by the circumference of the outermost circle: it is the limiting case of reality, the last consequence of the expansion of the One, and so possesses only the ideal existence of a boundary.

Between the One and Matter lie three descending grades of reality—the World-mind (*nous*), the World-soul (*psyche*), and Nature (*physis*). The descent is marked by increasing individuation and diminishing unity. The World-mind resembles Aristotle's Unmoved Mover: it is thought-thinking-itself, an eternal lucidity in which the knower and the known are distinguishable only logically; within it lie the Platonic Forms, which are conceived not as inert types or models but as a system of interrelated forces, differentiations of the one Mind which holds them together in a single timeless apprehension (*noēsis*). The dualism of subject and object, implicit in the self-intuition of Mind, is carried a stage further in the discursive thinking characteristic of *Soul: because of its weaker unity, Soul must apprehend its objects successively and severally. In doing so it creates time and space; but the World-soul is itself eternal and transcends the spatio-temporal world which arises from its activity. The lowest creative principle is Nature, which corresponds to the immanent World-soul of the Stoics (*see* STOICISM): its consciousness is faint and dreamlike, and the physical world is its projected dream.

Man is a microcosm, containing all these principles actually or potentially within himself. His consciousness is normally occupied with the discursive thinking proper to Soul: but he has at all times a subconscious activity on the dreamlike level of Nature and a superconscious activity on the intuitive level of Mind; and his conscious life may lapse by habituation to the former level or be lifted by an intellectual discipline to the latter. Beyond the life of Mind lies the possibility of unification (*henōsis*), an experience in which the Self by achieving complete inward unity is momentarily identified with the supreme unity of the One. This is the Plotinian doctrine of ecstasy. The essays in which he expounds it, on the basis of personal experience, show extraordinary introspective power and are among the classics of mysticism. It should be observed that for Plotinus unification is independent of divine grace; is attainable very rarely, as the result of a prolonged effort of the will and understanding; and is not properly a mode of cognition, so that no inference can be based on it.

Plotinus also made important contributions to psychology, particularly in his discussion of problems of perception, consciousness, and memory; and to aesthetic, where for Plato's doctrine that Art 'imitates' natural objects he substitutes the view that Art and Nature alike impose a structure on Matter in accordance with an inward vision of archetypal Forms (*see* ART, ANCIENT ATTITUDES TO). His most original work in ethics is concerned with the question of the nature and origin of evil, which in some passages he attempts to solve by treating evil as the limiting case of good, and correlating it with Matter, the limiting case of reality.

Plouton *See* HADES.

Ploutos *See* PLUTUS.

Plutarch (Lucius (?) Mestrius Plutarchus) of Chaeronea; b. before AD 50, d. after AD 120; philosopher and biographer. Most of Plutarch's life was spent in his home town of Chaeronea in Boeotia. For the last thirty years of his life, he was a priest at *Delphi. A devout believer in the ancient pieties and a profound student of its antiquities, he played a notable part in the revival of the shrine in the time of Trajan and Hadrian; and the people of Delphi joined with Chaeronea in dedicating a portrait bust of him 'in obedience to the decision of the Amphictions' (*see* AMPHICTIONY). Plutarch was a prolific writer on a wide variety of subjects. Extant are 78 miscellaneous works and 50 *Lives*. Delphi is the scene of four dialogues, all concerned with prophecy, *daimones*, and divine providence; and it is in these (together with *Isis and Osiris*) that the greater part of Plutarch's philosophical and religious speculation is to be sought.

He was a Platonist (*see* PLATONISM, MIDDLE), and a teacher of philosophy; and the more technical side of this activity is to be seen in his interpretation of the *Timaeus* and a series of polemical treatises against the Stoics and Epicureans (*see* STOICISM; EPICURUS). We possess also important antiquarian works—*Roman Questions* and *Greek Questions*, mainly concerned with religious antiquities. As understanding of his learning

and the aims and methods of his writing has deepened, he has come to be seen, not as a marginal figure, but as a thinker whose view of the classical world deserves respect and study.

Pluto, Pluton *See* HADES.

Plutus Wealth, originally and properly abundance of crops, hence associated with *Demeter at *Eleusis. He is son of Demeter and *Iasion according to *Hesiod, but at Athens, where he had an important role in the *Mysteries, he is attested simply as son of Demeter. Demeter and Kore (*see* PERSEPHONE/KORE) send him to those whom they favour, especially of course Eleusinian initiates. Unlike the fertility god Plouton (*see* HADES), he is only a personification, never the object of formal worship. In Eleusinian art he is represented in the company of Demeter and Kore usually as a boy a few years old, naked, holding a cornucopia or bunch of grain stalks, and wearing (in the Classical period) a loosely draped himation, as in the Great Eleusinian Relief. At a climactic moment in the Mysteries he evidently made a dramatic appearance.

Outside the Mysteries he is found in a variety of popular traditions and is associated with several gods and goddesses, including *Eirene and *Dionysus. In one tradition, represented by Aristophanes' *Plutus*, he personifies wealth in general, appearing in the form of a blind old man.

[Hesiod, *Theogony* 969–74; *Homeric Hymn to Demeter* 488–9; Aristophanes, *Plutus*]

Plynteria, an Attic festival (*see* ATTIC CULTS AND MYTHS) celebrated (in Athens) near the end of the early summer month Thargelion, at which the ancient image of *Athena Polias was undressed and washed (*plynō*) by women of the *genos* Praxiergidai; it was probably taken in procession to the sea. The day of the cleansing counted as impure, and temples were closed. The festival is probably old Ionian in origin, as several Ionian communities have a month-name Plynterion. *See* IONIAN FESTIVALS.

pneuma (Lat. *spiritus*) is connected etymologically with *pneō*, breathe or blow, and has a basic meaning of 'air in motion', or 'breath' as something necessary to life. In Greek *tragedy it is used of the 'breath of life' and it is the 'Spirit' of the New Testament. In early Greek thought *pneuma* is often connected with the *soul; in *Aristotle it frequently denotes 'warm air', sometimes 'heat', and the term is also used of seismic winds which are trapped within the earth. Its precise meaning, then, must always be determined in its context. The word may have been used first by *Anaximenes of Miletus to describe both elemental air in motion in the world, and 'psychic air' in man. 'Psychic *pneuma*' also constitutes the soul and underlies sensory and motor activities in a number of ancient medical theories. In Hippocratic and post-Hippocratic writings it is widely used of inspired air or breath inside the body, with no apparent reference to any particular theory. *Pneuma*-theory forms a cornerstone of Stoic physics (*see* STOICISM), and the Stoics are particularly associated with the doctrine that *pneuma* provides the universe both with cohesion and its dynamic properties.

polis (pl. *poleis*), the Greek city-state. The *polis* is the characteristic form of Greek urban life; its main features are small size, political autonomy, social homogeneity, sense of community and respect for law. It can be contrasted with the earlier Mycenaean palace economy, and with the continuing existence of tribal (*ethnos*) types of organization in many areas of northern Greece. (For a different sense of 'tribe' see below.) Socially the citizens comprised an ethnically homogeneous or limited group, organized according to 'tribes' (*phylai*) and smaller kinship groups, such as *phratries, demes (local settlements) and families; new cities would replicate these, and they were often reorganized more or less artificially to serve new civic functions. Each city had a specific patron deity and a religious calendar (*see* CALENDAR, GREEK) with other lesser cults and festivals; the older priesthoods belonged to specific aristocratic families, later ones were often appointed by the people (*see* PRIESTS). Animal sacrifice (*see* SACRIFICE) was accompanied by equal distribution of the meat at civic festivals, which from the 6th cent. became the focus for city-organized competitions in sport, dancing, and theatre (*see* AGŌNES). New cities required religious authorization, traditionally from the oracle of Apollo at Delphi (*see* DELPHIC ORACLE); sacred fire was brought from the mother city, and established at the *prytaneion*, which in all cities acted as the common hearth, where magistrates and others took meals provided at public expense; the *founder of a new city was given heroic honours after death, with a tomb within the walls and public rites. See HEROCULT. Important and prominent as they were, however, religious and social institutions were not autonomous, but were continually being adapted to conform to the needs of *polis* organization, which was directed towards broadly 'political' ends.

Polites, in mythology, son of *Priam by *Hecuba, a swift runner and consequently employed as a scout. He takes a minor part in the fighting. In *Virgil's *Aeneid* he is killed by *Neoptolemus.

[Homer, *Iliad* 2. 791 ff., 13. 533, 15. 339, 24. 250; Virgil, *Aeneid* 2. 526 ff.]

pollution, the Greek concept of Societies create order by stigmatizing certain disorderly conditions and events and persons as 'polluting', that is, by treating them metaphorically as unclean and dangerous. Very roughly, the pollutions generally recognized by the Greeks were birth, death, to a limited degree sexual activity, homicide except in war, and sacrilege; certain diseases, madness above all, were also sometimes viewed in this way, while mythology abounds in instances of extreme pollutions such as incest, parricide, and *cannibalism.

Different pollutions worked in different ways (local rules also varied). We get some indication of the attendant complications from, above all, a long code from Cyrene and the rules of purity attached to certain Coan priesthoods (*see* EPIGRAPHY). To give some illustrations: contact with a dead person of one's own family pollutes for longer than with an unrelated person; a person entering a house of birth becomes polluted, but does not transmit the pollution further; sexual contact only requires purification if it occurs by day.

Pollution has a complicated relation to the sacred. In one sense they are polar opposites: the main practical consequence of (for instance) the pollutions of birth and death was that the persons affected were excluded from temples for a period of days, and *priests and priestesses had to observe special rules of purity. But offenders against the gods became 'consecrated' to them in the sense of being made over to them for punishment; and such negative consecration (which could also be imposed by a human curse) was comparable to a pollution. This is why *agos* and *enagēs*, words that appear to be related to a root *ag* conveying the idea of sacredness, to some extent overlap in usage with *miasma* and *miaros*, the standard terms for pollution and polluting. In consequence, the boundaries are blurred between the concepts of 'pollution' and of 'divine anger'.

Since some pollutions are natural and inescapable, rules of purity are obviously not simply rules of morality in disguise. But the very dangerous pollutions were those caused by avoidable (if sometimes unintentional) actions such as bloodshed and sacrilege. In theory, one man's crime could through such pollution bring disaster to a whole state. There is a common mythological schema (best seen at the start of *Sophocles, King Oedipus*), whereby pollution causes plague, crop-failure, infertility of women and of animals. Such pollution is fertility reversed, which is why such powers as the Eumenides (*Erinyes) are double-sided, agents of pollution and also givers of fertility (see above all *Aeschylus, *Eumenides*). Orators often attempted to brand political opponents as pol-

luting demons, the source of the city's misfortunes; and a question actually put to the *oracle of *Zeus at *Dodona shows that this conception of the polluting individual was not a mere anachronism in the historical period: 'is it because of a mortal's pollution that we are suffering the storm?'

But pollution is also often envisaged as working more selectively. According to Antiphon's *Tetralogies*, for instance, murder pollution threatens the victim's kin until they seek vengeance or prosecute, the jurors until they convict. Thus the threat of pollution encourages action to put right the disorder.

Fear of pollution is often said by modern scholars to be absent from the world of *Homer; the emergence of such anxieties becomes therefore a defining mark of the succeeding centuries. But it is wrong to interpret pollution beliefs, an ordering device, as primarily a product of fear; and the natural context for, for instance, a doctrine of blood pollution of the type discussed above is a society such as Homer's where legal sanctions are weak. As we have seen, pollution belief is a complex phenomenon, a vehicle for many different concerns: it has no unified origin or history. *See also* PURIFICATION, GREEK.

Pollux Mythical character. *See* CASTOR AND POLLUX, TEMPLE OF; DIOSCURI.

Polyboea, (1) name of several mythological heroines; (2) a goddess, sister of *Hyacinthus, identified with *Artemis and Kore (*Persephone).

[Pausanias 3. 19. 4]

Polybus, (1) a king of Corinth married to Merope. Being without sons, they adopted the infant *Oedipus and reared him as their own. (2) A king of Sicyon who died without sons and left his kingdom to *Adrastus, the son of his daughter who had married Talaus, king of Argos.

[(1) Sophocles, *King Oedipus* 1016 ff. (2) Herodotus 5. 67. 4]

Polycarp (*c.*AD 69–*c.*155), bishop of Smyrna

and correspondent of Ignatius of Antioch. His martyrdom at the age of 86 is described in a letter from the Smyrnaean church to that at Philomelium, Phrygia, but presents certain textual and chronological problems. His extant letter to the Philippians (a warning against apostasy) speaks of Ignatius as dead in ch. 9, but implies that he is not yet known to be dead in ch. 13; the view that it conflates two letters has commended itself to many scholars.

Polydamas, in mythology, son of *Panthous. In the *Iliad* he takes some part in the fighting, but is chiefly noteworthy for his sage advice, which *Hector rejects to his cost. His death is nowhere recorded and he seems to be thought of as surviving the war.
[Homer, *Iliad* 18. 249 ff.]

Polydeuces (i.e. Pollux) *See* CASTOR AND POLLUX, TEMPLE OF; DIOSCURI.

Polydorus, in mythology youngest son of *Priam, by Laothoë or Hecuba. In the *Iliad* he is killed by*Achilles. But according to *Euripides' *Hecuba*, Priam had sent him with much gold to be kept safe by Polymestor, a Thracian king, who murdered him for the gold after the fall of Troy; and Hecuba avenges his death by blinding Polymestor and killing his two sons. This tradition is adopted by *Virgil.
[Homer, *Iliad* 20. 407–18, 21. 84–91; Euripides, *Hecuba*; Virgil, *Aeneid* 3. 22 ff.]

Polyeidus, a seer, one of the Melampodidae, a Corinthian (*see* MELAMPUS). When Glaucus, son of *Minos, was drowned in a honey-jar, Polyeidus, after passing a test imposed by Minos, found the body and afterwards restored it to life by using a herb revealed by a snake.
[Hyginus, *Fables* 136]

Polynices *See* ANTIGONE (1); ETEOCLES; OEDIPUS; SEVEN AGAINST THEBES.

Polyphemus *See* CYCLOPES; GALATEA.

Polyxena, in mythology a daughter of *Priam and *Hecuba, though she is not mentioned by *Homer. In the *Cypria* (*see* EPIC CYCLE) she is mortally wounded at the fall of Troy by *Diomedes (2) and *Odysseus and buried by *Neoptolemus. In the *Iliu Persis* (again, *see* EPIC CYCLE) and later she is sacrificed on the tomb of *Achilles by Neoptolemus to appease the ghost of Achilles and thus to raise winds to take the Greek ships home. Later, the story arose that Achilles, during his life, had been in love with her.

In art she is often shown present in scenes of *Troilus ambushed at the fountain and pursued by Achilles.
[Euripides, *Hecuba* 35 ff., 220 ff., 534 ff.; Hyginus, *Fables* 110]

pomerium—explained in antiquity as meaning what comes after, or before, the wall—was the line demarcating an augurally constituted city. It was a religious boundary, the point beyond which the *auspicia urbana* (*see* AUSPICIUM) could not be taken, and was distinct both from the city-wall and the limit of actual habitation, although it might coincide with the former and was often understood as the strip inside or outside the wall. Almost every aspect of the history of the *pomerium* of Rome is debatable. Our sources refer to an original Palatine *pomerium*, later extended by Servius *Tullius and then unchanged until Sulla's day; Tacitus, perhaps following the emperor Claudius, describes a circuit round the *Palatine. Although this circuit has been thought to result from confusion with the circuit of the *Lupercalia, recent excavations on the north-east slope of the Palatine have revealed a series of ditches and walls from the regal period, which seem from their size to be more of symbolic value than a real system of defence and thus perhaps confirm the literary tradition. *Varro's account of the city of the four regions may correspond to the *pomerium* at some early date. Gellius (quoting the augur Marcus Valerius Messalla 'Rufus', consul 53 BC), mentions extensions by Sulla—perhaps to be connected with the boundary-stones to the Campus Esquilinus—and also by *Caesar. On the other hand, *Augustus' silence in his catalogue of achievements, the *Res gestae*, suggests that he made none, despite the statement of Tacitus. Later extensions were made by Claudius, who was the first to include the *Aventine, and by Vespasian . The boundary stones dating from Hadrian seem only to be restorations, while the account of Aurelian's later extension is doubtful. The imperial *pomerium*, as loosely defined by the boundary stones, is thought to have coincided on the east with the republican wall, breaking away to include the Aventine and the Emporium, the southern half of the *Campus Martius and all the Pincian hill, at the last point extending beyond Aurelian's later wall.

[Varro, *On The Latin Language* 5. 46–54, 143; Livy 1. 44; Tacitus, *Annals* 12. 23; Aulus Gellius, *Attic Nights* 13. 14. 4–7]

Pomona, Italo-Roman goddess of *poma*, i.e. fruits, especially such as grow on trees (apples etc.). Her *flamen* (*see* FLAMINES) was lowest in rank of all, corresponding apparently to the small importance of her province. She had a sacred place, *pomonal*, 20 km. (12½ mi.) out of Rome on the via Ostiensis, but no known festival. *Ovid has a story (unconnected with facts of cult and clearly his own or another comparatively late author's invention) that *Vertumnus loved her, pleaded his own cause in disguised shape, and finally won her. In another version she is the spouse of *Picus.

[Ovid, *Metamorphoses* 14. 623 ff.]

pontifex/pontifices, one of the four major colleges of the Roman priesthood. The college of *pontifices* was a more complicated structure than the other three, containing as full members the *rex sacrorum* (the republican priest who took over the king's religious functions) and the three major *flamines* as well as the *pontifices* proper; the Vestals (*see* VESTA) and the minor *flamines* together with the pontifical scribe were also part of and under the authority of the college. The *pontifices* themselves were originally three in number, all patricians; new members were co-opted by the old ones. In an archaic priestly order, the

rex and the *flamines* take precedence over the *pontifex*, but this may reflect the situation of the regal period, not that of the early republic.

The college's duties were wide-ranging: they had general oversight of the state cult—sacrifices (*see* SACRIFICE), games (*see* LUDI), *festivals and other rituals; they advised magistrates and private individuals on the sacred law and kept books which recorded their rules and decisions; they had special areas of concern in relation to families and lineages (*gentes*)—the control of adoptions, burial law, the inheritance of religious duties (*sacra familiaria*); some argue that their legal role originally extended far more widely into the civil law. They had no authority over priests outside the college; and their relationship with the state remained an advisory one—their rulings had to be put into effect by magistrates or by the assemblies.

The *pontifices'* position evolved gradually during the republic: the *lex Ogulnia* of 300 BC abolished the monopoly of the *patricians and added extra places for the plebeians. From then till the end of the republic the college, together with the augurs (*see* AUGURES), had as its members the dominant figures in the ruling élite, including Julius *Caesar, Marcus Aemilius Lepidus the triumvir, and *Augustus himself.

The leading member of the college—the *pontifex maximus*—who had originally been selected by the college, was from the mid-3rd cent. BC onwards elected by a special procedure (only seventeen of the thirty-five tribes voted), which was later extended to the rest of the college—and the other colleges—by the *lex Domitia* of 104 BC. He acted as spokesman for the college, particularly in the senate; but could be overruled by his colleagues. Perhaps as a result of the selection by popular vote, the *pontifex maximus* came to be seen as the most prominent and influential of the priests; but it was not until Augustus united the position with other priesthoods and with the power of the *princeps*, that the *pontifex maximus* came to resemble a 'High Priest'. From then on the position was always held by the reigning emperor until Gratian (AD 367–83) refused to accept it.

Pontius Pilatus, prefect of *Judaea AD 26–36. A famous inscription from Caesarea attests to the name of his post. Offences against religious sentiment, perhaps not deliberate, created several serious disturbances which Pilatus handled badly. He yielded to determined protests against image-bearing standards being brought into *Jerusalem by troops. Shields set up in the palace, treated also as iconic, were removed at Tiberius' behest. Control of a crowd objecting to the use of Temple funds for the building of an aqueduct was achieved with heavy violence. A military attack on Samaritans gathering at Mt. Gerizim finally led to accusations before Lucius Vitellius, legate of Syria, and then to Pilatus' recall. A reliable account of his conduct of the trial of Jesus, mentioned also in *Josephus, cannot be extracted from the conflicting Gospel accounts. John's portrayal of him giving judgement from a tribunal in front of his official residence is plausible. Later Christian tradition and an apocryphal literature proliferated around him and his wife.

[Josephus, *Jewish Antiquities* 18. 55–89; *Jewish War* 2. 169–77; Philo, *Legatio* 299–306; Matthew 27; Mark 15; Luke 23; John 18: 28, 19]

Poplifugia An obscure Roman festival on 5 July. Its name resembles that of the equally puzzling *Regifugium. The ancients explained it as the flight of the people at the death of *Romulus or the ritual routs of Latin armies celebrated by offerings to Vitula on 8 July. Scholars have implausibly linked it to Jupiter, or conjectured that it and the Regifigium involved some ritual to evoke terrible powers whose presence must be avoided.

[Dionysius of Halicarnassus, *Roman Antiquities* 2. 56. 5; Plutarch, *Romulus* 29; Macrobius, *Saturnalia* 3. 2]

Porphyry (AD 234–c.305), scholar, philosopher, and student of religions. He was a devoted disciple of *Plotinus with whom he studied in Rome (263–268 AD), and whose works he edited.

Among his own varied writings, the metaphysical works are almost entirely lost but included treatises on the principles, matter, the incorporeal, the soul and the surviving *Sententiae*, a succinct, but probably incomplete, introduction to Plotinian metaphysics which displays some divergences from Plotinus. An anonymous commentary on the *Parmenides*, even if not by Porphyry himself, suggests strongly that Porphyry is the ultimate source for some important developments in the concepts of being, existence, and transcendence with particular reference to the One and Mind. It can no longer be held that Porphyry made no original contribution to philosophy.

Although Porphyry's publications on religion have been commonly interpreted as pointing to an intellectual development from credulous superstition to critical rejection, a fairer assessment of the evidence demonstrates a consistent interest and respect for most traditions allied to a searching but constructive critique of the workings and significance of many pagan rituals. *On Abstinence* (a treatise on vegetarianism); and the *Letter to Marcella* show a traditional piety, *On Statues* a conventional interest in ritual symbolism, *Philosophy from Oracles* acceptance of ritual with some questioning, the *Letter to Anebo* a searching critique of ritual religion, and *De regressu animae* a limitation of the scope of *theurgy. Porphyry raised but did not solve the problem of the relationship of philosophy to religion. In *Against the Christians* he used historical criticism e.g. to establish the lateness of the Book of Daniel. Elsewhere he similarly proved the 'Book of Zoroaster' to be a forgery. Also interesting are his *Life of *Pythagoras*, and his allegorizing interpretation of the *Cave of the Nymphs* in the *Odyssey* (see CAVES, SACRED).

Porsen(n)a, Lars, king of Clusium, who besieged Rome at the beginning of the republic in a vain attempt to reinstate the exiled *Tarquinius Superbus. The standard version of the story is that Porsenna was so impressed by the heroism of Romans such as *Horatius Cocles and Gaius Mucius Scaevola that he gave up the siege and made peace with the Romans. He withdrew from Rome, and instead sent his forces, under the command of his son Ar(r)uns, against the Latin town of *Aricia. This expedition ended in failure, however, when Arruns was defeated and killed by the Latins and their allies from Cumae. The survivors of his army made their way back to Rome, where they were hospitably received. There are many contradictory elements in this romantic tale, which is further complicated by an alternative tradition which maintained that the Romans had surrendered to Porsenna, and that he imposed a humiliating treaty on them. This unflattering version, which is unlikely to have been invented by the Romans, has given rise to a modern theory that Porsenna used Rome as a base from which to launch his attack against the Latins, and that it was his defeat at Aricia that finally caused him to withdraw. The battle of Aricia is probably an authentic event, since it appears to have been independently recorded in Greek sources, but it is unlikely that Porsenna's original aim was to restore the Tarquins. Since Tarquinius Superbus was closely associated with Porsenna's enemies, the Latins and Aristodemus, it is more probable that, so far from attempting to restore the Roman monarchy, Porsenna actually abolished it, and that the republic emerged after his withdrawal.

[Livy 2. 9–15; Tacitus, Histories 3. 72; Pliny, Natural History 34. 139]

portents may be defined as phenomena seen as in some way indicating the future, which are generally believed to be of divine origin. Such signs frequently occur spontaneously, although they may be sought. Roman theory thus distinguished the two types respectively as *oblativa* and *impetrativa* (see AUGURES). Some sort of belief in portents was general (though not universal) in antiquity, but scepticism on particulars was

widespread; there was much room for disagreement on what constituted a portent and on what it portended, as well as on its importance in relation to other factors.

Already in *Homer we can observe much that is characteristic of portents in the Greek world. Signs from the behaviour of birds are frequent, and are sometimes explicitly said to come from *Zeus; they may simply confirm something that has been said or they may use symbolism to convey a more complex message. Typical of the latter kind is the portent in book 12 of the *Iliad*, where an eagle is bitten by a snake it is carrying and forced to drop it. This is interpreted by *Polydamas to mean that the Trojans will eventually fail in their attack on the Achaean ships. Scepticism is shown by *Hector, who regards such signs as trivial ('one omen is best, to fight for your country')—but events will prove him wrong. Other portentous events in Homer include thunder and sneezing. Most of the portents recorded from later periods, Greek and Roman, conform to basically similar types. They are drawn from meteorological or astronomical phenomena (strange types of rainfall, *eclipses—also earthquakes), from the behaviour of animals (birds, swarms of bees), and from the involuntary actions or unknowing words of humans. Other sources include the entrails of sacrificial victims, the unusual appearance of statues, and (especially in Rome) deformed births, human or animal. Wishing to interpret such an event, Greeks might consult a professional *mantis* (seer) or even send to an oracle, or they might, like Polydamas, draw their own conclusions. As with other forms of prophecy, much latitude was possible here. Xenophon relates, for instance, that when a Spartan expedition was demoralized by an earth tremor their leader and king Agesipolis interpreted it to indicate *Poseidon's approval, since the expedition was already under way. Once he had achieved part of his aim, however, he was prepared to accept a thunderbolt and a lobeless sacrificial liver as signs that the expedition should be disbanded.

Similar phenomena were regarded as portentous in the Roman world, but were conceived in a different way. Whereas certain signs, as among the Greeks, were simple indicators of the future, in particular of the success or otherwise of an undertaking, the more unusual or sinister-seeming—rains of blood, monstrous births—were classified as *prodigia* and seen as signs of divine anger. Rather than exact interpretation, what was needed therefore was expiation, and the matter was likely to be the concern of the state. Prodigies were reported to the consuls, who prepared a list for the senate; the senate then decided which were authentic and of public concern. It might then take immediate action or more usually refer the matter to the *pontifices* (*see* PONTIFEX) or **haruspices*, or arrange a consultation of the Sibylline Books (*see* SIBYL). With this elaborate state mechanism in place, it is not surprising that perhaps even more than in Greece portents were closely connected with politics and could be the subject of manipulation, conscious or unconscious. Such *publica prodigia* decline in frequency during the 1st cent. BC, but omens and portents of other types continue to be reported throughout antiquity and beyond.

See also DIVINATION; PROPHECIES.

[Homer, *Iliad* 12. 200 ff.]

Portunus, god worshipped in the **Tiber harbour at Rome (festival, the Portunalia, 17 August; a *flamen* is attested (*see* FLAMINES)). Originally linked with 'ways in' in the wider sense, his cult came to concern harbours in general, and at Rome was associated, probably from the 6th cent. BC, with the Corinthian sea-faring cults of Palaemon (*see* ISTHMIA; MELICERTES) and Leucothea (*see* INO-LEUCOTHEA). His temple at the head of the Pons Aemilius, long wrongly known as that of Fortuna Virilis, one of the best-preserved in Rome, is part of the monumental remodelling of the waterfront of the Tiber harbour by members of the *gens Aemilia* in the mid-2nd cent. BC.

Poseidon 'All men call Poseidon god of the sea, of **earthquakes, and of horses', wrote **Pausanias in the 2nd cent. AD, describing the three principal aspects of one of the most widely, and anciently, worshipped of the Greek gods. Pausanias' term for god of the sea, *pelagaios*, is descriptive, not cultic, but his epithets for the earthquake god, Asphaleios, 'He who keeps things steady', and god of horses, Hippios, were common cult titles. In the form Posedaon (= *Poseidaōn*, as in epic poetry) he is attested on Mycenaean tablets from the palace archives at Cnossus on Crete and at Pylos in Messenia, where there are more references to him than to any other divinity; he has a sanctuary (Posidaion) and Posidawes (cult personnel?), while a female figure, Posideia, owes her name to him. His local importance at Pylos is reflected in **Homer's *Odyssey*, where **Nestor and nine groups of 500 Pylians sacrifice nine black bulls to the god on the seashore, and in later traditions of the Neleids in Athens and Ionia, who claimed descent from Pylian kings (*see* NELEUS). According to Homer, in a division of realms, **Zeus received the sky, Poseidon the sea, and **Hades the underworld, while all three shared **Olympus and earth. He is a powerful figure, resistant to pressure from his brother Zeus while acknowledging the latter's seniority; this is in contrast to **Hesiod's story of Zeus being the last child of **Cronus and Rhea. In Homer he is largely the god of the sea, aside from the implications of earthquake in the epithets *enosichthon, ennosigaios* ('earth-shaker'). He causes storms and calms the waters; his wife is Amphitrite, a sea-creature. Poseidon supports the Greeks in the Trojan War (*see* TROY, MYTHS OF), but is hostile to **Odysseus, the supreme seafarer. Eventually Odysseus will establish the god's cult far from the sea where an oar is mistaken for a winnowing fan.

Poseidon begets various monstrous figures such as Odysseus' enemies the **Cyclopes. He is not associated, in myth or cult, with civic institutions. The violence of natural phenomena, sea and earthquake, are central to the Greek conception of him. In art he is always a grave, mature male, indistinguishable from Zeus when not accompanied by attributes.

Numerous sanctuaries of the god on coastal sites, such as the 5th-cent. BC marble temple on the promontory of *Sunium in Attica, where quadrennial boat races were held in his honour, and the oracular shrine at *Taenarum in Laconia which boasted a passage to the underworld, show that his ties to the sea were also prominent in cult, as do the dedications of sailors and fishermen. Many coastal settlements were named after him.

But there were also important cult places inland where clefts in rocks, pools, streams and springs were signs of his activity. Heliconius, his title as common god of the Ionians at the *Panionium near Mycale, and similar epithets on the Greek mainland (cf. also Mt. *Helicon in Boeotia with its spring Hippocrene), may refer to the blackness of deep waters. A concern with fertility is seen in the worship of Poseidon Phytalmios ('of plants') which was said to be almost universal among the Greeks. This aspect of the god may have stemmed from his association with fresh waters and lightning, for which the trident was an instrument. There is, however, in general an emphasis on masculinity and potency in his myths and cults (so stallions, bulls, and uncastrated sheep are sacrificial victims).

Mating with grim figures (a single Erinys (*see* ERINYES) in Boeotia, with *Demeter Erinys at Arcadian Telphusa (*see* ARCADIAN CULTS AND MYTHS), she in the form of a mare, he as a stallion), he begets the marvellous horse *Arion and, at Telphusa also a daughter with a secret name. Again in Arcadia, at Phigaleia, Black Demeter is represented with a horse's head and her child by Poseidon is *Despoina, which is also the public name of the daughter of Demeter and Poseidon Hippios at Lycosura. With the Gorgon Medusa (*see* GORGO) he begets Chrysaor and the winged horse *Pegasus whose name was connected with the springs (*pēgai*) of Ocean. He had herds of horses in Arcadian

Pheneus, and horses were sometimes sacrificed to him. In his sanctuary at Onchestus in Boeotia a horse with chariot but no driver was allowed to run loose and if the chariot crashed it was dedicated to the god. This close association with the horse has led to the theory that he was introduced to Greece along with the horse by the speakers of an ancestral form of Greek early in the second millennium BC. Whatever the reasons for the original connection, the aristocratic and non-utilitarian associations of the horse were appropriate for a god often named as the ancestor of aristocratic families.

He was worshipped widely in inland Arcadia and Boeotia ('All Boeotia is sacred to Poseidon', says an ancient scholarly source) and he had important cults around the Saronic Gulf. In the Archaic period, on the island of *Calauria off Troezen, his sanctuary was the centre of an *amphictiony of originally five small *poleis* (*see* POLIS) on the Argolic and Saronic gulfs, together with Athens and Boeotian Orchomenus (Poseidon's son *Theseus moves in myth, as his cult may have moved historically, from Troezen to Athens). The organization seems to have lapsed in the Classical period but revived briefly in the Hellenistic. The Athenian orator and statesman Demosthenes killed himself in the sanctuary while fleeing from the Macedonians in 322 BC. Corinth, not a member of the amphictiony, developed the open-air shrine of the god on the Isthmus, dating from the Dark Age, into a major regional and then panhellenic sanctuary (*see* ISTHMIA) with one of the earliest ashlar-built temples (mid-7th cent. BC) and, in the early 6th cent., a biennial festival with games (*see* ISTHMIAN GAMES). It was the seat of the Hellenic League first formed at the time of Xerxes' invasions and revived more than once by the Macedonian kings. The sanctuary was destroyed by the Romans in 146 BC and rebuilt by them more than a century later. On the southern tip of Euboea was the sanctuary of Poseidon Geraistius.

In Athens Poseidon was shown contending with *Athena for the patronage of the city in the west pediment of the *Parthenon. He bore the epithet *Erechtheus while Erechtheus himself (originally a local form of the god?) was regarded as a heroized early king of the city. The same Attic *genos ('clan') provided the priest of Poseidon Erechtheus and the priestess of Athena Polias (the goddess of the Acropolis). Even so, no major Athenian festival was celebrated in his honour. The annual Posideia, held in the winter month of Posideon, is more likely to have been concerned with his agricultural than his maritime role. His priest, along with the priestess of Athena, also marched to Sciron, west of Athens, the site of a sacred ploughing.

The etymology of the name is not certain. The first two syllables seem to contain the Greek word for 'Lord', 'Husband', cf. Sanskrit (*pátī-*). *da*, in the second part of his name, may be an alternative form of Ga = Gē, Earth (see GAIA), for which the Pindaric epithet (see PINDAR) Ennosidas and the first syllable of Damater (Demeter) may provide support. He would then be 'Husband of Earth' (cf. the epic epithet *gaieochos*, 'holder of the earth').

[Homer, *Iliad* 15. 184–99, *Odyssey* 3. 4 ff.; *Homeric Hymn to Apollo* 229–38; Pausanias 7. 21. 7, 8. 7. 2, 14. 5–6, 25. 4–5, 37. 9–10, 42. 1–2]

possession, religious That a human being might become possessed by a supernatural power was a fairly common ancient belief. The effect might be a prophetic frenzy as in the case of the Pythia (see DELPHIC ORACLE). Plato further distinguishes between telestic (inspired by *Dionysus), poetic (inspired by the *Muses), and erotic (inspired by *Aphrodite and *Eros) possession. Words expressing the notion 'possessed by (a) god', such as *theolēptos* or *theophorētos*, carried an ambivalent meaning. On the one hand they referred to terrifying pathological experiences, as for instance epileptic strokes or various types of insanity. On the other, possession involved direct contact with a god and thus could effect a kind of sacralization. Around 400 BC inscriptions mention Archedemus from Thera, *ho*

nympholēptos ('seized by the nymphs'), who withdrew to a cave to devote himself to a monk-like worship of the *Nymphs (see CAVES, SACRED). Closely related are the various *katochoi* or *katechoumenoi* of later pagan and Christian creeds, especially in Asia Minor and Egypt: people who retired from the world to become the possession of their gods, whom they served in complete submission. Belief in the pathological connotations of possession, especially possession by demons, grew stronger in the post-Classical period (cf. the many stories about demoniacs in the NT) and reports of magical cures and exorcisms, pagan and Christian, abound. *See* ASCETICISM.

[Plato, *Phaedrus* 244a ff.; Virgil, *Aeneid* 6. 45–101]

pottery In both the Greek and Roman world, pottery is a primary source of evidence, being pervasive and almost indestructible. It can thus tell us much about settlement patterns and individual building complexes, including *sanctuaries. Fine pottery, particularly the Athenian black-figure and red-figure vases of the 6th and 5th cents. BC, offers among its repertoire of painted scenes a great variety of mythological subjects, in which the figures are often identified in writing, and thus provide an invaluable source of information. Sometimes they attest the existence of a story which is known in literary sources only from much later. (*See* IMAGERY.) Although gold and silver vessels (see PLATE, PRECIOUS) were naturally more prestigious than pottery, fine painted vases of this type were also sought after, and painted amphoras were given as prizes at the *Panathenaea.

Praeneste (mod. Palestrina), with interesting polygonal walls, occupied a cool, lofty spur of the Apennines 37 km. (23 mi.) east-south-east of Rome. Traditionally founded in the mythical period, the oldest finds belong to the recent bronze age. It was well-known as the seat of the ancient *oracle which Roman emperors, foreign potentates, and others consulted in the huge temple of *Fortuna Primigenia, perhaps Italy's largest sanctuary. Its impressive remains probably belong to the second half of the 2nd cent. BC, and it was still venerated in the 4th cent. AD: sweeping ramps carry the edifice up the hillside in a series of terraces.

[Polybius 6. 11; Virgil, *Aeneid* 7. 678]

Praetextatus, Vettius Agorius (c.AD 320–84), pagan senator, a resolute opponent of Christianity and friend of *Symmachus, who held many high state offices and various priesthoods, both in the traditional public cults and in the so-called '*oriental' cults such as *Isis, Magna Mater (see CYBELE), and *Mithras. His joint epitaph with his wife Aconia Fabia Paulina, in which husband and wife address one another, shows how a synthesis of pagan cults was attempted in face of the common enemy *Christianity; Praetextatus is said to have saved his wife from the fate of death by her initiations into the mysteries. Like other anti-Christians, Praetextatus was attached both to philosophy and to the ancient writers, 'by whom the gates of heaven are opened'. He produced a Latin version of Themistius' adaptation of *Aristotle's *Analytics*, and his work in translating Greek prose and poetic works into Latin and in revising their texts is also mentioned on his epitaph. He also used his public offices to promote the interests of his religion. Having held both the prefecture of Rome (367–8) and the praetorian prefecture of Italy (384), Praetextatus died as consul designate for 385. It is debated whether he rather than Nicomachus Flavianus is the subject of the anonymous *Carmen contra Paganos*.

Praxidikai, 'the exactors of justice'; goddesses worshipped at Haliartus in Boeotia. Their temple was roofless (it is common for *oaths to be taken in the open air) and they were sworn by, but not lightly. They were daughters of *Ogygus, i.e. ancient Boeotian. In the singular Praxidike is an epithet of *Persephone.

[Pausanias 9. 33. 3]

prayer Prayer was the most common form of expression in ancient religion. It could be formal or informal and was often accompanied by other acts of worship, e.g. *sacrifice or vow (the Greek word *euchē* meant both prayer and vow). The earliest instance of an independent formal prayer, namely the prayer of the priest Chryses to *Apollo in Homer's *Iliad*, presents a complete set of the fixed constitutive elements of ancient prayer. These are: (1) *invocation*. The god is addressed with his (cult) name(s), patronymic, habitual residence, functions, and qualities. This part serves both to identify and to glorify the god. (2) The *argument*, consisting of considerations that might persuade a god to help, e.g. a reminder of the praying person's acts of piety, or a reference to the god's earlier benefactions or his natural inclination to help people. This part often expanded into a eulogy with narrative aspects, especially in *hymns. (3) The *prayer* proper, the petition. For the great majority of both private and public prayers contain a wish. There is a large variation in 'egoistic' motifs. Drought, epidemics, or hail, for instance, can be prayed away, but also passed on to enemies or neighbours. This comes very close to the *curse, which, too, may contain elements of prayer: the Greek term *ara* denoted both prayer and curse. Although feelings of gratitude were not lacking, the prayer of gratitude was extremely rare. It did exist but instead of terms for gratitude (*charis*, *gratia*) expressions of honour (*timē*, *epainō*, *laus*) were generally employed, glorification being the most common expression of gratitude, as in human communication. Private prayer often lacked these formal aspects, but in public cultic prayer too very simple invocations occurred, as e.g. in the famous Eleusinian prayer (see ELEUSIS): *hye kye* ('rain, conceive'). There were also linguistically meaningless sounds which accompanied certain dances and processions and which could be interpreted as invocations of the god, such as *ololugē, thriambe, euhoi, paian* (see PAEAN). They could even develop into the name of a god: the cry *iakche* became the divine name *Iacchus.

Although Greek influence is noticeable, especially with respect to the formal aspects, Roman, and generally Italic, prayers (*preces*) distinguished themselves by their elaborate accuracy. Prayers for individual use were often equally formulaic, but both officially and privately less elaborate prayers occurred as well, e.g. *Mars vigila* ('Mars, wake up').

Ancient prayer used to be spoken aloud. Silent or whispered prayer was reserved for offensive, indecent, erotic, or magical uses, but was later adopted as the normal rule in Christian practice. Kneeling down, though not unknown, was unusual, the *gesture of entreaty being outstretched arms, with the hands directed to the god invoked (or his cult-statue).

[Homer, *Iliad* 1. 37 ff.]

Precatio terrae, Precatio omnium herbarum, two short anonymous prayers of uncertain date to Mother Earth and to all herbs; the second may show Christian influence.

prejudice *See* INTOLERANCE, RELIGIOUS; SEMITISM, ANTI-.

Presocratic philosophers, thinkers who lived not later than *Socrates. Several among them commented on religious matters. *See* e.g. ANAXAGORAS; ANAXIMANDER; ANAXIMENES; EMPEDOCLES; PARMENIDES; PRODICUS; PROTAGORAS; PYTHAGORAS; XENOPHANES.

Priam (*Priamos*), in mythology son of *Laomedon and originally called Podarces; king of *Troy at the time of its destruction by *Agamemnon. When Laomedon refused to pay *Heracles the promised reward for saving *Hesione from the sea-monster, Heracles killed Laomedon and all of his sons except Priam, whom he spared and made king of Troy. Priam's principal wife was *Hecuba, though he had other wives and concubines. He was father of fifty sons, including *Hector, *Paris, *Deiphobus, *Helenus, *Troilus, *Polydorus, and *Lycaon, and daughters including *Cassandra and *Polyxena (though the latter is not mentioned by

*Homer). When the Greeks came to Troy with Agamemnon, Priam was already an old man. Homer depicts him as an amiable character, tender to *Helen although he disapproves of the war and its cause, respected even by his enemies for his integrity and esteemed by most of the gods (though *Hera and *Athena are hostile) for his piety. He takes part in the treaty and has returned to the city before it is broken. He tries to persuade Hector to come to safety within the walls after the rout of the Trojans and after his death goes to the Greek camp to ransom his body, moving *Achilles to pity. The lost *Iliu Persis* (*see* EPIC CYCLE) told of his death at the fall of Troy, killed by *Neoptolemus while taking refuge at the altar of *Zeus Herkeios in his own palace. The most powerful description in surviving literature is *Virgil's. Priam's name became almost proverbial for a man who had known the extremes of contrasting fortunes.

Neoptolemus killing Priam at the altar is a popular scene in art from the early 6th cent. on, as a separate scene or as the centre of a Sack of Troy, and is often associated with the death of *Astyanax. Priam is also shown coming to ransom Hector's body from Achilles.

[Homer, *Iliad*, esp. books 3, 22, 24; Virgil, *Aeneid* 2. 506 ff.]

Priape(i)a are poems about the phallic god *Priapus, addressed to him, spoken by him, or invoking him. The genre is well represented in Hellenistic and later epigram, but the range of topics is limited. It was enriched and developed by the Romans, whose Priape(i)a are distinguished from Greek exemplars by their focus on the god's aggressive, anally-fixated, sexuality, by the absence of any discernible religious sentiment, and by the almost invariable treatment of Priapus as a figure of fun.

Priapus, an ithyphallic god most familiar from the sportively obscene short poems (Greek and Latin) called Priape(i)a: in these he typically threatens to punish by penetration any male or female intruder into the garden of which he is guardian. He was said to be a son of *Dionysus (the god he is most closely linked to in cult) by a *nymph or *Aphrodite. He is first mentioned in the 4th cent. BC (in the title of a comedy *Priapus*) and allusions become common in the 3rd, when his cult seems to have spread rapidly out from the Lampsacus region in Asia Minor, probably absorbing some pre-existent ithyphallic deities on the way; he was later to be well known almost throughout the Roman empire. He is associated with sexuality, human fertility, gardens, herds, in Greek texts with fishermen and occasionally in Roman texts with tombs; a text of the 3rd cent. BC presents him simply as a bringer of wealth and a general helper. His image was typically sited in a garden or house, though temples are sometimes also attested. His preferred victim in Lampsacus was the lustful donkey, but elsewhere he received animal sacrifice of more normal type or, very commonly, offerings of fruit, flowers, vegetables (and fish).

In the *Priape(i)a he presents himself as a minor and disreputable god, and in texts of all kinds he is humorously handled. It has often been suggested that this embodiment of generative power had once been treated with more reverence. But the prurience, embarrassment, depreciation, and humour associated with him are appropriate responses to that image of sexuality which, as much as of fertility, he presents. The association between ithyphallic display and protection of territory is also found among primates; how to fit this analogy into a broader account of the god is uncertain. *See* PHALLUS; BAUBO.

[Strabo 13. 1. 12; Pausanias 9. 31. 2]

priests (Greek and Roman) Cities in the Graeco-Roman world always had men and women, often of high rank, specially chosen for the service of the gods and goddesses. They might be serving for life or for a fixed term; they might be holding a hereditary position, or be publicly elected or selected by some other method, or the office might (at least in the Greek world) be put up for sale. The offices always carried honour, but often too, especially in later periods, the expectation of high expenditure by the holders. The duties varied a great deal, from quite humble to high authority and power.

Greek and Latin have several terms referring to these positions—*hiereis* and *sacerdotes* are only the most common; in English, 'priest' is used as a generic term for all of them, but implies a potentially misleading unity of conception and an analogy with the roles of priesthood in later religions. Pagan priests did not form a separate group or caste and seldom devoted their whole lives to religious activity; characteristically, they performed their religious duties on special occasions or when required and otherwise continued with the same range of social or political activities as other members of their social groups. Above all, there was no religious community, separate from the civic community, with its own personnel or power-structure. Nor did priests monopolize religious action or communication with the gods and goddesses: fathers of families, leaders of social groups, officials of the city, all had the power of religious action, with priests as advisers or helpers. So far as the city itself was concerned, it might well be the city authorities who took the religious decisions and the magistrates (elected officials), not the priests, who took religious actions on the city's behalf.

To this extent, there was not much difference between the pagan practice of Greece and of Rome; but differences appear on a more detailed examination. Greek cities have female as well as male priests, generally but not always female for goddesses, male for gods. They do not form priestly groups or colleges, but are attached to particular cults and even to particular temples, sanctuaries, or festivals; there is an alternative pattern where priesthood is carried in families. Priests seldom act as advisers to individuals, who consult ritual experts (*exēgētai; see* EXĒGĒTĒS) or diviners (*see* DIVINATION). They seem not to have been consulted on religious issues by the state, except the priests of an oracle speaking on behalf of a god or when special *purifications or remedies were needed and a religious expert might be brought in.

In Rome on the other hand priests are (with the exception of the Vestal Virgins; *see* VESTA) males, formed into colleges or brotherhoods (*see* SODALES). They are not attached to particular deities or temples, but rather to special festivals (as the Luperci to the *Lupercalia) or areas of religion (the *augures to the taking of auspices). The *flamines are a spectacular exception, perhaps preserving a more archaic and far closer relationship between priest and deity; they therefore provide the model for the priesthood of the emperors after death (the Divi; *see* RULER-CULT). The most senior colleges were above all expert advisers, consulted by the senate when religious problems were to be dealt with. The *pontifices* (*see* PONTIFEX/PONTIFICES) are also available to private individuals, in need of advice on the religious law (*see* HIEROMNĒMONES).

In both Greece and Rome, the powers associated with priesthood were narrowly defined. They superintended particular cultic activities, but the financing of these activities was often carefully controlled by state officials and the priests controlled no great temple incomes or resources, as equivalent officers did in other parts of the ancient world. The city would often vote funds for religious expenditure and might regard the treasures stored in temples as state reserves to be used in case of emergency and repaid later. There might also at all periods be city officials taking overall responsibility for state religious expenditure.

In the imperial period, both in the east and west, priesthood became closer than ever to the expression of public power. The flaminate in its new guise of an imperial priesthood became widespread in the provinces and cities, held by the leading members of the local élites as a mark of their authority and an opportunity for public generosity. Meanwhile, the emper-

or's image in priestly garb became one of the empire-wide expressions of his rule.

Apart from these official civic priesthoods, there was a great range of religious expertise available for private consultation—diviners of all sorts, magicians, and astrologers; these had no official recognition and often attracted criticism. The mystery-cults (*see* MYSTERIES) also had their priests, who might attain to great authority within a less controlled cultic environment than that of the civic priests; religious groups devoted to a particular cult might appoint priests of their own; the Bacchist movement of 186 BC (*see* BACCHANALIA) had priests and priestesses, differentiated from lay magistrates in the senate's decree; but the clearest example of this development is the figure of the *Isis priest in *Apuleius' novel (*The Golden Ass* 11), who acts as mentor and spiritual adviser to the hero after his rescue from the spell that turned him into a donkey. It seems clear that there were new currents within pagan religious life that corresponded to, if they were not imitating, the new religious types evolving at the same time amongst Jews and Christians. Nothing, however, in pagan religious life corresponded to the Christian hierarchic structure of deacons, priests, and bishops. *See* CHRISTIANITY; JUDAISM; ORACLES; QUINDECIMVIRI SACRIS FACIUNDIS.

Priscillianists The Priscillianists were members of a Christian ascetic movement which flourished in Spain and Aquitaine during the last quarter of the 4th cent. AD. Its founder, Priscillian, was a well-educated Spanish layman, possibly of senatorial standing. From *c*.375 his teachings spread rapidly, attracting a considerable following and powerful opposition. Affinities with *Gnosticism and *Manichaeism laid the Priscillianists open to charges of heresy. Priscillian was consecrated bishop of Avila in 380, but condemned by the council of Bordeaux in 384. After an appeal by Priscillian and his associate Instantius, their opponents bishops Ithacius and Hydatius accused them of sorcery and the case was tried as a criminal rather than ecclesiastical matter. Using confessions acquired by torture, they were found guilty. Despite the protests of Martin of Tours, Priscillian was executed and Instantius banished to the Isles of Scilly (385). The condemnation of clerics by a lay tribunal and episcopal complicity in prosecuting a capital case shocked contemporaries. Ithacius and Hydatius were forced to resign their sees while Priscillian's followers hailed him as a martyr. The Council of Toledo (400) reconciled moderate Priscillianists, but the movement remained strong in Galicia until *c*.600.

Priscillian's teachings included advocacy of celibacy, vegetarianism, lay spirituality, and the spiritual equality of men and women. Priscillianist theology exhibits a fondness for apocryphal scriptures, numerology, and esotericism. Priscillian's followers included wealthy aristocrats and common people alike. The movement represents both the theological variety and social turmoil which characterized the ascendancy of *asceticism in the west.

proagōn The *proagōn* at Classical Athens was an official theatrical presentation which took place a few days before the Great *Dionysia began. It was held in the Odeum, a building east of the theatre reconstructed by Pericles *c*.445 BC, where the poets appeared before the public with their choruses, actors, and presumably *chorēgoi* (*see* CHORĒGIA), to give an exposition of some kind of the dramas with which they were to compete, perhaps little more than an indication of their general plot or subject-matter. Those involved in the forthcoming competitions were thereby identified before their civic peers: for, though garlanded, actors and choruses appeared without costumes or masks. We hear only of *tragedy being presented in this way, but the procedure may have included comedy.

Proba, Faltonia Betitia, Christian poet and wife of Clodius Celsinus Adelphius, prefect of Rome in AD 351. She composed a lost epic on the civil war between Constantius II and Magnentius (under whom her husband held his prefecture), and later an extant Virgilian cento (a poem produced by rearranging lines and phrases from Virgil) on the creation of the world and the life of Christ.

processions are an extremely common feature of Greek and Roman religious practice. It is above all in the procession that a group may ritually display its cohesion and power to itself and others. And the route taken may express the control of space. The group may embody the whole community, as in the splendid festivals of the Greek *polis*—the Panathenaic procession (*see* PANATHENAEA) represented on the *Parthenon frieze, for example, with its various subgroups of virgins, youths, old men, musicians, chariots, and so on. Smaller groups form processions at funerals, weddings, and the like. Or a great procession may be centred around a single individual, as in the Roman *triumph. The procession almost always leads up to some action at its destination, frequently animal *sacrifice in a precinct (with the victims led in the procession); but also mystic *initiation (*see* MYSTERIES), as in the mass of initiands proceeding on the sacred way from Athens to *Eleusis; theatrical performances, as at the Athenian City *Dionysia; the offering of a robe to the deity, as at the Panathenaea; fire ritual on a mountain top, as at the Boeotian Daedala; games, as in the Roman circus procession; and so on. Special types of procession include those which escorted a deity (generally *Dionysus) into the city, as at the Anthesteria, and those conducted by children collecting contributions. Among the objects carried in processions were phalloi (*see* PHALLUS), baskets, the sacred objects of the mysteries, and branches hung with wool and fruit (*eiresionai*; *see* PYANOPSIA). Detailed accounts survive of magnificent processions at Alexandria (the procession of Ptolemy II Philadelphus) and at Rome (preceding the Ludi Romani; *see* JUPITER). Christian antipathy to pagan festivals is expressed in the idea of the *pompa diaboli* (devil's procession).
[Athenaeus 196a–203b; Dionysius of Halicarnassus, *Roman Antiquities* 7. 72]

Proclus, Neoplatonist philosopher (AD 410 or 412–485; *see* NEOPLATONISM). After some study in Alexandria, came to Athens in search of philosophical enlightenment, where he spent the rest of his life, and succeeded Syrianus as head of the Platonic school (*diadochos*) in 437. His importance as a creative thinker has sometimes been exaggerated: most of the new features which distinguish his Neoplatonism from that of *Plotinus, such as the postulation of triadic 'moments' within each hypostasis, or of 'henads' within the realm of the One, are traceable, at least in germ, to *Iamblichus or Syrianus. But he is the last great systematizer of the Greek philosophical inheritance, and as such exerted a powerful influence on medieval and Renaissance thought, and even, through Hegel, on German idealism. His learning was encyclopaedic and his output vast.

Procne *See* PHILOMELA.

Procris, an Attic heroine (*see* ATTIC CULTS AND MYTHS; HERO-CULT), best known for her stormy marital relationship with *Cephalus. When the disguised Cephalus discovered her willingness to be unfaithful, she fled in shame to Crete, where she cured *Minos of his childlessness and, being a great huntress, was presented by him with a hound which never missed its mark, which in turn she gave to Cephalus. Having then tricked her husband with his own method, she remained suspicious of him, and was accidentally killed by him while spying on him as he was hunting. Her father *Erechtheus then buried her and prosecuted Cephalus.

[Hesiod, *Theogony* 985–7; Apollodorus 2. 4. 7, 3. 14. 3, 15. 1]

Procrustes, familiar epithet of one of *Theseus' adversaries on his journey from Troezen to Athens, also known as Damastes, Polypemon, and perhaps Procoptas. He was a brigand who lived between *Eleusis and Athens. Having overcome his victims he would force them to lie down on a bed, or on one of two beds; if they were too short, he would hammer them out or rack them with weights to fit the longer bed, if too tall he would cut them to fit the shorter. Theseus disposed of him in like manner.

[Diodorus Siculus 4. 59. 5; Apollodorus, *Epitome* 1. 3. 4; Hyginus, *Fables* 38]

Prodicus of Ceos, a sophist and contemporary of *Socrates. Little is known about his life. We learn from *Plato that he served on diplomatic missions and that he took advantage of the opportunities these afforded to build up his clientele and to demand high fees. He was chiefly a teacher of rhetoric, with a special interest in the correct use of words and the distinction of near-synonyms. Plato represents Socrates as being on friendly terms with him and paying tribute to the value of his teaching, though usually with a touch of irony. Of his writings all that survives is Xenophon's paraphrase of his myth of the Choice of *Heracles between Virtue and Vice. He gave naturalistic accounts of the origin of religion, in some respects anticipating *Euhemerus, and is counted as an atheist by some sources. *See also* ATHEISM; CULTURE-BRINGERS.

prodigies *See* PORTENTS.

Proetus, the first king of Tiryns, who quarrelled with his brother *Acrisius in their mother's womb. (*See also* BELLEROPHON.) The only other important myth, which is fragmented into various local traditions, concerns his daughters, the Proetides. These insulted the statue of *Hera, or refused the rites of *Dionysus. They were driven mad by the offended deity and wandered about the country 'with all sorts of indecent behaviour'. In particular, they took themselves for cows and roamed the Peloponnese mooing. *Melampus, being asked to heal them, demanded a share of the kingdom; this was refused, and they went madder still, now being joined by all the other women who had killed their own children. Finally, Proetus agreed to Melampus, although his terms had been raised. The women were then caught by Melampus and a band of youths at Sicyon and cured, except one, Iphinoe, who had died. Melampus married one of the daughters and became king. The myth with its 'mooing' girls, a stay outside the city, a chase by youths and a concluding marriage strongly suggests a background in initiation. As daughters of the primeval king, the Proetides were the exemplary initiates; see INITIATION.

[Homer, Iliad 6. 157 ff.]

Prometheus, divine figure associated with the origin of *fire and with *Hephaestus, developed by *Hesiod into a figure of greater weight. The name, of unknown significance, was given the sense 'Forethought' by Hesiod, who added a contrasting figure Epimetheus ('Thinking after the event'). His father is *Iapetus.

Local Myth and Cult: (1) At Athens Prometheus and Hephaestus are worshipped by potters (because of the firing of clay?) and in the area called Academy (Akadēmeia or Hekadēmeia). A *torch-race in honour of Prometheus probably formed part of a ritual renewal of fire. (2) In Thebes one of the *Cabiri is named Prometheus and his son is Aetnaeus ('of Mt. Etna', where Hephaestus and the *Cyclopes worked as smiths). (3) *Deucalion is the son of Prometheus, and after the flood first lived at Opus (just north of Boeotia in Locris). Prometheus has a memorial at Opus, as also at Sicyon. (4) At Panopeus (just west of Boeotia in Phocis) a building housed a statue of Asclepius or possibly Prometheus. The mythic inhabitants of Panopeus were the Phlegyes ('Blazing men'), etymologically identical with the Indian Bhṛgus, a priestly clan responsible for sacrificial fire received from a divine being Mātariśvan.

In the *Theogony* of the Boeotian Hesiod, Prometheus is bound to a pillar, his liver eaten daily by an eagle and nightly renewed until finally he is freed by *Heracles. This is traced back to a meal shared by men and gods where Prometheus tricks the gods into feasting on bones and fat, explaining the division of victims after *sacrifice and also

the distance which now separates men and gods. *Zeus in anger removes fire from men, but Prometheus steals it and gives it to man, who is then further punished by Hephaestus' creation of woman, foolishly accepted by Epimetheus (*see* PANDORA). The portrait of Prometheus was developed by later authors: (Pseudo-?) *Aeschylus' *Prometheus Bound* makes him yet more of a culture hero, responsible for man's skills and sciences. There is also a persistent tradition that Prometheus created man from clay, as commonly in mythologies, and this might lie behind Hephaestus' creation of woman in Hesiod.

Prometheus' defiance of the gods captured the romantic imagination and has profoundly influenced most modern artistic and literary genres, notably because of the monumental nobility in the *Prometheus Bound* of Prometheus chained to the rock, hurling defiance at Zeus, and despising mere thunderbolts. The trickery with which Hesiod characterizes this culture-hero has attracted interest in the light of trickster heroes in other mythologies, notably North American. In any case, myths of the origin of fire and of man bring Greek myth closer than usual to world mythologies and folk-tale.

His release by Heracles is depicted in art since Archaic times; his theft of fire and creation of man are later and less frequent.

[Hesiod, *Theogony* 506–616; Pindar, *Olympian* 9. 55; Aeschylus, *Prometheus Bound*; Pausanias 2. 19. 8, 9. 25. 6, 10. 4. 4]

pronoia See PROVIDENTIA.

prophecies, texts purporting to be the work of inspired sages, had an important role in Graeco-Roman thought. Collections of prophecies, which are attested as early as the 6th cent. BC, might be attributed to a divine or semi-divine character such as *Orpheus, *Bacis, or a *Sibyl; they could be presented as accounts of moments where an individual was seized by a prophetic fit, or collections of significant oracles that either emanated, or were claimed to have emanated, from major oracular shrines. The priests of *Delphi are said to have assembled such a collection for the Lydian king Croesus in the 6th cent. BC, *Porphyry assembled such texts in the 3rd cent. AD to explain cult practices, and Christians took over parts of these collections to illustrate intimations of Christian truth in pagan texts.

The purveyors of such texts, usually called *chresmologoi* in Greek and by a number of different titles in Latin (including *vates*, *prophetes*, and *hariolus*), ordinarily did not claim inspiration for themselves, and it is impossible to know what role they played in the actual composition of such works. Evidence from Egyptian sources (most importantly the *Oracle of the Potter*) and from the manuscript traditions of the Sibylline Oracles does, however, suggest that there was considerable fluidity in their texts.

Recitation of these prophecies is often noted at times of public unrest. Thucydides, Aristophanes, and *Plutarch provide a sample of such prophecies (and parodies of the same) during the Peloponnesian War (431–404 BC); *Phlegon of Tralles preserves a number of anti-Roman texts that circulated in the east during the 2nd and 1st cents. BC; and Cassius Dio provides several examples of their use in the imperial period. Other authors (e.g. Plutarch and *Pausanias) show that the appearance of such writings was not an epiphenomenon of crisis, but rather that they were in general circulation at all times.

The most significant extant collections of prophecies are the corpus of *Sibylline Oracles*, the *Chaldaean Oracles*, the *Tübingen Theosophy*, a Syriac collection of the 6th cent. AD, and in Phlegon of Tralles. There are obvious connections in theory and use, if not necessarily in form or content, between the prophecies of the classical world and the ancient near east, especially the so-called 'Akkadian Apocalypses', the books of the Hebrew Prophets, and some Egyptian Wisdom Literature. *See also* APOCALYPTIC LITERATURE; DIVINATION.

[Herodotus 1. 91; Thucydides 2. 8. 2, 54. 2; 5. 26. 4; 8. 1. 1; Aristophanes, *Knights* 61, *Peace* 1065; Plutarch, *Nicias* 13; Dio 56. 25]

prophētēs, the title of the mortal who speaks in the name of a god or interprets his will. It is properly used only of seers and functionaries attached to an established oracular shrine; the unattached seer is called *mantis* or *chresmologos*. And it is more often used of the officials who presided over oracular shrines than of the actual receivers of mantic inspiration: a fragment of *Pindar distinguishes the two functions, inviting the Muse (*see* MUSES) to 'prophecy, and I will be your mouthpiece (*prophētēs*)'. At Delphi (*see* DELPHIC ORACLE) and *Didyma the immediate reception of the divine revelation was a woman, while the 'prophets' were males who oversaw the oracular session: at Didyma, an annually elected magistrate, at Delphi (where the title was not official) two priests who served for life. The distinction is not absolute, however, as the term *prophētis* was also sometimes applied to the inspired woman. It used to be supposed that at *Claros a male *prophētēs* spoke the oracles, but according to a recent suggestion the *thespiōdos*, 'oracular singer', did so instead.

Propylaea A propylon is a monumental roofed gateway: the derivative term, propylaea, is applied to more complex structures, specifically the Periclean gateway to the Acropolis of Athens designed by Mnesicles and built between 436 and 432 BC. It made an appropriately grand setting for the arrival of *processions. Much admired in antiquity, the building was part-replicated in the (2nd cent. AD) 'Greater Propylaea' at *Eleusis.

Proserpina, Proserpine *See* PERSEPHONE.

proskynēsis Prostration before a superior, whether human or deity, generally treated by Greeks as a demeaning practice typical of barbarians. The word is sometimes used of Greek worship, and it has been suggested that here it may rather have the meaning of blowing a kiss, which would suit the etymology. *See* RULER-CULT, *Greek*.

prostitution, sacred is a strictly modern, not ancient, term and misleading in that it transfers to the institution, or rather a variety of institutions, an adjective which in ancient sources denotes only the status of the personnel involved (sometimes also their earnings, which likewise became sacred on dedication). In the cult of *Aphrodite at Corinth, Strabo, admittedly writing long after the city's destruction in 146 BC, gives a total of over 1,000 *hetairai* ('companions') dedicated by both men and women. Much earlier *Pindar, in a *scolion* or drinking-song which explicitly anticipates a degree of moral opprobrium and seeks to forestall this with a coy invocation to 'necessity', celebrates the dedication of up to 100 by the contemporary Xenophon of Corinth (the figure given is strictly a total of limbs rather than of persons). The modern view that their professional activities were ritually significant is not borne out by the down-to-earth, matter-of-fact ancient term 'earning from the body', elsewhere and no less casually also used of wet-nursing. Dedication is also emphasized by Strabo in the cult of Aphrodite at *Eryx in Sicily (once again a thing of the past by his time), some women being sent from outside the island; Diodorus Siculus emphasizes relaxation and entertainment rather than religious solemnity. In the cult of Ma (*Bellona) at Comana Pontica, Strabo says most but not all such women were sacred. In all these cases, the adjective denotes no more than manumission by fictive dedication of a kind already attested in the cult of *Poseidon at *Taenarum in the 5th cent. BC.

A quite distinct institution, reported only from the margins of the Greek world, is the practice of pre-marital sex with strangers, sometimes sustained over a period of time, sometimes strictly delimited, but invariably presented as followed by a lifetime of strict conjugal fidelity, the *locus classicus* being Herodotus' often hilarious description of Babylon (not confirmed but not contradicted by cuneiform sources; some distinctive features repeated in the *Septuagint version of Jeremiah 42–3, *c.*300 BC). This is a one-off rite, compulsory for all,

in the service of the goddess *Mylitta, to whom earnings are dedicated, the act itself (by contrast with Corinthian practices) involving a strictly religious obligation. Other sources give similar descriptions located in Cyprus and Sicca Veneria, Numidia. By contrast, Herodotus' picture of Lydian girls earning their dowries by prostitution (and giving themselves away in marriage) could be a strictly secular (economic) phenomenon; in the same source, not only did the Lydians invent coined money, they were the world's first 'hucksters'.

Distinct again but poorly attested (that is to say indirectly and in the rather suspect context of tyrannical misdeeds) is the vow supposedly taken by the citizens of Locri Epizephyrii (South Italy) to prostitute all their unmarried girls (*virgines*) in the event of victory over Rhegium in 477/6 BC, a one-off and clearly desperate measure which must if authentic be explained in quite different terms, perhaps connected with the highly unusual circumstances of the city's foundation. But oriental origins (or influence), so often invoked to exorcise the Hellenist's embarrassment at the Corinthian data, the real problem remaining the fact of their reception (and naturalization), however comforting on the Greek mainland, are certainly not applicable to Locri.

[Strabo 6. 2. 6, 8. 66. 20, 12. 3. 36; Diodorus Siculus 4. 83. 6; Herodotus 1. 199; Jeremiah 42–3 (LXX); Justin, *Epitome of Pompeius Trogus* 21. 3. 2]

Protagoras of Abdera (*c.*490–420 BC), the most celebrated of the sophists. He travelled widely throughout the Greek world, including several visits to Athens, where he was associated with Pericles, who invited him to write the constitution for the Athenian colony of Thurii. The ancient tradition of his condemnation for impiety and flight from Athens is refuted by *Plato's evidence (in *Meno*) that he enjoyed a universally high reputation till his death and afterwards. *See* ATHEISM; INTOLERANCE, RELIGIOUS. He was famous in antiquity for agnosticism concerning the existence and nature of the gods, and for the doctrine that 'Man is the measure of all things', i.e. the thesis that all sensory appearances and all beliefs are true for the person whose appearance or belief they are; on the most plausible construal that doctrine attempts to eliminate objectivity and truth altogether. It was attacked by Democritus and Plato (in the *Theaetetus*) on the ground that it is self-refuting; if all beliefs are true, then the belief that it is not the case that all beliefs are true is itself true. In the *Protagoras* Plato represents him as maintaining a fairly conservative form of social morality, based on a version of social contract theory; humans need to develop social institutions to survive in a hostile world, and the basic social virtues, justice and self-control, must be generally observed if those institutions are to flourish.

Protesilaus, leader of a Thessalian contingent at *Troy. According to the *Iliad*, he was the first of the Greeks to disembark and was immediately killed, 'and his wife was left tearing her cheeks and his house half-built'. This is later elaborated, mainly (to our knowledge) in Latin authors. Here Protesilaus had offended the gods by failing to sacrifice before he began his house. An oracle prophesied that the first man ashore at Troy would die and he deliberately sacrificed himself. His wife Laodamia grieved so for his loss that the gods allowed her to see him for three hours, after which she killed herself; or she spent so much time with an image of him that her father burnt it and she flung herself on the fire.

[Homer, *Iliad* 2. 698–702; Catullus 68. 73–130; Ovid, *Heroines* 13; Hyginus 103–4]

Proteus, a minor sea-god or 'Old Man of the Sea', herdsman of seals. In the *Odyssey*, *Menelaus encounters him on the island of Pharos off the coast of Egypt. The god takes on various shapes in an effort to escape (his shape-changing became proverbial), but Menelaus holds him fast and forces him to answer questions. This episode must have been the subject of *Aeschylus' *Proteus*, the satyr-play of the *Oresteia*. Later writers, including *Virgil, associate the god with Chalcidice.

In Herodotus, however, Proteus is not a god but a virtuous Egyptian king, who keeps *Helen with him for the duration of the Trojan War. This is followed by *Euripides in his *Helen*.

[Homer, *Odyssey* 4. 349–570; Virgil, *Georgics* 4. 387–529; Herodotus 2. 112–20; Euripides, *Helen* 1 ff.]

Providentia, learned term for *prudentia*, 'foresight', the capacity to distinguish good from bad, which became, under the influence of the *pronoia* ('forethought') of *Stoicism, a virtue of statesmen. *Providentia Augusti* became the object of cult at the beginning of the Principate. It expressed the wise forethought of *Augustus in regulating the succession in AD 4, before being extended to other fields of imperial forethought. The altar of Augustan *Providentia* was sited in the *Campus Martius near the *Ara Pacis Augustae. Its anniversary fell on 26 June, date of the adoption by Augustus of the future emperor Tiberius. The date of the altar's construction is unknown. It was already in existence by AD 20. The *Providentia Augusti* was invoked on the discovery of conspiracies and was a frequent theme in imperial coinage. From the time of Hadrian, *Providentia deorum*, the foresight of the Gods, protectress of the imperial family and the empire, was invoked alongside *Providentia Augusti*.

Prudentius, Aurelius Clemens (AD 348–after 405), greatest of the Christian Latin poets, was a native of the Ebro valley in north-east Spain and abandoned a distinguished administrative career for Christian poetry. His works are (*a*) lyrical: *Cathemerinon*, 'Hymns for the day' and *Peristephanon*, 'Crowns of the martyrs'; (*b*) didactic: *Apotheosis*, 'The divinity of Christ', *Hamartigenia*, 'The origin of sin', *Psychomachia*, 'Battle of the Soul' (an allegory), and the *Dittochaeon*, four-line poems on biblical topics; (*c*) polemic: *Contra Symmachum*, 'Against Symmachus', in two books, based on the Altar of Victory controversy in 384 (*see* SYMMACHUS).

Prudentius adapted classical poetic forms and metres to convey the Christian message, introducing into Christian poetry the literary hymn, the allegorical epic, and the Christian ballad. His work profoundly influenced medieval art and Church liturgy as well as poetry.

prytaneion, symbolic centre of the **polis,* housing its communal hearth (*koinē hestia*), eternal flame, and public dining-room where civic hospitality was offered; usually in or off the **agora.* A facility of ancient origin (the Athenian *prytaneion* was allegedly founded by **Theseus), it probably took its name from the post-regal magistracy of the *prytaneis,* with whom it sometimes remained closely linked (e.g. at Ephesus); in Dorian cities its functions could be housed in the offices of the *hierothytai* ('sacrificers'), as on Hellenistic Rhodes and (after *c.*192 BC) at Sparta. The privilege of permanent maintenance (*sitēsis*) in the *prytaneion* was highly honorific and, in Classical times, sparingly conceded; less honorific was the once-only invitation to a meal (*deipnon, xenia*). Excavated *prytaneia* tend to be architecturally modest, as might have been the fare, at least at democratic Athens. *See* HESTIA.

[Athenaeus 4. 137e]

pseudepigraphic literature Antiquity has left us a number of writings which evidence, internal or external, proves not to be the work of the authors whose names are traditionally attached to them. The most frequent cases are of rather late date and connected with the enthusiasm for producing evidence of the doctrine one favoured being of great age. For instance, the numerous Neopythagorean treatises (*see* NEOPYTHAGOR-EANISM) are regularly attached to the names of prominent early Pythagoreans, including **Pythagoras himself, despite the fairly constant tradition that he wrote nothing. The Sibylline oracles (*see* SIBYL) are an outstanding instance of this; Phocylides is the alleged author of a long set of moralizing verses pretty certainly the work of an unknown Jew and of late date. Christian literature has some glaring examples of this practice, notably the Clementine Recognitions and Homilies, most certainly neither by **Clement of Rome nor any contemporary, and the works attributed to **Dionysius the Areopagite, really produced some four centuries after his death. *See also* APOCALYPTIC LITERATURE; HERMES TRISMEGISTUS; PHYSIOLOGUS.

psyche is the Greek term for '*soul', but modern concepts like psychology or psychiatry wrongly suggest that the Greeks viewed the soul in the modern way. In our oldest source, **Homer, we still find a widespread soul system, in which *psyche* was the 'free-soul', which represented the individual personality only when the body was inactive: during swoons or at the moment of death. On the other hand, psychological functions were occupied by 'body-souls', such as *thymos* and *menos.* It is also the *psyche* that leaves for **Hades and the dead are indeed frequently, but not exclusively, called *psychai*; on black-figure vases of *c.*500 BC we can see a little person, sometimes armed, hovering above the dead warrior. Towards the end of the Archaic age two important developments took place. First, **Pythagoras and other philosophers introduced the notion of reincarnation (*see* TRANSMIGRATION). The development is still unexplained, but it certainly meant an upgrading of the soul, which we subsequently find in **Pindar called 'immortal'. However, it would only be in post-Classical times that this notion became popular. Second, *psyche* started to incorporate the *thymos* and thus became the centre of consciousness. This development culminated in the Socratic notion that man had to take care of his *psyche* (*see* SOCRATES). In Greek philosophy, except **Aristotle, care for and cure of the soul now became an important topic of reflection. From the Hellenistic period onwards **Eros is often pictured with a girl and it is attractive to see here a model for **Apuleius' fairy-tale-like story *Amor and Psyche.* Unfortunately, Psyche's ancestry still remains very much obscure.

Ptah, the mummiform Egyptian god primarily of Memphis whom, as a creator-god, patron of craftsmen, the Greeks recognized as *Hephaestus. The great temple at Memphis also contained the enclosure of the *Apis bull and other sacred animals, considered as different embodiments of Ptah. It was here that the Ptolemies were crowned, at least from the reign of Ptolemy V Epiphanes.

Ptoion, sanctuary of *Apollo located in the territory of Acraephnium in Boeotia. The ruins of the *oracle on Mt. Ptoon consist of the remains of a temple, a grotto and spring, and various sacred buildings. Excavations have found rich dedications of Archaic date, especially statuary. The cult dates at least from the 8th cent. BC, and was marked by a male prophet who gave responses in a state of *ecstasy. Apollo was associated with a female goddess or heroine. *Pindar and Herodotus constitute the earliest literary evidence for the origin of the cult. The sanctuary, but not the oracle, flourished until the 3rd cent. AD.

[Pindar, *Paian* 7; Herodotus 8. 135]

Ptolemaeus of Mende, a priest, wrote on the Egyptian kings in three books. He wrote before Apion (first half of the 1st cent. BC), who refers to him. He attributes the Hebrew Exodus under Moses to the time of King Amosis (founder of the 18th dynasty).

Ptolemy (Claudius Ptolemaeus) wrote at Alexandria, between AD 146 and c.170, definitive works in many of the mathematical sciences, including astronomy and geography. His *Apotelesmatika* (*Astrological Influences*) or *Tetrabiblos* (from its four books) was the astrological complement to the astronomical *Almagest*, and although not as dominant, was influential as an attempt to provide a 'scientific' basis for astrological practice (*see* ASTROLOGY). *Karpos* (*Fruit*, Lat. *Centiloquium*), a collection of 100 astrological aphorisms, is spurious. In his *Harmonics*, though in part criticizing the Pythagoreans (*see* PYTHAGORAS AND PYTHAGOREANISM), he extends harmonic analysis to the structures of all perfect beings, especially the *soul and the heavens. Ideas from book 1, modified and abbreviated, survived into the Middle Ages through *Boethius' paraphrase.

Pudicitia, the personification at Rome of women's *chastity and modesty, interestingly identified originally as specific to patrician women until the cult of Pudicitia Patricia in the forum Boarium was challenged (296 BC) by one Virginia, a patrician lady married to a plebeian consul, who established a cult of Pudicitia Plebeia in part of her home. The cult was also exclusive of all but women who had married only once. Livy laments the decline in moral standards of participants in the cult by his time.

[Livy 10. 23. 6–10]

pulvinar, a cushioned couch on which images (or representations, *struppi*, bundles of herbs) of gods were placed at a *lectisternium*, either inside or in front of a temple or *altar (also loosely used to denote a podium or temple). Most but apparently not all gods had *pulvinaria*. Later *pulvinaria* figured among other tokens of divine honours voted by the senate.

[Livy 21. 62. 5, 24. 10. 13; Cicero, *Philippics* 2. 110; Suetonius, *Julius The God* 76; Tacitus, *Annals* 15. 23. 3]

purification, Greek (*katharmos*). The concept of 'purification', like that of *pollution, was applied in very diverse ways in Greek *ritual. Many purifications were performed not in response to specific pollutions, but as preparation for particular events or actions or on a regular calendar basis. The Athenian assembly, for instance, was purified at the start of meetings (by carrying the body of a sacrificed piglet around it), and temples could be treated similarly; individuals purified themselves by washing before approaching the gods. Most drastically, some whole cities of ancient Ionia, not excluding Athens, were purified annually by the expulsion of human scapegoats (*see* PHARMAKOS) at the festival *Thargelia.

There were many different techniques of

purification: by washing or sprinkling, by fumigation (with sulphur above all), by 'rubbing off' with mud or bran; all admitted various degrees of symbolic elaboration (the use of sea-water, or water from a special spring, or even from seven springs, for instance). *Sacrifice too, or modified forms of it, often functioned as a purification: the corpse might be carried around the place to be purified (see above), while the blood supposedly sticking to a killer was 'washed off with blood' by pouring that of the animal victim over his hands. Where actual pollutions are concerned, however, these issues of technique and symbolism are less important than the question of the circumstances in which purification was permitted and deemed effective. Even minor and inescapable pollutions such as contact with a death could not be removed immediately: the major pollution of bloodguilt required a period of exile before the killer could (if at all) be readmitted to the community after purification. (The fullest regulation of degrees of bloodguilt is *Plato's in *Laws*.) Thus the most powerful of all purifying agents was in a sense time.

Purification was related to medicine in two distinct ways. On the one hand, seers professed to be able to cure certain diseases, epilepsy above all, by purifications of religious type. On the other, theories about the need to 'purify' different organs of the body had considerable importance in early Greek scientific medicine. Much though 'scientific' doctors despised purifiers (see Hippocrates, *On the Sacred Disease*), their theories in a sense represent a transposition of traditional religious ideas into a secular key.

Purification was given heightened significance by the other-worldly movements in Greek thought, *Orphism and Pythagoreanism (*see* PYTHAGORAS AND PYTHAGOREANISM). For them, purification signified an escape not just from particular pollutions but from man's fallen condition, his imprisonment in the body. This was a new metaphorical extension of the traditional idea; but adherents of these movements also underwent purifi-

cations and observed abstinences of a more conventional type (*see* FASTING), so that the new 'purification' had a considerable psychological continuity with the old.

The god who presided over purification from blood guilt was *Zeus Catharsios, 'Of purification'; this role derived from his general concern for the reintegration into society of displaced persons (cf. Zeus 'Of suppliants' and 'Of strangers'). *Apollo by contrast was not formally called Catharsios; he could, however, be seen as a 'purifier of men's houses' (in *Aeschylus' words) because his oracle at Delphi (*see* DELPHIC ORACLE) regularly gave advice on such matters. On a more everyday level, similar advice was available to Athenians from publicly-appointed 'exegetes' (*see* EXĒGĒTĒS).

purification, Jewish *See* JUDAISM

purification, Roman *See* LUSTRATION.

Pyanopsia, an Attic festival of *Apollo, celebrated at Athens on the 7th of the month Pyanopsion (i.e. roughly late October). It was probably once a widespread Ionian festival, to judge from the diffusion of the month name Pyanopsion. The attested activities are (1) carrying and dedication of the *eiresiōnē (a branch wound with wool and hung with fruit) (2) preparation—and no doubt dedication and consumption—of a dish of boiled beans and other vegetables and cereals, from which the festival derives its name, 'Bean-boiling'. Like the Oschophoria, celebrated within a few days of it, the Pyanopsia was linked mythologically with the homecoming of *Theseus. *See* ATTIC CULTS AND MYTHS; IONIAN FESTIVALS.

Pygmalion, name (perhaps Phoenician) of two legendary eastern Mediterranean kings: (1) king of Cyprus, father-in-law or grandfather of Cinyras, with whom he shared a devotion to the cult of *Aphrodite-Astarte. It was originally an ivory cult-statue of the goddess for which he conceived a fetishistic passion; but in *Ovid's version the king himself carves the image of his ideal woman, who is then brought to life by Aphrodite, becomes his wife, and bears a daughter, eponym of the town of *Paphos. (2) king of Tyre and brother of Elissa (*Dido), whose husband Sychaeus (or Acherbas) he killed in the hope of seizing his fortune.

[(1) Apollodorus 3. 14. 3; Ovid, *Metamorphoses* 10. 243 ff. (2) Virgil, *Aeneid* 1. 343 ff.]

pygmies, dwarves who live in Africa, India, Scythia, or Thrace. They are usually discussed in Greek mythology in connection with their fight against the cranes. *Homer says that the cranes flee before the winter to the (southern) stream of Oceanus and bring death to the Pygmies. *Hecataeus (1), who located the pygmies in southern Egypt, Ctesias, and the writers on India (e.g. Megasthenes) considerably elaborated the story. Pygmies disguise themselves as rams, or ride on rams and goats. They battle with the cranes to protect their fields (perhaps a reflection of the farmer's life), and conduct operations to destroy the cranes' eggs and young. Other *mythographers invented explanations for the struggle, tracing the enmity to a beautiful pygmy girl transformed into a crane. *Philostratus tells of an unsuccessful pygmy attack on *Heracles after he killed *Antaeus.

The crane fight is often shown in Greek art, first on the François vase c.570, where the pygmies are shown as midgets battling with clubs, hooked sticks, and slings, and riding goats. On later Archaic and Classical vases they become podgy and grotesquely proportioned. Some 4th-cent. vases show them with pelts and poses like giants; like them, they were earth-born (hence their defence of Antaeus). Pygmies appear on Hellenistic drinking cups and, in isolated groups, on gems. In Hellenistic and Roman art, they occur on Campanian wall-paintings as fully armed warriors with no *deformity, and in Nilotic paintings and mosaics deformed, often in humorous confrontations with crocodiles or hippopotami.

[Homer, *Iliad* 3. 3–6; Athenaeus 9. 393e–f; Philostratus, *Eikones* (*Descriptions of pictures*) 2. 22]

Pylaemenes, a minor Iliadic character (*see* HOMER), king of the Paphlagonian Enetoi, fighting on the Trojan side. He is chiefly notorious for appearing alive in book 13, after he has been killed in book 5, a famous inconsistency in ancient criticism.

Pyramus and Thisbe, hero and heroine of a love-story almost unknown except from *Ovid, who says that it is not a common tale. They were next-door neighbours in Babylon, and, as their parents would not let them marry, they talked with each other through the party-wall of the houses, which was cracked. Finally, they arranged to meet at Ninus' tomb. There Thisbe was frightened by a lion coming from its kill; she dropped her cloak as she ran and the lion mouthed it. Pyramus, finding the bloodstained cloak and supposing her dead, killed himself; she returned, found his body, and followed his example. Their blood stained a mulberry-tree, whose fruit has ever since been black when ripe, in sign of mourning for them.

[Ovid, *Metamorphoses* 4. 55 ff.]

Pyrgi, modern Santa Severa, was the main port of the Etruscan city Caere, and famous as the site of a wealthy sanctuary (*see* ETRUSCAN RELIGION) sacked by Dionysius of Syracuse in 384 BC. Excavation (1957 onwards) has revealed two Archaic temples: B (c.500) is a Graeco-Tuscan compromise, and A (c.480–470) is typically Tuscan. Both were destroyed in the 3rd cent. BC. Three inscribed gold tablets were found between the two temples in 1964: one is the only Phoenicio-Punic text known in the Italian peninsula; the other two are in Etruscan. All three concern the dedication of Temple B by the Etruscan ruler of Caere to the Phoenician goddess Astarte (*see* PHOENICIAN RELIGION); they demonstrate the close ties that enabled Carthage to influence the internal politics of the cities of Etruria c.500. A line of small rooms along one wall of the sanctuary is fully contextual with Temple B, and has been connected with sacred prostitution rites of Phoenician type (*see* PROSTITUTION, SACRED); these cubicles could equally well have served as pilgrim shelters.

Pyrrhus *See* NEOPTOLEMUS.

Pythagoras and Pythagoreanism

1. Pythagoras Pythagoras, son of Mnes-archus, one of the most mysterious and influential figures in Greek intellectual history, was born in Samos in the mid-6th cent. BC and migrated to Croton in *c.*530 BC. There he founded the sect or society that bore his name, and that seems to have played an important role in the political life of Magna Graecia for several generations. Pythagoras himself is said to have died as a refugee in Metapontum. Pythagorean political influence is attested well into the 4th cent.

The name of Pythagoras is connected with two parallel traditions, one religious and one scientific. Pythagoras is said to have introduced the doctrine of transmigration of *souls into Greece, and his religious influence is reflected in the cult organization of the Pythagorean society, with periods of initiation, secret doctrines and passwords (*akousmata* and *symbola*), special dietary restrictions, and burial rites. Pythagoras seems to have become a legendary figure in his own lifetime and was identified by some with the *Hyperborean *Apollo. His supernatural status was confirmed by a golden thigh, the gift of bilocation, and the capacity to recall his previous incarnations. Classical authors imagine him studying in Egypt; in the later tradition he gains universal wisdom by travels in the east. Pythagoras becomes the pattern of the 'divine man': at once a sage, a seer, a teacher, and a benefactor of the human race.

The scientific tradition ascribes to Pythagoras a number of important discoveries, including the famous geometric theorem that still bears his name. Even more significant for Pythagorean thought is the discovery of the musical consonances: the ratios $2:1$, $3:2$, and $4:3$ representing the length of strings corresponding to the octave and the basic harmonies (the fifth and the fourth). These ratios are displayed in the *tetractys*, an equilateral triangle composed of 10 dots; the Pythagoreans swore an oath by Pythagoras as author of the *tetractys*. The same ratios are presumably reflected in the music of the spheres, which Pythagoras alone was said to hear.

In the absence of written records before Philolaus in the late 5th cent., it is impossible to tell how much of the Pythagorean tradition in mathematics, music, and astronomy can be traced back to the founder and his early followers. Since the fundamental work of Walter Burkert, it has been generally recognized that the conception of Pythagorean philosophy preserved in later antiquity was the creation of *Plato and his school, and that the only reliable pre-Platonic account of Pythagorean thought is the system of Philolaus. *Aristotle reports that for the Pythagoreans all things are numbers or imitate numbers. In Philolaus we read that it is by number and proportion that the world becomes organized and knowable. The basic principles are the Unlimited (*apeira*) and the Limiting (*perainonta*). The generation of the numbers, beginning with One in the centre, seems to coincide with the structuring of the cosmos. There must be enough cosmic bodies to correspond to the perfect number 10; the earth is a kind of heavenly body, revolving around an invisible central fire. This fact permitted Copernicus to name 'Philolaus the Pythagorean' as one of his predecessors.

Plato was deeply influenced by the Pythagorean tradition in his judgement myths, in his conception of the soul as transcending the body, and in the mathematical interpretation of nature. The *Phaedo* and the *Timaeus*, respectively, became the classical formulations for the religious and cosmological aspects of the Pythagorean world view. In the *Philebus* (16c) begins the transformation of Pythagoras into the archetype of philosophy. This view is developed by Speusippus, who replaces Plato's Forms by Pythagorean numbers. Hence Theophrastus can assign to Pythagoras the late Platonic 'unwritten doctrines' of the One and the Infinite Dyad, and these two principles appear in all later versions of Pythagorean philosophy.

In the 1st cent. BC, Publius *Nigidius Figulus revived the Pythagorean tradition in Rome, while in Alexandria the Platonist Eudorus attributed to the Pythagoreans a supreme One, above the two older principles of One and Dyad. This monistic Platonism was developed by the Neopythagoreans (see NEOPYTHAGOREANISM). Their innovations were absorbed into the great Neoplatonic synthesis of *Plotinus, and thereafter no distinction can be drawn between Pythagoreans and Neoplatonists. Porphyry and Iamblichus both composed lives of Pythagoras in which he is represented as the source of Platonic philosophy.

There is an important *pseudepigraphic literature of texts ascribed to Pythagoras, Archytas, and other members of the school. This begins in the 3rd cent. BC and continues down to Byzantine times. A number of these texts have survived, thanks to the prestige of their supposed authors.

2. Pythagoreanism (Religious Aspects)

Pythagoreanism is the name given to the philosophical and religious movement(s) allegedly derived from the teachings of Pythagoras. Reliable tradition on the early form of Pythagoreanism, coming chiefly from *Aristotle and his school, presents Pythagoras and his followers as a religious and political association in southern Italy (chiefly Croton) where they gained considerable political influence, until their power was broken in a catastrophe in about 450 BC. From then on, Pythagoreanism survived in two distinct forms, a scientific, philosophical form (the so-called *mathēmatikoi*) which in the 4th cent. manifested itself in the thinking of Philolaus and Archytas of Tarentum and the Pythagoreans whom Plato knew and followed, and a religious, sectarian form (*akousmatikoi*, those following certain oral teachings, *akousmata* or *symbola*) which manifested itself in the migrant Pythagoristai of Middle Comedy. After the analysis of Walter Burkert, it is universally recognized that scientific Pythagoreanism is a reform of its earlier, religious way ascribed to Hippasus of Metapontum around 450 BC.

Despite the fact that many pseudepigraphical Pythagorean writings are dated to Hellenistic times, the continuity of any form of Pythagoreanism after the Classical age is disputed. Neopythagoreanism existed at any rate in the late Hellenistic (the Roman Publius Nigidius Figulus, founder of Neoplatonism according to Cicero) and early imperial epochs (*Apollonius of Tyana); through the alleged derivation of Pompilius *Numa's teaching from that of Pythagoras, it gained popularity in Rome. It continued into the related Neoplatonist movement (see NEOPLATONISM); prominent Neoplatonists such as *Porphyry and his pupil *Iamblichus wrote on Pythagoreanism. The hexametrical collection of life rules, under the title Golden Words, ascribed to Pythagoras himself, appears at the same date.

While among the philosophical disciplines of the mathematici, arithmetic, theory of number and music are prominent and influential, the doctrines of the *akousmatikoi* laid down rules for a distinctive life style, the "Pythagorean life". The originally oral *akousmata*, collected by later authors, contained unrelated and often strange answers to the questions 'What exists?', 'What is the best thing?', 'What should one do?' Prominent among the rules of life is a complicated (and in our sources not consistent) vegetarianism, based on the doctrine of *transmigration and already ascribed to Pythagoras himself during his life-time by *Xenophanes; total vegetarianism excludes participation in sacrifice and marginalizes those who profess it, at the same time all the more efficiently binding them together in their own sectarian group. Transmigration and, more generally, an interest in the afterlife connects Pythagoreanism with Orphism; Plato associates vegetarianism with the Orphic life-style, and authors from about 400 BC onwards name Pythagoreans as authors of certain Orphic texts.

See ORPHIC LITERATURE; ORPHISM.

[Ovid, *Metamorphoses* 15. 60–496; Iamblichus, *On the Pythagorean Life*]

Pythia *See* DELPHIC ORACLE; WOMEN IN CULT.

Pythian Games Originally the Pythian festival at *Delphi took place every eight years, and there was a single contest, the singing of a hymn to *Apollo accompanied by the cithara. After the First Sacred War (early 6th cent.) the festival was reorganized under the control of the *amphictiony, and further musical and athletic contests (*see* AGŌNES) were added. These games were next in importance to the *Olympian Games, and were held quadrennially in late August of the third year in each Olympiad. The Pythiads were reckoned from 582 BC. The musical contests consisted in singing to the cithara (lyre), cithara-playing, and flute-playing, and the athletic contests resembled those at Olympia. The horse races were always held below Delphi in the plain of Crisa. The stadium lies above the sanctuary under Mt. *Parnassus, and the gymnasium and palaestra are near the temple of *Athena Pronaia. The prize was a crown of bay leaves cut in the Valley of Tempe.

quindecimviri sacris faciundis, one of the four major colleges (*see* COLLEGIUM) of the Roman priesthood (*see* PRIESTS). The size of the college increased gradually, starting at two (*duoviri*), reaching ten (*decemviri*) in 367 BC, fifteen, and finally sixteen (though the name remained *quindecimviri*) in the late republic. Like the other colleges, they lost the right to select their own members through the *lex Domitia* of 104 BC, but continued to be recruited by popular election from the noblest families. Their main functions throughout their history were to guard the Sibylline books (Greek oracles, dating supposedly from the reign of King Tarquin (*Tarquinius Superbus), and consisting for the most part of ritual texts, not prophetic utterances; *see* SIBYL); to consult the books when asked to do so by the senate, particularly in response to prodigies (*see* PORTENTS) or other disasters; and to provide the appropriate religious remedies derived from them. Their recommendations led to the importation, from the 5th cent. BC onwards and especially in the 3rd, of Greek cults and rituals, over which they maintained at least some oversight. They reached particular prominence in the early empire as the responsible authorities for the *Secular Games, radically reconstructed from the republican series to suit the new regime's ideas.

Quinquatrus, Roman festival on 19 March

which opened the army's new campaign season. It was later connected with Minerva. [Ovid, *Fasti* 3. 809 ff.]

Quirinus, a Roman god claimed as Sabine in origin by the ancients. Except that his functions resembled those of *Mars and that he had sacred arms, we know little of him; he regularly forms a third with *Jupiter and Mars; his *flamen* (*see* FLAMINES) is the lowest of the three *flamines maiores* and the third *spolia opima* belong to him. His *flamen*'s activities are known only in the service of other deities. His festival is on 17 February; his cult-partner is Hora, of whom nothing is known. He may first have appeared as a local deity of a community on the Quirinal hill, but the most plausible etymology is still the suggestion that the name was originally *co-uirium*, 'assembly of the men', hence also *Quirites*. His function is much debated. Even if he is sometimes identified as Mars, or as the god of the first furrow, a founder assimilated to *Romulus, the most satisfying solution is to see him as a sort of peaceful 'double' of Mars, a god of the 'organized social totality', with its activities both political and military. From the 3rd cent. BC on, he was assimilated to Romulus.

[Livy 8. 9. 6; Ovid, *Fasti* 2. 475 ff, 4. 910; Aulus Gellius 7. 77. 7, 13. 23. 2]

Qumran *See* DEAD SEA SCROLLS.

rabbis The Hebrew term 'rabbi' which means 'my master', was a term of respect among Jews which by late Hellenistic times seems to have been particularly applied to religious teachers. According to the Gospels, Jesus was called 'rabbi' by some who addressed him. The term is also found in Greek transliteration on epitaphs from the late Roman period. But after AD 70 its main use was with reference to the religious authorities whose sayings are found in the *Mishnah and *Talmuds and who came to dominate Judaism by the end of antiquity.

Later rabbinic tradition attributes the foundation of rabbinic Judaism to the efforts of Yohanan ben Zakkai and a few colleagues in their academy at Jamnia (Yavneh) in Judaea after the destruction of the Jerusalem Temple in AD 70. Rabbis taught primarily in Judaea from AD 70 to the *Bar Kokhba war (AD 132–5), and mostly in Galilee from AD 135 to c.200. In the following centuries smaller centres of rabbinic activity were found elsewhere in Palestine, especially Caesarea and southern Judaea, but the main competition to the Galilean schools was from those in Babylonia, which was under Sasanian control. Evidence for rabbis teaching in any of the Jewish diaspora communities within the Roman empire is sparse.

Rabbinic Judaism differed from earlier forms of Judaism primarily in its emphasis on study as a form of worship. The rabbis of late antiquity evolved a complex legal structure, based on the Hebrew bible and shaping both religious and secular aspects of Jewish life. Legislation evolved partly through *midrash on scriptural passages, partly through sophisticated forms of logical argument similar to those used in contemporary Greek rhetoric.

The stages of development of rabbinic law can be traced from one generation to the next only with difficulty. The evidence is complicated by occasional pseudepigraphic attributions and by the rabbis' assumption that the law is unchanging, and that the views of each sage were therefore implicit in the sayings of his predecessors. Particular concerns of the rabbis in the late 1st and the 2nd cents. AD according to the extant evidence were the rules for sacrifices in the Jerusalem Temple (already a theoretical topic, since it had been destroyed in AD 70), the sources of pollution, and the correct tithing of agricultural produce. These interests coincide with those of the *Pharisees before AD 70 according to some sources. It is thus reasonable to assume that the rabbis may have continued some of the traditions of Pharisaism, especially since figures revered in the rabbinic sources from the family of Hillel, such as Rabban Gamaliel, are described in other sources as Pharisees. However, it is noteworthy that the rabbis never called themselves Pharisees, preferring the self-designation '*hakham*' ('sage'). Whatever the precise relationship between Pharisaism and rabbinic Judaism, it is highly likely that the developed rabbinic theology found in the Talmud differed greatly from the teachings of the Pharisees three or four centuries previously.

The extent of rabbinic control over the Jews of late antiquity is debated. The rabbis assumed that they spoke for all Israel, but they themselves sometimes referred to Jews who did not follow their teachings. One important factor in the eventual supremacy of rabbinic Judaism may have been the rabbis' control of the calendar, an important matter in a religion with a strong sense of sacred time.

Another factor was the role of the patriarch (*nasi*) in Palestine. Confined almost exclusively to the wealthy descendants of the 1st-cent. AD sage Hillel, this post was accorded great prestige within rabbinic circles, although political disagreements between sages and patriarch are also recorded. Judah haNasi, patriarch at the end of the 2nd cent., was the compiler of the Mishnah. By the late 4th cent., if not before, the patriarch was recognized by the Roman state as the main representative of Jews throughout the Roman empire and granted the status of an honorary praetorian prefect. The patriarchate came to an end in AD 429. *See* JEWS; JUDAISM.

Rea Silvia *See* ROMULUS AND REMUS.

Regia, traditionally the home of King *Numa was situated at the east end of the *forum Romanum, between the *via Sacra and the precinct of *Vesta. Under the Republic it was the seat of authority of the *pontifex maximus* and contained his archives (*see* PONTIFEX/PONTIFICES); also shrines dedicated to *Mars (which held the sacred shields carried in procession by the *Salii) and to *Ops Consiva. Excavations in the 1960s revealed that archaic huts on the site were in the late 7th cent. replaced by a stone building around a courtyard, recalling the palaces of Etruria. Rebuilt several times, the structure took on its definitive plan at the end of the 6th cent.; this was then preserved throughout antiquity, despite several reconstructions, notably in the 3rd cent. and again in 148 BC. Following a fire in 36 BC, the Regia was rebuilt in marble, once again on the traditional plan.

Regifugium, Roman festival falling on 24 February, associated with the expulsion of the kings (*reges*). Of unclear origins: its calendar note *Q(uando) R(ex) C(omitiavit) F(as)* ('when the king sacrificed in the *comitium*') was misunderstood in antiquity as *Q(uod) R(ex) C(omitio) F(ugerit)* ('that the king fled the *comitium*'). When there was an intercalary month, it fell six days before the March Kalends.

[Ovid, *Fasti* 2. 685–856, 5. 727–8; Plutarch, *Roman Questions* 63]

relics, the remains (complete or partial) or property of a dead person (real or fictional) which were imbued with the power to benefit their possessor. Inevitably, the veneration of relics in ancient Greece occurs within the context of *hero-cult.

There are numerous examples of relics, which fall into three main categories: first, those put into a certain place on purpose and subsequently worshipped there; second, those brought from one place to another for worship at the latter; third, those found by chance, given an identity, and venerated.

Examples of the first group are (*a*) oikists' tombs (*see* FOUNDERS, CITY), (*b*) the tombs of fallen warriors (e.g. the fallen at Plataea; Glaucus at Thasos); in the second group belong (*a*) the bones of *Orestes brought to Sparta from *Tegea, (*b*) those of *Melanippus to Sicyon from Thebes, (*c*) those of *Theseus from Scyros to Athens; of the third (*a*) the so-called tombs of the *Seven against Thebes at *Eleusis (these were probably the Bronze Age tombs disturbed in the Geometric period, walled in and venerated), (*b*) the 'sceptre of *Agamemnon' found near Chaeronea.

The practice goes back at least to the Geometric period, persisted throughout antiquity, and has survived within the Catholic and Orthodox churches.

[Plutarch, *Aristides* 21. 3–6, *Theseus* 36. 1–4; Herodotus 1. 67–8, 5. 67; 2. 22. 2–3 (Tantalus); 8. 9. 3, 8. 36. 8 (Arcas); 9. 40. 11–12 (sceptre)]

Remus *See* ROMULUS AND REMUS.

revenge *See* CURSES; ERINYES; NEMESIS.

rex, the Latin word for king, has an Indo-European root which is found also in Celtic and Indo-Iranian languages. Traditionally Rome itself was ruled by kings during its earliest history, but curiously the literary sources are reticent about kingship among other Italic peoples, including the Latins. Apart from a few isolated examples such as king Acron of Caenina (*see* SPOLIA OPIMA), early Latin kings are rare in the sources, which tend to suggest that the Latin cities were ruled by aristocracies, even during the Roman monarchy. By contrast kings are much better attested among the Etruscans. *Rex* is however found as a priestly title at *Aricia, where the priesthood of *Diana was held by the *rex nemorensis* ('king of the wood'), a runaway slave who had killed his predecessor in single combat and held office for as long as he could defend himself against aspiring successors. At Rome too there was a priest known as the *rex sacrorum* (or *rex sacrificulus*), who in the Republic was confined to minor ritual duties connected with the calendar, but was believed once to have been the most important figure in the priestly hierarchy. The traditional explanation of the *rex sacrorum* is that he was a priest created at the beginning of the Republic to carry out the religious tasks previously performed by the real king. If this is correct the office of the *rex sacrorum* can be added to the list of relics of monarchy that survived into the Republic (e.g. the *interrex*, the *Regia).

That early Rome was ruled by kings is virtually certain, even if none of the traditional kings has yet been authenticated by direct testimony such as a contemporary inscription (*see* ROME, MYTHS OF). There were supposedly seven kings, whose reigns spanned nearly 250 years, from the founding of the city to the expulsion of Tarquinius Superbus. This is far too long, and there are other reasons too for doubting the chronology of the regal period (*see* TARQUINIUS SUPERBUS) and for treating the traditional list of kings as an artificial construct. Alter-native traditions preserved the names of kings (*see* TATIUS, TITUS), who were not included among the famous seven, and of these latter the first, *Romulus, is clearly no more than a legendary figure who gave his name to Rome. Of the others, who may be authentic, one (Tullus *Hostilius) was Latin, two (*Numa Pompilius, Ancus *Marcius) were Sabine, and two (the Tarquins) were Etruscan (*see* TARQUINIUS PRISCUS and SUPERBUS). The origin of Servius *Tullius was disputed.

According to tradition the Roman monarchy was not hereditary but elective. Under the regular procedure the patricians nominated the king through tenure of the office of *interrex*, but their choice had to be ratified by a vote of a special assembly and by favourable signs from the gods at an inauguration ceremony. It is noteworthy that none of the traditional kings was a patrician; most of them were in some sense outsiders, some indeed foreigners. This feature, which has many parallels in other historical monarchies, should not be dismissed as fictitious, nor should it be assumed that the accession of an Etruscan (Tarquinius Priscus) occurred because Rome had been the victim of an Etruscan conquest. The last two kings, Servius Tullius and Tarquinius Superbus, are presented in the sources as usurpers who adopted a tyrannical style of rule. This is quite possibly historical, given the close contacts between Rome and the Greek world in the 6th cent. BC.

The powers of the king cannot be reconstructed in detail. The accounts of the sources presuppose that the king's power was enshrined in the concept of *imperium*, which was taken over by the magistrates of the republic. It is probable enough that the trappings of power, which symbolized the absolute authority of the holder of *imperium*, go back to the time of the kings; they include the *fasces*, purple robes, and the *sella curulis*, which were supposedly borrowed from the Etruscans. The ceremony of the *triumph, in which the victorious general bore all the regal insignia, was probably also a relic of the monarchy (it too was of Etruscan origin). It seems likely that the king commanded in war and exercised supreme jurisdiction; on the other hand he probably had to work with an advisory council (the senate) and a popular assembly (the *comitia curiata*), both of which seem to have existed in the regal period.

The religious authority of the kings is more problematic. Even if the king, and his Republican surrogate, the *rex sacrorum*, held the highest priestly position, tradition also traces other major priesthoods, such as the pontiffs and the augurs (*see* PRIESTS; PONTIFEX/PONTIFICES; AUGURES), back to the regal period. This must imply that the king did not have a monopoly of priestly authority. Conflict between king and priest is clearly evident in the story of Tarquin the Elder and the augur Attus Navius.

On the other hand, a well-known theory maintains that the king retained his religious authority longer than his other powers, and that the *rex sacrorum* of the Republic was in fact the real king who had been gradually reduced to a purely ceremonial figure by a gradual process of change during the Archaic period. On this view the king's military and judicial powers were taken over by a secular magistrate, either an annual dictator or *magister populi*, or by a supreme *praetor maximus*. Only at a secondary stage, variously dated to *c*.450 or even 367 BC, did the Romans institute the collegiate office of two equal consuls. The traditional story, however, which most scholars are inclined to accept in broad outline, is that at the end of the 6th cent. the last king was expelled by a group of aristocrats, who set up a republic under two annually elected consuls.

[Livy 1; Dionysius of Halicarnassus, *Roman Antiquities* 3. 70–1; Cicero, *On Divination* 1. 31–2]

rex nemorensis, the 'king of the grove', i.e. *Diana's grove near *Aricia, in central Italy. This priest was unique among religious officials of the Roman world, in being an escaped slave who acquired office by killing his predecessor, after issuing a challenge by plucking a branch from a particular tree in the grove. The 'mystery' of the priest of Nemi is the starting point of J. G. Frazer's *The Golden Bough*.

[Ovid, *Art of love* 1. 259–60; Strabo 5. 3. 12, 239; Suetonius, *Caligula* 35]

rex sacrorum On the expulsion of the kings from Rome (*see* REX; TARQUINIUS SUPERBUS) their sacral functions were partially assumed by a priest called *rex sacrorum* 'the king for sacred rites' (and his wife, the *regina*, 'queen'). He sacrificed on the Kalends; on the Nones he announced the days of *festivals, *feriae*; and he celebrated the rite of *Regifugium. A patrician, born of a particular form of marriage, he ranked first among the priests, but was subordinate to the *pontifex maximus* (*see* PONTIFEX/PONTIFICES). He served for life, and might hold no other post.

[Dionysius of Halicarnassus, *Roman Antiquities* 4. 74. 4; Ovid, *Fasti* 1. 333–4, 2. 20–2; Plutarch, *Roman Questions* 63]

Rhadamanthys, in mythology usually the son of *Zeus and *Europa, although an obscure tradition gives the genealogy Cres (*eponymous hero of *Crete)–*Talos(1)–*Hephaestus–Rhadamanthys. He did not die but went to *Elysium, where the most blessed mortals live in bliss. There he is a ruler and judge. He is universally renowned for his wisdom and justice, and is one of the judges of the dead in the underworld, along with his brother *Minos and *Aeacus. In *Virgil he presides over *Tartarus and punishes the wicked for their sins. It is sometimes said that he married *Alcmene after the death of *Amphitryon and lived in exile at Ocaleae in Boeotia.

[Diodorus Siculus 5. 84; Apollodorus 2. 4. 11, 3. 1. 1, 3. 1. 2; Pindar, *Olympian* 2. 75 ff.; *Pythian* 2. 73 f.; Virgil, *Aeneid* 6. 566]

Rhamnus, a community of moderate size on the north-east coast of Attica, overlooking the narrow waters to Euboea. A road lined with a series of monumental tombs runs inland from the acropolis to the *sanctuary of *Nemesis with its two 5th-cent. temples. The late 5th-cent. temple of Nemesis is relatively well preserved, and it has been possible to reconstruct its upper portion and a large part of the famous cult *statue, with its base.

[Pausanias 1. 32. 2–8; Pliny, *Natural History* 36. 17]

rhapsodes were professional reciters of poetry, particularly of *Homer but also of other poets. The name, which means 'song-stitcher', is first attested in the 5th cent., but implies the formulaic compositional technique of earlier minstrels. Originally reciters of *epic accompanied themselves on the lyre, but later they carried a staff instead. Both are shown on vases; *Plato distinguishes rhapsodes from citharodes, but classes Homer's Phemius as a rhapsode. In the 5th and 4th cents. rhapsodes were a familiar sight, especially at public festivals and games, where they competed for prizes. They declaimed from a dais, and hoped to attract a crowd by their conspicuous attire and loud melodious voice. They would be likely to own texts of Homer, but recited from memory. They were carefully trained, and preserved a traditional pronunciation of Homer down to Alexandrian times, probably under the influence of the Homeridae, who were looked up to as authorities and arbiters. A good rhapsode might be filled with emotion while reciting, and communicate it to his audience, and there was felt to be a kinship between him and the actor; but he is not to be confused with the 'Homerist', the low-class actor of Homeric scenes who was later popular. Though despised as stupid by the educated and a byword for unreliability, rhapsodes continued to practise their art and compete at games at least down to the 3rd cent. AD.

[Plato, *Ion*; Xenophon, *Memorabilia* 4. 2. 10, *Symposium* 3. 6; Athenaeus 14. 620]

Rhea, in mythology, a *Titan, daughter of *Uranus and *Gaia (Earth). She married *Cronus, and bore him six children. Cronus ate the first five at birth, but Rhea managed to give birth safely to the last, *Zeus, on Crete; Zeus (as prophesied by Gaia) then overthrew Cronus. In an Arcadian legend (*see* ARCADIAN MYTHS AND CULTS), Poseidon was saved at birth by Rhea, who put him among a flock of sheep, told Cronus that she had given birth to a horse and got him to swallow a foal.

[Homer, *Iliad* 14. 200–4, 15. 187–8; Hesiod, *Theogony* 132–6, 453–506; Apollodorus 1. 1. 3–7; Pausanias 8. 8. 2–3, 8. 36. 2–3, 8. 41. 2, 9. 2. 7, 9. 41. 6]

Rhea Silvia *See* ROMULUS AND REMUS.

Rhesus, a Thracian ally of *Priam. The *Iliad* (a post-Homeric addition) tells how *Odysseus and *Diomedes (2), learning of his arrival before Troy from the Trojan spy Dolon, stole into his camp, killed him and twelve of his men, and carried off his magnificent horses. Other authors told of a prophecy that, if his horses had fed or drunk at Troy, the city could not have fallen, or alternatively credited him with some fighting at Troy before his death. The story is also the subject of the *Rhesus* attributed to *Euripides. While the *Iliad* makes Rhesus the son of Eïoneus, the play makes him the son of the river Strymon and a Muse (*see* MUSES). The Muse appears with his body at the end, and declares that he will live on as a demigod.

[Homer, *Iliad* 10; Euripides, *Rhesus*; Virgil, *Aeneid* 1. 469–73]

Rhodes, cults and myths The island was sacred to *Helios who claimed it before it rose from beneath the sea. He had seven sons (Haliadae) with the *nymph Rhodos (who gave her name to the island), and three grandsons, the eponymous heroes (*see* EPONYMOI) of the chief Rhodian cities Camirus, Ialysus, and Lindus. The brilliant panhellenic Halieia were celebrated quinquennially with great pomp and games. Expensive gifts to the god included the the Colossus of Rhodes, one of the seven wonders of the ancient world, and every year a *quadriga* (chariot), horses and all (with which the god circled the world), was thrown into the sea in his honour. The festival replaced the Tlapolemeia of the founding hero and son of *Heracles, whose myth records the island's Dorian settlement. Heracles Bouthoinas had a cult at Lindus with curious rites resembling the *Attic Bouphonia. The Sminthia at Lindus celebrated *Apollo 'mouse killer', well known in that function, and *Dionysus, as destroyers of mice which attacked the vines.

On Mt. Atabyris bronze bull votives were offered to *Zeus. The animals were said to bellow when evil befell Rhodes. The mountain cult and legend connect Zeus Atabyrius with Crete, but *Athena Lindia's cult was older, possibly Mycenaean. In legend the Danaides (see DANAUS AND THE DANAIDS) founded her sanctuary during their flight to Argos. The goddess received unburnt sacrifice, because the Haliadae forgot to bring fire when they came to pay their respects. In Hellenistic times Egyptian cults, notably of *Sarapis and *Isis, were imported to Rhodes and Lindus.

[Pindar, *Olympian* 7; Herodotus 2. 182; Athenaeus 445A–B, 561F; Xenophon of Ephesus 5. 11; Lactantius, *Divine Institutes* 1. 21. 31]

rider-gods and heroes The representation of a deity on horseback is relatively rare in the central areas of the Graeco-Roman world. The best example is provided by the *Dioscuri. Rider-gods, albeit with varying regional characteristics are more frequent around the periphery, in Hellenistic-Roman Egypt, Syria, Asia Minor, and north Africa.

Rider-gods were extremely popular in the Eastern Balkans, where they often appeared as a hunter on horseback. This kind of votive monument is known as *Thracian Rider* and is not to be confused with the *Danubian Rider*— mostly votive tablets of smaller format. The latter belongs to a mystery cult with Mithraic elements found in the lower and middle Danube area in the 2nd and 3rd cents. AD. The central figure of a goddess is flanked by one or two riders. An example of the rider-god from the Rhine area is the Jupiter-rider.

Common features are difficult to distinguish, but it seems that rider-gods frequently fulfilled the function of helper and saviour. Finally, cult-heroes, too, were represented as riders or in connection with horses. The depiction of the deceased as a hero on horseback was especially popular. In the Thracian area these representations were assimilated to the figures of the *Thracian Rider*. Hence they seem to suggest deification of the person thus depicted. *See* THRACIAN RELIGION.

rites of passage is the term first used by A. van Gennep in his classic study *The Rites of Passage* (1909) for mainly those rituals which dramatize passages in the life-cycle and the calendar. According to Van Gennep, these rites were characterized by a separation from the old status, a liminal phase 'betwixt and between', and the incorporation into the new condition. More importantly, an analysis of these rituals shows which transitions were deemed important, which parts of these transitions, which symbols were used, and what they signify.

The main passages in the ancient life cycle were birth, *initiation, *marriage and death (*see* DEAD, DISPOSAL OF), although in Rome initiation must have been abolished at a relatively early period because only traces of these institutions have survived. It is much harder to see which parts of the transitions received attention in which periods. Whereas on Attic black-figure vases of the late Archaic Age the public procession of the couple to the bridegroom's home received all attention, the red-figure vases focused on the relationship of bride and groom: a nice illustration of a shift in attention from public to private. Unfortunately, our information about the rites is usually so fragmentary that development within these (as in other) rites is often hard to document.

Important symbols in the transitions were bathing or washing, change of clothes and hairstyle, and the use of *crowns. It is important to look at the timing and the shape of the symbol: the occurrence of a particular haircut; black or white clothes; crowns of fertile or fruitless plants. It is only the combination of symbols which gives meaning, not the individual symbols: both the dead and grooms wear white clothes, but they have different crowns. And when the Greek dead wear crowns but the mourners do not, it is the contrast which supplies meaning, not the crown itself.

Regarding the *calendar, the most important change was the transition from Old to New Year, which took place via one or more festivals: the break was felt to be too big to take place in just one day as in modern times. In Athens, the typical New Year month was inaugurated by the Cronia, the scene of role reversals between masters and slaves, and only then came the Synoikia, the commemoration of the foundation of Athens. The Roman first month was preceded by the sombre month of February, the month of purification (*februare* means 'to purify'); *see* LUSTRATION. In other words, for a right understanding of the calendar we have to analyse carefully the meaning and mood of the various festivals and not look at them in isolation.

ritual Both definition and interpretation of ritual are highly debated among social scientists. On a minimal definition (at least in the context of Greek and Roman cultures), ritual could be seen as symbolic activity in a religious context. A ritual (or ceremony) is composed of several single acts, the rites. Ritual is an activity whose imminent practical aim has become secondary, replaced by the aim of communication; this does not preclude ritual from having other, less immediate practical goals. Form and meaning of ritual are determined by tradition; they are malleable according to the needs of any present situation, as long as the performers understand them as being traditional. As to interpretation, in an era where often loosely associated Frazerian meanings dominated the field, the seminal work of A. van Gennep (1909; see the preceding entry) made it clear

that rituals with seemingly widely different goals have common structures; this developed the insight, deepened by structuralism, that in ritual, structures are prior to meaning. French sociology (E. Durkheim) and British social anthropology (E. E. Evans-Pritchard) saw society as the main frame of reference for the interpretation of ritual meaning; V. Turner analysed the anti-structural aspects of Van Gennepian ritual. Insights from social anthropology have been applied to classical studies by a variety of scholars. *See* ANTHROPOLOGY AND THE CLASSICS.

The study of ritual in Greek and Roman religion, as in most religions of the past, is hampered by lack of sufficient data. Social anthropology developed its interpretative models with societies where the rituals are documented in all their details, both the ordinary and the uncommon ceremonies and rites. Ancient sources, local historians and antiquarians, as well as sacred laws, recorded only the exceptional and aberrant rituals, not the familiar and ordinary ones which were part of daily life; and because they recorded only the salient features, entire scenarios are very rare. Further, instruction in the correct performance of ritual was part of an oral tradition, from generation to generation or from priest to priest, esp. in the Greek sacerdotal lineages like the Eumolpidae in *Eleusis or the Iamidae in *Olympia (*see* EUMOLPUS; IAMUS), or in the *collegia* (*see* COLLEGIUM) in Rome. (*See* PRIESTS.) Elaborate ritual texts such as those known from near-eastern, notably Hittite sources, are therefore absent in Greece and Rome. The exception, the Greek magical papyri, confirm the rule; magical rituals were transmitted in books from one practitioner to another one because these individual practices lacked any organizational form. But the magical papyri, combining different religious traditions, are of only limited value for a study of Greek and Roman ritual; *see* MAGIC.

Neither Greek nor Roman cultures analysed ritual as a specific category of religious activity. In Greek, the closest equivalent is *teletē*, but this term tended to be used in a much narrower sense for specific rituals of an exceptional nature, like those of the mystery cults; other terms, as the frequent *hiera*, 'sacred things', or (*theon*) *therapeia*, 'service (of the gods)', are much wider; a term often used in Attic texts, *ta nomizomena*, 'what is customary', underscores the importance of tradition. In Rome, the closest equivalents are *caerimonia* and *ritus*; both, however, rather mean subjectively the 'manner of a religious (or profane) observance'. *See* GREEK RELIGION, TERMS RELATING TO, and ROMAN RELIGION, TERMS RELATING TO.

In modern discussions of ancient ritual, the dichotomy Olympian (*see* GREEK RELIGION) versus *chthonian often plays an important role: rituals destined for Olympian gods would be categorically distinguished from those of chthonian gods or heroes. This dichotomy is the product of late antique scholarship, not of observation of religious usage; it might have some explicatory value in late antiquity, much less for the Archaic and Classical epochs.

The central rite of Greek and Roman religion is animal *sacrifice. Whatever the theories about its origin, Greek and Roman analysis understood it as a gift to the gods; the myth of its institution by the trickster *Prometheus explained less its function as communication between man and god than the deficiency of something which should have been a nourishing gift from man to god. Beyond this indigenous interpretation, ordinary animal sacrifice with its ensuing meal repeated and reinforced the structure of society and was used to express the societal values; changes of ritual reflected changes in values. Specific significations went together with specific forms of the ritual: the change from ordinary sheep or goat sacrifice to extraordinary sacrifice of bovines expressed a heightening of expense, festivity, and social status (religious reformers exposed the fundamental lack of moral values in such a differentiation); more specific animals were used for specific deities,

chiefly as a function of their relationship to the central civic values (dog sacrifice to Enyalius (*see* ARES), *Hecate, or *Robigus). Holocaust sacrifice, which destroyed the entire animal, was offered in marginal contexts, but not only with extraordinary animals. *See* ANIMALS IN CULT.

Besides animal sacrifice, there existed different kinds of bloodless sacrifice. A common gift was the cake (*see* CAKES), in specific forms which again were determined by the character of the divinity and its position in society. Other sacrifices comprised fruits or grains, often mixed and even cooked as a specific ritual dish (*kykeōn* in Eleusis, 'hot-pot' of *Pyanopsia or *Thargelia, *puls* in Rome), as a function of the specific value of the festival. *Libation was used combined with animal sacrifice, but also as a ritual of its own. Again, the use of different liquids was determined by the function of the ritual; the main opposition was between mixed wine, the ordinary libation liquid as it was the ordinary drink, and unmixed *wine, *milk, *water, oil (*see* OLIVE), or *honey. Already post-Aristotelian postcultural theory explained many of the substances as survivals from an earlier period without wine libations and animal sacrifice (see *Porphyry, *On Abstinence*).

Another important group are purificatory rituals (*see* PURIFICATION; LUSTRATION). Their aim is to remove *pollution, either on a regular basis, as in the ritual of the *pharmakos* of the Greek Thargelia or in the festivals of the Roman month Februarius which derived its name from *februa*, a twig bundle used in purificatory rites, or in specific cases, to heal misfortune caused by pollution, as in the rites to cure epilepsy (see pseudo-Hippocrates, *On the Sacred Disease*); or in the many rites instituted by oracles to avert a plague. Cathartic rituals precede any new beginning; therefore, they belong to New Year cycles (Februarius precedes the new beginning of the Kalends of March) or initiatory rites. The forms of apotropaic rituals vary from ritual washing to holocaust sacrifices, and many forms used are not specific to cathartic rituals. A common idea, though, is to identify the pollution with an object and then to destroy it, by either burning it entirely (holocaust sacrifice of pigs) or expelling it (*pharmakos*; cure of epilepsy, where the *katharmata*, the unclean substances, are carried beyond the borders of the community).

A further group of rituals which has attracted scholarly interest is *initiation rituals, or rather rituals which can be seen as transformation from rituals which, in a hypothetical earlier phase of Greek or Roman society, fulfilled the function tribal initiation fulfils in ethnological societies; in them, the Van Gennepian tripartite structure is particularly visible (*see* RITES OF PASSAGE). In historical Greece, the possible transformations were many. One group of rituals retains the function of introducing the young generation into the community; beside the rituals in the archaic Spartan and Cretan societies, the institution of the *ephēbeia* belongs to this group. Other rituals concentrate upon a few elected members, like the Arrephori in the cult of the Athenian Athena (*see* ARREPHORIA), or the Roman *Salii where some rites preserve traces of their respective practical functions, namely to initiate women into weaving as the main female technology, or to initiate young men into armed dancing as training for hoplite combat. A specific group of rituals whose roots, at least partly, lie in initiation, are the *mystery cults of Eleusis, *Samothrace, and the Theban and Lemnian *Cabiri; here, earlier initiation into a family group or a secret society has been transformed into a panhellenic ritual by emphasizing and elaborating the anti-structural aspect. See also previous entry.

The social function of ritual was used by Hellenistic kings and Roman emperors alike to legitimate and base their rule on a religious foundation; in ruler cult, traditional forms like sacrifice were taken up to express these new concerns; modern negative judgements of such cults misunderstand the fundamental social and political meaning of much of ancient religion, where refusal of such rites by Christians was rightly understood as refusal to recognize the political supremacy of the ruler. *See* RULER-CULT; CHRISTIANITY.

river-gods Rivers and seas are ultimately derived from Oceanus, the father of all rivers (*see* OCEANUS). As personifications of animate powers river-gods such as Scamander in the Trojan plain may assume human form (conversation with *Achilles) but attack as gushing waters. River-gods also assemble in the council of *Zeus. Rivers are ancestors of 'older' heroes (Inachus, father of Io), articulating a differentiation of the landscape and humanity's link with it. Rivers can function as guardians: the river Erasinus refused to abandon the citizens of Argos to the Spartan king Cleomenes. One tenth of the property of the traitors of Amphipolis (the city 'surrounded by river') was dedicated to the river.

River-gods, such as the Nile or the *Tiber, are quintessentially male, and are often represented as bulls (also as horses and snakes) and appear thus—or as humans with bull-attributes, sometimes swimming—on coins (especially from Sicily). Live bulls, a natural metaphor for the roaring waters, were occasionally sacrificed by throwing them into the river (horses too, sometimes). *Ritual acts and cult seem to have been ubiquitous. Before crossing a river one must, says *Hesiod, pray and wash the hands. A vision of rivers is a sign of offspring, according to the dream book of *Artemidorus. River shrines, such as Spercheius', were located at river-banks. Scamander had a special priest; Trojan maidens are said to have entered its waters and asked the god to take their virginity as a gift. Hair was consecrated to rivers at puberty, e.g. at Phigaleia, and their function as 'youth-nourishers' (*kourotrophoi*) is attested early (*see* KOUROTROPHOS). Oaths are sworn by invoking rivers. During a battle the diviners (*manteis*) would offer sacrifices to the river.

*Achelous was perceived as the archetypal river; it had a shrine by the Ilissus in Attica (with the *nymphs). A son of Oceanus and *Tethys, it wrestled with *Heracles for *Deianira; when it metamorphosed into a bull, Heracles won by breaking one of its horns. Achelous was a father of several nymphs associated with water, such as Castalia (the spring at *Delphi), or the *Sirens. In Italy, we are best informed about the Tiber, which by contrast developed little mythology. Neither did it possess a temple; prayers were addressed and offerings made directly to the river itself. Its cult was particularly concerned with purification (*see* LUSTRATION) and healing.

Robigus, Roman spirit of wheat rust. His festival (Robigalia) was on 25 April, at the fifth milestone of the via Claudia; the flamen Quirinalis (*see* FLAMINES; QUIRINUS) offered a red dog and a sheep, praying to avert the rust. The red dog of the July moveable festival *augurium canarium* implies a connection. *See* RITUAL.

[Ovid, *Fasti* 4. 901–42]

Roman religion The history of Roman religion might be said to begin with *Varro's *Human and Divine Antiquities* (47 BC), of which the second half, 16 books on Divine Antiquities, codified for the first time Roman religious institutions: priests, temples, festivals, rites, and gods. This work, which may have had the unsettling effect of enabling people to see how imperfectly the existing system corresponded to the 'ideal', was extremely influential on traditionalists, and provided ammunition for Christians such as *Augustine in the *City of God*. Nineteenth-cent. scholarship on Roman religion, in attempting a diachronic history down to the age of Varro, assumed an ideal phase, in which religion was perfectly attuned to the agricultural year, from which republican religion was a sorry decline: politics increasingly obtruded on religion, and scepticism was rife. This decline model, which underlies the older handbooks, has become increasingly unpopular. In its place scholars now prefer to stress the dynamic changes of republican religion, including its position in public

life, and also the continuing significance of public religion in the imperial age.

Defining 'Roman religion' is harder than it might seem. The emphasis of scholars has generally been on the public festivals and institutions, on the ground that they provided the framework within which private rituals were constructed; only those committed to a protestant view of personal piety will argue that public rituals lack real religious feeling or significance. The geographical focus of the phrase changes radically over time, from the regal period when Rome was an individual city-state through to Rome's acquisition of an empire stretching from Scotland to Syria. Two related themes run through that expansion: the role of specifically Roman cults outside Rome, and the religious impact of empire on Rome itself.

Our knowledge of the early phase of Roman religion is patchy, and subject, like all early Roman history, to later mythmaking. For the regal period archaeology casts some light, for example on the extent of Greek influence in the area; the principal festivals of the regal *calendar are all attested, in all probability, in the calendar of the late republic. For the republic, archaeological evidence, for example of temples, remains important, and the literary tradition becomes increasingly reliable, especially from the mid-4th or 3rd down to the 1st cent. BC. It becomes possible to produce a diachronic history of the changes to the public cults of the city of Rome, such as the introduction of the cult of Mater Magna (204 BC; *see* CYBELE), the suppression of the *Bacchanalia (186 BC), the creation in Italy and the provinces of *coloniae* whose religious institutions were modelled on those of Rome, and the increasing divine aura assumed by dynasts of the late republic.

The Augustan 'restoration' of religion (*see* AUGUSTUS) was in reality more a restructuring, with the figure of the emperor incorporated at many points. Some 'ancient' cults were given a fresh impetus, while Augustus also built major new temples in the city (*Apollo; *Mars Ultor), which expressed his relationship to the divine. This Augustan system remained fundamental to the public religious life of Rome to the end of antiquity. The religious life of the city also became increasingly cosmopolitan under the empire, with a flourishing of associations focused on gods both Roman and foreign, some within individual households, others drawing their membership from a wider circle. In the high empire the civic cults of Rome operated alongside associations devoted to *Isis, *Mithras, Jahveh, or Christ. Outside Rome, civic cults of the Greek east continued to offer a sense of identity to Greeks under Roman rule, but hardly fall under the rubric 'Roman religion'; civic cults in the Latin west, however, took on a strongly Roman cast. Pre-Roman gods were reinterpreted and local pantheons modelled on the Roman (*see* INTERPRETATIO ROMANA). In the 3rd and 4th cents., there was an increasing conceptual opposition between Roman religion and *Christianity, but elements of the Roman system proved to be very enduring: in Rome the *Lupercalia were still celebrated in the late 5th cent. AD.

Roman religion, terms relating to Latin *religio* was likened by the ancients to *relegere*, to 'go over again in thought' or to *religare*, 'to bind', and designates religious scrupulosity as well as the sense of bonds between gods and humans. Knowledge of these bonds incites men and women to be scrupulous in their relations with gods, notably by respecting their dignity and moral obligations towards them: the term *religio* is thus defined as 'justice rendered to the gods', *iustitia erga deos*, and is parallel to *pietas*, the justice rendered to parents. But *pius, pietas*, which correspond fairly closely to Greek *eusebes* and *eusebeia*, apply equally to the religious domain: *Virgil's Aeneas is *pius* because he observes right relations to all things human and divine. Generally *religio* has a good meaning, but *religiosus* designates frequently an exaggerated scrupulosity towards the gods and approaches *superstitiosus* in sense (*see* SUPERSTITIO). There exists no idea of 'the sacred' in Rome. In its proper sense, i.e. in Roman sacred law, *sacer* signifies 'consecrated to, property of' the gods, in contrast to what belongs to humans and the di *manes (*res religiosa*). A temple is *sacer*, likewise a duly consecrated object, a sacrificial victim after *immolatio* (*see* SACRIFICE, ROMAN), or a man consecrated to a deity after a crime. The meanings 'entitled to veneration' or 'accursed' are secondary. *Sanctus* is that which is guaranteed by an oath—thus what is inviolable, e.g. the walls of a city, certain laws, the tribunes of the plebs, deities. *Profanus* is an ambiguous term. It qualifies sacred objects rendered suitable for human use by a ritual (*profanare*), like the meat of a sacrificial victim consumed by the participants; in a secondary sense *profanus* and *profanare* signify that which is not consecrated or is 'made profane', i.e. unduly removed from divine ownership, and submitted to violence. But in certain texts concerning the cult of *Hercules or that of *Mercurius *profanare* means—without doubt more widely—'to sacrifice'. *Ritus* serves to qualify, not religious acts *tout court* (these are called *religiones, caerimoniae*, or *sacra*; and note *sacra facere*, 'to perform a religious ceremony'), but the manner of celebrating religious acts (*Romano ritu, Graeco ritu*, 'by the Roman/ Greek rite'). *See* GREEK RELIGION, TERMS RELATING TO.

Romanization and religion

1. In the west This term describes the processes by which indigenous peoples incorporated into the empire acquired cultural attributes which made them appear as Romans. Since the Romans had no single unitary culture but rather absorbed traits from others, including the conquered, the process was not a one-way passing of ideas and styles from Roman to indigene but rather an exchange which led to the metropolitan mix of styles which characterized the Roman world. Styles of art and architecture, town-planning and villa-living, as well as the adoption of Latin and the worship of the Roman pantheon, are all amongst its expressions. The result of Romanization was not homogeneity, since indigenous characteristics blended to create hybrids like Romano-Celtic religion or Gallo-Roman sculpture.

Its manifestations were not uniform, and there is debate over the relative importance of directed policy and local initiative. Rome promoted aspects of her culture to integrate the provinces and facilitate government with least effort. Provincial centres like Tarraco (Tarragona) and Lugdunum (Lyon) were created to promote loyalty to the state through the worship of Roman gods, and their priesthoods became a focus for the ambitions of provincials. Tacitus states that Agricola in Britain promoted religious and secular public building and education for these purposes. Roman culture was also spread less deliberately by Roman actions. In Gaul local aristocrats were obtaining Roman citizenship in the Julio-Claudian period, establishing for themselves a new status in relation to Rome and their own peoples. Emulation of Roman customs and styles accompanied their rise. Thus in Claudian Britain, Tiberius Claudius Cogidubnus almost certainly constructed the highly sophisticated Roman villa at Fishbourne, and presided over a client kingdom where a temple of Neptune and Minerva was built. This copying of things Roman by locals was probably the most important motive for these cultural and religious changes.

2. In the east No ancient writer provides any general description or explanation of the impact of Roman culture and institutions on the eastern provinces of the empire. The term Romanization is best applied to specific developments which can be traced to the patterns of Roman rule. Specifically Roman cults, such as that of *Jupiter Optimus Maximus or of the Capitoline Triad (see CAPITOL) made little impact on the Greek east outside military camps. The Roman *ruler-cult, however, whose origins lay in a collaboration between the Roman authorities, especially provincial governors, and the upper classes of the eastern provinces, and which evolved a new form of politico-religious expression within the framework of imperial rule, had an enormous impact. Imperial temples and other buildings often dominated the cities; priesthoods and other offices concerned with the cult became the peak of a local political career; games and festivals in honour of the emperors dominated civic calendars. Much of the 'Romanness' of a city of the eastern provinces during the imperial period could therefore be traced directly to the institution of emperor-worship.

Rome, myths of *Mythology at Rome was rather different from general Greek myths (e.g. Hesiodic-style cosmology), but was similar to the local mythologies of individual Greek cities in its focus on the site of Rome. Stories were told of the visit of *Hercules to the place that was to be Rome (inhabited then by *Evander and the Arcadians). The foundation of Rome was also of great importance. The developed version of the story contained two main legends, those of *Aeneas and *Romulus, which were artificially combined at an unknown date (but certainly before 300 BC). Although both legends are very ancient, they are, as far as we can tell, quite unhistorical, although certain incidental details (e.g. the idea that Romulus founded his settlement on the *Palatine) are consistent with the archaeological facts.

According to the sources the city was originally ruled by kings, which is likely enough, but no confidence can be placed in the complex dynastic history or the dating of the canonical seven: Romulus, *Numa, Tullus *Hostilius, Ancus *Marcius, *Tarquinius Priscus, Servius *Tullius, and *Tarquinius Superbus (see REX). With the exception of the *eponymous Romulus these names may be those of genuine kings, but the notion that their reigns occupied the whole of the period from the 8th cent. BC to the end of the 6th is unacceptable. The conventional foundation date, fixed at 753 BC by *Varro, is the result of artificial manipulation, and does not accord with any archaeological starting point; the earliest settlement is much earlier than 753, and the formation of an urbanized city-state considerably later. It is necessary to suppose either that the regal period was much shorter than the conventional 250 years, or that there were more kings than the conventional seven As it happens there are good reasons for doing both, since alternative traditions record the names of kings not in the canonical list (e.g. Titus *Tatius and Mastarna).

The detailed narratives of their reigns must be regarded largely as fictitious elaboration; but it is nevertheless possible that some elements are based, however dimly, on genuine memory. For instance, accounts of the Roman conquest of the Alban hills region (traditionally attributed to Tullus Hostilius) and the lower Tiber valley (Ancus Marcius) describe an extension of Roman territory that must have occurred before the end of the 6th cent. Similarly the organization of the calendar and the major priesthoods, traditionally the work of Numa, can be dated with some confidence to the 6th cent. or even earlier. The belief that the Roman monarchy was elective rather than hereditary is unlikely to be an invention, and many institutions associated with the election process, and the ceremony of inauguration, were probably genuine relics of the time of the kings. The earliest institutions of the state, the three pre-Servian tribes and the thirty curiae, of which only residual traces survived in the later republic, almost certainly go back to the early monarchic period (tradition ascribes them to Romulus). The centuriate reform attributed to Servius Tullius, as it is described in the surviving narratives, belongs to the middle republic, but a simpler system dividing the citizens according to their capacity to arm themselves may well be a genuine reform of the 6th cent.; it is also likely that the innovation of local tribes is of pre-republican origin.

The last two kings are presented as tyrants—illegal usurpers who adopted a flamboyant and populist style of rule similar to that of the contemporary Greek tyrants. Like the latter, they pursued an ambitious foreign policy, patronized the arts, and embarked on extensive and grandiose building projects. *See* CASTOR AND POLLUX, TEMPLE OF; FORUM ROMANUM; OVID; REX; ROME (TOPOGRAPHY).

See also GENEALOGICAL TABLES (6) HOUSE OF ROME.

Rome (topography) Archaeology has revealed the presence of bronze-age settlement on the Capitol, and Iron-Age settlements here and on many of the other hills, notably the Palatine, Esquiline, and Quirinal. During the regal period, it grew to become one of the most substantial cities in the Mediterranean. Projects associated with the kings include the *Regia in the Forum, the temple of Jupiter Capitolinus, the temple of *Diana on the *Aventine, and the *pons Sublicius* which replaced the Tiber ford. *See further* FORUM ROMANUM.

Most of the surviving monuments of ancient Rome are largely the work of the emperors, whose rebuildings or additions transformed or eclipsed the older monuments. *Augustus built a new *forum Augustum, decorated with statues of Roman heroes and members of the gens Iulia; his palace on the *Palatine was associated with the new temple of *Apollo, while many new monuments in the *Campus Martius, including the Mausoleum, were erected by him or Marcus Vipsanius Agrippa. The combination of Saepta, *Pantheon, and Agrippa's baths rivalled Pompey's theatre and portico for scale and grandeur. The eastern end of the Forum Romanum was remodelled, with the temple of the Divine Iulius a new focal point, but ancient cult buildings were respected and in many cases restored; and the city was divided into fourteen new regions. Tiberius' contributions to the urban landscape were limited, the Castra Praetoria on the outskirts of the Viminal reflecting the growing importance of the praetorian guard. Gaius and Nero, however, both sought to expand the imperial palace beyond Augustus' relatively modest habitation; Gaius linked it to the Forum by means of the temple of *Castor and Pollux. When Nero's first palace, the Domus Transitoria, was destroyed in the fire of AD 64, he built another, the lavish Golden House, on a site which extended from the Palatine to the Esquiline. The effect of these building schemes was to drive the residential quarters off the Palatine to the villas and parks of the Quirinal, Pincian, and Aventine, and to make both emperors highly unpopular with the Roman élite; the Flavians spent much energy in returning the site of the Golden House to the people of Rome, by replacing it with the Colosseum and baths of Titus, and removing many of its treasures to the new temple of Peace (*see* TEMPLUM PACIS). Later, the baths of Trajan were built on the site. Domitian rebuilt the Palatine palace, further extending it to overlook the Circus Maximus; two new fora were built by Nerva and Trajan. The centrepiece of the latter was Trajan's Column and temple to the Deified Trajan, probably of Hadrianic date; the complex also included the 'Markets of Trajan', which deliberately separated the commercial functions of the Forum from the ceremonial. Hadrian sought to establish parallels between his rule and that of Augustus (and thereby legitimate his authority) by erecting a new Mausoleum, and rebuilding the Pantheon and baths of Agrippa in the Campus; his creation of a new temple to Venus and Rome (a deity worshipped in the provinces, but not previously in the city) demonstrated that Rome had now become the capital of an empire, not Italy alone.

Then followed a pause in building activities: the Antonines could afford to live upon the prestige of their predecessors, adding only triumphal monuments and temples of the deified emperors. Later building schemes, apart from repairs, take the form of isolated monumental buildings, chiefly utilitarian in scope; typical among these are the great baths. These tended to be on the outskirts of the city, near residential areas.

The city had by the early 4th cent. reached the climax of its development; soon it was to give way to Constantinople as imperial capital.

Romulus and Remus, mythical founders of Rome. In its normal form, the story runs thus. Numitor, king of Alba Longa, had a younger brother Amulius who deposed him. To prevent the rise of avengers he made Numitor's daughter, R(h)ea Silvia, a Vestal virgin (*see* VESTA). But she was violated by *Mars himself, and bore twins. Amulius, who had imprisoned her, ordered the infants to be thrown into the Tiber. The river was in flood, and the receptacle in which they had been placed drifted ashore near the Ficus Ruminalis. There a she-wolf (Plutarch adds a woodpecker, both being sacred to Mars; *see* PICUS) tended and suckled them, until they were found by *Faustulus the royal herdsman. He and his wife *Acca Larentia brought them up as their own; they increased mightily in strength and boldness, and became leaders of the young men in daring exploits. In one of these Remus was captured and brought before Numitor; Romulus came to the rescue, the relationship was made known, they rose together against Amulius, killed him, and made Numitor king again. The twins then founded a city of their own on the site of Rome, beginning with a settlement on the Palatine; Romulus walled it, and he or his lieutenant Celer killed Remus for leaping over the walls. He offered asylum on the *Capitol to all fugitives, and got wives for them by stealing women from the *Sabines, whom he invited to a festival. After a successful reign of some forty years he mysteriously vanished in a storm at Goat's Marsh and became the god *Quirinus.

Their legend, though probably as old as the late 4th cent. BC in one form or another (the Ogulnii dedicated a statue of the she-wolf with the twins in 206 BC), cannot be very old nor contain any popular element, unless it be the almost universal one of the exposed children who rise to a great position. The name of Rōmulus means simply 'Roman', Remus (who in the Latin tradition replaces the Rhōmos of most Greek authors), if not a back-formation from local place-names such as Remurinus ager, Remona, is possibly formed from *Roma* by false analogy with such doublets as *Kerkyra, Corcyra*, where the o is short. The origin of the legend of Romulus and Remus has long been debated. The discussion focuses above all on three problems: the antiquity of the myth, its meaning, and the death of Romulus. The majority opinion today is that the legend of the twins already existed by the beginning of the 3rd cent. BC, but some scholars have no hesitation in dating its origin to the first quarter of the 6th cent., while the comparativists liken it to the Vedic Nāsataya-Aśvin or the creation. Interpretations vary. While all scholars recognize that the myth narrates the foundation of Roman institutions, one version even making Romulus a Greek *ktistēs* (*see* FOUNDERS, CITY), historians stress variously the schemata known from *anthropology (e.g. the bands of youths), the Indo-European concept of twins, or the political realities of the republican period. As to the different versions of the death of Romulus (sudden disappearance, or murder followed by dismemberment), the light has yet to penetrate. The assimilation of Romulus to the god *Quirinus could go back, like the tradition about his apotheosis, to the 3rd cent. BC. Romulus did not receive cult.

See also GENEALOGICAL TABLES (6) HOUSE OF ROME.

[Livy 1. 3. 10 ff.; Dionysius of Halicarnassus, *Roman Antiquities* 1. 76. 1 ff.; Ovid, *Fasti* 4. 807–62; Plutarch, *Romulus* 3 ff.]

Rosalia or Rosaria (generally neut. plur., occasionally fem. sing., plur. Rosaliae). The Romans regularly used roses on festal occasions, at banquets both official (Arval Brothers, *see* FRATRES ARVALES) and private. Thus rose festivals were common, but were never fixed and public except locally. Best-known were commemorations of the dead, also called *dies rosationis*, when presumably family members met at the grave and decked it with roses. Violets were also used, hence *uiolatio, dies uiolares* or *uiolae*. Rose festivals appear in various documents, none earlier than Domitian, and extending as late as the Roman calendar of AD 354 (23 May) and a Campanian calendar of AD 387, on dates from early May to mid-July, precisely when various rose species would bloom or re-bloom. These festivals did not develop from the cult of the dead; rather, these honours were a particular case of inviting them to a feast or other entertainment at which the survivors were also present, or simply a development of the custom of decking graves with flowers. Rose festivals occurred in Romanized contexts throughout the empire: e.g. the *Rosaliae signorum* in the calendar of a Roman cohort at Dura Europus (31 May), when offering of *incense was prescribed; the legionary *standards probably received rose garlands.

Rufinus of Aquileia, Christian writer, translator, and monastic leader, born *c.*AD 345 of good family, boyhood friend of *Jerome, whose education he shared, baptized at Aquileia *c.*371, studied in Egypt for eight years under Didymus the Blind and desert hermits, presided over a monastery on the Mount of Olives, and from 393 onwards became involved in the Origenist controversy (*see* ORIGEN), returning to Italy in 397. He there produced many translations or adaptations from the Greek, including *Eusebius' *Church History*, which he extended to 395 by adding two extra books; also Origen's *De Principiis*, commentaries on the Song of Songs and on Romans, and numerous homilies, the *Clementine Recognitions*, selected sermons of *Gregory of Nazianzus and *Basil of Caesarea, and the Sentences of Sextus. He had an important influence on the development of western monasticism both personally and through his translations (Basil's *Rule*, the *Historia Monachorum*, writings of Evagrius Ponticus). His original works included the *De Adulteratione

Librorum Origenis (which he appended to a translation of Pamphilus' Apology for Origen), defences of his own orthodoxy to Pope Anastasius and against Jerome, and a commentary on the Apostles' Creed. He died in 411 in Sicily, whither he had fled from the Gothic invasion.

ruler-cult

Greek The essential characteristic of Greek ruler-worship is the rendering, as to a god or hero, of honours to individuals deemed superior to other people because of their achievements, position, or power. The roots of this lie in Greece, though parallels are to be found in other near eastern societies.

In the aristocratic society of the Archaic age, as in the Classical city-state of the 5th cent., no person could reach a position of such generally acknowledged pre-eminence as to cause the granting of divine honours to be thought appropriate: posthumous heroization (*see* HERO-CULT), rather than deification, was the honour for city-*founders. The first case of divine honours occurred in the confused period at the end of the Peloponnesian War (404 BC), when the Spartan Lysander, the most powerful man in the Aegean, received divine cult on Samos. There are some other, 4th-cent. examples.

Ruler-cult in a developed form first appears during the reign of Alexander the Great, and is directly inspired by his conquests, personality, and in particular his absolute and undisputed power. Alexander's attempt to force the Greeks and Macedonians in his entourage to adopt the Persian custom of prostration before the king (*proskynēsis*), which for the Persians did not imply worship, was an isolated and unsuccessful experiment without consequence. Much more important is his encounter with the priest of *Ammon at *Siwa in 331 BC. The priest seemingly addressed Alexander as the son of Amon-Ra, the traditional salutation due to any Pharaoh of Egypt, but the prestige which the oracle of Ammon then enjoyed throughout the Greek world had a decisive

effect, not only on the Greeks, but also and in particular on the romantic imagination of the young king himself. It is probably the progressive development of these emotions which caused Alexander in 324, when he ordered the restoration of political exiles, to apply pressure on the Greek cities to offer him divine cult; some cities certainly responded, though contemporary evidence remains thin. Alexander also secured heroic honours for his dead intimate Hephaestion as official recognition of his outstanding achievements.

The cults of Alexander's successors are found in various different contexts. The principal context was that of the Greek cities dependent on particular kings, both ancient cities and those founded by the king himself. The cities acknowledged benefactions received from a king by the establishment of a cult, with temple or altar, priest, sacrifices, and games, modelled on that granted to the Olympian gods (*isotheoi timai*). Rulers were also honoured by having their statues placed in an already existing temple. The king was thought to share the temple with the god (as *sunnaos theos*, 'temple-sharing god'), and thus to partake in the honours rendered to the deity and, on occasion, in the deity's qualities.

The other main context was that of the court itself. The Greek monarchies of the east in time created their own official cults. The dynastic cult of the Ptolemies at Alexandria in Egypt (a cult founded by 285/4) in its developed form by the end of the 3rd cent. BC consisted of priests of Alexander, of each pair of deceased rulers, and of the reigning king and queen. In the Seleucid kingdom of Syria, in 280 Antiochus I deified his dead father Seleucus I and dedicated to him a temple and precinct at Seleuceia in Pieria; Antiochus III extended a court cult throughout his newly reconquered Seleucid empire, with high priests of the living king and his divine ancestors in each province of the empire. In the later dynastic cult of the Attalids of Pergamum the kings were deified only after death.

Cults are also found outside strictly Greek contexts. In Commagene (south-eastern Turkey) a complex cult, organized by Antiochus I (1st cent. BC; *see* NEMRUT DAG) round different cult centres, was a blend of Greek and Persian traditions. In Egyptian temples cult of the Ptolemies continued on the model of Pharaonic practice. Incorporation of Greek practice might, however, be controversial: the erection of a statue of the Seleucid *Antiochus IV in the Temple at Jerusalem stimulated the writing of the Book of Daniel, with its attack on Nebuchadnezzar's demand for worship, and was one factor that provoked the Maccabean Revolt (*see* MACCABEES).

Even within Greek contexts, at the outset there were debates about the propriety of divine honours for human beings, though the cults gradually became an accepted practice. That it became accepted does not prove it was essentially a political and not a religious phenomenon: to press the distinction is to deny significance to the creation of a symbolic system modelled on the cult of the gods. Those responsible for the cults, whether at court or in cities, were attempting to articulate an understanding of the power of the king.

Roman The offering of divine honours to humans was not indigenous to Italy. The Romans had long sacrificed to the ghosts of the dead (*Manes*) and conceived of a semi-independent spirit (*genius*) attached to living people. But the myth of a deified founder, *Romulus, was invented only in or after the 4th cent. BC, under Greek influence, and developed in the new political circumstances of the late Republic. From the time of Marcus Claudius Marcellus' conquest of Syracuse in 212 BC, Roman officials received divine honours in Greek cities; a notable instance is the 'liberator' of Greece, Titus Quinctius Flamininus (c.191 BC), whose cult survived into the imperial period. At Rome such honours are met only from the late 2nd cent. BC, and then exceptionally, e.g. those offered privately to Caius Marius (101 BC) and

popularly to the demagogue Marius Gratidianus (86 BC). Under Stoic influence the idea that worthy individuals might become divine after death appeared in *Cicero's *Somnium Scipionis* (c.51 BC) and in the shrine he planned for his daughter Tullia (d. 45 BC). Though the evidence is controversial, *Caesar as dictator in 45–44 BC probably received divine honours, based on Roman models (cults of Alexander the Great and Hellenistic kings took different forms). After his assassination the triumvirs, supported by popular agitation, secured from the senate his formal deification in 42 BC as Divus Iulius.

Worship of emperors and members of their families has two aspects, the worship of the living, including identification with the gods, and the apotheosis of the dead. It took different forms in different contexts: Rome; provincial assemblies; towns; and in private. At Rome *Augustus and later 'good' emperors avoided official deification in their lifetimes; Gaius Caligula and Commodus were exceptional in seeking to emphasize their own divinity. Augustus was *divi filius* (son of the deified one), and enjoyed a mediating role with the divine, as implied by his name, and as a result of becoming *pontifex maximus* in 12 BC (*see* PONTIFEX/PONTIFICES). He also in 7 BC reorganized the cults of the 265 wards of the city: henceforth the officials of the wards, mainly freedmen, worshipped the Augustan *Lares and the Genius of Augustus. The worship appropriate for a household was now performed throughout the city. Poets played with the association of Augustus with the gods, and assumed that he would be deified posthumously. In AD 14 Augustus' funeral managed both to evoke, on a grand scale, traditional aristocratic funerals and to permit his formal deification by the senate; it was the precedent for all subsequent emperors up to *Constantine. After Livia Drusilla in AD 41, imperial relatives, male and female, could also be deified posthumously. After Constantine's avowal of *Christianity, it became increasingly difficult for traditional practices to continue: Christ alone had combined human and divine, and the prevalent doctrine, formulated by *Eusebius, was that the emperor ruled by divine favour.

Provincial councils (*concilium*/*commune* in the west; *koinon* in the east) had an important role in ruler-cult outside Rome. The councils held (?annual) meetings attended by representatives from the constituent communities of part or all of a province or even several associated provinces. Their chief functions were (1) to represent their provinces to the centre not only diplomatically, but also on matters of substance, notably complaints against unsatisfactory governors but also routine requests for clarification of legal and administrative procedure; and (2) to organize the provincial ruler-cult, a function so central that the presiding official often doubled as imperial high priest (*archiereus* in the east, *flamen* or *sacerdos* in the west); the councils could orchestrate provincial oaths of loyalty, as with the Panachaean League in AD 37. In the Greek east provincial assemblies were permitted to establish cults of Roma and Augustus: the precedent was set in Asia at Pergamum and in Bithynia at Nicomedia in 29 BC. In 'civilized' western provinces provincial assemblies followed the Roman model, on the precedent of Hispania Tarraconensis which was granted permission to establish a temple and *flamen* (*see* FLAMINES) to Divus Augustus at Tarraco (mod. Tarragona) in AD 15. Assemblies in more recently conquered western provinces had cults of the living Augustus and Roma (Three Gauls at Lugdunum (mod. Lyon), 12 BC; Germany near Cologne (Colonia Agrippinensis), 8–7 BC?); these centred on *altars, not temples, and had *sacerdotes* not *flamines* (the title indicating that they were not Roman priesthoods). Shorn of the imperial cult, the councils survived the reforms of Diocletian and Constantine into the 6th cent. AD, by when their membership included the provincial bishops.

Below the provincial level different forms of cult are found, depending in part on local traditions. In the (non-Greek) Egyptian temples Augustus and other emperors were accorded the position of high priest, like the Ptolemies and the Pharaohs before them. In Greek contexts, in Egypt and the rest of the Greek east, emperors were generally accommodated within the context of the ordinary cult of the Olympian gods. In cities throughout the east living emperors were granted temples and cult statues, priests and processions, sacrifices and games. At first the cult focused specifically on Augustus, and then often became a general cult of the emperors. Though some cults of Hellenistic kings did survive through to Roman times, the imperial cult was more varied and more dynamic than Hellenistic cults had been. Towns in Italy and the west also established cults of the living Augustus (not his *genius*) and his successors; some, especially *coloniae*, chose to follow the Roman model.

Private households in Rome and elsewhere included associations of worshippers of Augustus, who will mainly have been the slaves and freedmen of the house. *Ovid in exile makes great play of his piety in praying at dawn each day before his household shrine with images of Augustus, Livia, Tiberius, and Drusus. In Italy and the west there were also the *Augustales*, a high-ranking status for Roman freedmen, whose officials are sometimes associated with the imperial cult.

The significance of the imperial cult has been much debated. Was it a form of *Graeca adulatio* (divine honours to a human as Greek adulation), a system that was really political and not religious? On the other side it has been argued that to impose a distinction between religion and politics is anachronistic and Christianizing, and that it is illegitimate to undercut the implicit meanings of the rituals by claims about insincerity and flattery. The way forward is to investigate the different ritual systems that honoured the emperor in their different social and cultural contexts. As the cult was in general not imposed from above, it is essential to examine the contexts from which it sprang and which gave it meaning. There is a profound difference between a Greek city with its stable Olympian pantheon within which the emperor was accommodated and a town in Gaul whose pre-Roman pantheon was re-structured on Roman models before the emperor found a place in it. Focus on actual divinization of the emperor is also too narrow. There was a whole range of religious honours, only some of which placed the emperor unambiguously among the gods. In some sense there was no such thing as 'the imperial cult'. *See* CHRISTIANITY.

Rumina, an obscure Roman goddess, whose significance depends on her name's etymology. Some, following *Varro, connect her with *ruma* (breast) and hence suckl-ing. This is appropriate for her shrine and sacred fig-tree (*ficus Ruminalis*; *see* FIG) near the Lupercal (*see* LUPERCALIA), where milk, not wine, was offered. Others accept an Etruscan connection, thus relating her to Roma, the city's deity.

[Ovid, *Fasti* 2. 412]

Sabazius, a god first attested in several slighting allusions in Aristophanes' comedies; there are also 4th-cent. references to his unofficial cult in Attica. Aristophanes treats him as a Phrygian; the bulk of the surviving dedications derive from Anatolia, particularly from Phrygia; Attalus III of Pergamum in 135/4 BC claimed to be incorporating 'Zeus Sabazios' (*see* ZEUS) into the state cult of Pergamum (a rare instance of official recognition for Sabazius) as an 'ancestral god' of his mother, Stratonice of Cappadocia. Later, Sabazius also appears as an 'ancestral god' of Thrace (*see* THRACIAN RELIGION). Except in Attica, the cult is little attested until the late Hellenistic period; it eventually penetrated almost every corner of the Roman empire, normally at the level of private associations. From Rome itself, it seems, the *praetor peregrinus* had already in 139 BC expelled 'the Jews who had tried to contaminate Roman traditions through the worship of Jupiter Sabazius' (*see* JUPITER). Specific rites and beliefs are hard to identify, since reports are few and hostile. It is not certain that the disreputable initiations and purifications lampooned by Demosthenes are Sabazian; Diodorus tells of rites celebrated at night because of their shameful character; Christian polemicists speak of snake-handling. The murals and inscriptions of the tomb of Vincentius in the *catacomb of Praetextatus at Rome show that in the late 3rd or early 4th cent. AD a devotee of Sabazius could nourish hopes for the afterlife. In art, Sabazius appears either in Phrygian costume or with the attributes of Zeus/Jupiter, with whom he was, from the time of Attalus III, regularly identified. A typical form of Sabazian monument is the votive hand, making a sign of blessing, and adorned with numerous cult symbols.

Sabini, people of ancient Italy. The Sabines occupied an area to the north-east of Rome along the western side of the *Tiber valley and extending to the Apennine uplands. Their main centres in the Tiber valley were Cures, Eretum, and Trebula Mutuesca, and in the central Apennines Reate, Amiternum, and Nursia. Tradition maintained that the Sabines were the ancestors of all the 'Sabellian' peoples including the Picentines and Samnites, who migrated from the Sabine heartland in a series of sacred *springs. They also play an important part in the legends of early Rome. The rape of the Sabine women, and the subsequent war and reconciliation, leading to the integration of the Sabines into the community under the joint rule of *Romulus and Titus *Tatius are central elements in the story of how the city of Rome was formed. The legends have been variously interpreted. For some they represent a historicized version of an Indo-European myth, in which a complete society of gods is formed from the fusion of two opposing but incomplete groups, one possessing magical strength and bravery, the other wealth and fecundity, as in the Icelandic myth of the Aesir and the Vanir, who correspond in the Roman story to the Romans and Sabines respectively. Others have suggested that the story is a projection back into the prehistoric past of events that occurred centuries later, namely the incursions of Sabines into Latium in the 5th cent. BC and their incorporation in the Roman state in 290. But the majority of scholars are prepared to accept that the legends reflect a historical fact, namely the presence of a significant Sabine element in the Roman population from the earliest times. The peaceful infiltration of Sabines in the 6th cent., e.g. the migration of the Claudii, may have been going on for a long time; other clans, such as the Valerii, claimed a Sabine origin, and two of the kings, *Numa Pompilius and Ancus *Marcius, were Sabine—or three if one counts Titus Tatius.

[Livy 1. 13; Ovid, *Fasti* 3. 199–258]

Sacred Wars Four wars declared by the Delphic *amphictiony (*see* DELPHI) against states allegedly guilty of sacrilege against *Apollo.

The *First* involved Solon of Athens and resulted in Cirrha's destruction as a punishment for 'brigandage' and impious treatment of pilgrims and dedications (early 6th cent.). Claims that this is a pseudo-historical event, invented in the 340s, are dubious given a reference in 373/2.

The *Second* arose when Athens placed the sanctuary under Phocian control. Sparta intervened to restore Delphian authority and Athens countered by restoring Phocis (*c*.448). The Phocians lost control again after 446. The affair is obscure; Sparta's intervention in Doris in 458 is probably part of the background.

The *Third*. Phocian intentions were suspect in 363, but it was a Delphian denunciation (357) for cultivation of the Crisaean plain (between Delphi and the coast) which precipitated war. Phocis ignored a large amphictionic fine and, with financial and moral support from Athens and Sparta, Philomelus seized the sanctuary (summer 356). Within the year the amphictiony declared a war which re-energized post-Leuctra politico-military divisions but eventually helped transform the political scene, when a Theban invitation permitted Philip II to

win Hellenic status by championing Apollo's cause and destroying Phocis (346). The conflict (disfigured by atrocities on both sides) has three periods corresponding to the generalships of (*a*) Philomelus, (*b*) Onomarchus, and (*c*) Phayllus and Phalaecus, and was largely fought in the Cephissus Valley (355, 351–348) and western Boeotia (354–347). (Phocis was theoretically vulnerable from all directions. But western Locris and Doris were neutralized immediately and the northern approaches controlled by conquests in eastern Locris (354, 351); Thessaly was anyway distracted by civil war.) It was prolonged by Theban and Macedonian failure to exploit victories at Neon (355) and Crocus Field (353/2). Liberation of Delphi was not a consistent absolute priority (Thebes also pursued Peloponnesian interests, for example), and people only slowly appreciated the implications of Phocian pillaging of Delphian treasuries (over 10,000 talents, the majority under Phayllus): this permitted unprecedentedly large-scale state-employment of mercenaries (general and army actually came to supersede the state's authority), and following Persian disbandment of forces in the 350s there were many professionals available to fill dead men's shoes, especially at rates 50–100 per cent above normal. (Thebes, by contrast, was financially strained and diverted troops to Anatolia in 355/4 to raise money.)

The *Fourth*. When Amphissa proposed that Athens be fined for rededicating Persian Wars booty taken from the Thebans (340), Aeschines denounced Amphissa's cultivation of Cirrhaean land. Official inspectors destroyed some buildings, but were physically attacked, whereupon an extraordinary amphictiony meeting (winter 340/339) declared war. Military attack led to a fine, removal of the guilty parties, and restoration of exiles, but when Amphissa failed to pay and reversed the other arrangements Philip II was invoked as commander (autumn 339). The upshot was occupation of Elatea and the campaign which ended at Chaeronea (338). How far the whole war had been provoked to provide Philip an *entrée* to central Greece is disputed.

sacrifice, Greek Sacrifice was the most important form of action in *Greek religion, but we should note at once that there is no single Greek equivalent to the English word 'sacrifice'. The practices we bring together under this heading were described by a series of overlapping terms conveying ideas such as 'killing', 'destroying', 'burning', 'cutting', 'consecrating', 'performing sacred acts', 'giving', 'presenting', but not at all the idea present in 'it was a great sacrifice for him'. As occasions for sacrifice the philosopher Theophrastus distinguished 'honour, gratitude, and need', but his categories do not correspond to fixed types, and in fact the rite could be performed on almost any occasion. Vegetable products, savoury *cakes above all, were occasionally 'sacrificed' (the same vocabulary is used as for animal sacrifice) in lieu of animals or, much more commonly, in addition to them. But animal sacrifice was the standard type. The main species used were sheep, goats, pigs, and cattle. In a few cults fish and fowl were offered, wild animals still more rarely; dogs and horses appear in a few sacrifices of special type that were not followed by a feast. Human sacrifice occurred only in myth and scandalous story. The choice between the main species was largely a matter of cost and scale, a piglet costing about 3 drachmae, a sheep or goat 12, a pig 20 or more, a cow up to 80. Within the species symbolic factors were sometimes also relevant: the virgins *Athena and *Artemis might require unbroken cattle; fertile Earth a pregnant sow. (*See* ANIMALS IN CULT.) The most important step-by-step accounts of a standard sacrifice are a series of Homeric scenes. Attic practice differs or may have done from Homeric in several significant details, but the basic articulations of the rite are the same in all sources. Vase-paintings and votive reliefs provide extremely important supplementary evidence, though by their nature they very rarely depict the full succession of actions as a sequence. Three main stages can be distinguished:

1. Preparatory. An animal was led to the altar, usually in *procession. The participants assembled in a circle, rinsed their hands in lustral water, and took a handful of barley grain from a basket. Water was sprinkled on the victim to force it to 'nod' agreement to its own sacrifice. The main sacrificer (not necessarily a priest) then cut hair from the victim, put it on the *altar fire, and uttered a *prayer which defined the return that was desired (e.g. 'health and safety') for the offering. The other participants threw forward their barley grains.

2. The kill. The victim's throat was cut with a knife; larger victims had been stunned with a blow from an axe first. Women participants raised the cry known as *ololygē*. In Attic practice it was important to 'bloody the altar'; small animals were held over it to be killed, the blood from larger ones was caught in a bowl and poured out over it.

3. Treatment of the meat, which itself had three stages. First the god's portion, typically the thigh bones wrapped in fat with (in Homer) small portions of meat cut 'from all the limbs' set on top, was burnt on the altar fire. *Wine was poured on as it burnt. (Further portions for the gods were sometimes put on a table or even on the knees or in the hands of their statues; in practice, these became priests' perquisites.) Then the entrails were roasted on skewers and shared among all the participants. Finally the rest of the meat was boiled and distributed (normally in equal portions); in contrast to the entrails, this boiled meat was occasionally taken away for consumption at home, though a communal feast on the spot was the norm (*see* DINING-ROOMS). Omens were often taken both from the burning of the god's portion and from the condition of the entrails.

A distinction is drawn in Herodotus between sacrifice to the gods, *thyein*, and to heroes, *enhagizein* (*see* HERO-CULT). It used to be common to draw a contrast between the normal Olympian sacrifice outlined and a 'chthonian' type which supposedly diverged from the other systematically: the victim would be dark, not light; it would be killed with its head pressed down into a low pit or hearth, not drawn back over a high altar; the accompanying libations would be 'wineless'; and, above all, the animal's flesh would not be eaten. But it is now clear that these divergences from the standard type more often occurred individually than as a group, and also that they might be present in 'Olympian' sacrifice, absent (largely or wholly) from sacrifice to chthonian gods or heroes. (*See* CHTHONIAN GODS; OLYMPIAN GODS.) There were also certain 'quasi-sacrifices' which contained several of the actions listed above and could be described by some, though not all, of the group of words that denote sacrifice. The killing of animals to ratify an oath, for instance, followed many of the stages mentioned under 1 and 2 above; stage 3, however, was omitted entirely, the carcass being carried away or thrown in the sea. (*See* OATHS.) And similar quasi-sacrificial ritual killings occurred in certain *purifications and before battle.

Explicit early reflection on sacrifice is sparse. The division whereby men received most of the meat was explained by a trick played on *Zeus by the man-loving god *Prometheus at the time of the first sacrifice. The rite of *Bouphonia (part of the Attic festival Dipolieia; *see* ATTIC CULTS AND MYTHS) raised the issue of the institution's moral legitimacy: an ox sacrifice was followed by a 'trial' at which guilt for the killing was eventually fixed on the sacrificial axe or knife. Plato's Euthyphro no doubt echoes popular usage in describing sacrifice as a form of 'gift' to the gods. Recent interpretations are largely divided between those which see sacrifice (perhaps with reference to its hypothetical origins among prehistoric hunters) as a dramatization of killing, violence, and the associated guilt, and those for which by contrast it is a way of legitimizing meat-eating by treating the taking of life that necessarily precedes it as a ritual, i.e. a licensed act: the

former approach stresses that rituals such as the Bouphonia raise the issue of sacrificial guilt, the latter that they resolve it. Sacrifice is normally killing followed by eating, but where does the emphasis lie? In the vast majority of cases, clearly, on the eating; but all the uneaten sacrifices and quasi-sacrifices have to be set aside if the institution is to be understood by reference to the communal feast alone.

[Homer, *Iliad* 3. 245–313, 19. 250–68; *Odyssey* 3. 430–63; Hesiod, *Theogony* 535–61; Euripides, *Electra* 774–843; Aristophanes, *Birds* 938 ff.]

sacrifice, Roman Roman sacrificial practices were not functionally different from Greek, although there are no sources for them earlier than the 2nd cent. BC, and the *modalités* of Roman sacrifice were complex, since several rites existed (Roman, Greek, and Etruscan). In any case, as in the Greek world, sacrifice was a central act of religion. The expression *rem divinam facere*, 'to make a thing sacred', often abridged to *facere* ('to sacrifice'), and the etymology of the words designating sacrificial activity, *sacrificare*, *sacrificium* (*sacrum facere*, 'to perform a religious ceremony'), show the importance of these acts and signal that sacrifice was an act of transfer of ownership. On its own or part of larger celebrations, the typical sacrifice embraced four phases: the *praefatio*, the *immolatio*, the slaughtering, and the banquet.

1. After the purification (*see* LUSTRATION) of the participants and of the victims (always domestic animals) chosen in accordance with the divinity's function and the context, a *procession led them to the *altar of the divinity. There the presiding figure celebrated the *praefatio* ('preface') on a portable hearth (*focus, foculus*) set up beside the sacrificial altar (*ara*). This rite consisted of offering *incense and *wine, and, according to the ancient commentators, was the equivalent of a solemn salutation affirming the superiority of the gods. At the same time this rite opened a ritual space and announced what was to follow.

2. The second stage of the sacrifice was

the *immolatio*. The presiding figure poured wine on the victim's brow, sprinkled its back with salted flour (*mola salsa*, whence *immolare*), doubtless prepared by the *Vestals, and finally passed a sacrificial knife over the victim's spine. According to ancient commentators and the *prayer spoken during this rite, immolation transferred the victim from human possession into the divine.

3. Once this transfer was effected, the sacrificers (*popae, victimarii*; cf. Gk. *mageiroi*) felled the victim, butchered it, and opened the corpse, now on its back. The presiding figure then performed the *extispicina*, the inspection of the *exta* (vital organs: the peritoneum, liver, gall bladder, lungs, and, from the beginning of the 3rd cent. BC, the heart), to decide if they were in the good shape which would signal the deity's acceptance (*litatio*) of the sacrifice. If the victim was unacceptable, the sacrifice had to begin again.

4. The banquet comprised two phases. Once acceptance was obtained, the sacrificers beheaded the victim, set aside the *exta*, and prepared them for offering: the *exta* of bovines were boiled in cooking pots (*ollae extares*), those of ovines and the pig-family were grilled on spits. This cooking done, the *exta* were offered to the divinity (*porricere*; *pollucere* for Hercules), i.e. burnt, basted with *mola salsa* and wine, sometimes along with pieces of meat designated on the victim in advance (*magmentum*). This was done on the altar if celestial divinities were in question; offerings to aquatic deities were thrown into the water, those for epichthonic or chthonic divinities were placed on the ground or in ditches. Offerings for the *di* *manes* were made on a pyre itself resting on the ground. When the offering to the deity had been consumed, the rest of the victim was seized (*profanare*) by the presiding figure, no doubt by imposition of hand, and thus rendered fit for human consumption. In principle all sacrifices, except those addressed to divinities of the underworld, were followed by a sacrificial banquet (*cena, visceratio*). But the procedures at these

banquets are ill-understood, because of both the complexity of communal banquets in Rome's strongly hierarchical society, and the enormous numbers having the right to take part (e.g. the citizens). Sometimes the banquet was celebrated (doubtless on behalf of all) by just the immediate participants and their helpers, along with those possessing privileges in a particular sanctuary (e.g. the flute-players at the temple of Jupiter); sometimes the banquet united the chief sections of society (e.g. the Roman élite for the *epulum Jovis*); sometimes the meat was sold in butchers' shops (i.e. it was accessible to all); sometimes, finally, it was eaten at great communal banquets, ultimately financed by benefactors. At the *ara maxima* of *Hercules, sacrificial meat had to be eaten or burnt before nightfall, a requirement giving rise to a very generous form of sacrificial banquet even if the cult's foundation-myth barred one of the families in charge of the cult, the Pinarii, from taking part.

In public sacrifices conducted in accordance with Greek ritual (*Graeco ritu*), the details of which are very poorly known, the conduct of the presiding figure was different. While in the Roman rite he wore the purple-bordered *toga praetexta*, draped in such a way as to allow a flap of cloth to cover the head, in the Greek ritual he sometimes removed the *praetexta* before proceeding with the *immolatio*, and for the rest of the proceedings; he certainly sacrificed with head uncovered, sometimes wearing a laurel-wreath. The commentators on the *Secular Games show that sacrifice according to the Greek rite was no different functionally from the Roman rite. Only the *immolatio* differed, since the presiding figure burnt hairs cut from the animal's brow and offered crowns, and in addition the *exta* were called *splanchna*; but it is not known whether the rules for the division of the victims differed from the 'Roman' ones. At any rate, Roman sacrifices according to the 'Greek ritual' were much more complicated than has been thought, although the state of the sources prevents a full understanding of them. Of sacrifices according to Etruscan ritual we know even less, save that the inspection of the *exta* (*haruspicatio*) permitted *divination. Even if they had no special name, the sacrificial rituals of certain cults of the imperial age differed from traditional sacrifices, at least to judge from the evidence of imagery. If we are to believe the sources, the *taurobolium* (or *criobolium*) in some way reproduced the myth of *Attis, by creating a central role for blood and for the setting aside of the testicles of the sacrificial victim. Of Mithraic sacrifice, represented on numerous altars of *Mithras, too little is known for comparison with traditional Roman sacrifice. All that can be said is that Mithraic imagery emphasizes violence where representations of traditional sacrifice underline calm.

Communal sacrifices were celebrated by those who exercised power in the community in question: the head of the household, magistrates and *priests, and the presidents (*magistri*) of *clubs. In spite of a few exceptions, women could not sacrifice on behalf of the whole community. Many sacrifices were part of much larger celebrations, and in certain cases the sacrifices themselves were celebrated in more spectacular fashion (e.g. at the *lectisternium). Occasions for sacrifice were innumerable, from regular acts of homage shaped by sacred calendars and the ritual obligations of the city and its constituent associations to thanks-offerings or contractual sacrifices (*vota*, vows). Faults and involuntary oversights committed in the celebration of the cult, or the involuntary deterioration of the patrimony of the gods, were expiated by *piacula*, sacrifices the purpose of which was to present excuses for past or imminent action (e.g. maintenance works in a sanctuary). By way of a global view of what traditional Roman sacrifice articulated and realized, it can be understood as establishing—with the help of a solemn sharing of food—a hierarchy between three partners: gods, humans, and animals (*see* ANIMALS IN CULT). To the gods was assured absolute priority in the course of a symbolic feast, during which they shared with

humans an animal victim or a vegetable-offering. The different Roman myths which commented on sacrificial practices—those concerning the *instauratio* of the cult of the Ara Maxima, the two groups of Luperci (*see* LUPERCALIA), and the *Vinalia, as well as those revealing the origin of sacrifice—all insist on the fact that, by the privilege of priority, essential in Roman society, and the quality of the offerings (the *exta*, seat of the animal's vitality, the incense and the pure wine, all reserved for the immortals), sacrifice fixed the superiority and immortality of the gods, along with the mortal condition and the pious submission of their human partners, at the expense of the animal victims. At the same time the sacrificial rite was capable of expressing, by the right to take part in the banquet and by the privilege of priority, the hierarchy among mortals.

Sadducees, a religious group within Judaism attested in Judaea from the 2nd cent. BC to the 1st cent. AD. The Sadducees are described by Josephus and are mentioned in the New Testament and in rabbinic texts, usually as opponents of the *Pharisees in matters concerning law or theology. According to the generally unfavourable picture given by Josephus, their distinctive tenets consisted in a refusal to accept the unwritten religious traditions championed by the Pharisees, an unwillingness to ascribe human fortunes to the operations of fate, and unwillingness to accept the notion of life after death. Josephus also accused them of harshness in judgement and claimed that they had little influence over the people.

Josephus stated that most Sadducees came from the rich and powerful part of Judaean society. This assertion, together with the evidence of Acts of the Apostles and the probable derivation of the name 'Sadducees' from Zadok, the ancestor of the high priests in earlier times, has led many scholars to identify the Sadducees with the ruling priests in Jerusalem. Some overlap between these groups is certain, but some influential priests (including high priests) were not Sadducees, and there is no reason to doubt that some Sadducees were not priests.

Some of the legal views ascribed to Sadducees in early rabbinic texts have been paralleled in sectarian writings found among the *Dead Sea Scrolls, but the view that the Qumran sectarians should be classified as a type of Sadducee is debated. See JUDAISM.

Salii (from *salire*, 'to dance'), an ancient ritual *sodalitas* (see SODALES) found in many towns of central Italy, usually in association with the war-god. Outside Rome, they are heard of at *Lavinium, Tusculum, *Aricia, Anagnia, and especially at Tibur where they were attached to *Hercules. Their attachment at Rome was to *Mars, though it is a possibility that one of the two companies of twelve (Palatini and Collini) belonged originally to *Quirinus. Salii had to be of patrician birth and to have both father and mother living. They wore the dress of an archaic Italian foot-soldier: *tunica picta* (painted tunic), with breastplate covered by the short military cloak (*trabea*), and the *apex (a conical felt cap). They also wore a sword and, on the left arm, carried one of the *ancilia*; the original *ancile* fell from heaven as a gift from *Jupiter to *Numa Pompilius, but many copies were made to conceal which was the original; in the right hand they carried a spear or staff. The Salii played a prominent part in the *Quinquatrus of 19 March: it is much more doubtful whether they also did so at the *Armilustrium of 19 October. During March and October the Calendars note that the *ancilia* were moved, presumably involving *processions by the Salii. When they processed they halted at certain spots and performed elaborate ritual dances (*tripudium*), beating their shields with staves and singing the *Carmen Saliare, of which fragments are preserved. The idea that their activities marked the opening and closing of a symbolic campaigning season is modern theorizing, open to question. See also RITUAL.

[Ovid, *Fasti* 3. 365–92; Dionysius of Halicarnassus 2. 70; Plutarch, *Numa* 13]

Sallustius, author of a brief manual of Neoplatonic piety known as *On the Gods and the World* (see NEOPLATONISM). He is probably to be identified with the emperor *Julian's friend, Flavius Sallustius, consul 363. His book echoes the language and ideas of *Iamblichus and Julian, and seems to have been written during Julian's reign (AD 361–3) in the service of the pagan reaction against Christianity.

Salmoneus, a son of *Aeolus. *Homer calls Salmoneus 'blameless', but post-Homeric tradition pictures him as the eponymous king of Salmone in Elis, who in a case of *hubris pretended to be *Zeus, flinging torches for lightning and making a noise like thunder with his chariot; Zeus killed him with a real thunderbolt. Sophocles wrote a Salmoneus satyr play. See SATYRIC DRAMA.

[Homer, *Odyssey* 11. 235 f.; Apollodorus 1. 9. 7]

Salus, a deified 'virtue', the safety and welfare of the state (akin to, and perhaps influenced by, the Greek *Soteria), with a temple on the Quirinal vowed in the Samnite War in 311 and dedicated in 302 BC. Her feast (*natalis*, 'birthday') was on 5 August. There may have existed an earlier cult of Salus; her association with Semonia (related to the Semunes of the archaic *Carmen arvale) suggests Salus as protectress of the sowing (on some imperial coins she holds corn-ears). From the 2nd cent. BC she became identified with the Greek *Hygieia, 'Health'. *Salus Augusta* or *Augusti*, the 'Health' and 'Saving Power' of the emperor, frequently appears on inscriptions and coins (enthroned, holding sceptre and dish, often feeding the snake). Public and private vows for the *salus* of the emperor (often associated with the *Salus Publica*, esp. in the records of the Arvals; see FRATRES ARVALES), and the oaths by his *salus*, became ubiquitous events. Particularly numerous are dedications to Salus in Spain, and by the imperial cavalry bodyguard. With the *augurium salutis* the goddess Salus does not appear to be connected.

Samothrace, a mountainous island in the northern Aegean. Inhabited from Neolithic times, it was settled *c.*700 BC by Greeks who intermingled with the local Thracian population. A member of both Athenian maritime alliances, Samothrace gained its fame as a cult centre which was heavily patronized by the Macedonian royal house and their successors. Control of the island passed among several Hellenistic dynasts, and under the Romans it became a free city. The popular cult of twin gods, the *Cabiri, was centred in a major sanctuary near the northern coast. The sanctuary was open to all visitors, and initiates sought protection, moral improvement, and the promise of immortality. During the Hellenistic era the sanctuary was lavishly endowed by royal patrons, who constructed several grand buildings.

sanctuaries Sanctuaries in the Greek world (*see also* TEMENOS) were areas set aside for religious purposes and separate from the normal secular world. The boundary (*peribolos*) might be an actual wall, but more often would be indicated by boundary markers. Traditional Greek and Roman worship was not restricted to initiates (except for the *mysteries at *Eleusis and elsewhere) who had to be accommodated in closeable buildings suitable for private ritual: the open space of the sanctuary was where the worshippers congregated to observe and participate in the ritual which was enacted on their behalf; for this, the main requisite was sufficient space.

The *festivals which were the occasion for such worship were normally annual, though sanctuaries would be accessible for individual acts of worship and the performance of vows. Within the sanctuary space were the buildings and other structures dedicated to the use of the god, especially the *altar at which the burnt *sacrifice, essential to the religious functioning of the sanctuary, was made. Other buildings responded to various religious needs, and are not always found. There is normally a *temple to house the

image which was the god, which watched and so received the sacrifice. The temple was itself both an offering to the god, and a store room for *votive offerings. The open area of the sanctuary round the altar was the place where, at the god's festival, worshippers would witness the sacrifices. The meat from these was then divided amongst them, and normally consumed within the sanctuary: some sanctuaries had laws which stipulated that the meat had to be consumed within their boundaries. Most worshippers seem to have feasted alfresco, but certain sanctuaries had special *dining-rooms (*hestiatoria*) for a privileged section of the worshippers. Other religious functions accommodated include contests of song and dance, as well as athletic ones (*see* AGŌNES). Specialized structures (theatres, odeions, stadia) eventually developed for these.

The size and arrangement of a sanctuary depended on the importance and nature of the cult. In large sanctuaries it is often possible to distinguish between an innermost sacred area round the altar as place of sacrifice and the temple as the abode of the god, and an outer area given over to human activity, the feasting and contests. As a result theatres and stadia are often on the periphery. In healing sanctuaries, such as the Asclepieion at *Epidaurus, or the sanctuary of *Amphiaraus at Oropus, buildings where those seeking the god's cure might spend the night in the sanctuary (*see* INCUBATION) were normally adjacent to the temple itself. In some sanctuaries the distinction between the two areas is clearly marked: at Olympia a wall was eventually built round the innermost sanctuary, leaving outside gymnasia, stadium, and the course for the chariot races. Here and at Epidaurus a vaulted passage leads from the inner area into the stadium. In other sanctuaries the distinction is not so clear cut. At the sanctuary of *Poseidon at *Isthmia the original running track has been found very close to the temple; later it was removed to a nearby valley which perhaps afforded a better locality for the spectators.

Though undoubtedly there were shrines and religious places in the Greek settlements of the Mycenaean civilization, the sanctuaries of the Classical period develop at the earliest in the 8th cent. BC, as far as can be judged from the archaeological evidence. Reasons for the choice of a sanctuary site are quite unclear. Some are based on places of late Bronze-Age occupation, though it is not known whether this in any way denotes continuity of cult or rather a sense of awe inspired by the visible remains of an earlier age. Natural features such as *springs may be the attraction; *water is an important element in the performance of cult. A spring in the sanctuary, or its vicinity, was often embellished with a fountain house. Water may have to be provided artificially, as at Perachora, or by the construction of wells. It was needed for ritual *purification, but also, when feasting buildings were provided, for more normal cleaning purposes. Sometimes the reason for the location of a sanctuary may be nothing more than an awareness of some unusual character of a place. Shrines in Minoan Crete, in the palaces and elsewhere, were often aligned with 'peak sanctuaries' on a prominent visible mountain top; the idea that similar alignments may explain classical sanctuaries has been promoted, but is unconvincing (see MINOAN AND MYCENAEAN RELIGION). Some sanctuaries are developed for particular communities, and each community would possess one of major significance to it, dedicated to its protecting deity. Others belong to less important gods, or serve only limited sections of the community, classes in society, or villages outside the urban centre of the state. Within the state-context, the location of major extra-urban sanctuaries (see HERAION) could serve to demarcate a community's territory in the face of competing claims by neighbours. Other sanctuaries develop to serve more than one community, up to the 'international' sanctuary such as *Delphi or *Olympia which attract support and worshippers from all over Greece.

The earliest stages of the sanctuaries, where known, are often small and simple. Increasing popularity, larger numbers of worshippers, and the acquisition of greater wealth lead to discernible expansion. Control over the sanctuary, and responsibility for its development, rests extensively with the community at large (see POLIS), through its political bodies, supervising finance, approving and supporting building programmes, and passing all necessary legislation for the conduct of its affairs. Immediate direction is often vested in groups of officials (who have a religious function but are not *priests; see HIEROMNĒMONES): in democratic Athens, and elsewhere, the accounts were scrutinized and published as inscriptions. Smaller sanctuaries were of lower, or minimal, public concern. Many major sanctuaries were not limited to single cults. The acropolis of Athens within the surrounding walls and the gateway, the Propylaea, was a sacred area, the pivot of which was the altar to *Athena. Pausanias lists a whole succession of cult-places within the sacred area, including, for example, a precinct of Brauronian Artemis (see ARTEMIS and BRAURON). (See ATHENS, RELIGIOUS TOPOGRAPHY.) Asclepius at Epidaurus shared his sanctuary with his father, Apollo (probably the original owner), as well as Hera.

The sanctuary would contain 'sacred property'. This might include the utensils and other paraphernalia of sacrifice and feasting, recorded on inscriptions. These both belonged to the god and were used by the god, or his worshippers. They include, at times, valuable *plate, in gold or silver, which in itself constitutes a special offering, but is still essentially a possession to be used. Other offerings are often described as votives, strictly gifts made in response to the successful outcome of a vow, but even with these there may be a related purpose. A statue may well constitute an offering (see STATUES, CULT OF), but is also a commemoration, of service by priests or priestesses (especially those whose office was temporary), of successful achievement whether by the community in war or the individual in athletic contest. In 'international' sanctuaries, individual cities might dedicate *thesauroi*; the term means treasury, but this is a misleading translation, since they are not mere storehouses but offerings in their own right, often dedicated to the god to commemorate a victory in war. Some sanctuaries are oracular and thus needed to provide for the appropriate consultation process; these might require modification of the temple plan (as at Delphi) with perhaps, in addition, special office-type buildings, as at *Didyma.

The sanctuaries of the Roman period represent an essential continuation of these concepts. An important right, confirmed by the Roman authorities in a limited number of cases, is that of asylum, though strictly all sanctuaries, being sacred places, offered potential refuge. In the early 5th cent. BC the regent Pausanias, condemned by his fellow Spartiates, sought refuge in the sanctuary of Athena Chalcioecus, where he could not be put to death, or even allowed to die when he was starved out. In form, Roman sanctuaries are often more regularly planned, a characteristic inherited from Hellenistic architectural concepts, typified by the sanctuary of Artemis at Magnesia ad Maeandrum in its redeveloped, 2nd-cent. BC form. Such sanctuaries are normally a strict rectangle in plan, surrounded by porticos round the boundaries, and with formal gateway buildings which can be closed. The temple, with its altar directly in front, is placed within the resulting courtyard, and often situated to the back of it. The Severan marble plan of the city of Rome shows several such sanctuaries for which other archaeological evidence is inadequate; but this form also characterizes the so-called imperial fora, such as those of Caesar, Augustus, and Trajan, which are essentially courtyard sanctuaries. (*See* FORUM, various entries; ROME (TOPOGRAPHY)). This concept, of the chief temple in its precinct, which continues over a road and frequently a barrier to form the civic *forum, is typical of towns in the western Roman provinces.

In Roman Syria these precincts assume a complex form: large rectangles with formal entrances on all four sides, the principal 'Golden Gate' to the east and the whole structure embellished with towers. The formalism of such sanctuaries may owe something to local cult needs, and the political significance of the priests who control them, but the underlying concepts are general to the entire classical world. *See* ALTARS; DINING-ROOMS; PRIESTS; TEMPLUM; ALBANUS MONS; ARDEA; ARICIA; AVENTINE; LATINI; LAVINIUM; PIETRABONDANTE; PYRGI. *See also* LAWS, RELIGIOUS.

Sandas, an indigenous god of Tarsus, whose symbols (club, bow) and fire-ritual probably account for his Hellenization (i.e. his Greek form) as *Heracles. The cult recurs in Lydia (where he was the consort of *Cybele), Cappadocia, and other nearby regions.

Sarapis (Lat. Serapis), the Hellenized (Gk.) form of Egypt. *wsir ḥp*, *Osiris-*Apis (Osorapis, Oser-), the hypostasis of Osiris and of Apis-bulls entombed at Saqqara. The cult was performed in the temple complex rebuilt by Nectanebo I and II (380–343 BC) above the 'great chambers', later called the Memphis Serapeum. This rebuilding was probably in recognition of the crowds of pilgrims, including many foreigners, who sought healing by incubation, oracles, and *dream-interpretation. Excavation has shown that officials, priests, and poor alike were buried around the Serapeum way. The cult's importance was immediately grasped by the Macedonian occupiers left by Alexander the Great. Ptolemy I made an extra loan of 50 talents for the burial of the Apis-bull and rebuilt the temple approach route.

To provide themselves with a divine Graeco-Egyptian patron, the early Ptolemies (I, II, and III are all cited in the sources: the archaeological evidence suggests all three had a hand) founded a Serapeum on the hill of Rhacotis at Alexandria. The account of Ptolemy's dream and discovery of a statue of ?Pluto at 'Sinope' is a pious fraud based on Osorapis' regular mode of communication; there were quite different traditions, one of which made 'Sesostris' responsible. The discordant interpretations by Hellenistic writers, equating Sarapis with Osiris, *Dionysus, Pluto (*Hades), *Zeus, *Asclepius, etc., suggest something of the creative fusion or melting of categories that Sarapis evoked in Alexandria and beyond: the cult-statue, whose attribution to the sculptor Bryaxis has been needlessly disputed, combined the traits of a benign Pluto with an Osirian deviation, the *kalathos* with ears of grain on his head. In Memphis, Sarapis remained essentially Osorapis, lord of the underworld, demiurge 'from the grave', providing oracles and cures through dreams. But in Alexandria, or Canopus, he was free to be reinterpreted according to political, local, or individual requirement. Certainly Alexandrian Sarapis was at first a god with close connections at court, only later acquiring a following among the Hellenized inhabitants of the Egyptian countryside.

At Memphis, and elsewhere in Egypt, Sarapis 'detained' individuals as *katochoi* in the Serapeum. The fullest subjective account of this status derives from the archive of Ptolemaeus (172–152 BC). This confinement had a religious grain, even if individuals' motives for surrendering their freedom of movement varied. Outside Egypt, analogous self-dedication in the temple is also found; but devotion to Sarapis generally took a different form, membership of a *thiasos* which met for worship and feasting (*sarapiastai*). It was the cult of Sarapis which often inspired the initial Hellenistic expansion of Egyptian cults into the Aegean (Apollonius on *Delos sang daily paeans in honour of his miracles). A gradual decline of dedications (2nd cent. BC–2nd cent. AD) is associated with the growing predominance of Isis, who appears in the royal oath of Ptolemy III Euergetes (246–222 BC) as the secondary element of the pair, but in the Maroneia eulogy of *Isis (*c.*100 BC) as the active partner, selecting Sarapis as her consort. Plutarch, in his *On Isis and Osiris*, hardly mentions Sarapis, presumably because he was so closely aligned with Osiris and had no separate myth. The cult of Sarapis is also secondary in Italy, and much of the western empire, where he appears mainly as a transcendent god, as Zeus, *megas*, *dominus*, *conservator*, *invictus*. This emphasis descends directly from the Ptolemaic cult associating the ruling sovereign with Sarapis as guarantor of royal power, which was transferred to the Roman emperors after 31 BC (cf. Vespasian as 'new Sarapis', and the repeated evocation of Sarapis in relation to Hadrian in AD 130). The dominance of the theme in the west, and the revival of an old link with *Helios (2nd–3rd cents. AD), seems to coincide with an erosion of Sarapis' association with the underworld. This also gave him some value in imperial iconography, especially in the coinage of Commodus and Caracalla, though its significance has been exaggerated.

[Plutarch, *On Isis and Osiris*; Tacitus, *Histories* 4. 83 f.; Apuleius, *Metamorphoses* 11. 19]

sarcophagi A sarcophagus is a coffin for inhumation which in ancient times was often richly decorated. In Minoan Crete and Mycenaean Greece two standard shapes of terracotta coffin—the bath-tub and the chest on four legs with a gable roof—were in use especially from the 14th to the 12th cents. BC, and some, including the famous Haghia Triada sarcophagus, were richly painted. In the late Archaic period sarcophagi of painted clay and rectangular or trapezoidal form were made at or near Clazomenae in western Asia Minor. Sculptured stone sarcophagi appear first in the 5th cent. BC: the finest anthropoid and casket sarcophagi with sculptured reliefs were made by Greek craftsmen for the kings of Sidon in Phoenicia from the 5th cent. to about 300 BC; anthropoid sarcophagi are also known from other sites on the Mediterranean and Black Sea coasts. A distinctive type of sarcophagus with ogival roof was made in Lycia (southwest Asia Minor). Some Hellenistic wooden sarcophagi with painted decoration have survived in the southern Ukraine.

The Etruscans used sculptured sarcophagi of clay and stone from the 6th cent. BC; the two commonest forms are the casket with gabled lid and the type with a reclining effigy of the dead. A few families of republican Rome buried their dead in sarcophagi: that of Lucius Cornelius Scipio Barbatus (consul 298 BC) imitates the form of a contemporary altar. The prevailing rite of cremation in Rome gave way to inhumation in the early 2nd cent. AD, when the rich series of Roman sculptured marble sarcophagi begins. These were made all over the Roman world; two of the best-known centres were in Athens and Docimium (Phrygia), where large sarcophagi were made with figures set between columns. At Rome, especially in the 3rd cent. AD, roughly cut chests were imported from the Greek island quarries of Thasos and Proconnesus to be decorated to the taste of local clients. In some areas with no local supply of stone decorated lead coffins were made, notably in Syria-Palestine and in Britain, where they were often set inside plain stone chests.

See ART, FUNERARY, ROMAN; DEAD, DISPOSAL OF.

Sarpedon, in *Homer's *Iliad* the son of *Zeus and Laodamia, the daughter of *Bellerophon; he was commander of the Lycian contingent of *Priam's allies. He is one of the strongest warriors on the Trojan side and takes a prominent part in the fighting, killing *Heracles' son *Tlepolemus, leading an assaulting group of the allies on to the Greek wall, and making the first breach. The story of his death at the hands of *Patroclus is narrated in detail: Zeus, knowing that he is fated to die, wishes to save his beloved son, but, rebuked by *Hera, allows his death and marks it by causing bloody rain to fall. There is a great fight over Sarpedon's corpse, until *Apollo rescues it on Zeus' instructions; it is then carried back home to Lycia by Sleep and Death (*Hypnos and *Thanatos; subject of a famous late-Archaic Attic vase by Euphronius) and given honourable burial. Post-Homeric accounts make

Sarpedon one of the sons of Zeus and *Europa, explaining the chronological discrepancy by supposing that Zeus allowed him to live for three generations, or by making the Cretan Sarpedon, driven out from Crete to southern Asia Minor by his brother *Minos, grandfather of the Iliadic hero. Ancient critics had already noticed that the Cretan connection was secondary (some made the difference of time six generations). There was a *hero-cult of Sarpedon in Lycia of great antiquity (his hero-shrine is mentioned, for instance, by ancient commentators on the *Iliad* and a Sarpedonium is attested at 1st-cent. BC Xanthus), with which the Homeric story of his burial is presumably to be connected.

[Homer, *Iliad* 2. 876, 5. 628–62, 12. 101 ff., 290 ff., 16. 419–683; Apollodorus 3. 1. 2]

Saturnus, Saturnalia Saturnus is one of the most puzzling gods in Roman cult. His festival (below) was part of the 'Calendar of Numa' (*see* NUMA), and its position, 17 December, midway between Consualia and Opalia, is intelligible if we suppose, as has commonly been done that his name (Sāturnus, also Saeturnus) is to be connected with *sătus* and taken as that of a god of sowing, or of seed-corn. Other historians derive the god from the Etruscan Satre. But neither of these explanations resolves the difficulties raised by the cult of Saturn. The god, whose temple was sited by the north-west corner of the *forum Romanum, is now considered as an Italo-Roman deity (his name is mentioned in the *Carmen Saliare*) who underwent a Hellenizing i.e. Greek *interpretatio* (*see* INTERPRETATIO ROMANA) from the end of the 3rd cent. BC. The difficulty arises from the fact that the cult was celebrated according to the Greek rite, i.e. with the head uncovered (*see* SACRIFICE, ROMAN). To account for these facts, along with the other rites of the Saturnalia of 17 December, notably the fact that the statue of Saturnus, bound for the rest of the year, was freed for this day, as well as other inversion-rituals, the god's function has been defined as that of liberation, one which the obscure Lua Saturni might amplify.

Of the early history of his festival nothing is known: Livy speaks as if it originated in 496 BC, which is obviously not so. At most, some modification of the ritual in the direction of Hellenization took place then. In Cicero's day, at any rate, the festival lasted for seven days. *Augustus reduced it to three, but from the reigns of Gaius and Claudius it attained five days, quite apart from the fact that everyone continued to celebrate for seven days. The Saturnalia were celebrated down to the Christian age and beyond (under the name of *Brumalia*). In the Chronographer of AD 354 (*see* FILOCALUS) the vignette of December represents a person celebrating the Saturnalia, and it is in this context that the famous work of Macrobius entitled *Saturnalia* must be placed. The Saturnalia were the merriest festival of the year, 'the best of days' (Catullus). Slaves were allowed temporary liberty to do as they liked, presents were exchanged, particularly wax candles and *sigilla* (*see* SIGILLARIA). There was also a sort of mock king, *Saturnalicius princeps*, 'leader of the Saturnalia', who presided over the feasts and amusements. As a general rule, Romans at this time adopted a comportment inverting their normal conduct. The social order was inverted, slaves dined before their masters and could allow themselves a certain insolence, leisure-wear (*synthesis*) was worn instead of the toga, as well as the felt bonnet proper to slaves (*pilleus*), and the time was spent eating, drinking, and playing. There is a debate about the claims of Christian writers that gladiators were linked to Saturn and that they were a form of human sacrifice.

[Seneca, *Apocolocyntosis* 8. 2; Epictetus, *Discourses* 1. 25. 8; Lucian, *Saturnalia*]

satyric drama In the Classical period it was normal for a satyr-play to be written by each tragedian for performance after his set of three tragedies at the Athenian City *Dionysia. The chorus is composed of satyrs (see next entry), and is closely associated

with their father Silenus. One complete satyr-play 709 lines long (Euripides' *Cyclops*), survives, together with numerous fragments, notably about half of Sophocles' *Ichneutai* ('Trackers') preserved on papyrus, and numerous vase-paintings inspired by satyr-plays, notably the Pronomos vase, which displays the entire cast of a victorious play. The themes were taken from myth (sometimes connected with the theme of the trilogy), and the earthy preoccupations of the satyrs may have had the effect of reducing the dignity of various heroes, as happens to *Odysseus in the *Cyclops*. Odysseus' speech is, metrically and stylistically, virtually indistinguishable from tragic speech, and even that of the satyrs and Silenus, though lower in tone, remains much closer to tragedy than to comedy. Horace describes tragedy as like a matron who does not descend to uttering trivial verses as she consorts modestly with the impudent satyrs at a festival. There is a set of typical motifs, notably the captivity (explaining their presence in various myths) and eventual liberation of the satyrs, marvellous inventions and creations (of wine, the lyre, fire, etc.), riddles, emergence from the underworld, the care of divine or heroic infants, and athletics. Some of them may reflect the activities of the satyrs in cult (notably initiation into the Dionysiac *thiasos* (*see* DIONYSUS; THIASOS)). *Aristotle reports that tragedy developed from the *satyrikon* (satyr-play-like); *see* TRAGEDY. And it seems that satyric drama was thereafter formally instituted in the festival to preserve what was being lost from tragedy as it turned to non-Dionysiac stories (the first satyric dramatist was said to be Pratinas of Phlius, early 5th cent. BC). Certainly it is too simple to see the function of satyric drama as merely to alleviate the effect of the seriousness of tragedy with comic relief, which could after all have been provided by comedy. Less universal in its appeal than tragedy and comedy, satyric drama had by the mid-4th cent. become detached from the tragic contest. But we hear of a production as late as the 2nd cent. AD, and there is good evidence for its performance in Rome.

satyrs and silens are imaginary male inhabitants of the wild, comparable to the 'wild men' of the European folk tradition, with some animal features, unrestrained in their desire for sex and wine, and generally represented naked. The first mention in literature of 'silens' is as making love to *nymphs in caves; of 'satyrs' it is as 'worthless and mischievous'. On the Attic François vase (c.570 BC) the horse–human hybrids accompanying *Hephaestus (with *Dionysus) back to *Olympus are labelled as silens. It seems that in the course of the 6th cent. BC the (Attic-Ionic) silens were amalgamated with the (Peloponnesian) satyrs (so that the names were used interchangeably) to form, along with nymphs or maenads, the sacred band (*thiasos) of Dionysus. It is a thiasos of young satyrs that, in the 5th cent., forms the chorus of *satyric drama, with Silenus (in keeping with the ancient belief in individual silens) as father of the satyrs. In vase-painting satyrs are at first present in a limited number of myths (the Return of Hephaestus, the Battle of the *Giants, etc.), but in the 5th cent. this number grows considerably, at least partly under the influence of satyric drama.

People dressed up as satyrs, e.g. at the Athenian *Anthesteria, where their frolics are depicted on the 'Choes' vases. Also at the Anthesteria was the procession in which Dionysus arrived in a ship-cart accompanied by satyrs, who are prominent also in great *processions at Alexandria and Rome. In contrast to this public presence, satyrs also conducted mystic *initiation (e.g. the paintings at the Villa of the Mysteries at Pompeii; see MYSTERIES). To be initiated might be to join a satyric thiasos, a community of this world and the next. Hence the occurrence of satyrs in funerary art throughout most of antiquity.

Analogous to this contrast is the ambiguity of the satyrs as grotesque hedonists and yet the immortal companions of a god, cruder than men and yet somehow wiser, combining mischief with wisdom, lewdness with skill in music, animality with divinity. In satyric drama they are the first to sample the creation of culture out of nature in the invention of *wine, of the lyre, of the pipe, and so on. Silenus is the educator of Dionysus. King *Midas extracted from a silen, whom he had trapped in his garden, the wisdom that for men it is best never to have been born, second best to die as soon as possible. And *Virgil's shepherds extract from Silenus a song of great beauty and wisdom. This ambiguity is exploited in Alcibiades' famous comparison of Socrates to the musical satyr Marsyas.

At first somewhat equine, the satyrs become progressively more human in appearance (though from the Hellenistic period more caprine than equine, perhaps through association with *Pan), and may decorate a pastoral landscape or embody, for the visual artist, the charm of a not quite human body, as in the sculpted sleeping satyr known as the 'Barberini Faun'. Popular belief in the presence of satyrs in the wild no doubt persisted throughout antiquity, as did the practice of imitating them in urban festivals, which was banned in Constantinople in AD 692.

[Homeric Hymn to Aphrodite 262–3; Plato, Symposium 215; Virgil, Eclogues 6]

scapegoat See PHARMAKOS

Scheria, the land of the Phaeacians, at which *Odysseus arrives after his shipwreck. It is a fertile country, apparently an island, having an excellent, almost landlocked harbour, by which its city stands, at least one river, and a mild climate (fruits grow all the year round). The population are enterprising and very skilful seafarers, great gossips, boastful, and rather impudent, not very warlike or athletic, fond of pleasure, but kindly and willing to escort strangers in their wonderful ships. Various real places have been suggested as the original of Scheria, the most popular in ancient and modern times being Corcyra (Corfu); but as that is within some 80 miles of Ithaca, whereas Scheria is distant a night's voyage for one of the magical Phaeacian ships, the identification is unlikely. That details of real places have been used for the picture is likely.

[Homer, *Odyssey* 5. 451 ff., 6. 204, 263 ff., 7. 117 ff.]

Sciron or Sciros, names of several related heroic figures connected with Attica, Salamis, and Megara. The name suggests a possible connection with *Athena Sciras and the *Scirophoria, and this is borne out by the cult-places: at Sciron on the Sacred Way, the destination of the Scirophoria procession, and at Phaleron near the sanctuary of Athena Sciras (in an inscription the pair receive *sacrifice at the same altar). From a later period, presumably, comes the integration into Attic mythology, largely through the figure of *Theseus. The Thesean saga distinguishes two figures. Sciron of Megara was one of the many brigands killed by Theseus on his journey to claim his Athenian inheritance; he presumably derives from a Megarian hero, since Plutarch reports the Megarian tradition making him a just man. Sciros king of Salamis helped Theseus by giving him skilled navigators for the voyage to Crete. Another mythical Sciros, identified by Pausanias with the hero buried at Sciron, fought with the Eleusinians against *Erechtheus; *see* ELEUSIS.

Scirophoria or Scira, an Athenian religious festival celebrated on 12 Scirophorion (June), primarily by women. It featured a procession, including the priestess of *Athena, the priest of *Poseidon-*Erechtheus, and perhaps that of *Helios, from the Acropolis to a sanctuary of Athena Sciras at Sciron on the road to *Eleusis near the crossing of the *Cephissus. The ceremony involved the 'carrying of the skira' which may have been a large sunshade (*skiron*) or an image of Athena made of gypsum (*skira*). At Sciron there was a sanctuary of *Demeter, Kore (*see* PERSEPHONE), Athena, and Poseidon, quite likely the site of the festival. Some think that there the

women performed rites preliminary to Demeter's later *Thesmophoria, but the evidence is garbled and inconclusive. In any case the deities and location of the festival suggest an amalgamation of Eleusinian and Athenian cults.

sculpture, Greek

Origins (c.1000–c.600 BC) Of Dark-Age sculpture, only small bronzes and terracottas survive; unpretentious at first, by the 8th cent. they tend to favour the rigorously analytical forms of contemporary vase-painting. Some wooden cult images certainly existed, though most were perhaps aniconic or semi-iconic. Yet *Homer describes an *Athena at *Troy that was probably lifesize and fully human in form; and a half-lifesize *Apollo, a *Leto, and an *Artemis, bronze-plated over a wooden core, survive from Cretan Drerus as confirmation (c.750). This technique is near-eastern in origin.

The Cretan city-states were socially and politically precocious, and their eastern trade, in which Corinth soon joined, set off a new cycle of experimentation c.700. In sculpture, the most popular of these orientalizing styles is usually called 'Daedalic' after the mythical founder of Greek sculpture (*see* DAEDALUS). Diffused through terracotta plaques and popular in a wide variety of media and scales, Daedalic is characterized by a strict frontality and an equally strict adherence to stylized, angular forms; coiffures are elaborately layered in the Syrian manner. When employed on temples (Gortyn, Prinias), it often follows near-eastern precedent in both placement and iconography.

Meanwhile, Cycladic sculptors were looking to Egypt, receptive to foreigners from 664. After c.650 the walking, kilted Egyptian males were adapted to form the *kouros* type, nude and free-standing—supposedly a 'discovery' of *Daedalus. Marble was the preferred medium, and adherence to the shape of the quarried block tended to make the finished work look like a four-sided relief. The type soon spread to east

Greece and the mainland. In the earliest *kouroi*, as in their draped female counterparts, the *korai*, the Daedalic style predominated, but by *c*.600 its rigid stylization was breaking down as sculptors sought new ways of communicating male and female beauty, to delight the gods or to commemorate the dead.

Archaic sculpture (c.600–c.480 BC) Archaic sculpture seeks exemplary patterns for reality, somewhat akin to the formulae of Homeric and archaic poetry. The aim was still to make sense of the phenomenal world, to generalize from experience, but in a more flexible and direct way. Each local school developed its own preferences in ideal male beauty.

Korai offered fewer opportunities for detailed physical observation, but just as many for displays of beauty appropriate to their subjects' station in life and value to a male-dominated world. Their sculptors concentrated upon refining the facial features, creating a truly feminine proportional canon, and indicating the curves of the body beneath the drapery.

Both types could be adapted for cult statues (*see* STATUES, CULT OF), and the sources recount much work in this genre, often associated with the new stone *temples that now served as focal points of city-state religion. Gold and ivory (chryselephantine) statues also begin to appear; several have been found at Delphi. From *c*.600, temple exteriors were often embellished with architectural sculpture, first in limestone, then in marble; treasuries for votives were soon enhanced in the same way. Mythological narratives first supplemented, then supplanted primitive power-symbols like gorgons and lions (Corcyra (mod. Corfu), 'Hekatompedon', and Hydra pediments at Athens). Sculptors soon adapted their subjects to their frames, whether triangular (see above), rectangular (Ionic friezes at Ephesus, Samos, and *Delphi), or square (metopes of the Sicyonian treasury at Delphi and temples at Paestum and Selinus); to

carve pediments in higher relief and even in the round ('Old temple' pediments at Athens; Apollo temple at Delphi); and to dramatize the story by judicious timing, lively postures and gestures, and compelling rendering of detail.

Classical sculpture (c.480–c.330 BC) 'The dynamic of the subject-matter'—the living body, unencumbered by arcane symbolism or religious inhibitions—had always played an important part in modifying the formulaic style, and surely contributed signally to its abandonment, but other factors also helped. Three stand out: a strong commitment to credible narration, prompting sculptors to think of the body as an integrated organism, not a mechanism assembled from discrete parts; a feeling that naturalism was a mixed blessing, requiring corrective measures to preserve the statue's monumentality; and a new quest for interiority, for exploring man's inner self. Around 480 even the automaton-like kouros gave way to more subtly mobile, narrative-oriented figures, monumental in physique and grave of countenance, pausing as if to think, like the 'Critius' boy, or resolute in action, like the Tyrannicides.

This more flexible, holistic, and contextual view of man was abetted by a simultaneous repudiation of late Archaic 'excess' in decorative patterning in favour of a rigorously applied doctrine of formal restraint. The new style strongly recalls the *sōphrosynē* or 'wise moderation' urged by the poets. This was an ethic much in vogue after the replacement of aristocracies at Athens and elsewhere by limited democracies, and particularly after the spectacular defeat of the hubristic and excessive Persians in 490 and 480.

Sōphrosynē is best exemplified in the sculptures of the temple of *Zeus at *Olympia, carved between 470 and 457. Their themes bespeak insolent violence overcome by divinely-inspired wisdom, and the participants act out their characters like participants in a tragedy. The expansive rendering brings power to the narrative, while a self-imposed economy of means allows bold distinctions in characterization, unhampered by distracting clutter. The same is true of bronzes like the Zeus from Artemisium and Riace Warrior A (one of two bronzes recovered in the 1970s from ancient shipwreck), whose carefully calculated postures are eloquent, respectively, of divine might and heroic potency; and of works known only in copy like the Discobolos of Myron, whose swinging curves capture the essence of athletic endeavour.

Throughout, the aim is to find forms or modes that express the general or typical, yet are open to some variation for individuality's sake: witness the differences between the two Riace warriors. Further progress was the work of two geniuses, Polyclitus of Argos and Phidias of Athens (active c.470–420).

Polyclitus was remembered as supreme in the rendering of mortals, Phidias as the unsurpassed interpreter of the divine, master of chryselephantine, and propagandist for Periclean Athens. In his Athena Parthenos and Zeus at Olympia he sought to convey the majesty of the gods by subtle manipulation of the rendering, and by surrounding them with mythological sagas to demonstrate their power. On the *Parthenon (447–432) he extended this technique to the exterior sculpture. Athena's power and reach are proclaimed by a closely co-ordinated programme of narratives, and her chosen people, the Athenians, are exalted by a rendering unsurpassed in Greek sculpture for its fluency, grace, harmony of body and clothing, and perfection of formal design. In this way the typical became the citizen ideal.

Phidias' followers, active during the Peloponnesian War (431–404) both pressed his style to its limits and turned it to other ends. Paeonius' *Nike and the parapet of the Nike Temple on the Athenian Acropolis manipulate drapery to create a surface brilliance that seduces the spectator into believing that what he sees is truth: victory scintillates before his eyes.

Whereas in the Peloponnese the war only benefited the conservative pupils of Polyclitus, in postwar Athens, demand for sculpture was virtually restricted to gravestones, revived around 430 (see ART, FUNERARY, GREEK). Not until c.370 could the Athenians celebrate recovery by commissioning a bronze Eirene and Plutus (Peace and Wealth) from Cephisodotus, a work that exudes Phidian majesty and harmony. Also seeking new ways to the divine, Cephisodotus' son Praxiteles created his revolutionary Aphrodite of Cnidus, proclaiming the power of the love goddess through total nudity and a beguiling radiance of feature and surface. Meanwhile, his contemporary Scopas sought to perfect an acceptable formula for conveying the passions of gods and men.

Scopas was a leading sculptor in the team engaged by Mausolus of Caria for his gigantic tomb, the Mausoleum. Its unparalleled magnificence announced the advent of the Hellenistic world; a pointer, too, was the hiring away of the best artistic talent by a '*barbarian' patron. The real revolutionary, though, was Lysippus of Sicyon (active c.370–310), who radically transformed Greek sculpture's central genre, the male nude.

Hellenistic Sculpture (c.330–c.30) The phenomenal expansion of the Greek world under Alexander created a bonanza of opportunity for sculptors. Lysippus' pupils and others were hired to create commemorative, votive, and cult statues for the new kingdoms. Portraitists were particularly in demand to render and where necessary improve the features of Successor kings, generals, and dignitaries.

The devastating wars of the years around 200 mark a watershed in Hellenistic sculpture. Following Pergamene precedent, the victorious Romans looted hundreds of statues and began to entice Greek sculptors west to work directly for them; realistic portraiture and Athenian neo-Classical cult-images were most in demand. As the Roman market grew, Greek workshops also began to respond with decorative copies and reworkings of Classical masterpieces for direct shipment to Italy.

Meanwhile the main beneficiaries of Rome's intervention, Pergamum and Achaea, celebrated in style. Eumenes II of Pergamum built the Great Altar, probably after Macedon's final defeat in 168, embellishing it with a 'baroque' Battle of the *Giants and a quasi-pictorial inner frieze narrating the life of the city's mythical founder, *Telephus. He also installed a copy of the Athena Parthenos in the Pergamene library to advertise his claim to rule the 'Athens of the east'. Attalus III of Pergamum willed his domains to Rome in 133, bringing its sculptural tradition to a close, but the most crushing blow was dealt by the Mithradatic Wars (88–66), which left Greece and Asia devastated and impoverished. Though some striking work was still produced, largely in portraiture, sculptors now moved to Italy in large numbers, creating the last of the great Hellenistic schools, but now on foreign soil and pledged to foreign masters. When the Carrara quarries opened c.50 and *Augustus officially endorsed imperial classicism after Cleopatra VII's defeat in 31 BC, the west at last reigned supreme. See IMAGERY; SCULPTURE, ROMAN.

sculpture, Roman Roman sculpture was produced in a variety of materials (bronze, marble, other stones, precious metals, terracotta) but it is marble that is seen as typically Roman because so much that survives is in this medium. Sculpture was used for commemorative purposes (for display in public and in private contexts, especially the tomb), for state propaganda, in religious settings, and for decorative purposes, and various different forms were developed: statues and busts, relief friezes and panels, and architectural embellishments. The taste for sculpture in the Classical Greek style was fostered by the Augustan regime (see AUGUSTUS), and had periodic revivals, most notably in the reign of Hadrian, but from the late republic onwards there were developments

in subject matter and style that are distinctly Roman, though owing much to Greek precursors. This is seen for example in the development of portraiture in late republican Rome.

Perhaps the most original Roman developments occurred in the series of historical reliefs used to decorate major state monuments and to express current ideologies. The taste for the representation of contemporary events first appears in the late republic (e.g. the relief from the so-called 'altar of Domitius Ahenobarbus' in the Louvre, with its scene of a *sacrifice at the closure of the census): such a documentary approach continues under the empire, and can be seen at its most developed on the columns of Trajan and Marcus Aurelius, where the stories of Rome's wars with the barbarians are represented on a long relief spiralling round the column. Realism and allegory appear side by side on one of the most complex and subtle Roman propaganda monuments, the *Ara Pacis Augustae, where 'realistic' procession scenes are placed next to mythological, allegorical, and decorative panels to express the ideals of the Augustan regime. Later state reliefs might combine the two approaches, as in the panels inside the arch of Titus representing the Judaean *triumph (see JEWS): the carrying of the spoils of Jerusalem is represented in a realistic (if dramatic) way, whereas the emperor in his triumphal chariot is accompanied by deities and allegorical figures.

In the provinces local styles and schools of sculpture developed. The sculptors of the eastern provinces, especially Greece and Asia Minor, continued and developed the Classical and Hellenistic styles: they travelled widely around the empire, working on major monuments such as the 'Sebasteion' at Aphrodisias or the forum of Septimius Severus at Lepcis Magna. In the northern and western provinces Celtic traditions fused with Roman to produce interesting hybrids, such as the pediment of the temple of Sulis Minerva at Bath (*Aquae Sulis). See ART, ANCIENT ATTITUDES TO; IMAGERY.

Scylla (1), fantastic monster with twelve feet and six heads who lurked in a cave situated high up on the cliff opposite Charybdis, darting her necks out like a kind of multiple moray eel to seize dolphins, sharks, or passing sailors. Her voice is the yelp of a newborn pup (etymologizing on *skylax*, dog), and she has other canine elements: three rows of teeth, like a shark (*kyōn*), and a mother who in the *Odyssey* is called Crataiïs but whom *Hesiod and *Acusilaus identify as *Hecate, the underworld goddess associated with a pack of savage hounds; a passage in the *Odyssey* shows that *Apollonius Rhodius was right to identify the two. In art (e.g. coin of Acragas, late 5th cent.) and later literature the dog-heads are transposed to her waist, an iconography also attested for Hecate in the 5th cent., thus freeing her upper body to become an alluring woman, while her lower body becomes fishy. Later authors elaborate, equipping her with an earlier human existence (which leads to a frequent conflation with *Scylla (2), the daughter of *Nisus (1), as in *Virgil) from which she had been metamorphosed by a jealous love-rival—Circe, according to *Ovid. The Hellenistic poet Lycophron knows a story that she was killed by *Heracles but restored to life by her father *Phorcys, who scorched her corpse with torches (another Hecate motif).

[Homer, *Odyssey* 11. 597, 12. 85 ff., 245 ff.; Lucretius 5. 892 f.; Virgil, *Eclogues* 6. 74–7; Ovid, *Metamorphoses* 13. 730 ff., 14. 1 ff.]

Scylla (2) *See* NISUS (1).

Scythian religion Scythia is the broad term used by Greeks and Romans to characterize the lands to their north and east, roughly from the Danube to the Don, Caucasus, and Volga. Typically, classical writers present Scythia as a chill wilderness, an 'otherness' of savages and uncivilized practices (from blinding, scalping, and flaying through tattooing to the drinking of wine unmixed with water). Scythians and Scythian customs (including religion) were a favourite literary theme from Herodotus and Pseudo-Hippocrates onwards. The histor-

icity of such accounts remains the subject of scholarly debate, but their ideological function has been established beyond doubt. Classical writers were particularly interested in Scythian nomadism, uncivilized but attractive in its primitive simplicity. Accordingly, Scythia might be imagined as a source of ignorance. But it can also be a source of wisdom, as personified by the legendary figure of the wise Scythian prince *Anacharsis.

[Herodotus 4. 59–70]

Secular Games, theatrical games (*ludi scaenici*; *see* LUDI) and sacrifices (*see* SACRIFICE, ROMAN) performed by the Roman state to commemorate the end of one saeculum and the beginning of a new one. The saeculum, defined as the longest span of human life, was fixed in the republic as an era of 100 years. The ceremony took place in the Campus Martius, near the Tiber. The explanatory myth was that one Valesius, who wished to save his children from the plague, inadvertently fulfilled an oracle by giving them water to drink from an altar of Dis Pater and *Persephone, at a spot which was known as Tarentum or Terentum; in thanks for their cure he established here three nights of sacrifices and games. Republican celebrations of the Secular Games are not well attested. Those ascribed to the consulship of Valerius Corvus, 348 BC, who belonged to the same *gens* as the mythical Valesius, may be mythical; the Secular Games of 249 BC, are probably the first authentic ones. The celebration, resulting from consultation of the Sibylline Books (*see* QUINDECIMVIRI; SYBIL), was under the direction of the *decimviri* (later *quindecimviri*) *sacris faciundis*. Many scholars believe that the ceremony was actually introduced in 249 from Tarentum, though the connection of the games with the south Italian city is by no means certain. The next celebration took place in 146 BC (a date attested by contemporary writers, and therefore more trustworthy than Livy's date of 149). A century later there was concern about the ending of the saeculum and games may have been planned. None were held, but the messianic expectations of *Virgil's Fourth Eclogue arose from speculations about Caesar's relation to the saeculum.

*Augustus' plans to celebrate the saeculum were known in the 20s BC, and were referred to by Virgil in the *Aeneid* ('aurea condet saecula'). At Augustus' request, the *quindecimviri* consulted the Sibylline Books and discovered a prophecy sanctioning Secular Games with many novel features. The *ludi* of 17 BC are fully recorded in an inscription, set up at the Tarentum (above). The saeculum was now fixed at 110 years. The *ludi* retained three nights of sacrifices and games, but Dis Pater and Persephone were replaced by the Moerae (*Fates), the Eileithyiae (Goddesses of Childbirth, *see* EILEITHYIA), and Terra Mater (Mother Earth), and three daytime celebrations were added, to *Jupiter, *Juno, and *Apollo and *Diana. The Augustan games marked not the passing of an era, but the birth of a new age. Other novelties include the addition of seven supplementary days of more modern entertainment in theatre and circus, and *sellisternia* held by 110 matrons for Juno and Diana. After the offerings on the third day, 27 boys and 27 girls (*see* CAMILLUS) sang Horace's Secular Hymn, first at the temple of Apollo and then on the *Capitol. In the hymn Horace brings into great prominence Augustus' patron god Apollo in his new Palatine temple.

The antiquarian emperor Claudius next celebrated games, in AD 47, on a new cycle, the eight-hundredth birthday of Rome. Taking their lead from Claudius, games were also held the following two centuries, in AD 148 and 248, but these were not counted in the official numbered sequence of games. The next games on (or nearly on) the Augustan cycle were celebrated by Domitian in AD 88 (six years early) and Septimius Severus in 204 (back on the Augustan cycle). Another inscription from the Tarentum records this celebration (which included a new secular hymn). It was to be the last celebration, as games were not held in AD 314 by *Constantine I, newly converted to *Christianity.

Securitas, often with epithets like 'publica', 'Augusta' or 'temporum' (of the times), associated with the emperor or the state as a 'virtue' or 'desirable state'. Securitas was invoked when some imminent danger had been averted or on an occasion like 10 January AD 69, when the Arval Brothers (*see* FRATRES ARVALES) sacrificed to her among other gods on Galba's adoption of his heir. On coins her characteristic attribute is the column on which she leans.

Sedulius (fl. AD 435). His *Paschale Carmen,* five books of hexameters (with prose paraphrase) on Christ's life and miracles, is mainly an adaptation of the Gospels with an emphasis on the status of Christ. Thick with Virgilian echoes, and perhaps intended to rival the *Aeneid*, it long proved popular. Two hymns also survive.

seers *See* AUGURES; DIVINATION; IAMUS; LAMPON; MELAMPUS (1); MOPSUS; PROPHECIES; TIRESIAS.

Selene, Greek moon-goddess, was according to *Hesiod daughter of the Titans (*see* TITAN) *Hyperion and Theia, sister of *Helios and *Eos; she later became Helios' daughter, in recognition apparently of the idea that the moon shines by borrowed light. Selene drives the moon chariot, drawn by a pair of horses or oxen, or she rides on a horse or mule or ox. In myth, she is best known for her love for *Endymion, which caused Zeus to cast him into an eternal sleep in a cave on Mt. Latmus, where Selene visits him (first in Sappho); similar stories attach to Eos, the Dawn. In another myth she was lured into the woods by amorous *Pan. Actual worship of Selene, as of Helios, is treated by Aristophanes as characteristic of barbarians in opposition to Greeks. Like Helios, if in lesser degree, she seems to have infiltrated cult from the late Hellenistic period onwards. A more important way in which the moon had a place in religious life was through the identification with it (but not necessarily with the mythological Selene) of major goddesses such as *Artemis (first in *Aeschylus) or *Hecate (*Sophocles); *see also* MĒN.

[Hesiod, *Theogony* 371; Aristophanes, *Peace* 406; Virgil, *Georgics* 3. 391–3]

sellisternium, a religious banquet at which the goddesses sat on chairs (*sellae:* *Juno and *Minerva at the *epulum Iovis,* 'the banquet for *Jupiter'), whereas at the *lectisternium* they reclined (at least originally) together with the gods on couches. *Sellisternia* were commonly offered by women (for Juno, and at the *Secular Games for Juno and *Diana). Also in the cult of *Hercules at the Ara Maxima ('The Greatest Altar') only chairs were used at banquets.

Semele, a daughter of *Cadmus of Thebes, seduced by *Zeus, who visited her unseen, and by whom she conceived a child. At the urging of *Hera, she persuaded Zeus to show himself to her: he appeared in the form of a thunderbolt, which killed her. Zeus removed the embryo from the corpse, sewed it into his own thigh, and eventually gave birth to *Dionysus, whom *Hermes handed over to Semele's sister Ino, to rear. The story is summarized by *Apollodorus. *Homer's version, although brief, implies that the birth was normal ('Semele gave birth to Dionysus'); so does Hesiod. As a cult figure, Semele possessed a *sēkos*—an open-air enclosure, formerly her bridal chamber—on the Cadmeia at Thebes, which was the focal point of the sanctuary of Dionysus Cadmeus (note also the *sēkos* of Ino at Chaeronea). There is no agreement about Semele's origins: divine or human, Greek or non-Greek; Thraco-Phrygian, Semitic, and Egyptian etymologies compete, but without conviction.

[Apollodorus 3. 4. 3; Homer, *Iliad* 14. 323–5; Hesiod, *Theogony* 940–2]

Semiramis in history was Sammu-ramat, wife of Shamshi-Adad V of Assyria, mother of Adad-nirari III, with whom she campaigned against Commagene in 805 BC. Her inscribed stela stood with stelae of kings and high officials in Aššur. In Greek legend, she was the daughter of the Syrian goddess Derceto at Ascalon, wife of Onnes (probably the first Sumerian sage Oannes) and then of Ninos, eponymous king of Nineveh; she conquered 'Bactria' and built 'Babylon' (the historian Berossus denied this). In Armenian legend, she conquered Armenia (ancient Urartu), built a palace and waterworks, and left inscriptions.

Semitism, anti- The anti-Jewish movements of Graeco-Roman antiquity have led to scholarly debate over (*a*) their causes and (*b*) their relationship to 'anti-Semitism'—i.e. the modern (and mainly western) phenomenon of ideologically driven prejudice against *Jews and the Jewish religion (*see* JUDAISM). The episodes most discussed are the measures of *Antiochus (1) IV and his successors in Judaea, the conflicts between Jews and 'Greek' citizens in the eastern Roman provinces (above all Syria and Alexandria), and the series of expulsions of Jews from Rome. As to (*a*), scholarly argument focuses on how far, if at all, ancient anti-Jewishness in essence was a response to the religious and cultural otherness of Jews, described with varied reactions (sympathy included) by classical writers from *Hecataeus (2) on (the 'substantialist' model); or whether (the 'functionalist' model) it was grounded in concrete, localized conflicts (at Alexandria, Jewish aspirations to Greek citizenship; Greek resentment of Roman protection of the Jews). As to (*b*), many scholars see 'anti-Semitism' as a modern concept unsuited for retrojection to antiquity; others claim to recognize a unique type of ancient antipathy directed at the Jews alone, prefiguring the (in some ways related) phenomenon of Roman hostility to and persecution of early *Christianity.

Semo Sancus Dius Fidius, a deity of puzzling origin, nature, and name, said to be Sabine, *see* SABINI (e.g. Propertius identifies him with *Hercules, apparently from the interpretation of Dius Fidius as Iovis filius, 'son of *Jupiter'). The name of the god is thought to be Sancus (sometimes Sanctus), from *sancire*, 'sanction'. Some scholars accept the affirmation of one ancient source that sancus is the Sabine word for 'sky'. Semo has no clear meaning. It was once thought to be a generic name like *genius, but the view today is that a seed-god is in question, although his relation with Sancus is unexplained. In any case Dius Fidius, whose name locates him in Jupiter's ambit (the Oscan and Umbrian Fisius Sancios makes this explicit), in the historical period is firmly united with Sermo Sancus, and is worshipped with him in the temples in Rome on the Quirinal hill and on the Tiber island. In everyday speech Sancus was the name used, in the language of the calendars Dius Fidius (5 June). In historical times SSDF is connected with oaths and treaties, hence the common oath *medius fidius* and the deposition of the treaty with Gabii in the Quirinal temple. Hence he has some connection with thunder. Christians believed that dedications 'to Semo Deus Sanctus' (Semoni deo Sancto) referred to the deification of Simon the mage.

[Ovid, *Fasti* 6. 213–18]

Semos of *Delos (*c*.200 BC), Greek antiquarian, was a careful, scholarly compiler, whose geographical and antiquarian works include: *Delias*, an 8-book survey of the geography, antiquities, institutions, and products of Delos; *Nesias*, a work on islands; *On Paros*; *On Pergamum*; and a *Periodoi*. From his *On *Paeans*, a valuable fragment survives describing the masks, dress, and performance of 'improvisers', 'erect phalli', and 'phallus-bearers'.

septemviri epulones, the latest addition to the four major colleges of Roman *priests. They were instituted by law in 196 BC and were then three in number (*tresviri*), all apparently plebeians. Their first responsibility, from which they take their name, was the organization of the *epulum Iovis* (Feast of Jupiter), a great feast at the games (*see* JUPITER; LUDI), attended by the senate and people and presided over by the images of the Capitoline deities (*see* CAPITOL). The number of priests increased from three to seven and later ten, though the seven remained their title.

Septizodium (or Septizonium), a freestanding ornamental façade and nymphaeum dedicated by Septimius Severus in AD 203 closing the vista of the via Appia and screening the south-east corner of the *Palatine hill at Rome. It was designed like the rear scenery of a theatre, with a series of large semi-circular niches, framed by three storeys of Corinthian columns and decorated with statuary. Although part of the building appears on the Severan marble plan of Rome and the east end survived into the 16th cent., the exact reconstruction is debated. Earlier examples of septizodia occur in Rome and north Africa. The adjective 'seven-statued' (heptazōnos) was applied to the seven planets which governed the days of the week, but it is not clear what astronomical or astrological significance was attached to these structures.

Septuagint (in abbreviation, LXX), the collection of Jewish writings which became the Old Testament of the Greek-speaking Christians. They are mainly translated from the Hebrew (or Aramaic) scriptures but include also some other pieces composed by Jews in the Hellenistic period, some in Greek and others translated from lost Semitic originals.

The name is derived from a story preserved in Greek, the *Letter of Aristeas* (probably of the mid-2nd cent. BC) relating that Ptolemy II Philadelphus, the contemporary king of Egypt, asked for a translation of the Jewish Law (the Torah, i.e. the Pentateuch), and was sent from Jerusalem 72 learned Jews who on the island of Pharos near Alexandria made a Greek translation of it for the royal library. (The number 70 became a popular alternative to 72 probably because of the widespread use of this number elsewhere in Jewish tradition.) The story which at first had some verisimilitude was embellished by later writers with legendary elements and was extended to include beside the Pentateuch the other translated books. The LXX was authoritative for Philon, who claimed that the translators had been divinely inspired.

The translation was evidently done by different hands at different times between the 3rd cent. BC and the beginning of the Christian era. It was intended primarily for those Jews who having migrated into Egypt and other Greek-speaking lands became more at home with the Greek language than with the Hebrew. The Septuagint early became the Bible of the Christian movement and is quoted in the New Testament and in later Christian writers as well as by the Jews Philon and Josephus, although even before the Christian era some Jews had begun to revise it in the light of the Hebrew text. Apart from Jews and Christians few ancient writers show any knowledge of it. Greek and Roman references to things Jewish are not derived directly from it. The citation of Genesis in the anonymous treatise On the Sublime is a single exception that proves the rule. The influence of the LXX is probably first manifest in less literary circles, as in the *Corpus Hermeticum* (*see* HERMES TRISMEGISTUS) and in the magical papyri. Translations of the Old Testament into Latin and some other languages were chiefly based upon the Greek, so that *Jerome's decision to use the Hebrew in preparing the Latin Vulgate was revolutionary.

The Greek translations of the several books or parts of them vary in style and in degree of literalness. When not influenced by the original Semitic idiom, their Greek, as in the New Testament, and in non-literary documents of the period, represents the vernacular Hellenistic (koinē).

Since the Hebrew from which the LXX was translated is older than the major Hebrew MSS known to us and than the standardized (Masoretic) text of the Old Testament, its apparent differences reflect some variation in the underlying Hebrew. The discovery of the *Dead Sea Scrolls shows that such differ-

ences existed before AD 70. These early MSS sometimes agree with the Septuagint against the Masoretic text, sometimes vice versa, and (in the Pentateuch) sometimes with the Samaritan Hebrew. Sometimes they contain a text different from all other known texts. Just what is the history of such variant texts is still under debate.

In like manner the Greek MSS show variation, suggesting that they were corrupted in copying or were deliberately edited or revised. This variation also is the object of continuing study. Again, limited finds near the Dead Sea or elsewhere of fragmentary early Greek MSS of parts of the Old Testament have provided fresh grounds for conjecture in this field, particularly from the evidence of Theodotion-type readings in the Greek Minor Prophets scroll from Nahal Hever. Each form of text, whether Hebrew or Greek, had its own associations and history to the extent that it may be misleading to refer to the LXX as if a single original text had once existed.

Perhaps just because the Christians used the LXX, later Jews, if they wished a Greek translation at all, made new ones or revived earlier ones. Three of these are attached to the names of Theodotion, Aquila, and Symmachus, and were copied in columns parallel to the Hebrew and the Septuagint in the famous Hexapla of Origen in the 3rd cent. of the Christian era. They are no longer extensively preserved. *See* JEWISH-GREEK LITERATURE.

Serapis *See* SARAPIS.

Set (called Typhon by the Greeks) was a god of Upper Egypt. He appears in the myth of *Osiris as the wicked brother who murders the great god of the underworld and wounds his son *Horus. The role of Set in this myth was well known to the Greeks, hence he is the wicked Typhon in Plutarch's essay concerning *Isis and Osiris. The Greek *Typhon was a wicked son of *Gaea and *Tartarus who was overcome by *Zeus, just as Horus finally overcame Set.

[Plutarch, *On Isis and Osiris*]

Seven against Thebes, myth. *Oedipus' curse upon his sons *Eteocles ('True Glory') and Polynices ('Much Strife') results in their dispute over the throne of Thebes and in Polynices calling upon his father-in-law *Adrastus, King of Argos, and five other heroes (in the epic, *Tydeus, Capaneus, *Parthenopaeus, Mecisteus, and the seer *Amphiaraus). These seven heroes fight at, and match, the mythical seven gates of Thebes. In particular, Zeus strikes Capaneus with a lightning-bolt, the two brothers slaughter each other, the seer Amphiaraus (who joins the expedition through the treachery of his wife Eriphyle) is swallowed up by the earth, and Tydeus is denied immortality when Athene finds him devouring the brains of *Melanippus. This failed expedition was recounted in three epic Thebaids (1) around 700/600 BC, in *c.*7,000 lines, (2) by Antimachus, so long-winded that it took 24 books to reach Thebes, (3) by Statius in 1st cent. AD. *See* EPIC CYCLE. Corinna too wrote a lyric *Seven against Thebes*. Capaneus, Tydeus, Amphiaraus and Adrastus provided material for various lesser tragedians. In the case of *Sophocles we only know of an *Amphiaraus*. *Euripides' *Phoenician Women* is set in Thebes during the conflict, *Hypsipyle* drew on an episode at Nemea as the Argive army advanced towards Thebes and the *Suppliant Women* presents Adrastus and the mothers of the fallen, unburied, Argive heroes appealing to *Theseus and Athenian civilized values. Aeschylus' *Seven against Thebes* was the last play of his Theban trilogy (467 BC), following the *Laius* and *Oedipus*. It focuses on Eteocles' acceptance of the task of fighting his own brother and the impact of their deaths on the family—a catastrophic end to the House of Laius. It was an esteemed play, whose text appears to have been rehandled, particularly to allow a final view of *Antigone in the light of Sophocles' *Antigone*. *See also* EPIGONI.

[Apollodorus 3. 6. 1–7. 1; Aeschylus, *Seven against Thebes*; Euripides, *Phoenician Women, Suppliant Women*; Statius, *Thebaid*]

seven wonders of the ancient world, canon of seven 'sights' of art and architecture. First attested in the 2nd cent. BC, the canon comprises the pyramids of Egypt, the city walls of Babylon, the hanging gardens of *Semiramis there, the temple of Artemis at Ephesus, the statue of Zeus at *Olympia, the Mausoleum of Halicarnassus, and the colossus of Rhodes (*see* HELIOS). The concept was developed in individual references to a single wonder and especially in complete lists of seven, sometimes drawn up to celebrate an 'eighth' wonder. Later lists keep the number, but not always the identity of the wonders. Other wonders like the Pharus of Alexandria, the *Labyrinth, Egyptian Thebes, and the temple of Zeus at Cyzicus first feature in Pliny's list, the altar of horns at *Delos, first in Martial, the Ecbatana palace of Cyrus, first in Ampelius, the Asclepieum of Pergamum and the *Capitol of Rome, first in a late epigram. Christian authors replace pagan sanctuaries with Noah's ark and Solomon's temple or add the Hagia Sophia church in *Constantinople, eventually listing up to sixteen to accommodate both traditional and new wonders.

sexuality and religion *See* ASCETICISM; POLLUTION.

shamans *See* ABARIS; ARISTEAS; EMPEDOCLES; EPIMENIDES; PYTHAGORAS AND PYTHAGOREANISM; ZALMOXIS.

shame *See* NEMESIS; PUDICITIA.

Sibyl The word Sibylla, of uncertain etymology, appears first in Heraclitus (6th cent. BC) and was used as a proper name by the 5th cent. BC. Specific oracles relating to events in the 4th cent. appear to have been attributed to the Sibyl by the historian Ephorus. Originally the Sibyl seems to have been a single prophetic woman, but by the time of Heraclides Ponticus (4th cent. BC) a number of places claimed to be the birthplace of Sibylla, traditions concerning a number of different Sibyls began to circulate, and the word came to be a generic term rather than a name. There are a number of Sibylline catalogues, of which the most important was that compiled by *Varro for his *Res Divinae*. It lists ten:

(1) Persian; (2) Libyan; (3) Delphic; (4) Cimmerian (in Italy); (5) Erythraean (named Herophile); (6) Samian; (7) Cumaean; (8) Hellespontine; (9) Phrygian; (10) Tiburtine. Other sources mention Egyptian, Sardian, Hebrew, and Thessalian Sibyls. The most important discussion of different traditions, which emphasizes the local connections of Sibyls, is given by *Pausanias. Inscriptions from Erythrae record sacrifices to the Sibyl and a sacred grove theoretically marking Herophile's birthplace. There are coins commemorating local Sibyls from Erythrae, Cumae, and Gergis.

The nature of Sibylline inspiration is diversely reported. *Virgil offers a famous description of the Cumaean Sibyl uttering ecstatic prophecy under the inspiration of *Apollo, but texts from Erythrae or recorded in various ways by Phlegon of Tralles, Plutarch, and Pausanias clearly state that the Sibyl spoke under her own inspiration. The evidence for Sibylline inspiration provided by the extant corpus of Sibylline oracles is inconsistent. Until the 4th cent. AD, the format is consistent: all but one of the extant texts are in Greek hexameter verse. Latin translations of Greek texts, and, possibly, some original Latin compositions date from the 4th cent. or later, as does the Greek archetype of the prose oracle of the Tiburtine Sibyl (subsequently much adapted in Latin, Arabic, and Old French down to the 12th cent.).

Widespread interest in Sibyls throughout the Mediterranean world probably stems from the connection between the Sibyl and Rome that dates to, at the very latest, the early 5th cent. BC. Legend has it that the collection first came to Rome in the reign of *Tarquinius Priscus, who is said to have bought three books from the Cumaean Sibyl and placed them in the care of a priestly college (see QUINDECIMVIRI SACRIS FACIUNDIS), to be consulted only at the command of the senate; the senate could also vote to add new books to the state's collection after inspection by the college. This collection was housed in the temple of Capitoline Jupiter (see CAPITOL), where it was destroyed in the burning of the Capitol in 83 BC. After this the senate commissioned a board of three to make a collection from various places. Augustus subsequently moved this collection to the temple of *Palatine Apollo. The last known consultation of these books (to which additions had been made from time to time) was in AD 363; they were destroyed in the early 5th cent. The books were consulted by order of the senate in times of crisis, and the one extant example, preserved by *Phlegon of Tralles, suggests that the oracles contained a statement of the problem, followed by various remedies. Sibylline texts in Latin, of quite different style, in the hands of members of the Roman aristocracy, were consulted in AD 536/7.

The Sibyl's intimate connection with Rome made her a natural choice for Christians who sought evidence from pagan sources for the truth of their beliefs. Her earliest appearance is in the vision of *The Shepherd of Hermas*; with the development of the apologetic tradition, she begins to appear with more frequency. Belief that Virgil's Fourth Eclogue (modelled on sibylline prophecy) was in fact inspired by the Cumaean Sibyl combined with this interest to elevate the Sibyl to a position of remarkable importance in Christian literature and art.

Two collections of Sibylline oracles survive from late antiquity, one dating to the end of the 5th cent. AD, the other to the period just after the Arab conquest of Egypt in the 7th cent. One contains texts numbered 1-8, the other includes oracles numbered 11-14. The material in these collections is extremely diverse. Some is manifestly Christian, other passages are almost certainly Jewish, and yet other material is pagan. The subject matter ranges from Christian doctrine and predictions of woe for cities and peoples to Roman history and sibylline biography.

[Pausanias 10. 12; Virgil, *Eclogues* 4]

Sicily and Magna Graecia, cults and mythology Greek settlers in Sicily and Magna Graecia (south Italy) brought with them the principal cults of old Greece. Those of *Demeter and *Persephone are particularly widespread and conspicuous in the archaeological evidence, reflecting perhaps the urgency of ensuring fertility and survival in a new environment. Rural and extra-urban shrines helped to mark the claims of the communities to the land. The degree of interaction with the cults of indigenous peoples is questionable, but note the association of Demeter and Persephone with the Sicel centre of Enna.

The geographical position of the western Greeks accounts in part for the importance of *Zeus Olympios (e.g. at Syracuse and Locri Epizephyrii); his great sanctuary at *Olympia in the north-western Peloponnese more than any shrine in Italy or Sicily served them as a common cult centre. More complex are the reasons for the popularity of *Hera (notably at Croton and Poseidonia/Paestum), though both with her and Persephone (especially at Locri, which produced a rich repertoire of terracotta plaques) female rites of passage seem to have been important.

While common Greek cults naturally predominate in the new cities of mixed origin there are exceptions. The Megarian cult of (Demeter) Malophoros was established outside the town soon after the foundation of Selinus. But alongside her sanctuary was that of Zeus *Meilichios, a figure associated with familial and personal welfare, worshipped widely (though not in the west) and sometimes, as here, for the most part aniconically. At Metapontum a comparable cult, of Apollo Lykeios, is plausibly associated with male rites of passage.

There are various indications of an interest in Orphic and Dionysiac eschatology beginning in the Classical period, but Pythagorean doctrines, known from literary sources, have yet to appear in the epigraphic or artistic evidence (see ORPHISM; DIONYSUS; PYTHAGORAS AND PYTHAGOREANISM). A scarcity of inscriptions and the absence of a Pausanias leave some of the great temples insecurely identified. For myth as well as cult, *Heracles is important in the west (cf. his adventures in capturing the cattle of Geryon, recounted by *Stesichorus). Less is known about other heroes. Leucaspis, perhaps originally Sicel, seems to have been brought to Attica. The heroization of city *founders was common (see HERO-CULT). From Taras (Tarentum) there are many representations of an anonymous reclining hero. In general, the spate of archaeological evidence has outstripped all attempts at synthesis. See also PALICI; SIRENS.

Sigillaria, the fair on the last of the seven days of the Saturnalia (see SATURNUS), when pottery figurines (sigilla) were given as gifts; as well as these, other trifling wares were sold. It was usual to give dependants money for this fair. The origin of the custom is not known.

silens, Silenus See SATYRS AND SILENS.

Silvanus, Roman god of the countryside. Apparently of ancient origin, he is rarely attested before the Augustan period, but during the empire was one of the most popular deities in the western and Danubian provinces, where he appears in over 1,100 inscriptions. He was associated primarily with forests (as reflected in his name) and agriculture, to a lesser extent with hunting and herding. Although in ancient literature he is sometimes linked or confused with *Faunus and *Pan, he lacks their prophetic abilities and wild personalities. Instead, he generally appears in inscriptions and monuments as a benign anthropomorphic deity, accompanied at times by female deities named Silvanae or Nymphae. In some areas (e.g. southern France) he was regularly identified with local gods, while in others (e.g. Romania) he apparently retained his purely Roman character. Silvanus never received any public cult either in Rome or in the provinces, although a number of *collegia were organized in his name. Most of the dedications to the god were erected by individuals, of whom fewer than 10 per cent seem to have been members of the élite. His cult was thus essentially popular in character.

silver Silver was extensively used for statuettes (but rarely for larger sculpture), for *votive offerings, and for the domestic plate of wealthy Greeks and Romans.

Silvius, son of *Aeneas and Lavinia, father of Silvius Aeneas and ancestor of the Alban royal house of Silvii. A legend due to the name, but unknown to Virgil, told that Lavinia, fearing the jealousy of *Ascanius, fled to the woods and there gave birth to her son.
[Virgil, *Aeneid* 6. 760–7; Livy 1. 3; Dionysius of Halicarnassus 1. 70]

sin The modern term has no equivalent in either Greek or Latin. The Christian concept of sin accommodates two basic and coherent senses: offence against moral codes, and action against the laws or the will of God. It presupposes conscious voluntariness, while remorse may be associated with its consequences, interpreted as an expression of estrangement from God. Although some of these characteristics can be found in the archaic and classical religions of Greece and Rome, as a whole this complex is not clearly represented. Various aspects are denoted by different terms such as Greek *adikia* (wrongdoing, injustice), *anomia* (lawless conduct), *hamartia, hamartēma* (failure, fault, error), or Latin *vitium* (fault, blemish), *scelus* (evil deed, crime), *peccatum* (fault, error), etc. The term *syneidēsis* (Lat. *conscientia*), originally 'awareness, consciousness', developed the sense 'consciousness of right and wrong, conscience' (adopted by early Christianity) only in the Hellenistic and more especially imperial period. The Greek term *hamartia* approximates most closely (but cannot be identified with) our concept 'sin' and was adopted in the *Septuagint and early Christian scriptures for rendering and developing the biblical concept of sin (cf. Lat. *peccare, peccatum,* etc.).

Three of the most remarkable ancient characteristics as opposed to modern ones, are:

1. In the earlier period voluntary and involuntary offences against moral or divine laws were both equally reprehensible and hence liable to divine vengeance. Evil intention is not necessarily implied in the ancient definition of wrongdoing. The Greek concept of *atē* (delusion, infatuation, through which 'the evil appears good': Sophocles), which in the early period was often held responsible for human error, was either understood as divinely inspired—thus providing an escape from the problem of human responsibility, though not from divine punishment—or as rooted in personal (and condemnable) rashness, being a corollary of *hubris.

2. Closely related is the ancient belief that as far as effects are concerned no clear distinction can be drawn between offences against ethical, legal, and social prescriptions on the one hand and violation of ritual rules on the other.

3. Accordingly, it is often impossible to draw a sharp line between the state of impurity (*see* PURIFICATION) as result of a ritual fault and the state of moral blemish. Murder is a case in point. The earliest phases of (Greek and Roman) civilization did privilege an emphasis on the ritual aspects, and through the ages a gradual development can be perceived toward a more personally felt ethical experience of guilt. That said, even in our earliest source, Homer, there are unmistakable traces of ethical codes warranted by the gods.

Greece In Homer it was especially *Zeus who had the domain of guarding the laws of hospitality in the house and the court and of protecting strangers and suppliants. What happened on the other side of the boundary did not affect him, except in cases of either ritual offence or personal acts of hubris defying his honour. *Dikē* (man's duty to his fellows) is not synonymous with *themis* (man's duty according to divine institution).

But the two may coincide, e.g. in the sin of hubris or disregard of the right of others (both mortals and gods). However, Hesiod pictures *dikē* as Zeus' central responsibility, even making Dikē the daughter of Zeus. He also presents an interesting mixture of ethical and ritual aspects. In his view, divine vengeance will equally follow both transgression of a certain branch of moral offences, such as ill-treatment of orphans or one's own parents, and purely ritual offences such as omitting to wash one's hands before pouring libation. In fact the core of his poem is an appeal to the justice of Zeus: whoever offends human or divine laws will encounter divine anger.

Divine punishment Early Greece made impressive attempts to bracket together two eternal problems: that of the cause of illness and disaster and that of *theodicy, the question of the justice of the gods. In the expression 'By day and night diseases of themselves come upon man, and do him harm silently, for cunning Zeus took out their voice' (Hesiod), Zeus can be seen as a designation of blind fate or fortune, making man a plaything of an arbitrary and unfathomable divine power. Otherwise illness is a penalty for evil acts, sent by Zeus in his quality of divine judge. Both options were eagerly exploited, the first being a typical expression of so-called 'archaic pessimism', so characteristic of much Greek lyric poetry, the latter providing an explanation that permits control, in cases of sudden unaccountable illness, more especially of epidemics. These disasters were often seen as caused by the sin of one person (Hesiod), even by a sin unwittingly committed: 'Not willingly am I detained, but I must have sinned (*alitesthai*: the Homeric term for offending a god) against the deathless gods', says *Odysseus in the *Odyssey*. An oracle then might be consulted as to the nature of the unknown sin and the manner of its expiation.

The interpretation of illness as the punishment of sin cannot but raise another question of theodicy: what if patent sinners do not fall ill? 'How, O son of Cronus, does your mind manage to award the same portion to evil-doers and just men?' (Hesiod). By way of solution, Archaic literature offers three variations on the theme of temporary postponement: evildoers will be punished but not always immediately (Hesiod), or the penalty will strike a later generation (Hesiod; Solon). Combinations occur (Homer; Hesiod). Although these solutions share the belief that the sinner literally must 'pay' (the common word for being punished), it is obvious that no uniform and consistent doctrine can be vindicated for Archaic and Classical Greece. Various options concerning sin and retaliation coexisted, sometimes in the mind of one person. This is particularly marked in the third variant: the idea of retaliation in the afterlife and the netherworld.

Punishment in the hereafter As early as in Homer three different conceptions are faintly discernible: (1) the netherworld as a cheerless and gloomy place where all souls assemble, without any connotation of retaliation or reward; (2) the *Islands of the Blest, reserved for the (heroic) happy few, likewise without clear references to any ordeal; and (3) a place where the divine judges *Aeacus, *Minos, and *Rhadamanthys judge the dead. However, with one exception in the *Iliad* (general punishment of perjury in the netherworld), the only condemned persons mentioned, *Orion, *Tityus, *Tantalus, and *Sisyphus, are sentenced not for 'normal' moral offences, but as a result of their defying the gods. Their offence is an act of hubris against the honour of the Homeric gods. Remarkably enough the early doctrine of the Eleusinian mysteries (*see* ELEUSIS), as represented in the *Homeric Hymn to Demeter* (c.700 BC), though promising the initiated a blissful stay in the underworld, did not require any proof of good behaviour; from a later period we learn that in this respect there was only one requirement: not to have impure hands tainted with blood. On the other hand, we hear that the Samothracian mysteries (*see* CABIRI) required a confession of sins as a preliminary to the initiation: nothing more was apparently needed, the confession being an expiation of the state of sinfulness and impurity.

Most probably it was the Orphic movement (see ORPHISM) that helped two different solutions to develop: the first was the construction of something that can be called 'hell', with penalties through eternal suffering in mud, etc. Basically different, and no doubt inspired by influences from Pythagoreanism (see PYTHAGORAS AND PYTH-AGOREANISM), was the idea that evil was a corollary of bodily existence, the body being the prison for the *soul, which is thus punished for sins in previous lives. If these sins are not expiated during one incarnation, the soul transmigrates to another body (see TRANSMIGRATION). Thus, this doctrine of reincarnation provided an elegant solution to the dilemma of divine justice and human suffering. Moreover, it opened an avenue to personal responsibility and an escape from the ritualist group solidarity which involved vicarious suffering for another's fault. Overall, however, the idea of punishment in the afterlife never attained the refinement and popularity that it later enjoyed in Christianity.

Classical developments The 5th and 4th cents. BC reflected and expanded on earlier Archaic initiatives. We can only indicate superficially the most important tendencies. Fifth-cent. Greek tragedy problematized all existing ideas on sin, retaliation, and theodicy. *Aeschylus (esp. in his *Oresteia*), fascinated by the idea of hereditary curses, tested ways in which a descendant from a doomed house could escape his fate. *Sophocles explored both the question of guiltless guilt (*King Oedipus*) and the tensions between human and divine law (*Antigone*). *Euripides added a theological critique: gods who make unfair demands cannot be gods. Like other thinkers under the influence of the ideas of the sophists, he demonstrated that gods and ethics are often very difficult to reconcile. In the late 5th cent. this could (but in only a few scattered instances actually did) lead to athe-

istic expressions (*Diagoras). In this same period the debate about the distinction between the laws of man and those of the gods begins. It is argued that the unwritten laws are in the hands of the gods and carry their own unavoidable punishment, whereas penalties resulting from violation of human law are avoidable. Others argued that the gods were the invention of a clever politician in order to bind people to laws which could not otherwise be enforced (most emphatically in the satyr play *Sisyphos* (see SATYRIC DRAMA) by Euripides or Critias.

From the 4th cent. onwards the major philosophical schools inherited from Plato's *Socrates the basic conviction that 'no one sins willingly', wrongdoing being regarded as an error of judgement. *Stoicism especially puts the emphasis on individual autonomy within a human communion whose cement is the divine principle of Reason (*logos*) which permeates the whole. Here universal laws are identical with divine laws, human life being a divine service. Sin is error, the violation of cosmic laws.

Confession of sins A wrongdoer was either punished by the law or by the gods (or not at all), but (public) confession of sins was not in vogue in Greek culture. The earliest hints of something of this kind (apart from recognition of *hamartia* in tragedy) can be found in the 4th-cent. cures of *Epidaurus: cure-inscriptions detailing the healing miracles of *Asclepius (see INCUBA-TION). In the same period curse tablets (see CURSES) develop a special variant: the prayer to the gods for (judicial) help in cases of theft, black magic, slander, etc., where sometimes the wish is added that the culprit should publicly confess his misdeed. The same idea takes pride of place in the so-called confession inscriptions from Maeonia (Lydia and the bordering area of Phrygia, 2nd and 3rd cents. AD), where we read accounts of private offences resulting in punishment by the god, redress of the crime or a sacrifice of atonement, and public confession, followed by praise of the power of the god. The influence, either of indigenous Anatolian traditions or of *oriental cults is probable, as the sin- and guilt-culture of, for instance, the cult of *Atargatis, including sackcloth and ashes, seems to be related.

Rome For early Rome a similar state of things can be detected to that of early Greece. Legends abound about the grave consequences resulting from wholly accidental *vitia* in ritual matters. In the Roman *ius divinum* ('divine law'), as in the secular law, a casual slip in a ceremonial action or utterance might entail dire consequences comparable to those assigned to arrogant neglect of the deity. One of the earliest attestations of a movement towards more enlightened views can be found in the archaic Twelve Tables: they make provision for lenient treatment of a merely accidental homicide. In Rome no independent reflection on the nature and origin of evil or disaster developed; but from the 2nd cent. BC onwards *Stoicism (see above) deeply influenced Roman thought in the field of (social) ethics. *See also* CHRISTIANITY.

Sinis, a son of *Poseidon who waylaid travellers at the Isthmus of Corinth and was killed by *Theseus on his way from Troezen to Athens. He was called Pityocamptes (pine-bender), either because he made his victims hold down a bent pine tree which sprang back and flung them through the air or because he tied them between two bent pine trees which tore them apart.

[Bacchylides 18. 19–22; Apollodorus 3. 16. 2]

Sinon, character in literature and mythology, a Greek who claimed falsely to have deserted from the Greek forces at Troy and who inveigled the Trojans into taking the Trojan Horse inside the walls of Troy; he then later released the Greek heroes from the Horse and joined them in sacking the city. This story is related by *Virgil in the *Aeneid*, but was treated earlier in the cyclic *Little Ilias* and *Iliu Persis* (*see* EPIC CYCLE) and in the *Sinon* of *Sophocles; it is found in a number of later texts.

[Virgil, *Aeneid* 2. 57–194]

Sinuri, sanctuary of, in Caria, south of Mylasa, patronized by the 4th-cent. BC local Hecatomnid satraps Hecatomnus, Idrieus, and Ada. Sinuri was an indigenous god, who gave his name to the sanctuary, but the many inscriptions are in Greek. Most, apart from the Hecatomnid material, are of the 2nd or 1st cent. BC.

Sirens, enchantresses who live on an island near *Scylla and *Charybdis in *Homer's *Odyssey*. Sailors charmed by their song land and perish; their meadow is full of mouldering corpses. They attempt to lure *Odysseus by claiming omniscience, but on *Circe's advice he has himself bound to the mast and stops his comrades' ears with wax. Likewise *Orpheus saves the *Argonauts by overpowering their song with his lyre. In some versions they die or commit suicide if a mortal can resist them. The escape of Odysseus or of Orpheus leads to their death, as does their defeat in a singing contest with the *Muses. They also have power to calm the winds.

In Homer there are two Sirens, later often three, whose names vary. They are the daughters of *Phorcys, of Earth, *Gaia, of *Achelous and Sterope, or of one of the Muses. They are often associated with death in both literature and art. They are companions of *Persephone at her rape, and in their search for her are turned to birds with girls' faces, or are punished with bird form for their failure to guard her. Alcman equates Muse with Siren, and Plato has eight celestial Sirens producing the harmony of the spheres, a Pythagorean idea (*see* PYTHAGORAS AND PYTHAGOREANISM). They were located or received cults in various parts of Sicily or southern Italy, especially Naples (ancient Neapolis), Surrentum, and Tereina in Bruttium.

In art they are usually represented as birds with women's heads, though some of the earliest examples are bearded. They are often shown crowning tombs, and also with musical instruments or in musical contexts. A frequent type from the 8th cent. BC onwards is the Siren as attachment to a bronze cauldron. They are common on vases from 600 BC, especially in scenes with Odysseus, and their suicide is already implied on some 6th-cent. BC examples. They also appear with *Dionysus and the *satyrs. Early Sirens have claws like vultures or eagles, but in Classical and Hellenistic art they become beautiful, melancholy creatures, representative of music almost as much as the Muses.

The Sirens were allegorized by both Classical and Christian writers as representing the lusts of the flesh, the insatiable desire for knowledge, the dangers of flattery, or as celestial music drawing souls upwards to heaven. Odysseus bound to the mast even came to be seen as an allegory of Christ on the cross.

[Homer, *Odyssey* 12. 39–54, 158–200; Apollonius Rhodius, *Argonautica* 4. 891–919; Ovid, *Metamorphoses* 5. 552–63]

Sisyphus, son of *Aeolus (1), and king and founder of Corinth, of legendary cunning, a trickster who cheated death, and one of the sinners punished in *Hades in Homer: he is pushing a large boulder up a hill, and it keeps rolling back, and he has to start again. One way he cheated death was by persuading the underworld deities to let him return to the upper world for some reason and then not returning below. In one version *Zeus sent *Thanatos to him as punishment for revealing to Asopus that Zeus had abducted his daughter, but Sisyphus bound up Thanatos so that no one could die, until *Ares freed Thanatos and handed Sisyphus over to him. But before he died he instructed his wife not to give him the proper funerary rites and then persuaded Hades to allow him to return to complain; when in the upper world he refused to return and died in old age.

In one version, he founded the *Isthmian Games in honour of Palaemon/*Melicertes. In some post-Homeric versions he is *Odysseus' real father. He stopped *Autolycus from stealing his cattle by attaching to their hooves lead tablets on which was inscribed 'Autolycus stole them', and thus tracking them.

[Homer, *Odyssey* 11. 593–600; Apollodorus 1. 9. 3]

Siwa, large and fertile oasis in Egypt's western desert, c.540 km. (c.335 mi.) south-west of Alexandria, home in antiquity to a populous community of farmers (the Ammonioi) ruled by local chiefs, nominally subject to Egypt's rulers. The well-preserved remains of the famous oracular temple of *Ammon, built in the Egyptian style under (probably) the pharaoh Amasis, are at modern Aghurmi, with the ruins of a second sanctuary of Ammon near by. Excavations at the site of El-Maraki have revealed a Graeco-Egyptian sanctuary with a small Doric temple (also known from early travellers) and a (Greek) inscription recording building work by local landowners under Trajan. Siwa remained a bastion of paganism until at least the 6th cent. AD.

sleep See DREAMS; HYPNOS; INCUBATION; MORPHEUS; PALINURUS.

snakes were regarded in Greek and Roman religion mostly as guardians, e.g. of houses, tombs, springs, and altars. Snakes appear as attributes of bell-shaped idols in Minoan houses and small sanctuaries; coiled terracotta snakes were found in Mycenaean palaces, perhaps indicating their later, attested function as domestic guardians. (*See* MINOAN AND MYCENAEAN RELIGION.) Probably evoking their hidden, secretive natural habitat of crevices and the world of 'under' in general, snakes were associated with *chthonian powers. They were linked either with what emerges from the earth, such as trees or springs, or what is placed inside it, such as foundations of houses and altars, or graves.

Snakes guard sacred places (the garden of the Golden Apples of the *Hesperides) or objects (the Golden Fleece; *see* JASON (1)). *Apollo killed the Python which guarded *Delphi for its patron goddess, Earth (Gē, *Gaia); the sacred snake of Athena is said to have abandoned the Acropolis when the

Athenians left for Salamis. In art and ritual snakes often appear coiled around sacred trees, at the foot of altars, on tombstones, and as guardians of caves facing dedicants who present them with sacred *cakes (the *oracle of *Trophonius). In fantastic compositions we find men-snakes (*Cecrops, *Erichthonius), or metamorphoses: *Thetis took on the form of a snake to escape *Peleus; Cychreus, king of Salamis, was worshipped by the Athenians as a snake. As an attribute of gods, snakes were close to *Demeter with her serpent-chariot, used also by *Athena (and *Medea). As healing powers, they were associated with *Asclepius, especially in Hellenistic and Roman religion.

Feared for their deadly venom, perhaps striking archetypal psychological chords of terror, the frightening aspect of snakes finds expression more in myth and art than in cult. Snakes (or 'dragons') were born of the earth or of the drops of Titans' blood (see TITAN); they are entwined in the Gorgon's hair (see GORGO), coiled around the body of *Cerberus, accompany the Furies (see ERINYES), and sent by *Hera to kill baby *Heracles and his twin. To strike terror they were depicted on hoplites' shields or, as an expression of victory, on commemorative monuments (the Serpent Monument, dedicated at *Delphi as a thank-offering after the Persian Wars). At Sparta snakes were the holy animals of the *Dioscuri, perhaps originally house-gods. Real house-snakes may have been regarded as the Divine Twins attending a *theoxenia, the participation of gods in a meal reception. See also ANIMALS IN CULT; NAASSENES.

Socrates (469–399 BC), Athenian public figure and central participant in the intellectual debates so common in the city in the middle and late 5th cent. His influence has been enormous, although he himself wrote nothing.

Socrates' circle included a number of figures who turned against democracy in Athens. This may well have been the under-

lying reason why he himself was tried and put to death by drinking hemlock in 399 BC. He was charged with impiety, specifically with introducing new gods and corrupting young men (see ATHEISM). This charge may have masked the political motives of his accusers, since the amnesty of 403 BC prohibited prosecution for political offences committed before that date.

Socrates' execution prompted *Plato and Xenophon to create portraits intended to refute the formal charge under which he was tried and to counter his popular image, which may have been inspired by Aristophanes' *Clouds*. Aristophanes had depicted Socrates engaged in natural philosophy and willing to teach his students how 'to make the weaker argument stronger'—a commonplace charge against the sophists. Both Plato and Xenophon were intent on distinguishing Socrates as radically as possible from other members of the sophistic movement, with whom he may actually have had some affinities. But their strategies differ. In both authors, Socrates devotes himself, like the sophists, to dialectical argument and the drawing of distinctions. In both, he refuses, unlike the sophists, to receive payment. In Xenophon, however, he uses argument to support, in contrast to the sophists, a traditional and conventional understanding of the virtues. In Plato, on the other hand, it is a serious question whether he holds any views of his own, and his main difference from the sophists is that, unlike them, he never presents himself as a teacher of any subject.

Plato's and Xenophon's portraits, inconsistent as they are with Aristophanes', are also inconsistent with each other. This is the root of 'the Socratic problem', the question whether we can ever capture the personality and philosophy of the historical Socrates or whether we must limit ourselves to the interpretation of one or another of his literary representations. For various reasons, in the mid-19th cent. Plato replaced Xenophon as the most reliable witness for the historical Socrates, even though it is accepted that our knowledge of the latter can be at best a matter of speculation. And, though recent attempts to rehabilitate Xenophon are not lacking, most contemporary scholars turn to Plato for information on Socrates' ideas and character.

Socrates often, in both Plato and Xenophon, referred to a 'divine sign', a daimonion, which prevented him from taking certain courses of action—he attributes his reluctance to participate in active politics to this sign's intervention. His religious views, even though they sometimes overlapped with those of tradition (he acknowledged the authority of *Apollo, for example, when he received the *Delphic oracle), must have been quite novel, since he appears to have thought that the gods could never cause evil or misery to each other or to human beings. He also seems, as we see in Plato's *Euthyphro*, to claim that the gods' approval or disapproval does not render actions right or wrong. On the contrary, rightness and wrongness are established independently, and the gods, knowing what these are, both engage in the former and shun the latter and approve of human beings for acting likewise.

sodales are either 'companions, mates', or else 'members of a single college or fraternity'. Examples of the latter sense are the secondary religious groups of Rome: these include the *fetiales, who made treaties and declared war; and three *sodalitates* that were concerned with performing specific annual rites—the *Salii, active in March and perhaps October; the Luperci, whose festival was the *Lupercalia of February; and the best-recorded of them all, the *fratres arvales, whose cult of *Dea Dia was originally agrarian and concerned with boundaries, later with the celebration of the imperial house.

Some of these were formed of one (Sodales Titii) or more (Luperci Faviani and Luperci Quintiliani) of the ancient lineages (*gentes*). It is not, however, clear that *sodalitates* were always based on lineage links. New ones were formed when a new cult was brought to Rome, for instance those of the Great Mother (Mater Magna, *Cybele) when the cult was introduced from the east in 204 BC (*see* PESSINUS); or those of the new Divi under the empire, the Sodales Augustales after the death of *Augustus, the Sodales Flaviales, Hadrianales, and Antoniniani under later dynasties.

The discovery of an archaic dedication to *Mars at Satricum by the *suodales* of Poplios Valesios (Publius Valerius) has raised new questions about the origins of the institution: one possibility is that this was a religious fraternity like the Roman ones already discussed; another that these *sodales* were the clients of a *gens*, like the Fabian clients who fought at the battle of the Cremera, led by a war-leader (whether or not Valerius himself was a Roman). There is evidence both from Italy and elsewhere of groups of comrades, sometimes bound by oath, supporting leaders in peace and war. It is clear that there were different types of *sodalitates*; less clear how far the types overlapped.

Sol The name of the Sun is given to two utterly different deities in Rome. The older is Sol Indiges, of whom we know that he had a sacrifice on 9 August, while *calendars for 11 December, give AG(onium) IND(igetis). Nothing more is known with any certainty; the indication for 11 December is supplemented by a late source which says that the festival was in honour of Helios. This cult was native, apparently, and is perhaps to be connected with the agricultural calendar. There existed at the Circus Maximus a temple of Sol and *Luna, which may date from the 3rd cent. BC. A sacred grove of Sol Indiges is attested at *Lavinium. Much later and certainly foreign (Syrian) was the worship of deus Sol Invictus (the invincible Sun-god (*see* ELAGABALUS)), to give him his most characteristic title. Eastern sun-gods had been making their way in the west, helped by the current identification of *Apollo with *Helios, for some time; but the first attempt to make the Sun's the chief worship was that of Elagabalus (AD 218-22), who introduced the god of Emesa in Syria, whose priest and, apparently, incarnation he was, El Gabal. Elagabalus' excesses and consequent unpopularity and assassination checked the cult, but the emperor Aurelian (270-5) reintroduced a similar worship, also oriental; he was himself the child of a priestess of the Sun. This remained the chief imperial and official worship till *Christianity displaced it, although the cult of the older gods, especially *Jupiter, did not cease, but rather the new one was in some sort parallel to it, the Sun's clergy being called *pontifices Solis* (see PONTIFEX/PONTIFICES), a significant name which was part of a policy of Romanizing the oriental god. Sol had a magnificent temple in the campus Agrippae; its dedication day was 25 December.

Somnus *See* PALINURUS; HYPNOS.

Sophocles, Athenian tragic playwright (c.495-406 BC). He wrote more than 120 plays, and won at least 20 victories, 18 at the City Dionysia: he was thus markedly the most successful of the three great 5th-cent. playwrights. He was apparently a priest of the hero Halon (see HERO-CULT) and welcomed the new cult of the healing god *Asclepius and the *snake which symbolized him into his own house while a sanctuary was built (probably in 420-19). After his death he was given the honours of a hero cult himself, with the new name Dexion.

*Aristotle in the *Poetics* makes much use of the idea of 'recognition' (*anagnōrisis*) in his analysis of the tragic effect. The idea is not of much help in reading *Aeschylus and of intermittent usefulness in Euripides. But in Sophocles (as arguably in *Homer's *Iliad*) it is an illuminating critical tool. In play after play, one or more characters is brought to a realization that he or she has misperceived the nature of reality and the realization is almost always associated with pain, suffering, and death. The idea of recognition is more often than not also associated with relationships between man and divinity. Between the two worlds of gods and men there is communication, in the imagined world of Sophoclean theatre: it comes in the form of dreams, oracles, and the reading of signs by seers such as *Tiresias. Men and women try to guide their decisions by their understanding of such communications. But such understanding is almost always false: the language and the signs used by divinity are everywhere ambiguous, however simple in appearance, and they are systematically and readily misunderstandable, even if they are to hand.

In *Ajax*, at a crucial moment, men learn too late of the seer's reading of Athena's intentions and Ajax dies; in *Trachiniae* both Deianira and Heracles only perceive the true meaning of a series of oracles and non-human communications when it is too late and the recognition cannot save them from the consequences of catastrophically mistaken action. In *Antigone*, both Antigone and Creon believe that they are acting as the gods require of them: Antigone dies with that belief shaken and perhaps foundering and Creon confronts his misreading of the requirements of divinity only when not just Antigone but his son and wife also are already dead. In *Philoctetes* the oracle is never brought sharply into focus but none the less haunts the play; in *King Oedipus* the simplicities of the oracle's language become utterly opaque when read through the lens of Oedipus' 'knowledge' of the truth about himself. The recurring pattern of Sophoclean tragedy is that all falls into place and coheres only in retrospect: recognition comes after the event. *See also* TRAGEDY.

Soracte, mod. Soratte, the isolated mountain 691 m. (2,267 ft.) high to the north of Rome, from which it is sometimes visible. Celebrated by Horace, there were priests here called Hirpi, resembling Roman Luperci (*see* LUPERCALIA). They worshipped *Apollo Soranus by walking over hot coals; the pestiferous cave alluded to by an ancient commentator in describing the origin of the Hirpi has been located.

[Horace, *Odes* 1. 9; Virgil, *Aeneid* 7. 697, 11. 785 ff.]

Soter (fem. Soteira), a title of several deities (e.g. *Zeus Soter, *Artemis Soteira), expressing their power to save people from danger. It has no Latin equivalent, except perhaps for Juno Sospita. Christian ideas of the Saviour must not be projected onto pre-Christian usage. 'Soter' comments on function, and does not imply divine status. But from early times the word was used by analogy of humans who performed extraordinary deeds worthy of divine cult. In the Hellenistic period it was often used of kings: Antigonus Doson was called Euergetes (Benefactor) in his lifetime, Soter after his death; Ptolemy I Soter is perhaps the most famous holder of the title. It became a commonplace of honours to Roman officials in the east. *See* RULER-CULT.

Soteria The term was applied to a sacrifice or festival celebrating deliverance from danger, on behalf of individuals or a community. The gods in general or a particular god could be the recipient of the sacrifice. *Soter, 'the Deliverer', was especially an epithet of *Zeus, as appropriately as at the seaport of Piraeus. Recently heroized men regarded as deliverers, such as Aratus at Sicyon and Philopoemen at Megalopolis, could be associated with Zeus Soter and his Soteria. (*See* HERO-CULT.) In the Hellenistic period a number of regular annual or quadrennial festivals with this name were instituted (*see* AGŌNES). Of the sixteen known, the most famous was that established at *Delphi shortly after the gods were said to have appeared and turned back the Celts under the command of Brennus in 279/8 BC. These Soteria are known from Delphic inscriptions and from the inscribed acceptances to Delphic invitations to participate by a number of Greek cities. They were reorganized by the Aetolian Confederacy *c*.246 BC. In addition to athletic events musical competitions were conspicuous. *See also* SALUS.

soul The term in Greek nearest to English 'soul', *psychē* (Latin *anima*), has a long history and a wide variety of senses in both philosophical and non-philosophical contexts. In *Homer, the *psychē* is what leaves the *body on death (i.e. life, or breath?), but also an insubstantial image of the dead person, existing in *Hades and emphatically not something alive. But some vague idea of *psychē* as the essence of the individual, capable of surviving the body (and perhaps entering another) is well-established by the 5th cent., though without necessarily displacing the older idea and even being combined with it. Simultaneously, in medical contexts and elsewhere, *psychē* begins to be found regularly in contrast with *sōma*, suggesting something like the modern contrast between 'mind' and body.

All of these ideas are found, separately or in combination, in the philosophers. *Democritus stresses the interconnectedness of *psychē* ('mind') and body, while *Socrates regards the *psychē* primarily as our essence *qua* moral beings. Socrates was probably agnostic about whether it was something capable of surviving death; Plato, by contrast, offers repeated arguments for the immortality of the *psychē*, which he combines with the (originally Pythagorean) idea that it transmigrates, after the death of the person, into another body, human or animal. (*See* PYTHAGORAS AND PYTHAGOREANISM; TRANSMIGRATION). Sometimes he represents the *psychē* as something purely (or ultimately) rational, sometimes as irrevocably including irrational elements. At the same time his myths include many aspects of Homeric eschatology, which may have retained an important place in popular belief. Aristotle is at the furthest remove from non-philosophical attitudes, adopting a largely biological approach which says that the *psychē* is the 'form' of the living creature, i.e. the combination of powers or capacities to do the things which are characteristic of its species.

In philosophical contexts, the primary connotations of *psychē* are probably life, consciousness, and 'self-caused' movement. *Psychē*, or an aspect of it, is typically made the ultimate cause of all or most movement, whether in the shape of a world soul, as in Platonism, or of god, as in Aristotle and *Stoicism. The chief exception is Epicureanism (see EPICURUS), which makes the movements of atoms themselves primary. It was also the Epicureans, among the philosophers, who most resolutely opposed the idea of an immortal *psychē* (even Aristotle allowed that the highest aspect of reason might be immortal and divine). Outside philosophy, until the Christian era, the idea, or notions more or less vaguely resembling it, are found chiefly in the context of mystery or ecstatic religion (see ECSTASY; MYSTERIES), and in literature reflecting influence from such sources. See also FLIGHT OF THE MIND.

Sparta, myths of The rule of *Menelaus at Sparta was crucial to the Spartans (see SPARTAN CULTS). The myth of the *Heraclidae (the descendants of *Heracles) to the Peloponnese was the justification for the unique dual kingship of Sparta.

[Pausanias 3]

Spartan cults The three greatest Spartan festivals, the ones that attracted visitors, all honoured *Apollo: the *Carnea, the Gymnopaedia (at which choirs competed for long hours in baking heat), and the Hyacinthia. This last comprised choral performances (again), spectacle, and feasting, spread over several days only some of which were tinged with melancholy; it honoured Apollo of *Amyclae and his dead lover *Hyacinthus. The importance of *Artemis Orthia is clear from the 100,000 or so small dedications found at her shrine; hers was a celebrated festival at which youths undergoing the Spartan military training sought to steal cheese from the altar and were whipped if caught, and it may have been ephebes again who wore the various masks found in her precinct. Other prominent cults honoured *Menelaus and *Helen, who were revered 'like gods' at the *Menelaion a couple of miles to the south-east of the city; the daughters of Leucippus, Phoebe and Hilaeira (see LEUCIPPIDES), who like Helen were probably closely linked with the choral training that constituted education for young Spartan girls; the *Dioscuri, glamorous local heroes many dedications to whom have been found; Athena of the Bronze House, whose bronze-plated temple occupied the lowly Spartan acropolis; and *Poseidon of Taenarum, who in wrath at a violation of sanctuary supposedly caused the great earthquake of the 460s. Lycurgus too, the *founder of the Spartan system, was worshipped 'as a god', though we do not know on what scale. And there were many Spartan *herocults, as we learn both from literary sources and from a distinctive type of hero-relief found throughout Laconia; *Agamemnon, *Orestes, *Talthybius, and the ephor Chilon were among those so honoured. (See RELICS.) Many further archaic-sounding cults have some prominence in post-classical sources, but one must beware of the 'invention of tradition' in prosperous Roman Sparta.

Spartoi See CADMUS. Their descendants had a birth-mark in the shape of a spearhead, by which they could be known.

Spes, the personification of hope (with particular reference to the safety of the younger generation) worshipped at Rome by the 5th cent. BC and given a temple in the forum Holitorium (remains survive, built into the church of S. Nicola in Carcere) by the consul of 258 BC. Destroyed by arson in 31 BC, the temple was restored by Germanicus, the emperor Tiberius' son, appropriately, since the cult of Spes (Augusta) was now concerned principally with the imperial succession.

sphinx, a hybrid creature, like the *Chimaera and the griffin. Illustrations can be traced back to Egypt and Mesopotamia in the mid-3rd millennium BC (impossible to accord priority, although the Egyptian version is known to be a late-comer to local iconography). Basically the sphinx possessed the body of an animal (usually a lion) and a human head (male or female). Variations include wings (common) and horns. The

Egyptian and Mesopotamian sphinx is depicted in religious and/or heraldic contexts, from the monumental (i.e. the sphinx at Giza) to the minute. The Egyptian is held to embody the king as *Horus supplicating the sun god Re. Both are sometimes shown slaying humans, presumably enemies of the king.

Sphinxes appear in Minoan and Mycenaean art, in Crete and the mainland, the ultimate inspiration probably Egypt. The sphinx later becomes a popular figure in Greek art—monumental and funerary—of the archaic and later periods. This is an extension of her role as guardian spirit.

The only literary references are to the Greek sphinx, whence the name, which came from a monster of Theban legend, (s)phix, that inhabited a mountain at the western edge of Theban territory, waylaid passers-by, and wrought havoc on the Cadmeans (see CADMUS; the story is referred to in *Hesiod's *Theogony*, where she is daughter of *Echidna and Orthos, and sister of the Nemean lion). Popular Greek etymologizing derived the name from the verb *sphingein* ('bind/ hold fast'), perhaps influenced by the story.

Her hostility to the Thebans may be connected with the traditional war between Minyan Orchomenus and Cadmean Thebes, which was begun and ended near Mt. Phicion, at Onchestus and the Teneric plain respectively. She would have been performing her accustomed role as guardian, this time of Minyan territory (it is to be remarked that as one approaches the mountain from the west—that is, from the direction of Orchomenus—it resembles in outline a crouching beast: this might have caused the connection to be made). Eventually she met her match in *Oedipus, who either answered her riddle, causing her to commit suicide, or actually killed her. The attachment of the sphinx to the Oedipus legend is regarded as secondary, and may have been grafted on to it from its original place in the story of the war.

[Hesiod, *Theogony* 326–9; Sophocles, *King Oedipus*; Euripides, *Phoenician Women*]

spolia opima were spoils offered by a Roman general who had slain an enemy leader in single combat. The practice was traditionally instituted by *Romulus, who fought a victorious duel against King Acron of Caenina, stripped him of his armour, and dedicated it in the newly built temple of *Jupiter Feretrius. The only other recorded instances were in 437 BC, when the military tribune Aulus Cornelius Cossus killed Lars Tolumnius of Veii, and in 222, when Marcus Claudius Marcellus overcame the Celtic chieftain Viridomarus. Interest in the *spolia opima* revived in 29 BC when Marcus Licinius Crassus killed Deldo, king of the Bastarnae, and claimed the right to dedicate the spoils. Octavian (see AUGUSTUS) rejected the claim on the (probably spurious) grounds that only the commander of the army was entitled to the *spolia opima*, and backed his argument by the 'discovery' that Cossus had been consul when he slew Tolumnius. Livy, who gives us this information, also makes it clear that Octavian's view was contradicted by that of all earlier historians.

[Livy 1. 10; Plutarch, *Romulus 16*]

springs, sacred Contrary to common belief, not every *sanctuary had access to running *water (e.g. *Aphaea, on Aegina did not), nor, in all likelihood, was every spring sacred. A thing, place, or person became 'sacred' (*hieros*) by being placed under the tutelage and control of a deity. It was a matter of function or utility, rather than ontology. Thus, Cassotis at *Delphi was a sacred spring because it was held to convey the power of divination from the god to the person who drank of it. Similar examples abound of springs performing similar functions, some oracular (see ORACLES), others merely inspirational (such as Acidalia, Hippocrene on Mt. Helicon, Aganippe), artists being held themselves to be human vessels transmitting divine messages.

At sanctuaries where cleanliness (e.g. *Asclepius and other medical gods) and purity (*mystery sanctuaries, as at *Eleusis and the

Theban Cabirium; *see* CABIRI) were import-ant, water—from springs and elsewhere—was an essential element, and in this sense the springs concerned would have been regarded as sacred.

The waters of springs served as means of *purification at the critical points of life: birth, *initiation, marriage, and death, but this function was shared by rivers, that is, by any source of fresh, running water. In the Mediterranean world, where this re-source is often at a premium, its availability is singularly important. It does not of course follow that the source itself is sacred for its own sake in the sense given above. On the other hand, the strategic location of a spring, as for example at a settlement site or a caravanserai, might be sufficient to imbue it with divine power (the sacred spring at Corinth and the Boeotian spring Tilphossa *en route* to Delphi are examples of each).

Sacred springs were a feature of the Roman landscape, urban and rural. For example, inscriptions refer to a god Fonta-nus and goddess Fontana: the deified Fons had an altar on the Janiculum; outside the Porta Capena was a grove with a spring of the Casmenae to which the Vestal virgins (*see* VESTA) resorted daily; and on 13 October the Romans celebrated *Fontinalia, a rite to honour natural springs (Horace's Ode to the spring Bandusia has been linked with the Fontinalia). Another important complex of springs and sanctuaries was to be found in Umbria at *Clitumnus (elegantly described by Pliny the Younger). *See also* RIVER-GODS.

In general sacred springs were presided over by female spirits—*nymphs—but it is not certain that every such spring had its attendant nymph.

[Horace, *Odes* 3. 13; Pliny, *Letters* 8. 8]

stadium, running track, about 200 m. (656 ft.) long. Athletic activity often antedates the surviving stadia (e.g. at *Nemea); presum-ably any area of flat ground was used. One of the earliest definable stadia, that in the sanctuary of *Poseidon at *Isthmia, consists

simply of a starting gate on the relatively level ground of the sanctuary, with a bank raised artificially to one side for spectators. The architectural development of stadia can be seen by the 4th cent. BC with the running track and seats to one or, preferably, either side. Early examples may have both ends straight or near straight (*Olympia, *Epi-daurus). Later the end is semicircular. Double races (the *diaulos*) and other long-distance races, however, started at a straight starting line at this closed end. This definitive form is still used in structures of the Roman period. *See* ATHLETICS; SANCTU-ARIES.

standards, cult of Every permanent station of a Roman military unit, especially legionary, and every camp regularly con-structed contained a chapel, which, at least in imperial times, was under the charge of the first cohort, or headquarters company. This cohort kept both the statues of gods worshipped by the troops and of the em-perors and also the standards of the unit and its component parts; all received divine or quasi-divine honours. They were anointed and otherwise tended on feast-days (*see* ROSA-LIA). A suppliant might take refuge at them; an altar was on occasion dedicated at least partly to them or at all events to the most important, the eagle of the legion; the *natalis* of the eagle, presumably the anniversary of the day when the unit was first commis-sioned, was celebrated; sacrifice was made to them particularly after a victory. The Christian apologist *Tertullian even says, rhetorically exaggerating, that the soldiers venerated them beyond all gods. They are not precisely gods, but are associated, according to Tacitus, with *genius* and *virtus*, and are 'the legions' particular spirits'.

statues, cult of

Prehistory There is no unequivocal evidence for the worship of statues in prehistory. Neo-lithic marble figurines and figures from the Cyclades, with their stylized and exagger-ated female attributes, are funerary and votive in character, rather than embodying the essential nature of any cult (as previously thought). Large wheel-made, hollow-bodied figures from late bronze age shrines at Phylakopi on Melos, Mycenae, and elsewhere are religious in character, although whether they represent deities is unclear, since their raised arms may indicate a votary. *See* MINOAN AND MYCENAEAN RELIGION.

Greece There is no certain evidence for the cult of statues in the dark ages. Pausanias remembered an aniconic period, and in his day stones sacred to individual deities could be seen in Greece, although their date is guesswork. The veneration of images of deities was well-established by the 7th cent. BC, when monumental temples to house a cult's principal statue became common (possibly the earliest such 'cult-statues' extant are from Drerus on Crete, *c.* 700 BC); in the manufacture of colossal cult-statues in precious metals from the 5th cent. BC sculptors like Phidias may have sought to visualize the divine attributes of brightness and abnormal height. *Prayer was offered to statues of deities, including cult-statues as such, which probably were more accessible to worshippers than once thought. Hand-held images were a feature of some cults; borne by priests or acolytes, they presided over ritual. Divine effigies could even be vehicles for political protest, as when one at Athens spat blood at *Augustus.

From the later 6th cent. BC on there are critiques of the use of statues. Those dealt with cultural relativism (Xenophanes), involved larger philosophical agenda (Heraclitus, Zeno), or focused on barbarians' lack of images.

Rome According to *Varro, the earliest Romans lacked cult images. While archaeological evidence such as figurines of the di Penates (*see* PENATES, DI) contradicts this, an archaic de-emphasis is plausible because of the amorphous quality of *numen, a spiritual force common at all periods in Roman religion. Aniconic worship continued in the cases of a special stone, and Jupiter Elicius.

Statues had special uses too. Élite Roman families kept wax images of their ancestors which they displayed in funeral processions. Some thought movement and appearance of statues constituted significant divine communication; in the myth of *Pygmalion the statue came to life. In the later empire appears literary and papyrological evidence of theurgic methods of animating statues of divinities to facilitate communication, Such animation should not be considered 'magical' but, rather, religious. *See* THEURGY.

Judaeo-Christian Worship of graven images was religiously forbidden in Judaism (Exodus 20: 4, 34: 17, Deuteronomy 27: 15, Jeremiah 10: 3–5; *see* JUDAISM). The continued denunciation bespeaks early Judaism's tendency towards such worship. This bemused pagans. Christianity appropriated the Jewish view (1 Corinthians 8: 4, 12: 2). Further, worship of statues not only became part of anti-pagan polemic but also theurgic animation could be charged against a heretic such as Simon Magus; idolatry could be charged against rival sects.

Stentor, a man who became proverbial from *Homer's statement that he had a 'brazen voice' equal to that of fifty other men. He died after his defeat by *Hermes in a shouting contest.

Sterope or Asterope, (1) one of the Pleiads (*see* PLEIADES), wife of *Oenomaus; (2) daughter of Cepheus king of Tegea. *Heracles gave her some of the hair of Medusa (*see* GORGO), bidding her lift it three times above the city wall, to put attackers to flight.

Stesichorus, Greek lyric poet from south Italy, active *c.*600–550 BC. Stesichorus' works were collected in 26 books; nothing now survives but quotations and some fragmentary papyri. His poems represented a kind of lyric epic, which covered a whole range of major myths: *Helen, Wooden Horse, Sack of Troy, Homecomings,* and *Oresteia* belong to the Trojan cycle, *Geryoneis, Cycnus,* and *Cerberus* to the adventures of *Heracles, *Eriphyle,*

Europia, and the untitled fragment about *Eteocles and Polynices to the Theban story (*see* SEVEN AGAINST THEBES); *Boar-hunters* was concerned with *Meleager, *Funeral Games for Pelias* with the *Argonauts. The poems sometimes deliberately reworked Homeric stories. One fragment reworks the departure of *Telemachus from Sparta; Geryones borrows rhetoric from *Sarpedon and dies like Gorgythion, his mother speaks as *Hecuba (*see also* HELEN). Stesichorus's influence has been suspected in the metopes of the *Heraion at Paestum, and in Attic vase-painting of the later 6th cent.; a Roman monument of the 1st cent. AD (the Tabulae Iliacae) claims to represent his *Sack of Troy*.

stoa The name stoa is applied to various types of building, comprising essentially an open colonnade, generally in the Doric order, and a roof over the space to a rear wall. In their simplest form they provide shade and shelter, whether for people watching religious activities in a sanctuary (the stoa at the Samian *Heraion, of the 7th cent. BC) or engaged in the various activities of the *agora; these can be political, judicial, or social, whether philosophical discussions (*see* STOICISM) or feasting (the south stoa of the Athenian agora has a series of rooms behind its double-aisled facade clearly arranged to accommodate dining couches). *See* BASILICA.

Stoicism, philosophical movement, founded by Zeno of Citium, who came to Athens in 313 BC, and, after studying with various philosophers, taught in his own right in the Stoa Poecile (Painted Porch). Zeno developed a distinctive philosophical position divided into three parts, logic, physics, and ethics. We know little of the institutional organization of the school, except that at Zeno's death one of his pupils, *Cleanthes, took over the 'headship' of the school. He was not, however, the most famous of Zeno's pupils, and the original position got developed in different directions. Ariston of Chios stressed ethics to the exclusion of physics and logic; Herillus emphasized

knowledge at the expense of moral action. Cleanthes stressed a religious view of the world, interpreting Stoic ideas in works like his Hymn to Zeus. Stoicism was in danger of dissolving into a number of different positions, but was rescued by Cleanthes' pupil Chrysippus of Soli. He restated and recast Zeno's position in his voluminous writings, defending it with powerful arguments. It was correctly thought later that 'if there had been no Chrysippus there would have been no Stoa'; the work of Zeno's earlier pupils came to be seen as unorthodox, and Chrysippus' works became the standard formulation of Stoicism. Although Chrysippus claimed to adhere to Zeno's ideas, modern scholars have often held that there are divergences between them; but this is hazardous given the fragmentary state of our sources. Chrysippus' own innovations were mainly in the technical area of logic.

In the later period Stoicism survived in its standard form, as we can see from a textbook like Hierocles, and continued to be an object of philosophical discussion; some of the Church Fathers, such as *Tertullian, were influenced by it. We also find writers less interested in philosophical argument than in presenting Stoicism as an attitude or way of life. The letters and essays of Seneca the Younger, the essays of Musonius Rufus, the reported lectures of Epictetus and the meditations of the emperor *Marcus Aurelius are examples of this. They tend to edifying and moralizing discussion and give little indication of the philosophical structure of their positions.

stones, sacred There are two kinds of sacred stone: stones embedded in the earth, and free-standing stones. The first kind is found in mystery sanctuaries: the Mirthless Stone of *Eleusis, the special stones of the Theban Cabirion (*see* CABIRI), one or more of the 'rock altars' at *Samothrace. These are natural rock formations, whose function in cult was to provide a visible and tangible link between the upper and nether worlds. Far better known is the free-standing variety, which ranges from the Delphic Omphalos (*see* DELPHI) to various unworked lumps of rock set up in sanctuaries. Between the two extremes are rocks or heaps of rocks placed at doorways of houses and at crossroads, to act as talismans, guides, or averters of evil. Some of these were said to have fallen from the skies, and some were worshipped as cult objects. The ancient Hebrews regarded stone worship as an evil to be eradicated, while Greeks acknowledged it with embarrassment as a sign of superstition, or even madness. The Romans, on the other hand, took it very seriously indeed, particularly in their worship of the boundary stone as the god *Terminus. There are other indications that stone worship was an important feature of early religious sentiment (see e.g. the roughly shaped stele from Metapontum, 6th-cent. BC, inscribed 'I am [the stone, or image?] of *Apollo Lyk[ios], [property] of Theages [and] Byros [?]'). On the whole, therefore, it is best to be sceptical about the evidence for stone worship in Greece and resist the temptation to see it as a survival from high antiquity as a form of fetishism.

strenae, originally the luck-bringing (mostly laurel) twigs (from the grove of the goddess Strenia), also figs, honey-cakes, and dates, later any gifts, lamps, coins, and even gold, exchanged by the Romans (and accompanied by good wishes) on New Year's Day. In the case of the houses of the *rex sacrorum* and the major *flamines*, the temple of Vesta, and the *curiae*, the laurel branches were placed there on 1 March, the old New Year. Hence the meaning of strena as 'good omen' (already in Plautus). The custom was (unsuccessfully) combated by the Church.

[Ovid, *Fasti* 1. 175–226, 3. 137–42]

Stymphalus, city-state of north-east Arcadia, situated in a long, narrow, enclosed upland basin. The basin, with no outward surface drainage, floods and produces a lake of varying size, famous in antiquity as the home of the man-eating Stymphalian birds

killed by *Heracles. An older settlement (not securely located) was replaced in the 4th cent. BC by a fortified, orthogonally planned, town on the north shore of the lake. Stymphalus' limited resources gave it only modest political influence. By the 2nd cent. AD Stymphalus, like neighbouring Alea, was linked to the Argolid rather than Arcadia.

Styx, eldest of the daughters of Ocean (*see* OCEANUS) and *Tethys, located at the bottom of *Tartarus. Having helped *Zeus against the Titans (*see* TITAN), she became the 'great oath of the gods'. In later writers, the Styx is the river of the underworld (*see* HADES). Herodotus and other authors place the Styx in Arcadia. The Arcadians took *oaths by the waters of the Styx, which was believed to have harmful properties. Since the 19th cent., the Styx has been identified with the falls of Mavronero, which flow down the length of a rocky slope near the village of Solos, at the foot of the highest peak of Mt. Chelmos. The myth's origins must lie in geography.

[Hesiod, *Theogony* 400, 775–806]

Summanus, Roman god who sends nocturnal thunderbolts. Some scholars derive the cult from an omen during the war with Pyrrhus when a temple was founded (?276 BC), located 'at the Circus Maximus'. Wheel-shaped *cakes called *summonalia* were offered to him. Late authors identified him with Dis Pater. In AD 224 Summanus Pater received black victims (*see* SACRIFICE, ROMAN) in an expiation of nocturnal thunderbolts.

[Ovid, *Fasti* 6. 729–32]

Sunium, the name of the southernmost part of Attica including the bold promontory with its temples to *Poseidon and *Athena and its fort. There are Early Helladic finds from the promontory, but the sanctuary seems to date from the 7th cent., at the end of which several *kouroi* (*see* SCULPTURE, GREEK) were dedicated, one of them colossal. The early 5th-cent. Ionic temple to Athena was of unusual asymmetrical design; the well-preserved Doric temple to Poseidon was architecturally closely related to the temple of *Nemesis at Rhamnus.

suovetaurilia (*suovi-*), a purificatory sacrifice at the conclusion of *lustratio* of three (generic) victims: pig, sheep, bull (*sus, ovis, taurus*). *Suovetaurilia lactentia* ('sucking') consisted of *porcus, agnus, vitulus*, male pig, lamb, calf, and were employed at the *lustration of private fields. At public lustrations (at the census, of the army) the *suovetaurilia maiora* ('greater') were used consisting of full-grown victims, *verres, aries, taurus*, boar, ram, bull. The term *solitaurilia* Quintilian regarded as a corruption of *suovetaurilia*; others (in antiquity and recently) have proposed various etymologies, none fully convincing.

superstitio designated for the Romans a negative attitude. At first positive, the term *superstitio* became pejorative from the end of the 1st cent. BC. Superstition meant a free citizen's forgetting his dignity by throwing himself into the servitude of deities conceived as tyrants. The civic ideal of piety (*see* PIETAS) envisaged above all honouring the gods while preserving one's freedom—that is, with restraint and measure. Thus the superstitious were supposed to submit themselves to exaggerated *rituals, to adhere in credulous fashion to *prophecies, and to allow themselves to be abused by charlatans. The reproach was addressed to women as well as to the members of the social and intellectual élite portrayed by Cicero in his *On the Nature of the Gods* and *On Divination*. This conception corresponded to that conveyed by the Greek *deisidaimonia, as it is discussed by Plutarch in the *On Deisidaemonia*. As a general rule the Romans considered strangers, and especially barbarians, as superstitious, either because they celebrated monstrous cults, like the Gauls, or because they were terrified by every exceptional happening and attributed it to divine wrath. But one could equally be considered superstitious, like the Jews, in submitting without flinching to the prophesies of sacred books (*see* JUDAISM). With the coming of *Christianity, two new forms of superstitious aberration appeared, which both could be described as 'the cult of the wrong gods'. One was the retention, despite all the strong disapproval of the doctors of the Church, of purely pagan beliefs. The other was the use of Christian names, holy books, etc. in *magic. *See* ROMAN RELIGION, TERMS RELATING TO.

supplication, Roman (*supplicationes*) When calamity struck (pestilence, defeat) or danger threatened, the senate, advised by priests, often decreed adoration by all the people, or part of it, especially women of all or certain gods (often placed on *pulvinaria* (*see* PULVINAR), with the temples open) to expiate transgressions (*obsecratio*) or to ensure future support. *Supplicationes* were also decreed to render thanks (*gratulatio*) for a signal victory. This double character of the rite favours the etymological connection with *placo*, 'give satisfaction', rather than with *plico*, 'to bend' (one's knees). Originally lasting one day, they reached 12 days for Pompey, 50 for *Caesar, and 55 supplications with the total of 890 days for *Augustus. Apparently it was an old Roman rite, but it fell under Greek influence: more than half of expiatory supplications were held at the suggestion of *decemvirs* (and the Sibylline books; *see* QUINDECIMVIRI; SIBYL); they were occasionally associated with a *lectisternium, and the participants frequently wore wreaths (*see* CROWNS).

Symmachus (Quintus Aurelius Symmachus, *c.*AD 340–402), Roman senator, orator, and letter-writer, and leading proponent of the pagan religious cause against the Christian emperors, was educated by a Gallic teacher and enjoyed a highly successful political career. After visiting the court of Valentinian I in 369–70, where he delivered the three panegyrics of which fragments survive and made the lasting acquaintance of Ausonius, he was proconsul of Africa (373) and prefect of Rome (383–4). Despite his support in a lost panegyric for the usurper Magnus Maximus, he was made consul in 391. In the last decade of his life, through his extensive correspondence and personal contacts he tirelessly promoted the interests of his family and friends; the letters in which he arranged the praetorian games of his son are of special interest. He died in 402, shortly after leading an embassy to the imperial court at Ravenna during the first occupation of north Italy by Alaric. The letters of Symmachus were edited by his son Quintus Fabius Memmius Symmachus, who arranged them after the manner of the younger Pliny, in nine books of private letters, the tenth being composed of letters addressed to the emperor. These include the 49 *relationes* addressed to Valentinian II during Symmachus' tenure of the urban prefecture, the most famous being *Relatio* 3, in which he argued for the restoration of the Altar of Victory to the senate-house. Symmachus failed to win over Valentinian against the influence of *Ambrose of Milan, whose own two letters on the subject are also extant. Symmachus' religious attitudes seem to focus upon the maintenance of the public cults of Rome and their priesthoods. In this he would contrast—though this may be a misleading impression—with the more varied religious tastes of *Praetextatus, and he did not follow his intimate friend Nicomachus Flavianus into armed opposition to *Theodosius I in 393/4. Nevertheless, Symmachus' public career is marked by a high level of integrity and courage, in which he was not afraid to speak directly in criticism to emperors. His correspondence, for long dismissed as artificial and highly formal without much substantial content, is a fine monument to the character of senatorial influence and the literary culture of senators, though it reveals much less than one would wish of Symmachus' private tastes. Among his 130 known correspondents (others are anonymous), Symmachus included many of the most important political figures of his day, from cultivated court officials to barbarian generals. Symmachus' son, the editor of the letters, married a granddaughter of Nicomachus Flavianus, and his daughter married Flavianus *iunior*.

The names of the two families are preserved on the two leaves of an ivory diptych, respectively in the Victoria and Albert, and Cluny, Museums.

Symplegades, the 'Clashing Rocks' which, according to legend, guarded the entrance at the Bosporus to the Black Sea; they are also regularly called 'Dark (Kyaneai) Rocks'. They ceased clashing together when *Jason's ship, the *Argo* (*see* ARGONAUTS) succeeded in passing between them. The name 'Symplegades' occurs first in *Euripides; *Pindar speaks of 'rocks that run together'. They were presumably originally identified with the Planktai, 'Wandering Rocks', which the Homeric *Circe (*see* HOMER) says were safely navigated by the *Argo* with *Hera's help, but these were later sited in the western Mediterranean (usually in the Aeolian islands near Sicily) and distinguished from the Symplegades. *Apollonius of Rhodes has a marvellous description of the Argo's passage through the Symplegades.

[Homer, *Odyssey* 12. 59–72; Apollonius of Rhodes, *Argonautica* 2. 549–606]

synagogue (Gk. *synagōgē*), the name used by Greek-speaking Jews to describe both their communities in the diaspora and their meeting places for regular public recital and teaching of the Torah (the Law of Moses, as embodied especially in the Pentateuch).

The belief of Jews that they have a duty to hear the law being read at least on occasion can be found already in Nehemiah 8: 1–8, composed probably in the 4th cent. BC, but the first evidence of Jews dedicating buildings to this or a similar institution is found in Ptolemaic Egypt, where Jewish inscriptions recording the erection of prayer-houses (*proseuchai*) have been found, dated to the 3rd cent. BC and after. Josephus' use of the term *proseuchē* to describe the building in Tiberias in Galilee where sabbath meetings were held during the revolt against Rome in AD 67 confirms the identity of the *proseuchē* with the *synagōgē*. The New Testament and *Philon (1) take synagogue meetings for granted as part of Jewish life in the 1st cent.

AD both in Galilee and in the east Mediterranean diaspora. A 1st-cent. AD inscription records the erection of a synagogue in *Jerusalem by a certain Theodotus. Rather more tentative should be the identification as synagogues of public buildings dated before AD 70 at Gamla (on the Golan), Masada and Herodium (in Judaea), and at *Delos.

The term *proseuchē* ('prayer') found in the Egyptian evidence suggests that public prayer may have been part of the function of synagogues, alongside the reading and teaching of the law, at least in the diaspora. However, there is no evidence of a formal public liturgy in synagogues in the land of Israel until the late Roman period. Rabbinic texts of the 2nd cent. AD are silent about any such liturgy, and according to the Gospels (Matthew 6: 5) it was a sign of hypocrisy to pray publicly in the synagogues in order to be admired. Literary references to prayer suggest that it was a private business. It is possible that proximity to the Jerusalem Temple, where formal liturgy accompanied sacrifices, discouraged the use of synagogues for similar purposes in the land of Israel, but the evidence is inconclusive.

By contrast, distance from the Jerusalem Temple may have encouraged treatment of diaspora synagogues as sacred places as far back as the Hellenistic period. Thus the synagogue in Antioch in Syria was described by Josephus as a temple (*hieron*). Synagogues in Palestine were described on inscriptions as sacred places only in late Roman and Byzantine times, when Jews began to erect numerous synagogues in Judaea, Galilee, and the Golan in monumental style and often with elaborate mosaics. Synagogue architecture was very varied even within Palestine, and in the diaspora the wall frescoes of the Dura-Europus synagogue, and the huge basilica found at Sardis, have no parallel.

In Babylonia and the land of Israel the teaching function of synagogues was fulfilled by weekly recitation of the Pentateuch in a regular (eventually annual) cycle.

Explanation took the form of translation into Aramaic (targum) and elucidation and elaboration (*midrash). In the western diaspora, the law was often read in Greek, either in the *Septuagint or in one of the later versions.

Among diaspora Jews the synagogue often functioned as a community centre as well as a place for worship. The archisynagōgos ('ruler of the synagogue') was often the senior magistrate of the community. He and other synagogue officials enforced discipline and adjudicated between members in cases of dispute. *See* JUDAISM.

syncretism The word has been used to denote the process whereby various god-names and god-natures are mingled so as to unite the creeds of different peoples. But the obscurity of the processes at work has meant that the term's real value lies in its imprecision. Two basic types are to be distinguished in the ancient world, 'internal' and 'contact'. Internal syncretism is typical of ancient Egyptian (and Vedic) religion, as much the result of popular piety as of temple theology. Each god appears in a variety of forms and functions. Forms, names, and epithets diversify and intermingle with boundless energy. Gods, often in triads, co-exist or co-habit within one another, remaining separate at the level of cult.

Contact syncretism itself occurs in several modes, three of which may be highlighted:

1. The construction of the 'traditional' Greek and Italo-Roman pantheons took the form of variable fusion in the proto-historic period between the incomers' deities and the religions of the indigenous populations. Consciousness of this fusion had in the historical period mostly faded, but a version of it ('*Pelasgians', etc.) was used to note local idiosyncrasy. A parallel process on a small scale appears in the course of Archaic Greek colonization.

2. The identification or interpretation of others' gods in Greek or Roman terms, i.e. the assertion of significant similarity in one

or more respects. From the Graeco-Roman point of view, this may be a simple familiarizing device, as generally in Herodotus or Strabo, but the religious statement may also be linked to political claims, e.g. to common origins, the possibility of cultural symbiosis, *evocatio*, the subjection of inferiors, the stripping of unacceptable elements of cult. Both in the Hellenistic world and the Roman empire native divinities quite rapidly acquired Greek or Roman identities. From the point of view of the conquered élites, acceptance of the new name was one index of their loyalty; moreover, the translation valorized local divinities, in Syria, Anatolia, Africa, Gaul or along the Danube, by aligning them with the gods of the imperial power. The counterpart of *interpretatio graeca* or *romana* (the tendency to identify foreign gods with known Greek or Roman ones; *see* INTERPRETATIO ROMANA; THRACIAN RELIGION) was thus the 'spontaneous' restructuring of indigenous religious systems.

3. Graeco-Roman polytheism was always marked by integrating devices (political control; poetic interpretation; shared iconography; *oracles; historical writing) to counteract its inherent fissility. Such fragmentation is particularly marked in the Hellenistic world and the Principate. Several new integrating devices were developed (e.g. cumulative assimilation, listing devices, *di Augusti*). But themes from highly-developed non-Graeco-Roman religious traditions were also used, esp. the promotion of a god, in a particular context, to universal status, by combining the name with other divine names (polyonomy), or by the locution 'One ...'. The first is typical of *Isis, but extends to other gods; the second derives from near-eastern hymn- and acclamation-formulae. The practice is pushed furthest in mystic or philosophical religion, e.g. theosophical oracles from *Claros, the magical papyri, the orations of the emperor Julian. But it is never exclusive, remaining primarily an invocatory device.

Synesius of Cyrene, *c*.AD 370–413, Christian Neoplatonist (*see* NEOPLATONISM) and bishop of Ptolemais 410–13. A pupil of Hypatia at Alexandria, he tended towards oratory and poetry. Nine hymns, 156 letters, and a series of discourses are extant. Of the latter, the Dion is a powerful attack on the contemporary decline of humane culture, whether in the form of exaggerated Christian *asceticism or superstitious pagan *theurgy. He shared Neoplatonic interest in the occult (e.g. the Chaldaean oracles) and wrote on *divination by *dreams. His wife and brother were Christians; he himself was probably a catechumen as early as 399. He spent three years in Constantinople (probably 397/8–400) as ambassador of his city requesting tax reductions, during which he became greatly involved in imperial politics.

Syrian deities Almost all the deities worshipped in Greek and Roman Syria were Semitic. In spite of regional differences, a few main types of cult can be distinguished. One group comprises the cults of high places, of waters and springs, of trees and of stones, especially meteorites. Secondly, the close associations between some animals and certain anthropomorphic deities—particularly the bull, lion, horse, camel, snake, dove, and fish—may imply earlier identifications. The largest group consists of deities in human form. These are often divinities of agriculture and fertility, of the sky and thunder; they may be protectors, or bringers of military and commercial success; they may represent the sun, moon, or stars. Annual death and resurrection occur in some cults. Most characteristic of Syrian religion were the 'Lord' and 'Lady', the Ba'al and his consort the Ba'alat (or El and Elat), pairs of deities who could take many of the above-mentioned forms. Each pair originally protected a Semitic tribe; when the tribe settled, the divine pair were regarded as owning the tribal territory, and sometimes their influence spread beyond it.

Ancient Mesopotamian deities (such as Bel and Nebo) often constituted a part of the syncretistic mixture and certain religious developments reveal the continuing influence of the Babylonian astrologers, the 'Chaldaeans'. Deities were frequently grouped into triads (god, goddess, son; Bel, sun, moon, etc.). Furthermore, when the cyclical nature of the movement of the heavenly bodies was recognized, deities of the skies and stars (e.g. Ba'alshamin) became omnipotent masters of the universe and eternity, and so of the whole of human life and the after-life. Finally, in the Roman period, the Syrian deities were welded into one eternal and omnipotent power, manifest in the Sun. This trend may be regarded as 'solar henotheism'.

Worship included ritual banquets, *processions in which symbols or statues of the deity were carried, dancing, *libations, and *sacrifices, *divination, sacred prostitution (see PROSTITUTION, SACRED), and *mysteries. Imposing temples in the traditions of Syrian Hellenistic architecture still stand at Palmyra, Baalbek, etc.; others, at Hierapolis-Bambyce, Edessa, etc., have now disappeared.

The deities of human form are usually depicted in Hellenistic or Roman guise, although many symbols from the ancient near-eastern iconographic tradition (e.g. astral signs) and occasional items of costume survive. At the same time there remain in some areas traces of an older austere aniconic theology (Nabataean and, of course, Jewish), though western influence could not be totally resisted.

Many Semitic deities received approximate Greek or Roman identifications: Bel–*Zeus, Allat–*Athena, Nergal–*Heracles, etc. The local Ba'al was often romanized as *Jupiter (Dolichenus, Heliopolitanus, Damascenus; Ba'alshamin as Jupiter Caelestis). Syrian cults were carried west especially during the Severan period, usually by soldiers, slaves, and merchants. The emperors Elagabalus and Aurelian attempted to establish Syrian solar cults as supreme in Rome. See ATARGATIS; ELAGABALUS, DEUS SOL INVICTUS (the deity); ORIENTAL CULTS AND RELIGION; SOL.

[Lucian, *On the Syrian Goddess*]

Syrinx, a nymph loved by *Pan. She ran away from him and begged the earth, or the river nymphs, to help her; she became a reed-bed, from which Pan made his pipe (syrinx). See also HERMES.

[Ovid, *Metamorphoses* 1. 689–712]

Tabulae Iguvinae At Gubbio (Iguvium) in Umbria there were discovered in 1444 seven bronze tablets of varying sizes (the largest measure 86 by 56.5 cm. (33⅕ by 22⅕ in.), the smallest 40 by 28 cm. (15¾ by 11 in.)), engraved on one or both sides with Umbrian texts, partly in the native, partly in the Latin alphabet. These are the famous Iguvine Tables. They range in date probably from *c*.200 BC to the early 1st cent. BC and are the main source of our knowledge of Umbrian.

The texts contain the proceedings and liturgy of a brotherhood of priests, the *frater atiieřiur* 'Atiedian Brothers', not unlike the Roman Arval Brothers (*see* FRATRES ARVALES). The name is clearly to be linked with *atiieři-ate* (dative sing.), the name of one of the family groupings (*fameřias*) within Iguvine society; it had two subdivisions, which may correspond to two *lineages* mentioned in rituals as having sacrifices performed on their behalf.

The ceremonies include the purification of the Fisian Mount (the city of Iguvium), in which sacrifice is offered to the triad Jupiter Grabovius, Mars Grabovius, and Vofionus Grabovius (cf. the Roman triad *Jupiter, *Mars, *Quirinus) before the three gates of the city and to Treba Jovia/Trebus Jovius, Fisus Sancius (cf. Lat. *Dius Fidius, Sancus*), and Tefer Jovius (perhaps a god of the hearth) behind the three gates of the city; the *lus-tration of the *poplo* of Iguvium (the military levies, the original meaning of Lat. *populus*, people), in which sacrifice is offered to the triad Çerfus Martius (Çerfus being etymologically connected with Lat. *Ceres*), Prestota Çerfia of Çerfus Martius, and Torsa Çerfia of

Çerfus Martius (these and other double names probably mark functional or ideological connections rather than genealogical relationships), and a threefold circuit of the assembled *poplo* is made (cf. the Roman *lus-tratio* in which sacrifice was offered to Mars); sacrifices in the event of unfavourable auspices offered to Dicamnus Jovius, Ahtus Jupiter, and Ahtus Mars (Jupiter and Mars as oracles; cf. Lat. *aius locutius); a private sacrifice of a dog on behalf of the *gens Petronia* to Hondus (cf. Gk. *chthonios*, and *see* CHTHONIAN GODS) Jovius; sacrifices at the festival of *Semo on behalf of the *fameřias* of the Iguvine people offered to Jupiter Sancius; a procession through the fields to a grove where sacrifice is made to Jupiter, to Pomonus Poplicus, and to Vesona of Pomonus Poplicus. In scope, content, and antiquity the Iguvine Tables surpass all other documents for the study of *Italic religion, even though the interpretation of several passages remains uncertain. In many details they show resemblance to Roman ritual and cult but such analogies must be used with extreme caution, particularly since the Tables record a relatively developed stage of Iguvine religion.

Taenarum (Gk. *Tainaron*, more rarely *Tainaros*). The central peninsula of the south Peloponnese (mod. Mani) and its terminal cape, near which stood a temple of *Poseidon of which scanty traces remain. Through a cave nearby, *Heracles traditionally dragged up *Cerberus from *Hades. The sanctuary enjoyed a right of asylum (inviolability), and private slaves were manumitted there.

Tages, a figure of Etruscan mythology, an example of *puer senex*, 'aged child', childlike in appearance but of divine wisdom. He sprang out during ploughing from a furrow near Tarquinii, and revealed (to *Tarchon or to the twelve *lucumones*—Etruscan priests) the art of Etruscan *disciplina*, i.e. *divination, especially haruspicy (the books of Tages, *libri Tagetici*), and immediately died. *See* HARUSPI-CES; ETRUSCAN RELIGION; TARQUITIUS PRIS-CUS (all on Etruscan *disciplina*).

Talmud The greatest achievement of rabbinic Judaism in late antiquity, the Talmuds are compendia of legal opinions, sayings, and stories by and about the *rabbis of the first five centuries of the Christian era. Two quite separate Talmuds are extant: the Palestinian (or Jerusalem) Talmud, redacted in Palestine in *c*.AD 400, and the Babylonian Talmud, redacted in Mesopotamia in *c*.AD 500. Both Talmuds are organized as commentaries on the *Mishnah, tractate by tractate; for some tractates a commentary is found only in the Babylonian Talmud. The commentary (termed *gemarah*, lit. 'completion') attempts harmonization of conflicting views expressed in the Mishnah, and elucidation of obscure passages, in order to produce a complete, unified account of Jewish law. In the process the editors included much extra material of only tangential relevance to the Mishnaic passage under discussion. This extra material consists partly in homiletic narratives about rabbis, partly in independent literary units containing disputes over legal interpretation, partly (but less frequently) in *midrash of biblical texts.

The Mishnaic text quoted within each Talmud is in Hebrew, as are some sayings (*beraitot*) composed, or purporting to have been composed, by rabbis before the compilation of the Mishnah (i.e. in the 1st and 2nd cents. AD). The rest of both Talmuds is in Aramaic, expressed in a style so elliptic and formulaic that the meaning of many passages is only apparent with the help of the medieval commentaries traditionally used

by Jews engaged in study of the Talmud. The obscurantism of Talmudic discourse appears to be deliberate, reflecting the origin of the text in scholarly discussions within rabbinic academies, where both the main premisses of the subject debated, and the types of argument permitted on either side, were taken for granted.

The Talmuds deal with civil, criminal, and matrimonial law as well as more strictly religious matters. They have less discussion about the sacrificial rites in the *Jerusalem Temple than does the Mishnah; conversely, they contain more information about the operation of rabbinic academies. The Babylonian Talmud quotes the views of many Palestinian scholars, and vice versa, but the two compilations do in general reflect differences in outlook between the two centres of rabbinic learning. It is also sometimes possible to discern the distinct views of particular rabbinic schools or groups.

The rabbis quoted in the *gemarah* date from the 3rd to 4th cent. (Palestinian Talmud) or the 3rd to 5th cent. (Babylonian Talmud), but the extent to which their sayings are correctly reported is debated. Medieval traditions ascribing the editing of the Talmuds to particular rabbis are worth little, but some scholars have perceived evidence of a strong editorial hand in the statements transmitted anonymously as a commentary on the discussions recorded (the *stam*) and in the shaping of individual tractates. It is certain that some sayings were wrongly attributed to particular rabbis on the principle that, in the light of his other views as recorded elsewhere, this is what that rabbi would have said if he had given an opinion.

The prolonged interest by Jews in the Babylonian Talmud as an authoritative legal source has ensured that this huge document from late antiquity survives more or less intact, but there are numerous references by medieval commentators to textual variants no longer attested in the extant manuscripts, and the argumentative style of the Talmud, with the preservation of divergent views on many topics and a tendency to pseudepigraphy, makes its use as a source for the history of *Jews and *Judaism complex.

Talos (*Talōs*) (1) An animated bronze man, in the usual account made by *Hephaestus to guard *Europa; later the guardian of Crete. There are several variant accounts of his origin and function. He kept strangers off by throwing stones, or burned them, or heated himself red-hot and clasped them in his arms. His vital fluid was kept in a magic membrane in his foot; *Medea cast him into a magic sleep and cut the membrane, thus killing him.

(2) Nephew of *Daedalus, sometimes called Kalos or Perdix (the latter is also given as his mother's name). Daedalus was jealous of his inventive talent and so killed him. According to *Apollodorus, his invention was to make a saw from a snake's jaw-bone.

[(1) Apollonius Rhodius 4. 1638–88; (2) Apollodorus 3. 15. 8]

Talthybius, *Agamemnon's herald. For some reason his name remains familiar in later writings, while his comrade Eurybates is forgotten. He was the *eponym of a herald-clan at Sparta, the Talthybiadae. *See* SPARTAN CULTS.

[Homer, *Iliad* 1. 320; Herodotus 7. 134. 1]

Tanaquil was wife of *Tarquinius Priscus. In Livy she fosters Priscus' ambition, encourages his emigration to Rome, and interprets an eagle omen as portending his future kingship. She subsequently similarly explains a fire portent concerning Servius *Tullius (and in other accounts the previous appearance of a *phallus that led to Servius' birth) and engineers Servius' succession after Priscus' assassination. Tanaquil's role in the Tarquin dynasty and her prophetic powers probably belong to the earliest Roman literary accounts, but only Livy develops her as a masterful political figure; other traditions apparently stressed her domestic rectitude. That she originated as a human double of *Fortuna is unsubstantiated speculation,

and though her name is Etruscan, her portrayal probably reflects Greek literary models and Roman male preoccupations rather than an enhanced role for women in Etruscan society.

[Livy 1. 34 ff.; Pliny, *Natural History* 8. 194]

Tantalus, legendary king of Sipylus on the borders of Phrygia and Lydia, son of *Zeus and father of *Pelops and *Niobe; like other Asian rulers (*Midas, Croesus) he was proverbial for his wealth, as the phrase 'the talents of Tantalus' in the lyric poet Anacreon shows. Along with *Lycaon (3), *Tityus, *Ixion, and *Sisyphus he belongs to the group of archetypal violators of the laws laid down by Zeus for the conduct of human society, criminals whose exemplary punishment stands as a moral landmark for posterity. His offence was to abuse the great privilege he enjoyed, as one of the first generation of mortals, in being allowed to dine with the gods. Either he blabbed about the divine policy discussions he had overheard; or he stole and distributed to mortals the nectar and *ambrosia served at the feast; or, most commonly, he tested the gods by killing and cooking his son Pelops to see whether they would detect the forbidden food. Only *Demeter, distracted by sorrow for her missing daughter, ate a piece of shoulder from the stew; this meant that when the child was reconstituted and brought back to life an ivory prosthesis was necessary. In the *Odyssey*, Tantalus suffers eternal and condign punishment, 'tantalized' by having to stand in a pool which drains away when he tries to drink, with fruit dangling before his eyes which are whisked away as soon as he reaches for them; other authors, including *Pindar, describe a rock teetering overhead, adding terror to the pains of hunger.

See also GENEALOGICAL TABLES (5) DESCENDANTS OF TANTALUS.

[Homer, *Odyssey* 1. 583 ff.; Pindar, *Olympian* 1]

Tarchon, companion, son or brother of Tyrrhenus, founder of Tarquinii, also of Pisa and Mantua. The scene on a bronze mirror from Tuscania does not refer to him, but rather to his son, Avl(e) Tarchunus: with his cap of a haruspex (*see* HARUSPICES) thrown onto his back, he watches the youthful Pava Tarchies (not to be identified with Tages) examining a liver for omens.

Tarpeia in the war between *Romulus and Titus *Tatius supposedly betrayed the *Capitol to the *Sabini for what they wore on their left arms, but instead of being rewarded with the gold bracelets she expected, was crushed to death by their shields. This cautionary tale of female treachery (and, remarkably, Sabine luxury) goes back to Fabius Pictor and borrowed Hellenistic motifs to provide an aetiology of the Tarpeian Rock. Lucius Calpurnius Piso Frugi, however, inferred from the public sacrifice made at the supposed tomb of Tarpeia that she was a national heroine, attempting to disarm the Sabines by trickery.

[Livy 1. 11; Dionysius of Halicarnassus, *Roman Antiquities* 2. 387–9]

Tarquinius Priscus, Lucius, the fifth king of Rome (traditionally 616–579 BC), was believed to be the son of Demaratus of Corinth, who fled Tarquinii to escape the tyranny of Cypselus. Tarquin himself migrated to Rome with his entourage, including his wife *Tanaquil, and became the right-hand man of Ancus *Marcius. When Marcius died, Tarquin was chosen, by the regular procedure, as his successor. The story provides interesting examples of the horizontal mobility that characterized élite society in the Archaic period, when high-ranking individuals and groups could move freely from one community to another without loss of social position. This phenomenon, which is documented in the Etruscan cities by contemporary inscriptions, is consistent with the Demaratus story, which is in any case made plausible by archaeological evidence of cultural and trade relations between Etruria and Greece (especially Corinth). It also makes the traditional account of Tarquin's accession at Rome far more likely than the alternative

modern theory of an Etruscan conquest of Rome, for which there is no supporting evidence. On the other hand, the connection between Demaratus and Tarquin may be artificial; it cannot be historical if the two Tarquins who ruled at Rome were father and son, as the oldest tradition maintained. As king, Tarquin is said to have increased the size of the senate and raised the number of cavalry centuries from three to six; and he conducted successful wars against the Latins (*see* LATINI), Sabines (*see* SABINI), and Etruscans. Dionysius of Halicarnassus makes him conquer the Etruscans, but this version, which is not found in Livy, is doubtless exaggerated. He is also said to have started the construction of the temple of Jupiter Capitolinus, a task completed by his son; but this is probably a compromise designed to overcome the fact that the same building was attributed by different versions of the tradition to both Tarquins. This process of duplication is evident elsewhere, for instance in the case of the drainage works they are both said to have carried out. Tarquin was assassinated by the sons of Ancus Marcius, but their bid for the throne was thwarted by Tanaquil, who secured it for her favourite Servius *Tullius. This bizarre story is made all the more odd by the fact that Tarquin himself is credited with two sons, Lucius (*Tarquinius Superbus) and Arruns. Of his two daughters, one married Servius Tullius, the other Marcus Brutus and thus became the mother of Lucius Iunius Brutus, the founder of the republic.

[Livy 1. 35 ff.; Dionysius of Halicarnassus, *Roman Antiquities* 4. 1 ff.; Pliny, *Natural History* 36. 107]

Tarquinius Superbus, Lucius, traditionally the last king of Rome (534–510 BC). According to the oldest sources he was the son of *Tarquinius Priscus, although on the traditional chronology that is impossible. It follows either that Superbus was in fact the grandson of Priscus, or, more probably, that the traditional chronology of the regal period is unsound. Tarquin is said to have pursued an aggressive foreign policy;

he captured several Latin towns and re-organized the Latin League (see LATINI) into a regular military alliance under Roman leadership, a state of affairs that is reflected in the first treaty between Rome and Carthage (509 BC). The text of the treaty he made with Gabii is supposed to have survived until the time of *Augustus. He is also famous for having completed the temple of Capitoline Jupiter (see CAPITOL), and notorious for his tyrannical rule which eventually led to his downfall. Terracottas from the temple site at Sant'Omobono may belong to the reign of Superbus; in any event they confirm that the later Roman kings were flamboyant rulers who modelled themselves on contemporary Greek tyrants. This proves that Superbus' reputation as a tyrant is not (or not entirely) the result of secondary elaboration in the annalistic tradition in an artificial attempt to assimilate Rome and Greece.

For the story of his accession see TULLIA, for that of his fall see LUCRETIA. After his expulsion from Rome Tarquin fled to Caere, and persuaded Veii and Tarquinii to attack Rome. After their defeat at Silva Arsia, he appealed to Lars *Porsenna, whose assault on Rome is said to have been aimed at restoring Tarquin to power; but this cannot have been so if Porsenna succeeded in taking the city, and it is hard to reconcile with the story that Tarquin then turned to his son-in-law Octavius Mamilius, dictator of the Latins (see LATINI), since the Latins had vanquished Porsenna. After the defeat of Mamilius at Lake Regillus, Tarquin took refuge with Aristodemus of Cumae, where he died in 495 BC.

[Livy 1. 40 ff.; Dionysius of Halicarnassus, *Roman Antiquities* 4. 41 ff.; Polybius 3. 22]

Tarquitius Priscus, an authority on 'Etruscan lore', *Etrusca disciplina* (see ETRUSCAN RELIGION). He appears to have lived at the end of the republic. *Macrobius quotes a passage from his book, translated from *Ostentarium Tuscum* ('Etruscan Prognostications'), on the felicitous omen of the ram with reddish or golden hue, and another from *Ostentarium arborarium* ('Prognostication from Trees'), concerning unfruitful and unlucky trees (*arbores infelices*). Pliny the Elder lists him among his sources for books 2 and 11, and Ammianus Marcellinus mentions the 'books of Tarquitius'.

[Macrobius, *Saturnalia* 3. 7. 2, 20. 3]

Tartarus, son of *Gaia (Earth) and *Aither (Sky; see NYX); and father of *Typhon by (again) Gaia, his own mother. Tartarus was also the name for the deepest region of the underworld, lower even than *Hades. There is an alternative neuter plural form Tartara. See also DEATH, ATTITUDES TO; STYX; TITAN.

[Hesiod, *Theogony* 119, 822; Homer, *Iliad* 8. 13 ff.]

Tatian, Greek-speaking Christian philosopher from Mesopotamia, pupil of *Justin Martyr in Rome. After Justin's death he split from the Roman community (c.AD 172) and returned to the east where he lived as an ascetic (see ASCETICISM). He is the author of the *Oration to the Greeks* (an attack on pagan philosophy and culture and in praise of the 'barbarian philosophy' of the Christians) and of the *Diatessaron*, an edition of the Gospels in a single narrative.

Tatius, Titus, king of the Sabines (see SABINI), who led an attack on Rome after the rape of the Sabine women (see SABINI) and captured the *Capitol (see TARPEIA). After the women had reconciled them, the Romans and Sabines formed a single community under the joint rule of Titus Tatius and *Romulus. Tatius was assassinated while sacrificing at *Lavinium, in suspicious circumstances (some sources hint at Romulus' involvement). The legend of their joint rule has been variously interpreted, most famously as prefiguring the collegiate magistracy of the republic.

Telamon, in mythology son of *Aeacus and Endeis, and brother of *Peleus. He and Peleus were banished for killing their bastard half-brother, *Phocus; and Telamon settled in Salamis, on Cyprus, where he became king. He was one of the *Argonauts, and a participator in the Calydonian boar-hunt (*see* MELEAGER). By his wife, Eriboea or Periboea, he fathered the great *Aias (1). By his slave-concubine, *Hesione, the daughter of King *Laomedon of *Troy and given him by *Heracles for his help in taking Troy, he fathered *Teucer (2). When Teucer returned home from the Trojan War without Aias, Telamon banished him. Telamon's *hero-cult is well attested.

[Apollodorus 3. 12; Euripides, *Helen* 91 ff.; Herodotus 8. 64. 2]

Telchines, an ancient race of Nibelung-like godlings, inventors of the craft of metal-work (*see* CULTURE-BRINGERS); associated chiefly with the islands of Rhodes, Cyprus, Ceos, and Crete (*see* CRETAN CULTS AND MYTHS), but traces of their folklore are also found in Boeotia, where, according to *Pau-sanias, *Athena Telchinia was worshipped, Sicyon, and elsewhere on the mainland. Their 'magical' skill brought with it allega-tions of wizardry, the blighting of crops with their sulphur and foul water, and the evil eye. Hence their reputation as spiteful, jeal-ous gnomes whom *Zeus attempted to drown or scatter; hence too, most famously, *Callimachus' pillorying of his literary enemies under their name.

[Callimachus, *Aetia* fr. 1, cf. frs. 75, 64; Ovid, *Metamorphoses* 7. 365 ff.; Strabo 14. 654]

Telemachus, the son of *Odysseus and *Penelope in *Homer's *Odyssey*, where he plays a prominent part, with the narrative showing his development from a timid and unenterprising youth, quite unable to re-strain the unruly suitors, to a self-reliant and resourceful young man who helps his father to kill them. In books 1–4, inspired by *Athena, he sails from *Ithaca to the main-land to inquire after his father at the courts of *Nestor at Pylos and *Menelaus and *Helen at Sparta. He sails home by a differ-ent route, thus avoiding an ambush laid for him by the suitors. After reaching Ithaca once more, he is reunited with his father in the hut of *Eumaeus the swineherd, and father and son together plot the suitors' de-struction. Telemachus fights valiantly beside Odysseus in the final battle where all the suitors are killed.

According to *Hyginus, *Palamedes put the baby Telemachus in front of his father's ploughshare, or, according to *Apollodorus, threatened him with a sword, so as to expose Odysseus' pretended madness. Odysseus saved his son and thus gave himself away. According to the *Telegonia* (*see* EPIC CYCLE), after Odysseus' death Telemachus married *Circe and was made immortal by her.

[Homer, *Odyssey*, esp. bks. 1–4, 16–24; Hyginus, *Fables* 95. 2; Apollodorus, *Epitome* 3. 7]

Telemus, in mythology, a prophet who foretold to Polyphemus the *Cyclops that *Odysseus would one day blind him.

[Homer, *Odyssey* 9. 507 ff.]

Telephus, an Arcadian hero. He was son of *Heracles and of Auge, daughter of Aleus king of Tegea and priestess of *Athena Alea. The baby was hidden by his mother in Athena's sanctuary, and in consequence the land became barren. To get rid of his daugh-ter and her son, Aleus decided to set them adrift at sea, but they reached King Teuthras in Mysia. In some versions deriving from Arcadian tradition Auge alone was exiled to Mysia, while Telephus was exposed on Mt. Parthenion, where he was suckled by a hind (his name contains *elaphos* 'deer' or 'hind') and rescued by shepherds. Fourth-cent. coins of Tegea show Telephus with the hind, and there was a precinct sacred to him on Mt. Parthenion. When he grew up, Telephus consulted the *Delphic oracle and was reunited with his mother; Teuthras made him his heir. Later, when the Greeks stopped in Mysia on their way to Troy, Tele-phus killed many of them, but as he fled from *Achilles in the Caïcos plain he caught his foot in a vine placed there by Dionysus and was wounded by him. The episode is depicted on the west pediment of the temple of Tegea. Eight years later, following an oracle, Telephus was healed by Achilles' spear, and led the Greeks to Troy. The story of Telephus was taken up by the Attalids, and represented on the small frieze of the altar of Pergamum.

[Apollodorus 2. 7. 4; Strabo 13. 1. 69]

Telesphorus, a healing deity associated with *Asclepius, with a speaking name ('bringing fulfilment'), son of Asclepius in an Athenian hymn (dating from after AD 250). He is always represented as a boy in a hooded cloak.

Telesphorus must have originated around AD 100 in Pergamum, where he had been introduced by an oracle, as a personification of the hopes for healing, equivalent to the Epidaurian daughter of Asclepius, *Akesis*, 'Healing' (*see* EPIDAURUS). His first known statue was dedicated in AD 98/102 by a treasurer of the emperor Trajan; under Hadrian (reigned 117–38) his image appears first on Pergamene, then on other Anatolian coins; Publius Aelius *Aristides, permanent invalid in Pergamum after AD 145, often acknowledges his help. His popularity rose rapidly during the 2nd cent. when first *Epidaurus, and later other places, adopted his cult. Representations, especially small statuettes and coins of the boyish Telesphorus are frequent in Anatolia and the Danube provinces.

teletē Being related to *telein* (accomplish, finish), this word properly means no more than 'accomplishment', 'performance'. However, already at its earliest occurrence (*Pindar), it had a special meaning: the accomplishment of a ceremony with a religious nature or connotation. So Pindar uses it of the *Olympian Games and of Athenian festivals including athletic contests. In *Euripides *teletē* often means a rite, in particular a more or less eccentric or orgiastic rite. Aristophanes uses it for religious celebrations of any kind. But from the 5th cent. onwards it tends to be used especially for *mysteries and mystic cults, sometimes, as for example in *Plato, with special reference to the initiatory parts of mysteries or to *initiation in general. From the Hellenistic period onwards the word also acquires a more general meaning as a rite containing some hidden philosophic or gnostic mean-

ing. It can also signify a magical or supernatural action or even force. This finally develops, especially in *Philon (1) of Alexandria, into the sense of 'inner meaning', or even 'allegorical interpretation'.

Tellus, the Roman earth-goddess, probably very old, though her temple on the Esquiline dates only from 268 BC. She should not be confused with *Ceres. According to *Ovid, Tellus was patroness of the place of cultivation, Ceres of cultivation's origins; and while Terra describes the element 'earth', Tellus is the name of its protecting deity, according to the commentator Servius. Terra mater, 'Mother Earth', is only attested from the 2nd cent. BC. The question of Greek influence on her ritual has been much debated. She is associated in cult with Tellumo, with Altor ('Feeder') and Rusor ('Ploughman'?), perhaps with the doubtful Tellurus. No festival is named after her and she has no *flamen* (*see* FLAMINES); but she is the deity concerned in the *feriae sementivae* (*see* FESTIVALS, ROMAN); the *Fordicidia of 15 April (the offering, a cow in calf, is typical for powers of fertility); and the sacrifice of a sow, the *porca praecidanea* (together with Ceres), a sin-offering for neglect of rites, especially those of the dead.

[Ovid, *Fasti* 1. 657 ff., 671 ff., 4. 629 ff.; Servius on *Aeneid* 1. 171; 12. 778; Varro in Augustine, *City of God* 7. 23; Aulus Gellius, *Attic Nights* 4. 6. 8; Martianus Capella 1. 49]

temenos, a demarcated sacred land, subject to rules of purity, reserved as a sanctuary (*hieron*) and containing an altar (*bōmos; see* ALTARS) and optional edifices, such as *temples, treasuries, and priests' houses. *Temenos* kept its original meaning of an estate, the result of the community 'cutting off' (*temnein*) and allocating choice lands to prominent men: the Lawagetas and Wanax in Mycenaean Greek (*te-me-no*), Homeric kings and heroes, and exceptional kings in the Classical period (the Battiads at Cyrene). In *Homer, the verb of possession, *nemein*, preserves the sense of allocation. Beginning with Homer we also find the ritual '*temenos* and fragrant altar', giving the impression of rather small sites compared with the revenue-bearing estate-*temenē*.

What was indispensable for Greek cult was the altar alone, constituting a 'sacred spot'. All the physical landscape could be perceived by Greeks as imbued with the presence of gods and punctuated with landmarks of sacred sites (and altars). With no need for demarcation, many did not constitute *temenē*. The Homeric *alsos*, sacred grove, need not have implied an artificially demarcated spatial perception. The public sacrifice to *Poseidon at Pylos (in *Odyssey* bk. 3) took place on the beach, not in a precinct. The transition to the sacred 'space', the precinct with its clearly demarcated boundaries (cf. the terms *herkos*, *sēkos*, *anaktoron*), delimited against other private and public lands, developed in the context of the rise of the 8th-cent. political community. In ritual terms people set up (*hidruein*) altars (to *Apollo *Archegetes at Naxos in Sicily, a sacred spot in a new land); depending on the context, they also marked around it (*horizein*) the *temenos*. The larger precinct allowed the community to gather inside it, in contrast, for example, to the tiny early temples of Dreros and Prinias in Crete. It implied a relation of the sovereign community with the gods, less dependent on royal or aristocratic mediation. The *temenos* became indispensable for small communities (not colonies) living among foreigners, as at Naucratis (Egypt) and Gravisca (Etruria). The addition of the spatial dimension to that of the 'sacred spot' also emphasized the new value attached to landownership as an expression of citizenship and participation in the *polis*, the community of the city: gods too had become sharers in the city, possessing plots of land. In 8th-cent. colonies land was initially parcelled and plots (*klēroi*) allocated both to settlers and to the gods (*temenē*). In the context of the *polis, the *temenos* was probably linked to the emergence of the *agora, a public, differentiated, 'political' (and to a degree also sacred) space.

Urban *temenē* were usually smaller than extra-urban ones, which sometimes served as revenue-bearing estates for the finances of cult (the exception, lands whose tilling was forbidden as at *Eleusis or *Delphi, illustrates the rule). In the synoecized city (that is, where villages had merged into one political unit) *temenē* tended to converge towards the centre (Athens, Corinth); by contrast, in the colonies (Syracuse, Thasos) more sub- and extra-urban sanctuaries were created. It has been claimed (with the clearest examples from colonies) that extra-urban *temenē*, located near boundaries, were created to proclaim territorial sovereignty and to constitute the 'foundation' of the *polis*. However, since such *temenē* were in fact created later than the foundation, since colonies had no boundaries but open-ended frontiers, and since safer lands (nearest the settlement) were needed for the settlers, it seems rather that extra-urban sanctuaries were initially reserved (*exairein*) as (potential) revenue-bearing estates; in religious terms the division of the 'whole' land was analogous to the division of sacrificial meat: a whole divided between humans and gods, the humans receiving edible meat—the gods the fat and fragrance. It also seems probable that sometimes (the Argive *Heraion? *Perachora?) peripheral locations enhanced a function of social mediation between various communities.

The distinction between public *temenē* and public lands (*chōria*), first made explicit by Solon in the 6th cent. BC, makes it clear that the two were not synonyms. *Aristotle speaks of selling and leasing *temenē dēmosia* (public *temenē*) at Byzantium, mentioning also *temenē thiasiōtika* (serving cults of particular groups) and *temenē patriōtika* (perhaps of ancestral, or heroic cults). The *temenos*, then, acquired its sacred character gradually, when particular sacred functions (a communal sacrifice or a source of sacred revenues), or monuments (an altar or temple containing a cult image), were attached to it. Mostly it expressed the intimate links of the gods with the soil, simultaneously separating sacred and profane and making the

Greek community a unity of both gods and men. *See* SANCTUARIES.

[Homer, *Odyssey* 3. 1–68; Thucydides 6. 3. 1]

Temenus of Argos, a Heraclid (*see* HERA-CLIDAE), son of Aristomachus, ancestor of the Macedonian royal house. He was a leader of the successful Heraclid/Dorian invasion of the Peloponnese, at the conclusion of which he received Argos as his portion. The tyrant Pheidon, who was believed to be Temenus' descendant, presented his expansionist policies in the guise of claiming the heritage of Temenus.

Temenus' sons arranged his murder because he had favoured their sister *Hyrnetho and her husband *Deiphontes (apparently representing non-Dorian groups) over them. A descendant of Temenus called Perdiccas or his son Archelaus founded the royal house of Macedonia. Temenus received *hero-cult at his grave at Temenion.

[Apollodorus 2. 8. 2–5; Pausanias 2. 19. 1–2, 38. 1; Herodotus 8. 137–8; Strabo 8. 6. 2]

temple The Greek temple was the house of the god, whose image it contained, usually placed so that at the annual festival it could watch through the open door the burning of the sacrifice at the altar which stood outside (*see* STATUES, CULT OF). It was not a congregational building, the worshippers instead gathering round the altar in the open air, where they would be given the meat of the victims to consume (*see* SACRIFICE, GREEK). *Orientation was generally towards the east, and often towards that point on the skyline where (allowing for the vagaries of ancient Greek calendars) the sun rose on the day of the festival. The temple also served as a repository for the property of the god, especially the more valuable possessions of gold and silver plate (*see* VOTIVE OFFERINGS).

The core of the temple is the cella, a rectangular room whose side walls are prolonged beyond one end to form a porch, either with columns between them (in antis) or in a row across the front (prostyle). More prestigious temples surround this with an external colonnade (and are described as

peripteral). They generally duplicate the porch with a corresponding prolongation of the walls at the rear of the cella, *without*, however, making another doorway into the cella (the opisthodomus, or false porch). Some temples, such as the *Parthenon, have a double cella with a western as well as an eastern room, in which case the porch has a door in it.

The origins of this are uncertain. No provable temples exist (excluding the very different shrine buildings of the late bronze age) before the 8th cent. BC.

By the end of the 7th cent. the rectangular form is normal. Cut stone replaces the earlier mudbrick structures, and important temples are peripteral 'hundred footers' (*hekatompeda*); the 6th cent. sees a handful of exceptionally large 85-metre examples, such as *Artemis at Ephesus and the Samian *Heraion. From the 6th cent. stone-built temples are normal; marble begins to be utilized where readily available. Doric temples generally stand on a base (*crēpis*) with three steps, though the enlarged dimensions of the building make these excessively high for human use; they have to be doubled at the east-end approach, or replaced there by a ramp; Ionic temples often have more steps. Roofs are generally now of terracotta tiles; gutters occur infrequently in Doric temples, regularly in Ionic. Marble tiles (introduced first in Ionic) are used in the Parthenon. The roof is supported on beams and rafters. Wider buildings require internal supports within the cella; these may also be added as decoration, even when the span is too small to require their support. Some of the very large Ionic temples do not seem to have had internal supports in their cellas, which must therefore have been unroofed or 'hypaethral', though the surrounding colonnades were roofed up to the cella wall.

There are recognizable regional variations, even within the broad distinctions of Doric and Ionic. Approach ramps at the east end are regular in Peloponnesian temples, which often restrict carved decoration in the Doric metopes to those of the inner entablatures over the porch. Sicilian Doric temples may have four rather than three steps, and frequently have narrower cellas, without any internal supports.

Only exceptional buildings, such as the Parthenon, have full pedimental sculpture, let alone carved figures on every metope of the external entablature, while the frieze which replaces the metope frieze over the prostyle porches, and is continued along both sides of the cella, is a unique additional embellishment.

Roman temples derive from Etruscan prototypes, themselves possibly influenced by the simple Greek temples of the 8th and 7th cents. BC. They stand on high *podia*, with stepped approaches only at the front (temples of the Roman period in the Greek part of the empire often continue the tradition of the lower Greek stepped *crēpis*). Roofs are steeper (reflecting perhaps the wetter climate of Etruria); more lavish carved decoration may derive from western Greek taste. The Corinthian order, used for some Hellenistic temples, became the preferred form. Marble is common in the Augustan period, white, with fluted columns; later polished smooth shafts of variegated marbles, granites, etc. are preferred. Regional variations continue to be important. The western provinces generally follow the example of Rome. *See* SANCTUARIES; TEMENOS.

temple officials Greek and Roman temples served as the houses of gods and goddesses, but also as centres of religious activity, meeting-places, storehouses for dedications, and secure locations for the keeping of valuables. They do not seem in general to have played as great a role in the social and economic life of the cities as did the great temples of Egypt and the near east, but all the same they must have required regular control, care, and funding in fulfilling their tasks and maintaining their fabric.

In Greece we have a picture of how the temples operated. There were normally *priests or priestesses in charge of each; in any large temple they would be assisted by minor officials. *Aristotle distinguishes three types of these: first, there were cult officials who assisted in the sacrifices and rituals (*hieropoioi*), who would have received their share of the sacrificial meat and other perquisites; secondly, there were wardens or caretakers (*neōkoroi, naophylakes*) who controlled access to the sanctuary, carried out purifications of those entering, and cleaned the sanctuary; thirdly, there were treasurers (*hierotamiae*), who assisted with financial administration, took care of treasures and votives, and oversaw the raising of revenue. The detail of all this varies greatly from sanctuary to sanctuary and from city to city; there was much overlapping in the functions of the officials and many more titles occur in the rich record of the inscriptions (cantors, musicians, sacred *heralds, libation-pourers, etc.).

For Rome and central Italy it is less clear how temple administration worked. In Rome, at least, priests were not normally attached to temples or responsible for them; exceptions occur when foreign cults were introduced, as with the Greek priestesses of the Greek *Ceres or the priestly personnel who accompanied the cult of the Magna Mater (*see* CYBELE). The only temple official we hear of is the *aedituus; many other religious officials are known—*victimarii (sacrificers), *tibicines* (flute-players), *pullarii* (keepers of sacred chickens)—some of whom would have had functions similar to the Greek *hieropoioi*, but these are not directly attached to temples, work with magistrates as well as with priests, and form groups or colleges of their own (*see* COLLEGIUM). The work corresponding to that of the Greek temple officials must have been done by the slaves and freedmen of the *aeditui*, but nothing of their work is recorded.

[Aristotle, *Politics* 6. 1322^b]

templum, an augural term denoting (*a*) the field of vision defined by a ritual formula (*templum in aere*) to observe the (impetrative) auspices (*see* AUSPICIUM) from the flight of birds; lightning was observed in the semicircular celestial *templum*; (*b*) the quadrangular area delimited and inaugurated by the **augures*. Many official state functions had to take place in a *templum* (especially the senatorial meetings and observations of the impetrative auspices); most shrines (*aedes sacrae*) were *templa* (but not that of **Vesta*), also the Curia (senate-house) and the Rostra ('speaker's platform').

[Varro, *On the Latin Language* 6. 91, 7. 6–13]

templum Pacis, later called forum Pacis or Vespasiani, was the precinct of the temple of Peace at Rome, dedicated by Vespasian in AD 75. The area (145 × 100 m. (476 × 328 ft.)) was surrounded by marble porticoes within an enclosure wall of peperino and laid out as a garden. The temple, a rectangular hall in the centre of the east side set flush with the portico, housed the spoils from **Jerusalem*. It was flanked by a library, the bibliotheca Pacis, and various other halls. One of these carried the Forma Urbis, a marble plan of the city from after AD 203, and may have housed the office of the urban prefect. After a fire under Commodus the complex was restored by Septimius Severus.

Tenes or Tennes, eponymous hero (*see* EPONYMOI; HERO-CULT) of the island Tenedos and owner of a **sanctuary* there. Son of **Apollo* or of Cycnus, king of Colonae in the Troad, he was falsely accused of rape by his stepmother, and Cycnus set him and his sister **Hemithea* adrift in a chest which landed at Tenedos. Later, Cycnus discovered the truth and attempted a reconciliation, but Tenes with an axe cut the moorings of his boat when Cycnus visited Tenedos, hence the proverb 'Tenedian axe' for a refusal to be addressed. Tenes was finally killed by **Achilles* while defending Hemithea; this was the mythological explanation for the taboo on the name Achilles at the hērōon of Tenes, just as flute-players were forbidden entry because a flute-player had denounced Tenes to Cycnus. Both types of taboo can be paralleled elsewhere.

[Plutarch, *Greek Questions* 28 (*Moralia* 297d–f)]

Tereus *See* PHILOMELA.

Terminus, a boundary-marker; in Roman religion, the god who protected these markers, which were set up with ceremony, sacrifices being made and blood and other offerings, with the ashes of the fire, put into the hole which was to constitute the *terminus*. Enunciation of the function of both god and markers was repeated by means of a yearly sacrifice and feast by the neighbours, on 23 February (Terminalia). On the same day a public sacrifice, celebrated on the sixth milestone of the via Laurentina, affirmed the symbolic limit of the *ager Romanus antiquus*, the earliest territory of Rome. According to myth, the Terminus on the **Capitol* had been there before the temple of **Jupiter* Optimus Maximus was built, and refused to move; he therefore was left inside the temple, with an opening in the roof above, as he had to be under the open sky; but this is just an interpretation of elements linked with the cult of Jupiter.

[Ovid, *Fasti* 2. 638 ff., 669 ff.]

terracottas Among objects made of fired clay were those of religious significance, commonly votive offerings, but also cult images. The relative status of terracotta was low; thus **Apollonius* of Tyana preferred 'to find an image of gold and ivory in a small shrine, than a big shrine with nothing but a rubbishy terracotta thing in it'.

Representational terracottas of large size were sometimes made in Greece as votives (**Olympia*); in Etruria they were common. Corinth in Greece, and Veii in Etruria seem to have been especially productive. The Etruscan repertory was largely religious, but also included **sarcophagi* with life-size figures reclining on the lid. In Sicily large busts of the Eleusinian deities were favoured. Small-scale representational terracottas—**masks*, reliefs, and figurines—were made as votives for sanctuaries, graves, and house-shrines. Relatively few and chiefly religious types were made in the 5th cent. BC.

Votive plaques (Locrian, Melian) were popular. In the 4th cent. the craft flourished, especially in Athens and Boeotia (Tanagra). The repertory contained few religious types (*Aphrodite and *Eros), and many of theatrical genre (actors and comic figures). Later Hellenistic types were varied, including new religious themes, imaginative genre, and echoes of sculpture. The most active centres were in Asia Minor. Roman workshops continued the Hellenistic repertory with local additions, but with the establishment of Christianity, the craft ended completely in the 5th cent. AD. *See* VOTIVE OFFERINGS.

[Philostratus, *Life of Apollonius* 5]

Tertullian (Quintus Septimius Florens Tertullianus, *c.*AD 160–240), born in or near Carthage, the son of a centurion. The tradition that he was a lawyer rests chiefly on the questionable authority of *Jerome. None the less, he uses brilliant gifts of advocacy, rhetoric, and irony in favour of the rigorist party among the Carthaginian Christians. From the first he was steeped in the spirit of the martyrs. His *Ad martyres*, *Ad nationes*, and *Apologeticus* (all written *c.*197) defended Christianity against pagan charges of atheism, black magic, and sedition, while maintaining that only in martyrdom could the Christian be assured of his salvation. Next (198–205) he devoted himself largely to Christian ethical problems. His *De oratione*, *Ad uxorem*, *De paenitentia*, and *De baptismo* all make high demands on the Christian life.

Tertullian's sole authority, apart from his verbal and intellectual acumen, was the Bible. Where, as in the *De anima*, he cites Stoics with approval, it is as the confirmation, not the source, of his beliefs (*see* STOICISM). His *De testimonio animae* is a classic exposition of the view that all men have innate knowledge of God; yet heresy is found, in his *De praescriptione haereticorum*, to result from the illegitimate substitution of philosophy for the 'rule of faith'. This was followed by works against the followers of the Platonizing Christian Valentinus, and

(between 207 and 211) five books against the arch-heretic Marcion. Against Marcion's belittlement of the Old Testament and violent emendation of the New, he argues for the integrity of scripture and a unity of purpose between the 'just' Father and the 'good' Son.

At some time he joined the Montanists (*see* MONTANISM), disciples of a new era of the Spirit, from whom they claimed to be receiving immediate direction. His action may have been precipitated by disgust with Catholic laxity, and perhaps by a dispute with the clergy at Rome. Yet, to judge by his subsequent reputation, there was never a formal schism. The transition seems to have taken place by 207. Believing that it was time for man to regain his unfallen image, he wrote his *Ad Scapulam* (212) to a local pagan governor in defence of religious freedom; his *De fuga in persecutione* and *De corona militis* against Christians who complied with the authorities; and his *De ieiunio* and *De monogamia* to enjoin a rigour in discipline that went beyond scriptural teaching. *See* FASTING.

His important doctrinal writings of this period are the *De carne Christi*, *De resurrectione carnis*, *De anima*, and *Adversus Praxean*, all notable for their hostility to dualistic thought. Body and soul are one, God himself is a body (though its matter is Spirit), and the body of Christ that died on the cross is identical with the risen one. His last surviving work, *De pudicitia*, was probably directed against measures by Callistus, bishop of Rome (217–22), to relax the Christian penitential system. The work is fundamental for its theology of a gathered Church and the study of the western doctrine of the Holy Spirit.

Tertullian seems to have lived to a ripe old age, and finally to have broken with the Montanists to found his own sect of Tertullianists, more rigorous than they. With the possible exception of *Minucius Felix, he is the first Latin churchman, and, as a favourite of both *Cyprian and *Augustine, exercised a great and abiding influence upon Christian theology in the west. He shares with his contemporary *Hippolytus (2) a hatred of Callistus, an aversion to all philosophy, a rebellious spirit harnessed to a strong ecclesiology, and a belief in the importance of distinguishing the persons of the Godhead (see *Adversus Praxean*). The affinity illustrates the close relations between north Africa and the capital in this period; he is, however, unparalleled in both the originality and the difficulty of his Latin style.

Tethys, in mythology, daughter of Earth (*Gaia) and Heaven, sister of Ocean (*see* OCEA-NUS); becomes the consort of Ocean and bears the Rivers, also the three thousand Oceanids (*see* NYMPHS), whose work it is to aid the rivers and *Apollo to bring young men to their prime, and *Styx, chief of them all.

[Hesiod, *Theogony* 136, 337 ff.]

Teucer (*Teukros*) (1) In mythology son of the river Scamander and a *nymph Idaea, and ancestor of the Trojan kings. He married his daughter Bateia (or Arisbe) to *Dardanus, and from this marriage was born Erichthonius, father of Tros (the genealogy is in *Apollodorus).

(2) Son of *Telamon by *Hesione. Throughout *Homer's *Iliad* he is a valiant archer, and faithful comrade of his half-brother, the greater Ajax (*Aias (1)). His character is similarly depicted in later works, e.g. the *Ajax* of *Sophocles. He was absent at the time of Ajax's suicide, but returned in time to take a leading part in the struggle to secure him honourable burial. After his banishment (*see* TELAMON) he founded Salamis in Cyprus.

[(1) Apollodorus 3. 12. (2) Sophocles, *Ajax*; Horace, *Odes* 1. 7. 27 ff.]

Thamyris or Thamyras, in the *Iliad*, a Thracian bard, who boasted that he would win a contest even if the *Muses opposed him, whereat they blinded him and made him forget his skill. Later authors attribute musical inventions to him.

[Homer, *Iliad* 2. 594 ff.]

Thanatos, mythological figure personifying death, the son of *Nyx or Night. In *Homer he is not an agent of death. He and his twin *Hypnos carried *Sarpedon's corpse to Lycia for burial, an incident represented in art which also inspired the creation of images on white-ground vases in which the two carry the corpse of ordinary people, representing the notion 'good death'. Thanatos is winged and usually has an ordinary regular face, but sometimes he has an ugly rough one. In post-Homeric times he is the agent of death, most notably in Euripides' *Alcestis*, where he has a prominent role (and where he is also metaphorically described as, 'winged *Hades'); also, in one version of *Sisyphus' myth Sisyphus bound up Thanatos when the latter came to collect him so that no one could die, until *Ares freed Thanatos—and handed Sisyphus over to him.

[Hesiod, *Theogony* 211–12; Homer, *Iliad* 16. 671–5]

Thargelia, a festival of *Apollo and held in Athens (7th of Thargelion, late May), some Ionian cities (*see* IONIAN FESTIVALS), and their colonies; it dates to a time before colonization. Scholars in antiquity explained its name from a *first-fruits sacrifice, a pot with the first cereals which was offered in Athens; the festival marks the beginning of the harvest season. At the same time, it had a manifestly cathartic character (*see* PURIFICA-TION), which explains the presence of Apollo: on the previous day in Athens, in the course of the festival in the Ionian towns, the citizens expelled the *pharmakos*, the 'scapegoat'. The rite is well attested with only minor local variations: the city fed a marginal person, often a criminal, for a certain time; during the festival he was decked out, led around the town, and driven out or even thrown from a cliff. At a crucial junction of the year, the expulsion of a member of society cleanses the town and prepares for the new harvest.

Theagenes (or Theogenes) of Thasos, 5th-cent. BC victor in the *Olympian Games, given cult at Thasos. *See* HERO-CULT.

theatre *see* DIONYSUS; FESTIVALS.

Thebes, myths of Thebes was founded by
*Cadmus, although Thebans also claimed
*Ares as an ancestor. Cadmus' daughter *Se-
mele was the mother of *Dionysus by Zeus,
but her nephew *Pentheus sought in vain to
prevent the worship of the new god. Thebes
was where *Alcmene gave birth to *Heracles, who as its champion freed it from the
tribute imposed by the king of Orchomenus
(*see also* AMPHITRYON). The legend of Heracles
reflects the essence of Boeotian politics,
which were moulded in the rivalry between
Thebes and Orchomenus. The other main
Theban cycle concerns the descendants of
Labdacus—the story of *Oedipus and, especially, the strife between Oedipus' sons
*Eteocles and Polynices for the throne of
Thebes, which resulted in the expedition
of the *Seven against Thebes. The sons of
the Seven, the *Epigoni, restored Polynices'
son *Thersander to the throne.

See also GENEALOGICAL TABLES (3) HOUSE OF
THEBES; BOEOTIA, CULTS; DIRCE.

[Pausanias 9. 5–17]

Themis, daughter of *Gaia and *Ouranos.
She is associated with Gaia in the myth of
previous owners of the *Delphic oracle. Her
identification with Gaia in the *Prometheus
Bound* (where Themis is Prometheus' mother
and utters prophecies) is a theological statement, not a reflection of cult. In *Pindar she
gave a prophecy to *Zeus and *Poseidon. On
a red-figure cup she is represented as the
Pythia (*see* DELPHIC ORACLE), delivering
prophecies while sitting on a tripod holding
a laurel-branch. She is a primordial goddess,
but she is closely associated with *Zeus'
order, and with justice, with right, law, ordinances. In *Hesiod she is Zeus' second wife
and she bore him the Hours (*Horae), Good
Order (*Eunomia), Justice (*Dike), Peace
(*Eirene), and the Fates (*see* FATE). In a fragment of the historian Ephorus *Apollo and
Themis founded the oracle together, to
guide and civilize humanity. The conceptual
association between the two is also
expressed in the Homeric *Hymn to Apollo,

where Themis fed the new-born Apollo
nectar and *ambrosia.

[Hesiod, *Theogony* 135, 901–6; *Homeric Hymn to Apollo*
124–5; Pindar, *Isthmians* 8. 31–6; [Aeschylus],
Prometheus Bound 211 ff.]

Themisto, name of several heroines, the
main one being the daughter of Hypseus,
wife of *Athamas. One version makes her
his first wife and mother of several children,
including Phrixus and Helle.

theodicy is the effort to explain (*a*) phenomena appearing to demonstrate a divinity's hostility to virtuous people or to people
whose actions suggest that they should
expect to be recipients of divine favour, or
(*b*), more generally, reasons for divine anger
with humanity. Theodical explanations are
well attested in Egyptian and Mesopotamian
literature, and they form the basis for significant portions of the Hebrew Bible. Theodicy
is particularly important in societies that
view divine forces as guarantors of good.
*Hesiod is the most important early source
for Greek theodicies. The story of *Pandora,
which explains the existence of evil in the
world as a response to *Prometheus' deceit,
is one such, another is that *Zeus decided to destroy the human race as a result
of its *hubris. Early Greek elegy contains
other examples in, for instance, Solon's
poem on the subject of *Dikē. The notion
that a good person can be punished for the
evil of an ancestor or ancestors is seen in
the Delphic explanation (*see* DELPHIC
ORACLE) of the fall of the semi-mythical
Lydian king Croesus, who is told that his
misfortune is the consequence of the crime
of Gyges. *Aeschylus' *Oresteia* and *Sophocles' *King Oedipus* are strong explorations of
the theme.

The fundamental Greek concern with
divine punishment is most plainly evident
in the preoccupation with ritual purity and
impurity (*see* PURIFICATION, GREEK; POLLU-
TION). A society that does not ensure the
punishment or purification of individuals
who had incurred *miasma* (pollution) invites
divine punishment for the society as a

whole. The prosecution of individuals for *asebeia* (impiety) is another illustration of this problem, raising the question of a society's responsibility for thoughts that the gods might consider offensive as well as for actions. See INTOLERANCE, RELIGIOUS.

In republican Rome, theodicy is intimately connected with conceptions of impiety or *impietas* and *vitium* (error). Both concepts provided powerful explanations for disasters affecting society as a whole. If *vitium* went undetected in the taking of the *auspices or at a *sacrifice, it could be taken as a sufficient explanation for military disaster, and the senate would take charge of the examination of ritual actions during a magistrate's term in office to determine the point at which *vitium* had occurred. Favourable signs observed after *vitium* had occurred would be taken as a sign of a divinity's determination to punish the previous error by leading a magistrate into a fatal situation. In such cases blame for disaster could be diffused quite widely through Roman society. Cases of open *impietas*, the wilful flouting of divine authority (the story that Publius Claudius Pulcher, consul of 249 BC, threw sacred chickens into the sea before the battle of Drepanum) are less common, though in such cases blame for disaster could be fixed upon an individual.

Theodical explanations for social disorder are common in the literature of the late republic and early empire. Horace, for instance, offers a theodicy based upon the story of Rhea Silvia's execution (see ROMULUS), the preface to Lucan's *Pharsalia* suggests that the civil wars were the result of the general immorality of the Roman people, and *Jupiter's explanation of the Hannibalic War as a necessary event for the regeneration of the Roman people in Silius Italicus' *Punica* is overtly theodical. Tacitus describes various disasters connected with the civil war of AD 69 as manifestations of the anger of the gods against the human race, and Ammianus Marcellinus presents the disaster at Adrianople as divine revenge upon Valens for his crimes.

Theodical ideas were not restricted to the realm of magistrates and intellectuals. Thus, according to Cassius Dio, there was considerable unrest in the reign of Nero, resulting from his matricide, which could be taken as an explanation for the Great Fire of 65. Various natural disasters resulted in the persecution of Christians, whose presence in a community could be thought to attract divine anger (see CHRISTIANITY), and the sack of Rome in 410 was widely interpreted (by *pagans) as a manifestation of divine anger at a society that had fallen away from its proper religious customs.

Some fascinating examples of direct divine intervention in the lives of the common people of Phrygia (see PHRYGIA, RELIGION OF) have survived in two series of 'confession plaques', one from the sanctuary of *Apollo Lairbenos in Phrygian Hierapolis, another from north-east Lydia. These texts were carved at the expense of people who had been shown by a god (often regarded as the ruler of the community) to have committed a crime. It is impossible to know if these confession texts reflect attitudes towards divine judgement outside the immediate area where they were discovered, since the procedure is not attested elsewhere.

In Christian society, concern with divine judgement is widely attested. In the first three centuries, its most important direct application was probably as an explanation of persecution. After the conversion of *Constantine I, the most important and wide-ranging exposition of a theodical explanation for good and evil in the world appears in *Augustine's *City of God*. See SIN.

[Hesiod, *Works and Days*, 47–105; Solon, fr. 13; Herodotus 1. 91; Horace, *Odes* 1. 2; Lucan, *Pharsalia* 1 ff.; Silius Italicus, *Punica* 3. 153–5, 573–5; Tacitus, *Histories* 1. 3; Cassius Dio 62. 18; Ammianus Marcellinus 29. 2. 20, 31. 1. 3; Cyprian, *De lapsis* 11; Augustine, *City of God* 1. 1, 11. 16–18, 12. 1–9]

Theodoret, c.AD 393–466. After a good education he became a monk and from 423 bishop of Cyrrhus in Syria. From 428 he supported his friend Nestorius in the Christological controversy against *Cyril of Alexandria, of whom he became a leading critic. Deposed by the monophysite council of Ephesus, he was rehabilitated at Chalcedon despite strenuous protests (451), but his attacks on Cyril were condemned under Justinian at the council of Constantinople (553). His elegant letters are informative about both secular and ecclesiastical matters. His *Graecarum Affectionum Curatio* supplies unique testimonia on the lives and teachings of pagan philosophers. His *Church History* from *Constantine I to 428 includes many invaluable documents; the *Religious History* contains biographies of *ascetics. His Pauline commentaries (*see* PAUL, ST) are notable for their notion of *psychagōgia* (winning of souls).

Theodorus, Samian architect, sculptor, and metalworker, active *c.*550–520 BC. He made two massive silver craters dedicated by the Lydian king Croesus at *Delphi, Polycrates' famous ring, and a golden vine eventually owned by Darius I of Persia. He also built a hall at Sparta, and assisted in the construction of the *Heraion at Samos (upon which he wrote a book) and the Ephesian Artemisium. He is said to have collaborated with Telecles on a statue of Pythian *Apollo (i.e. Apollo of Delphi) for Samos, which was proportioned in the Egyptian fashion.

Theodosius I, 'the Great', emperor 379–395, was brought to the throne at a time of major crisis. He was a pious Christian and, unlike his predecessor Valens, an adherent of the Nicene creed, an allegiance which he owed to his origin and upbringing in the west. He was also surrounded by westerners, relatives and others, to whom he gave advancement, many of them individuals of intense personal piety. He was baptized very early in his reign, during a serious illness at Thessalonica. On 27 February 380 (before he had come to Constantinople) he issued a constitution declaring that the faith professed by Pope *Damasus and by Peter, bishop of Alexandria, was the true Catholic

faith. He deposed Demophilus, the Arian bishop of Constantinople (*see* ARIANISM), and recognized as bishop the Nicene protagonist, *Gregory (2) of Nazianzus. On 10 January 381 he ordered that all churches be surrendered to the Catholic bishops as defined by himself. He then called a council of about 150 bishops at Constantinople, which ratified Theodosius' action but refused to accept Gregory of Nazianzus. Theodosius asked them to produce a shortlist and chose Nectarius, a former senator of Constantinople, as bishop. Theodosius was very severe against heretics, issuing eighteen constitutions against them; he even ordained the death penalty for some extremist sects. Towards the *pagans his policy was at first ambivalent. He did not forbid *sacrifice, but was so severe against *divination as to prevent it. He did not close the temples, but allowed fanatical Christians, including his own praetorian prefect Cynegius, to destroy them, or granted them to petitioners. In a law issued at Milan in 391 he abruptly closed all temples and banned all forms of pagan cult. This step was probably taken under the influence of *Ambrose, bishop of Milan, who had obtained great ascendancy over him since his arrival in the west. Late in 388 Ambrose forced him to leave unpunished the bishop of Callinicum, who had burned down a *synagogue, and in 390, when Theodosius ordered retributive killings at Thessalonica to avenge the death in a riot of the general Butheric, he refused him communion until he had done penance.

Theodosius' death was followed by what is often seen as the formal division of the Roman empire into eastern and western parts. His settlement with the Goths had long-term effects, as under their leaders the Goths installed themselves ever more intimately into the political structure and society of the Roman empire. His religious policies mark a significant step in the developing alliance between Church and State, and were greeted with delight by Christian writers like *Orosius and *Augustine, and with dismay by Eunapius.

theogony An account of the origins and the genealogical relations of the Gods, usually in close association with the origins of the world itself, of which the Gods are a personification or, somehow, an explanation. The earliest surviving example is the *Theogony* of *Hesiod, dating to perhaps the end of the 8th cent. BC. This work became the standard treatment of the early ages of the world and is our main source for myths about *Gaia and *Uranus, *Cronus and *Rhea, and the conflict between *Olympian Gods and *Titans. The other main surviving examples of theogonies are those labelled 'Orphic', which in part follow Hesiod's scheme, but incorporate additions and important changes of emphasis: *see* ORPHIC LITERATURE.

See also GENEALOGICAL TABLES (1) GREEK GODS.

Theophilus (1), bishop of Antioch, author of the three books *To Autolycus* (written shortly after AD 180), which include a defence of basic Christian doctrines (*see* APOLOGISTS, CHRISTIAN) and an attack on paganism, in particular Greek poetry and philosophy. In addition, the second book contains an exegetical treatment of the early chapters of Genesis. Theophilus' numerous other writings are known by their titles only.

Theophilus (2) of Alexandria, patriarch AD 385–412, was no thinker but a zealous pastor who vigorously suppressed Egyptian paganism (he was instrumental in destroying the great temple of *Sarapis at Alexandria in 391) and advanced the power of his see by opposing John *Chrysostom of Constantinople. He is presented in hostile spirit in the writings of *Jerome but in a kind light in *Synesius' letters.

theophoric names *See* NAMES, RELIGIOUS.

Theophrastus (372/1 or 371/70–288/7 or 287/6 BC) of Eresus in Lesbos, associate and successor of *Aristotle, shared in, continued, and extended Aristotle's activity in every subject. He rejected Aristotle's Unmoved Mover, and argued—though not necessarily against Aristotle—that teleological explanation could not be applied to every aspect of the natural world. He retained a belief in the divinity of the heavens and the eternity of the universe; the evidence for his rejecting the fifth, heavenly element (the *aithēr*) and regarding fire as fundamentally different in kind from the other sublunary elements is uncertain. His arguments in favour of vegetarianism, used extensively by *Porphyry, may represent one side of a debate rather than his personal opinion. His best-known surviving work, the *Characters*—a series of sketches of thirty more or less undesirable types of personality, preserves some interesting information on religious practice, especially the section on *deisidaimonia*.

theōrika, 'spectacle' grants, paid by the state to the citizens of Athens to enable them to attend the theatre at the major *festivals. Attributions of these grants to Pericles (who introduced payment for jurors) and to Agyrrhius (who introduced payment for attending the assembly) are both undermined by the silence of Aristophanes on the subject, and the likeliest attribution is to Eubulus and Diophantus after the Social War of the 350s BC. In peacetime the fund received not only a regular allocation (*merismos*) but also any surplus revenue, and became rich enough to pay for a variety of projects; this, together with the fact that the treasurer of the fund was elected and could be re-elected, and shared with the council the oversight of the old financial committees, made the fund and its treasurer very powerful.

The term is found also in Roman Egypt, where it seems to denote funds for local religious festivals, which had to be supplied by taxation.

theōroi, 'observers', a word originally applied to sight-seeing travellers and to the attendants at festivals of distant cities. It became an official title given to a city's representatives at another city's festival. The great panhellenic festivals (*see* AGŌNES;

PANHELLENISM) were attended by theoric delegations (*theōriai*) from every Greek state. Cities to which *theōroi* regularly came assigned the duty of receiving them to official *theōrodokoi*. At the festivals the *theōroi* offered sacrifices in the name of their cities, and so the title was likewise given to the envoys that a city sent to a distant shrine to offer sacrifice in its name and to the envoys that it sent to consult a distant oracle. The envoys that were sent round to announce the coming celebration of a festival and, after the creation of new panhellenic agonistic festivals in the 3rd cent. BC and later, to announce the new games to all the Greek states were also called *theōroi*. It thus became the accepted title of all sacred envoys. The religious functions of *theōroi* eventually obscured the original purpose of their office; although Greek cities continued to dispatch festival-embassies into the 3rd cent. AD, under the Principate another term, *synthutēs* ('co-sacrificer'), usually described their personnel.

theos is the common Greek word denoting a god, especially one of the great gods (*see* OLYMPIAN GODS for list). Although often referring to an individual deity in his anthropomorphical representation, the term is rarely used to address a god: no vocative exists. The term is often used instead of the proper name of a god, e.g. when the god's name is under certain restrictions or reserved for direct dealings with the deity, as in the mysteries: *tō theō* ('the gods' in the dual form) is the normal expression there for *Demeter and Kore (*Persephone), *ho theos* and *hē thea* (the god and the goddess) are Pluto (*Hades) and Persephone. It is also employed when identification of an individual god is precarious, for instance in the case of an *epiphany or vision, or as a comprehensive reference to any inarticulate, anonymous divine operator (*theos tis*, *theoi*: 'some god', 'the gods'); it alternates in Homer with **daimōn* to denote some unidentifiable divine operator. Later *to theion* ('the divine power') becomes an equivalent,

which, from Herodotus onwards, refers to occurrences that cannot be explained by natural causes. Accordingly, the term is often used in a predicative way to denote events or behaviour which are beyond human understanding: 'recognition of your own kin is *theos*'. No plausible etymology of the word has been proposed.

theoxenia ('theoxeny'), in myth and cult the entertaining of a god or gods by humans, usually at a meal. The thought pattern is old, and reaches beyond the Graeco-Roman world. In Homer, the gods are said to 'meet' or be present at a sacrifice; more specifically, at one point in the *Odyssey* they are said to roam the earth in disguise, testing the moral qualities of mortals. This is the germ of the typical theoxeny myth, in which a deity is given—or refused—hospitality, and after an *epiphany effects a reward or punishment. 'Failed' theoxenies are exemplified by the story of *Pentheus, while successful ones form an aetiology for very many cults, especially of *Demeter and *Dionysus. In this pattern the host is often worshipped as a hero (*see* HERO-CULT), having been instructed by the deity and thus become the cult's first priest or the introducer of a new technique such as viticulture (*see* CULTURE-BRINGERS). The reception of Demeter at *Eleusis, narrated in the Homeric *Hymn to Demeter*, has elements of both success and failure. But perhaps the best-known literary version, probably deriving ultimately from local Anatolian sources, is the story of *Baucis and Philemon in *Ovid.

In ancient usage, the term *theoxenia* is confined to cult, where as a festival name it indicates a specific type of worship in which a table is spread and a banqueting couch laid out for the divine guest or guests. The meal is commonly shared by the worshippers, thus contrasting with normal sacrifice, which distinguishes human from divine portions. One of the best-known examples was the Theoxenia of Delphi, which attracted delegates from all over Greece as well as numerous gods, among whom Apollo was predominant. The rite seems to be particularly characteristic of the cult of the *Dioscuri, for whom Theoxenia are celebrated not only in the Peloponnese and in Dorian-speaking areas, but also, for instance, in Attica and on Paros. A parallel ritual, partly influenced by Greek custom, is the Roman *lectisternium.

[Homer, Odyssey 17. 485–8; Homeric Hymn to Demeter; Ovid, Metamorphoses 8. 618–724]

Thermum, religious and political centre of Aetolia (see AETOLIAN CULTS AND MYTHS). Situated north-east of Lake Trichonis on a natural rock-castle, it commanded the central plains of Aetolia and formed the meeting-place for the Aetolian Confederacy. Extensive excavation has revealed its occupation from the bronze age and its importance as a cult centre for the worship of *Apollo Thermios, Apollo Lykeios, and *Artemis; oval houses, a horseshoe-shaped building surrounded by wooden posts (Megaron B, probably of Geometric date), and three Archaic temples are the most important discoveries.

Thersander, name of five mythological characters; the one of most importance in terms of *genealogy is son of Polynices and Argela, from whom the tyrant Theron of Acragas claimed descent. He was one of the *Epigoni.

Thersites, according to Homer the ugliest man at Troy, lame, bow-legged, round-shouldered, almost bald, who abuses Agamemnon until beaten into silence by *Odysseus. Here, evidently, he is of low birth; but in post-Homeric tradition he is of good family, son of Agrius brother of *Oeneus, and therefore related to *Diomedes. So, when he is killed by *Achilles for jeering at him because of his supposed love for the dead *Penthesilea (in the Aethiopis—see EPIC CYCLE), a dispute arises and Achilles sails to Lesbos to be purified (see PURIFICATION).

[Homer, Iliad, 2. 212 ff.]

Theseus, a legendary king of Athens, who came to embody many of the qualities Athenians thought important about their city. Apparently originating without special Attic connections, he may perhaps have merged with a local hero of northern Attica, where several of his myths are situated, and his prominence in Athenian tradition seems not to pre-date the 6th cent. BC, deriving at least in part from an epic or epics; the developed tradition of his life indicates a very different figure from older Athenian heroes such as *Cecrops or *Erechtheus. Detailed accounts of his life are given in *Apollodorus and in *Plutarch's Life of Theseus. See also GENEALOGICAL TABLES (5) DESCENDANTS OF TANTALUS.

Theseus' claim to membership of the Athenian royal line is somewhat shaky, since his father king *Aegeus was probably a late addition to the stemma, made precisely to accommodate Theseus. The alternative version, that his real father was *Poseidon, scarcely helps. In either case, his mother was *Aethra, daughter of *Pittheus of Troezen. With her, Aegeus left instructions that if on reaching manhood their son was able to lift a certain rock under which Aegeus had placed sandals and a sword, he was to take the tokens and travel to Athens. This Theseus did, choosing the dangerous land-route, on which he encountered and defeated many dangerous brigands and monsters, such as *Procrustes, *Sciron, and the wild sow of Crommyon. On arrival in Athens, Theseus faced more dangers from *Medea, his father's new wife, and from his cousins the Pallantidae, but escaped their respective attempts at poisoning and ambush. He next defeated the troublesome Marathonian bull; it was on this expedition that he was given hospitality by *Hecale. But the major exploit of this part of his life was the journey to Crete and killing of the Minotaur (see CRETAN CULTS AND MYTHS). In revenge for the death of his son *Androgeus, *Minos had laid upon Athens an annual tribute of seven youths and seven maidens to be given to the Minotaur (for which see MINOS); Theseus now travelled to Crete as one of the youths and killed the beast, escaping from the *labyrinth in which it was kept, with the help of a thread given him by Minos' daughter *Ariadne. He then fled Crete with Ariadne, but for reasons variously given abandoned her on Naxos. On his return to Athens with his companions, he was unwittingly responsible for his father's death, by forgetting to hoist the white sails indicating his survival; Aegeus, thinking his son was dead, hurled himself off the Acropolis or into the sea.

Theseus thus became king. His greatest achievement as such was the 'synoecism' of Attica—the conversion of numerous small towns into one political unit centred on Athens. This was accomplished by persuasion, but other exploits, not all respectable, relied on force. Like (sometimes with) *Heracles, he undertook an expedition against the *Amazons, winning Antiope or Hippolyte for himself, but provoking an Amazon invasion of Attica, which was finally defeated. His friendship with the Lapith *Pirithous led him to join the fight against the *Centaurs, and later to attempt to carry off *Persephone from the underworld (here Plutarch records a rationalizing alternative). In the usual version, after their failure and imprisonment, Theseus was rescued by Heracles, but Pirithous remained below. Theseus also kidnapped the child *Helen and kept her in the care of his mother until she should mature—though *Iphigenia was said by *Stesichorus and others to be the child of this union. In either case, he was forced to hand her back to her brothers the *Dioscuri when they invaded Attica. This gave Theseus' enemies, headed by *Menestheus, their chance, and in the ensuing political confusion Theseus sent his sons *Acamas and *Demophon to Euboea and himself fled to Scyros, where he was treacherously killed by King Lycomedes.

The formation of this tradition has clearly been influenced at several points by the figure of Heracles, notably in the monster-killing episodes at the beginning of his career (which, according to Plutarch, he undertook in emulation of his great contemporary). Evidently the developed Theseus saga was built up from pre-existing snippets to satisfy Athenian desire for a home-grown and clearly non-Dorian hero of Heraclean type, a process which should be dated to roughly the last quarter, even the last decade, of the 6th cent., when there is a dramatic increase in the popularity of Theseus in the visual arts (see below). It is quite possible that the interest of the tyrant Pisistratus and/or his sons may have been a factor contributing to this growth, but it seems very likely that the political significance of the 'new' hero soon became linked with Cleisthenes, whose regional reforms could be seen as similar in spirit to the synoecism. Later, it seems we can trace a connection with the family of Miltiades and Cimon, culminating in the latter's transferral of the hero's bones from Scyros to Athens (see RELICS). But by the time of the tragedies of the last 30 or so years of the 5th cent., far from being the property of any one party Theseus is clearly a universally respected figure, the heroic representative of his city's greatness. True, *Euripides' Hippolytus presents him as incautious and mistaken (and outside drama, the distinctly negative traditions of the rape of Helen and the attempt on Persephone survived) but the usual picture of him in tragedy is of a strong, fair-minded, and compassionate man presiding with perfect confidence over a proto-democracy, the antithesis of the tragic tyrant.

Coming to prominence relatively late, Theseus had few major sanctuaries in Attica. This was explained by the view that the living Theseus had handed over all, or almost all, of his lands (temenē; see TEMENOS) to Heracles, whose cult is in fact clearly older in Attica. On the other hand, Theseus became deeply embedded in the festival cycle. As well as having his own festival, the Theseia, on 8th Pyanopsion, he was honoured to a lesser extent on the eighth day of every month (the day also sacred to Poseidon). Moreover, his journey to and return from Crete came to be associated with several cult-complexes and *rituals. Among these were the *Oschophoria, where ritual *transvestism was explained by the story that two of the 'girls' sent to Crete had been young men in disguise, and the juxtaposed cries of joy and grief by the coincidence of Theseus' return with Aegeus' death; and the *Pyanopsia, an Apolline festival (*see* APOLLO) said to derive from Theseus' *sacrifice in payment of a vow. It is possible to see Theseus here and elsewhere as the heroic prototype of the young men whose transition to adulthood seems to be one concern of the rites. Outside Athens, Theseus was said on his return from Crete to have established various sacrifices and the 'crane-dance' on *Delos, a tradition helpful to the Athenians in their claim to Ionian primacy.

The fight with the Minotaur, the only Theseus story regularly shown in Archaic art, is among the most popular of all scenes, continuing to imperial times in many media. The Minotaur is shown with bull's head (early, with human head), being killed; on the Amyclaean throne (mid-6th cent.), it was merely captured (*see* AMYCLAE). Roman paintings often show the aftermath rather than the fight.

From the late 6th cent. a cycle of Theseus' adventures on the road from Troezen appears, perhaps derived from poetry, or the adoption of Theseus as hero of the new democracy, resulting in the creation of a complementary series of 'Labours' to those of the Pisistratid hero, Heracles. Such cycles appear on the metopes of the late Archaic Athenian treasury at Delphi, the Hephaesteion in Athens *c.*450 (*see* ATHENS, RELIGIOUS TOPOGRAPHY), and the frieze of Gjölbaschi-Trysa (Lycia), *c.*370. Several vases depict cycles, but the scenes generally appear in groups or individually, mostly *c.*520–420. Theseus may be naked or wear a short cloak, and his weapons vary; his opponent is bearded and naked. Frequently, rocks and trees suggest Theseus' travels.

The lifting of the rock appears also on imperial Campana reliefs (also *Sinis, *Sciron, the Marathonian bull) and gems. On Classical vases, Theseus attacks a woman who may be *Medea (rather than Aethra), and Medea may be identified watching Theseus and the Marathonian bull on a series of late Classical vases; her attempt to poison Theseus is shown on Classical vases and Roman copies of Classical reliefs.

Theseus in the underworld was painted in the Cnidian Lesche or club-house for the people of Cnidus at Delphi; in the Stoa of Zeus with Democracy and the Demos (People); in the Painted *Stoa fighting the Amazons (also on the temple of Apollo at *Eretria, the Zeus at *Olympia, Athena Parthenos, Trysa, and some Classical vases), and rising from the plain of Marathon; and in the Theseion. The visit to the sea in the latter appears on Classical vases (*see* TRITON). Euphranor and Parrhasius painted Theseus. *Pausanias notes sculptures of Sciron, the Minotaur, the Marathonian bull, and Theseus in the Calydonian boarhunt; *see* MELEAGER.

[Apollodorus 3.16.1, *Epitome* 1. 24; Plutarch, *Theseus*; Pausanias 1. 31. 1, 24. 1, 27. 9–10; 8. 45. 6; 10. 29. 9–10]

Thesmophoria, a women's festival in honour of *Demeter, common to all Greeks, celebrated in the autumn (on 13th Pyanopsion in Athens), before the time of sowing. Men were excluded and the women camped out, sometimes at a little distance from the town, for three days. At Athens the first day was the *anodos*, 'way up', the second *nēsteia*, 'fasting', the third *kalligeneia*, referring to a goddess of 'Fair Birth'. Pigs were thrown into pits or caves, such as have been found at some Demeter shrines. The putrified remains brought up by 'Balers', *antlētriai*, and placed on altars of Demeter and Kore (*see* PERSEPHONE), ensured a good harvest when mixed with the seed corn. (It is uncertain when the pigs were cast down. The suggestion of the festival of *Scirophoria, in summer after harvest, is far from certain.) The festival included obscenity and a sacrifice. Otherwise, the secrets of the Thesmophoria have been well kept, as Aristophanes' uninformative play, *Thesmophoriazousae*, shows.

Thestius, in mythology, king of Pleuron, father of Lynceus and Idas (*Argonauts and hunters of the Calydonian boar (*see* MELE-AGER)) and of Althaea, wife of *Oeneus.

[Ovid, *Metamorphoses* 8. 304, 446]

Thestor Of the five persons so called, the least obscure is the father of *Calchas. He has no old legend, the tale in *Hyginus being manifestly late romance.

[Homer, *Iliad* 1. 69; Hyginus, *Fables* 190]

Thetis, a sea-*nymph, daughter of *Nereus, wife of *Peleus, and mother of *Achilles. The *Cypria* (*see* EPIC CYCLE) accounted for her marriage to Peleus by saying that she refused the advances of *Zeus to avoid offending *Hera and that Zeus, in anger, swore that she must marry a mortal. According to *Pindar, however, she was desired by both Zeus and *Poseidon, but *Themis revealed that Thetis was fated to bear a son stronger than his father, and for this reason she was married off to Peleus. This version was exploited in the *Prometheus* plays attributed to *Aeschylus, where *Prometheus knew of the prophecy about Thetis and used the knowledge as a bargaining counter.

Before marrying Thetis, Peleus had to capture her while she assumed different forms to escape him. The wedding was attended by the gods, who brought gifts (described for instance in Catullus 64). Both the capture and the wedding are very popular subjects in Greek art.

Most sources say that Thetis abandoned Peleus after her unsuccessful attempt to make the infant Achilles immortal; but *Homer sometimes implies that she stayed with him. She plays a crucial role in the *Iliad* as intermediary between Achilles and the gods, interceding with Zeus on his behalf, commissioning new armour for him, and bringing him the gods' command to release *Hector's body.

[Homer, *Iliad* 1. 348–430, 493–533; books 18–19; 24. 77–142; Pindar, *Isthmians* 8. 26–57; Aeschylus, *Prometheus Bound* 757–70, 907–27; Ovid, *Metamorphoses* 11. 221–65]

theurgy was a form of pagan religious *magic associated with the *Chaldaean Oracles* and taken up by the later Neoplatonists. It covered a range of magical practices, from rain-making and cures to animating statues of the gods. Like other forms of *magic, theurgy was based on a theory of cosmic sympathy but in theurgy, as in Neoplatonist metaphysics, sympathy was thought to extend beyond the material world and to unite it with a higher, divine world. Theurgy was accordingly believed to promote the union of the human soul with the divine. Plotinus shows no interest in theurgy but in the next generation it became the focus of a dispute between *Porphyry and *Iamblichus. Iamblichus' *On the Mysteries* argues, against Porphyry, that the human soul cannot attain union with the divine purely by its own efforts of philosophical contemplation; such union requires the assistance of the gods, which can be brought about by theurgy. Most of the later Neoplatonists accepted Iamblichus' position, although they varied in the emphasis they placed on theurgy. It has often been thought that the 5th- and 6th-cent. Neoplatonists of Alexandria were less committed to theurgy than their Athenian contemporaries. In fact, of the pagan Neoplatonists at Alexandria, Ammonius son of Hermeias is notably silent about both theurgy and the *Chaldaean Oracles* but the rest share the views of the Athenian school. Theurgy continued to attract the interest of the Byzantine Neoplatonists, particularly Michael Psellus. *See* NEOPLATONISM.

thiasos, a group of worshippers of a god. Permanent *thiasoi* are attested epigraphically (*see* EPIGRAPHY) from the Hellenistic period in much of the Greek world: they are associations centred, at least in theory, on the worship of a particular god or hero, and are not clearly distinguishable from other Hellenistic forms of religious or pseudo-religious club. Earlier, *thiasoi* appear in literary sources in connection with *Dionysus and with other ecstatic cults (*see* ECSTASY). How these earlier *thiasoi* were organized is unknown; possibly they were brought together for no longer than the duration of a particular rite. However that may be, the members were united by a strong sense of undergoing an experience in common: *Euripides in his *Bacchae* speaks, obscurely, of 'entering the *thiasos* in soul'.

Some and possibly all Attic *phratries were also subdivided into *thiasoi* by the early 4th cent. It is not known whether these phratry *thiasoi* had the religious function that the name seems to suggest; possibly the hereditary 'thiasoi of *Heracles' that are mentioned in the orator Isaeus, without further details, are instances of such phratry segments. A 'law of *Solon' guaranteed the right of association to groups of thiasōtai (of what type?). See CLUBS.

Thracian religion Accounts in Greek and Latin authors are an important source of information for the religion of Thrace. Herodotus writes that the Thracians worshipped only *Ares, *Dionysus, and *Artemis, though their kings also had a cult of *Hermes. No doubt this is a typical case of *interpretatio Graeca*, 'Greek interpretation'. That is, the functions of these deities were meant to illustrate the nature of the Thracian gods for a Greek audience. Ares suggests the existence of a war-god, Dionysus probably stood for a deity of orgiastic character linked with fertility and vegetation, while Artemis was an embodiment of the female principle. One may assume the worship of a Great Goddess, which may have shown similarities with the Artemis cult in Asia Minor or the cult of *Cybele. This Great Goddess was introduced to Athens as the Thracian goddess *Bendis in the 5th cent. BC. Herodotus understood Hermes to be a dynastic deity, worshipped as the ancestor of royal lines. The combination of gods in Herodotus was probably restricted to the southern parts of Thrace. Its interpretation is still much disputed. On the whole there seems to have existed a strong particularism in religious beliefs and practices. Thus *Zalmoxis is only attested for the Getae along the lower Danube. According to Herodotus he was worshipped as the only god and had extremely celestial features. According to a Hellenized (i.e. Greek) version Zalmoxis once upon a time did live on earth. This may reflect the idea of heroization prevalent in Thracian thought, which in pre-Roman times was restricted to members of the nobility and the royal family. *Rhesus, the mythical king of Thrace, on his death was given a cult as a human *daimōn in the Pangaeus mountains.

The existence of a cult of *Helios has been postulated on the evidence of a fragment of a play by *Sophocles and archaeological and numismatic finds. This assumption is further supported by the myth of *Orpheus. Still, the dualism of the orgiastic Dionysus cult and the more moderate *Apollo/Helios cult of this myth seems to suggest local cult-constellations from the south of Thrace.

The second important source for Thracian religion is the archaeological monuments of pre-Roman times. Tumuli and edifices illustrate the native nobility's idea of heroization (see HERO-CULT). A clear example is the mural paintings in the grave of a prince in Sveshtari near Razgrad (early 3rd cent. BC). The deceased is depicted as a hero on horseback, the *rider-god, attested as a hunter from the 5th cent., who plays an important part in Thracian metalwork. There are also monuments that represent a rider receiving insignia of power from a goddess or holding these insignia.

Female deities with their attributes do appear in Thracian silver *plate. It is still not clear whether these are representations of functionally different types of the same Great Goddess or altogether separate deities. The double depiction of a god driving a chariot adorned with feathers (silver pitcher of Vratsa) may be associated with the Apollo myth of the *Hyperboreans.

The third source is the monuments of the Roman imperial period, chiefly votive reliefs and small statues representing, in the manner of conventional Graeco-Roman iconography, *Asclepius and *Hygieia (occasionally *Telesphorus), Apollo, *Zeus, *Hera, Hermes, Artemis (sometimes on a hind), *Heracles, the *nymphs, Cybele, *Hecate, *Demeter, to name but the most important. The occasional Thracian epithet, numerous native dedicants, and rural cult places suggest that a few older features of Thracian religion survived in Greek or Roman guises. In addition there are *c.*2,500 votive monuments in stone representing a rider, often hunting. Here, too, the local character is shown by Thracian *epithets mentioned in the Greek votive inscriptions. The so-called *Thracian Rider* was most frequently identified as Apollo or Asclepius. There are also connections and for some parts identifications with Dionysus, *Silvanus, *Sabazius, Pluto (*see* HADES), the *Dioscuri, and other deities. The iconographical formula stems in principle from the Greek hero-relief. Consequently the oldest monuments of the Thracian Rider are Hellenistic and come from the Greek *poleis* (cities) along the Aegean and western Pontic coast. This kind of votive monument flourished in the latter half of the second and the first half of the third century BC.

Other grave monuments show that the deceased, like a god, was represented as a rider-god, and that furthermore the idea of heroization had reached a wider spectrum of the population.

Thrasyllus, Tiberius Claudius, of Alexandria, a distinguished astrologer patronized by the emperor Tiberius, who wrote also on music and philosophy. He is frequently cited by *Vettius Valens and other astrologers. *See* ASTROLOGY.

Thrasymedes, a son of *Nestor with a minor part in *Homer's *Iliad*. He was one of the Greeks in the Wooden Horse, and later with his father he welcomed *Telemachus at *Pylos.

[Homer, *Iliad* 10. 255, 16. 321 ff.; *Odyssey* 3. 39]

Thyestes *See* AEROPE; ATREUS.

Thyia, apparently the same word as *thyias*,

a Bacchante (*see* DIONYSUS; MAENADS). There being a spot so named at *Delphi, she is occasionally heard of as the *nymph of the place.

[Herodotus 7. 178. 2]

Tiber, central Italy's greatest river, forming the eastern border of Etruria and the northern boundary of Latium, was probably regarded as sacred from early times, and the Pons Sublicius had special religious significance. In the Hellenistic period the cult of the river became assimilated to that of Greek *river-gods. There was a shrine of the river-god on the Tiber Island in Rome, and a festival Tiberinalia is attested from late antiquity.

[Dionysius of Halicarnassus, *Roman Antiquities* 3. 44; Virgil, *Aeneid* 8. 18–80]

time *See* AION.

time-reckoning Ancient culture knew a range of expedients for dividing the twenty-four hours of the day, for marking the succession of days in the month or year, and for dating important historical events. *Hesiod already used the rising of particular *constellations to mark the changing seasons, and ascribed auspicious and inauspicious qualities to the days of the month that corresponded to the phases of the moon. By the 5th cent. BC, Athenian astronomers—like their Babylonian colleagues—knew that the lunar month is approximately $29\frac{1}{2}$ and the tropical year approximately $365\frac{1}{4}$ days long, and could divide the day and night up into twelve 'seasonal' hours that varied with the length of daylight. Astronomers developed increasingly accurate luni-solar cycles and learned to explain and predict solar and lunar *eclipses. They also created *parapēgmata*, or public calendars, which traced the risings and settings of stars and predicted weather throughout the year. Civil practices, however, were never guided solely by astronomical expertise. Most people continued to divide the day and night into rough sections rather than precise hours. The Athenian calendar's failure to correspond with the actual movements of the moon was notorious, while the Roman months, before *Caesar reformed the calendar, deviated by a quarter of a year and more from what should have been their place in the seasons. Intercalation was often practised for political rather than calendrical ends. Only in the 1st cent. BC and after, when the spread of *astrology made it urgent to know the year, day, and hour of an individual's birth, did an interest in precise calendar dates become widespread outside scientific circles. The chief motive for interest in the calendar lay, normally, in its days of ritual or ominous import rather than in its technical basis.

Historical events were at first normally dated, by both Greeks and Romans, by the year of a given priest or magistrate into which they fell: rough lengths for a single generation were used to date past dynasties of rulers. Even in the 2nd cent. BC, *Apollodorus used an *acme* system to date famous but poorly attested individuals like philosophers and historians; that is, he assumed that an individual reached his *acme* (conventionally put at age 40) at the date of some well-known external event which had occurred in the life of that individual. From the end of the 4th cent. BC, however, when the Seleucid era of 312/11 BC came into widespread use, more precise eras and methods gradually came into use. Scholars tried to co-ordinate historical dates from different societies by measuring their distance from some single, common era, like that of the first *Olympian Games in 776 BC or the founding of Rome in 753/2 BC. Other eras sometimes used included that of the Trojan War (normally given as 1183/2 BC) and the astronomers' era of Nabonassar, 26 January 747 BC. *See also* CALENDAR, GREEK and ROMAN.

Tiresias, legendary seer, whose ghost was consulted by *Odysseus. He was the resident *mantis* (seer) of the Cadmeans of Thebes, surviving from the time of *Cadmus (when he was, according to *Euripides, *Bacchae*, already old) to that of the *Epigoni, that is, seven full generations. He was a pivotal figure in the Theban plays of *Sophocles and Euripides, and is presented by *Pindar as an outstanding interpreter of the will of *Zeus.

A tradition which goes back at least to *Pherecydes (2) links Tiresias closely to the Theban legendary aristocracy, making him a descendant of Udaeus, one of the *Spartoi. This same source tells how he was blinded because he caught sight of *Athena bathing: his mother Chariclo was a favourite of the goddess, and he was with her at the time. At her entreaty, Athena granted Tiresias the gift of prophecy (*see* DIVINATION, *Greek*) in compensation. This is the version elaborated by *Callimachus.

According to the pseudo-Hesiodic *Melampodia*, the blinding and the gift of prophecy came from *Hera and Zeus respectively: the goddess was displeased because Tiresias said that women enjoyed sexual intercourse more than men. The gods had asked his opinion, as he was in an excellent position to give an accurate assessment, having been both man and woman: Tiresias had wounded copulating snakes on Mt. Cyllene in Arcadia and been turned into a woman; later, he saw them in action again and was turned back into a man.

Callimachus locates the blinding of Tiresias on Mt. *Helicon, and it is at the base of the Helicon massif, at the spring Tilphossa, that Tiresias met his death. He was leading the Cadmeans from Thebes after its capture by the *Epigoni, and died from drinking the water of the spring. He was buried nearby. The location of his tomb there, as well as the tradition of an *oracle of Tiresias at Orchomenus, suggest that Tiresias had connections with the region at an early date, and was not exclusively a Theban figure, even to begin with.

[Homer, *Odyssey* 10. 490–5, 11. 90–9; Pindar, *Nemean* 1. 60–1; Callimachus, *Hymn* 5; Apollodorus 3. 6. 7]

Tisamenus *See* ORESTES.

Titan, name inherited by *Hesiod for gods

of the generation preceding the Olympians (*see* OLYMPIAN GODS for list). There is no plausible etymology, unless once it meant 'king'. Apart from *Cronus, there is practically no cult. Hesiod seems to have padded them out into a set of twelve: *Oceanus, Coeus, Crius, *Hyperion, *Iapetus, Theia, Rhea, *Themis, Mnemosyne, *Phoebe, *Tethys, *Cronus. Some other Titan names are found in other texts. *See also* GENEALOGICAL TABLES (1) GREEK GODS.

Mythologically, it is no less important to have former gods (Titans) than to have former people (*Pelasgians) so that the current order may be defined, hence the battle between the two sides, the 'Titanomachy'. Hittite mythology too had its 'former gods' and the imprisonment of the Titans in *Tartarus by *Zeus has its parallel (at least) in Marduk's treatment of the children of Tiamat in the Babylonian creation-epic, Enūma Eliš.

In 'Orphic' theology (*see* ORPHISM), as known to *Plato and even more to Neoplatonic commentators (*see* NEOPLATONISM), the Titans destroyed the child *Dionysus as he played with toys and were blasted by Zeus' thunderbolt. We are, however, partly made out of their soot and as a result have a compulsive tendency to crime, to destroying the Dionysus within us, re-enacting the crimes of the Titans.

In Roman poets, Titan and Titanis are Hyperion and Phoebe, Sun and Moon. Our modern word 'titanic' derives from the monstrous power and size of the creatures preceding the rule of Zeus.

[Hesiod, *Theogony* 132–8 and *passim*]

tithe, *dekatē*, the tenth part of a revenue offered as thank-offering to a god; the sense is often the same as that of *votive offering, *aparchē*. For example, in a 5th-cent. BC inscription a certain Aeschines offered a statue to Athena as *dekatē*. Best known are the tithes which the Athenians brought to the Eleusinian goddesses (*see* DEMETER; ELEUSIS; PERSEPHONE) and in a 5th-cent. decree exhorted all Greeks to bring.

Tithonus *See* EOS.

Tityus, a son of Earth (*Gaia), whom *Odysseus saw in *Hades, covering nine acres of ground, while two vultures tore at his liver, as a punishment for assaulting *Leto. The seat of desire is appropriately punished. He was killed by *Zeus, *Apollo, *Artemis (in the Hellenistic poet Euphorion, she was defending herself, not her mother), or Apollo and Artemis. There are many variants in his story.

[Homer, *Odyssey* 11. 576–81; Pindar, *Pythian* 4. 90; Apollonius Rhodius 1. 759 ff.; Apollodorus 1. 4. 2; Hyginus, *Fables* 55]

Tlepolemus, son of *Heracles (by Astyoche or Astydamia) and founder of the Rhodian cities. On reaching maturity he killed his father's uncle *Licymnius, either accidentally or in a quarrel, and fled to Rhodes (according to Pindar, by oracular instruction). He led troops to *Troy, and was killed by *Sarpedon, though wounding him severely.

[Homer, *Iliad* 2. 661 ff., 5. 628 ff.; Pindar, *Olympian* 7. 31 ff.]

Tmolus, the deity of the Lydian mountain so named. He appears, with *Midas, as judge of the contest between *Apollo and *Pan, and as a coin-figure.

[Ovid, *Metamorphoses* 11. 156 ff.]

tolerance *See* INTOLERANCE, RELIGIOUS.

torch-race (*lampadedromia*), a spectacular ritual race, normally a relay, in which fire was taken from one altar to another. Most of the evidence comes from Athens, where three main torch-races were held, at the *Panathenaea, the Hephaestea (*see* HEPHAESTUS), and the Promethea (*see* PROMETHEUS); three more are attested before the end of the 4th cent., for *Pan, for *Bendis (on horseback—a great novelty), and for *Nemesis of Rhamnus, and several others emerge in the Hellenistic period. It was the form of ritual activity most distinctively associated with the *ephēboi*, a matchless competitive display of dexterity and speed.

[Xenophon, *Ways and Means* 4. 52]

tragedy The production of tragedy was not confined to Attica, but it was in Attica that tragedy acquired its definitive form, and it is from Attica that we have almost everything that we know about it. From the end of the 6th cent. BC, if not before, tragedies were performed in the Athenian spring *festival of *Dionysus Eleuthereus, the City Dionysia. This remained the main context for tragic performances, although they occurred also at the Rural Dionysia, and (probably in the 430s) a competition for two tragedians each with two tragedies was introduced into the *Lenaea. In all these festivals the tragic performances were one feature of a programme of events which, at the City Dionysia, included processions, sacrifice in the theatre, libations, the parade of war orphans, performances of dithyramb and comedy, and a final assembly to review the conduct of the festival.

At the City Dionysia three tragedians generally competed each with three tragedies and a satyr-play. In charge of the festival was a leading state official, the eponymous *archon* (see ARCHONTES), who chose the three tragedians (perhaps after hearing them read their plays). He also appointed the three wealthy *chorēgoi* who bore the expenses of training and equipping the choruses (see CHORĒGIA). Originally the tragedian acted in his own play, but later we find tragedians employing actors, as well as the appointment of protagonists by the state. This last method may have been instituted when prizes were introduced for actors in 449 BC. In a preliminary ceremony called the *proagōn* it seems that each tragedian appeared with his actors on a platform to announce the themes of his plays. Ten judges were chosen, one from each of the tribes (see PHYLAI), in a complex process involving an element of chance. The victorious poet was crowned with ivy in the theatre.

The normal choice of subject-matter was from the heroic past; it must have come naturally to tragedians to use the habits familiar to the lyric poets and to contemporary vase-painters and sculptors. Epic story-telling by rhapsodes must have been a shared experience, and many of the heroes continued to be deeply implicated in Greek life through their worship in cult. It is no accident that Athenian tragedy often deals with heroes who were the object of cult in Attica: *Theseus, *Heracles, *Aias (1), *Erechtheus and his family, *Iphigenia, *Oedipus. The tragedians of the 5th cent. seem to have aimed at a balance between displacement (through the choice of a time and place different from the here and now) and the explicit linking of the play with the audience's world, as in the use of aetiology (e.g. the foundation of the Areopagus in *Aeschylus' *Eumenides* or the prophecy of Athenian and Ionian prosperity at the end of Euripides' *Ion*) and in appeals through *ritual to their sense of community (e.g. the burial procession at the end of *Sophocles' *Ajax*).

The study of ritual practice and of ritual patterns in drama has helped to redefine the questions that it is appropriate to ask about the gods in Greek tragedy. As in Homeric epic, the gods are everywhere, but the plays are not about theology, and critics are less ready than they used to be to identify the religious beliefs of the individual dramatists. Even a more than usually god-focused play like *Euripides' *Heracles* asks questions rather than finding answers, combining sceptical challenges to divine morality with aetiological reminders of Attic hero-cult. But it would be wrong to underestimate the religious intensity of plays like Aeschylus' *Agamemnon*, Sophocles' *Oedipus at Colonus*, or Euripides' *Bacchae*; as always, it is through the use of language that the plays achieve their deepest effects. Existential issues like time and mortality, and questions that apply to individuals as well as to communities (such as 'Who am I?' and 'How should I behave?') are strongly represented in tragedy alongside questions relating to contemporary society. This must have been an important factor in the spread of the medium beyond Attica and even outside the Greek-speaking world.

transmigration The belief that on death,

some aspect of us—usually identified with the '*soul' (Gk. *psychē*)—survives to enter another body, is connected with the idea of immortality, supplying one possible destination for the disembodied soul. It is particularly associated with Pythagoreans (*see* PYTHAGORAS AND PYTHAGOREANISM), and later (?) with 'Orphics' (*see* ORPHISM); in the 5th cent. it is attested in *Pindar, *Empedocles, and Herodotus (who claims, probably wrongly, that Greeks borrowed it from Egypt). For Pythagoreans, the transmigrating entity retains its individual identity, but *Plato, who inherited the general idea from the Pythagoreans, specifies that souls do not remember previous bodily existences. 'Transmigration', or (in late sources) 'metempsychosis' (or *metensōmatōsis*), is different from *palingenesia*, which strictly refers to the periodic recurrence of events in *Stoicism. *Caesar reports that the Gallic druids (*see* CELTIC RELIGION) believe that 'souls (*animae*) do not perish, but after death pass from their original owners to others'; Diodorus Siculus directly connects Gaulish with Pythagorean beliefs.

[Pindar, *Olympian* 2. 56–80; Herodotus 2. 123; Caesar, *Gallic War* 6. 14. 5; Diodorus Siculus 5. 28. 6]

transvestism, ritual, the wearing of a dress of the opposite gender during *ritual. Ritual transvestism belongs to rituals of reversal where the values of ordinary life are temporarily abandoned; it is often combined with functionally similar rites, as in Dionysiac rituals (*see* DIONYSUS). It is a special case of ritual change of dress; a structural equivalent is the taking up of freedmen's dress by Roman citizens during the Saturnalia (*see* SATURNUS). In Greece it occurs in many rituals, among them those which were understood as transformations from initiatory rituals (e.g. *Oschophoria; *see* INITIATION) where a temporary role reversal was characteristic for marginality. Persons who perpetually live on the margins of society might perpetually wear transvestite attire, as did the eunuch priests of *Cybele (*see* EUNUCHS IN RELIGION).

travel Travel for religious purposes occurred in various contexts in the ancient world, usually in order to attend a *festival in another location or to consult an *oracle. The travel-book of *Pausanias gives an indication of the importance which visiting sanctuaries might have even on more 'touristic' trips. *See* PILGRIMAGE; THEORIA.

treasuries *See* SANCTUARIES.

trees, sacred Trees have been involved in cult in the Aegean world since the bronze age (*see* MINOAN AND MYCENAEAN RELIGION). They perhaps symbolized the renewal of life, appearing as central features in a sanctuary or associated with anthropomorphic deities. The (probably genuine) ring of Nestor shows a Tree of Life. Sometimes single boughs stand inside the horns of consecration (e.g. Psychro plaque). The tree continued in Classical cult: *Dionysus stands before a Minoan-type tree sanctuary on a red-figure vase from Gela. He received cult as *Dendritēs*, *Endendros* (both names derived from the Greek for 'tree') throughout Greece, although he specialized in the cultivation of the vine. At Symi in Crete *Hermes Kedrites emerged from bronze age cult: he is shown sitting in a tree which represented the force of life and vegetation. The same significance may in part lie behind the curious myths of *Helen *dendritēs*, who was hanged from a tree in Rhodes, and *Artemis *apanchōmenē* (hanged Artemis) in Arcadian Caphyae.

Some trees were associated with particular divinities for special reasons, like the mantic (oracular) oak of *Zeus at *Dodona, Athena's *olive, which symbolized the source of Athens' prosperity, or the laurel of Apollo with its apotropaic and purifying properties. The palm was sacred to *Leto on *Delos; in Laconian Boeae, Artemis Soteira was worshipped in the form of a myrtle, and she had a cult as Kedreatis in Arcadian Orchomenus. In popular belief trees housed some kind of 'soul'; spirits of the woods and mountains lived in them. Some were revered for their age. The *nymphs haunted sacred groves, which were the first natural sanctuaries of the gods. *Poseidon had a sacred grove at Onchestus in Boeotia (see BOEOTIA, CULTS), Athena on Phaeacia in the *Odyssey* (see SCHERIA). At Curium on Cyprus the sanctuary of Apollo Hylates arose from a sacred grove.

A sacred fig-tree stood in the Roman Forum near the sanctuary of Rumina the goddess of nurture or nursing; cf. the cornel-tree which grew from *Romulus' javelin on the *Palatine.

[Homer, *Iliad* 2. 506, 20. 8, *Odyssey* 6. 321, 10. 350; *Homeric Hymn to Aphrodite* 264–8; Pausanias 3. 19. 10, 22. 12, 8. 23. 6; Plutarch, *Romulus* 4]

Triopas, a Dorian culture-hero, usually the son of *Helios, but sometimes of *Poseidon, and associated with Cnidus. 'Concerning the genealogy of Triopas many historians and poets disagree', says Diodorus, which is certainly true. Strong links with Thessaly perhaps reflect the pre-Dorian population of the islands. According to *Diodorus, he fled to Cnidus after cutting down a grove of *Demeter at Dotium in Thessaly and there founded the Triopion, a temple of *Apollo and site of an important *Dorian festival. Better known is the version in which his son, *Erysichthon, committed this outrage against Demeter and was punished with unquenchable hunger.

[Diodorus Siculus 5. 61. 3]

Triptolemus, one of the princes of *Eleusis in the *Homeric Hymn to Demeter*, to whom the goddess teaches her *mysteries. Athens claimed that he was given corn and the arts of agriculture by *Demeter, and then taught these to other nations. He is frequently portrayed in Attic art from the mid-6th cent. BC onwards receiving Demeter's gifts and setting out on his travels on a wheeled car, which is sometimes winged. *Sophocles' *Triptolemus* (of which only fragments survive) perhaps contributed to his popularity. He was worshipped at Eleusis, was regarded as a lawgiver, and became one of the judges in the underworld.

[*Homeric Hymn to Demeter* 153, 474; Plato, *Apology* 41a]

Triton The meaning of the name is unknown. Tritons sometimes play a subordinate part in a legend: a triton in human form appears to the *Argonauts at Lake Tritonis and gives them a clod of earth which was the pledge of future possession of Cyrene; *Virgil tells of a triton who, furious at the presumption of the human trumpeter Misenus in daring to challenge him to a contest playing the conch, drowns him. *Pausanias had seen what were represented as bodies of tritons.

In art, the fish-tailed Triton wrestles with *Heracles, assuming the iconography of *Nereus around the mid-6th cent. BC; the scene is rare after *c.*510. It has been suggested that the story, unknown in literature, alludes to Athenian maritime success under the Pisistratids. Triton is probably shown on two Archaic pediments on the Athenian Acropolis (see ATHENS, RELIGIOUS TOPOGRAPHY). On three 5th-cent. vases, he supports *Theseus on his visit to the Ocean. He and Nereus watch *Peleus wrestling *Thetis. Later, Triton is often shown blowing a conch.

[Virgil, *Aeneid* 6. 171–4; Pausanias 9. 20. 4, 21. 1]

tritopatores, tritopatreis The spirits of the collective ancestors of a gentilitial group (such as a *genos*, 'clan') or of a community, they were concerned with its propagation and continuation. Known from Attica (see ATTIC CULTS AND MYTHS), *Delos, Troezen, Selinus, and Cyrene, they corresponded to the unnamed body of ancestors elsewhere. The most important source is the Attic historian Phanodemus (see ATTHIS). Their generative force is indicated by Athenian sacrifice and prayers to them at marriage and by Philochorus' description of them as the 'parents of mankind'. The historian Demon identified them with the impregnating winds. In the Orphic *Physikos* they are given names and called guardians of the winds.

triumph, the procession of a Roman general who had won a major victory to the temple of *Jupiter on the *Capitol. The word came to the Romans from Greek (*thriambos*) via Etruscan and appears in Etruscan form (*triumpe*) in the *Carmen arvale*. The origin of the triumph cannot be recovered. In Roman tradition, all the kings except for the peaceful Pompilius *Numa celebrated triumphs, followed by the founding consul, Publius Valerius Poplicola, but in its developed form it owed much to Etruscan influence, and Etruscan paintings show similar rituals which we cannot fully interpret. In classical times, the procession entered Rome through the *porta triumphalis* ('triumphal gate') through which no one else might enter. (It may have been part of the porta Carmentalis: *see* CARMENTIS OR CARMENTA.) It made its way to the Capitol by a long route including open spaces where large numbers could see it. It comprised, essentially, the *triumphator* (dressed in the costume said to have been the kings' and close to Jupiter's) on a four-horse chariot, with any sons of suitable age as outriders; eminent captives (normally destined for execution) and freed Roman prisoners of war dressed as the *triumphator*'s freedmen; the major spoils captured; his army; and animals for sacrifice. The whole senate and all the magistrates were supposed to escort it. Increasingly costly and elaborate details were added from *c*.200 BC, including banners, paintings of sieges and battles, musicians, and torch-bearers. The *triumphator* was preceded by his lectors (attendants bearing the ceremonial axes), and a slave rode with him, holding a laurel wreath over his head and reminding him that he was mortal. The soldiers chanted insulting verses, no doubt to avert the gods' displeasure. The right to triumph depended on a special vote of the people allowing him to retain his military *imperium* or supreme power in the city, and so in fact on the senate's decision to ask for this vote.

In the Republic the prerequisites for expecting such a decision were a victory in a declared war over a foreign enemy, with at least 5,000 of them killed and the termination of the war; the *triumphator* must have fought under his own *auspicia* (*see* AUSPICIUM) in his own province and as a magistrate. But interpretation of entitlement was elastic and subject to intrigue, and the senate might even be bypassed. From the 3rd cent. BC, some generals refused a triumph celebrated one at their own expense in a procession to Jupiter Latiaris on the Alban Mount (*see* ALBANUS MONS), probably after the supposed precedent of such ceremonies in the days of the Latin League (*see* LATINI). If the entitlement was judged defective, the general might be awarded a 'lesser triumph' called *ovatio*. This has been claimed to be an old pre-Etruscan form of triumph, but in Roman tradition it was a lesser substitute, first celebrated in 503 BC. All forms of triumph could be equally counted in the record of a man's career, but the Capitoline triumph was the summit of a Roman aristocrat's ambition.

Trivia, Latin translation of *Trioditis*, title of *Hecate as goddess of cross-roads. Since the identification of Hecate with *Artemis and *Selene was popular in Hellenistic times and *Diana was identified with Artemis, the epithet is often used of Diana.

Troilus, in mythology son of *Priam and *Hecuba, though sometimes said to be son of *Apollo. In *Homer's *Iliad* he is mentioned only as being dead. Later accounts, however, starting with the *Cypria* (*see* EPIC CYCLE; PROCLUS), specify that he was killed by *Achilles. This was clearly a popular story, for Achilles' ambush of Troilus (accompanied by *Polyxena) at the fountain, the pursuit, the slaughter of the boy on the altar of Apollo, and the battle over the mutilated body, are favourite subjects in Archaic art from the early 6th cent. and found occasionally later. From Homer on, Troilus tends to be associated with horses: Homer gives him the epithet 'fighting from a chariot'; in art he is often shown fleeing on horseback from Achilles pursuing on foot; in *Sophocles' lost *Troilus* he was exercising his horses when Achilles ambushed him; in *Virgil he has a chariot, but his horses bolt and he is dragged along in the dust behind, still holding the reins. A late mythographer records a prophecy that Troy would never be taken if only Troilus lived to the age of 20, so this may have been Achilles' motive for killing him.

'Troilus and Cressida' (i.e. *Chryseis) is a purely medieval fiction and has no connection with antiquity (the line runs from the *Roman de Troie* to Boccaccio, *Filostrato*, to Chaucer, *Troilus and Criseyde*, to Shakespeare's *Troilus and Cressida*).

[Homer, *Iliad* 24. 257; Apollodorus 3. 12. 5]

Trojan War *See* TROY, MYTHS OF.

trophies (Gk. *tropaia*, Lat. *trophaea*, from *tropē*, a turning i.e. rout of the enemy). The act of dedicating on the field of battle a suit of enemy armour set upon a stake is a specifically Greek practice. Originally intended as a miraculous image of the *routing god* who had brought about the defeat of the enemy, a trophy marked the spot where the enemy had been routed. Trophies were also dedicated in the sanctuary of the deity to whom victory was ascribed. They appear in art at the end of the 6th cent. BC and were certainly in use during the Persian Wars (490–479 BC). From the 4th cent. onwards and in Roman practice they became permanent monuments.

Trophonius, son of Erginus, was with his brother Agamedes a renowned master-builder whose work included the lower courses of *Apollo's first temple at Delphi, the treasury of Augeas, and the treasury of Hyrieus. The last, a variation of the story of the Egyptian king Rhampsinitus told by Herodotus, provides the connection with Trophonius as cult figure and son of Apollo. While building the treasury, the brothers left a stone loose, so that they could make off with the treasure bit by bit. Hyrieus set a trap, which caught Agamedes. Trophonius cut off his brother's head, and ran off with it, pursued by Hyrieus. At Lebadea, the ground opened up and swallowed Trophonius. He lived on underground as an oracular god (a fate similar to that of *Amphiaraus: in

both cases an underground oracular god— the ritual of consultation is basically identical—is identified with a figure of heroic tradition; *see* ORACLES).

The oracle must have been functioning by the 6th cent. BC. It was at Lebadea in western Boeotia, separated from the town by the river Hercyna, whose eponymous nymph was said to have been Trophonius' daughter (this probably is derived from the group carved by the 4th-cent. BC sculptor Praxiteles in which the pair resembled *Asclepius and *Hygieia). The cult complex—oracular male and spring *nymph at the foot of a hill or mountain—is repeated in several other sanctuaries dotted around lake Copais.

Early consultations attested by Herodotus for non-Greeks like Croesus and Mys may be apocryphal, but the oracle was certainly well known to Athenians by the second half of the 5th cent. (e.g. *Euripides, *Ion*, passing references in Aristophanes, several comedies about Trophonius). What caught the imagination was the bizarre means of consultation: there was no medium; instead the consultant, after suitable and lengthy preliminaries, descended underground and confronted the god himself (a consultation of Trophonius was called *katabasis*: 'descent'). The experience was spectacular, frightening, notorious, and expensive.

Towards the end of the 3rd cent. BC, the town of Lebadea, as part of a huge rebuilding programme, moved the oracular cave from the grove by the gorge of Hercyna to the top of the hill on which they began to build a large temple of *Zeus Basileus. The temple project foundered, but the oracle prospered at its new site (*Pausanias and other sources explicitly locate the oracle on the mountain above and beyond the grove).

Pausanias gives a detailed description of the site and its monuments, and a graphic account of consultation in his day (he wrote from personal experience). The oracle functioned at least until the 3rd cent. AD.

[Euripides, *Ion* 300–2, 404–9; Pausanias 9. 39. 2–14]

Troy, myths of Troy was founded by *Ilus

son of *Dardanus. Ilus' son *Laomedon was notorious for his deceit, reneging on his promises first to *Apollo and *Poseidon, who had built the city walls for him, and then to *Heracles. But the principal myth is that of the Trojan War, which is central to the epics of *Homer and other early epics (see EPIC CYCLE). Here Laomedon's son *Priam is king. He is married to *Hecuba, and father of (sons) *Deiphobus, *Helenus, *Hector, *Lycaon (1), *Paris, *Polydorus, *Troilus, and (daughters) *Cassandra and *Polyxena. The theft of *Helen from her husband *Menelaus by Paris occasioned the war, which ended in Trojan defeat and the capture of the city.

See also GENEALOGICAL TABLES (2) HOUSE OF TROY.

truce See LIBATIONS.

Tubilustrium, Roman festival on 23 March and 23 May, whose 'trumpet purification' readied the army for war. Calendars added Q(uando) R(ex) C(omitavit) F(as): the *rex sacrorum made a nefastus day into fastus (i.e., public business could be transacted: see FASTI). It was celebrated in the atrium Sutorium. See LUSTRATION.

[Ovid, Fasti. 3. 849 ff.]

Tullia, younger daughter of Servius *Tullius, supposedly impelled her brother-in-law *Tarquinius Superbus to murder her husband and sister, marry her, and seize power by killing her father. The narrative probably goes back to the early Roman historian Qunitus Fabius Pictor and forms part of a depiction of the last three Roman kings in Greek 'tragic' style, as a political dynasty that ultimately wreaks its own self-destruction. Its detailed development incorporates a series of topographical aetiologies or 'historical' explanations of cults, linked particularly to *Diana and Virbius (= *Hippolytus) and the traditions of the slave *rex nemorensis at *Aricia. These are based on Servius' supposed slave origins and his creation of the federal Latin cult of *Diana on the *Aventine.

[Livy 1. 46–8]

Tullius, Servius, the sixth king of Rome (conventionally 578–535 BC), murdered by *Tarquinius Superbus at the instigation of his daughter *Tullia. Claudius identified him with the Etruscan adventurer Mastarna, but Roman sources, deriving Servius from servus ('slave'), made him the son of a Latin captive Ocrisia and brought up in the household of *Tarquinius Priscus. Because of his supposed slave ancestry he was credited with the enfranchisement of freedmen, the creation of the Compitalia (see LARES), a close association with *Fortuna, and perhaps the establishment of the (certainly archaic) federal Latin sanctuary of *Diana on the *Aventine (whose dedication date coincided with a slave festival). As the penultimate king he was credited with political and military institutions that were deemed fundamental to the republic but believed to antedate it: the centuriate organization, the first territorial tribes, and the census. Although their initial phases may well date from the 6th cent., the form in which our sources present these innovations is anachronistic, as is the associated ascription to Servius of the first Roman coinage, direct taxation, and army pay. The 'Servian wall' of Rome dates from the early 4th cent. (earlier 6th-cent. defences have not been securely identified) but two phases of the Sant'Omobono sanctuary (with which Servius was associated) do belong to the 6th cent. (see MATUTA MATER). Accius already celebrated Servius as establishing 'liberty' for the citizens, but later writers offer varying interpretations of his reforms: as concentrating political power in the hands of the wealthy, as creating a timocratic socio-political hierarchy, or simply as the work of a skilful pragmatic populist. Recent speculation has seen him as (in part) attempting to combat the power of the nascent patriciate.

[Livy 1. 39 ff.; Dionysius of Halicarnassus, Roman Antiquities. 4. 1 ff.]

Turnus, Italian hero, in *Virgil son of Daunus and the *nymph Venilia and brother of the nymph Juturna; the Greek tradition calls him 'Tyrrhenus', suggesting an Etruscan link. His role as *Aeneas' rival in Italy is well established before Virgil. In the *Aeneid* he is king of *Ardea and the Rutulians and favoured suitor, not fiancé, of *Latinus' daughter Lavinia; rejected in favour of Aeneas and maddened by *Juno's intervention, he rouses the Latins (*see* LATINI) against the Trojans. In the war he fights bravely as the Latin commander and can elicit sympathy, but is sometimes rash; his highhanded appropriation of the sword-belt of the dead *Pallas (2) leads tragically at the very end of the poem to his own death at the hands of Aeneas.

[Dionysius of Halicarnassus 1. 64. 2; Livy 1. 2. 1–5; Virgil, *Aeneid* 7, 9–12]

Twelve gods *See* OLYMPIAN GODS.

Tyche, fate, fortune both good and bad. The connection with the Greek verb *tynchanein*, to happen, chance, always remains evident, reinforcing the sense of sudden change and fortuitous happenings in the individual's life. Archaic and Classical writers paint various pictures. Like Moira (*see* FATE), Tyche gives everything to mortals from birth. The mightiest of the Moirai in *Pindar, she is the child of *Zeus Eleutherius. A splendid lyric fragment praises noble Tyche who dispenses more good than evil from her scales: grace shines about her golden wing, and she lights up the darkness. Though ambivalent by nature, she tends to be favourable (*Aeschylus makes her the saviour and guide of the Achaeans), comparable with the *Agathos Daimōn. *Oedipus is the child of beneficent Tyche, according to a choral ode in *Sophocles. She is divine spirit, mind, forethought and the only god who governs human affairs. Tyche looks upon the deeds of gods and men and grants each his rightful share. Similar sentiments were expressed by the orators, but the idea of Chance as ruling principle found less favour in philosophy, least of all with the Stoics (*see* STOICISM) for whom *heimarmenē*, *fate, was the cause of all things. *Plato set *tychē* beside *theos* (god),

kairos (opportunity), and *technē* (skill). Tyche's personified identity remains vague, however. In tragedy she rarely rises above the basic concept of change, unexpected happening mostly sent by the gods. Occasionally she becomes a *daimōn* herself, especially in *Euripides.

Tyche was unknown to *Homer. She had no myth to speak of. According to *Pausanias, her name occurred first in *Homeric *Hymn to Demeter* as one of the Oceanids (*see* NYMPHS) and companions of *Persephone. The list derived from *Hesiod: she is daughter of *Tethys and Oceanus (*see* OCEANUS), sister of *Peitho and Eudore (cf. sister of Peitho and Eunomia and daughter of Promatheia (Forethought), in the lyric poet Alcman). Tyche assumed a higher profile with the decline of the traditional gods. The momentous events of the 4th cent., the rise of Macedonian power leading to rapid change in the world order in east and west, fostered a belief in the random and irrational working of Fate. Tyche became synonymous with a general *automaton* i.e. accidental, spontaneous, although *Aristotle distinguished between a comprehensive *automaton* and *tychē* which applied to human affairs only.

The popular view of a capricious, malignant Tyche emerges from New *Comedy: she was dangerous, senseless, blind, wretched, etc. In romances she figures large as a convenient plot device. Negative in Thucydides as blows of Fate (*tychai*), or an inscrutable element that confuses human affairs, she plays a larger role in Polybius, where cunning Tyche is sudden, changeable, jealous. Nevertheless the historian contrasts this popular image of all-powerful Chance with what can be expected as reasonable historical development, like Rome's rise to power.

Tyche's cults spread widely from the 4th cent. at Thebes, Athens, Lebadea in Boeotia, Megara (image by Praxiteles), Sicyon (Tyche Akraia on acropolis), and her latest sanctuary at Hermione. An altar—appropriately to Good Luck—stood in the Altis at *Olympia. She was represented with a rudder, carrying child *Plutus or a cornucopia, and standing on a sphere. Tyche functioned as City Goddess (*Turrigera*: 'turret-crowned') similar to the old Polias in Greece, the islands, and most frequently in the east, where she successfully competed with her Semitic counterpart Gad and with *Isis.

See also FATE; FORTUNA/FORS.

Tydeus, son of *Oeneus, legendary warrior of the generation before the Trojan War. Leaving his homeland in Aetolia (*see* AETOLIAN CULTS AND MYTHS), he came to *Argos, where *Adrastus gave him his daughter Deipyle in marriage; she bore him *Diomedes (2), who is always conscious at Troy of the need to match his father's exploits. Enrolled as one of the *Seven against Thebes, he first—according to *Homer's *Iliad*, drawing and no doubt embroidering upon earlier *Thebaid* traditions, *see* EPIC CYCLE—took part in an embassy to the city, triumphed over the locals in a series of games, then killed all but one of a fifty-strong band sent to ambush him on his return. In the war itself, he proved himself a fierce fighter in spite of his stocky build; his thirst for slaughter, vividly described in *Aeschylus' *Seven against Thebes*, drove him to put the Theban princess Ismene ruthlessly to the sword, a scene shown on a Corinthian wine bowl in the Louvre, and even in his own death-throes to try to eat out the brains of the wounded *Melanippus—an act that cost him the immortality which Athene had arranged.

[Homer, *Iliad* 4. 372 ff., 5. 801 etc; Aeschylus, *Seven against Thebes* 377 ff.]

Tyndareos (*Tyndareōs*), in mythology husband of *Leda and father, real or putative, of *Helen, *Clytemnestra, the *Dioscuri, Timandra, and Philonoe. His brothers were said to be Leucippus, Aphareus, and Icarius, and sometimes Hippocoön. Hippocoön drove him from Sparta, but he returned and succeeded to the throne after *Heracles had invaded the land and killed Hippocoön and his twelve sons. When suitors came, wishing to marry Helen, Tyndareos made them take an oath to protect the marriage-rights of the chosen bridegroom,

which led in due course to the Trojan War (*see* TROY, MYTHS) when the Greek leaders marshalled troops to fetch back Helen after she deserted *Menelaus for *Paris. *Hesiod says that when sacrificing to the gods Tyndareos forgot *Aphrodite, so the goddess in anger made his daughters unfaithful, Helen with Paris, Clytemnestra with *Aegisthus, and Timandra, who had married Echemus, with Phyleus. Tyndareos in due course bequeathed his kingdom to Menelaus. *Euripides has him live long enough to bring the charge of matricide against *Orestes.

[Apollodorus 3. 10. 3–9, *Epitome* 2. 16; Euripides, *Orestes*]

Typhon, monster and adversary of *Zeus. *Hesiod's Typhoeus has 100 snake-heads, eyes blazing fire, and voices that cover the gamut of gods and animals. The final child (by *Tartarus) of Earth (*Gaia), he is blasted down to the place Tartarus by Zeus' thunderbolt, but remains the source of hurricanes ('typhoon' merges Chinese *ta fĕng*, 'big wind', with Greek myth). *Homer knows that Typhoeus lies amongst the Arimi (in Cilicia). In *Apollodorus, the gods flee to Egypt in panic, turning themselves into animals (referring to Egyptian theriomorphism, *see* EGYPTIAN RELIGION); Zeus with thunderbolts and an adamantine sickle wounds Typhon at Mt. *Kasios in Syria, but is overpowered, his sinews cut out and both he and his sinews put in 'the Corycian cave' in Cilicia. *Hermes and Aegipan ('Goat-*Pan') steal the sinews and refit Zeus (or *Cadmus tricks the sinews from Typhon). The geography of the story includes Syria and Cilicia and its motifs link it to Hittite myths of Illuyankas ('Dragon'). *See also* SET.

[Hesiod, *Theogony* 823–35; Homer, *Iliad* 2. 783; Apollodorus 1. 6. 3]

Tyro, in mythology, daughter of *Salmoneus and mother (by Cretheus) of *Jason (1)'s father Aeson and (by *Poseidon) of the twins *Pelias and *Neleus. Tyro loved the river *Enipeus, but Poseidon tricked her by assuming that river's form and lay with her.

According to a later tradition dramatized by *Sophocles, Tyro exposed the twins who, however, survived to be reunited with their mother and punish their stepmother, Sidero, who had maltreated Tyro. Her name is often connected with *tyros*, 'cheese', because of her soft whiteness.

[Homer, *Odyssey* 11. 235–59; Menander, *Epitrepontes* (*Arbitration*) 325–33]

Tyrrhenus, eponym of the Tyrrhenians (i.e. Etruscans). In Dionysius of Halicarnassus he is son of King Atys and comes from Maeonia (Lydia); elsewhere, he is Atys' grandson; son of *Heracles, or of *Telephus; apparently god of the Tyrrhenian sea. He invented trumpets.

[Dionysius of Halicarnassus, *Roman Antiquities* 1. 27–8; Valerius Flaccus 4. 715; Hyginus, *Fables* 274. 20]

Uranus (Gk. *Ouranos*), the divine personification of the sky in Greece. Scarcely known in cult, his best-known appearance is in *Hesiod. He is produced by *Gaia (Earth), then becoming her consort, but hating their children, he causes them to remain confined within her. At the instigation of Gaia, he is castrated by their son *Cronus; the severed genitals are cast into the sea and engender *Aphrodite.

[Hesiod, *Theogony* 126 ff.]

utopias *See* EUHEMERUS; FANTASTIC LITERATURE; GOLDEN AGE.

Varro, (Marcus Terentius Varro 116–27 BC), had completed 490 books by the start of his 78th year: 55 titles are known in all, and his *œuvre* has been estimated to include nearly 75 different works totalling *c*.620 books. His works include: *Antiquitates rerum humanarum et divinarum* (41 books: 47 BC). Of the first 25 books, on human (i.e. Roman) antiquities, little is known: the introductory book was followed by four segments of (probably) six books each, on persons (*de hominibus*: the inhabitants of Italy), places (*de locis*), times (*de temporibus*), and things (*de rebus*). The remaining sixteen books, dedicated to *Caesar as *pontifex maximus, took up the human construction of the divine: another book of general introduction, then five triads, on priesthoods (27-9), holy places (30-2), holy times (33-5), rites (36-8), and kinds of gods (39-41).

vates, 'prophet', 'seer', used by Ennius as an insulting term for his predecessors became by the Augustan period a central term for the inspired poet with an assumed social role as 'master of truth' and generated a constant interplay between the roles of poet and prophet.

Vatican, an extramural area of the city of Rome, on the right bank of the river *Tiber around the Vatican hill. In the early empire the Vatican was the site of an imperial park, and of entertainment structures, the *Naumachiae*, where mock sea-battles were exhibited, and the Vatican circus, where the emperor Gaius set up a great obelisk from Heliopolis and which was traditionally the site of the martyrdom of St Peter. There was also an important shrine of *Cybele (or the Mater Magna) attested in inscriptions; and along the two roads that crossed the area, the via Cornelia and the via Triumphalis, were cemeteries. A group of mausolea on the foot-slopes of the mons Vaticanus were excavated under St Peter's in the 1940s, and within this cemetery (directly under the high altar of St Peter's) was found a small 2nd-cent. shrine, marking the probable burial-site of Peter, apostle and first bishop of Rome.

With *Constantine I's conversion, and capture of Rome in 312, the importance and appearance of the Vatican area were transformed by the building of a huge five-aisled *basilica in honour of St Peter, some 250 m. (820½ ft.) long including its atrium and preceding steps. The high altar of this church was sited directly over the shrine and probable body of the saint, which required closing a functioning cemetery and a tremendous task of levelling to create a flat platform for the new building. The importance of this church gradually attracted other new buildings around it. Mausolea, including that of the Honorian dynasty, were built immediately to the south, and the church was linked to the main part of the city by a new porticoed street leading to the pons Aelius. This street clearly became a Christian sacred way, culminating in St Peter's, since it was here, rather than in the forum, that two new imperial triumphal arches were erected in the years around AD 400.

Ve(d)iovis, Roman god, a form of *Jupiter, with a festival on 21 May, and temples on the *Tiber island and between the two summits of the Capitoline hill (*see* CAPITOL). Important remains of the latter, including the marble cult-statue, have been explored under the Palazzo Senatorio, revealing several rebuildings. The cult had important links with the *gens Iulia* (an ancient altar at suburban Bovillae dedicated by its members), and was the object of considerable antiquarian speculation in antiquity. Associations with both youth and the underworld appear to be present.

[Ovid, *Fasti* 3. 429–58]

Vegoia *See* ETRUSCAN RELIGION.

Venantius Honorius Clementianus Fortunatus (*c*.AD 540–*c*.600), Christian Latin poet, born near Treviso in northern Italy and educated at Ravenna, he left Italy in 565 and later lived at Poitiers, where he knew St Radegunda and ultimately became bishop. He is best known for his numerous poems on secular and especially religious themes, including the great Passion hymns, *Pange lingua* and *Vexilla regis*, and is arguably both the last classical and the first medieval Latin poet.

vengeance *See* CURSES; ERINYES; NEMESIS.

Venus The debate over the original nature of this goddess, who does not belong to Rome's oldest pantheon but is attested fairly early at *Lavinium, has been partly resolved. It is now accepted that the neuter *venus*, 'charm', cannot be separated from the terms *venia*, *venerari*, *venenum* ('gracefulness', 'to exercise a persuasive charm', 'poison'). How this neuter was transformed into a feminine, a process attested for the Osco-Umbrian goddess Herentas (cf. ITALIC RELIGION) is ill-understood in the absence of evidence. One view is that it took place at the federal sanctuary of Lavinium, a city with old and well-attested links with the Greek world and the legend of Troy. Whatever the case, from the 3rd cent. BC, Venus was the patron of all persuasive seductions, between gods and mortals, and between men and women (Venus Verticordia). Because of her links with the extraordinary power of

*wine, Venus is presented in the rites and myth of the *Vinalia as a powerful mediator between *Jupiter and the Romans. The first known temple is that of Venus Obsequens ('Propitious'), vowed in 295 BC and built some years later. During the Punic Wars (264–146 BC), the tutelary and diplomatic role of Venus grew continually, in proportion to the process of her assimilation to Greek *Aphrodite. In the 1st cent. BC she even acquired a political value. She was claimed by Sulla as his protectress (his extra name Epaphroditus means 'favoured by Venus'), as by Pompey (Venus Victrix) and *Caesar (Venus Genetrix), while the city of Aphrodisias in Caria benefited progressively from important privileges. Under the empire Venus became one of the major divinities of the official pantheon.

There were the following temples of Venus in Rome: Venus Obsequens; Venus Erucina on the Capitol, built in 215 BC; Venus Victrix, dedicated in 55 BC; Venus and Roma, consecrated in AD 121, completed after 137, rebuilt by Maxentius in 307.

[Lucretius 1. 30–41; Ovid, *Fasti* 4. 1–162]

ver sacrum, 'the sacred spring', a ritual practised in Italy, particularly by the Sabellic tribes. In times of distress all produce of the spring (or the whole year) was consecrated to a deity, primarily *Mars. The animals were sacrificed; the humans, when of age, were sent away. This controlled over-population; led by a god or totemic animal the *sacrani* (the 'devoted') founded new communities: so originated the Picentes (from *picus*, 'woodpecker'), Samnites, Mamertines (Men of Mars). In Rome the only recorded *ver sacrum* was vowed (to *Jupiter) in 217 BC; human offspring were not included.

Verginia was traditionally killed by her own father to save her from the lust of the decemvir Appius Claudius Crassus Inregillensis Sabinus. This event prompted a secession of the *plebs* to the *Aventine and ultimately led to the overthrow of the decemvirs (449 BC). Verginia herself resembles *Lucretia, and her name seems too good to be true; but it does not follow that the story is a late invention. The poetic details, clearly evident in Livy's magnificent narrative, led Macaulay and others to postulate a traditional ballad. In Diodorus, whose account may represent an early version of the story, the protagonists are not named, but referred to simply as 'a maiden' and 'one of the decemvirs'. The notion that in the original version Verginia was a patrician is based on a mistranslation of Diodorus' text.

[Livy 3. 44–8; Diodorus Siculus 12. 24. 2–4]

Vertumnus (Vortumnus), supposedly an Etruscan god, according to *Varro and Propertius, who says he came from Volsinii, but nothing proves this view, which may just be speculation based on the resemblance of his name to that of *Voltumna and the fact that his temple on the *Aventine (its anniversary 13 August) displayed a painting of M. Fulvius Flaccus, conqueror of Volsinii in 264 BC. His statue stood in the vicus Tuscus in Rome, and Propertius indicates that the shopkeepers there made frequent offerings to him. Nothing is known of his functions, since all ancient interpretations played with the various meanings of the verb *vertere*, from which they derived the god's name. The hypothesis that his name can be connected with the Etruscan family *ultimni*, Latinized Veldumnius, is not acceptable. More interesting, but lacking decisive proof, is the theory that we should see here an 'introducing god' akin to Roman *Janus, who would be of Umbrian origin. *See also* ETRUSCAN RELIGION.

[Propertius 4. 2; Ovid, *Metamorphoses* 14. 623–771]

Vesta, Vestals Vesta was the Roman goddess of (the hearth-) fire, 'guardian of the flame' (*Ovid), one of the twelve Di *Consentes. The cult is also known from Pompeii and Latium: it was believed to have been introduced into Rome by Pompilius *Numa—or *Romulus—from *Alba Longa. An ancient etymology linked Vesta to Greek *Hestia: her cult expressed and guaranteed Rome's permanence. Vesta's main public shrine, never inaugurated with the ordained formula and so never a true *templum, was a circular building just south-east of Augustus' arch in the *forum Romanum (the original 7th-cent. BC shape is unknown). In the late republic its form was taken to be that of a primitive house, intimating a connection between public and private cults of the hearth. In the historical period, the state cult (Vestalia, 9 June) effectively displaced private cults. There was no statue of Vesta within the shrine: it contained only the fire and, in the inner sanctum, the 'sacred things that may not be divulged'—esp. the *Palladium, and the *fascinum*, the erect *phallus that averted evil. On being elected *pontifex maximus* in 12 BC, Augustus created another shrine for Vesta on the *Palatine.

Though she bore the title *mater*, Vesta was thought of as virgin, by contrast with her sisters *Juno and *Ceres. She was 'the same as the earth', which also contains *fire, and was sacrificed to on low altars; she protected all altar-fires. Her character gains contour from a contrast with *Volcanus. The sacral status of the six *sacerdotes Vestales*, the Vestal virgins (the sole female priesthood in Rome), was manifested in many ways. Though they were required to maintain strict sexual purity during their minimum of 30 years' service, their dress (*stola*, *vittae*) alluded to matrons' wear, their hair-style probably to a bride's. They were excised from their own family (freed from their father's legal authority, ineligible to inherit under the rules of intestacy) without acceding to another. It was a capital offence to pass beneath their litter in the street.

There were several restrictions upon eligibility; most known Vestals are of senatorial family. Though they had many ceremonial roles, their main ritual tasks were the preparation of the grain mixed with salt (*mola salsa*) for public sacrifices and the tending of Vesta's 'undying fire' (*ignis inextinctus*). The extinction of the fire provided the prima facie evidence that a Vestal was impure: impurity spelled danger to Rome. The last known case of living entombment in the Campus Sceleratus (near the Colline gate) occurred under Domitian in AD 89(?). The last known chief Vestal (*vestalis maxima*) is Coelia Concordia (AD 380); the cult was finally abandoned in 394.

[Dionysius of Halicarnassus, *Roman Antiquities* 2. 64. 5 ff.; Ovid, *Fasti* 6. 249–318; Pliny, *Letters* 4. 11]

Vettius Valens, Greek astrologer from Antioch, wrote (between AD 152 and 162) the *Anthologies*, an extant nine-book treatise on *astrology, preserving the only major collection of Greek horoscopes (*c*.130) outside the papyri; it was heavily used in the Middle Ages.

via Sacra, the 'sacred way', street connecting the *forum Romanum with the Velia, affording access to the *Palatine. According to *Varro and Pompeius Festus, the stretch of road popularly known as via Sacra lay between the *Regia and the house of the *rex sacrorum*, which was at a point known as Summa Sacra Via; as properly defined, however, the road led from the Sacellum Streniae (*see* STRENAE) on the Carinae to the Arx. The location of Summa Sacra Via is, however, disputed by modern scholars, being identified either with the area adjacent to the so-called 'Tempio di Romolo', or near the arch of Titus. In AD 64, Nero planned the street anew as a noble colonnaded avenue, leading from the forum to the entrance to the Golden House, which was flanked by shops for jewellers, and other luxury-traders.

Vibenna, Caelius (or Caeles), an Etruscan adventurer who, according to Roman tradition, came to help *Tarquinius Priscus (*Romulus according to *Varro) and settled with his followers on the hill which later bore his name (the Caelian hill). He and his brother, Aulus, were also well-known figures in Etruscan tradition. They are represented on funerary urns from Chiusi and a bronze mirror from Bolsena, but most famously in the François tomb-painting from Vulci (late 4th cent. BC) which shows Caeles Vibenna being released by his friend Mastarna, while Aulus Vibenna and other companions dispatch their adversaries, who include a

Cnaeus Tarquinius from Rome. The name *Aules V(i)pinas* appears on a 5th-cent. Etruscan red-figure cup of unknown provenance, and may be evidence of a hero-cult; on the other hand, a votive bucchero vase from Veii inscribed *Avile Vipiiennas* dates from the mid-6th cent., and is therefore contemporary with Aulus Vibenna, who may indeed have dedicated it in person.

[Tacitus, *Annals* 4. 65]

victimarius, sacrificial slaughterer; *see* SACRIFICE, ROMAN. The magistrate in charge of a sacrifice did not himself perform the act of killing; he performed symbolic acts and pronounced the prayers, but a *victimarius* took over the killing and butchering from him. In imperial times, we know that they formed a *collegium of their own.

Victoria, the Roman equivalent of *Nike. There is no evidence that she is anything more, mentions of an early cult of Victory being referable to Vacuna or Vica Pota. She is associated in cult with *Jupiter (Victor), oftener with Mars, also with other deities. She was worshipped by the army, as was natural, and hence is given surnames associating her with particular legions and more commonly still with emperors. Her temple on the clivus Victoriae leading up to the *Palatine dates from 294 BC; from 204 BC it housed temporarily the sacred stone of her future neighbour, the Mater Magna (*see* CYBELE; PESSINUS). In 193 BC Marcus Porcius Cato added a shrine (*aedicula*) to her temple; in the early Principate both sanctuaries celebrated their anniversary on 1 August, no doubt because of Octavian's victory in Alexandria in 30 BC (*see* AUGUSTUS). Her most famous monument was perhaps her altar in the senate-house, put there by Augustus in 29 BC, removed under Constantius II, replaced by the pagan party in Rome, removed again by Gratian in 382, replaced for a short time by Eugenius and perhaps once more by Stilicho, and finally vanishing with the other vestiges of pagan cult.

Vinalia, Roman wine festivals on 23 April (*Priora*), 19 August (*Rustica*). The *Priora* probably offered *Jupiter new wine at the time of sale. *Varro substitutes *Venus, chronologically difficult since her first temple (Venus Obsequens) was dedicated 295 BC, understandable from its 19 August dedication. The *Rustica* propitiated the weather; Pliny: 'they feared three times of year for the crops'.

[Ovid, *Fasti* 4. 863–900]

Virgil, (Publius Vergilius Maro 70–19 BC), Latin poet who became the Roman *Homer, the *Aeneid* in particular serving as the great Roman classic against which later epic poets and in a sense all Latin poets had to situate themselves. As with Homer, all human learning came to be seen as condensed in the *Aeneid*, a view which finds full expression in Macrobius' *Saturnalia*: the ancient biographical tradition already shows a tendency to see Virgil as a *theios anēr*, a divine genius, and this became pronounced in the Middle Ages, with the legends of Virgil the Magician. The text of the *Aeneid* was consulted as an *oracle in the *sortes Vergilianae*.

The Literary Works The *Eclogues* (published 39–38 BC): ten short hexameter poems (the longest is 111 lines long) in the pastoral genre. One of the *Eclogues* came to have particular significance for later readers: *Eclogue 4*, with its description of the birth of a child whose lifetime will see a return of the world to the *golden age. There were several possible candidates for the identification of the child even for contemporary readers, but the poem can equally be read as a broader allegory of renewal; Christian readers naturally saw reference to the birth of Jesus. The influence of Jewish messianic writing on the poem is nowhere a required hypothesis, but is not in itself unlikely.

The *Georgics*: a didactic poem in four books on farming (book 1: crops, book 2: trees and shrubs, book 3: livestock, book 4: bees).

Aeneid: Virgil's final work was the *Aeneid* (in Latin *Aeneis*), an account in twelve books

of hexameter verse of the flight of *Aeneas from Troy and his battles in Italy against *Turnus to found a new home, the origin of Rome. As an epic, the *Aeneid* occupies the summit of ancient generic classification. Epic was the sustained narration of great events ('kings and heroes' according to Callimachus) by an inspired, omniscient, but distanced narrator (*see* VATES); it was also the genre in which the anxiety of influence was greatest, since any epic was inevitably read against Homer's *Iliad* and *Odyssey*, by common consent the greatest poems of antiquity. Intertextuality with both poems is intense. Two other epics are also of importance: the *Argonautica* of *Apollonius Rhodius and Ennius' *Annales*. But the range of material whose traces may be interpreted in the *Aeneid* is vast.

Although the particular version of the Aeneas legend presented in the *Aeneid* has become canonical, the versions of the myth in the preceding tradition were many and varied, and the reconstruction of the matrix of possibilities against which the *Aeneid* situates itself has always been a standard critical procedure. It is clear that many of the details offered by Virgil were by no means the standard ones in his day, that his 'sources' were multiple, and that there was no compunction against free invention. The *Aeneid* is not therefore a 'safe' text to use for the investigation of early Latin history and cult. The story as told by Virgil takes the reader, as in the *Odyssey, in medias res*. Aeneas on his way to Italy is blown off course to North Africa by a storm instigated by Juno (book 1). There he meets *Dido, and tells her the story of the fall of Troy (book 2; *see* TROY, MYTHS OF) and his subsequent wanderings (book 3). He and Dido become lovers, and he forgets his mission; Mercury is sent to remind him, and his departure leads to Dido's tragic suicide (book 4). In book 5, the threat of another storm forces Aeneas to put into Sicily, where funeral games are celebrated for his dead father *Anchises; after Juno instigates the Trojan women to burn the ships, part of the group are left behind in Sicily and Anchises appears in a dream to urge Aeneas to visit the *Sibyl of Cumae (near Naples). The first half of the epic concludes with the consultation of the Sibyl and their visit to the underworld, where Aeneas meets his father and receives a vision of the future of Rome (book 6).

The events of the second half are described by Virgil as a 'greater work'. Landing in Latium, Aeneas sends a successful embassy of peace to the Latin king *Latinus; but Juno uses the Fury Allecto (*see* ERINYES) to stir up the young Rutulian king *Turnus and Latinus' wife Amata to encourage war. Aeneas' son Iulus kills a pet stag while hunting, and from that small spark a full-blown war develops. Before battle commences we are given a catalogue of Italian forces (book 7). In book 8 Aeneas, advised by the god of the river *Tiber in a dream, visits the Arcadian king *Evander, who is living on the future site of Rome; Evander's young son Pallas (*see* PALLAS (2)) joins the Trojan forces, and Aeneas receives a gift of armour from his mother Venus, including a shield which again depicts future events in the history of Rome, most notably the battle of Actium (book 8). In the succeeding books of fighting, emphasis falls on the terrible cost of the war, as the young lovers *Nisus (2) and Euryalus die in a night expedition (book 9), Turnus kills Pallas, and Aeneas kills both the equally tragic youth Lausus and his father the evil *Mezentius (book 10), and Turnus' ally the female warrior *Camilla is killed by an arrow to her breast (book 11). Finally in book 12 Aeneas and Turnus meet in single combat, despite Juno's attempts to delay the duel; Aeneas is victorious, and hesitates over sparing Turnus until he sees the sword-belt that Turnus had taken from the dead Pallas. In a paroxysm of love and anger, he slaughters Turnus.

Throughout the *Aeneid*, as this summary suggests, there is a strong narrative teleology, reaching beyond the events of the story to the future Rome. 'Fate' is a central concept; it coincides with the will of Jupiter, though the exact relationship is kept vague.

Juno, pained and angry at past events, attempts always to retard the progress of the story, as a sort of 'counter-fate'. She is always doomed to failure; at the end of the epic she is reconciled to the fate of Aeneas but we know that this is only temporary. Onto the opposition between the king and queen of heaven may be projected many other oppositions in the poem: heaven and hell, order and disorder, reason and emotion, success and failure, future and past, epic and tragedy. The treatment of these oppositions has been the central issue in the criticism of the *Aeneid*. It is clear that although many of them coincide, the contrast is never absolute: if Juno naturally turns to Allecto and the underworld, Jupiter god of the bright sky also uses the infernal Dirae (*see* ERINYES) as the instruments of his wrath; if Aeneas like *Hercules represents reason and self-control, he also concludes the epic with an act of passion. It is possible to see these inconsistencies as 'energizing contradictions' which forge a successful viewpoint on the world; or to see them as undermining or subverting the claims to dominance of Roman order, as in the 'two-voices' school of criticism; or more generally to see the oppositions (like all oppositions) as inherently unstable and liable to deconstruction. Naturally, simple appeal to the text or its historical setting cannot settle which of these approaches is adopted.

Three particular aspects of the debate may, however, be mentioned. First, the opposition between Jupiter and Juno is a gendered one, and many of the other contrasts drawn relate to ancient (and modern) conceptions of typically male or female characteristics, such as reason and emotion. Women in the *Aeneid* feature predominantly as suffering victims opposed to the progress of history (Juno, Dido, Amata, Camilla, Juturna), and this may be read either as an affront to the values of martial epic or as reinforcing them. At any rate, Virgil's treatment of gender is distinctive and central to the interpretation of the poem, though it is idle to use it to speculate about his own sexuality.

Second, the political aspects of the oppositions are more than implicit. The hero of the epic is *pius Aeneas* (*see* PIETAS; ROMAN RELIGION, TERMS RELATING TO), a man marked out by attachment to communal values who at the fall of Troy turns away from individual heroism to save his father and in Carthage rejects personal happiness for the sake of his son's future and the destiny of Rome. This subordination of the individual to the collective is often seen as a prime component of Roman ideology, and its embodiment in Aeneas a central feature of the epic. At the same time, as in Virgil's earlier work, the pain and loss suffered by individuals are at least equally as prominent in the poem. The question of the relationship between individual and community is raised in a different form by the question of the poem's relationship to the new autocratic rule of Augustus. The purpose of the *Aeneid* was commonly seen in antiquity as to praise Augustus, who receives explicit eulogy from Jupiter, Anchises, and the primary narrator in the description of Aeneas' divine shield. Much of the imagery of the *Aeneid* can be related to Augustan symbolic discourse, and there are many typological links between Augustus and Aeneas and other figures such as Hercules. On the other hand, many have again seen the poem's tragic elements as incompatible with a celebration of power. It is impossible to separate the question of the *Aeneid*'s political tendency—in its crudest form, whether we make it pro- or anti-Augustan—from the wider ideological issues mentioned above, and again the debate cannot be resolved by an appeal to text or history.

Volcanus (Volkanus, Vulcanus), an ancient Roman god of destructive, devouring *fire, in both the human environment and in nature: e.g. in volcanoes (worshipped at the *Solfatare* of Puteoli, and associated with fire coming out of the ground near Mutina), which explains why his temple should always stand outside a city, on the authority of the Etruscan *haruspices*. He was associ-

ated with *Maia (2), the goddess of the irrepressible development of the fire, and was worshipped at Rome from the earliest-known times, having a *flamen* (*see* FLAMINES) and a festival, the Volcanalia, on 23 August. His shrine, the Volcanal, stood in the Area Volcani in the *forum Romanum at the foot of the *Capitol; it may therefore go back to a time when the Forum was still outside the city. A newer temple (before 214 BC) stood in the *Campus Martius. His name is certainly not Latin, the nearest to it in sound being the Cretan *Welkhanos*, who, however, seems to have no resemblance to him in functions. There are also Etruscan names sounding like Volcanus. It is thus possible, but unproved, that he came in from the eastern Mediterranean, through Etruria. He seems to have been worshipped principally to avert fires, hence his by-name Mulciber ('qui ignem mulcet', 'he who mitigates fire'), his title Quietus, and his association with Stata Mater, apparently the goddess who makes fires stand still. On the Volcanalia, when sacrifice (*see* SACRIFICE, ROMAN) was also made to Juturna, the *Nymphs, *Ops Opifera, and *Quirinus, he was given a curious and (at least for Rome) unexampled sacrifice, live fish from the *Tiber being flung into a fire (*see* CALENDARS, ROMAN). This also can be readily explained as an offering of creatures usually safe from him to induce him to spare those things which at so hot a time of year are particularly liable to be burned. He had a considerable cult at Ostia at the mouth of the Tiber, where he seems to have been the chief god. In classical times he is fully identified with *Hephaestus. *See* TUBILUSTRIUM.

Voltumna, an Etruscan goddess, at whose shrine the Etruscan federal council met. Nothing more is known of her and the site of the shrine is uncertain (traditionally at the original site of Volsinii). Some connection with *Vertumnus etymologically is likely.

votive offerings are voluntary dedications to the gods, resulting not from prescribed ritual or sacred calendars but from *ad hoc* vows of individuals or communities in circumstances usually of anxiety, transition, or achievement. Votives display a considerable number of constant features in both Greek and Roman religions. Dedications consisted in renunciation and long-term symbolic investment in the divine, in expectation of good things to come. Unlike *sacrifice, where one 'destroys', by depositing a perceptible object in a sanctuary one both loses it and makes it eternal. One of the primary functions of *temples was to house expensive dedications; the temple itself was a communal dedication, *anathēma*, to the god.

On a personal level, just like prayers, votive offerings emphasize the individual's 'if-then' relations with the gods. The gift to the sanctuary both mediates and serves as testimony to the occasion of the vow. 'If my ship arrives safely, if I recover from illness, if my crop succeeds, etc.... I shall dedicate a statue, a *tithe, a temple', and so on. One of the earliest Greek inscriptions (*c*.700 BC, on a bronze statuette) says: 'Mantiklos, has dedicated me to the Striker from Afar with the Silver Bow [*Apollo]... grant in exchange, Phoebus, an agreeable reward'.

Votive offerings punctuate life's passages (*see* RITES OF PASSAGE): emerging from puberty, boys and girls dedicate toys or locks of their hair (girls: also girdles to *Artemis), thus 'letting go' of a part of their changing body to the god. Retiring craftsmen may 'give up' tools of their trade: what sustained one's passing life is now renounced to become 'sacred' and permanent at a sanctuary. Personal victory at competitions could be followed by an offering of the prize: *Hesiod, for example, dedicated the tripod he won at the competition in Chalcis to the *Muses at *Helicon, where they first taught him 'the way of clear song'. Such dedications could become compulsory: the victors in the Triopia (*see* TRIOPAS) were compelled to leave their tripods as dedications to Apollo. War served as occasion for both individual and collective offerings. *Hector swears to hang the arms of his foe in the temple of Apollo.

After victories over the Persians and Carthage in 480 BC, Themistocles of Athens and Gelon of Syracuse dedicated temples. Similarly, in 296 Appius Claudius Caecus vowed a temple to *Bellona Victrix, in 195 Marcus Porcius Cato fulfilled his vow to *Victoria Virgo, and so on. Collective dedications in the form of a tithe (*dekatē*) or the 'top' of the piles of booty (*akrothinia*), a percentage from the sales of prisoners, and so on, became common from the Archaic period. Treasuries in the panhellenic sanctuaries contained dedicated memorials of victories won over centuries, serving as reminders of fluctuating fortunes and animosities.

The vow as well as the act of giving was made publicly, accompanied by *euchē*, a word signifying both cry, *prayer, and vow (the Latin formula *ex voto* was so common as to become a noun). The dedicated object, such as a mask or a figurine, would be deposited at the shrine. Sometimes paintings or sculptural reliefs portray (vowed?) acts of sacrifice (which leave no traces). The perpetuation of the gift could be enhanced by an inscription: 'Mnasithales dedicated me [= the vase] to Antiphamos' (the hero-*founder of Gela in Sicily), reads the text on a 5th-cent. cup. The variety of dedicated objects could be enormous, depending on occasion and function of the deity. Representations of limbs (e.g. hands, legs, penises) were deposited at healing sanctuaries; *cakes, garments, *masks, arms, and especially figurines were common (e.g. about 100,000 excavated at the sanctuary of *Artemis Orthia at Sparta). Most prominent and well known for their artistic value were the statues (not cult-images) 'set up' (*anathēmata*) in sanctuaries, advertising the donors and evoking the god. *See* next entry; *also* SANCTUARIES.

votum, a vow. Both Greeks and Romans habitually made promises to gods, in order to persuade them to grant a favour stipulated in advance. If the gods fulfilled their part, the vower fell under the obligation to do as he had promised. Although the practice was no less popular in Greece, the vow developed an institutional form especially in Rome, due to the practical and juridical nature of Roman religion. Expressions such as v(otum) s(oluit) l(ibens) m(erito) ('NN has paid his vow with pleasure and deservedly'), mainly in private votive gifts, and voti reus, voti damnatus ('obliged to fulfil his vow'), mainly in public vows, belong to the fixed formulas. In the private sphere *prayers for recovery and good health, crops, childbirth, safe return from an expedition, etc. were, in case of fulfilment, answered by a great variety of *votive offerings. In public votive religion it was the magistrate who in the name of the state undertook to offer to a god or gods sacrifices, games, the building of a temple or an altar etc., if the god on his side would give his assistance in such basic collective crises as war, epidemics, and drought. Formulas had to be pronounced in public and were very strict: mistakes required the repetition of the whole ceremony. In addition to these extraordinary vows there were also regular vota, pronounced for a definite period: e.g. the annually renewed vota of the magistrates for the welfare of the state on 1 January before the first regular sitting of the senate, and the vota at the termination of the lustrum (see LUSTRATION). Such vows found their direct continuation under the empire in the vota pro salute imperatoris (for the health or safety of emperor and his family) and became periodical: vota quinquennalia, decennalia (for five, ten years). Extraordinary vows (for the safe return of the emperor from an expedition, for the recovery of the empress in cases of sudden illness) continued to exist into late antiquity. The text of the votum was officially fixed in the presence of the pontifices (see PONTIFEX / PONTIFICES), and the document went into the archives.

Vulcan See VOLCANUS.

Vulgate, Latin version of the Bible. The first Latin translations of scripture (Vetus Latina, Old Latin) appeared in the 2nd cent. AD. But by a variety of processes the texts in use began to diverge more and more, and by the 4th cent. the situation was chaotic. An attempt to impose order was made in the early 380s by Pope *Damasus, who commissioned *Jerome to revise the Latin text of the Gospels, and perhaps of the whole of the Bible, in the light of the Greek. The gospel revision was completed in 384, and during his early years in the Holy Land (386–c.390) Jerome went on to produce versions of the Psalter (the 'Gallican Psalter') and of other books of the Old Testament on the basis of the *Septuagint. But around 390 Jerome became convinced that a translation of a translation would not do, particularly when arguing points of scripture with Jews, and during the next fifteen years or thereabouts he produced a completely new translation of the Hebrew books of the Old Testament on the basis of the original, and with the aid of the Greek versions of Aquila and Symmachus. At the request of friends, and with the aid of an interpreter, he also translated from the Aramaic the books of Tobit and Judith, which he did not recognize as part of the canon.

Jerome's revision of the Gospels was essentially conservative; in his preface he maintained that he had altered the Old Latin text only when it seemed absolutely necessary, retaining in other cases what had become familiar phraseology. This principle, though by no means rigorously observed throughout, explains inconsistencies in practice (e.g. 'high priest' is usually translated in Matthew and Luke by princeps sacerdotum, in Mark by summus sacerdos, and in John by pontifex). His own new translations from the Hebrew also display apparent contradictions: at times they are slavishly literal, at others extremely free. At no point, however, did Jerome attempt to render Scripture in a stylish, classicizing Latin: what mattered was not the literary packaging but the content, and the word of God should be written in language ordinary people could understand and appreciate.

Though it took centuries to win complete acceptance by the Church, Jerome's translation of the Hebrew Old Testament, together with his revision of the Gospels, came to form the backbone of the Vulgate, which coalesced around the 8th cent. and became the standard Latin text of the Bible. The Vulgate also included the Gallican Psalter (preferred to the version from the Hebrew), Jerome's translations of Tobit and Judith, and the remaining books of the Apocrypha and New Testament in versions not by Jerome; the revision from the Old Latin of *Acts, Epistles, and Revelation may be attributable to Jerome's follower, Rufinus the Syrian.

war, rules of These, like much other international law, depended on custom and showed a constant conflict between the higher standards of optimistic theory and the harsher measures permitted by actual usage, while passion and expediency frequently caused the most fundamental rules to be violated. Thus, the temptation to profit from a surprise at times led to the opening of hostilities without a declaration of war. Probably the law most generally observed was that of the sanctity of *heralds, for heralds were essential to communications between belligerents. Nor did Greeks frequently refuse a defeated army a truce for burying its dead, for the request of such a truce meant an admission of defeat and was usually followed by retreat. Beyond this there were few restraints except humanitarian considerations and the universal condemnation of excessive harshness. Plundering and the destruction of crops and property were legitimate, and were carried on both by regular armies and fleets, and by informal raiding-parties and privateers, and even the sanctity of temples was not always respected. Prisoners, if not protected by special terms of surrender, were at the mercy of their captors, who could execute them or sell them into slavery.

warfare, attitudes to *See* ARES; MARS.

water, in the mostly arid Mediterranean climate by its local availability shaped patterns of settlement and, as erratic rainfall, determined harvest-fluctuations and food-shortages. In mythology spring-water had sacred power; in real life springs often prompted cult (*see* NYMPHS; SPRINGS, SACRED). Together with *fire, water was widely used in cult for *purification (including bathing), in *libations, and in *sacrifice; extra-urban *sanctuaries were as concerned as cities to secure a good supply. Purificatory water was also used in rites of birth, marriage, and death, the dead being considered 'thirsty'. In the so-called 'Orphic' texts on gold plates (*see* ORPHISM), the soul is 'parched with thirst' and wants to drink the water of Memory; in the eschatological myths of *Plato and *Virgil the *souls drink the water of Oblivion. Finally, water was a primal element in cosmogonic thought; this applies equally to philosophy and to the early mythical cosmogonies (*Oceanus as the source of all). *See also* NEPTUNUS; RIVER-GODS.

werewolves *See* LYCANTHROPY.

wind-gods are attested as the object of anxious cultic attention as early as the Mycenaean period, when a priestess of the winds (*anemōn hiereia*) is recorded on the Linear B tablets from Cnossus; a late lexicon provides the names *Anemokoitai* 'Windbedders' and *Heudanemoi* 'Windlullers' for specialized *priests at Corinth and Athens respectively. Most *rituals (for which hilltops were the favoured site) aimed at pre-emptive placation of these powerful forces, though the conjuring of beneficent winds also had its place (priests on Ceos who summon the Etesian winds; *Achilles' prayer in the *Iliad* to *Boreas and Zephyrus to blow on *Patroclus' pyre). At Methana, the *sacrifice of a white cock sought to protect the budding vines from the onslaught of the *Lips*, the SW gale, while a black lamb is a suitable victim to appease 'Typhos' in Aristophanes' *Frogs*. Persian magi (*see* MAGUS) are described by Herodotus as quelling the devastating storm off Sepias in 480 BC by casting spells and sacrificing to *Thetis and the Nereids (*see* NEREUS). As violent aerial *daimons, the female wind-spirits called *Aellai* or *Thyellai* are close to the Harpies or *Harpyiae (one of whom, Podarge, bore Achilles' wind-swift horses to Zephyrus), and may bring sudden death to women by snatching them up—a fate for which *Penelope and *Helen long in Homer. More kindly breezes waft the souls of heroes from their pyre, whence no doubt their appearance as a motif on Roman sarcophagi. Male winds like Boreas have the power of impregnating mares, and are themselves thought of as winged stallions. The precise naming of winds from various quarters of the compass led naturally to personification: Homer adds Eurus, the East wind, to the triad of Zephyrus (W), Boreas (N), and Notus (S) catalogued by *Hesiod. But epic may conceive of them, as convenient, either as minor gods who feast in their own palaces or as unruly elemental forces who are controlled by *Aeolus from his floating prison-island and can be confined in a leather bag. At Rome the power of the winds was recognized by the dedication of a temple to the *Tempestates* (Storm Winds) in 259 BC. *See* BOREAS.

[Homer, *Iliad* 6. 345 ff., 16. 150 ff., 20. 222 ff., 23. 194 ff., *Odyssey* 5. 295, 10. 1 ff.; Hesiod, *Theogony* 378–80]

wine (Greek and Roman) Viticulture had become fully established in the Greek world by Mycenaean times, as it had even earlier in its near-eastern neighbours. By the earliest historical period wine had already become a fundamental component of classical culture. *See* DIONYSUS; SACRIFICE, GREEK and ROMAN.

witchcraft, witches *See* AMULETS; CURSES; MAGIC.

wolf, wolves *See* APOLLO; LUPERCALIA; LYCANTHROPY; LYCUS; ROMULUS AND REMUS.

women in cult Women played a prominent part in the public religious life of the Greek cities, their roles being in many respects different from those of men. Most, though not all, cults of a female deity were served by a female rather than a male priest, each local sanctuary following its own tradition here. A few cults of male deities, as for instance frequently those of *Dionysus, were also served by priestesses (*hiereiai*). Some cults stipulated that the priestess must be virgin (thus a little girl), a few that she have 'finished association with men', but the majority made no such provision; thus Lysimache was priestess of *Athena Polias in Athens for 64 years in the 5th cent. The role of a priestess was exactly parallel to that of a priest (*see* PRIESTS). Both sexes mediated between worshippers and worshipped, principally by presiding over *sacrifices. A woman would not normally deal the fatal blow to the sacrificial victim, but except in the case of very small cults, neither did a male priest; that act was the preserve of a special official. Women other than the priestess also normally had a special role in the act of sacrifice: the basket containing the sacrificial knife was carried in the procession by an unmarried girl (*kanēphoros*), while the moment of the victim's death was marked by ululation (*ololygmos*) from all women present. A few local cults, however, banned the presence of women altogether.

Some women who were not priestesses as such had also special religious roles to play, the best-known example perhaps being that of the Pythia at *Delphi, an elderly woman who, probably in a trance-like state, became the medium for *Apollo's prophecy (*see* DELPHIC ORACLE). In Athens the wife of the basileus (*see* ARCHONTES) performed various sacred functions, including becoming in some way the bride of Dionysus at the *Anthesteria (*see* MARRIAGE, SACRED). Far less exclusive were the 'women's festivals', annual celebrations known all over the Greek world, from which men were rigorously excluded. Some of these, like the *Arrhephoria and the Brauronian bear-ritual (*see* BRAURON) in Attica, involved unmarried girls and almost certainly developed from *initiation ceremonies in which the girls in ritual seclusion were symbolically prepared for marriage and motherhood. Others, of which the very widespread *Thesmophoria may be seen as typical, were largely the concern of married women and seem to have been particularly concerned with fertility—vegetable, animal, and human. Such festivals also gave symbolic expression to the ambiguous position of women in relation to the community. Other types of celebration, such as some of the wilder forms of Dionysiac ritual (*see* DIONYSUS; MAENADS), or the 'unofficial' Adonia (*see* ADONIS) which became popular in Athens at the end of the 5th cent., seem to have involved women in a more overtly emotional, perhaps sometimes ecstatic, form of religious experience. Women's participation in cults open to both sexes is also amply attested by *votive offerings and literary references.

Despite some Greek influence from Sicily and southern Italy, the Roman state presented a radically different form of religious organization, and the place of women was correspondingly different. Most of the major priesthoods, even of female deities, were held by men. In contrast to normal Greek custom (the priestly couples of some cults in Asia Minor are closer) the wives of some of these priests held a quasi-sacerdotal office by virtue of their marriage; notable is the wife of the *flamen dialis*, known as *flaminica*, whose assistance was necessary at certain public rituals and whose death compelled her husband to relinquish office (*see* FLAMINES). An even more clearly priestly role was taken by the Vestals, unmarried women who served the cult of *Vesta for thirty years from before puberty, whose peculiar status gave them elements akin to both married women (*matronae*) and to men. Their presence was required at many public religious rites, at some of which they undertook parts of the sacrificial process which normally seem to have been barred to women. Like the Greek cities, however, Rome had its women's festivals, although it is argued that such celebrations were marginal to the city's religious life. One among several known to us was the festival of the *Bona Dea, celebrated with great secrecy in the house of the highest magistrate present in Rome, which attained notoriety when Publius Clodius Pulcher attempted to gain entry to *Caesar's house on this occasion (prompting the latter's remark that his wife must be above suspicion). Women were often more conspicuous in cults with a 'foreign' tinge, ranging from the city cult of *Ceres (originating from south Italy) which was served by a priestess, to the prominence of female devotees of *Isis (although until the imperial period all Isiac priests were apparently male, in conformity with Egyptian usage). Mithraic initiation (*see* MITHRAS) was confined to men (although dedications by women have been found in Mithraea), but there is ample testimony also of the interest many Graeco-Roman women took in *Judaism and *Christianity. The epistles of *Paul, among other sources, demonstrate the difficulties faced by the new religion in assigning an agreed role to women.

wreaths *See* CROWNS AND WREATHS.

wrestling This was a popular exercise among the Greeks. They used a wide variety of holds and throws, many of which are illustrated in vase-paintings and statuettes of wrestlers. The object was to throw an opponent to the ground, and generally three throws were required for victory. In the major *agōnes wrestling was both a separate event and the last of the events of the *pentathlon; though weight was an advantage, general athletic ability was required too. *See* ATHLETICS.

Xenophanes of Colophon, poet, theologian, and natural philosopher, left Ionia at the age of 25, probably after the Persian Conquest in 545 BC, and led a wandering life for 67 years, as he tells us himself in a preserved passage from an elegiac poem. He lived in several cities in Sicily, and is reported to have composed an epic on the colonization of Elea, but the tradition that he was the teacher of *Parmenides is doubtful. He is credited with being the first author of satirical verses (*Silloi*). The extant fragments, in various metres and genres, include two long elegiac passages on how to conduct a civilized symposium and on the civic importance of his own work and wisdom (*sophiē*).

A skilful poet in the wisdom-moralizing tradition, Xenophanes carried the Ionian intellectual enlightenment to south Italy. His natural philosophy is a somewhat simplified version of the new Milesian cosmology, supplemented by interesting inferences from observed fossils. The origin of things is from earth and water; meteorological and celestial phenomena (including sun, moon, and stars) are explained by clouds formed from the sea. In theology and epistemology he was an original and influential thinker. He attacks *Homer and *Hesiod for portraying the gods as behaving in ways that are blameworthy for mortals. He mocks anthropomorphic conceptions of deity, and undermines the supernatural interpretation of natural phenomena. In place of the Homeric pantheon he offers the vision of a supreme god, 'greatest among gods and men, like unto mortals neither in body nor in mind', who without effort sways the universe with his thought. Moderns have imagined him a monotheist, but he seems rather to have preached a harmonious polytheism, without conflict among the gods. In our ignorance of Milesian speculation about the gods, Xenophanes appears as the first thinker systematically to formulate the conception of a cosmic god, and thus to found the tradition of natural theology followed by *Plato, *Aristotle, and the Stoics (*see* STOICISM). Pursuing a theme of Archaic poetry, Xenophanes is the first to reflect systematically on the distinction between human opinion or guesswork and certain knowledge.

Xuthus, a mythological figure connected with the perceived racial divisions among the Greeks. According to *Hesiod, he was son of *Hellen and brother of Dorus and *Aeolus (2), who gave their names to the Dorians and Aeolians; his sons by the Athenian Kreousa, *Ion and Achaeus, gave their names to the Ionians and Achaeans. This version reflects Athenian claims to Ionian primacy, but originally Xuthus may have been Euboean. The variant making Ion son of *Apollo and Creusa is later and may even be Euripidean innovation; here, Xuthus' true sons are Dorus and *Achaeus.

[Euripides, *Ion* 1589–94]

years *See* CALENDAR.

Zagreus *see* DIONYSUS.

Zalmoxis According to Herodotus, a god of the Getae in Thrace ('also called Gebeleizis') who promised immortality to his devotees; the tribe communicated with him by despatching a messenger-victim every four years. Also offered is an alternative, euhemeristic version (cf. EUHEMERUS) in which Zalmoxis was a charlatan who imported ideas picked up from *Pythagoras, whose slave he had been, and faked a 'resurrection' by reappearing from a hidden underground chamber after three years. Later, Plato presents him as a divinized king to whom, like *Abaris, healing spells were ascribed. *See* THRACIAN RELIGION.

[Herodotus 4. 94–6; Plato, *Charmides* 156d–158b]

Zealots, a Jewish political group in the 1st cent. AD. According to Josephus the Zealots were one of the three factions who controlled *Jerusalem in the last years of the Jewish revolt against Rome (AD 66–70). In 68 the Zealots attacked the existing leaders of the rebel Jewish state, seized control of the Temple and, despite reverses at the hands of other Jewish factions, maintained an independent role until the capture of Jerusalem by Titus in AD 70.

Josephus' depiction of the excesses of the Zealots when in power in Jerusalem is deeply hostile, but he none the less described their leaders as priests of distinguished lineage. Their supporters included country people from northern Judaea. They signalled a break from the previous leadership in Jerusalem by execution of political opponents and by appointing a high priest from a non-traditional family. The name *zēlōtēs* was apparently a self-designation.

The relationship between the Zealots and other movements in 1st-cent. Jewish society as described by Josephus, especially the *sicarii* ('dagger-men') and the Fourth Philosophy (which opposed foreign rule), is debated. Members of all these movements at times sought religious justification for a strongly anti-Roman stance. Josephus sometimes suggested a connection between them and condemned them all equally, but at other times he was at pains to distinguish each group as separate.

Zephyrus *See* WIND-GODS.

Zetes *See* CALAIS.

Zethus *See* AMPHION.

Zeus, the main divinity of the Greek pantheon (*see* OLYMPIAN GODS; GREEK RELIGION) and the only major Greek god whose Indo-European origin is undisputed.

His name is connected with Latin *Iu-p-piter*, Rigveda *Dyaus pitar*, derived from the hypothetical root *diéu-*, 'day (as opposed to night)' (Lat. *dies*), '(clear) sky'; as the Rigveda and Latin parallels suggest, his role as father, not in a theogonical or anthropogonical sense, but as having the power of a father in a patriarchal system, is Indo-European too. Thus in *Homer, Zeus is both *patēr*, 'father', and *anax*, 'king' or 'lord'. His cult is attested in bronze-age Greece (*see* MINOAN AND MYCENAEAN RELIGION); the Linear B texts attest several sanctuaries (Pylos, Chania) and, at Minoan Cnossus, a month name or a festival. Another Cnossian text attests the *epithet Dictaeus, Zeus of Mt. Dicte, which remained an important place of cult in the first millennium. A text from Chania gives a common cult of Zeus and *Dionysus, a Pylos text one of Zeus, *Hera, and (a figure later unknown) Drimios son of Zeus, which suggests Hera as the consort of Zeus, as in later mythology.

Zeus, the Indo-European god of the bright sky, is transformed in Greece into Zeus the weather god, whose paramount and specific place of worship is a mountain top. Among his mountains, the most important is Mt. *Olympus, a real mountain which was already a mythical place before Homer. Many mountain cults are reflected only in an epithet, which does not necessarily imply the existence of a peak sanctuary. Few such sanctuaries are excavated (e.g. on Mt. Hymettus in Attica); those attested in literature are mostly connected with rain rituals (Zeus Hyetios or Ombrios); the sanctuary on the Arcadian Mt. Lycaeum had an *initiatory function as well (see ARCADIAN CULTS AND MYTHS). As 'the gatherer of clouds' (a common Homeric epithet), he was generally believed to cause rain (comic parody in Aristophanes' Clouds). With the god of clouds comes the god of thunder and of lightning; a spot struck by lightning is inviolable and often sacred to Zeus Kataibatēs, 'He who comes down'. As the master of tempest, he is supposed to give signs through thunder and lightning and to strike evildoers, as at the beginning of his reign he struck the *Giants and the monstrous *Typhon.

But already for the early Archaic Greeks (as, presumably, for the Mycenaeans), Zeus had much more fundamental functions. According to the succession myth in *Hesiod's Theogony (whose main elements are also known to Homer), Zeus deposed his father *Cronus, who had deposed and castrated his father *Uranus; after his accession to power, Zeus fought the Giants and the monster Typhon who challenged his reign, and drew up the present world-order by attributing to each divinity his or her respective sphere: to his brothers *Poseidon and *Hades-

Pluton, he allotted two-thirds of the cosmos, to the one the sea, to the other the netherworld, to his sisters Hera (also his wife) and *Demeter, and to his many divine children their respective domains in the human world; mankind had existed before Zeus' reign. Thus, Zeus became the ruler over both the other gods and the human world; the order of things as it is now is Zeus' work.

Closely related succession myths are attested from Hittite Anatolia (see ANATOLIAN DEITIES) and from Mesopotamia. In Hittite mythology, the succession passes through Anu, 'Sky', who is deposed and castrated by Kumarbi, finally to Teshub, the Storm God, who would correspond to Zeus; other myths narrate the attacks of Kumarbi and his followers on Teshub's reign. Myths from Mesopotamia present a similar, though more varied structure; the Babylonian Enūma Elish moves from a primeval pair, Apsu and Tiamat, to the reign of Marduk, the city god of Babylon and in many respects comparable to Ba'al and Zeus; a later version of the Typhon myth locates part of it on Syrian Mt. Kasion, seat of a peak cult of Ba'al Zaphon (Zeus *Kasios). The conception of Zeus as the kingly ruler of the present world is unthinkable without oriental influence. In a similar way, the shift from Indo-European god of the bright sky to the Greek master of sky and storms is inconceivable without the influence of the weather gods of Anatolia and Syria-Palestine with whom he was later identified (Zeus Beelsamēm).

Zeus is a king, not a tyrant. One of his main domains is right and justice: any transgression of his cosmic order is injustice; if necessary, Zeus punishes transgressors. Human kings are under his special protection, but they have to endorse his justice (Hesiod, Theogony). Zeus himself protects those outside ordinary social bonds—strangers, suppliants and beggars; cult attests Zeus Xenios and Zeus Hikesios. To preserve his order, he is himself subject to it: he is committed to Fate.

In many instances (e.g. the Trojan War), human affairs follow the plan of Zeus despite apparent setbacks. He might hasten perfection, if asked in prayer to do so, and he might signal his will, either asked for or unasked, in dreams, augural signs, thunder and lightning, but also by provoking ominous human utterances (thunder and utterance). In cult, this function is expressed in rare epithets like *Phantēr*, 'he who signals', *Terastios*, 'he of the omens', *Phēios* or *Klēdonios*, 'who gives oracular sayings'.

In these cases, the prophetic power of Zeus is occasional and accessory. It becomes central in the only Greek *oracle of Zeus, *Dodona in Epirus, reputed to be the oldest Greek oracle, known already to Homer. It was active until late-Hellenistic times; though consulted by cities too, its main clients were private individuals from northwestern Greece. Zeus is here paired with *Dione, mother of *Aphrodite in ordinary Greek myth. Homer mentions the Selloi as prophets, 'barefoot, sleeping on the earth'. They disappear without a trace; Herodotus knows only of priestesses; later authors add that they prophesy in *ecstasy. Zeus manifested himself in the sounds of the holy oak-tree and in doves, whose call from the holy oak-tree or whose flight are used as divine signs; other sources know also *divination by lots (cleromancy), water vessels (hydromancy), and by the sounds of a gong.

Zeus has only a few major civic *festivals; and though he often is called *Polieus*, he has no major temple on an acropolis, unlike the Roman *Jupiter Capitolinus. A few month names attest early festivals: the bronze-age month Diwos (Cnossus) to which corresponds the Macedonian, Aetolian, and Thessalian *Dīos*, the Attic Maimakterion which pertains to the festival of a shadowy Zeus *Maimaktēs*, and the Cretan (W)elchanios which derives from the Cretan (Zeus) Welchanos. Of some importance for the cities in question were the sacrifice of a bull of Zeus Polieus on Cos and the festival of Zeus Sosipolis at Magnesia ad Maeandrum, both attested in Hellenistic sacred laws. Athenian festivals of Zeus are less self-asserting. The Diisoteria featured a sacrifice and a procession for Zeus Soter and Athena Soteira—it was a festival to honour Zeus 'Saviour of the City'. As to date and place, however, it was more marginal than the Coan festival: it was celebrated outside the city in the Piraeus, although with the participation of the city. Closer to the centre were the Dipolieia (*see* ATTIC CULTS AND MYTHS; BOUPHONIA) and *Diasia. The Dipolieia featured the strange and guilt-ridden sacrifice of an ox on the altar of Zeus Polieus on the acropolis, the Bouphonia; they belong among the rituals around New Year. Aristophanes thought it rather old-fashioned: the ritual killing of the ox, the myth which makes all participants guilty, with the ensuing prosecution of the killer with the formal condemnation of axe and knife, enacts a crisis, not a bright festival.

The Diasia, 'the greatest Athenian festival of Zeus', had an even less auspicious character. The festival took place in honour of Zeus *Meilichios who appears in reliefs in the shape of a huge *snake. His cult took place outside the town, with animal sacrifice or bloodless *cakes; the sacrificial animals were burnt whole. This meant no common meal to release the tension of the sacrifice; instead, there were banquets in small family circles and gifts to the children: the civic community passes through a phase of disintegration, characteristic of the entire month, Anthesterion, whose festival, the *Anthesteria, had an even more marked character of uncanny disintegration.

This apparent paucity of civic festivals is not out of tune with the general image of Zeus. The city-state has to be under the protection of a specific patron deity, *Athena or *Apollo, while Zeus is the overall protector and cannot confine himself to one city only; his protection adds itself to that of the specific civic deities. From early on, he is prominent as a Panhellenic deity. The founding hero of Dodona, *Deucalion, father of Hellen, discloses the oracle's panhellenic aspirations. But Zeus' main Greek festival is the penteteric *Olympian Games with the splendid sacrifice to Zeus Olympios and the ensuing Panhellenic *agōn* (*see* AGŌNES). Their introduction in 776 BC, according to tradition, marked the end of the isolation of the Dark-Age communities; the common festival took place at a spot outside an individual city-state and under the protection of a superior god. Analysis of the sacrifices points to an origin in *initiation rituals of young warriors which had been widened and generalized in an epoch not too distant from the Homeric poems, with their own universalist conception of Zeus.

In the city-state at large, Zeus' own province is the *agora, where he presides, as Zeus *Agoraios*, over both the political and the commercial life of the community; thus, he can be counted among the main divinities of a city, like *Hestia Prytaneia and Athena Poliouchos or Polias. Among the smaller social units, he is one of the patrons of phratries (brotherhoods) and lineages (Zeus *Phratrios* or *Patrōios/Patrios*, sometimes together with Athena Phratria or Patr(o)ia). He also protects individual households: as Zeus *Herkeios*, he receives sacrifices on an altar in the courtyard (every Athenian family had to have one), as Zeus *Ephestios*, on the hearth of a house. *See* HOUSEHOLD, WORSHIP OF.

There are functions of Zeus at the level of the family which are easily extended both to individuals and to the community. Since property is indispensable for the constitution of a household, Zeus is also protector of property (*Ktēsios*); as such, he receives cults from families (Thasos: Zeus Ktesios Patroios), from cities (Athens: a sacrifice by officials in 174/3 BC) and from individuals (Stratonicea: to Zeus Ktesios and *Tyche). In many places Zeus Ktesios has the appearance of a snake (Athens, Thespiae): property is bound to the ground, at least in the still agrarian mentality of ancient Greece, and its protectors belong to the earth. The same holds true for Zeus Meilichios. For the individual, Xenophon attests his efficiency in providing funds, while in many communities Zeus Meilichios protects families or clans; in Athens, he receives the civic festival of the Diasia; here also and elsewhere, he has the

form of a snake. And finally, one might add Zeus *Philios*, protector of friendship between individuals and also between entire communities.

As the most powerful god, Zeus has a very general function which cuts across all groups and gains in importance in the course of time: he is *Sōtēr*, the 'Saviour' par excellence (*see* SOTER). As such, he receives prayers and dedications from individuals, groups, and entire towns. These dedications reflect different possible situations of crisis, from very private ones (where Zeus competes with *Asclepius Soter, see e.g. Zeus Soter Asclepius in Pergamum) to political troubles, natural catastrophes (earthquake) or military attacks (*Delphi, *Soteria after the attack by the Celts).

The Zeus cults of Crete fit only partially into this picture. Myth places both his birth and his grave in Crete: according to *Hesiod, in order to save him from Cronus, Rhea gave birth to Zeus and entrusted the baby to *Gaia, who hid it in a cave near Lyctus, on Mt. Aegaeum. Later authors replace Gaea by the *Curetes, armed *daimones*, whose noisy dance kept Cronus away, and name other mountains, usually Mt. Ida or Mt. Dicte. This complex of myths reflects cult in caves, which partly go back to Minoan times, and armed dances by young Cretan warriors like those attested in the famous hymn to Zeus from Palaikastro (sanctuary of Zeus *Diktaios*), which belong to the context of initiatory rituals of young warriors; in the actual oaths of Cretan young men, Zeus plays an important role. In this function, Zeus (exceptionally) can be young—the Palaikastro hymn calls him *kouros*, 'youngster'; the statue in the sanctuary of Zeus Dictaeus was beardless, and coins from Cnossus show a beardless (Zeus) Welchanos. There certainly are Minoan (and presumably Mycenaean) elements present in the complex, but it would be wrong to separate Cretan Zeus too radically from the rest of the Greek evidence; both the cults of Mt. Lycaeum and of Olympia contain initiatory features. *See* CRETAN CULTS AND MYTHS.

Already in Homer (much more than in actual cult), Zeus had reached a very dominant position. During the Classical and Hellenistic age, religious thinkers developed this into a sort of 'Zeus monotheism'. To *Aeschylus, Zeus had begun to move away from the object of simple human knowledge ('Zeus, whoever you are …') to a nearly universal function ('Zeus is ether, Zeus is earth, Zeus is sky, Zeus is everything and more than that'); *Sophocles sees Zeus' hand in all human affairs ('Nothing of this is not Zeus'). The main document of this monotheism, however, is the hymn to Zeus by the Stoic philosopher *Cleanthes; Zeus, mythical image of the Stoic logos (*see* STOICISM), becomes the commander of the entire cosmos and its 'universal law', and at the same time the guarantor of goodness and benign protector of man. This marks the high point of a development—other gods, though briefly mentioned, become insignificant besides this Zeus.

Neoplatonist speculation marks something of a regression: in the elaborate chains of divine beings, Zeus is never set at the very top; the Neoplatonists allegorize the succession from Uranus through Cronus to Zeus and consequently assign him to a lower level. *See* NEOPLATONISM.

Zeus in art Although 8th-cent. figurines may represent Zeus, he does not assume a type until early Archaic, when he strides with thunderbolt and, rarely, eagle. In the Classical period, Zeus is quieter, often seated and with a sceptre: the prime example is Pheidias' cult statue at *Olympia, familiar from literature, coins, gems, and echoes on vases. The type continues in the Hellenistic period. Zeus participates in many scenes. The east pediments of Olympia and the *Parthenon centred on him. He fights in the Battle of the *Giants from Attic and South Italian Archaic and Classical vases to the Hellenistic Pergamum altar frieze. On Classical vases and sculpture, his pursuits include Aegina (the eponymous heroine of Aegina, *see* EPONYMOI) and *Ganymedes. His transformations occur, particularly in depictions of his seduction of Europa from early Archaic, and *Leda from late Classical. He is common on coins. Zeus was favoured by Alexander the Great and some Roman emperors, especially Hadrian (*see* OLYMPIEUM).

[Homer, *Iliad* 11. 772 ff., *Odyssey* 6. 207 f., 9. 296 ff., 14. 57 ff., 20. 95 ff., 22. 334 ff.; Hesiod, *Theogony* 80 ff., 468 ff.; Aeschylus, *Agamemnon* 160 ff.; Xenophon, *Anabasis* 7. 8. 1 ff.; Apollodorus 1. 5–7, 2. 1]

Zodiac, twelve signs of the *See* CONSTELLATIONS AND NAMED STARS.

Zoroaster is the Greek form of Iranian Zarathuštra. It is not clear whether Zarathuštra was a reformer or the creator of a new religion, a prophet. In the oldest part of the Avesta, the 17 Gāthās, ascribed to Zoroaster himself, he is called a *manthrān*, 'he who possesses the sacred formulas'. The Gāthās portray a dualistic system in which *aša* (truth, rightness) is opposed to *druj* (lie, deceit) with *Ahuramazda as the supreme deity. It is occasionally doubted whether he was a historical figure. Of the various dates for Zoroaster, that of the 6th cent. BC is based on a late Zoroastrian tradition, that of *c*.1000 BC is arrived at by linguistic arguments and therefore preferable. The Greeks had heard of Zoroaster as early as the 5th cent. BC. By the time of Plato and Aristotle they had some notion of the contents of his teaching. He is often called a *magus and regarded as a sage. Legendary details of all sorts accumulated about him. He was (incorrectly) credited with the authorship of numerous works on theology, natural science, *astrology, and *magic. *See* MITHRAS; PERSIAN RELIGION.

Maps

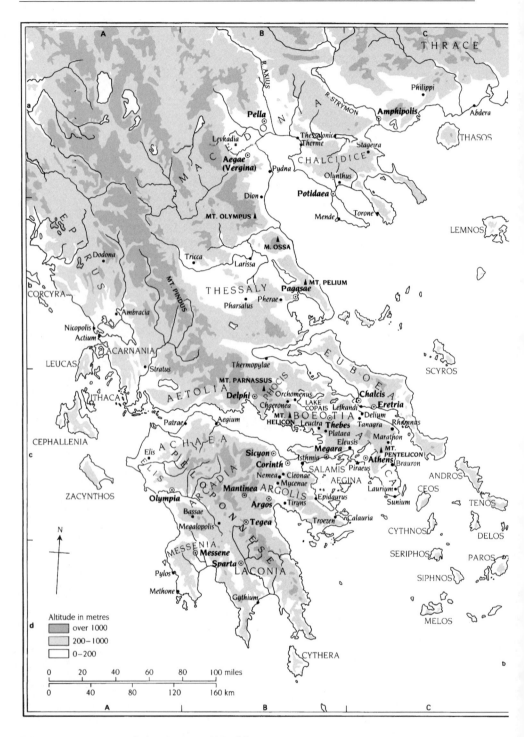

Map 1.   Greece and the Aegean World

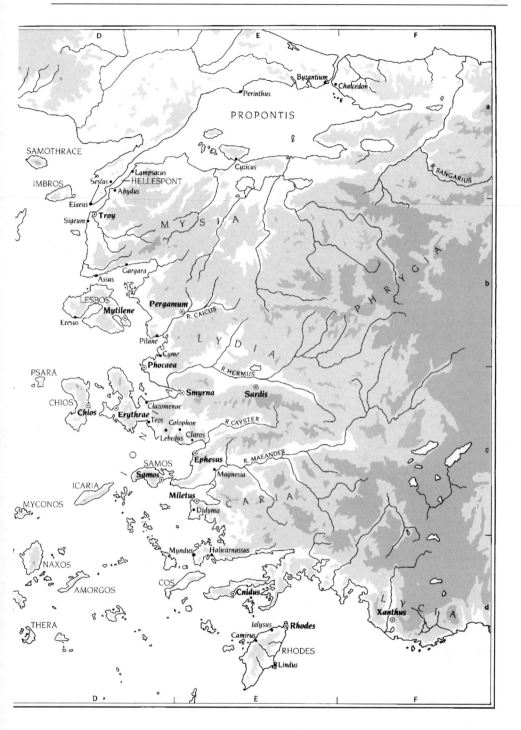

Map 2. Italy

Map 3. The Central and Eastern Mediterranean World

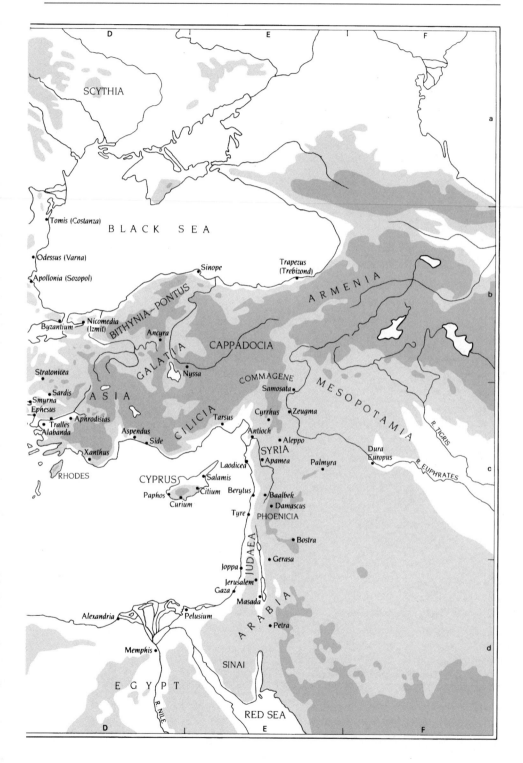

SCYTHIA

BLACK   SEA

Tomis (Costanza)

Odessus (Varna)

Apollonia (Sozopol)

Sinope

Trapezus
(Trebizond)

ARMENIA

BITHYNIA-PONTUS

Nicomedia
(Izmit)

Byzantium

Ancyra

GALATIA

CAPPADOCIA

Nyssa

COMMAGENE

MESOPOTAMIA

Stratonicea

Sardis

Smyrna
Ephesus

ASIA

Aphrodisias

Tralles
Alabanda

Xanthus

Aspendus

Side

CILICIA

Tarsus

Samosata

Cyrrhus

Zeugma

Antioch

Aleppo

SYRIA

Apamea

Palmyra

Dura
Europus

R. TIGRIS

R. EUPHRATES

RHODES

CYPRUS

Laodicea

Salamis

Paphos

Citium

Curium

Berytus

Baalbek

Damascus

Tyre

PHOENICIA

Bostra

JUDAEA

Gerasa

Joppa

Jerusalem

Gaza

Masada

ARABIA

Petra

Alexandria

Pelusium

Memphis

SINAI

EGYPT

R. NILE

RED SEA

Genealogical Tables

1. Greek Gods (according to Hesiod)

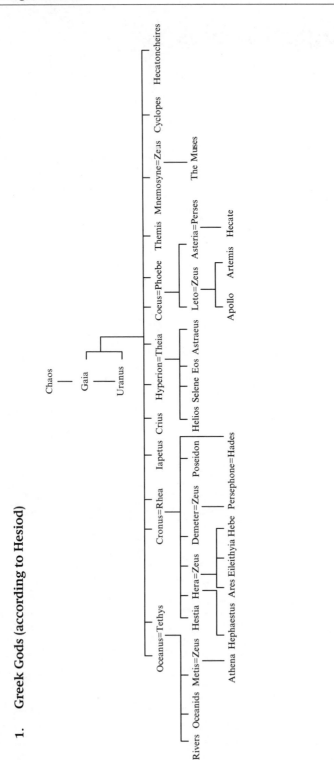

2. House of Troy

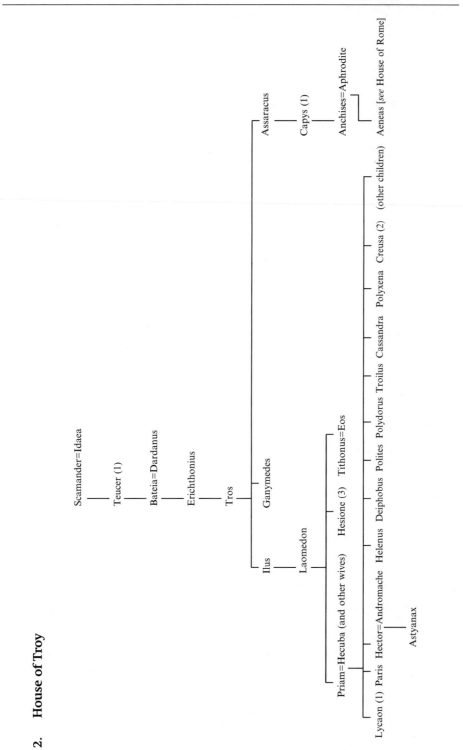

3. House of Thebes

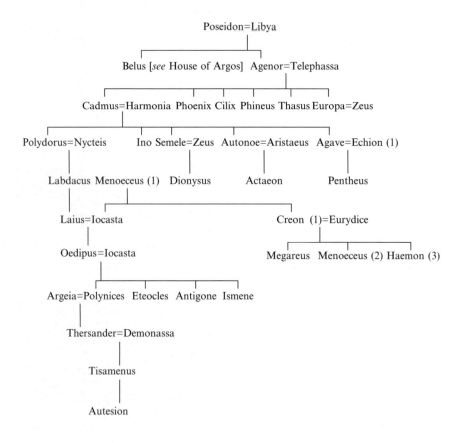

4. House of Argos

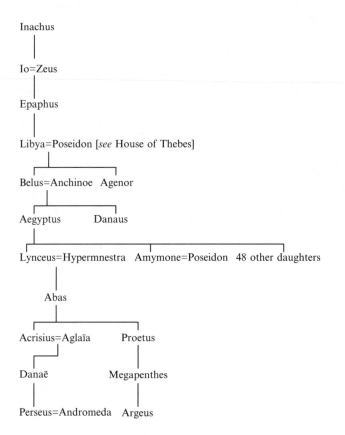

Inachus

Io=Zeus

Epaphus

Libya=Poseidon [*see* House of Thebes]

Belus=Anchinoe   Agenor

Aegyptus   Danaus

Lynceus=Hypermnestra   Amymone=Poseidon   48 other daughters

Abas

Acrisius=Aglaïa   Proetus

Danaë   Megapenthes

Perseus=Andromeda   Argeus

5. Descendants of Tantalus

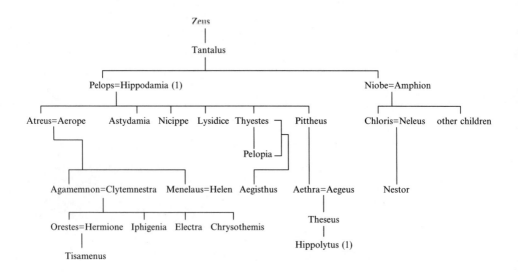

6.   House of Rome

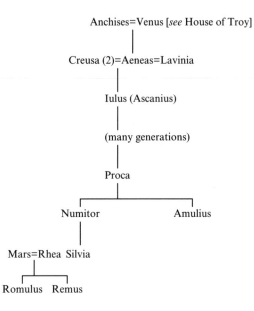

Anchises=Venus [*see* House of Troy]

Creusa (2)=Aeneas=Lavinia

Iulus (Ascanius)

(many generations)

Proca

Numitor   Amulius

Mars=Rhea Silvia

Romulus   Remus